Databases: Design, Development & Deployment

Using Microsoft® Access

Databases: Design, Development & Deployment

Using Microsoft® Access

Second Edition

Peter Rob
Elie Semaan

Boston Burr Ridge, IL Dubuque, IA Madison, WI New York San Francisco St. Louis
Bangkok Bogotá Caracas Kuala Lumpur Lisbon London Madrid Mexico City
Milan Montreal New Delhi Santiago Seoul Singapore Sydney Taipei Toronto

The McGraw·Hill Companies

DATABASES:
DESIGN, DEVELOPMENT & DEPLOYMENT USING MICROSOFT® ACCESS
Published by McGraw-Hill/Irwin, a business unit of The McGraw-Hill Companies, Inc., 1221 Avenue of the Americas, New York, NY, 10020.

This book is printed on acid-free paper.

domestic 1 2 3 4 5 6 7 8 9 0 QPD/QPD 0 9 8 7 6 5 4 3
international 1 2 3 4 5 6 7 8 9 0 QPD/QPD 0 9 8 7 6 5 4 3

ISBN 0-07-282658-4

Publisher: *George Werthman*
Sponsoring editor: *Dan Silverburg*
Developmental editor: *Lisa Chin-Johnson*
Marketing manager: *Greta Kleinert*
Senior producer, Media technology: *David Barrick*
Senior project manager: *Kari Geltemeyer*
Production supervisor: *Gina Hangos*
Designer: *Kami Carter*
Senior supplement producer: *Vicki Laird*
Senior digital content specialist: *Brian Nacik*
Typeface: *10/12 New Aster*
Compositor: *GAC Indianapolis*
Printer: *Quebecor World Dubuque Inc.*

Library of Congress Cataloging-in-Publication Data

Rob, Peter.
Databases : design, development & deployment / Peter Rob, Elie Semaan.-- 2nd ed.
p. cm.
ISBN 0-07-282658-4 (alk. paper) -- ISBN 0-07-121506-9 (international : alk. paper)
1. Database design. 2. Database management. I. Semaan, Elie. II. Title.

QA76.9.D26R625 2004
005.75'65--dc21

2003046394

INTERNATIONAL EDITION ISBN 0-07-121506-9

www.mhhe.com

To Anne, who remains my best friend after 41 years of marriage. And to the students who made me remember that teaching is a noble profession.

Peter Rob

To Peter Rob, from whom I learned how to be a database professional and who gave me the opportunity to coauthor this book.

Elie Semaan

Brief Contents

Contents

Preface

Three years—a database applications lifetime—have elapsed between the publication of this edition and the previous one. During those three years, much has changed in the applications development arena. The current version of Microsoft Access reflects many of those changes. For example, the development of data pages is easier and better than ever, thus making it possible to explore Web database applications development and management. (If you'll take a peak at the screen pictures that accompany many of the problems in Chapter 9, you'll see why we are excited about the many learning and teaching opportunities that are to be found in the development of the Access data pages.)

This book, like its predecessor, includes a wide-ranging and in-depth coverage of Microsoft Access. Yet we do not consider this book to be *just* an Access book. Instead, we believe that this book's most important contribution lies in its role as a practical, hands-on database design, implementation, and applications development guide. Our argument is simple: No matter how well you learn Access, if you apply it to a poorly designed and badly implemented database, you will wind up with a poor end-user product. To use an analogy, hiring better bricklayers to lay the brick for a badly designed building is not going to improve the building much.

IF YOU WANT TO SING THE SONG, YOU HAVE TO KNOW THE WORDS AND THE MELODY

Important database concepts and technical database vocabulary come into play even in the early stages of Access applications development. For example, what on earth does Access mean when it asks whether you want to enforce referential integrity? Or whether you intend to declare a primary key? Why do you need a primary key in the first place? What, for that matter, is a primary key? What kinds of relationships exist, and what is their function in the database environment? The answers to such questions will help dictate the results of your attempts at database applications development. The almost limitless development opportunities found in the Web's database environment make it more important than ever that the database's architecture be respected. If the database applications developer does not understand the basic components of the database structure, (s)he has an unprecedented opportunity to let end users use computers to make bigger mistakes faster.

Learning Microsoft Access database applications development without first building a solid foundation of database vocabulary, design concepts, and implementation principles seems to be only marginally useful and potentially dangerous. That's why we first build a solid working knowledge of the necessary database vocabulary and concepts. Then we carefully cover database *design* concepts and principles, followed by a detailed look at the modeling tools that help database professionals produce successful database design blueprints. Finally, we examine how the blueprint can be implemented properly. Only after this crucial foundation has been put into place do we provide finely detailed coverage of the applications development process, using Microsoft Access.

IF YOU WANT TO PLAY THE GAME, GO AHEAD AND PLAY

While the knowledge of database vocabulary, concepts, and design is useful, such knowledge fades quickly if it is not reinforced through application. Therefore, we show—in fine detail—the development of a point-of-sale (POS) database system for a mail-order business. The POS database development process is sufficiently complex to serve as the basis for building valuable database design, implementation, and applications development skills, yet the complexity is not overwhelming. (After all, you already have a basic knowledge of sales transactions and inventory management. You have purchased many products and realize that these purchases generate revenue for the seller and decrease the seller's product inventory.) And because the database design is done in modular form, one module at a time, even the more complex components are easily handled.

Unless you know how to *begin* the database systems development process and how to fit the components into a meaningful framework, knowing "how to do the pieces" is not particularly useful. Therefore, our database development process matches the typical real-world scenario. To make sure that you learn how to build a database system from the ground up, we begin by crafting a detailed description of operations from which the business rules are distilled. We then show how these business rules help define the database components. Next we show how the business rules are incorporated into the database design. (Because real-world database professionals are required to exercise professional judgment, we also show how the design components are often shaped by competing requirements such as design efficiency, transactions speed, and information requirements.) We then verify the design against the business rules, normalize the design, and show how the database design is implemented with Microsoft Access. Finally, we show how the end-user applications are developed to meet the end-user needs.

It is useful to keep in mind that users of a database system don't see the intricacy and efficiency of the underlying database design. They just want the database system to work. They want the system to be easy to use and manage, to perform the required transactions, and to generate the necessary information. But even if the database system performs all of its intended functions perfectly, end users tend to "grade" database professionals by the end-user interface and the attractiveness of the forms and reports. That's why we made sure that we also adequately addressed presentation format and quality.

IT'S A MULTIPLE-DATABASE WORLD OUT THERE

Real-world databases have the unfortunate habit of never quite fitting any single example. That's why familiarity with a wide range of database environments is beneficial when you're trying to develop real-world database design and implementation skills. Therefore, although the POS is the primary recipient of this book's database design, implementation, and applications development effort, we also illustrate how specific database design practices and procedures can be addressed in many database environments. In short, the examples throughout this book cover a wide variety of database types. We also reinforce database design skills by providing an opportunity to apply them to a wide variety of database problems. That's why you will see database designs that include a consulting company, an aircraft-rental company, a trucking company, an aircraft museum, a service organization, and a consignment sales business.

WHAT MAKES THIS BOOK SO SPECIAL?

Much of the database book market seems to be divided into two main categories: conceptual and applications oriented. Conceptual coverage is very important because concepts provide the underpinning for good applications development. Applications-driven coverage is important because the end users of a real-world database just want to use the system's products, such as forms and reports.

Unfortunately, purely conceptual database coverage provides little opportunity to discover an awful truth: What works well in theory may not work very well in practice. Even if you have perfect knowledge of concepts, *applying* them turns out to be a different proposition. Perhaps you can learn the basic movements of ice-skating on the living-room floor, but you'll have a real surprise or two when you first venture out on the ice. On the other hand, the applications-oriented approach tends to be focused on the "how to do this and that, using ________" without adequately fitting the applications into a proper conceptual framework. That "how-to" approach tends to lead to the many data integrity problems that conceptual knowledge helps prevent. Perhaps it ought to be obvious that even a collection of well-constructed car parts does not necessarily allow you to drive to work.

This book is special because it provides *both* the crucial and in-depth conceptual knowledge base and the hands-on component that makes the conceptual knowledge useful. Knowing and understanding the database concepts is good, but seeing those concepts come to life in the actual implementation of end-user applications is better. Seeing the applications development process from start to finish, yielding useful and attractive interfaces and applications, is better still. In spite of the fact that we provide detailed and in-depth conceptual coverage, our Access applications coverage is both wide and deep.

If you actually apply the database concepts to a properly developed design, implementing that design can teach you many valuable lessons. One of those lessons is that successful database implementations are defined by competing requirements such as transaction speed, information type and extent, design efficiency, and system navigation. To make the necessary trade-offs, one needs to exercise professional judgment. This book is unique because it does address such judgment issues at all levels: design, implementation, and applications development.

We do not claim that this book dispenses instant wisdom or professional judgment. But we do address many issues that are resolved through the application of professional judgment within a proper conceptual framework. Perhaps our coverage will, at the very least, sensitize the reader to the notion that database design, implementation, and applications development seldom succumb to the blind application of rules. Although the "database business" tends to be science driven, there's a lot of art in this business.

In short, we wrote this book for a simple reason: If you want to "grow" database professionals, you need both conceptual and applications-oriented coverage, and the two coverage types must be well integrated. You also need a book that at least introduces the notion of professional judgment and then shows you how such judgment can affect database design and implementation efforts. We couldn't find a book that did the job. So we wrote one.

MANAGING THE DATABASE

This book is also dedicated to the notion that database professionals do more than design databases and end-user applications. They also *manage* databases. Therefore, whether you use Access, SQL Server, or Oracle, coverage of database administration and security issues is important. Database back ends and front ends, password protection, workgroups, users, and permissions flourish in the professional database environment. And, yes, database administrators tend to encounter the Web with increasing frequency. That's why you'll find these topics addressed in this book.

DATABASE TYPE SELECTION

Our database design, implementation, and applications development coverage is focused on the database type known as a production database. We made this choice for what we believe are sound reasons.

- Production databases are familiar. If your students have ever bought a product, enrolled in a course, applied for a loan, earned a driver's license, or paid taxes, they are acquainted with at least one aspect of the end-user side of the production database. Being somewhat familiar with the production database's end product becomes a valuable asset when students are introduced to unfamiliar database concepts and tools. The "Eureka!" principle works best when at least a portion of the database work fits into a familiar framework.
- Given the pervasive presence of the production database, its design, implementation, and application development skills are especially valuable.
- Production databases serve as a prime data source for decision support databases such as the data warehouse. Therefore, the production database's proper design and implementation spread benefits far and wide.
- Although decision support databases and production databases are subject to different operational requirements, the skills learned for the latter translate well to the skills required in the former.
- The production database transaction environment lends itself well to demonstrating how implementation issues are tied to database design.
- The Access applications development tools are particularly well suited to the production database environment.

THE RELATIONAL DATABASE SELECTION

The production database we develop in this book, a mail-order company point of sale (POS) system, is based on the relational database model. This choice, too, was an easy one. First, Access is a relational DBMS, so it fits our relational database coverage well. Second, the POS system's transaction environment fits well into the relational model's framework. Finally, the relational model is easily the most frequently encountered database model in the production database applications arena.

MICROSOFT ACCESS SELECTION

Whether you deal with database design, applications development, the Web, or database security, you'll have to actually put the concepts to the test by implementing them. We chose Microsoft Access as the basis for a real hands-on learning environment. We made this choice for some simple reasons:

- Access is a fine relational database product that enables teachers to explore a wide range of real-world design, implementation, and applications development issues quickly and easily. In short, Access is a great teaching tool.
- Thanks to Microsoft's educational initiatives, Access is widely available at low cost. Cost and availability matter to teachers and their students.
- Many organizations, ranging from not-for-profit to small business to Fortune 500 to government, discovered long ago that Access makes it possible to prototype database applications quickly and efficiently. Therefore, Access applications development skills are marketable.

DESIGN TOOL SELECTION

Given the POS structure and its implementation in a relational database environment, the entity relationship diagram (ERD) is an appropriate database design tool. Therefore, Chapters 1 and 3 provide detailed coverage of the ERD. Its components tie easily into the relational database model, which, in turn, fits Access's implementation and applications work well. Therefore, there are no logical gaps between design, implementation, and applications development.

TOPICAL COVERAGE AND APPROACH

We believe that a database course ought to be taught the way a database is created. In other words, design before you build. Therefore, we begin—in Chapters 1 and 2—by developing database design skills. These skills must be, and are, based on a solid conceptual foundation. And, naturally, we build a professional database vocabulary to make precise transmission of information possible.

A real database must reflect the business data and information requirements accurately. Therefore, we use Chapter 3 to show how a detailed description of operations yields the business rules that help define the database design components. Because Chapter 3 deals with real-world design issues faced in building a POS system, we make sure that the design components are treated as modules. Once the design modules—invoicing, shipping, back ordering, and so on—are successfully completed, they are laced together to produce the complete design. This carefully scripted approach helps to moderate the complexity of a real-world database design process.

After translating the business requirements into a database design, we implement that design in Chapter 4. This chapter provides many practical illustrations of the conceptual material. For example, the database implementation requires the creation of the relationships that were defined in the ERD and the enforcement of entity and referential integrity as the relationships are built.

Once the database has been implemented and the data are properly stored in the database tables, we show (in Chapter 5) how queries known as "select" queries are used to retrieve the data. We also demonstrate how such queries may be used to transform data into information. (The select queries are also the foundation for most forms and reports that are generated from the database contents.) In addition, we demonstrate the use of parameter queries, thus producing an interactive query environment. And we show how update and delete queries are used to modify and manage the data in the database tables.

In Chapters 6 and 7, we turn our attention to forms and reports. Because end users tend to evaluate the database professional's expertise on the basis of the interface and the report detail and presentation quality, our coverage reflects the end-user expectations.

When Chapters 1 through 7 are completed, all the proper database components are ready for use. Unfortunately, these components are now standing alone, thus making it difficult for end users to navigate through the database's many parts. What is needed at this point is some way to link the components. That job is accomplished by the detailed macro coverage in Chapter 8. We'll show how the macros are used to develop the prototype of a fully functioning database *system*.

Chapter 9 introduces the student to Web database applications. Like the other chapters in this book, we focus our attention on the Web implementation and application development issues. To let students concentrate on Web-specific issues, we use components of the familiar POS system we developed in the previous chapters. Our feedback indicates that this chapter is generally considered to be the reward for lessons well learned. Students will have an opportunity to design and implement database-driven colorful Web pages that make use of the many pictures we have supplied.

Chapter 10 covers basic database security issues. Because the best security system includes multiple layers, we start with simple password protection. Then we move on to the database administrator's security environment, covering the Admin function, workgroups, groups, and users within the groups. We demonstrate all the Admin security options, including the assignment of permissions to use individual objects within the database. We also show how a database applications system can be made more secure by creating a front-end component that stores the applications and a back-end component that houses the database. Once again, the practical aspects of database learning become obvious in this area.

PRACTICAL NORMALIZATION COVERAGE THAT WORKS

Avoiding data redundancy is an important principle in production database design. Therefore, we provide brief, but thorough and solid coverage of normalization principles and procedures. Because we learned a long time ago that visual cues are an important learning tool, we use dependency diagrams to diagnose normal forms. Those same dependency diagrams perform a valuable role in normalizing lower normal forms to higher normal forms. Our use of dependency diagrams is easily explained: They work well, and their use makes normalization a snap.

CLASS TESTED

The POS database supplied with this edition has been used successfully in a classroom setting during the past several years. Students and faculty members have had plenty of opportunity to pick apart the design and the implementation coverage. They have also had a chance to dissect the applications development. Such classroom testing means that the "gotcha" element is minimized.

CONVERSATIONAL WRITING STYLE

Database design, implementation, and application development are wonderfully interesting and satisfying professional activities. But if you want to translate concepts into a working database, you'll discover many challenges. Such challenges must not become unnecessarily difficult because they are hidden in a complex language box. That's why we use a light, conversational writing style. We discovered long ago that a simple, one sentence analogy often yields a better grasp of complex material than a long and convoluted paragraph. Sometimes, corny works!

NO PROGRAMMING

Building on the successful previous edition, we continue to focus our attention on database design, implementation, and applications development. The SQL queries are written through the Access Query by Example (QBE) interface, with the help of the Access Expression Builder. Access writes the code that is the foundation for the forms and reports. The Web applications are generated very well with the help of the Access Wizards that write the necessary HTML and XML code.

Although Visual Basic (VB) programming is particularly well suited to applications development, we use the many Microsoft Access tools to produce useful database system prototypes. The addition of VB programming coverage would either dilute the book's focus or add too much material to fit within a one-semester database course. In fact, VB programming usually is taught as a separate course. Naturally, a VB programming course could use the interfaces developed in this book as primary programming targets.

INSTRUCTOR SUPPORT

All database problem solutions are found in the teacher databases that are part of the Instructor Resource Kit (IRK). Therefore, the instructor can demonstrate each solution to a query, form, or report problem. If a required macro in Chapter 8 yields student questions, the macro group—or a specific macro within that macro group—can be shown. If you want to demonstrate the effect of a change in an object name or a path designation in any of the Chapter 9 Internet database page applications, you can do that easily. In short, we have tried to minimize the instructor's class preparation workload. (Given the hands-on quality of this book, such an instructor support feature is a real time saver!)

Each chapter has its own complete set of databases and applications. For example, if you are covering query development in Chapter 5, all of the databases for that chapter are found in that chapter's folder and all the databases in that folder have a Ch05 prefix. In short, finding the database material has become much easier than it was in the previous edition.

To avoid information overload and unnecessary clutter, each chapter's databases contain *only* the components covered in that chapter. For example, the query development coverage in Chapter 5 uses databases that contain only the queries that were developed in the text and only the queries that are required to solve the end-of-chapter problems. The Ch05 databases do not contain forms, reports, or macros. The form development coverage in Chapter 6 means that the Ch06 databases include only the forms and the queries that provide the data for those forms, but there are no reports or macros. And so on. (With apologies to Nissan, each chapter has everything you need, nothing you don't.)

The student and instructor database application input and output match the figures in the chapters. Therefore, you will no longer have to search for approximate matches to discover which application components are being discussed. When possible, we have specified the names of the queries, forms, reports, and macros in the problem sets. Therefore, you will find it much easier to select a specific problem solution and, of course, it will be much easier to grade student work when you know what to look for on a student-supplied diskette.

Instructors will also appreciate the extensive problem sets that accompany each chapter. No problem is trivial, and the sheer quantity of the end-of-chapter problems makes it possible to cover different problems in different semesters. Combine the extensive problem sets with the large number of databases, and you'll see why this book can be used for several semesters or quarters without duplicating the homework assignments.

To help instructors prepare class presentations and use the databases and the extensive problem sets effectively, the IRK also includes a CD that includes:

- An attractive PowerPoint slide show that contains the book's coverage of design vocabulary, concepts, and design issues.
- A detailed instructor's manual that includes problem solutions and additional discussion material, as well as alternative design and applications development examples.
- A large test bank developed by McGraw-Hill.
- All of the databases for each of the chapters.

THE MARKET

Because this book covers applications development within a framework of conceptual database design, it can be used in a wide variety of markets. Given this book's coverage type and extent, it is particularly well suited to database courses that emphasize the practical aspects of the database systems development, rather than the theoretical side. Therefore, it should especially appeal to community college, college, and university programs that are technically oriented. The book's practical approach also makes it the perfect text for off-campus courses that target businesses or for technical courses offered by seminar groups. In addition, the book's material lends itself very well to advanced corporate training programs. Finally, if only a single high-level theory-based course is offered, this book may be used to supplement the theoretical coursework.

If an institution offers a two-semester or two-quarter database course sequence, the first semester or quarter may be devoted to the theoretical database framework, using a text that focuses on theoretical issues. The second semester or quarter may then be used to tackle implementation and applications development, using this book. If the first semester or quarter is devoted to database back-end topics and the second semester or quarter covers database front-end topics, this book will fit the latter coverage well.

WHAT'S DIFFERENT ABOUT THIS EDITION? (WE REALLY DID LISTEN TO YOU!)

We have had the opportunity to check almost three years' worth of feedback from students and teachers. To make sure that we did not lose the messages reflected in the feedback, we created a matrix to store the feedback themes and their frequencies. This edition reflects our responses to your comments and suggestions. Several major themes helped guide our rewriting efforts:

1. Finding many of the database components is often a problem.

   Response: That problem has been eliminated. Please note the description in paragraphs 2 and 3 of the "Instructor Support" section in this preface.

2. There were too many cases—especially in Chapter 5—in which the chapter figure and the actual database output format were significantly different, thus causing confusion.

   Response: We have made sure that this is no longer a problem. That is, the database output format and the format shown in the text will match. (Our response to comment 1 above made this task much easier.)

   But do keep in mind that time-sensitive output *values*—such as "years employed"—will change as time marches on. For example, an employee who was hired on February 15, 1991 has a "years employed" value of 11 on February 15, 2002. That value will become 12 when an update query is run on—or after—February 15, 2003. Also, if an incorrect value is used in the text for discussion purposes and that error is subsequently corrected, only the corrected value will occur in the database. (You can, of course, easily change the value in the database to make it incorrect and then demonstrate the correction process. Storing multiple correct/incorrect versions of the same database objects creates lots of confusion, especially when the incorrect database object values are subsequently corrected!)

3. The Internet chapter was out of synch with the rest of the book in that it did not have the hands-on coverage of the other chapters.

   Response: Problem solved. Please take a look at Chapter 9 and note that the development of the data pages matches the development of the forms and reports in previous chapters. That is, every step in the development process is shown. The problem section reflects this major chapter revision.

4. The book lacks the important coverage of picture objects that are dynamically linked to the database records. (Examples: Employee photo to match employee record; product picture to match product record; etc.)

   Response: We have added this coverage and we have made sure that picture objects are always properly linked to their originating records through proper path definition. Note particularly the coverage found in Chapter 6, "Form Development"; Chapter 8, "Macros and Macro Groups"; and Chapter 9, "Access and the Internet" for good examples. The AC_Museum database problems in Chapters 6, 8, and 9 and the JewelCo database problem in Chapter 9 are particularly nice illustrations. The linking technique demonstrated in these chapters can easily be extended to other objects such as audio, video, text, and so on. (Student feedback indicates that they really like this new coverage!)

5. The text needs composite index coverage when you discuss queries. Show examples of enforcing unique records.

   Response: Done. Note particularly the new and detailed coverage of composite indexes in Chapter 4, section 4.5.1.

6. Two macro chapters? Get rid of the advanced macro coverage in Chapter 9. Just give us the advanced macros in databases that actually show the macro execution and then I can simply project the

macro from the actual database. There is too much confusion when I go from text to database. Much of that macro coverage is rendered moot by the use of data pages on the Web. (You have heard of the Web?)

Response: Done. The old Chapter 9 is gone and we have put data page coverage in the new (Internet) Chapter 9. We have also included three completed databases—with their advance macros—in the teacher's IRK. (Check the **Complete DB** folder.)

These six major points and our responses to them indicate that we have taken your comments and suggestions seriously. There are, of course, many other improvements. For example, in Chapter 5 we have included better coverage of the outer join queries and we have added running sum and union query coverage in that chapter.

A WORD OF CAUTION

Each book has a CD that contains all the student databases and objects necessary to complete some of the applications. Giving students a set of databases to let them practice their new-found skills can lead to some interesting problems. Please read the following words of caution before you try to use the AC_Museum database in Chapters 6 and 8 and all of the databases in Chapter 9. (Naturally, *all* of the databases are subject to the requirement in the first bullet.)

- The databases on the CD are subject to the **Read-Only** property. If you simply copy the databases to your disks and then try to modify any component, your efforts will be denied. Simple problem, simple solution: After the database has been copied from the CD to the disk, right-click on the database filename and uncheck the **Read-Only** property.
- The aircraft museum database used in Chapters 6 and 8 requires the use of the **\AC_Museum** folder in which two additional folders, **\AC_Pictures** and **\Database**, are stored. Note that the **\AC_Museum** folder is stored in the root. Specifically, the folder organization looks like this:

  \AC_Museum

  \AC_Pictures (the photos used by the database are stored in this folder)

  \Database (the AC_Museum database is stored in this folder)

  The **AC_Museum** database's PHOTO table uses a PHOTO_LOCATION path that reads

  \AC_Museum\AC_Pictures

  to ensure that the applications can find the photos that are stored in the **\AC_Pictures** folder. (Because no drive is designated in the applications, you can copy the **\AC_Museum** folder to any drive and the application will run OK.) *If the path to the photo object does not match the object location, you will generate errors when the database application cannot find the picture objects*. To avoid such problems, copy the entire **\AC_Museum** folder to your drive and *do not make changes in either the folder names or their locations*.[1]

  If you *do* want to use a different set of folder names and/or locations, make sure that the path to the photos in the PHOTO table and the actual photo object locations match before you try to run the application. In addition, make sure that you also change the path that is specified in the image used on the form to show the photos.
- When you are using the (Web) page component of an Access database, Access performs quite a few system housekeeping chores in the background. If you change *any* component of the path to the database folder or you make any change(s) in the application component names, Access will no longer be able to find the affected application component(s). Therefore, the data pages in Chapter 9 lead to a whole host of errors *if the data pages and the links are not properly matched to the database objects*.

  If you copy the databases for Chapter 9 to a folder different from the one used in the application, all the paths in the data pages and any links located on those pages must be edited to reflect the new object locations. Actually, this is a very valuable exercise, but it's probably more rewarding *initially* to use the folder and path designations that we have used! *These kinds of problems and their solutions are covered in depth in section 9.10 of Chapter 9.*

  If you are a teacher, your completed applications—the solutions to the problems—are located on the teacher's CD. Copy the folders that contain the databases and data pages without making changes in the folder names, the access paths, or the database names. For example, the applications in the **Ch09_POS_2nd** database assume the use of the following path:

  C:\Rob-Semaan-2ndEdition\Databases (Teacher)\Ch09\Ch09_POS_2nd

  The Chapter 9 databases on the student CD do not include any data pages. These pages must be

[1] The AC_Museum database and its derivatives are subsets of Peter Rob's F_100 database project. Peter Rob retains the rights to the full use of this database and all the aircraft pictures used in the illustrations.

created during the coverage of Chapter 9. We recommend that you use the same database names, folder names, and paths that are used in the database material stored on the CD. For example, we will assume that the **Ch09_POS_2nd** database applications use the following path:

C:\Rob-Semaan-2ndEdition\Databases(Student)\Ch09\Ch09_POS_2nd

If the students use object locations different from the ones illustrated in the text or stored on the CD, the data pages automatically reflect those locations. If the student work is then copied to another folder, you will (again) generate data page and link errors. *These kinds of problems and their solutions are covered in depth in section 9.10 of Chapter 9.*

ACKNOWLEDGMENTS

Like its preceding edition, this book reflects the valuable input we received from many sources. First, several years' worth of class testing of the first edition gave us the opportunity to ask our students to grade our efforts, and the students responded well to the challenge. They found errors and omissions. Best of all, they told us what worked and what didn't work for them. When we rewrote material or changed our presentations, they provided instant feedback, thus causing us to rewrite some chapters and/or sections up to a dozen times between 1998 and 2002. We particularly thank Sonja Hunolt, Diane Grandstaff, and Richard Ted Moores, Jr., Loai I. Alammar, Dongming Qin, Adrian Araya, Jessica Porter, and Carolyn Oliver. You have earned our heartfelt thanks for your comments, thoughtful questions, and suggestions, always delivered with style and a sense of humor. Students like you made our work especially satisfying, and we hope that a *little* bit of us will travel with you as you develop your careers.

This edition is built on the solid foundation of its predecessor. McGraw-Hill distributed our initial book drafts to other class testers, who took the time and effort to provide very important feedback and whose very positive comments helped ensure that this book would survive the review process. We remain particularly indebted to Dr. Kent L. Jones at Whitworth College in Spokane, Washington. His thorough, detailed, and well-written chapter-by-chapter reviews and his practical and useful suggestions have left a lasting imprint on the first edition and provided a guide to the development of this second edition.

We would like to thank all the people at McGraw-Hill for making the second edition a reality, especially George Werthman, publisher; Dan Silverburg, sponsoring editor; Lisa Chin-Johnson, development editor; Kari Geltemeyer, project manager; Gina Hangos, production supervisor, and last but not least, Kami Carter, designer. This superb team made the writing/editing/production process smooth and trouble-free for the authors. After more than 25 years of writing for various publishers, I think I can safely argue that the members of this team are top-of-the-line in all respects. Thanks much for you hard work, your "can do" approach, and your unfailing good cheer.

Finally, I thank Anne, who has always been my life's harbor. She cheerfully put up with the long hours that are the by-product of an author's endeavors. Although she had some initial misgivings about my work on yet another book, she was also quick to note that this book occupied a special place in the writer's portion of my heart. As always, my work is dedicated to her.

Peter Rob

Chapter **One**

Database Vocabulary, Concepts, and Design Tools

Preview

We realize that you probably want to get your hands on the Access software as soon as possible in order to learn the very marketable Access applications development skills. However, it is useful to remember that good brick-laying skills are not going to improve a badly designed building much. Similarly, Access applications development skills are of limited value unless and until you learn the proper way to design and implement a database. That's why we introduce some very important design concepts and tools in this chapter and in Chapters 2 and 3. These concepts and tools will serve you well, regardless of which database software you will use later.

Before you can learn to produce a good database design, you must first know what a database is, what its components are, and how those components interact. Therefore, we start by introducing the necessary database vocabulary. Next we'll introduce you to the database concepts that provide the foundation for good database design. Finally, we'll show you how to use a database design tool to produce the database design's blueprint.

Objectives

After you have mastered the material presented in this chapter, you will know the answers to these questions:

- What are data and what is the difference between data and information?
- What is a database and what are its components?
- What is a database system?
- What are entities, entity sets, attributes, and relationships?
- What attribute types exist and how do they affect database design?
- What are database tables and how are they (conceptually) presented?
- What are primary keys and foreign keys and what is their purpose?
- What are candidate keys and secondary keys and why do they exist?
- What are the entity and referential integrity rules and what is their function?
- What relationship types exist and how do they affect database design?
- What are connectivities and cardinalities and what role do they play?
- What are optionalities and how do they affect the database design and implementation?
- What are supertypes and subtypes and how are they used in database design?
- What are recursive relationships and how do they fit into the database design?
- What entity types exist and how are they implemented?
- What is an ERD and what are its components?
- What is a description of operations and what role does it play in the database design process?
- What are business rules and how do they influence the database design process?

1.1 DATA AND INFORMATION

The first four letters in the word *database* provide the focus for our initial discussion. Data are facts about people, places, things, or events.[1] Business data are likely to include facts about employees, customers, vendors, products, inventories, and so on. For example, employee data are likely to include Social Security numbers, names, dates of birth, hiring dates, year-to-date (YTD) salaries and wages, YTD Social Security (FICA) tax payments, YTD federal income tax (FIT) payments, and YTD benefit co-payments. Similarly, customer data are likely to include customer names and addresses, phone numbers, account balances, purchase histories, and so on.

Data are recognized as an important business asset because data constitute the raw material from which information is derived. In fact, **information** is usually defined as *processed* data. As important as any raw material is, it requires *processing* to render it useful. For example, iron ore is a raw material that is processed to become raw steel that is processed to become car parts, pots and pans, and numerous other items we consider to be useful in our daily lives. Until it is processed, the iron ore has no value to us. Yet we value it highly in its various processed forms. Similarly, a sales manager probably has a rather limited use for a 1000-page computer printout containing data about 252,518 customers unless these data have been processed to yield descriptive summaries, such as the one shown in Table 1.1.

In the summary in Table 1.1, the data processing was limited to a simple cross tabulation that required only creating the age and gender categories and then counting the number of people who fit the table's intersections.

Data processing may also yield graphical summaries such as bar graphs, pie charts, point plots, and time-series lines. In fact, graphical presentations such as the one shown in Figure 1.1 are the basis for idea formulation.

Data processing may be, and usually is, much more complex than cross tabulating or graph presentation. For example, statistical modeling may yield time-series models used in forecasting and multivariate-regression models used to predict market movements or control production processes. Regardless of the processing extent and complexity, without data no data processing can take place. And without processing the data are of very limited value.

Information is important because it forms the foundation for decision making. The decision to expand a product's sales promotion depends on information concerning its likely customers; the likely effectiveness of the anticipated sales promotion; the nature, type, and extent of the competitive environment; and so on. The decision to buy new production equipment depends on the effectiveness of the current equipment, the acquisition and operating costs of the new equipment, the payoff probability, and so on. Make enough bad decisions based on incomplete or incorrect information, and you'll be out of business. Make enough good decisions based on timely, correct, and relevant information, and you'll prosper. No wonder that information generation and management has become so important to business managers everywhere. The realities of the global marketplace make information a key to survival.

TABLE 1.1 A Customer Cross Tabulation by Gender and Age

	Age Distribution						
	Under 25	**25–30**	**31–40**	**41–50**	**51–60**	**Over 60**	**Total**
Female	20,871	33,894	25,778	18,339	15,092	14,396	128,370
Male	22,947	30,049	24,115	19,243	16,731	11,003	124,088
Total	43,818	63,943	49,893	37,582	31,823	25,399	252,458

FIGURE 1.1
A Simple Bar Graph

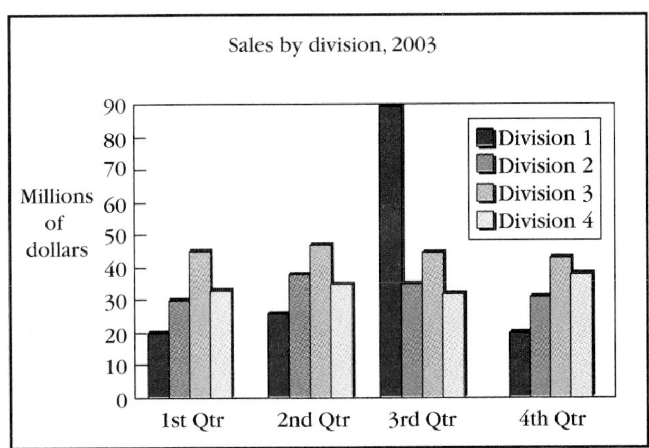

Given the relationship between data and information, it requires little imagination to conclude that you cannot generate good information from bad data. Therefore, how data are generated, stored, and processed is the subject of much discussion. In fact, you'll discover that how and in what format data are stored in various databases will help determine how usable and useful the data will be. Given the important role that databases play, their design, implementation, end-user applications interface development, and management have become a key to business survival in an increasingly competitive global business environment. No wonder that database professionals smile a lot these days.

1.2 THE DATABASE AND THE DATABASE MANAGEMENT SYSTEM (DBMS)

Conceptually, a database is a highly specialized electronic cabinet in which data, kept in electronic folders, are stored in the electronic cabinet's drawers. The electronic cabinet also contains a special drawer in which **metadata,** or data about data, are kept in a data dictionary. The **data dictionary** is a compilation of the data components, their names, and their characteristics. The data dictionary also contains the definition of the relationships between the data within the electronic folders and within the electronic drawers and between the folders and between the drawers. We examine the data dictionary's contents more thoroughly after considering data types and relationship types later in this chapter.

The database contents are managed through a **database management system,** or **DBMS.** The DBMS performs the following services:

- It manages the metadata in the data dictionary. Of special importance to us is that the DBMS automatically funnels all database activities through the database's data dictionary. The most important effect of this funneling activity is that it provides efficient access to the data within the database. In practice, the DBMS takes care of all physical storage details, data structures, relationships, and so on. Therefore, the DBMS greatly simplifies the tasks of database design, implementation, applications development, and management.
- It produces the complex data storage constructs, and it automatically transforms input data to conform to the data dictionary's requirements.
- It maintains an environment in which security is created and enforced.
- It manages the complex structures created by the multiuser environment.
- It ensures and enforces data integrity at all levels. (We examine specific data-integrity issues later in this chapter.)

In short, the DBMS is what makes the database practical. Given the many and often complex tasks performed by the DBMS, it requires a considerable amount of computing power. Fortunately for us, today's microcomputers have sufficient

Note

A full-blown data dictionary tracks all of the data and database components. This tracking feature is very useful. For example, if you change a data component name, the DBMS will cascade that change throughout the system. Therefore, all parts of the database that use this data component will be updated automatically, too. The Access DBMS is not quite that complete. You will discover later that making even minor changes in one component may require you to make changes in many of the *other* components that access the *changed* component.

random access memory (RAM) and secondary storage capacity to make the DBMS available at the most affordable computing level.

1.2.1 The Relational Database and the Relational Database Management System (RDBMS)

By far the most commonly encountered database today is the relational database. (Access is a relational database.) The **relational database** takes its name from E. F. Codd's work, published in 1970.[2] Dr. Codd's use of the word *relation* stems from the mathematical set theory from which he derived his database model. Too many database professionals believe—incorrectly—that the relational database's name stems from the use of relationships between the database components. Actually, all databases make use of relationships, including the relational database's predecessors, the hierarchical and network database models. In fact, the database professionals who designed and implemented those hierarchical and network databases in the 1970s and 1980s are all too well aware of the difficulties they endured while trying to define the relationships at the physical level!

What made Dr. Codd's relational database model so valuable was that it eliminated the need to specify the very complex physical level constructs that made the hierarchical and network databases so difficult to use and manage. Conceptually, the relational database model lets the users think of data in a simple matrix or table format apparently unfettered by structural storage details. Because Dr. Codd used the table structure as the embodiment of the mathematical set theory's relation, the word *table* is generally used as a synonym for *relation*. In any case the relational database's tables can be linked through the use of commonly held components, thereby implementing relationships that are easy to visualize. We examine the details of the construction and use of such tables in section 1.3.

To render the relational database simple to visualize and use, the **relational database's DBMS,** the **RDBMS,** must handle the creation, use, and management of the relational database's very complex physical details. Therefore, the RDBMS requires much more computing power than the conventional DBMS requires. In fact, when Dr. Codd published his work, the common reaction was that it was nice, but impractical. After all, the available computing power was too limited and too expensive to handle the huge RDBMS overhead. Today's microcomputers handle the RDBMS's requirements without difficulty, illustrating just how far we've come since the 1970s.

1.2.2 Database Types: Production Databases and Decision Support Databases

There are many different kinds of databases, designed to perform different functions. The most commonly encountered database is the production database. The

production database is transaction intensive; that is, frequent and complex transactions characterize its use. A **transaction** is a logical unit of work that reads from or writes to a database. A transaction may either involve a single action or consist of multiple actions. For example, a simple credit sales transaction requires at least three actions: the sale decreases the inventory by the number of units bought; adds the sales amount to the seller's credit sales total; and adds the sales amount to the customer's balance.

You encounter a production database whenever you make a purchase, enroll in a college, or apply for a driver's license. Because the production database is the most common database, we focus our efforts on the design, implementation, applications development, and management of such databases. Therefore, we will make extensive use of a design tool expressly created for the transaction-intensive database. This design tool, known as the entity relationship diagram (ERD), is covered extensively later in this chapter

You should recall that information is processed data. Because information lies at the core of the decision-making process, the increasingly competitive business environment requires more extensive information generation and management capabilities than the production database can offer. Therefore, specialized **decision support system (DSS) databases** focus on the information requirements, rather than on the transaction requirements that characterize production databases. The most common DSS databases are known as data warehouses.[3] As its name implies, the **data warehouse** is primarily a data storage facility dedicated to using the existing data to generate information. The data warehouse and its many variants rely on data extraction and loading, rather than on transactions, to generate the data stored within them. Much of the data warehouse's data is extracted from various production databases. Therefore, the production database's design is important to the data warehouse database, too. After all, if the production database's data are corrupted because of poor design and bad transaction management, the data warehouse's data will reflect this corruption. And the information drawn from such data will be useless.

Data warehouse databases tend to be huge, often expanding into the multiterabyte range. Their end-user interface is dedicated to information generation, so it must be optimized to handle complex queries efficiently and quickly. (A **query** is a question. The answer to a query is designed to yield information. The data warehouse structure can handle very complex queries such as, How do the sales of product X, sold to customers in the Northeast region, compare to the sales of that product in the Southwest and Midwest regions during the third quarters of 2001 and 2002?) Given the query-intensive environment, the design of the DSS DBMS tends to support data modeling and presentation tools, data analysis tools, and query generation and optimization tools. Because there are few transactions to support, data warehouses tend to be characterized by relatively infrequent data updates. When data updates do occur, they usually involve massive data append procedures as data are extracted and loaded from various data sources.

Because DSS databases such as the data warehouse databases do not serve the same purpose as production databases, their structures differ substantially, too. Therefore, the production database's ERD design tool is of limited use in the DSS database environment. Instead, the design of DSS databases usually relies on multidimensional modeling tools to produce structures known as star schemas and their many variants.

In this book we focus our efforts on the production database, using the relational database model. Therefore, the remainder of this book deals with the design, implementation, application development, and management of relational databases. Our focus on the relational model's production databases is appropriate for several reasons:

1. The production database is the most frequently encountered database.
2. The production database serves as the most frequent data source for data warehouses, so the production database's design is critical to the success of either database environment.
3. The data warehouse structure would be difficult to understand without a firm grounding in the database concepts and structures encountered in the production database. Therefore, even if you are primarily interested in the data warehouse, knowing the production database environment is crucial.

In addition, because we want you to see the complete development of a working database, covering both types of databases is impractical in a single book. So from this point forward, when you see the word *database*, think relational database and production database.

1.3 THE INFORMATION SYSTEM

Because information is such a crucial component of the decision-making process, its generation, use, and management require a carefully structured environment. This environment is created in an information system. This system requires the components shown in Figure 1.2. Note that an information system requires people, hardware, and software.

The database is the foundation for the information system in Figure 1.2. Because the database is indispensable to the proper functioning of the information system, this book is dedicated to the proper design and implementation of the database.

1.4 DATABASE BUILDING BLOCKS: ENTITIES, ENTITY SETS, AND ATTRIBUTES

Databases store data about entities and their attributes. An **entity** may be a person, place, thing, event, or even a concept. It may be tangible, or it may be intangible. In short, an entity can be anything you want to keep track of. In a business environment you are most likely to encounter entities such as employees, invoices, departments, customers, products, and vendors. For example, Jeanine B. Cahill and George R. Cachenko are EMPLOYEE entities. A Vegematic food processor, priced at $39.95, and a GE electric can opener, priced at $24.99, are PRODUCT entities. The Good Stuff company, located at 125 East Windham Road

FIGURE 1.2
The Information System

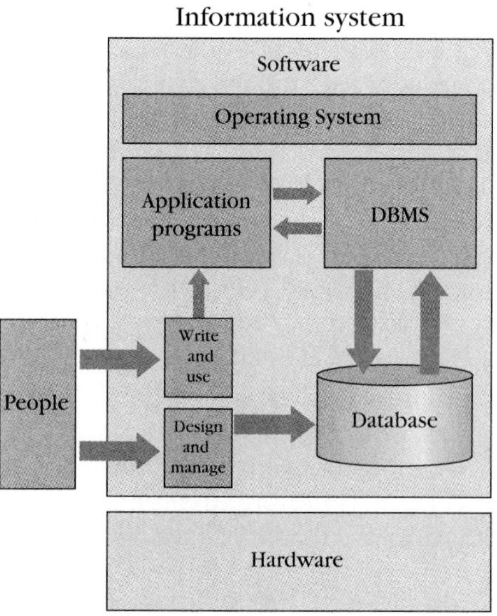

FIGURE 1.3 Five EMPLOYEE Entities and Their Attributes

EMP_NUM	EMP_LNAME	EMP_FNAME	EMP_INITIAL	EMP_ADDRESS	EMP_PHONE	DIV_CODE	DEPT_CODE	EMP_EMAIL
504	Graham	Georgette	E	1234 Trident Lane, Eaton, MA 12345	234-234-6789	G5	ACTG	GEG4@gge.com
506	Smith	Alex		4321 Hill Drive, Dalton, GA 23456	123-456-7890	E2	MKTG	AlexS3@tds.com
507	Thieu	Robert	E	5678 Crescent Lane, Dalton, GA 2345(	123-457-1123	E2	ACCT	RobET1@tds.com
510	Chen	Alice	L	3456 Lake Drive, Nashville, TN 37654	456-333-9876	B3	INFO	AChen1@gge.com
512	Alazar	George	D	2345 Oak Drive, Nashville, TN 33123	456-456-7654	B3	INFO	GDA8@tds.com
0								

in Memphis, Tennessee, is a VENDOR entity. The summary of a sales transaction is an INVOICE entity.

An **entity set** is a named collection of related data. The data within an entity set are related through their classification. For example, the data in an EMPLOYEE entity set are related by the fact that only employee data are stored in this set. In other words, the EMPLOYEE entity set contains a collection of EMPLOYEE entities. You should not expect to find product entities in an EMPLOYEE entity set.

Each entity has characteristics known as **attributes.** For example, a STORE entity is likely to have attributes such as a store identification code, a store name, a store location, and so on. Similarly, an EMPLOYEE entity is likely to have an employee first name, an employee initial, an employee last name, an employee address, and an employee home phone number as its attributes. And a PRODUCT entity is likely to have attributes such as product code, product name, product minimum quantity on hand, product reorder quantity, product current quantity on hand, and product price. Figure 1.3 shows a screen capture of an EMPLOYEE entity set containing five EMPLOYEE entities and their attributes. These attributes are employee number, employee first name, employee initial, employee last name, employee home address, employee home phone number, employee company division, employee department, and employee e-mail address. You'll discover later why some of these attributes lack desirable database qualities. (Incidentally, note that the e-mail address is a hyperlink, indicated by the pointing finger that is displayed whenever you place the cursor over any hyperlink. Chapter 4 explains that Access enables you to declare a hyperlink data type.)

1.5 DATABASE TABLES AND THEIR COMPONENTS

Entities are stored in a database table. So for all practical purposes, a database table is the equivalent of an entity set. Conceptually, a database **table** is a matrix composed of intersecting rows and columns. The table columns and rows must have these characteristics:

- Each column is named for an attribute and contains the attribute values for the attribute it represents. For example, a column named EMP_NUM must contain only employee number values, whereas a column named EMP_PHONE must only contain employee phone number values.
- Each row, also known as a **tuple,** is uniquely identified by an attribute known as a **primary key (PK).** For example, an employee number or a Social Security number might uniquely identify an employee. Because a vehicle identification number (VIN) uniquely identifies each automobile, the VIN is a proper PK.

1.5.1 Composite Primary Keys

A PK may be a single attribute or may be composed of a combination of attributes. A PK that consists of a combination of attributes is known as a **composite primary key.** For example, Figure 1.4 shows an invoice line table in which the PK

FIGURE 1.4
A Sample Invoice LINE Table

Table name: LINE

	INV_NUM	LINE_NUM	PROD_CODE	LINE_UNITS	LINE_PRICE	LINE_AMOUNT
▶	100541	1	SME-123456	8	$10.05	$80.40
	100541	2	FRT-765432	1	$6.50	$6.50
	100542	1	DFR-345678	1	$24.95	$24.95
	100543	1	SME-123456	4	$10.05	$40.20
	100543	2	DFR-345678	1	$24.95	$24.95
	100543	3	GRD-998877	4	$6.50	$26.00
*	0	0		0	$0.00	$0.00

is the combination of the invoice number (INV_NUM) and the line number (LINE_NUM). This combination is required because an invoice may list many products, each appearing on a separate invoice line. For instance, note that INV_NUM = 100541 occurs twice, and INV_NUM = 100543 occurs three times. Therefore, the invoice number alone does not uniquely identify each row. But the combination of INV_NUM = 100541 and LINE_NUM = 1 occurs only once.

1.5.2 Candidate Keys

As you examine Figure 1.4, you may note that the combination of INV_NUM and PROD_CODE also uniquely identifies each row. Therefore, although we designated the combination of INV_NUM and LINE_NUM to be the PK, the combination INV_NUM and PROD_CODE might also be used as a PK. If any attribute or combination of attributes that could serve the role as PK is not selected to be the PK, that attribute or combination of attributes is known as a **candidate key.** (You will learn later in this chapter why we created the LINE_NUM attribute to become part of the PK.)

To designate a proper PK, you must use the minimum number of attributes to do the job of uniquely identifying each row. Therefore, although the combination of INV_NUM, LINE_NUM, and PROD_CODE uniquely identifies each row, this combination of attributes is not a proper PK. That's because the combination of INV_NUM and LINE_NUM is sufficient to identify each row uniquely, thus making the PROD_CODE redundant as a PK component. (You will discover later in this chapter what the role of the PROD_CODE attribute is and why it was included in the invoice line table.) *In any case a PK must never contain redundant attributes.*

1.5.3 Secondary Keys

Finding a specific row (record) in a database table is easy—if you know the PK value. However, if you don't know the PK value, some other attribute or combination of attributes may be used to find what you are looking for. Using the EMPLOYEE table in Figure 1.3 as an example, if you don't know that Mr. George Alazar's employee number is 512, you can still find the record by using the combination of the last name and the first name. This kind of non-PK search key is known as a **secondary key.**

Keep in mind that secondary keys do not necessarily yield unique matches. For example, suppose that you have three employees named John Smith in your EMPLOYEE table. A secondary key composed of the employee last and first names will yield three records in this case. However, if all three records are displayed on your computer screen, it's easy to find the specific record by asking, Are you the John Smith whose phone number is . . . ? or by asking additional questions that will let you select the appropriate record.

Secondary keys are especially handy when you are searching large database tables without knowing the appropriate PK values. For example, suppose you are trying to find the record of a customer who does not know his or her customer number. Fortunately, that customer is likely to know his or her last name, first name, and ZIP code, so you can use that combination as a secondary key.

Note

Microsoft Access uses the old file terminology to identify table rows and columns. For example, it identifies table rows as **records.** Therefore, the LINE table in Figure 1.4 contains six records, and the EMPLOYEE table in Figure 1.3 contains five records.

Microsoft Access identifies the columns (attributes) as **fields.** Therefore, the LINE table in Figure 1.4 has six fields, and the EMPLOYEE table in Figure 1.3 has nine fields.

Naturally, the more attributes you include in the secondary key, the more likely you are to find the relevant records. However, adding attributes to the secondary key slows down the computer's search process. Therefore, try to use a secondary key that contains as few attributes as possible. From a computer resource use point of view, it may be better to use a minimal secondary key to get three or four records on your screen than to use a huge secondary key that finds an exact match.

1.5.4 Foreign Keys

The relationship between the tables is established through the use of foreign keys. The **foreign key (FK)** in one table is an attribute that matches the PK in the table to which it points. The role and nature of PKs and FKs are most easily understood by examining the two database tables in Figure 1.5.

As you examine Figure 1.5, note that

- The PKs of the STORE and REGION tables are, respectively, STORE_CODE and REGION_CODE. The STORE table's records are all uniquely identified by the STORE_CODE attribute values. The REGION table's records are all uniquely identified by the REGION_CODE attribute values.
- The STORE table's FK is the REGION_CODE that points to the REGION table. We are thus able to establish that the Nanosecond, ANSI, and OLE stores are located in the East region.
- All STORE REGION_CODE FK values reference existing REGION_CODE PK values in the REGION table.

1.6 ENTITY INTEGRITY AND REFERENTIAL INTEGRITY

If all the rows of a database table are uniquely identified, the table is said to display **entity integrity.** To identify each row uniquely, a table's PK values must all

FIGURE 1.5
Table Components

Table name: STORE

STORE_CODE	STORE_NAME	REGION_CODE
1	Megabyte	2
2	Nanosecond	1
3	EISA Bus	2
4	Kilobyte	2
5	Baud Rate	4
6	ASCII Code	4
7	ANSI	1
8	Byte by Byte	3
9	Bit by Bit	4
10	URL	2
11	IDE	4
12	OLE	1
(AutoNumber)		0

Table name: REGION

REGION_CODE	REGION_NAME
1	East
2	West
3	North
4	South
(AutoNumber)	

Note

The (AutoNumber) designation at the bottom of each table reflects the Access way of indicating the data type for the next record to be created. As its name suggests, the AutoNumber data type automatically generates a new STORE_CODE value each time a new STORE record is created.

be unique. In Figure 1.5 each of the STORE table's PK values is unique, so the STORE table exhibits entity integrity. And because the REGION table's PK values are all unique, the REGION table also exhibits entity integrity. You will discover in Chapter 4 that Microsoft Access automatically enforces entity integrity when you declare a PK.

Because a PK must have a unique value, it can never be null. (A **null** is created by making no entry at all, so a null denotes the *absence* of a value. *A null is not a blank*, because a blank, generated by tapping the space bar, has an ASCII value.) The problem with nulls is that a null can have any of the following meanings:

- The value does not exist.
- The value exists, but it is not known.
- The value is not applicable.
- The value is unknown, or it is not applicable.

In short, because nulls can have many meanings, they cannot occur in a PK. You will discover in Chapter 4 that the Access RDBMS does not permit you to use a null as a PK "value."

Proper FK values in one table must either match PK values in the related table or must be null. If a table's FK values meet the "match or null" requirements, they are said to exhibit **referential integrity.** Referential integrity ensures that it will be impossible to point to PK values that do not exist. You will discover in Chapter 4 that Microsoft Access allows you to specify the enforcement of referential integrity when you create the relationships between the tables.

1.7 PUTTING IT ALL TOGETHER IN A SMALL DATABASE

Now that you know what PKs and FKs are, let's take a look at how they fit into the wider database picture by creating the small database shown in Figure 1.6. As you examine the database's table contents, note that the database enables you to track the customer purchasing activities.

Tracking the sales transactions shown in Figure 1.6 requires you to follow the route pointed out by the FKs. For example, to track Ms. Chasteen's sales transactions, trace these steps:

1. Look at the CUSTOMER table and note that Ms. Chasteen's customer number is 112. A sales transaction is recorded in the INVOICE.
2. Look for the CUS_NUM = 112 in the INVOICE table. Note that this value occurs twice: once for INV_NUM = 100541 on INV_DATE = 11-Jun-2002, for a total of $93.85, and once for INV_NUM = 100543 on INV_DATE 12-Jun-2002, for a total of $98.44. Both invoices were paid in full. Each invoice contains invoice lines, one for each product purchased.
3. Move to the LINE table and look for the INV_NUM values 100541 and 100543. Note that INV_NUM = 100541 occurs twice in the LINE table, indicating that two products, PROD_CODE = SME-123456 and PROD_CODE = FRT-765432, were recorded on the invoice, one per invoice line. The INV_NUM value 100543 occurs three times in the LINE table, indicating that three products,

Note

Although the definition of referential integrity accepts nulls as a valid foreign key "value," you will discover that nulls create many problems when you run certain types of queries or when you try to establish relationships between entities. Therefore, we advise you to avoid nulls to the greatest extent possible. There are, of course, some (rare) situations in which a null is acceptable. For example, some people do not use a middle initial in their names. Therefore, a middle initial null "value" is quite appropriate. (It is unlikely that a person's middle initial will ever be used as part of a foreign key.)

FIGURE 1.6
A Small Invoicing System

Table name: CUSTOMER

CUS_NUM	CUS_LNAME	CUS_FNAME	CUS_INITIAL	CUS_ADDRESS	CUS_CITY
112	Chasteen	Anne	R	1234 Rose Lane	Murfreesboro
114	Williamson	Kirby	T	2345 Grove Street	Nashville
115	Quahtoty	hrman		3456 Waterford Rd.	Nashville
118	Smith	Mary	M	4567 Oleander Blvd.	Owensboro
122	Taylor	Christopher	F	5678 Treeline Rd.	Murfreesboro
123	Trevors	Anne	K	6789 Sweetwater Dr.	Louisville
0					

CUSTOMER table, continued

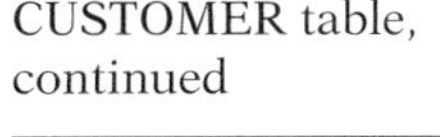

CUS_STATE	CUS_ZIP	CUS_AREACODE	CUS_PHONE	CUS_BALANCE
TN	37130	615	123-2345	$0.00
TN	32001	615	234-5678	$235.68
TN	32008	615	239-9876	$415.53
KY	38345	652	456-6543	$376.97
TN	37130	615	238-3344	$0.00
KY	39932	654	654-9001	$300.22
				$0.00

Table name: INVOICE

INV_NUM	INV_DATE	CUS_NUM	INV_SUBTOTAL	INV_TAX	INV_TOTAL	INV_PAYMENT	INV_BALANCE
100541	11-Jun-2002	112	$86.90	$6.95	$93.85	$93.85	$0.00
100542	11-Jun-2002	122	$24.95	$2.00	$26.95	$26.95	$0.00
100543	12-Jun-2002	112	$91.15	$7.29	$98.44	$98.44	$0.00
0		0	$0.00	$0.00	$0.00	$0.00	$0.00

Table name: LINE

INV_NUM	LINE_NUM	PROD_CODE	LINE_UNITS	LINE_PRICE	LINE_AMOUNT
100541	1	SME-123456	8	$10.05	$80.40
100541	2	FRT-765432	1	$6.50	$6.50
100542	1	DFR-345678	1	$24.95	$24.95
100543	1	SME-123456	4	$10.05	$40.20
100543	2	DFR-345678	1	$24.95	$24.95
100543	3	GRD-998877	4	$6.50	$26.00
0	0		0	$0.00	$0.00

Table name: PRODUCT

PROD_CODE	PROD_DESCRIPTION	PROD_COST	PROD_PRICE	PROD_QOH	PROD_MIN_QUANT
DDE-876543	Torque wrench & socket set	$15.40	$21.05	67	50
DFR-345678	Cordless drill, 1/4-in. chuck	$18.00	$24.95	23	15
FRT-765432	Pipe wrench, adjustable head	$3.85	$6.50	44	35
GRD-998877	Screwdriver, ratchet head	$3.52	$6.50	61	40
KLG-325421	8-in. saw blade, carbide tips	$8.19	$14.45	32	25
SME-123456	16-in. chain saw bar	$5.95	$10.05	49	30
		$0.00	$0.00	0	0

Assignment

Give a full description of the sales transaction recorded in the INVOICE table for invoice number 100542

PROD_CODE = SME-123456, PROD_CODE = DFR-345678, and PROD_CODE =GRD-998877, were recorded on the invoice.

4. Go to the PRODUCT table and note that PROD_CODE = SME-123456 matches a 16-inch chain saw bar and that PROD_CODE = FRT-765432 matches a pipe wrench with an adjustable head. By tracking the FK values in the various tables, you now know that Ms. Chasteen bought eight 16-inch chain saw bars for $80.40 and one pipe wrench with an adjustable head for $6.50 on 11-Jun-2002. You also know that she paid $6.95 in sales taxes and that she paid the $93.85 total in full. You can track the three product purchases made on 12-Jun-2002, the same way.

As you examine the database in Figure 1.6, note that the database meets both entity and referential integrity requirements.

1. All entities (table rows) are uniquely identified by their PK values, thus preserving entity integrity.
2. All FK values match existing PK values, thus preserving referential integrity. Note, for example, that
   a. The INVOICE table's CUS_NUM values match existing CUS_NUM values in the CUSTOMER table.
   b. The LINE table's PROD_CODE values match existing PROD_CODE values in the PRODUCT table.
   c. The LINE table's INV_NUM values match existing INV_NUM values in the INVOICE table.

1.7.1 Data Inclusion: Historical Accuracy Requirements

The small database in Figure 1.6 allows you to make some very important preliminary observations and judgments. For example, you may think that storing the item prices in the LINE table is unnecessary. After all, isn't the item price already stored in the PRODUCT table? Actually, there is an excellent reason for copying the item price from the PRODUCT table into the LINE table when the invoice line is generated at the time of the sale. To keep the sales transaction record historically accurate, *the sales price must be the one that was current when the sale was made*. Suppose, for example, that we fail to store the item price in the LINE table when the sale is made and the item price is later changed in the PRODUCT table. This price-change scenario demonstrates that we will no longer be able to retrieve the historically accurate sales price by looking at the price currently stored in the PRODUCT table. Therefore, if you don't store the product price in the LINE table at the time of the purchase, you will lose crucial information. In short, the LINE_PRICE and the PROD_PRICE are only equal at the time of the actual sale, and they will be quite different when the PROD_PRICE is changed sometime in the future.

Historical accuracy is also the argument for storing the derived attribute INV_TAX amount in the INVOICE table. If the tax percentage is changed at some later date, the tax charged at the time of the sale must remain what it was at the time of the sale. If you fail to include the tax amount in the INVOICE, you may not be able to get an accurate accounting of the collected taxes later.

1.7.2 Data Inclusion: Evaluation of Derived Attributes

Some database professionals insist that attributes whose values can be computed from existing attribute values should not be stored in a database table. However, practical considerations often require the storage of such computed attributes, known as **derived attributes.** For example, the decision to store the derived variables INV_SUBTOTAL and INV_TOTAL is easily defended by noting that query speed is enhanced by not having to compute these values from the LINE table at the time of report generation. If a large department store's invoice lines must be totaled each time a sales report is to be generated, it may take quite a bit of time to recalculate the amounts when there are millions of LINE records. In addition, the query construction is much simpler when the totals are already available in the INVOICE table. Designers of real-world information management systems are always making decisions that involve trade-offs among transaction/retrieval speeds, design elegance, and simplicity.

1.7.3 Data Inclusion: Line Numbers

Why use the "artificial" attribute LINE_NUM in the LINE table of Figure 1.6? After all, the combination of INV_NUM and PROD_CODE will make a fine PK, so the LINE_NUM seems redundant. While this argument is valid, it overlooks two important practical considerations.

- Suppose you used the composite PK based on INV_NUM and PROD_CODE. Now suppose that you made the partial LINE table entries shown in Figure 1.7. (To keep the example as simple as possible, we have shown only the composite PK entries. Also, you may assume that we've used PROD_CODE values that reflect corresponding new entries in the PRODUCT table, thus preserving referential integrity.)
- The entries in Figure 1.7 are proper, and the PK based on these entries shows that the entity integrity requirement is met. But suppose you are talking to a customer who has a question about the third line in invoice number 100879. You pull the invoice information onto the computer screen, producing the output shown in Figure 1.8.
- Remember, the customer is looking at the third invoice line in Figure 1.7 in which product AAA-32456 appears. You are looking at the third invoice line in Figure 1.8 in which the product DDD-21334 shows up. *Although both lines are correct, they are not shown in the same sequence.* What happened? What happened is that the DBMS will index any attribute that participates in the PK. Therefore, the indexed order is different from the order in which the customer made the purchases—which is the order in which the invoice was originally printed. Sure, you'll eventually get back in tune with the customer, but you have wasted time, and you may have made a customer unhappy. By using the "artificial" LINE_NUM attribute in Figure 1.9, you make sure that the order in which the products were input and the order in which they are output will always be the same.

FIGURE 1.7
Partial LINE Table Input

	INV_NUM	PROD_CODE
▶	100879	ZZZ-32453
	100879	DDD-21334
	100879	AAA-32456
	100879	EEE-43234
	100879	EEE-12345
	100879	AAA-12311
	100879	LLL-38976
*	0	

FIGURE 1.8
Partial LINE Table Output

	INV_NUM	PROD_CODE
▶	100879	AAA-12311
	100879	AAA-32456
	100879	DDD-21334
	100879	EEE-12345
	100879	EEE-43234
	100879	LLL-38976
	100879	ZZZ-32453
*	0	

FIGURE 1.9
Partial LINE Table Input That Will Match the Output

	INV_NUM	LINE_NUM	PROD_CODE
▶	100879	1	ZZZ-32453
	100879	2	DDD-21334
	100879	3	AAA-32456
	100879	4	EEE-43234
	100879	5	EEE-12345
	100879	6	AAA-12311
	100879	7	LLL-38976
*	0	0	

• The second reason for using the LINE_NUM attribute in the LINE table also has to do with indexing. Because the LINE_NUM values include fewer characters than the PROD_CODE values, indexing the LINE_NUM values takes less time than indexing the PROD_CODE values. When you are talking about large tables, indexing and re-indexing speeds become important. Remember, transaction speed is one of the database design objectives.

1.8 DOCUMENTATION: SELECTING AND NAMING THE ATTRIBUTES

We store data in database tables because, sooner or later, we want to generate information from such data. Clearly, to get a well-rounded picture of the entities within each entity set, we need to select a sufficient number of useful attributes for each entity set. For example, if you intend to create a company phone directory for your employees, surely you will include the employee names and phone numbers in the EMPLOYEE table. Similarly, if you intend to keep track of each product's price, minimum quantity on hand, and actual quantity on hand, you must include those attributes in a PRODUCT table. In short, the selection of appropriate attributes is important and you must spend considerable time thinking about the information needs that each database table satisfies.

When you start implementing database designs, and particularly when you begin developing the database's end-user applications, you will discover that documentation is crucial. Basically, documentation is a process that yields a precise definition and description of the database's components and the relationships between those components. In other words, good documentation produces a map by which you can navigate through the system. Therefore, good documentation facilitates system maintenance and modification. In contrast, lack of proper documentation hampers system maintenance and modifications.

One of the important ingredients in successful documentation involves the use of self-explanatory names for all system components. At this point we have focused on entities and their attributes. You should recall that entities are stored in entity sets. In the relational database environment, tables store the entity sets, so it is useful to establish naming conventions that readily identify the database tables. In turn, the attributes (fields) associated with those tables should be named to identify both their function and their location. We have found the following naming conventions very useful in our database work:

• The tables that contain the entity sets are named after the entities they contain. Table names are singular, and they are capitalized. For example, a table named STUDENT contains student entities. Similarly, a table named INVOICE contains invoice entities, a table named PRODUCT contains product entities, and so on. Under this naming convention we know that a table named CUSTOMER contains customer entities. The table names describe their contents. Naming a table CFWQUT is not a good idea, because few people can figure out what that table is likely to contain. (Note that table names are all nouns.)

• Table column (attribute) names consist of two parts. The first part (that is, the prefix) identifies the table, and the second part identifies the attribute (field) stored in that column. Although the names must be descriptive, they must be as short as practical. Very long attribute labels affect output spacing and, when Access tables are exported to other DBMSs, very long attribute labels are likely to be truncated. Therefore, the attribute name REGION_YEAR_TO_DATE_SALES is probably less desirable than REG_YTD_SALES. Given the label length constraint, an attribute name's prefix ought to be limited to three to six characters, and the attribute name's second part should be abbreviated, too. Again, the key to success is using sufficiently descriptive labels. Attribute names (that is, table column names or "fields") are also singular and capitalized. For example, the following attribute names meet the naming standards:

EMP_LNAME = employee last name, stored in the EMPLOYEE table.
EMP_DOB = employee date of birth, stored in the EMPLOYEE table.
EMP_YTD_FICA = year-to-date FICA taxes paid, stored in the EMPLOYEE table.
REG_YTD_SALES = year-to-date sales, stored in the REGION table.
STU_GPA = student grade point average, stored in the STUDENT table.
PROD_CODE = product code, stored in the PRODUCT table.
CUST_LNAME = customer last name, stored in the CUSTOMER table.
INV_NUM = invoice number, stored in the INVOICE table.
VEND_NUM = vendor number, stored in the VENDOR table.

The sample database shown in Figure 1.6 adheres to these naming conventions. For example, the prefix CUS indicates attributes "native" to the CUSTOMER table. Similarly, the prefix INV indicates the INVOICE table attributes, the prefix LINE indicates the LINE table attributes, and the prefix PROD indicates the PRODUCT table attributes. This convention enables us to produce very useful self-documentation:

- The attribute (field) name CUS_LNAME can easily be identified as being located in the CUSTOMER table and storing the customer's last name.
- All field names that use INV as a prefix are native to the INVOICE table. Therefore, if you encounter the field name CUS_NUM in the INVOICE table, you will know immediately that its CUS prefix does not "belong" to the INVOICE table. Therefore, the INVOICE table's CUS_NUM field must be a FK that must point to the CUS_NUM PK in the CUSTOMER table.

Given our naming convention, *an attribute name whose prefix is not clearly related to the name of the table in which it is located will always be a FK.* Therefore, you can determine a table's FK just by looking at its attribute names. For example, if you examine Figure 1.6 again, you will see that all attributes that belong to the LINE table carry the LINE prefix. Therefore, the PROD_CODE in the INV_LINE table is clearly the FK to the PRODUCT table, while the INV_NUM in the LINE table is the FK to the INVOICE table.

Keep in mind that labels that are considered sufficiently descriptive in some organizations may appear exotic to those who are unfamiliar with the standard technical abbreviations those organizations use. Database designers simply must become familiar with the technical and specialized vocabularies used within the organizations for which they design the databases. For example, if you produce a database design for an aviation-oriented organization, you will encounter abbreviations such as TTAE, which stands for "total time, airframe and engine," TTAF, which stands for "total time on the airframe," and TTEL, which stands for "total time on the left engine." Similarly, AC is the standard abbreviation for aircraft. Therefore, the attribute name AC_TTEL clearly describes the aircraft's total left-engine time, stored in the AIRCRAFT table.

1.9 ATTRIBUTE CHARACTERISTICS

Selecting and naming attributes is an important aspect of the database design process, especially when the design is to be implemented. However, the attribute *characteristics* are crucial to the successful use of the database. To make it easier to draw information from the database, the attributes should, to the greatest practical extent possible, be *simple* and *single valued.*

1.9.1 Simple (Atomic) and Composite Attributes

A **simple** or **atomic attribute** is one that cannot be further divisible into its components. For example, an employee's gender is a simple attribute because it cannot be further subdivided into meaningful components. In contrast, an employee attribute name such as EMP_NAME is not simple, because the name can be further subdivided into a first name, an initial, and a last name. An attribute that can be further subdivided is known as a **composite attribute.**

It is generally a good practice to use simple attributes. Just think of how difficult it would be to create an employee telephone directory if we stored the employee names in the composite EMP_NAME attribute. By splitting the EMP_NAME into its components, EMP_LNAME, EMP_FNAME, and EMP_INITIAL, creating a telephone directory would become much easier. Similarly, it would be useful to separate the telephone area code from the phone number itself. Thus, it would probably be a good idea to use EMP_AREACODE and EMP_PHONE as two separate attributes.

On the other hand, how useful would it be to further subdivide the phone number 123-4567 into its prefix (123) and extension (4567)? Let the extent of atomism be determined by the information requirements and a bit of common sense. Therefore, if you have a reason for separating employees by prefix, go ahead and separate the telephone number's prefix and the extension. If there is no requirement to do so, leave the prefix and the extension as a single attribute. In short, use atomic attributes to the greatest practical extent possible.

1.9.2 Single-Valued and Multivalued Attributes

As the label "single valued" implies, a **single-valued attribute** can have only one value. For example, you have only one first name, only one birth date, and only one Social Security number. On the other hand, an employee can have many degrees, so EMP_DEGREE is a **multivalued attribute.**

Good database designs generally ensure that single-valued attributes are stored in the database tables. Unfortunately, there are several bad ways of converting multivalued attributes into single-valued attributes. For example, we could put all of the possible multivalued attribute values into a single string. Thus the EMP_DEGREE attribute might contain such strings as shown in Figure 1.10. (Note that employees 459 and 460 do not have degrees.)

To get only the employees with BS degrees out of Figure 1.10, you would have to do a complex string search, so the string storage shown in Figure 1.10 is not desirable. On the other hand, the listing in Figure 1.10 is a better solution than the listing in Figure 1.11, in which multiple simple attributes store the possible multivalued attribute outcomes.

The "solution" in Figure 1.11 yields a really bad situation:

- The proliferation of nulls, that is, no values at all, is undesirable. Nulls, you should recall from section 1.6.3, can mean many things. For example, a null in Figure 1.11 can mean that the employee has no degree; the employee has a degree, but the specific degree is not known; we don't know whether the employee has a degree; and so on.
- The use of multiple attributes to handle multivalued attributes produces flexibility problems. What, for example, will happen if an employee earns a fifth degree? We are now faced with a problem: Either we ignore the possibility that employees can earn more than four degrees, and therefore we lose information,

FIGURE 1.10
Handling Multivalued Attributes through Strings

	EMP_NUM	EMP_LNAME	EMP_FNAME	EMP_INITIAL	EMP_DEGREE
▶	458	Renselaer	Randolph	D	BA
	459	Freeman	William	H	
	460	Hartog	Susanne	M	
	462	Appleton	Anne	M	BBA, MBA, MFA
	463	Randall	Herman	A	BE
	464	Hernandez	Olanzo	R	BS, MS, MBA, Ph.D.
	465	Oszwicki	James	P	BS, MS
*	0				

FIGURE 1.11 **Handling Multivalued Attributes through Multiple Attributes**

	EMP_NUM	EMP_LNAME	EMP_FNAME	EMP_INITIAL	EMP_DEGREE1	EMP_DEGREE2	EMP_DEGREE3	EMP_DEGREE4
▶	458	Renselaer	Randolph	D	BA			
	459	Freeman	William	H				
	460	Hartog	Susanne	M				
	462	Appleton	Anne	M	BBA	MBA	MFA	
	463	Randall	Herman	A	BE			
	464	Hernandez	Olanzo	R	BS	MS	MBA	Ph.D.
	465	Oszwicki	James	P	BS	MS		
*	0							

or we add yet another attribute, EMP_DEGREE5, which produces yet another set of nulls for the remaining employees.

We can solve the dilemma created by the use of multivalued attributes by taking these actions:

- Move the EMPLOYEE table's degree attributes, EMP_DEGREE1 through EMP_DEGREE4, into a separate DEGREE table in which each degree has its own record.
- Create a new table, EDUCATION, that links the two tables, EMPLOYEE and DEGREE, through its FKs. Such a linking, or bridging, table is known as a **composite table** or a **bridge table.** (It is called a "composite" table because it contains components from the other two tables.) This composite table may also include additional attributes, such as the institution from which the degree was earned and the data on which the degree was earned.

The process that leads to the use of a composite table is best illustrated through the example in Figure 1.12.

As you examine the three tables in Figure 1.12, note the following features:

- The composite table's PK is the combination of the PKs of the tables to which it points. (Remember, a PK must identify each record uniquely. Taken individually, neither the EDUCATION table's EMP_NUM nor its DEGREE_CODE do the job. However, the combination of EMP_NUM and DEGREE_CODE yields

FIGURE 1.12 **Creating a Composite Table**

Database name: CH1_EMPEDUC

Table name: EMPLOYEE

	EMP_NUM	EMP_LNAME	EMP_FNAME	EMP_INITIAL
▶	458	Renselaer	Randolph	D
	459	Freeman	William	H
	460	Hartog	Susanne	M
	462	Appleton	Anne	M
	463	Randall	Herman	A
	464	Hernandez	Olanzo	R
	465	Oszwicki	James	P
*	0			

Table name: EDUCATION

	EMP_NUM	DEGREE_CODE	EDUC_EARNED	EDUC_INSTITUTION
▶	458	BA	1993	U. of Kentucky
	462	BBA	1985	U. of Massachussetts
	462	MBA	1989	UCLA
	462	MFA	1996	U. of Memphis
	463	BA	1992	U. of Florida
	464	BS	1981	Florida State University
	464	MBA	1991	Penn Sate University
	464	MS	1986	Penn State University
	464	Ph.D.	1999	Michigan State University
	465	BS	1985	Cal Tech
	465	MS	1986	Cal Tech
*	0			

Table name: DEGREE

	DEGREE_CODE	DEGREE_NAME
▶	BA	Bachelor of Arts
	BBA	Bachelor of Business Administration
	BS	Bachelor of Science
	MBA	Master of Business Administration
	MFA	Master of Fine Arts
	MS	Master of Science
	Ph.D.	Doctor of Philosophy
*		

Note

The order in which data entries are made is crucial. For example, suppose that an employee has earned a master of education degree, which is not currently listed in the DEGREE table in Figure 1.12. If the degree code and name are not first entered into the DEGREE table, an entry in the EDUCATION table that references such a degree will yield a referential integrity error. In short, if you are going to reference a degree, make sure it exists in the DEGREE table!

unique outcomes.) Any PK based on a combination of attributes is known as a **composite PK.** In this case, the composite EDUCATION table's composite PK is EMP_NUM 1 DEGREE_CODE.

- Each PK component in the EDUCATION table is an FK that points to a table. For example, EMP_NUM points to the EMPLOYEE table, and DEGREE_CODE points to the DEGREE table.
- The number of tables it connects through its FKs defines the composite table's minimum number of attributes. Because our composite table connects two tables, it must have a minimum of two attributes.
- In addition to the minimum number of attributes required to define its PK, a composite table allows you to also keep track of as many other attributes as you like. For example, Figure 1.12 illustrates that we can even keep track of when each degree was earned and from what institution it was earned.
- Employees 459 and 460 do not have degrees, so they do not occur in the EDUCATION table.

The use of the composite EDUCATION table has eliminated all the problems associated with multivalued attributes. We have eliminated the nulls, and we have made it easy to draw information from the tables. In addition, the use of a composite table has introduced unlimited flexibility. For example, if employees earn additional degrees, all we need to do is enter additional records in the EDUCATION table. And if employees earn additional degrees that are not currently stored in the DEGREE table, all we need to do is enter such degrees in the DEGREE table and then make the entry in the EDUCATION table to indicate that the employee has earned this new degree. Finally, the EDUCATION table can easily be modified to give us the flexibility to store additional information about the degree: when it was earned, from which institution it was earned, and so on.

We have just shown you how to avoid nulls through the use of composite tables. However, you cannot always easily or even reasonably avoid nulls. For example, some customers do not have a middle initial, so CUS_INITIAL may be a null. A customer may not (yet) have an e-mail address, so CUS_EMAIL may be null. A driver who has not yet returned from a trip cannot have signed in, so the DRIVER_RETURN may be null. In each of these cases, null avoidance is easily accomplished through so-called **dummy variable values.** (A dummy variable value is one that has no operational meaning. For example, to indicate that a customer does not yet have an e-mail address, that customer's CUS_EMAIL value may be set to "No E-mail Address." Trying to send e-mail to that "address" demonstrates that it has no operational meaning!) However, keep in mind that some "null avoidance" techniques may not be practical when the desire to eliminate nulls becomes extreme. For example, is it really reasonable to use a 9 to indicate "no middle initial" for the CUS_INITIAL attribute? Besides, as you begin the database design process, you will discover that there are instances in which the desire to avoid nulls greatly adds to the complexity of the database design. Database professionals must exercise professional judgment.

1.10 RELATIONSHIP TYPES

Figure 1.12 shows three database tables that are related through the use of FKs. Before we can properly design databases, we must know what relationship types exist. Database designers encounter three relationship types: one-to-one, one-to-many, and many-to-many, usually expressed as 1:1, 1:M, and M:N.

The next few subsections explain what these relationships are and what they look like at the table level. Actually, you have already seen 1:M and M:N relationships. But you must now learn how to recognize them and how to fit them into the database picture. You will also learn how these relationship types may be further classified as optional or mandatory, weak or strong. And you will be introduced to recursive relationships.

1.10.1 The 1:1 Relationship

As its name implies, the 1:1 relationship indicates that one entity is related to only one other entity. For example, at least in the United States, one spouse can be related to only one other spouse. Although 1:1 relationships are rare and are often caused by a misidentification of an attribute as an entity, they can serve a very useful purpose. For example, suppose that you are designing a database for an airline. When you take a look at the airline's EMPLOYEE entity, you discover that there are many different kinds of employees and some, such as pilots, have many characteristics not shared by other employees. For instance, pilots have special licenses, medical requirements, and training requirements. Therefore, if we store the pilot attributes in the EMPLOYEE table, we will introduce many nulls for the many employees who are not pilots. (See Figure 1.13.)

On the other hand, pilots have many attributes, such as names and addresses, in common with other attributes. Therefore, we should not create a special employee table for pilots because that action will create common employee data (names, addresses, and so on) in different locations. The solution is to store the unique attributes in one table and then to link this table to the one that contains the common attributes. Because both tables refer to attributes for the same pilot, the two tables are related in a 1:1 relationship as shown in Figure 1.14. (Each PILOT table entry is related to one and only one EMPLOYEE table entry.)

As you examine the tables in Figure 1.14, note the following features:

- Both tables use the EMP_NUM as the PK.
- The PILOT table's PK is also the FK to the EMPLOYEE table.
- Neither table contains nulls.

The 1:1 relationship shown in Figure 1.14 is also known as a **supertype/subtype relationship.** The **supertype** contains the entity's common (shared) attributes. Because the EMPLOYEE table contains the common (shared) EMP_LNAME attribute, the EMPLOYEE table represents the supertype. (All employees have a last name; therefore, EMP_LNAME is an attribute that is shared by all employees.) The **subtype** is the entity that contains the attributes that are unique to that entity. Because the PILOT table contains the attributes that are characteristic of pilots only, the PILOT table represents the subtype.

FIGURE 1.13 An EMPLOYEE Table with Many Nulls

	EMP_NUM	EMP_LNAME	EMP_LICENSE	EMP_MED_TYPE	EMP_MEDICAL	EMP_FLT_CHECK
▶	1205	Smith	ATP	1	16-Feb-1999	22-Mar-1999
	1211	Jones				
	1212	Hernandez	ATP	1	23-Apr-1999	19-May-1999
	1213	Wuizicki	COM	2	18-Dec-1998	15-Jul-1999
	1216	Anderson				
*	0					

FIGURE 1.14 Eliminating Nulls with a 1:1 Relationship

Table name: EMPLOYEE_SUPERTYPE

EMP_NUM	EMP_LNAME
1205	Smith
1211	Jones
1212	Hernandez
1213	Wuizicki
1216	Anderson
0	

Table name: PILOT

EMP_NUM	EMP_LICENSE	EMP_MED_TYPE	EMP_MEDICAL	EMP_FLT_CHECK
1205	ATP	1	16-Feb-1999	22-Mar-1999
1212	ATP	1	23-Apr-1999	19-May-1999
1213	COM	2	18-Dec-1998	15-Jul-1999
0				

1.10.2 The 1:M Relationship

Evidence of a 1:M relationship is found when an entity in one table may be related to many other entities in another table. For example, one customer can generate many invoices, but each invoice is generated by only one customer. Similarly, a department usually has many employees, but an employee is assigned to only one department. The 1:M relationship is the most common of the three relationships. In fact, the 1:M relationship is the relational database design standard.

Figure 1.15 shows two tables, CUSTOMER and INVOICE. You can easily tell that the CUS_NUM 32219 occurs only once in the CUSTOMER table and more than once in the INVOICE table. Therefore, the CUSTOMER table represents the "one" side, and the INVOICE table represents the "many" side of the relationship. Note also that the "many" side contains the FK that establishes the relationship between the CUSTOMER and INVOICE tables.

Figure 1.12, in which we related the EMPLOYEE and DEGREE tables through the composite EDUCATION table, also illustrates the 1:M relationship. Note that Figure 1.12 includes two 1:M relationships:

- One degree, such as the BA in the DEGREE table, can occur many times in the EDUCATION table. Therefore, the relationship between DEGREE and EDUCATION is 1:M.
- One employee, such as employee number 464 in the EMPLOYEE table, can occur many times in the EDUCATION table. Therefore, the relationship between EMPLOYEE and EDUCATION is also 1:M.

Figure 1.12 illustrates how solving the problems created by multivalued attributes yields several 1:M relationships. You will discover in section 1.10.3 that 1:M relationships are also used to eliminate the problems created by M:N relationships. In short, the 1:M relationship is often used to solve design problems. It bears repeating that most real-world relationships are likely to be of the 1:M variety. (A photographer can take many photos, but each photo is taken by one photographer; a police officer can write many tickets, but each ticket is written by one police officer; and so on.)

FIGURE 1.15 The 1:M Relationship between CUSTOMER and INVOICE

Table name: CUSTOMER

CUS_NUM	CUS_LNAME	CUS_FNAME	CUS_INITIAL	CUS_BALANCE
32219	Zabo	Eric	G	$1,505.22
32220	Smith	Annelise	A	$1,228.76
32221	Andrews	Kathryn	K	$2,114.55
0				$0.00

Table name: INVOICE

INV_NUM	CUS_NUM	INV_DATE	INV_TOTAL
100347	32220	12-May-2002	$233.67
100348	32219	12-May-2002	$387.19
100349	32219	12-May-2002	$122.06
100350	32220	12-May-2002	$1,005.34
100351	32221	12-May-2002	$34.88
100352	32220	13-May-2002	$68.71
100353	32221	13-May-2002	$106.09
0	0		$0.00

Note

The *unnecessary* duplication of data creates a condition known as data redundancy. In turn, such data redundancy produces the data anomalies that will make it difficult to properly manage the data or to produce consistent information. However, if it is *necessary* to store multiple occurrences of an attribute value, such a condition does *not* produce a data redundancy. For example, take a look at the EDUCATION table in Figure 1.12. Although the EMP_NUM 462 occurs three times in the EDUCATION table, the EMP_NUM is part of the composite PK, EMP_NUM + DEGREE_CODE. Therefore, the combinations (462,BBA), (462,MBA), and (462, MFA) are unique. Because 462 is a required part of each unique PK value, it is not redundant. The same nonredundant repetition occurs in the LINE table in Figure 1.6. Note that the LINE table's PK is composed of INV_NUM + LINE_NUM. Therefore, the combinations (100543,1); (100543,2); and (100543,3) are unique. Again, 100543 it is not redundant because it is a required part of each unique PK value.

1.10.3 The M:N Relationship

The M:N relationship exists when an entity can occur more than once on both sides of the relationship. For example, an employee may have earned many degrees: a BA, an MBA, an MFA, and so on. And many employees may have earned a BS or an MBA degree. Figure 1.16 illustrates how the implementation of the M:N relationship will yield serious problems.

As you examine the EMPLOYEE table in Figure 1.16, note that it contains **redundant data,** that is, data that turn out to be *unnecessarily* replicated. For example, to show that Anne M. Appleton had earned the BBA, MBA, and MFA degrees, we had to repeat the *same* EMP_NUM, EMP_LNAME, EMP_FNAME, and EMP_INITIAL values three times. And because the EMP_NUM value has been repeated, it is no longer unique, so we have lost the PK, too.

The redundancy illustrated in Figure 1.16 creates serious problems known as *anomalies*. (An **anomaly** is anything that fails to follow the general rule. In database terms the *needless* replication of data fails to follow the general rule that prohibits such replication.) For example, suppose that Anne M. Appleton decided to get married and requested a last name change to "Dornberg." We would have to change the Appleton last name each time it occurred, thus producing a **modification anomaly.** We would also have to make sure that each "correction" would be uniform. If the new name is entered in three different records as Durnberg, Dornburg, and Dornborg, the computer sees these entries as three different people. Or suppose we enter a new employee with six degrees into the database. Given the structure you see in Figure 1.16, we would have to enter that employee's last name, first name, and initial six times, thus producing an **insertion anomaly.** Not to mention the fact that we would have to make very sure

FIGURE 1.16
M:N Redundancy Problems

Table name: EMPLOYEE

EMP_NUM	EMP_LNAME	EMP_FNAME	EMP_INITIAL	EMP_EDUCATION
458	Renselaer	Randolph	D	BA
459	Freeman	William	H	
460	Hartog	Susanne	M	
462	Appleton	Anne	M	BBA
462	Appleton	Anne	M	MBA
462	Appleton	Anne	M	MFA
463	Randall	Herman	A	BE
464	Hernandez	Olanzo	R	BS
464	Hernandez	Olanzo	R	MS
464	Hernandez	Olanzo	R	MBA
464	Hernandez	Olanzo	R	Ph.D.
465	Oszwicki	James	P	BS
465	Oszwicki	James	P	MS
0				

Note

We showed you how to create composite tables when we used one to eliminate the nulls that occurred in Figure 1.11. Note that in Figure 1.12 EDUCATION is a composite table that breaks the M:N relationship between EMPLOYEE and DEGREE into two sets of 1:M relationships. The relationship between EMPLOYEE and EDUCATION is 1:M because an employee can occur in the EMPLOYEE table only once but in the EDUCATION table many times. For example, employee 462 occurs only once in the EMPLOYEE table but three times in the EDUCATION table. Similarly, the relationship between DEGREE and EDUCATION is 1:M because a degree can occur in the DEGREE table only once but in the EDUCATION table many times. For example, the BA degree occurs once in the DEGREE table but twice in the EDUCATION table.

The composite table must always contain the FK attributes that point to existing PK values in each table connected by it. For example, note that the composite EDUCATION table contains the EMP_NUM attribute to connect it to the EMPLOYEE table and the DEGREE_CODE attribute to connect it to the DEGREE table. In this case, the composite EDUCATION table has a composite PK, composed of the two FKs, EMP_NUM and DEGREE_CODE. Although such a composite PK is often used in a composite table, you will discover later that it is usually desirable to create a PK based on a single attribute, thus making the combination of FK attributes a candidate key.

that the data entries were all correct and uniform. And what about deleting Anne M. Appleton when she gets a better job elsewhere? We would have to find and delete three records, thus producing a **deletion anomaly.**

You can imagine the extent of the anomalies when you have tens of thousands of customers and hundreds of sales representatives who handle the company's customer transactions. If we design the CUSTOMER table to include each customer's sales representative's name and telephone number, we have a real problem when a sales representative quits, changes a name, or changes a telephone number!

Avoiding anomalies is simple if you heed this advice: Do not implement M:N relationships. Instead, break up each M:N relationship by creating a composite table to produce sets of 1:M relationships. Then implement those 1:M relationships.

The composite table can be used to solve two major problems. In section 1.9.2 we used a composite table to eliminate nulls and to produce far greater data flexibility in the case of multivalued attributes. And now you know that composite tables are also used to eliminate the data redundancies created by M:N relationships.

1.10.4 Optional and Mandatory Relationships

An **optional relationship** exists when an entity occurrence on one side of the relationship does not require a corresponding entity occurrence on the other side of the relationship. For example, an employee may have one or more dependents, but we cannot require an employee to have dependents. Note that in Figure 1.17 employees 458, 459, and 463 do not claim dependents; employee 460 claims two dependents; employee 462 claims three dependents; employee 464 claims one dependent; and employee 465 claims four dependents.

As you examine Figure 1.17, note the following features:

- There is a 1:M relationship between EMPLOYEE and DEPENDENT. (The EMP_NUM may occur many times in the DEPENDENT table.)
- DEPENDENT is optional to EMPLOYEE. An employee is not required to have one or more dependents. Note that some of the EMP_NUM values in EMPLOYEE do not occur in DEPENDENT.

1.10.5 Weak and Strong Entities

Figure 1.17 also illustrates that the entities may be classified as weak or strong. A weak entity meets two criteria:

FIGURE 1.17 An Optional Relationship between EMPLOYEE and DEPENDENT

Table name: EMPLOYEE_F1_17

EMP_NUM	EMP_LNAME	EMP_FNAME	EMP_INITIAL
458	Renselaer	Randolph	D
459	Freeman	William	H
460	Hartog	Susanne	M
462	Appleton	Anne	M
463	Randall	Herman	A
464	Hernandez	Olanzo	R
465	Oszwicki	James	P
0			

Table name: DEPENDENT

EMP_NUM	DEP_NUM	DEP_FNAME	DEP_DOB
460	1	James	05-Sep-1990
460	2	Robert	05-Sep-1990
462	1	Rudolph	25-Dec-1992
462	2	Beth	19-Aug-1968
462	3	Herman	23-Apr-1995
464	1	Marie	22-Jun-1948
465	1	Suzanna	15-Oct-1963
465	2	William	11-Jan-1988
465	3	Robert	30-Sep-1991
465	4	Jeanne	27-Nov-1996
0	0		

- It is **existence dependent** on another entity. That is, the entity cannot exist without the related entity's presence. In this case, DEPENDENT is existence dependent on EMPLOYEE. That is, a dependent cannot exist without an employee.
- Its PK is at least partially derived from the related entity's PK. In this case, the EMPLOYEE table's PK is EMP_NUM, and the DEPENDENT table's PK is a composite primary key, EMP_NUM + DEP_NUM. Note that the DEPENDENT table "borrows" part of its PK, the EMP_NUM, from the EMPLOYEE table on which it is dependent. If both conditions exist, that is, the dependent entity is existence dependent and borrows at least part of its PK from the entity on which it is dependent, that dependent entity is a **weak entity.**

Note that EMPLOYEE is not existence dependent on DEPENDENT. You can, after all, be an employee even if you don't have one or more dependents. And the EMPLOYEE could not have inherited its PK from DEPENDENT because, from the employer's database perspective, a dependent cannot exist in the database unless the employee existed already. Therefore, EMPLOYEE is a **strong entity.**

In Figure 1.17's EMPLOYEE-DEPENDENT relationship, the weak entity happened to be optional, too. However, a weak entity does not have to be optional. For example, if you examine the small invoicing system in Figure 1.6, you'll see that the LINE "borrows" part of its PK, INV_NUM + LINE_NUM, from the INVOICE, whose PK is INV_NUM. Clearly, an invoice line cannot exist apart from an invoice, so LINE is existence dependent on INVOICE. Therefore, because LINE is both existence dependent on INVOICE and derives part of its PK from INVOICE, LINE is a weak entity. But LINE is mandatory to INVOICE because an invoice must contain at least one invoice line.

1.10.6 Composite Entities

You already know that composite (bridge) tables are used to transform the M:N relationship into a set of 1:M relationships. For example, if you reexamine Figure 1.12, you will see that the composite EDUCATION table was used to transform the M:N relationship between EMPLOYEE and DEGREE into two 1:M relationships. (One 1:M relationship was created between EMPLOYEE and EDUCATION and one 1:M relationship was created between DEGREE and EDUCATION.) The composite table is the implementation of a composite entity. In other words, the composite EDUCATION entity is the conceptual view of the EDUCATION table. (In fact, any table is the implementation of its corresponding entity.)

Because a composite entity's PK is the combination of the PKs of the two entities that are "connected" by that composite entity, the composite entity is clearly existence-dependent on the two original entities. For example, the EDUCATION entity cannot exist without the presence of the EMPLOYEE and DEGREE entities. And because the composite entity's PK is composed of the PKs of the two related entities, the composite entity is also a weak entity. There is no need to further identify the composite entity as weak, because it is weak by definition!

FIGURE 1.18
A Recursive M:N Relationship in a COURSE Table

CRS_NUM	CRS_NAME	CRS_CREDIT	CRS_PREREQ
CIS200	Intro. To Microcomputing	3	
CIS300	Visual Basic	3	CIS200
CIS330	Spreadsheets	3	CIS200
CIS335	Intro. To Systems Analysis	3	CIS200
CIS480	Production Database Back End	3	CIS200
CIS480	Production Database Back End	3	CIS335
CIS490	Production Database Front End	4	CIS200
CIS490	Production Database Front End	4	CIS335
CIS490	Production Database Front End	4	CIS480
CIS495	Data Warehousing	4	CIS200
CIS495	Data Warehousing	4	CIS335
CIS495	Data Warehousing	4	CIS480
CIS495	Data Warehousing	4	CIS490
		0	

1.10.7 Recursive Relationships

Recursive relationships, although quite important, are frequently overlooked. A **recursive relationship** exists if an entity can be related to itself. If you are a student, you are already familiar with recursive relationships. For example, quite a few courses require one or more other courses as prerequisites. That is, the course entity is related to another course entity. In this example, illustrated in Figure 1.18, the recursive relationship "course is a prerequisite to course" also happens to be an M:N relationship; after all, a course can have more than one prerequisite, and a course can be a prerequisite to many other courses.

You already know that M:N relationships must not be implemented. You also know that the composite table is the way to break up the M:N relationship. This technique does not change just because you are dealing with recursive relationships. In this case, note that we have created the implementable 1:M relationship between the COURSE and PREREQ tables shown in Figure 1.19.

As you examine Figure 1.19, note that the course description is no longer repeated, thus eliminating that redundancy. If, as would be true in the real-world case, the COURSE table would also include a relatively detailed course description, you begin to appreciate the extent to which the redundancies have been eliminated. In fact, the courses are likely to be kept in a university catalog, thus requiring the identification of departments, too. In any case, you should appreciate how many data anomalies are likely to be prevented by the implementation of the recursive relationship in Figure 1.19.

Athletic events often display recursive relationships, too. After all, teams usually play other teams. Production scheduling sees many recursive relationships, too. For example, a mechanical component probably contains other components.

FIGURE 1.19
An Implementable Recursive Relationship

Table name: COURSE

CRS_NUM	CRS_NAME	CRS_CREDIT
CIS200	Intro. To Microcomputing	3
CIS300	Visual Basic	3
CIS330	Spreadsheets	3
CIS335	Intro. To Systems Analysis	3
CIS480	Production Database Back End	3
CIS490	Production Database Front End	4
CIS495	Data Warehousing	4
		0

Table name: PREREQ

CRS_NUM	PRE_CRS
CIS300	CIS200
CIS330	CIS200
CIS335	CIS200
CIS480	CIS200
CIS480	CIS335
CIS490	CIS200
CIS490	CIS335
CIS490	CIS480
CIS495	CIS200
CIS495	CIS335
CIS495	CIS480
CIS495	CIS490

Note

In Figure 1.18 we could, of course, have also shown CRS_PREREQ as a multivalued attribute, using the string format illustrated in Figure 1.10. However, such a structure would be subject to the caveats expressed in section 1.9.2, making a composite table desirable. Similarly, the M:N relationship that was originally present in Figure 1.18's COURSE table created the data redundancies that were eliminated through the use of the PREREQ composite table in Figure 1.19.

Information requirements, sometimes mandated by law, often require the use of recursive relationships to enable managers to track every part in every assembly in every component of every product. In short, in spite of the fact that academic texts usually omit coverage of recursive relationships, they are very important; you should know what they are and how they must be implemented.

All the relationship types and conditions are applicable to the recursive relationships. That is, within the recursive relationship environment you may encounter optional and mandatory relationships; 1:1, 1:M, and M:N relationships; weak and strong entities, and so on. Therefore, all the concepts and techniques that were introduced in the preceding sections are just as applicable to recursive relationships.

1.11 DATABASE DESIGN: CREATING A BLUEPRINT WITH AN ERD

Just as you need a blueprint to build a house, you will need a database blueprint before you can successfully implement a database. Although a database blueprint can be created in many ways, the most enduring database design tool has been the **entity relationship diagram,** or **ERD.** The ERD uses symbols to indicate entity sets, relationships, and relationship types to produce an easily read, easily organized, and easily expanded database blueprint.

In section 1.1 we made a distinction between entity sets and entities. This distinction properly reflects the mathematical origin of relational database concepts. However, for unknown reasons ERD designers do not draw a distinction between entity sets and entities. Instead, they refer to entity sets as entities and to the entities within the entity sets as *occurrences*. We have summarized these distinctions in Table 1.2.

We will be bound by the naming convention summarized in Table 1.2. Therefore, we will describe the data shown in Figure 1.20 as an EMPLOYEE entity containing four occurrences. Because each of the ERD's entities will be implemented as a database table later, it is appropriate to begin thinking of them as tables here.

Because the Chen model is a common basis for ERD development, we will use its basic structures and conventions in the development of our designs.[4] To make the ERD easier to read, we have added self-documenting features such as naming conventions, the placement of relationship type labels, and entity occurrence labels. Therefore, the ERDs will be based on the following features. (Each feature is illustrated in Figure 1.21.)

TABLE 1.2 ERD Naming Conventions: Entities

Mathematical Term	ERD Designer Term
Entity Set	Entity
Entity	(Entity) Occurrence

FIGURE 1.20
The EMPLOYEE Table as the Implementation of the ERD's EMPLOYEE Entity

EMP_NUM	EMP_LNAME	EMP_FNAME	EMP_INITIAL
458	Renselaer	Randolph	D
459	Freeman	William	H
460	Hartog	Susanne	M
462	Appleton	Anne	M
0			

- An entity name is always a noun. For example, entity names such as REGION, EMPLOYEE, DEGREE, DEPARTMENT, and STORE are appropriate. Descriptive names help the ERD's users understand what is going on. In short, descriptive names help document the design.
- All entity names are capitalized.
- The ERD uses a diamond to represent a relationship. A line connects the relationship to the entity.
- All relationship names are written in lowercase, and they must be active or passive verbs. Again, for documentation purposes use descriptive names. For example, relationship names such as "employs" or "is employed by" work just fine.
- A relationship is always read from the 1 side to the M side. For example, the 1:M relationship labeled "generates" between CUSTOMER and INVOICE is read as "CUSTOMER generates INVOICE" and not as "INVOICE generates CUSTOMER."
- A circle written next to, above, or below any ERD entity indicates an optional relationship also known as an **optionality.**
- A single character, known as a **connectivity,** is written next to each entity to indicate its relationship type. For example, in Figure 1.21 the 1 next to CUSTOMER indicates that the CUSTOMER is the "one" side of the relationship between CUSTOMER and INVOICE, and the M next to the INVOICE indicates that

FIGURE 1.21
A Collection of ERD Symbols and Designs*

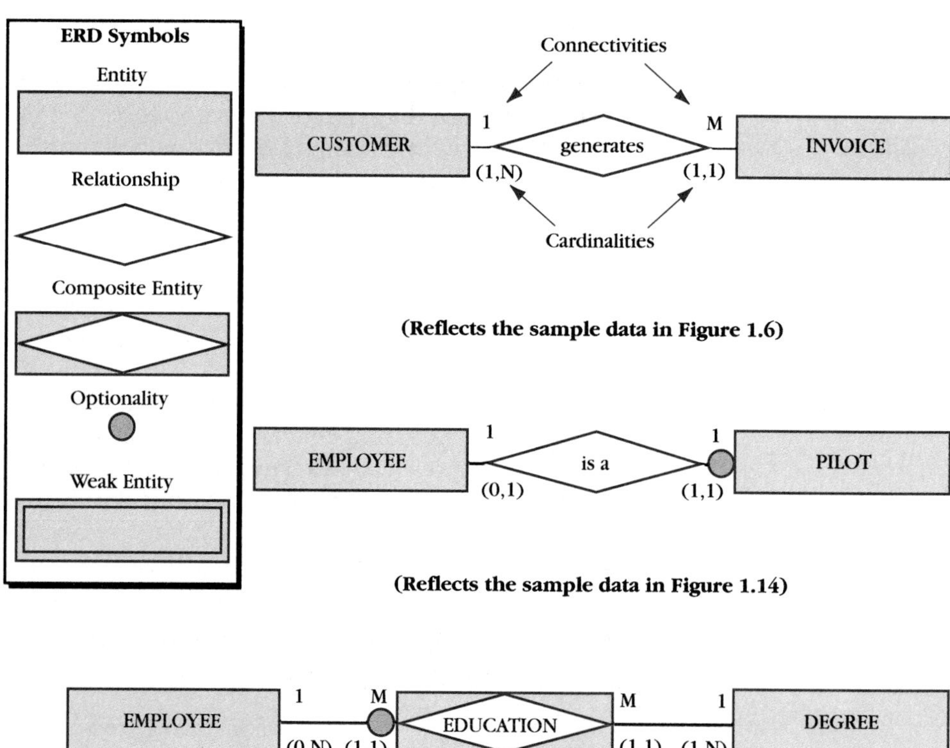

*Reflects the sample data in Figure 1.12.

Assignment

Trace the other ERDs in Figure 1.21 just as we have done here.

the INVOICE is the "many" side of the one-to-many (1:M) relationship between CUSTOMER and INVOICE.

- Each entity is also labeled to indicate its **cardinalities.** To understand the cardinality concept, remember that a relationship is always defined by having one entity reference the related entity. For example, the cardinality (1,N) next to CUSTOMER (see Figure 1.21) indicates that the (related!) INVOICE entity will contain one or more references to the CUSTOMER. (Remember that a customer can generate many invoices.) The INVOICE's (1,1) cardinality indicates that each INVOICE record contains one and only one reference to the related CUSTOMER. (After all, each invoice was generated by one and only one customer.) The first cardinality value always indicates the lower limit, and the second cardinality value indicates the upper limit.

Examine the three designs in Figure 1.21 carefully. To help clarify the connectivities and cardinalities, make sure you relate them to the sample data referenced in each ERD. For example, trace the third ERD's components this way:

- Any employee will occur in the EMPLOYEE table only one time. An employee who has one degree will occur in the EDUCATION table once, but an employee with more than one degree will occur in the EDUCATION table more than once. Because an employee can occur only once in the EMPLOYEE table but many times in the EDUCATION table, the relationship between EMPLOYEE and EDUCATION is 1:M. The placement of the connectivities thus accurately reflects the 1:M relationship.
- Any degree will occur in the DEGREE table only once. However, a degree, if earned by more than one employee, can occur many times in the EDUCATION table. Because a degree can occur only once in the DEGREE table but many times in the EDUCATION table, the relationship between DEGREE and EDUCATION is 1:M. The placement of the connectivities thus accurately reflects the 1:M relationship.
- The optionality symbol is placed next to the EDUCATION entity. This placement indicates that, because some employees do not have degrees, they will not occur in the EDUCATION table. Therefore, EDUCATION is optional to EMPLOYEE.
- The (0,N) cardinality written next to EMPLOYEE indicates that an employee may occur 0 times or up to N times in the EDUCATION table. Similarly, the (1,N) cardinality written next to the DEGREE indicates that each degree occurs one or more times in the EDUCATION table.
- The (1,1) cardinalities written on each side of the EDUCATION entity indicate that each occurrence of an employee and a degree in the EDUCATION table references one and only one employee and one and only one degree.

1.11.1 Putting the Design Picture Together: The ERD, the Tables, and the Relational Schema

A **relational schema** shows how the ERD's entities are related to each other by connecting the entity FKs to their respective PKs. An example of a relational schema is shown in Figure 1.22. Note that the relational schema is a simple

FIGURE 1.22 The Database Design and Implementation Components

ERD 

Tables (CH1_EMPEDUC.mdb database)

Table name: EMPLOYEE

EMP_NUM	EMP_LNAME	EMP_FNAME	EMP_INITIAL
458	Renselaer	Randolph	D
459	Freeman	William	H
460	Hartog	Susanne	M
462	Appleton	Anne	M
463	Randall	Herman	A
464	Hernandez	Olanzo	R
465	Oszwicki	James	P
0			

Table name: DEGREE

DEGREE_CODE	DEGREE_NAME
BA	Bachelor of Arts
BBA	Bachelor of Business Administration
BS	Bachelor of Science
MBA	Master of Business Administration
MFA	Master of Fine Arts
MS	Master of Science
Ph.D.	Doctor of Philosophy

Table name: EDUCATION

EMP_NUM	DEGREE_CODE	EDUC_EARNED	EDUC_INSTITUTION
458	BA	1996	U. of Kentucky
462	BBA	1985	U. of Massachussetts
462	MBA	1989	UCLA
462	MFA	1998	U. of Memphis
463	BA	1992	U. of Florida
464	BS	1981	Florida State University
464	MBA	1991	Penn Sate University
464	MS	1986	Penn State University
464	Ph.D.	1999	Michigan State University
465	BS	1985	Cal Tech
465	MS	1986	Cal Tech
0			

Relational Schema

listing of each entity's attributes, using lines to connect the FKs to their PKs. Figure 1.22 also puts all the database design and implementation components together to give you a bird's-eye view of the process.

Carefully review the three components in Figure 1.22—the ERD, the database tables, and the relational schema—to see how the ERD is translated into a database. Note the following:

- The EMPLOYEE entity is the 1 side of the "EMPLOYEE earns EDUCATION" relationship. Note that each EMPLOYEE number occurs only once in the EMPLOYEE table.
- The EDUCATION entity is the M side of the "EMPLOYEE earns EDUCATION" relationship. Note that the EDUCATION table contains several of the EMP_NUM values more than once.
- The DEGREE entity is the 1 side of the "DEGREE occurs in EDUCATION" relationship. Note that each DEGREE code occurs only once in the DEGREE table.
- The EDUCATION entity is the M side of the "DEGREE occurs in EDUCATION" relationship. Note that the EDUCATION table contains several DEG_CODE values more than once.
- Several DEGREE options (BEd., MEd.) do not occur in the EDUCATION table, and several EMPLOYEE numbers (10043, 10046) do not occur in the EDUCATION table. Clearly, EDUCATION is optional to both EMPLOYEE and DEGREE, reflecting the fact that an employee is not required to have a degree and some degrees have not (yet) been earned by any employee.

FIGURE 1.23
Degree Required, Some Degrees Not (Yet) Earned

By examining how the FK values relate to the PK values in each table, you'll understand how the connectivities and cardinalities are written. Note particularly that the cardinalities reflect the number of occurrences in the related entity. For example, the cardinality (0,N) written next to the EMPLOYEE entity indicates that an EMPLOYEE may occur between 0 and N times in the EDUCATION entity.

Keep in mind that an organization's actual procedures and practices determine the ERD's presentation. For example, if a company's policy is to recruit only employees who have degrees—but some degrees have not (yet) been earned by any employee—the optionality occurs only on the DEGREE side of the EDUCATION entity. Figure 1.23 reflects such a requirement.

It is worth reemphasizing that the ERD is a well-used and well-regarded design tool for the so-called production databases. Remember that a production database is based on transactions such as the sale of a product, the payment of a loan, and the enrollment of a student. In short, the production database is the one you are most likely to encounter in your daily life. Because this book focuses on production databases, the ERD is our design tool of choice.

It is also worth reemphasizing that production databases are optimized for transactions. Therefore, it sometimes becomes difficult to generate the very complex queries that can be used to extract multidimensional (time, place, type, and so on) information. The modern business DSS requires access to multidimensional information. Therefore, to support the DSS, a new kind of database, known as the data warehouse, was developed. (Bill Inmon, who is widely known as the "father of the data warehouse," created this concept.) Data warehouse design uses a process known as multidimensional modeling, instead of the ERD.

Because the data warehouse uses the production database as its primary data source, good production database design becomes critical to DSS, too. In short, the ERD continues to play a crucial role in the modern database environment.

Because the ERD will be implemented as a database, the proper identification of its components is crucial to successful database design. The ERD must reflect precisely the business operations for which it serves as the blueprint. To define the business operations precisely, the database design process actually starts with a very detailed and accurate description of those operations. In turn, the description of operations yields a very detailed set of business rules on which the database design will be based.

1.12 BUSINESS RULES

The ERD's components are derived from business rules. **Business rules** are short and concise statements that establish the existence and composition of entities, attributes, relationships (expressed in terms of connectivities and cardinalities), and constraints. For example, the following declarations are business rules:

1. A customer may be assigned a sales representative.
2. No more than one sales representative can be assigned to a customer.
3. Each sales representative must be assigned at least one customer.
4. A driver may be assigned to many trips.
5. A driver may not drive more than 10 hours in any 24-hour period.

Note that the first business rule establishes an optional relationship between the customer and the sales representative (rep). Specifically, the word *may*

Note

Not all business rules can be expressed in the database design. For example, the ERD cannot show the implementation of business rule 5. A business rule that specifies an automatic backup procedure every night at midnight can't be shown in the ERD, either. Such constraints are best handled at the applications level.

Some business rules, if implemented, can create operational inefficiencies. For example, making INVOICE mandatory to CUSTOMER means that the entry of a new customer into the CUSTOMER table must be tied to an invoice. However, the new customer may not yet have made a purchase, thus making such a reference improper. Naturally, you can create a dummy INVOICE record to indicate "no purchase" and a $0.00 invoice amount to be charged to the customer, then use the new customer's PK as the FK entry in the INVOICE's dummy record. The dummy-record solution allows the mandatory relationship to be implemented, but this solution is awkward, to say the least. Clearly, declaring INVOICE to be optional to CUSTOMER yields a more flexible and elegant solution.

indicates that SALESREP is *optional* to CUSTOMER because it is possible for a customer not to have a sales rep assigned to him or her. The second and third business rules establish a 1:M relationship between SALESREP and CUSTOMER. The combination of the first three business rules establishes that the CUSTOMER's cardinality is (0,1) and that the SALESREP's cardinality is (1,N).

Although the preceding discussion of business rules is sufficient to serve as the basis for your initial database designs, you will need to know how to develop a proper description of operations from which the business rules are derived. We give you a precise outline of the description of operations in Chapter 3.

1.12.1 Implementing Business Rules into Designs: Sample ERDs

To learn how to translate business rules into database designs, practice makes perfect. Therefore, we think that the following sets of business rules and their translation into ERDs will prove to be very helpful. Let's begin by looking at a simple invoicing system:

- A CUSTOMER may generate many INVOICEs over time.

Discussion: If your customer list includes potential customers, some of the customers on your customer list may not yet have bought anything from you. Therefore, INVOICE is optional to CUSTOMER. We'll use this assumption in our ERD.

- An INVOICE contains at least one invoice LINE.

Discussion: This relationship is mandatory on both sides. If an invoice is generated, it must be because a product was bought, and that product is referenced in an invoice line.

- Each invoice LINE records the sale of one or more units of a PRODUCT.

Discussion: A customer can buy many products, and a product can be bought by many customers. For example, if you sell 500 boxes of TufStuf cereal today, the product "TufStuf" will have been sold to many customers. And, of course, a customer may buy products other than TufStuf cereal. This "CUSTOMER buys PRODUCT" M:N relationship is implemented by breaking it up into two 1:M relationships, using LINE as the composite entity. Some products in inventory may never be sold and may, therefore, never show up in an invoice line. Therefore, the ERD in Figure 1.24 shows LINE as optional to PRODUCT.

The relational schema in Figure 1.24 helps you understand how the database design is implemented. By looking at each entity's PK and FK attributes, you can see how the ERD's relationships are translated into the database's implementation.

The ERD in Figure 1.24 contains the composite entity named LINE. By showing LINE as a composite entity, you'll know that LINE table's PK uses the INVOICE and PRODUCT PKs as its FKs.

FIGURE 1.24
A Simple Invoicing System

The ERD

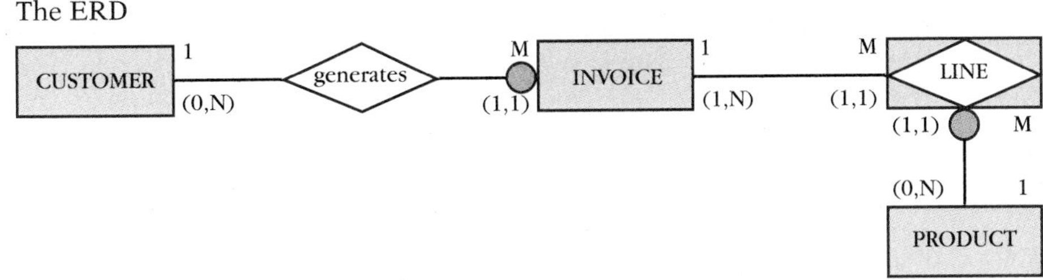

The Relational Schema

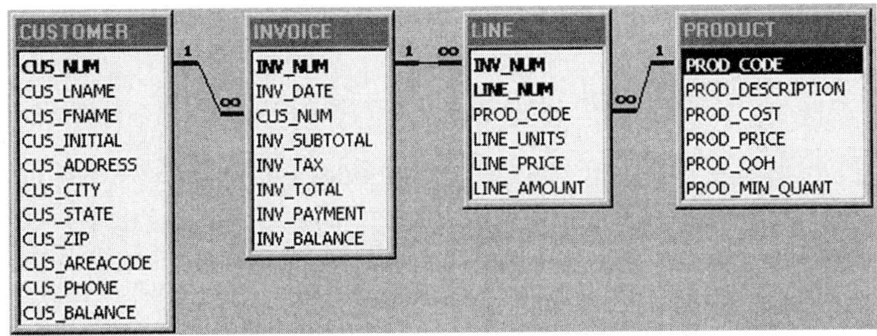

Keep in mind that all types of relationships may be used within an ERD. For example, suppose you want to design a database for your county's Little League baseball program. In this case, the recursive M:N relationship TEAM plays TEAM is implemented through a composite entity named GAME. The following business rules are created:

- A CITY sponsors one or more TEAMs, but each TEAM is sponsored by only one city.
- A TEAM has many PLAYERs, but each player plays for only one TEAM.
- It takes at least eight PLAYERs to make a TEAM.
- Each TEAM plays each of the other TEAMs twice, once at home and once as the visiting team.

  Discussion: Here's the recursive M:N relationship TEAM plays TEAM. This M:N relationship is broken into 1:M relationships through the composite entity GAME.

The preceding business rules are reflected in the ERD in Figure 1.25. As you examine the relational schema in Figure 1.25, note that the team number shows up twice in each GAME entity, once as GAME_HOME_TEAM and once as GAME_VISIT_TEAM. After all, it takes two teams to make a game. (As you examine Figure 1.25, examine how the ERD's GAME entity is translated into the relational schema's GAME table structure. In turn, the GAME table structure is reflected in the sample GAME table data.) Note also that the (8,N) cardinality in the relationship TEAM uses PLAYER indicates that a team must have a minimum of eight players. Finally, although we have not shown optionalities in this ERD, keep in mind our earlier comments about the occasional need to declare optionalities for operational reasons.

To eliminate the synonyms in the design shown in Figure 1.25, remember how the M:N relationship between INVOICE and PRODUCT was handled through the creation of the composite LINE entity. In the case of the baseball games, the solution is to create a GAME_DETAIL entity to contain the game results. This solution is shown in Figure 1.26.

As you examine the design in Figure 1.26, keep in mind that each team's play status—home team or visitor—and results are stored as records, rather than as attributes. (Note also that the placement of the ERD's entities is a matter of

Note

The relational schema in Figure 1.25 includes synonyms. A **synonym** is a word that has the same meaning as another word. In the database context, the synonym indicates that different attribute names are used to label the same attribute. In this case, the GAME_HOME_TEAM foreign key and the GAME_VISIT_TEAM foreign key in the GAME table both refer to the same TEAM_NUM primary key in TEAM. As a general rule, you should avoid the use of synonyms within a table, because they reflect the same poor table structure that was created by the multivalued "solution" found in Figure 1.11.

choice, *but make sure that the layout is easy to read*. Minimize the travel of the relationship lines and try to ensure that the relationship lines do not cross one another. The less ERD clutter, the better. Always remember that the relationship is read from the 1 to the M side and from the supertype to the subtype.) Figure 1.27 illustrates how the data are stored in the GAME and GAME_DETAIL tables.

Note that the modified design shown in Figure 1.26 has eliminated the synonyms that were present in the design shown in Figure 1.25. The modified design also yields the additional bonus of design *flexibility*. For example, you will be able to easily modify the GAME_DETAIL table to add DETAIL_RUNS and DETAIL_ERRORS.

To further illustrate the implementation of business rules, let's examine a portion of a database design for a car dealership. We'll focus on the car maintenance program.

FIGURE 1.25
An Example of a Recursive Relationship in a Design

The ERD

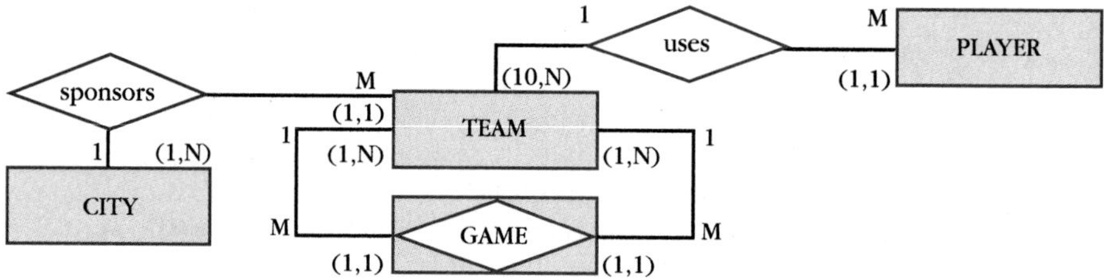

The Relational Schema

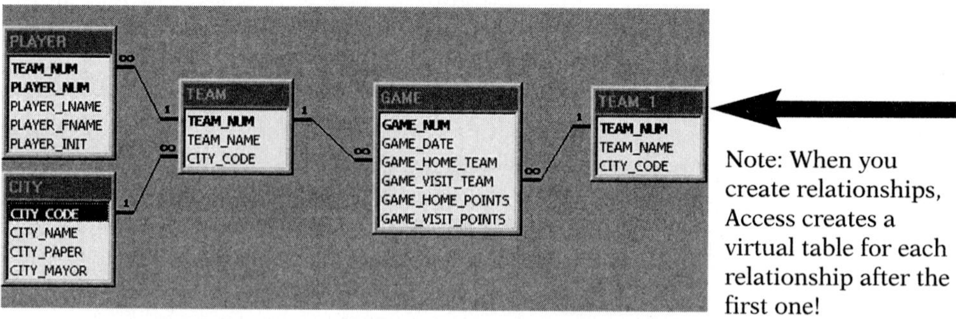

The Game Table

GAME_NUM	GAME_DATE	GAME_HOME_TEAM	GAME_VISIT_TEAM	GAME_HOME_POINTS	GAME_VISIT_POINTS
1	12-May-2002	1	3	2	5
2	15-Apr-2002	3	1	4	1
3	15-Apr-2002	2	1	3	8
4	17-Apr-2002	1	2	4	2
5	19-Apr-2002	3	2	4	3
6	22-Apr-2002	2	3	5	2
(AutoNumber)		0	0	0	0

FIGURE 1.26
Changing the Design to Eliminate the Synonyms

The ERD

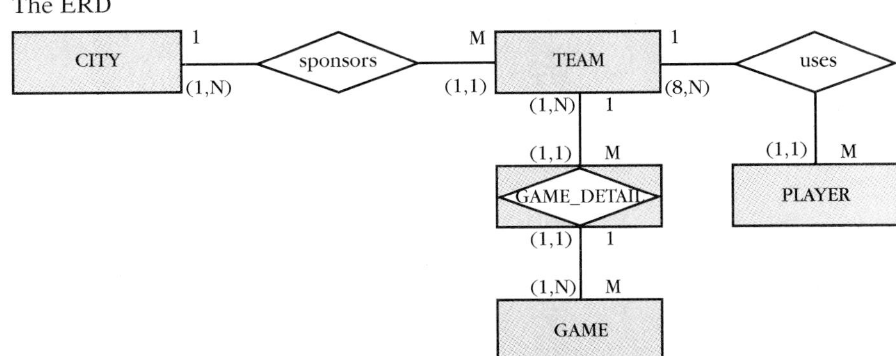

The Relational Schema

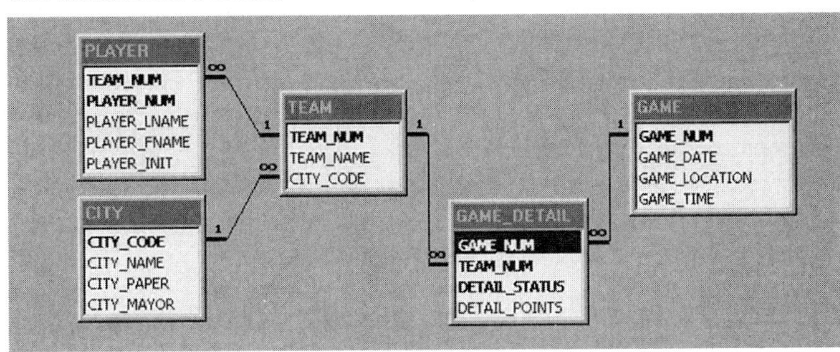

- A CUSTOMER may own one or more CARs.

Discussion: Even if the car is held in joint ownership, it will be likely that one of the owners is designated to be responsible for making sure that the car payments are made. In addition, it is very likely that all maintenance procedures are billed to only one customer. After all, the division of any billing amount among the various parties is not something in which most managers would want to be involved. Therefore, from the database perspective, you can write the second portion of this business rule as shown in the next bullet.

- Only one CUSTOMER owns each CAR.
- A CAR may require maintenance, thus causing the car data to be entered into a maintenance log.

Discussion: If the car requires maintenance, this log, named MAINT_LOG, is written before the car is put in the maintenance shop. This log allows the car dealer to track the maintenance summary for any car. Each time a car requires

FIGURE 1.27 Sample Data in the GAME and GAME_DETAIL Tables

The GAME Table Contents

GAME_NUM	GAME_DATE	GAME_LOCATION	GAME_TIME
1	12-May-2002	Brandon Field	5:30 PM
2	15-Apr-2002	Memorial Field	7:00 PM
3	15-Apr-2002	Memorial Field	6:30 PM
4	17-Apr-2002	Brandon Field	4:30 PM
5	19-Apr-2002	Memorial Field	7:00 PM
6	22-Apr-2002	Brandon Field	7:30 PM
0			

The GAME_DETAILS Table Contents

GAME_NUM	TEAM_NUM	DETAIL_STATUS	DETAIL_POINTS
1	1	Home	2
1	3	Visitor	5
2	1	Visitor	1
2	3	Home	4
3	1	Visitor	8
3	2	Home	3
4	1	Home	4
4	2	Visitor	2
5	2	Visitor	3
5	3	Home	4
6	2	Home	5
6	3	Visitor	2
0	0		0

maintenance, it requires a maintenance log entry. Therefore, a car may generate many maintenance log entries over time. But each maintenance log entry refers to one and only one car.

Based on this discussion, two business rules can be written:

1. A CAR may enter a MAINT_LOG many times.
2. Each MAINT_LOG entry refers to one and only one CAR.

- Each EMPLOYEE has one (primary) JOB classification.

Discussion: Job classifications can include such entries as mechanic, accountant, secretary, manager, and so on.

- Any given JOB classification can be assigned to many EMPLOYEEs.

Discussion: It is very likely that the car dealership employs more than one mechanic or more than one janitor. Therefore, job classifications such as "mechanic" and "janitor" can be assigned to many employees.

- An employee, who must be a mechanic, writes the maintenance log entry.

Discussion: It is possible to use an EMPLOYEE is a MECHANIC supertype/subtype relationship to enforce the requirement that only a mechanic can write a maintenance log entry. However, the applications software can also enforce such a restriction. The existence of the "JOB is assigned to EMPLOYEE" relationship makes it possible to restrict the maintenance log entries to only those employees who have a job classification of "mechanic."

- Each MAINT_LOG contains at least one repair entry, MAINT_LINE.

Discussion: Note how this set of entities reflects the same relationship as the one displayed by the INVOICE and LINE entities in Figures 1.24 and 1.25. As a matter of fact, the MAINT_LOG and MAINT_LINE entities will generate the car dealership's invoice contents. In this case, the invoice is a printed report, rather than a part of the database!

- Each MAINT_LINE may reference a PART.

Discussion: A repair may or may not require parts. For example, tightening a hose clamp does not require a part. Therefore, PART is optional to MAINT_LINE.

- Some parts are never used in a maintenance procedure. Therefore, MAINT_LINE is optional to PART.

Discussion: Perhaps they were placed in inventory for eventual use, but they were never needed. In any case, operational requirements make this optionality desirable.

- Some employees have one or more certifications. More than one employee may have earned any given certification.

Discussion: These two business rules indicate the existence of a M:N relationship between EMPLOYEE and CERTIFICATE. This M:N relationship must be broken up into two 1:M relationships through the use of a composite entity. We have named this entity QUALIFICATION. To make the design "data flexible," we will assume that CERTIFICATE includes various certifications and licenses. Therefore, CERTIFICATE may include certified public accountant or CPA, as well as such licenses as a mechanic's license, certification as an electrician, and so on.

- Some certifications require periodic training.

Discussion: A hazardous waste management certificate may require training once a year, while other certifications may require even more frequent training. To track all such training, the TRAINING entity exists. Table 1.3 shows some sample data entries in the TRAINING table.

As you examine these entries, note that this composite table uses a PK composed of EMP_NUM, CERT_CODE, and TRAIN_DATE to ensure that each row entry is unique. For example, employee 105 took the HAZ-1 training on 12-Mar-2001 and again on 15-Mar-2002. Because the PK requires the combination of

TABLE 1.3 Sample TRAINING Table Contents

EMP_NUM	CERT_CODE	TRAIN_DATE	TRAIN_SCORE
105	HAZ-1	12-Mar-2001	95
109	GTR-2	23-Jun-2001	87
111	HAZ-1	26-May-2001	92
105	HAZ-1	15-Mar-2002	98
105	ELC-1	27-Jun-2002	78
109	HAZ-1	15-Jul-2002	94

these three attribute values to be unique for each row, the use of this PK will prevent duplicate data entries.

The ERD in Figure 1.28 incorporates the preceding business rules. You'll have a chance to expand this design and add an appropriate relational schema in the end-of-chapter problems.

1.13 CONFLICTING DATABASE DESIGN GOALS

As you embark on the database design process, you must always keep in mind that your design must meet information, transaction speed, redundancy control, expandability, and maintainability requirements. These requirements may be in conflict, and the designer's job is to reconcile the conflicting requirements to the greatest extent possible. In short, database design is exciting because it requires the exercise of professional judgment as well as the skill to wield the design tools we have discussed in this chapter. Follow the design rules carefully, yet be mindful of the trade-offs that your database environment may require you to make!

1.14 A SAMPLE DATABASE DESIGN'S DEVELOPMENT PROCESS

This book uses Microsoft Access as the database implementation and application development environment. However, regardless of which database software you

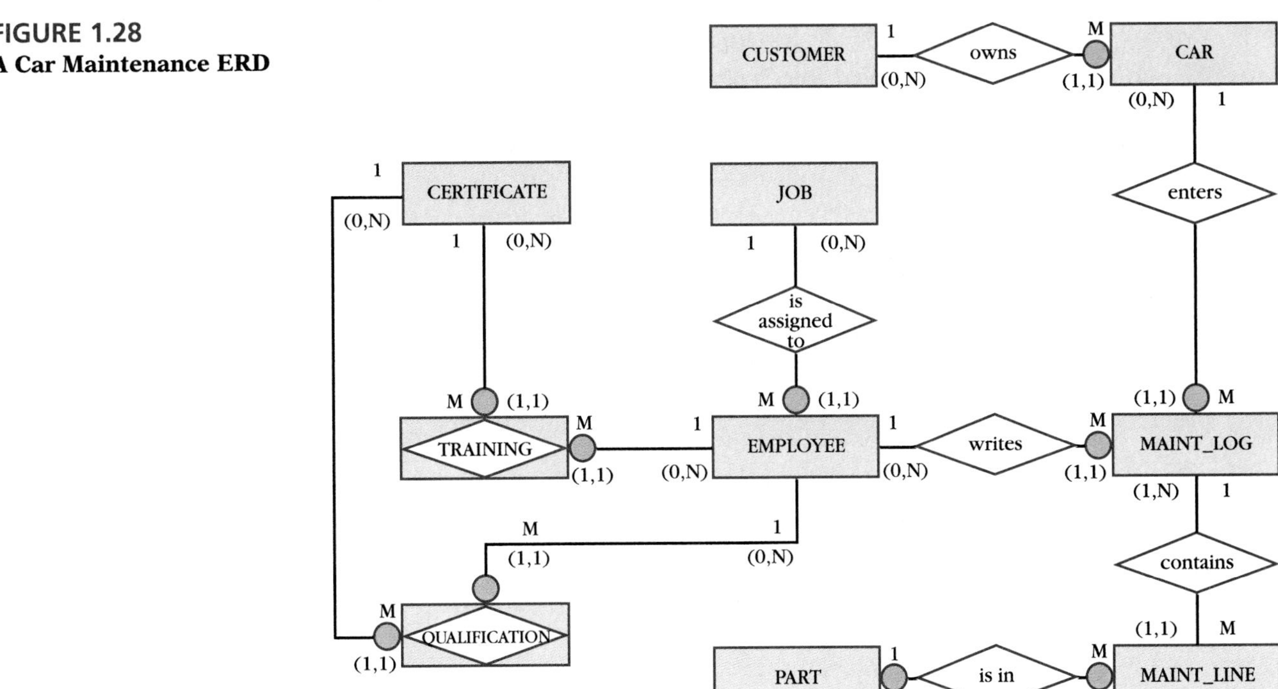

FIGURE 1.28
A Car Maintenance ERD

Note

The TRAINING table structure reflected in Table 1.3 shows a composite table. This structure works fine, and we have already noted that it prevents duplicate record entries. However, you will discover later that it is often desirable to create an "artificial" single-attribute PK. In this case, the new PK might be the TRAIN_NUM attribute shown in Table 1.4. Note that the combination of the EMP_NUM, CERT_CODE, and TRAIN_DATE remains as the candidate key. You will learn in Chapter 4 that you can use an index to avoid the duplication of records in this revised table structure.

The change in the table structure also changes the presentation of the TRAINING entity in the ERD, because the entity is no longer composite. (The PK is TRAIN_NUM, rather than the original composite PK composed of EMP_NUM + CERT_CODE + TRAIN_DATE.)

TABLE 1.4 Sample Revision of the TRAINING Table Contents

TRAIN_NUM	EMP_NUM	CERT_CODE	TRAIN_DATE	TRAIN_SCORE
1001	105	HAZ-1	12-Mar-2001	95
1002	109	GTR-2	23-Jun-2001	87
1003	111	HAZ-1	26-May-2001	92
1004	105	HAZ-1	15-Mar-2002	98
1005	105	ELC-1	27-Jun-2002	78
1006	109	HAZ-1	15-Jul-2002	94

will use in your professional career, the success of database implementation and end-user applications development rest on your ability to properly design the database. Therefore, you'll find it useful to review the development of the ERD presented in this section before you try to tackle the problems at the end of this chapter or to even think about applications development.

To design an effective database for any organization, you must at least know what the organization does, how it is organized, what its data environment is, and what its information requirements are. In short, you must have a precise description of operations from which to distill the business rules. Because we want to focus your attention on the design process in this chapter, we have summarized the essential processes and components for you in the following development of a service organization database. We show you how to produce a complete description of operations in Chapter 3.

1.14.1 A Service Organization Database

Organization Type

Located at Tiny University, the XYZ organization's members and pledges provide community services. Because XYZ is officially certified as a Tiny University service organization, all of its members and pledges must be at least part-time Tiny University students.

Objectives

The XYX organization's objectives are threefold:

1. To provide community services free of charge.
2. To provide its members an opportunity to contribute to the community in which they live.
3. To provide its members an opportunity to develop practical leadership skills.

XYZ considers the last two objectives to be an important extension of the educational process.

Organizational Membership and Management

To earn membership, a student must serve a one-semester trial period as a pledge, during which (s)he demonstrates a commitment to XYZ's service philosophy. Once the pledge period has been successfully completed, the pledge becomes a member. XYZ keeps all current member and pledge data in a single member file.

Assignment

As you read the following material, keep track of all identifiable entities and attributes. (Use a high-tech device like a pencil or pen to record your ERD impressions on a piece of paper.) Try to determine what types of relationships exist and convert all M:N relationships into 1:M relationships through composite entities. Identify all optional relationships, connectivities, and cardinalities. The completed ERD is presented at the end of this section. (But don't look at the solution until you've completed your own design!)

If a member leaves in good standing, that member becomes an alumnus. Alumni are classified as active or inactive. Active alumni are those who pay their alumni dues. Active alumni may participate in all XYZ activities, but they are not required to do so. Alumni data are kept in a separate file.

All XYZ activities are managed through officers who are elected from the membership during the second week of each academic year. Officers serve for one academic year and are eligible for reelection. XYZ's officers include a president, a vice president, a pledge director, a treasurer, a secretary, and a newsletter editor.

- The president provides the leadership necessary to set short-term and long-term organizational goals and is the liaison between XYZ and the community it serves.
- The vice president directs XYZ's activities when the president is not available. In addition, the vice president assists the president in community liaison activities. Finally, the vice president is responsible for organizing the recycling drives that provide funds for the XYZ service budget.
- The pledge director supervises the pledges and their activities. The pledge director also tracks the academic progress of all pledges and serves as the pledges' academic counselor. Pledge aides assist the pledge director in his or her duties. The pledge director may appoint as many pledge aides as necessary to help ensure the pledges' academic success and the pledges' service activities.
- The treasurer is responsible for collecting and recording dues, handling contributions, and making disbursements. The treasurer must make a monthly report of all financial transactions.
- The secretary records and maintains the minutes of all meetings. The minutes recorded at each month's meeting are reported at the subsequent month's meeting for approval by the membership. The secretary also conducts all alumni activities.
- The newsletter editor produces a monthly newsletter and maintains the XYZ Web page.

A member may hold only one officer position at a time. For example, a member cannot be president and treasurer at the same time.

Basic Operations

On-campus XYZ members and pledges provide basic tutoring as well as orientation programs that help incoming freshmen adjust to university life. Off-campus XYZ members and pledges conduct buddy programs, staff after-school programs for the local school system, conduct fund-raisers for the local school and library, and staff literacy and library reading programs.

The XYZ organization does not charge for any of its services, and its members and pledges staff the organization and its services on a volunteer basis. However, XYZ supplies funding for materials, supplies, and programs that are required to conduct its service operations. In addition, XYZ funds its own supply

TABLE 1.5 Members, Pledges, and Active Alumni

Year	Members	Pledges	Active Alumni	Inactive Alumni
1997	14	8	0	0
1998	21	12	5	2
1999	29	17	11	5
2000	34	15	15	9
2002	40	22	21	14
2003	47	30	28	20

and operations budget to support its service mission. Members, pledges, and alumni fund the service support budget through recycling drives, membership dues, and contributions.

In addition to performing volunteer work, XYZ pledges and members attend monthly organizational meetings, weekly socials, and monthly training sessions. These activities are designed to develop organizational and other skills that contribute to the success of XYZ's mission. Although members and pledges are encouraged to match their interests and their volunteer services, XYZ does reserve the right to assign volunteers to assure proper service coverage.

The Data Environment

Five Tiny University students started the XYX organization on August 12, 1997. Table 1.5 provides a summary of the membership, pledges, and active alumni growth. The year 2003 values are estimated.

The data in Table 1.5 must be examined in the light of the following conditions:

- Some members graduate each semester.
- Many of the graduating members become active alumni. Active alumni pay yearly dues and may participate in any of XYZ's activities.
- Graduating members who do not pay alumni dues are classified as inactive.
- Any member who leaves XYZ in good standing is an alumnus. For example, some students may not graduate, yet they earn the alumnus status by their past membership in good standing. If such an alumnus returns to Tiny University to continue work on a degree, that alumnus may elect to become an active member again.
- Most pledges successfully complete their pledge period to become members.
- Pledges who fail to meet membership requirements are dropped from the XYZ files. Such pledges may reapply, but they must begin at the start of a new pledge activity cycle and complete all requirements within that cycle.

Member and pledge data are currently kept in a member file. When a member becomes an alumnus, the membership record is archived to an alumni file. Although the alumni file contains most of the original membership data, it also contains data that are typical of alumni only. For example, alumni data include status, active or inactive.

Members pay $20 yearly dues, while pledges pay $10 yearly dues. Pledges also pay $32 to cover the cost of certificates and membership patches when they are initiated as members. Active alumni pay $25 yearly dues.

When a pledge is initiated, XYZ assigns him or her a membership number. Once a membership number has been assigned, it can never be reused. From a data perspective a member has a membership number and a membership type classification of M. A pledge has a membership number and a membership classification of P. When a pledge becomes an active member, the membership number is retained and the membership classification is changed to M.

Pledges become XYZ members by successfully completing a sufficient number of service commitments to gain a cumulative score of at least 300 points during

Note

Table 1.5 presents summary information. Such information is derived from one or more tables in the database, using queries you'll learn to construct in Chapter 5. In short, the table contents shown in this section do not necessarily match any single table in the database design. Descriptions of operations typically include data summaries, reports, and proposed information formats that help define database components. Based on the condensed description of operations presented in this section, you must decide on the appropriate entities and their attributes.

The table contents shown in typical descriptions of operations do not necessarily reflect proper table structures. Therefore, you must decide how to store the data in proper table structures. Database design involves a lot of professional decision making.

Finally, you will discover that this description-of-operation summary contains similar information spread over several different descriptive segments. For example, service and contribution activities are described separately for members, pledges, and alumni, yet the tracking requirements are the same. Therefore, you must make decisions about which data to combine from what sources.

the pledge semester. The points must be earned in any combination of service activities sanctioned by XYZ. Table 1.6 gives a summary of activities and point counts.

To earn points in any category, a pledge must serve a minimum number of hours before any points are counted. Once the minimum hour requirement has been satisfied in a category, each additional hour generates 10 percent of the category points. Using Table 1.6 as a guide, if a pledge chooses the Literacy category, that pledge is committed to at least 15 hours of work in the Literacy category for the semester. If a pledge completes fewer than 15 hours, (s)he earns no points. If 20 hours have been allocated, the point count is $18 + (5 \times 2) = 28$ points. If applied to the Orientation category, the 20-hour work allocation would yield $10 + (10 \times 1) = 20$ points. Because the 300-point minimum score is required to become a member, tracking all activities for all pledges by date, category, and hours is crucial.

To maintain their active membership status, members must select at least two service categories and serve at least the minimum number of hours in each selected category. Using Table 1.6 as a guide, if a member selects the Buddy and Library categories, a minimum of $12 + 15 = 27$ hours must be invested. All member activities must be tracked. To simplify data tracking, members and pledges have their service activities recorded in the same file. However, although service point totals are recorded for members, they are used for special commendation purposes only.

All member and pledge fees and voluntary contributions are tracked in a contribution file. This file contains the contribution date, amount, and purpose. To facilitate dues payments, these payments may be made in installments. All dues must be paid in full within the first academic semester of each year.

TABLE 1.6 Sanctioned Service Activities

Category	Points	Minimum Hours
Service Fund-raising	8	10
Orientation	10	10
Buddy	15	12
After School	15	12
Literacy	20	15
Library	20	15

XYZ currently keeps track of 35 XYZ alumni, 21 of whom are active. Each active alumnus pays a yearly fee of $25 to cover the cost of incidental mailings. Any alumnus may make additional financial contributions to help fund XYZ's service budget, and all such contributions must be tracked. Inactive alumni are kept on the XYZ alumni roster; they are periodically encouraged to become active alumni.

Although alumni are not required to participate in any of the approved service activities, XYZ urges them to remain active in the service arena. Alumni are not subject to the minimum hour requirement listed in Table 1.5. However, if alumni accumulate at least 100 service hours in any of the approved service categories during any year, XYZ recognizes them by publishing their names in the monthly newsletter honor roll. In addition, XYZ sends a special letter of commendation. Therefore, alumni activities must be carefully tracked.

Currently, XYZ maintains its membership, alumni, and pledge data in a single member file. The member file records the member's XYZ membership number, pledge date, membership date, name, home address, campus address, academic department, home phone, campus phone, and e-mail address. Alumni data include graduation date if applicable, degree earned if applicable, degree's major field and department if applicable, and any special distinctions earned by each alumnus.

Inactive alumni are those who have not paid their alumni dues for 2 consecutive years. The data for such alumni are archived into a special "inactive" file. Inactive alumni do not participate in any of XYZ's activities and, therefore, the "inactive" file contents are not subject to any activity-tracking requirements.

Transaction and Information Requirements

XYZ's operations require detailed activity tracking and reporting. The main transactions involve service activities by members and pledges and financial transactions. The latter transactions include all assessments, contributions, and disbursals.

Service Activities

The database must enable designated XYZ officers to track all service activities by all members and pledges to generate ad hoc query capability and formal end-of-semester summaries. (An ad hoc query enables the end user to produce spur-of-the-moment answers to questions. For example, if a pledge walks in and asks, How many service points did I earn last month? you will have to use an ad hoc query to generate the answer.) The following data must be tracked for members and pledges: activity date, activity type (see Table 1.6), number of hours spent on this activity on this date, and activity points. The system must be able to generate point counts and totals for each activity type for each member and pledge for any date interval. Table 1.7 shows a few sample tracking entries.

TABLE 1.7 Activity Tracking

Date	Member or Pledge	Service Category	Unit Points	Time (Hrs.)
11/22/2002	Jeanine B. Bernard	Buddy	15	1.5
11/22/2002	Fred K. Jeppeson	Buddy	15	1.2
11/22/2002	Phillip D. Rothman	Literacy	20	2.6
11/22/2002	Melanie E. Klauber	After School	15	1.8
11/23/2002	James G. Etuchevski	Literacy	20	1.1
11/23/2002	Arnold D. Washington	After School	15	2.4
11/23/2002	Fred K. Jeppeson	After School	15	2.5
11/23/2002	Jeanine B. Bernard	Buddy	15	1.9
11/23/2002	Melanie E. Klauber	Orientations	10	3.7
11/24/2002	Jeanine B. Bernard	Literacy	20	2.0

TABLE 1.8 Service Fund Categories

Category
Dues
Fees
Orientation
Buddy
After School
Literacy
Library
General

Financial Transactions

Although all contributions are deposited into a single service fund account, XYZ's treasurer must keep track of all contributions by service fund category. Contributions may be made to any of the designated category areas shown in Table 1.8. If the contributor designates no specific service category, the deposit is recorded as "general" and is available for expenditure in any service category. Because services are also funded via the deposit of dues and fees, these are recorded as service fund categories. However, dues and fees must be tracked individually to ensure that members, pledges, and alumni get proper credit.

The treasurer must be able to account for all checks by service category. Therefore, the database must enable the treasurer to generate reports for all contributions and expenditures by service category for any selected period of time.

The treasurer must also be able to track all individual contributions by donor, date, amount, and category and be able to provide summary reports by donor, service category, or any combination thereof. Table 1.9 shows a few sample contribution entries.

Hardware and Software Resources

The XYZ organization leases a one-room office. This office contains an Intel Pentium IV–based microcomputer (2.20 GHz) with 512 MB of RDRAM, a 120-GB hard drive, a CD-RW drive, a 3.5-inch HD floppy drive, and a 100-MB Zip drive. Peripherals include a laser printer, a dedicated fax machine, a telephone, and a copy machine.

XYZ uses the Microsoft Office XP Small Business Edition suite to conduct its operations. Most of XYZ's operational data have been managed through Excel spreadsheets. To date, the use of Access has been limited to membership data. However, the spreadsheet-based applications have not been able to yield the desired transaction management and reporting capability. Therefore, several XYZ members who major in computer information systems have presented a proposal to create a true database environment based on the Access DBMS software.

TABLE 1.9 Contribution Tracking

Date	Contributor	Service Category	Amount
10/20/2002	Jane H. Harmond	Literacy	$50.00
10/20/2002	Whitney D. Travera	Buddy	$25.00
10/28/2002	George H. Tracker	Literacy	$35.00
10/11/2002	Anton G. Grimaldi	After School	$10.00
10/23/2002	Charles F. Smithson	General	$100.00
10/04/2002	Jane H. Harmond	After School	$25.00
10/15/2002	James S. Valercheck	After School	$35.00
10/16/2002	Anne J. Jamison	General	$100.00
10/23/2002	Marie T. Dobson	General	$25.00
10/04/2002	Elijah B. Jones	Literacy	$75.00

Business Rules

Before you write the business rules that govern XYZ's activities, it is useful to examine three critical transaction types. These transactions define how XYZ conducts its operations:

1. XYZ members, pledges, and alumni perform services. These services must be tracked by service type, who performed the service, when, and for how long. The MEMBER table contains data common to members, alumni, and pledge data, while data that are peculiar to alumni are stored in an ALUMNUS table. (Remember that entity names—and, therefore, table names—are nouns and are singular.) The SERVICE table stores the service types, service points, and other service-related data.
2. XYZ members, pledges, and alumni pay dues, fees, and may make contributions to a fund from which XYZ and service expenses are funded. The FUND table stores the fund type that enables XYZ to track all activities related to the funding environment.
3. XYZ members and pledges attend organizational meetings, training sessions, and socials. The MEETING table stores the meeting type and description. XYZ must be able to track attendance records for each of these activities.

The preceding three transaction types are crucial because their proper recording and tracking define XYZ's operational requirements. There are, of course, additional data requirements. For example, we hope that you noticed the inclusion of a department attribute for members and pledges. Because you want to avoid data redundancy problems, it will be useful to store the department code, department description, and campus address in a DEPARTMENT table. Such departmental data are also useful for notification purposes.

Given this summary and the preceding very brief description of operations, you'll be able to see where the following business rules were generated. Pay particular attention to the sample data shown in Tables 1.5 through 1.9. Only a few of the most critical business rules are shown here. Reread the description of operations to write additional business rules to complete the design components.

1. A MEMBER may provide many SERVICEs, and each SERVICE can be provided by many MEMBERs.

   Discussion: Check Table 1.3 to see the evidence of this M:N relationship. Keep in mind that the M:N relationship must be broken up into two 1:M relationships, using a composite table named ACTIVITY. From an operational point of view, it's a good idea to make the ACTIVITY optional to MEMBER and SERVICE. After all, you don't want to be forced to make an activity entry when you enroll a new pledge when that new pledge has not yet had an opportunity to provide a service. It's useful to remember that operational requirements make some optionalities desirable even when they are not dictated by the nature of the transaction.
2. An ALUMNUS retains membership status.

   Discussion: Because alumni may—and are, in fact, encouraged to—participate in service activities and make special contributions, their efforts must be traceable. Attributes that are peculiar to alumni, such as graduation dates, should be stored in the ALUMNUS table. However, although alumni do not attend chapter meetings, many of their activities are tracked just as those of members are tracked. Therefore, the attributes that are common to members and alumni are stored in the MEMBER table. The status of each MEMBER entity may be established by creating a MEM_STATUS attribute, whose values, P = Pledge, M = Member, and A = Alumnus, may then be used for differentiation purposes. The relationship between MEMBER and ALUMNUS is one of supertype and the (optional) subtype. (All alumni are members, but not all members are alumni.)

   Although you might be tempted to create a supertype/subtype relationship between members and pledges, the addition of an entity and a relationship complicate the design without yielding many benefits. The only attribute not shared by pledges is the membership date. Therefore, it hardly seems worthwhile—from both operational and design perspectives—to create a table and a relationship just to store one attribute. The decision to keep this pledge attribute in the MEMBER table does, of course, introduce a null for each pledge. However, there are not that many pledges, and the null is only temporary.

3. A MEMBER may make contributions to many FUNDs, and each FUND may receive contributions from many MEMBERs.

Discussion: Break this M:N relationship into two 1:M relationships by creating the CONTRIBUTION table. Remember that the FUND includes membership and pledge dues and fees. Again, for operational reasons, it's a good idea to make the CONTRIBUTION optional to MEMBER and FUND. (Remember that the inclusion of active alumni data in the MEMBER table allows you to track alumni activities, too.)

4. Members attend many meetings, and many members attend each meeting.

Discussion: To minimize the number of tables, the MEETING table contains both the social and professional meeting types. Because attendance must be tracked for all members and pledges, an ATTENDANCE composite table provides the bridge between MEMBER and MEETING. Because a new pledge cannot yet have attended a meeting, it is operationally useful to ensure that ATTENDANCE is optional to MEMBER. And because you want the ability to add a new meeting type without having to generate an attendance record for it, ATTENDANCE should be optional to MEETING, too.

5. Each MEMBER is enrolled in a DEPARTMENT, and one DEPARTMENT can have many MEMBERs enrolled in it.

Discussion: Remember that the MEMBER table contains both member and pledge data. There is a 1:M relationship between DEPARTMENT and MEMBER. Because a member must be enrolled in a department, DEPARTMENT is mandatory to MEMBER. However, some departments may not have any XYZ members enrolled in them, so MEMBER is optional to DEPARTMENT.

These five business rules are sufficient to lay out the database design shown in Figure 1.29. Additional design details can be generated by writing additional

FIGURE 1.29
The XYZ Database Design

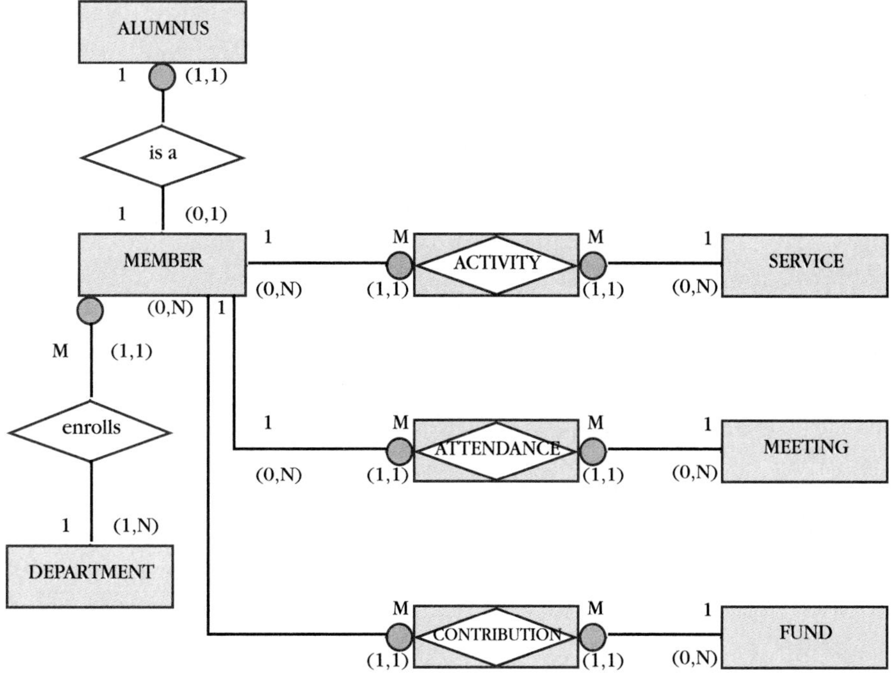

business rules. Most of these business rules will depend on how you interpret the description of operations. Therefore, in a real-world design, you'll wind up asking a lot of questions as you begin to generate the design details.

The ERD in Figure 1.29 is a good first design effort. However, as you reread the description of operations, you are likely to see a need for possible ERD modifications. In fact, such modifications will become part of the design-verification process as you begin to learn how to normalize the tables (Chapter 2), how to implement database designs (Chapter 4), and how to develop the queries (Chapter 5) that help transform stored data into information.

Keep in mind that even designs that appear logically sound are not always implementable. For example, you might wonder why we created the 1:1 relationship between MEMBER and ALUMNUS, rather than creating additional relationships between ALUMNUS and ACTIVITY and CONTRIBUTION. After all, if you make MEM_NUM the PK for both the MEMBER and the ALUMNUS, the ACTIVITY table's MEM_NUM might be used as the FK to both ALUMNUS and MEMBER. Unfortunately, this "solution" yields referential integrity problems. (When you have mastered the material in Chapter 4, try this approach and see what happens when you try to establish both relationships between ACTIVITY and MEMBER and between ACTIVITY and ALUMNUS.)

There are, of course, other design and implementation considerations. For example, rather than creating the ALUMNUS entity, you might use an attribute named MEM_STATUS in the MEMBER table to record P for Pledge, A for alumnus, and M for member. But this solution eliminates the possibility of recording and tracking all sorts of data that are unique to alumni, such as the graduation date. (Current members and pledges have not yet graduated.) And now you know that you should not store such unique alumni data in the MEMBER table, because that solution would yield nulls.

As you begin to consider the attributes that are to be kept in each table, remember that a very precise description of operations must be the source of such details. The very brief description of XYZ's operations is very far from complete at this point. (You will learn how to write a more comprehensive description of operations in Chapter 3.) Although our description of XYZ's operations lacked the requisite detail, the relational schema shown in Figure 1.30 contains the min-

FIGURE 1.30 The Relational Schema for the XYZ Database Design

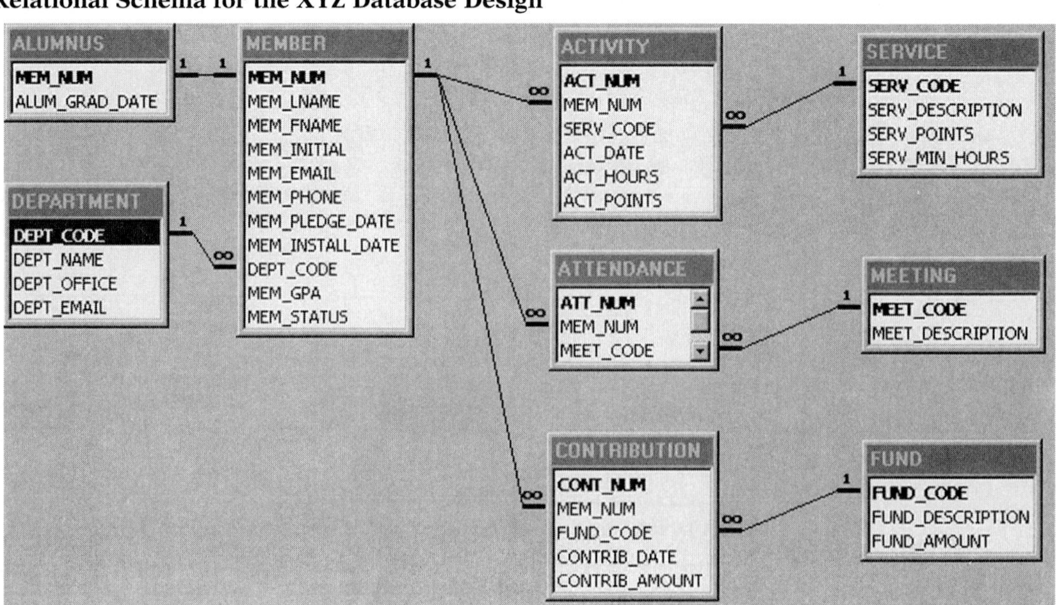

FIGURE 1.31
The Enhanced Chen ERD

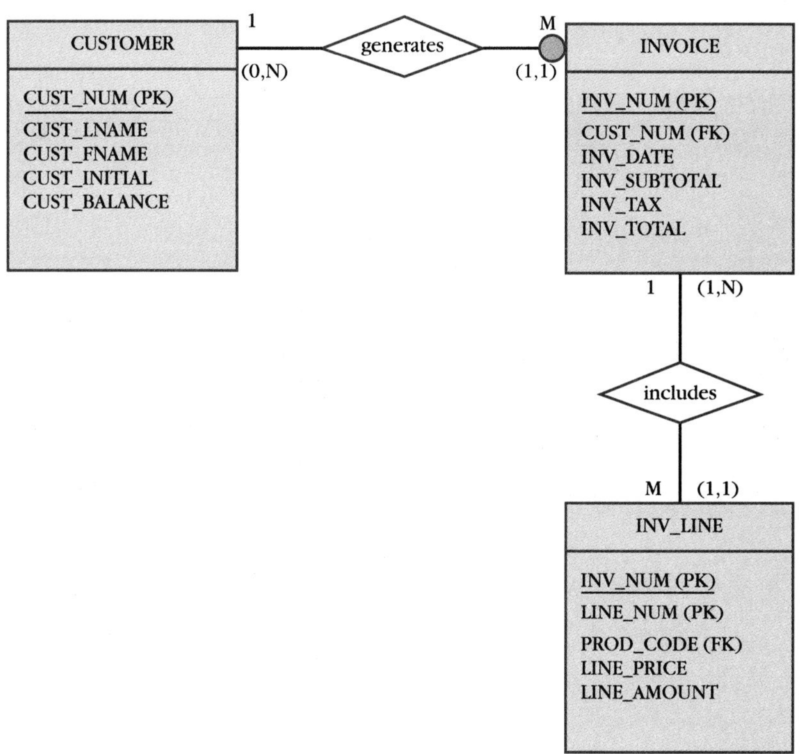

imum number and types of attributes that make the design implementable and usable. To save space, we have omitted many attributes. For example, we left out member home and campus addresses.

1.15 ENHANCED ERDS

The Chen ERDs we have shown thus far are very useful conceptual views of the database's architecture. Ultimately, the purpose of the design is to produce a good database implementation. And database implementation requires that you know what attributes are to be stored in which entities.

1.15.1 The Enhanced Chen ERD

The conceptual Chen ERDs are wonderful modeling tools, but they don't get you to the point where you can *implement* the design—unless you also develop the relational schema to go with the ERD. Therefore, many designers prefer to use an enhanced Chen ERD. The **enhanced Chen ERD** includes for each entity the attributes that describe it. In other words, the enhanced Chen ERD combines the purely conceptual model with the relational schema. An example of an enhanced Chen ERD is shown in Figure 1.31.

1.15.2 The Crow's Foot ERD

The Crow's Foot ERD is a popular alternative to the Chen ERD. The **Crow's Foot ERD** gets its name from its presentation of relationships; the "many" side of the relationship is depicted as a three-pronged unit that resembles a crow's foot. The Crow's Foot ERD's symbolic representation of relationships gives it some features that make it easier to automate the design process through the use of visual design tools. To make the comparisons between the enhanced Chen ERD and the Crow's Foot ERD easy, Figure 1.32 depicts the same design segment as Figure 1.31.

FIGURE 1.32
The Crow's Foot ERD

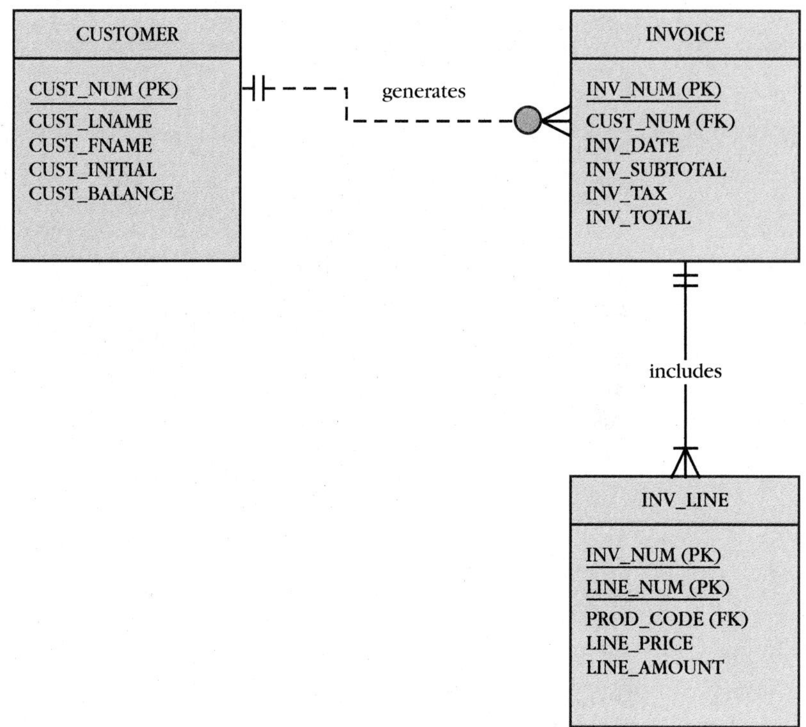

As you compare the Crow's Foot ERD in Figure 1.32 to the enhanced Chen ERD in Figure 1.31, note the following differences in the Crow's Foot ERD:

- The 1 side of the relationship is represented by a slash.
- The M side of the relationship is represented by a three-pronged "crow's foot."
- The relationship line is dashed.
- The relationship name is not depicted in a diamond.
- The connectivities and cardinalities are combined (see Figure 1.33).
- The cardinalities represent the occurrences in the entity itself, rather than in the related entity. This difference is the most significant of the Crow's Foot and Chen distinctions.

FIGURE 1.33
Connectivities and Cardinalities in a Crow's Foot ERD

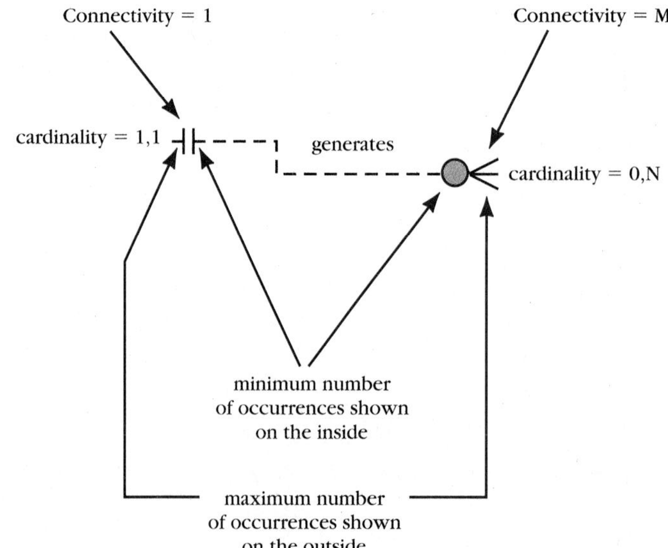

1.15.3 Creating the ERDs

Regardless of which ERD format you prefer, you can easily create it with the help of PowerPoint. You can even produce a set of PowerPoint templates and ERD components that you can cut-and-paste together quickly. However, quite a few database design tools are available. Many of those tools also provide automatic updates of foreign keys and other enhancements when you create relationships. For example, Microsoft's Visio Professional produces a wide range of ERD formats, including the Crow's Foot, automatic FK generation, reverse engineering, and design implementation.

Problems

1.1 Identify the attribute type for each database table attribute in Figure P1.1. The first line has already been completed. Note that the attribute named STU_NUM is both simple and single valued. Note also that the STU_AGE is a function of the current date. For example, on Mach 12, 2003, JoAnne R. Hilliard turns 31. Clearly, the STUDENT table shown in Figure P1.1 needs to be updated. You will learn how to let Access perform such an update in Chapter 5. (*Note:* This table is located in the **Ch01_PROBLEMS.mdb** database that is located on the student CD in the **\Databases(Student)\Ch01** folder.)

FIGURE P1.1
The STUDENT Table Structure and Contents

	STU_NUM	STU_NAME	STU_MAJOR	STU_DOB	STU_HOURS	STU_STATUS	STU_GPA	STU_AGE
▶	21223	JoAnne R. Hilliard	CIS	12-Mar-1972	102	SR	3.20	26
	21226	John. H. Smith	ACCT	23-Jun-1980	79	JR	2.98	18
	21227	Ralph J. Dean	SOC, HIST	18-May-1978	93	JR	3.50	20
	21232	Marie G. Imani	MATH, PHYS	19-Aug-1975	60	JR	2.92	23
	21239	Kathy K. Gill	EDU	29-Jul-1979	15	FR	3.89	19
	21245	Lieu L. Chen	CIS	01-Mar-1977	28	FR	3.35	21
*	0				0		0.00	0

Attribute	Simple	Single Valued	Composite	Multivalued	Derived
STU_NUM	_X_	_X_	___	___	___
STU_NAME	___	___	___	___	___
STU_MAJOR	___	___	___	___	___
STU_DOB	___	___	___	___	___
STU_HOURS	___	___	___	___	___
STU_STATUS	___	___	___	___	___
STU_GPA	___	___	___	___	___
STU_AGE	___	___	___	___	___

1.2 A consulting company tracks its contracts with the help of the CONTRACT table shown in Figure P1.2. Given the CONTRACT table's structure and contents, answer questions (*a*) and (*b*). (*Note:* This table is located in the **Ch01_PROBLEMS.mdb** database that is located on the student CD.)

FIGURE P1.2
The CONTRACT Table's Structure and Contents

	CONTRACT_NUM	CUS_NUM	CONTRACT_AMOUNT	CONTRACT_DATE	EMP_NUM
▶	29012	294	$20,028,500.00	12-Aug-2002	453
	29013	109	$1,983,450.00	12-Aug-2002	304
	29014	385	$2,500,000.00	18-Aug-2002	298
	29015	294	$3,675,500.00	21-Aug-2002	453
	29016	220	$12,500,500.00	25-Aug-2002	304
	29017	192	$789,000.00	27-Aug-2002	453
	29018	109	$4,095,000.00	01-Sep-2002	453
	29019	294	$325,000.00	01-Sep-2002	304
	29020	220	$1,005,000.00	02-Sep-2002	298
*	0	0	$0.00		0

a. The primary key(s) is (are) ____________________

b. The foreign key(s) is (are) ____________________

1.3 Given the CONTRACT table structure and contents in problem 1.2, define the likely relationship type (1:1, 1:M, or M:N) between the contract entity and the

a. CUSTOMER entity. ______________

b. EMPLOYEE entity. ______________

1.4 Using the information provided in problems 1.2 and 1.3, and assuming that only *some* of the consulting company's employees are authorized to write contracts, draw the ERD. Show all entities, relationships, optionalities, connectivities, and cardinalities.

1.5 The owner of a jewelry store sells jewelry on a consignment basis. Each time a piece of jewelry is sold, the piece's creator must be properly credited. All jewelry pieces in inventory are traceable to the jewelers who created them. At the end of each month, each jeweler receives a check based on the pieces sold. The jewelry store owner also maintains a cumulative sales record for all jewelry pieces sold for each of the jewelers.

The jewelry pieces are unique creations. Therefore, each piece has a unique serial number. For example, a piece of jewelry coded AMJ1-0056 indicates a piece of jewelry created by a jeweler whose initials are AMJ, serial number 0056. The 1 following the initials indicates the first jeweler whose initials are AMJ. If another jeweler has the initials AMJ, the code would begin with AMJ2. The sample table contents of the JEWELRY table are shown in Figure P1.5. (*Note*: This table is located in the **Ch01_JewelCo.mdb** database that is located on the student CD.)

FIGURE P1.5
The JEWELRY Table Structure

JWLRY_CODE	JWLR_NUM	JWLRY_NAME	JWLRY_SALES_PRICE	JWLRY_JWLR_PRICE
AMR1-0001	1	Baracuda	$250.00	$120.00
AMR1-0002	1	Unending Waves	$340.00	$204.00
AMR1-0023	1	Lightning Bugs	$250.00	$150.00
AMR1-0045	1	Blue bird	$320.00	$150.00
AMR1-0049	1	Madonna	$250.00	$150.00
BS1-001	11	First Impression	$350.00	$175.00
BS1-002	11	Untitled	$350.00	$175.00
BT1-001	16	Administrative Nightmare	$375.00	$125.00
BT1-002	16	Untitled	$375.00	$125.00
CC1-001	14	Untitled	$280.00	$120.00
CC2-002	14	Pensive Look	$280.00	$120.00
CC2-003	14	Outrageous Character	$900.00	$460.00

a. Evaluate the JEWELRY table structure, concentrating on such details as the nature of the attribute (composite, simple, single valued, etc.) and the existence of possible data redundancies.

b. Given this brief description of the activity and information requirements, draw the ERD for a database that can support the requirements. Show all entities, relationships, connectivities, optionalities, and cardinalities. (You will implement this database design, named JewelCo.mdb, in Chapter 4.)

1.6 Suppose you are shown the attributes in the (poorly) constructed EMPLOYEE_PROB1_6 database table shown in Figure P1.6. (*Note*: This table is located in the **Ch01_PROBLEMS.mdb** database that is located on the student CD.)

FIGURE P1.6
The EMPLOYEE Table Structure for Problem 1.6

Name	Skill	DOB	Veteran
John R. Dempsey		02-Dec-1970	No
Susan B. Smithson	Network Admin., Database Systems Design	11-Apr-1964	Yes
James D. Smith	Database Systems Design	23-Sep-1973	No
Anne W. McDermott		28-Nov-1975	No
George Cheng	Network Administration	09-Jul-1971	Yes
Marie J. Jackson	Systems Analysis, Statistical Modeling	16-Oct-1971	No
James D. Smith	Database Systems Design, Data Analysis, DSS	23-Apr-1965	No

Given this information, place a check mark matching each attribute to its characteristics. For example, if you (wrongly!) think that the "Name" attribute is Simple and Multivalued, place a check mark in the blanks next to "Name" and below the headers "Simple (atomic)" and "Multivalued".

	Simple (atomic)	Single Valued	Composite	Multivalued
Name	___	___	___	___
Skill	___	___	___	___
DOB	___	___	___	___
Veteran	___	___	___	___

1.7 Given the EMPLOYEE table structure and contents shown in problem 1.6, show an alternate way to store the Skill data in the database table. Show only the table structure as it is defined by its attributes. For example, the EMPLOYEE table structure in problem 1.6 is defined by its attributes this way:

Name	Skill	DOB	Veteran

(*Hint*: The alternative way does not use a single composite skill attribute. Instead, it stores the skill attribute components as separate attributes.)

1.8 Recognizing that the EMPLOYEE table structures used in problem 1.6 and the one you created in problem 1.7 are undesirable, you decide to break up the EMPLOYEE table's structure to form three tables. These three tables must have structures that

- Minimize the likelihood of nulls.
- Do not require structural changes to accommodate additional skills.
- Do not place a limit on the number of skills that can be accommodated.
- Maximize the information-capable component of the database.
- Simplify the queries.
- Meet entity and referential integrity requirements.
- Contain attributes whose names conform to the naming conventions that were developed to improve the database's self-documentation properties.

Show the table structures and include the contents to show that no data will be "lost" as a consequence of the structural changes you made.

1.9 Write the appropriate cardinalities next to each of the entities in the ERD shown in Figure P1.9.

FIGURE P1.9
The ERD for Problem 1.9

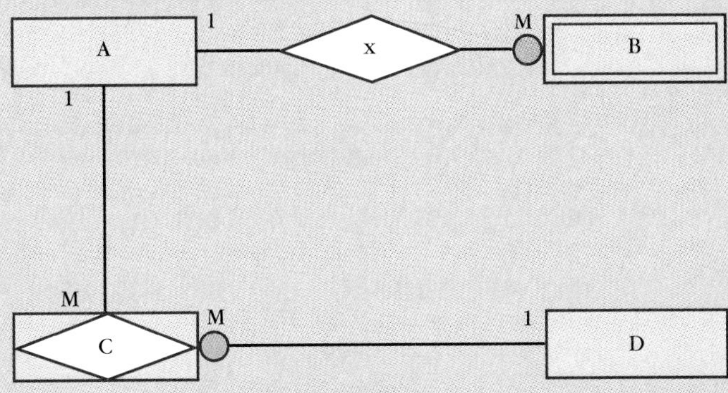

1.10 Given the ERD shown in problem 1.9:

a. The entity C is most precisely described as a ________________ entity.
b. The entity B is most precisely described as a ________________ entity.
c. *At least* what two attributes must be contained in entity C?

1.11 Use the following business rules to create the ERD for a small consulting company named ConsultCo. (The ERD will be implemented as the ConsultCo database in Chapter 4.) Show all entities, relationships, optionalities, connectivities, and cardinalities.

- A client can contract many projects, but one client contracts each project.
- A project may have many (consulting company) employees assigned to it, and each employee may be assigned to many projects.

- Some employees are not assigned to any project. (Such employees run the consulting company's daily operations.)
- One employee leads each project.
- An employee may lead more than one project at a time.
- One employee coordinates each project.
- An employee may coordinate more than one project at a time.
- Some employees never lead or coordinate projects.
- Many of the consulting company employees have multiple job skills. (For example, an employee may be qualified as a systems analyst *and* as a network administrator.)
- Each job description—systems analyst, database designer, accountant, and so on—can fit many employees. (For example, the consulting company is likely to have several database designers, systems analysts, etc.)
- All work done by the employees for any project is charged to that project, using an hourly charge based on the job skill applied by the employee to that project. Each charge to a project must be documented by the date, the employee who performed the work, the job skill applied, the hourly rate for that job skill application, the number of hours—to the nearest 1/10 of an hour—and the total charge for that work. (The total charge, a derived attribute, is computed by multiplying the hours worked and the hourly charge. In Chapter 5 you will learn how to let Access do this computation and storage job for you.)

1.12 Use the following information, in addition to the information provided in the discussion that accompanies Figure 1.27 (a car maintenance ERD), to create a database design for the LUXmobile custom automobile shop. LUXmobile modifies cars and maintains them. Make sure that your design does not require the use of synonyms and that it does not generate any null entries through any of its transactions.

- Each car belongs to a single customer.
- A customer can own more than one car.
- A customer can bring in a car for customization and/or repair work many times.
- LUXmobile employs 23 employees. Of these employees, 14 are mechanics. Three of the mechanics have inspection authorization. Mechanics have licenses and are certified in at least one of five specialties: body work, electrical work, engine work, brake work, and transmission work.
- Each time a car is brought in for repair or customization work, a mechanic with inspection authorization opens a maintenance log. The maintenance log contains the log number, the customer number, the log starting date, a brief description of the work to be done, and the log closing date. The log is closed when the work is completed and a mechanic with inspection authorization has inspected the work.
- When a work log is started, the log form becomes the cover page for the repair and maintenance form. This form contains the details of the work. Each line on the repair and maintenance form provides a precise statement of the work done, the time it took to complete the work, the part(s) used, if any, and the employee number of the mechanic who performed the work. (A mechanic need not have an inspection authorization to sign off on a repair and maintenance form line.)
- More than one mechanic may work on a given car, and a mechanic may work on several cars during any given work period.
- When all necessary repair and/or maintenance work has been completed, a mechanic with inspection authorization inspects all work. If the work is satisfactory, this mechanic closes the procedure by writing the completion date and his/her employee number on the log form. The customer receives a copy of all paperwork and a list of all parts used.
- Most customers pay the bills with a credit card or by writing a check. Some customers pay cash. A few customers are authorized to charge the work to a LUXmobile account. Such customers may make partial payments on a monthly basis or they may pay the entire bill when it is mailed to them. LUXmobile tracks all payments and payment types. The LUXmobile manager receives a monthly summary of all payments by type.

1.13 The RentAll Company wants you to design a database that will enable the company to track all rental transactions by customer and equipment. In addition, your database design must support the company's invoicing, equipment inventory management, and repair. The database design must also support a reporting program that will enable the RentAll management to track the repair history of any piece of equipment. (Such reports are used to decide whether to repair or replace equipment.)

1.14 Design a database for a town library. The database must enable the librarians to check books in and out and to assess fines based on late returns. The librarians must also be able to check which books are on loan and when these books are to be returned. In addition, the librarians want to be able to get a use summary for all books by type: history, romance, suspense, among others. Finally, your database must enable the librarians to manage the book inventory.

1.15 Expand the database design of the Little League baseball program in Figure 1.26 to include the following business rules and information requirements:

- Each team has at least one sponsor, and each sponsor may sponsor more than one team.
- Each team has at least three coaches, and each coach can coach only one team.
- In addition to storing the team scores, hits, runs, and errors for each game, all individual player statistics—hits, runs, and errors—must be stored. (Such data will then yield information summaries for each player and for each team.)

1.16 Identify the attribute type for each database table attribute in Figure P1.16 by placing an X in its blank below each attribute type. (*Note:* The table shown in Figure P1.16 is found in the **Ch01_PumpCo.mdb** database that is located on the student CD. The table shown here reflects the PumpCo company's initial—and unsuccessful—attempt to create a useful database. The VENDOR column contains values that are supposed to reference vendor names, vendor addresses, vendor phone numbers, vendor contact persons, vendor e-mail addresses, and so on. Some parts are produced in-house and, therefore, do not have a vendor reference.)

FIGURE P1.16 The CH1_PumpCo Database's PART_INITIAL Table Structure and Contents

PART_CODE	PART_DESCRIPTION	PART_COST	PART_QOH	VENDOR
BB5	Ball bearing, mod IS5 impeller, 1.5 mm, 997 steel	$3.06	2088	V5, V8
BH5	Bottom housing, mod IS5 impeller, vv3 cast, 1045A aluminum	$27.45	392	
BO5	Bolt, mod IM5-1&2 assembly, 994 steel, 2.5 mm dia, 4 cm length	$3.99	406	V2, V5, V6, V12
BR5	Bearing retainer, mod IS5 impeller	$23.91	385	V2, V5, V6
BS5	Bearing sleeve, mod IS5 impeller	$27.88	408	V2, V5, V6
EM5	Electric motor, mod IM5-1 assembly, 24v	$102.66	364	V4, V5
GA5	Gasket, mod IM5-1&2&3 assembly, 1 mm cre5 cut	$3.52	411	
IC5	Impeller cap, self-locking, 991 steel, mod IS5 impeller	$2.35	379	V2, V5, V6, V12
IM5	Impeller, IM5-1 assembly, RH2-112 composite, 4 cm dia.	$45.94	367	
IP5	Inlet pipe, mod IM5-1 assembly, 2.5 mm dia, threaded, lock ring	$8.76	397	V2, V5, V6
IS5	Impeller shaft, mod IS5 impeller, 994 steel, 2 mm dia, 10 cm length	$11.47	401	
LN5	Lock nut, 994 steel, mod IS5 impeller	$2.78	426	V1, V2, V6, V9
NU5	Nut, mod IM5-1&2 assembly, 994 steel, fits BO5, self-locking	$2.87	400	V2, V5, V6, V12
OP5	Outlet pipe, mod IM5-1 assembly, 2.5 mm dia, threaded, lock ring	$9.03	386	V2, V5, V6
TH5	Top housing, mod IS5 impeller, vv3 cast, 1045A aluminum	$23.18	389	
WA5	Washer, mod IM5-1&2 assembly, self-locking, 1 mm, fits BO5 bolt	$0.55	896	V2, V5, V6, V12
		$0.00	0	

Attribute	Simple	Single Valued	Composite	Multivalued	Derived	PK	FK
PART_CODE	___	___	___	___	___	___	___
PART_DESCRIPTION	___	___	___	___	___	___	___
PART_COST	___	___	___	___	___	___	___
PART_QOH	___	___	___	___	___	___	___
VENDOR	___	___	___	___	___	___	___

1.17 From a database design and implementation perspective, the PART_INITIAL table shown in problem 1.16 contains an attribute with undesirable characteristics. Identify this attribute and explain why its characteristics are undesirable. Be very specific!

1.18 Given your response to problem 1.17, draw the ERD that will eliminate the undesirable characteristics. Show and label all the appropriate entities, relationships, optionalities, connectivities, and cardinalities. (*Note*: The PumpCo vendor list contains some vendors that have never received a PumpCo order. And because some parts are made in-house, they are never ordered from a vendor.)

1.19 Draw the relational schema that correctly fits the ERD you drew for problem 1.18.

1.20 The Aircraft Museum (AC_Museum) has been dedicated to preserve the complete historical record of an aircraft known as the North American Aircraft (NAA) F-100 Super Sabre. This aircraft, the first of the so-called Century Series Fighters, was the first production aircraft to fly supersonically in horizontal flight. You have been asked by the Aircraft Museum (AC_Museum) to design a database that will meet the following requirements and specifications:

- The museum personnel must be able to find and/or track all aircraft data for each model. (Many aircraft reference each model. For example, many aircraft are classified as model F-100D, many aircraft are classified as model F-100C, etc.) Each aircraft is identified by its serial number. (Examples: 54-1328, 56-0080, 55-2897.) Aside from the serial number, aircraft data include the date of manufacture and a copy of the release test flight results. Aside from the model code, model data include performance data such as maximum gross take-off weight, range, maximum speed, stalling speed, and engine.
- The AC_Museum keeps a detailed photographic record for many of the aircraft in its database. In fact, multiple photos are available for many of the aircraft. For example, more than 20 photos depict aircraft 56-2319. (Unfortunately, some aircraft do not have a photographic record at all; AC_Museum is still trying to acquire additional photographs!)
- The AC_Museum also keeps a detailed record of all donated personal stories of the pilots who flew each of the aircraft and of the mechanics who worked on them. Because many people have flown and/or worked on each aircraft, any given aircraft may have multiple stories associated with it. Therefore, any given donor may have donated multiple stories for more than one aircraft. The AC_Museum must be able to match the donated aircraft photos, artifacts, and personal histories to each aircraft.
- The AC_Museum must be able to track all photo, artifact, and story donations to donors. Each donor may have contributed many photos, artifacts, and/or stories. All photos, artifacts, and stories are related to specific aircraft. Each story may reference one or more photos of one or more aircraft. Each donor receives periodic AC_Museum updates about scheduled activities and new acquisitions.
- The AC_Museum also tracks all money donated by each donor. The donor may select two donation categories: the library/research center or the museum collection. Over time, a donor may make multiple donations to one or both categories. The AC_Museum must be able to generate periodic reports that show—for each donor who made monetary contributions—all donations, the total amount donated, and the average donation amount. (*Note:* The total and average amounts donated are computed from the data stored in the contribution table. Therefore, these computed amounts are not stored in the table.)

Given this brief summary of requirements and specifications, draw the fully labeled ERD. Show all entities, relationships, attributes, connectivities, and optionalities.

1.21 Redraw the ERD for problem 1.20 to conform to the enhanced Chen ERD format (see Figure 1.31). Make sure that you use at least the minimum number and types of attributes to make it possible to implement the design.

1.22 Redraw the ERD you produced in problem 1.21 to conform to the Crow's Foot format.

End Notes

1. Technically speaking, a single fact is a *datum*. The plural of datum is *data*. Therefore, we will use data in the plural when we refer to more than a single fact. In short, data *are*, rather than data *is*.
2. E. F. Codd, "A Relational Model of Data for Large Shared Data Banks," (San Jose, CA: IBM Research Laboratory, 1970). *Communications of the ACM* 13, no. 6 (June 1970), pp. 377–87. Dr. Codd expanded the relational model in his "Extending the Relational Database Model to Capture More Meaning," *ACM Transactions on Database Systems* 4,

no. 4 (December 1979), pp. 397–434. Reprinted in the *Proceedings of the International Conference on Management of Data*, June 1979.

3. Bill Inmon is generally considered to be the father of the data warehouse. If you want to examine the data warehouse environment more carefully, read Bill Inmon and Chuck Kelly's "The 12 Rules of Data Warehousing for a Client/Server World," *Data Management Review* 4, no. 4 (May 1994), pp. 6–16.
4. P. Chen, "The Entity Relationship Model: Toward a Unified View of Data," *ACM Transactions on Database Systems*.

Chapter Two

Normalizing the Database Table Structures

Preview

In Chapter 1 you learned some very important design concepts, and you learned how to use the ERD as a design tool. The objective was and remains to create a blueprint that would serve as the framework for database implementation and applications development. In this chapter we close the design circle by introducing a process known as normalization. This process, designed to reduce data redundancy, will fine-tune the table structures that were created during the ERD phase of the database design.

We begin by examining different types of dependencies between a table's attributes. We then show you how to map those dependencies, using a tool known as a dependency diagram. Next we show you how to use those dependency diagrams as the basis for diagnosing poor table structures that lead to redundancies. Dependency diagrams are useful tools when you must transform poor table structures into good ones.

You will learn that normalization is part of the database design process and that it is used concurrently with ERD work. Normalization cannot show relationships between entities; on the other hand, the ERD cannot show relationships between attributes within those entities. Therefore, it takes both normalization and ERD to create database designs that can be effectively implemented and that can serve as the basis for useful end-user applications development.

Objectives

When you have mastered the material in this chapter, you should know

- What dependencies are.
- What data anomalies are.
- What normalization is.
- How to determine normal forms (1NF, 2NF, and 3NF).
- How to create and use dependency diagrams.
- How to change a table structure from 1NF to 2NF to 3NF.
- How to use the ERD to model the normalized table structures.

2.1 DEPENDENCIES

To understand the normalization process, you have to understand the concept of dependencies. As its name implies, a **dependency** is established when the value of one attribute is dependent on the value of another attribute. Putting it another way, the attribute X is dependent on the attribute Y if the value of attribute Y *determines* the value of attribute X. That is, Y is the **determinant** of X. This relationship is usually written as

```
Y →X
```

If Z is also dependent on Y, the dependency may be written as

```
Y →X, Z
```

The dependency concept is best illustrated with the help of some data. For example, in the CUSTOMER data in Figure 2.1, if the CUS_NUM value is 30213, you will also know that the CUS_LNAME = Orlando, the CUS_FNAME = Carlos, the CUS_INITIAL = H, and the CUS_ZIPCODE = 38219. In other words,

```
CUS_NUM →CUS_LNAME, CUS_FNAME, CUS_INITIAL, CUS_ZIPCODE
```

The dependencies in Figure 2.1 are desirable because they are all based on a proper primary key (PK), CUS_NUM. (You should remember from Chapter 1 that a PK *must* determine all other attribute values for each record.)

The INVOICE data in Figure 2.2 shows several types of dependencies. The first dependency is properly based on the (composite) PK composed of the combination of INV_NUM and LINE_NUM. Therefore, if you know both the INV_NUM and the LINE_NUM values, all other attribute values will be known, too. For example, if you know that INV_NUM = 1057 and LINE_NUM = 2, you will also know that PROD_CODE = BK-AVC-T455 *and* PROD_TITLE = Boeing 777 Journey *and* CUS_NUM = 30213 *and* UNITS = 1.

Given the existence of the PK in Figure 2.2, the dependency statement may be written as

```
INV_NUM, LINE_NUM →PROD_CODE, PROD_TITLE, CUS_NUM, UNITS
```

The composite PK performs its intended function because it requires *both* the INV_NUM value and the LINE_NUM value to establish the remaining attribute values. For example, if you know that INV_NUM = 1058 and LINE_NUM = 2, you will also know that PROD_CODE = BK-SC-CO213. The entire composite PK is needed to establish the PROD_CODE. If you only know that INV_NUM = 1058, the PROD_CODE value may be either BK-AVC-T455 *or* it may be BK-SC-CO213. Therefore, it is clear that an INV_NUM value by itself does *not* determine the PROD_CODE value.

However, Figure 2.2 displays two dependencies in addition to the PK-based dependency. The first of these dependencies

```
INV_NUM →CUS_NUM
```

is based on only a *part* of the PK. A dependency based on only part of the PK is known as a **partial dependency.** For example, if you only know that INV_NUM = 1057, you will also know that CUS_NUM value = 30213. Similarly, if you know that INV_NUM = 1060, you will also know that CUS_NUM = 19896. Clearly, you can determine the CUS_NUM values by knowing only part of the PK.

FIGURE 2.1
Some Sample Data to Illustrate Dependency

	CUS_NUM	CUS_LNAME	CUS_FNAME	CUS_INITIAL	CUS_ZIPCODE
▶	28914	Robinson	Anne	K	37215
	30213	Orlando	Carlos	H	38219
*	0				

FIGURE 2.2
Dependency Based on a Multiple Attribute Combination

	INV_NUM	LINE_NUM	PROD_CODE	PROD_TITLE	CUS_NUM	UNITS
▶	1057	1	CD-AVM-MB41	F16 at Farnborough	30213	1
	1057	2	BK-AVC-T455	Boeing 777 Journey	30213	1
	1057	3	BK-SC-CO213	Caribbean Cruise Ships	30213	3
	1058	1	BK-AVC-T455	Boeing 777 Journey	28914	1
	1058	2	BK-SC-CO213	Caribbean Cruise Ships	28914	2
	1059	1	CD-CT-DR905	Turbine Cars II	30213	1
	1060	1	BK-SC-CO213	Caribbean Cruise Ships	19896	1
	1060	2	BK-AVC-T455	Boeing 777 Journey	19896	1
	1060	3	CD-AVM-MB41	F16 at Farnborough	19896	2
	1060	4	BK-AVM-B2001	F18 On Station at Zebra	19896	1
*	0	0			0	0

The second dependency shown in Figure 2.2

PROD_CODE → PROD_TITLE

is based on an attribute, PROD_CODE, that is not even part of the PK. A dependency based on an attribute that is not part of the PK is known as a **transitive dependency.**

2.2 DATA REDUNDANCY

Partial and transitive dependencies should generally be avoided because their existence indicates the presence of data redundancies. A **data redundancy** exists when two conditions are met:

1. Multiple values of an attribute exist within a table.
2. The multiple values are not required to establish the relationships between tables.

The second condition means that multiple foreign key (FK) values are not redundant, because the FK values are required to *implement* the relationships between related tables. Putting it another way, values that are *required* cannot be redundant.

If you examine the INVOICE data in Figure 2.2, you'll see that it contains data redundancies based on the partial and transitive dependencies. For example, if you look at the partial dependency INV_NUM → CUS_NUM, you'll note that, *in this single table structure,* the INV_NUM is not a FK, yet several INV_NUM values occur multiple times, as do several CUS_NUM values. Similarly, if you examine the transitive dependency PROD_CODE → PROD_TITLE, you will see that both the PROD_CODE and PROD_TITLE values occur more than once. For example, note that the PROD_TITLE Boeing 777 Journey occurs three times within Figure 2.2, yet it cannot possibly serve as an FK in that figure's data environment. Such data redundancies are likely to lead to data anomalies.

2.2.1 Data Anomalies

Webster's dictionary defines an **anomaly** as "a departure from the regular arrangement or usual method; abnormality." The database data storage standard requires that, except for foreign key and replicated data requirements, data must occur in only one place at one time.[1] Any departure from this standard is considered to be an anomaly. In other words, the structure in Figure 2.2 is considered to be "abnormal" because it contains multiple copies of the same data without adhering to the requirements that govern multiple data copies.

Data redundancies produce unusual and undesirable data management problems caused by data anomalies. For example, suppose you want to change the PROD_CODE's BK-AVC-T455 product description in Figure 2.2 from "Boeing 777 Journey" to "Boeing Saga: Development of the 777." The data redundancy problem in Figure 2.2 requires you to make this change in three places. In a real-world database, invoicing typically includes thousands or even hundreds of thousands of entries, so the changes are likely to be required in thousands of records. This kind of multiple-record-update problem is labeled an update anomaly. (This kind of problem also exists if you merely want to add new records. Will the product title always be entered correctly?) Or suppose that you want to delete the product BK-AVC-T455 from the database because you no longer stock this product. Deleting the records containing the PROD_CODE = BK-AVC-T455 values causes you to lose all the other data in each deleted record, too, thereby producing a **deletion anomaly.**

Data redundancies may yield unacceptable information penalties, too. For example, suppose you failed to update all the records in which the product title "Boeing 777 Journey" appeared. If you then search the table for matches on the title "Boeing Saga: Development of the 777," you'll not find the records containing the original title, thereby losing relevant information.

Given the management and information penalties associated with data anomalies, preventing their occurrence through the removal of data redundancies is clearly a desirable database design goal. Therefore, removing the partial and transitive dependencies is part of the database design process. You will discover in the next section that partial and transitive dependency removal will break up the table structures that included them, thus producing new table structures.

2.3 THE NORMAL FORMS

A table's normal form is determined by the type(s) of dependencies it may exhibit. The lowest implementable normal form is labeled **1NF,** for **first normal form.** A database table is in 1NF when these conditions are met:

- The PK entity integrity requirements are met.
- Each row/column intersection can contain one and only one value. (This characteristic does not prevent the storage of multivalued attribute values—as long as those values are entered as a single string.)
- All of the table's attributes are dependent on the PK.

The data shown in Figure 2.2 meet these conditions, so Figure 2.2 is in 1NF. However, the 1NF condition does not preclude the existence of partial and transitive dependencies.

Some of the 1NF data redundancy is removed by changing the table structure from 1NF to 2NF, or **second normal form.** A table is in **2NF** if

- All 1NF conditions are met.
- The partial dependencies have been removed.

However, a table in 2NF still contains transitive dependencies. Therefore, it still contains data redundancies.

To remove the data redundancies from tables in 2NF, they must be converted to **3NF,** or **third normal form.** A table in 3NF is one that

- Meets all the 2NF conditions.
- Contains no transitive dependencies.

Changing table structures to increase their normal form rating from 1NF to 2NF to 3NF requires a process known as **normalization.** This process is most easily accomplished with the help of dependency diagrams.

2.3.1 Dependency Diagrams

People tend to work most efficiently in a visual environment. Dependency statements such as

```
INV_NUM, LINE_NUM → PROD_CODE, PROD_TITLE, CUS_NUM, LINE_UNITS
```

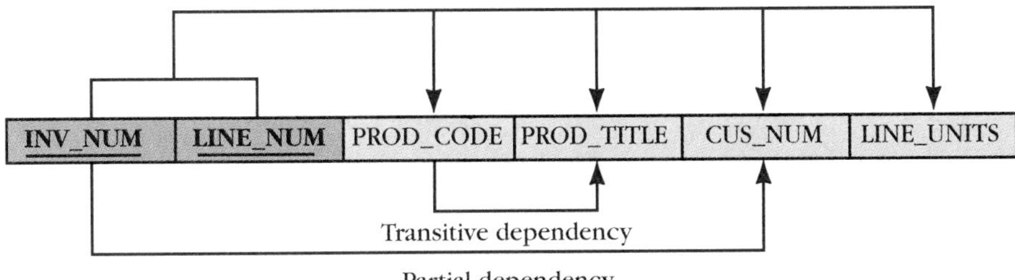

FIGURE 2.3
The Dependency Diagram for the Table Structure in Figure 2.2

tend to hide as much as they reveal. Therefore, mapping the various kinds of dependencies is best done with visual aids known as dependency diagrams.

Dependency diagrams are structures that display all dependencies and their sources. For example, converting the table structure in Figure 2.2 into the dependency diagram shown in Figure 2.3 allows you to answer these questions at a glance:

- What attributes are involved in the dependencies? All attributes are listed by name, and each appears in a rectangle to match its header. PK components are in boldface type and underlined.
- What dependency types exist? The desirable PK-based dependencies are shown above the attribute list. The undesirable partial and transitive dependencies are shown below the attribute list.
- Which attributes are the determinants, and which attributes are dependent? The arrows emerge *from* the determinant, and the arrowheads point *to* the dependent attributes.

Because the initial dependency diagram shown in Figure 2.3 will be broken up to form a new set of tables, the normalization process is known as **decomposition.** In other words, to change the 1NF structure to higher-level structures, we will decompose it.

To change any 1NF structure to higher-level normal forms, follow these three steps:

1. Identify the PK in the initial dependency diagram. In this case, Figure 2.3 shows that the PK is composed of two attributes: INV_NUM and LINE_NUM. Write each PK attribute on a separate line and then write the composite PK components on the last line. (See Figure 2.4.) Each of these attributes *may* become the PK of a new table. Given the structure shown in Figure 2.3, this procedure potentially yields three tables.

FIGURE 2.4
Normalization: The First Decomposition Step

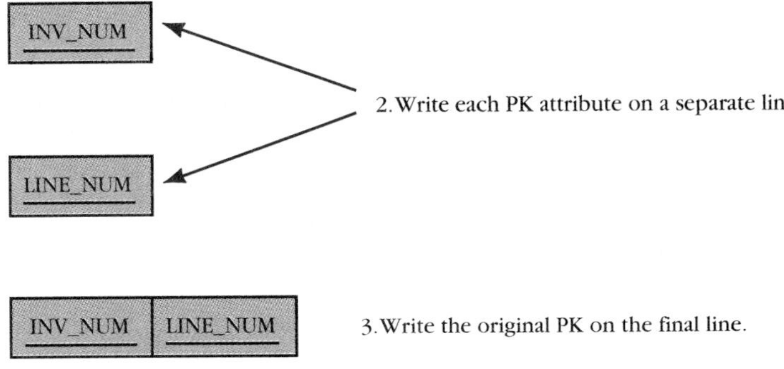

FIGURE 2.5
Normalization: The Second Decomposition Step

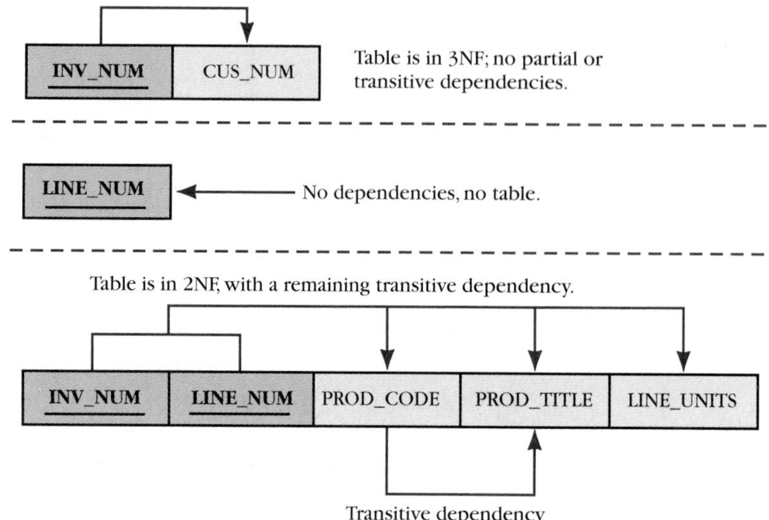

2. Using the basic template developed in step 1, write the dependent attribute(s) next to each PK you identified in Figure 2.4 to create Figure 2.5. Then show the dependencies in each of Figure 2.5's structures. In this case, no attribute was solely dependent on the LINE_NUM attribute.

Note that the second step may leave some structures in 2NF, so you may have to move to the third step.

3. Break out all transitive dependencies to become new table structures. Each transitive dependency is based on a determinant, and this determinant will become the PK in the new table structure. But leave a copy of the determinant in the original table structure to become the FK to the new table structure. In this case, the only transitive dependency in Figure 2.5 was based on the PROD_CODE attribute, so leave PROD_CODE in Figure 2.5's original structure to become the FK to the new PRODUCT table shown in Figure 2.6.

As you examine Figure 2.6, note that all table structures are in 3NF. Note also that we have named the new table structures to match the table names when these tables are implemented in the database. (You will learn how to create and implement tables in Chapter 4.) Finally, note that we have changed a few attribute names to conform to the attribute naming conventions we established in Chapter 1.

After normalizing the tables, it is appropriate to examine whether or not the attributes meet all the information requirements. For example, if the PRODUCT

FIGURE 2.6
Normalization: The Third Decomposition Step

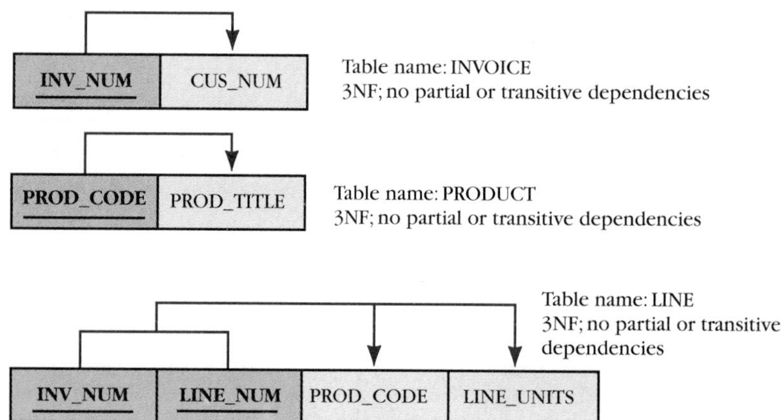

FIGURE 2.7
The ERD for the Normalized Tables

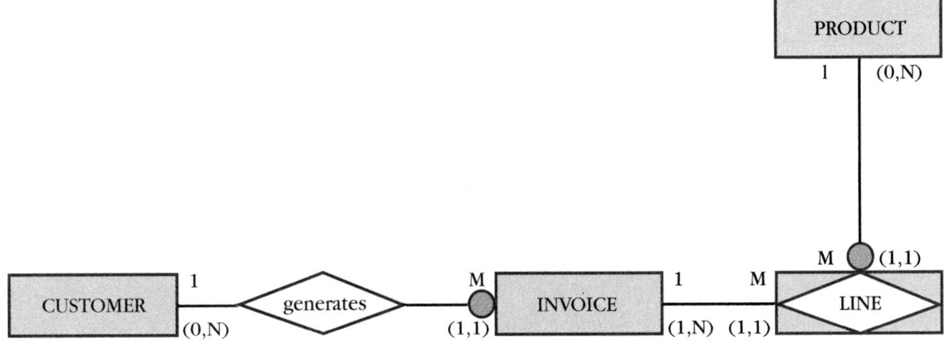

table will serve an inventory maintenance role, it ought to *at least* include the product price, quantity on hand, and minimum quantity on hand. Similarly, the INVOICE table ought to at least include the invoice date and, if reporting speed is important, the invoice total and taxes paid. After all appropriate attributes are included, check the normal forms again and revise the ERD (see Figure 2.7) before you try to implement the tables in the database. (We've added the CUSTOMER to complete the invoicing process.)

As always, the ERD reflects business rules. For example, in Figure 2.7 the ERD indicates that the customer table must also include some potential customers who have not yet bought anything and who, therefore, do not yet show up in the INVOICE table. Similarly, the optionality shown in LINE indicates that a product is not necessarily sold, so it may not show up in the LINE table. You should recall from Chapter 1 that these optionalities may also be used to avoid having to create dummy records. For example, if you make the LINE table mandatory to PRODUCT, you won't be able to enter a product into the PRODUCT table unless you also create a LINE entry for it. Making LINE optional to PRODUCT avoids that awkward situation.

In Figure 2.7 the ERD shows the LINE entity to be a composite entity. Knowing which entities are composite helps to focus the database modeler on the need for multiple FKs in the composite entity. However, keep in mind that some higher-level databases have data dictionaries that require all relationships to be named. Therefore, you may have to alter the ERD in Figure 2.7 to create the variant shown in Figure 2.8.

2.4 THE QUEST FOR HIGHER NORMAL FORMS

Although higher normal forms are almost always better than lower normal forms (3NF beats 2NF, which beats 1NF), sometimes 2NF is preferred over 3NF for performance reasons. In fact, in spite of vigorous debates concerning the legitimacy of 2NF implementations, these debates have largely been rendered academic by

FIGURE 2.8
The Revised ERD, Using Named Relationships

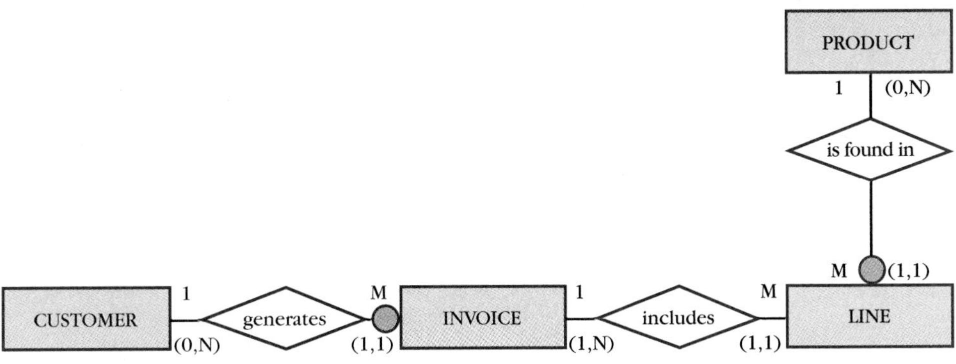

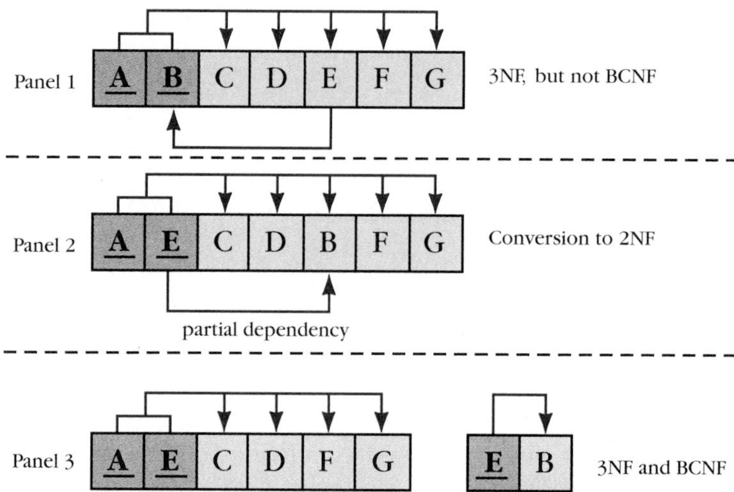

FIGURE 2.9
Normalizing a Table Structure: BCNF

the emergence of the data warehouse database structural standards that *require* 2NF structures.

Normal forms higher than 3NF tend to be of greater interest in the academic world than in most business applications. Because the primary focus here is on the practical aspects of database design and implementation that most business database professionals face, 4NF, 5NF, domain key, and even higher normal forms are beyond the scope of this book. However, there is one additional normal form—known as the Boyce-Codd normal form—that is worth examining.

2.4.1 The Boyce-Codd Normal Form

Most database professionals consider the **Boyce-Codd normal form,** or **BCNF,** to be a special case of the 3NF. In fact, all the 3NF structures in this chapter meet the BCNF requirements.

To understand the difference between BCNF and 3NF, keep in mind that a table is in 3NF when it meets the 2NF requirements and it contains no *transitive* dependencies. *But a transitive dependency exists only when a non-key attribute determines another non-key attribute.* (A **non-key attribute** is one that is neither a PK nor a part of a PK.) However, it is possible for a non-key attribute to be the determinant of a PK or part of a PK without violating the 3NF requirements. For example, panel 1 in the dependency diagram in Figure 2.9, meets 3NF requirements *because there are no transitive dependencies*. But panel 1 fails to meet BCNF requirements because it shows that a non-key determinant, E, determines B, which is a portion of a PK.

To remove panel 1's dependency, switch attributes B and E to let E become a part of panel 2's composite key. This action is quite logical because

- E determines B.
- B is part of the PK.
- Therefore, E can just as well serve as part of the composite PK as B can. (After all, E *determined* B!)

However, this switch does create a partial dependency in panel 2. Use the standard normalization procedures to remove the partial dependency to ensure that the tables meet both 3NF and BCNF requirements. (See panel 3.) Note that attribute E is the FK in the structure on the left to point to the PK in the structure to the right.

If you use our four-step normalization process, you should find the BCNF violation to be rare. Nevertheless, violations of the BCNF requirements are possible, and these violations do set the stage for the undesirable data redundancies that

TABLE 2.1 PROJECT Data Summary Table

Attribute (Field)	Record 1	Record 2	Record 3
PROJ_NUM	25	33	34
PROJ_NAME	Glass Cat	Brass Dog	Lot Lizard
PROJ_LEADER	132	115	132
PROJ_COORDINATOR	115	156	115
PROJ_EMPLOYEE_1	109	134	1213
PROJ_EMPLOYEE_2	134	145	141
PROJ_EMPLOYEE_3	123		156
PROJ_EMPLOYEE_4	141		
CUST_NUMBER	1004	1004	1007
CUST_REP_NAME	John Smith	Anne Jones	John Smith
CUST_REP_PHONE	615-899-1234	615-899-1234	904-432-7654

can produce data anomalies. Therefore, make sure that you know how to produce structures that meet both 3NF and BCNF requirements.

2.5 NORMALIZATION LIMITATIONS: THE ERD'S ROLE

Although normalization is an important database table design tool, you should not rely on it *alone* to produce good database designs. For example, if you examine the table structure and contents in Table 2.1, you will conclude that the table is in 3NF because it contains neither partial nor transitive dependencies. (Note: Because the attribute list is too large to fit on the page horizontally, we have written each of the three records shown in Table 2.1 in vertical format.)

Why did we conclude that the structure shown in Table 2.1 conformed to 3NF requirements? The three PROJECT records in Table 2.1 enable us to draw the following conclusions:

- The PK, PROJ_NUM, properly identifies each of the attribute values uniquely. For example, if you know that PROJ_NUM = 25, you will also know that PROJ_NAME = Glass Cat, PROJ_LEADER = 132, PROJ_COORDINATOR =115, PROJ_EMPLOYEE_1 = 109, and so on.
- The customer number does *not* determine the customer representative. The records clearly indicate that the CUST_NUM value 1004 can either indicate John Smith or Anne Jones. In other words, the customer number 1004 does not *uniquely* identify the customer representative's name, so the CUST_REP_NAME attribute value is not dependent on the CUST_NUM value.
- The CUST_REP_NAME does *not* determine the CUST_REP_PHONE value. Note that two different companies employ a John Smith as customer representative and that the same company could employ two persons named John Smith as customer representatives. (Because names are not unique, they cannot be PKs.) In short, knowing that the CUST_REP_NAME = John Smith will not necessarily tell you the CUST_REP_PHONE value.
- The CUST_REP_PHONE value does *not* determine the CUST_REP_NAME values. For example, 615-899-1234 can identify either John Smith or Anne Jones.

Yet in spite of its 3NF structure, the PROJECT table structure shown in Table 2.1 fails to meet design requirements. For example, the PROJECT table uses the very undesirable multivalued attribute implementation we discussed in section 1.3.3. (Note that the use of PROJ_EMP1 through PROJ_EMP4 produces nulls. You would need to add attributes PROJ_EMP5 through PROJ_EMP10 if six additional employees were assigned to some project. You can imagine the problem if 100 employees were assigned to any project: Think of the number of nulls and the attributes that must be assigned to the table!)

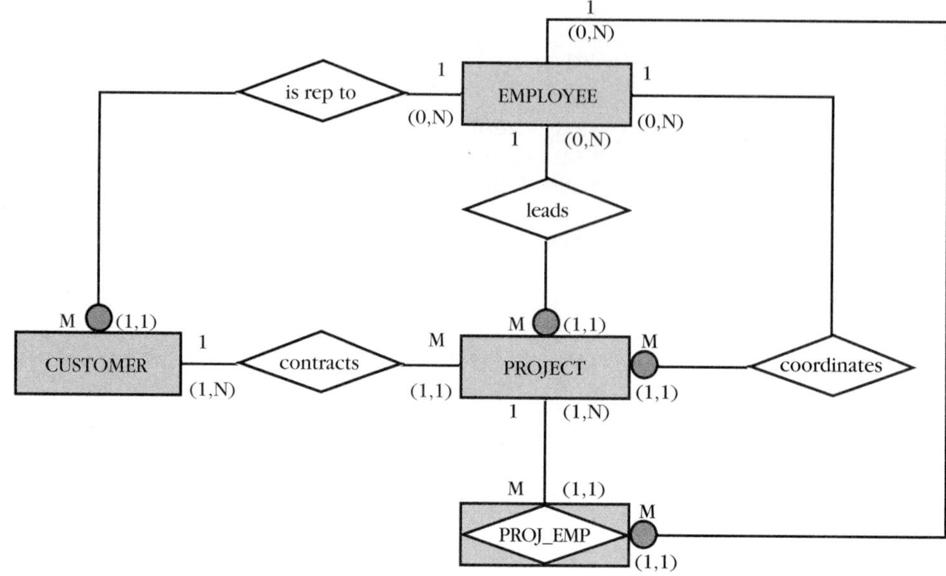

FIGURE 2.10
The ERD for the Revised PROJECT Management System

To produce a viable database design from the bits and pieces distributed through the PROJECT table in Table 2.1, we will have to assemble them into structures that are dictated by the ERD shown in Figure 2.10. We can use ERD techniques to create a set of tables that can be implemented successfully.

Figure 2.10 also provides additional information. For example, the ERD in the figure also tells us that

- All customers have a customer representative who is an employee of the consulting company. (A customer representative is known as a "rep.") Therefore, EMPLOYEE is mandatory to CUSTOMER in the *"is rep to"* relationship.
- An employee can serve as a rep to many customers, but each customer has only one rep. Therefore, a 1:M relationship exists between EMPLOYEE and CUSTOMER in the *"is rep to"* relationship.
- Not all employees serve as customer representatives. Therefore, CUSTOMER is optional to EMPLOYEE in the *"is rep to"* relationship.

Although an ERD contains a wealth of information, the discussion presented in this section does not suggest that ERDs are all you need to design databases successfully. Even using the best ERD techniques, you will still have to fit attributes into tables, and that means you must use normalization procedures to help eliminate data redundancies created by undesirable dependencies. In turn, normalization is likely to produce additional tables, thus causing revisions in the ERD. Our point is simple: It takes a *combination* of ERD techniques and normalization procedures to produce a well-designed database system. And this combination yields an iterative process: produce an initial ERD, normalize, revise the ERD, check normalization, and make final revisions as needed.

Problems

2.1 Using Figure P2.1, label all transitive and partial dependencies.

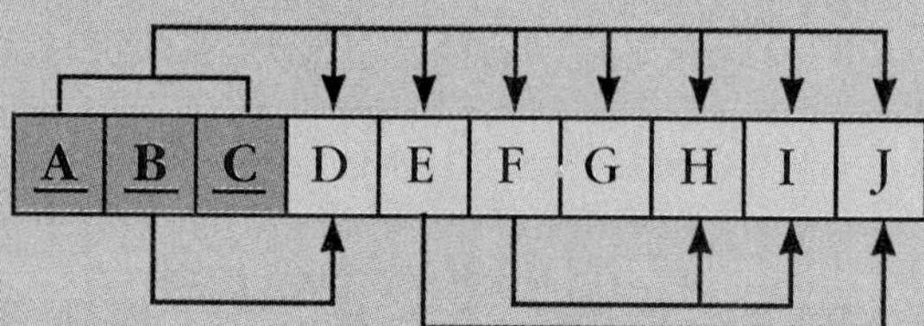

FIGURE P2.1
The Dependency Diagram for Problem 2.1

2.2 Using the dependency diagram in problem 2.1 as the basis for normalization procedures, use properly labeled dependency diagrams to complete the normalization process through step 3. (*Hint*: Your structures will include tables in 2NF.)

2.3 Use the solution in problem 2.2 to complete the normalization process. When you are done, all the tables should be in 3NF.

2.4 Draw the dependency diagram and indicate all dependencies for the table structure and contents in Figure P2.4.

FIGURE P2.4
STUDENT Table Structure and Contents

STU_NUM	STU_LNAME	STU_FNAME	COLL_NAME	DEPT_NUM	DEPT_NAME	STU_CREDITS	STU_CLASS	STU_GPA
21458	Travis	Anne	Business	12	Info. Systems	84	Junior	3.22
21479	Dionne	Randolph	Business	15	Accounting	57	Sophomore	2.79
21480	Becker	Paul	Arts & Science	32	History	81	Junior	3.01
21493	Williamson	Hortense	Business	12	Info. Systems	48	Sophomore	3.08
21495	Chavez	Maria	Business	15	Accounting	54	Sophomore	3.23
21496	Smith	John	Arts & Science	35	English	120	Senior	3.35
21502	Brandeis	Aaron	Education	52	Secondary Ed.	108	Senior	3.95
21511	Smith	Juliette	Arts & Science	41	Mathematics	93	Junior	2.67
21512	Jamaya	Jamal	App. Science	22	Egineering	55	Sophomore	2.85
21533	Kruger	Herman	Arts & Science	23	Psychology	72	Junior	3.21
21534	Smith	Robert	Business	15	Accounting	112	Senior	2.09
21537	Jones	Marsha	Arts & Science	40	Physics	54	Sophomore	2.16
21538	Ramsey	Thomas	App. Science	22	Engineering	78	Junior	2.87
21546	O'Toole	Elisabeth	Business	19	Economics	69	Junior	3.09
21548	Roberts	Melanie	Arts & Science	32	History	51	Sophomore	2.98
0				0		0		0.00

2.5 Normalize the STUDENT table structure shown in problem 2.4 to produce a set of tables in 3NF.

2.6 Use the solution in problem 2.5 to create the ERD.

2.7 Given the structure shown in Figure P2.7,

FIGURE P2.7
The Dependency Diagram for Problem 2.7

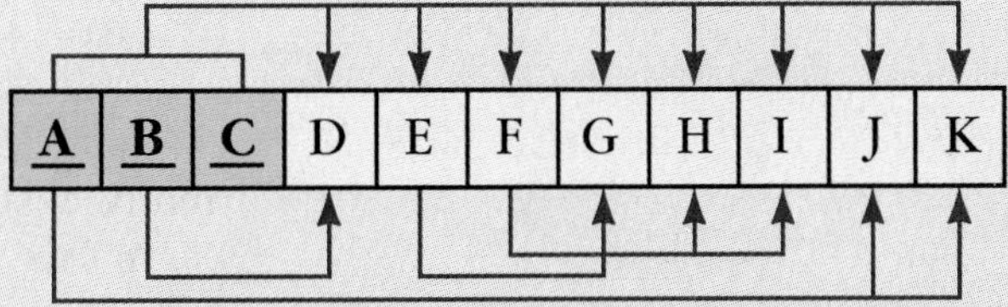

a. Identify all partial and transitive dependencies.

b. Identify the table's normal form: ______.

c. Decompose the table structure to produce a set of table structures that are all in 3NF.

2.8 AVIARS, Inc., has created the table structure shown in Figure P2.8 to keep track of aircraft rental transactions.

FIGURE P2.8
Aircraft Rental Transaction Data

RENT_NUM	CUS_NUM	CUS_LNAME	AC_NUM	AC_TTAF	MOD_CODE	MOD_CHG_HR	RENT_HOURS	RENT_CHARGE
1	25	Smith	2085V	1965.2	PA28-181	$68.75	1.2	$82.50
2	56	Goodpasture	1479P	4001.5	C-172	$64.00	1.6	$102.40
3	38	Troyano	3428Y	3245.8	C-172	$64.00	0.9	$57.60
4	67	Rembacher	2217E	5722.3	C-152	$58.50	1.1	$64.35
5	45	Herrara	2085V	1966.4	PA28-181	$68.75	1.4	$96.25
6	41	Jones	6586K	3289.6	C-152	$58.50	1.3	$76.05
7	62	Williams	2217E	5723.4	C-152	$58.50	1.6	$93.60
8	56	Goodpasture	1479P	4003.1	C-172	$64.00	1.5	$90.00
9	71	McDonald	5032S	3003.3	PA28-200	$84.50	1.1	$92.95
10	54	Robertson	2122R	6784.5	Be76	$175.00	1.9	$332.50
11	38	Troyano	2217E	5725.0	C-152	$58.50	0.8	$46.80
12	49	Krukewski	6586K	3290.9	C-152	$58.50	1.2	$70.20
13	67	Rembacher	3428Y	3246.7	C-172	$64.00	2.7	$172.80
14	41	Jones	2217E	5725.8	C-152	$58.50	3.8	$222.30
15	25	Smith	2085V	1967.8	PA28-181	$68.75	2.2	$151.25
16	45	Herrara	2122R	6786.4	Be76	$175.00	1.0	$175.00
17	56	Goodpasture	1479P	4004.6	C-172	$64.00	1.4	$89.60
18	25	Smith	3428Y	3249.4	C-172	$64.00	1.5	$96.00
19	59	Chen	2085V	1970.0	PA28-181	$68.75	1.2	$82.50
(AutoNumber)	0			0.0		$0.00	0.0	$0.00

a. Given this table structure, identify all dependencies, including transitive and/or partial. (Make sure you take *all* data redundancies into account!) Draw the dependencies based on the PK above the table and draw all other dependencies below the table. (*Hint*: Note that aircraft total airframe hours, AC_TTAF, is updated each time the aircraft is flown. For example, RENT_NUM = 1 shows that aircraft 2085V started with 1965.2 airframe hours and was flown for 1.2 hours. When RENT_NUM = 5, AC_TTAF = 1966.4.)

b. Identify the table's normal form: ______.

c. Break up the table structure to produce a set of tables in 3NF.

d. Create the fully labeled ERD for the structures you created in (*c*). Show all ERD entities, relationships, connectivities, cardinalities, and optionalities.

2.9 AVIARS, Inc., keeps track of its customer aircraft maintenance transaction with the help of the data set in Figure P2.9. The data in Figure P2.9 display the following characteristics:

FIGURE P2.9
AVIARS, Inc., Maintenance Data

	LOG_NUM	LOG_DATE	LINE_NUM	CUS_NUM	CUS_LNAME	AC_NUM	AC_TTAF	MOD_CODE	PART_CODE	PART_PRICE	UNITS_USED	LINE_HOURS	EMP_NUM
▶	1	06-Jul-2002	1	563	Camaro	1197G	2578.9	PA28-181	WR/342-1	$98.66	3	0.5	32
	1	06-Jul-2002	2	563	Camaro	1197G	2578.9	PA28-181	QW-398G	$456.79	1	3.6	32
	1	06-Jul-2002	3	563	Camaro	1197G	2578.9	PA28-181	FR-TR651	$23.45	1	0.6	21
	2	06-Jul-2002	1	215	Smith	3890Y	3002.1	C-172	GT-8875R	$40.00	1	1.9	32
	2	06-Jul-2002	2	215	Smith	3890Y	3002.1	C-172	WR/342-1	$98.66	2	0.4	35
	3	06-Jul-2002	1	306	Carter	2178M	2987.2	PA28-200	GL-321/E	$132.99	1	2.3	36
	3	06-Jul-2002	2	306	Carter	2178M	2987.2	PA28-200	KF3/123H	$28.67	1	3.1	36
	3	06-Jul-2002	3	306	Carter	2178M	2987.2	PA28-200	PO-879R2	$89.75	4	0.8	36
	3	06-Jul-2002	4	306	Carter	2178M	2987.2	PA28-200	DFR-32945	$50.89	1	1.2	32
	4	07-Jul-2002	1	433	Grabowski	3290R	2245.5	C-172	GHT-33R9	$156.78	1	2.5	32
	5	07-Jul-2002	1	563	Camaro	2009T	5009.6	Be76	H5-788591	$62.75	1	1.3	21
	5	07-Jul-2002	2	563	Camaro	2009T	5009.6	Be76		$0.00		2.2	21
	6	07-Jul-2002	1	398	Weisermann	1986D	1875.0	C-152	WR/342-1	$98.66	2	0.4	32
	6	07-Jul-2002	2	398	Weisermann	1986D	1875.0	C-152	QW-398G	$456.79	1	3.7	22
	6	07-Jul-2002	3	398	Weisermann	1986D	1875.0	C-152		$0.00	0	2.1	36
	7	07-Jul-2002	1	215	Smith	3890Y	3004.3	C-172		$0.00	0	0.6	35
	7	07-Jul-2002	2	215	Smith	3890Y	3004.3	C-172	WR/342-1	$98.66	1	0.5	35
	8	08-Jul-2002	1	374	Travis	2987M	4087.4	A36TC	FR-TR651	$25.99	2	0.8	32
	8	08-Jul-2002	2	374	Travis	2987M	4087.4	A36TC		$0.00	0	2.9	21
*	0		0	0			0.0			$0.00	0	0.0	0

Maintenance data, continued

All attribute values are dependent on the combination of the LOG_NUM value and the LINE_NUM value. For example, if you know that the LOG_NUM = 2 and the LINE_NUM = 1, you will also know that the remaining attributes have the following values:

```
LOG_DATE = TUESDAY, JULY 06, 2002
CUS_NUM = 215
CUS_LNAME = SMITH
AC_NUM = 3890Y
AC_TTAF = 3,002.1
MODEL = C-172
PART_CODE = GT-8875R
UNIT_PRICE = $40.00
UNITS = 1
HRS = 1.9
MECHANIC = 32
```

The maintenance data are subject to the following business rules:

- A customer can own many aircraft, but a single customer owns each aircraft. (If a partnership owns the aircraft, the partnership will be billed as the owner.)
- An aircraft is referenced by one model, but each model references many aircraft.
- Each time an aircraft requires maintenance, its identification number and its owner identification (customer number) are entered in a maintenance log. Each log entry is numbered. Therefore, each log number identifies a single aircraft and a single aircraft owner, but an aircraft number and its owner can be entered into the log many times.
- Each maintenance log entry must be made by a mechanic.
- When a log entry is made, a form containing the log entry's number is opened. All individual maintenance actions are recorded on this form, one line per maintenance action.
- Some maintenance does not require parts. For example, tightening a set of bolts does not require parts.

Given this information,

a. Draw the table's dependency diagram.

b. Decompose the dependency diagram you drew in (*a*) through step 3 in the text's normalization procedures. Your new dependency diagrams will contain at least one structure in 2NF.

c. Complete the normalization process to produce a set of structures that are all in 3NF.

d. Use the results in (*c*) to produce a fully labeled ERD. Show all ERD entities, relationships, connectivities, cardinalities, and optionalities.

2.10 Identify all transitive and partial dependencies by labeling them in the dependency diagram in Figure P2.10.

FIGURE P2.10
The Dependency Diagram for Problem 2.10

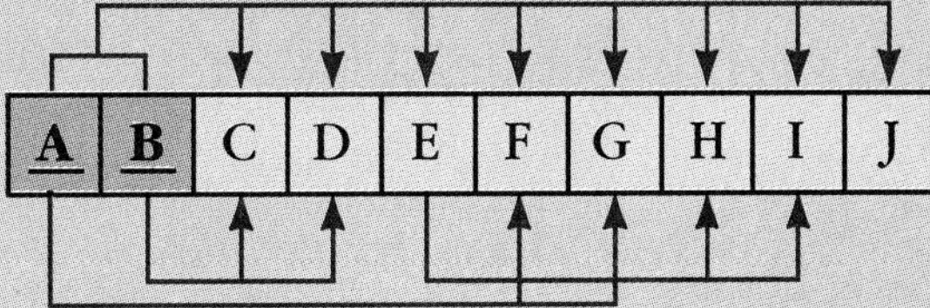

2.11 Decompose the dependency diagram shown in problem 2.10 into a *collection* of dependency diagrams that shows both 2NF and 3NF structure(s). *Label each dependency diagram.*

2.12 Decompose the 2NF dependency diagram(s) shown in problem 2.11 to produce the appropriate 3NF diagrams.

2.13 Create the dependency diagram for a table that contains the record shown next. Make sure you identify all partial and/or transitive dependencies by labeling them in the dependency diagram.

Attribute (Field)	Record
EMP_NUM	442
DRIVER_LICENSE_1	B2118932TN
DRIVER_LICENSE_1TYPE	TRUCKS/BUSES UNDER 26,000 LBS., TRAILERS UNDER 10,000 LBS.
DRIVER_LICENSE_1DATE	21-MAR-1996
SCHOOL_CODE1	23
SCHOOL_NAME1	ACE DRIVERS
DRIVER_LICENSE_2	A3281222KY
DRIVER_LICENSE_2TYPE	COMBINATION VEHICLES OVER 26,000 LBS.
DRIVER_LICENSE_2DATE	28-JUL-2000
SCHOOL_CODE2	18
SCHOOL_NAME2	BIGTRUCKS, INC.
ENDORSE_CODE1	S
ENDORSE_CODE1_DESCR	SCHOOL BUS
ENDORSE_CODE1_DATE	12-AUG-2001
ENDORSE_CODE2	T
ENDORSE_CODE2_DESCR	DOUBLE/TRIPLE TRAILERS
ENDORSE_CODE2_DATE	25-May-2002

2.14 Decompose the dependency diagram you drew in problem 2.13 to produce a collection of dependency diagrams in 3NF.

2.15 Given the record contents shown in problem 2.13 and the 3NF table structures developed in problem 2.14, draw the ERD. Show only the entities and the relationships.

Note: Use the following description of operations to work problems 2.16 through 2.19.

The TrustUs Commercial bank provides commercial loans to start up computer-related businesses. To help ensure that those businesses can succeed, TrustUs requires each business to develop a well-defined business plan that includes a detailed analysis of its technology infrastructure—hardware, software, training, and so on. To help its business clients with their business plans, TrustUs management maintains a list of approved consultants. These consultants must have the proper credentials. For example, if a consultant specializes in networks and database systems, he/she must have network and database certification. (*Hint*: Clearly a consultant may be certified in many specialties such as networking, decision support systems, systems analysis, etc. And naturally, there are many consultants who are certified in each of those specialties.) Although the consultants are independent operators and do consulting work with clients who are not TrustUs customers, TrustUs does maintain the list of contracts between its clients and the consultants. (*Hint*: Note that each client can generate more than one contract, but that each contract is generated by a single client.)

To facilitate the interaction between its customers and the consultants, TrustUs usually suggests that consultants and customers be located in the same region, to help ensure that the consultants are thoroughly aware of regional business environment differences. Although this "regional format" is preferred, there are, of course, many exceptions. For example, although there may be many consultants in any given region, a consulting specialty may not be available in that region, or the consultants in that region may be booked. (*Hint*: Note that each region can contain many consultants, but each consultant is located in a single region. Similarly, each region can be home to many clients, but each client is located in a single region.)

TrustUs tracks clients, contracts, consultants, and so forth in its own database. Because TrustUs management has had trouble with its database, you have been called in to solve the database problems. As you open the first database table, you look at the following three records in a (very poorly constructed) database table. (We have listed the table record contents vertically in order to fit the records to the page width.)

Attribute (Field)	Record 1	Record 2	Record 3
CLIENT_NUM	1003	1015	1003
CLIENT_NAME	Anne G. Traynor	George G. Itaki	Anne G. Traynor
CLIENT_REGION	SE	SW	SE
CONTRACT_NUMBER	1562	1328	1579
CONTRACT_DATE	06/03/1999	11/25/1998	06/22/1999
CONTRACT_AMOUNT	$25,000.00	32,000.00	22,500.00
CONSULTANT_NUM1	231	178	178
CONSULTANT_NAME1	James D. Hide	Kathy F. Smith	Kathy Smith
CONSULTANT1_REGION	SE	SW	SW
CONSULTANT_NUM2	109	231	109
CONSULTANT_NAME2	Maria J. Hernando	Herman H. Jones	Maria J. Hernando
CONSULTANT2_REGION	SE	SW	SE
CONSULTANT_NUM3		109	101
CONSULTANT_NAME3		Maria Hernando	Karl Gofar
CONSULTANT3_REGION		SE	SE
CONSULTANT_NUM4		236	
CONSULTANT_NAME4		Clyde R. Romanov	
CONSULTANT4_REGION		SW	
CERTIFICATION_1	Network	Systems Analysis	Systems Analysis
CERTIFICATION_2	Internet	Network	Statistics
CERTIFICATION_3	Database Design	Database Design	
CERTIFICATION_4	Database Management		

Given the TrustUs information presented here, complete problems 2.16 through 2.19.

2.16 Draw the dependency diagram for the table structure shown here. Clearly indicate and label all dependencies.

2.17 Break up the dependency diagram you drew in problem 2.16 to produce dependency diagrams that are all in 3NF. (*Note*: You may have to create some new attributes to ensure that the table structures are complete and that they can meet the TrustUs information requirements. Also, make sure that the attribute names you used in the new dependency diagrams meet the proper naming conventions.)

2.18 Because you are aware that the normalization procedures you used in problem 2.17 cannot yield a complete and implementable database, you decide to use an ERD to produce the appropriate design. (Now you know why you need both normalization and entity relationship modeling to design a real database!) Draw the appropriate ERD, including the necessary composite structures. (You should have noted that the original table structure was clearly designed to deal with multivalued attributes.) Make sure you label all optionalities, connectivities, and cardinalities.

2.19 Given the results of problems 2.17 and 2.18, create the relational schema. Indicate all relationships and label them to indicate the relationship type.

Use the dependency diagram shown in Figure P2.20 to work problems 2.20 through 2.22.

FIGURE P2.20
The Initial Dependency Diagram for Problems 2.20 through 2.22

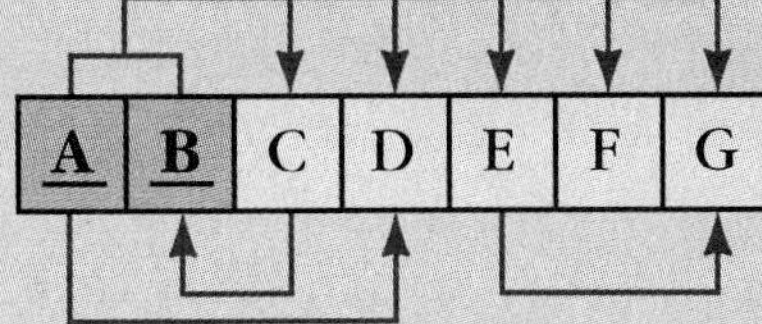

2.20 Break up the dependency diagram to create two new dependency diagrams, one in 3NF and one in 2NF.

2.21 Modify the dependency diagrams you produced in problem 2.20 to produce a set of dependency diagrams that are all in 3NF. To keep the entire collection of attributes together, copy the 3NF dependency diagram from problem 2.20 and then show the new dependency diagrams that are also in 3NF. (*Note*: One of your dependency diagrams will be in 3NF, but not in BCNF.)

2.22 Modify the dependency diagrams in problem 2.21 to produce a collection of dependency diagrams that are all in 3NF and BCNF. To ensure that all attributes are accounted for, copy the 3NF dependency diagrams you showed in problem 2.21 and then show the new 3NF dependency diagrams.

End Note

1. Data are commonly replicated when, for safety reasons, at least one copy of the database exists as a backup. Data replication also is used in distributed databases.

Chapter Three

The POS Database Design Process

Preview

In Chapters 1 and 2 you learned important database design vocabulary and concepts. You also learned how to produce simple entity relationship diagrams (ERDs). And you learned how to use normalization techniques to prevent the occurrence of destructive data redundancies. In short, you became well acquainted with the basics of the database design process.

In this chapter the knowledge you gained in Chapters 1 and 2 becomes the foundation for practical database design. In many ways this chapter turns out to be the key to successful database implementation and end-user applications development. After all, if you don't know how to create a proper database design, learning the Access implementation and applications development skills is likely to become an exercise in futility. You can't implement a database that doesn't exist. The query skills you'll develop in Chapter 5 are of limited value in a badly designed and implemented database. The pretty forms and reports you'll learn to create in Chapters 6 and 7 are of little use if a badly designed database renders their output useless. And so on.

To illustrate the database design process, we will develop the database design for a point of sale (POS) system for a small mail-order company. This POS system will be sufficiently complex to provide a realistic and useful learning experience but simple enough to be practical. We will show you how the POS database design process begins with a detailed description of operations from which precise statements, known as business rules, will be distilled. These business rules form the ERD's foundation.

You will learn how to easily create a complex ERD by building it as a set of modules. Each completed module defines an important set of business transactions. For example, you will learn how to precisely describe the sales transactions to develop an invoicing system, how to update the inventory, how to create a back-ordering system, how to handle defective products, and so on. The advantage of a modular approach is that you will be able to implement the modules one at a time, thus allowing you to produce even a complex system in relatively small and easy stages. When the modules are complete, they can be put together to form the blueprint for a fully functioning database system.

Objectives

When you have mastered the material in this chapter, you will know how to

- Create a description of operations.
- Write appropriate business rules.
- Translate the business rules into ERD components.
- Assemble the ERD components into ERD modules.
- Assemble the ERD modules into a fully implementable ERD.

3.1 DATABASE SYSTEM DEVELOPMENT

To make the POS—or for that matter, any production database system—a reality, you must follow a carefully defined plan. This plan reflects the notion that a database's successful design, its implementation, and its applications development require the successful completion of the following steps:

1. Write a detailed and accurate description of business operations.
2. Develop an extensive and precisely written set of business rules based on the description of business operations.
3. Define the major transaction modules. In the POS system these modules define sales, inventory management, shipping, back ordering, and product returns.
4. Define the entities, attributes, relationships, connectivities, cardinalities, and constraints for each module defined in step 3. Use the business rules developed in step 2 as the source for your component definitions.
5. Create the initial ERD segments to model the modules you defined in step 4. Remember that each of the ERD's entities will be implemented through a database table. The coverage of ERDs in Chapter 1 will be your guide to completing this step successfully.
6. Create a basic data dictionary for all the components found in each ERD segment. At the initial design stage, the **data dictionary** is a document that precisely describes each attribute's characteristics. Table 3.1 shows a few sample data dictionary entries. Keep in mind that the amount of detail in the data dictionary is important. More detail is always better than less detail. (Note that items of special interest are highlighted.)

   Check the data definitions to make sure that they are appropriate. For example, if a PK attribute (field) in one table is numeric, make sure that the FK that references it is also numeric. If you use a date attribute, make sure you select the (Julian) date format so that you can perform date arithmetic, such as finding the number of days within a date range, finding the number of years an employee was employed, and so on.
7. Perform the appropriate normalization checks based on the data dictionary contents. The successful completion of this step requires the knowledge you gained in Chapter 2.
8. If necessary, modify the ERD segments you developed in step 5 to reflect the normalization findings in step 7.
9. Link all the ERD segments created in step 5 and (possibly) modified in step 8 to produce the initial ERD for the entire database. You will use the techniques learned in Chapter 1 to complete this step.
10. Check the normal forms again to make sure that they are appropriate.
11. Complete the final ERD.
12. Perform a final review of the data dictionary contents. Examine all table structures, all attribute characteristics, and the relationships as expressed by FKs.
13. Implement the database based on steps 11 and 12. Make sure that entity integrity and referential integrity are maintained. You will learn how to implement a database in Chapter 4.
14. Create the end-user interface to "connect" the end user to the database. This step requires the creation of the basic end-user components: forms, queries, and reports. You will learn how to accomplish these tasks in Chapters 5, 6, and 7.
15. Create the database system by connecting all the system components. In Chapter 8 you will learn how to use macros, stored in macro groups, to do this job.
16. Verify the implementation and applications development for each module against the business rules and the end-user requirements derived from the description of operations. In Chapter 8 you will see how to approach this task.

Note

Keep in mind that steps 4 and 5 are concurrent. That is, you'll model an ERD segment and then examine the attributes you defined for it in step 4. You may then modify the step 4 attributes and characteristics based on your ERD segment. One of the many advantages of ERD modeling is that it yields a far clearer picture of the logical relationships exhibited between and within the entities.

TABLE 3.1 Sample Data Dictionary Entries for the Two Entities

INVOICE	Description	Data Type	Data Format	Sample Value	PK?	FK?	Derived Attribute?
INV_NUM	Invoice number	Numeric	Autonumber	10010	Yes	No	No
INV_DATE	Invoice date	Date	dd-mmm-yyyy	03-Jan-2003	No	No	No
CUST_NUM	Customer number	Numeric	Long integer	5403	No	Yes (CUSTOMER)	No
INV_SUB	Invoice subtotal	Numeric	Currency	$50.00	No	No	Yes, sum of invoice line amounts
INV_TAX	Invoice tax	Numeric	Currency	$3.00	No	No	Yes, INV_SUB times tax rate
INV_TOT	Invoice total	Numeric	Currency	$53.00	No	No	Yes, INV_SUB plus INV_TAX

LINE	Description	Data Type	Data Format	Sample Value	PK?	FK?	Derived Attribute?
INV_NUM	Invoice number	Numeric	Long integer	10010	Yes	Yes, INVOICE	No
LINE_NUM	(Invoice) line number	Numeric	Integer	1	Yes	No	No
PROD_CODE	Product code	Character	Text	HE-2135-W	No	Yes, PRODUCT	No
LINE_PRICE	(Invoice) line price (from PRODUCT)	Numeric	Currency	$50.00	No	No	Yes, Copied from PRODUCT
LINE_UNITS	(Invoice) line units sold	Numeric	Integer	2	No	No	No
LINE_AMT	(Invoice) line amount	Numeric	Currency	$20.00	No	No	Yes, LINE_UNITS times LINE_PRICE

PRODUCT	Description	Data Type	Data Format	Sample Value	PK?	FK?	Derived Attribute?
PROD_CODE	Product code	Character	Text	HE-2135-W	Yes	No	No
PROD_DESCRIPT	Product description	Character	Memo	Band saw, 2-inch	No	No	No
PROD_PRICE	Product price	Character	Text	HE-2135-W	No	No	No
PROD_QOH	Product quantity on hand	Numeric	Integer	122	No	No	No

17. Create a security system to protect the database from improper and/or unauthorized use. You will learn how to create a full-blown database administrator's security environment in Chapter 10.

18. Test the system thoroughly. This step requires that you put your own database through its paces. We suggest that you let other testers use your database system for a while to see how well it works. It's always best to discover and fix problems before you deliver the final product!

Once you know how to create a functioning database system, Chapter 11 shows you how to display database reports on the Web. We examine steps 1 through 12 in this chapter. Therefore, let's begin by taking a look at the description of operations.

3.2 THE DESCRIPTION OF OPERATIONS

The description of operations is the field in which the seeds of the database design are planted. If this field is not prepared properly, the database design is likely to fail. After all, if you don't know precisely what the business organization's data environment is, how can you hope to design an appropriate database for it? As obvious as this point would seem to be, this crucial component is often shortchanged, thus leading to problems downstream.

A good description of operations contains at least a detailed and accurate picture of the business type, business objectives, organizational hierarchy, data environment, available resources, current operations, current problems and proposed solutions, and limitations. Although several components contain overlapping segments, it is often useful to examine these segments from different perspectives offered by end users ranging from system operators to managers.

3.2.1 Business Type

The business type must be classified and described precisely because it helps determine the

- Number and types of entities.
- Data type(s) and characteristics.

In short, the business type helps establish the data requirements. An airline and a library have different data requirements, as do a law enforcement agency, a grocery chain, a mail-order company, and a bank. Because the database is a data repository, the data types and the data characteristics clearly will have an effect on how you structure the database and its components.

The POS database you develop while you are mastering the contents of this book is transaction oriented. You'll get your first indication of the POS *transaction* focus by examining the following (*very* abbreviated) business type description of the RobSem Company.

RobSem's Business Type

RobSem's business type is classified as specialty retail catalog sales. RobSem's specialty is serving customers whose primary hobby interests are aircraft, ships, and cars, both civilian and military.

To support its sales, RobSem stocks an inventory of specialty books, CDs, videos, and models. RobSem's sales are supported through a POS system, characterized by high-volume, low-cost transactions. Because each sales transaction affects inventory, inventory updates are frequent.

The competitive nature of the specialty retail catalog sales business makes customer satisfaction a particularly high-priority item. Therefore, rapid shipment and efficient management of back order and return transactions are a major business focus. RobSem needs on-demand and detailed reporting capability to establish sales and product composition trends and to manage inventory effectively.

A brief examination of RobSem's business type description establishes that the database structure must support the heavy transaction focus. Although information requirements are very important, they are not the primary determinant of the database structure.

Brief as it is, the preceding business type description helps establish several types of transactions: sales, inventory, back order, and shipment. Each transaction will generate a set of procedures supported by a database design module, and within each module a set of entities will be defined. For example, the sales module clearly must contain customer, invoice, and product entities. (You need a customer to make a sale, each sale is recorded in an invoice, and each sale involves a product.)

Although the transaction details have yet to be established precisely, a bird's-eye view is beginning to emerge already. The remaining description of operations will add the required detail and will help define other processes, entities, attributes, relationships, and so on. You will also discover that the remaining description of operations sections often cover the same ground, but from a different perspective and with different levels of detail. This apparent duplication is very useful because it provides context. To use an analogy, just because you have described an eye precisely doesn't mean that you know the face.

3.2.2 Business Objectives

For a business to succeed, its business objectives must be synchronized with its business type. Therefore, the business objectives must be described precisely and in detail. Because the business objectives are so closely tied to the business type, they help audit the initial database components. For example, while the business objectives are likely to add attributes and entities to the database design, they should not yield database components that are in conflict with those required by the business type. In fact, if such conflicts develop, it's time to examine whether the objectives support the business type. Or if the objectives support the business type, yet yield different basic database structures, it's time to reexamine the initial database modules and structures.

An abbreviated description of RobSem's business objectives follows. Note that this set of objectives supports the basic modules and module components defined by the business type. But also note that the business objectives suggest *additional* database structures and components.

RobSem Company Objectives

Given RobSem Company's sustained sales growth in a highly competitive environment, the company's stated objectives have been and remain:

1. To maintain and manage *sustainable* sales growth. This objective requires designing RobSem operations to foster customer loyalty and to attract new customers by
   a. Maintaining an inventory of products that meet customer needs.
   b. Maintaining and improving order response time.
   c. Delivering ordered products quickly and efficiently.
   d. Maintaining customer contact through follow-up actions.
   e. Maintaining price competitiveness through operational cost control. (Lower costs can be passed on to the customer in terms of lower prices without sacrificing target profit margins.)
2. To maximize net sales returns by maintaining and improving cost controls through
   a. Efficient data access and data-to-information transformation to improve inventory management.
   b. The customer order process.
   c. The vendor order process.

d. The shipping process.
e. The back-order process.
f. The product return process.

Again note that if the organization's primary business objective is efficient *transaction* management, the database's tables, their structures, and their contents are likely to be different from those required by an organization whose primary focus is on *information* management. For example, if the focus is on transaction efficiency and management, the database structure is that of a production database. If the primary focus is on decision support, information management becomes the dominant requirement, thus making a data warehouse database structure more appropriate.

3.2.3 Organizational Hierarchy

Knowing the organization's structure helps define information (reporting) requirements in terms of frequency, detail, and format. Therefore, information requirements help define table contents and may even give rise to additional tables and relationships. In addition, knowing who reports to whom helps define database access requirements and, therefore, security constraints.

An abbreviated description of RobSem's organizational structure follows. A full description would require the complete job description of each job and would include the information required by each manager in the hierarchy. In fact, even nonmanagement personnel may have formal information requirements. For example, the people who prepare the shipments must have a copy of the invoice to pull the products and place them in the shipping boxes.

RobSem Company Organizational Hierarchy

The RobSem Company management consists of a general manager, a sales director, a shipping supervisor, a chief accountant, an information systems manager, and a general services manager.

- The *general manager* makes both strategic and tactical business decisions. The general manager also supervises the activities and monitors the performance of the four department managers.
- The *sales director* supervises a staff of 11 salespersons who solicit, take, and process orders. The sales director also monitors inventory requirements, creates and manages special sales, manages the back-order process, specifies the catalog contents and format, and manages the advertising process. The sales director reports directly to the general manager.
- The *shipping supervisor* manages a staff of four shipping clerks who process and pack the orders. The shipping supervisor coordinates and controls the shipping process and negotiates shipping contracts. The shipping supervisor also manages the shipping department's inventory, including boxes, labels, and other packing materials. The shipping supervisor reports to the sales director.
- The *chief accountant* supervises two accountants and manages the budgeting and payroll processes. The chief accountant also interprets price and cost data and makes both tactical and strategic recommendations to the company owner and president.
- The *information systems manager* supervises two technical (customer) support representatives who monitor the use of existing applications software; modify existing interfaces; and create additional queries, reports, and interface expansions as required. (*Note*: Customer support refers to a process in which the company system's users are the "internal" customers.) The technical (customer) support representatives also troubleshoot hardware and software, install new software, and train the end users on the company's software. The information

FIGURE 3.1
The RobSem Company's Organizational Hierarchy

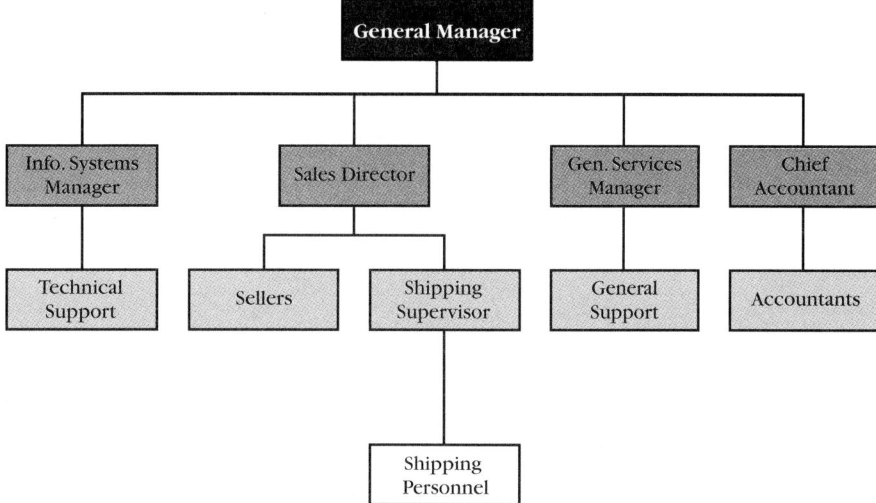

systems manager also monitors system performance, performs database systems design functions, and when necessary, contracts database systems consultants. The information systems manager makes both tactical and strategic technology recommendations to the general manager.

- The *general services manager* supervises all personnel in the general support department. This department houses the general support personnel and a human resources specialist. The general support team, comprised of two secretaries, three clerks, and one janitor, performs secretarial, janitorial, and similar nontechnical services. General support personnel services are available to all departments.

The general services manager and the human resources specialist handle all personnel matters not expressly related and dedicated to the operational processes. (The operational processes include sales, ordering, inventory management, data processing and technical support, and so on.) Therefore, this small human resources team handles personnel relations, including the grievance process, and personnel benefits.

Figure 3.1 summarizes the RobSem Company's current organizational hierarchy.

3.2.4 Data Environment

How much data will the database contain? How frequently are the data updated? What data types exist? Although this description of operations component is related to the business type, keep in mind that even businesses involved in similar activities may have very different data requirements. For example, an aircraft-rental business and a video-rental business both use rental transactions. However, the aircraft-rental business faces a very pervasive set of federal regulations and reporting requirements compared to the video-rental business. In addition, the aircraft-rental company is likely to have a far lower transaction frequency than the video business has. (There are many more video renters than aircraft renters! And individual video renters tend to rent multiple videos during a given period of time.) In any case, even similar businesses may have different data requirements. Therefore, although data requirements are often related to the business type, the data requirements section usually has its own section in the description of operations.

An abbreviated version of the RobSem data environment follows.

TABLE 3.2 Product Classification and Stock

Product Class	Product Type	Product Category	Titles	Units	Type Total	Class Total
Book	Aircraft	Military	62	1,206		
		Civilian	24	897	2,103	
	Ships	Military	32	324		
		Civilian	18	231	555	
	Cars	Military	11	202		
		Civilian	67	1,563	1,765	4,423
Video	Aircraft	Military	34	783		
		Civilian	12	228	1,011	
	Ships	Military	15	187		
		Civilian	9	173	360	
	Cars	Military	2	117		
		Civilian	3	112	229	1,600
CD	Aircraft	Military	16	157		
		Civilian	11	109	266	
	Ships	Military	8	121		
		Civilian	3	98	219	
	Cars	Military	3	46		
		Civilian	7	83	129	614
Model	Aircraft	Military	78	1,319		
		Civilian	56	1,228	2,547	
	Ships	Military	21	996		
		Civilian	16	358	1,354	
	Cars	Military	12	301		
		Civilian	85	1,220	1,521	5,422

RobSem Company Data Environment

Customer Base. The RobSem Company's customer base currently stands at 18,843, a growth of 16 percent since 2001. The customer base is expected to grow at a rate of 12 percent per year during the next 2 years.

Product Mix. As of June 2002, the RobSem Company maintains an inventory of 605 products, including 214 book titles, 75 video titles, 268 model types, and 48 CD titles. The number of products has grown 28 percent since 2001 and is expected to grow at an annual rate of 15 percent during the next 2 years. To track the details of its sales, the RobSem management uses the product classification system shown in Table 3.2.

The summary in Table 3.2 is derived from the most recent product inventory check. Note the difference between titles and units. A military aircraft book title such as *The F-18 Hornet* might have 5 copies in stock and a military aircraft book title such as *The F100D Saga* might have 10 copies in stock. These two titles thus account for 15 military aircraft book units. The Table 3.2 summary provides a quick look at the product mix and current inventory. For example, Table 3.2 shows that 62 military aircraft book titles and that 1,206 military aircraft books are in stock. In addition, a glance at Table 3.2 confirms that RobSem has 2,103 aircraft books, 555 ship books, and 1,765 car books, for a total of 4,423 books.

Sales Transactions. Daily sales transactions have grown from an average of 177 per day to 288 per day. Table 3.3 provides a summary of the company's customer sales transactions.

Back Orders. If customers order products that are not available or are available in quantities less than desired by the customers, RobSem places a back order for

TABLE 3.3 Customer Sales Transactions

	2000	2001*	2002 (est.)	2003 (est.)
Customers	16,229	18,843	21,104	23,637
Sales Transactions				
Total/Year	53,128	63,689	73,864	88,639
Daily**	177	204	240	288
Per Customer/Year	3.27	3.38	3.50	3.75
Items (Total)	847	1,084	1,247	1,396
Books	635	742	816	898
Videos	78	105	126	151
Models	103	179	233	303
CDs	31	58	64	70

*As of June 2001.
**Based on 300 business days per year.

these products. Careful inventory control has kept back orders to the values shown in Table 3.4.

Product Returns. Customers may return defective products or products that do not conform to the customers' expectations. Product returns are summarized in Table 3.5.

Stock Replacement. Most stock replacement orders are processed on a weekly basis, based on each product's minimum quantity-on-hand requirements. However, back-order requirements are handled on a daily basis to reflect RobSem's interest in maintaining and improving order response time and delivering products

TABLE 3.4 Back Orders

Product Class	Product Type	Product Category	2000	2001	2002
Book	Aircraft	Military	32	28	21
		Civilian	5	4	5
	Ships	Military	18	11	7
		Civilian	23	19	14
	Cars	Military	0	2	1
		Civilian	10	12	8
Video	Aircraft	Military	42	30	24
		Civilian	29	22	19
	Ships	Military	9	8	5
		Civilian	15	13	4
	Cars	Military	3	1	2
		Civilian	8	14	11
CD	Aircraft	Military	33	20	15
		Civilian	17	15	11
	Ships	Military	14	10	7
		Civilian	11	7	5
	Cars	Military	9	5	6
		Civilian	11	12	9
Model	Aircraft	Military	56	33	23
		Civilian	78	54	45
	Ships	Military	39	32	21
		Civilian	36	29	22
	Cars	Military	4	3	3
		Civilian	4	0	1

TABLE 3.5 Product Returns

Product Class	Product Type	Product Category	2000	2001	2002
Book	Aircraft	Military	39	41	33
		Civilian	8	11	11
	Ships	Military	14	14	8
		Civilian	25	28	18
	Cars	Military	6	6	3
		Civilian	15	10	8
Video	Aircraft	Military	49	33	24
		Civilian	33	31	21
	Ships	Military	12	14	9
		Civilian	19	25	14
	Cars	Military	11	12	9
		Civilian	18	14	11
CD	Aircraft	Military	38	40	33
		Civilian	21	23	15
	Ships	Military	22	21	18
		Civilian	11	12	21
	Cars	Military	17	11	12
		Civilian	14	19	15
Model	Aircraft	Military	21	30	23
		Civilian	32	28	24
	Ships	Military	30	26	20
		Civilian	23	18	22
	Cars	Military	17	19	11
		Civilian	19	15	15

quickly and efficiently. Regardless of the reason for the product orders, such orders are all bundled by vendor to avoid unnecessary ordering sequences.

Employee Data. RobSem's "people base" is summarized in Table 3.6.

Personnel attributes can be found in the Ch03_POS_2.mdb database that is located on the CD in the **\Databases(Student)\Ch03** folder.

3.2.5 Available Resources

The availability of resources is likely to help you decide the extent to which the database can be developed and used. Therefore, the available resources have an effect on the database design. For example, although you may have a large and

TABLE 3.6 RobSem Employee Count

Job Class	2000	2001	2002
General Manager	1	1	1
Sales Director	1	1	1
Shipping Supervisor	1	1	1
Chief Accountant	1	1	1
Information Systems Manager	1	1	1
General Services Manager	1	1	1
Sales Personnel	6	8	11
Shipping Clerks	2	3	4
Accountant	1	2	2
Technical Support Reps	1	1	2
Secretary	1	2	2
Clerk	2	2	3
Janitor	1	1	1
Human Resource Specialist	0	1	1

complex database in mind, the lack of resources may force you to limit the design and implementation to one or two modules. (That's another reason for modular design: it's good to design a limited database structure that can be expanded easily as additional resources become available!) In any case, make a careful inventory of the available resources. What computers are in use? How many computers are in use? Are the computers networked? What kind of networks? What is the primary operating system? What database software is in use? Is there a professional information systems (IS) staff? How large is it? Does a database administrator manage the database? What resources are available for database design and implementation? Is the resource inventory sufficient to warrant the database design efforts? Let's face it, a single-proprietor business with 10 transactions per day does not require a very extensive database design. *It's useful to remember that a $100,000 solution to a $100 problem is not a solution.*

3.2.6 Current Operations

A very precise and detailed description of current operations is perhaps the most important part of the description of operations. This section is where all the transactions are defined. And these transactions have a profound impact on the number and types of tables, the number and extent of relationships, and the attributes that are used. What types of transactions take place? How many different types of transactions are there? What is the transaction extent?

The current operations portion of the database is very likely to constitute the bulk of the description of operations. Each operational segment requires a precise rendition of actual processes and procedures. Therefore, flow diagrams and/or other graphic displays may be very helpful. Make sure that all forms, reports, policies, and other supporting documents are included. For example, if you describe the shipping process, include a sample label, tracking documents, training syllabus, procedure manual, and so on. Nothing is too trivial to be included. If there is a hard copy of something, include it.

After you have gathered all the relevant documentation and have written a comprehensive transaction statement, use it to review what actually happens. Take a look at what the procedure manual or the verbal descriptions specify. Then track the actual practice. You may be amazed at the difference between the two.

If the practice and the requirements appear to be in conflict, find out precisely why and how. One of the many advantages of having a precisely written set of current operations segments is that it forces careful assessment of the procedures. The procedures in place may actually be detrimental to business operations, so you might have an opportunity to fix operational problems as you develop a sound basis for your database design. If you do this job right, you may truly impress your future clients. *In any case, do not design the database segments that cover the current and/or proposed transactions unless and until there is no longer a conflict between what actually happens and what is supposed to happen.*

RobSem's transaction management environment is largely described by three sets of transactions:

1. Invoicing (customer order processing).
2. Product ordering (replacement and new order).
3. Product returns.

The invoicing process always triggers a shipping process and may trigger a back-order process. To save considerable text space, we include only a portion of the RobSem invoicing process. However, this small example should be sufficient to give you the flavor of the required level of detail in the crucial current operations segment.

TABLE 3.7 Customer/Catalog Scenarios

Previous Customer?	Customer Number Known?	Current Product Catalog	Scenario Action
No	NA	No	2a
No	NA	Yes	2b
Yes	No	No	2c
Yes	Yes	Yes	2d
Yes	No	Yes	2e
Yes	Yes	No	2f

RobSem Current Operations

Invoicing. The invoicing process is triggered by customer orders and conforms to the following event sequence:

1. A customer calls to place an order.
2. A seller responds to the call and initiates the invoicing process by opening the invoice form. The customer's order is subject to the scenarios shown in Table 3.7.

   Given the outcomes in Table 3.7, the scenario actions are described next:

   a. The caller has never placed a RobSem order and has no current product catalog. The seller must first record the relevant customer data on a customer form. The seller records the customer number on the invoice form, verifies the customer address, and verifies the shipping address if it is different from the customer address. The seller gathers enough product information (product class, type, category, title, or some combination) to search the product database to determine the appropriate product number for each invoice line.

   b. The caller has never placed a RobSem order but has a current product catalog. The seller must first record the relevant customer data on a customer form. (See Appendix A for customer attributes.) The seller records the customer number on the invoice form, verifies the customer address, and verifies the shipping address if it is different from the customer address. The seller requests the product number for each product to be ordered from the catalog.

   c. The caller has ordered from RobSem before but does not know his or her customer number. The customer does not have a current product catalog. The seller must first request the customer's last name, first name, and phone number to find the customer number. The seller records the customer number on the invoice form and verifies the customer address and, if different, the shipping address. The seller gathers enough product information (product class, type, category, title, or some combination) to search the product database to determine the appropriate product number for each invoice line.

   d. The caller has ordered from RobSem before and knows his or her customer number. The customer has a current product catalog. The seller records the customer number on the invoice form and verifies the customer address and, if different, the shipping address. The seller requests the product number for each product to be ordered from the catalog.

   e. The caller has ordered from RobSem before but does not know his or her customer number. The customer has a current product catalog. The seller must first request the customer's last name, first name, and phone number to find the customer number. The seller records the customer number on the invoice form and verifies the customer address and, if different, the

TABLE 3.8 Back-Order Scenarios

Product in Stock?	Customer Response to Back Order
Yes, insufficient quantity	Accept available quantity; no back order
Yes, insufficient quantity	Accept available quantity and back order the balance
Yes, insufficient quantity	Cancel order line; continue orders for other products
Yes, insufficient quantity	Cancel invoice if the product is the only one to be ordered and the back order is not accepted
No	Accept back order; continue orders for other products
No	Cancel order line; continue orders for other products
No	Cancel invoice if the product is the only one to be ordered and the back order is not accepted

shipping address. The seller gathers enough product information (product class, type, category, title, or some combination) to search the product database to determine the appropriate product number for each invoice line.

f. The caller has ordered from RobSem before and knows his or her customer number. The customer does not have a current product catalog. The seller records the customer number on the invoice form and verifies the customer address and, if different, the shipping address. The seller must request product information (product class, type, category, title, or some combination) to search the product database to determine the appropriate product number for each invoice line.

3. When the desired product has been identified, the seller enters the product code, verifies the product description and price, and enters the number of units. If the product is not in stock, the seller asks the customer if the product may be back ordered. If the customer accepts the back order, a back order for the product is generated. If the product is in stock but is below the customer order quantity, the seller asks whether the customer will accept the currently available quantity and accept a back order for the balance. The answers to these two questions determine whether a back order is generated. Assuming that the product was in stock or has been back ordered, the seller action sequence completes a single invoice line. Each completed invoice line adjusts the product inventory. The seller then asks for the next product order and repeats the invoice line process. This invoicing sequence is repeated until the order is complete. Table 3.8 summarizes the back-order scenarios.
4. When all order lines are completed, the seller asks the customer what shipment mode is desired and informs the customer of the shipping charge.
5. The seller verifies the product orders and gives the customer each order line subtotal, the order subtotal, the shipping charges, the tax amount, and the order total. If the customer wishes to change any invoice item, the seller makes the required changes and repeats the verification process.
6. If step 5 has been successfully completed, the seller verifies the customer's shipping address and makes whatever shipping address changes are appropriate to ensure that the order is delivered properly.
7. If step 6 has been successfully completed, the seller transmits the invoice to the shipping department. This action automatically generates the shipping label. A shipping department clerk uses the invoice lines to pull the products from inventory, boxes the products, places the shipping label on the box, seals the box, and places the box in the appropriate shipping container for transport to the customer.

3.2.7 Current Problems and Proposed Solutions

If you are designing a new database or you are modifying the design of an existing database, it's a fair assumption that your work is related to the fact that the current data environment is creating problems. (A perfectly functioning database doesn't need your design skills!) You must know precisely what kinds of problems the end users face because you don't want the new (or modified) database to duplicate the existing problems or to increase the number and extent of the problems! And if you cannot define precise solutions to the problems, it's difficult to design a database that reflects those solutions.

A few sample problems and solutions statements follow. The problems and solutions statements may generate additional entities and/or attributes and/or relationships at the database design level. For example, the solution for problem 1 suggests the addition of a product classification hierarchy to make the "pyramid search" possible. Therefore, the PRODUCT table must include additional attributes to cover product class and category. Similarly, the solution to problem 4 requires the inclusion of a supertype/subtype relationship between EMPLOYEE and SELLER. Therefore, the problems and solutions statement generates an additional entity, a new relationship, and some new attributes.

Several of the following problems and solutions statements cause the database designer to modify the database design. However, the most likely impact of problems and solutions statements is on the applications development phase.

RobSem Company Current Problems and Solutions

Problem 1. If the customer does not have access to the current sales catalog and does not know the product code, product information is difficult to track. Because the applications software is not able to provide detailed search key information, the seller does too much time-consuming manual searching and often fails to find the product data in time to complete the sale. Customer callbacks are frequent and costly, especially in terms of lost time.

Solution to Problem 1. Create applications software that enables the seller to perform detailed product searches during the invoicing process. The search routines must enable the seller to perform the search on the basis of a pyramid of information. That is, the search keys must enable the seller to search on the basis of information ranging from minimal to complete. Because incomplete search keys are likely to generate multiple possible matches, the basic information for each of the matches must be shown. The seller can then make a selection from those multiple matches to produce the matching product profiles. The proposed product search keys are the

1. Product number.
2. Product class: book, video, model, and CD.
3. Product category: military and civilian.
4. Product author (if appropriate).
5. Product title.
6. Product producer or publisher.

Because the product search must be enabled during the invoicing process, as well as during a simple customer inquiry, it must be callable via command buttons located on the invoice form and on the product menu.

Problem 2. If a customer purchase is tax exempt, the customer's tax status must be entered and verified with each purchase. This process is time-consuming and is subject to evaluation error.

Solution to Problem 2. Modify the CUSTOMER table to store customer tax-exemption status, verifiable through the customer's state tax number. The invoice application can then automatically look up the tax status through the customer profile and make the necessary adjustments in the invoicing process.

Problem 3. After the applicable state sales taxes have been collected, the current system requires state sales tax collection summaries to be generated periodically. The summaries are then used to write manual checks. The state internal revenue service addresses are stored in a separate file that generates the mailing labels. This approach requires three different actions, several of which are manual. Not surprisingly, the system has led to errors and omissions.

Solution to Problem 3. Store the state internal revenue addresses in the same tax table that is used to look up the tax percentage during the invoicing process. When the periodic tax report is run, one of the reporting options will be Pay Required Taxes. The selection of this option will, for each state, write the appropriate check and generate the state internal revenue office's address label. We suggest the inclusion of a hyperlink in the TAX table to enable the system to transmit the taxes due electronically.

Problem 4. The RobSem Company sales manager cannot track the sales performance of individual sellers. In addition, if there are complaints about an invoice or a shipping problem, RobSem has no way to determine which employee wrote the invoice or the shipping release.

Solution to Problem 4. Store the characteristics that are unique to the seller in a separate table based on a supertype/subtype relationship between employee and seller. The seller identity will be entered on the invoice and on the shipping release to support the required tracking. The SELLER subtype table can then store sales data to track each seller's sales performance.

3.2.8 Available Resources

Resources include people, buildings, computer hardware and software, peripherals, available funds, and so on. Such resources help determine the feasible database solutions. For example, suppose you operate a small business out of a single room in your private residence, using a single stand-alone microcomputer attached to a single printer, and you have $2,000 available for a database application. Given these conditions, a $100,000 system running on a 100-node client/server network is not likely to be a feasible solution. (Fitting a 100-node network into a single room would be a sufficient challenge even without a database design!) In any case, a careful survey of the available resources helps define the extent of the database ballpark.

People

Table 3.6 (in section 3.2.4) shows a 2002 employee count of 26, with an estimated 2003 end-of-year count of 32. RobSem Company's information systems department is small; the information systems manager supervised a single technical support rep in 2002 and is expected to hire an additional technical support rep in the fourth quarter of 2003. Given such a limited staff, the information systems department focuses most of its efforts on internal customer support operations such as applications software installations and upgrades, basic maintenance of computers and peripherals, and staff training.

The information systems manager has a business administration degree with a management major and an information systems minor. In addition, the information systems manager is network certified and has recently earned Microsoft certification. Given this educational background, the information systems manager is well qualified to manage the RobSem Company's network and to conduct staff training and supervision in the use of Microsoft applications software. The information systems manager also manages the current database system's basic operations, including backups, access management, and security.

FIGURE 3.2
The RobSem Company's Building Layout

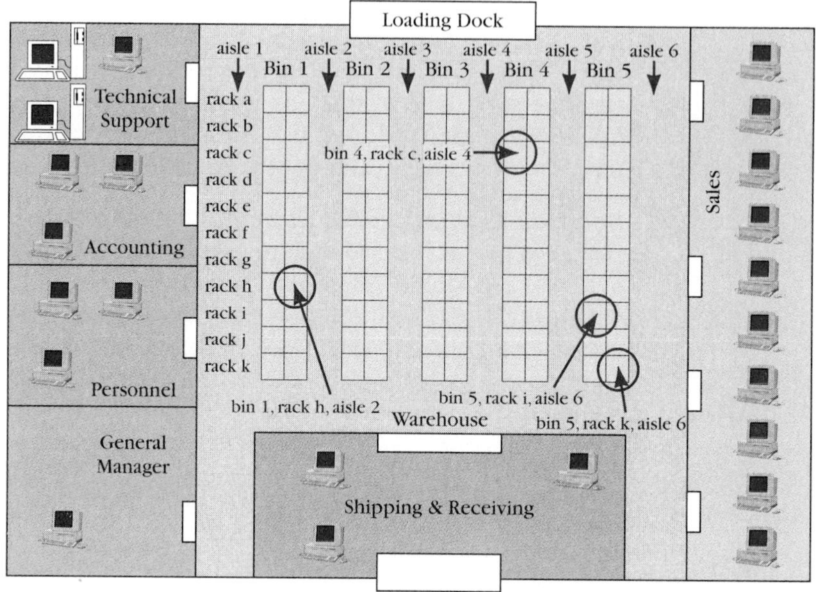

Because the information systems manager has extensive operational duty requirements, consultants and vendor representatives handle major network and database system problems and upgrades. The information systems manager has insufficient database design skills to modify the database systems environment. Therefore, consultants handle all RobSem Company database design modifications and upgrades.

The technical support rep has a community college degree with an emphasis on computer information systems. Given this educational background, the technical support rep is able to perform most day-to-day applications software training, troubleshooting, and upgrading. In addition, the technical support rep handles basic computer and peripheral device maintenance.

Building Facilities

The RobSem Company operates from a 10,000-square-foot building that is partitioned into sales, shipping, data processing, and warehousing areas. The company has a 5-year lease on the building. The company owns all computer and peripheral hardware and software used in its operations.

Figure 3.2 illustrates the physical layout. Incoming products are unloaded at the loading dock and are logged into the company's inventory by the shipping supervisor. All log-in processes are handled in the shipping and receiving office. Once the inventory items are logged in, they are distributed to various locations in the warehouse. Bin, rack, aisle, and shelf designations are used to tag warehouse locations.

As you examine Figure 3.2, note that the product locations are easily found, thus simplifying warehouse management and training. (Several locations are marked and labeled in Figure 3.2. Note, for example, the location of bin 1, rack h, aisle 2. Because Figure 3.2 is a two-dimensional layout, the shelf locations cannot be shown. However, each bin/rack location contains five shelves. Therefore, if a product is located in aisle 3, rack e, bin 5, and shelf 2, it can be located quickly and efficiently. Each product's storage location is kept in the product file

Phone and other orders are processed in the sales office. Completed sales transactions are transmitted to the shipping and receiving department for shipment processing and pickup. The shipping and receiving office handles all product returns.

TABLE 3.9 Computers and Peripherals

Department	PCs	Printers	Bar-Code Readers	Modems
Accounting	3	1	0	3
Personnel	3	1	0	3
Sales	10	1	0	8
Shipping	3	2	2	2
Technical Support	3	1	1	3
Manager	1	1	0	1
Total	**23**	**7**	**3**	**20**

Computer Hardware, Peripherals, and Network

Table 3.9 summarizes the distribution of RobSem's computers and peripheral devices. Two of the three computers located in the technical support office (see Figure 3.2) are network servers.

The RobSem computers and peripherals are connected through a local area network. This network enables the departments—and the people within those departments—to share information and resources. The primary reason for maintaining and operating the network is to share identical, "live" (real-time) data that are always available to and modifiable by different people simultaneously. For example, the RobSem inventory must be current after each sales transaction—and different sales personnel using different workstations may complete different sales transactions at the same time.

The network consists of computers that are connected through network interface cards, networking software, and networking cabling. Each of the 23 RobSem PCs has a unique network address and a unique name to distinguish it from other devices on the network.

The network includes an *adapter* (network interface card, or NIC). This adapter tells each node how to operate as a part of the network and controls the data exchange between all hardware components on the network. In addition, each network device has one or more connectors called *ports*. Network cables are plugged into the adapter (NIC) ports to provide high-speed data transmission. (The adapter type plays a major role in determining the network's type and speed.)

RobSem uses a *client/server network* layout, as shown in Figure 3.3. Note that this network uses two servers. The servers handle almost all of the system's storage requirements and have more disk space, faster CPUs, and more RAM than the other computers. Both servers are *dedicated;* that is, their *sole* purpose is to function as the network server.

FIGURE 3.3
The RobSem Client/Server Network Layout

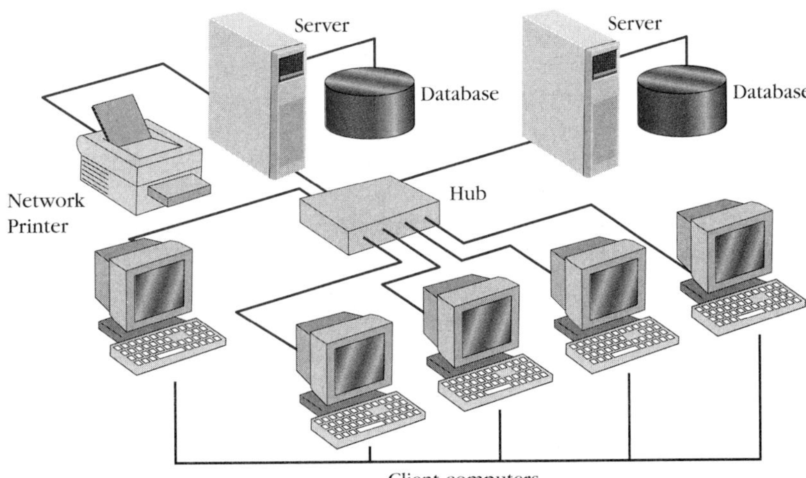

Note

The specifications listed here describe a client/server system, which is typically found in a business environment. The **client** is the source of the end user request for various services. The requested services include data delivery, printing, fax, and so on. The **server** is the computer that provides the requested services. In a "pure" client/server application, all requests are processed on the server side and the results are sent back to the clients. Depending on the extent to which the server handles the client requests, the system may be described as "fat" or "thin."

In contrast to a client/server system, a file system runs all the processes on the user desktop. Access databases run as file systems and do not operate as a client/server application. Even when an Access database application is launched from a network, all processes run on the user desktop.

The two network servers—located in the technical support office—include one database server and one file server. The backend database will be stored on the database server and the front end will be stored on the file server. Every night both servers are backed up to a tape drive for security reason.

RobSem's network environment is defined by the following components:

- Twenty-one workstations each based on a 1.80 GHz Intel processor, 128 MB of RAM, 40 GB hard drive.
- Two servers, each based on Intel processor 850 MHz, 128 MB of RAM, 120 GB SCSI hard drive.
- A hub to connect the network devices.

Computer Software

RobSem runs Windows XP on the servers. The *operating system* handles the data transmission protocols, contains the network management tools, and performs all the tasks that are required to make the network perform its tasks properly.

Each workstation on the network has its own operating system, using also Windows XP. All client computers use the current version of Microsoft Office as the applications software standard.

3.3 EDITING THE DESCRIPTION OF OPERATIONS

The first draft of a description of operations is never the last draft. Once you begin the design efforts, you will discover that there may be missing pieces of information. Or you are likely to discover that the description of operations yields contradictory business rules, thus reflecting an incorrect description of operations component. The beauty of the design process is that the blueprint provides a far clearer logical view of the data environment and the business processes than hundreds of pages of text provide. Therefore, the design process will force you to return to the description of operations and verify and correct its components. (You may have already discovered that what end users *say* they do and what they *actually* do are often very different things.) Then you return to the design—and back to the description of operations if need be. By the time you have completed the first rough draft of your database design, your description of operations may have gone through many editing cycles.

By the time you have honed your description of operations to perfection, you are likely to discover that the design based on it yields undesirable normal forms. Therefore, you are likely to revise your ERD several times. Database design requires lots of attention to detail, and those details must be correct. However, all this work pays off when you implement the design and discover that it's smooth sailing! It's much easier to fix a design problem at the design stage than to fix it after it has been implemented.

Now that you know what the basic components of a description of operations are, let's take a look at an example. However, keep in mind that a real description of operations may be hundreds of pages long and may contain many technical appendixes to provide additional details, especially of the transactions. In addition, a real description of operations contains all of the available forms, policy papers, procedures, and so on. Clearly, such a description of operations cannot be included in a textbook. (For one thing we suspect that you don't want to carry or pay for a 900-page book!) Therefore, we will severely limit our description of operations coverage. However, you will at least see what the basic components are. Your knowledge of those components will help you become a better database designer.

3.4 BUSINESS RULES AND THE ERD SEGMENTS

Business rules are concise statements that are derived from the description of operations. The business rules establish the existence of entities, attributes, relationships, connectivities, cardinalities, optionalities, and constraints. Although not all business rules can be expressed in an ERD, most can and will be.

The RobSem POS system's ERD will be based on the following business rules. Although we have not shown you a complete description of operations, these business rules are derived from such a document. The business rules you see here will become ERD components. To help you understand how the ERD is built, the business rules are logically sequenced to define the database system modules. We then show you the ERD segments for each module. When the process is complete, all the modules are connected to create a complete ERD.

We start by reminding you of the invoicing segment found in the description of operations. You should recall that RobSem includes the following groups of people in its CUSTOMER table:

- Those who have purchased RobSem products in the past.
- Those who have called in the past to make product inquiries.
- Those whose names and addresses have been purchased from commercial lists of hobby magazine subscribers.

In short, RobSem includes potential as well as actual customers in its CUSTOMER table.

3.4.1 The Invoicing Module

The invoicing module will be based on the following business rules:

1. A customer is someone who *may* have made a purchase in the past and who, therefore, *may* have generated at least one invoice.

   Comment: This business rule establishes two entities: CUSTOMER and INVOICE. This business rule also establishes an optional relationship between CUSTOMER and INVOICE. More precisely, INVOICE is optional to CUSTOMER because a customer may not yet have bought anything from RobSem. If you have not yet made a purchase, you cannot have generated an invoice.

2. An invoice is generated only when a customer makes a purchase.

   Comment: This business rule establishes that CUSTOMER is mandatory to INVOICE. (You cannot generate an invoice unless a customer buys something.)

3. A customer may generate many invoices, but each invoice is generated by only one customer.

   Comment: This business rule establishes that the relationship type between CUSTOMER and INVOICE is 1:M.

4. Each invoice must be written by a seller.

   Comment: This business rule establishes a new entity: SELLER. It also establishes that SELLER is mandatory to INVOICE. Although an invoice must be

Special Note

Optional relationships are often established even when they are not dictated by specific business rules. The practical reason for establishing optional relationships is to make it easier to avoid referential integrity errors when new records are entered. For example, if the INVOICE entity is not optional to SELLER, entering a new seller into the SELLER table requires the entry of an INVOICE record to reference that seller, which requires the generation of an INVOICE even though that seller has not yet written an invoice. Generating invoice dummy records just to enable the end user to enter a new seller is clearly undesirable.

Summarizing the effects of business rules 4 and 5, note that the 1:M relationship between SELLER and INVOICE is—from an operational point of view—further refined by ensuring that:

- INVOICE is optional to SELLER
- SELLER is mandatory to INVOICE

written by a seller, it is useful to remember the contents of the note below business rule 5. For example, if an employee has just been made a seller, that seller will not yet have written an invoice. It is inadvisable to generate a dummy invoice record just to create a seller. Therefore, it is useful to make the INVOICE optional to the SELLER just to enable the end user to create new sellers! (However, do keep in mind that all invoices must be written by *existing* sellers. Therefore, SELLER is mandatory to INVOICE.)

5. Each seller may write many invoices, but each invoice is written by one seller.

Comment: This business rules establishes a 1:M relationship between SELLER and INVOICE.

6. A seller is an employee, but not all employees are sellers.

Comment: This business rule establishes that the SELLER entity is optional to EMPLOYEE entity. It also establishes a 1:1 supertype/subtype relationship between EMPLOYEE and SELLER. (Each seller is an employee, and an employee can only be one seller. Only some employees are sellers, so SELLER is optional to EMPLOYEE.)

Before we continue generating more business rules, let's pause to create an ERD segment based on the preceding six business rules. We don't want you to lose track of the many design components that create a complete ERD. Besides, developing the ERD in segments is a good idea for several reasons:

- The design process is easier to follow when you develop the design in stages.
- The ERD modules can be implemented one at a time, thus making it easier to test the implementation. The modules can be connected later to form a complete system.
- It is easier to check the ERD modules to see whether they reflect the business rules accurately when those rules are still fresh in your memory and still few in number. (Sometimes it's easy to get overwhelmed by the sheer number of business rules.)
- Discrepancies are best taken care of before they cascade throughout the complete ERD.

In any case examine Figure 3.4 and note that its contents accurately reflect the six business rules.

Having created the initial ERD segment based on the first six business rules, let's continue the ERD development process by defining additional business rules.

7. An invoice may contain many purchased products, and any product may be found in many invoices.

Comment: This business rule establishes a new entity named PRODUCT and establishes an M:N relationship type between INVOICE and PRODUCT. Because

Note

It bears repeating that optional relationships are often established even when they are not dictated by specific business rules. The practical reason for establishing optional relationships is to make it easier to avoid referential integrity errors when new records are entered. For example, if the INV_LINE entity is not optional to PRODUCT, entering a new product requires the entry of an INV_LINE record to reference that product, which requires the generation of an INVOICE even though that product has not yet been sold. Generating dummy records just to enable the end user to enter a new product is clearly undesirable.

FIGURE 3.4
The Initial Invoicing ERD Segment

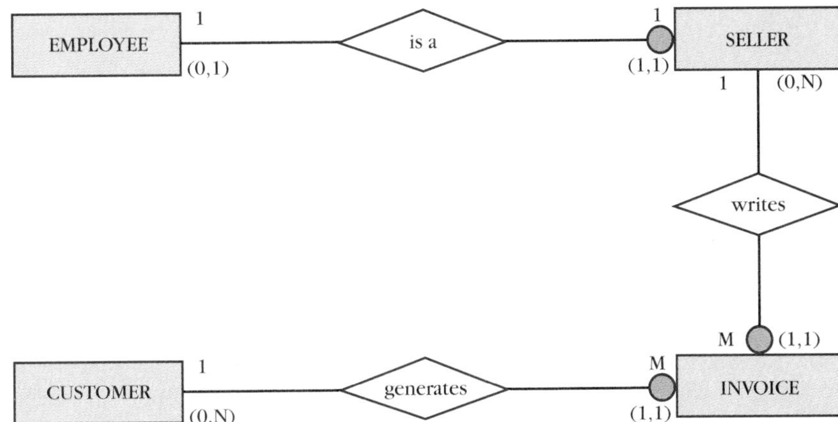

the M:N relationship must not be implemented in a relational database system, the discovery of the M:N relationship forces immediate remedial action to decompose the M:N relationship into two 1:M relationships with the help of a composite entity. The next two business rules provide the solution.

8. An invoice contains at least one invoice line and each invoice line belongs to a specific invoice.

Comment: This business rule establishes a new entity named INV_LINE and establishes a 1:M relationship type between INVOICE and INV_LINE. In addition, the relationship is mandatory in both directions: An invoice line cannot exist independent of an invoice, and an invoice must contain at least one invoice line to reflect the sale of at least one product.

9. Each invoice line references one product, but a product may be found in many invoice lines.

Comment: This business rule establishes a 1:M relationship between INV_LINE and PRODUCT. Because each invoice line references a product and each invoice line is also associated with a given invoice, the INV_LINE must be the connector between the INVOICE and PRODUCT entities. Therefore, INV_LINE must be a composite entity that relates INVOICE to PRODUCT.

10. A product that is never ordered by a customer is never sold and, therefore, will never appear on an invoice line.

Comment: This business rule establishes an optional relationship between INV_LINE and PRODUCT. Specifically, because an unsold product never appears in an invoice line, INV_LINE is optional to PRODUCT.

Now check Figure 3.5 to see how business rules 7 through 10 are translated into an ERD segment.

As you examine Figure 3.5, note that the relationship between INVOICE and INV_LINE in Figure 3.5 is not named. Many designers would argue that the relationship is implied by the composite entity's existence and does not need to be

Note

The composite entity (INV_LINE) in the ERD segment shown in Figure 3.5 requires that the INV_LINE's PK to be the combination of the invoice number, INV_NUM, and the invoice line number, LINE_NUM. Therefore, the composite INV_LINE entity reflects the relationship between INVOICE and INV_LINE. Also, keep in mind that the INV_LINE entity is existence-dependent on INVOICE, because the invoice line cannot exist independent of the invoice. And, because the INV_LINE entity's PK inherits part of its PK from INVOICE, the INV_LINE entity is also a weak entity relative to INVOICE.

The PRODUCT's PK, PROD_CODE, is used as a FK in INV_LINE. Therefore, the relationship between PRODUCT and INV_LINE is represented by a diamond containing the "is written in" relationship name. Because the INV_LINE entity's PK does not include the PROD_CODE, the INV_LINE entity is *not* weak relative to PRODUCT.

FIGURE 3.5
The Second Invoice ERD Segment

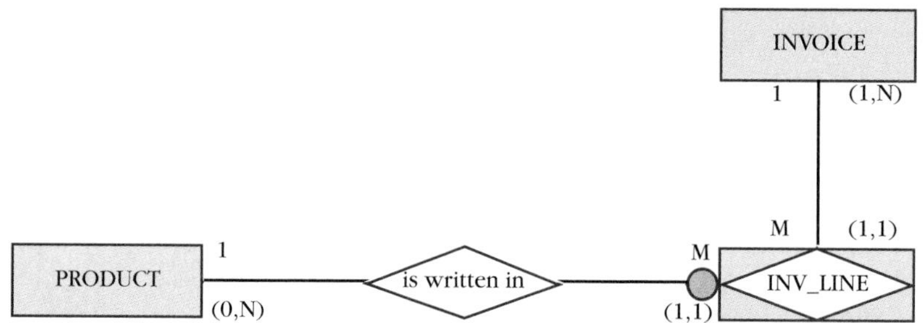

named. However, many design tools require that all relationships be named, whether or not they are implied. In fact, all data dictionaries include the names for all relationships; if you don't name the relationships, the DBMS will do it for you. However, if you let the DBMS create the relationship name, you may not recognize its function later as you examine the data dictionary. (Finding out what a "name" such as TTRU87866785 indicates may be a bit of a chore.) Therefore, the ERD segment shown in Figure 3.5 may be modified as depicted in Figure 3.5A. (We will omit the relationship names when page spacing limitations in the text and in the PowerPoint slides make it convenient to do so.)

When you compare the ERD segments in Figures 3.4 and 3.5, note that they have the INVOICE entity in common. Therefore, you can paste the segments together to create the completed invoice ERD shown in Figure 3.6. This ERD will serve as the basis for the INVOICE module when you implement the database design.

3.4.2 The Product Order Module

To sell products to customers, those products must have first been ordered from vendors. Business rules 11 through 14 define the ERD components for the product order module.

FIGURE 3.5A
The Second Invoice ERD Segment: Alternate Presentation

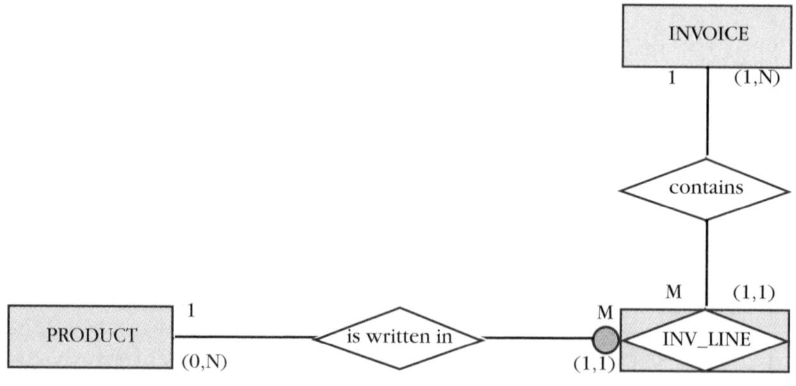

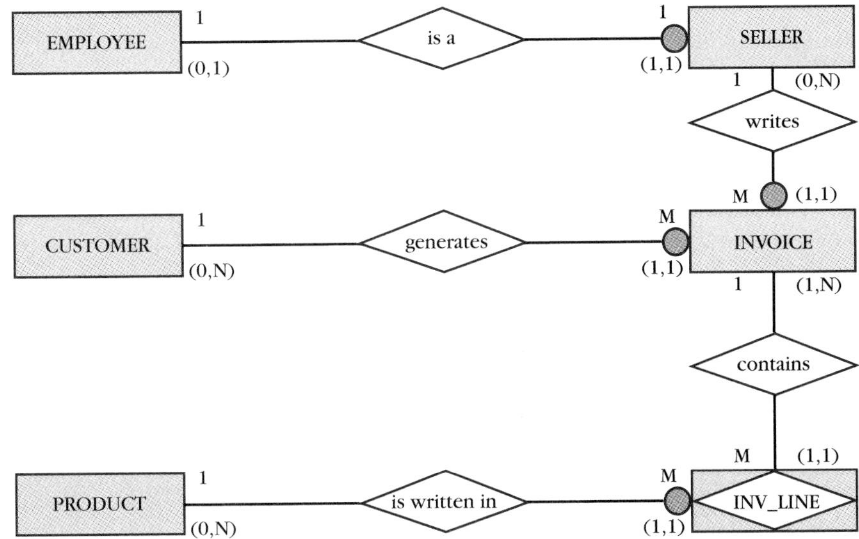

FIGURE 3.6
The Completed Invoice ERD Segment

11. All products are ordered from a vendor.
Comment: This business rule establishes a new entity named VENDOR.

12. The RobSem Company writes a product order to order products from a vendor.
Comment: This business rule establishes a new entity named ORDER.

13. Some vendors on the vendor list have not yet received an order.
Comment: This business rule reflects the RobSem practice of including *potential* vendors in its vendor list. Given this practice the ORDER entity is optional to the VENDOR entity. The practical side of this optionality is that it permits RobSem to add vendors to its VENDOR table without having to write an ORDER entry.

14. A vendor may supply many products, and a product may be supplied by many vendors.
Comment: This business rule establishes the M:N relationship between VENDOR and PRODUCT. This M:N relationship must not be implemented. Instead, it is useful to remember that the product-ordering process essentially mirrors the "customer buys product" process. Therefore, the product-ordering process is modeled by essentially duplicating the invoicing process shown in Figure 3.6. In this case, an ORDER entity performs the same role as the INVOICE entity and the order's order line (the ORDER_LINE entity) performs the same role as the invoice's invoice line (the INV_LINE entity). It will be useful to keep the ORDER_LINE optional to PRODUCT, thus allowing the entry of PRODUCT records without having to generate corresponding ORDER_LINE records.

Figure 3.7 shows how business rules 11 through 14 are translated into the product order ERD module. Because the RobSem product purchase and sales transactions are governed by the same logical procedures, you should not be surprised to discover that Figures 3.6 and 3.7 are similar.

3.4.3 The Back-Order Module

If a product is out of stock when a customer want to buy it, the system must automatically generate a back order. The back-order process is defined by business rules 15 through 17.

15. A back order may be generated when the invoice is written.
Comment: This business rule establishes a new entity named BACK_ORDER. Because products are not usually out of stock, most invoices do not

FIGURE 3.7
The Product Order Module's ERD Segment

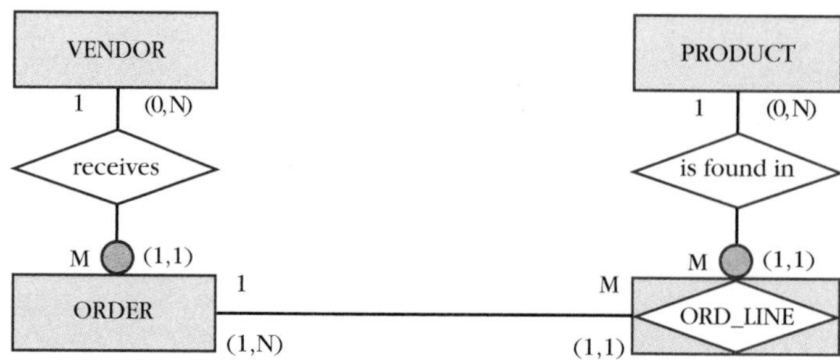

generate back orders. Therefore, BACK_ORDER will be optional to INVOICE. (Note that the business rule specifies that a back order *may* be generated.)

16. An invoice may generate many back orders.

Comment: This business rule reflects the possibility that a customer may want to buy *several* products that are (temporarily) out of stock. Therefore, a 1:M relationship exists between INVOICE and BACK_ORDER. Remember that this relationship is optional because an INVOICE can be generated without a BACK_ORDER.

17. A product may occur in many back orders, and a back order may include many products.

Comment: If a customer wants to buy several products that are currently out of stock, the back order will include those products. Also, if several customers want to buy a product that is currently out of stock, that product will appear in several back orders. Therefore, the M:N relationship exists between BACK_ORDER and PRODUCT. Because the M:N relationship must not be implemented, a composite entity must be created. In fact, the BACK_ORDER entity performs the same role as the INVOICE entity, and the BACK_ORD_LINE will be the composite entity that breaks up the M:N relationship between the PRODUCT and BACK_ORDER entities.

Business rules 15 through 17 yield the back-order ERD module shown in Figure 3.8.

3.4.4 The Product Return Module

If a customer wants to return an unsatisfactory product, the system must be able to handle this situation. Therefore, the design must include this product return transaction. Business rules 18 through 23 will become the basis for the product return ERD module.

18. A DEFECTIVE_PRODUCT record cannot be generated without an INVOICE number.

Comment: The customer must obtain a return authorization before shipping the defective product back. This return authorization is issued only when the customer supplies the invoice number. Therefore, INVOICE is mandatory to DEFECTIVE_PRODUCT.

FIGURE 3.8
The Back-Order Module's ERD Segment

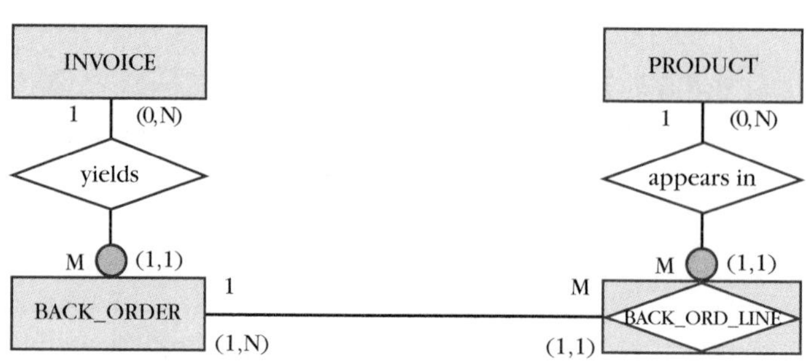

Note

The ERD shown in Figure 3.10 is partially implemented in the **Ch03_POS_2nd.mdb** database that is located on the CD that was bundled with this book. (Look in the **\Databases(Student)\Ch03** folder.) The design in Figure 3.10 will be fully implemented by the time you have reached Chapter 9.

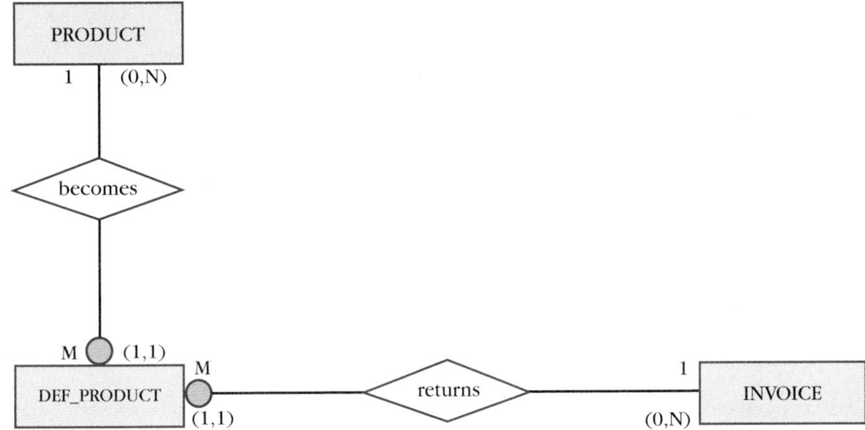

FIGURE 3.9
The Product Return Module's ERD Segment

19. Any DEFECTIVE_PRODUCT record must have a PRODUCT code to be generated.
Comment: Therefore, PRODUCT is mandatory to DEFECTIVE_PRODUCT.
20. Each product can generate multiple defective product returns.
Comment: For example, the PRODUCT inventory may include many aircraft videos, several of which turn out to be defective. Therefore, a 1:M relationship exists between PRODUCT and DEFECTIVE_PRODUCT.
21. Not all products yield defective products.
Comment: DEFECTIVE_PRODUCT is optional to PRODUCT.
22. Only some invoices reflect the shipment of defective products.
Comment: One would hope that only very few defective products are sold. Therefore, DEFECTIVE_PRODUCT is optional to INVOICE.
23. It is possible for more than one defective product to be shipped on a single invoice.
Comment: A 1:M relationship exists between INVOICE and DEFECTIVE_PRODUCT.

Business rules 18 through 23 generate the ERD module shown in Figure 3.9.

3.4.5 Putting the ERD Segments Together

Each of the major RobSem transaction modules shown in this chapter can be implemented and operated independently. However, all the modules must work together to actually operate the business. Therefore, the modules must be pasted together to complete the database design process. This task is accomplished in Figure 3.10. This design is the basis for the following implementation and applications development chapters.

3.5 DESIGN LIMITATIONS

We will limit the database design, its implementation process, and its applications development to the description of operations and the derived business rules

FIGURE 3.10 The RobSem POS ERD

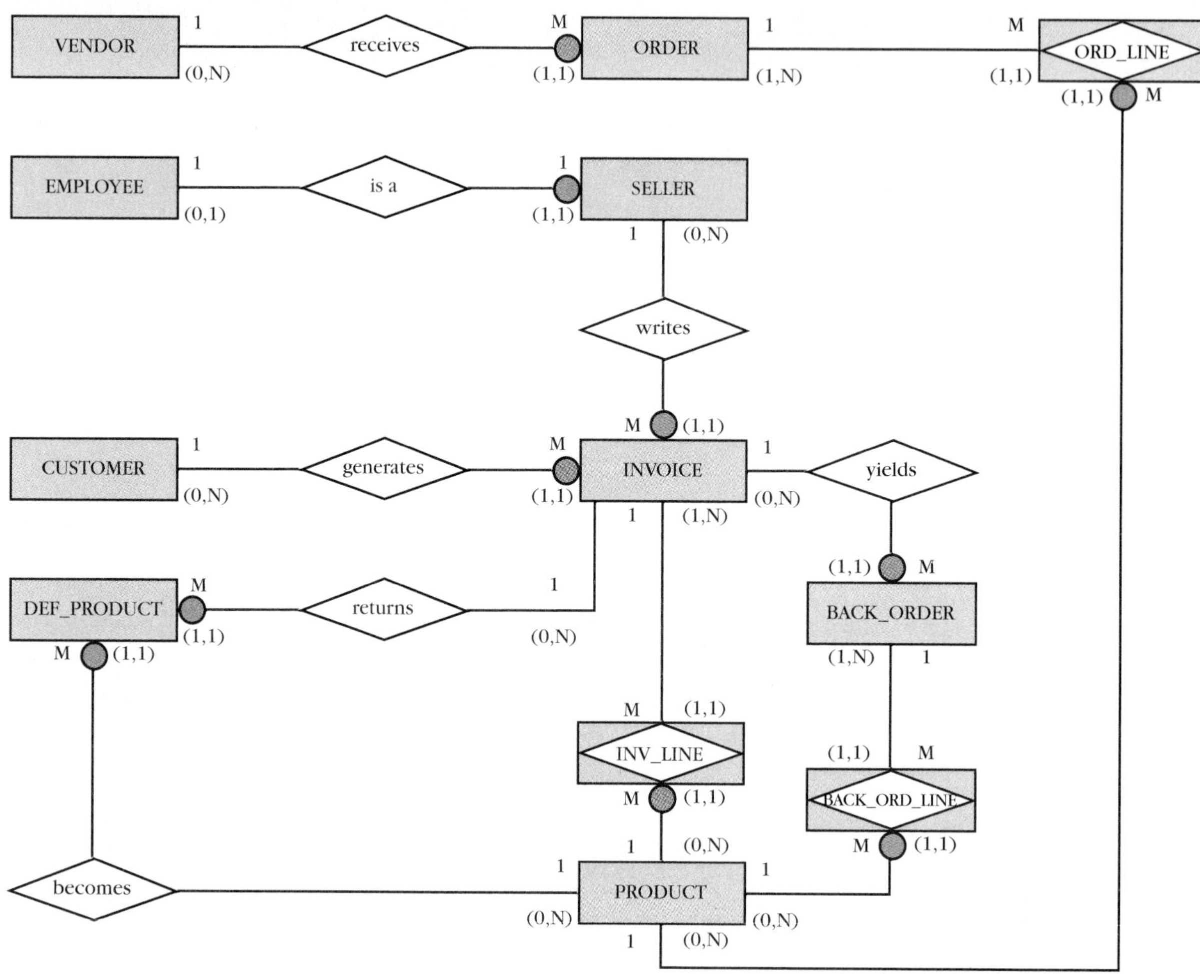

we have offered in this chapter. This design is sufficiently realistic and detailed to enable you to develop practical database skills. Adding personnel management functions, a payroll system, a detailed financial function, and so on, merely increases the book's bulk (and, therefore, its cost) without adding significant value to the learning process. If you understand the database system we have developed thus far, you can add other functions without further coaching!

Problems

3.1 Modify the ERD shown in Figure 3.9 to include the following business rules:

- An employee must have a job classification.
  Comment: For example, an employee may be classified as an accountant, a technical support representative, a janitor, a clerk, and so on.
- Any job classification may be assigned to one or more employees.
  Comment: RobSem Company can surely employ more than one clerk, more than one accountant, and so on.
- Some job classifications have not been assigned to an employee.
  Comment: Some job classifications may not yet have been filled. Also, you must be able to take into account that an employee resignation leaves a job vacancy. Just because your only database administrator resigned does not mean that the job classification no longer exists!

Note

Properly licensed means that a driver must have earned a commercial trucker's license from an insurance-approved commercial driver's school. There are several levels of commercial driver's licenses. For example, a level 1 license allows drivers to drive all vehicles owned by TruckCo, including heavy equipment. A level 2 license allows commercial driving but excludes driving certain types of vehicles, such as tandem trailer, double-axle trucks. TruckCo currently keeps track of the commercial driver's license number, the date on which the license was earned, and the school from which the license was earned. A list of insurance-approved commercial drivers' schools is kept in a separate table. TruckCo also keeps track of the insurance-approved school from which each driver earned the license!

3.2 Create an ERD based on the following description of operations:

TruckCo Trucking, Inc., currently operates a fleet of vehicles. Each vehicle is located at a single base, while each base is the "home" of many vehicles. Each vehicle is classified by type. That is, some are classified as utility vehicles, some as tandem trailer, double axle, and so on. TruckCo does not yet have all listed types represented in its vehicle fleet. (For example, TruckCo does not have a double-axle dump truck in its fleet yet, but this type is currently listed in a TruckCo type sheet.)

Over time, many drivers will drive a given vehicle, and a driver will drive many different vehicles. All drivers must be properly licensed.

Drivers must be TruckCo employees. That is, TruckCo does not hire contract drivers. TruckCo keeps track of all relevant employee data, including data about possible employee dependents. Upon hiring, each TruckCo employee is assigned to a base.

3.3 The manager of the FlyHigh Aircraft Rental Company has asked you to develop a database that will allow FlyHigh to track the use of rental aircraft and customers. (FlyHigh promises to give you additional work if you can produce the currently required database segment.) The following brief description of operations must serve as your guide to the initial database design.

FIGURE P3.3A
Available Aircraft

		AC_NUM	MOD_CODE	AC_TTAF	AC_TTEL	AC_TTER	AC_100HRS	AC_YTDHRS	AC_SINCE100
▶	+	1085Q	C-152	4143.8	1338.2	0.0	06-Dec-02	283.2	27.8
	+	1440P	Be76	4191.2	281.8	1578.7	01-Jul-02	141.8	55.8
	+	1550P	C-172	3002.4	1120.5	0.0	21-Jan-03	300.7	81.2
	+	1998V	C-172	4195.9	1324.2	0.0	03-Nov-02	322.0	76.3
	+	2085V	PA28-181	2011.8	519.0	0.0	05-Feb-03	309.3	83.0
	+	2284W	C-152	4078.7	1114.3	0.0	04-Apr-03	310.4	57.0
	+	2323G	A36	451.6	301.0	0.0	06-Jan-03	185.5	66.3
	+	2873R	C-152	3521.8	784.8	0.0	04-Dec-02	398.0	45.8
	+	3122K	C-152	3436.5	894.3	0.0	25-Feb-02	224.0	78.2
	+	3319R	C-172	4971.7	1123.8	0.0	12-Jan-03	376.0	56.1
	+	5827Y	PA28-200	2279.9	324.7	0.0	26-Dec-02	215.0	90.4
*				0.0	0.0	0.0		0.0	0.0

FlyHigh provides flight instruction and aircraft-rental services to customers, using the fleet of aircraft shown in Figure P3.3A.

FlyHigh's hourly rental charges depend on which aircraft model is flown. The aircraft MODEL table, shown in Figure P3.3B, is a good place to store attribute values that are common to aircraft that "belong" to a given model.

(*Hint*: Note that the AIRCRAFT table uses the MOD_CODE attribute as the FK to MODEL. The existence of the recurring MOD_CODE value in the AIRCRAFT table indicates that the MOD_CODE represents the "M" side in the 1:M relationship between MODEL and AIRCRAFT. The MODEL table's MOD_RETRACT attribute indicates whether or not a model has a retractable landing gear.)

Qualified customers may rent either single-engine or multiengine aircraft. To rent FlyHigh's multiengine aircraft, customers must have a commercial pilot's license, at least 500 hours of total pilot-in-command (PIC) flight time, and at least 100 hours of multiengine aircraft flight time. To rent single-engine aircraft, customers must have at least a private pilot's license. New customers with pilot's licenses are required to

Note

Any business for which you are likely to design databases will use terminology and acronyms that are typically used in that business. (One of your first jobs as a database professional is to learn the jargon used in the business for which you design databases!) In the FlyHigh company's aviation business, the acronym AC_TTAF means "aircraft total time, airframe," which is measured to the nearest 1/10 of an hour. Therefore, the aircraft identified by AC_NUM 5 1085Q has logged 4029.1 hours on its airframe. The acronym AC_TTEL means "aircraft, total time on the left engine." Because the AIRCRAFT table includes both twin-engine and single-engine aircraft, the single-engine aircraft engine times are maintained in the AC_TTEL field. Naturally, the AC_TTER (right-engine total time) field value is set to 0.0 for single-engine aircraft. The AC_100HRS field indicates the date on which the 100-hour inspection was performed on the aircraft. The AC_SINCE100 field indicates the hours flown since the 100-hour inspection. Because 100-hour inspections may be performed *before* the 100-hour limit is reached, the AC_SINCE100 field value is not necessarily based on 100-hour increments. (For example, if an aircraft requires repair after it has flown 70 hours, FlyHigh may perform the 100-hour inspection at that time.)

FIGURE P3.3B The MODEL Table Contents

MOD_CODE	MOD_NAME	MOD_TYPE	MOD_MANUFACTURER	MOD_ENGINES	MOD_SEATS	MOD_RETRACT	MOD_CHG
A36	Bonanza	Single engine	Beechcraft	1	4	☑	$95.50
B55	Baron	Multi-engine	Beechcraft	2	6	☑	$265.00
Be76	Duchess	Multi-engine	Beechcraft	2	4	☑	$175.00
C-152	Commuter II	Single engine	Cessna	1	2	☐	$58.50
C-172	Skyhawk	Single engine	Cessna	1	4	☐	$64.00
C-182	Skylane	Single engine	Cessna	1	4	☐	$65.00
C-210D	Centurion	Single engine	Cessna	1	6	☑	$95.50
PA-28-151	Warrior	Single engine	Piper	1	4	☐	$65.75
PA28-181	Archer II	Single engine	Piper	1	4	☐	$68.75
PA28-200	Arrow II	Single engine	Piper	1	4	☑	$84.50
PA-31-350	Navajo Chieftain	Multi-engine	Piper	2	8	☑	$387.75
PA-32	Cherokee 6	Single engine	Piper	1	6	☐	$72.00
PA-38-112	Tomahawk	Single engine	Piper	1	2	☐	$55.00
PA-44-180	Seminole	Multi-engine	Piper	2	4	☑	$168.00
				1			$0.00

demonstrate their flight proficiency by passing a FlyHigh flight proficiency check. Customers must hold a current medical certificate and must have satisfied a biennial flight check requirement.

Customers may hold multiple licenses and ratings. For example, a customer may have a commercial license with instrument and multiengine ratings. The license and rating descriptions are shown in Figure P3.3C.

FIGURE P3.3C License and Rating Descriptions

CERT_CODE	CERT_DESCRIPTION
ATP	Airline Transport Pilot
COMM	Commercial Pilot
I	Instrument rating
MEL	Multi-Engine, Land
PVT	Private Pilot
SEL	Single Engine, Land

Over time, customers may rent many different aircraft, and each aircraft can be rented to many different customers. The rental transaction requires that you track the customer, the aircraft, the date, the hours flown, the rental charge per hour, the total rental charge, the tax paid, and the total rental charge.

FlyHigh wants your database design to accommodate all invoicing activities, aircraft use, and customer rental activity. FlyHigh wants to track rentals—both hours and revenues—by aircraft model, by aircraft, and by customer.

When a customer returns the aircraft, the time flown, measured by a Hobbs meter located in the aircraft, must be used to update the aircraft total airframe time, the aircraft total engine time, the aircraft year-to-date (YTD) hours flown, the aircraft hours flown since the 100-hour inspection, and the customer hours flown.

Making use of all of the information given, produce the fully labeled ERD on which the database implementation will be based. Show all entities, relationships, optionalities, connectivities, and cardinalities.

3.4 Create the relational schema for the design you produced in problem 3.3.

3.5 Expand the ERD created in problem 3.2 to include the following description of operations.

The TruckCo Company: Driver and Mechanic Licensing, Endorsements, and Company Testing Requirements

For both insurance and legal reasons, TruckCo requires detailed tracking of licenses and endorsements earned by its drivers and mechanics. TruckCo also subjects its drivers to company testing procedures to ensure knowledge of and/or compliance with company, state, and federal rules and regulations.

Drivers

TruckCo's drivers may have any one of four license types: A, B, C, or D. License type A provides types A, B, C, and D privileges. License type B provides types B, C, and D privileges. License type C provides types C and D privileges. And License type D restricts the driver to the privileges of a type D license. The LICENSE table's contents are shown in Figure P3.5A.

FIGURE P3.5A
Driver Licenses

LIC_TYPE	LIC_DESCRIPTION
A	Combination vehicles over 26,000 lbs.
B	Trucks/Buses under 26,000 lbs., trailers under 10,000 lbs.
C	Trucks/Buses 26,000 lbs. and over. Requires special endorsements.
D	Vehicles under 26,000 lbs. Requires special endorsements.

TruckCo keeps track of all licenses earned for each of its drivers. All licenses must have been earned from insurance-approved commercial driver schools. Therefore, if driver J. G. Hill earned a type D license on 02/12/1997 from the Great Trucks Driver's Institute and a type C license on 09/23/2001 from the XYZ Trucking School, TruckCo wants to be able to track these facts. Because all licenses are awarded after the candidate has passed a practical examination and a written examination, the scores of these examinations are also tracked. TruckCo also keeps the most recently earned license number, the date on which that license was earned, the (insurance-approved) school's code, and the required license renewal date in the DRIVER table.

The driver licenses must also carry endorsements that describe specific activities. For example, endorsement P allows the license holder to transport more than 15 occupants including the driver, endorsement T allows the license holder to drive double and triple trailers, endorsement H allows the license holder to carry hazardous materials, and so on. The endorsement types are shown in Figure P3.5B. The driver license endorsements, too, must have been earned from the list of insurance-approved driver schools. (Driver endorsements are indicated as D in the **ENDORSE_TYPE.**)

FIGURE P3.5B
Driver Endorsements

ENDORSE_CODE	ENDORSE_TYPE	ENDORSE_DESCRIPT
B	M	Brake Systems
D	M	Diesel
E	M	Electrical
F	D	For hire (commercial status)
H	D	Hazardous materials. Requires at least one year driving experience.
I	M	Inspector (Includes D, T, B, and E endorsements)
N	D	Tanker, over 1,000 gallons. Requires at least one year driving experience.
P	D	More than 15 occupants, including driver.
S	D	School bus
T	D	Double/Triple trailers
T	M	Transmission/Drive Train
X	D	Driver endorsements N and H

All drivers must take and pass a yearly battery of tests created by and for the TruckCo Company. These tests, listed in Figure P3.5C, must be passed with a minimum score of 70.

FIGURE P3.5C
Company Driver Exams

TEST_CODE	TEST_NAME
1	Hazardous materials
2	Company regulations
3	Driving regulations
4	Driving road test
5	Maneuvering test
6	Drug Test
0	

If a driver fails the drug test (test code 6), that driver must be placed on immediate probation and will be subject to more frequent random drug testing. If the driver fails the drug test a second time, the driver is suspended immediately and permanently. If a driver fails any remaining test (codes 1–5), that driver may not be assigned to driving duties until he or she earns a passing score. Retesting (codes 1–5) must be done within 3 days of the date of failure. If a test (codes 1–5) is not successfully completed after three attempts, the driver is suspended from driving duties; the base manager has the option to assign the driver to other duties or to terminate that driver. TruckCo tracks all test results, maintaining records of the test code, the test date, and the test score for each test for each driver.

Mechanics

Mechanics may have earned their licenses from any number of sources: apprenticeship, schools, special training programs, and so on. Unlike drivers, who can earn multiple licenses, mechanics earn only a single license. Because there are no insurance-specified license sources, TruckCo does not track the mechanics' license source. Instead, TruckCo keeps the mechanics' license number, the date on which the license was awarded, and the license renewal date in its MECHANIC table.

Like drivers, mechanics may earn endorsements to their licenses. However, unlike the endorsements earned by drivers, mechanics may earn their endorsements from any number of sources: apprenticeship, schools, special training programs, and so on. Because there are no insurance-specified endorsement sources, TruckCo does not track the endorsement source for its mechanics. (Figure P3.5B shows that mechanics' endorsements are indicated as M in the **ENDORSE_TYPE.**)

TruckCo tracks all endorsements earned by its mechanics. Therefore, if mechanic J. G. Doe earns a B endorsement on 02/25/1995, an R endorsement on 06/19/1996, and an E endorsement on 10/05/2001, TruckCo wants to be able to track these facts. Because all endorsements are awarded after the candidate has passed a practical examination and a written examination, the scores of these exams are also tracked.

Maintenance

All TruckCo maintenance is performed in house. When a vehicle requires maintenance, it is entered into a maintenance log. The log entries are numbered sequentially, and each log entry consists of an entry date, the vehicle identification, the general description of the maintenance required, and the identity of the mechanic who signed the vehicle into the maintenance log. (The mechanic who signs the vehicle into the maintenance log must have an inspector endorsement.)

After the maintenance-log entry has been completed, it becomes the cover sheet for the maintenance detail lines. Each detail line contains one *and only one* maintenance procedure. For example, if a maintenance-log entry indicates that a vehicle requires a brake inspection and wheel balancing, two detail lines will be associated with the maintenance log. (*Hint*: Do you see a resemblance to an invoice and its invoice lines here?) Each detail line contains the line number, the precise procedure description, the identification of any part(s) used, and the time—to the nearest 1/10 of an hour—required to complete the procedure. In addition, the mechanic who performed the procedure must sign each completed line.

When all maintenance procedures have been completed, the vehicle is released for use. The release is indicated on the maintenance log, which contains the release date and the identity of the mechanic who released the vehicle. (The mechanic who releases the vehicle must have an inspector endorsement.)

3.6 Given the following simplified description of operations for the ProdCo company, draw the ERD that can yield an implementable database. Show all entities, relationships, connectivities, optionalities, and cardinalities.

Note

By requiring mechanics to sign their work, TruckCo ensures that all work is traceable. In fact, in many transportation-related industries traceability, or tracking, is now a legal requirement. Clearly, such requirements have an effect on the database design.

If you pursue a career as a database professional, you are likely to discover that the basic design-for-tracking process described in this problem is beginning to spread across an ever-growing variety of industries.

The ProdCo company manufactures and sells two fuel pump models. Each fuel pump is composed of an impeller housing that contains an impeller assembly powered by a small electric motor. The impeller housing is composed of a top housing shell and a bottom housing shell that are bolted together. An impeller housing gasket is used to ensure that the assembled impeller housing does not leak. Given their critical performance requirements, each fuel pump has a unique serial number to ensure ProdCo's ability to trace its installation and use.

ProdCo manufactures some of the required parts, such as the impeller housing shells, the impeller housing gasket, and the impeller. All other parts used in the assembly of the fuel pumps are ordered from vendors. Most vendor-ordered parts may be ordered from many vendors, and each vendor may receive orders for many parts. Some of the vendors on ProdCo's vendor list have not yet received a ProdCo order. ProdCo's management wants to be able to track all outstanding and delivered orders. If parts are, for one reason or another, unusable, they are returned to the vendor. ProdCo's management wants to be able to track all returned parts.

Some complex parts, such as the fuel pump's impeller assembly, contain other parts. For example, an impeller assembly is composed of the impeller, two sets of bearing sleeves, a shaft, four washers, and bearing sleeve retainers. Although some of the critical parts—such as the impellers—have a unique serial number to enable ProdCo to track their installation and use, most parts are generic.

When ProdCo sells its products, it writes an invoice to record its sales. Customers may pay the invoice amount or, if they have a ProdCo customer charge account, they may charge all or part of the invoice amount to that account. If purchases are charged to the account, ProdCo ensures that the new account balance does not exceed the maximum authorized balance. Customers who have a charge account may make many separate payments to that account. Although several customers on the customer list have not yet bought a ProdCo product, most of ProdCo's customers have bought at least one ProdCo product.

If a customer returns a ProdCo product, the customer account is updated. If the product return value exceeds the current customer account balance, the customer may request the difference in the form of a check or leave the difference in the account to fund future purchases.

3.7 Show the relational schema that corresponds to the ERD in problem 3.6.

3.8 Create a (simplified) data dictionary for the design you created in problem 3.6 as reflected in the relational schema in problem 3.7. (*Hint*: Your data dictionary should at least show the collection of all appropriate attributes associated with each entity and the basic characteristics of these attributes. A sample data dictionary is shown in Table 3.1.)

3.9 The AC_Museum is very pleased with your database design work. (See Problem 1.20 in Chapter 1.) Therefore, its management has asked you to expand the design to include the following requirements:

- The AC_Museum must be able to track the entire assignment history for each of the aircraft. For example, aircraft 56-2319, a model F-100D, might have been assigned to the 435 TFS of the 479 TFW on 02-Jun-1956, to the 309 TFS of the 31 TFW on 12-Aug-1959, and to the Arkansas ANG on 11-Dec-1964. On 04-Feb-1968, this aircraft was flown to the Pima, Arizona, Bone Yard for storage. On 15-Jun-1999 this aircraft was donated to the AC_Museum. (*Note*: TFW = Tactical Fighter Wing; TFS = Tactical Fighter Squadron. Each wing has at least one squadron, but each squadron "belongs" to one wing.)

- Because active Air Force aircraft assignments are made to a wing and then, within that wing, to a squadron, each aircraft assignment specifies a wing and a squadron. However, the final aircraft assignment may be to a museum, an Air Force storage facility, a scrap yard, a weapons research program, or a NASA research program.
- An officer commands each wing and squadron. The AC_Museum wants to keep a complete record of all command assignments to all wings and squadrons. Each wing and/or squadron assignment must include the officer's name, rank, serial number, and a brief biography. Over time, many officers have commanded each wing and squadron. An officer may be assigned to command a given wing or squadron more than once. The officer's rank and biography are likely to change from one assignment to the next.

Chapter **Four**

Implementing the Database Design

Preview

In this chapter we show you how to implement the database design we developed in Chapter 3. We start by defining the database location on the computer's hard drive. Next we show you how to create the database structure in which the database components—tables, relationships, and so on—are stored.

After you create the database structure, we show you how to define the field data types—numeric, date, text, memo, and so on—within the table structures. Then we show you how to designate the PKs and FKs within the tables and how to save the table structure.

Once the table structures have been created and saved, we show you how to establish the appropriate relationships between the tables by generating the database's relational schema, how to enforce the referential integrity requirements, and how the ERD is reflected in the relational schema. We also show you how you can use the table's field definitions to help the end user enter the data correctly.

You'll learn how to guide the end user to proper data entry by using input masks, default data values, validation rules, and validation text. When the database, its tables, and the relationships between the tables have been created, you will be ready to perform some data entry work. These data will become the raw material for the queries you'll learn to develop in Chapter 5 and for the forms and reports you'll encounter in Chapters 6 and 7.

Objectives

When you have mastered the material in this chapter, you should know how to

- Create a database structure.
- Create the table structures within the database.
- Define primary keys (PKs) to enforce entity integrity.
- Designate foreign keys (FKs).
- Create relationships between tables.
- Enforce referential integrity.
- Use input masks to control data entry input format.
- Establish data entry validation through the use of validation rules and text.
- Establish outer joins.

Note

Many database professionals, who do not necessarily use Windows, still use the terms *folders* and *directories* as synonyms. This convention is derived from the conceptual view of the file storage architecture. Therefore, the **C:\MSOffice\Access\Databases** *folder* might be referred to as the **C:\MSOffice\Access\Databases** *directory*. To be precise, **\Databases** is actually a subdirectory (subfolder) of the **C:\MSOffice\Access** directory (folder), because—at least conceptually—**\Databases** is stored as a branch of the **C:\MSOffice\Access** directory. Similarly, **\Access** is a subdirectory (subfolder) of the **C:\MSOffice** directory (folder.) We will use the terms *directory* and *folder* as synonyms.

4.1 PREPARATIONS: SELECTING THE DATABASE'S STORAGE LOCATION

Before you can store a database, you must decide on its name. We recommend that you use a short but descriptive name. Because the database design in Chapter 3 reflects a point of sales (POS) system, the name would reasonably include the label POS. The POS system we developed in Chapter 3 is actually a second version of our corporate-training database. Therefore, we've decided to name the database POS_2nd. (In order to have a chapter-specific database for each chapter, we will name the database used in this chapter **Ch04_POS_2nd**.)

The database must be stored *somewhere* on the disk. To make it easy to remember where the **Ch04_POS_2nd** database is stored, we have created a folder named **Ch04** within a folder we have named **C:\MSOffice\Access\Databases** (see Figure 4.1).

As you examine Figure 4.1, keep in mind that your directory structure will contain different directories and subdirectories. In fact, if you are working on a computer lab or class computer, you may be required to save your database work on a floppy disk located in drive A. In that case, create a directory (folder) named Ch04 on your floppy disk before continuing. Now that we have a place in which to store the **Ch04_POS_2nd** database, let's create the **Ch04_POS_2nd** database structure with the help of Access.

4.2 CREATING THE NEW DATABASE

Before you can create and Access database, you must first use **Start/Programs** and then select **Microsoft Access** as shown in Figure 4.2.

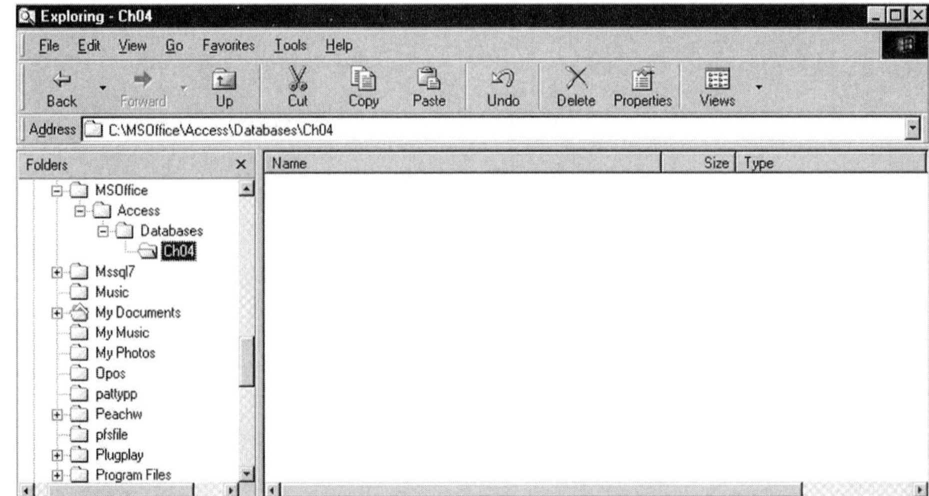

FIGURE 4.1
The Ch04 Subdirectory That Will Contain the Ch04_POS_2nd Database

Note

This book is about database design, database implementation, and database applications development with Access. It is not about learning Windows. However, because the Access database software runs under Windows, your computer must be equipped with this operating system. To keep our focus on database, we will assume that you are familiar with the Windows environment. Therefore, you should know what click, double-click, and right-click accomplish. You should also know what a window is and what message boxes and dialog boxes are. You should also know to create folders (directories), how to copy files, how to minimize, maximize, and restore, how to drag and drop, and so on. If you are not familiar with the Windows terms and procedures, first invest in a simple Windows tutorial and learn Windows before trying to tackle the database work done in this book.

FIGURE 4.2
Start Access

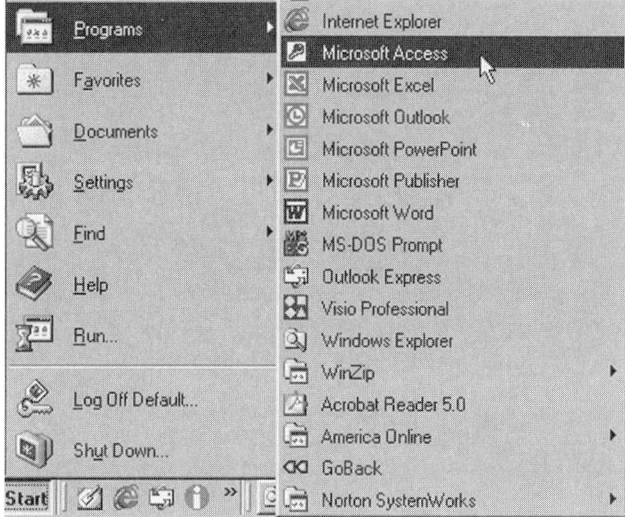

The actions indicated in Figure 4.2—select **Start**, then select **Programs**, and then select **Microsoft Access**—will generate the Access opening screen shown in Figure 4.3.

The **Open a file** section shown in Figure 4.3 lists the four most recently used databases. Because these databases reflect the contents of the active disk drive, in this case, ours, your screen will show a different listing than the one shown in Figure 4.3. If no databases have yet been created, this section will not contain any **.mdb** files. (The **.mdb** file extension indicates a **M**icrosoft **d**ata**b**ase.)

Because we have not yet created our database structure, we will *not* select the **More files** option. Instead, we will select the **New** section's **Blank Database** option to create a new database structure. (If you move the cursor over this option, the cursor will change to the hand you see in Figure 4.3.) The selection of the **New/Blank Database** option will cause Access to produce the screen shown in Figure 4.4.

The **File New Database** dialog box in Figure 4.4 shows your computer's default database folder, named **My Documents**. Note that the database default name, **db1.mdb,** is shown at the bottom of the screen, next to the **File name** label.

If you are working on a lab computer, chances are that your instructor will ask you to save your work on your own 3.5-inch floppy drive or on your own 100-Mb ZIP drive. Figure 4.5 shows the floppy drive selection.

Using the **File New Database** window shown in Figure 4.4, locate the Ch04 folder we created in Figure 4.1 and type **Ch04_POS_2nd.mdb** as the database

Note

The **Database Wizard** option will give you less of a chance to explore the database creation process, so we will not use it here. In fact, we suggest that you always use the "hands-on" approach to give you maximum control over the database creation process.

FIGURE 4.3
The Access Opening Screen

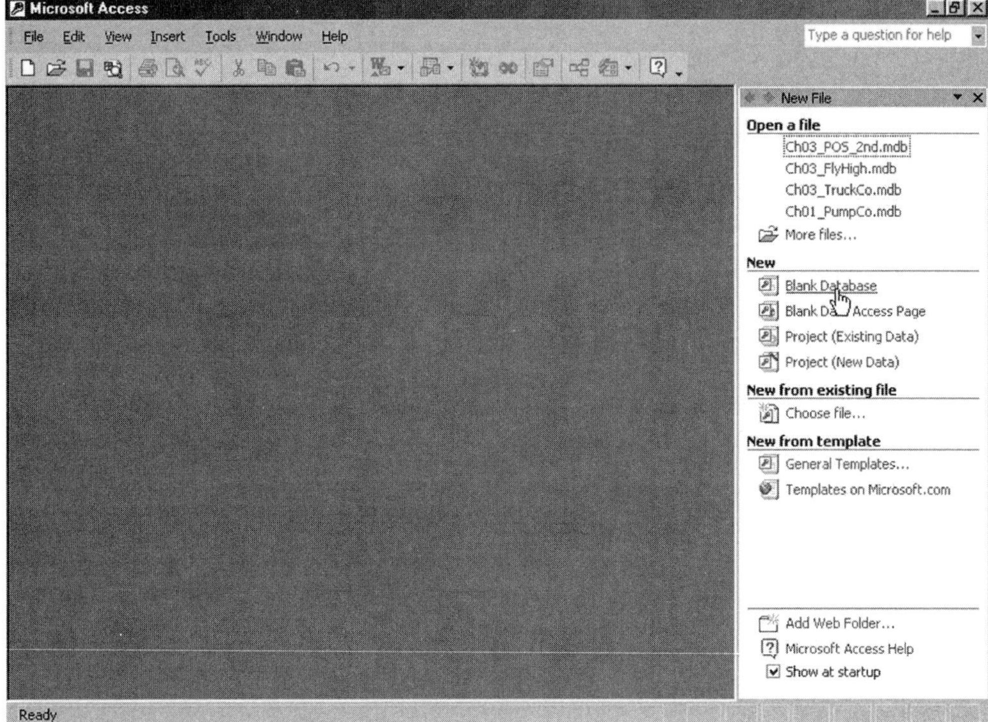

name in the **File name** space at the bottom of the screen as shown in Figure 4.6. Click the **Create** button in the lower right corner of the **File New Database** dialog box when you have finished typing the database name in the **File name** space.

FIGURE 4.4
The Default Database Folder

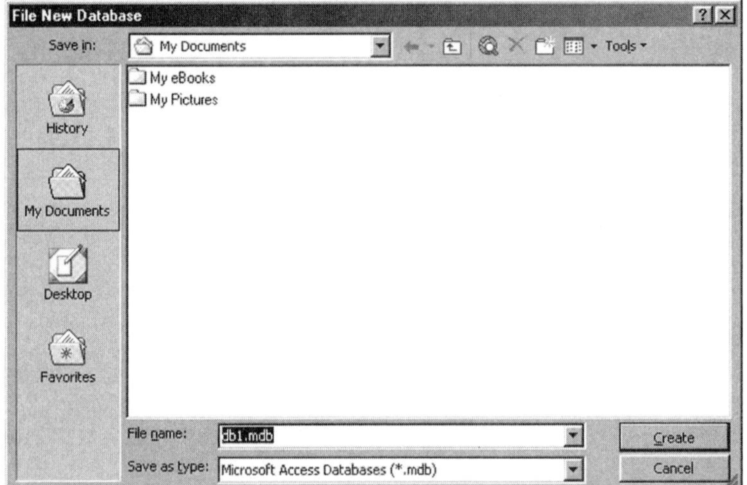

Note

If you use Windows NT rather than Windows, the window in Figure 4.4 has a slightly different "look" to it. Also, you may have selected a different Windows default view, thus changing the Windows presentation format. Fortunately, the database creation procedure will not be affected by such presentation differences.

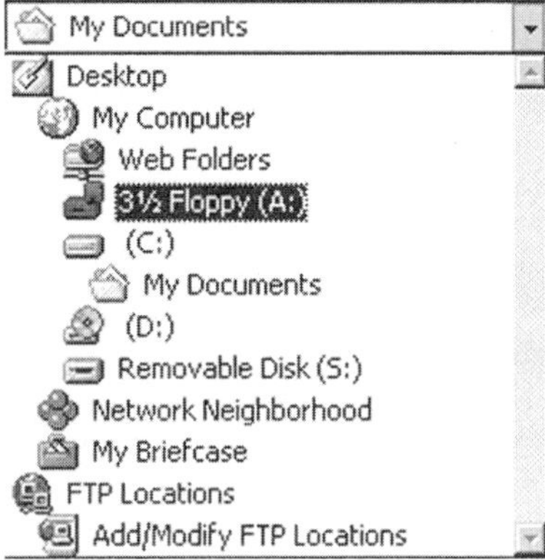

FIGURE 4.5
The Database Storage Area Options

Clicking the **Create** button in Figure 4.6 produces the database window shown in Figure 4.7.

As you examine the new database window in Figure 4.7, note that the database can contain seven kinds of objects: **Tables**, **Queries**, **Forms**, **Reports**, **Pages**, **Macros**, and **Modules**. Because we will focus our attention on the implementation of the database design, we will cover the **Tables** option in this chapter. With the exception of modules, the remaining options are examined in detail in the following chapters.

As you examine Figure 4.7, observe the various options on the top left of the database window: **Open**, **Design**, **New**, and the **X** (delete). The **Open**, **Design**, and the **X** are grayed out at this point, indicating that these options are not available at this point. (Because we have not yet created a database table that can be opened, modified in the design view, or deleted, only the **New** option is

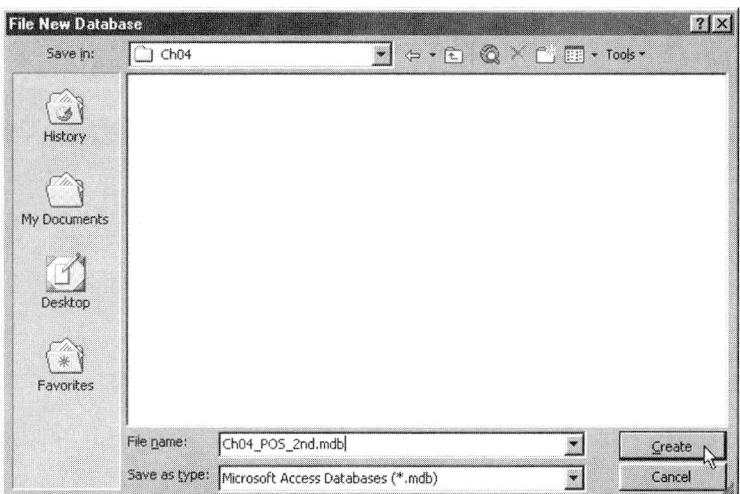

FIGURE 4.6
Selecting the Database Storage Location

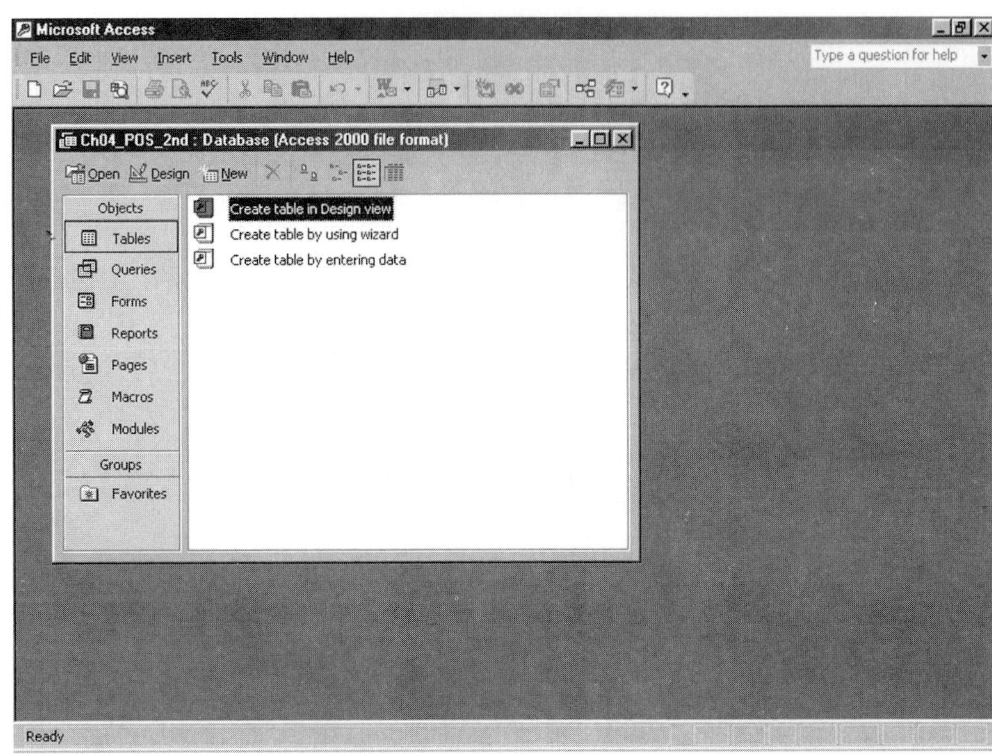

FIGURE 4.7
The New Ch04_POS_2nd Database Window

available.) All the options will be available after the first table structure has been created and saved.

4.2.1 Changing the Default Folder

To change the default database folder shown in Figure 4.3, follow these steps:

1. From the database window, select **Options** from the **Tools** drop-down menu as shown in Figure 4.8.
2. The selection of the **Options** in Figure 4.8 will generate the screen shown in Figure 4.9. Using this screen, select the **General** tab and type the new path in the **Default database folder**. Note that, at this point, **C:\MSOffice\Access\Databases** is the default database folder.

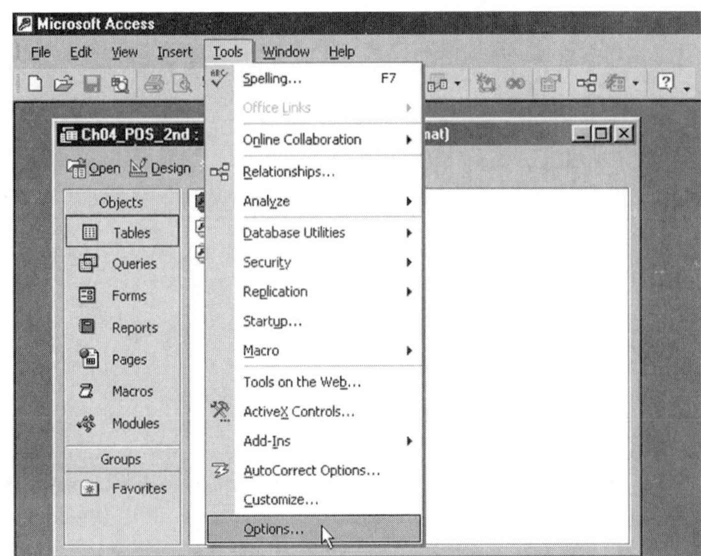

FIGURE 4.8
Changing the Default Database Folder—Step 1

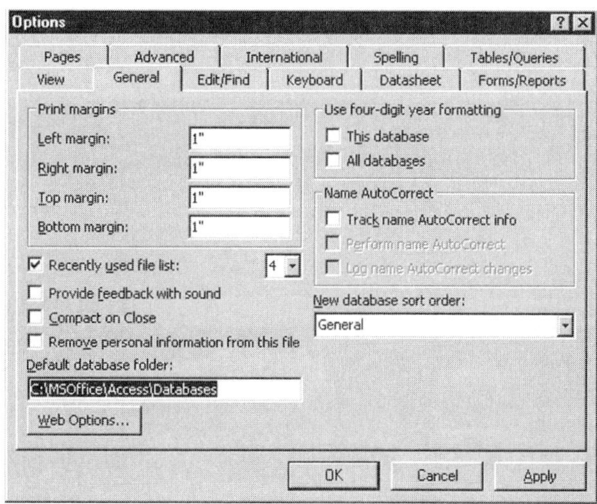

FIGURE 4.9
Changing the Default Database Folder—Step 2

These two steps complete the process of creating a new default folder. The next time you open or save a new database, the default folder specified by you will be selected. The new default database folder is shown in Figure 4.10. You can, of course, change this default folder any time. (Note that the database storage location in Figure 4.9 is **C:\MSOffice\Access\Databases**. If you have decided to use a different folder, substitute that folder name for the one we have shown here.)

4.3 CREATING THE TABLES WITHIN THE DATABASE STRUCTURE

To build a table structure, click the **New** option as shown in Figure 4.7 to generate the **New Table** dialog box shown in Figure 4.11. (Note that the default selection is **Datasheet View**. Because you want to design a table structure, select **Design View** and then click **OK**.

Selecting the **Design View** in Figure 4.11 will produce the screen in Figure 4.12. Note that the table's default name is Table1.

You are now ready to create the EMPLOYEE table structure. Incidentally, as you examine Figure 4.12, note that the cursor is on the **Field Name**. (Clicking in the **Field Name** column causes the small dark triangle ▶ to be displayed in the small tab located at the selected **Field Name**'s left margin.) The cursor location causes the large square box in the window's lower right corner to describe the field name characteristics. Access even provides context-sensitive help; press F1 if you want to examine the other available data types.

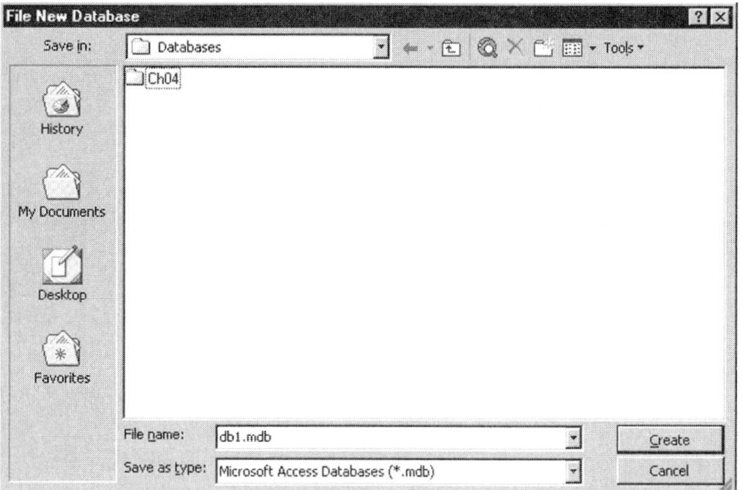

FIGURE 4.10
The New Default Database Folder

Note

Figure 4.6 shows that you can select many different ways to create a table. Because we want to make sure that you know how to work with the table components, we will cover only the **Design View** option.

FIGURE 4.11
Creating the First Table: Using the Design View

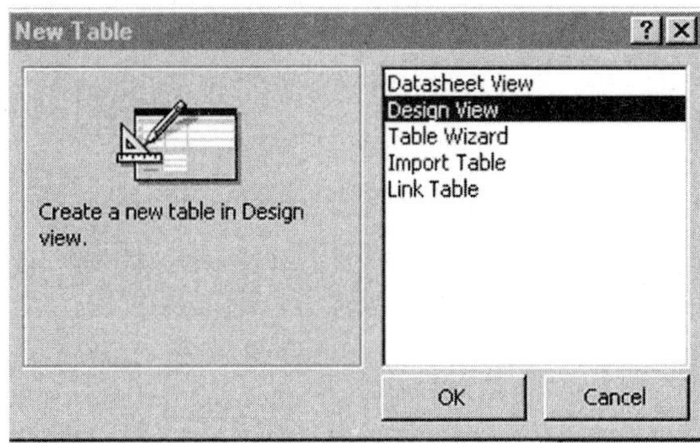

4.3.1 Creating Fields for the Table

We are now ready to define the EMPLOYEE table's components, starting with the EMP_NUM attribute. (Remember, Access uses the word *field* instead of *attribute*. Therefore, we will use the words *field* and *attribute* as synonyms.) The field definition process requires the following steps: create the field name, define the data type, and write a field description.

Step 1: Create the Field Name

Using Figure 4.12 as your template, type the first of the EMPLOYEE table's attribute names, EMP_NUM, under **Field Name** (see Figure 4.13).

Step 2: Define the Data Type

After typing EMP_NUM in the field name column, press the Tab key to move to the **Data Type** column (see Figure 4.13). Note that the default selection is **Text**. Because the cursor is located on the **Text** data type, its field properties are displayed to indicate its default values. At this point,

FIGURE 4.12
The Table Design View

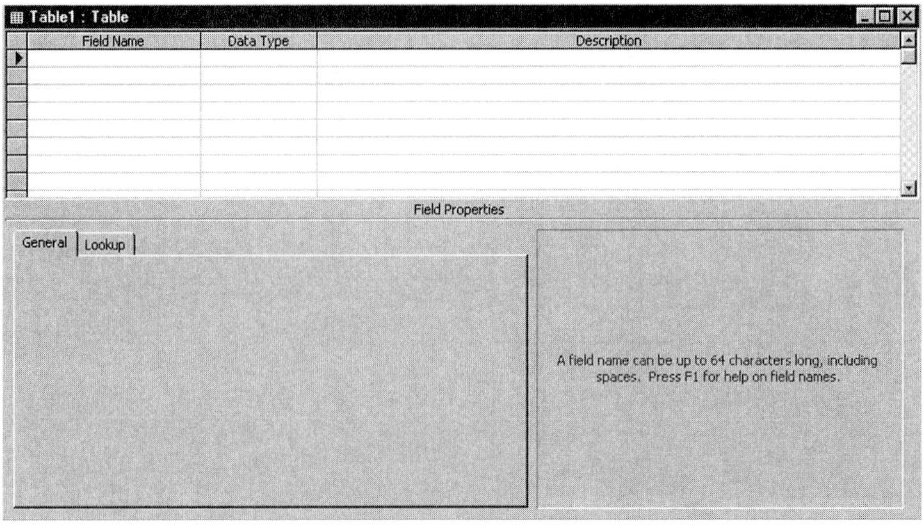

FIGURE 4.13
Initial Attribute Entry

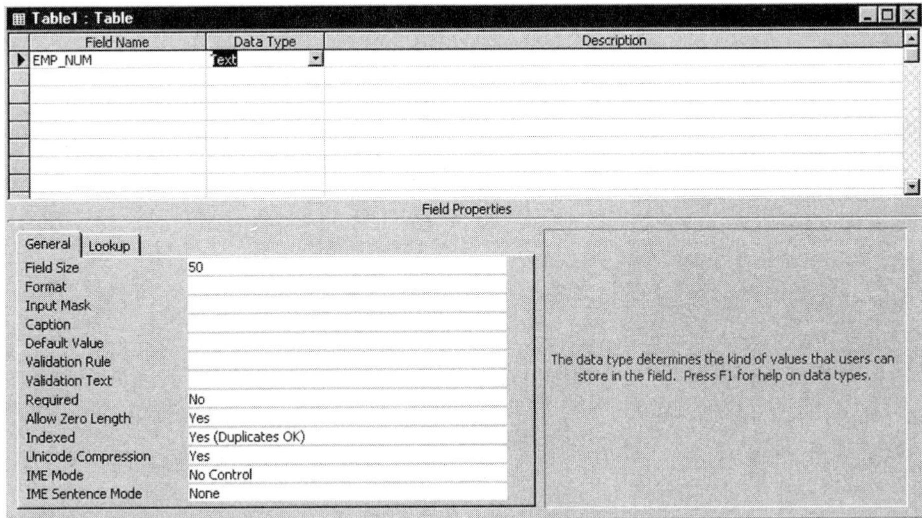

- The text field size default value is 50; that is, a text string may be up to 50 characters long.
- A text field value is not required; therefore, a null entry would be accepted.
- A zero-length string size is not allowed.
- The text field value will be indexed, but duplicates will be allowed. This property is useful when you are using employee last names because there are potentially many employees named Smith. However, duplicates must *not* be allowed when the specified field defines a PK, because PKs must *uniquely* identify each record. (You will discover later that the PK designation will automatically reset the PK field's default property to "no duplicates allowed.")
- The remaining characteristics (format, input mask, caption, etc.) are left undefined.

To avoid the always-present danger of information overload, we discuss these field properties and modify them as they become relevant.

As you examine Figure 4.13, note also that the large square in the lower right corner provides additional information and an option to get help by pressing the F1 key. The information in this box is context sensitive, so it changes whenever you change the cursor location.

To see what additional data types are available, click on the down arrow displayed next to the (default) **Text** entry in the **Data Type** column to generate the pick list shown in Figure 4.14.

FIGURE 4.14
Displaying the Available Data Types

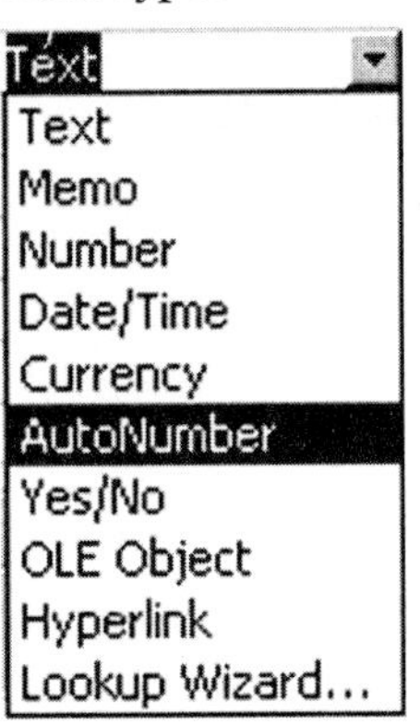

As you examine Figure 4.14, note that we have moved the cursor down to the **AutoNumber** data type. We have selected the **AutoNumber** data type because we will use its ability to automatically generate unique numbers with each entry of a new record. Therefore, this data type helps us to enforce entity integrity rules with no effort on our part.

When you select the **AutoNumber** data type, the field properties change to match this selection. For example, if you look at Figure 4.15, you see that the **Field Properties** component now shows the **Field Size** property is **Long Integer** and the **New Values** property is **Increment**. Also, note that the **AutoNumber** data type is automatically indexed.

Step 3: Write a Field Description

Having selected the **AutoNumber** data type as shown in Figure 4.15, press the Tab key to move to the attribute's **Description** column. Although the EMP_NUM label is probably sufficiently descriptive to make a more detailed description unnecessary, making an entry in the **Description** column is a good habit to

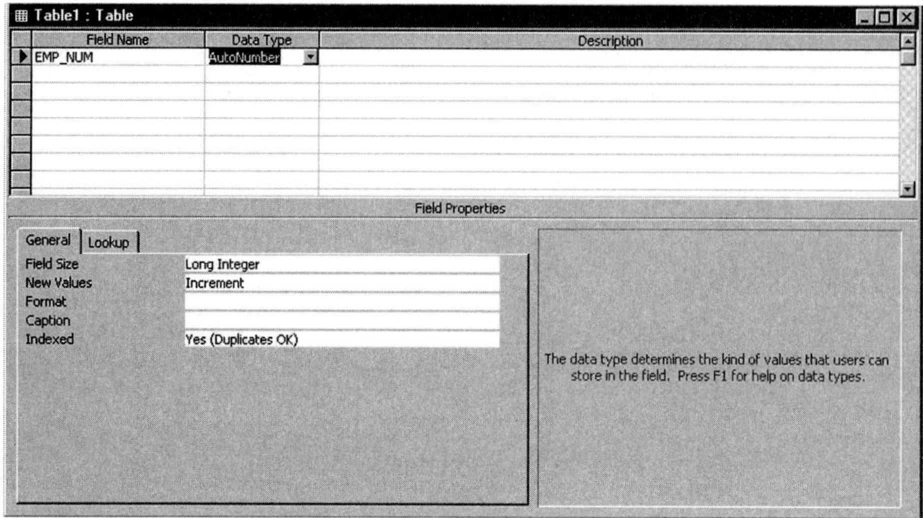

FIGURE 4.15
AutoNumber Field Properties

develop, so go ahead and type Employee number (Primary key) as shown in Figure 4.16. The PK designation indicates that the EMP_NUM attribute will be the PK for the EMPLOYEE table. (We show you how to create the PK in the next section.)

Figure 4.16 also shows the EMP_TITLE field and its characteristics. (Complete the just-discussed three steps to get the job done.)

As you examine Figure 4.16, note that we have altered some of the EMP_TITLE's field properties. (The text field's original default properties are shown in Figure 4.13.) To make any alterations in the listed field properties, put the cursor on the field property and type in the desired entry. As you compare the text field properties in Figure 4.13 with those shown in Figure 4.16, note that

- We have changed the field size to 4, because the longest EMP_TITLE string is Mrs., which contains four characters: three letters and a period.
- The **Required**, **Allow Zero Length**, and **Indexed** field properties in Figure 4.16 have been set to **No**.

4.3.2 Saving the Table and Setting the Primary Key

At this point we have created the EMPLOYEE table structure with only two fields in it, so we're not quite done. Nevertheless, it is a good idea to save your work

Table1 : Table

Field Name	Data Type	Description
EMP_NUM	AutoNumber	Employee number (Primary key)
EMP_TITLE	Text	Employee title (Mr. Ms., Mrs.)

Field Properties

General | Lookup

Field Size	4
Format	
Input Mask	
Caption	
Default Value	
Validation Rule	
Validation Text	
Required	No
Allow Zero Length	No
Indexed	No
Unicode Compression	Yes
IME Mode	No Control
IME Sentence Mode	None

The maximum number of characters you can enter in the field. The largest maximum you can set is 255. Press F1 for help on field size.

FIGURE 4.16
Defining the EMP_TITLE Field Size

FIGURE 4.17 Saving the Table Structure

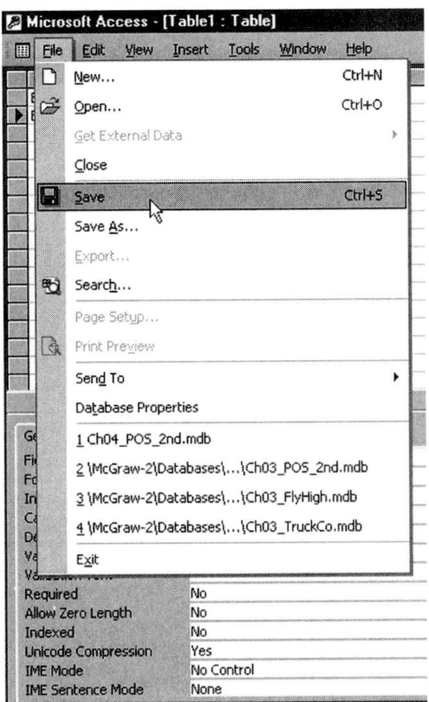

FIGURE 4.18 A Reminder to Save the Table

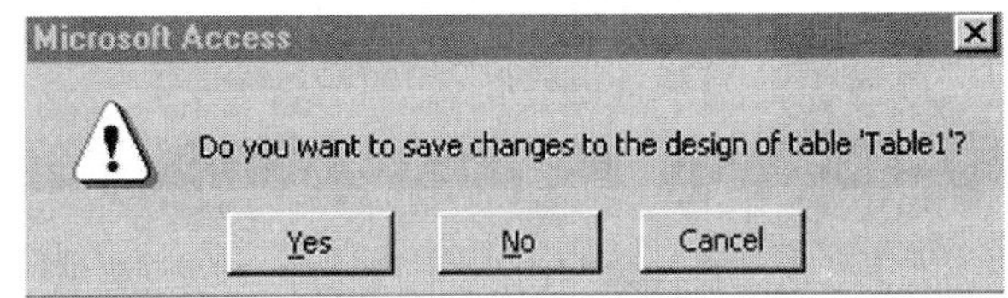

FIGURE 4.19 A Prompt to Name and Save the Table

FIGURE 4.20 Primary Key Reminder

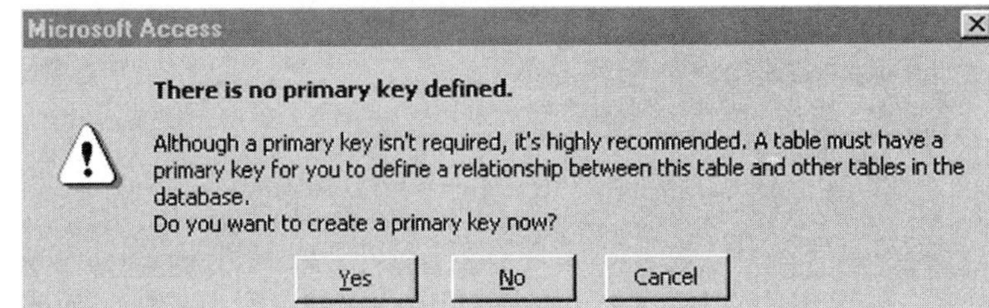

from time to time, so we'll go ahead and save the work that has been completed thus far. (Actually, we have forgotten to define the table's PK, and that's something you may, sooner or later, also forget to do. Therefore, it is useful to see how Access will react to our omission and to see how we can correct the oversight.)

As usual, Access permits us to save the table in many different ways. In this illustration we have elected to use the **File** option from the menu bar at the top of the screen. As you can tell by looking at Figure 4.17, we clicked on the **File** option and then selected **Save** from the menu.

If you forget to save the table before closing it, Access will remind you to do so using the dialog box shown in Figure 4.18.

Whether you select the **File/Save** option shown in Figure 4.17 or you click the **Yes** button in Figure 4.18, Access will produce the **Save As** dialog box shown in Figure 4.19. Actually, this reminder will initially contain the table default name, **Table1**, but we have already typed in the proper table name, EMPLOYEE.

Clicking **OK** in the **Save As** dialog box will cause Access to remind you of a critical omission. This reminder takes the form of the message box shown in Figure 4.20.

Because we want to create the PK at the design level, select the **Cancel** button shown in Figure 4.20 to return to the table design window, a small portion of which is illustrated in Figure 4.21. Click on the EMP_NUM field name to place the cursor on it. Note that this action causes a small, right-pointing triangle to be displayed in the field name tab located to the left of the EMP_NUM field as shown in Figure 4.21.

FIGURE 4.21 Marking the Primary Key Field

Table1 : Table

	Field Name	Data Type
▶	EMP_NUM	AutoNumber
	EMP_TITLE	Text

Note

If you select **No** from the dialog box in Figure 4.18, Access will save the table without a PK. If you select **Yes** from the dialog box in Figure 4.15, Access will automatically create a new field, named ID, and assign it as the PK. Neither choice is a good one, so **Cancel** is the best option here.

FIGURE 4.22
Creating the Primary Key with the Edit Menu

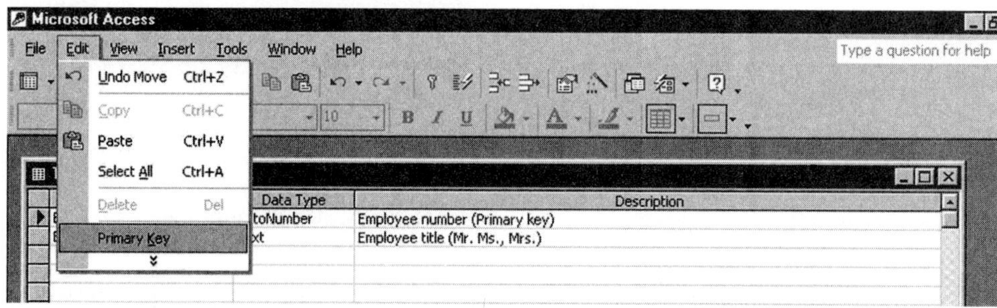

Next, click on the small tab at the left margin of the EMP_NUM field. This action will highlight the entire line, indicating the selection of the EMP_NUM field. Now move to the menu bar at the top of the screen and select **Edit**; then double-click the **Primary Key** option as shown in Figure 4.22.

The action sequence illustrated in Figure 4.22 completes the PK creation process. Note that the EMP_NUM field in Figure 4.23 now is marked by a small key symbol, located on the tab just to the left of the field name.

The PK can also be defined via the table's toolbar. If the toolbar is not located at the top of your screen, select the **View/Design View/Toolbars/Table Design** sequence shown in Figure 4.24. (If the toolbar already exists, the **Table Design** option will have a check box next to it.)

The actions illustrated in Figure 4.24 will put the toolbar shown in Figure 4.25 at the top of your screen. (You may turn off the toolbar by going through the same sequence, this time deselecting the **Table Design** option by clicking on the check box in front of it.)

To create the PK with the help of the toolbar shown in Figure 4.25, select the EMP_NUM field just as you did for the **Edit/Primary Key** sequence in Figure 4.22. Then use the toolbar shown in Figure 4.25 and click on the button that shows the key symbol. This action will place a key symbol in the small tab at the left margin of the EMP_NUM field, indicating that the selected field is now the PK field.

Because the EMPLOYEE table now has a proper PK, go ahead and save it again. (See Figure 4.17 if you need a reminder about the saving procedure. Or use the **Save** button at the top of the screen. Naturally, this time you will not see the

FIGURE 4.23 The Primary Key Designation

Table1 : Table

Field Name	Data Type	Description
EMP_NUM	AutoNumber	Employee number (Primary key)
EMP_TITLE	Text	Employee title (Mr. Ms., Mrs.)

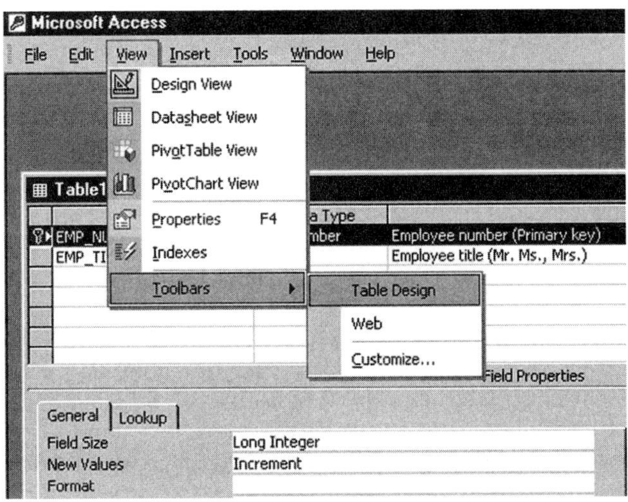

FIGURE 4.24
Selecting the Table Design Toolbar

FIGURE 4.25 The Table Design Toolbar

PK warning.) When the EMPLOYEE table structure has been saved, Access will return you to the database window shown in Figure 4.26. Note that the EMPLOYEE table shows up as an object in the **Tables** folder.

4.3.3 Composite Primary Keys

Suppose that some employees are required to take periodic tests. For example, commercial drivers may be required to periodically demonstrate their knowledge of hazardous materials (HAZMAT) handling and Department of Transportation regulations (DOTREG). Conceptually, there is an M:N relationship between EMPLOYEE and TEST; that is, an employee may take many tests and many employees may take each test. Because the M:N relationship cannot be properly implemented, it must be broken up through the creation of a new entity—we'll

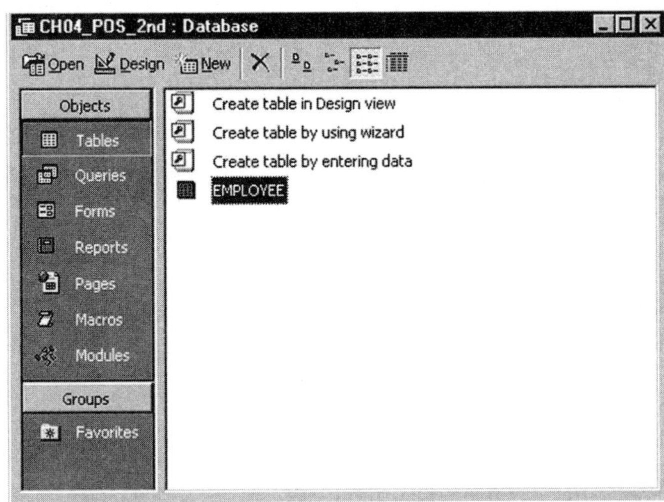

FIGURE 4.26
The EMPLOYEE Table in the Database Window

FIGURE 4.27
The EMPLOYEE Table Contents

EMP_NUM	EMP_LNAME
101	Okoski
102	Jones
103	Tavares
104	Stone
105	LeBreau
0	

FIGURE 4.28
The TEST_RESULT Table Contents

EMP_NUM	TEST_CODE	TEST_RESULT_DATE	TEST_RESULT_GRADE
101	DOTREG	10-Jan-2002	87
101	DOTREG	18-Jan-2003	91
101	HAZMAT	21-Dec-2001	90
101	HAZMAT	28-Jun-2002	92
101	HAZMAT	15-Dec-2002	93
103	DOTREG	18-Nov-2002	89
103	HAZMAT	21-Jul-2002	95
103	HAZMAT	25-Jan-2003	97
0			0

FIGURE 4.29
The TEST Table Contents

TEST_CODE	TEST_TITLE	TEST_FREQUENCY	TEST_MIN_GRADE
DOTREG	Dept. of Transportation Commercial Driver Regulations	Yearly	70
HAZMAT	Hazardous Materials Handling	Every six (6) calendar months	85
			0

name it TEST_RESULT—to create two 1:M relationships. You learned in Chapter 1 that one way to get this job done is to create a TEST_RESULT table to link the EMPLOYEE and TEST tables. This approach is illustrated in Figures 4.27 through 4.29. Note that this approach requires the use of a composite PK in the

Note

The three database tables shown in Figures 4.27 to 4.29 are located on the student CD. Look for the database named **Ch04_Composite_Practice**. Note that the database tables include various data types, including calendar dates. You will learn how to create such fields later in this chapter.

Keep in mind that the material on the CD is **Read Only**; that is, you cannot make changes in those files. Because you want to be able to edit the database material, first copy the databases from the CD to your drive, then select the file properties—right-click on the filename as shown in the window in Figure 4.30—and uncheck the **Read Only** property. Then click **Apply** and **OK** to let you edit the file contents whenever you like.

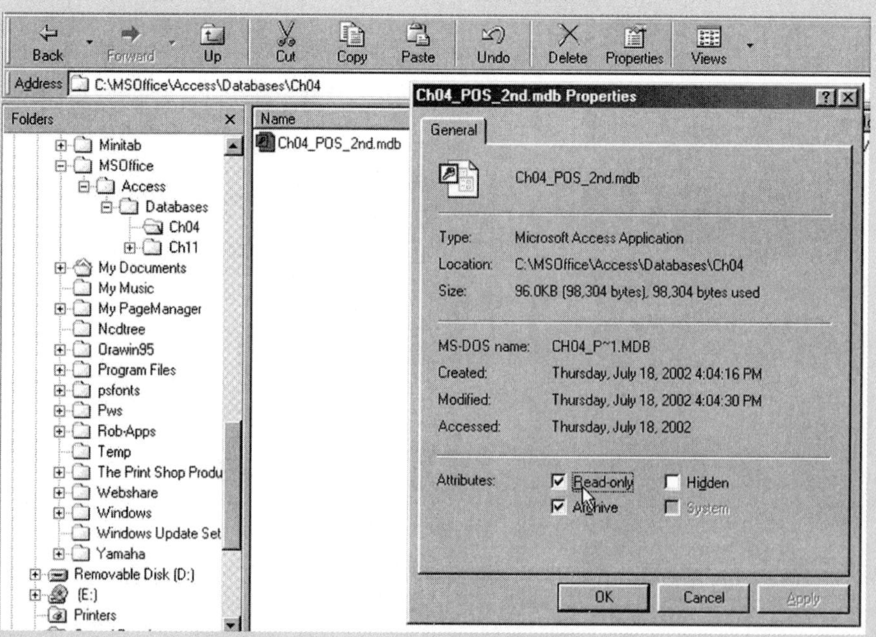

FIGURE 4.30
Changing the File Properties

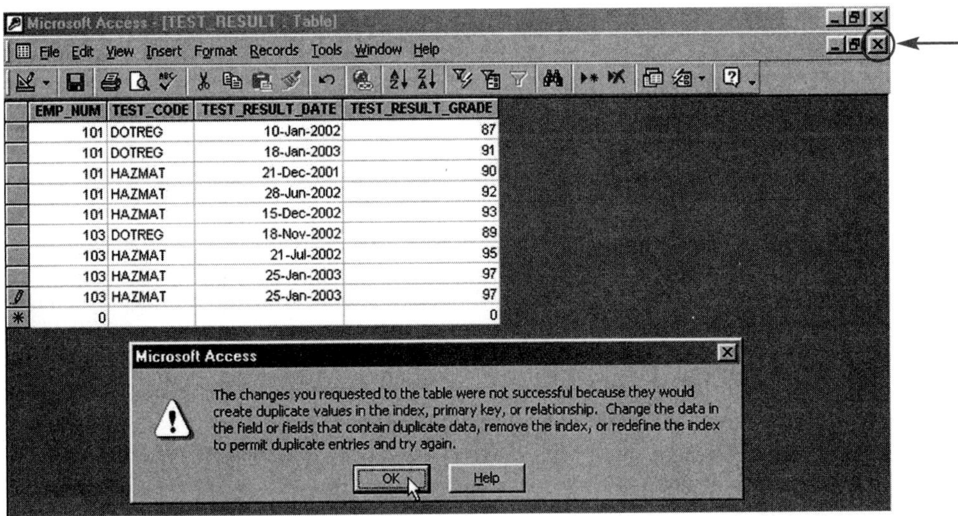

EMP_NUM	TEST_CODE	TEST_RESULT_DATE	TEST_RESULT_GRADE
101	DOTREG	10-Jan-2002	87
101	DOTREG	18-Jan-2003	91
101	HAZMAT	21-Dec-2001	90
101	HAZMAT	28-Jun-2002	92
101	HAZMAT	15-Dec-2002	93
103	DOTREG	18-Nov-2002	89
103	HAZMAT	21-Jul-2002	95
103	HAZMAT	25-Jan-2003	97
103	HAZMAT	25-Jan-2003	97
0			0

FIGURE 4.31
The Error Message Produced by a Duplication of a Record

TEST_RESULT table. This composite PK consists of EMP_NUM + TEST_CODE + RESULT_DATE. *Note that the date must be included in this composite PK to ensure that the PK is always unique.* (The EMP_NUM and TEST_CODE combination would not yield unique results, because each test may be taken more than once by the same employee.)

As you examine the TEST_RESULT table in Figure 4.28, note that the PK prevents the duplication of test results records, because the PK enforces entity integrity. Figure 4.31 illustrates what happens if you try to duplicate the last record in the TEST_RESULT table.

If you click **OK** on the message shown in Figure 4.31, you will have a chance to correct your data entry. For example, if you meant to enter a new HAZMAT test result for employee 103 for June 23, 2002, but you accidentally entered January 25, 2003, just put the cursor back on the date field and make the correction. *As long as the PK is not duplicated, the records you enter will be saved.* If you did not mean to enter a new record, but you accidentally added the duplicate record, click **OK** on the error message shown in Figure 4.31, then close the table by clicking on the second (lower) **Close** button **X** at the upper right-hand corner of the screen. (We have maximized the screen. If you click on the *first* **Close** button, you will close the database rather than the table.)

When you click on the **Close** button to close the table, Access will produce the message shown in Figure 4.32.

Clicking **OK** on the reminder message shown in Figure 4.32 will produce the message shown in Figure 4.33.

Click on the **Yes** button shown in Figure 4.33 to terminate the process and to restore the database table contents to their original values.

To create the TEST_RESULT table's composite PK, use the standard Windows conventions. For example, in this case, the first three attributes (fields) are to be used as a composite primary key. Therefore, select the first attribute by clicking on the tab in front of it, and then select the third attribute while holding the keyboard's Shift key down. This action will select the first through the third attributes. Having selected the three attributes, click on the button bar's primary key button (see Figure 4.34).

Save the table with its new PK to make the change permanent. When you open the table in design format again, you will see that all three attributes are marked with a PK symbol. (See the key pictures on the left-most tabs of the EMP_NUM, TEST_CODE, and TEST_RESULT_DATE in Figure 4.35.)

FIGURE 4.32
The Reminder Message

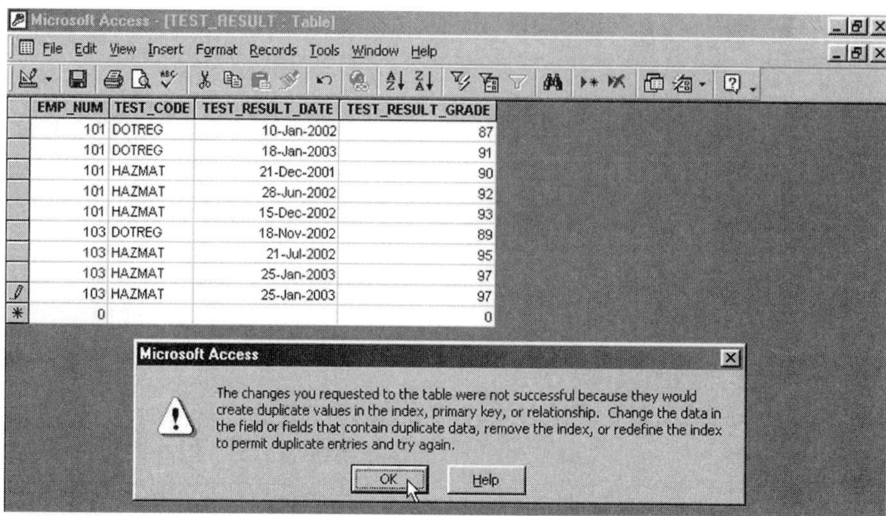

EMP_NUM	TEST_CODE	TEST_RESULT_DATE	TEST_RESULT_GRADE
101	DOTREG	10-Jan-2002	87
101	DOTREG	18-Jan-2003	91
101	HAZMAT	21-Dec-2001	90
101	HAZMAT	28-Jun-2002	92
101	HAZMAT	15-Dec-2002	93
103	DOTREG	18-Nov-2002	89
103	HAZMAT	21-Jul-2002	95
103	HAZMAT	25-Jan-2003	97
103	HAZMAT	25-Jan-2003	97
0			0

FIGURE 4.33
The No Save Message

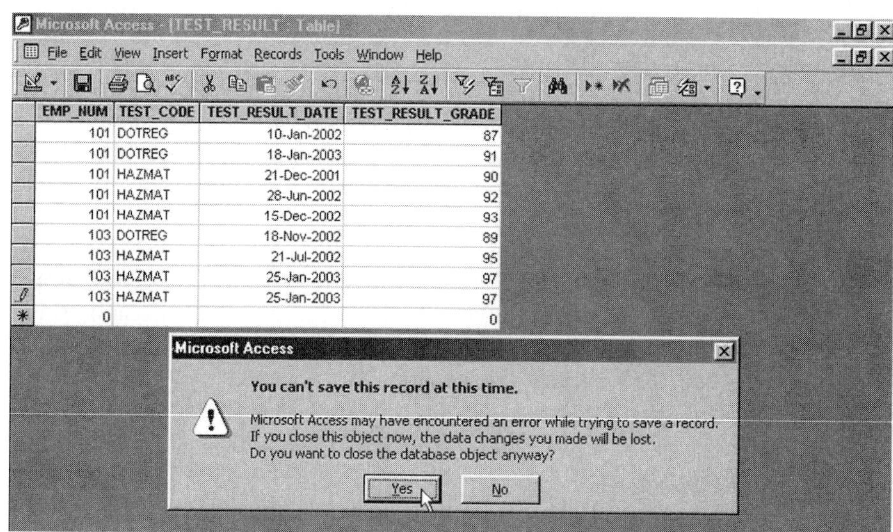

EMP_NUM	TEST_CODE	TEST_RESULT_DATE	TEST_RESULT_GRADE
101	DOTREG	10-Jan-2002	87
101	DOTREG	18-Jan-2003	91
101	HAZMAT	21-Dec-2001	90
101	HAZMAT	28-Jun-2002	92
101	HAZMAT	15-Dec-2002	93
103	DOTREG	18-Nov-2002	89
103	HAZMAT	21-Jul-2002	95
103	HAZMAT	25-Jan-2003	97
103	HAZMAT	25-Jan-2003	97
0			0

FIGURE 4.34 Selecting Multiple Attributes for the PK

Field Name	Data Type	Description
EMP_NUM	Number	
TEST_CODE	Text	
TEST_RESULT_DATE	Date/Time	
TEST_RESULT_GRADE	Number	

FIGURE 4.35 The Composite PK

Microsoft Access - [TEST_RESULT : Table]

File Edit View Insert Tools Window Help

Field Name	Data Type	Description
EMP_NUM	Number	
TEST_CODE	Text	
TEST_RESULT_DATE	Date/Time	
TEST_RESULT_GRADE	Number	

If a table's composite primary key consists of its first attribute, its fourth attribute, and its sixth attribute, select the first attribute, and then hold the keyboard's Ctrl key down while you select the fourth and sixth attributes. Having selected the attributes, set the primary key as usual; that is, click on the button bar's primary key button to create the primary key or select the **Edit/Primary** key sequence.

4.4 MODIFYING THE TABLE STRUCTURE

Now that the EMPLOYEE table has been safely stored on disk, you may return to it to make modifications. Just open the EMPLOYEE table in the design format by clicking on the **Design** button shown in Figure 4.26 to return to the EMPLOYEE table structure. You may make these modifications:

- *Add an attribute*. You can append an attribute to the field list by moving to the first open field line. Then follow steps 1 through 3 in section 4.3.1. You may insert an attribute between existing attributes by marking an existing attribute and pressing the Ins (insert) key on your keyboard.
- *Delete an attribute*. You can delete an attribute by marking it and pressing the Del (delete) key on your keyboard.
- *Modify an attribute*. You may modify an attribute by clicking on its field name and then selecting any of its components for modification. (Use the standard Windows conventions. For example, if you want to change the text field length for the EMP_LNAME field, put the cursor on the current field length value and type in the desired field length.)

Once you are satisfied that the changes are appropriate and that you want to save the modified table structure, use any of the saving options available to you. (That is, select the menu bar, then **File/Save**; or click on the **Save** button on the toolbar.)

4.4.1 Date Fields: Date Formats

The EMPLOYEE table contains several date fields, so it is appropriate to examine various date formats. We must make one point emphatically: *Don't* store dates as strings.

- Strings do not allow you to do simple date arithmetic. Questions such as How many days elapsed between 12-Apr-1998 and 23-Jan-2003? are difficult to answer, even when you know how to use the many string functions Access makes available to you.
- String storage makes it next to impossible to convert the date segments to a common format requested by end users. For example, your end users may want to know how many sales were made on Mondays. Or they may want to know what the average absentee rates are on the various weekdays. What day of the week was 10-Jan-2003 again?
- Unless strings are stored in a year/month/day (yy/mm/dd) format—which is not how we usually think of dates—you will find it easy to get wrong date string comparisons. For example, if you store dates in the commonly used mm/dd/yy string format, you will discover that the computer "thinks" that 01/01/03 occurred *before* 12/31/02. (Given the ASCII coding scheme, string comparisons are made from left to right. Therefore, 01/01/03 is seen as "less than" 12/31/02 because 01 is less than 12.)

Fortunately, Access supports the Julian date format. Better yet, this format is available in many format options, and it is accompanied by a wealth of functions. The Julian date format makes date arithmetic simple. Therefore, questions such as On what date will this bill be more than 90 days overdue? are easy to answer.

Assignment

Modify the EMPLOYEE table to add the following attributes:

- EMP_LNAME
- EMP_FNAME
- EMP_INITIAL
- EMP_ADDRESS
- EMP_STATE
- EMP_ZIPCODE
- EMP_EXTENSION
- EMP_AREACODE
- EMP_HOMEPHONE
- JOB_CODE

Take a look at this chapter's version of the POS_2nd database (Ch04_ POS_2nd) to identify the properties for each of the fields. Remember to save the EMPLOYEE table when you are done.

(Just add 90 to the date in question.) Given this wealth of possibilities, always select an Access date format whenever you have a date field.

To create the proper date format for a date field, modify the **EMPLOYEE** table by adding the EMP_HIREDATE field. (You can find all attribute characteristics in the Ch04_POS_2nd database on your CD. Use section 4.3.1, steps 1 through 3 to enter the new attribute. This time, select the **Date/Time** option from the **Data Type** list—see Figure 4.14 if you need a reminder—when you define the data type.)

Having selected the **Date/Time** format to define the EMP_HIREDATE data type, you will discover that many date format options are available. For example, if you click on the **Date/Time** field property for the EMPLOYEE's EMP_HIREDATE, you will see the options listed in Figure 4.36.

We will use the medium date format, so put the cursor on the **Medium Date** option and click to make this selection the date property of the EMP_HIREDATE. This format ensures that a date such as January 15, 2003, will be shown as 15-Jan-03.

As you can tell by looking at the many date/time options listed in Figure 4.36, you have considerable control over the date/time presentation format. In fact, you can even define your own presentation format. For example, if you examine the property box of the EMP_HIREDATE field shown in Figure 4.37, note that we have typed in the presentation format dd-mmm-yyyy to show all four year digits. This format ensures that the input 1/22/03 will be shown as 22-Jan-2003. If you want the entire month name shown, just add an "m" to the string—dd-mmmm-yyyy—thus yielding 22-January-2002. If you want to show only the last two year digits and the first three letters of the month, use dd-mmm-yy. And so on.

We will use dd-mmm-yyyy throughout the text to ensure that our end users will see all four year digits when a record is opened. Even if the end user types in a date such as 1/15/03, the screen will show 15-Jan-2003 the next time the record is shown. We can also force the proper data entry format through an input mask. We examine various input masks in the next section.

FIGURE 4.36
Date Format Options

General Date	6/19/94 5:34:23 PM
Long Date	Sunday, June 19, 1994
Medium Date	19-Jun-94
Short Date	6/19/94
Long Time	5:34:23 PM
Medium Time	5:34 PM
Short Time	17:34

FIGURE 4.37
The EMP_HIREDATE User-Formatted Date Field Property

EMP_HIREDATE	Date/Time	Date of hire
EMP_DOB	Date/Time	Employee date of birth
EMP_SERVICE	Yes/No	Does the employee perform public se

Field Properties

General | Lookup

Format	dd-mmm-yyyy
Input Mask	
Caption	
Default Value	Date()
Validation Rule	
Validation Text	
Required	No
Indexed	No

The disp

4.4.2 Controlling Data Input: Validation, Input Masks, and Default Values

Each time you select an attribute's data type, you have the option to specify which values and data format are acceptable. We begin by examining how to control which values may be entered, using a validation rule. To see how a validation rule can be created, let's examine the EMP_TITLE field, whose properties are shown in Figure 4.38. (The original default properties were shown in Figure 4.16.)

As you examine Figure 4.38, note the following alterations to the default format.

- We have created a validation rule to limit data entries to three possibilities: Mr., Ms., or Mrs. Note that the format of this validation rule is defined by the **In()** function. The options are all text entries, and they are therefore enclosed in quotes. In addition, each entry is separated from the others by a comma. Therefore, we typed **In ("Mr.","Ms.","Mrs.")**. Enter this validation rule by placing the cursor on the line next to the **Validation Rule** text box and then type the rule as shown. This validation rule will ensure that *only* the *specified* strings can be entered. Data entries such as **CD**, **X**, or **123** will not be accepted.
- To make sure that the end user understands why an incorrect entry is not accepted, it is useful to show an appropriate error message. Such an error message will be generated by specifying its contents in the **Validation Text** property. As you examine Figure 4.38, note that the validation text, **Please use Mr., Ms., or Mrs.**, is typed without quotes. Whatever you type as the validation text will be

FIGURE 4.38
EMP_TITLE Field Properties

General | Lookup

Field Size	4
Format	
Input Mask	>L<CCC
Caption	
Default Value	
Validation Rule	In ("Mr.","Ms.","Mrs.")
Validation Text	Please limit your entry to Mr., Ms.,or Mrs.
Required	No
Allow Zero Length	Yes
Indexed	No
Unicode Compression	Yes
IME Mode	No Control
IME Sentence Mode	None

TABLE 4.1 Validation Rules For Different Data Types

Data Type	Validation Rule	Sample Validation Text
Numeric	[MOD_ENGINES] between 1 and 4	All of our aircraft have between 1 and 4 engines.
Numeric	[MOD_SEATS] >= 1	All of our aircraft have at least one seat!
Date	[FLT_DATE] >= #01/01/2002# and <= #12/31/2002#	Please limit flight dates to any date within 2002.

written in a message box when you make a data entry that fails to conform to the requirements listed in the validation rule. (We illustrate the effects of the validation rule and text when we describe the data entry procedures in section 4.5.)

Validation rule formats depend on the data type used. For example, numeric and date data types use field names enclosed in square brackets as well as mathematical delimiters such as between, <, >, <>, =, <=, or >=. Table 4.1 shows rules for some of the attributes found in a database designed for an aircraft-charter company.

As you examine Table 4.1, it is useful to note the following:

- The attribute (field) name is enclosed in square brackets. For example, the attribute named FLT_DATE is shown as [FLT_DATE].
- The use of *between* is actually inclusive, allowing the MOD_ENGINES values 1 and 4. This limitation might also be written as [MOD_ENGINES] >= 1 and <= 4.
- The # symbol is used as a date delimiter.
- Field names are case sensitive. For example, if you have stored the number of engines as MOD_ENGINES and you write the validation rule as

```
[MOD_ENGINES] >= 1
```

Access will tell you that the specification is invalid. Because Access does not require the use of the field name as long as the specification is written in the context of the table structure, you could simply write the validation rule for the MOD_ENGINES field property as

```
>= 1 AND <= 4
```

without specifying the field name at all.

We can fine-tune the data entry by forcing the end user to conform to a desired data format. The data format control is handled through the input mask, which can be specified in the **Field Properties** box. As you examine Figure 4.38 again, note that its **Input Mask** property is set to

```
>L<CCC
```

This property ensures that the first letter is always capitalized while the remaining characters will be lowercase. In other words, characters following > will be capitalized, and characters following < will be lowercase regardless of how they are entered. In short, if the end user types MR. or mr., the entry will be shown as Mr. Similarly, the entries ms. or MS. will be shown as Ms. And such entries as MRS., mrs., Mrs., or mRs. will be shown as Mrs. By combining the validation rule and the input mask, we have created a data entry environment in which the end user is forced to enter the data properly. Figure 4.38 currently indicates that the EMP_TITLE field is not required, thus allowing the end user to skip data entry for this attribute. By setting the **Required** property to **Yes**, we will also ensure that the end user actually makes a data entry.

An example of the input mask help screen is shown in Figure 4.39. In this example, the telephone number default format would yield an input requirement of an area code and the phone number to match the input mask (___) ___-____.

Note

The characters L and C we have used in the EMP_TITLE's input mask have a precise meaning. The L indicates that the character must be a letter. The C indicates that any character may be used, including a period. We used >L<CCC to ensure that the period after Mr. or Ms. would not be rejected in a four-character data entry field. If we had used >L<LLL, all three characters following the capitalized first letter must be letters, thus causing entries such as Mr. or Ms. to be rejected because they end with a period.

Remember that Access will provide context-sensitive help on any topic. For example, to see what characters are available for input masking, put the cursor on the property box's **Input Mask**, then tap the F1 key on your keyboard. This action will generate the screen shown in Figure 4.39. Use the scroll bars to look at all of the help screen's text. If you want to see more detailed information, put the cursor on the Show All text in the upper right-hand corner. This action will change the cursor shape to a hand. Then click to produce the desired additional detail.

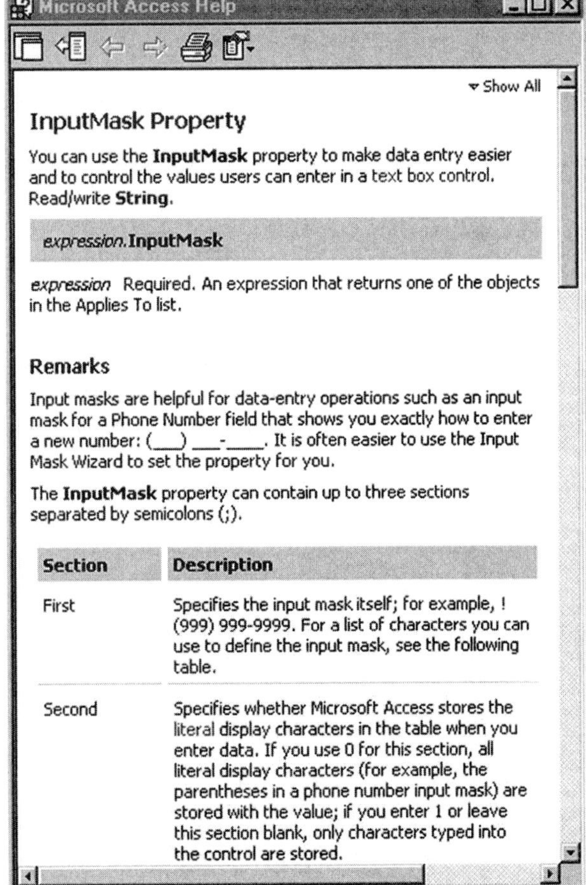

FIGURE 4.39
The Input Mask Help Screen

Using the instructions provided by the input mask help screen, let's create an input mask for the EMP_HIREDATE field. (We have already specified an *output* format of dd-mmm-yyyy. However, we have not specified how to *input* a date. A data entry of either 1/15/03 or 15-Jan-2003 would be accepted as a valid input.) But suppose that you want to force the end user to input a date such as January 15, 2003, as 01/15/2003, using a long date format. As you examine the input mask in Figure 4.40, note that it is composed of three parts and each part is separated from the others by a semicolon (;) delimiter.

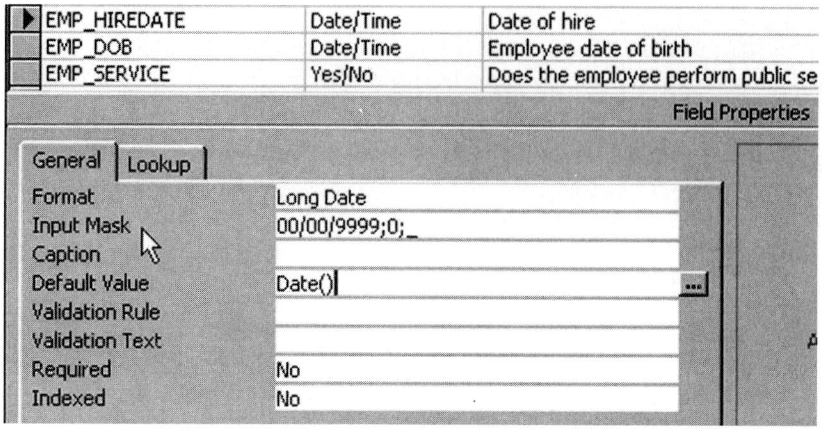

FIGURE 4.40
The EMP_HIREDATE Input Mask

EMP_HIREDATE	Date/Time	Date of hire
EMP_DOB	Date/Time	Employee date of birth
EMP_SERVICE	Yes/No	Does the employee perform public se

Field Properties

General | Lookup

Format	Long Date
Input Mask	00/00/9999;0;_
Caption	
Default Value	Date()
Validation Rule	
Validation Text	
Required	No
Indexed	No

- The 00/00/9999 specifies the input mask itself.
- A zero (0) following the first delimiter specifies whether Access actually stores the value in the database table. If you use 0, all characters will be stored, including all display characters such as a slash (/) or a comma (,). If you type a 1 or leave it blank, only the characters you have actually typed will be stored.
- The underline (_) is the character that will be displayed on the screen. In this case, the underline symbol appears in the data entry field to indicate where the data are to be typed.

Using the 00/00/9999;0;_ input mask, you will see the entry prompt __/__/____. (The end user does not type the slashes between the date components.) Similarly, if you want to store phone numbers in the format (999) 999-9999, use the input mask (999) 999-9999;0;_ to produce the input prompt (___) ___-____. (The end user does not type the parentheses around the area code.)

Use an input mask >LL for the state codes. Table 4.2 summarizes the use of input mask characters.

TABLE 4.2
Input Mask Characters

Character	Effect
0	Numerical values 0–9, entry required, + and – not allowed.
9	Numerical values 0–9 or a space, entry optional, + and – not allowed.
#	Numerical values 0–9 or a space, entry optional; spaces are shown as blanks in edit mode, but blanks are not saved, + and – allowed.
L	Letters A–Z, entry required.
?	Letters A–Z, entry optional.
A	Letter or numeric value, entry required.
A	Letter or numeric value, entry optional.
&	Any character or a space, entry required.
C	Any character or a space, entry optional.
.	Decimal place holder.
,	Thousands delimiter.
:	Date and time separator.
;	Date and time separator.
-	Date and time separator.
/	Date and time separator.
<	Converts all characters following it to lowercase.
>	Converts all characters following it to uppercase.
!	Causes characters to fill the input mask from left to right.
\	Causes the character(s) following it to be displayed as the literal character. \X will be displayed as X.

Assignment

Using your own database, complete the EMPLOYEE table's structure. Use appropriate validation rules, input masks, and default values. Next, create the table structures for the CUSTOMER and the INVOICE. (You should use the **Ch04_POS_2nd** database on your CD as your field structure source.)

Take another look at Figure 4.40 and note that we have also used a **default value** in this date field. In this case, the **Date()** function automatically enters the current date, thus relieving the end user from having to type it. Relieving the end user's workload is always desirable. Suppose, for example, that your table includes (currency) fields such as year-to-date pay and year-to-date withholding. If a new employee is entered into the database, these values will be zero, so why not select the data type to be **Currency** and set the default values to 0? If the data entry involves a current time, why not use a **Time()** function as the default? *(Remember, use the F1 key on your keyboard to examine the many options Access makes available to you!)*

4.5 INDEXES

Suppose you wanted to find every occurrence of the phrase *referential integrity* in this book. A very inefficient way to find this phrase would be to read every page, starting on page 1. Or you could simply go to the back of the book, find the index, look up the desired phrase, and go directly to the page numbers that are listed in the index. What makes the search even easier is that the index lists all of its words and phrases in alphabetical order.

In theory, a database table index works like an index for any book. The creation of an index for any field creates a pointer file for that field. For example, if the **Indexed** property for the EMPL_LNAME field is set to **Yes**, a pointer file would be created for that field. Therefore, to find the employee whose last name is Smith in the EMPLOYEE table, the EMP_LNAME index would move the index pointer directly to the occurrence of "Smith." If the EMP_LNAME field is not indexed, the search for Smith requires a scan of all of the table contents to find the Smith occurrences. The computer index works just as well with numbers, dates, or other data formats.

Using an index makes finding a matching value more efficient. However, there is a penalty to be paid for using indexes. For example, if you use frequent data updates by adding, deleting, or modifying records, the index pointer files must be updated to reflect the changes. Such updates require time. In short, use indexes when their search efficiency can be justified even in the face of update inefficiency.

If you look at any PK's field property, you'll note that its index is defined as **Yes (No duplicates)**. The **No Duplicates** property reflects the requirement that each PK must be unique to preserve entity integrity. Because the PK is always the record's prime locator, an index is automatically created for each PK.

4.5.1 Composite Indexes

Quite aside from the fact that indexes yield more efficient data retrieval, they can also be used to help avoid data duplication. Let's use the Ch04_Composite_Practice database to illustrate the procedure. Figure 4.41 shows an alternate version of the original TEST_RESULT table. This new table is named TEST_RESULT_VERSION2. Note that its PK is a single attribute named TEST_RESULT_NUM. (The original TEST_RESULT table's composite PK was

FIGURE 4.41
The Alternate Version of the TEST_RESULT Table

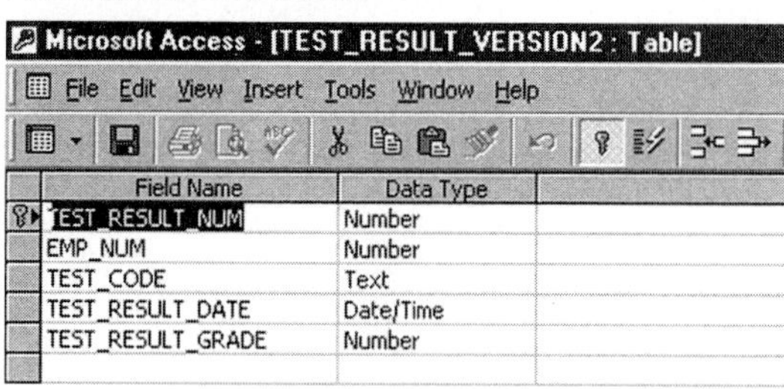

FIGURE 4.42
Selecting the Indexes Option

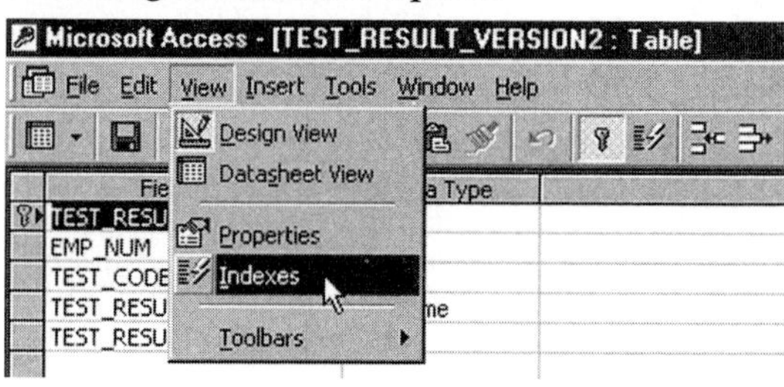

EMP_NUM + TEST_ CODE + TEST_RESULT_DATE, and one of its tasks was to avoid data duplication. Review section 4.3.3 if necessary.)

What is the advantage of the single attribute PK in the TEST_RESULT_VERSION2 table? You will discover later that a foreign key in a related table cannot reference a composite PK. In short, a composite PK works just fine—as long as such a relationship is not required in the database implementation. Because you cannot always guarantee that such relationships will not be necessary sometime in the future, the use of a composite PK is generally not recommended. (We covered composite PKs for some good reasons. First, you will encounter them from time to time. Therefore, you should know what they are and how to work with them. Second, if the existence of a composite PK creates a problem in establishing relationships between tables, you should know how to deal with that problem. If you don't know what the problem is, the problem will be hard to solve. Finally, if relationships between FKs and composite PKs are not likely to occur, the composite PK does no harm.)

Keep in mind (take another look at Section 4.3.3) that one of the very important benefits of the composite PK is its ability to help the end user avoid duplication of existing records. How can you get that benefit and yet keep the single attribute PK? The answer lies in the development of a composite index. To create such an index, perform the following procedures:

Step 1

Select the **Indexes** option from the **View** menu (see Figure 4.42).

The **View/Indexes** selection will show you all the currently existing indexes (see Figure 4.43). Note that the primary key, TEST_RESULT_NUM, is identified and that we have already created indexes for the EMP_NUM, TEST_CODE, and TEST_RESULT_NUM. (Declaring a PK automatically indexes the field(s) used in the PK.)

FIGURE 4.43
The Current Indexes

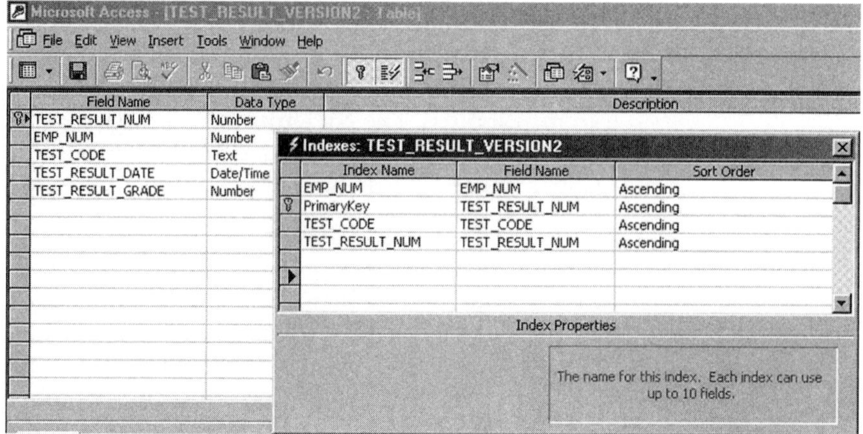

Note

At this point, we have kept the (default) **No** settings for each of the three fields (EMP_NUM, TEST_CODE, and TEST_RESULT _DATE) that are to be used in the composite index field named AVOID_DUPLICATES. The default settings are shown in Figure 4.44:

Primary	No
Unique	No
Ignore Nulls	No

The selection of these default settings is based on the following reasons:

1. None of the three fields is part of the PK. Therefore, the **Primary** option is **No** for each of the three fields.
2. *Taken individually*, none of the three fields is unique. An employee may take the same test multiple times on different dates. Therefore, *each* of the EMP_NUM, TEST_CODE, and TEST_RESULT_DATE values may occur multiple times in the TEST_RESULT_VERSION2 table. (Note the original listing in Figure 4.28, which showed the test results for several employees. The TEST_RESULT_VERSION2 table contains the same test result data, with the difference that its PK consists of a single attribute.) Therefore, the **Unique** selection must be **No** for *each* of the three fields. Given the nature of default values, this default setting is also shown in the AVOID_DUPLICATES index (see FIgure 4.44). As you will see shortly, the failure to modify this inherited default value will cause a problem.
3. Although each of the three attributes may occur multiple times, *each combination of those three attribute values must be unique.* Nulls are undefined. Therefore, if any null test dates or employee numbers or testing dates exist, no unique combinations can be defined. (The nulls yield ambiguous results.) Therefore, nulls must *not* be ignored; that is, the end user must be prevented from leaving a null in any EMP_NUM, TEST_CODE, and TEST_RESULT_DATE field in the TEST_RESULT_VERSION2 table. In short, the **Ignore Nulls** option is kept at its **No** default value.

Step 2

Type the new index name on an empty line below the **Index Name** column. We have used the index name AVOID_DUPLICATES in Figure 4.44.

Step 3

Select the field name to be indexed. When you examine Figure 4.44, you'll see that clicking on the **Field Name** line produces a drop-down list that contains all the available fields. Click on the field name you want to use in the index. We will use all the FK fields—EMP_NUM, TEST_CODE, and TEST_RESULT_DATE—in order to trap duplicate data entries. Therefore, start by clicking on the EMP_NUM field to place it in the **Field Name** column.

Now move the cursor to the next line and select the TEST_CODE field, then move the cursor to the next line and select the TEST_RESULT_DATE field. When all three fields have been entered, your index looks like Figure 4.45. (Note that the default sort order is **Ascending**. Naturally, you can change this sort order to

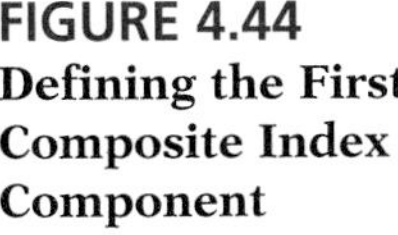

FIGURE 4.44
Defining the First Composite Index Component

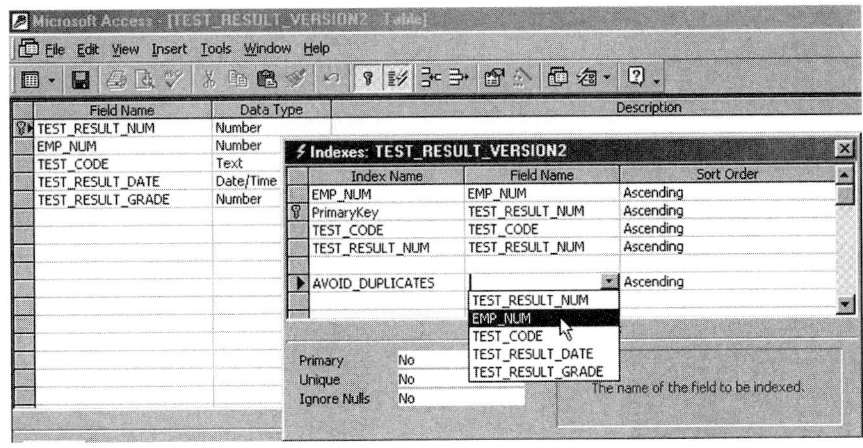

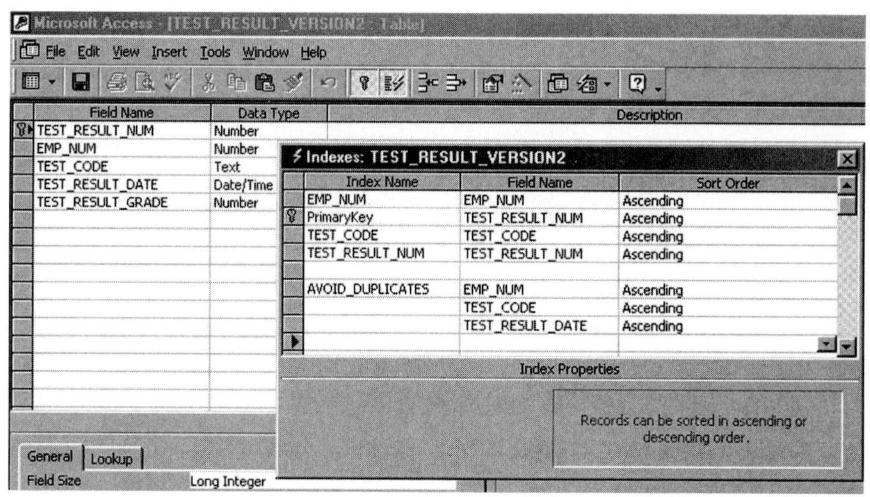

FIGURE 4.45
The Remaining Composite Index Components

Descending, if you like. However, because the standard index option is **Ascending**, that's what we'll use.)

Step 4

Save the index. If you forget to do this, Access will prompt you, as shown in Figure 4.46.

If you now open the table, you will discover that the data records can still be duplicated. *Why didn't this composite index work?* The answer is disarmingly simple: We failed to specify that the composite index must be *unique* if duplicate records are to be caught. To fix this problem, open the TEST_RESULT_VERSION2 table in its design format, select the **View/Indexes** option again, and select **Yes** to the **Unique** option for the AVOID_DUPLICATES index. (See Figure 4.47.) But remember from the discussion in the previous note that the *individual attributes* (fields) that were used to create this AVOID_DUPLICATES index are *not* unique!

Save the change after you have fixed the problem. If you now try to duplicate a record, the composite index will trap the duplicate, causing Access to produce the message shown in Figure 4.48.

4.6 DATA ENTRY

Having completed the EMPLOYEE table structure, you are ready for data entry. The data entry will demonstrate how the validation rules, the input masks, and the default values do their jobs. To begin data entry, return to the database window, click on the EMPLOYEE table name, and then select the **Open** button to

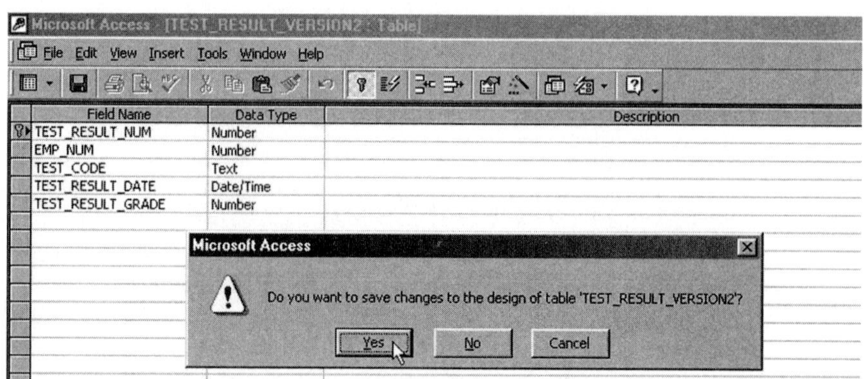

FIGURE 4.46
Saving the Composite Index

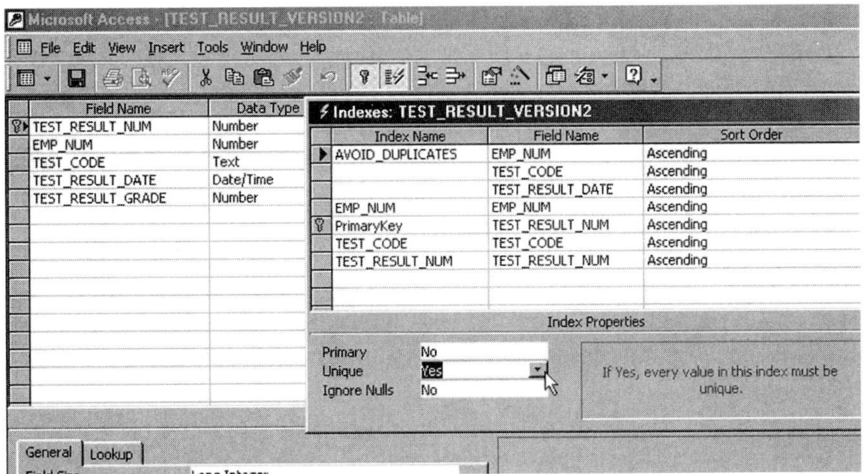

FIGURE 4.47
Setting the Composite Index to Unique

show the EMPLOYEE table in edit mode. The edit mode, shown in Figure 4.49, shows only the attributes that fit on the screen. To see the other attributes, use the left/right scroll bars at the bottom of the screen.

As you examine Figure 4.49, note the navigation buttons at the lower left of the screen. The current location of the record pointer is at record 1.

To start entering the first record, keep in mind that the cursor *default* location is just below the first field, labeled EMP_NUM. Because the EMP_NUM's data type is **AutoNumber**, you will *not* make a data entry in that field. Instead, move the cursor to the space below the EMP_TITLE field header by pressing the Tab key or by pressing the Enter key to enter the EMP_TITLE value. To illustrate that the EMP_TITLE's field properties (see Figure 4.38 again) work as intended, try entering the (incorrect) string value MG (see Figure 4.50).

Note the following features in Figure 4.50:

- Any time we change a record, the pencil-shaped symbol indicates that we are editing the record.
- The attempt to enter MG caused the uppercase G to be entered as a lowercase g. That's the >L<CCC input mask at work.
- The data entry space was delimited by an underline, covering four characters. That's the input mask again.

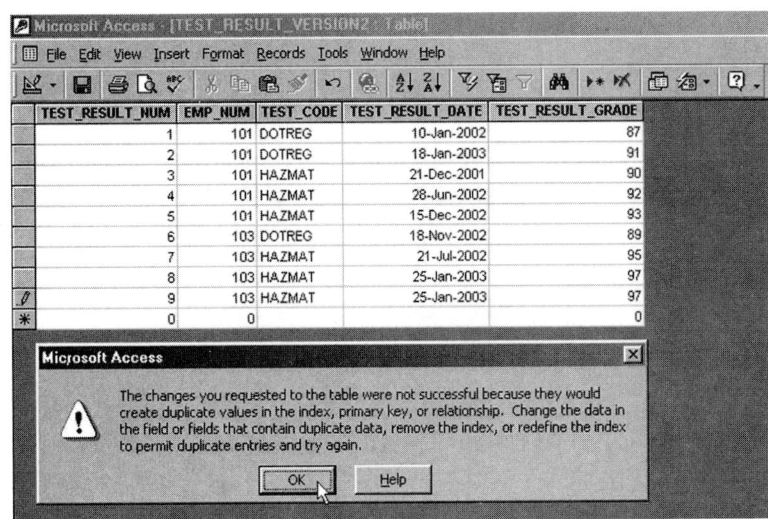

TEST_RESULT_NUM	EMP_NUM	TEST_CODE	TEST_RESULT_DATE	TEST_RESULT_GRADE
1	101	DOTREG	10-Jan-2002	87
2	101	DOTREG	18-Jan-2003	91
3	101	HAZMAT	21-Dec-2001	90
4	101	HAZMAT	28-Jun-2002	92
5	101	HAZMAT	15-Dec-2002	93
6	103	DOTREG	18-Nov-2002	89
7	103	HAZMAT	21-Jul-2002	95
8	103	HAZMAT	25-Jan-2003	97
9	103	HAZMAT	25-Jan-2003	97
0	0			0

FIGURE 4.48
Data Duplicates Are Avoided with the Composite Index

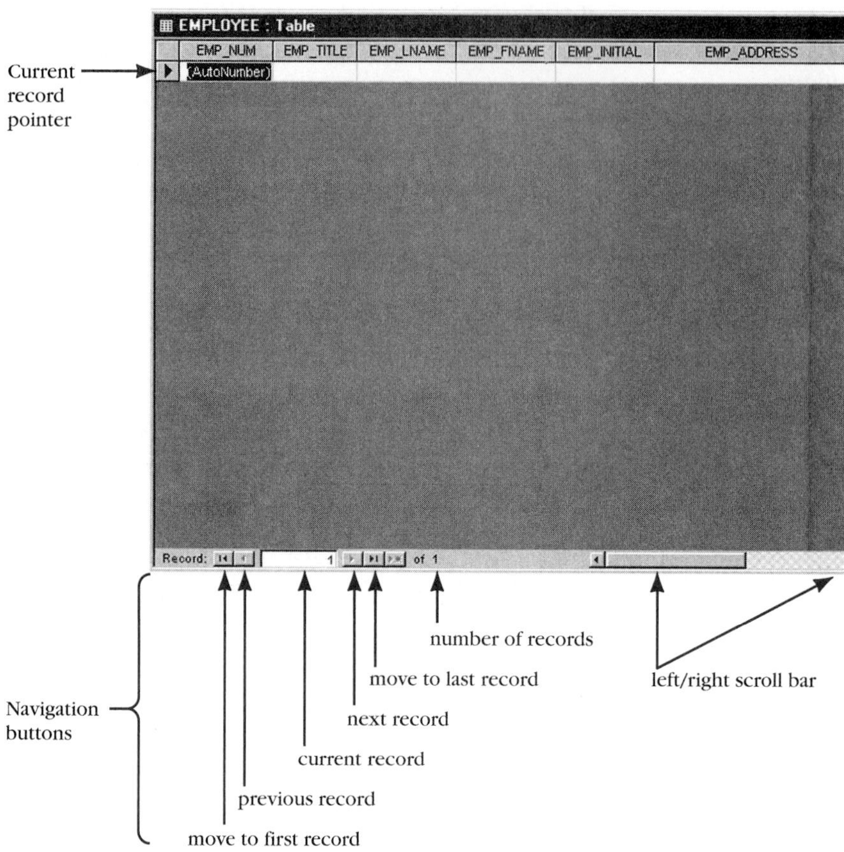

FIGURE 4.49
The Data Entry Opening Screen

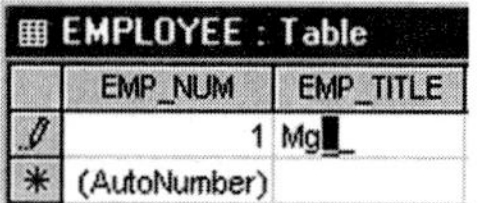

FIGURE 4.50
Initial Data Entry into the EMP_TITLE Field

- The EMP_NUM value shows up as 1, even though you made no data entry into the EMP_NUM field. That's the **AutoNumber** function at work. (Remember, we gave EMP_NUM an **AutoNumber** data type.)

When you try to use the Tab key to move from the EMP_TITLE field to the next field, EMP_LNAME, Access will display the message box shown in Figure 4.51. This message box illustrates that the data validation rule worked as intended.

Just click **OK** to return to data entry and then use one of the correct options: Mr., Ms., or Mrs. Now enter three records, making a few intentional errors to trigger the various data validation rules, default values, and input masks. For example, when you get to the EMP_HIREDATE field, note that the date default, Date(), put the current date into the field. (See Figure 4.52. As you can tell by looking at the date default value, we created this record on March 18, 2002.)

If you try to enter only the last two year digits, you'll generate the error message shown in Figure 4.53, courtesy of the input mask. (We entered the date of birth 02/14/1940 incorrectly. Did you notice that the input mask automatically produced the field entry format ___/___/____ for you?)

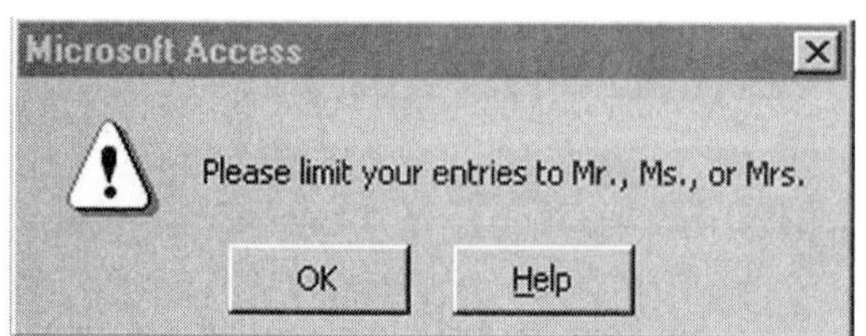

FIGURE 4.51
The EMP_TITLE Data Validation Rule Is Enforced

Assignment

Experiment with the navigation buttons and the left/right scroll bar. (See Figure 4.49 for their use.) Using the navigation buttons, go to the last record, move back a record, move one record forward, go to the last record, and go to the first record. Move the scroll bar to check all the field values for the three records. (Note that we have selected the first record in Figure 4.55.) Now save the records, using either the menu bar (**File/Save**) at the top of the screen or the **Save** on the button bar.

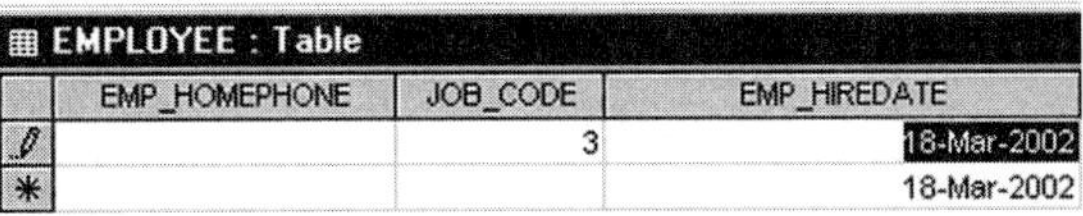

EMPLOYEE : Table

	EMP_HOMEPHONE	JOB_CODE	EMP_HIREDATE
✎		3	18-Mar-2002
*			18-Mar-2002

FIGURE 4.52
The Default Date Format for the EMP_HIREDATE Field

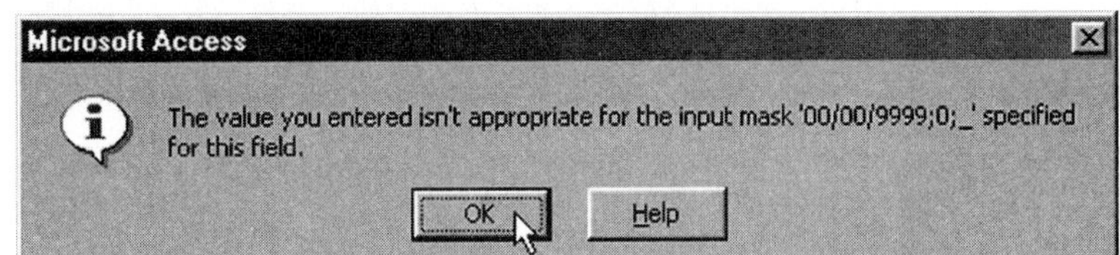

FIGURE 4.53
Date Input (Format) Entry Error

Just click **OK** and then correct the entry by deleting the incorrect entry and typing 02/14/1940. Press the Tab key or the Enter key to move to the next field. This action will convert the date field you have just typed to the presentation format shown in Figure 4.54. You also wind up in the EMP_SERVICE field, which was defined as a *logical* field. Therefore, Access presents it as a check box. If you click on this check box, the data entry is yes, indicated by the automatic insertion of the check mark.

As you continue entering the values for the fields in the EMPLOYEE table, note that they are automatically scrolled into the screen. If a field is not wide enough to fit the field value, the value will be entered even if it scrolls past the field limits. (Of course, you can always drag the field limits to make them wider.)

When you have entered the value for the last field in the EMPLOYEE table, pressing the Enter key will automatically move the cursor to the next record. After entering three records, note that the navigation buttons at the bottom of the screen indicate the table's status (see Figure 4.55).

You can always produce the desired toolbars by going to the menu bar and selecting the **View** option. From this point forward, we spell out the selection sequences from the menu bar, rather than show you the screens. Each menu bar option produces its own menu selections, and the selection sequences either produce additional submenus or execute the selected option (see Figure 4.56). To indicate the sequence shown in Figure 4.38, we can use **View/Toolbars/Table Datasheet**.

4.7 EDIT AND DELETE

You can change the table structure and its contents by editing them. You can also delete table components (fields), and even delete the tables.

	JOB_CODE	EMP_HIREDATE	EMP_DOB	EMP_SERVICE
✎	3	18-Mar-2002	14-Feb-1940	☑
*		18-Mar-2002		☐

FIGURE 4.54
Data Entry into a Logical Field

Note

If you can't find the **Save** button, use the menu bar at the top of the screen to produce the appropriate toolbar. The selection sequence is **View/Datasheet View/Toolbars/Table Datasheet**, and it is shown in Figure 4.56.

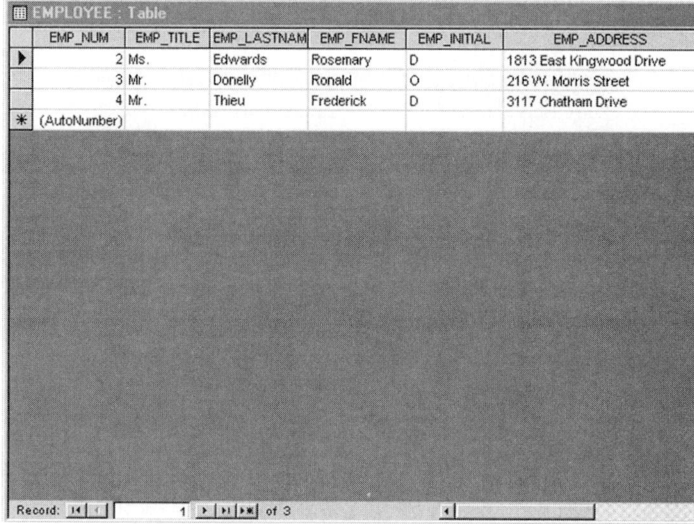

EMPLOYEE : Table

	EMP_NUM	EMP_TITLE	EMP_LASTNAM	EMP_FNAME	EMP_INITIAL	EMP_ADDRESS
▶	2	Ms.	Edwards	Rosemary	D	1813 East Kingwood Drive
	3	Mr.	Donelly	Ronald	O	216 W. Morris Street
	4	Mr.	Thieu	Frederick	D	3117 Chatham Drive
*	(AutoNumber)					

Record: 1 of 3

FIGURE 4.55
The EMPLOYEE Table with Three Records

4.7.1 Editing Table Components

To edit a table's components, first select the table from the database window, using the **Design** button. (Check Figure 4.57 to review the database window's contents. Remember that clicking on the **Open** button lets you see the selected table's contents and clicking on the **Design** button lets you see the selected table's structure.) In this case, select the EMPLOYEE table by clicking on it; then select the design mode by clicking on the **Design** button to produce Figure 4.58.

To illustrate the editing process, we have changed the EMP_LNAME field name to EMP_LASTNAME as shown in Figure 4.58. To make this change,

FIGURE 4.56
Producing the Toolbar via the Menu Bar Selection

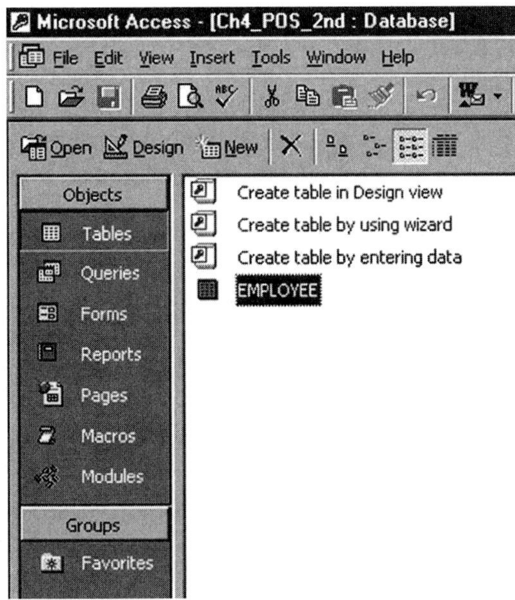

FIGURE 4.57
The Database Window: Tables

- We put the cursor on the EMP_LNAME Field Name, just after the letter L in EMP_LNAME.
- We typed in the insert AST to change LNAME to LASTNAME.
- Using the same editing technique, you may change the Field Size to 20.
- Put the cursor on the current Field Size 15.
- Delete the current value.
- Type in the desired value 20.

You may even change the field data types. For example, the current EMP_SERVICE data type is logical, using the **Yes/No** format shown in Figure 4.59. You may change this logical data type to **Text** by clicking on the **Data Type** down arrow to select **Text** from the pick list.

After selecting **Text** from the **Data Type** pick list, you can modify the EMP_SERVICE **Field Properties** box as follows:

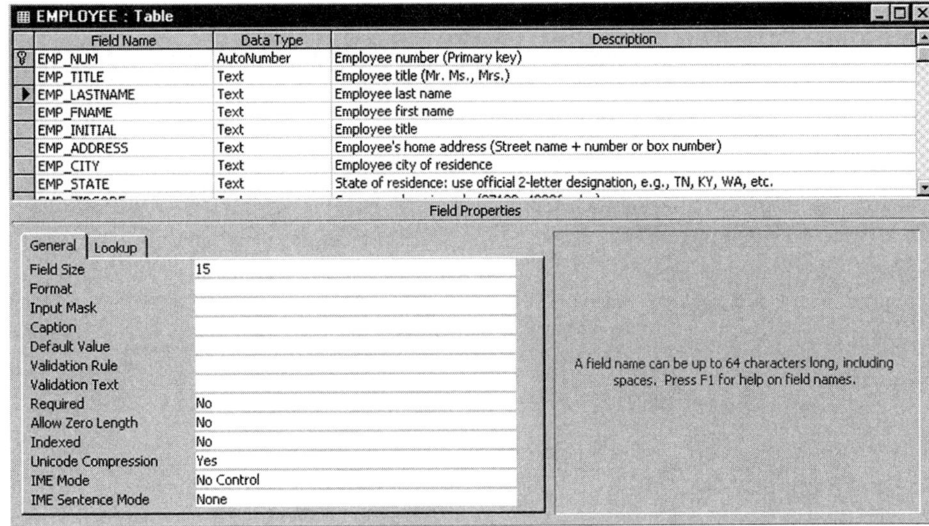

FIGURE 4.58
Editing the EMPLOYEE Attributes

FIGURE 4.59
Editing a Logical Data Type

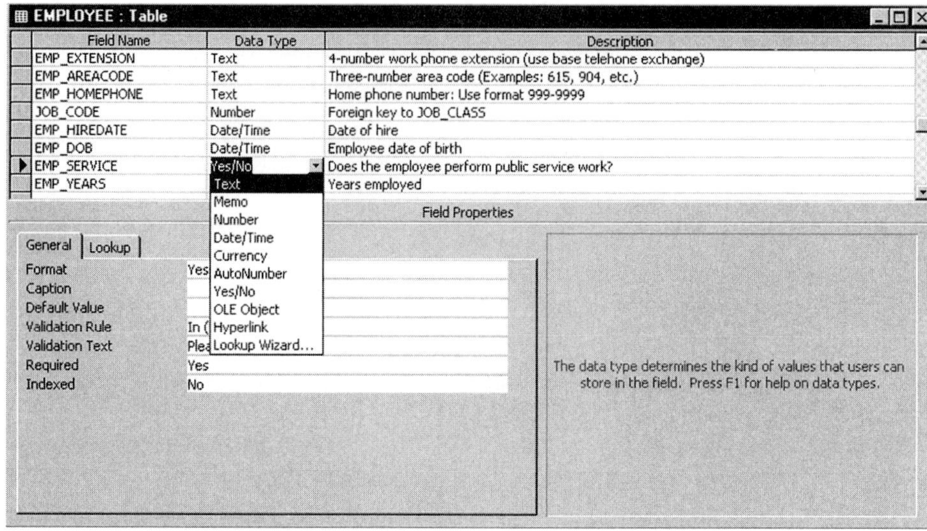

- Select a **Field Size** of 1.
- Create an **Input Mask** that specifies >L.
- Create a data **Validation Rule** that specifies **In ("Y","N")**.
- Create a **Validation Text** that specifies **Please limit your entry to Y or N**.
- Set **Required** to **Yes**.

When you are done, the **Field Properties** box contains the entries shown in Figure 4.60.

As you clicked on each field property, you probably noticed that Access used a down arrow (shown in the **Required** property of Figure 4.60). If you place the cursor on the **Validation Rule**, you will see a **Build** button like this one: Clicking on the down arrow always produces a list of the available choices. Clicking on the build button opens the Expression Builder. Although we have not used the Expression Builder to make the simple changes we have made here, you will discover that the Expression Builder is a very powerful tool in the Access applications development arsenal. As always, to avoid information overload, we will explore the details of any feature when we actually need it.

When you are done with the editing chores, save the file by selecting **File/Save** from the menu bar or by selecting the **Save** button from the toolbar. If you forget to save the changes and you close the table, Access will remind you of your oversight by printing the message box shown in Figure 4.61.

Clearly, your editing changes can be quite extensive while you are in edit mode. In fact, you can even make changes that make no sense. For example, you may decide to change the EMP_FNAME to a numeric data type. However, if you do, Access will print the warning shown in Figure 4.62 when you try to save such changes.

FIGURE 4.60
The Edited EMP_SERVICE Field Properties

General | Lookup

Field Size	1
Format	
Input Mask	>L
Caption	
Default Value	"Y"
Validation Rule	In ("Y","N")
Validation Text	Please limit your entries to Y or N.
Required	Yes
Allow Zero Length	No
Indexed	No
Unicode Compression	No

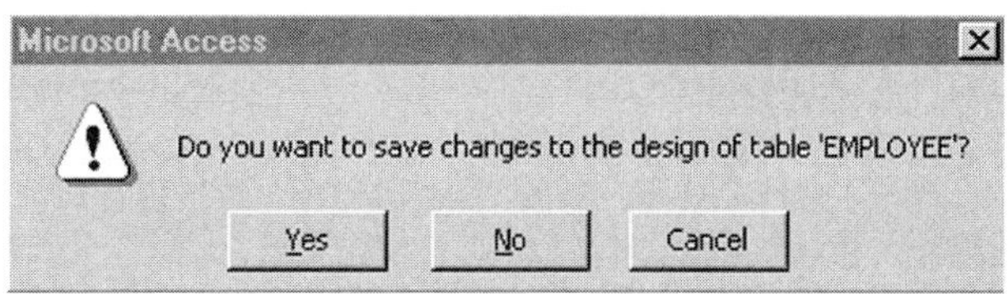

FIGURE 4.61
A Reminder to Save

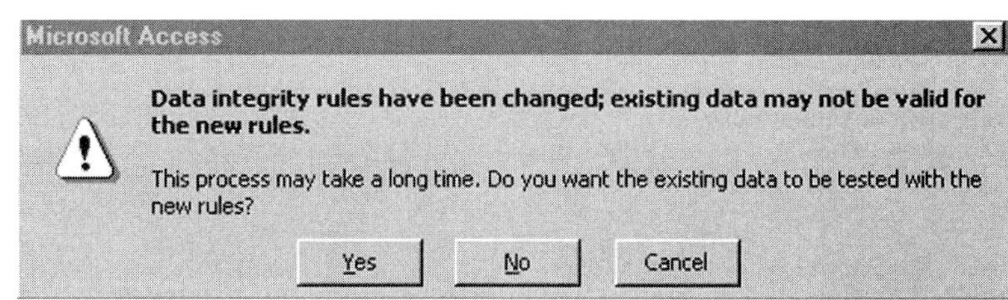

FIGURE 4.62
A Warning about Possible Data Loss

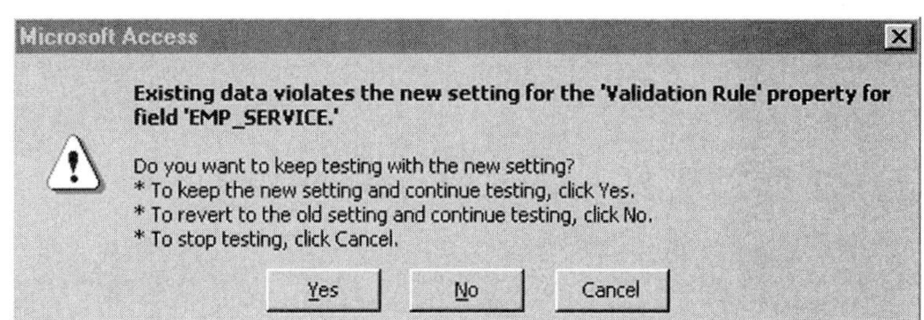

FIGURE 4.63
A Final Confirmation

FIGURE 4.64
Removing the Primary Key

Selecting **No** from the message box shown in Figure 4.62 will generate the message box shown in Figure 4.63. This selection means that the original data type and its characteristics were preserved. In this case, we kept the EMP_SERVICE's logical (**Yes/No**) data type in its original format.

There is one major restriction on data type selection: You can have only one **AutoNumber** field format per table. Therefore, because the EMP_NUM field already has been defined as having an **AutoNumber** data type, you cannot change any other field format in the EMPLOYEE table to have an **AutoNumber** data type.

As long as a table is not related to another one, you may remove the PK by marking the PK field and then selecting the **Edit** option from the menu bar (see Figure 4.64). Remember, you mark the field by clicking on the tab located at its left margin.

As you examine the **Primary Key** option in Figure 4.64, note that it is checked. To deselect the PK, click on the **Primary Key** selection to remove the check mark from the check box. After you have made your selection, note that the PK symbol has been removed from the EMP_NUM field.

You can designate another field to be the PK the same way: Just mark the field and then select the **Edit** option from the menu bar. (Review the procedures illustrated in Figures 4.22 through 4.25 if necessary.)

4.7.2 Deleting and Inserting Fields

To delete a field, select the table in design mode. Then mark the field to be deleted by clicking on the tab in front of it. (Using the standard Windows conventions, you can, of course, select a block of fields by marking the first field and then selecting the last field while holding down the keyboard's Shift key. Figure 4.65 shows the EMP_TITLE field highlighted and ready to be deleted.

After selecting the field to be deleted, press the Delete key or select the **Edit/Delete** option from your menu bar. Either method will generate the screen shown in Figure 4.66.

Note

We have just shown you how to remove a PK, but that does not mean that it's a good idea to save a table without a PK. Therefore, do *not* save these changes! There will be rare occasions that require you to remove a PK to create a *different* PK.

FIGURE 4.65 Selecting a Field to Delete

EMPLOYEE : Table

Field Name	Data Type	Description
EMP_NUM	AutoNumber	Employee number (Primary key)
EMP_TITLE	Text	Employee title (Mr. Ms., Mrs.)
EMP_LASTNAME	Text	Employee last name
EMP_FNAME	Text	Employee first name
EMP_INITIAL	Text	Employee title

Because we do not want to delete the selected fields at this time, click on the **No** button as shown in Figure 4.66.

4.7.3 Editing the Table Contents

You can change the attribute (field) *values* by selecting the **Open** option from the database window. Simply place the cursor on any value and make the desired changes. For example, to change the address shown in the first record in Figure 4.67, scroll to the EMP_ADDRESS field as shown, mark the parts to be modified, and type the corrections. In this example, we have marked the street portion of East Kingwood Drive. Typing **Avenue** will produce the edited address, which will then read 1813 East Kingwood Avenue.

A logical field value (**Yes/No**) has a value **Yes** when the check box contains a check mark (see Figure 4.54). To change this value to **No**, simply click on the check box's check mark to delete it.

Although Access will give you a lot of leeway to edit field values, there are two major restrictions:

1. Values of any field defined as having an **AutoNumber** data type *cannot* be changed. Therefore, you cannot change the EMP_NUM value 3 to 4, 10, or to any other number.
2. If the table has a relationship with another table, its FK values cannot be changed to values that will violate referential integrity. (We show you how to

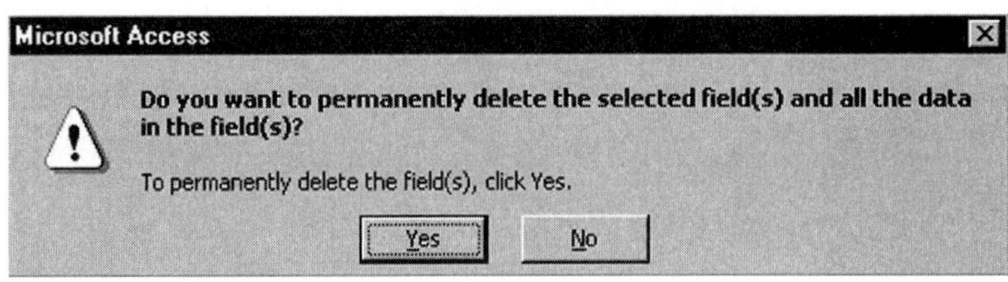

FIGURE 4.66
Delete Message Box

FIGURE 4.67
The EMPLOYEE Table Contents Ready for Editing

EMPLOYEE : Table

EMP_FNAME	EMP_INITIAL	EMP_ADDRESS	EMP_CITY	EMP_STATE
Rosemary	D	1813 East Kingwood Drive	Murfreesboro	TN
Ronald	O	216 W. Morris Street	Murfreesboro	TN
Frederick	D	3117 Chatham Drive	Smyrna	TN

Assignment

Edit all the tables you created in the previous assignment. Change field names, change field characteristics, and insert new fields. Next, open the table in the data sheet view to show all the records, and then edit the field values. Save all of the changes to see the dialog boxes associated with the editing process. Finally, delete all of the tables you have created. When you are done, the database window will not show a single table.

FIGURE 4.68
The Record Deletion Message

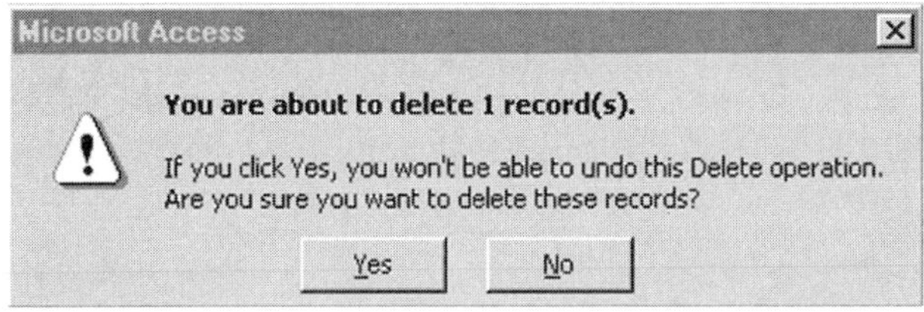

FIGURE 4.69
Deleting a Table via the Menu Bar

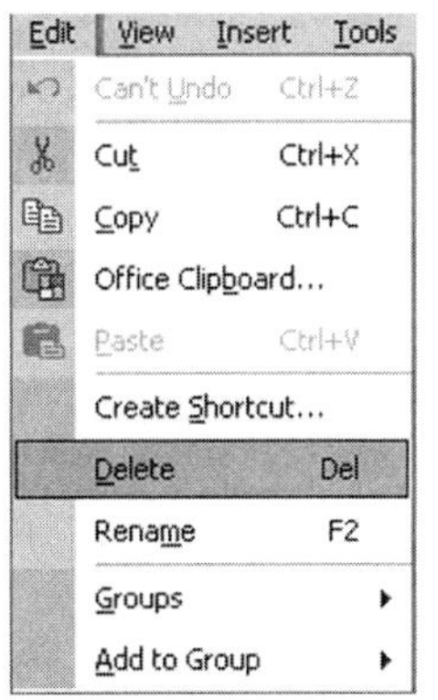

create relationships and what will happen if you violate referential integrity in section 4.9. Review Chapter 2 if you do not quite remember what referential integrity means.)

4.7.4 Deleting Records

To delete records, open the table from the database window, mark the record(s) to be deleted, and press the keyboard's Delete key. Or use the **Edit/Delete** option from the menu bar. In either case, Access will produce the message box shown in Figure 4.68. (Remember that the EMPLOYEE table contained three records. Go ahead and mark the second one for deletion.)

Clicking the **Yes** button will remove the second record.

4.7.5 Deleting Tables

As long as tables are not related to other tables in the database, you may delete them. Select the table from the database window and then select the **Edit/Delete** option shown in Figure 4.69.

The table deletion is not actually done until you click on the **Yes** button shown in Figure 4.70. We have selected the **Yes** option because we will import the complete EMPLOYEE table in the next section.

4.8 IMPORTING AND EXPORTING TABLES

To import tables, you need the table source and you need a storage place—the database—to store the imported tables. The table source may be another directory on your disk, a floppy disk, a CD, or an Internet URL. Regardless of the source, the import sequence requires the completion of the following steps:

1. Open the destination database. We will use the **Ch04_POS_2nd** database we have created in this chapter.

FIGURE 4.70
Table Deletion Message

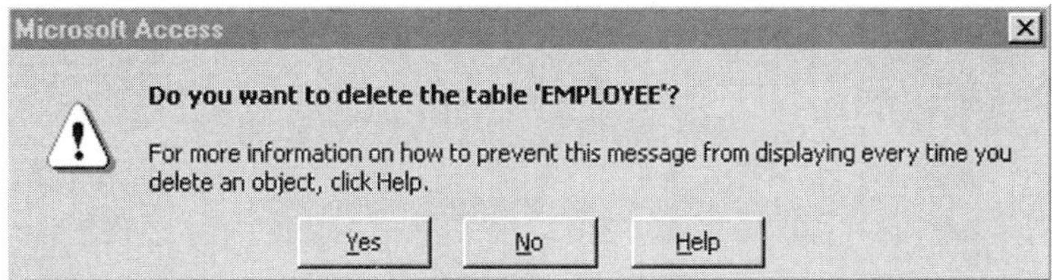

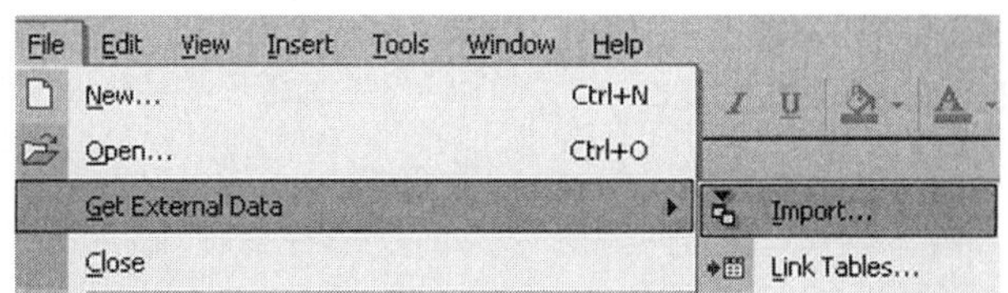

FIGURE 4.71
Selecting the File/Import Option

FIGURE 4.72
The Data Source for the Import Sequence

2. Delete all the tables you created in the **Ch04_POS_2nd.mdb** database. (Note the preceding assignment.)

3. Copy the **Ch04_POS_2nd.mdb** database from the student CD into the **C:\MSOffice\Access\Databases\Ch04** folder and name it **Ch04_POS_2nd Backup .mdb**. You are now ready to copy tables from the **Ch04_POS_2ndBackup** database into your **Ch04_ POS_2nd** database.

4. Select the **File/Get External Data/Import** option from the menu bar as shown in Figure 4.71.

The **Import** option shown in Figure 4.71 will open the source window shown in Figure 4.72.

5. Locate the **Ch04_POS_2ndBackup.mdb** in the C:\MSOFFICE\Access\Databases**Ch04**\ folder to generate the screen shown in Figure 4.72.

6. Select the import option by clicking the **Import** button in Figure 4.72 to generate the screen shown in Figure 4.73. Select the tables to be imported by marking them. We will import the five tables as marked in Figure 4.73.

7. After marking the tables as shown in Figure 4.73, click on the **OK** button to complete the import sequence. Your database will contain the tables shown in Figure 4.75 when the import process has been completed.

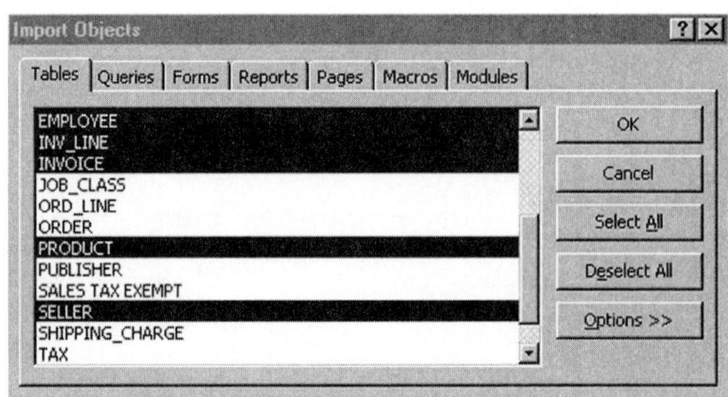

FIGURE 4.73
Tables Marked for Import

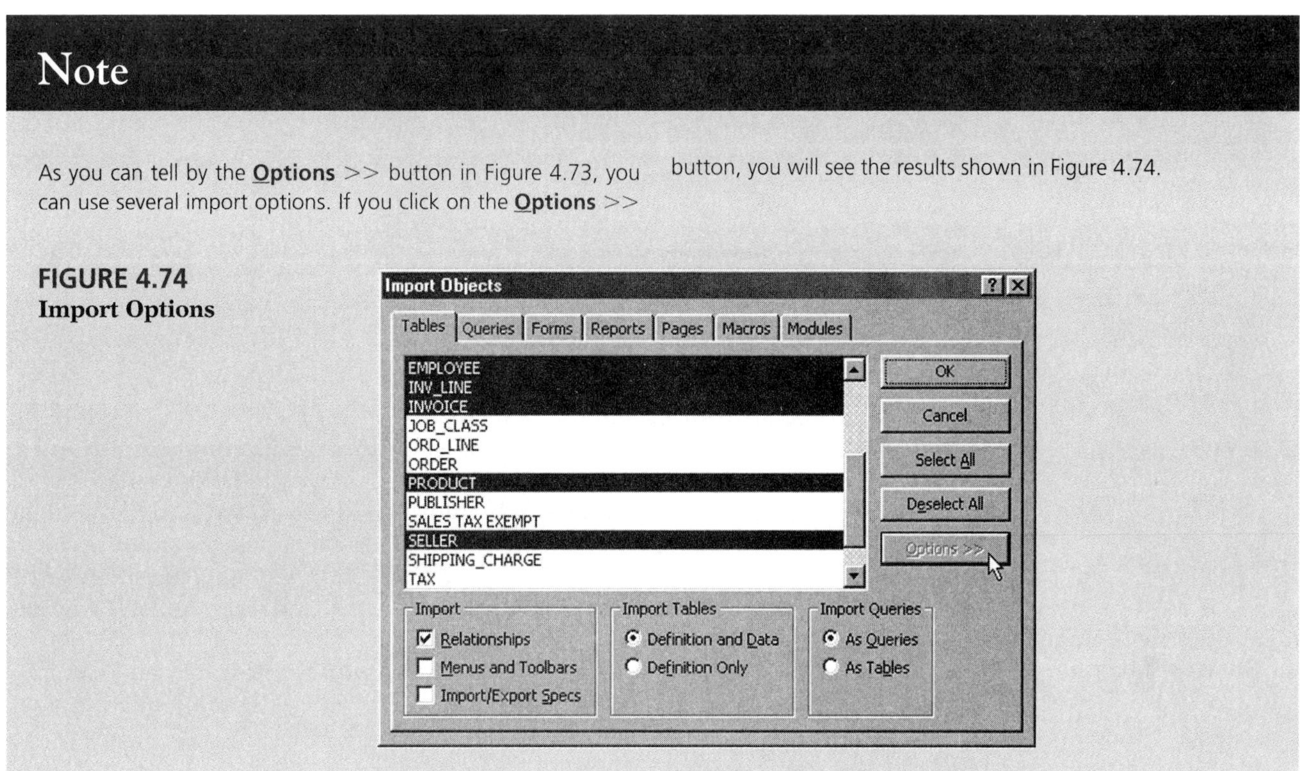

Note

As you can tell by the **Options >>** button in Figure 4.73, you can use several import options. If you click on the **Options >>** button, you will see the results shown in Figure 4.74.

FIGURE 4.74
Import Options

You can import any and all database objects: queries, forms, reports, macros, and modules just as you imported the tables. To do so, select the desired object type from the screen shown in Figure 4.73 and use the same import sequence that you used to import tables.

You can export Access objects as easily as you imported them. Just start with the menu bar's **File/Export** option shown in Figure 4.76 to generate the dialog box shown in Figure 4.77. Also, you can use the shortcut menu by selecting the table and right-click on the mouse as shown in Figure 4.77.

Although the default export data type is Access, you can save the exported object in many different formats. (Note the partial listing in Figure 4.78. As you produce this screen on your computer, go ahead and scroll down this list to see the amazing number of export formats that are available to you.)

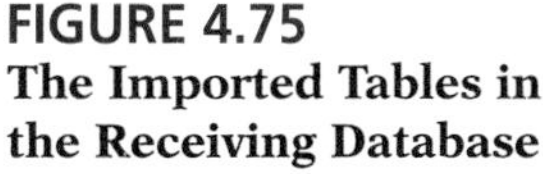

FIGURE 4.75
The Imported Tables in the Receiving Database

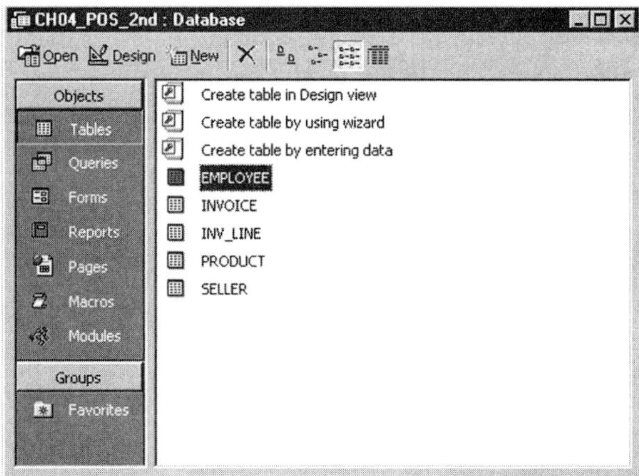

FIGURE 4.76
The File/Export Option

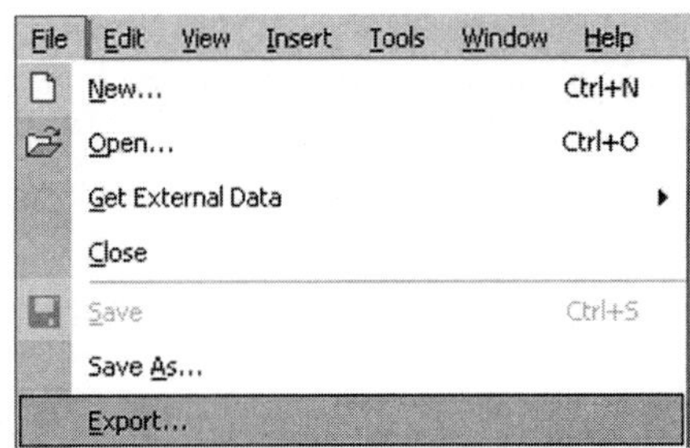

4.9 CREATING RELATIONSHIPS BETWEEN TABLES

You should recall from Chapter 1 that the strength of the relational database model is its ability to link (join) related tables through their common attributes, thus minimizing data redundancy. In fact, given its ability to let us combine data from two or more tables, the relational join is usually considered to be the relational database's crucial element. Because the relational database cannot perform its intended tasks without the proper joins, we will show you how to establish the appropriate relationships between the **POS_2nd.MDB** database tables. (You imported five of them in the previous section.)

Access permits two different types of joins: the *equijoin,* also labeled *inner join* by Access, and the **outer join**. Because Access lets you use both join types, you should know what they are and what they do.

FIGURE 4.77
Right-Click to Generate the Shortcut Menu

4.9.1 The Equijoin

As its name implies, the **equijoin** produces a listing of all records whose foreign key values are equal to the related table's primary key values. Each equijoin links two tables by letting the FK in one table point to the PK in the related table. If the FK in one table has the same value as the PK in the related table, the join can be completed. For example, the small database in Figure 4.79 shows a few customers who may or may not yet have a sales representative—an employee of the company that serves these customers—assigned to them. (This database is located on your CD.) Note that there are six customers, located in the CUSTOMER table, and three sales representatives, located in the EMPLOYEE table.

As you examine the CUSTOMER table in Figure 4.79, note that customer 1005 does not (yet) have a sales representative assigned to him or her. Only five records in the CUSTOMER table have a match in the EMPLOYEE table. The equijoin would, therefore, show only the five records listed in Figure 4.80.

FIGURE 4.78
The Export Destination

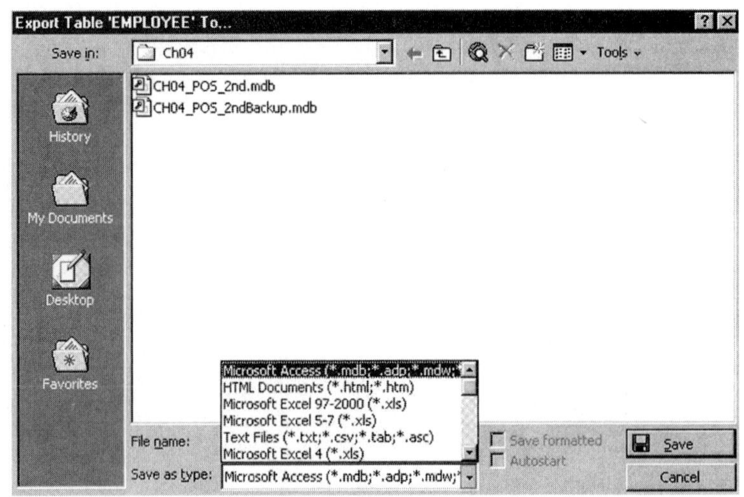

FIGURE 4.79
The Ch04_Relationships_ Demo Database

CUSTOMER Table

CUST_NUM	CUST_LNAME	EMP_NUM
1001	Roberts	101
1002	Rodriquez	103
1003	Smith	101
1004	Jones	101
1005	Okovski	
1006	Schwaben	103
0		0

EMPLOYEE Table

EMP_NUM	EMP_LNAME
101	Romanov
102	Hastings
103	Altair
0	

FIGURE 4.80
The Equijoin Results

CUST_NUM	CUST_LNAME	EMP_NUM	EMP_LNAME
1001	Roberts	101	Romanov
1003	Smith	101	Romanov
1004	Jones	101	Romanov
1002	Rodriquez	103	Altair
1006	Schwaben	103	Altair

FIGURE 4.81
Selecting the Relationships Option

To establish the equijoin in Access, we need the following elements:

- The tables to be joined.
- The relationship type. (You should remember from Chapter 1 that 1:1 or 1:M relationships are implementable, whereas M:N relationships must be decomposed into pairs of 1:M relationships.)

In addition, you must decide whether or not the relationships must enforce referential integrity. (We will almost always want to select such enforcement. In Chapter 10, "Database Security," we examine a few occasions in which referential integrity may need to be broken at the administrative level.)

To illustrate the way in which relationships are created, we'll use the **Ch04_POS_2nd** database with the tables we imported previously. To select the tables to be joined, make sure that the database window is open and that it contains the tables you want to join. Select the **Relationships** button shown in Figure 4.81 to display the **Relationships** screen shown in Figure 4.82.

Selecting the **Relationships** option will generate the screen shown in Figure 4.82. (We right-clicked in the open space to generate the small menu shown in the **Relationships** screen.)

Select the **Show Table** option from the menu in Figure 4.82 to open the **Show Table** dialog box in Figure 4.83.

FIGURE 4.82
The Initial Relationships Screen

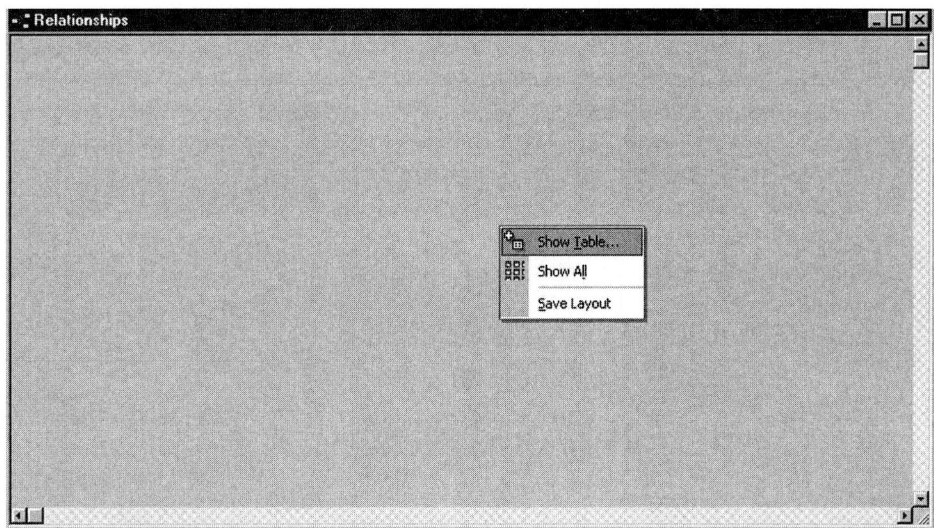

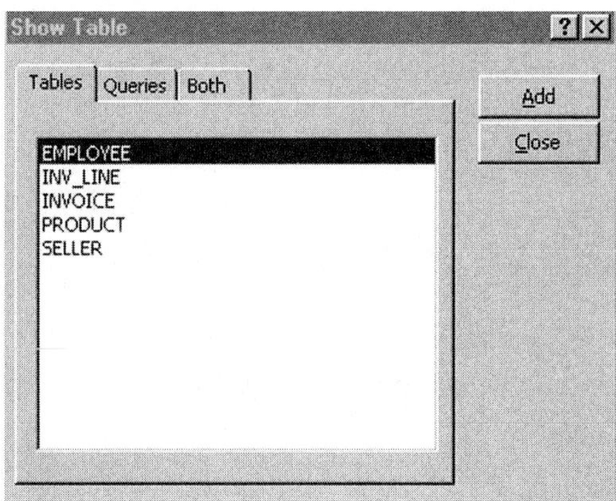

FIGURE 4.83
The Show Table Dialog Box

From the **Show Table** dialog box, you can place the selected table(s) into the **Relationship** screen by clicking the **Add** button or by double-clicking each table name. When the tables have been transferred to the **Relationships** screen, it will resemble Figure 4.84.

Each table shown in Figure 4.84 may be moved by clicking on its title bar and then dragging it to the desired location. You can also size the table boxes by dragging their borders.

You may delete any table inside the **Relationships** screen by clicking on it to select it; then press the keyboard's Delete key or select the **Edit/Delete** option from the menu bar. Figure 4.85 shows the **Relationships** screen after we deleted two tables and resized the remaining three.

You can restore the deleted tables by right-clicking anywhere on the **Relationships** screen and selecting the **Show Table** option from the pop-up menu (see Figure 4.82).

Let's create the first relationship based on the SELLER and INVOICE tables shown in Figure 4.85. The relationship between SELLER and INVOICE is a 1:M relationship. (A SELLER can write many INVOICEs, but each INVOICE is written by one SELLER.) To produce this 1:M relationship, select the PK attribute from the SELLER table, drag the attribute to the FK attribute of the related table, and drop it. In this case, drag the SELLER table's EMP_NUM to the INVOICE table's EMP_NUM and drop it. This action will generate the **Relationships** dia-

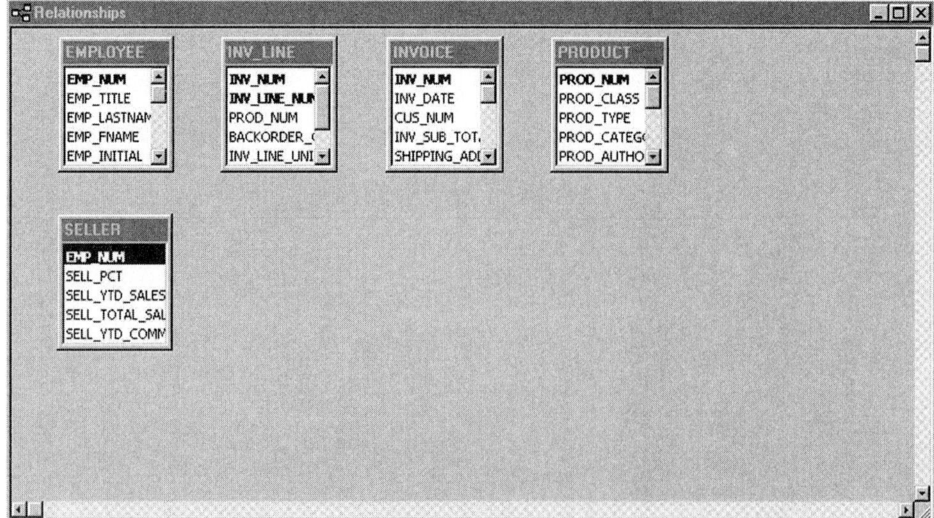

FIGURE 4.84
The Selected Tables in the Relationships Screen

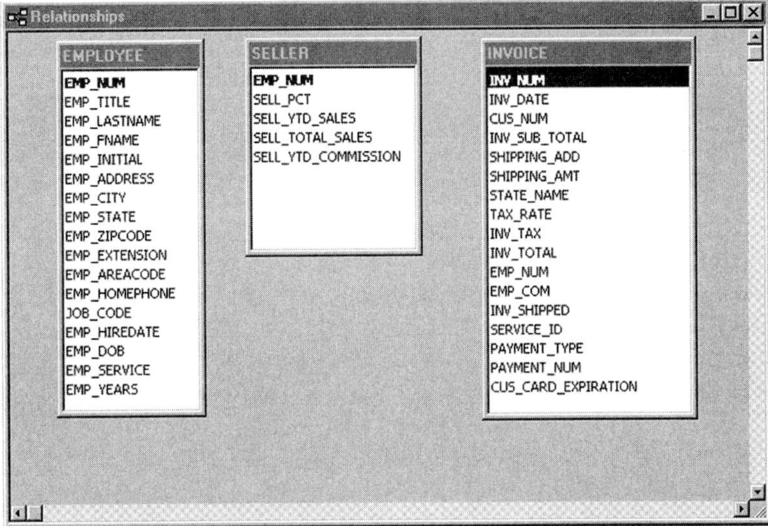

FIGURE 4.85
The Revised Relationships Screen

log box shown in Figure 4.86. (Note that the default **Relationship Type** here is **One-To-Many**, which matches the relationship between SELLER and INVOICE.)

As you examine Figure 4.86, note that our attribute (field) naming convention makes it easy to see which fields are involved in the relationship, what the PK is, and what the FK is. Because the SELLER is an employee, the SELLER table's EMP_NUM must be the PK and the INVOICE table's EMP_NUM must be the FK.

In Figure 4.86 we have checked the **Enforce Referential Integrity** box. Referential integrity is important because it ensures that a FK value can never point to a PK value that does not exist. The practical significance of referential integrity is that the system's pointers can't become stuck because of an inability to match rows of related tables, thereby causing the application to fail.

Until recently, it took countless hours and complex programming techniques to enforce referential integrity. Fortunately, Access enables you to get the job done by merely clicking a button. Better yet, the referential integrity enforcement action takes place at the table level, thus freeing all applications from having to perform this task.

Yet, no matter how desirable the enforcement of referential integrity is, there are times when it must be suspended temporarily, either through the use of system-triggered applications software or by the actions of the database administrator who manages the database environment. The reason for such suspensions is largely grounded in the database cascading environment, examined in the following paragraph.

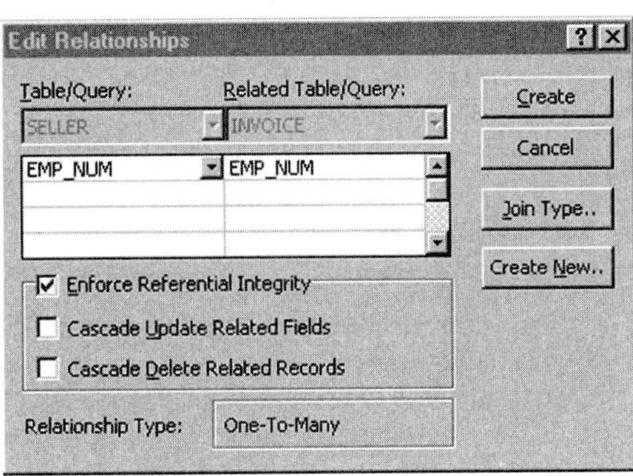

FIGURE 4.86
The Relationships Dialog Box

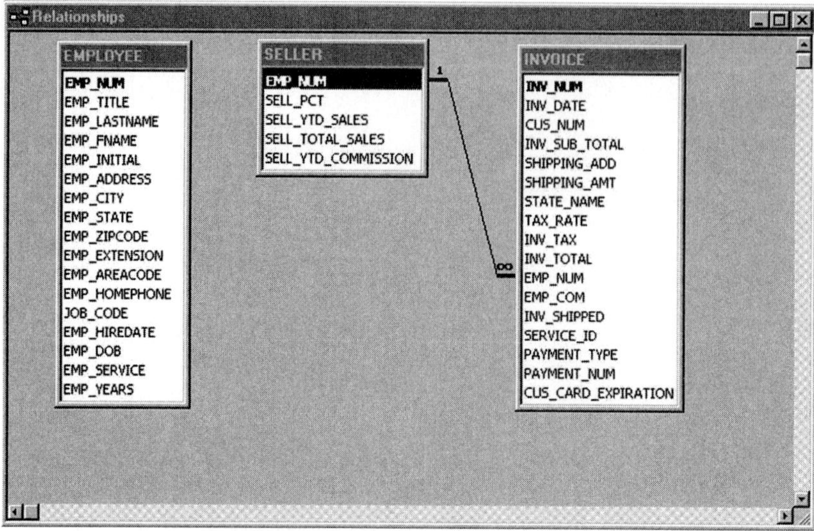

FIGURE 4.87
The 1:M Relationship between SELLER and INVOICE

Note that we have not checked either **Cascade** option in Figure 4.86. Cascades must be used carefully because their implementation can easily have unintended side effects. In this case, if we select the **Cascade Delete Related Records** option, Access will delete all invoices related to a seller when we delete the seller. Clearly, this action is undesirable because it means that we will lose all invoice data related to the deleted seller. (If a seller has left the business or was reassigned to another job, we cannot reasonably conclude that the seller's past sales never took place. We still must have access to the historical details of the business transactions.) On the other hand, keeping the seller's EMP_NUM in the INVOICE when it has been deleted from SELLER means that a violation of referential integrity has occurred, thus triggering an Access error message. Ideally, the deletion of the seller should set all the INVOICE's EMP_NUM values for that seller to null. (In fact, the "on delete set to null" FK option is available in large DBMSs such as Oracle, SQL Server, Informix, and DB2. We will have to enforce this requirement at the form level, using macros. You will learn how to get this job done by writing macros in Chapter 8. In any case, use of the cascade option requires careful professional judgment. And here is yet another reason for understanding the database concepts. (*Knowing Access without understanding the database environment in which it is applied is a recipe for disaster.*)

When you click on the **Create** button in Figure 4.86, Access will display the **Relationships** screen shown in Figure 4.87. Note that the "many" side of the relationship is indicated through the use of the mathematical infinity symbol, ∞. (Each SELLER can write *many* INVOICEs, remember?)

To save the relationship you have just created, select the **File/Save** option from the menu bar or click on the toolbar's **Save** button. If you close the **Relationships** screen without saving first, Access displays the dialog box shown in Figure 4.88. If you click on the **Yes** button, the relationships are saved; clicking on **No** will close the **Relationships** screen without saving, and selecting **Cancel** will return you to the **Relationships** screen.

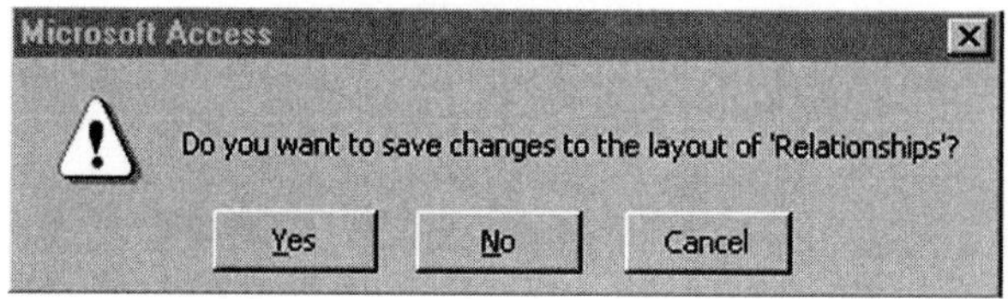

FIGURE 4.88
A Reminder to Save the Relationships

Note

Because all Save routines work the same way, we will omit further references to the Save routines.

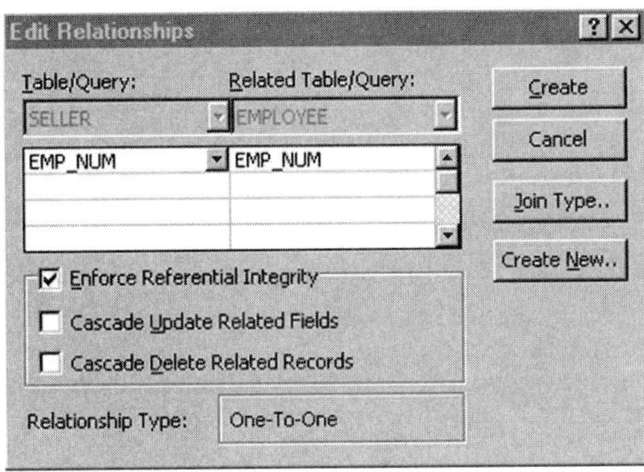

FIGURE 4.89
Establishing the 1:1 Relationship between EMPLOYEE and SELLER

You can also use the just-described techniques to create the 1:1 relationship between the supertype EMPLOYEE and the subtype SELLER. Remember to drag from the PK in EMPLOYEE to the FK in SELLER. (Also remember that in a supertype–subtype relationship, the subtype's PK is also its FK.) This action will generate the screen shown in Figure 4.89.

As you examine Figure 4.89, note that the default **Relationship Type** is now **One-To-One**. Clicking on the **Create** button will generate the screen shown in Figure 4.90. (Remember that you can move and size the table boxes shown in Figure 4.90.)

Given the 1:1 supertype–subtype relationship between EMPLOYEE and SELLER, it was easy to establish the relationship because it caused Access to select a 1:1 relationship type default. However, if you want to establish a 1:1 relationship between two tables that do not contain a supertype and subtype, respectively, you must first make sure that the FK in the related table has an index property that specifies *unique* values. (Otherwise, the relationship type will

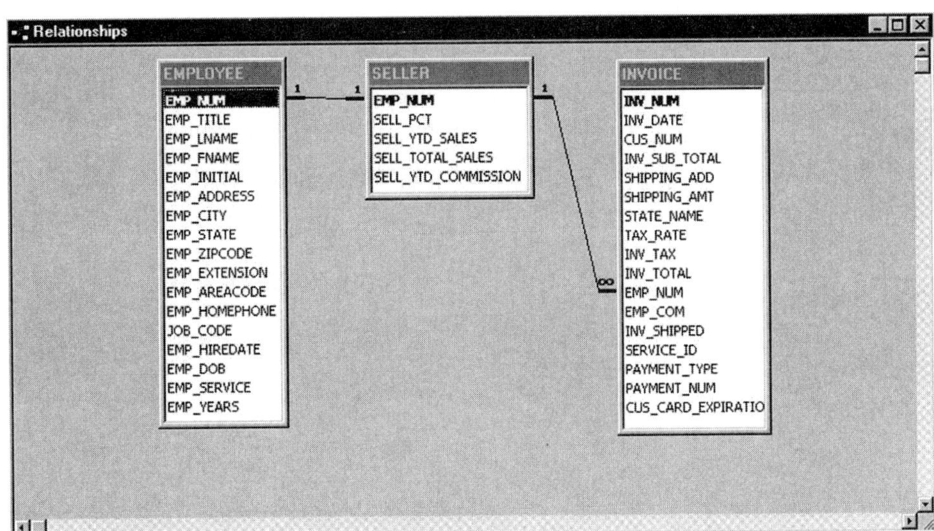

FIGURE 4.90
Two Sets of Relationships in the Relationships Screen

FIGURE 4.91
A STORE and EMPLOYEE ERD Segment

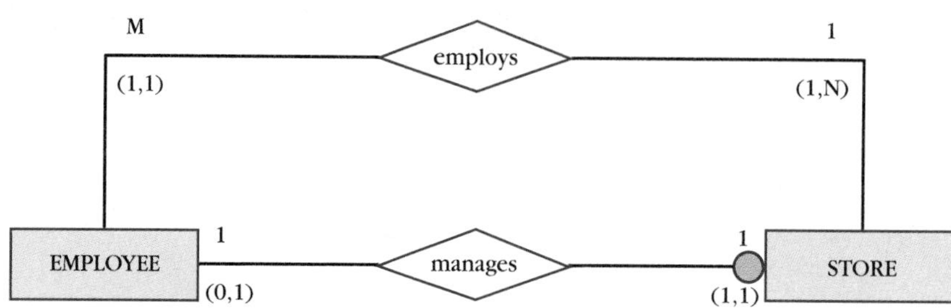

default to 1:M! It will default to 1:1 *only* if the FK values are unique, as they would be in a supertype–subtype relationship.) Failing to meet this "unique value" requirement may frustrate you when Access properly defaults to the 1:M relationship and you cannot put the cursor on the relationship type option to change it.

Although 1:1 relationships not based on supertype–subtype relationships are rare, they do exist and you should know how to implement them. For example, suppose you work in a database environment in which there are many stores, each managed by one of the many employees who work there. Figure 4.91 shows the ERD for this database segment.

As you examine Figure 4.91, note that there are two relationships between STORE and EMPLOYEE:

- 1:M—a STORE employs many employees, and each EMPLOYEE is employed by only one store.
- 1:1—a STORE is managed by one employee, and each EMPLOYEE who is a manager manages only one store. (Note that not all employees manage a store and that no employee is required to manage a store. Therefore, STORE is optional to EMPLOYEE in the *manages* relationship.)

The EMPLOYEE manages STORE relationship is clearly *not* a supertype–subtype relationship, but it *is* a 1:1 relationship. Both relationships are encountered in the small database, named **Ch04_DEMO_1.MDB**, whose two tables are shown in Figure 4.92.

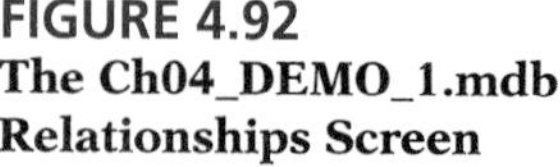
FIGURE 4.92
The Ch04_DEMO_1.mdb Relationships Screen

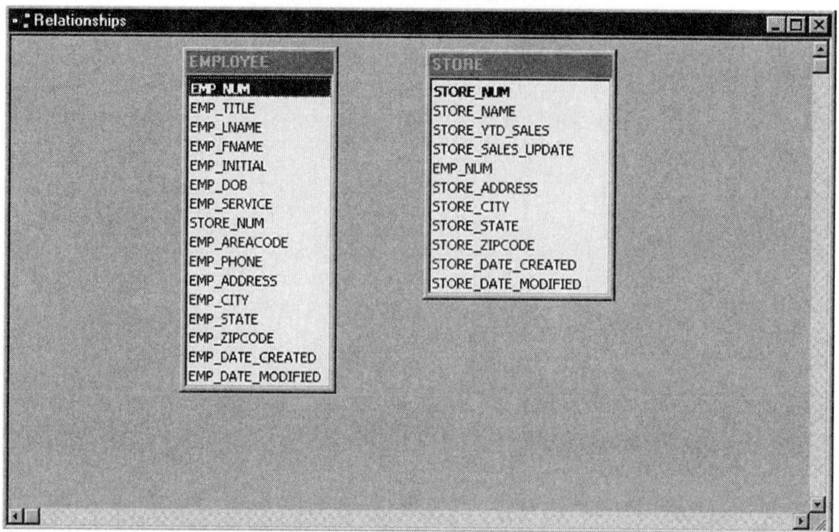

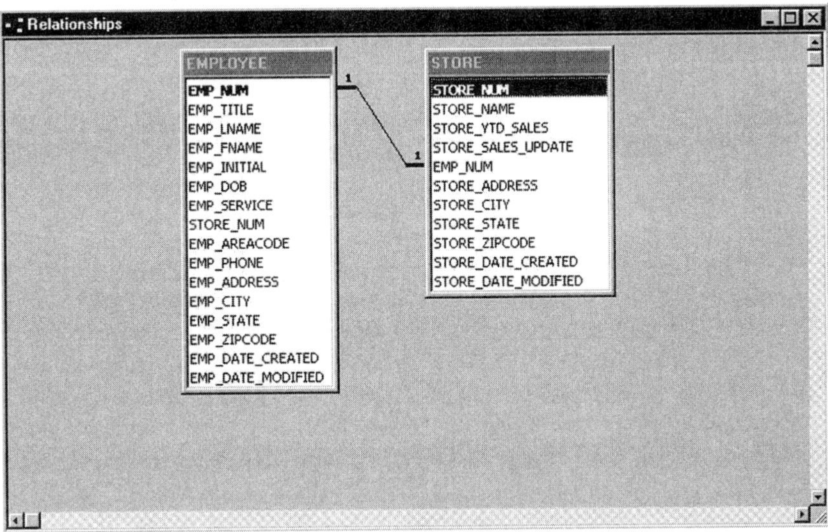

FIGURE 4.93
The 1:M Relationship between STORE and EMPLOYEE

To see how Access handles the relationships in Figure 4.92, start by establishing the 1:M relationship between STORE and EMPLOYEE. No problem: Just drag and drop the STORE's PK, STORE_NUM, to the EMPLOYEE's FK, STORE_NUM, and then use the **Relationships** dialog box you first encountered in Figure 4.66. Figure 4.93 shows the results of these efforts.

Having established the 1:M relationship between STORE and EMPLOYEE in the STORE *employs* EMPLOYEE relationship, let's now create the 1:1 relationship in the EMPLOYEE *manages* STORE relationship. While you are in the **Relationships** screen shown in Figure 4.93, drag and drop the EMPLOYEE's PK, EMP_NUM, to the STORE's FK, EMP_NUM. Because there is already a relationship between STORE and EMPLOYEE, Access produces the dialog box shown in Figure 4.94.

We want to create an *additional* relationship, so click on the **No** button shown in Figure 4.94. This action causes Access to produce the **Relationships** dialog box shown in Figure 4.95.

Unfortunately, as you examine Figure 4.95, you will note that the **Relationships Type** has defaulted to **One-To-Many** because the EMP_NUM FK in STORE was not uniquely indexed. You cannot modify the **One-To-Many** Relationship type in Figure 4.95 by editing it. Instead, you must return to the STORE table in design format and change the EMP_NUM FK index property, set by default to **Yes (Duplicates Allowed)**, to **Yes (No Duplicates)**, as shown in Figure 4.96.

Save the change in the **Indexed** property and then return to the **Relationships** screen. This time, when you drag and drop the EMPLOYEE table's EMP_NUM on the STORE table's EMP_NUM, the **Relationships** dialog box in Figure 4.97 will show a 1:1 relationships default. (Remember, you'll first see the dialog box shown in Figure 4.94 again. Select **No** from this dialog box.)

Creating the new 1:1 relationship produces the screen shown in Figure 4.98. As you examine Figure 4.98, note that Access has automatically placed a second EMPLOYEE table structure, labeled EMPLOYEE_1, on the screen. This table

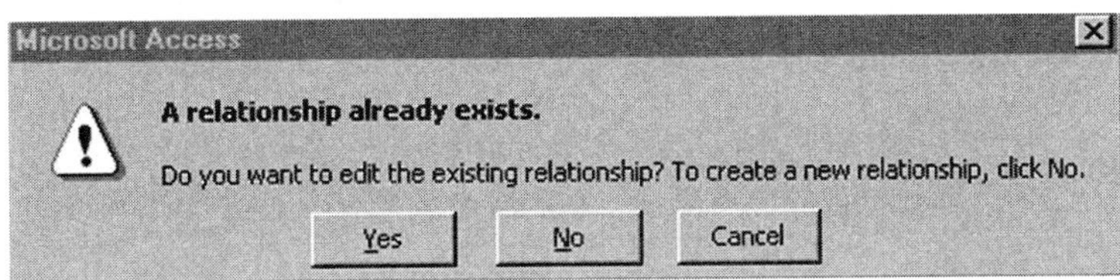

FIGURE 4.94
A Multiple Relationship Dialog Box

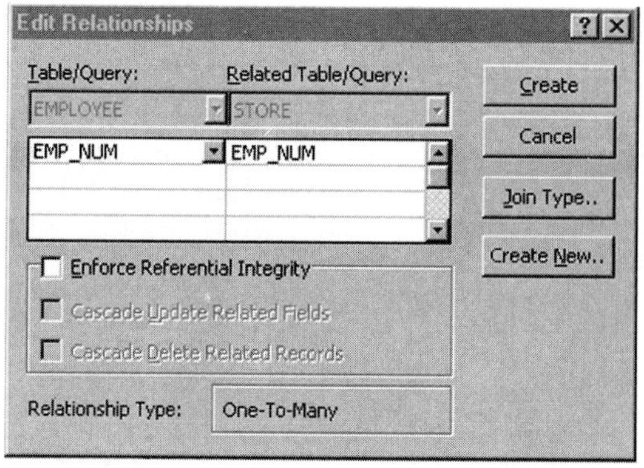

FIGURE 4.95
The 1:M Relationship Type Default

FIGURE 4.96
Changing the FK Index Property

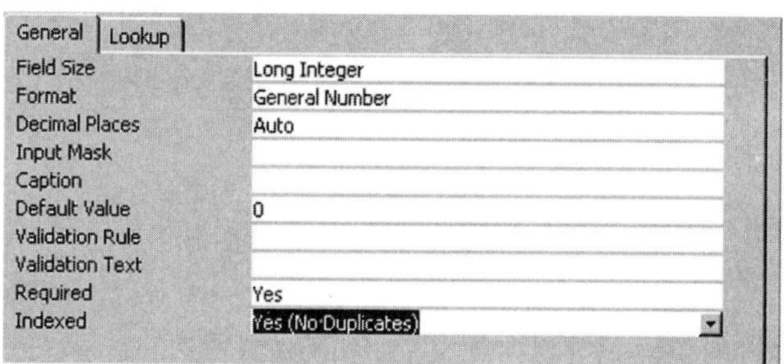

structure serves only to indicate the new 1:1 relationship; *it does not exist in the database*. (If you check the table listing later, you'll not see a table named EMPLOYEE_1.)

As you examine Figure 4.99, keep in mind that Access will place the table structures and relationships anywhere on the screen. Drag the presentation elements where *you* want them and size them to fit your needs. (That's what we did to create the presentation in Figure 4.99.)

4.9.2 Referential Integrity Enforcement and Field Properties: Unintended Consequences?

We strongly recommend that you always select referential integrity enforcement when you establish relationships between tables. However, you may run into interesting problems that seem difficult to solve if you don't consider the ramifications of the choices you make. For example, suppose that the STORE and EMPLOYEE tables in Figure 4.98 each have properties box entries in which FKs are set to **Required** = **Yes** and **Default Value** = **0**. If the FK is *required* and the

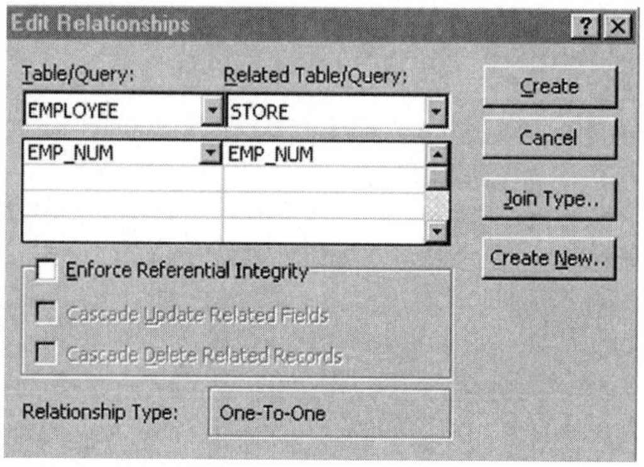

FIGURE 4.97
The 1:1 Relationship Default

Note

Figure 4.98 shows the properly implemented 1:1 EMPLOYEE *manages* STORE relationship. However, if you close the **Relationship** window and then open it again later, you may see that Access has rearranged the 1:1 relationship presentation shown here. For example, you may see the original EMPLOYEE and STORE tables, but the virtual table may be a structure labeled as STORE_1. In short, the 1:1 relationship may be pictured either from STORE to EMPLOYEE or from EMPLOYEE to STORE. Actually, if you had created the 1:1 relationship *before* the 1:M relationship, you would have seen the STORE_1 virtual table structure in the first place! (See Figure 4.99.) Either presentation is correct.

The Access **Relationship** window exhibits some strange quirks. For example, if you edit the window in Figure 4.98 to delete the EMPLOYEE_1 and you reestablish the same relationship later, you may see TWO virtual tables, named EMPLOYEE_1 and EMPLOYEE_2, the next time you open the **Relationship** window. There will be no operational effect on the 1:1 EMPLOYEE *manages* STORE relationship, but the **Relationship** window sure looks strange. Finally, you'll suffer some occasional frustrations when you discover that your **Relationship** window edits were not saved even though you used the **Save** option. Keep on trying: The **Save** option will work sooner or later. Access contains some minor, but annoying, bugs.

FIGURE 4.98
The Multiple Relationship Screen

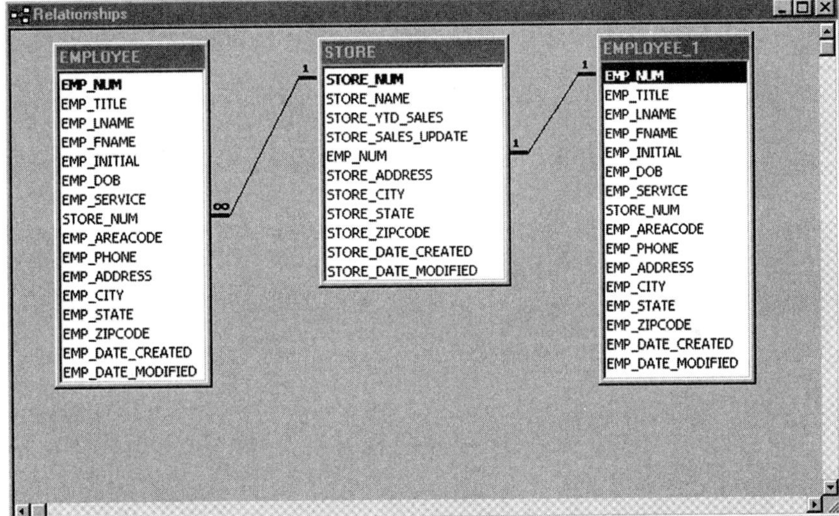

FIGURE 4.99
An Alternative Presentation of Multiple Relationships

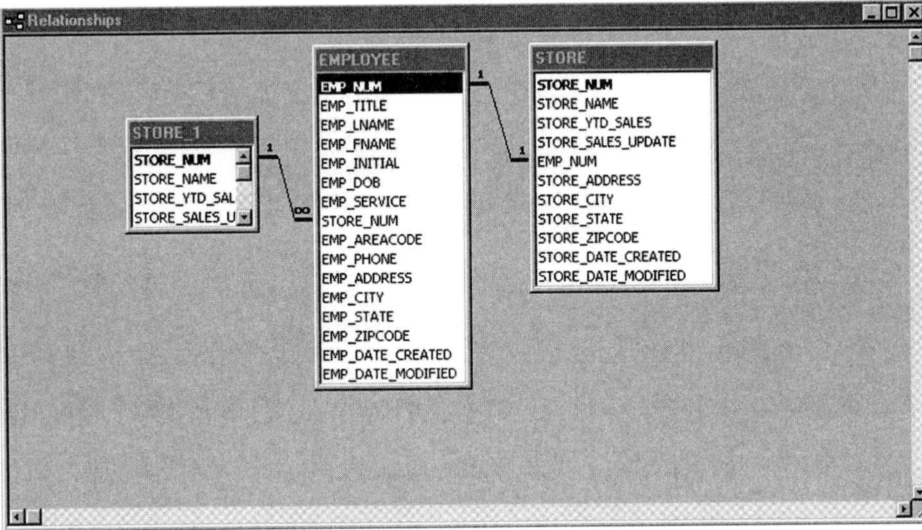

Note

Managing the multiple relationships adds complexity to the *implementation* and *management* of the design. Therefore, many database designers would prefer to change the structure of the design we illustrated in Figure 4.90. For example, you can assign a primary job code (store manager, clerk, department manager, etc.) to each employee in the EMPLOYEE table, and then create a JOB table to store the details of each primary job code. In fact, given a choice, this is how we would design the database. The relationship between EMPLOYEE and JOB enables you to determine who each store manager is, thus eliminating the need for the 1:1 relationship created by the "EMPLOYEE manages STORE" ERD segment. Nevertheless, because you are likely to encounter combinations of 1:M and 1:1 relationships in a real-world environment, it is useful for you to know how to create and manage such multiple relationships. (And now you know how to propose an alternate solution!)

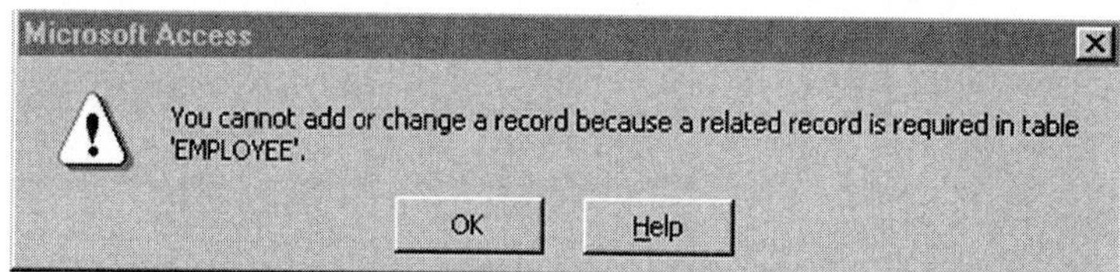

FIGURE 4.100
Referential Integrity Error Message

referential integrity enforcement option is selected for *both* relationships shown in Figure 4.91's ERD, you will be caught in a data entry trap. To see why this trap exists, you can easily trace the problem in the following scenario in which you try to enter a new EMPLOYEE who will manage a new STORE.

To enter employee data in the EMPLOYEE table, you must include the new store's STORE_NUM because the new employee is employed by a store. Unfortunately, the store number does not yet exist, because you have not yet created the store record in STORE. You also cannot enter a new STORE record, because the new employee who will *manage* that store does not yet exist in EMPLOYEE. The only way to add a new store record is to make sure that the new store's manager is an *existing* employee. In this case, the referential integrity enforcement, coupled with the FK field properties, will mean that no data can be entered in either table!

Given the just-described conditions, try to enter a new store record in the STORE table, selecting an employee number for an employee who does yet not exist in the EMPLOYEE table. Your reward will be the error message shown in Figure 4.100.

Clicking **OK** will get you back to datasheet view, ready to reenter the employee number value in the STORE table. Access will not let you continue, no matter how often you try, until you enter a valid employee number. Finally, if you give up, click **OK**, and then close the table. Access will tell you that the record that violated the referential integrity requirement will not be saved (see Figure 4.101). Click **Yes** to return to the STORE table without saving the record you tried to enter.

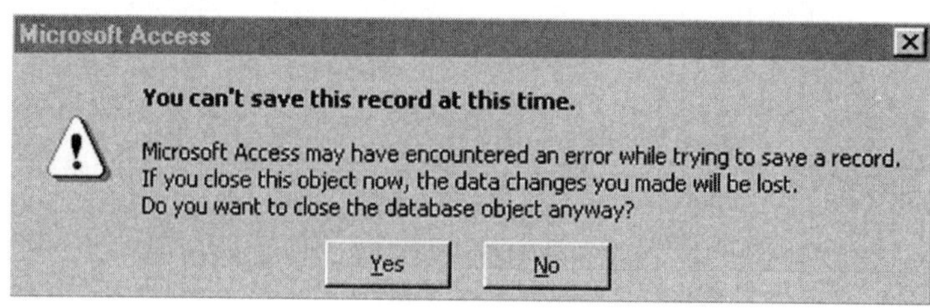

FIGURE 4.101
A Referential Integrity Error Message Upon Closing the Table

Assignment

Using the **Ch04_POS_2nd.MDB** database, generate a referential integrity violation message (see Figure 4.90) by referencing (in the INVOICE) a seller who does not exist. After generating the error message, close the INVOICE table to see a message similar to the one shown in Figure 4.101.

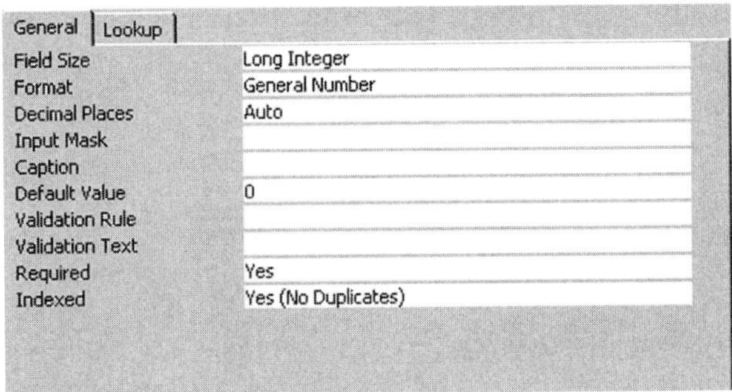

FIGURE 4.102
EMP_NUM Properties in the STORE Table

General	
Field Size	Long Integer
Format	General Number
Decimal Places	Auto
Input Mask	
Caption	
Default Value	0
Validation Rule	
Validation Text	
Required	Yes
Indexed	Yes (No Duplicates)

To solve the problem, take a look at the STORE table's EMP_NUM property (shown in Figure 4.102) and note the two properties we mentioned earlier:

1. The EMP_NUM is required.
2. The EMP_NUM default property was set to 0.

By setting the EMP_NUM **Default Value** entry shown in Figure 4.102 to null by deleting the 0 and by changing the **Required** selection from **Yes** to **No**, the problem disappears. This time, when you enter the STORE table's first record, just press the Enter key when you encounter the EMP_NUM field in the STORE table. (Recall from Chapter 1 that no referential integrity violation occurs when the FK "value" is null.) Of course, you will still encounter referential integrity violations if you enter a nonnull FK value that does not match the PK in the related table. And that, of course, is what you *want* to happen!

Keep in mind that the data trap existed because we created two relationships between two tables. However, whether or not multiple relationships exist and whether or not the design requires FK values, you will always want to receive a warning when improper FK values are entered.

4.9.3 Editing the Relationships

Although we strongly advise you to create relationships that include referential integrity enforcement before you enter the first record in any table, you may sometimes want to change the nature of the relationship, usually on a temporary basis.

To edit any relationship, open the **Relationship** screen and then click on the relationship line for the relationship to be edited. Note that the line thickens (see Figure 4.103) when you select it. Having selected the relationship line, right-click to generate the pop-up menu shown in Figure 4.103. (Only a small portion of the now-familiar screen is shown.)

FIGURE 4.103
Editing the Relationship via the Pop-up Menu

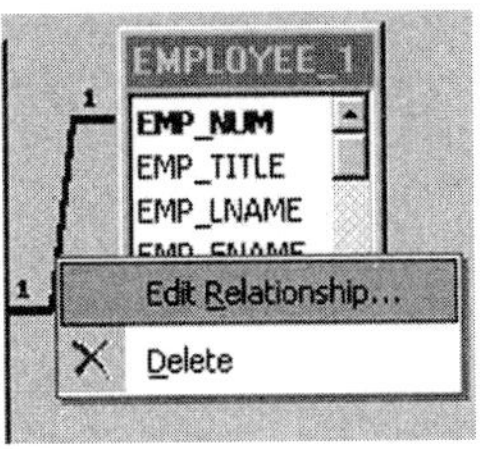

The **Edit Relationship...** selection made in Figure 4.103 causes Access to return to the familiar **Relationships** dialog box shown in Figure 4.104. Note that we have clicked off the **Enforce Referential Integrity** box.

Removal of the referential integrity option causes the relationship line to change its composition. The effect is shown in Figure 4.105.

Note

You will always be able to tell that referential integrity will be enforced by looking at the relationship lines in the **Relationship** window. For example, look at the relationship lines in Figure 4.98 and note two main features:

1. The relationship lines are thick and dark.
2. The nature of the relationships (1:1 and 1:M) is labeled, using a 1 on the one side and an infinity symbol (∞) on the many side.

If you do not elect to enforce referential integrity when the relationship is created, the relationship line is thin and lacks the labeling of the relationship type.

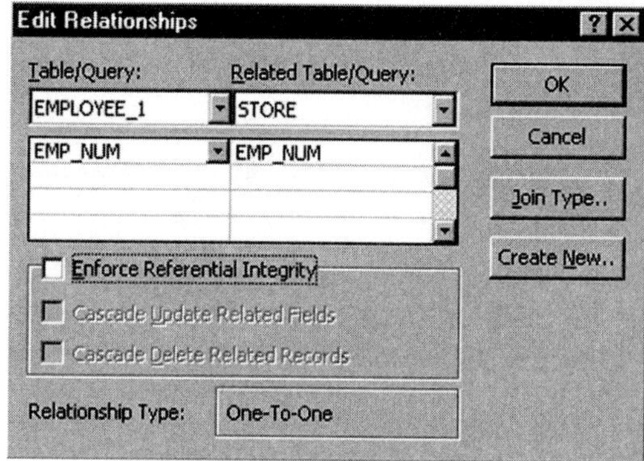

FIGURE 4.104
The Relationships Dialog Box

As you examine the relationship line in Figure 4.105, note that it is much thinner than it was before and that the relationship type labels have disappeared. Instead, a small nub anchors the relationship line to the two tables.

After changing the 1:1 EMPLOYEE *manages* STORE relationship by removing its referential integrity enforcement option, you will be able to enter data into the STORE even if the FK is required. Because referential integrity is no longer enforced in this 1:1 relationship, it will be possible to enter STORE records even when you enter an invalid employee number as the store manager.

You may also delete a relationship. Just select the **Delete** option shown in Figure 4.103 to generate the screen shown in Figure 4.106. Select **Yes** to delete the relationship. (You can always reestablish the relationship by using the procedures illustrated in Figures 4.85 through 4.87.)

4.9.4 Managing the Effects of the Relationships

You can always delete a relationship. However, if you try to delete a record in a table that contains the PK to which the FK in another table points, you will gen-

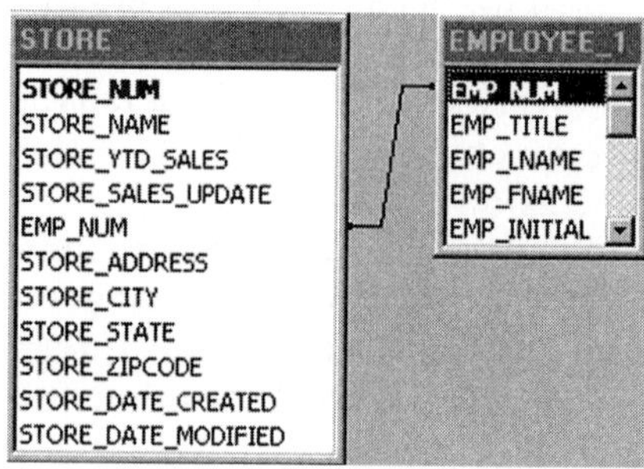

FIGURE 4.105
A Relationship without Referential Integrity Enforcement

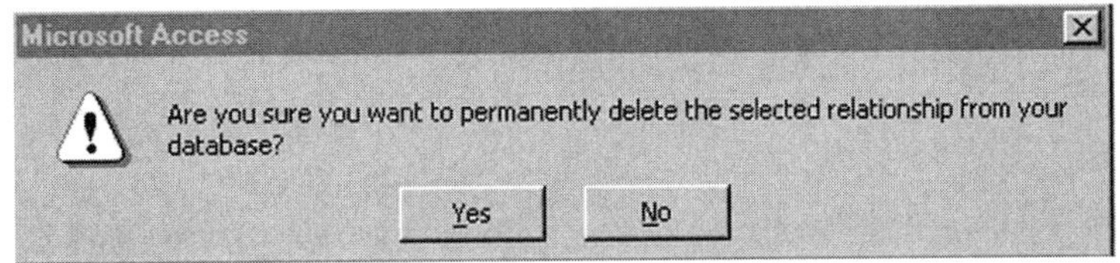

FIGURE 4.106
The Delete Relationships Dialog Box

erate a referential integrity violation message. (The deletion of the record includes the deletion of its PK value, thus causing one or more of the other table's FK values to point to the just-deleted PK value.) For example, if you delete a STORE record, all the EMPLOYEE records that reference this store through their FK, STORE_NUM, will have several FK values that no longer match a PK in the STORE table. Therefore, the deletion triggers a referential integrity violation, and Access will not allow you to make the deletion as long as the relationship exists and the FK's **Required** property is set to **Yes**.

But suppose you do need to eliminate a store from the database? If the relationship between STORE and EMPLOYEE is defaulted to mandatory, that is, the FK value in EMPLOYEE is *required,* there are several ways to manage the store deletion. (Business needs and personnel management policy determine the appropriate option.)

- Reassign the employees from the STORE to be deleted to other stores. In other words, if store 3 is to be deleted, first change all the EMPLOYEE STORE_NUM values from 3 to 1, 2, or another existing store number. Once the employees have been reassigned, none of the EMPLOYEE table's FK values will be pointing to the STORE record that is to be deleted.
- Open the EMPLOYEE table in the design format; then change the **Required** property of the EMPLOYEE's FK, STORE_NUM, to **No** and make sure that its default value is set to null. (Just delete whatever value is there.) After making these changes, return to the EMPLOYEE table in datasheet format and change the affected STORE_NUM values to null by deleting them. In other words, if store 3 is to be deleted, change all the EMPLOYEE STORE_NUM values from 3 to null by deleting the STORE_NUM value 3 in each affected record. (At this point you will have to manually find every EMPLOYEE record in which STORE_NUM = 3. You will learn how to do this job much more efficiently in the next chapter.)
- Edit the relationship between STORE and EMPLOYEE in the *employs* relationship. You can either change the referential integrity requirement or you can delete the relationship. Because referential integrity enforcement is so important, this fix is not permanent. But it will allow you to delete the STORE record, after which you can use either of the preceding solutions. (Naturally, reset the referential integrity option after using either solution.)

4.9.5 Outer Joins

In section 4.9.1 you learned that the equijoins, also known as inner joins, perform a crucial role in the database environment. The equijoin allows you to drastically reduce or even eliminate the data redundancy problems created by having the same data occur in more than one place at one time. As you will discover in Chapter 5, the equijoin enables you to combine the data from multiple tables to provide information in usable form. The equijoin works on a simple principle: Link records in the various tables by checking to see whether the FK values in one table *equal* the PK values in another table.

There are, however, many instances when you will want to know which FK values are *not* equal to PK values. For example, suppose you have imported some database tables and you discover that your attempt to create a relationship

FIGURE 4.107
The ERD for the Ch04_DEMO_2.mdb Database

One vendor may supply many products
If a product is supplied by a vendor, it is supplied by only one vendor
Some products are not supplied by a vendor

triggers a referential integrity violation. Wouldn't it be nice to find out quickly and efficiently which FK values do not match existing PK values? Or suppose you want to find out how may FK values are set to null? This feature would be particularly useful if you want to find out how many—and which—customers do not yet have a sales representative assigned to them, which products were not bought from a vendor, which students have not yet declared a major, or which employees have not yet been assigned to a project or a department. Finding the answers to such questions efficiently is clearly desirable.

The outer join is tailor-made to spot and report the FK/PK inequalities. This section examines two types of outer joins: the right outer join and the left outer join. To learn how such joins work and to see their effects, let's start by examining a small database, named **Ch04_DEMO_2.MDB**. The **Ch04_DEMO_2.MDB** database contains two tables, PRODUCT and VENDOR, and it is based on the ERD shown in Figure 4.107. The table contents are shown in Figures 4.108A and 4.108B.

As you examine the ERD and the VENDOR and PRODUCT table contents in Figures 4.107, 4.108A, and 4.108B, note the following conditions:

- VENDOR is optional to PRODUCT, and vice versa. These optionalities explain why the VENDOR table may contain several VEND_CODE values (1, 4, 6, 7, and 8) that have no match in the PRODUCT table and why the PRODUCT table does not reference all VEND_CODE values in the VENDOR table. (In this case the vendor list contains *potential* vendors, as well as vendors who have actually supplied products in the past.)
- The PRODUCT table contains a null VEND_CODE in its third record. This condition does not violate referential integrity, because referential integrity exists when FK values point to existing PK values or the FK values are null.
- The PRODUCT table contains the VEND_CODE value 9 (in the seventh record) that does not match any VEND_CODE value in the VENDOR table. This

FIGURE 4.108A
The VENDOR Table in the Ch04_DEMO_2.mdb Database

VEND_NUM	VEND_NAME	VEND_CONTACT	VEND_PHONE
1	CompuDark, Inc.	H. D. Cable	(123) 333-4567
2	MooComp, Inc.	A. A. Grassfield	(234) 543-8902
3	Gettum Supply	C. F. Inthere	(433) 456-7654
4	PC Country	I. M. Formerly	(234) 214-8790
5	Dill Computer, Inc.	I. B. Pickle	(901) 786-3338
6	Outeredge Supply	D. N. Whammy	(501) 778-9345
7	Compuck, Inc.	C. C. Rider	(433) 190-2229
8	Toshboo Supply	H. D. Eyestrain	(344) 996-3124
(AutoNumber)			

FIGURE 4.108B
The PRODUCT Table in the Ch04_DEMO_2.mdb Database

PROD_CODE	PROD_DESCRIPTION	PROD_PRICE	PROD_QOH	VEND_NUM
COCBLPAR6	6 ft. parallel cable, shielded metal case	$14.34	63	5
DRSUCR44MX	Removable cartridge, 44MB, Maxell	$45.95	23	3
DRSUCR88MX	Removable cartridge, 88MB, Maxell	$52.99	41	
DRSUDI12-3M	3.5" HD/DS Diskettes, 1.44 MB formatted, IBM, 12/box, 3M	$5.99	95	5
DRSUDI50-3M	3.5" HD/DS Diskettes, 1.44 MB formatted, IBM, 50/box, 3M	$16.43	108	2
DRSUTC3490E	tape cartridge, 1,100ft, 36-track, AS400-3480-3490E	$21.75	22	2
PRCTCANBC02	Canon color cartridge, BJ-100, 2200, 210, 230	$36.57	102	9
PRCTHPDJ56	HP DeskJet Plus, 500C, 550C, 600	$26.95	89	3
PRCTLEX4072	IBM (Lexmark) 4072 ExecJet cartridge	$22.95	127	5
		$0.00	0	0

Note

Using Structured Query Language (SQL), the standard SQL code for this inner join would read:

```
SELECT PRODUCT.PROD_CODE,
   PRODUCT.DESCRIPTION,
   VENDOR.VEND_NUM, VENDOR.VEND_NAME
      FROM PRODUCT, VENDOR
         WHERE PRODUCT.PROD_CODE =
               VENDOR.PROD_CODE;
```

The SQL's WHERE clause makes it easy to see why this is called an *equijoin*. You will discover in Chapter 5 that you don't have to know SQL to generate queries, because Access will produce the appropriate SQL code for you.

FIGURE 4.109
The VENDOR/PRODUCT Equijoin (Inner Join) Results

PROD_CODE	PROD_DESCRIPTION	VEND_NUM	VEND_NAME
DRSUDI50-3M	3.5" HD/DS Diskettes, 1.44 MB formatted, IBM, 50/box, 3M	2	MooComp, Inc.
DRSUTC3490E	tape cartridge, 1,100ft, 36-track, AS400-3480-3490E	2	MooComp, Inc.
DRSUCR44MX	Removable cartridge, 44MB, Maxell	3	Gettum Supply
PRCTHPDJ56	HP DeskJet Plus, 500C, 550C, 600	3	Gettum Supply
COCBLPAR6	6 ft. parallel cable, shielded metal case	5	Dill Computer, Inc.
DRSUDI12-3M	3.5" HD/DS Diskettes, 1.44 MB formatted, IBM, 12/box, 3M	5	Dill Computer, Inc.
PRCTLEX4072	IBM (Lexmark) 4072 ExecJet cartridge	5	Dill Computer, Inc.
*		(AutoNumber)	

condition violates referential integrity, and you will trigger an error message when, *after entering these data*, you try to establish the relationship between PRODUCT and VENDOR with a referential integrity requirement.

• Although we did establish the relationship between VENDOR and PRODUCT in this database, we have not yet selected the referential integrity enforcement option in order to show you how outer joins can be used to find unmatched FK values.

Using the **Ch04_DEMO_2.MDB** database, we first select the equijoin to show how its output is limited to *matches* between the FK and PK values. Therefore, some of the records are not accounted for in the equijoin. For example, if you examine Figure 4.109, you will note that

• The PRODUCT table's third record (see Figure 4.108B) contains a null VEND_CODE, which does not have a matching VEND_CODE value in the VENDOR table. Therefore, it does not show up in Figure 4.109's equijoin.

• VEND_CODE = 9 does not exist in Figure 4.108A's VENDOR table. Therefore, Figure 4.108B's PRODUCT table VEND_CODE = 9 does not show up in Figure 4.109's equijoin.

In contrast to the inner join results, the outer join will yield all of the table rows, whether or not a match occurs. The right outer join shown in Figure 4.110 will yield all the PROD_CODE values in the PRODUCT table, and the left outer join will yield all the VENDOR records.

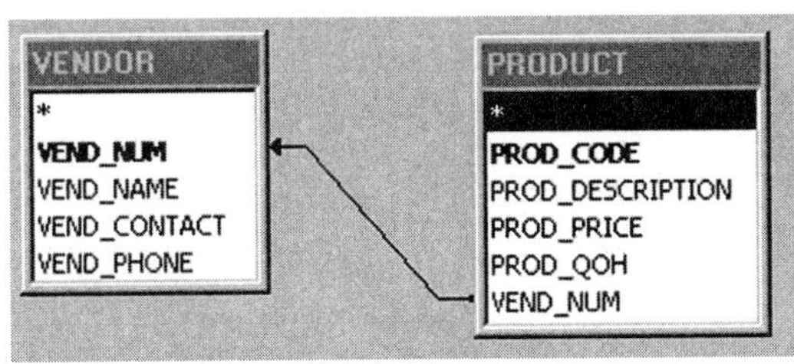

FIGURE 4.110
The Right Outer Join

Note

The "left" and "right" outer join designations are based on the SQL code that generates such joins. Because we let Access generate all the SQL code for us, you will not write SQL commands. Therefore, the "left" and "right" outer join designations we have used in this chapter—and in Chapter 5—make more sense if you always put the "1" side (in this case, the VENDOR) on the left and the "many" side (in this case, the PRODUCT) on the right, as shown in Figure 4.110. The right outer join will have the arrow emerging from the "many" side on the right, while the left outer join will have the arrow emerging from the "1" side on the left, as shown in Figure 4.113. In Chapter 5 we will show you how the appropriate queries are created and executed.

FIGURE 4.111
The Right Outer Join Output Results

	VEND_NUM	VEND_NAME	PROD_CODE	PROD_DESCRIPTION
▶			DRSUCR88MX	Removable cartridge, 88MB, Maxell
	2	MooComp, Inc.	DRSUDI50-3M	3.5" HD/DS Diskettes, 1.44 MB formatted, IBM, 50/box, 3M
	2	MooComp, Inc.	DRSUTC3490E	tape cartridge, 1,100ft, 36-track, AS400-3480-3490E
	3	Gettum Supply	DRSUCR44MX	Removable cartridge, 44MB, Maxell
	3	Gettum Supply	PRCTHPDJ56	HP DeskJet Plus, 500C, 550C, 600
	5	Dill Computer, Inc.	COCBLPAR6	6 ft. parallel cable, shielded metal case
	5	Dill Computer, Inc.	DRSUDI12-3M	3.5" HD/DS Diskettes, 1.44 MB formatted, IBM, 12/box, 3M
	5	Dill Computer, Inc.	PRCTLEX4072	IBM (Lexmark) 4072 ExecJet cartridge
			PRCTCANBC02	Canon color cartridge, BJ-100, 2200, 210, 230
*	(AutoNumber)			

The execution of the right outer join yields the output shown in Figure 4.111. Note that the right outer join illustrated in Figure 4.111 is very valuable, because it shows how many products do not have a matching vendor. In this case, the matching failure detected by the right outer join has two reasons:

1. The PRODUCT table lacked a VEND_NUM entry in its third record. (Note the null VEND_NUM in Figure 4.108B's PRODUCT table. This record, PROD_CODE = DRSUCR88MX, shows up in Figure 4.111's first output line.
2. Figure 4.108B's PRODUCT table also contains an incorrect VEND_NUM value 9 for PROD_CODE = PRCTCANBC02. (This VEND_NUM = 9 value does not have a match in the VENDOR table, thus violating referential integrity.)

The output in Figure 4.111 lets us zero in on match failures, thus enabling us to find the reason for referential integrity errors. If no referential integrity errors are generated, the output tells us which of the PRODUCT table's VEND_CODE entries are null. In short, the outer joins deliver very useful management tools!

To produce an outer join, note that Access allows us to select a **Join Type** when the relationship is created. (Check the **Join Type** button in any **Relationships** dialog box such as the one presented in Figure 4.103.) You can also elect to edit an existing join (see Figure 4.103). To produce the right outer join shown in Figure 4.110, the **Join Type** selection yields the dialog box shown in Figure 4.112.

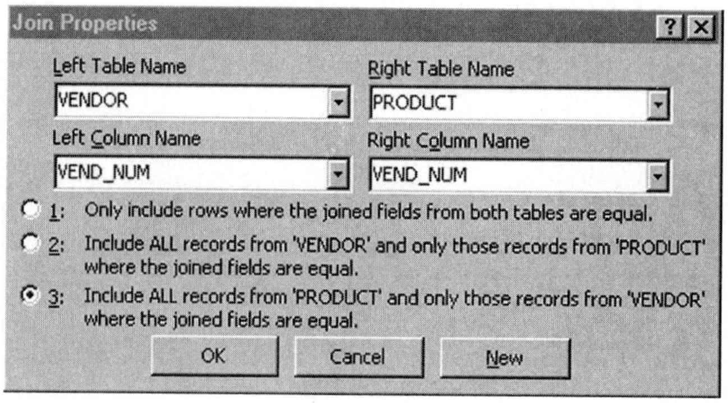

FIGURE 4.112
The Join Type Dialog Box Right Outer Join

Join Properties
Left Table Name: VENDOR
Right Table Name: PRODUCT
Left Column Name: VEND_NUM
Right Column Name: VEND_NUM
1: Only include rows where the joined fields from both tables are equal.
2: Include ALL records from 'VENDOR' and only those records from 'PRODUCT' where the joined fields are equal.
3: Include ALL records from 'PRODUCT' and only those records from 'VENDOR' where the joined fields are equal.
OK | Cancel | New

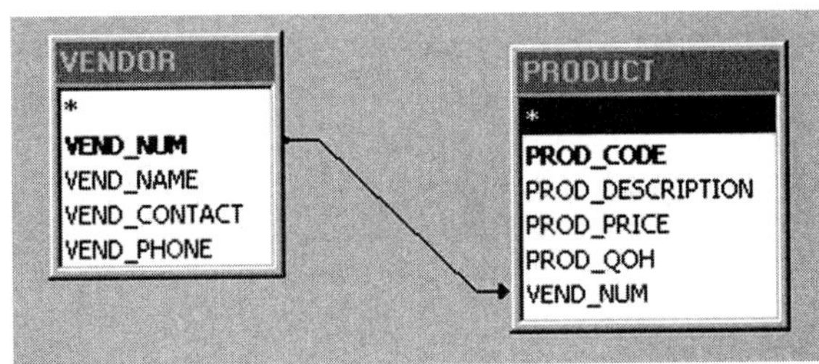

FIGURE 4.113
The Left Outer Join

To select the left outer join, click the middle radio button in Figure 4.112. (Include ALL records from "VENDOR" and only those from "PRODUCT" where the joined fields are equal.) This selection yields the join shown in Figure 4.113.

Executing the left outer join shown in Figure 4.89 will produce the output shown in Figure 4.114.

Figure 4.114 shows that there are no matching PROD_CODE values for vendors 1, 4, 6, 7, and 8. Therefore, the left outer join allows us to examine which vendors have never supplied a product to us. You could use the same technique to find out which customers have never placed an order, which faculty advisors do not have student advisees assigned to them, and so on. So, like the right outer join, the left outer join turns out to be a useful data management tool.

FIGURE 4.114
The Left Outer Join Output Results

VEND_NUM	VEND_NAME	PROD_CODE	PROD_DESCRIPTION
1	CompuDark, Inc.		
2	MooComp, Inc.	DRSUDI50-3M	3.5" HD/DS Diskettes, 1.44 MB formatted, IBM, 50/box, 3M
2	MooComp, Inc.	DRSUTC3490E	tape cartridge, 1,100ft, 36-track, AS400-3480-3490E
3	Gettum Supply	DRSUCR44MX	Removable cartridge, 44MB, Maxell
3	Gettum Supply	PRCTHPDJ56	HP DeskJet Plus, 500C, 550C, 600
4	PC Country		
5	Dill Computer, Inc.	COCBLPAR6	6 ft. parallel cable, shielded metal case
5	Dill Computer, Inc.	DRSUDI12-3M	3.5" HD/DS Diskettes, 1.44 MB formatted, IBM, 12/box, 3M
5	Dill Computer, Inc.	PRCTLEX4072	IBM (Lexmark) 4072 ExecJet cartridge
6	Outeredge Supply		
7	Compuck, Inc.		
8	Toshboo Supply		
(AutoNumber)			

Problems

4.1 Create a database named Ch04_SaleCo.MDB. Within the Ch04_SaleCo.MDB database, create the appropriate table structures for the tables based on the ERD in Figure 4.71 and the discussion that accompanies Figures 4.72 through 4.78.

a. Use appropriate input masks and defaults.

b. Do not yet enter any data into the tables, but do create the appropriate relationships and make sure that referential integrity is enforced.

c. Start entering data into the database. If you encounter referential integrity errors, explain why they occurred and how these errors may be avoided. Once you have explored the options, make sure that you select the one that yields enforced referential integrity. (Hint: Remember the role of defaults, required FK values, and FK nulls?)

d. Explore cascade options and explain why (or why not) you would use them in this database.

e. Edit each table's attributes. Change names, properties, descriptions, and so on. Insert fields, delete fields, and modify fields. Edit relationships. If you generate error messages, explain their cause and respond appropriately.

f. Delete the tables from the database. What problems did you run into? Why? Respond to the error messages and complete the deletions.

g. Import the two tables into your database structure, using the tables provided by your instructor.

Note

All the databases referenced in this problem set are found on the student CD. Before you try to complete each problem, open the database for that problem and take a look at the tables, attributes, relationships, and other components that are pertinent to the implementation of the database. Then create your own database structure and save it in a different folder. You might even add the prefix *My* to the database name, to indicate that this is your database implementation. For example, you might name the **Ch04_SaleCo.MDB** database in problem 1 **My_Ch04_SaleCo.MDB**. Once you have created the database (see section 4.2) you can create the table structures and relationships using the techniques you learned in this chapter. You might also try to import several of the database components, using the techniques discussed in section 4.8. (Try clicking the **Options** >> button shown in Figure 4.73 to see what import options you have. For example, you may import the table structures only, the complete tables, or the complete tables and all the relationships between the tables you will import.)

4.2 Implement the **Ch01_XYZ** database from Chapter 1, using the information presented in Figures 1.14 and 1.15 as your database design. Name the implemented database **Ch04_XYZ.MDB**.
   a. Make sure that the referential integrity requirements are enforced.
   b. Make sure that you use input masks, default values, and validation rules. Use appropriate validation texts to alert end users to data entry errors caught by the validation rules.
   c. Enter some sample records. Make some deliberate data entry errors to check whether (*a*) and (*b*) work as intended.

4.3 Using the database design you created for problem 1.5, implement the database. Name the database **Ch04_JewelCo.MDB**.
   a. Make sure that the referential integrity requirements are enforced.
   b. Make sure that you use input masks, default values, and validation rules. Use appropriate validation texts to alert end users to data entry errors caught by the validation rules.
   c. Enter some sample records. Make some deliberate data entry errors to check whether (*a*) and (*b*) work as intended.

4.4 Using the database design you created for problem 1.11, implement the database. Name the database **Ch04_ConsultCo.MDB**.
   a. Make sure that the referential integrity requirements are enforced.
   b. Make sure that you use input masks, default values, and validation rules. Use appropriate validation texts to alert end users to data entry errors caught by the validation rules.
   c. Enter some sample records. Make some deliberate data entry errors to check whether (*a*) and (*b*) work as intended.

4.5 Modify the ERD in problem 4.4 to enable ConsultCo management to track all work done for each project. The work transactions must enable the managers to track who worked on each project, for how many hours, and at what cost. A sample work transaction record might include this information:
   Work transaction number: 5
   Work date: 12-Jan-2003
   Project number: 125
   Employee number: 6
   Employee job code: DSD
   Number of hours worked on this project on this date: 9.8
   Hourly charge: $175
   Total charge for this work transaction: $1715
   Complete the ERD modifications and then implement the design changes.

4.6 Using the database design you created for problem 1.12, implement the database. Name the database **Ch04_LuxMobile.MDB**.
   a. Make sure that the referential integrity requirements are enforced.

b. Make sure that you use input masks, default values, and validation rules. Use appropriate validation texts to alert end users to data entry errors caught by the validation rules.
c. Enter some sample records. Make some deliberate data entry errors to check whether (*a*) and (*b*) work as intended.

4.7 Using the database design you created for problem 1.13, implement the database. Name the database **Ch04_RentAll.MDB**.
a. Make sure that the referential integrity requirements are enforced.
b. Make sure that you use input masks, default values, and validation rules. Use appropriate validation texts to alert end users to data entry errors caught by the validation rules.
c. Enter some sample records. Make some deliberate data entry errors to check whether (*a*) and (*b*) work as intended.

4.8 Using the database design you created for problem 1.14, implement the database. Name the database **Ch04_Library.MDB**.
a. Make sure that the referential integrity requirements are enforced.
b. Make sure that you use input masks, default values, and validation rules. Use appropriate validation texts to alert end users to data entry errors caught by the validation rules.
c. Enter some sample records. Make some deliberate data entry errors to check whether (*a*) and (*b*) work as intended.

4.9 Using the database design you created for problem 1.15, implement the database. Name the database **Ch04_L_League.MDB**.
a. Make sure that the referential integrity requirements are enforced.
b. Make sure that you use input masks, default values, and validation rules. Use appropriate validation texts to alert end users to data entry errors caught by the validation rules.
c. Enter some sample records. Make some deliberate data entry errors to check whether (*a*) and (*b*) work as intended.

4.10 Using the database design you created for problem 3.3, implement the database. Name the database **Ch04_FlyHigh.MDB**.
a. Make sure that the referential integrity requirements are enforced.
b. Make sure that you use input masks, default values, and validation rules. Use appropriate validation texts to alert end users to data entry errors caught by the validation rules.
c. Enter some sample records. Make some deliberate data entry errors to check whether (*a*) and (*b*) work as intended.

4.11 Using the database design you created for problem 3.5, implement the database. Name the database **Ch04_TruckCo.MDB**.
a. Make sure that the referential integrity requirements are enforced.
b. Make sure that you use input masks, default values, and validation rules. Use appropriate validation texts to alert end users to data entry errors caught by the validation rules.
c. Enter some sample records. Make some deliberate data entry errors to check whether (*a*) and (*b*) work as intended.

4.12 Your school's IS department chair has asked you to design and implement a database, to be named **Ch04_DeptKey.MDB**, that enables the IS department's secretary to keep track of all keys to all buildings, offices, supply cabinets, and so on. The following business rules and end-user requirements exist:
- Each key has a unique key code. (Example: 12114.)
- A key can be used to open and lock a building door, an office, a supply cabinet, or a classroom. Some sample KEY records are shown in Figure P4.12.

FIGURE P4.12
Some Sample KEY Records

KEY_CODE	KEY_BLDG	KEY_ROOM	KEY_ROOM_TYPE
12111	REB	501	O
12112	REB	502	O
12113	REB	503	O
12114	REB	504	O

Note

These are just sample listings. Your reports—you will learn how to generate them in Chapter 7—will show different output, depending on what records you created in your transactions. Keep in mind that information requirements such as these help drive the database design process!

Note that key 12111 fits the lock on room 501 in the Ralph E. Brown building. Code O indicates that this room is an office. A classroom would be coded C, a supply cabinet would be coded S, and a building key would be coded B. If the key is a building key, rather than an office, a supply cabinet, or a classroom key, its KEY_ROOM value is K.

- There are multiple copies of each key. For example, three faculty members might each have a key to classroom 601 in the REB building. The key that fits this classroom is 12130, so each of the three faculty members has a copy of key number 12130.
- Keys may be checked in or out. The secretary must be able to track which keys were checked in or out, on which dates, and by whom.
- The secretary must be able to generate reports on all keys in inventory and on all keys currently checked out. Key reports must be available by key code and by employee. For example:

Building	Room	Type	Key Number	Key Copy	Employee
REB	501	O	12111	2	Blount
				5	Peterson
				1	Willis
REB	505	C	12116	1	Willis
				3	Sumner
				4	Blount
etc.					

Employee	Key Code	Key Number	Building	Room	Type
Blount	12111	2	REB	501	O
	12116	4	REB	505	C
	12123	1	KLB	203	C
Willis	12111	1	REB	501	O
	12116	1	REB	505	C
	12123	6	KLB	203	C
	12188	2	REB	309	S
etc.					

- You must also be able to generate reports that show all transactions—return (R) or check out (O) keys—by selected date range, by employee, and by key.

Make sure that your database meets these requirements:

a. The referential integrity requirements are enforced.

b. Use input masks, default values, and validation rules. Use appropriate validation texts to alert end users to data entry errors caught by the validation rules.

c. Enter some sample records. Make some deliberate data entry errors to check whether (*a*) and (*b*) work as intended.

4.13 The FlyHigh Aircraft Rental Company (see problem 4.10) has been bought out by the FlyHigher Company. The FlyHigher Company's management is impressed with your FlyHigh database design and implementation and has now asked you to expand your original FlyHigh database to encompass FlyHigher Company's operations. These operations include counter sales—sales of pilot supplies such as maps and flight plotters—flight instruction, and aircraft maintenance.

FlyHigher Organization

FlyHigher's operations are conducted by three divisions: The flight department, managed by the chief flight instructor, conducts all aircraft rental and flight instruction operations. The sales department, managed by the sales manager, conducts all pilot supply sales and provides general service support to the organization. The maintenance department, managed by the maintenance manager, conducts all maintenance for FlyHigher Company's rental aircraft and customer-owned aircraft. All three department managers report directly to FlyHigher's owner.

Flight Department

The flight department manages all aircraft flight operations, aircraft rental, and flight instruction. Flight instruction is given to customers who want to pursue private pilot and commercial pilot licenses. Flight instruction charges are based on the type of instruction given. Flight instruction may be given in FlyHigher's rental aircraft or in the customer's own aircraft.

Ground school is conducted in classes of at least five students. Flight instruction is on an individualized basis. Although customers usually receive all of their flight instruction from one instructor, customers may elect to conduct their flight training with two or more instructors. (Instructor selection may be affected by availability of the instructor or because of customer preferences.) Sample charges are shown in Figure P4.14A.

FIGURE P4.14A
Instruction Charges

CHG_NUM	CHG_DESCRIPTION	CHG_AMOUNT
1	Ground school, private pilot	$8.50
2	Ground school, commercial pilot	$10.00
3	Ground school, instrument	$12.50
4	Private pilot flight training	$18.75
5	Commercial pilot flight training	$22.50
6	Instrument flight training	$25.00
7	Multi-engine flight training	$28.75
(AutoNumber)		$0.00

All flight instructors are FlyHigher employees; there are no "contract" flight instructors. Flight instructors must have at least a commercial pilot's license, a certified flight instructor license, and a class 2 medical certificate (see Figure P4.14B).

FIGURE P4.14B
Licenses and Certifications

CERT_CODE	CERT_DESCRIPTION
AERO	Aerobatics Endorsement
ATP	Airline Transport Pilot License
CFI	Certified Flight Instructor
CFII	Certified Flight Instructor, Instrument
CFIMEL	Certified Flight Instructor, Multi-engine
COMM	Commercial license
INSTR	Instrument rating
MED1	Class 1 Medical
MED2	Class 2 Medical
MED3	Class 3 Medical
MEL	Multi-Engine, Land rating
PVT	Private Pilot License
STU	Student Pilot License

Customers may have a student pilot's license and receive instruction toward a private pilot's license, or they may already have a private pilot's license and receive instruction toward a commercial license or toward various ratings such as the instrument rating or the MEL rating. Private and student pilots must have at least a class 3 medical certificate, good for 2 years. (A class 2 medical certificate is good for 1 year and a class 1 medical certificate, required for all pilots who exercise the privileges of the airline transport pilot [ATP] license, is good for 6 months.)

To rent a FlyHigher company aircraft, customers must have passed a flight competency check by a FlyHigher instructor, have at least a private pilot's license, a current class 3 medical certificate, and a current biennial flight review. (A biennial flight review is taken every 2 years and is conducted according to Federal Aviation Regulations, or FARs.)

Note

You will learn how to access photos that are located in a separate folder, that is, *outside* the database, in Chapter 6, "Form Development." At this point in the implementation process, just create the path to that folder as an attribute in the PHOTO table. Make sure that you create a default folder location in the PHOTO table. For example, the default PHOTO_LOCATION might be written as **\Ch04\AC_Museum\AC_Pictures**. (Create that folder first!)

Maintenance

FlyHigher Company's maintenance procedures correspond to those used by the TruckCo Company (see problem 3.5). Therefore, an aircraft maintenance procedure begins with a maintenance-log entry, which triggers the use of the log lines that "belong" to the log. A mechanic with inspection authorization must do the log entries. The mechanic who did the work must sign off the log's lines. The company must account for all maintenance procedures and parts used. The keys in aircraft maintenance are traceability and accountability.

FlyHigher requires its mechanics to have at least an airframe and powerplant (A&P) license. (In official aviation jargon *powerplant* means "engine.") Two mechanics also hold inspector certification, which authorizes them to inspect and sign off on work done by any mechanic, if necessary, and to make aircraft maintenance-log entries.

Rental aircraft are subject to stringent maintenance requirements. Such aircraft must pass 100-hour inspections that cover both airframe and power plant(s). In addition, each rental aircraft must pass an annual inspection. (Customer aircraft are not used "for hire" and require only an annual inspection.) All aircraft must pass a yearly emergency locator transmitter (ELT) inspection that covers the ELT battery, cables, connectors, and antenna. In addition, all aircraft must pass a 24-month pitot-static system inspection. (The aircraft's indicated airspeed is generated by measuring the difference in pressure between the "ram" air entering the pitot tube and the "static" air source.) The pitot-static system check also covers the aircraft's transponder, a device that can enhance and encode a ground-based radar signal to give controllers a higher-definition radar image on their radarscopes.

To preserve the integrity of all maintenance-related data, the invoicing is done separately from the aircraft rental, flight instruction, and counter sales. The maintenance invoice total is the sum of all maintenance line charges and the parts used. A copy of the maintenance log and the associated maintenance log lines accompany the customer's invoice.

Counter Sales

As the name implies, counter sales are made over the counter in FlyHigher's main office. Such sales include pilot supplies such as visual flight rule (VFR) and instrument flight rule (IFR) maps and charts, plotters, flight computers, flight-planning software, fuel strainers, and warning strips. FlyHigher's database environment must include an inventory management module to ensure item tracking and item ordering. Sales reports include sales per selected date range, by product, and by employee. A sample report structure might look like Table P4.13.

TABLE P4.13
Sample Report Structure

Product Code	Product Description	Units Sold	Price	Gross Revenue	Tax
20012SC	Receiver/scanner	12	$150.00	$1,800.00	$144.00
E6BA	Flight computer	9	$ 59.95	$ 539.55	$ 43.16
			Total	**$2,339.95**	**$187.16**

4.14 Implement the DONOR, AIRCRAFT, MODEL, PHOTO, and DONATION entities and relationships you defined in the **AC_Museum** database design in problem 3.10 of Chapter 3. Name this database **Ch04_AC_Museum**. The DONATION table must enable the end user to link each donation to a specific donor and an aircraft. (Remember that each donor can make many donations and supply many aircraft photos. However, each donation and each aircraft photo is donated by one donor.)

Chapter Five

Queries

Preview

It is said that a renowned guru was once asked to name the most important business asset. The answer: data. The guru was then asked to name the greatest danger to a business. The answer: data. Both answers are correct. Data are the crucial raw ingredients for *information* creation. Without timely and accurate information, poor decisions are likely to be the norm. On the other hand, incomplete, inaccurate, or "polluted" data yield poor information on which equally poor decisions are based. You have already learned that data redundancies are a prime source of bad data. You have also learned how to eliminate data redundancies through good database design. And you have learned how to use entity and referential integrity enforcement to avoid serious data storage and retrieval errors that lead to inaccurate data.

Well-designed databases are created to protect the integrity of stored data. But even properly stored and protected data are useless unless they can be *accessed* easily and efficiently. And even if data retrieval meets the ease and efficiency test, data are not particularly useful unless we can create *information* from such data. Fortunately, very precisely structured and powerful query languages such as **Structural Query Language (SQL)** exist to facilitate data retrieval and to help transform data into useful information. Because SQL coding is often complex, Access provides an easy to use interface, known as **Query by example (QBE),** to handle the SQL code generation. In this chapter you will learn how to use the Access QBE interface to retrieve and organize data.

Objectives

After studying this chapter, you should be able to retrieve, organize, and update data with the help of the QBE interface. To help you perform these data management tasks, you will learn to

- Use the query tools.
- Develop and use a wide variety of Select queries, including parameter queries.
- Develop and use Crosstab queries.
- Develop and use Action queries.

5.1 QUERY BASICS: ROLE AND TYPE

A query is a question. For example, the following questions are queries:

- Which employees have worked for our company more than five years?
- How many aircraft books have we sold during the past three months?
- How many items are currently on back order?
- What is the dollar value of sales in the various product categories?

The answers to such questions can help manage the organization's operational environment. Naturally, asking the right questions is a key to management success. Getting the correct answers to the right questions is the second part of the success equation.

Our job as database professionals is to make sure that these questions are translated into a format that the database can handle efficiently. Getting the correct answers to questions requires efficient data retrieval and organization. Fortunately, Access not only allows us to ask the questions but also helps us get the correct answers through the QBE interface. As the name suggests, the QBE interface allows us to specify an example of the expected output by placing the desired output elements into a grid. The output elements are usually fields selected from various tables, but they may be calculated values or even constants.

Regardless of what kinds of output elements we select, we must specify their source(s). Data sources for the queries include both tables and other queries. Access makes source selection easy because it lets us use the QBE interface to select the data sources via dialog boxes. Next, Access lets us drag and drop the desired attributes into a grid. Finally, Access enables us to format the output and to organize it in various ways. And then the magic begins: When we direct Access to execute the query, Access automatically generates the complex SQL code to get the answer.

Queries constitute the basis for much of the work we will do within the database environment. Two basic query types exist: *select queries* and *action queries.* **Select queries** are queries that are designed to extract (select) and organize data to produce information. Select queries may also be used to produce input for

- Forms you will learn to construct in Chapter 6.
- Reports you will learn to produce in Chapter 7.
- More complex queries you will learn to construct later in this chapter.

Action queries are queries that perform a wide variety of actions such as table updates, deletes, and appends. We examine these query types and their generation in the following sections.

5.2 SELECT QUERIES

As the name suggests, a select query selects and displays records for one or more tables. The record selection may be limited by

- Restricting the number of fields to be displayed; for example, list all records in the EMPLOYEE table, but show only the EMP_LNAME and EMP_FNAME fields.
- Restricting the record selection based on some specified limitation; for example, show the employee records for all employees whose last name is Smith. You may also use multiple restrictions; for example, list all records for employees who were employed before January 1, 1995, and whose job code is 3.
- Restricting the number of fields to be displayed and the record selection based on some combination of the first two items.

Note

Because you cannot write to the student CD, none of the material on that CD can be altered. That is, all of the CD databases are subject to the **Read-only** property. When you copy the databases from the CD to your computer, these databases *still* have that **Read-only** property. Because you must be able to alter the database contents to work with the databases in this chapter—and, for that matter, in all remaining chapters—you must change this **Read-only** property after you have copied the material from the CD. We will show you how to do this in the following example.

5.2.1 Creating a Simple Select Query

The simplest kind of select query requests a list of only a few of the many available fields in a table. For example, you may ask Access to list the EMPLOYEE table's EMP_LNAME, EMP_FNAME, EMP_INITIAL, EMP_AREACODE, and EMP_PHONE.

No matter what kind of query you want to create, you will discover that the Access Query by Example (QBE) screen makes the job simple and effective. To let you practice all of this chapter's query techniques, we have created a database for you. This database is located on the student CD that is packaged with this book. Before you continue studying the material presented in this chapter, make sure that you copy this chapter's practice database from the CD to your own computer.

But before you copy any database from the CD, make sure that you have a proper directory (folder) available to help you organize your data environment. Although you can, of course, use any directory (folder) structure that makes sense to you, we will assume that you have organized your database environment to match the examples in Chapter 4. For example, using the techniques you learned in Chapter 4, first create a folder named **Ch05** in the **C:\MSOffice\Access\Databases** folder. You can then store all of the Chapter 5 databases in this folder. Go ahead and copy the **Ch05_POS_2nd.mdb** from the student CD to this new folder.

To make sure that you can alter—edit, append, and so on—the database you have copied from the student CD, you must uncheck its **Read-only** property. To get that job done, complete the following three steps:

1. Using the Windows Explorer, find the **CH05_POS_2nd.mdb** you have just copied to your disk and right-click on its name to generate the menu in the center of Figure 5.1.

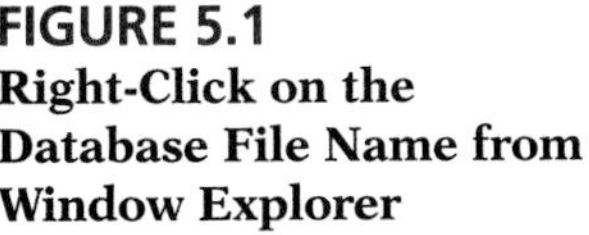

FIGURE 5.1
Right-Click on the Database File Name from Window Explorer

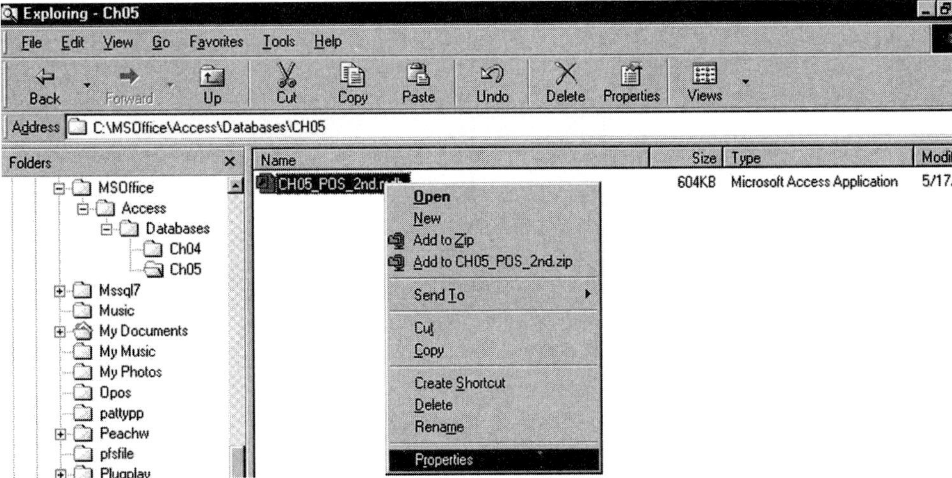

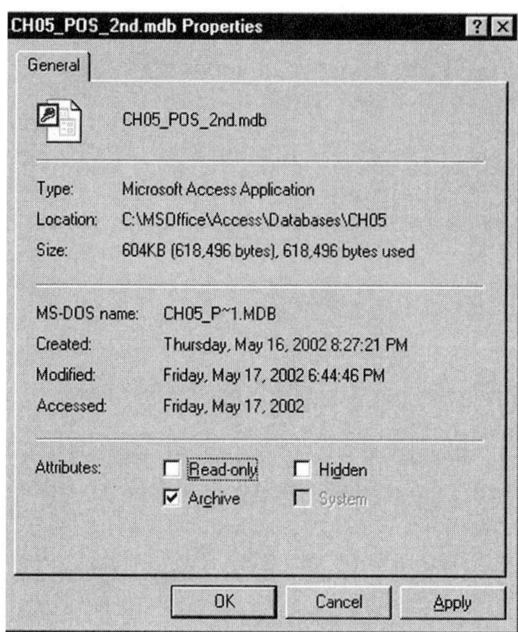

FIGURE 5.1A
Uncheck the Read-only Check Box

2. Using the window shown in Figure 5.1, select **Properties** to generate the screen shown in Figure 5.1A. When you first examine Figure 5.1A, the **Read-only** attribute will have a check mark in the little square, known as a check box, before it. Uncheck the **Read-only** property by clicking on that check box. (Figure 5.1A shows that we have already done that, so the check box no longer shows a check mark.)

3. When you have unchecked the **Read-only** check box, click on the **Apply** button shown in Figure 5.1A, then click **OK**.

Once you have completed the preceding three steps, you have an updatable database. Open the Ch05_POS_2nd.mdb to generate its database window. (The default will be the **Tables** tab. The database window's **Tables** tab will show all the tables found in the **Ch05_POS_2nd.MDB** database.) Click on the database window's **Queries** tab and then click on the **New** button to generate the screen shown in Figure 5.2. (If you examine Figure 5.2, you will see that we've placed the cursor on this button to show the button's function.) Because we have not yet created a query, the database window is still empty.

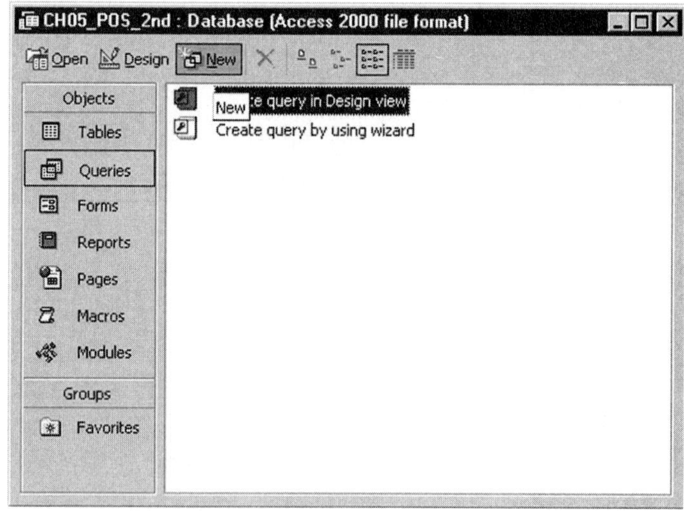

FIGURE 5.2
The Initial Query Tab in the Database Window

Note

The QBE screen in Figure 5.4 shows the tables that are currently in the database. Therefore, if you have a different set of tables in your database, the **Show Table** dialog box will list *that* set of tables, rather than the ones you see in Figure 5.4.

FIGURE 5.3
The New Query Dialog Box

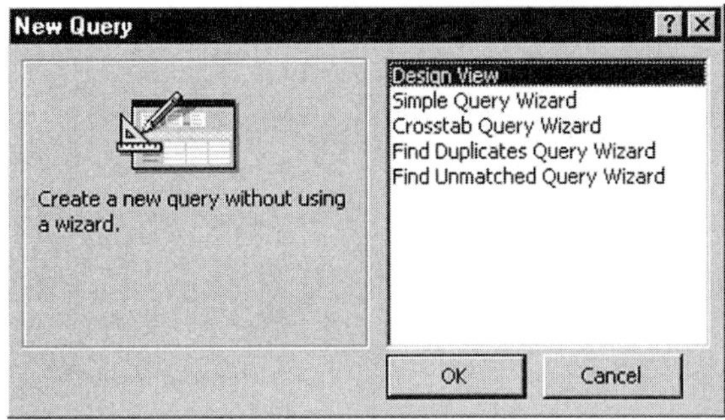

Clicking on the **New** button in Figure 5.2 will produce the **New Query** dialog box shown in Figure 5.3.

Click on the **OK** button shown in Figure 5.3 to open the query in **Design View.** This action will produce the initial QBE screen shown in Figure 5.4.

As you examine Figure 5.4, note that a **Show Table** dialog box is superimposed on the QBE screen. This dialog box defaults to the first selection, EMPLOYEE, in the **Tables** folder. You can add any of the tables shown in the dialog box to the QBE screen by double-clicking on it or by selecting each table and

FIGURE 5.4
The Initial QBE Screen

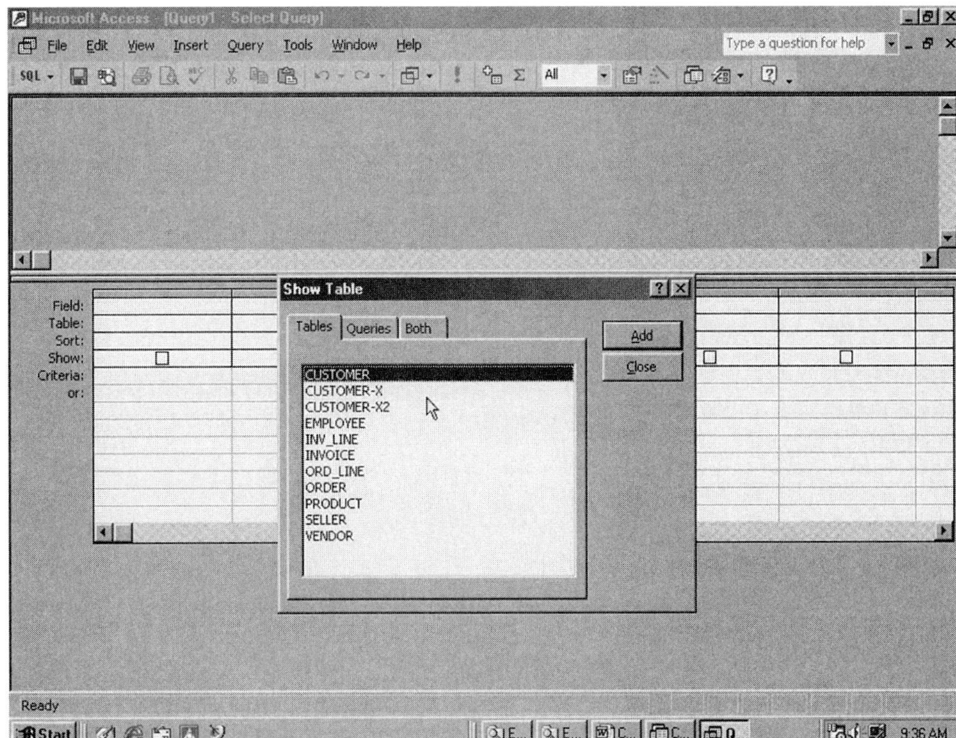

Note

If you check Figure 5.4, you will see the notation **Select Query** in the upper-left corner. Because you will be working on select queries, make sure that this query type has been specified. If Access has not defaulted to the **Select Query** option, select the **Query Type** option from the menu in Figure 5.5 to generate Figure 5.5A. In this case, the new menu shows that the **Select Query** option has been selected because the adjacent button is pushed in, thus producing the shaded segment.

Figure 5.5A also shows the other query type options, to be examined later.

FIGURE 5.5A
The Query Type Options

FIGURE 5.5
The QBE Menu Options

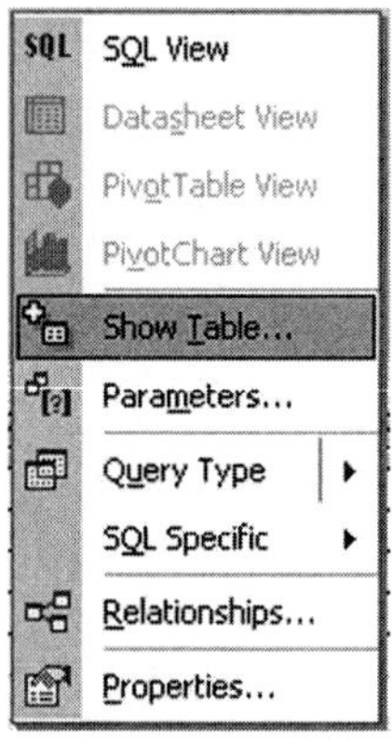

clicking on the **Add** button. Use the **Close** button once you have added the necessary table(s).

If the QBE screen is opened without the **Show Table** dialog box, just place the cursor on the **QBE data source** section—that's the blank section above the **QBE grid**—and right-click to produce the menu selections shown in Figure 5.5. Then select the **Show Table** option from this menu to display the screen shown in Figure 5.4.

From the **Show Table** dialog box in Figure 5.4, select the EMPLOYEE table and close the dialog box. This action puts the EMPLOYEE table structure in the **QBE data source** area (see Figure 5.6).

To see more of the QBE screen, maximize it and then drag the QBE screen's components to size them as you like. (As always, you can also size the EMPLOYEE table box to suit your needs.) Next drag and drop the following EMPLOYEE table fields to the field locations shown in the **QBE grid** at the bottom of the QBE screen.

```
EMP_TITLE, EMP_LNAME, EMP_FNAME, EMP_INITIAL, EMP_AREACODE,
EMP_HOMEPHONE
```

When you are done—and assuming that you have maximized the QBE screen—you will see Figure 5.7.

FIGURE 5.6
The EMPLOYEE Table as the QBE Screen's Data Source

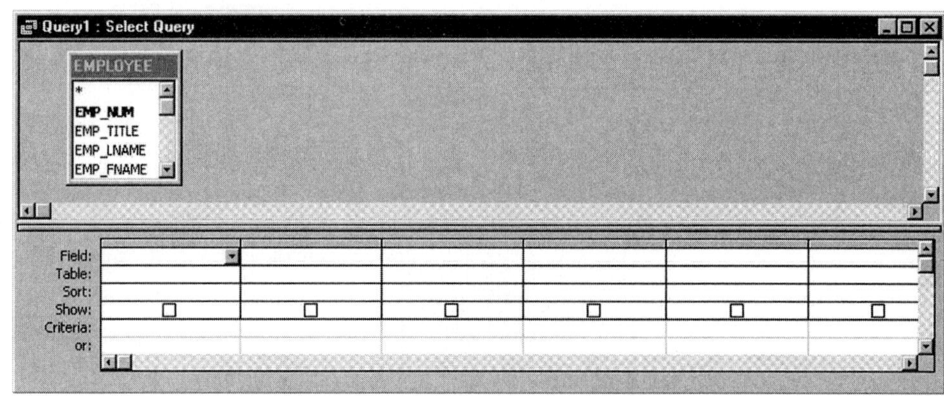

Note

Once you have experimented with the **Add** and **Delete** functions, restore the QBE grid to the format shown in Figure 5.7. You will be using these selections later.

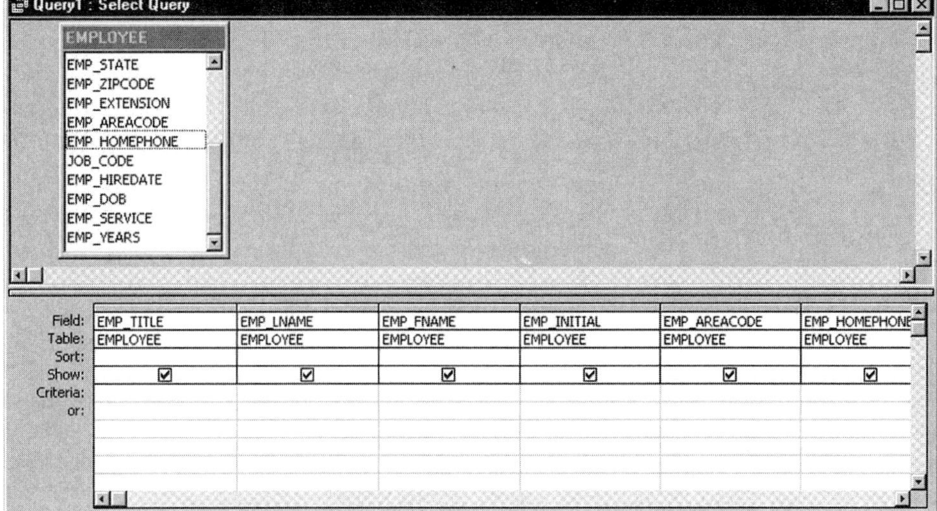

FIGURE 5.7
The EMPLOYEE Field Selections

Adding and Deleting Fields

If you did not enter all the fields shown in Figure 5.7's QBE grid, you can always add them. To add a field to the QBE grid, drag it from the data source—in this case, the EMPLOYEE table—and drop it into the desired location in the QBE grid. If you drop the new field on top of an existing field, Access will automatically insert the new field between this existing field and the next field. (To create a space between existing fields, you can also place the cursor on any field in the grid and press the Insert key on your keyboard. You can then drop the new field in the space you have created.)

To delete any field from the QBE grid, mark it by placing the cursor just above the field name and then click. The cursor shape will change to the arrow shown above the EMP_LNAME in Figure 5.7A. Clicking will mark the selected field by inverting its screen presentation as shown in Figure 5.7A's EMP_TITLE. Once the field has been marked, just press the keyboard's Delete key to complete the deletion process. (As always, you can use the standard Windows conventions to mark multiple fields for deletion by holding down the left mouse button and then dragging the cursor along the fields. Instead of using the keyboard's Delete key, you can always use the **Edit** menu and select the **Delete** option from it.)

Field:	EMP_TITLE	EMP_LNAME	EMP_FNAME	EMP_INITIAL	EMP_AREACODE	EMP_HOMEPHONE
Table:	EMPLOYEE	EMPLOYEE	EMPLOYEE	EMPLOYEE	EMPLOYEE	EMPLOYEE
Sort:						
Show:	☑	☑	☑	☑	☑	☑
Criteria:						
or:						

FIGURE 5.7A
Deleting Fields from the QBE Grid

FIGURE 5.8
The Save As Dialog Box

Saving the Query

After the fields have been selected, you are ready to save the results. As always, if you forget to save your work, Access will remind you to do so. Note that we have typed the query name into the **Save As** dialog box shown in Figure 5.8.

Keep in mind that preparing documentation is a crucial task and that proper naming conventions help you perform that task more efficiently. Therefore, we use query names that have the following characteristics:

- The prefix **qry** identifies the object as a query.
- The name is sufficiently descriptive to remind you of its purpose. Because we will use this query as the basis for a phone directory later, we chose the name **qryEmployeePhoneList**.
- The query name contains no spaces, and the name mixes upper- and lowercase letters. The first letter of each word in the description is capitalized to make the words stand out. We do this because it is easier to read **qryEmployeePhone List** than to read **qryemployeephonelist** or **QRYEMPLOYEEPHONELIST**.

Once the query has been saved, your database window will show the query name in the query folder. Double-click on the query to execute the query and to see its output or select the **Design** button to return to the QBE screen and make appropriate modifications.

Once the query has been saved, close the QBE screen to return to the database window. The database window will show the saved query. (A small segment of the database window is shown in Figure 5.9.)

5.2.2 Sorting Options

To make it easy to find an employee's phone number, the phone list requires that the listing be alphabetized. Therefore, we select the **Design** button from the database window shown in Figure 5.9 to return to the QBE screen shown in Figure 5.10.

As you examine Figure 5.10, note that we clicked on the **Sort:** blank under the EMP_LNAME field to display the down arrow shown on the right margin.

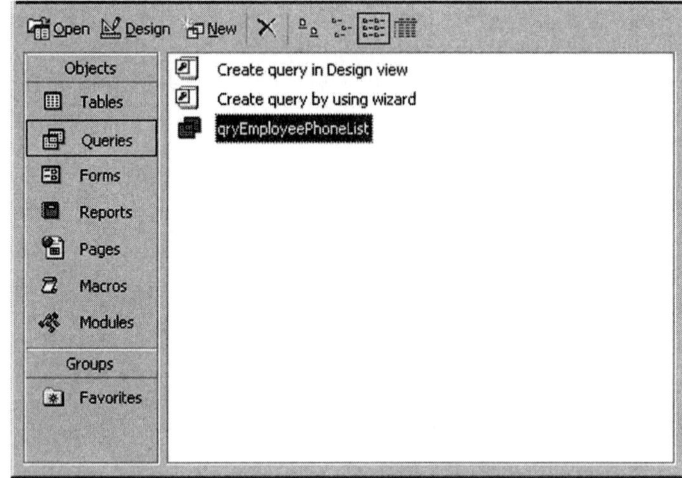

FIGURE 5.9
The Saved Query in the Database Window

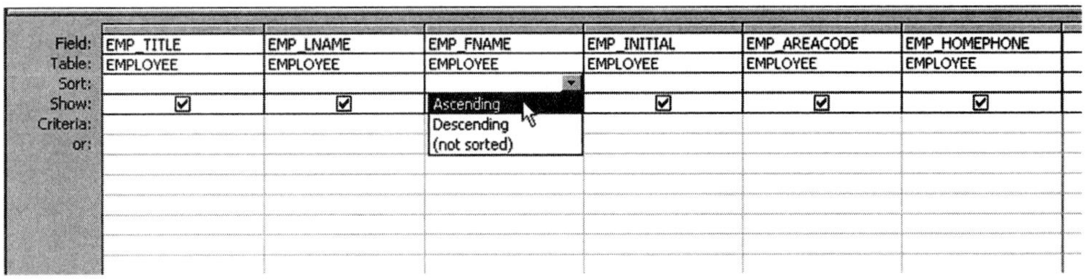

FIGURE 5.10
The Sort Options List

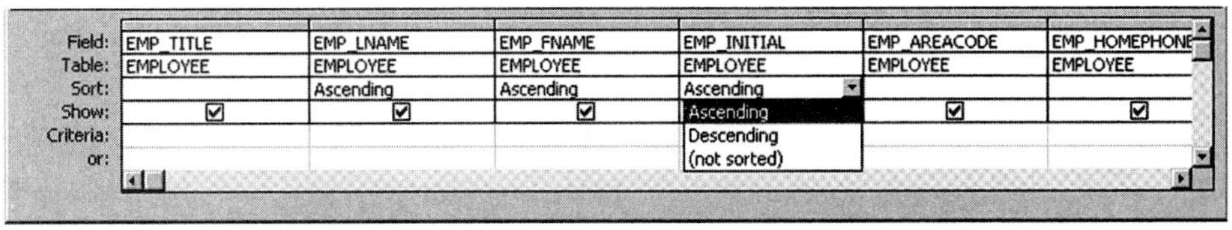

Field:	EMP_TITLE	EMP_LNAME	EMP_FNAME	EMP_INITIAL	EMP_AREACODE	EMP_HOMEPHONE
Table:	EMPLOYEE	EMPLOYEE	EMPLOYEE	EMPLOYEE	EMPLOYEE	EMPLOYEE
Sort:						
Show:	☑	☑	Ascending	☑	☑	☑
Criteria:			Descending			
or:			(not sorted)			

FIGURE 5.11
The Modified Phone List Query

Field:	EMP_TITLE	EMP_LNAME	EMP_FNAME	EMP_INITIAL	EMP_AREACODE	EMP_HOMEPHONE
Table:	EMPLOYEE	EMPLOYEE	EMPLOYEE	EMPLOYEE	EMPLOYEE	EMPLOYEE
Sort:		Ascending	Ascending	Ascending		
Show:	☑	☑	☑	Ascending	☑	☑
Criteria:				Descending		
or:				(not sorted)		

Click on this down arrow to display the options list, and then select the **Ascending** option.

Repeat this procedure for the EMP_FNAME and the EMP_INITIAL to display the query structure shown in Figure 5.11.

Save the modified query and then close the QBE screen to return to the database window. Now select the **Open** button from the database window to see a (partial) listing in Figure 5.12. Note that the names are listed alphabetically. (Depending on the editing you have done in the EMPLOYEE table, your listing may be different, of course!)

5.2.3 Output Formatting: The Properties Box

The phone list in Figure 5.12 is serviceable, but the use of field names as column headers is not desirable for several reasons. First, end users expect to see a clean and readable output. Therefore, they would expect to see the title header named Title rather than EMP_TITLE, the last name header named Last Name rather than EMP_LNAME, and so on. Second, because queries often become the input for forms and reports later, it is useful to control output formatting at the query level. (Forms and reports *inherit* the output formats that have been specified in the query.)

In Chapter 4 you learned that modifying a table's properties at the design level can control a table's field characteristics. Such control is standard across all Access objects. Therefore, you can also control all the query components (*at the design level!*) via the query properties. For example, to change the field properties of Figure 5.12's EMP_TITLE, do the following:

1. Put the query in the design format shown in Figure 5.11.
2. Put the cursor on the EMP_TITLE field.
3. Right-click.

These three steps will open the pop-up menu shown in Figure 5.13.

FIGURE 5.12
The Alphabetized Employee Phone Listing

EMP_TITLE	EMP_LNAME	EMP_FNAME	EMP_INITIAL	EMP_AREACODE	EMP_HOMEPHONE
Mr.	Ardano	James	G	615	278-6803
Ms.	Bahint	Elizabeth	B	615	896-6358
Mr.	Blalock	Andrew		615	355-1700
Mr.	Blalock	James	G	502	266-6836
Mr.	Brynnan	William	C	615	253-0019
Ms.	Dexter	Willa	N	615	277-8412
Mr.	Donelly	Ronald	O	615	278-3377
Ms.	Doornberg	Anne	D	615	867-0744
Ms.	Downes	Anne		615	278-1152
Ms.	Dubrien	Susanna	K	615	277-9546
Ms.	Edwards	Rosemary	D	615	863-9562
Ms.	Graztevski	Mary	B	615	291-9107

Note

In Figure 5.13 the **Table Names** option has been selected. Access defaults to this selection but double-check to make sure it is *still* selected! (You may have accidentally turned it off during a previous session.) Selecting the **Table Names** option means that you will always be able to see the data source when you are working with the query in design format. Failure to select the **Table Names** option will make it very difficult for you to track data sources when you develop more complex queries.

FIGURE 5.13
The Field Properties Menu Option

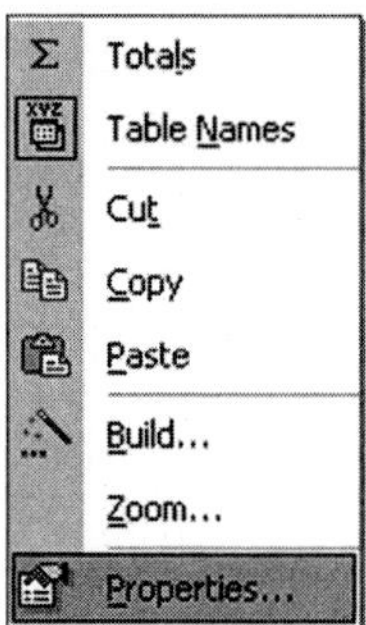

FIGURE 5.14
The EMP_TITLE Properties Box

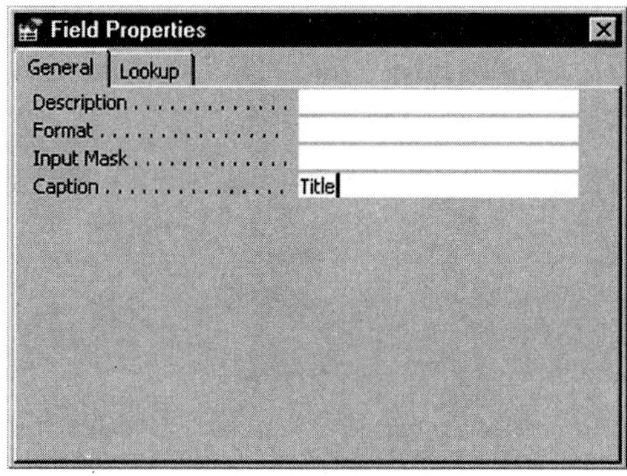

Click on the **Properties** selection in Figure 5.13 to display the Field Properties box shown in Figure 5.14. The properties box is always context sensitive. Therefore, because we selected the EMP_TITLE field, the properties box will reflect the EMP_TITLE properties.

Because we want to change the EMP_TITLE field's header (caption) from EMP_TITLE to Title, place the cursor on the **Caption** input line and type Title as shown in Figure 5.14. Move the properties box to an unused portion of the QBE screen, select the EMP_LNAME field (see Figure 5.11 again), and type the caption **Last Name**. Repeat the process for each field and then save the query again. When you reopen the query, you will see that the headers are changed as shown in Figure 5.15. (Note that we have also sized the field limits to fit the smaller headers.)

Up to this point, we have gone back and forth to save and open the query. Actually, you can work on the query and see the effects of your work without having to save your work and then reopening the query. You can switch back and forth between the **Datasheet View** and the **Design View** with the help of the **View** menu button, as shown in Figure 5.16.

At this point you should begin to see a familiar pattern emerge. For example, you learned in Chapter 4 that you could generate the appropriate table **Toolbars** via the **View** menu. Figure 5.16 shows you that the *same* menu, this time for the

FIGURE 5.15
The Modified Employee Phone Listing

Title	Last Name	First Name	Initial	Area Code	Home Phone
Mr.	Ardano	James	G	615	278-6803
Ms.	Bahint	Elizabeth	B	615	896-6358
Mr.	Blalock	Andrew		615	355-1700
Mr.	Blalock	James	G	502	266-6836
Mr.	Brynnan	William	C	615	253-0019
Ms.	Dexter	Willa	N	615	277-8412
Mr.	Donelly	Ronald	O	615	278-3377
Ms.	Doornberg	Anne	D	615	867-0744
Ms.	Downes	Anne	B	615	278-1152

FIGURE 5.16
The View Menu

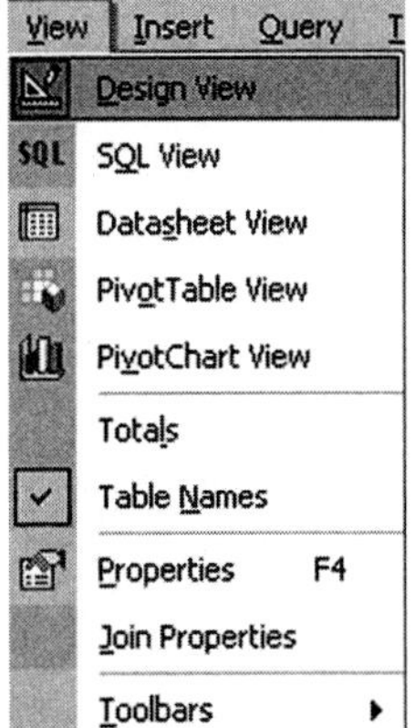

FIGURE 5.17 The Employee Phone List Access SQL Command Structure

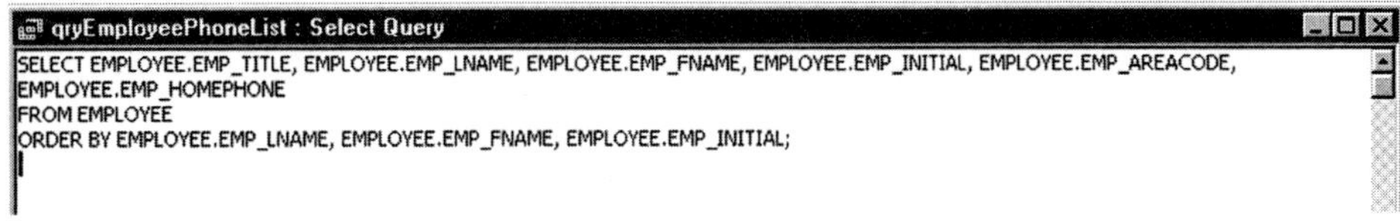

query environment, can be used to select the query design toolbar. All Access menus are context sensitive. Therefore, any menu selection automatically yields the appropriate options for the objects you are working on. For example, the **Toolbars** option for queries will produce the toolbar buttons appropriate for the query design; similarly, the option will produce the toolbar buttons that are appropriate for the table design if you are working on tables. Because Access keeps producing the same basic options tailored to the selected design environments, we will not continue to show the **View** menu options.

Although the **Datasheet View** and **Design View** options are our primary concern, Figure 5.17's **SQL View** shows you the SQL code that was generated by Access to produce the employee phone list. If you are interested in learning how to code in SQL, this option, whose results are depicted in Figure 5.15, may be helpful. Because we generate all of our queries via the QBE interface, we will not show additional SQL command structures in our query development.

5.2.4 Data Organization: Grouping

Thus far we have explored how QBE generates simple listings. As useful as this feature is, data summaries are often the basis for transforming data into information. For example, suppose the question is, How many employees fit into each job code? To create the query that will answer this question, start at the database window shown in Figure 5.2 and select the **New** button to begin a new query design. (Just follow the procedures in section 5.2.1 to place the EMPLOYEE table into the QBE screen's data source section.)

Having selected the EMPLOYEE table as the data source, look at Figure 5.18 and note that

1. We dragged and dropped the JOB_CODE and EMP_NUM fields into the field slots. (Scroll back and forth within the EMPLOYEE table structure until you see the fields you need.)

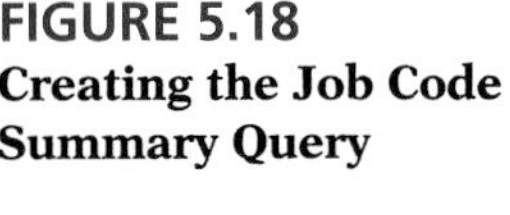
FIGURE 5.18
Creating the Job Code Summary Query

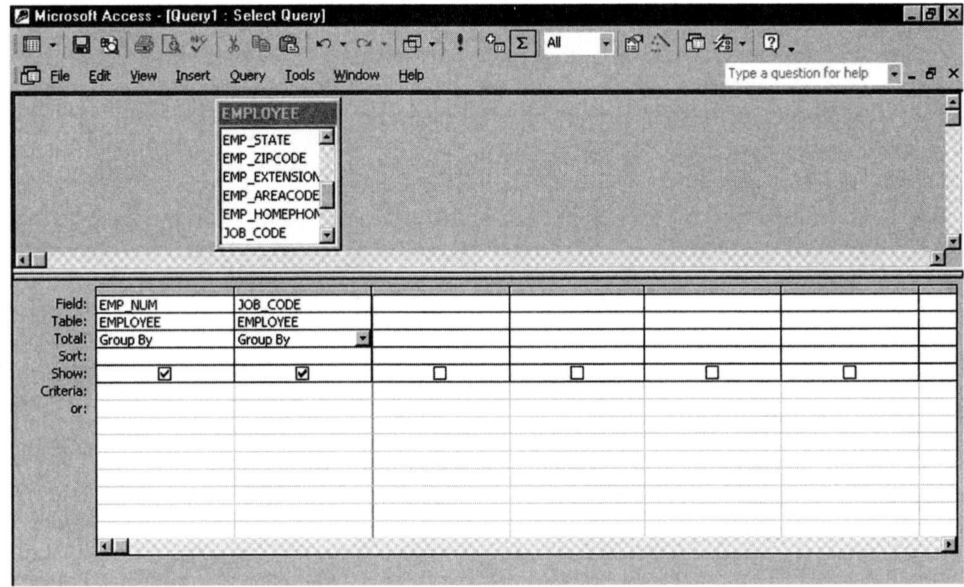

Assignment

Use the Field Properties box (see section 5.2.3) to create the headers **Job Code** and **Employee Count** for the output shown in Figure 5.21.

2. We clicked the **Totals** [Σ] button from the toolbar. (Remember, if the button bar is not shown on your screen, select the **View** menu [see Figure 5.16] and then select the **Toolbars** option.)

As you examine Figure 5.18, note that clicking the **Totals** button caused Access to write the message **Group By** next to the **Totals** slot in the QBE grid. (The down arrow shown *next* to the EMP_NUM's **Group By** notation was created by clicking on the EMP_NUM's **Total** line.) Click on the down arrow to produce the options shown in Figure 5.19. Because we want to count the number of employees in each job code, select the **Count** option.

FIGURE 5.19
The Count Option for the Group By Clause

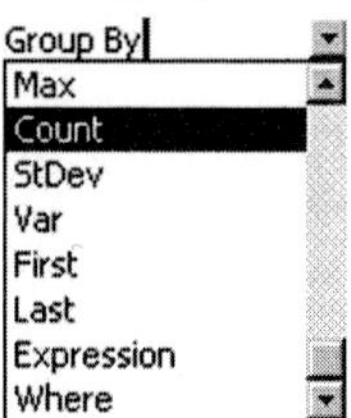

Selecting the **Count** option shown in Figure 5.19 will write **Count** into the EMP_NUM **Totals** slot as shown in Figure 5.20.

Save the new query as **qryEmployeeCountByJobCode** and then open the query to see the results shown in Figure 5.21.

FIGURE 5.20
The Completed QBE Grid

JOB_CODE	EMP_NUM
EMPLOYEE	EMPLOYEE
Group By	Count
☑	☑

By examining the job count output in Figure 5.21, you can readily see that 16 employees are classified as JOB_CODE 3. Note also that Access created its own header, **CountOfEMP_NUM,** for the second column's employee count.

FIGURE 5.21
The Job Count Output

JOB_CODE	CountOfEMP_NUM
1	1
2	1
3	16
4	1
5	4
6	1
7	2
8	1
9	2
10	1
11	1
12	2
13	2
14	1

5.2.5 Parameter Queries

The dictionary defines **parameter** as "a quantity whose value varies with the circumstances of its application." In database terms *parameter queries* are queries whose output extent is defined by specified constraints. For example, suppose you want to know how many employees have a last name Smith. Finding the answer requires a query that lists only the employee records for employees whose EMP_LNAME value is Smith. If you want to know how many employees were hired before January 1, 1995, you would use a query based on the date constraint, 01/01/1995. The output, one based on a last name and one based on a date, is very likely to be different in each case. In short, the output varies with the circumstances of its application.

Access allows you to place many different kinds of constraints in a single query. For example, the question How many employees named Smith were hired before January 1, 1995? is handled easily. You can place multiple constraints in different data sources. (We explore multiple data sources in section 5.2.6.) You can even check for *partial* string matches by using the standard wildcard characters * and ? in your query constraint section.

To see how parameter queries are created, let's examine the query that answers the question, How many employees have the last name Smith? As usual in the query design business, start at the database window, select the **New** button, and specify the data source. (Because the employee last names are stored in the EMPLOYEE table, we will use the EMPLOYEE table as the data source.) As you can tell by the screen shown in Figure 5.22, we have also limited the output to include only the fields EMP_NUM, EMP_TITLE, EMP_LNAME, EMP_FNAME, and EMP_INITIAL. Finally, note that we have specified the constraint "Smith" in the **Criteria** section.

Note

A string is any character or set of characters not to be used in any mathematical sense. Such characters are enclosed in quotes. For example, "Smith," "Y/WU32," and "615-898-1234" are strings. Wildcard characters are designed to be used on strings.

A wildcard character is one that may be substituted for any other character. The wildcard character "*" indicates that all characters following the current one will be included. The wildcard character "?" indicates any character in the ? position. Therefore,

- Smith* includes Smith, Smithson, Smithers, and any other string that leads with Smith.
- S* includes Smith, Summers, and Sorell, and any other string that leads with S.
- *son includes Wilson, Robertson, and any other string that ends in "son."
- Ard?more includes Ardemore, Ardomore, Ardumore, and any other string that contains a character between d and m.
- Nas??ill? includes Nashville, NaseBille, nasumilla, and any other string that has two characters between Nas and ill and a character following ill.

You will discover that Access's string searches and matches are not case sensitive *unless* you specify the constraint in terms of upper- and lowercase.

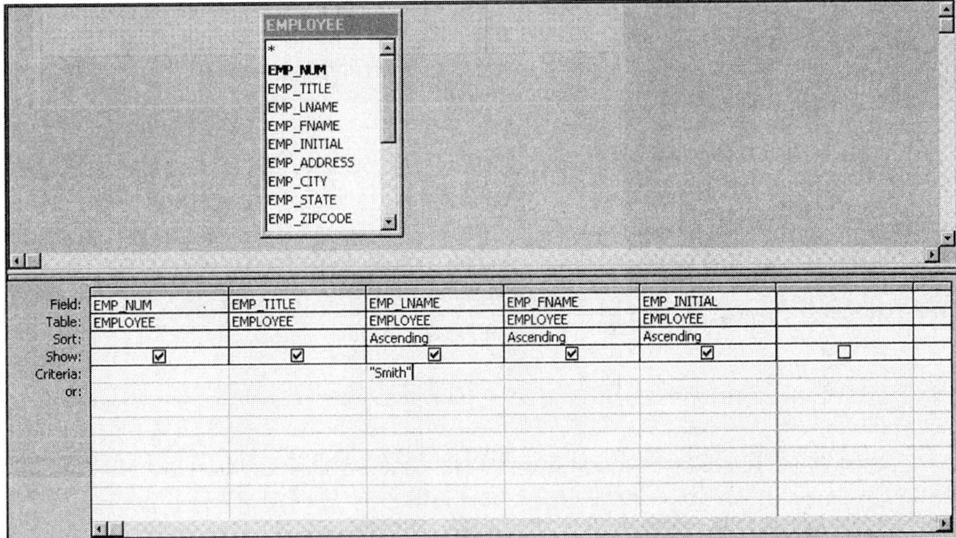

FIGURE 5.22
A Parameter Query Based on the Constraint EMP_LNAME = "Smith"

Save the new parameter query as **qryListEmployeeBySelectedLastName** and then open it to see the output produced in Figure 5.23.

If we want to include *any* names that *start* with Smith, substitute the string "Smith*" in Figure 5.22's **Criteria** section to produce the output shown in Figure 5.24.

You can add logical conditions with the help of the **or** line, just below the **Criteria** (see Figure 5.22). For example, suppose you want to have a listing for employees whose last names start with Smith or whose last name is Robertson. Figure 5.25 shows the properly entered constraints, and Figure 5.26 shows the output.

EMP_NUM	Title	Last Name	First Name	Initial
32	Ms.	Smith	Melanie	K
41	Mr.	Smith	Robert	A
47	Mr.	Smith	Robert	E
22	Mr.	Smith	Robert	T
(AutoNumber)				

FIGURE 5.23
The Last Name Parameter Query Output: EMP_LNAME = "Smith"

Note

Access automatically makes appropriate adjustments in your criteria. For example, if you forget to put quotes around Smith, Access will put them there while you're executing the query. If you insert a wildcard character by typing "Smith*", Access will add the wildcard string search **Like** constraint to execute the query. Therefore, when you have checked the output and return to design view, you will see the modification in Figure 5.25. (To save time, you did remember to toggle back and forth between **design view** and **datasheet view**, didn't you? Take another look at the options in the **View** menu.)

FIGURE 5.24
A Wildcard Character EMP_LNAME Constraint

EMP_NUM	Title	Last Name	First Name	Initial
32	Ms.	Smith	Melanie	K
41	Mr.	Smith	Robert	A
47	Mr.	Smith	Robert	E
22	Mr.	Smith	Robert	T
15	Ms.	Smithson	Elsa	K
44	Mr.	Smithson	George	D
(AutoNumber)				

FIGURE 5.25
Using the Logical OR Constraint

EMP_NUM	EMP_TITLE	EMP_LNAME	EMP_FNAME	EMP_INITIAL	
EMPLOYEE	EMPLOYEE	EMPLOYEE	EMPLOYEE	EMPLOYEE	
		Ascending	Ascending	Ascending	
☑	☑	☑	☑	☑	☐
		Like "Smith*"			
		"Robertson"			

FIGURE 5.26
The Logical OR Constraint's Output

EMP_NUM	Title	Last Name	First Name	Initial
7	Mrs.	Robertson	Elaine	W
32	Ms.	Smith	Melanie	K
41	Mr.	Smith	Robert	A
47	Mr.	Smith	Robert	E
22	Mr.	Smith	Robert	T
15	Ms.	Smithson	Elsa	K
44	Mr.	Smithson	George	D
(AutoNumber)				

Creating Dialog Boxes for Your Parameters

Although the parameter queries work as intended, they are rather clumsy. For example, suppose we want to have listings for different last names each time the query is run. Having to go back to the design stage each time is, to put it mildly, inefficient. Fortunately, Access makes it very easy to create dialog boxes; all that's needed is a prompt inside square brackets. (See the **Criteria** limitation on the EMP_LNAME field in Figure 5.27 and note that we have typed the prompt **[Search for this last name]**.)

If you run this modified parameter query, Access will automatically produce the **Enter Parameter Value** dialog box shown in Figure 5.28. Just enter the last name Smith, without quotes, to produce the same output you saw in Figure 5.23. (The dialog box input is not case sensitive; you will get the same output for the entries SMITH, Smith, or smith.)

You can add as many dialog boxes as you like. For example, if you want to search the EMPLOYEE table by both last name and first name, just add the second parameter prompt as a constraint with the EMP_FNAME. (See Figure 5.29).

Running this modified query will produce two dialog boxes, one for the last name and one for the first name. Try using the last name Smith and the first name Robert to see the three employees named Robert Smith in the EMPLOYEE table.

FIGURE 5.27
Specifying a Parameter Dialog Box

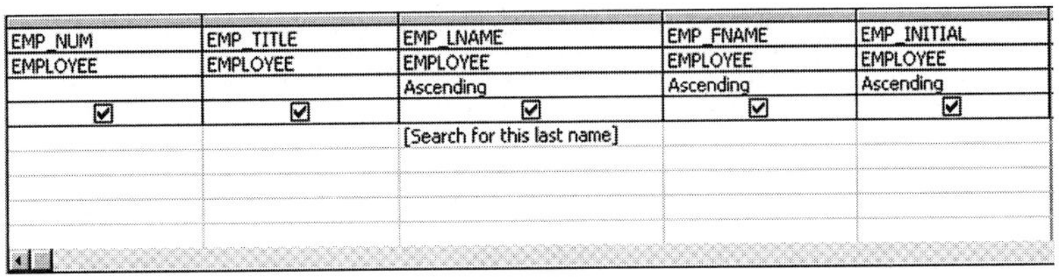

EMP_NUM	EMP_TITLE	EMP_LNAME	EMP_FNAME	EMP_INITIAL
EMPLOYEE	EMPLOYEE	EMPLOYEE	EMPLOYEE	EMPLOYEE
		Ascending	Ascending	Ascending
☑	☑	☑	☑	☑
		[Search for this last name]		

Segmented Searches

The parameter entries based on Figure 5.29 work fine as long as you have exact matches for the last and first names. Typing Smith in the **Last Name** dialog box and Robert in the **First Name** dialog box will yield all records for employees named Robert Smith. But suppose you don't know the employee's first name. Pressing the Enter key without entering a first name in the **First Name** dialog box, thereby creating a null, will yield no records because there are no employees named Smith who don't have a first name. Or suppose you know an employee's first name only. If you are looking for an employee whose first name is Robert, pressing the Enter key without typing a last name in the **Last Name** dialog box, thereby creating a null, and then typing Robert in the **First Name** dialog box will yield no records, because there are no employees named Robert who don't have a last name. In short, the dialog boxes created by the parameter criteria in Figure 5.29 are not particularly useful if you have incomplete information.

To create the more flexible search criteria demanded by the scenarios described in the previous paragraph, Access allows us to use wildcard characters in combination with the parameter criteria in Figure 5.29. For example, suppose we want to have the flexibility to conduct employee name searches subject to these conditions:

- First name unknown; last name known.
- Last name unknown; first name known.
- Both first name and last name unknown.
- Both first name and last name known.
- Only portions of the first and/or last names are known. (For example, we may know that the last name has "Smith" in it, but the last name may be Smithson, Wordsmith, Torsmithen, and so on. Or we may know that the first name contains "Robert", but it may be Roberto, or any other first name containing "Robert".

We can produce the required capability by substituting the parameter requests

```
LIKE "*" & [ENTER THE LAST NAME: ] & "*"
```

and

```
LIKE "*" & [ENTER THE FIRST NAME: ] & "*"
```

into Figure 5.29's EMP_LNAME and EMP_FNAME criteria. These modifications are shown in Figure 5.29A.

FIGURE 5.28
The Enter Parameter Value Dialog Box

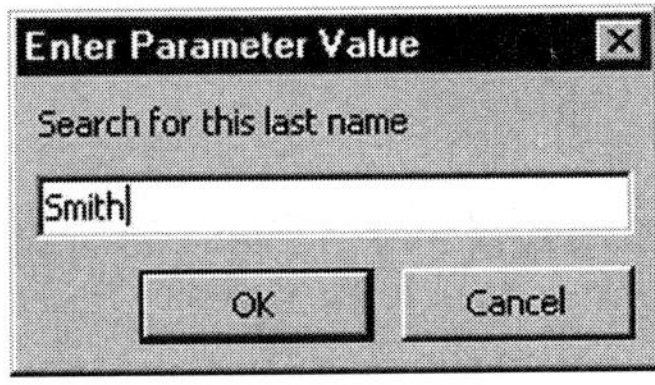

FIGURE 5.29
Generating a Second Parameter Dialog Box

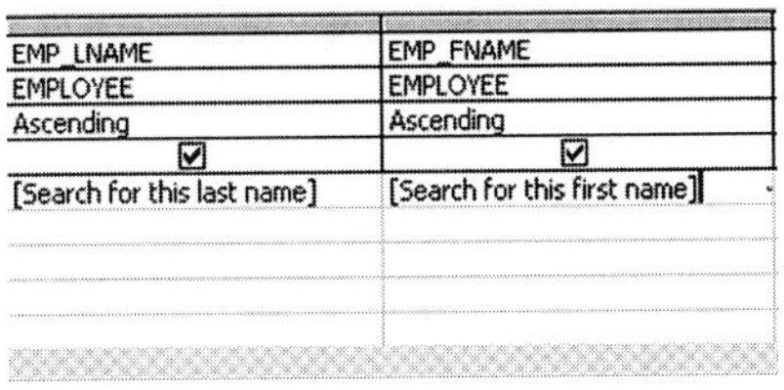

EMP_LNAME	EMP_FNAME
EMPLOYEE	EMPLOYEE
Ascending	Ascending
☑	☑
[Search for this last name]	[Search for this first name]

Assignment

Modify the query containing the two parameters criteria in Figure 5.29 by substituting the two parameters criteria we have just discussed. Save the changes and then run the query several times, using the following dialog box inputs:

- Enter Smith in the **Last Name** dialog box and make no entry in the **First Name** dialog box.
- Make no entry in the **Last Name** dialog box and enter Robert in the **First Name** dialog box.
- Enter Smith in the **Last Name** dialog box and enter Robert in the **First Name** dialog box.
- Make no entry in either dialog box; that is, just press the Enter key each time.

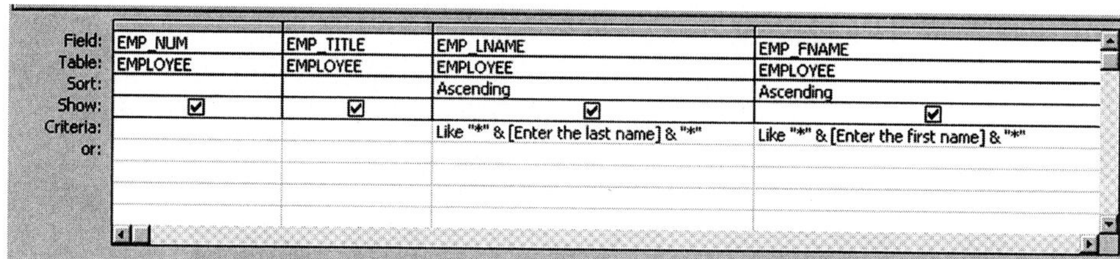

FIGURE 5.29A
Segmented Search Parameters

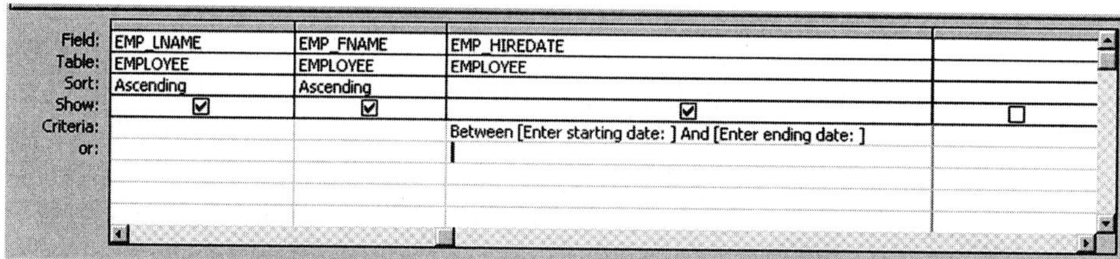

FIGURE 5.30
Generating Parameter Dialog Boxes for Date Constraints

Parameter Constraints Based on Nonstring Criteria

Thus far we have limited our examination of parameters to strings. However, you can place any kind of constraint on any nonstring fields such as date fields, money fields, numeric fields, and so on. You can even use *multiple* logical criteria within the *same* field. And you can do all of this with dialog boxes.

For example, suppose you want to get a listing of employees who were hired between January 1, 1998, and May 2, 2002. Let's examine how this query can be designed by looking at Figure 5.30. (Note that the query design includes the fields EMP_LNAME, EMP_FNAME, and EMP_HIREDATE, but that the constraints are placed on the EMP_HIREDATE.)

Executing the query shown in Figure 5.30 produces the dialog boxes shown in Figures 5.31 and 5.31A. (Because the output format is determined at the table level, the date input ranges may also be typed as 1/1/98 and 5/2/02 or 01-Jan-1998 and 02-May-2002 to produce the same output.)

FIGURE 5.31
The Dialog Box for Entering a Starting Date

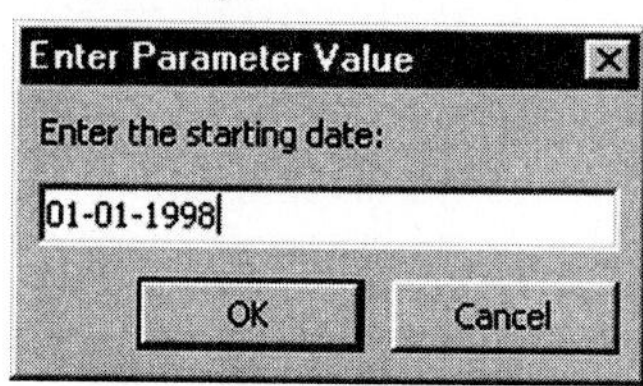

FIGURE 5.31A
The Dialog Box for Entering an Ending Date

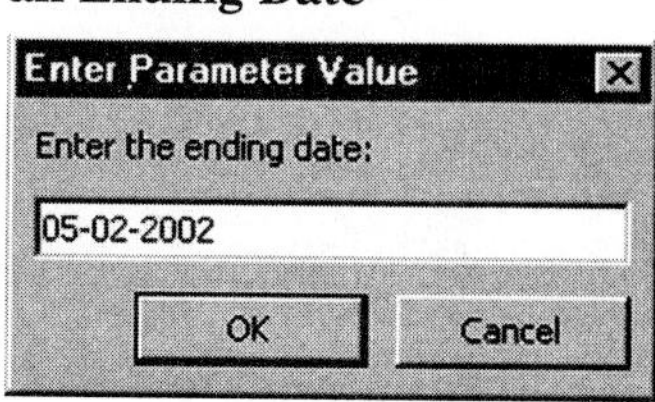

FIGURE 5.32
The Output for the Specified Date Range

EMP_NUM	Title	Last Name	First Name	EMP_HIREDATE
18	Ms.	Bahint	Elizabeth	08-Jan-1999
45	Mr.	Blalock	James	08-Aug-2001
49	Ms.	Doornberg	Anne	06-May-1999
52	Ms.	Downes	Anne	02-Feb-1998
17	Ms.	Dubrien	Susanna	01-Sep-1999
39	Mr.	Okomoto	Ronald	01-Aug-1999
47	Mr.	Smith	Robert	01-Jul-1999
41	Mr.	Smith	Robert	02-Feb-2002
44	Mr.	Smithson	George	01-Sep-2001
51	Mr.	Williamson	Charles	04-Apr-1998
(AutoNumber)				30-Oct-2002

The query yields the eight records shown in Figure 5.32. Note that all the records shown in Figure 5.32 have EMP_HIREDATE values that fall within the date range specified in Figures 5.31 and 5.31A. (Remember that the names in the original query were sorted by last name, first name, and initial. If you check the original EMPLOYEE table that you used in this query, you'll see that the two Robert Smith output lines reflect the results for Robert A. Smith, employee number 41 and Robert E. Smith, employee number 47. The **(Autonumber)** line reflects the default date that was current when the output was generated. As you can tell, we generated this output on October 30, 2002.)

Mathematical Delimiters

We used a logical constraint format based on SQL's **Between . . . And** in Figure 5.30. We wrote the constraint limits this way:

```
BETWEEN [ENTER STARTING DATE: ] AND [ENTER ENDING DATE: ]
```

(Incidentally, the two date limits are *inclusive* when you use this SQL-based set of constraints.) The constraints may also be written with the help of the mathematical delimiters shown in Table 5.1.

The date constraints shown in Figure 5.33 use the mathematical delimiters. (Note that strings are enclosed in quotes and dates are placed between # markers.)

Naturally, if you want the end user to have more flexibility in choosing the date constraints, you can use criteria entered via dialog boxes, just as you did in the sequence illustrated in Figures 5.30 through 5.31A. For example, you may use mathematical delimiters to write Figure 5.33's **Criteria** as

```
>= [ENTER THE STATING DATE: ] AND <= [ENTER THE ENDING DATE: ]
```

TABLE 5.1 Mathematical Delimiters and Their Meaning

Delimiter	Meaning
=	Equal to
<	Less than
<=	Less than or equal to
>	Greater than
>=	Greater than or equal to
<>	Not equal to

FIGURE 5.33
Date Constraints Based on Mathematical Delimiters

Field:	EMP_NUM	EMP_TITLE	EMP_LNAME	EMP_FNAME	EMP_HIREDATE	
Table:	EMPLOYEE	EMPLOYEE	EMPLOYEE	EMPLOYEE	EMPLOYEE	
Sort:			Ascending	Ascending		
Show:	☑	☑	☑	☑	☑	☐
Criteria:					>=#01-01-98# And <=#05-02-02#	
or:						

Note

The output shown in Figure 5.37 is based on the EMP_YEARS restriction. The EMP_YEARS values will change as time marches on. In fact, if you run an update query based on the current date (we'll show you how later) the EMP_YEARS values will change and, therefore, the number of records shown will change.

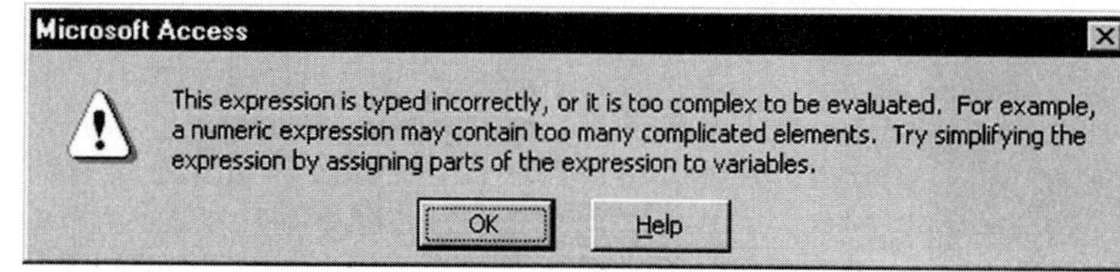

FIGURE 5.34
An Improper Date Entry Error Message

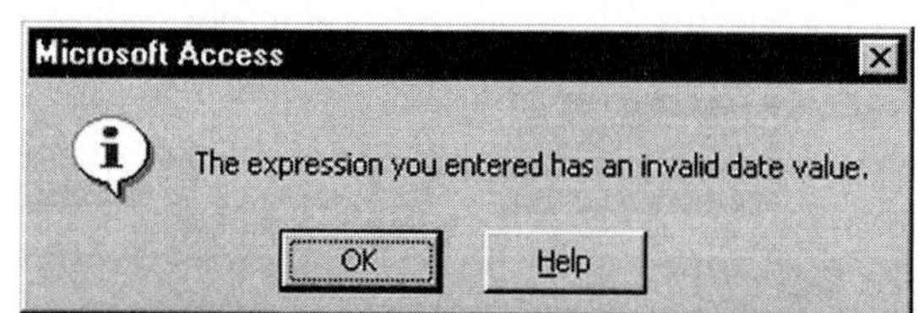

FIGURE 5.35
A Date-specific Error Message

to generate two date entry dialog boxes. Incidentally, Access will warn you when you are making improper entries. For example, try entering 02/30/2002 in the second dialog box. Because there is no February 30, Access will display the error message box shown in Figure 5.34.

The error message in Figure 5.34 covers a range of possible errors because the criteria are based on multiple constraints. If you had used a simple constraint such as <= **#02/30/2002#**, Access would have zeroed in on the problem by writing the date error message shown in Figure 5.35.

You can use the mathematical delimiters in Table 5.1 on any numeric field. For example, if you enter the fields and the criteria shown in Figure 5.36, you will generate the output shown in Figure 5.37.

Checking for Nulls

You may check for nulls with the **Is Null** function. (Remember that a null is *not* a blank. You would check for a blank by placing a blank between two quotes. In short, to look for blanks, you specify the delimiter "" in the QBE grid's criteria section.)

To generate a list of employees who do not have a middle initial, that is, whose middle initial is null, use the delimiter **Is Null** in the QBE grid's criteria for the EMP_INITIAL field (see Figure 5.38).

FIGURE 5.36
Mathematical Delimiters Placed on EMP_YEARS

Field:	EMP_NUM	EMP_TITLE	EMP_LNAME	EMP_FNAME	EMP_HIREDATE	EMP_YEARS
Table:	EMPLOYEE	EMPLOYEE	EMPLOYEE	EMPLOYEE	EMPLOYEE	EMPLOYEE
Sort:			Ascending	Ascending		
Show:	☑	☑	☑	☑	☑	☑
Criteria:						>=10 And <=15
or:						

FIGURE 5.37
Query Output for the Criteria in Figure 5.36

EMP_NUM	EMP_TITLE	EMP_LNAME	EMP_FNAME	EMP_HIREDATE	EMP_YEARS
3	Mr.	Donelly	Ronald	01-Jul-1987	15
2	Ms.	Edwards	Rosemary	23-Jul-1990	12
26	Mrs.	Herndon	Jill	18-Aug-1990	12
33	Mr.	Kruse	Herman	01-Aug-1988	14
30	Mr.	Orlando	Carlos	01-Aug-1988	14
37	Mr.	Orlof	Karl	01-Aug-1989	13
31	Ms.	Page	Katheryn	15-Dec-1986	15
22	Mr.	Smith	Robert	01-Aug-1992	10
8	Mr.	Thiako	Van	01-Aug-1989	13
4	Mr.	Thieu	Frederick	01-May-1992	10
25	Ms.	Williamson	Kathryn	15-Jun-1992	10
13	Mr.	Wilson	Todd	06-Nov-1990	11
(AutoNumber)				30-Oct-2002	0

FIGURE 5.38
Using the Is Null Delimiter

Field:	EMP_NUM	EMP_INITIAL	EMP_LNAME	EMP_FNAME	EMP_HIREDATE	EMP_YEARS
Table:	EMPLOYEE	EMPLOYEE	EMPLOYEE	EMPLOYEE	EMPLOYEE	EMPLOYEE
Sort:						
Show:	☑	☑	☑	☑	☑	☑
Criteria:		Is Null				<=20
or:						

FIGURE 5.39
Query Output for the Delimiters in Figure 5.38

EMP_NUM	EMP_INITIAL	EMP_LNAME	EMP_FNAME	EMP_HIREDATE	EMP_YEARS
3		Blalock	Andrew	12-Nov-1996	5
35		Jones	Hermine	01-Jan-1985	17
51		Williamson	Charles	04-Apr-1998	4
52		Downes	Anne	02-Feb-1998	4
(AutoNumber)				30-Oct-2002	0

As you examine Figure 5.38, note that we have combined the EMP_INITIAL field's **Is Null** limitation with a mathematical delimiter placed in the EMP_YEARS field criteria. In SQL terms, this placement of delimiters places the logical output limitation

```
WHERE EMPLOYEE.EMP_INITIAL IS NULL AND EMPLOYEE.EMP_YEARS <= 20
```

on the query output, shown in Figure 5.39.

5.2.6 Date Input and Output Formatting

In section 5.2.3 we showed you how to produce more attractive headers for the query output. Using the techniques based on Figures 5.13, 5.14, and 5.15, you can also control the presentation format for numerical fields and money fields. Such formatting is useful because the reports that will be based on such queries will inherit the query presentation formats, thus eliminating at least *some* output formatting work at the report level.

As useful as the presentation format is, output format has other functions. In fact, some query input/output (I/O) formatting turns out to be essential if the queries are to yield the information required by your end users. For example, suppose you want to find employee birthdays by month. Clearly, it would be useful to list the actual month *names*. For example, an end user is likely to prefer Nov or November to that month's number, 11. Similarly, June is likely to be preferred over that month's number, 06. To meet such format requirements, Access lets you use a format function to control both month input and output.

To illustrate the use of Access's format functions, let's use the EMPLOYEE table's date of birth (EMP_DOB) as the basis for the following queries. We begin by creating a select query, using the EMPLOYEE table as the QBE data source. Then drag the fields shown in Figure 5.40 to the QBE grid.

Note that the format statement

```
MONTH: FORMAT([EMP_DOB],"mm")
```

FIGURE 5.40
Month Number Format

Field:	Month: Format([EMP_DOB],"mm")	EMP_DOB	EMP_LNAME	EMP_FNAME	
Table:		EMPLOYEE	EMPLOYEE	EMPLOYEE	
Sort:					
Show:	☑	☑	☑	☑	☐
Criteria:					
or:					

shown in Figure 5.40 uses "**mm**" to generate the month *number* shown in the (partial) output presented in Figure 5.41.

If the query format in Figure 5.40 is changed to

```
Month: Format([EMP_DOB],"mmm")
```

the output is altered as shown in Figure 5.42.

If the query format in Figure 5.39 is changed to

```
Month: Format([EMP_DOB],"mmmm")
```

the output is altered as shown in Figure 5.43.

Incidentally, the four-m format "**mmmm**" will show the 11th month as November, the 5th month as May, and the 8th month as August. In short, using the format "**mmmm**" does not limit the output to four characters. (If you use the five-m format "**mmmmm**", the output will show both the month and the day of that month; for example: November 23.)

Remember that the formatting does not generate the output. It only controls the output presentation. Therefore, the query still requires the presence of the actual field *and* any restrictions placed on the output presentation. For example, the QBE screen segment shown in Figure 5.44 includes the EMP_DOB's **Where** restriction, followed by its condition **Like "6/*/*"**. Keep in mind that the **Where** clause is *not* shown, so the **Show:** box is *not* marked with an X in Figure 5.44.

To make the query output presentation more flexible, the **Where** portion shown in the preceding QBE screen segment may be changed to the parameter format shown in Figure 5.45.

As you examine the parameter query segment in Figure 5.45, keep in mind that two conditions must be met:

1. The **Where** clause requires its own format statement, even though the original query segment *started* with a format statement. (The *only* change we've made is in the **Where** portion of the QBE screen.)
2. The **Show:** box is *not* activated. (Note that the box is not marked with an X.)

FIGURE 5.41
Partial Output for the Month Number Format

Month	EMP_DOB	Last Name	First Name
07	03-Jul-1953	Edwards	Rosemary
10	02-Oct-1952	Donelly	Ronald
02	23-Feb-1948	Thieu	Frederick
06	20-Jun-1961	Robertson	Elaine
08	12-Aug-1951	Thiako	Van
01	16-Jan-1966	Blalock	Andrew
03	18-Mar-1939	Graztevski	Mary
06	12-Jun-1950	Holms	Anne
10	19-Oct-1966	Wilson	Todd
12	30-Dec-1967	Jones	Suzanne
09	13-Sep-1943	Smithson	Elsa
03	12-Mar-1970	Ardano	James
01	09-Jan-1970	Dubrien	Susanna
12	19-Dec-1971	Bahint	Elizabeth
06	19-Jun-1955	Smith	Robert
06	20-Jun-1940	Odondo	Roberto
11	17-Nov-1968	Williamson	Kathryn

FIGURE 5.42
A Partial Output for the Month Letter Format

Month	EMP_DOB	Last Name	First Name
Jul	03-Jul-1953	Edwards	Rosemary
Oct	02-Oct-1952	Donelly	Ronald
Feb	23-Feb-1948	Thieu	Frederick
Jun	20-Jun-1961	Robertson	Elaine
Aug	12-Aug-1951	Thiako	Van
Jan	16-Jan-1966	Blalock	Andrew
Mar	18-Mar-1939	Graztevski	Mary
Jun	12-Jun-1950	Holms	Anne
Oct	19-Oct-1966	Wilson	Todd
Dec	30-Dec-1967	Jones	Suzanne
Sep	13-Sep-1943	Smithson	Elsa
Mar	12-Mar-1970	Ardano	James
Jan	09-Jan-1970	Dubrien	Susanna
Dec	19-Dec-1971	Bahint	Elizabeth
Jun	19-Jun-1955	Smith	Robert
Jun	20-Jun-1940	Odondo	Roberto
Nov	17-Nov-1968	Williamson	Kathryn

FIGURE 5.43
A Partial Output for the Full Month Name Format

Month	EMP_DOB	Last Name	First Name
July	03-Jul-1953	Edwards	Rosemary
October	02-Oct-1952	Donelly	Ronald
February	23-Feb-1948	Thieu	Frederick
June	20-Jun-1961	Robertson	Elaine
August	12-Aug-1951	Thiako	Van
January	16-Jan-1966	Blalock	Andrew
March	18-Mar-1939	Graztevski	Mary
June	12-Jun-1950	Holms	Anne
October	19-Oct-1966	Wilson	Todd
December	30-Dec-1967	Jones	Suzanne
September	13-Sep-1943	Smithson	Elsa
March	12-Mar-1970	Ardano	James
January	09-Jan-1970	Dubrien	Susanna
December	19-Dec-1971	Bahint	Elizabeth
June	19-Jun-1955	Smith	Robert
June	20-Jun-1940	Odondo	Roberto
November	17-Nov-1968	Williamson	Kathryn

FIGURE 5.44
Date Parameter and Month Formatting

Field:	Month: Format([EMP_DOB],"mmmm")	EMP_LNAME	EMP_FNAME	EMP_DOB	
Table:		EMPLOYEE	EMPLOYEE	EMPLOYEE	
Total:	Group By	Group By	Group By	Where	
Sort:					
Show:	☑	☑	☑	☐	☐
Criteria:				Like "6/*/*"	
or:					

FIGURE 5.45
Date Parameter Formatting for the Parameter Dialog Box

Field:	Month: Format([EMP_DOB],"mm")	EMP_DOB	EMP_LNAME	EMP_FNAME	Format([EMP_DOB],"mm")
Table:		EMPLOYEE	EMPLOYEE	EMPLOYEE	
Total:	Group By	Group By	Group By	Group By	Where
Sort:					
Show:	☑	☑	☑	☑	☐
Criteria:					[Enter a 2-digit month number such as 06 or 11]
or:					

To help the end user decide what to enter, we've written the parameter request as a prompt. Therefore, the parameter box in Figure 5.46 reflects the prompt in Figure 5.45 when the query is run. The two characters in the "**mm**" format statement require two-digit numeric month values such as 01, 02, 03, . . . 10, 11, and 12.

The two-digit numeric format is desirable because it allows month sorting in the proper order. Given the nature of the ASCII code, characters are evaluated starting from the left. Therefore, because the value 3 is larger than 1, ASCII-based sorting would yield the conclusion that 12 is less than 3, because 12 starts with a 1. However, 03 starts with a 0, which is less than 1, so 03 would properly be seen as less than 12. The parameter entry in Figure 5.46 specifying the month 11, that is, November, generates the output shown in Figure 5.47.

Keep in mind that the **Where** format controls only the *input* requirements, whereas the *initial* **Group By** format controls the *output* presentation. *Therefore, the two format statements need not match.* For example, we used an "mm" format in the parameter request and an "**mmmm**" in the preceding input/output presentation.

Naturally, we have the option of selecting a different input format. For example, if the **Where** clause format had been written as

```
Month: Format([EMP_DOB],"mmmm")
```

the parameter prompt would have to be rewritten to produce the parameter box shown in Figure 5.48.

The dialog box in Figure 5.48 reflects the following change to the parameter prompt in Figure 5.45:

```
[Enter the month _ example: February ]
```

FIGURE 5.46
The Parameter Box, Formatted for the Month Number

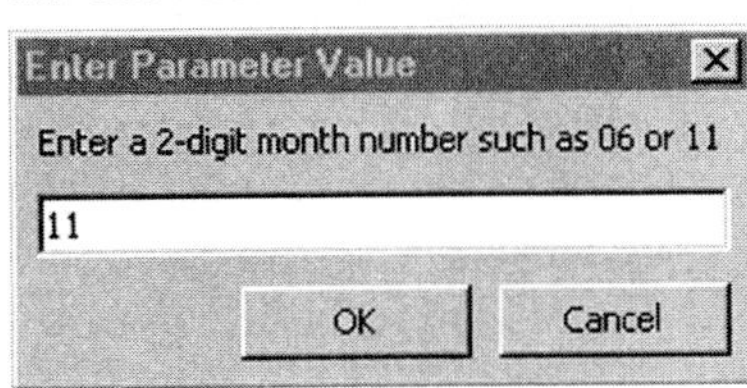

FIGURE 5.47
Query Output for the Date Parameter Input in Figure 5.46

Month	EMP_DOB	Last Name	First Name
11	17-Nov-1951	Teng	Weston
11	19-Nov-1955	Orlando	Carlos
11	26-Nov-1963	Zantaro	Sussette
11	17-Nov-1968	Williamson	Kathryn

FIGURE 5.48
The Parameter Box, Formatted for the Month Name

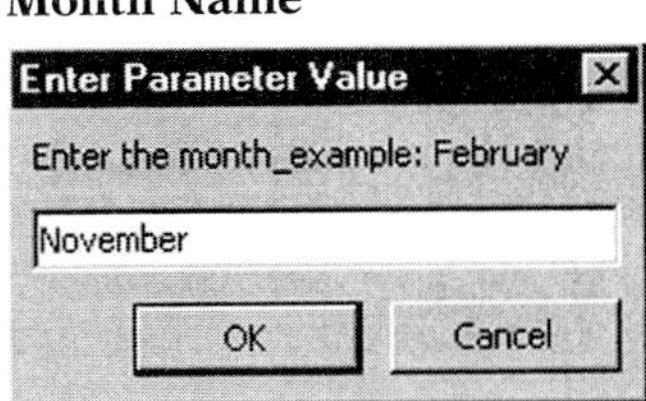

Note

The **Expr1:** and **Expr2:** labels are assigned by Access. You can, of course, change these labels with the help of the property box. (If necessary, review section 5.2.3 to see how that is done.)

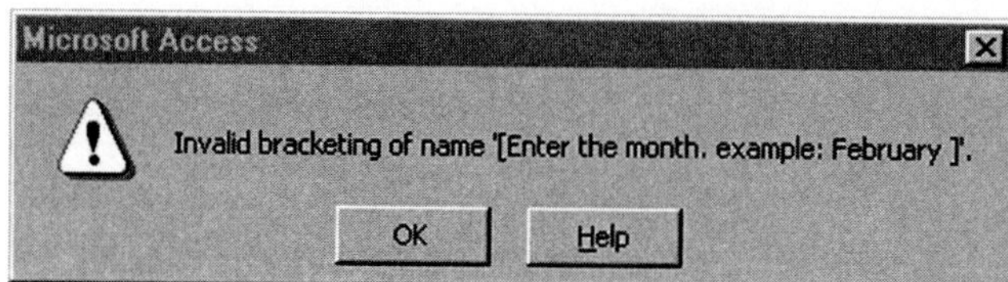

FIGURE 5.49
An Error Message Based on an Incorrect Parameter Prompt

This prompt helps the end user enter the correct information in the appropriate format. Incidentally, this format is *not* case sensitive, so the input **NOVEMBER** or **november** would have yielded the same output.

Remember that parameter prompting is subject to some restrictions. For example, if we had used a period in the prompt, writing it as

```
[Enter the month. Example: February ]
```

Access would have generated the error message shown in Figure 5.49.

Remember that string comparisons are made from left to right. Therefore, April, starting with an A, occurs before January, which starts with a J. Clearly, this property causes improper sort results by month. Fortunately, we can overcome this limitation by using the "**mm**" format to sort the month values *numerically,* after which we may control the output with either the "**mmm**" or "**mmmm**" format. (The month value for January is 01, the month value for February is 02, and so on.) Note that we have accomplished this output formatting task in Figure 5.50's QBE screen, using **Expr1:** to format the output.

Executing the query in Figure 5.50 yields the output shown (partially) in Figure 5.51. Note that we have used the properties box to modify the field headers and that the months are properly presented in ascending order.

Additional Date Formats

Years may also be formatted for input/output purposes. For example, to find out which employees were born in 1968, we can use the query format shown in Figure 5.52. Note that the formatting string now contains "**yyyy**", rather than "**mm**".

Figure 5.53 shows a portion of the output for the query in Figure 5.52. (Note again that we used the properties box to produce the **Year** header.)

Figure 5.54 shows that you may also format the EMP_DOB field for the day of the week.

The weekday format shown in Figure 5.54 yields the output shown in Figure 5.55. Note that the **Weekday** count begins at Sunday; that is, Sunday = 1, Monday = 2, Tuesday = 3, and so on.

FIGURE 5.50
Ensuring a Proper Month Sort through Formatting

Field:	Month: Format([EMP_DOB],"mm")	Expr1: Format([EMP_DOB],"mmmm")	EMP_DOB	EMP_LNAME
Table:			EMPLOYEE	EMPLOYEE
Total:	Group By	Group By	Group By	Group By
Sort:	Ascending			
Show:	☑	☑	☑	☑
Criteria:				
or:				

FIGURE 5.51
The Partial Query Output for Figure 5.50

Month	Month	EMP_DOB	Last Name	First Name
01	January	02-Jan-1955	Williamson	Charles
01	January	16-Jan-1966	Blalock	Andrew
01	January	09-Jan-1970	Dubrien	Susanna
02	February	23-Feb-1948	Thieu	Frederick
02	February	02-Feb-1960	Smith	Robert
03	March	18-Mar-1939	Graztevski	Mary
03	March	03-Mar-1944	Okomoto	Ronald
03	March	15-Mar-1945	Blalock	James
03	March	18-Mar-1960	Downes	Anne
03	March	12-Mar-1970	Ardano	James
05	May	24-May-1946	Smith	Melanie
05	May	16-May-1949	Kruse	Herman
05	May	25-May-1952	Orlof	Karl
05	May	17-May-1953	Dexter	Willa
06	June	20-Jun-1940	Odondo	Roberto
06	June	12-Jun-1950	Holms	Anne
06	June	19-Jun-1955	Smith	Robert
06	June	20-Jun-1961	Robertson	Elaine
07	July	04-Jul-1950	Jones	Hermine
07	July	03-Jul-1953	Edwards	Rosemary

FIGURE 5.52
Year Formatting

Field:	Year: Format([EMP_DOB],"yyyy")	Month: Format([EMP_DOB],"mmmm"	EMP_DOB	EMP_LNAME	EMP_FNAME
Table:			EMPLOYEE	EMPLOYEE	EMPLOYEE
Total:	Group By	Group By	Group By	Group By	Group By
Sort:	Ascending				
Show:	☑	☑	☑	☑	☑
Criteria:					
or:					

FIGURE 5.53
Year-formatted Query Output

Year	Month	EMP_DOB	Last Name	First Name
1939	March	18-Mar-1939	Graztevski	Mary
1940	June	20-Jun-1940	Odondo	Roberto
1943	September	13-Sep-1943	Smithson	Elsa
1944	March	03-Mar-1944	Okomoto	Ronald
1945	March	15-Mar-1945	Blalock	James
1946	May	24-May-1946	Smith	Melanie
1948	February	23-Feb-1948	Thieu	Frederick
1948	October	01-Oct-1948	Smithson	George
1949	May	16-May-1949	Kruse	Herman
1950	July	04-Jul-1950	Jones	Hermine
1950	June	12-Jun-1950	Holms	Anne
1951	August	12-Aug-1951	Thiako	Van
1951	November	17-Nov-1951	Teng	Weston
1952	May	25-May-1952	Orlof	Karl
1952	October	02-Oct-1952	Donelly	Ronald
1953	July	03-Jul-1953	Edwards	Rosemary
1953	May	17-May-1953	Dexter	Willa
1955	January	02-Jan-1955	Williamson	Charles
1955	June	19-Jun-1955	Smith	Robert
1955	November	19-Nov-1955	Orlando	Carlos

FIGURE 5.54
Weekday Formatting

Field:	Weekday: Format([EMP_DOB],"w")	Month: Format([EMP_DOB],"mmmm")	EMP_DOB	EMP_LNAME	EMP_FN
Table:			EMPLOYEE	EMPLOYEE	EMPLOY
Total:	Group By	Group By	Group By	Group By	Group B
Sort:	Ascending				
Show:	☑	☑	☑	☑	
Criteria:					
or:					

In fact, Access has numerous date format options. For example, if you substitute the format option

```
Day: Format([EMP_DOB],"d")
```

in Figure 5.54's first QBE grid column, the output in Figure 5.55 would show the actual *day* portion of the date. For example, if the EMP_DOB value is Sunday, August 12, 1951, the **Weekday** column would show the value **12.** If you modified the format option to read

```
Day: Format([EMP_DOB],"dddd")
```

Assignment

Click on each option in the Expression Builder screen to see what is available. (For example, to examine the third column's **Day** function, put the cursor on it and then click to place the item into the work area.) Clear the work area each time you have completed your examination. Check all of the Expression Builder's buttons to see what they do. After you have examined the available options and you have a working knowledge of the Expression Builder's environment, click the **Cancel** button to return to your QBE screen without saving any of your experiments.

Next open the query shown in Figure 5.54, click on the Criteria line under the EMP_YEARS, delete the current **Criteria** value, and then right-click to open the Expression Builder. Use the buttons below the work area to rebuild the criteria. Do *not* type the components >, =, **And**, <, and =. Just use the buttons! Click **OK** to save the entry when you have correctly entered **>= 10 And <= 15**.

FIGURE 5.55
The Weekday Format Output

Week	Month	Birth Date	Last Name	First Name
1	August	12-Aug-1951	Thiako	Van
1	August	29-Aug-1965	Herndon	Jill
1	December	19-Dec-1971	Bahint	Elizabeth
1	January	02-Jan-1955	Williamson	Charles
1	January	16-Jan-1966	Blalock	Andrew
1	July	19-Jul-1959	Page	Katheryn
1	June	19-Jun-1955	Smith	Robert
1	May	25-May-1952	Orlof	Karl
1	May	17-May-1953	Dexter	Willa
1	November	17-Nov-1968	Williamson	Kathryn
2	February	23-Feb-1948	Thieu	Frederick
2	June	12-Jun-1950	Holms	Anne
2	May	16-May-1949	Kruse	Herman
2	September	13-Sep-1943	Smithson	Elsa
3	February	02-Feb-1960	Smith	Robert
3	July	04-Jul-1950	Jones	Hermine
3	June	20-Jun-1961	Robertson	Elaine
3	November	26-Nov-1963	Zantaro	Sussette
4	October	02-Oct-1963	Doornberg	Anne
4	October	19-Oct-1966	Wilson	Todd

the **Weekday** column would show the value **Sunday**. (Naturally, you would see a different output list *order* than the one shown in Figure 5.55 because the sort is performed on a different date characteristic!)

You can investigate all date options by using the Expression Builder while you are working on the query design. To see which build options are available for any QBE grid field, click on it and then right-click to produce the menu shown in Figure 5.56.

Select the **Build...** option to display the Expression Builder screen shown in Figure 5.57. Note that the current date format field option is listed in the Expression Builder's work area. To select other build options, just delete the text in the work area.

FIGURE 5.56
Field Options

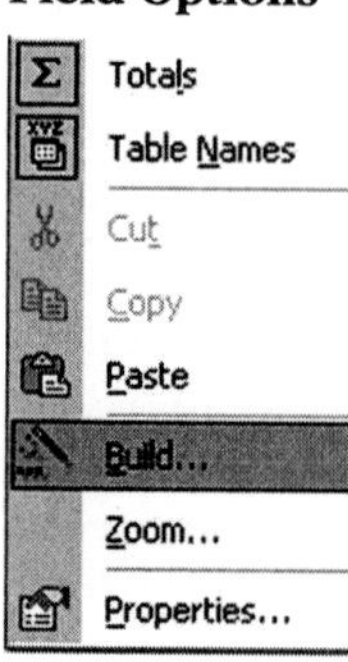

To see which functions are available, double-click on the **Functions** option shown in Figure 5.57 and then click on the function you want to use. In this example, we selected the **Date/Time** option shown in Figure 5.58.

When you start building more complex functions, you will discover that the Expression Builder is one of the most useful tools available to you. From now on, use it whenever you need to establish criteria, create a format, and so on. Use it even if you intend to type the simplest functions, constraints, and so on. For example, rather than entering

```
Year: Format([EMP-DOB],"yyyy")
```

in Figure 5.52's **Field** value, click on the (initially empty) field, right-click to open the Expression Builder, and then create the field format shown in the work area in Figure 5.59.

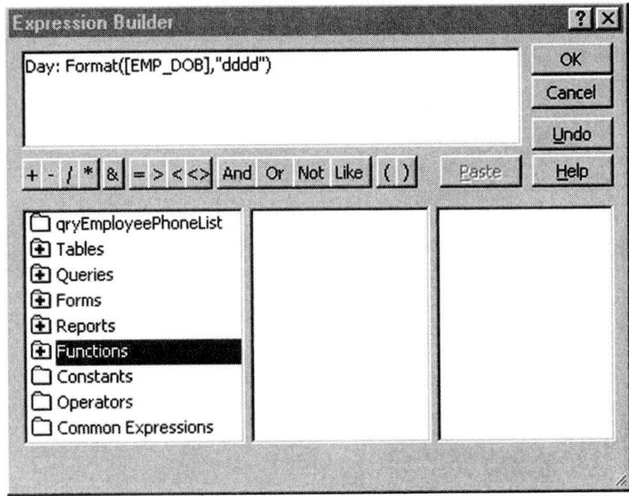

FIGURE 5.57
The Expression Builder Opening Screen

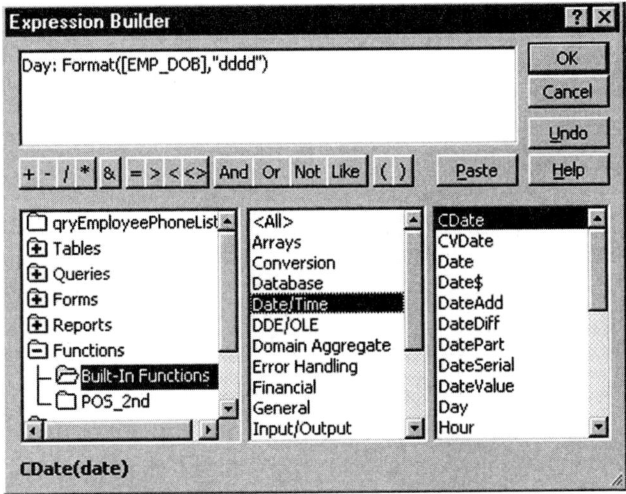

FIGURE 5.58
The Expression Builder's Function Selection Options

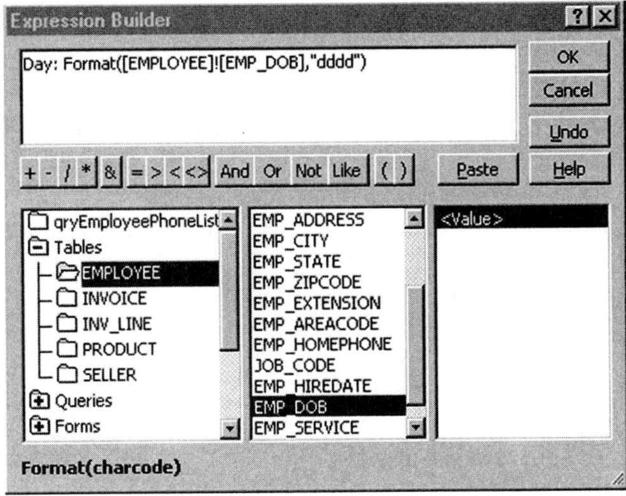

FIGURE 5.59
Using the Expression Builder to Format a Field

To produce the results shown in Figure 5.59, follow these steps:

1. Type **Format**.
2. Click on the (button. This action will produce the entry <<**Expre**>> to indicate that the Expression Builder expected to see a function before the parenthesis. Because we will not be using a function, delete the <<**Expre**>> portion and then continue with step 3.
3. Double-click on the **Tables** option in the first column below the work area and then double-click the EMPLOYEE table to produce the field list in the second column.
4. Scroll down the field list until you see the EMP_DOB; then double-click on it to move it to the work area. Note that the Expression Builder automatically added the field's location, the EMPLOYEE table, to the work area. The **[EMPLOYEE]![EMP_DOB]** entry is more precise than just the **[EMP_DOB]** that we used before. (Note the format. The EMPLOYEE table is enclosed in square brackets, as is the EMP_CODE field. The exclamation point separates the components. Such notation is standard, and you will see it in all complex Access objects.)
5. Type the comma to put the comma after the **]** bracket.
6. Type the segment "**yyyy**".
7. Click on the right parenthesis) button
8. Click **OK** to save the expression and move it to the **Query** field header.

Although it seems easier *at this point* to just type the relatively simple entries, getting used to the Expression Builder is a very worthwhile exercise. By the time you get to the more complex form- and macro-building activities, you'll discover how valuable your experience will be.

5.2.7 Queries Based on Multiple Sources

Thus far we have examined only single table queries. However, to get the best-structured and most comprehensive information out of the database, we usually wind up using multiple tables. We may use the results of other queries that may themselves be based on multiple tables. We can even mix queries and tables as data sources for yet other queries. In short, Access makes it possible to produce comprehensive information. If it's in the database, we can get it out in almost any desired format.

Queries Based on Multiple Tables

If you take another look at Figure 5.21, you'll note that the job code counts are correct. But you'll also note that the output is difficult to interpret. For example, just what might job code 3 mean? (There sure seem to be a lot of those around!) If we can get the job code descriptions into the output, the results would be much easier to interpret. Fortunately, we can use multiple tables and their relationships to get the job done.

To modify the **qryEmployeeCountByJobCode** query whose output was shown in Figure 5.21, open the query in the design format and then add the JOB_CLASS table to the QBE's data source area. (Remember: Right-click on an open spot in the data source area to produce the menu we showed in Figure 5.5 and then select the **Show Table** option.) If you did not save the query before, create it from scratch by selecting the **New** button on the database window's query folder. Then select both the EMPLOYEE and the JOB_CLASS from the **Show Table** window. Finally, select the fields from the two tables as shown in Figure 5.60.

As you examine Figure 5.60, note that it includes the relationship line between the two tables. The existence of this relationship line indicates that the relationships you established at the table level in Chapter 4 are inherited by the multitable query. Also, note that the relationship line shown in Figure 5.60 indicates

FIGURE 5.60
The QBE Design for the Two-table Query

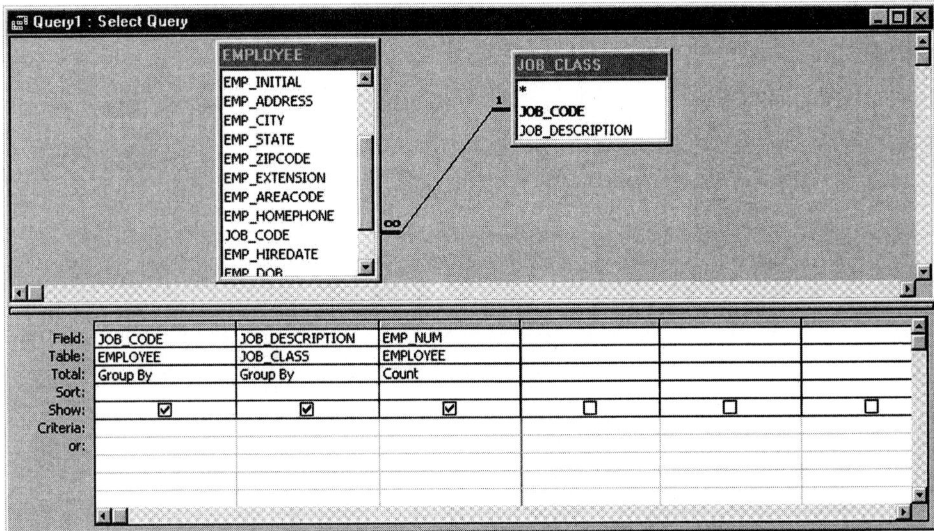

enforcement of referential integrity. (Review section 4.9.1 if necessary.) If your query screen lacks this relationship line, you have two options:

1. Return to the database window and then select the **Relationships** button to move to the **Relationships** screen. Create the desired relationship.
2. Create the relationship at the query level (shown in Figure 5.60) by dragging the JOB_CODE in the JOB_CLASS table to the JOB_CODE in the EMPLOYEE table. (If the EMPLOYEE table's JOB_CODE is not visible, scroll down the EMPLOYEE table until you can see it.) However, you will note that the relationship line created at the query level does not enforce referential integrity.

Save the query shown in Figure 5.60 and then run it to produce the output shown in Figure 5.61. Note how much easier it is to read this output compared to the output shown in Figure 5.21. (If you have not yet used the Field Properties box to produce the column headers, return to the design stage and follow the directions we gave you with the help of Figures 5.13 and 5.14.)

Queries Based on Other Queries

Queries may be based on other queries and combinations of tables and queries, so you will have a lot of flexibility when you need to draw information out of your database. For example, you may report the total employee count via the query that produced Figure 5.61's output. In this case, start the new query and then click on the **Queries** folder to display the available queries in Figure 5.61A's **Show Table** dialog box. (Your query list will not look like the one shown here, because Figure 5.61A only includes the queries that are necessary to illustrate this

FIGURE 5.61
Output for the Query Design in Figure 5.60

Job Code	Job Description	Employee Count
1	General Manager	1
2	Sales Director	1
3	Sales Rep	16
4	Shipping Supervisor	1
5	Shipping Clerk	4
6	Chief Accountant	1
7	Accountant	2
8	Tech Support Manager	1
9	Tech Support Rep	2
10	Personnel Manager	1
11	Human Resource Spec	1
12	Secretary	2
13	Clerk	2
14	Janitor	1

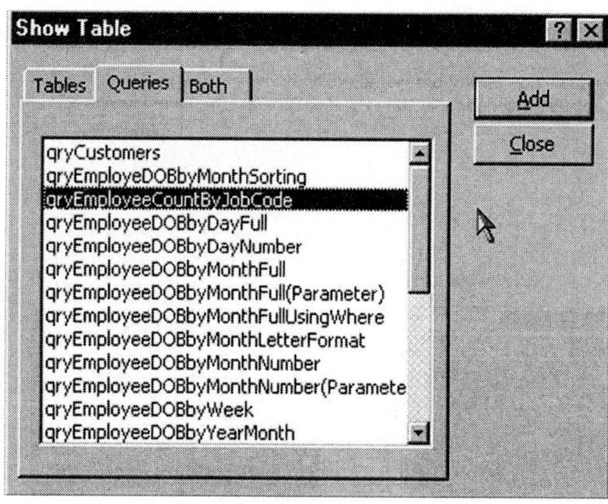

FIGURE 5.61A
Selecting a Query as the Data Source

section's query process. Because you have probably created all the queries in the preceding sections, your query list is far more extensive than the query list shown in Figure 5.61A.)

Selecting the query marked in the **Show Table** dialog box puts the query into the QBE data area. Next drag the desired query components to the QBE grid and drop them, just as you would do if you were working with a table. In fact, all of the familiar query-building actions and features are still available. Therefore, to get the total number of employees, select the **Group By** option and then select **Sum** from the option list to produce the results shown in Figure 5.61B. Note that although the QBE grid still says **Table**, it lists the **qryEmployeeCountByJobCode** as the data source.

Use the properties box to edit the header, thus producing the output shown in Figure 5.61C.

Using queries that are based on queries turns out to be a prime information management tool. For example, suppose that you are using the **Ch05_Store_Co** database and you want to know the details of the store and employee sales performance. Such details are not stored in the tables; instead, they are generated by so-called *nested queries*. The term **nested query** is derived from the structure of the SQL command set in which a query is executed on the query results that are

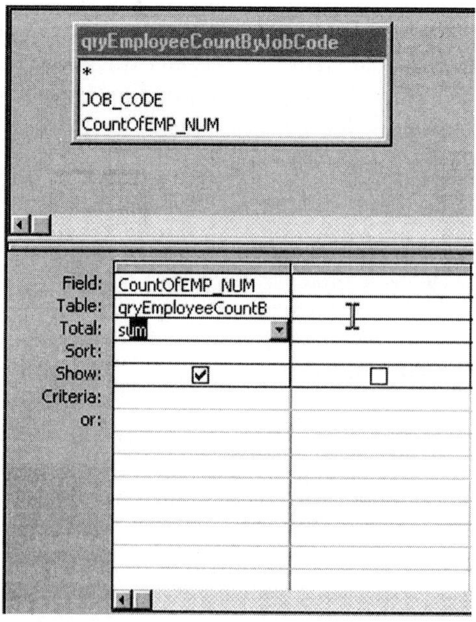

FIGURE 5.61B
QBE Screen for the Employee Count Query

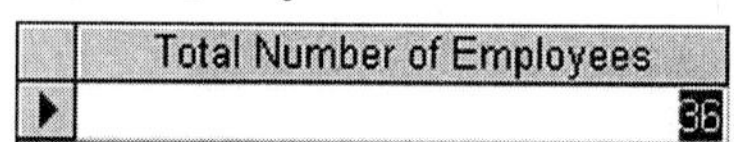

FIGURE 5.61C
Output for the Employee Count Query

FIGURE 5.61D The qryTotalSalesPerStoreAndPerEmployee Query in Design Format

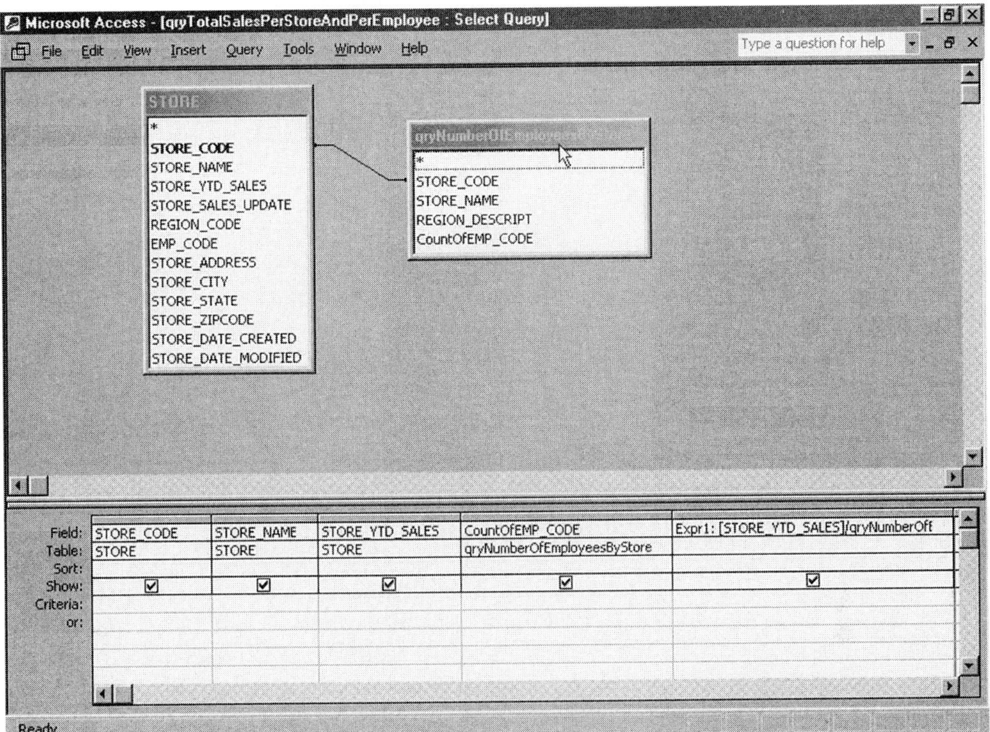

obtained by another query. If you are curious about the SQL syntax of a nested query, here is an example:

```
SELECT <Attribute(S)>
    FROM <Source>
        WHERE <Attribute =
            (SELECT <Attribute> FROM <Source>);
```

Because Access generates the SQL commands for you, you need to remember only that a nested query is simply a query based on the results of another query. After this aside, let's return to the question we are trying to answer: What are the average sales per employee for each store? To find the answer to this question, let's first lay out the arithmetic procedure:

1. Find the number of employees in each store.
2. Find the total sales in each store.
3. Divide the total sales in each store by the number of employees in each store.

You already know how to use the **Count** function to find the number of employees in each store. As you examine Figure 5.61D, note that the employee count is generated by the query named **qryNumberOfEmployeesByStore**. Each store's year-to-date sales value (STORE_YTD_SALES) is found in the STORE table.

As you examine Figure 5.61D, note that the **CountOfEMP_CODE** value was dragged to the QBE header from the query named **qryNumberOfEmployeesByStore**. The division of the store sales by the employee count is done in the last QBE column. If you want to enlarge this segment, use the **Zoom** option from the QBE field property (see Figure 5.61E). To generate the screen shown in Figure 5.61E, place the cursor on the QBE field—in this example, the **Expr1:** field—then right-click.

When you select the **Zoom** option shown in Figure 5.61E, you'll see the screen in Figure 5.61F. The **Expr1:** components are now much easier to read. (You

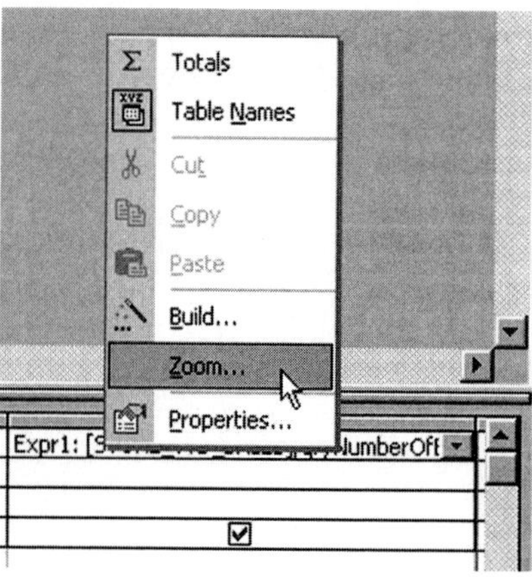

FIGURE 5.61E
Generating the Zoom Format for a QBE Field

can, of course, also use the Expression Builder to get a better view of the field contents.)

If you open the query you first saw in Figure 5.61D, you will see the results in Figure 5.61G. Information generated by this nested query can be used to evaluate the relative sales efficiency of each store's employees.

Remember that your output format can be controlled via the Properties box for each of the QBE fields. For example, Figure 5.61H shows that the currency format can be selected for the STORE_YTD_SALES and the **Expr1:** results. (Actually, the STORE table's STORE_YTD_SALES should already be formatted as **Currency** when you design the STORE table.)

5.2.8 Queries Based on Outer Join Relationships

In section 4.9.5 of Chapter 4 we discussed why outer joins are important to those who manage the database contents. We used the VENDOR and PRODUCT tables in the **Ch04_Demo_2.mdb** database to show that referential integrity requirements could not be met. (The PRODUCT table contained several vendor codes that did not exist in the VENDOR table.) Because you now know the basics of query design, we can turn our attention to how such outer joins are created at the query design level. To make sure that each chapter has its own database set, we have made a copy of the original **Ch04_Demo_2.mdb** database and this copy is named **Ch05_Demo_2.mdb** for use in this chapter.

To produce the right outer join, start by loading the **Ch05_Demo_2.mdb** database and then place the VENDOR and PRODUCT tables in the query design mode. Next, drag and drop the fields into the QBE grid. Finally, create the equijoin relationship by dragging the VEND_NUM from the VENDOR table and dropping it on the VEND_NUM in the PRODUCT table. Figure 5.62 shows the

FIGURE 5.61F
The Expr1: Components

FIGURE 5.61G
The Nested Query Output

Store Code	Store Name	YTD Sales	Number of Employees	Sales Per Employee
1	Access Junction	$1,403,455.76	5	$280,691.15
2	Database Corner	$1,821,987.39	3	$607,329.13
3	Tuple Charge	$1,386,783.22	5	$277,356.64
4	Attribute Alley	$1,344,568.56	6	$224,094.76
5	Primary Key Point	$3,330,098.45	3	$1,110,032.82

FIGURE 5.61H
Selecting the Output Format

Field Properties

General | Lookup

Description
Format
Decimal Places
Input Mask
Caption

Format	Example
General Number	3456.789
Currency	$3,456.79
Euro	€3,456.79
Fixed	3456.79
Standard	3,456.79
Percent	123.00%
Scientific	3.46E+03

STORE_YTD_SALES	CountOfEMP_CODE	Expr1: [STORE_YTD
STORE	qryNumberOfEmplo	
☑	☑	☑

results of these actions. (Note that the relationship line's format indicates that the referential integrity requirement was not met.

To produce a right outer join, click on the relationship line shown in Figure 5.62 and then right-click to access the join edit menu shown in Figure 5.63.

Select the **Join Properties** option in Figure 5.63 to produce the **Join Properties** dialog box shown in Figure 5.64.

Select option 3 from the **Join Properties** dialog box in Figure 5.64 and then click **OK** to produce the right outer join shown in Figure 5.65. (Note that the relationship line's arrow head points to the VENDOR, which is the 1 side of the 1:M relationship.)

Save the query as **qryProductNoVendorMatch** and then run it to produce the output shown in Figure 5.65A.

The left outer join originally illustrated in Figure 4.81 can be created with the same query design screen we just examined. Save the previous query as **qryVendorNoProductMatch** and then edit the relationship (join) line as shown in Figures 5.63 and 5.64. This time, select option 2 in the **Join Properties** dialog box (see Figure 5.64) to produce the left outer join shown in Figure 5.66.

FIGURE 5.62
A Query Based on the VENDOR and PRODUCT Relationship

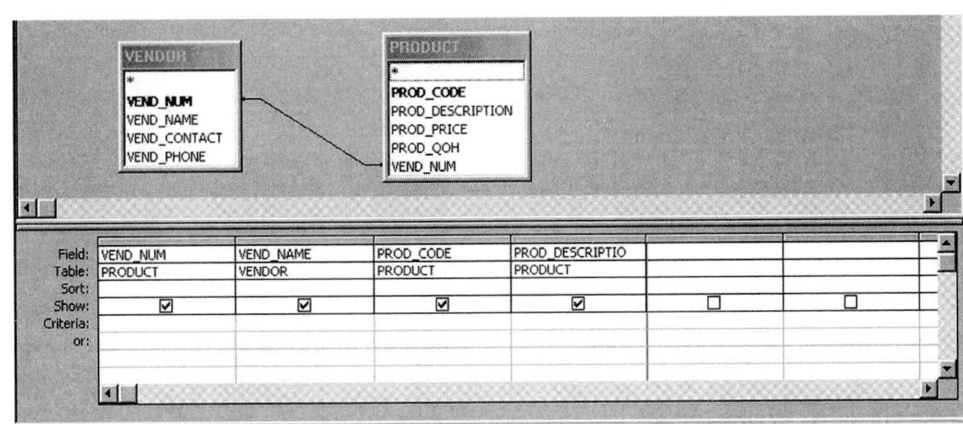

FIGURE 5.63
The Join Edit Option Menu

FIGURE 5.64 **The Join Properties Dialog Box**

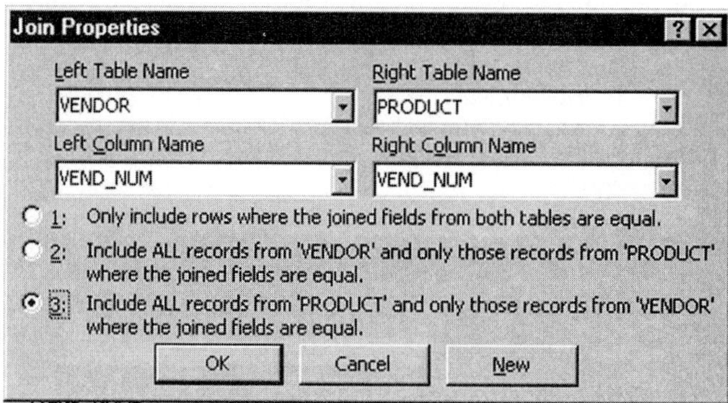

FIGURE 5.65
The Right Outer Join

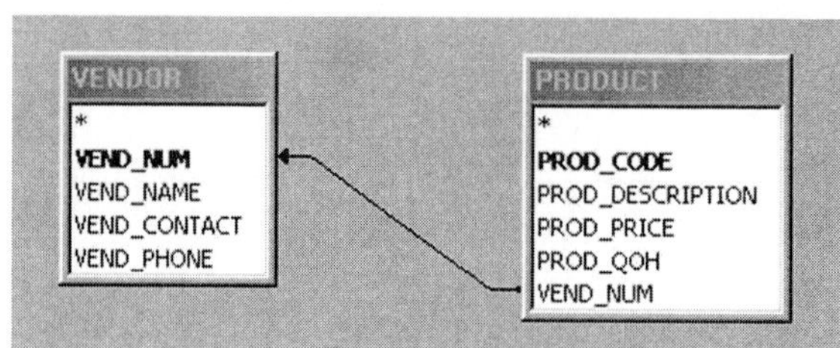

FIGURE 5.65A
The Right Outer Join Output

Microsoft Access - [qryProductNoVendorMatch : Select Query]

File Edit View Insert Format Records Tools Window Help

VEND_NUM	VEND_NAME	PROD_CODE	PROD_DESCRIPTION
		DRSUCR88MX	Removable cartridge, 88MB, Maxell
2	MooComp, Inc.	DRSUDI50-3M	3.5" HD/DS Diskettes, 1.44 MB formatted, IBM, 50/box, 3M
2	MooComp, Inc.	DRSUTC3490E	tape cartridge, 1,100ft, 36-track, AS400-3480-3490E
3	Gettum Supply	DRSUCR44MX	Removable cartridge, 44MB, Maxell
3	Gettum Supply	PRCTHPDJ56	HP DeskJet Plus, 500C, 550C, 600
5	Dill Computer, Inc.	COCBLPAR6	6 ft. parallel cable, shielded metal case
5	Dill Computer, Inc.	DRSUDI12-3M	3.5" HD/DS Diskettes, 1.44 MB formatted, IBM, 12/box, 3M
5	Dill Computer, Inc.	PRCTLEX4072	IBM (Lexmark) 4072 ExecJet cartridge
9		PRCTCANBC02	Canon color cartridge, BJ-100, 2200, 210, 230

FIGURE 5.66
The Left Outer Join

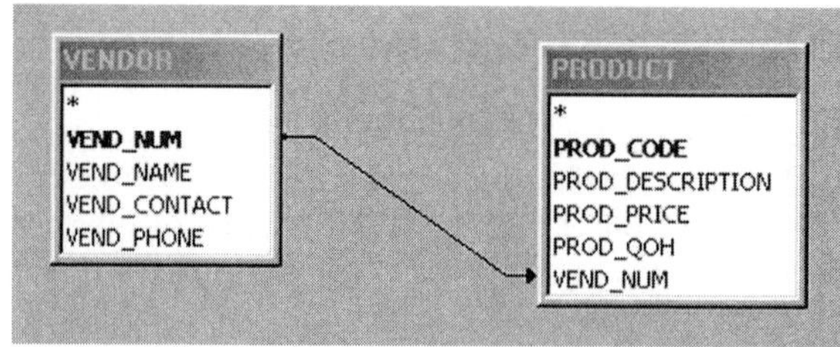

If you open the left outer join query, the output will look like Figure 5.66A.

Although the outer joins shown in Figures 5.65 and 5.66 are very useful, the output produced by these joins (see Figures 5.65A and 5.66A) may become unmanageable when you are working with large tables. It would be much better to report just the unmatched records, instead of all the records. Fortunately, outer join queries are easy to modify. For example, follow these steps to modify the **qryVendorNoProductMatch** (see Figure 5.66) to show its unmatched records:

1. Place the query in design mode.
2. Add the condition **Is Null** in the PROD_CODE's **Criteria** line.
3. Delete the no longer necessary PROD_DESCRIPTION field.

FIGURE 5.66A
The Left Outer Join Output

Microsoft Access - [qryVendorNoProductMatch : Select Query]

File Edit View Insert Format Records Tools Window Help

VEND_NUM	VEND_NAME	PROD_CODE	PROD_DESCRIPTION
1	CompuDark, Inc.		
2	MooComp, Inc.	DRSUDI50-3M	3.5" HD/DS Diskettes, 1.44 MB formatted, IBM, 50/box, 3M
2	MooComp, Inc.	DRSUTC3490E	tape cartridge, 1,100ft, 36-track, AS400-3480-3490E
3	Gettum Supply	DRSUCR44MX	Removable cartridge, 44MB, Maxell
3	Gettum Supply	PRCTHPDJ56	HP DeskJet Plus, 500C, 550C, 600
4	PC Country		
5	Dill Computer, Inc.	COCBLPAR6	6 ft. parallel cable, shielded metal case
5	Dill Computer, Inc.	DRSUDI12-3M	3.5" HD/DS Diskettes, 1.44 MB formatted, IBM, 12/box, 3M
5	Dill Computer, Inc.	PRCTLEX4072	IBM (Lexmark) 4072 ExecJet cartridge
6	Outeredge Supply		
7	Compuck, Inc.		
8	Toshboo Supply		
(AutoNumber)			

FIGURE 5.67
The Revised Left Outer Join Query

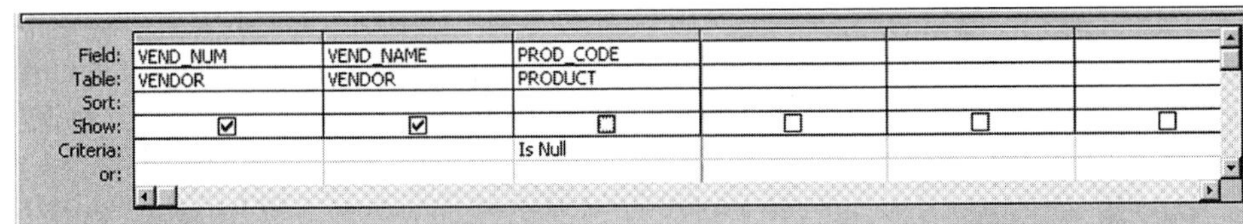

Field:	VEND_NUM	VEND_NAME	PROD_CODE			
Table:	VENDOR	VENDOR	PRODUCT			
Sort:						
Show:	☑	☑	☐	☐	☐	☐
Criteria:			Is Null			
or:						

4. Click off the PROD_CODE's **Show** check mark because you no longer need to show it.
5. Check the modified query's output by changing to datasheet view. Note that the output lists the vendors not found in the PRODUCT table.

The modified query and its output are shown in Figures 5.67 and 5.67A.

To save the modified query, use the **File/Save As** menu option. This option will preserve the original query and save the modified query by its new name. The **Save As** dialog box is shown in Figure 5.68.

The outer join's ability to detect and report unmatched records is very useful for several reasons. Consider, for example, the following scenarios:

- Your database contains a CUSTOMER table with 50,000 records. Each record in the CUSTOMER table includes a FK that references a sales representative through a REP_NUM field. Because many of the customers do not yet have a sales representative assigned to them, you want to know who those customers are. Finding the answer to that question is simple: Just run a query to see which CUSTOMER table REP_NUM values are null. But suppose you want to assign to those customers sales representatives who do not yet have a customer assignment? Finding the unassigned sales representatives is easy with an outer join.
- You have been given the task of converting a large table with many data redundancies to a set of normalized tables for which referential integrity must be enforced. (Review Chapter 3 if you are not quite sure what normalized tables are. Use Figures 3.1 through 3.4 as the example.) Using Chapter 4's table construction and editing procedures, you start the process this way:

FIGURE 5.67A **Output from the Revised Left Outer Join Query**

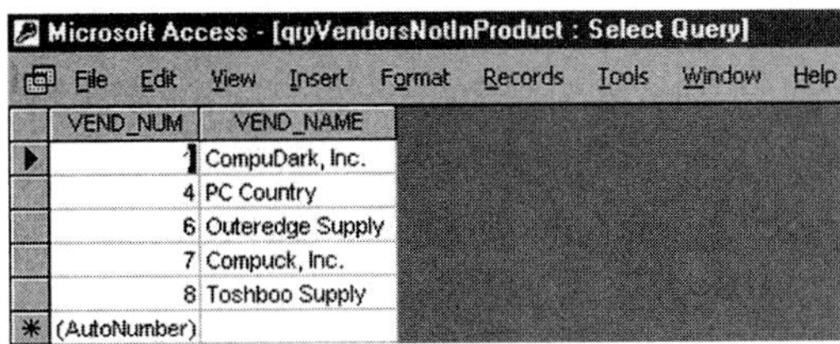

Microsoft Access - [qryVendorsNotInProduct : Select Query]

File Edit View Insert Format Records Tools Window Help

VEND_NUM	VEND_NAME
1	CompuDark, Inc.
4	PC Country
6	Outeredge Supply
7	Compuck, Inc.
8	Toshboo Supply
(AutoNumber)	

FIGURE 5.68 **The Save As Dialog Box**

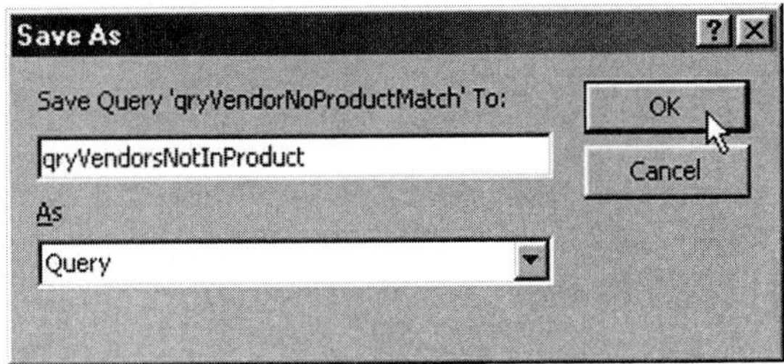

Assignment

Use the just-described techniques to modify the right outer join query named **qryProductNoVendorMatch**. You want to produce a listing of vendors referenced in the PRODUCT table that do *not* occur in the VENDOR table. Save the results as **qryProductVEND_NUMnotInVENDOR**. The output is shown in Figure 5.69.

According to the query results in Figure 5.69, vendor 8 does not exist, and PROD_CODE 101 and 102 have a null VEND_NUM.

FIGURE 5.69
Vendors Not Found in the VENDOR table

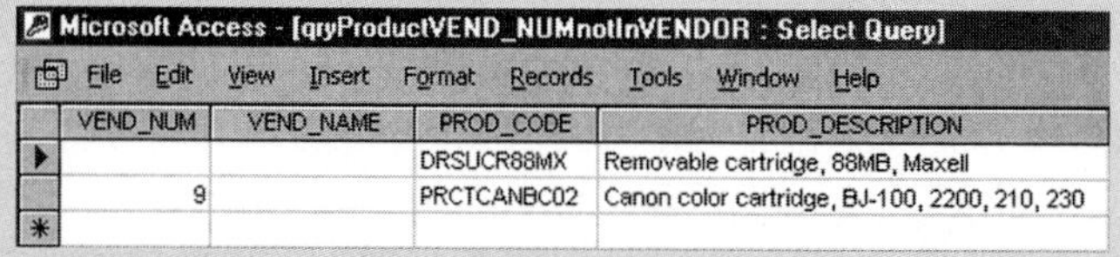

Microsoft Access - [qryProductVEND_NUMnotInVENDOR : Select Query]

File Edit View Insert Format Records Tools Window Help

VEND_NUM	VEND_NAME	PROD_CODE	PROD_DESCRIPTION
		DRSUCR88MX	Removable cartridge, 88MB, Maxell
9		PRCTCANBC02	Canon color cartridge, BJ-100, 2200, 210, 230
*			

1. Create the appropriate table structures, ORDER, CUSTOMER, PRODUCT, and ORD_LINE shown in Figure 3.4. Check for proper PKs and FKs, creating them where necessary for each normalized table. Set the referential integrity enforcement when you create the relationships between the tables.
2. Mark the field values for the parts of the nonnormalized table you want to copy, using **Edit/Copy**.
3. Insert the copied field values into the tables created in step 1, using **Edit/Paste**. Oops, you may discover that referential integrity errors are preventing the **Edit/Paste** routine from being completed.
4. If the referential integrity error is created in step 3, edit the relationships to remove the referential integrity enforcement. Repeat the **Edit/Paste** routine in step 3.
5. If step 4 turned out to be necessary, use the outer join to find out which unmatched record(s) produced the referential integrity error(s). Use the outer join's output to find and fix the unmatched FK values. Edit the relationship(s) to restore referential integrity error enforcement.

As the preceding discussion demonstrates, the outer join has many uses, and it turns out to be a powerful data management tool.

5.3 CROSSTAB QUERIES

One of the most useful (and certainly one of the most frequently used) data organization tools is the **cross-classification table.** Such a table depicts a two-dimensional summary of the available data, thereby providing its user with a quick impression of possible relationships between those two classifications. In addition, the cross-classification table's ability to summarize huge amounts of data in a very limited display area is a very attractive feature.

To see how Access can be used to produce a cross-classification table, we'll explore the **crosstab query.** We will use the PRODUCT table in our **Ch05_POS_2nd.mdb** database to illustrate the crosstab query's construction and use. The PRODUCT table, which contains product classifications (video, book, model, and CD) and product types (aircraft, cars, and ships), lends itself well to this exercise.

Before you attempt to design a cross-classification table with Access, lay out your two dimensions and think about what you want to know about them. Unless you do some pencil-and-paper work first, the Access instructions are likely to confuse you. In this example we start with the basic layout shown in Table 5-2.

After examining the components of Table 5.2, you will be able to respond to the Access prompts. Remember that the data source is the PRODUCT table and

TABLE 5.2
The Components of the PRODUCT Cross-Classification Table

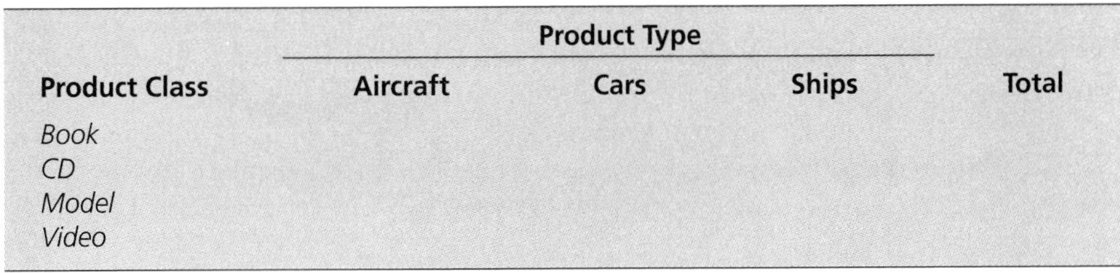

Product Class	Product Type			Total
	Aircraft	Cars	Ships	
Book				
CD				
Model				
Video				

the row headers (book, CD, model, and video) are defined by the product class field, PROD_CLASS. The column headers (aircraft, cars, and ships) are defined by the product type field, PROD_TYPE. The Total header shows that we want row totals. We will ask for a simple listing of the quantity on hand, PROD_QOH.

Now that we know what we want Access to do, let's select the **New Query** option to open the familiar **New Query** dialog box shown in Figure 5.70.

Using the dialog box in Figure 5.70, select the **Crosstab Query Wizard** to open the screen shown in Figure 5.71.

As you examine Figure 5.71, note that the **View** (data source) option is **Tables** and that we have placed the cursor on the PRODUCT table. You can either double-click on the PRODUCT table to move to the Crosstab Query Wizard's next screen, or you can click on the **Next** > button after selecting the PRODUCT table. In either case you will see the screen shown in Figure 5.72.

Using Figure 5.72 as your guide and remembering the layout in Table 5.2, you can place the PROD_CLASS row header into the **Selected Fields** section by

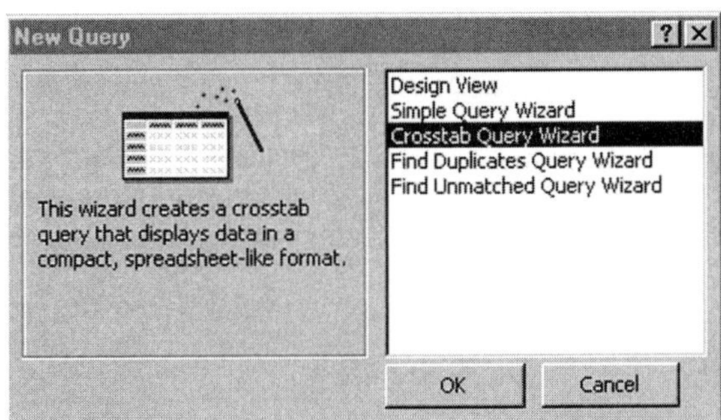

FIGURE 5.70
Selecting the Crosstab Query Wizard in the New Query Dialog Box

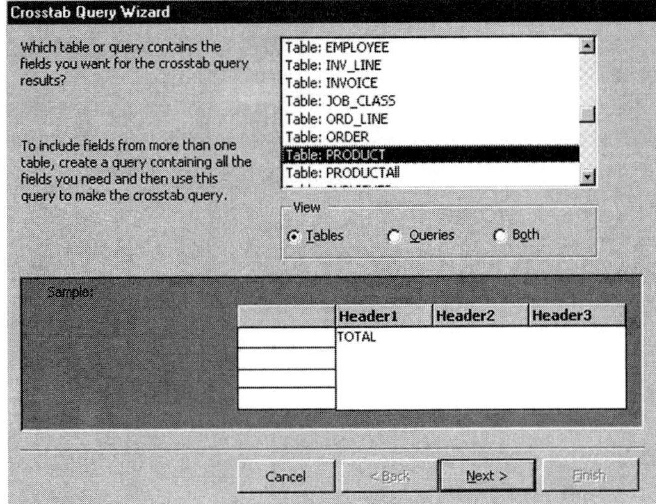

FIGURE 5.71
The Crosstab Query Wizard's Opening Screen

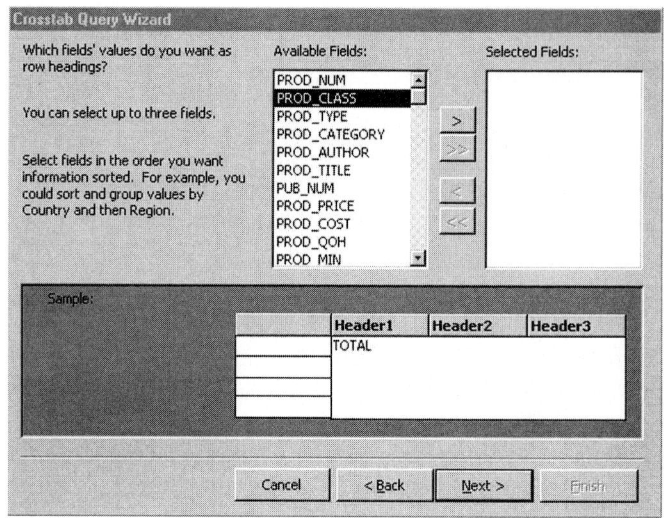

FIGURE 5.72
The Row Header Selection

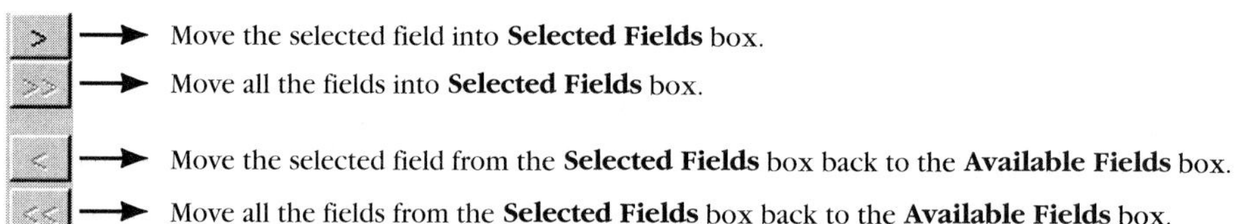

FIGURE 5.72A
The Move Buttons

double-clicking on it or by clicking on the > button after selecting the PROD_CLASS header. (The "move" buttons are described in Figure 5.72A.)

After you put the PROD_CLASS header into the **Selected Fields** box, the screen changes to reflect your selection (see Figure 5.73).

Click on the **Next** > button in Figure 5.73 to move to the column header selection screen shown in Figure 5.74.

As you examine Figure 5.74, note that the header selection from Figure 5.73 shows up in the **Sample** box. Note also that the (row) **TOTAL** is the default selection. Clicking on the **Next** > button moves you to the screen shown in Figure 5.75.

Because we will place the quantity on hand (PROD_QOH) into the cross-classification table (check Table 5.2 again if necessary), the screen in Figure 5.74

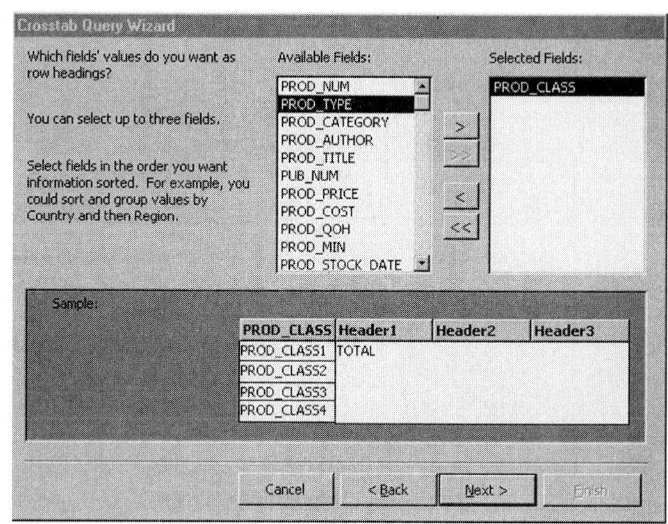

FIGURE 5.73
The Selected Fields Box after the PROD_CLASS Selection

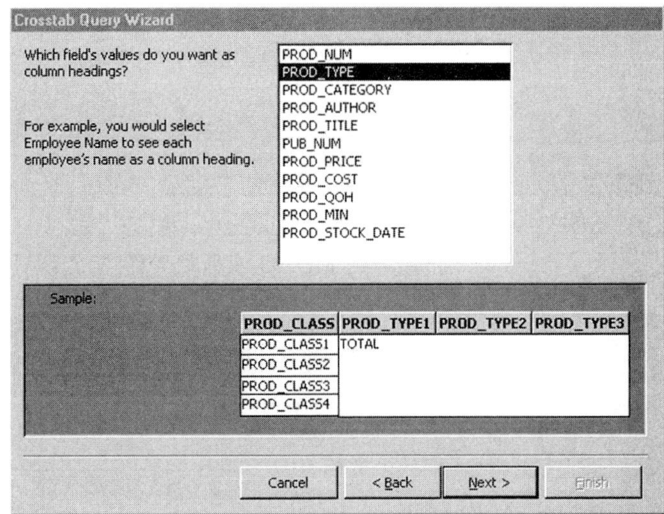

FIGURE 5.74
Selecting the Column Header

shows that we have selected this field. We selected **Count** in the **Functions** box because all we want to do is show the quantity on hand by the various cross-classifications. Finally, we checked the **Yes, include row sums** check box. Click on this selection to remove the check mark if you don't want to include the row totals. Finally, click on the **Next** > button to move to the final Crosstab Query Wizard screen shown in Figure 5.76.

As you examine Figure 5.76, note that the Crosstab Query Wizard used the default query name based on the table selection. Because we will save the new query as **qryProductTypeVsProductClass**, we'll type this name to replace the default name. Clicking the **Finish** button will show the output in Figure 5.77.

As you examine Figure 5.77, note how much information is presented in a very limited space. We can tell readily that our inventory includes 39 aircraft books, 17 aircraft CDs, 21 aircraft models, and 7 aircraft videos. The inventory includes 48 books: 39 aircraft books, 5 car books, and 4 ship books. We can also see that 84 of the items in inventory are based on aircraft: 39 + 17 + 21 + 7 = 84. We do not have any car CDs in stock, so we may have to plug that gap in our inventory by ordering car CDs if a cross-tabulation based on sales shows an interest in car CDs. (We may have to check what's on back order!) If you compare the output in Figure 5.77 with the simple PRODUCT table listing or even with a

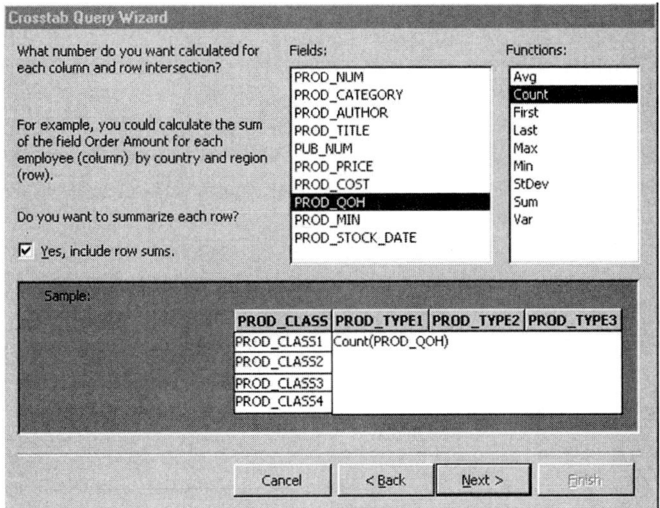

FIGURE 5.75
Selecting the Cell Contents

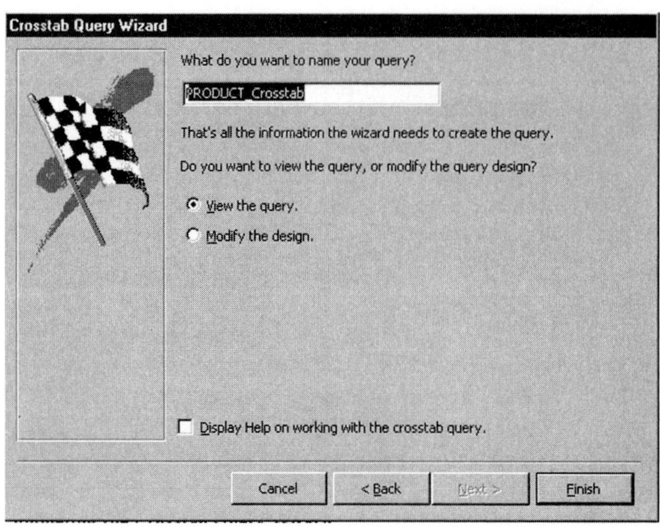

FIGURE 5.76 **Completing the Crosstab Query Wizard**

FIGURE 5.77 **The Crosstab Query Output**

PROD_CLASS	Total Of PROD_QOH	Aircraft	Cars	Ships
Book	48	39	5	4
CD	25	17		8
Model	29	21	4	4
Video	26	7	13	6

query that summarizes the PROD_TYPE in a single dimension, you will quickly see why the cross-classification table is such a powerful tool for decision makers.

To see which query design produced the cross-classification table in Figure 5.77, open the **qryProductTypeVsProductClass** in the design mode shown in Figure 5.78. You can modify the query as needed, just as you did with the previous queries.

FIGURE 5.78 **The Crosstab Query Design Format**

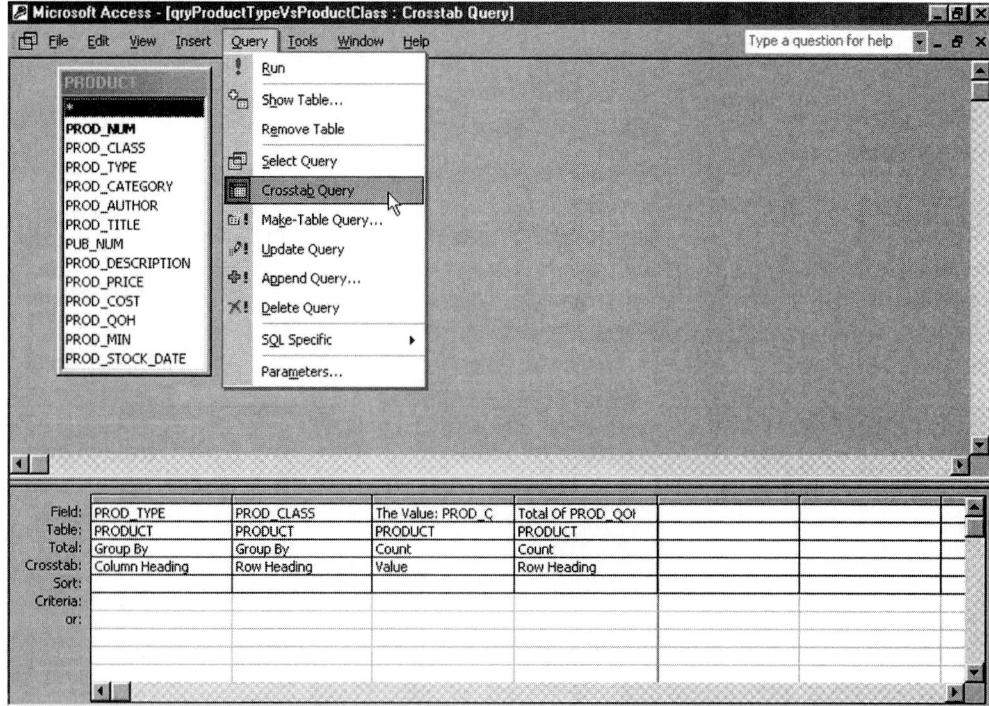

Assignment

Create a new cross-classification table, this time using the PRODUCT table's PROD_TYPE as the row header and the PROD_CLASS as the column header. Use the PROD_QOH as the summary characteristic to produce the Access crosstab output shown in Figure 5.79.

Note that the headers have been modified with the help of the field property boxes. Save the cross-classification table as **qryProductClassVsProductType**.

FIGURE 5.79
Product Class versus Product Type Cross-classification Output

Microsoft Access - [qryProductClassVsProductType : Crosstab Query]

File Edit View Insert Format Records Tools Window Help

Product Type	Total Units	Book	CD	Model	Video
Aircraft	84	39	17	21	7
Cars	22	5		4	13
Ships	22	4	8	4	6

Take a good look at Figure 5.78 and note that the query type is **Crosstab Query**. Make sure you select this option when you construct a crosstab query without the Wizard's help. (Just select the sequence **New/Design/Crosstab/select the table/select the fields/select the options**. In short, follow the usual crosstab design procedures if you don't want to use the Wizard.)

5.4 ACTION QUERIES

As its name implies, an **action query** performs an activity such as

- Updating a table by modifying its field values. Such an action query is known as an **update query.**
- Creating a table. This type of action query is known as a **make table query.**
- Adding (appending) records to a table. This action query is known as an **append query.**
- Deleting records from a table. This action query is known as a **delete query.**

Given the action query's ability to modify the data environment, it is an indispensable tool in the data management arena. The available query types are shown in the query menu in Figure 5.80.

FIGURE 5.80
Query Types Shown in the Query Menu

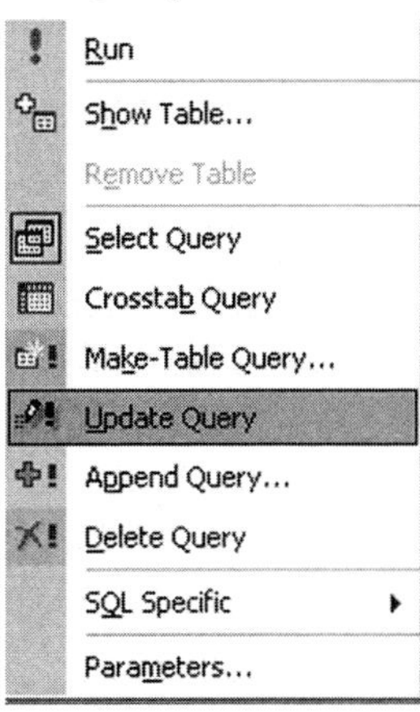

5.4.1 The Update Query

The update query is particularly useful because it allows us to modify many table records at a time. In addition, it permits us to insert calculated field values whose manual insertion would be prohibitively time-consuming. For example, suppose that we want to update the number of years each employee has worked in the company. If the company employs thousands of workers, preparing a manual update would be a real chore. Even for our small database, containing an EMPLOYEE table with only 36 records, a manual update would be undesirable. Aside from being time-consuming, manual updates have the potential for miscalculation, and finding such errors can be very difficult. The update query handles such updates quickly and efficiently.

To create an update query, we'll use the same initial—and by now familiar—procedures that we used to create the select queries. (See Figures 5.1, 5.2, and 5.3.) However, make sure you select the **Update Query** option from the menu in Figure 5.80. Selecting the **Update Query** option causes the QBE grid to be modified to include an **Update To:** line. Because you'll modify the EMPLOYEE table's EMP_YEARS field values, drag the EMPLOYEE table's EMP_YEARS field to the

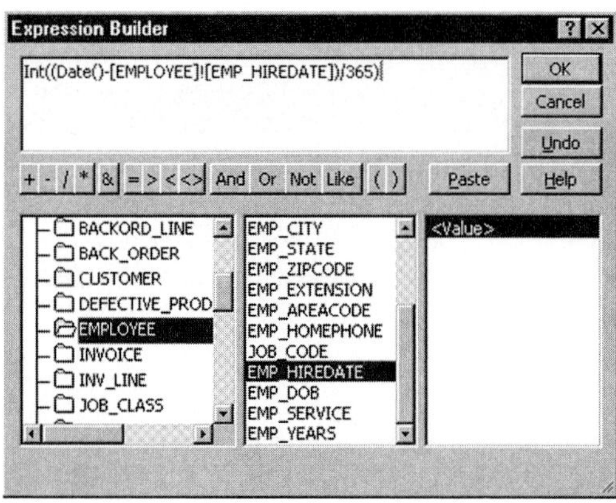

FIGURE 5.81
Calculating the Number of Years

QBE grid and drop it. Next plan the steps you need to accomplish the update. In this case the EMP_YEARS values can be calculated this way:

1. Subtract the EMP_HIREDATE from the current date, **Date()**, to find the number of days that elapsed between the current date and the date on which the employee was hired.
2. Assuming that a year has 365 days, dividing the number of days calculated in step 1 by 365 yields the number of years.
3. The number of years will be reported as an integer, so use the **Int()** function to report the desired results. (Using the Integer function is appropriate. Just think about how you report your age in years. If you will be 25 on January 12, 2003, you will report your age as 24 even when it is January 11, 2003.)

These three steps are completed in the Expression Builder shown in Figure 5.81. (You have kept practicing with the Expression Builder since it was introduced, haven't you? Remember that to update the EMP_YEARS field values, you must put the cursor on the QBE grid's **Update To:** line before you right-click to select the Expression Builder.)

Once you are done with the Expression Builder shown in Figure 5.81, click **OK** to transfer its computation procedures to the QBE grid's **Update To:** line. (See Figure 5.82.) Save the query as **qryUpdateEployeeYearsEmployed**.

Running this update query will produce the dialog boxes shown in Figures 5.83 and 5.83A. Figure 5.83 shows that Access will give you an option to change your mind about running the update query.

If you click on the **Yes** button shown in Figure 5.83, you will see the dialog box in Figure 5.83A.

The number of rows shown in the dialog box in Figure 5.83A—in this case, 36—reflects the number of records in the EMPLOYEE table that will be updated. Note that you are still given another option to change your mind about executing the update. (You can still select **No**.)

FIGURE 5.82 **The Completed Update Query**

Field:	EMP_YEARS				
Table:	EMPLOYEE				
Update To:	Int((Date()-[EMPLOYEE]![EMP_HIREDATE])/365)				
Criteria:					
or:					

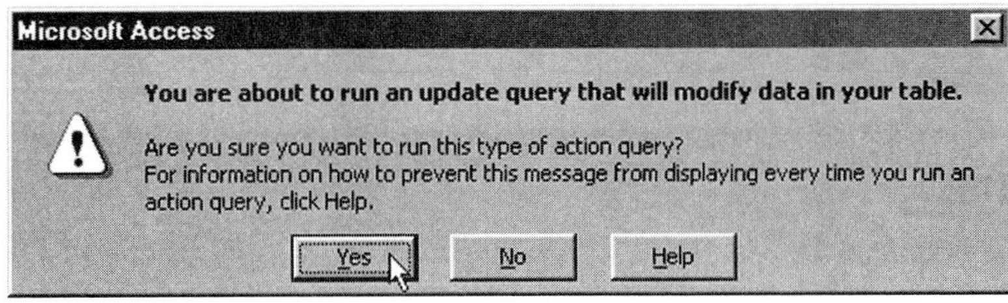

FIGURE 5.83
Update Query Execution Option

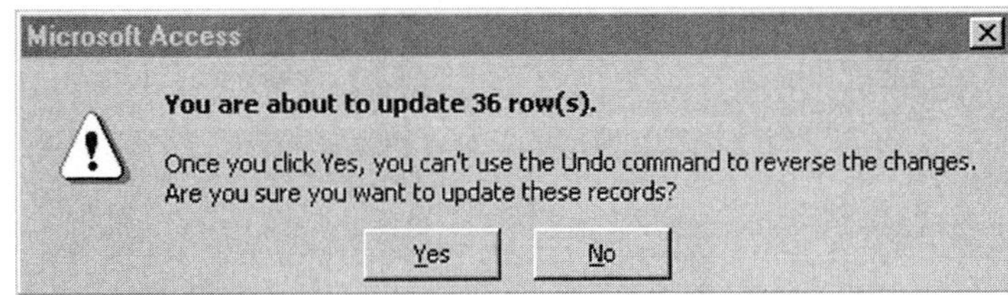

FIGURE 5.83A
Update Query Action Option

After clicking the **Yes** button in Figure 5.83, create a query based on the EMPLOYEE table to show just a few of the fields as illustrated in Figure 5.84. Although only a few of the employee records are shown in Figure 5.84, you can easily see that the update was successful. Keep in mind that the number of years of service is a function of the date on which the update query was run. We ran this query on October 30, 2002. Therefore, **EMP_YEARS** = **12** for the first record shown in Figure 5.84. The EMP_YEARS value for Ms. Edwards will not change to 13 until 23-Jul-2003.

Update queries can update many fields at the same time. To illustrate this point, we have added a field named EMP_UPDATED to the EMPLOYEE table to record the date of the last update. You could have updated the field values in this field to **Date()** by modifying the **qryUpdateEmployeeYearsEmployed** update query to include the EMP_UPDATED and setting its **Update To:** line to **Date()**. Running the modified query named **qryUpdateEmployeeYearsEmployedVersion2** would update both fields at the same time. The design view of this query is shown in Figure 5.84A.

If you run the query in Figure 5.84A, you'll generate the results shown in Figure 5.84B. In this example, we updated the EMP_YEARS values on October 30, 2002. Therefore, the EMP_YEARS_ UPDATED values are shown as 30-Oct-2002. (Only a few fields of a few records are shown to save space.)

The update queries are subject to the same flexibility and constraints as the select queries we examined earlier in the chapter. For example, you can combine a parameter query with the update query, as shown in Figure 5.84C. (We have used the **Ch05_Store_Co.mdb** database to generate the results shown here. We have named this query **qryUpdateStoreYTDsalesForAllStores**.)

(When you created the query shown in Figure 5.84C, you did make sure that you placed the cursor on the QBE's **Update to:** field before you used the Expression Builder, didn't you? If you left the cursor on the **Field:** line,

FIGURE 5.84
The Update Query Results (Only a Few of the 36 Records Are Shown)

EMP_LNAME	EMP_FNAME	EMP_DOB	EMP_HIREDATE	EMP_YEARS	EMP_YEARS_UPDATED
Edwards	Rosemary	03-Jul-1953	23-Jul-1990	12	30-Oct-02
Donelly	Ronald	02-Oct-1952	01-Jul-1987	15	30-Oct-02
Thieu	Frederick	23-Feb-1948	01-May-1992	10	30-Oct-02
Robertson	Elaine	20-Jun-1961	18-Oct-1983	19	30-Oct-02
Thiako	Van	12-Aug-1951	01-Aug-1989	13	30-Oct-02
Blalock	Andrew	16-Jan-1966	12-Nov-1996	5	30-Oct-02
Graztevski	Mary	18-Mar-1939	01-Aug-1978	24	30-Oct-02
Holms	Anne	12-Jun-1950	23-Feb-1978	24	30-Oct-02
Wilson	Todd	19-Oct-1966	06-Nov-1990	11	30-Oct-02
Jones	Suzanne	30-Dec-1967	05-Jan-1994	8	30-Oct-02
Smithson	Elsa	13-Sep-1943	16-Dec-1982	19	30-Oct-02

Note

Unlike the select query, the update query will not execute properly *unless you save it first.* Therefore, you cannot move back and forth between the design and datasheet views to check the results of your query efforts before saving the query!

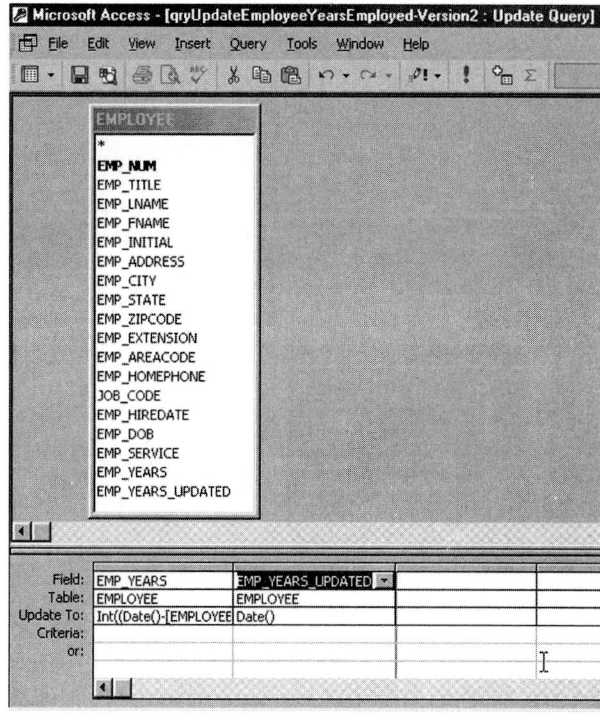

FIGURE 5.84A
The Design View of the Modified EMP_YEARS Update Query

you would have replaced the field that was supposed to be updated with the expression. If you made that error, Access would remind you to select a field to be updated!)

Run the update query twice; enter 1000000 once and inspect the effect on the STORE table's STORE_YTD_SALES values. Then run the query again, this time entering −1000000 to reset the STORE_YTD_SALES to their original values.

You can also add constraints to update queries to limit the number of records that will be updated. For example, you can modify the query shown in Figure 5.84C by adding the parameter query shown in Figure 5.84D to limit the update to a selected store.

Incidentally, no matter where you place the constraint, Access will move it to the last QBE field position after the query has been saved. In this example we

FIGURE 5.84B
The Results of Running the Modified EMP_YEARS Update Query

EMP_LNAME	EMP_FNAME	EMP_DOB	EMP_HIREDATE	EMP_YEARS	EMP_YEARS_UPDATED
Edwards	Rosemary	03-Jul-1953	23-Jul-1990	12	30-Oct-02
Donelly	Ronald	02-Oct-1952	01-Jul-1987	15	30-Oct-02
Thieu	Frederick	23-Feb-1948	01-May-1992	10	30-Oct-02
Robertson	Elaine	20-Jun-1961	18-Oct-1983	19	30-Oct-02
Thiako	Van	12-Aug-1951	01-Aug-1989	13	30-Oct-02
Blalock	Andrew	16-Jan-1966	12-Nov-1996	5	30-Oct-02
Graztevski	Mary	18-Mar-1939	01-Aug-1978	24	30-Oct-02
Holms	Anne	12-Jun-1950	23-Feb-1978	24	30-Oct-02
Wilson	Todd	19-Oct-1966	06-Nov-1990	11	30-Oct-02
Jones	Suzanne	30-Dec-1967	05-Jan-1994	8	30-Oct-02
Smithson	Elsa	13-Sep-1943	16-Dec-1982	19	30-Oct-02

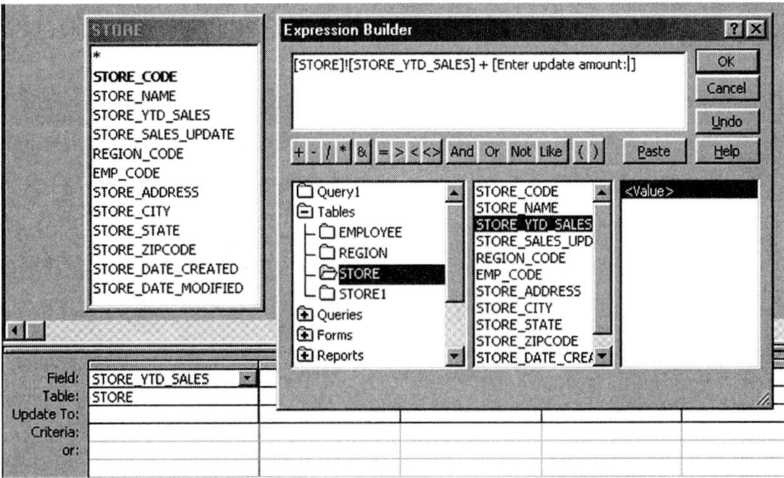

FIGURE 5.84C
The Initial Sales Update Query

dragged Figure 5.84D's STORE_NUM field to the first QBE field position, but Access moved it to the third position shown here when we saved the query.

Updates may be based on multiple data sources, just as they were in the select queries. For example, we have made a copy of the SALES table—naming it SALES1—and then used it to update the SALES table. The design view of this update is shown in Figure 5.84E. Note that the data source must be identified in the update.

Although the example in Figure 5.84E is very simple, it demonstrates the power of the update query. With just a little imagination, you can visualize updating a database's contents from other tables in the same database, from tables in another database, or from the Web. The major constraint is, of course, that the data types must be compatible. For example, you cannot update a currency field from a date field.

Speaking of constraints, updates may also use multiple constraint sources. For example, if you use the **Ch05_POS_2nd.mdb** database, you can change the SELLER table's SELL_PCT based on the EMPLOYEE table's EMP_YEARS values (see Figure 5.84F). Such update flexibility makes the update query a very powerful and useful management tool.

5.4.2 Delete Queries

The delete and append queries in this section will alter the data in the database tables. To save two copies of the CUSTOMER table, right-click on the

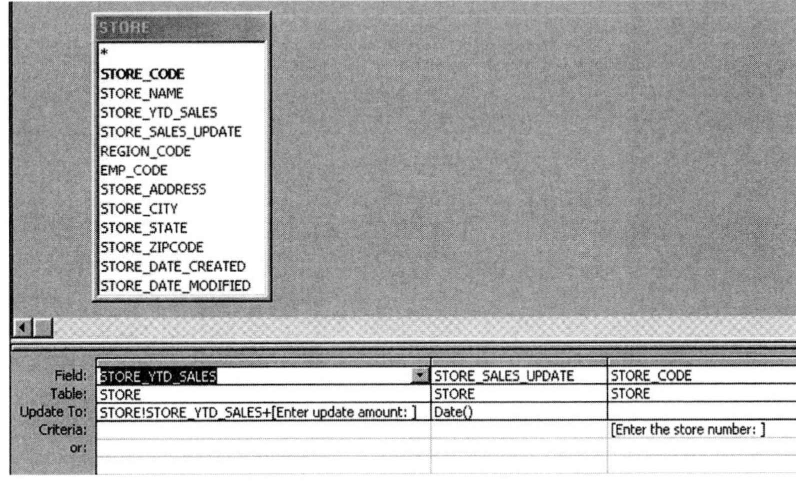

FIGURE 5.84D
The Modified Sales Update Query

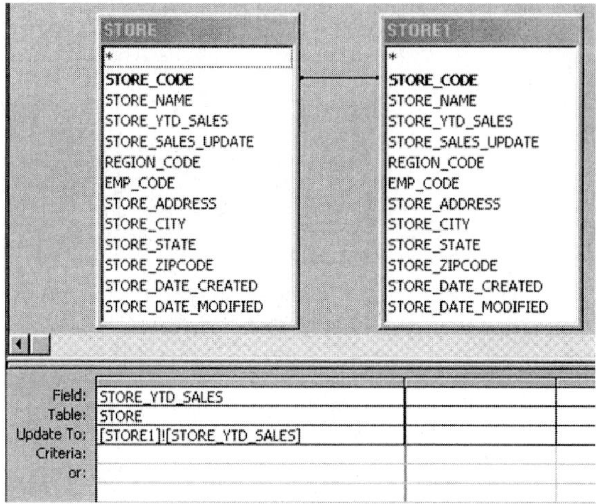

FIGURE 5.84E
An Update from Another Data Source

CUSTOMER table and select **Save As** as shown in Figure 5.85. This action produces the dialog box in Figure 5.86.

Type the copy name, CUSTOMER-X, over the **Copy of CUSTOMER** default entry in the dialog box shown in Figure 5.86 and then click **OK**. Use the same technique to make a second copy of the CUSTOMER table, naming it CUSTOMER-X2. Then run all your delete and update queries on the CUSTOMER-X and CUSTOMER-X2 tables, leaving the original CUSTOMER table intact as a backup table—just in case one of your experiments goes haywire.

The delete and append queries are constructed just like the update queries. Naturally, the QBE grid options change when you select the various query types. For example, after selecting the delete query, the QBE grid includes the **Delete:** line shown in Figure 5.87. (Note that we have selected the CUSTOMER-X table as the data source.)

In Figure 5.87 we have dragged the * from the top of the CUSTOMER-X table to indicate that *all fields are selected,* thus deleting all records. This selection also freezes the **Criteria:** line's choice to **From**. (Clicking on the **Delete:** line yields the short menu with two options: **From** and **Where**. However, the **From** option is the only one available when you select all the records. Therefore, in this case,

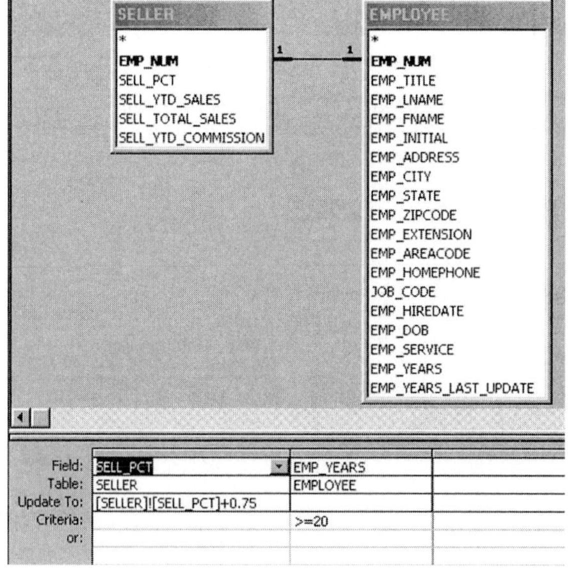

FIGURE 5.84F
An Update Based on a Constraint Found in Another Table

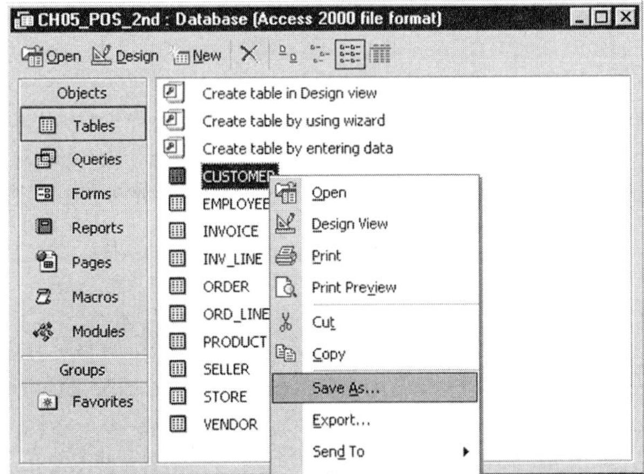

FIGURE 5.85
The Save As Option

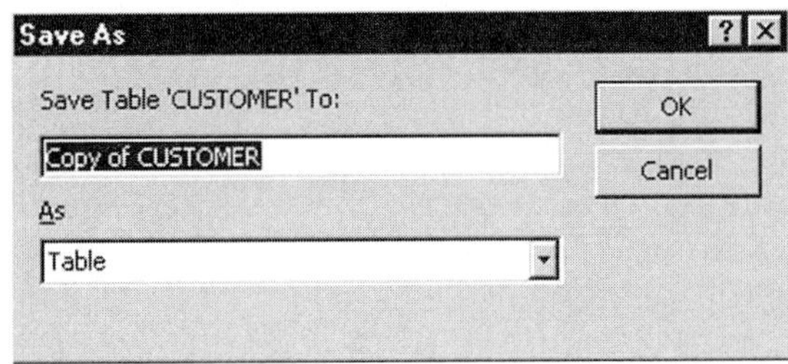

FIGURE 5.86
Making a Copy of the CUSTOMER Table

even clicking on the **Where** option will keep **From** on the delete line shown in Figure 5.87.)

You cannot execute the delete query by switching to the datasheet view, so save it first as **qryDeleteAllRecordsFromCUSTOMER-X**. After saving the query, open it to execute the deletion. The screens captured in Figures 5.87A and 5.87B show that Access gives you two opportunities to change your mind.

FIGURE 5.87
Record Deletion via the Delete Query

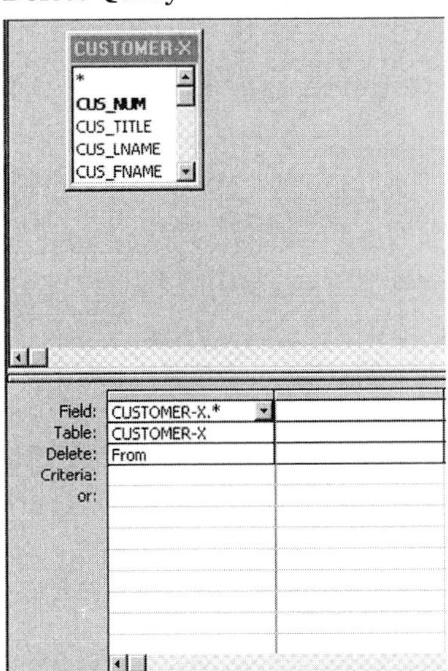

FIGURE 5.87A The First Deletion Warning Message

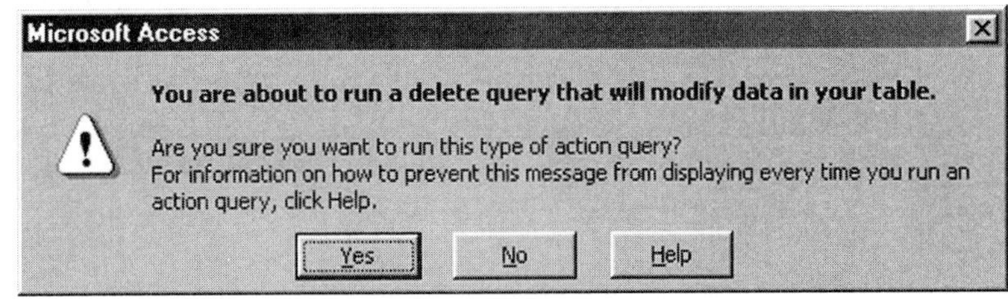

FIGURE 5.87B The Second Deletion Warning Message

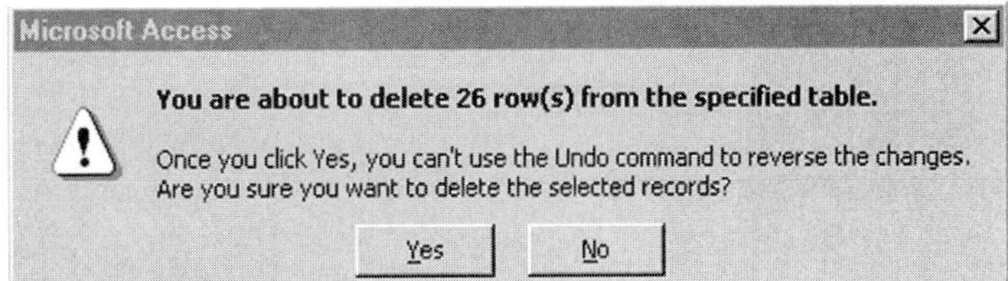

Note

If you try the delete query on a table that is related to one or more other tables, the deletion will be possible only as long as the referential integrity between these tables is not violated. *Access deletes only records whose deletion will not violate referential integrity.*

FIGURE 5.88
Delete Query Limited by a Parameter Value

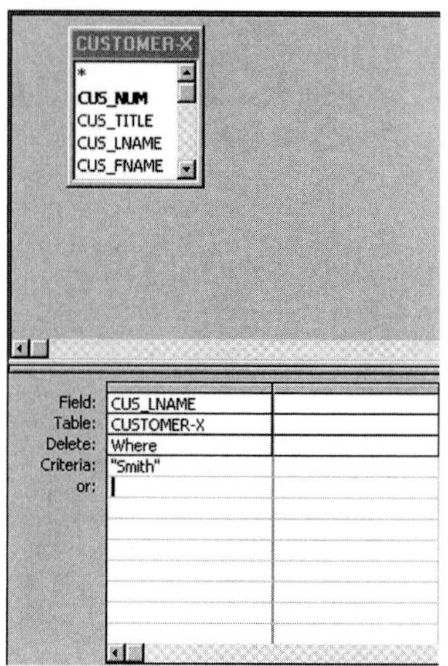

If you click on the **Yes** button in Figure 5.87B, all CUSTOMER-X records will be deleted. You can verify the deletion by returning to the database window; then open the CUSTOMER-X table and see that the table's records have been deleted. (After you have deleted records and verified the deletion, delete the CUSTOMER-X table. Then make another copy of the CUSTOMER table and save it as CUSTOMER-X again. This action will let you practice several additional deletion exercises.)

In the preceding example, we elected to delete all records. But suppose you want to control which records are deleted? You should remember from your study (and practice!) of the select query that you can add parameter limitations to any query. For example, Figure 5.88 shows that we dragged and dropped just one field from the CUSTOMER-X table to the QBE grid's **Field:** line and that we have limited the deletion to those customers whose last name is Smith.

The delete query shown in Figure 5.88 cannot be executed until you have saved it and opened it from the database window. Therefore, if you want to delete all customers named Smith, first save the parameter deletion query of Figure 5.88 as **qryDeleteAllCustomersNamedSmithFromCUSTOMER-X**. After you have saved the query, switch from the delete query's design view shown in Figure 5.87 to its datasheet view. Access will let you see which records will be tagged for deletion by printing the matching parameter values on the screen (see Figure 5.88A).

When you open the **qryDeleteAllCustomersNamedSmithFromCUSTOMER-X** delete query, you will see the same dialog boxes we showed you in Figures 5.87A and 5.87B. This time the dialog boxes will tell you that *four* records are about to be deleted. Go ahead and execute the query; then open the CUSTOMER-X table and note that the records for customers named Smith are actually deleted.

Keep in mind that if you drag and drop selected fields, you can specify which records are to be deleted by indicating the parameters for any one field *or for any combination of fields*. You can even make the deletion process interactive and more flexible by specifying the parameter

```
[Enter the last name: ]
```

In short, all the options that were available in the select queries are available in the delete queries. Incidentally, given the selection of specific fields, only

FIGURE 5.88A
Matching Delete Query Parameter Values

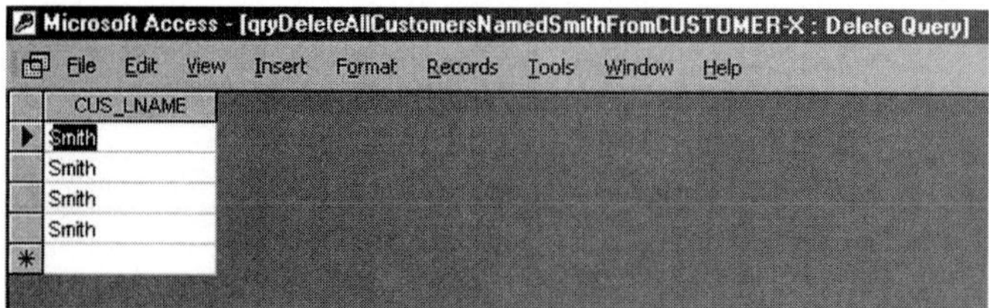

Assignment

Save the query named **qryDeleteAllCustomersNamedSmith-FromCUSTOMER-X** as **qryDeleteAllCustomersNamedSmith-FromCUSTOMER-X2** and then modify this query by using the parameter option

```
[Enter the last name: ]
```

we discussed in the previous paragraph. (Don't forget to substitute the CUSTOMER-X2 table for the CUSTOMER-X table in this query. If you forget to make this substitution, you will delete the records from the wrong table!)

After you have modified the query—and saved your modifications—run this modified query, entering the last name Smith. Check the CUSTOMER-X2 table after you have run the query to make sure that the four records for customers named Smith were actually deleted.

FIGURE 5.89
The Query List in the Database Window

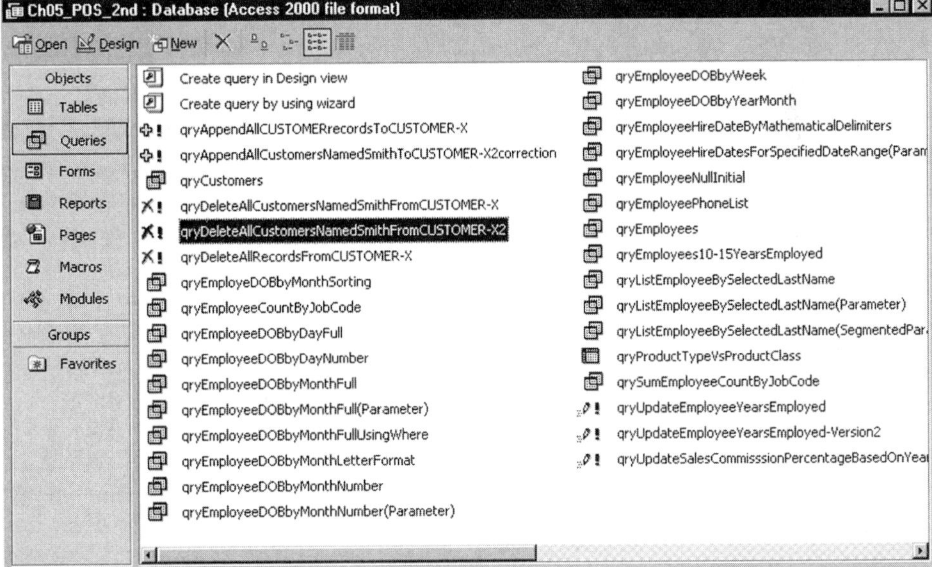

the **Where** option will be available to you, even if you click on the menu's **From** option.

You have now created several delete queries in addition to the other queries you have learned about in this chapter. You can recognize the various query types by examining the Access symbols before each query name. For example, your **Ch05_POS_2nd.mdb** database window's Queries folder should show most of the queries in Figure 5.89. (You will learn how to produce Append, Make Table, and Union queries in the following three sections of this chapter. If you check the symbols in the left margin, you'll learn to recognize which query symbol is used to label each query type. Because you know that the **qryDeleteAllCustomer-sNamedSmithFromCUSTOMER-X2** query is a delete query, you can check Figure 5.89 to see what the symbol for a delete query is.)

5.4.3 Append Queries

Append queries, as their name suggests, add data to tables. Like all the queries we have shown you, append queries may be controlled through the use of parameters. To show you how append queries work, we will again use the **Ch05_POS_2nd.mdb** database that we used to illustrate the delete queries.

FIGURE 5.90
The Append Query Option in the Query Menu

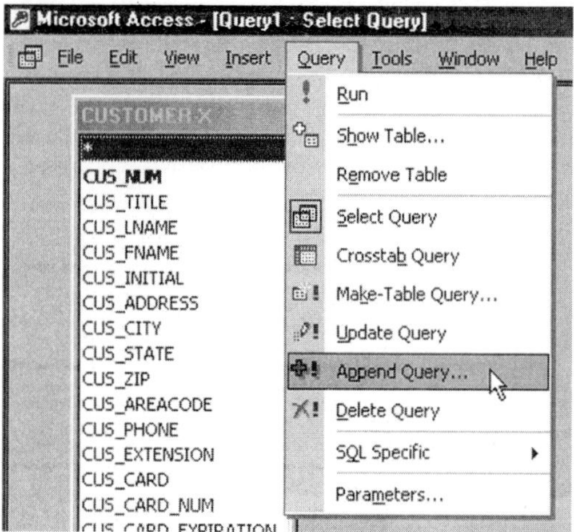

FIGURE 5.90A
The Append Dialog Box: Specifying the Data Destination

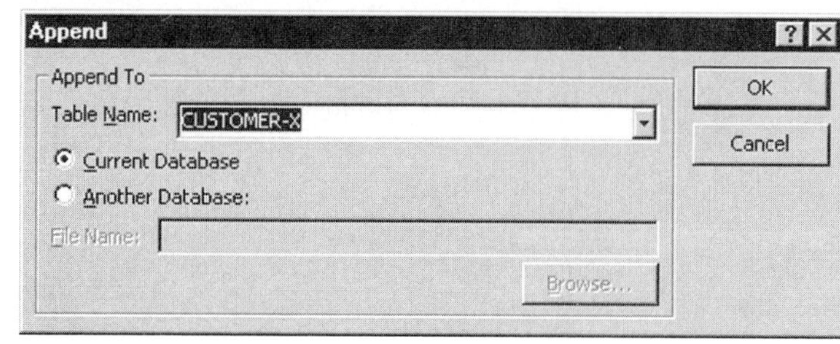

FIGURE 5.91
The Append Query: Date Source and Destination

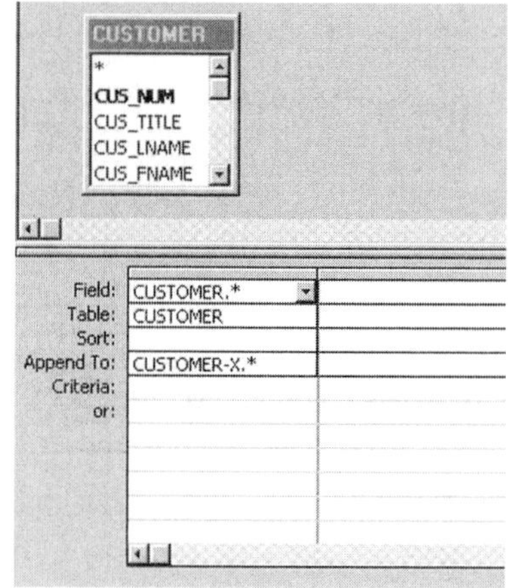

Let's see how the append query can restore the records to the CUSTOMER-X table. (First run the **qryDeleteAllRecordsFromCUSTOMER-X** query to ensure that the table contains no records at all.) To create an append query, select the **New Query** button to open the QBE screen. After selecting the **Query** button from the QBE tool bar, select the **Append Query** option from the by now-familiar menu shown in Figure 5.90.

Clicking on the append query option in the menu shown in Figure 5.90 will generate the Append dialog box shown in Figure 5.90A.

Because you want to append *all* of the CUSTOMER table's attribute values to the still-empty CUSTOMER-X table, drag the asterisk to the **Field:** selection. Select CUSTOMER-X to serve as the data destination. (See Figure 5.91. You do remember that you can always select a data source by right-clicking on the top portion of the QBE screen and then selecting the **Show Table** option from the menu, don't you?)

Save the new append query as **qryAppendAllCUSTOMERrecordsTo CUSTOMER-X**. If you open the append query you have just created, Access will generate the dialog boxes shown in Figures 5.92 and 5.92A.

Select the **Yes** button in Figure 5.92A to append the 26 records from the data source, CUSTOMER, to the data destination, CUSTOMER-X. When you return to the database window and open the CUSTOMER-X table, you will see that it contains the CUSTOMER table's 26 records.

As always, you can append records, or even parts of records, on the basis of parameter selections. For example, do you remember the customers named Smith that you deleted from the CUSTOMER-X2 table in the preceding assignment? We can copy those records from the original CUSTOMER table back into

FIGURE 5.92
The Append Confirmation Message

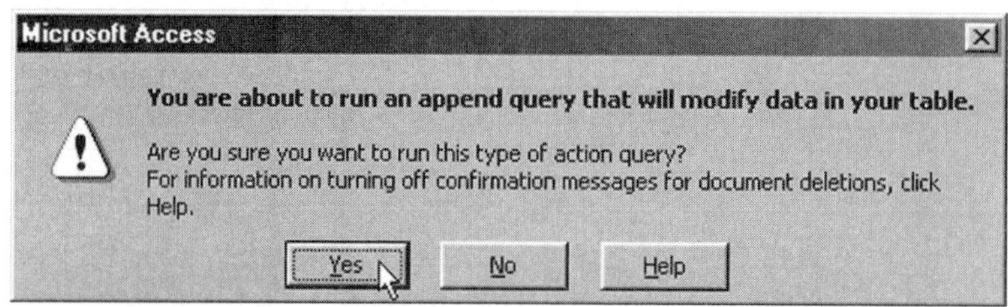

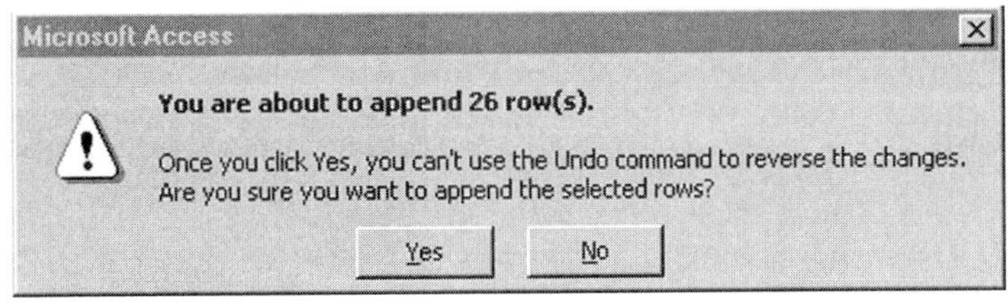

FIGURE 5.92A
The Append Results Confirmation Message

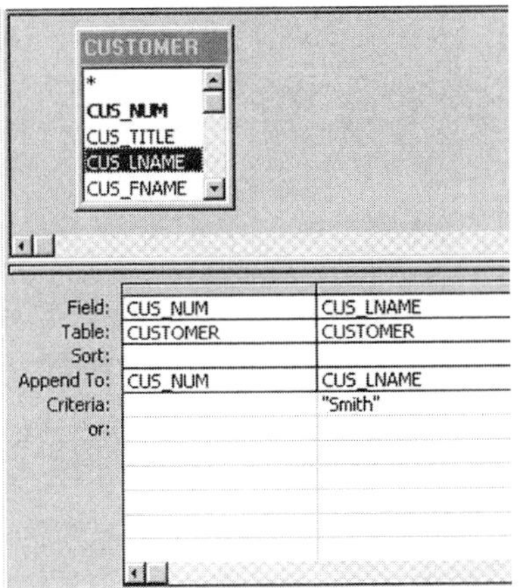

FIGURE 5.93
Appending Fields With a Parameter Specification

the CUSTOMER-X2 table by using the append query format shown in Figure 5.93.

Save the append query as **qryAppendAllCustomersNamedSmithToCUSTOMER-X2**. Executing this query from the database window yields the usual two confirmation messages, but you'll then see the surprise message shown in Figure 5.94 when you try to append the records.

The reason for the error message is simple. If you examine the QBE grid in Figure 5.93, you'll see that we included the CUS_NUM field. However, the CUS_NUM is based on an **AutoNumber** data type. Given this data type, once the three Smith CUS_NUM values were deleted from the CUSTOMER-X2 table, they could not be used again. Therefore, the **Append** function can only add CUS_NUM values larger than the CUS_NUM value of the CUSTOMER-X2 table's current last record.

To avoid the error message, create a new **Append** query *almost* like the query that just misfired. But this time, do not use the CUS_NUM field to avoid the error shown in Figure 5.94. Save the new query after and name it **qryAppendAllCustomersNamedSmithToCUSTOMER-X2correction**. The design view is shown in Figure 5.95.) If you run this new query, you will find that it can be successfully executed.

Given the **AutoNumber**'s characteristics, each time you run the delete query for Smith and then run the **qryAppendSmithRecordsToCUSTOMER-X2**, you will see that the CUS_NUM values for Smith have grown larger. Note, for example, that the CUSTOMER-X2 records displayed in Figure 5.95A have been through a delete and append cycle, so the appended Smith records now display the CUS_NUM values 37 through 40. (We have shown only a portion of the last few records to save space on the page.)

As you examine the customer listing in Figure 5.95A, note that only the Smith customer last names and were included in the append sequence. That's because only the CUS_LNAME field was included in the QBE grid in Figure 5.95. *If you want to include all the fields in the append sequence, include them in the QBE grid.*

Keep in mind that you can generate append error messages even if you don't use the **AutoNumber** data type. For example, suppose you had selected the **Number/Integer** data type to define the CUS_NUM values. Then suppose you had deleted customers with CUS_NUM values 5, 7, 8, 9, and 11. Given the Number/Integer data type, you can insert records that use these CUS_NUM values

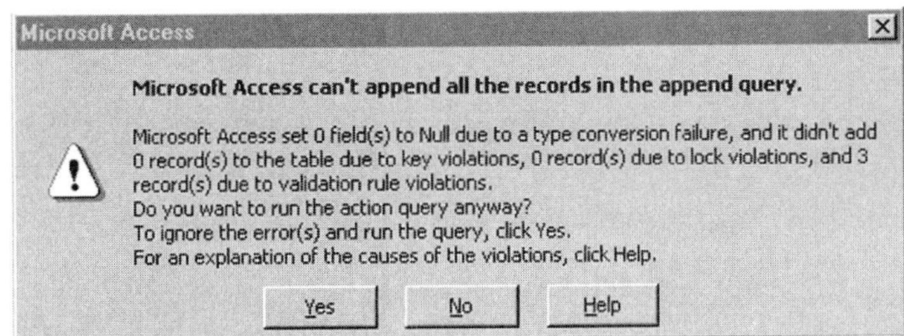

FIGURE 5.94
An Append Error Message

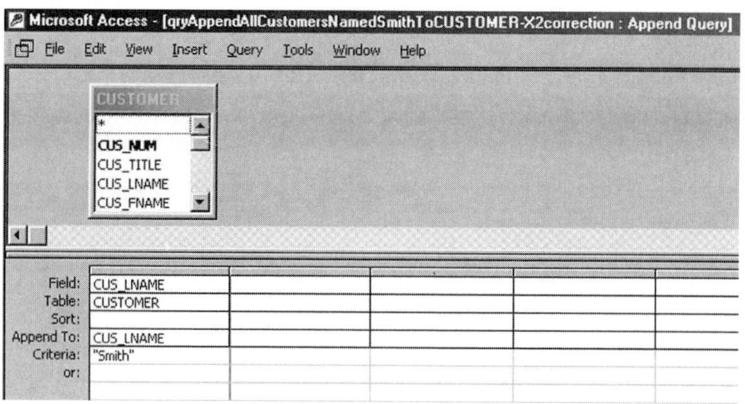

FIGURE 5.95
The Corrected Append Query

20	Mr.	Holder	Robert	B	208 Misty Drive
22	Mr.	Coltrain	Robert	C	Rural Route 66, Box 23
23	Mr.	Jennison	James	L	1234 Wild Haven Road
26	Mrs.	Spain	Elaine	M	656 Solley Ave
31	Mr.	Miller	Alex	J	34 Fountain Ave
32	Mrs.	McClean	Wanda	C	345 Snow Dog Drive
33	Mr.	Allenberger	George		4525 River Bend dr.
35	Mr.	Ghanem	Salim	A	815 Redwood Dr
36	Mr.	Moore	George	M	312 Hill Ave
37		Smith			
38		Smith			
39		Smith			
40		Smith			
(AutoNumber)					

FIGURE 5.95A
The CUSTOMER-X2 Records after a Delete and Append Cycle

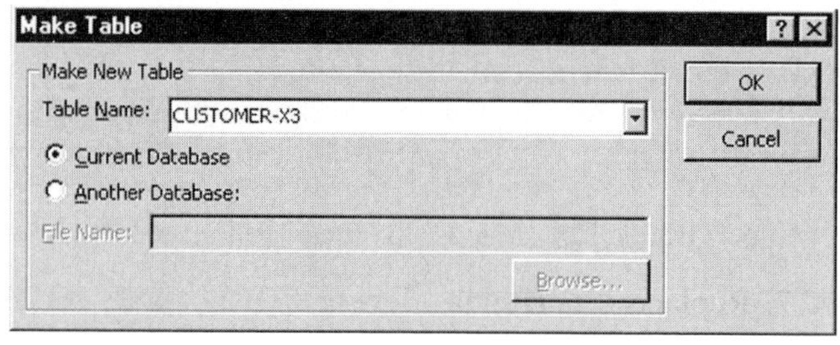

FIGURE 5.96
The Make Table Dialog Box

again. However, if you try to insert any one of the *existing* record numbers, you will create an entity integrity violation, thereby triggering an error message again. (Review Chapter 2 if you don't remember what *entity integrity* means.)

FIGURE 5.97
The Make Table QBE Screen

5.4.4 Make Table Queries

In sections 5.4.2 and 5.4.3 you learned how to use delete and append queries to modify data in existing table structures. The **Make Table** query can perform many of those functions even without existing table structures. In fact, the **Make Table** query creates the appropriate table structure(s) based on the fields that are placed on the QBE grid. For example, suppose you want to create a table, to be named CUSTOMER-X3, based on the CUSTOMER table's CUS_NUM and CUS_LNAME fields for customers named Smith. Select the **Make Table** query option from the QBE screen to open the **Make Table** dialog box shown in Figure 5.96.

Start the table-making process by typing the name of the new table in the **Table Name** text box. Then select the CUSTOMER table as the data source and drag and drop the CUS_NUM and CUS_LNAME as shown in Figure 5.97. Note that we have used the parameter value "Smith" to limit

FIGURE 5.98
The New CUSTOMER-X3 Table Contents

	CUS_NUM	CUS_LNAME
▶	12	Smith
	13	Smith
	14	Smith
	21	Smith
*	(AutoNumber)	

the number of records that will be created. (You could, of course, make the query more flexible through the use of the by-now-familiar dialog box. For example, the CUS_LNAME field's **Criteria** entry in Figure 5.97 may be altered to read

```
[Enter customer's last name: ]
```

to let you create tables based on any last name entered by the end user.)

Save the query as **qryMakeTableBasedOnSmith** and then open it from the database window. You'll see the customary dialog boxes. Answer **Yes** to each, and the new CUSTOMER-X3 table will be created according to the specified criteria. Open the table from the database window and you will see the contents displayed in Figure 5.98.

5.5 RUNNING SUM

Used in a query, the **Running Sum** function enables the user to see how each record affects the total of a current transaction. To illustrate the creation and use of a running sum in a query, we will continue to use the **Ch05_POS_2nd.mdb** database. After you have loaded the database, select the query tab, click on **New**, and then select the **Design View** from the **New Query** window. Use the ORD_LINE table as the query's data source and drop and drag the fields from ORD_LINE as shown in Figure 5.99. Note that the ORD_LINE_NUM values are sorted in ascending order. Save the query and name it **qryRunningSum**.

Using Figure 5.99 as your guide, click on the column *next* to the ORD_LINE_TOTAL and then click on the **Build** wizard to generate the Expression Builder window shown in Figure 5.100.

Using the Expression Builder, do the following:

1. Type **RunningSum:**
2. Select **Functions/Built-In Functions**
3. Select **Domain Aggregate**
4. Double-click on the **DSum** function
5. Delete <<**Expr**>> and replace it with "**[ORD_LINE_TOTAL]**"
6. Replace <<**domain**>> with "**[qryRunningSum]**"
7. Replace <<**criteria**>> with "**[ORD_LINE_NUM]<=" & [ORD_LINE_NUM] &** " "

FIGURE 5.99
The ORD_LINE Query

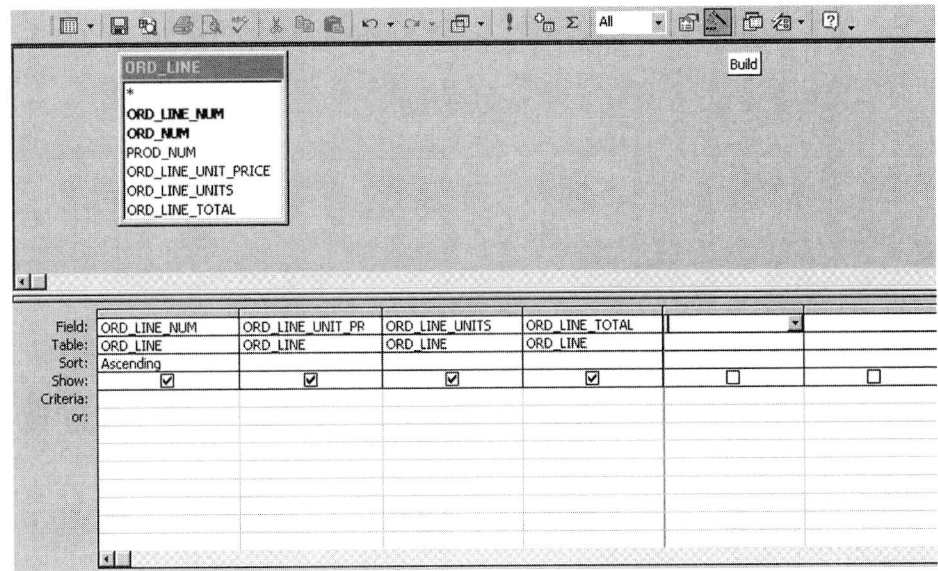

FIGURE 5.100
The Expression Builder Window

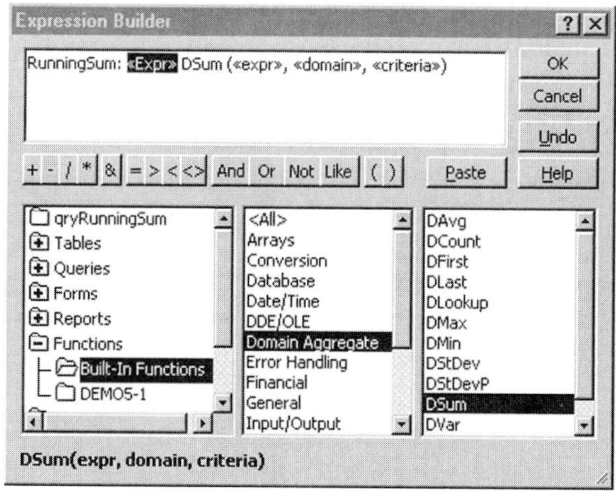

FIGURE 5.101
The RunningSum Function

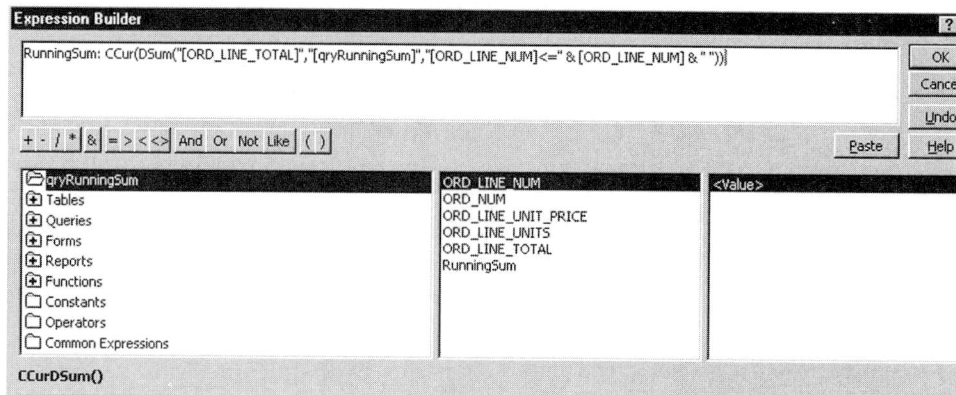

Finally, to ensure that the running total is presented in currency format, use the **CCur** function. Your completed Expression Builder command line is shown in Figure 5.101.

The **RunningSum** output is shown in Figure 5.102.

If you want to create a running sum for each order, insert a column prior to the **RunningSum** column, click on the **Build** wizard as shown in Figure 5.100, and in the Expression Builder window create the command line shown in Figure 5.103.

FIGURE 5.102
The RunningSum Output

Order Line Num	Order Num	Unit Price	Units	Total	Running Sum
4	4	$12.00	2	$24.00	$24.00
5	4	$41.25	3	$123.75	$147.75
6	4	$52.00	1	$52.00	$199.75
7	4	$86.35	1	$86.35	$286.10
8	5	$10.00	20	$200.00	$486.10
9	5	$10.00	12	$120.00	$606.10
10	5	$41.25	6	$247.50	$853.60
11	5	$86.96	8	$695.68	$1,549.28
12	6	$10.00	12	$120.00	$1,669.28
13	6	$10.00	20	$200.00	$1,869.28
14	6	$14.00	20	$280.00	$2,149.28
15	6	$52.00	25	$1,300.00	$3,449.28
16	7	$41.25	12	$495.00	$3,944.28
17	7	$11.00	25	$275.00	$4,219.28
18	9	$22.00	2	$44.00	$4,263.28
19	10	$0.00	12	$0.00	$4,263.28
20	11	$12.00	16	$192.00	$4,455.28
21	11	$41.25	0	$0.00	$4,455.28
22	12	$9.63	12	$115.56	$4,570.84
23	13	$41.25	12	$495.00	$5,065.84
24	13	$10.00	18	$180.00	$5,245.84
33	21	$14.00	6	$84.00	$5,329.84
(AutoNumber)	0	$0.00	0	$0.00	

FIGURE 5.103 The RunningSumByOrder Function

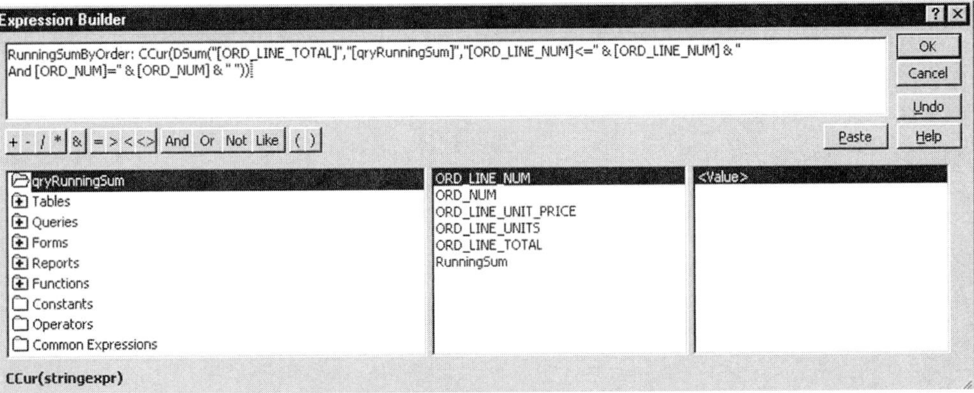

FIGURE 5.104 The RunningSumByOrder Output

Order Line Num	Order Num	Unit Price	Units	Total	Running Sum by Order	Running Sum
4	4	$12.00	2	$24.00	$24.00	$24.00
5	4	$41.25	3	$123.75	$147.75	$147.75
6	4	$52.00	1	$52.00	$199.75	$199.75
7	4	$86.35	1	$86.35	$286.10	$286.10
8	5	$10.00	20	$200.00	$200.00	$486.10
9	5	$10.00	12	$120.00	$320.00	$606.10
10	5	$41.25	6	$247.50	$567.50	$853.60
11	5	$86.96	8	$695.68	$1,263.18	$1,549.28
12	6	$10.00	12	$120.00	$120.00	$1,669.28
13	6	$10.00	20	$200.00	$320.00	$1,869.28
14	6	$14.00	20	$280.00	$600.00	$2,149.28
15	6	$52.00	25	$1,300.00	$1,900.00	$3,449.28
16	7	$41.25	12	$495.00	$495.00	$3,944.28
17	7	$11.00	25	$275.00	$770.00	$4,219.28
18	9	$22.00	2	$44.00	$44.00	$4,263.28
19	10	$0.00	12	$0.00	$0.00	$4,263.28
20	11	$12.00	16	$192.00	$192.00	$4,455.28
21	11	$41.25	0	$0.00	$192.00	$4,455.28
22	12	$9.63	12	$115.56	$115.56	$4,570.84
23	13	$41.25	12	$495.00	$495.00	$5,065.84
24	13	$10.00	18	$180.00	$675.00	$5,245.84
33	21	$14.00	6	$84.00	$84.00	$5,329.84
(AutoNumber)	0	$0.00	0	$0.00		

The query output generated by the command line in Figure 5.103 will look like Figure 5.104.

5.6 QUERY WRAP-UP

In this chapter you've learned how to create a number of query types. You saw the information generating power of the select and crosstab queries and you could, with a little imagination, appreciate the data management power of the various types of action queries.

The focus in this chapter was on technique, rather than on application. As the components of the **Ch05_POS-2nd.mdb** database come together in this book's last few chapters, you will have an opportunity to practice a higher level of query development based on what you learned in this chapter. By then you should also have learned enough about the applications development process to see and use the query types in their proper context and to understand and appreciate their power.

We started our discussion about queries by observing that they are powerful data management tools. In the context of the database system we will be developing in this book, you'll discover that we can trigger the use of appropriate queries automatically, thus decreasing the chance that end users forget to do the important data management chores. You will also learn that, in combination with other Access tools, such queries will play a crucial role in developing a well-organized and well-functioning system.

Problems

5.1 Modify the query created in section 5.2.5 to include a parameter request for the employee number. Make sure you use the **Like** function to include the employee number in the segmented search. (The basic format is shown in Figure 5.29A.) Using the **Like** function on the employee number that is based on the **AutoNumber** format will cause an entry such as 1 to produce all records containing a 1 in the employee number. Therefore, employee numbers 1, 11 through 19, 21, 31, and so on, will be included. Similarly, an entry of 11 would include all records whose employee numbers include 11. Also, include the employee initial in the output, but do not include the initial in the search. Sample input and output are shown in Figure P5.1. (The examples assume that you did not input anything in the last name and first name parameter requests. Note also that the output headers were modified with the help of the query's property boxes.)

FIGURE P5.1
Sample Employee Number Input and Output

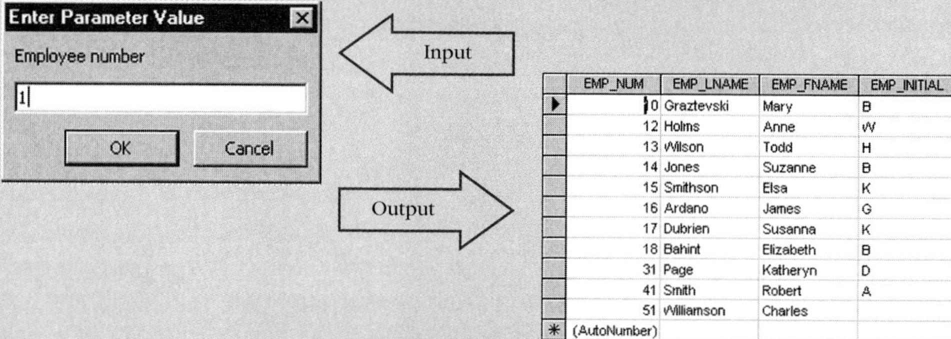

EMP_NUM	EMP_LNAME	EMP_FNAME	EMP_INITIAL
10	Graztevski	Mary	B
12	Holms	Anne	W
13	Wilson	Todd	H
14	Jones	Suzanne	B
15	Smithson	Elsa	K
16	Ardano	James	G
17	Dubrien	Susanna	K
18	Bahint	Elizabeth	B
31	Page	Katheryn	D
41	Smith	Robert	A
51	Williamson	Charles	
(AutoNumber)			

Save the query as **qryEmployeeSearch** and then open it several times to try the following input scenarios. (The notation *null* means that you make *no entry;* instead, you just press the keyboard's Enter key or you select **OK** from the parameter box without making an entry. Remember that a null does not mean a blank, so don't tap the keyboard's space bar before you select **OK**.)

Employee number: **2**	Last name: **null**	First name: **null**
Employee number: **null**	Last name: **Smith**	First name: **null**
Employee number: **null**	Last name: **null**	First name: **Robert**
Employee number: **null**	Last name: **Smith**	First name: **Robert**
Employee number: **null**	Last name: **null**	First name: **null**

(The last scenario will output *all* of the EMPLOYEE table records.)

Copy the **Ch05_TruckCo.mdb** database from the student CD in order to complete problems 5.2 through 5.16. (Remember, you have to uncheck the Read-only property to be able to work with the database.)

5.2 Use Access QBE to create a query to generate the output shown in Figure P5.2. Name the query **qryDriversByBase&License&School**. Note that the output attribute names have been changed with the help of the properties box. The drivers are listed in alphabetical order.

Note

Remember that you will always have a backup copy of the database on your CD. If you want to restore your database contents to the original, simply delete the database you have been working on and then copy the database from your CD. The backup copy is especially useful when you have experimented with update and append queries that did not quite run the way you intended!

FIGURE P5.2
Query Output for Problem 5.2

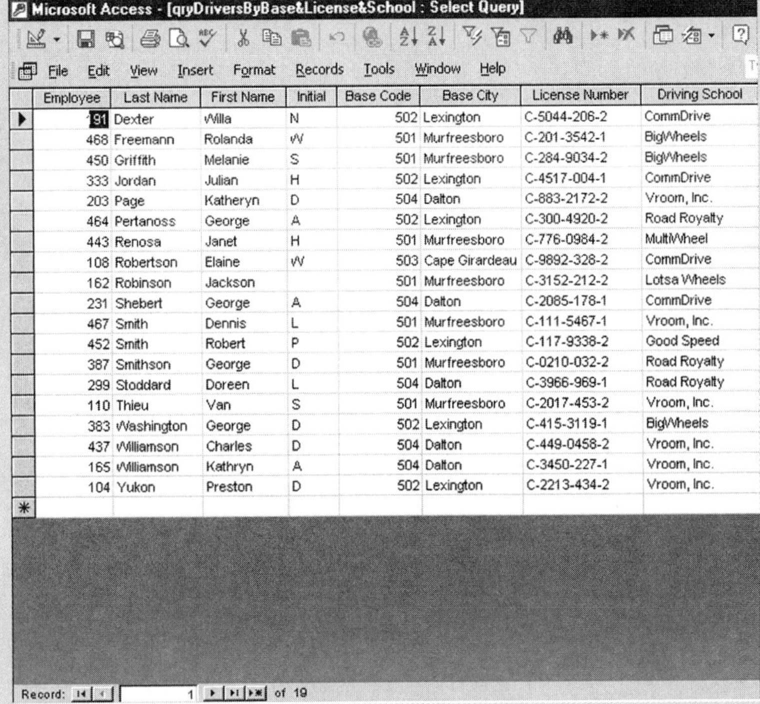

Microsoft Access - [qryDriversByBase&License&School : Select Query]

Employee	Last Name	First Name	Initial	Base Code	Base City	License Number	Driving School
191	Dexter	Willa	N	502	Lexington	C-5044-206-2	CommDrive
468	Freemann	Rolanda	W	501	Murfreesboro	C-201-3542-1	BigWheels
450	Griffith	Melanie	S	501	Murfreesboro	C-284-9034-2	BigWheels
333	Jordan	Julian	H	502	Lexington	C-4517-004-1	CommDrive
203	Page	Katheryn	D	504	Dalton	C-883-2172-2	Vroom, Inc.
464	Pertanoss	George	A	502	Lexington	C-300-4920-2	Road Royalty
443	Renosa	Janet	H	501	Murfreesboro	C-776-0984-2	MultiWheel
108	Robertson	Elaine	W	503	Cape Girardeau	C-9892-328-2	CommDrive
162	Robinson	Jackson		501	Murfreesboro	C-3152-212-2	Lotsa Wheels
231	Shebert	George	A	504	Dalton	C-2085-178-1	CommDrive
467	Smith	Dennis	L	501	Murfreesboro	C-111-5467-1	Vroom, Inc.
452	Smith	Robert	P	502	Lexington	C-117-9338-2	Good Speed
387	Smithson	George	D	501	Murfreesboro	C-0210-032-2	Road Royalty
299	Stoddard	Doreen	L	504	Dalton	C-3966-969-1	Road Royalty
110	Thieu	Van	S	501	Murfreesboro	C-2017-453-2	Vroom, Inc.
383	Washington	George	D	502	Lexington	C-415-3119-1	BigWheels
437	Williamson	Charles	D	504	Dalton	C-449-0458-2	Vroom, Inc.
165	Williamson	Kathryn	A	504	Dalton	C-3450-227-1	Vroom, Inc.
104	Yukon	Preston	D	502	Lexington	C-2213-434-2	Vroom, Inc.

Record: 1 of 19

5.3 Use Access QBE to create a query to generate the highest mileage for any vehicle in the VEHICLE table. (The output is shown in Figure P5.3.) Name the query **qryHighestMileageOnAnyVehicle**.

FIGURE P5.3
Query Output for Problem 5.3

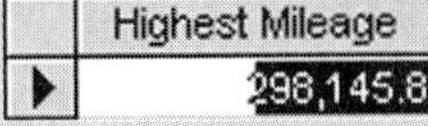

Highest Mileage
298,145.8

5.4 Use Access QBE to create a query to generate the output shown in Figure P5.4. Name the query **qryHighestMileageVehicle**.

FIGURE P5.4
Query Ouptut for Problem 5.4

Highest Mileage	Vehicle Number	Vehicle Type Code	Miles Driven	Base	Type Description
298,145.8	1013	3	298,145.8	Murfreesboro	Tandem trailer, single-axle

5.5 Use Access QBE to create a query to generate the input and output shown in Figure P5.5, using a mileage parameter. Name the query **QryListOfVehiclesDrivenMoreThanXMiles(ParameterQuery)**

FIGURE P5.5
Query Input/Output for Problem 5.5

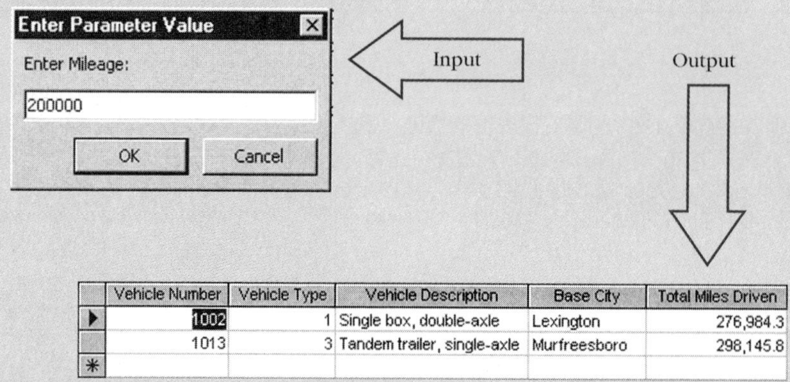

Vehicle Number	Vehicle Type	Vehicle Description	Base City	Total Miles Driven
1002	1	Single box, double-axle	Lexington	276,984.3
1013	3	Tandem trailer, single-axle	Murfreesboro	298,145.8

5.6 Use Access QBE to create a query to generate the output shown in Figure P5.6. Name the query **qryNumberOfEmployeesInEachJobDescription**.

FIGURE P5.6
Query Output for Problem 5.6

Job Code	Job Description	Number of Employees
1	Base Manager	4
2	Mechanic	18
3	Clerk	5
4	Driver	19
5	Secretary	4
6	Accountant	4
7	Customer Support Rep	4
8	Custodian	4
9	Database Manager	2
10	Technical Support Rep	4
11	Purchasing Agent	4

5.7 Use Access QBE to create a query to generate the output shown in Figure P5.7. Name the query **qryNumberOfEmployeesPerBaseAndBaseManagerName**.

FIGURE P5.7
Query Output for Problem 5.7

Base Code	Base City	Base Manager	Number of Employees
501	Murfreesboro	Edwards	22
502	Lexington	Ritula	16
503	Cape Girardeau	Matler	14
504	Dalton	Watson	20

5.8 Use Access QBE to create a query to generate the output shown in Figure P5.8. (*Hint:* Try using an outer join!) Name the query **qrySummaryOfDrivingSchoolsNotRepresentedInTheDRIVERtable**.

FIGURE P5.8
Query Output for Problem 5.8

School Number	School Name
7	Road Huggers
9	Safer Roads
10	Make'mSafe
11	Wide Turn
12	Comm Trucks
0	

5.9 Use Access QBE to create a parameter query that lets the end user specify a date range (by year) to produce the birthdays in the parameter output shown below the two dialog boxes in Figure P5.9. Name the query **qryEmployeeListByYearRange (Parameter Request)**.

FIGURE P5.9
Input/output Sequence for Problem 5.9

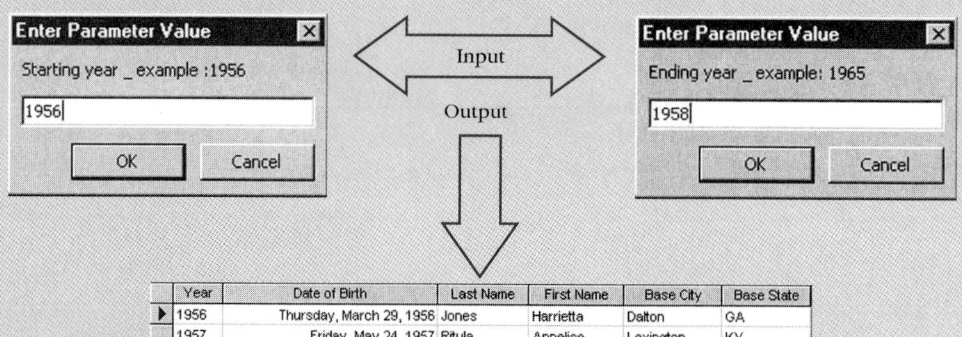

Year	Date of Birth	Last Name	First Name	Base City	Base State
1956	Thursday, March 29, 1956	Jones	Harrietta	Dalton	GA
1957	Friday, May 24, 1957	Ritula	Annelise	Lexington	KY

5.10 Using an end-user-selected date, create an update query to update the DRIVER table's DRIVER_YTD_MILES by the miles driven in the DRIVER_LOG and the DRIVER_YTD_HOURS by the hours logged in the DRIVER_LOG. The query must also update the VEHICLE table's VEHICLE_CURRENT_MILES by the miles logged in the DRIVER_LOG table. Name the query **qryUpdateDriverRecordsAfterTrip**.

Note 1: The driver cannot record miles and hours until the trip has been logged in. Therefore, use the DRIVER_LOG's ASSIGN_IN_DATE field as the target for your parameter's date entry.

Note 2: The ASSIGN_UPDATE_DONE field in the DRIVER_LOG must restrict the update. That is, the update can occur only if the field value is set to **No**, indicating that the record has not yet been used in an update.

5.11 Create two queries to show the vehicles that are not (yet) available for driver assignment. Name the two queries

a. **qryVehiclesStillNotReturnedFromTrip**
and

b. **qryVehiclesStillNotReleasedByMaintenance**
Combine the results of the two queries to show all of the vehicles that are not available for driver assignments. Name this query

c. **qryVehiclesNotAvailableForDriverAssignments**.

5.12 Create a parameter query to list a driver summary: total miles, average miles, average speed, and average number of hours for any selected driver. Name the query **qryDriverTotMiles,AvgMiles,AvgSpeed,AvgTimeBySelectedDriver.** Make sure that the parameter query lists the results for all the drivers if the end user makes no entry in the parameter dialog box and simply clicks **OK**, or taps the Enter key on the keyboard. (*Hint:* Remember the **Like** function and the "not null" criteria?) The input/output sequence is shown in Figures P5.12 and P5.12A.

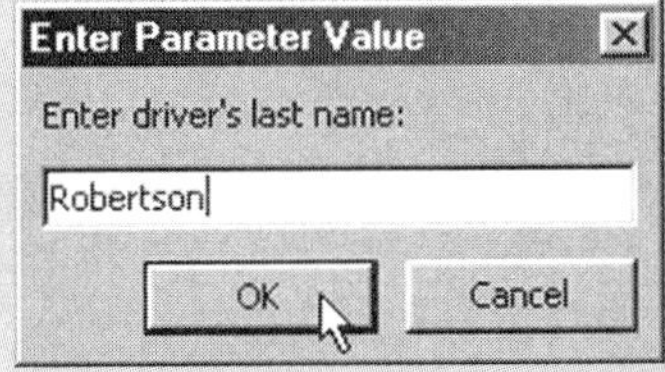

FIGURE P5.12
Sample Input for Problem 5.12

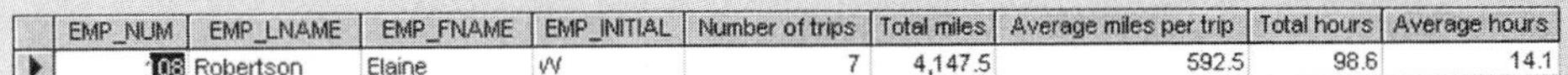

EMP_NUM	EMP_LNAME	EMP_FNAME	EMP_INITIAL	Number of trips	Total miles	Average miles per trip	Total hours	Average hours
108	Robertson	Elaine	W	7	4,147.5	592.5	98.6	14.1

FIGURE P5.12A
Sample Output for Problem 5.12

5.13 Create the query that lists the mileage between maintenance events for each vehicle in the maintenance log. Name this query **qryMilesBetweenMaintenanceFor Selected Vehicles**.

5.14 Create a starting and ending date parameter query to list the miles and hours driven for all drivers. Name this query **qryDriverMilesAndHoursBySelectedDateRange**. (*Hint:* The miles and hours for a trip cannot be listed unless the vehicle has returned from that trip.) As you examine Figures P5.14a through P5.14c, note that the date input format does not determine the output format, which was set at the table level. Naturally, the output format can be set at the query level, too—using the query's properties box.

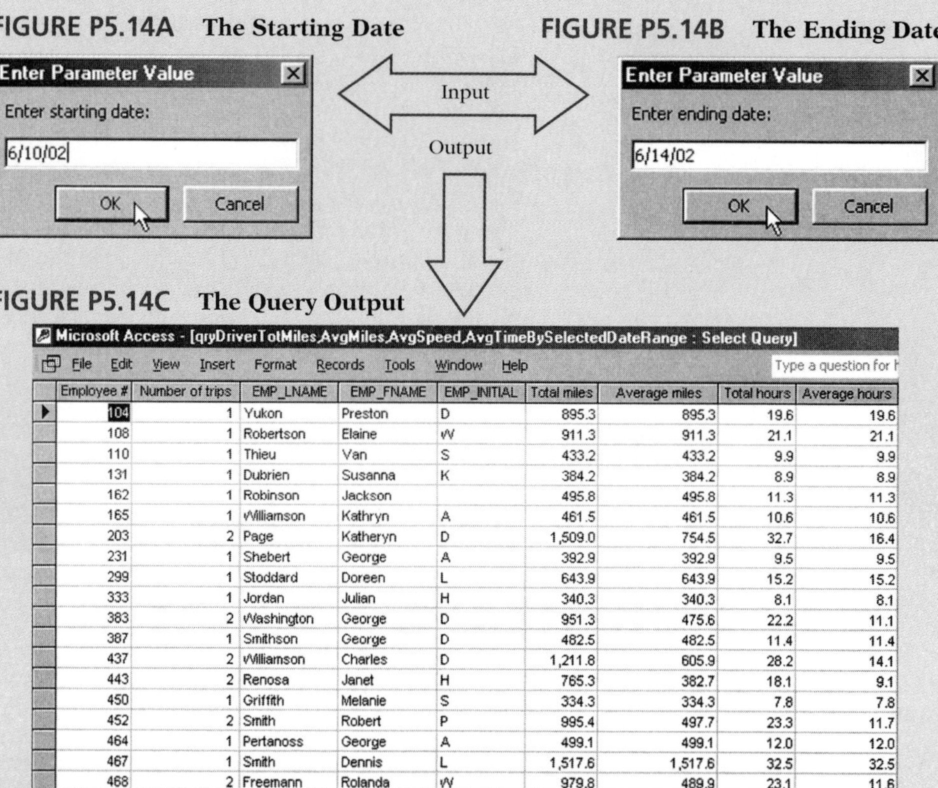

FIGURE P5.14A The Starting Date

FIGURE P5.14B The Ending Date

FIGURE P5.14C The Query Output

Employee #	Number of trips	EMP_LNAME	EMP_FNAME	EMP_INITIAL	Total miles	Average miles	Total hours	Average hours
104	1	Yukon	Preston	D	895.3	895.3	19.6	19.6
108	1	Robertson	Elaine	W	911.3	911.3	21.1	21.1
110	1	Thieu	Van	S	433.2	433.2	9.9	9.9
131	1	Dubrien	Susanna	K	384.2	384.2	8.9	8.9
162	1	Robinson	Jackson		495.8	495.8	11.3	11.3
165	1	Williamson	Kathryn	A	461.5	461.5	10.6	10.6
203	2	Page	Katheryn	D	1,509.0	754.5	32.7	16.4
231	1	Shebert	George	A	392.9	392.9	9.5	9.5
299	1	Stoddard	Doreen	L	643.9	643.9	15.2	15.2
333	1	Jordan	Julian	H	340.3	340.3	8.1	8.1
383	2	Washington	George	D	951.3	475.6	22.2	11.1
387	1	Smithson	George	D	482.5	482.5	11.4	11.4
437	2	Williamson	Charles	D	1,211.8	605.9	28.2	14.1
443	2	Renosa	Janet	H	765.3	382.7	18.1	9.1
450	1	Griffith	Melanie	S	334.3	334.3	7.8	7.8
452	2	Smith	Robert	P	995.4	497.7	23.3	11.7
464	1	Pertanoss	George	A	499.1	499.1	12.0	12.0
467	1	Smith	Dennis	L	1,517.6	1,517.6	32.5	32.5
468	2	Freemann	Rolanda	W	979.8	489.9	23.1	11.6

5.15 Create a query to list all the type codes that are not found in the VEHICLE table. Name this query **qryTypeCodesNotInTheVEHICLEtable**. (*Hint:* Remember outer joins?)

5.16 Use the results of the query created in problem 5.15 to produce a summary of the vehicle types not found in the VEHICLE table. Name this query **qrySummaryOfVehicleTypesNotInTheVEHICLEtable**.

Problems 5.17 through 5.27 are based on the Ch05_FlyHigh.MDB database. (Copy the database from the student CD attached to the book. Remember to uncheck the Read-only property of the file!) The output shown in the problems reflects the original database table contents. Naturally, if you make any changes in the table contents, those changes will be reflected in the query output. Therefore, use the query output shown in the problems as examples of the required query output format, rather than as a precise listing of your query output. Also, we have limited the query output in several problems to just a few of the records to save considerable space.

5.17 Create update queries to calculate and record the following RENTAL table attribute values: RENT_HOURS, calculated by subtracting RENT_HOBBS_OUT from RENT_HOBBS_IN. (*Hint:* Remember that you must select an update query format.) Then use the Criteria statement **[RENTAL]![RENT_HOBBS_RETURN]-[RENTAL]![RENT_HOBBS_OUT]** to update the RENTAL table's RENT_HOURS field values. (You did remember to use the Expression Builder, didn't you?) Name this update query **qryUpdateRentalHours**. Now run this update query.

To complete the update query series for the RENTAL table, you will need three additional queries.

a. Create an update query to calculate and update the RENTAL table's RENT_CHARGE values. (*Hint:* The RENT_CHARGE values are calculated by multiplying the RENT_HOURS you produced in the previous query and the RENTAL table's RENT_CHG_HOUR values.) Name this update query **qryUpdateRentalCharge**. Now run the query to perform the updates.

Note

The **qryUpdateRentalHours** update query teaches a vital lesson. If you merely perform the subtraction, the resulting calculations may be incorrect by a small fraction. (This problem is illustrated in Figures P5.17 through P5.17B. We have scrolled *down* to the 22nd record to preserve the headers. We have scrolled to the *right* in Figure P5.17A to show the remaining attributes in the RENTAL table.)

FIGURE P5.17 The Computed Rental Hour Value

Microsoft Access - [RENTAL : Table]

RENT_NUM	RENT_DATE	CUST_NUM	AC_NUM	RENT_HOBBS_OUT	RENT_HOBBS_RETURN	RENT_HOURS	RENT_CHG_HOUR	RENT_AI
22	06-May-2003	19	1440P	1008.4	1011.6	3.2	$175.00	$5
23	06-May-2003	13	2085V	1517.3	1519.3	2.0	$68.75	$1

FIGURE P5.17A Computed Rental Charge, Tax, and Total

Microsoft Access - [RENTAL : Table]

RENT_AMOUNT	RENT_TAX	RENT_TOTAL	RENT_CHG_UPDATED	RENT_CUS_UPDATED
$559.99	$44.80	$604.79	☑	☑
$137.50	$11.00	$148.50	☑	☑

As you examine Figure P5.17, you see that the RENT_HOURS value *appears* to be correctly calculated as 3.2. However, Figure P5.17A shows that the rental amount and, therefore, the total charge are incorrect—they are off by a penny (3.2 times $175.00 is *not* equal to $559.99). The reason for this error becomes clear when you look at Figure P5.17B.

FIGURE P5.17B The Recorded RENT_HOURS Value

Microsoft Access - [RENTAL : Table]

RENT_NUM	RENT_DATE	CUST_NUM	AC_NUM	RENT_HOBBS_OUT	RENT_HOBBS_RETURN	RENT_HOURS	RENT_CHG_HOUR	RENT_AI
22	06-May-2003	19	1440P	1008.4	1011.6	3.199951	$175.00	$5
23	06-May-2003	13	2085V	1517.3	1519.3	2.0	$68.75	$1

As you examine Figure P5.17B, you will see that the 22nd record in Figure 5.17B shows a RENT_HOURS value of 3.199951 when you place the cursor on this cell and click. (That will happen even though the RENT_HOURS attribute in the RENTAL table was properly defined to be a standard number with one decimal place.) Worse, if this calculated value is used in subsequent calculations such as the rental charge, you will discover that the rental charge will be off by a few pennies. Therefore, the tax may be miscalculated and, in any case, the total charge will be incorrect. That's the sort of thing that makes accountants *very* unhappy.

Such problems can be eliminated if you use the following **Round()** function **Round([RENTAL]![RENT_HOBBS_RETURN]-[RENTAL]![RENT_HOBBS_OUT],1)** in your update query's **Criteria** box for the RENT_HOURS attribute (see Figure P5.17C). Note that the **Round()** function format requires you to define what you are rounding and the number of decimal places—1, in this case—to which the value must be rounded.

FIGURE P5.17C Correctly Rounded Rental Hour Value

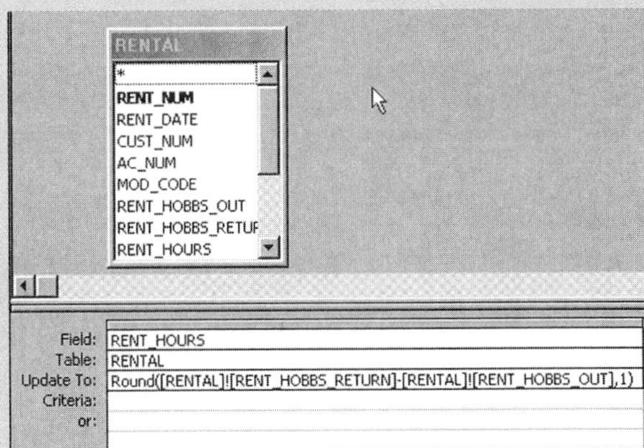

Go ahead and run the corrected **qryUpdateRentalHours** update query, then run (again!) the other update queries you created in this problem sequence. Now check the RENTAL table's 22nd record and you can see that the values are now correctly calculated. (We have already run this correction in the teacher's version.)

b. Create an update query to calculate the RENT_TAX on the rental charge. The tax rate is 8 percent. Name this query **qryUpdateTaxAmountOnRentalCharge**. Now run the query to perform the updates.

c. Create an update query to calculate the RENT_TOTAL in the RENTAL table. (*Hint:* The total rental charge is calculated by adding the RENT_CHARGE and the RENT_TAX values that were calculated with the help of the preceding update queries. Name this update query **qryUpdateTotalRentalCharge,IncludingTax**. Now run the query to perform the updates.

If you open the RENTAL table to see if the updates yielded correct results, you will get an unpleasant surprise when you examine the 22nd record. Read the following note carefully to see what happened and how you can correct the problem.

After creating and running the corrected update queries for this problem, create a parameter query named **qryRentalActivityBySelectedAircraft** to produce the input and output shown in Figures P5.17D and P5.17E. If the end user makes no input and simply clicks on the **OK** button shown in Figure P5.17D, the output for all aircraft must be shown. (*Hint:* Remember the **Like** option?)

FIGURE P5.17D
Query Input for Problem 5.17

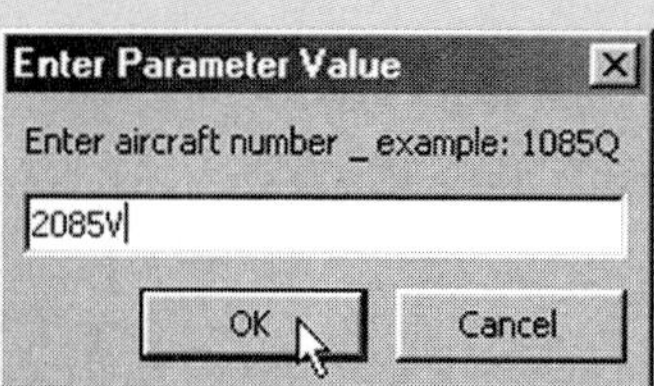

FIGURE P5.17E
Query Output for Problem 5.17

Microsoft Access - [qryRentalActivityBySelectedAircraft : Select Query]

File Edit View Insert Format Records Tools Window Help

Aircraft #	Rental Date	Model	Charge/Hour	Rental hours	Rental Charge	Tax	Total Charge
2085V	04-May-2003	PA28-181	$68.75	2.4	$165.00	$13.20	$178.20
2085V	05-May-2003	PA28-181	$68.75	2.0	$137.50	$11.00	$148.50
2085V	05-May-2003	PA28-181	$68.75	4.0	$338.00	$27.04	$365.04
2085V	06-May-2003	PA28-181	$68.75	2.0	$137.50	$11.00	$148.50
2085V	06-May-2003	PA28-181	$68.75	2.1	$144.37	$11.55	$155.92
2085V	06-May-2003	PA28-181	$68.75	3.5	$240.62	$19.25	$259.87
2085V	07-May-2003	PA28-181	$68.75	3.0	$206.25	$16.50	$222.75
2085V	07-May-2003	PA28-181	$68.75	4.0	$275.00	$22.00	$297.00
2085V	08-May-2003	PA28-181	$68.75	2.1	$144.37	$11.55	$155.92
2085V	09-May-2003	PA28-181	$68.75	1.0	$68.75	$5.50	$74.25
2085V	12-May-2003	PA28-181	$68.75	1.3	$89.37	$7.15	$96.52

5.18 Create a query named **qryQualificationsGroupedBySelectedCustomer** to produce the input and output shown in Figures P5.18 through P5.18B.

FIGURE P5.18
Last Name Input for Problem 5.18

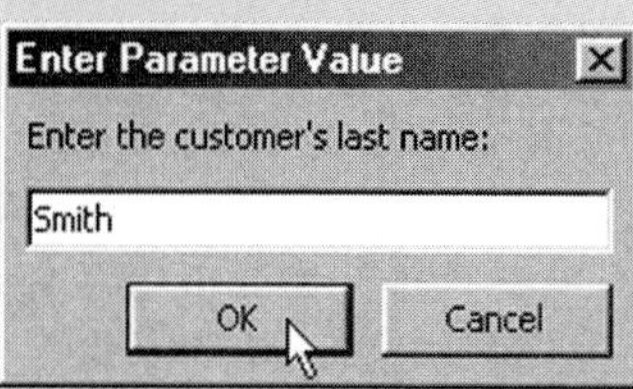

FIGURE P5.18A
First Name Input for Problem 5.18

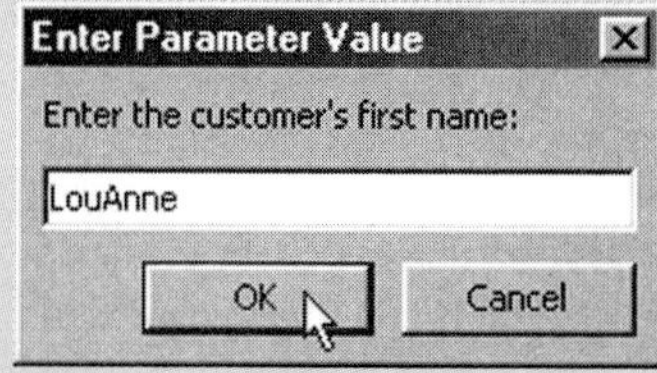

FIGURE P5.18B
Query Output for Problem 5.18

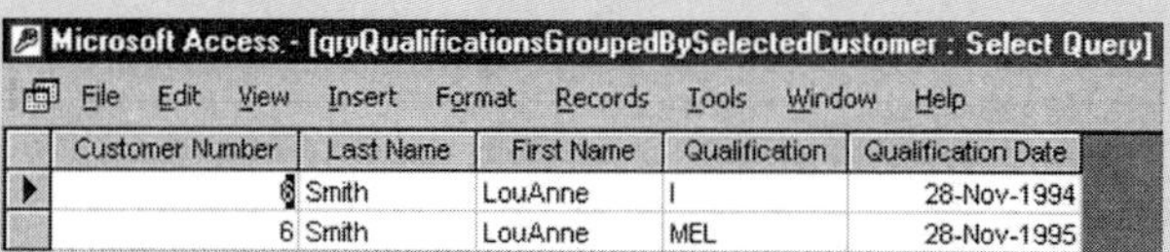
Microsoft Access - [qryQualificationsGroupedBySelectedCustomer : Select Query]

File Edit View Insert Format Records Tools Window Help

Customer Number	Last Name	First Name	Qualification	Qualification Date
6	Smith	LouAnne	I	28-Nov-1994
6	Smith	LouAnne	MEL	28-Nov-1995

5.19 Using a query named **qryQualificationsBySelectedCustomer,CascadingSearch**, create a parameter query to find the customer qualifications for selected customers. A sample search sequence, followed by the output, is shown in Figures P5.19 through P5.19C.

FIGURE P5.19
Customer Number Input for Problem 5.19

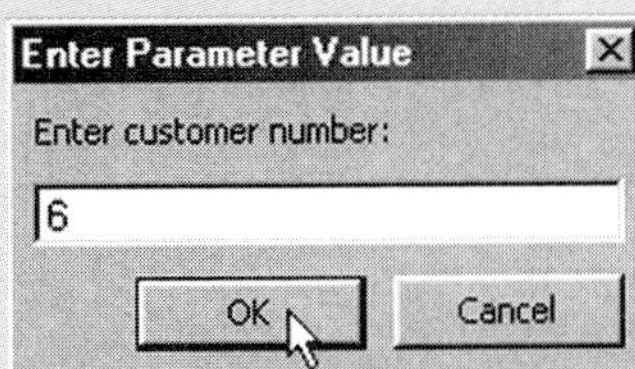

FIGURE P5.19A
Customer Last Name Input for Problem 5.19

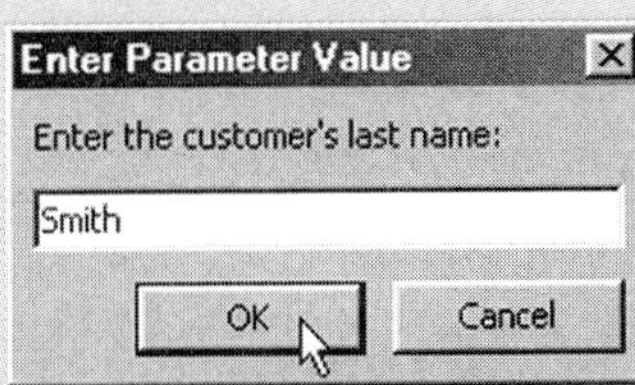

FIGURE P5.19B
Customer First Name Input for Problem 5.19

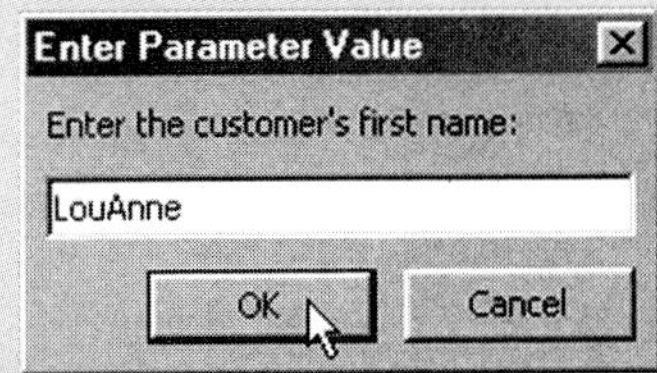

FIGURE P5.19C
Query Output for Problem 5.19

Microsoft Access - [qryQualificationsBySelectedCustomer,CascadingSearch : Select Query]

File Edit View Insert Format Records Tools Window Help

Customer Number	Last Name	First Name	Qualification	Qualification Date
6	Smith	LouAnne	I	28-Nov-1994
6	Smith	LouAnne	MEL	28-Nov-1995
10	Smith	William	COMM	07-Jan-2000
10	Smith	William	I	07-Jan-2002
10	Smith	William	MEL	18-Mar-2001
16	Smith	Mary	COMM	27-Mar-1997
16	Smith	Mary	PVT	03-Apr-1996
17	Smithson	John	COMM	28-Apr-1996
17	Smithson	John	I	30-May-1996
17	Smithson	John	PVT	28-Jul-1998
20	Smithlen	Jorge	I	12-Jul-2001
20	Smithlen	Jorge	MEL	15-Dec-2002
20	Smithlen	Jorge	PVT	27-Apr-2000

5.20 Create a query named **qryCustomersWithoutQualificationTableEntries** to find the customers for whom no entries have been made in the QUALIFICATION table. The query output is shown in Figure P5.20.

FIGURE P5.20
Query Output for Problem 5.20

Microsoft Access - [qryCustomersWithoutQualificationTableEntries : Select Query]

File Edit View Insert Format Records Tools Window Help

Customer	Last Name	First Name	Area Code	Phone	PIC Hours	MEL Hours
18	Weiskopf	Daphne	615	890-1122	567.0	352.7
21	Johnson	Peter	615	896-2218	456.7	0.0
(AutoNumber)			0		0.0	0.0

5.21 Create a query named **qryTotalRentalRevenuesAndTaxesByAircraft** to produce a revenue and tax summary for each aircraft rented by FlyHigh Company's customers. (*Hint:* Use the query you created in Problem 5.17 [named **qryRental ActivityByAircraft**] as the data source for this query.) The sample output is shown in Figure P5.21.

FIGURE P5.21
Query Output for Problem 5.21

Aircraft #	Rental Charge	Tax	Total Charge
1085Q	$941.85	$75.36	$1,017.21
1440P	$3,640.60	$291.20	$3,931.20
1998V	$652.80	$52.23	$705.03
2085V	$1,946.73	$155.74	$2,102.47
2284W	$982.80	$78.63	$1,061.43
2323G	$1,231.95	$98.56	$1,330.51
2873R	$386.10	$30.88	$416.98
3122K	$327.60	$26.21	$353.81
3319R	$953.60	$76.29	$1,029.89
5827Y	$895.70	$71.65	$967.35

5.22 Create a parameter query named **qrySelectedRentalsByAircraftNumber** to produce the output shown in Figures P5.22 and P5.22A. Note that the parameter query requires the end user to enter the aircraft number.

FIGURE P5.22
Query Input for Problem 5.22

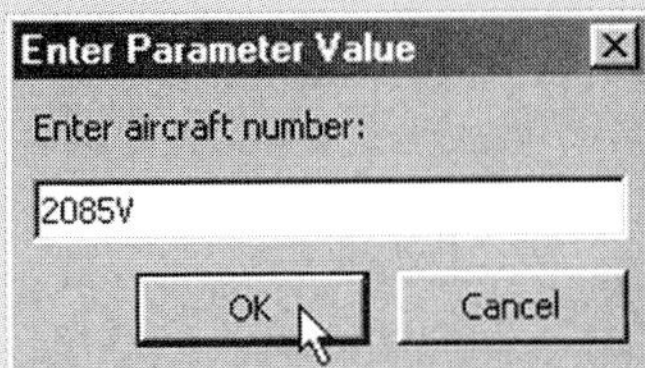

FIGURE P5.22A
Query Output for Problem 5.22

Aircraft	Rental Number	Rental Date	Rental Hours	Customer Last Name	Customer First Name
2085V	19	06-May-2003	2.1	Robertson	John
2085V	13	05-May-2003	2.0	Wilson	George
2085V	33	07-May-2003	4.0	Lopez	Jorge
2085V	37	07-May-2003	3.0	Treynor	Helen
2085V	29	06-May-2003	3.5	Embaum	Joseph
2085V	83	12-May-2003	1.3	Embaum	Joseph
2085V	23	06-May-2003	2.0	Williamson	George
2085V	16	05-May-2003	4.0	Barakat	Amin
2085V	4	04-May-2003	2.4	Ziade	George
2085V	58	09-May-2003	1.0	Smith	Mary
2085V	48	08-May-2003	2.1	Smithlen	Jorge
	(AutoNumber)				

5.23 Create a query named **qryNumberOfCustomersByQualification** to produce a count of the number of customers for each qualification. The sample output is shown in Figure P5.23.

FIGURE P5.23
Query Output for Problem 5.23

Qualification	Number of Customers
ATP	2
COMM	10
I	10
MEL	9
PVT	11

5.24 Create a query named **qryRentalHoursGroupedByCustomer** to produce the rental activity records for all customers. Some sample records are shown in Figure P5.24.

FIGURE P5.24
Query Output for Problem 5.24

Microsoft Access - [qryRentalHoursGroupedByCustomer : Select Query]

File Edit View Insert Format Records Tools Window Help

Customer #	Last Name	First Name	Rental Date	Rental Hours	Aircraft
1	Robertson	Steven	04-May-2003	1.2	1085Q
1	Robertson	Steven	07-May-2003	1.8	1440P
1	Robertson	Steven	09-May-2003	1.0	2323G
1	Robertson	Steven	09-May-2003	1.6	1440P
1	Robertson	Steven	10-May-2003	1.0	1440P
1	Robertson	Steven	11-May-2003	2.8	1440P
2	Drapfna	Anna	04-May-2003	2.2	5827Y
2	Drapfna	Anna	05-May-2003	0.8	3122K
2	Drapfna	Anna	08-May-2003	1.9	1998V
2	Drapfna	Anna	09-May-2003	1.0	2323G
2	Drapfna	Anna	09-May-2003	1.0	3319R
3	Fransisco	Mark	04-May-2003	3.1	3319R
3	Fransisco	Mark	06-May-2003	0.7	3122K
3	Fransisco	Mark	08-May-2003	1.0	2323G
3	Fransisco	Mark	10-May-2003	0.7	1085Q
3	Fransisco	Mark	11-May-2003	1.9	2323G
4	Robertson	John	05-May-2003	1.5	2284W
4	Robertson	John	06-May-2003	2.1	2085V
4	Robertson	John	09-May-2003	1.0	1440P
4	Robertson	John	09-May-2003	1.0	2323G
4	Robertson	John	10-May-2003	2.3	1085Q
4	Robertson	John	12-May-2003	3.2	5827Y
5	Wilson	George	05-May-2003	1.0	2873R
5	Wilson	George	05-May-2003	2.0	2085V
6	Smith	LouAnne	04-May-2003	3.8	5827Y
6	Smith	LouAnne	06-May-2003	3.3	3319R
6	Smith	LouAnne	07-May-2003	2.0	1085Q
6	Smith	LouAnne	09-May-2003	1.0	1440P
6	Smith	LouAnne	10-May-2003	1.0	2323G
7	Rosten	Peter	04-May-2003	1.0	2284W

Record: 1 of 82

5.25 Create a query named **qryTotalRentalHoursByCustomer** to produce the rental summary shown in Figure P5.25.

FIGURE P5.25
Query Output for Problem 5.25

Customer #	Last Name	First Name	Total Rental Hours
1	Robertson	Steven	9.4
2	Drapfna	Anna	6.9
3	Fransisco	Mark	7.4
4	Robertson	John	11.1
5	Wilson	George	3.0
6	Smith	LouAnne	11.1
7	Rosten	Peter	6.1
8	Damanov	Elise	6.2
9	Lopez	Jorge	7.2
10	Smith	William	10.1
11	Treynor	Helen	12.4
12	Embaum	Joseph	7.1
13	Williamson	George	10.6
14	Barakat	Amin	5.1
15	Ziade	George	8.0
16	Smith	Mary	4.8
17	Smithson	John	6.3
19	Mueller	Heinz	9.9
20	Smithlen	Jorge	3.2

5.26 Create a query named **qryRentalRevenue&TaxByCustomer** to produce the summary output shown in Figure P5.26.

FIGURE P5.26
Query Output for Problem 5.26

Microsoft Access - [qryRentalRevenue&TaxByCustomer : Select Query]

File Edit View Insert Format Records Tools Window Help

Cust. #	Last Name	First Name	Rental date	AC	Hrs.	Charge	Tax	Total Charge
1	Robertson	Steven	04-May-2003	1085Q	1.2	$70.20	$5.62	$75.82
1	Robertson	Steven	07-May-2003	1440P	1.8	$315.00	$25.20	$340.20
1	Robertson	Steven	09-May-2003	1440P	1.6	$280.00	$22.40	$302.40
1	Robertson	Steven	09-May-2003	2323G	1.0	$95.50	$7.64	$103.14
1	Robertson	Steven	10-May-2003	1440P	1.0	$175.00	$14.00	$189.00
1	Robertson	Steven	11-May-2003	1440P	2.8	$490.00	$39.20	$529.20
2	Drapfna	Anna	04-May-2003	5827Y	2.2	$185.90	$14.87	$200.77
2	Drapfna	Anna	05-May-2003	3122K	0.8	$46.80	$3.74	$50.54
2	Drapfna	Anna	08-May-2003	1998V	1.9	$121.60	$9.73	$131.33
2	Drapfna	Anna	09-May-2003	3319R	1.0	$64.00	$5.12	$69.12
2	Drapfna	Anna	09-May-2003	2323G	1.0	$95.50	$7.64	$103.14
3	Fransisco	Mark	04-May-2003	3319R	3.1	$198.40	$15.87	$214.27
3	Fransisco	Mark	06-May-2003	3122K	0.7	$40.95	$3.28	$44.23
3	Fransisco	Mark	08-May-2003	2323G	1.0	$95.50	$7.64	$103.14
3	Fransisco	Mark	10-May-2003	1085Q	0.7	$40.95	$3.28	$44.23
3	Fransisco	Mark	11-May-2003	2323G	1.9	$181.45	$14.52	$195.97
4	Robertson	John	05-May-2003	2284W	1.5	$87.75	$7.02	$94.77
4	Robertson	John	06-May-2003	2085V	2.1	$144.37	$11.55	$155.92
4	Robertson	John	09-May-2003	2323G	1.0	$95.50	$7.64	$103.14
4	Robertson	John	09-May-2003	2323G	1.0	$95.50	$7.64	$103.14
4	Robertson	John	09-May-2003	1440P	1.0	$175.00	$14.00	$189.00
4	Robertson	John	09-May-2003	2323G	1.0	$95.50	$7.64	$103.14
4	Robertson	John	10-May-2003	1085Q	2.3	$134.55	$10.76	$145.31
4	Robertson	John	12-May-2003	5827Y	3.2	$270.40	$21.63	$292.03
5	Wilson	George	05-May-2003	2873R	1.0	$58.50	$4.68	$63.18
5	Wilson	George	05-May-2003	2085V	2.0	$137.50	$11.00	$148.50
6	Smith	LouAnne	04-May-2003	5827Y	3.8	$321.10	$25.69	$346.79
6	Smith	LouAnne	06-May-2003	3319R	3.3	$211.20	$16.90	$228.10
6	Smith	LouAnne	07-May-2003	1085Q	2.0	$117.00	$9.36	$126.36
6	Smith	LouAnne	09-May-2003	1440P	1.0	$175.00	$14.00	$189.00

Record: 1 of 84

5.27 Using the query output you produced in problem 5.26 as your data source, create a query named **qryTotalRentalRevenue&TaxByCustomer** to produce the summary shown in Figure P5.27.

FIGURE P5.27
Query Output for Problem 5.27

Cust. #	Last Name	First Name	Rental Charge	Tax	Total
1	Robertson	Steven	$1,425.70	$114.06	$1,539.76
2	Drapfna	Anna	$513.80	$41.10	$554.90
3	Fransisco	Mark	$557.25	$44.59	$601.84
4	Robertson	John	$1,098.57	$87.88	$1,186.45
5	Wilson	George	$196.00	$15.68	$211.68
6	Smith	LouAnne	$919.80	$73.59	$993.39
7	Rosten	Peter	$361.80	$28.94	$390.74
8	Damanov	Elise	$369.85	$29.59	$399.44
9	Lopez	Jorge	$485.50	$38.84	$524.34
10	Smith	William	$791.80	$63.35	$855.15
11	Treynor	Helen	$809.60	$64.77	$874.37
12	Embaum	Joseph	$477.19	$38.18	$515.37
13	Williamson	George	$647.20	$51.77	$698.97
14	Barakat	Amin	$402.35	$32.19	$434.54
15	Ziade	George	$917.50	$73.40	$990.90
16	Smith	Mary	$495.25	$39.62	$534.87
17	Smithson	John	$416.55	$33.33	$449.88
19	Mueller	Heinz	$1,511.75	$120.89	$1,632.04
20	Smithlen	Jorge	$214.77	$17.18	$231.95

Problems 5.28 through 5.30 are based on the Ch05_ConsultCo database. (Copy the database from the student CD attached to the book. Remember to uncheck the Read-only property of the file!) The output shown in the problems reflects the original database table contents. Naturally, if you make any changes in the table contents, those changes will be reflected in the query output. Therefore, use the query output shown in the problems as examples of the required query output format, rather than as a precise listing of your query output. Also, we have limited the query output in several problems to just a few of the records to save considerable space.

5.28 Create a query to produce a listing of the assignment charges. The output is shown in Figures P5.28 and P5.28A. Name the query **qryProjectAssignment**. (Only the first 15 records are shown.)

FIGURE P5.28
Query Output for Problem 5.28, the First Six Fields

Charge_Num	Charge_Date	Proj_Num	Emp_Num	Job_Code	Job_Description
1	13-Jun-02	127	3	DSD	Database Systems Designer
2	13-Jun-02	123	6	SMO	Statistical Modeler
3	13-Jun-02	123	6	SAN	Systems Analyst
4	13-Jun-02	126	2	NAD	Network Administrator
5	13-Jun-02	128	7	DSS	Decision Support Systems Spec.
6	13-Jun-02	127	2	DSD	Database Systems Designer
7	13-Jun-02	123	7	DSD	Database Systems Designer
8	13-Jun-02	125	5	NAD	Network Administrator
9	13-Jun-02	124	3	DSD	Database Systems Designer
10	13-Jun-02	127	5	NAD	Network Administrator
11	13-Jun-02	123	3	DSD	Database Systems Designer
12	14-Jun-02	126	7	DAN	Data Analyst
13	14-Jun-02	127	6	SAN	Systems Analyst
14	14-Jun-02	125	3	DSD	Database Systems Designer
15	14-Jun-02	123	6	SMO	Statistical Modeler

FIGURE P5.28A
Query Output for Problem 5.28, the Remaining Fields

Job_Chg_Hour	Charge_Hours	Charge_Per_Hour	Charge_Amount
$175.00	2.6	$175.00	$435.00
$105.00	1.8	$85.00	$153.00
$145.00	2.0	$145.00	$290.00
$120.00	3.7	$120.00	$444.00
$79.50	3.2	$79.50	$254.40
$175.00	2.9	$175.00	$507.50
$175.00	2.9	$175.00	$507.50
$120.00	1.5	$120.00	$180.00
$175.00	2.3	$175.00	$402.50
$120.00	4.3	$120.00	$516.00
$175.00	3.8	$175.00	$665.00
$95.00	1.5	$95.00	$142.50
$145.00	5.0	$145.00	$725.00
$175.00	2.9	$175.00	$507.50
$105.00	3.8	$85.00	$323.00

5.29 Produce a query to list the total hours and charges by project. The query output is shown in Figure P5.29. Name the query **qryTotalHoursAndChargesByProject**.

FIGURE P5.29
Query Output for Problem 5.29

Project #	Project Name	Project Manager	Project Coordinator	Total Hours	Total Charge
123	Rock Veil	Smithson	Cheng	40.60	$4,677.45
124	Willow Branch	Hernandez	Smith	2.30	$402.50
125	Tin Roof	Jackson	Cheng	27.40	$3,417.50
126	Freeze	Cheng	Smithson	5.20	$586.50
127	Rumble Seat	Smithson	Jackson	19.80	$2,783.50
128	Fancy Flight	Cheng	Hernandez	7.30	$746.40
129	Soleil	Chen	Sanchez	16.10	$1,596.65
130	DataBuzz	Alammar	Cheng	20.90	$2,285.00
131	Take-Off	Callahan	Sen	7.50	$943.40
134	Sabre	Sen	Smithson	15.10	$1,762.95
135	Yellow Rose	Chen	Alammar	9.80	$1,262.50
136	Tulip Dawn	Sanchez	Hernandez	6.60	$524.70
137	Misty	Hernandez	Sanchez	3.90	$585.00

5.30 Produce a query to list the project characteristics by client. The query output is shown in Figure P5.30. Name the query **qryProjectSummaryByClient**.

FIGURE P5.30
Query Output for Problem 5.30

Client #	Client Name	Project Name	Project Opening Date	Project Cost	Manager	Coordinator
112	DataBuzz	Freeze	02-Mar-2002	$1,080,000.00	Cheng	Smithson
112	DataBuzz	Yellow Rose	25-Feb-2002	$850,000.00	Chen	Alammar
114	KPR & Co.	Fancy Flight	15-Apr-2002	$6,805,000.00	Cheng	Hernandez
114	KPR & Co.	Ropetrick	11-Feb-2002	$185,490.00	Sanchez	Alammar
114	KPR & Co.	Sabre	17-Feb-2002	$2,208,500.00	Sen	Smithson
114	KPR & Co.	Tin Roof	12-May-2002	$4,557,500.00	Jackson	Cheng
115	RadCo, Inc.	Koi Gardens	20-Apr-2002	$3,850,000.00	Chen	Sen
115	RadCo, Inc.	Misty	01-Mar-2002	$145,500.00	Hernandez	Sanchez
115	RadCo, Inc.	Soleil	22-Apr-2002	$208,500.00	Chen	Sanchez
118	CommCo, Inc.	DataBuzz	22-Apr-2002	$1,050,450.00	Alammar	Cheng
118	CommCo, Inc.	Rock Veil	12-May-2002	$2,707.00	Smithson	Cheng
118	CommCo, Inc.	Rumble Seat	12-Apr-2002	$3,010,000.00	Smithson	Jackson
118	CommCo, Inc.	Swordfish	11-Feb-2002	$205,314.00	Esterbach	Sanchez
118	CommCo, Inc.	Take-Off	30-Apr-2002	$75,800.00	Callahan	Sen
118	CommCo, Inc.	Tulip Dawn	26-Feb-2002	$48,500.00	Sanchez	Hernandez
122	DB 'R WE	Willow Branch	24-Aug-2001	$785,000.00	Hernandez	Smith

Problems 5.31 through 5.33 are based on the Ch05_JewelCo.MDB database. (Copy the database from the student CD attached to the book. Remember to uncheck the Read-only property of the file!) The output shown in the problems reflects the original database table contents. Naturally, if you make any changes in the table contents, those changes will be reflected in the query output. Therefore, use the query output shown in the problems as examples of the required query output format, rather than as a precise listing of your query output. Also, we have limited the query output in several problems to just a few of the records to save considerable space.

5.31 Produce a query to list the sales summary for each jeweler. The query output is shown in Figure P5.31. Name the query **qrySalesSummaryByJeweler**. (Note that the jeweler's share is a derived attribute, created by multiplying the invoice subtotal by the jeweler's percentage/100.)

FIGURE P5.31
Query Output for Problem 5.31

Jeweler #	Jeweler's Last Name	Jeweler's %	Invoice Subtotal	Jeweler's Share
1	Armado	60.00	$500.00	$300.00
1	Armado	60.00	$530.00	$318.00
1	Armado	60.00	$770.00	$462.00
3	Freeman	60.00	$450.00	$270.00
3	Freeman	60.00	$770.00	$462.00
7	Fortune	60.00	$430.00	$258.00
7	Fortune	60.00	$530.00	$318.00
7	Fortune	60.00	$840.00	$504.00
9	Semaan	60.00	$700.00	$420.00
11	More	65.00	$350.00	$227.50
12	Ziade	59.00	$560.00	$330.40
14	Clark	65.00	$280.00	$182.00
16	Coronel	60.00	$375.00	$225.00
18	Brown	54.00	$330.00	$178.20
18	Brown	54.00	$700.00	$378.00
19	Tillery	53.00	$900.00	$477.00
20	Morrison	57.00	$990.00	$564.30
22	Main	52.00	$500.00	$260.00

5.32 Produce a query to list the sales totals for each jeweler. The query output is shown in Figure P5.32. Name the query **qrySalesTotalsByJeweler**.

FIGURE P5.32
Query Output for Problem 5.32

Jeweler #	Jeweler's Last Name	Jeweler's %	Net Sales	Jeweler's Share
1	Armado	60.00	$1,800.00	$1,080.00
3	Freeman	60.00	$1,220.00	$732.00
7	Fortune	60.00	$1,800.00	$1,080.00
9	Semaan	60.00	$700.00	$420.00
11	More	65.00	$350.00	$227.50
12	Ziade	59.00	$560.00	$330.40
14	Clark	65.00	$280.00	$182.00
16	Coronel	60.00	$375.00	$225.00
18	Brown	54.00	$1,030.00	$556.20
19	Tillery	53.00	$900.00	$477.00
20	Morrison	57.00	$990.00	$564.30
22	Main	52.00	$500.00	$260.00

5.33 Produce a query to list the available jewelry by jeweler. A few sample query output records are shown in Figure P5.33. Name the query **qryJewelryListByJeweler**.

FIGURE P5.33
Query Output for Problem 5.33

Last Name	First Name	Initial	Jewelry Piece	Sales Price
Armado	Melanie	J	Baracuda	$250.00
Armado	Melanie	J	Lightning Bugs	$250.00
Armado	Melanie	J	Blue bird	$320.00
Armado	Melanie	J	Madonna	$250.00
Brown	Tania	T	Untitled	$250.00
Brown	Tania	T	Clear Sky	$330.00
Brown	Tania	T	Big Blue	$250.00
Burton	Scott	S	New Waves	$530.00
Burton	Scott	S	Shining Lights	$340.00
Clark	Jill	J	Untitled	$280.00
Clark	Jill	J	Pensive Look	$280.00
Coronel	Carlos	C	Untitled	$375.00

Problems 5.34 is based on the Ch05_POS_2nd.MDB database. (Copy the database from the student CD attached to the book. Remember to uncheck the Read-only property of the file!) The output shown in the problems reflects the original database table contents. Naturally, if you make any changes in the table contents, those changes will be reflected in the query output. Therefore, use the query output shown in the problems as examples of the required query output format, rather than as a precise listing of your query output. Also, we have limited the query output in several problems to just a few of the records to save considerable space.

5.34 Produce a query for running sum for the ORD_LINE table. The query output is shown in Figure P5.34. Name the query **qryOrderLineRunningSum**.

FIGURE P5.34
Query Output for Problem 5.34

Order Line Num	Order Num	Unit Price	Unit	Total	Running Sum by Order	Running Sum
1	3	$0.00	25	$748.75	$748.75	$748.75
2	3	$0.00	0	$0.00	$748.75	$748.75
3	3	$0.00	3	$59.85	$808.60	$808.60
4	4	$0.00	2	$64.00	$64.00	$872.60
5	4	$0.00	3	$59.85	$123.85	$932.45
6	4	$0.00	1	$19.95	$143.80	$952.40
7	4	$0.00	1	$100.00	$243.80	$1,052.40
8	5	$0.00	20	$1,599.80	$1,599.80	$2,652.20
9	5	$0.00	12	$239.40	$1,839.20	$2,891.60
10	5	$0.00	6	$192.00	$2,031.20	$3,083.60
11	5	$0.00	8	$880.00	$2,911.20	$3,963.60
12	6	$0.00	12	$240.00	$240.00	$4,203.60
13	6	$0.00	20	$1,599.80	$1,839.80	$5,803.40
14	6	$0.00	20	$1,599.80	$3,439.60	$7,403.20
15	6	$0.00	25	$498.75	$3,938.35	$7,901.95
16	7	$0.00	12	$240.00	$240.00	$8,141.95
17	7	$0.00	25	$498.75	$738.75	$8,640.70
18	9	$0.00	0	$0.00	$0.00	$8,640.70
19	10	$0.00	12	$240.00	$240.00	$8,880.70
20	11	$0.00	16	$720.00	$720.00	$9,600.70
21	11	$0.00	0	$0.00	$720.00	$9,600.70
22	12	$0.00	12	$1,200.00	$1,200.00	$10,800.70
23	13	$0.00	12	$240.00	$240.00	$11,040.70
24	13	$0.00	18	$1,439.82	$1,679.82	$12,480.52
25	14	$0.00	12	$252.00	$252.00	$12,732.52
26	14	$0.00	24	$478.80	$730.80	$13,211.32
(AutoNumber)	0	$0.00	0	$0.00		

Chapter **Six**

Form Development

Preview

The table structures we developed in Chapter 4 gave us flexible data-editing capabilities, allowing us to add, modify, or delete records "on the fly" via the datasheet view. The datasheet view also let us list each table's contents. Unfortunately, it was not possible to use the datasheet view to show data in more than one table at a time. We could not use logical constraints to limit output: the **Open** button would list all the records. If a record contained many fields, only a few of the fields would fit on the screen, so we had to use the scroll bars to see the remaining fields, a few at a time. Because Access set the datasheet's format, we could not control the output to fit the end users' needs. Finally, the datasheet view did not allow us to edit or add data in a related table.

The queries we developed in Chapter 5 let us examine data extracted from one or more tables. The queries also enabled us to use relationships between the tables and various data manipulation techniques (group, sum, count, and so on) to create useful information from the data stored in various tables. Queries also allowed us to format the output to make it more readable. In short, queries turned out to be very useful information management tools. We also used append, delete, and update queries as specialized data management tools. Yet as useful as queries turned out to be, they did not yield the visually attractive and flexible interfaces that end users demand. In addition, the query data management capabilities were limited because the query structures precluded their use to directly modify table-stored data one record at a time.

Fortunately, forms help fill the data management and information presentation gaps left by the datasheet and query presentations. In this chapter you will learn how to produce forms that vastly improve the visual appeal of the data presentation. We also show you how to make customized forms that let you show and modify data in several tables at once. And you will learn how to produce specialized forms known as menus that will become the visual basis for letting the database's end users access the many database components easily and effectively.

Objectives

When you have mastered the topics in this chapter, you should be able to

- Use the Form Wizard to create forms based on tables and/or queries.
- Identify all the components of a form: header, detail area, footer, text box, and label box.
- Modify a Wizard-created form by changing a form's basic presentation format, using the property boxes for each of the form's components.
- Create color groups, combo boxes, list boxes, and other devices designed to display data logically or to control end-user input choices.
- Create form/subform presentations to display data from multiple table and/or query sources.
- Use forms to input and/or modify data.
- Create forms to produce the menus that help pull the database application components together.
- Create command buttons that will later (in Chapter 8) be connected to macros to produce a user-friendly database application system.

6.1 FORMS: DEFINITION, USE, AND FUNCTION

Webster's dictionary defines the *form* as "the shape, outline, or configuration of anything. A printed document with blank spaces to be filled in." You are already familiar with forms as defined by Webster's because you have used them often. You filled out forms to enroll in school, to apply for or to renew a driver's license, to order a mail-order product, to apply for a loan, to apply for a credit card, and so on. Many of the forms you used were printed on paper, and you used a pen or pencil to enter the required data. Increasingly, forms are presented on a computer screen, and you use a keyboard, a light pen, or some other data-entry device to supply the required information.

Creating a sophisticated form for display on a computer screen used to be an incredibly complex task that required many hours of heavy-duty programming. You will discover, no doubt to your delight, that Access makes basic form creation a near-effortless task. In fact, we will show you how to use Access to create the forms that will produce an efficient and visually appealing end-user interface.

Forms play a crucial role in the database applications arena because they help connect the end user to the database. This crucial function is exercised in several ways:

- Forms are used to enter new data and to edit existing data. Although this function can, in a primitive way, be met through the use of the datasheet format, using the datasheet for data entry and editing lacks the safety features that forms can provide. In addition, end users demand logically connected and visually appealing interfaces that only forms can supply.
- Data entry and edit procedures are subject to human error. Although you learned (in Chapter 4) how to use input masks and validation rules to control at least some input formats and values, input errors must be controlled to an even greater extent. Fortunately, forms may be designed to extend the data validation rules through queries, value lists, and other input control devices.
- Forms are used to tie together the database components through menu structures. Therefore, forms enable the applications designer to control database access paths. The use of such access paths can then be controlled through password protection, read-only access, and other security measures. (We will examine security issues and the creation of security systems in Chapter 10.)

In short, it is difficult to conceive of a successful database environment in which forms do not play a dominant role.

6.1.1 Form Prerequisites

Although Webster's definition of "form" is simple enough, it does not try to specify what forms are based on or what their specific function is to be. In the Access environment, forms may be based on no data source at all, or they may be based on single or multiple data sources. Forms may be used to update table records, to trigger query output, or to call other forms. In short, forms are remarkably flexible devices.

Given the many roles played by forms and their many structures, you must always begin by defining the details of the conditions that govern form structure and use. Therefore, you should recognize the following possibilities and requirements:

1. A form may be based on one or more tables. The table(s) must exist before the form is created.
2. A form may be based on one or more queries. The query (or queries) must exist before the form is created.
3. A form may be based on a combination of tables and queries.
4. If the form is based on multiple tables, the relationships between those tables must be established before you try to create the form. (Naturally, if the forms are based on multiple-source queries, the relationships must be present at the

query level.) Those relationships are inherited from the tables or they are created at the query level as needed.

5. A form may include one or more unbound controls. An **unbound control** is a component that does not have a data source attached to it. (A data source is likely to be a table or a query, but it may also be a mathematical expression.) Unbound controls are commonly used to create input spaces, labels, and instructions.

6. Forms such as dialog boxes and menus do not use any record source. Such forms are created by selecting the **Blank Form** option from Access.

6.2 CREATING A FORM WITH THE FORM WIZARD

The most common form type is a single-source form, based on a tabular format. The single source may be a table or a query. To illustrate how such a form is created, we will use the EMPLOYEE table (use the **Ch06_POS_2nd.mdb** located in the Ch06 folder on the CD attached to the book) as the form's single (data) source in the following example.

As always, a new object, whether it is a table, a query, or a form, is created from the database window. Therefore, to create the form, start at the database window, select the **Forms** folder, and then select the **New** button to generate the **New Form** dialog box shown in Figure 6.1.

To make the form creation process as simple as possible, we have selected the **AutoForm: Columnar** option from the dialog box in Figure 6.1. The data source, the EMPLOYEE table, was selected from a list that was generated by clicking on the down arrow. Click **OK** on the **New Form** dialog box to set the Form Wizard into motion. It will take the Form Wizard just a few seconds to produce the form shown in Figure 6.2.

As you examine the form's contents in Figure 6.2, you'll see that the EMP_YEARS field—the number of years employed—has not yet been updated. This derived attribute will change its value as time goes by. Therefore, in a real-world environment, it would be a good idea to update this field periodically if, for example, its value helps determine retention bonuses or other time-derived values. You learned in Chapter 5 how to create the appropriate update query. (We have not updated the field to ensure that the form presentation remains the same for all users, regardless of the current date.)

As you examine Figure 6.2, note the following features:

- The fields for each EMPLOYEE table record are distributed across the screen, using a columnar format. Viewing each record's contents is now much easier than it was with the datasheet view selected from the **Tables** folder.
- The slide that fits along the left margin is the record selector. (Only a small segment is shown here.) By clicking on the record selector, you will

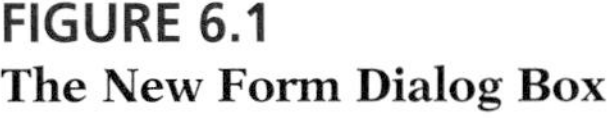

FIGURE 6.1
The New Form Dialog Box

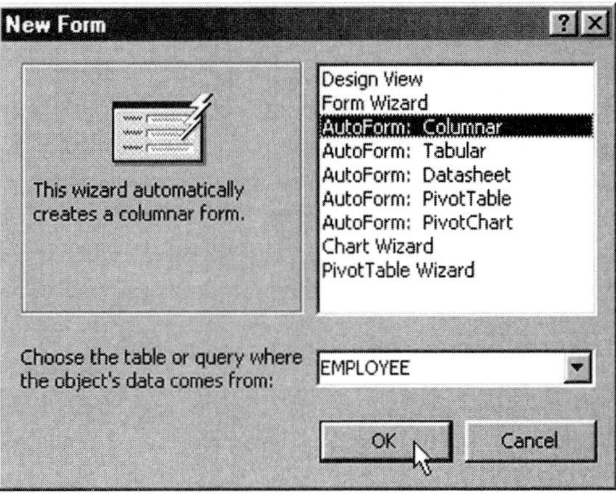

FIGURE 6.2 **The Wizard-created Employee Form**

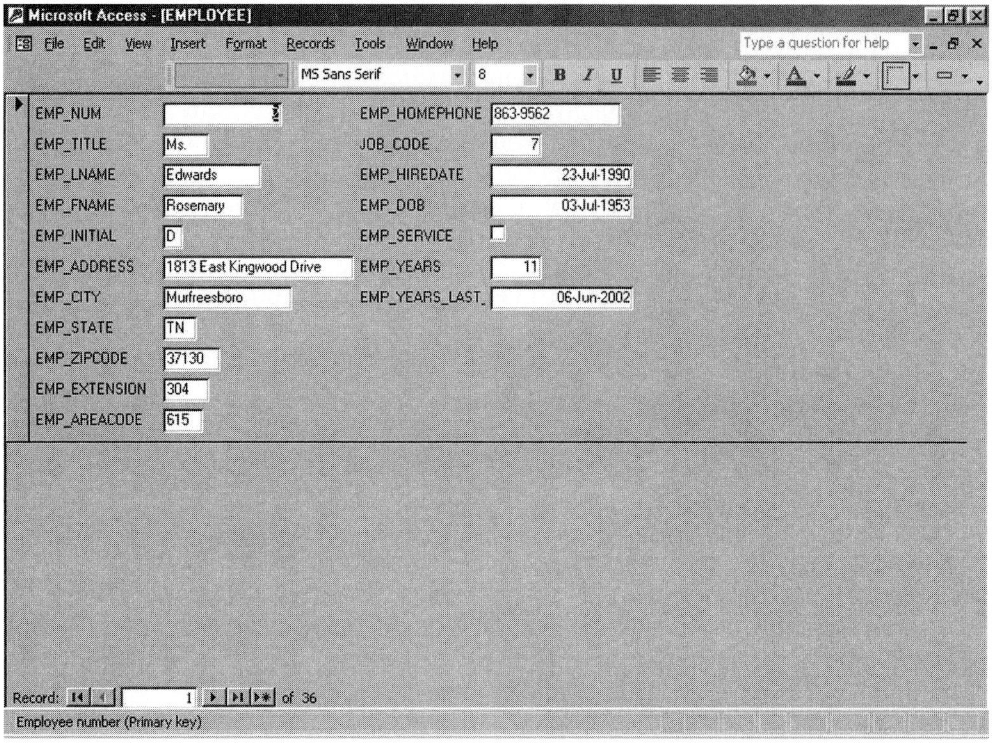

select the entire record, thus marking it for further use. For example, if you click on the record selector and press the keyboard's Delete button, you will delete the record.

- The form navigation buttons are located in the form's lower left corner (see Figure 6.3).

Save the form, then experiment with the navigation buttons. We will continue to use the naming conventions we established for queries (see Chapter 5). This time we will use the prefix **frm** to indicate that the object in question is a form. Also, remember that we used capital letters to designate tables. Because this form is based on the EMPLOYEE table, we will name it **frmEMPLOYEE**. (If this form had been based on a query named **qryEmployeeList**, the form would be named **frmEmployeeList**.) This naming convention makes it possible to easily determine what the object is (a form) and what its data component is (a table or a query). Using this naming convention, we made the **Save As** dialog box entry shown in Figure 6.4.

FIGURE 6.3
Form Navigation

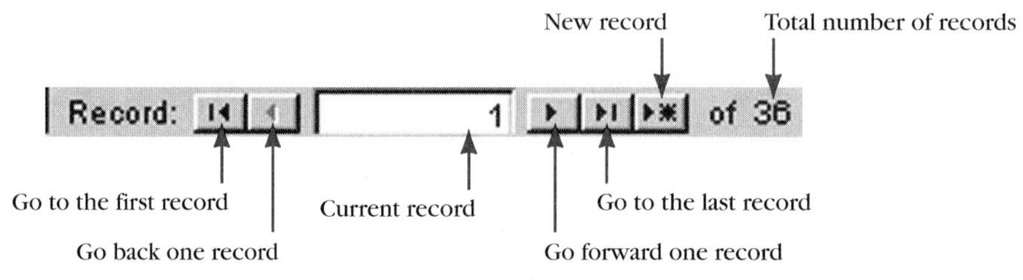

FIGURE 6.4
Naming and Saving the Form

Note

If you copied the **Ch06-POS_2nd** database from your CD, you'll see that we have stored this initial version of the form as **frmEMPLOYEE-initial** to make sure that you have the option to try various modifications while you are studying this chapter. We have also stored the **frmEMPLOYEE** form on your CD to show you what the final version looks like when you have completed the procedures discussed in this chapter. This support feature—available in all the chapters in which you create application objects—makes it possible for you to experiment freely. If an experiment fails to work out as intended, you can always delete the experimental form and replace it with the form found on your CD.

6.3 MODIFYING THE FORM'S PRESENTATION FORMAT

Although the form in Figure 6.2 is a vast improvement over the table's datasheet view, this form could stand improvement. For example, the field names are awkward from the typical end-user's point of view. (Using **Last name:** to label the employee's last name would seem more "finished" than using the field name EMP_LNAME.) Using labels to designate form components or to make sure that the form name stands out may also be desirable. In addition, enhancing the font size and format would help produce a more professional-looking form.

Giving end users the freedom to change the screen presentation is probably not a good idea. Therefore, it would be wise to remove the screen's **Min**, **Max**, and **Restore** buttons. We will discuss additional screen format features as we continue to modify the form in Figure 6.2.

Color is an important feature in any presentation. Therefore, it will be appropriate to add color, using it to brighten the screen's appearance and to separate the record's logical groupings from each other. Remember that end users often judge the application developer's professionalism by the appearance of the screen.

Finally, you will want to help end users enter appropriate and correct data. For example, the employee title is restricted to Mr., Ms., or Mrs. Therefore, having end users pick the correct entries from a list would be better than asking them to type such entries. Access provides a well-equipped toolbox that enables you to produce efficient, effective, and attractive forms.

Before we examine the many ways in which you can modify the Wizard-produced form, let's take a look at the form in its design format. Once again, you will find the initial design process familiar. Whether you deal with table design, query design, or form design, you always begin the design modification process at the database window. Because we're working on forms, start by selecting the database window's **Forms** folder. Next select the object to be modified—in this case, the **frmEMPLOYEE** you just saved—by clicking on it. Finally, select the design option by clicking on the **Design** button to produce Figure 6.5.

As you examine Figure 6.5, note that the field list and toolbox buttons have been activated. In this case, the form's toolbox is located on the form's right margin. We'll examine the toolbox options later in this chapter. We have dragged the field list—the attributes found in the EMPLOYEE table—to the right of the screen to leave the form's design completely visible.

Having placed the **frmEMPLOYEE** form in design format, we're ready to begin the modification process. We will begin by modifying the labels and text boxes.

6.3.1 Labels and Text Boxes

As you examine Figure 6.5, note that each field in the EMPLOYEE record is shown in two parts. The left part is called the *text label*, while the right part is the *text box*. The **label** merely identifies the text box. The **text box** contains the actual

Note

Although color is an important feature in any presentation, keep in mind that end users may be looking at your screen long and often. Therefore, to prevent end-user eyestrain, use soft colors and don't make the color contrasts too severe. Reserve bright colors, such as bright red and bright yellow, for warnings.

(The figures in this chapter are available on your student CD-ROM in full color. The black and white reproductions printed on these pages will serve as a guide to identify the elements of the forms, but you should refer to the CD to see how color affects the forms' effectiveness.)

FIGURE 6.5 The frmEmployee Form in Design Format

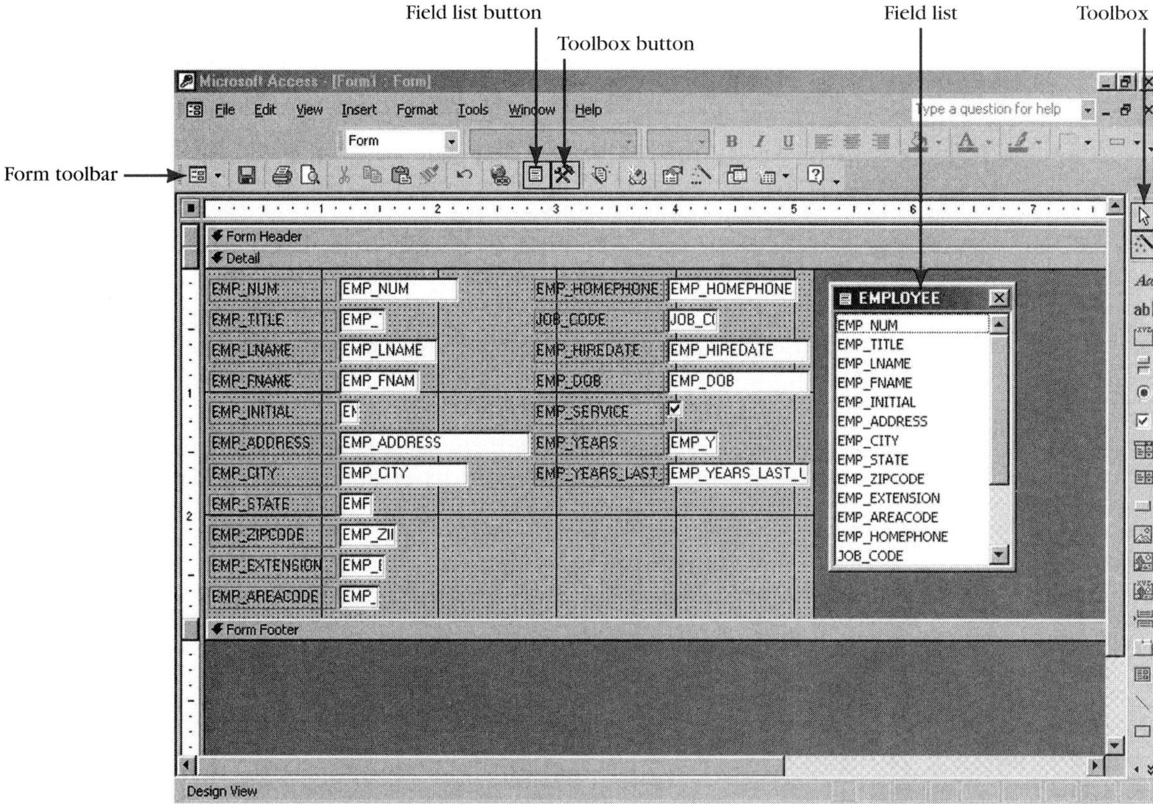

field value when the form is opened in the form view shown in Figure 6.2. (Remember that you can, as always, move back and forth between design view and form view by clicking on the **View** button and making the desired selection.)

With the form in design mode (see Figure 6.5), click on the EMP_NUM text box and note that the text box and text label portions are now marked with squares along their perimeters. Note particularly the larger squares in the upper left corner of the label box and the text box (see Figure 6.6). These larger squares are known as **move handles**. (As their name implies, move handles are used to move the text box and its label around the form.) The smaller squares or **selection markers** around the box perimeter indicate the text box's selection. The markers in Figure 6.6 indicate that the EMP_NUM text box was selected. Selecting the text box also marks the label with a move handle, indicating that the label is, at this point, attached to the text box.

If you move the cursor around the text box, you will notice that it occasionally changes to a hand with a pointing finger. The hand with the pointing finger, also

Note

Access conforms to the usual Windows conventions. For example, if you want to select multiple text and label boxes, click on each one while you hold down the keyboard's Shift key. You can also select multiple text and label boxes by holding down the left mouse button and dragging the cursor across the area containing the text and label boxes.

FIGURE 6.6
The Marked Textbox and Its Label

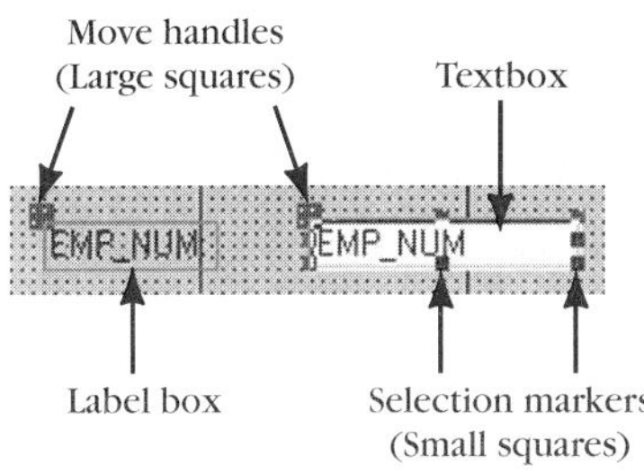

FIGURE 6.7
The Cursor Changes to a Pointing Finger

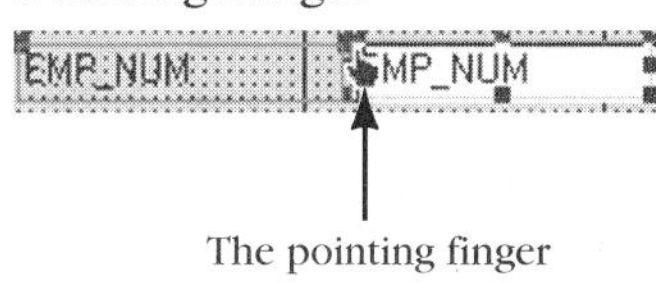

FIGURE 6.8
Marking the Box for Size Changes

known as an open hand, is shown in Figure 6.7. The open hand indicates that the text box and the label box will be moved *together* as you drag them to a different location on the screen. The hand symbol disappears when you move the cursor off the text box edge and reappears when you replace the cursor on the text box edge.

If you place the cursor on either of the move handles, the symbol changes to a pointing finger, indicating that the component can be moved separately from the other component. For example, Figure 6.7 shows that the pointing finger is on the text box move handle. Therefore, the text box can be moved—by dragging it—without moving the label box.

Finally, if you place the cursor on any small square, you will see the cursor shape change to a double-headed arrow, indicating that the selected box's size can be changed by dragging its border left or right. An example of the double-headed arrow is shown on the EMP_NUM text box's right margin in Figure 6.8.

You may select all text boxes and their associated labels in either the horizontal plane or the vertical plane by using the rulers at the screen margins. (These rulers are shown in the original form design format in Figure 6.5.) Placing the cursor on the ruler changes its shape to the arrow shown in Figure 6.6. The selection of the six text boxes and their labels (in the horizontal plane) was accomplished by placing the ruler's arrow next to the first label to be included (EMP_LNAME) and dragging it down to the last label to be included (EMP_INITIAL). Figure 6.9 shows that several text box/label combinations were selected this way.

If you want to mark a limited selection of text boxes and their labels in the vertical plane, place the cursor on the top ruler and then drag to make your selection. This procedure marks *all* text boxes and their labels in the selected portion of the vertical plane.

Editing the Labels and Text Boxes

Now that you know how to move the text boxes and labels around the form, let's edit them. One of the simplest and quickest ways to improve the form's appearance is to change the labels that are used to identify the text boxes. For example,

Note

Whether you select a single text box and/or label or a group of text boxes and their labels, you can move them with the help of the open hand (see Figure 6.6) or the pointing finger (see Figure 6.7). You can also change all text box and label sizes simultaneously by placing the cursor on any edge (see Figure 6.8) and dragging it to the desired size. We suggest that you practice moving and sizing the text boxes and labels before you start modifying their presentation characteristics.

FIGURE 6.9 Marking Text Boxes and Labels with the Rulers

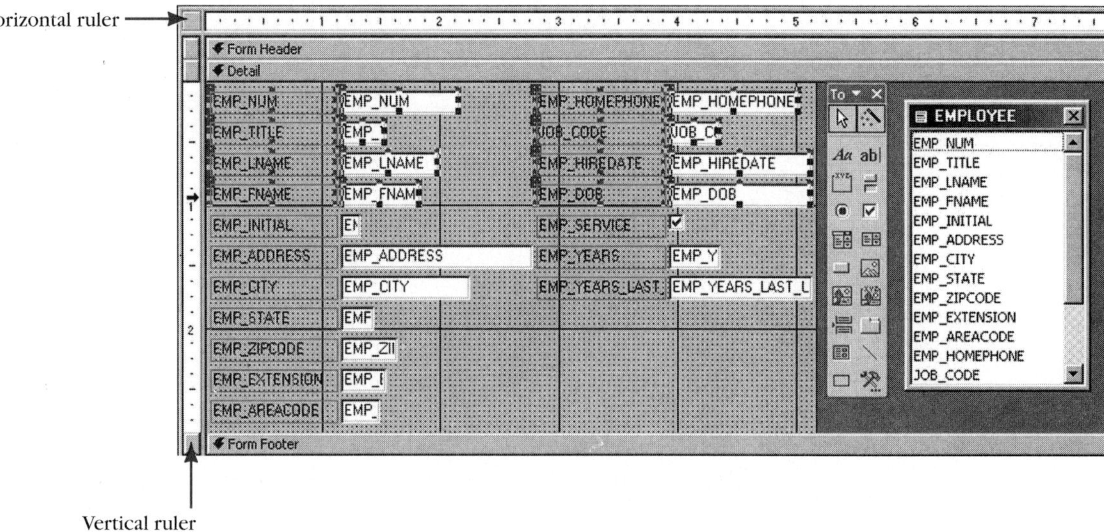

the labels EMP_NUM, EMP_TITLE, and EMP_FNAME produce a far less finished appearance than do the labels Number, Title, and First name.

To edit the EMP_NUM text box label, click on the label to select it. (Select the label portion only, so don't click on the EMP_NUM text box!) Then wait just a second before you place the cursor inside the label box and click. That's all it takes to place the label box in edit mode, so use the standard Windows conventions to do the editing. In this case, mark the EMP_NUM label for deletion and then type the new label as shown in Figure 6.10. When you have finished editing the label, just click outside the label box to deselect it and admire your handiwork. (Note that we have also edited the EMP_TITLE, EMP_LNAME, and EMP_FNAME labels in Figure 6.10. And we have selected the EMP_INITIAL label for the next edit.)

Now that we have created new labels, let's edit their fonts, too. You can control the font size, type, color, and so on, by selecting the label and then selecting the desired options from the tool bar at the top of the screen (see Figure 6.11). To ensure uniformity, we have selected the four label boxes as a group.

FIGURE 6.10 Several Edited Employee Form Labels

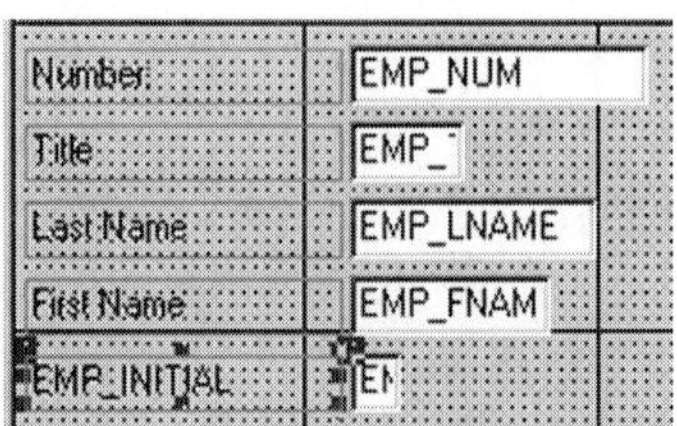

Note

Edit the labels only. Do *not* change the text box contents. They reference the table's fields to produce the field values in the datasheet presentation!

FIGURE 6.11 **Font Control**

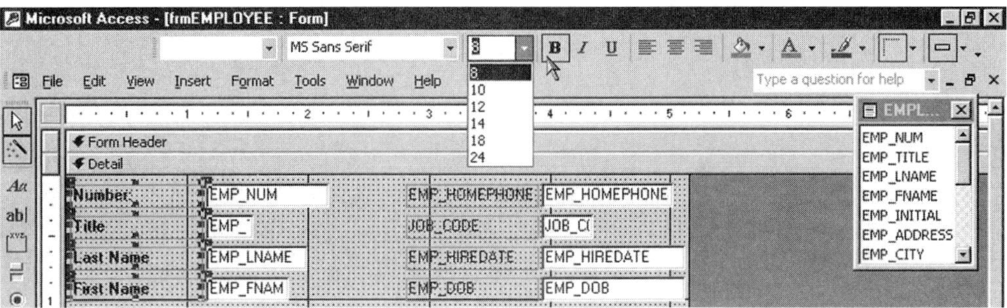

As you examine Figure 6.11, note that we have applied a boldface MS Sans Serif 8-point font to the labels. Although you should not change the text box contents, you can and should change the text box fonts to match the labels.

Note

If you do not see the form design and formatting tool bars shown in Figure 6.11, remember to click on the **View** button to select the **Toolbars** option, and then select whatever formatting options you need by clicking on each box to place a checkmark in it (see Figure 6.12). You have used this technique before, and you will use it again anytime you need a toolbar for any of the Access objects.

FIGURE 6.12
Selecting the Form Design Formatting Options

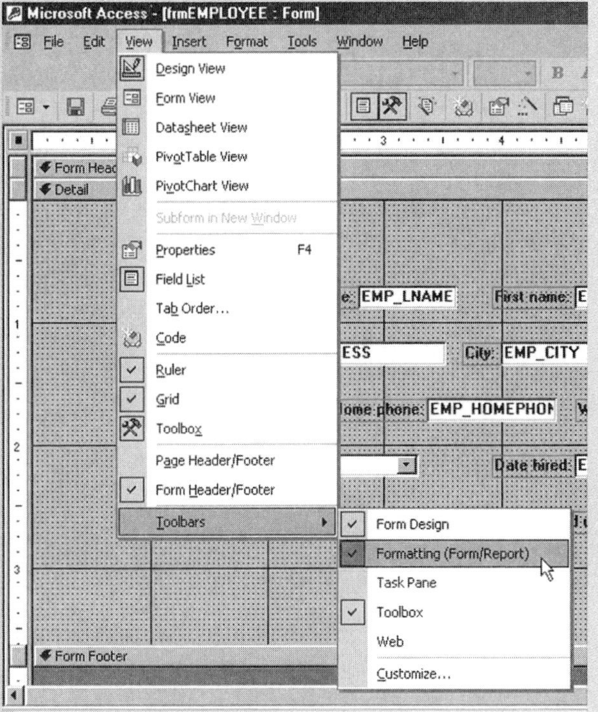

Assignment

Edit all the **frmEMPLOYEE** form's label boxes and then match the font specifications for the labels and text boxes. Move and size the text boxes and their labels. When you are done, your results should match Figure 6.13. Don't forget to save the form after you make the changes.

FIGURE 6.13 The Modified Employee Form

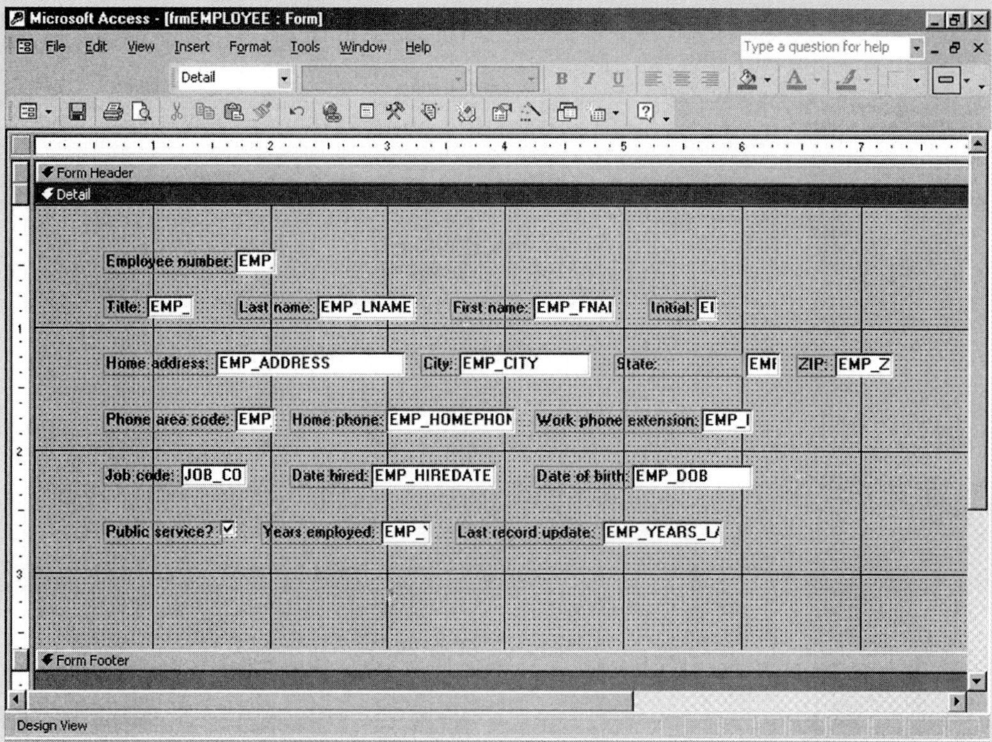

Controlling the Form Sections: Header, Detail, and Footer

So far we have worked in the form's detail section because that's where the Form Wizard placed all the text boxes and their labels. (Access labeled the **Form Header** and **Detail** as shown in Figure 6.5, just above the EMP_NUM label. The **Form Footer** label is shown just below the EMP_AREACODE label in the lower left corner.)

You can control the header, detail, and footer sizes by placing the cursor on their margins and dragging. Placing the cursor on the margins will change the cursor shape to a double-headed arrow. For example, if you place the cursor on the margin between the form header and detail segments, you'll see the arrow shown in Figure 6.14. When the arrow appears, drag down to produce the header space shown in Figure 6.15.

The header usually contains large labels, unassociated with text boxes, that identify the form's name and/or function. We show you how to produce such labels later. The header space may also hold text boxes and labels that are not to be edited and that are, therefore, not accessible to end users. For example, the employee number is not likely to be changed, so it is a good candidate for placement in the header. (After you have created the header space as shown in Figure 6.15, go ahead and drag the employee number text box to the new header.)

You can create the footer just as you created the header. Just place the cursor on the dividing line between the detail and the footer and then drag down to

FIGURE 6.14
The Double-arrow Cursor

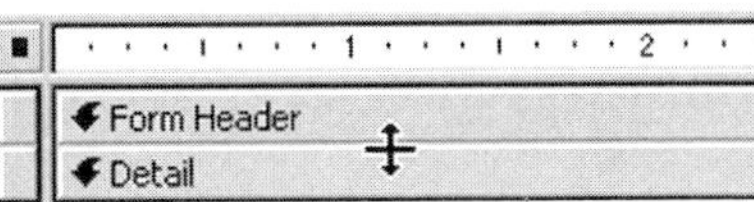

FIGURE 6.15
The Header Space After Dragging

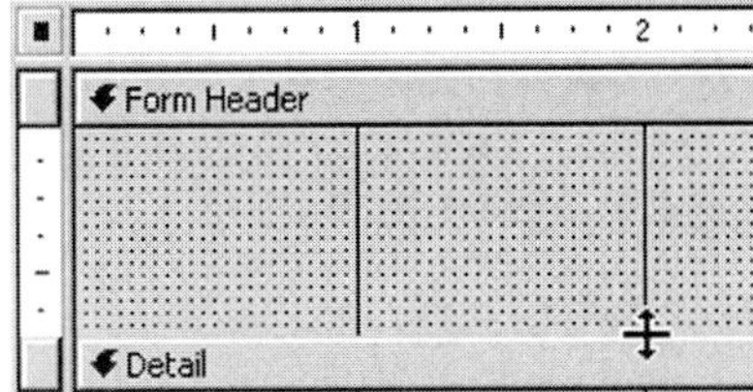

FIGURE 6.16
The Footer Space after Dragging

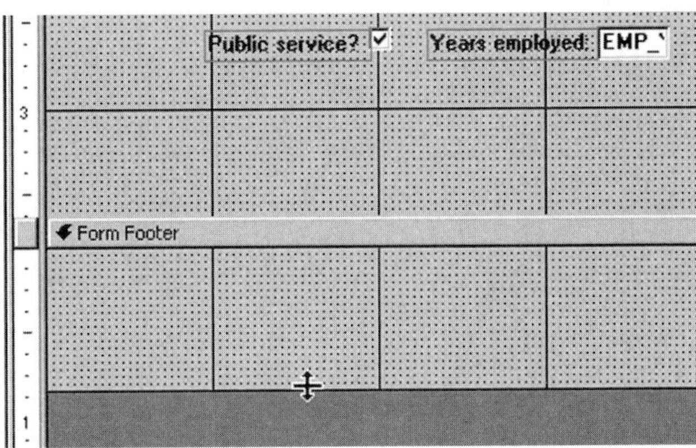

produce the footer space. The footer is usually reserved for the form's command buttons, help messages, and so on. Figure 6.16 shows the **frmEMPLOYEE** form's footer after its border has been dragged down to create it.

Figure 6.17 shows the **frmEMPLOYEE** form in form view after the header and footer have been created. Note that the form's sections—header, detail, and footer—are delineated by thin black lines at this point in the form design. Note

FIGURE 6.17 **The frmEMPLOYEE Form with a Header and a Footer**

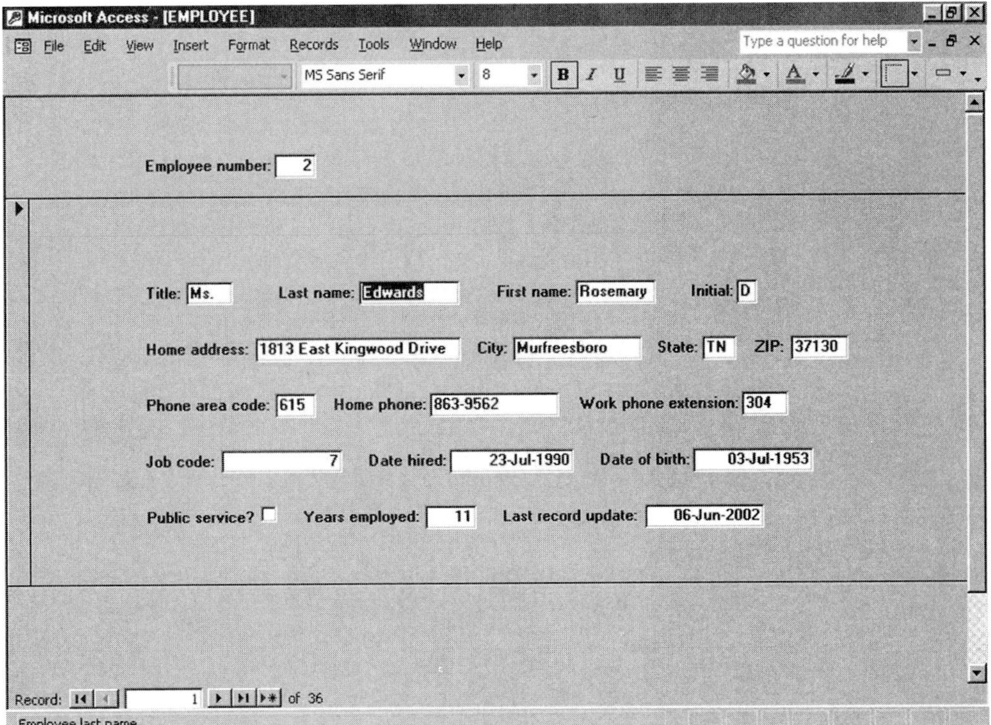

Note

If you pull the footer down too far, you will discover that the lower portion of the form's detail portion seems to disappear. For example, if we pull the footer limit shown in Figure 6.16 down a few more inches, part of the detail display seems to disappear (see Figure 6.18).

The "cut-off" illustrated in Figure 6.18 can be eliminated by reducing the footer size. If a part of the form you are designing seems to disappear, remember that you can eliminate that problem by changing the footer size.

FIGURE 6.18 The Effect of Creating a Large Footer

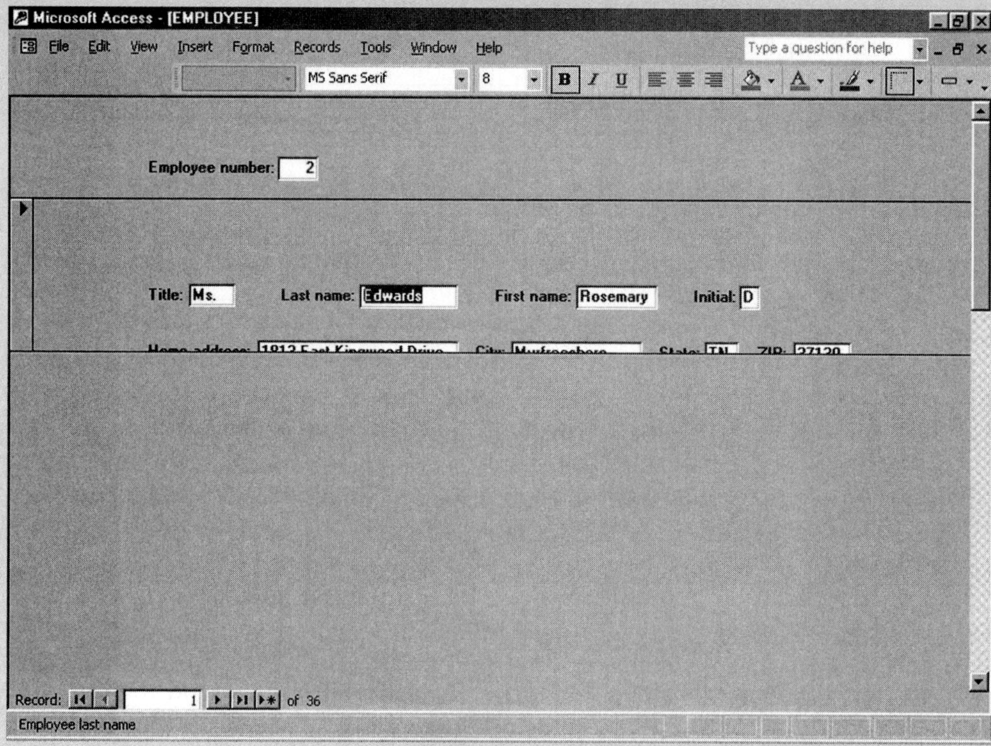

also that we have moved the EMP_NUM text box with its **Employee number:** label into the header and that we moved some of the other text boxes around the form's detail section. (Go ahead and practice such text box placements now.)

Finally, you can drag the form's right margin to increase the form's available space. Naturally, regardless of how far you drag the form's right limit, the form's size is ultimately limited by the available screen size. However, unless you want to place small forms in front of larger forms to produce a cascading effect, using a large form width is desirable because it gives you more space for the text boxes and labels.

Preparing for Form Customization: The Form Design Toolbox

To do really detailed custom design work on a form, you will need the Access tool*box*, not to be confused with the familiar tool*bar*. To make sure the form design toolbox is available, place the form in its design mode and then click on the **View** button. Select the **Toolbox** option as shown in Figure 6.19.

Selecting the **Toolbox** option will place the toolbox's button bar at the top of the screen (see Figure 6.20). To identify the various toolbox options, simply place the cursor on each button to display its label. As always, if you need a

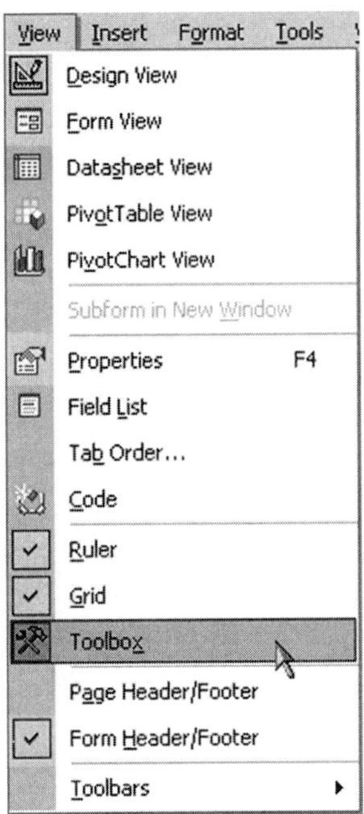

FIGURE 6.19 **Selecting the Toolbox Option from the View Menu**

FIGURE 6.20 **The Toolbox Buttons**

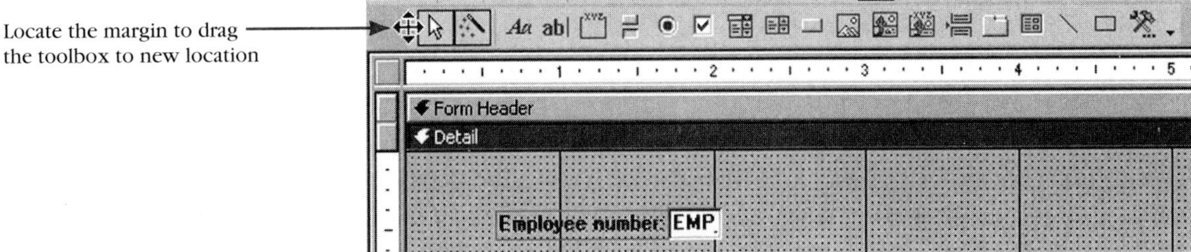

detailed explanation of any component, select it and then press the F1 key on your keyboard to generate the documentation.

If you want to move the toolbar to another location of the screen, place the cursor at the toolbox's margin. This action changes the cursor shape to the four-sided arrow you see in Figure 6.20. Then drag the toolbar to the desired location. (Actually, if you can locate any empty spot elsewhere on the toolbar, you can place the cursor on it and drag the toolbar to any desired location using that technique. Using this option, the cursor will not change its shape. However, it is sometimes hard to find a spot that will not activate a button, so you need to practice precise cursor placement.) Figure 6.21 shows the toolbox buttons after the toolbox has been dragged to the form's detail section.

Using standard Windows practice, you can change the shape of the toolbox by simply dragging its margins. You can also return the toolbox button bar to the screen's top margin by clicking on the header and dragging the bar back to the desired location. Naturally, you can also drag the toolbox contents to any location on the detail segment.

Using the Toolbox: Labels and Date Functions

We will assume that your **frmEMPLOYEE** form has a header section. If it does not yet have one, create it now, using the technique displayed in Figure 6.15. Using the form's header section as the destination, let's perform the following tasks:

- Write the label **Employee Profile** in this header.
- Place the current date in the header.

FIGURE 6.21
An Alternative View of the Toolbox Buttons

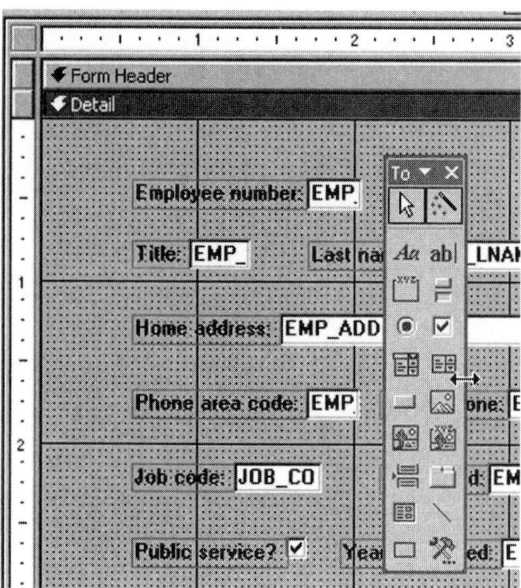

FIGURE 6.22
Label Placement in the Header Section

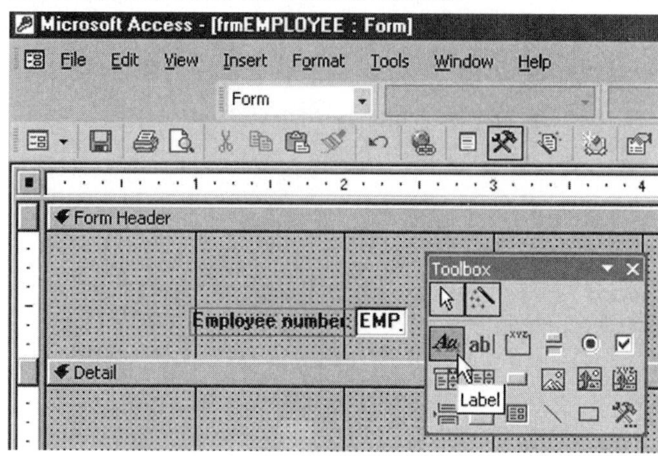

To create a label, first click on the toolbox's ***Aa*** (label) button as shown in Figure 6.22. Note that the employee number text box has already been dragged to the header and that we have changed the location and shape of the toolbox.

After you have activated the label button, click on the spot in the header section where you want to place the label. You can simply start typing at this point, or you can drag a space and then type the label. Figure 6.23 shows the results of this initial effort. Note that we have typed the label **Employee Profile** in the header.

After you have typed the label, click on any empty spot to leave the label box and to deselect the label. If you want to select the newly typed label box again, just click on it and you will see the now-familiar square markers as shown in Figure 6.23. You can treat the just-created **Employee Profile** label like any of the label boxes you created and edited earlier in the chapter. (Check Figures 6.10 and 6.11 again.) At this point, you can return the form to its form view and check the results of your efforts. If you want to edit the label, place the form in its design format again and then click on the **Employee Profile** label to select it. (We will edit this label later to add color, change its font size, and so on.)

FIGURE 6.23
The Initial Label

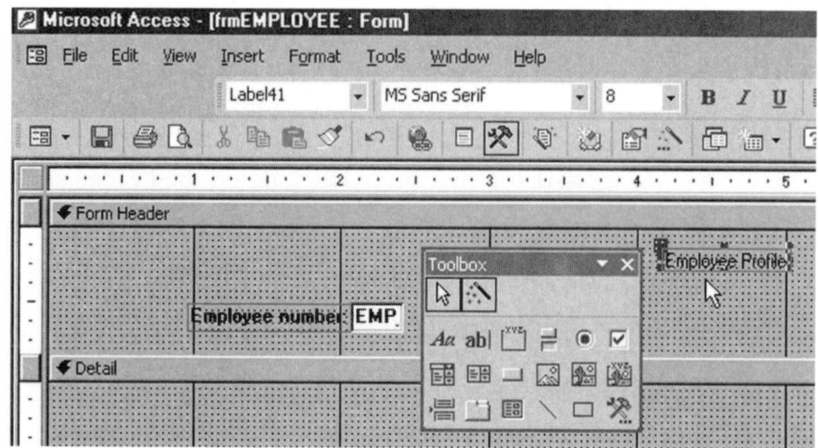

FIGURE 6.24
The Textbox Button

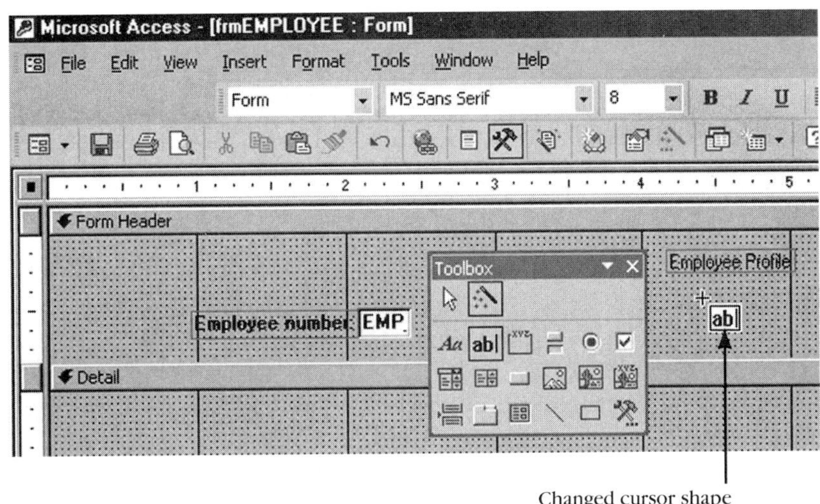

FIGURE 6.25 Selecting the Text Box Properties

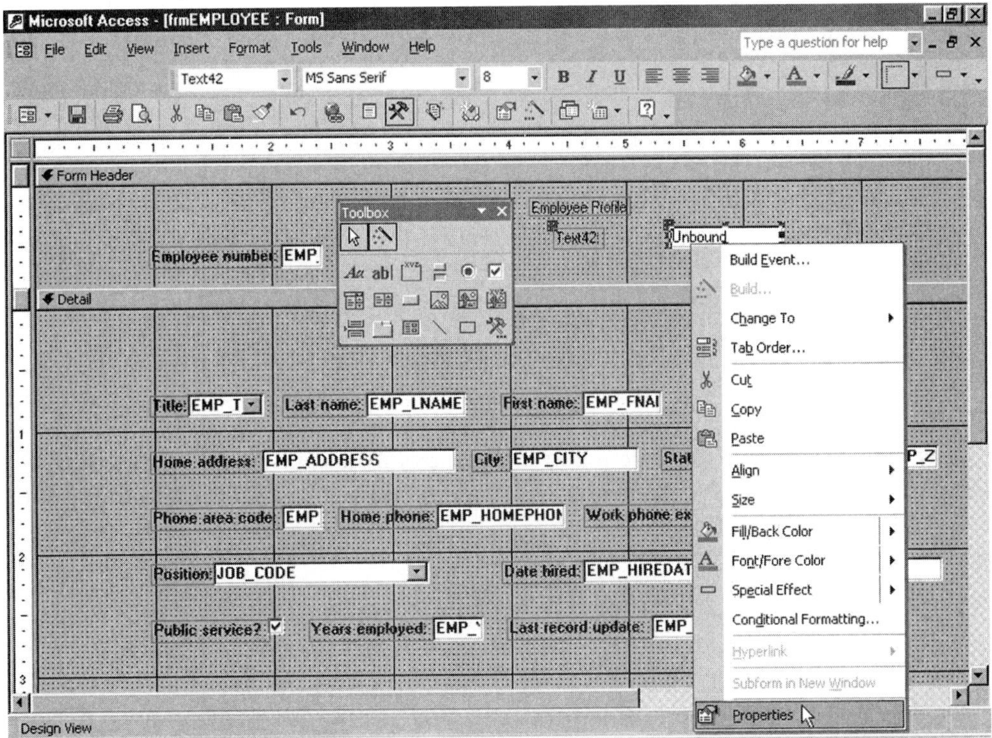

To produce the current date on the **frmEMPLOYEE** form's header, select the toolbox's text box button, marked **ab|**, by clicking on it. Next, place the cursor in the header section and note that the cursor changes its shape to reflect your selection (see Figure 6.24).

Drag the cursor shown in Figure 6.24 to create the text box limits shown in Figure 6.25. Note that the text box shown here is declared to be **Unbound**, because this text box does not have a data source, such as a field from a table, specified for it. Note also that our form's text box carries the label **Text42** to reflect that this is our 42nd text box creation in this database. (Your text box label will, of course, have a different number to reflect what you have done thus far.)

Note

Make sure that you have selected the newly created text box. If you click anywhere else on the form, *you will see the properties box for that selection.*

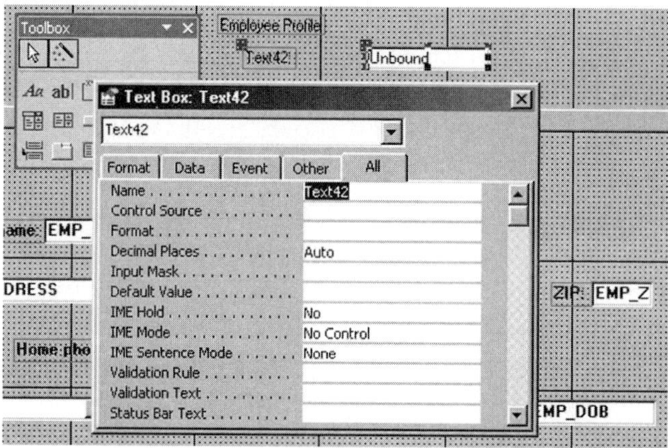

FIGURE 6.26
The Text Box Properties Box

After creating the text box shown in Figure 6.25, make sure that it is still selected—it must have the square handles at its margin—and right-click to produce the options menu shown in Figure 6.25. (If you have already clicked outside the text box to deselect it, just click on it to select it again.) Select the **Properties** option at the bottom of this option list.

Selecting the **Properties** option in Figure 6.25 will generate the **Text Box** properties box shown in Figure 6.26. You can also produce this result by simply double-clicking on the text box without first generating the drop-down window shown in Figure 6.25. (Naturally, you can use the standard Windows drag/drop/size conventions to change the size, shape, and location of the text properties box.)

Using the properties box shown in Figure 6.23, type **dd-mmm-yyyy** in the **Format** option, then type the current date function **Date()** in the **Default Value** option as shown in Figure 6.27.

As you examine Figure 6.27, note that the control source for the **Text42** properties box was left blank, because this text box is not tied to a data source in a

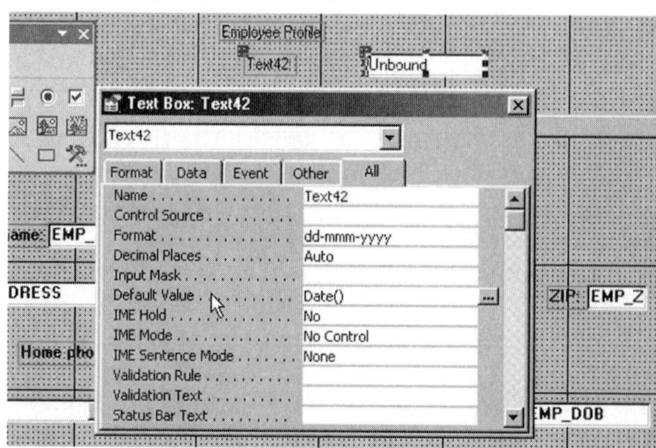

FIGURE 6.27
The Properties Box for the Text42 Text Box

Note

At this point, the unbound text box name shown in the property box in Figure 6.27 still carries the default name **Text42**. You will discover later that you will find it difficult to remember which text box is identified by this name when you use the Expression Builder to add various form features. Therefore, always edit the object names in a way that will help you remember them. For example, open the properties box for the **Text42** text box, and then change its name from **Text42** to **txtCurrentDate**. (Use **txt** as a prefix to differentiate between a label and a text box. A label box might use the prefix **lbl.**) The **txtCurrentDate** name will make it easy to remember that this unbound text box generates the current date. Such self-documentation helps organize the design process.

table or query. That is, the **Text42** text box is an **unbound text box**. In contrast, the employee number's text box is a **bound text box**, because its contents are determined by (i.e., are bound to) the EMPLOYEE table's EMP_NUM field.

To see the effect of the changes we have made on the **frmEMPLOYEE** form, open it in **Form View**. The results are shown in Figure 6.28. Note the **Employee Profile** label and the current date text box with its **Text42** label. As you can tell, we opened this form on July 25, 2002. (Naturally, you will see a different current date when you open the form.)

As you can tell from the form modification procedures we have just completed, the properties box plays an important role in the applications development process, and we will use it often. Each form component has its own set of properties, so you will discover that the properties box changes automatically to reflect the object you have selected. For example, if you place the employee form in its design mode and click on the **Employee Profile** label, you will discover that the properties box reflects the fact that you have selected a label. Similarly, if you

FIGURE 6.28 **The Modified Employee Form in Form View**

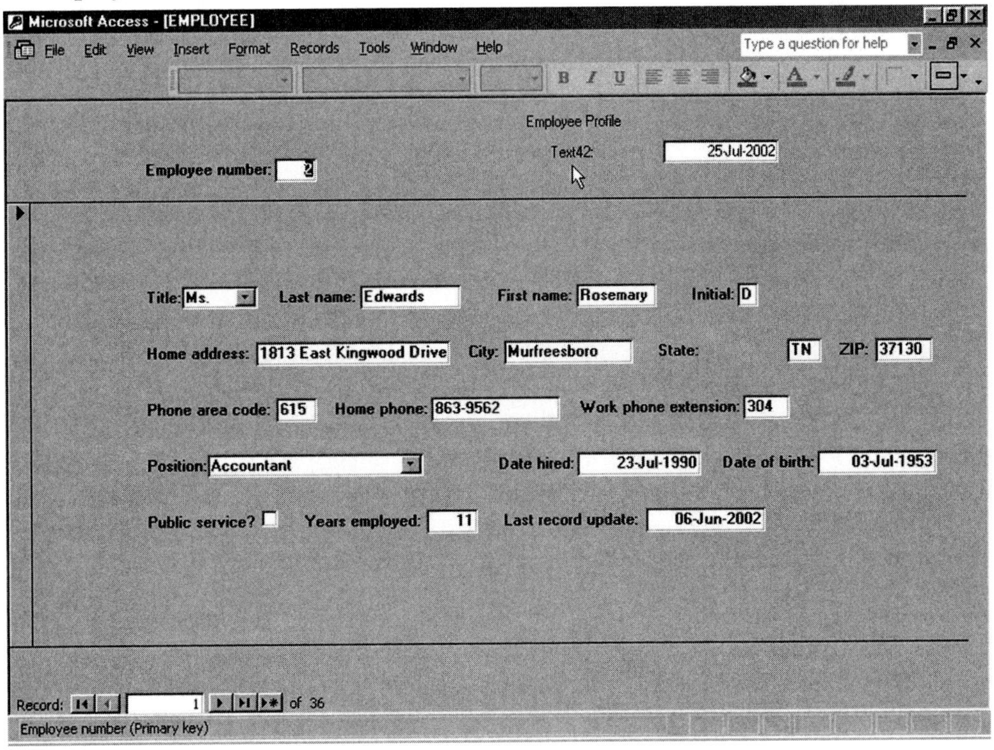

Assignment

Using the editing techniques you learned earlier, open the **frmEMPLOYEE** form in its **Design View** and change the format of the employee profile and current date labels. Make the print boldface and increase its font size. Drag the edges of the label and text boxes to make sure that the new labels and date values fit within the limits. Move the label and text boxes to give the header a more balanced look. When you are done, your header should look like Figure 6.29.

FIGURE 6.29 The Modified frmEMPLOYEE Form Header Contents

select the EMP_HIREDATE text box shown in Figure 6.30, the properties list will show the EMP_HIREDATE properties.

As you examine Figure 6.30, note that we control the date presentation format by typing the **Format** option as **dd-mmm-yyyy**. (If you want to show only the last two digits of the year, type the Format option as **dd-mmm-yy**. You can get the same presentation format by selecting the **Medium Date** option from the **Format** list as illustrated in Figure 6.30A. This option works fine at the table level, too.)

If you check the properties box in Figure 6.30, *note that a bound text box always has a named control source*—in this case, the EMP_HIREDATE field. And also note that the properties of a bound text box are inherited from the control source, so you won't have to type them in. (Of course, we are assuming that you properly specified the properties of each field when you created the EMPLOYEE table. However, if you did not define the EMP_HIREDATE format at the table level, you can still do that in the properties box.)

The bound text box's control source must always correctly reflect the text box's data source. If you were to delete the data source from the bound text box or if you modified the control source name to prevent the connection between the text box and its data source, the form would place a question mark on the form to indicate that the data source is not available.

FIGURE 6.30
The EMP_HIREDATE Text Box Properties Box

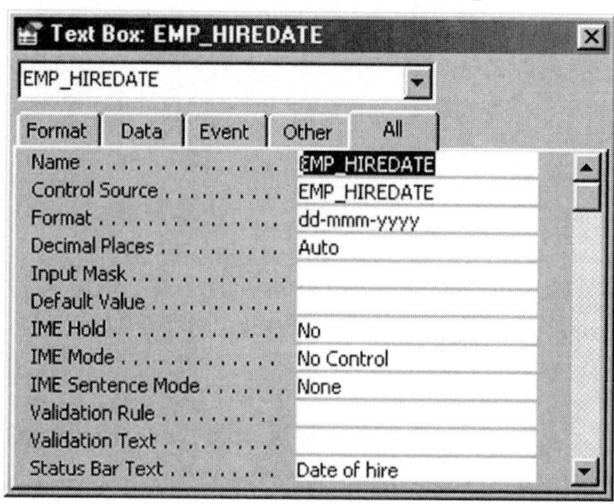

FIGURE 6.30A
An Alternate Date Format Selection

Text Box: EMP_HIREDATE

EMP_HIREDATE

Format | Data | Event | Other | All

Name . . . . EMP_HIREDATE
Control Source . . . . EMP_HIREDATE
Format . . . . Medium Date
Decimal Places . . . .
Input Mask . . . .
Default Value . . . .
IME Hold . . . .
IME Mode . . . .

General Date	6/19/94 5:34:23 PM
Long Date	Sunday, June 19, 1994
Medium Date	19-Jun-94
Short Date	6/19/94
Long Time	5:34:23 PM
Medium Time	5:34 PM
Short Time	17:34

You now know that all of the text labels and text boxes, both bound and unbound, reflect unique properties that are reflected in each object's properties box. The form's main divisions, header, detail, and footer are similarly endowed. To check this statement, place the form in its design format. Then click the cursor on any portion of the header not occupied by a label, a text box, or some other object, and you will see the **Section: FormHeader** properties box. Click on any unoccupied portion of the form's detail segment to generate the **Section: Detail** properties box. And clicking on any unoccupied section of the form's footer will produce the **Section: FormFooter** properties box. (Go ahead and try it now.)

You should not be surprised to discover that, if all of the form's components have their own properties boxes, the entire form is also governed by a set of properties. Generating the form's properties box is easiest when you scroll to any point *outside* the form's borders and then click to produce the form's properties box. In Figure 6.31 we placed the cursor outside the form's right margin. (The arrow-shaped cursor shows the location. We moved the properties box to show you the form's margin, which is the right edge of the dotted background.)

As you examine Figure 6.31, note that the **Record Source** shows that the form is based on the EMPLOYEE table. *Do not edit the record source*. The current **Caption** entry, EMPLOYEE, is reflected in Figure 6.28's open form. (Note that the label placed above the form in Figure 6.28 contains the message **Microsoft Access [EMPLOYEE]** to reflect this caption entry.) Although you may edit the caption, there is no need to do so. After all, the caption accurately reflects the form's data source, thus promoting the notion of self-documentation.

Go ahead and scroll through the Form properties box options to see the very long list of features that may be used. We will use many of these features as we develop the forms further and as we begin to tie them together to create a form-based system in Chapter 8. Given the number of possibilities, there is no practical way to cover them all in a single textbook. (You would probably dislike having to carry a 5,000-page book!) Fortunately, Access is, to a large extent,

FIGURE 6.31 **Selecting the Form Properties Box**

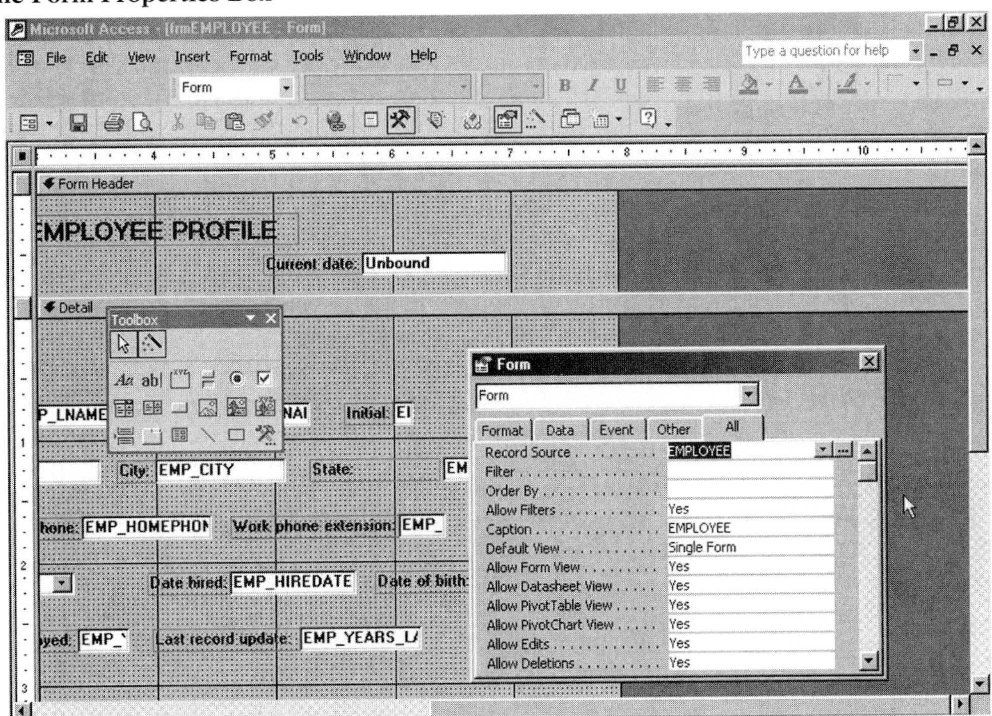

self-documenting. As always, you can select any component and press the F1 key on your keyboard to get context-sensitive information.

Controlling End-User Input: Combo Boxes

When we created the EMPLOYEE table, we placed some input quality controls into the table structure. For example, we made sure that the title input was controlled by the validation rule

```
In ("Mr.","Ms.","Mrs.")
```

when the EMP_TITLE field was created. We also used the input mask

```
>L<CCC
```

to ensure uppercase for the entry's first letter and lowercase entries for remaining letters. Although these table-level controls work well, end users still face the problem of having to type in the required data. It would be simpler for the end user to pick the appropriate entries from a list. Such a feature would be especially desirable if the entries were relatively complex. Fortunately, Access provides the tools to create such lists.

To demonstrate how a list is created on a form, let's create one for the EMP_TITLE field. To get the job done, follow these steps:

1. Open the employee form in its design mode.
2. Delete the current EMP_TITLE text box. (Just click on the text box and press the keyboard's Delete key; alternatively, click on the text box and right-click to generate the menu from which you can select the **Cut** option.)
3. Check the **Control Wizards** button to ensure that it activated.
4. Select the toolbox's **Combo Box** option. (If the toolbox has been turned off, restore it by selecting the **View/Toolbox** sequence shown in Figure 6.16.)
5. Go to the button bar at the top of the screen and then click on the **Field List** button to pop up the EMPLOYEE table's available fields (see Figure 6.32).
6. Click on the EMP_TITLE field to select it and then drag it to the form, placing the cursor on the desired final location. (Did you notice that the cursor changed its shape to become the combo box cursor as soon as you moved it off the toolbox button and that it changed to a small rectangle when you clicked on the field and started to drag?)
7. Release the mouse button to get the screen shown in Figure 6.33.
8. From the screen shown in Figure 6.33 select the **I will type in the values that I want** option and click **Next >** to get to the screen shown in Figure 6.34.

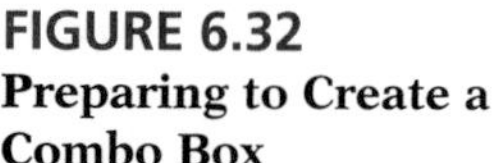

FIGURE 6.32
Preparing to Create a Combo Box

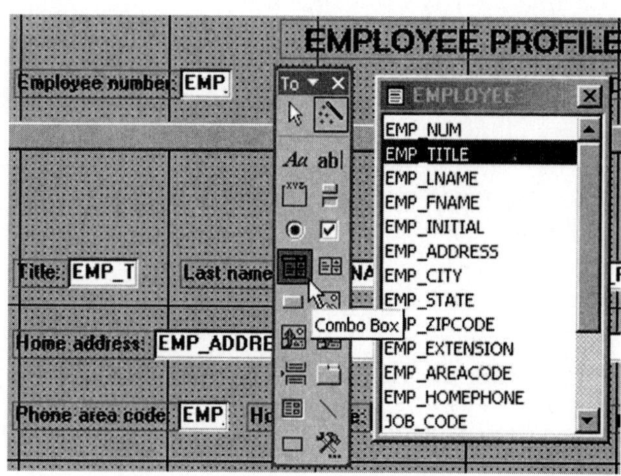

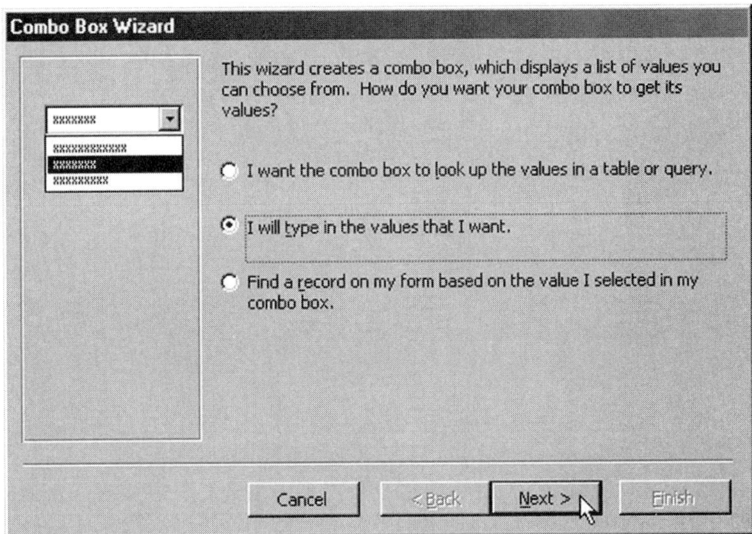

FIGURE 6.33
Selecting the "I will type in the values that I want" Option

FIGURE 6.34
Type the Values to Be Displayed in the Combo Box

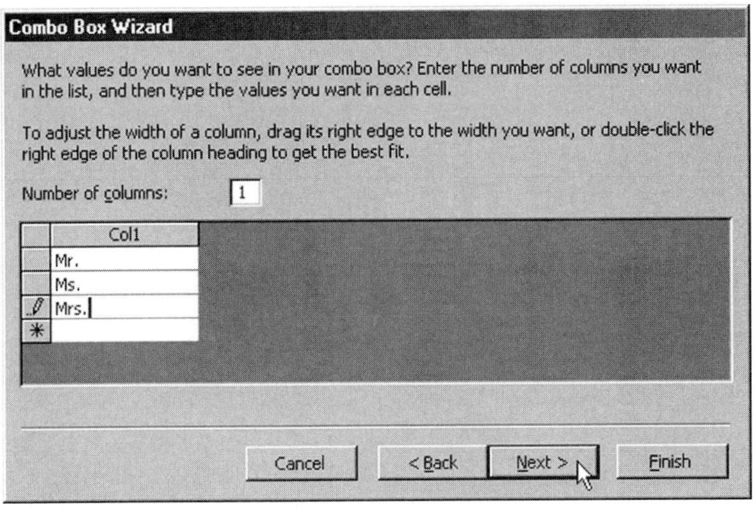

FIGURE 6.35
Select "Store that value in this field" and Select the EMP_TITLE

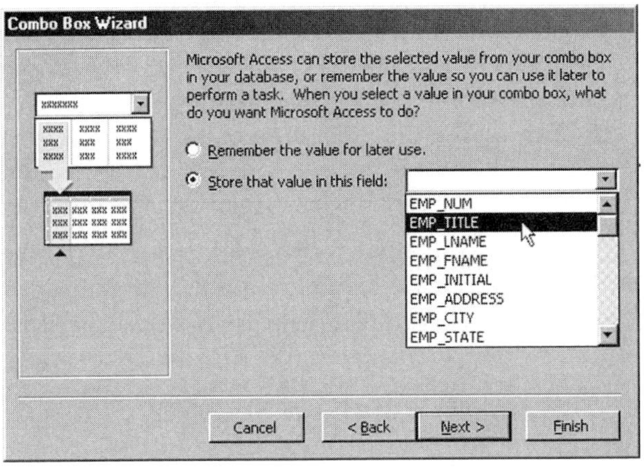

You will initially see only one row in the **Col1** header. Type **Mr.** and then use the mouse to click to the second row. (If you tap the Enter key, you will generate the next step in the combo box sequence. Figure 6.34 shows all of the entries.)

9. After typing the values in the screen shown in Figure 6.34, click **Next >** to generate the screen shown in Figure 6.35.

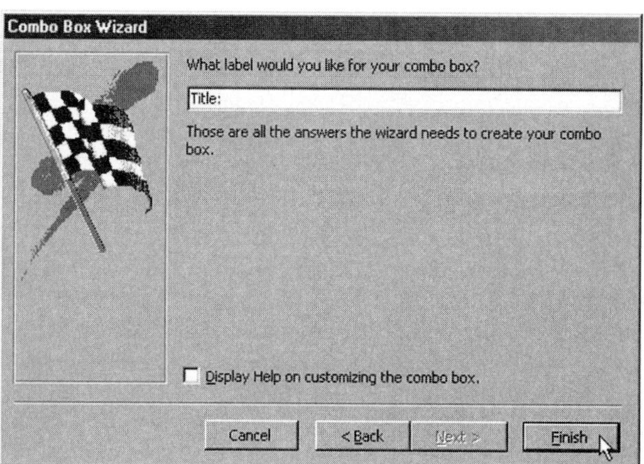

FIGURE 6.36
Name the Label of the Combo box

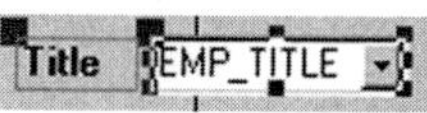

FIGURE 6.37
The EMP_TITLE Combo Box

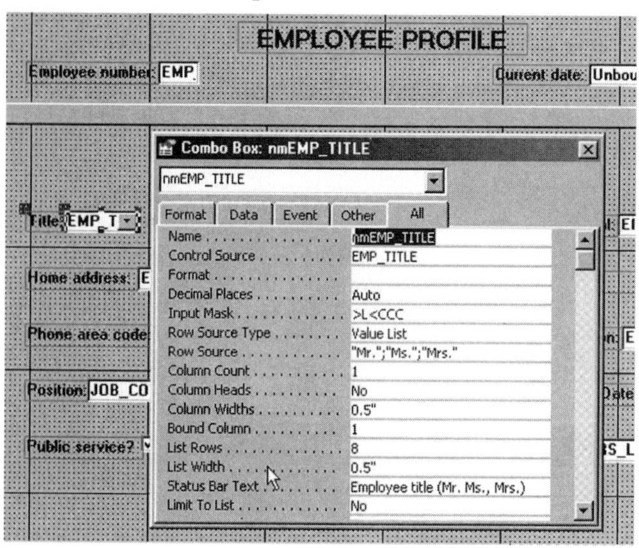

FIGURE 6.38
The Combo Box's Properties Box

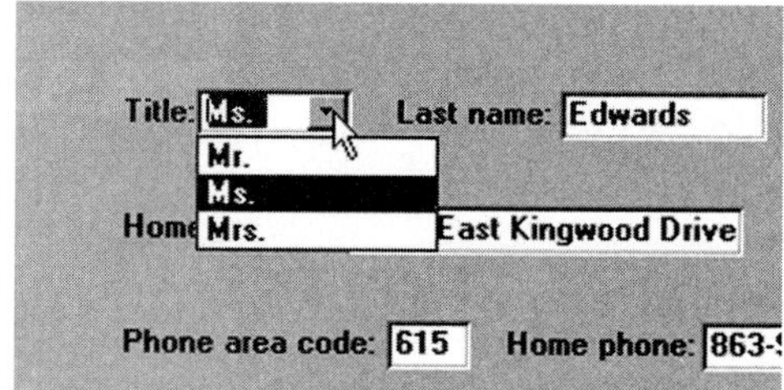

FIGURE 6.39
The Completed Combo Box

10. After selecting the **Store that value in this field** option shown in Figure 6.35, select the EMP_TITLE from the drop-down list and then click **Next >** to generate the screen shown in Figure 6.36.
11. After typing the label name **(Title:)** you want to display on the form in Figure 6.36, click **Finish** to complete building the combo box. You will now see the combo box on the form, which includes the down arrow shown in Figure 6.37.

After creating the combo box, select its properties box as shown Figure 6.38.

Now save the **frmEMPLOYEE** form again and then open it to see the results of your efforts. Figure 6.39 shows a small section of the form to illustrate the combo box effect. Although the form will normally show only the selected title option, we have clicked on the combo box's down arrow to show the available options.

As you examine Figure 6.39, you may decide that the list width is too great. Fortunately, you can edit the combo box components just as you can edit all the other form components. Return the **frmEMPLOYEE** form to the design view and select the combo box again; then open the combo box's properties box (see Figure 6.40).

As you examine Figure 6.40, note that we have changed the combo box name to **nmEMP_TITLE,** using the **nm** prefix to distinguish it from the **EMP_TITLE**

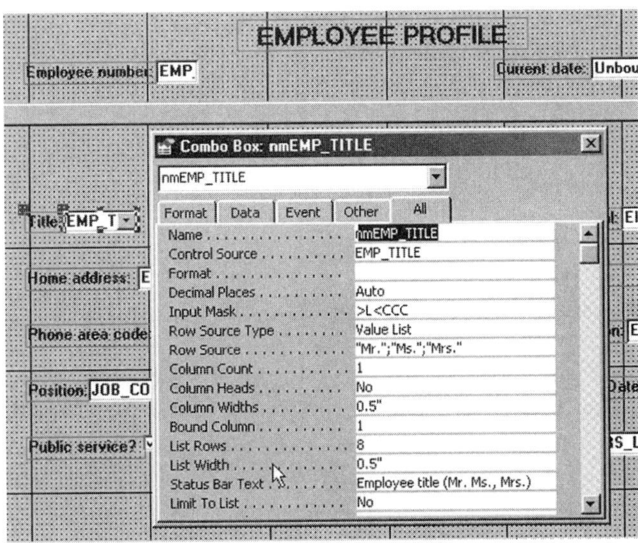

FIGURE 6.40
Editing the Combo Box

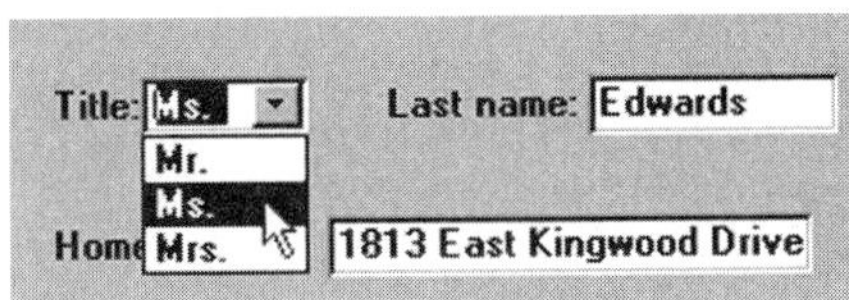

FIGURE 6.41
The Effect of a List Width Change

control source. At this point, the list width is 0.5″. Because we want to decrease the list width, we'll change it to 0.3″, then open the form in **Form View** mode to see the effect of the change. You can also try dragging the combo box width on the form to explore its effect. The results of these steps show up in Figure 6.41. Note that the combo box list width is narrower.

The properties box in Figure 6.40 includes some other important features:

1. The **Control Source** is EMP_TITLE, so you know that this combo box is clearly a bound text box.
2. The **Input Mask** value was inherited from the EMPLOYEE table's EMP_TITLE. We created the EMP_TITLE input mask when we defined the EMP_TITLE in the EMPLOYEE table in Chapter 3. Now you know that you can also specify the input mask by supplying it through the properties box at the form level.
3. The **Row Source Type** is a **value list**, which means that the values are supplied at the form design level as you type in a list of values for the **Row Source**. You will learn later that there are other ways, such as tables or queries, to supply appropriate values.
4. Because only one set of values is supplied for a single attribute, the **Column Count** is 1. You will learn later that you can actually show multiple columns in a combo box.
5. The default entry for **Column Heads** is **No**. If the row source had been a query or a table, you would have had the option of showing the attribute name above each column of the attribute values by declaring the **Column Heads** value to be **Yes**.
6. Because there is only one column of possible input values, only one **Column Width** is specified. If the combo box had been designed to show more than one column, you would have to supply a column width for each column.
7. The **Bound Column** is the EMP_TITLE column and there is only one column's worth of possible values. (See Figure 6.34.) Therefore, the **Bound Column**

default value is 1 to indicate that the first—and, in this case, *only*—column supplies the values for the EMP_TITLE field.

8. The **List Width** is the same size as the **Column Width** if you have only one column. If you have more than one column, the **List Width** is typically the sum of the **Column Width** values.

9. The **Limit to List** value is set to **No**. If you have values other than **Mr.**, **Ms.**, or **Mrs.**, they can be entered, unless you have already restricted the input values at the table level. You may, of course, specify **Yes** to make it possible to enter only the specified values. However, we limited the acceptable values at the EMPLOYEE table level when we created the EMP_TITLE field in Chapter 3. Therefore, you will *still* see the error message in Figure 6.42, even though the combo box's property box allows values other than the combo box's listed values. (Note that we entered **Prof**, rather than a selection from the list of specified values.) In short, the table-level specifications trump those defined at the form level.

Combo boxes may be created for more complex outcomes than the ones based on a value list. For example, it would be very useful to let end users select job codes from a list, rather than type the job codes into the employee form's job code field. Of course, seeing a list of job codes (1, 2, 3, 4, 5, and so on) does not give the end user a clue about the meaning of those entries, so it would be nice if we could provide the job description to go with the employee's job code. Fortunately, Access makes it very easy to produce the desired interface. All it takes is a table or a query that uses the JOB_CLASS table's JOB_CODE and JOB_DESCRIPTION. We won't even have to leave the form design mode to generate the appropriate query or to select the appropriate table.

To create a table-based combo box job list for the employee form, place the form in the design mode, delete the current job code text box, and follow the same steps that were used to create the EMP_TITLE combo box. Of course, this time we select the JOB_CODE field from the field list to produce the combo box properties and we select **I want the combo box to look up values in a table or query** as shown in Figure 6.43.

Click **Next >** on the window shown in Figure 6.40 to produce the window shown in Figure 6.44.

From the screen shown in Figure 6.44, select the JOB_CLASS table and click **Next >** to generate the screen shown in Figure 6.45.

From the screen shown in Figure 6.45 click on the >> button to move the JOB_CODE and JOB_DESCRIPTION from the **Available Fields** window to the **Selected Fields** window. The results are shown in Figure 6.46.

Click **Next >** in Figure 6.46 to produce the window shown in Figure 6.47.

Click **Next >** in Figure 6.47 to produce the window shown in Figure 6.48. Note that we selected JOB_CODE, because the form is supposed to supply the EMPLOYEE table's JOB_CODE value for the selected record. (Remember that the form was based on the EMPLOYEE table, which contains the JOB_CODE attribute as a foreign key.)

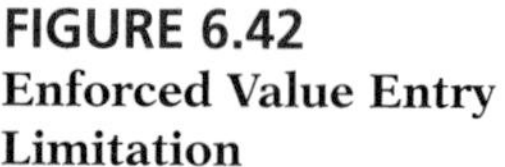

FIGURE 6.42
Enforced Value Entry Limitation

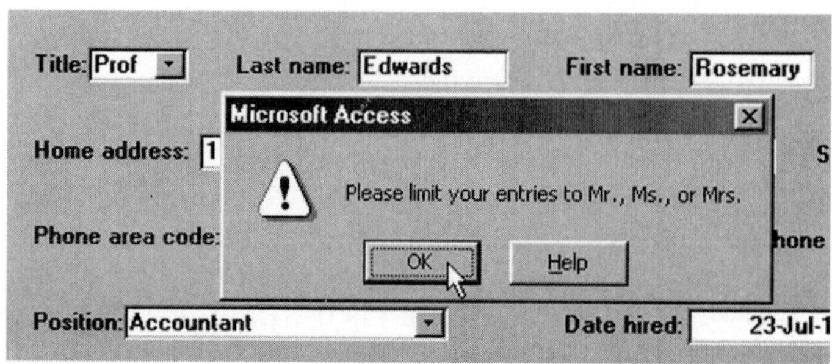

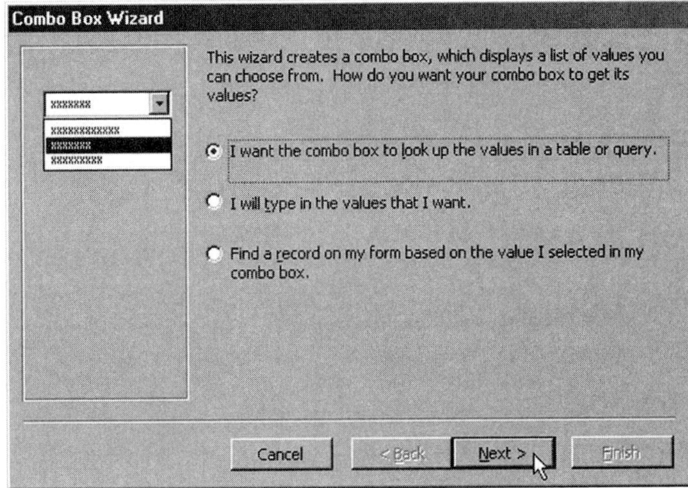

FIGURE 6.43
Selecting the "I want the combo box to look up values in a table or query" Option

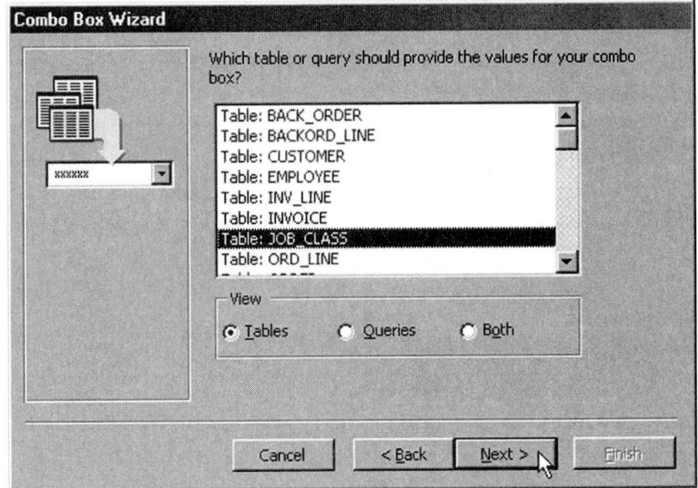

FIGURE 6.44
Selecting the JOB_CLASS Table from the Table Screen

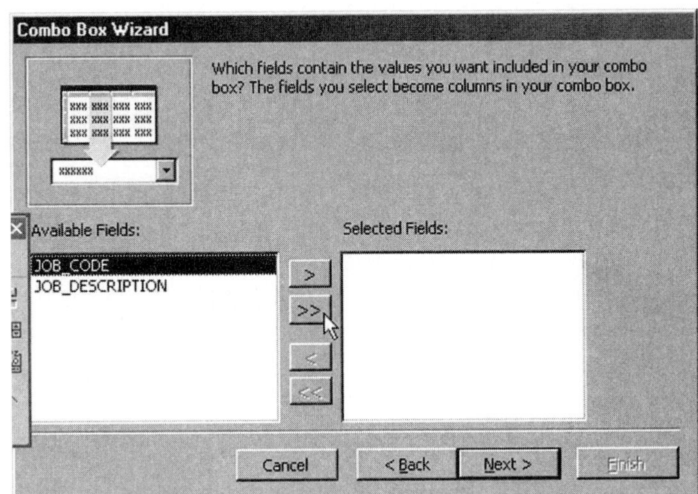

FIGURE 6.45
The Available Fields for the Combo List

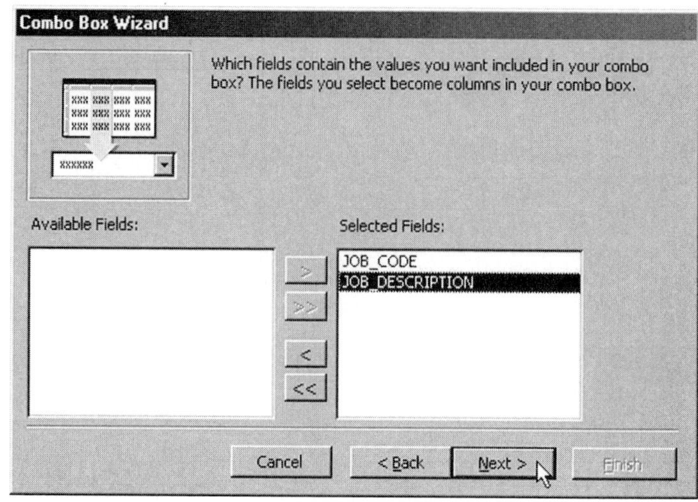

FIGURE 6.46
The Selected Fields

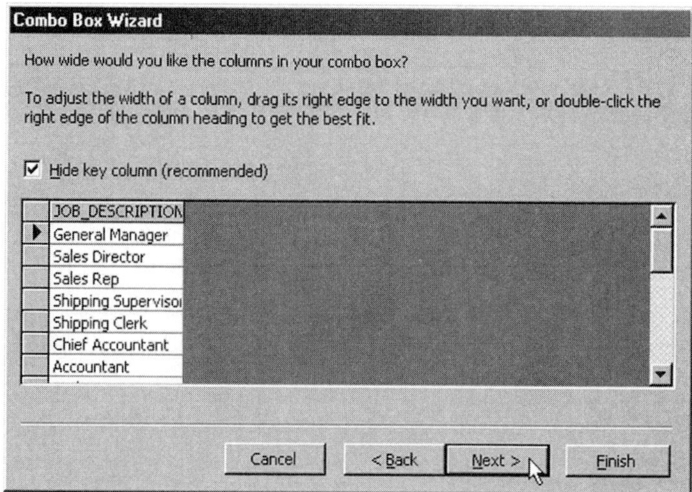

FIGURE 6.47
The JOB_DESCRIPTION in the Combo Box

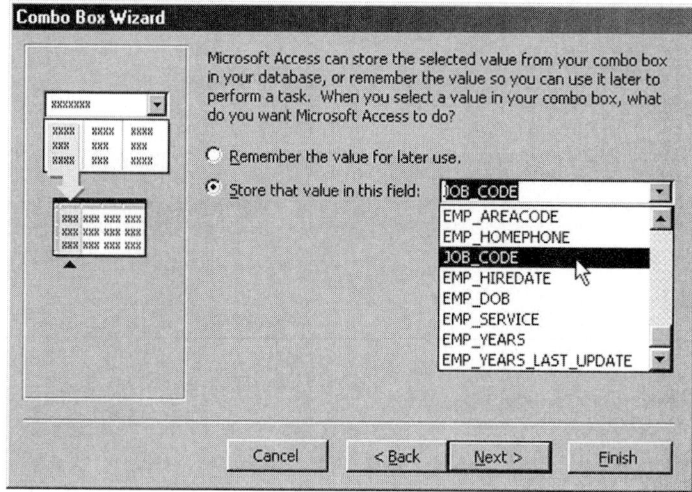

FIGURE 6.48
Field Selection for Value Storage

Now click the **Next >** button in Figure 6.48 to produce the window in Figure 6.49.

The default entry for the combo box label is JOB_DESCRIPTION. Type the label you want to show on the screen to replace the default entry, and then click the

FIGURE 6.49
The Combo Box Label

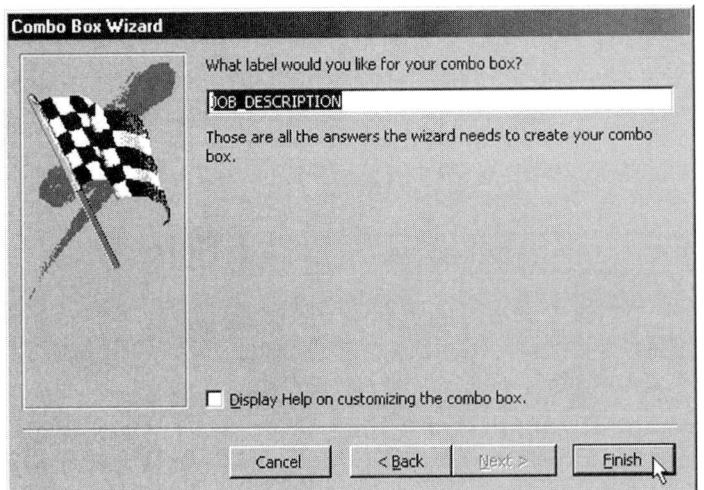

FIGURE 6.50
The Completed JOB_CODE Combo Box

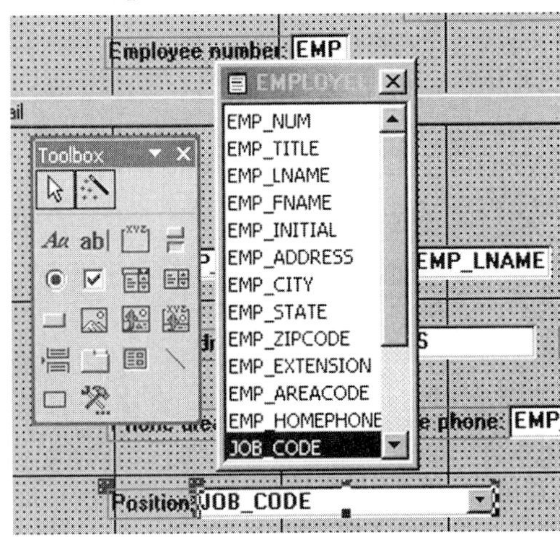

Finish button in Figure 6.49. As you can tell by looking at Figure 6.50, we used the label **Position:** to indicate the employee's job position. (We also moved the combo box to the spot that was vacated when we deleted the original JOB_CODE field from the form.)

As you review Figure 6.50, note that we have kept the **Toolbox** and the **Field List** on the form's design view. Go ahead and close these two design features; you can always restore them later with the **View** button when you do some additional editing on the form. Now go ahead and select the form's **Form View** to produce the screen shown in Figure 6.51.

FIGURE 6.51 **The Edited frmEMPLOYEE Form in Form View**

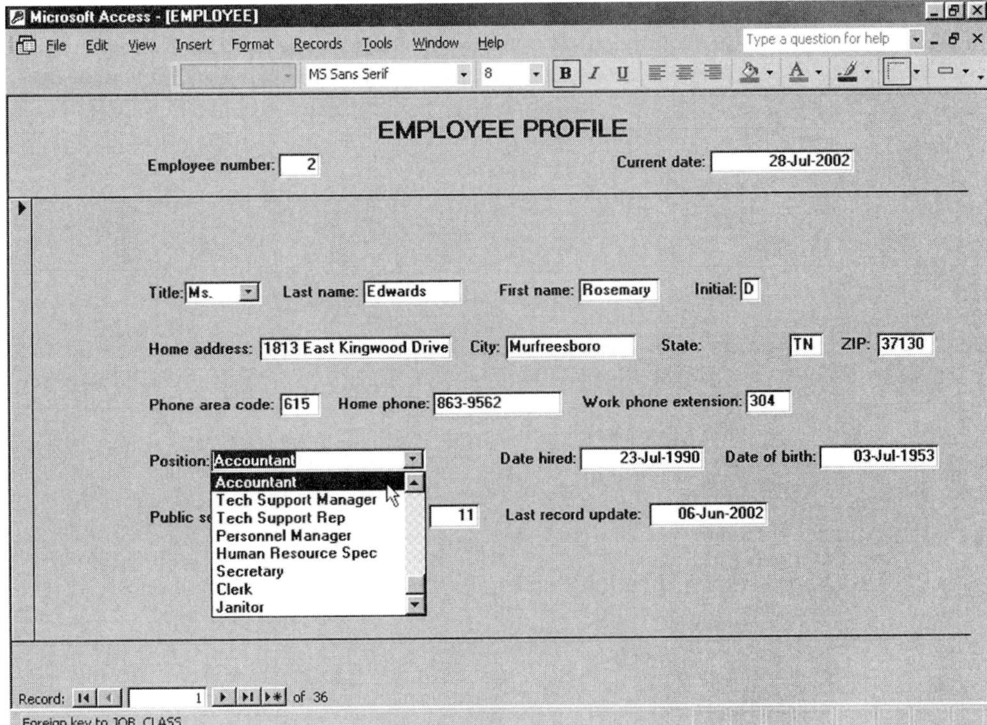

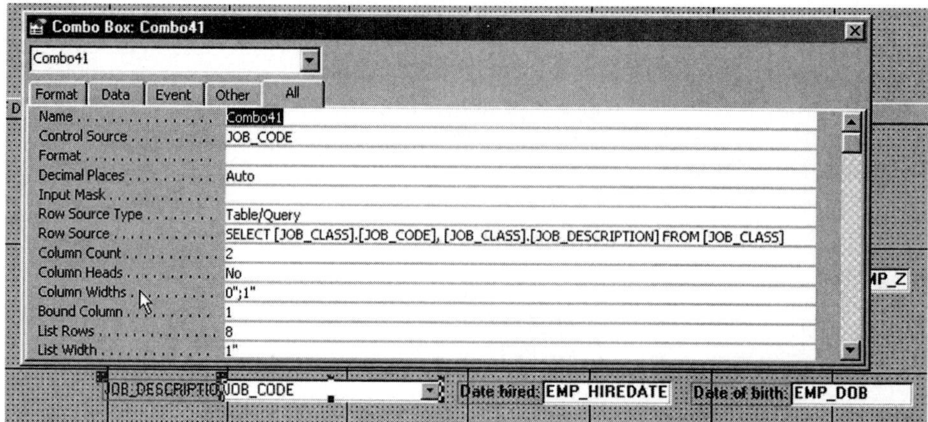

FIGURE 6.52
The JOB_CODE Combo Box Properties Box

As you examine Figure 6.51, note that only the JOB_DESCRIPTION is displayed. This occurs because the **Hide key column (recommended)** option was checked when the Wizard requested your preference (see Figure 6.47). If you had unchecked this option, both fields—JOB_CODE and JOB_DESCRIPTION—would have been displayed in the combo box list. (We'll take a look at that option later.)

To see what the properties of the new combo box are, select the **frmEMPLOYEE** form's **Design View** and open the JOB_CODE combo box's properties box to examine the screen shown in Figure 6.52.

As you examine Figure 6.52, note the following features:

- The Wizard wrote the **Row Source** query for you. If you do not use the Wizard, you must first create the query and then select this query at the combo box's properties box level. That's why we prefer to use the Wizard to produce the form and its contents. We can always edit the form later.
- Although only the job description showed up on the form in Figure 6.51, the column count is 2. That's because both the JOB_CODE and the JOB_DESCRIPTION were selected in Figure 6.46. There was a good reason for making this decision: Only the JOB_CODE is actually stored in the EMPLOYEE table, but the end user needs the JOB_DESCRIPTION in order to make sense out of the entry. (We'll show you how to list both fields later.)
- Because the first column—the JOB_CODE—is not shown on the form, its **Column Widths** value is 0.
- The **Bound Column** is column 1, the JOB_CODE. (The JOB_CODE attribute was the first one selected in Figure 6.46.) It is a bound column because the form's intended input is for the EMPLOYEE table's JOB_CODE field, which was a bound text box on the form.
- The **List Width** is at least the sum of the **Column Widths** values.

Once the basic form is completed, you can edit it to match the end-user requirements. Figure 6.53 illustrates the results of some basic editing done on the just-created combo box.

As you examine Figure 6.53, note these basic changes:

- The first column width is now set to 0.2″ to ensure that it will be shown on the screen.
- We have decreased the number of listed rows to 5. The combo box will have a slide that enables the end user to scroll down to all available entries.

These changes are reflected in Figure 6.54. (Only a small portion of the screen is shown here. Also, while we had the form in design view, we dragged the text box portion of the combo box to decrease its size.)

Combo Box: nmJOB_CODE

nmJOB_CODE

Format | Data | Event | Other | All

Name	nmJOB_CODE
Control Source	JOB_CODE
Format	
Decimal Places	Auto
Input Mask	
Row Source Type	Table/Query
Row Source	SELECT [JOB_CLASS].[JOB_CODE], [JOB_CLASS].[JOB_DESCRIPTION] FROM [JOB_CLASS]
Column Count	2
Column Heads	No
Column Widths	0.2";1.6"
Bound Column	1
List Rows	5
List Width	1.8"
Status Bar Text	Foreign key to JOB_CLASS

Position: JOB | Date hired: EMP_HIREDATE | Date of birth: EMP_DOB

FIGURE 6.53
Basic Property Box Edits for the JOB_CODE Combo Box

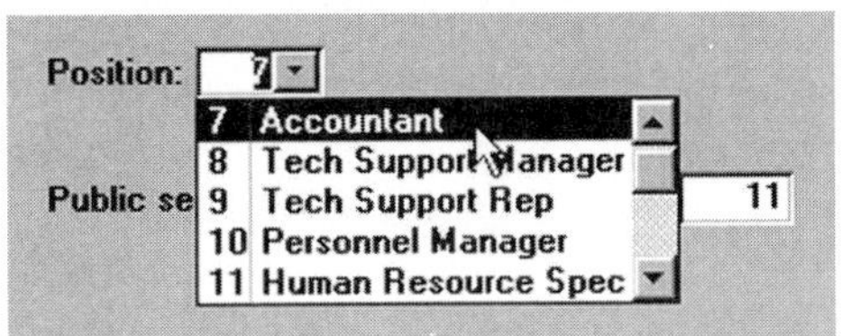

FIGURE 6.54
The Edited Combo Box in Form View

Using the Toolbox's Rectangle Option

The **frmEMPLOYEE** form contains two kinds of employee data:

1. Personal data such as the first name, last name, and home phone number.
2. Work-related data such as the job classification and the office extension number.

To make the distinction between the two data groups more obvious, it helps to place the fields that are characteristics of each group together. And the distinction becomes even more self-evident if they are each contained within a marked space. One good way to group a form's components is to enclose them. The toolbox's **Rectangle** button will make that task simple. Figure 6.55 shows the rectangle selection. (Check the button in the toolbox's lower left corner.) Note that the cursor placed on the form's detail section reflects the selection.

As you examine Figure 6.55, note that we have placed the cursor just above and to the left of the **Title:** text box. Also note that the cursor has changed its shape to reflect our selection. After placing the cursor as shown, drag a rectangle around the first grouping; then repeat the process for the second grouping. (Did you notice that we placed the **Position:** in the second, work-related grouping?) Figure 6.56 shows the results of our efforts in design view format.

As you examine Figure 6.56, note that we have selected the second rectangle: Its move and size handles appear on the screen. You can drag the rectangle edges to fit any grouping you like. Like all Access objects, you can select a rectangle and open its properties box to check and/or edit its characteristics. In short, you should feel comfortable with the various toolbox options at this point; their basic components and operations are remarkably similar.

Form Clean-up

At this point, the **frmEMPLOYEE** form makes it easy to examine, edit, and add data. However, it still has some features that are undesirable. For example, it is probably not wise to let end users use control boxes or to let them maximize and minimize the form at will. The form would probably look cleaner without the

FIGURE 6.55 The Rectangle Button Selection

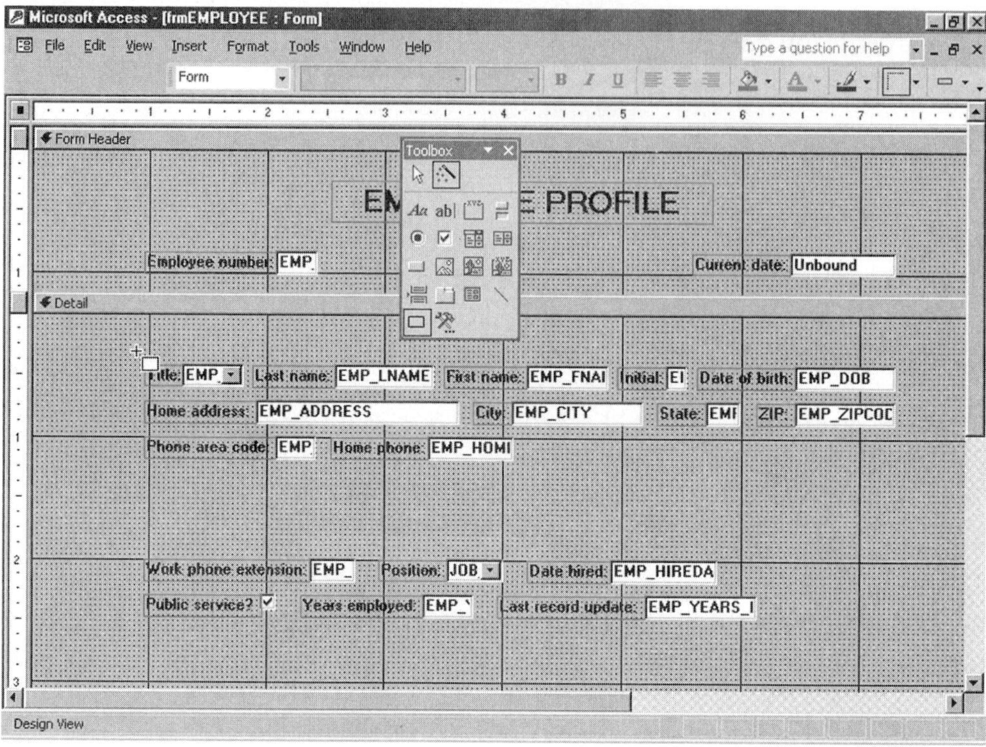

FIGURE 6.56 The Rectangles in Design View

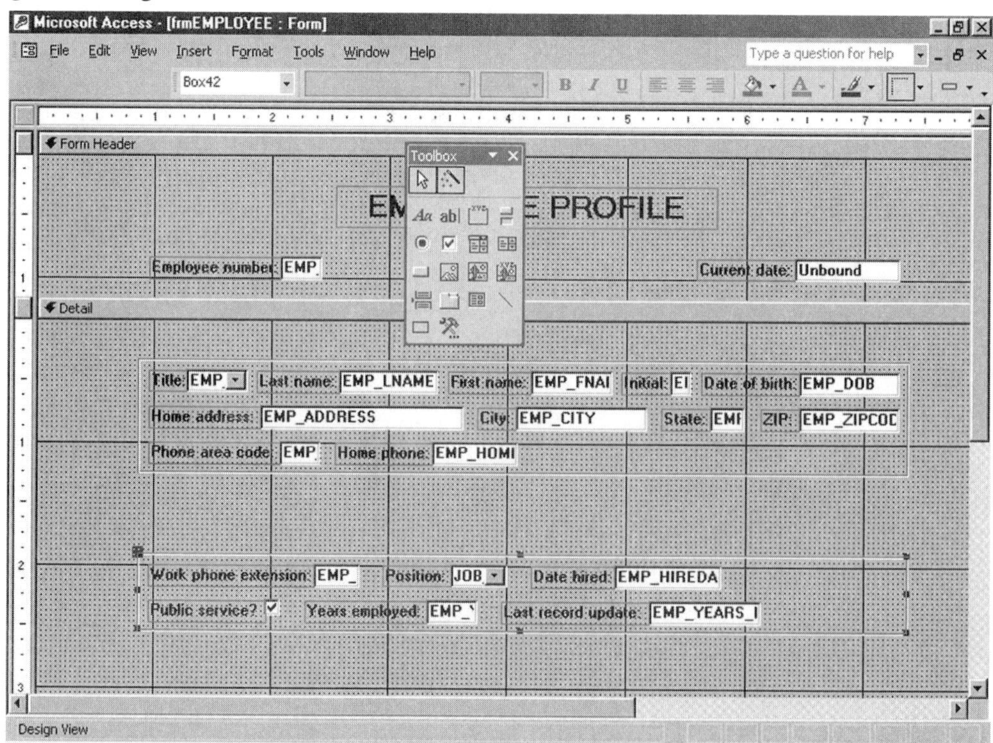

Note

In Figure 6.56 the rectangle uses the Access **Transparent** property default setting, so you can see the objects through it. If your default setting is not transparent, the objects will be hidden behind an opaque rectangle. Even if your rectangle is transparent at this point, selecting a color for it later will render it opaque, thus covering up the objects and making them invisible to you. Select the **Format/Send to Back** option shown in Figure 6.56A to ensure that the text boxes and their labels will not be hidden behind an opaque object.

FIGURE 6.56A
Sending the Rectangle Object to the Back

dividing lines. The form's properties box will let us define all those characteristics and more.

To see what options are available for the entire form, place the form in its design view and then click on any point *outside* the form's borders. (Note the location of the cursor in Figure 6.57. Use the scroll bars to move the form so that you can get to the point outside the form's borders.)

As you examine Figure 6.57, note that the properties box defines the *form* properties—look at the properties box header bar—for the **Scroll Bars**, the **Record Selectors**, the **Navigation Buttons**, the **Dividing Lines**, the **Control Box**, and the **Min Max Button**. (Remember that the properties box always reflects the object you have selected. If you click on a text box, the properties box will reflect the selected text box. If you click on a label, the properties box will reflect the selected label, and so on.)

The properties box shown in Figure 6.57 yields the form view shown in Figure 6.58. Note that we have also done some additional editing. For example, we have moved the text boxes to group them by function: personal information or work information. We have also changed the **Employee Profile** label's font size, we have altered several text box sizes, and we have moved the text boxes to make the grouping more obvious. You have already learned how to do such tasks, so go ahead and practice them to see if you can make your version of the form look like Figure 6.58.

6.3.2 Color and Form Organization

The employee data form in Figure 6.58 is a vast improvement over the original Wizard-generated form. The modified form's combo boxes, whether based on a value list or a query, make its use far simpler. The new labels are easier to read than the originals. And the revised organization of the text boxes yields a better

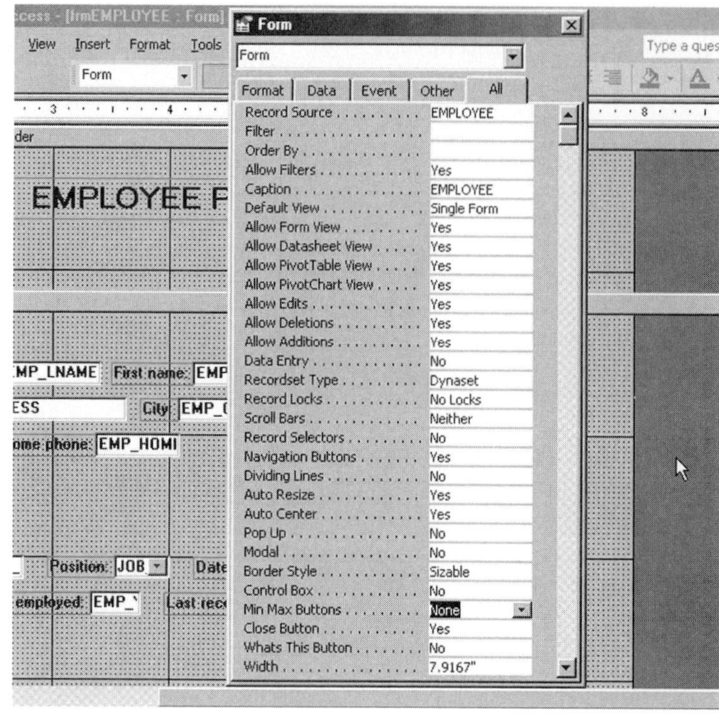

FIGURE 6.57 The Properties Box after Editing

FIGURE 6.58 The Edited Form in Form View

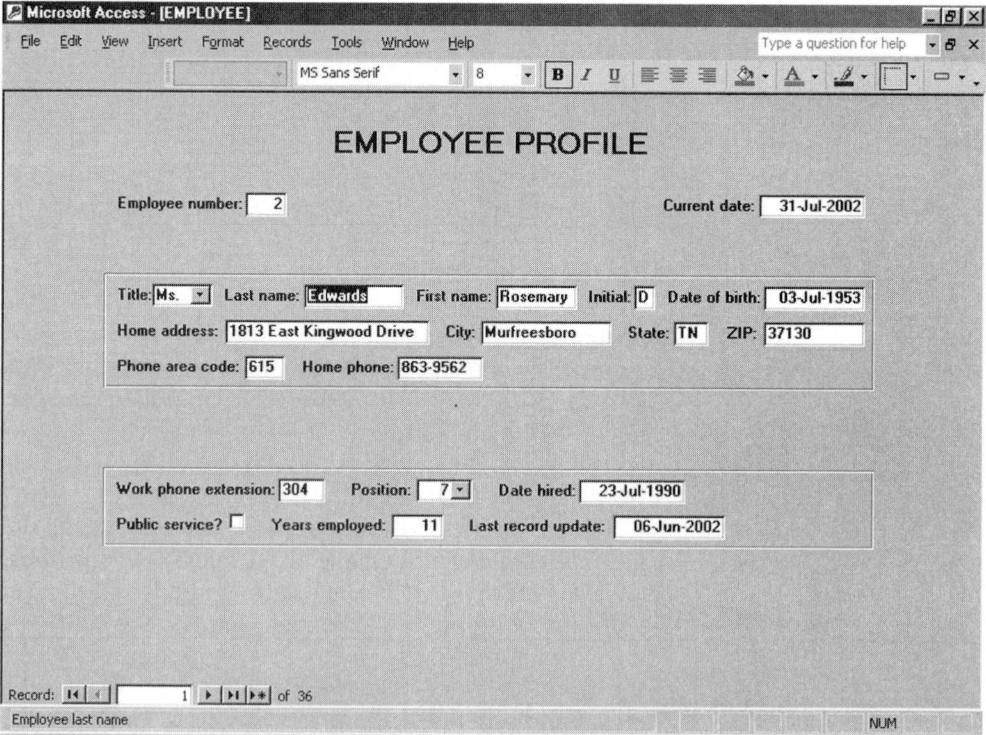

logical organization of the employee information. Yet in spite of the many improvements we've made on the form, it still has some major shortcomings:

- Color plays an important part in effective form presentation. At this point, the form's presentation is rather bland. However, a word of caution is in order.

Because many end users will spend long stretches of time looking at your forms, you'll want to make sure that their eyes are not strained by excessively bright colors or by sharp color contrasts. Use bright and sharply contrasting colors for warning purposes only.

- Forms are easier to read and interpret when their contents are grouped logically. For example, if customer forms display personal data, financial data, and shipping data, color can help you identify those categories. Although we have placed the **frmEMPLOYEE** form's text boxes into logical groupings and we have placed rectangles around them, those groupings would be far more obvious if we used different colors to delineate them. Incidentally, the order in which text boxes are displayed on the form need not reflect the order in which the fields are stored in the table, so you do have considerable flexibility in designing the form layout.

In this section we will show you how to make effective use of color. Naturally, you can select a different color format and presentation. Once you have learned the material in this section, you can let your own judgments and tastes determine the "look and feel" of your end-user interface.

Using the Color Palette

To modify the **frmEMPLOYEE** form, start by placing it in the design format. Next look at the button bar and note that the **Paint Bucket** button and the adjacent **Font** and **Line Color** button are not active at this point. (See Figure 6.59 and note that we have circled the three buttons in question.) If you do not see the button bar shown in Figure 6.59, select **View/Toolbars/Formatting(Form/Report)** to produce them on your screen.

As you examine Figure 6.59, note that we have moved the cursor over the **Paint Bucket** button—the down arrow is part of that button—to show the paint bucket options. These options are **Fill** color to place the color in any selected object and **Back** color to produce a background color. The two buttons next to the **Paint Bucket** button are used to color text and to define line color, respectively.

None of the color buttons are active until you select one or more form components to be colored. If you select a single form component that does not contain letters and/or numbers, such as an unoccupied portion of the form header, only the **Paint Bucket** button becomes active. If you select a text box or a label, both the **Paint Bucket** button and the **Font** button become active.

We'll begin by selecting the EMP_LNAME text box. As you look at the screen, you will see that the **Paint Bucket** button and the **Font** button are now active. Click on the small arrow next to the **Paint Bucket** button to display the color palette shown in Figure 6.60. The paint bucket selection will enable you to produce either a foreground or a background color. We'll use both options in this section.

Incidentally, you can move the color palette to any portion of the screen. Just move the cursor to the palette's upper limit—just where you see the double line—to change the cursor to the four-pointed arrow shown in Figure 6.61. Note that Access also spells out what this action will accomplish.

FIGURE 6.59 Color Tools

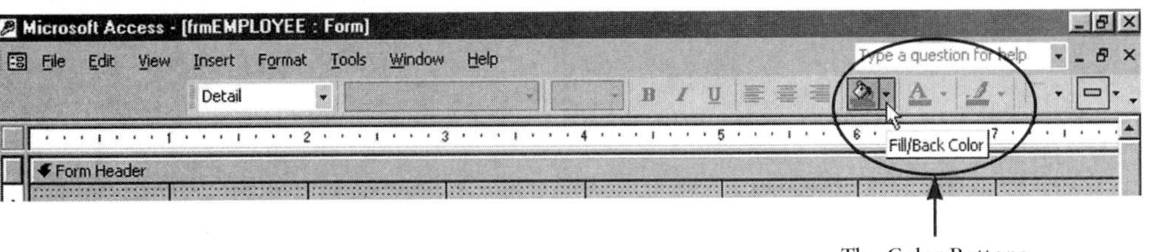

FIGURE 6.60 The Color Palette

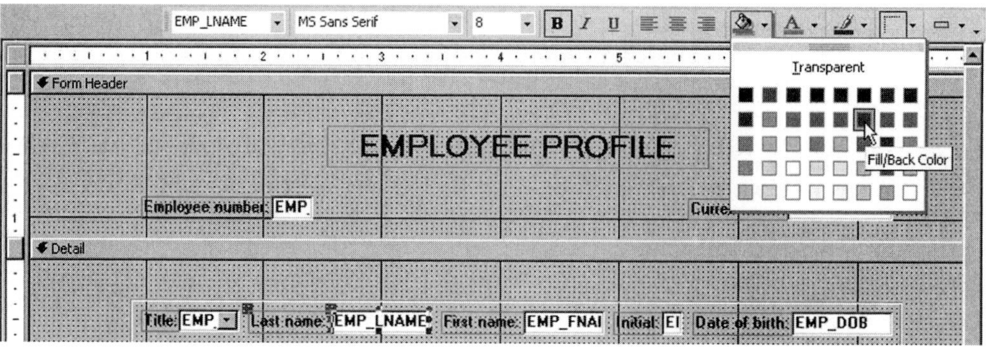

FIGURE 6.61
Move the Color Palette

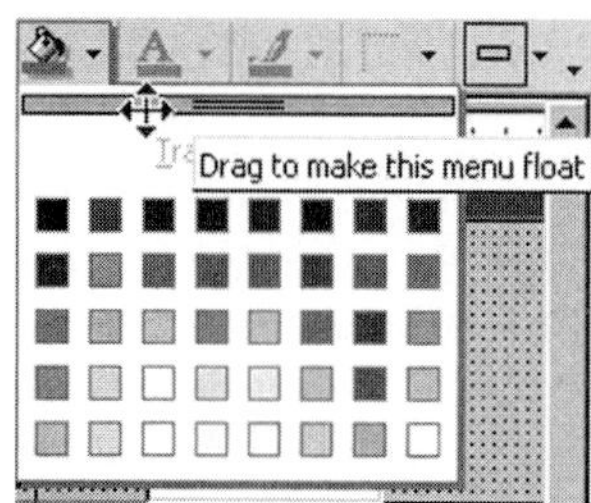

FIGURE 6.62
Coloring a Text Box and Its Label

Using Figure 6.60 as your guide, place your cursor on the blue color button and click. Note the effect of this action: The text box color will change to blue. Repeat this process for the text box label to change it to blue, too. The results are shown in Figure 6.62.

Now that the text box and its label are both blue, the black lettering is difficult to read. So let's change that lettering to white to provide better contrast. Select the EMP_LNAME text box and its **Last name:** label, then click on the **Font** button and move the cursor on the white square as shown in Figure 6.63. Note that the **Font** color palette looks just like the **Paint Bucket**'s color palette. Observe also that the previously selected blue color is now shown in the lower left corner of the palette. The latter feature helps you keep track of which colors were used to make it easier to match color selections.

Assuming that the EMP_LNAME text box and its **Last name:** label are still selected and that the cursor still rests on the white square as shown in Figure 6.63, select the white square by clicking on it and you'll see in Figure 6.64 that the font color has changed to white.

FIGURE 6.63
Selecting the Font Color

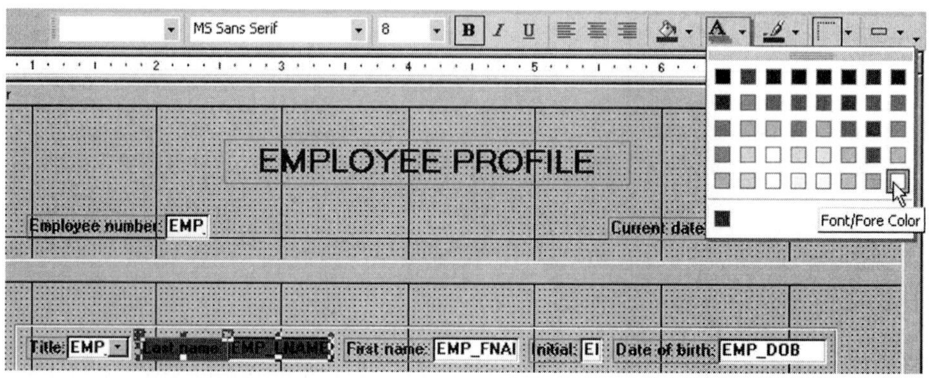

FIGURE 6.64
The Changed Font Color

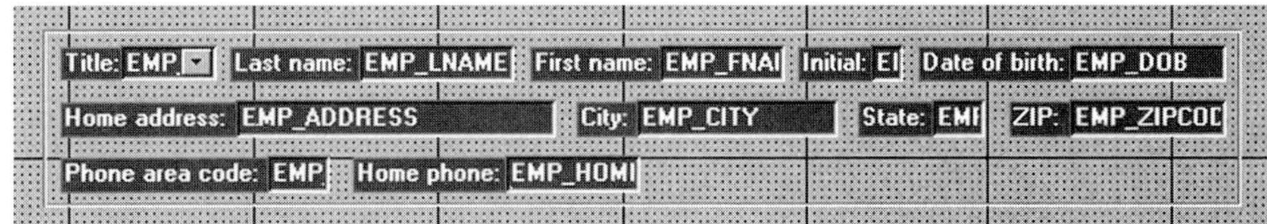

FIGURE 6.65
The Color Revision for the Employee Personal Data

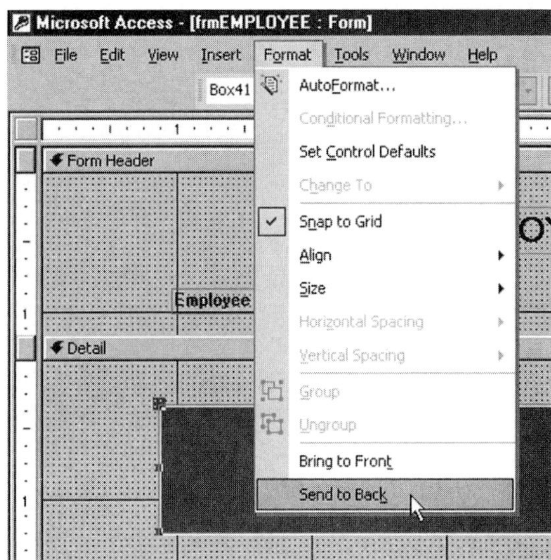

FIGURE 6.66
Sending the Rectangle to the Back

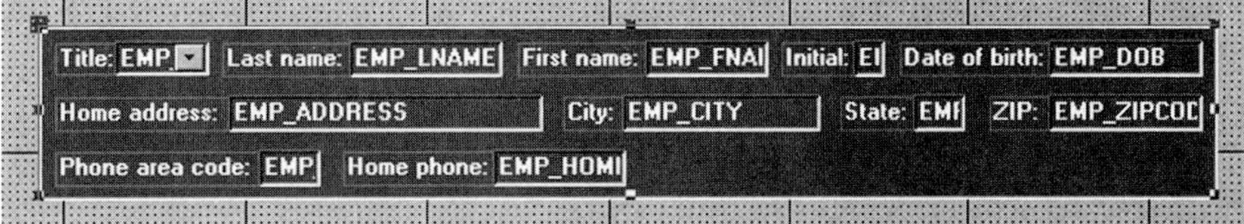

FIGURE 6.67
The Completed Personal Data Section

Repeat the process to change all the text boxes and their labels in the employee personal data section. (But do *not* select the rectangle yet!) When you are done, this section of the **frmEMPLOYEE** form will look like Figure 6.65.

To make the rectangle color match the label and text box backgrounds, click on the rectangle edge to select it. Then click on the **Paint Bucket** button and select the same blue **Fill/Back Color** that was used before. When you have completed this task, you will have a surprise if you have not already changed the rectangle format as illustrated in Figure 6.56A: The blue rectangle covers the text boxes and their labels, thereby making them impossible to read. To eliminate this problem, select the **Format/Send to Back** option shown in Figure 6.66 to generate the completed personal data section in Figure 6.67.

Although we have not changed the colors of the form's main components—the header, detail, and footer sections—you can use the paint bucket to color them just as you colored the rectangles and text boxes. For example, to change the header's background color:

- Place the form in Design format.
- Click on any unoccupied portion of the header.

Assignment

Using the just-described techniques, color the **frmEMPLOYEE** form's work-related data section maroon. Use white letters in this section. Also, use dark green and white letters to define the employee number and the current date in the form's header. Change the EMPLOYEE PROFILE label to blue and change its font size to 24. Move the sections to match the arrangement in Figure 6.68.

FIGURE 6.68 **The Modified frmEMPLOYEE Form**

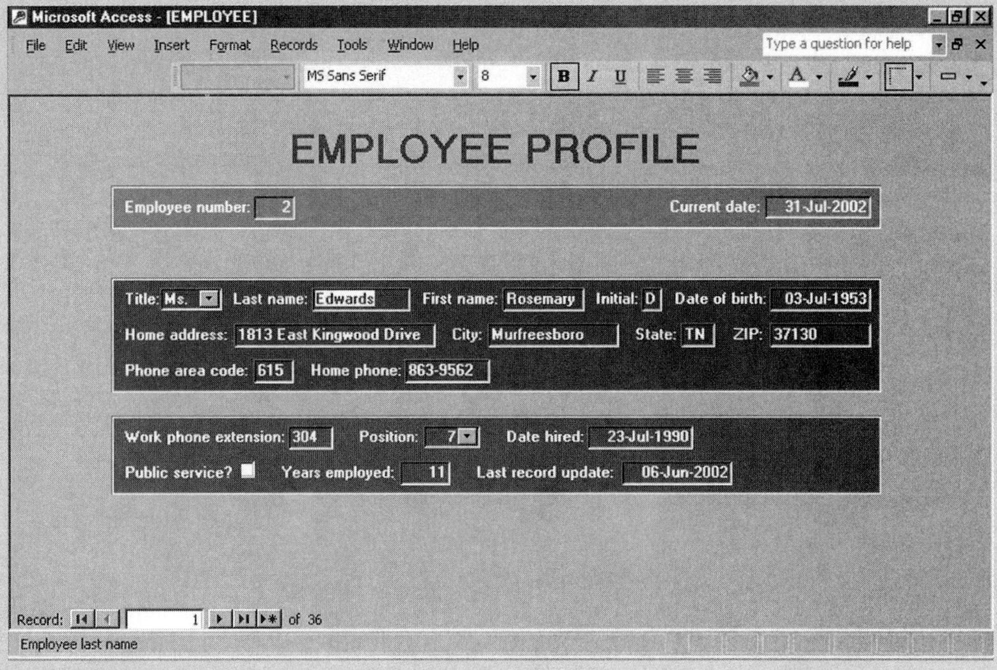

FIGURE 6.69
The Special Effect Menu

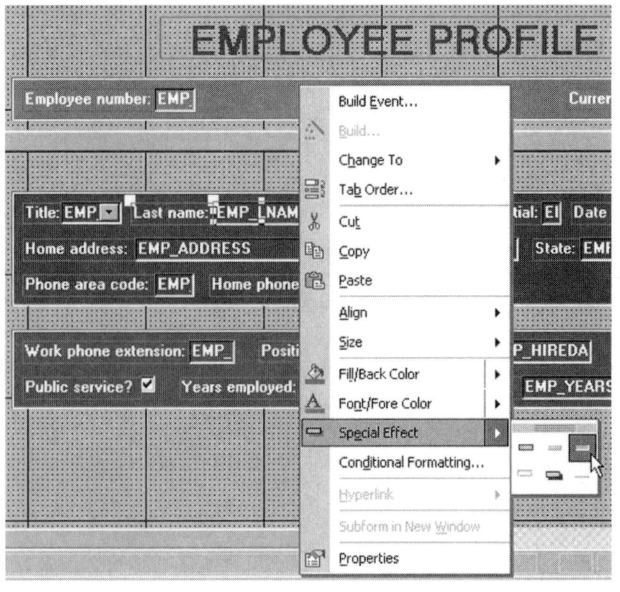

- Click on the **Paint Bucket.**
- Click on a desired color.

Using Special Effects

You can alter the form's appearance by using various special effects. For example, if you select any object and right-click, you will see the **Special Effect** menu in Figure 6.69. In this example, the menu selection indicates that the selected EMP_LNAME text box has a sculpted look. (We have placed the cursor arrow on the sculpted look option, which is the third square in the options box.)

The **Special Effect** options let you change any object's presentation appearance. For example, if you want the green rectangle in the frmEMPLOYEE form's header to have a shadow box effect, click on the rectangle to select it, then right-click to get its **Special Effect** menu with its options and click on the option you want to use. (If you look at Figure 6.69, you'll see a box with six special effects options. The shadow box option is located on the second tier, second button.) If you have

Assignment

Using the **frmEMPLOYEE** form, experiment with the various **Special Effect** menu options. Click back and forth between the form's design view and form view to evaluate the results of your selections. After you have explored the various options, do *not* save the changes. If you have accidentally saved the changes, restore the form to its original configuration.

FIGURE 6.70 The Shadow Box Effect

selected the shadow box option, the form view shows the results in Figure 6.70. (We have shown only the rectangle in the form's header. As always, the current date unbound text box shows the current date, so you can see that we took this screen picture on August 1, 2002.)

Tab Order

When you opened the **frmEMPLOYEE** form in its form view, you may have noticed that the tab was located on the employee's last name. If you use the keyboard's Tab key to move around the form, you are also likely to discover that the tab location does not change as you would expect it to. The reason for this problem is simple: We deleted several fields from the form in order to illustrate the development of various combo box options. When you delete a field from the form and then drag it back in via the menu bar's **Field** button, it is assigned a tab order value larger than the previous largest tab order value. For example, if the form's last field has a tab order value of 15, the next field dragged onto the form will be assigned a tab order value of 16, *regardless of where you place it on the form*.

To find the tab order value for any text box, open the form in the design mode and then double-click on the text box to open its properties box. (Remember that you can also do this job by clicking on the text box and then right-clicking to select the **Properties** option from the menu.) For example, when we opened the employee title combo box's properties box, the **Tab Index** value turned out to be 15, as shown in Figure 6.71. (Note that depending on the number of times you

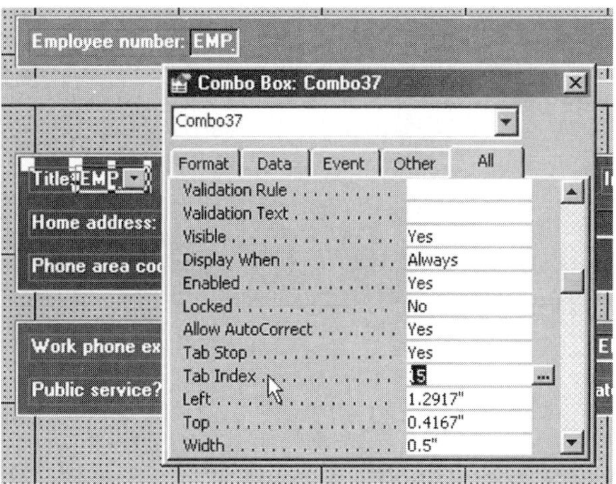

FIGURE 6.71 The Employee Title's Current Tab Order Value

deleted and replaced text boxes via the field list, your **Tab Index** value may be different from the one shown in Figure 6.71. Note also that we have used the slide along the property box's right edge to show the **Tab Index** value for the selected text box.)

The results shown in Figure 6.71 may surprise you. After all, the EMP_TITLE combo box is the first one encountered in the detail line. And if you remember that the employee's EMP_NUM text box was moved to the header, the logical tab order would be to first put the tab on the employee number, then on the employee title, and so on. In short, the tab order is clearly out of order. Fortunately, changing the tab order is easy. Access assigns tab index values, starting with 0 and ending with the number corresponding to the last text box. You can change the tab index values individually by selecting the properties box for each text box and typing the desired index value. For example, if you want the combo box's tab order to be second, select the tab index value 1. (Remember, the tab index values start at 0!) The results of this change are shown in Figure 6.72.

If you find it necessary to change the tab order of all the text boxes and combo boxes, it is much more efficient to select the form and then right-click to open the menu shown in Figure 6.73. (Click anywhere on an empty space on the form's detail section, but make sure that you do *not* click on an individual text box or label.)

Click on the **Tab Order** option shown in Figure 6.73 to open the **Tab Order** dialog box shown in Figure 6.74. Note that the **Section** shows the selection of the form's **Detail** portion.

Figure 6.74 shows the current tab order for the employee form's detail segment. You can select **Auto Order** to produce the tab index values that match the original order of the table's fields, or you can drag and drop selected text boxes. (Use the small tabs in front of the text boxes you want to select.) Whichever technique you use, do not forget to click **OK** when you are done. *Simply closing the dialog box will not save your changes.* You can use the same procedure to change the tab order for the form's header and footer objects.

The Power of the Properties Box

You can control all of the form's properties, not to mention the properties of all of its components, via the properties box. Therefore, the properties box turns out

FIGURE 6.72
The Employee Title Combo Box Revised Index Property

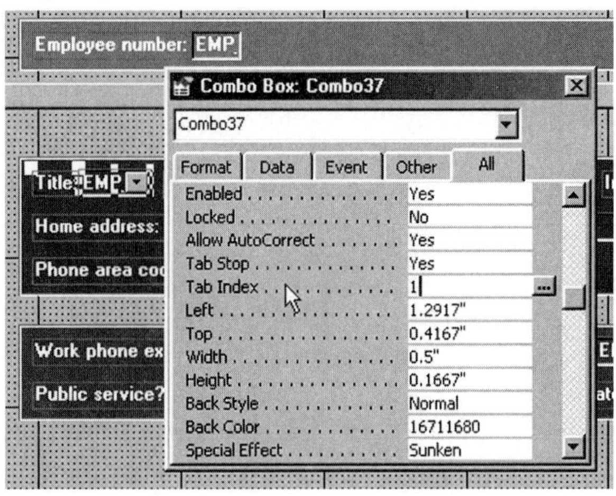

FIGURE 6.73
The Tab Order Menu Selection

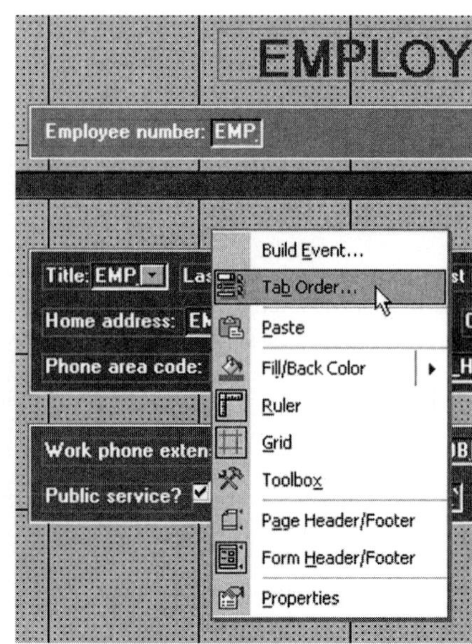

FIGURE 6.74
The Tab Order Dialog Box

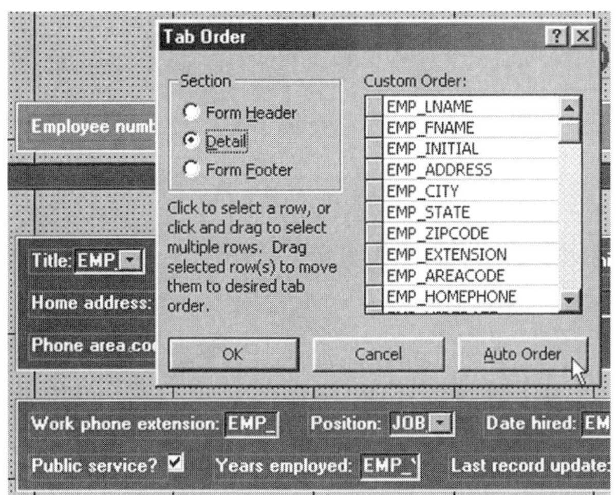

FIGURE 6.75
The EMP_NUM Tab Options

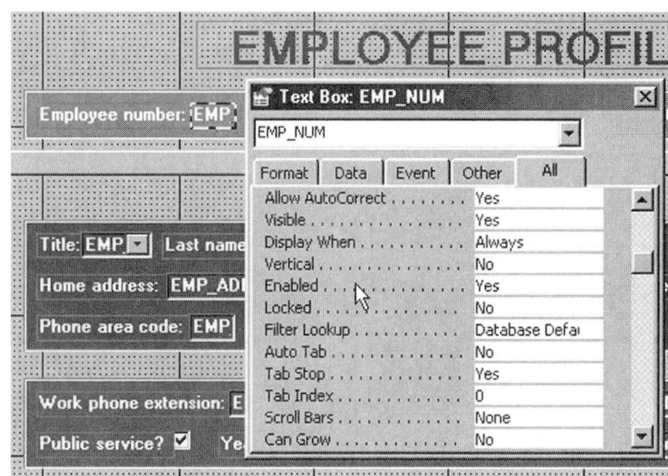

to be one of the most powerful tools available to you when you design and implement the database's end-user interface.

Controlling what end users can do with a form is always important. For example, you can use the properties box options to prevent end users from making a change in any of the form values or from placing the cursor on any specified location. Just select the object you want to protect; then use Figure 6.75 as your guide to select these options from the properties box:

Tab Stop: No
Enabled: No
Locked: Yes

Go ahead and try these options; then toggle between the design and form views to check the effects of your selections. (Given the preceding **Tab** option selection, you will see that you will not be able to make changes in the employee number. In fact, you will not even be able to place the cursor on the EMP_NUM text box.)

The possibilities created by the properties box options are almost endless. You can make objects visible or invisible to the end user. You can change the focus from one object to another. You can change the appearance and even the function of the form and its components. No matter what object you select, the properties box will always give you the available options for that selection. You can also use the properties box to help create a system from the many components you will have created. All it takes is the magic of macros (see Chapter 8) and the property box's ability to let you attach those macros to various objects.

Although the properties box is relatively new to you, just cursor through it and see how many options are available. If you are curious about a particular feature, click on it and then press the keyboard's F1 key to get a detailed explanation. Access even provides examples of the option you selected.

6.4 LIST BOXES ON FORMS

Forms may be based on tables, or they may be based on queries. (You should recall that the Form Wizard gave us an option to select the data source.) However, forms may also be constructed without specifying a data source at the time of their creation. Such forms may then be used to show query results, listing more than one record at a time. Creating such forms will satisfy two requirements. First, they will enable us to present query results more attractively. Second, they will enable us to use the query results as input for another form, a report, or even another query. This second function will be used to great advantage as we combine the forms we create in this chapter with the macros in Chapter 8 to produce the sophisticated multilevel search capabilities in the invoice interface.

Before we create the form, recall the segmented searches presented in section 5.2.5—see especially Figure 5.28A—and augmented in problem 5.1. The query, named **qryCreateEmployeeList**, was used to find employees on the basis of an employee number, a last name, and/or a first name and to print the matches. The ability to perform the required searches on the basis of incomplete information made the query especially useful. The results from this query will be reported in the form we develop next.

To create a form containing a list box, start by selecting the **New Form** option from the database window. Then select **Design View**, as shown in Figure 6.76. Do *not* select a data source before clicking **OK**.

Clicking **OK** on the **Design View** option in the **New Form** dialog box shown in Figure 6.76 generates the blank form shown in Figure 6.77.

FIGURE 6.76 **The Design View Selection in the New Form Dialog Box**

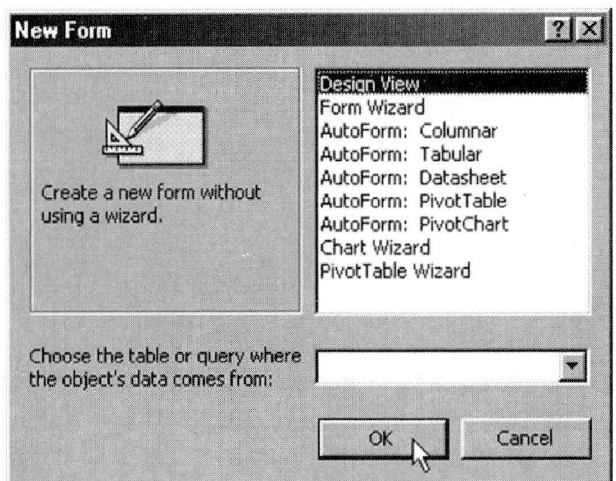

FIGURE 6.77 **The Blank Form**

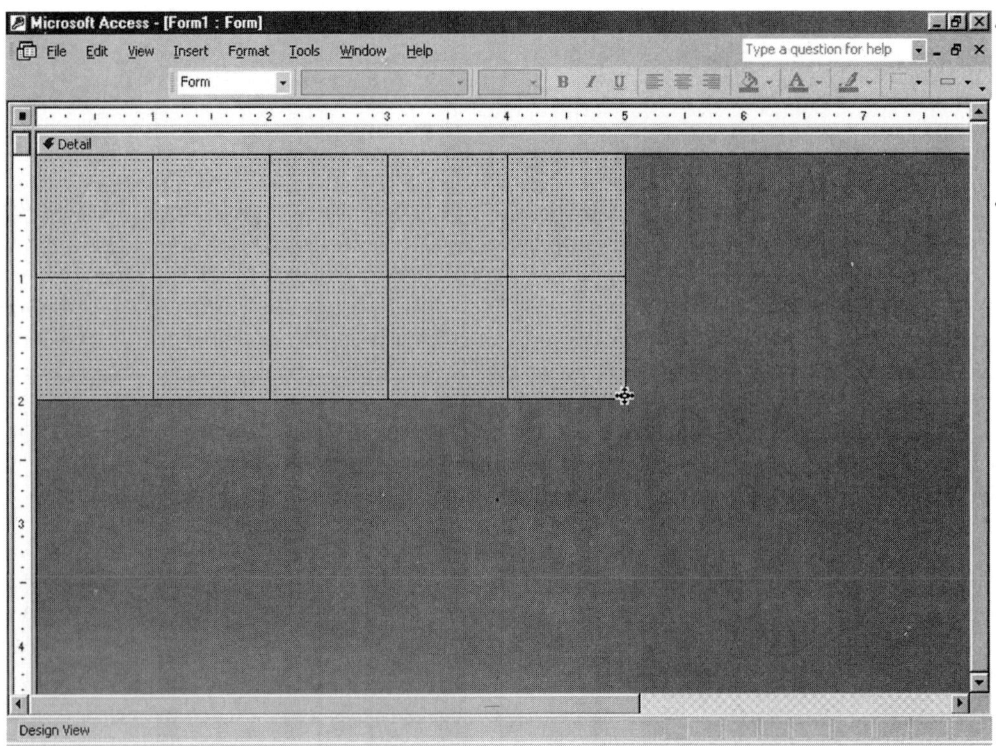

Note

Before you actually produce the list box, turn the **Wizard** button on the **Toolbox** off. You have already learned how to use the Wizard, so you are now ready to learn how to produce a toolbox-generated object at the design level.

FIGURE 6.78
The List Box Option

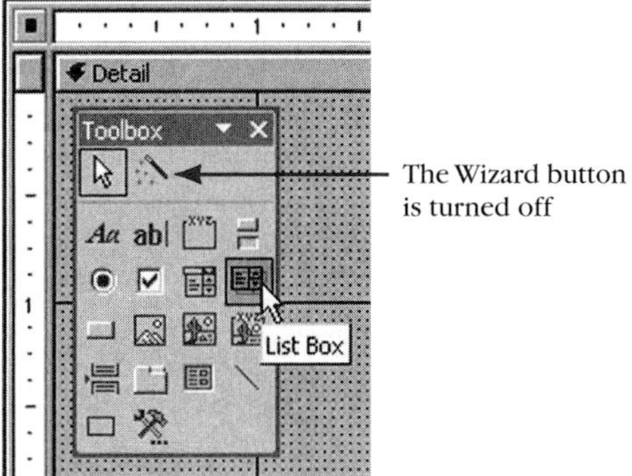

Using Figure 6.77 as your guide, place the cursor on the lower-right corner—note that the cursor changes its shape—and drag the form's detail limits to increase the form size. Next, click on the toolbox's **List Box** option (see Figure 6.78). Note that the cursor changes to a list box shape as you place it anywhere on the detail section.

With the cursor in the list box mode and the **Wizard** button turned off, drag the list box limits to create a large white rectangle, as shown in Figure 6.79.

The list label located next to the box's upper left corner, indicates that this object is, in fact, a list box. Because you will not need this label, delete it. Be careful

FIGURE 6.79 The Form's List Box Object

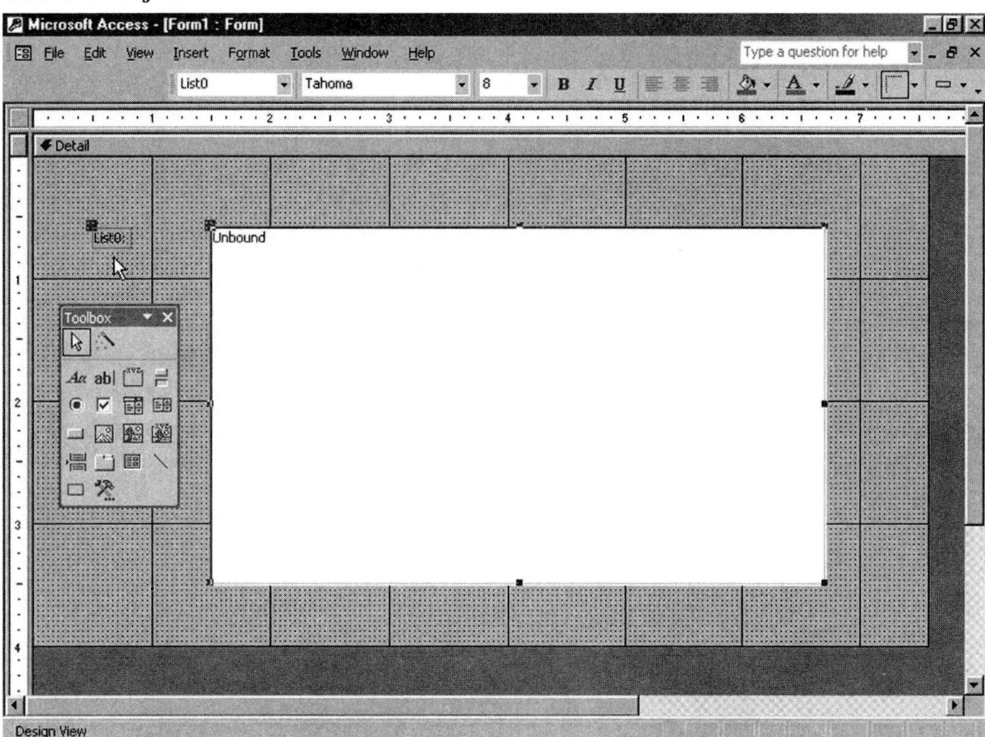

where you click before you delete: First click outside the list box; then click on the label portion only before you select the delete option. Remember, you want to delete the label, not the list box.

After deleting the list box label, turn your attention to the list box and note that Access has marked it as **Unbound**. In many respects, the list box behaves like a combo box, so you'll need to specify a data source. You should recall from our discussion that opened this section that the list box contents will be based on the query named **qryCreateEmployeeList**. This query is included in your **Ch06_POS_2nd** database and it produces the employee number, last name, first name, and initial. The list box must be wide enough to show all of the **qryCreateEmployeeList**'s attributes across the list box space.

As usual, it is the **List Box** properties box that lets us define its data source. Because we want the **qryCreateEmployeeList** output to be placed into the list box, step through this process:

- Open the **List Box** properties box and click on the **Row Source** option's right margin to select the **Builder** button (see Figure 6.80). Clicking on the **Builder** button opens the QBE screen shown in Figure 6.81. Note that we selected the **Queries** tab, as shown in Figure 6.81.

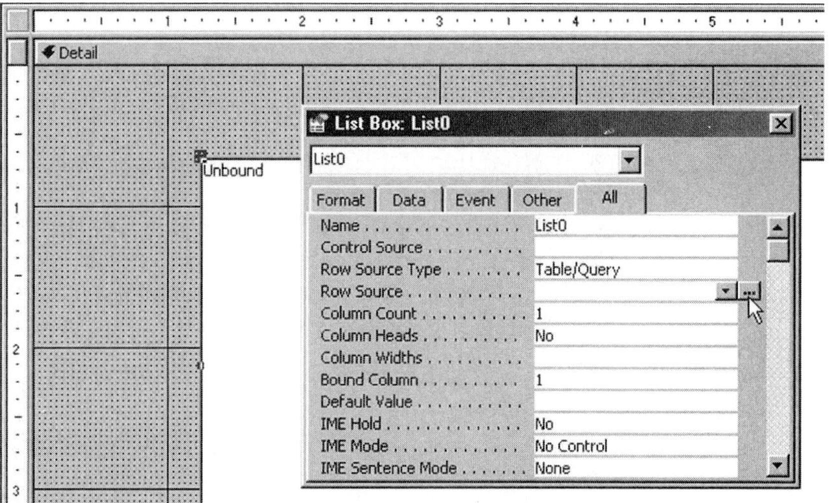

FIGURE 6.80
The List Box Row Source

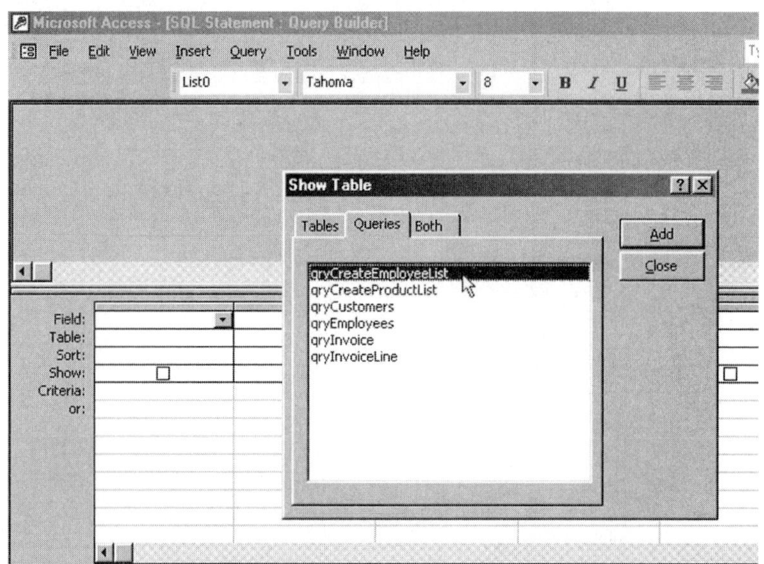

FIGURE 6.81
The Query Selection

- Because the **qryCreateEmployeeList** query is the list box's data source, place the query into the QBE data source section. Then drag each of the query's output fields into the QBE grid (see Figure 6.82).
- Close the **SQL Statement: Query Builder** format shown in Figure 6.82 and *don't forget to save it*. You have just created the row source data for the list box.
- Exit the QBE screen and save as usual to preserve the list box's data source and to return to the properties box. Note that the query specification is now shown as the **Row Source.** If you want to see the details of the SQL query, right-click on the **Row Source** contents—the SELECT statement—and use the **Zoom** option shown in Figure 6.83 to see the SQL statement in Figure 6.84.

Although the preceding **Row Source** selection sequence works well and yields an efficient generation of row source data, you can take a shortcut by simply clicking on the down arrow next to the **Row Source** in the list box's properties box. This action will show the list of all available tables and queries, so cursor down to the query you need and click it into the **Row Source** slot. (See

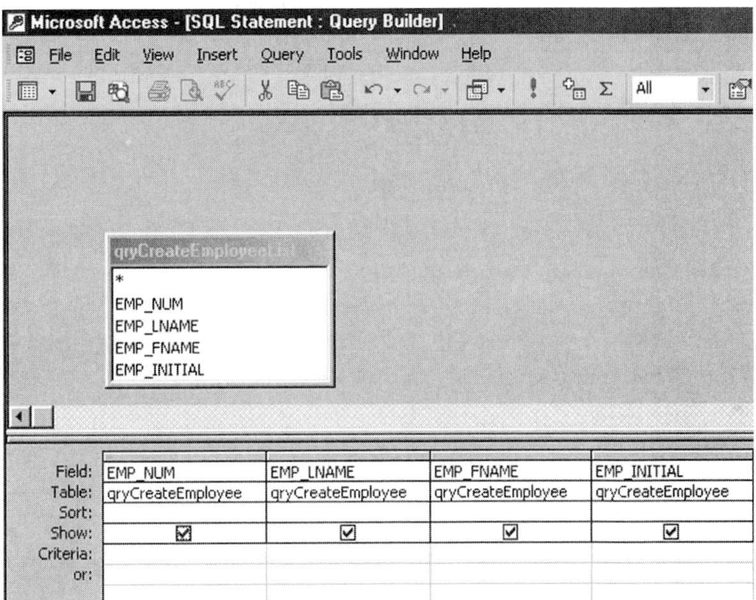

FIGURE 6.82
The Selected Fields for the List Box

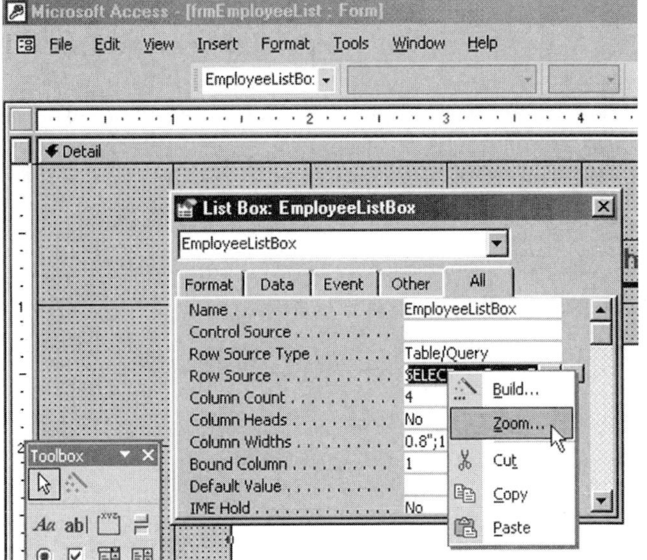

FIGURE 6.83
The Zoom Option to View the Row Source Contents

FIGURE 6.84
The Query Specification in the Row Source

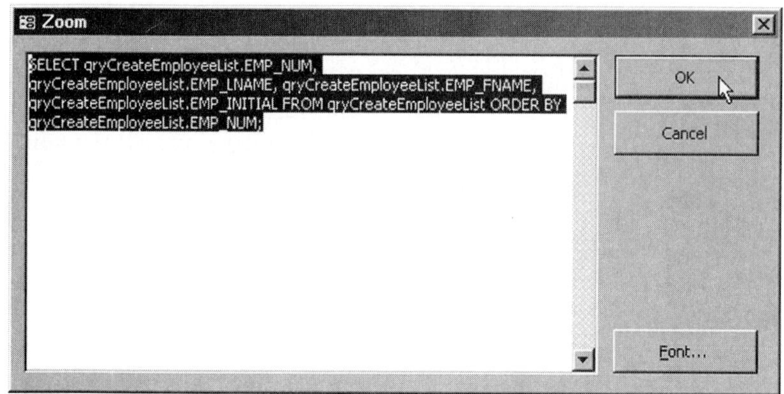

FIGURE 6.85
An Alternate Procedure for Selecting the Row Source

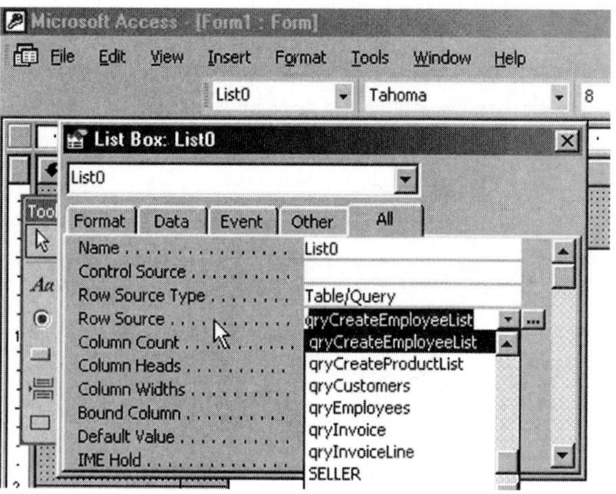

FIGURE 6.86
The Row Source Statement for the Alternate Row Source

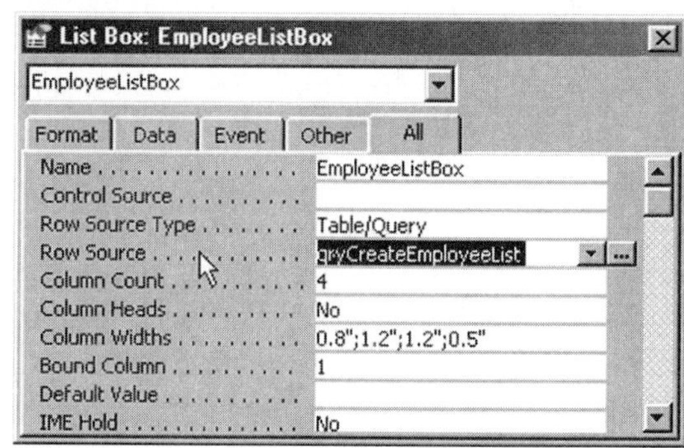

Figure 6.85 and note that we have selected the **qryCreateEmployeeList** query as the **Row Source**.)

Using either procedure, you will generate a proper list box data source. However, the selection in Figure 6.85 will yield the row source statement in Figure 6.86, which shows the query, rather than the query's structure.

As you examine Figure 6.86, note that the list box properties must be modified. For example, the list box name has been modified to **EmployeeListBox**. (The original **List0** name generated by Access would have made it difficult to identify the object in question when we do additional development work later.) Also, note that we have modified the column count to 4 and specified the column widths. If you forget to make these changes, you will see only a single column of employee numbers in your list box.

Keep in mind that you should cursor down the properties box to see the additional options that are available to you. Remove the form's scroll bars, the max/min buttons, the record selector, and the navigation buttons to clean up the screen. End users generally prefer clean screens!

Return to the form's design view and then use the toolbox **Label** button to produce the form identification and the output headers shown in Figure 6.87. Save the form as **frmEmployeeList** and then open it. You will see the same parameter query prompts that you saw in problem 5.1. This time the **qryCreateEmployeeList** parameter query places its output in the **frmEmployeeList** form as

Note

As you examine the **List Box** properties box, remember to scroll down to select the proper **Width** option, not shown here. The sum of the column widths is 0.8 + 1.2 + 1.2 + 0.5 = 3.7. The width must be at least as large as the sum of the column widths. However, if you select a width of 3.7, you'll discover that the list box will include horizontal scroll bars. If you don't want these scroll bars on your screen, select a width slightly larger than the sum of the column widths. (We selected a width of 3.8" to eliminate the scroll bar.)

FIGURE 6.87
Employee Number Prompt

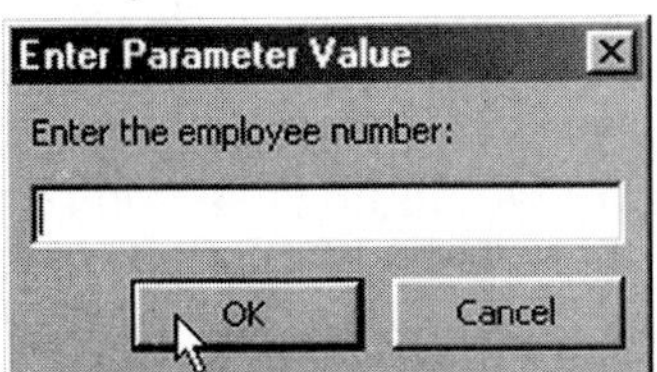

FIGURE 6.87A
Employee Last Name Prompt

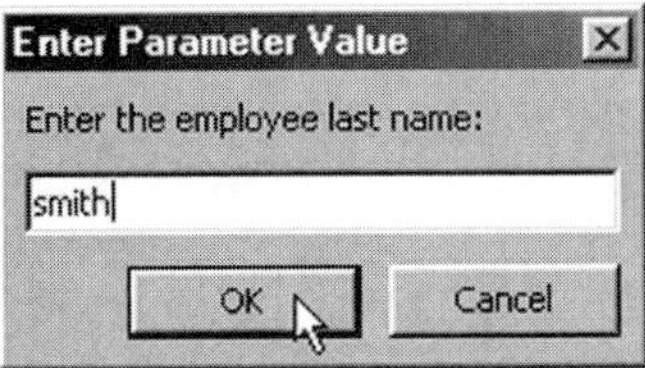

FIGURE 6.87B
Employee First Name Prompt

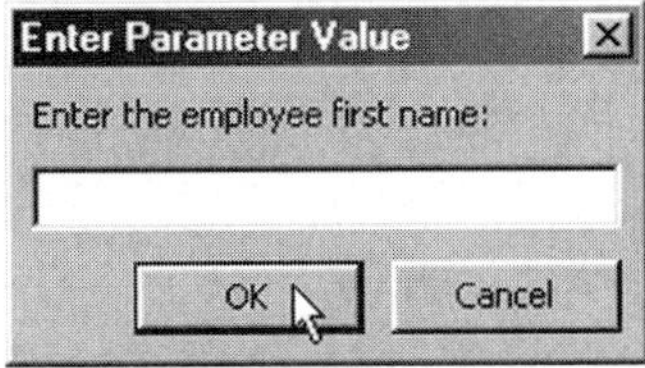

FIGURE 6.87C
Employee List Box Output

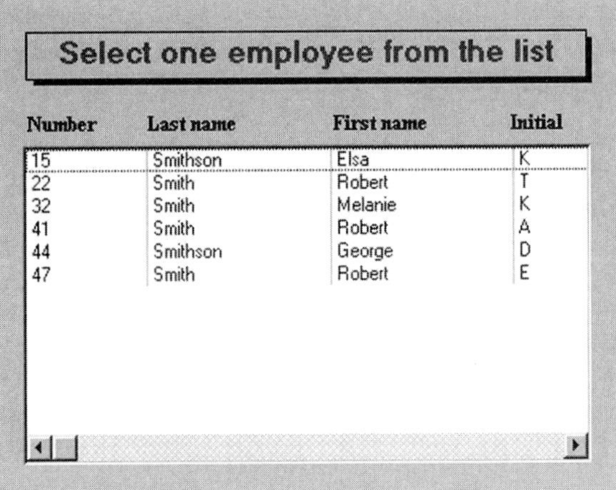

Number	Last name	First name	Initial
15	Smithson	Elsa	K
22	Smith	Robert	T
32	Smith	Melanie	K
41	Smith	Robert	A
44	Smithson	George	D
47	Smith	Robert	E

shown in Figure 6.87C. To produce the output shown in Figure 6.87C, we selected no entry for the employee number, Smith for the employee last name, and no entry for the employee first name. The query's **Like** command structure produces a match for any employee who has Smith as a last name component. Therefore, two employees named Smithson are included. If the EMPLOYEE table had included Ordsmith, Smithlein, or any other last name containing "smith," these employees would have been listed, too.

As you examine Figure 6.87C, note that the screen looks uncluttered because we removed the navigation buttons, the record selector, the min/max buttons, and all other nonessential screen elements. The form's properties box gives us a lot of control over how end users see the applications!

6.5 MAIN FORM/SUBFORM CREATION AND USE

One of the really useful form features is that forms may be linked to other forms to show data relationships on a single screen. The ability to display linked forms simultaneously is particularly useful when you have to process multilevel transactions. For example, if you want to perform invoicing transactions on the screen, it would be awkward to first open the invoice, make an entry, open the first invoice line, make an entry, close the line entry, open the invoice again, and so on, until you are done. You would have the same problem if you would want to examine the past invoices and all their invoice lines. Leaving the relevant invoice on screen while you are scrolling through its lines would be much better.

Fortunately, Access makes it easy to produce forms that contain subforms. Such forms are based on a so-called **main form** to represent one side of the relationship, while the **subform** represents the other side of the relationship. If the form portrays a 1:M relationship, the main form will contain the "one" side of the relationship and the subform will contain the "many" side of the relationship. For example, note the relationships expressed by the following two business rules

1. An INVOICE contains one or more INV_LINEs.
2. Each INV_LINE is related to one INVOICE.

These two business rules place the INVOICE on the "one" side and the INV_LINE on the "many" side of the relationship. Therefore, the main form would be based on the INVOICE table, and the subform would be based on the INV_LINE table.

The only limit to the number of subforms you place on a form is the available screen size. You will discover, for example, that the invoicing process in Chapter 9 contains an invoice form that contains customer data, seller data, tax data, and so on.

Because the 1:M relationship is most common, it will be the one you'll usually find on a form/subform setup. And these forms are becoming more intricate as the reporting requirements increase in various businesses. In fact, government rules and regulations dictate many end-user form formats. For example, in Chapter 2 the normalization procedures introduced an environment in which aircraft regulations require all maintenance to be tracked through log entries, each of which contains one or more maintenance actions. Each maintenance action may require the use of parts, and each part must be traceable to its source. The action taken must be traceable to the aircraft on which the action was performed, and to meet notification requirements, the aircraft's owner(s) must be traceable. In addition, each action, when completed, must be related to the person who completed it, and the log must be opened and closed by a person who must be traceable. Such an environment makes form/subform design and use a particularly productive activity.

Although we can choose from an almost limitless number of examples, we will use the POS invoicing environment as the basis for the creation of the main form/subform objects in this chapter. We will then be able to use the results of this chapter's efforts when we develop a detailed POS invoicing system in Chapter 8. Therefore, we will start with the main form, based on the INVOICE table.

6.5.1 Creating the INVOICE Main Form

Creating the main form requires the same procedures used to create the employee form in section 6.3. Therefore, begin by selecting the **New Form** option from the database window and then select the **AutoForm: Columnar** option from the **New Form** dialog box. Select the INVOICE table as the form's data source before you let the Form Wizard produce the form. Save the form when the Form Wizard is done, using the form name **frmINVOICE**.

After you have modified the invoice form to conform to the layout shown in Figure 6.88, it's time to show which invoice lines are associated with the invoice. By placing the invoice lines into the invoice screen, you will be able to examine the product purchases that make up the invoice amounts. (Remember that an INVOICE can have many INV_LINEs, each reflecting the purchase of a product.)

Assignment

Modify the Wizard-produced invoice form to produce the form shown in Figure 6.88. The form's basic background color is soft green and the lettering is white. Note the following features:

- The header and footer segment lines are shown.
- The tab order must be changed to control the tab stops.
- The cursor may not stop on the invoice number and on the invoice date.
- The end user must not be able to make changes in the invoice number

(*Hint*: Make sure you use the appropriate property boxes to select each object's properties.)

FIGURE 6.88 The Invoice Form: Main Form Segment

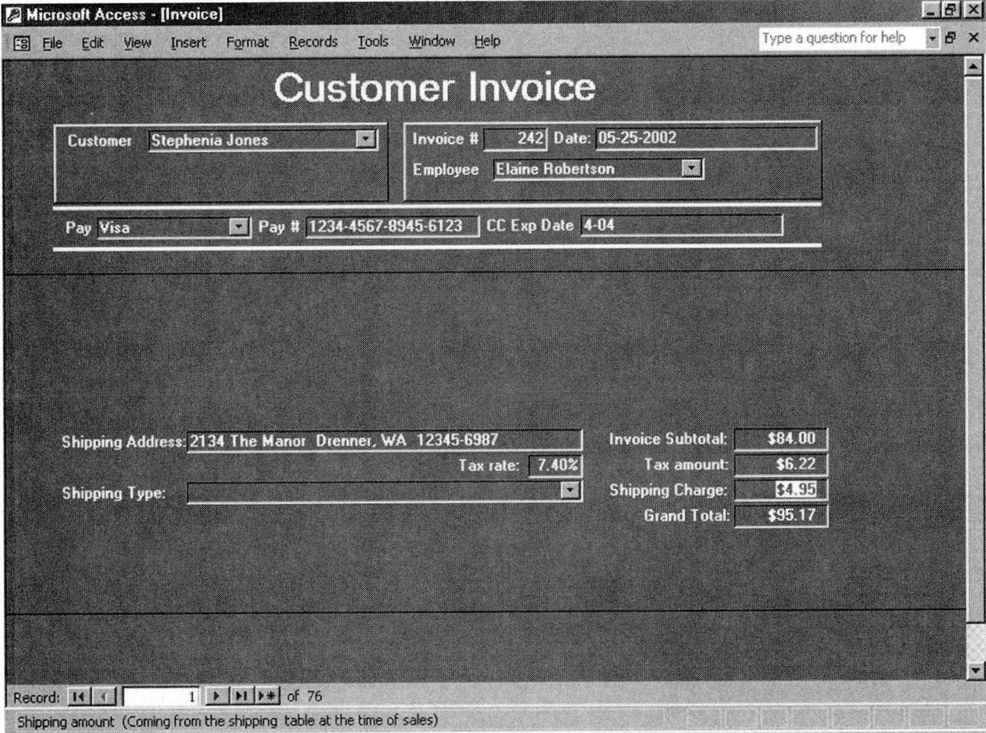

The segment that contains the invoice lines will become the subform to the invoice form. Because the invoice and its lines are related, the invoice lines will change each time the invoice number changes.

The invoice form's subform must have a data source. Because you'll want to control the data source presentation format, first create a form to contain the invoice lines. Usually, the subform format is presented as a tabular view, so we'll select the tabular format at the design stage. The New Form dialog box selections are shown in Figure 6.89. Note that the data source is the INV_LINE table.

Click **OK** in the **New Form** dialog box to generate the datasheet view in Figure 6.90. (Only a few lines are shown.) Save the new form as **frmInvoiceSubform**.

We are now ready to insert the form in Figure 6.91 as a subform into the invoice form shown in Figure 6.88. To create the subform, place the invoice form into its design mode, open the toolbox, and click on its **Subform/Subreport** button. (See Figure 6.92. Note that we have turned off the **Wizard** button.)

Assignment

Modify the invoice subform in Figure 6.90 to produce the results presented in Figure 6.91. (Only a few lines of output are shown here.) Note that the header labels have been changed and that the output spacing has been altered to yield a more balanced view of the data.

FIGURE 6.89 **The Invoice Line Subform Format Selection**

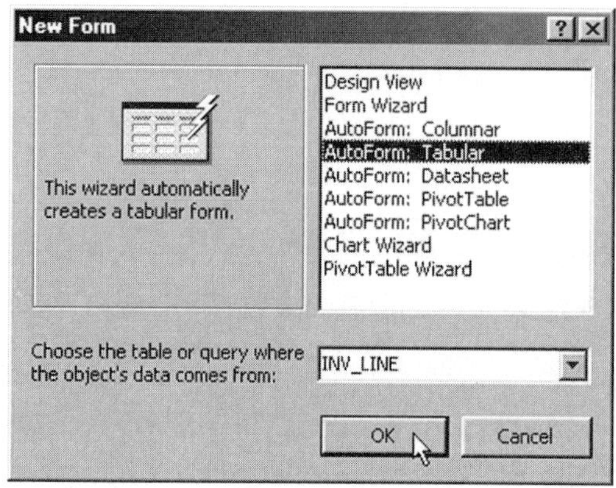

FIGURE 6.90 **The Datasheet View of the New Invoice Subform**

Microsoft Access - [INV_LINE]

File Edit View Insert Format Records Tools Window Help

'_NUM	INE_NUM	)_NUM	:R_QUANT_ORD	INV_LINE_UNITS	INV_LINE_PRICE	INV_LINE_TOTAL
242	1	2	0	2	$20.00	$40.00
242	2	1	0	1	$44.00	$44.00
242	3	3	3	0	$0.00	$0.00
243	1	4	2	0	$0.00	$0.00
243	2	5	0	1	$28.95	$28.95

FIGURE 6.91 **The Datasheet View of the Modified Invoice Subform**

Microsoft Access - [INV_LINE]

File Edit View Insert Format Records Tools Window Help

Invoice	Line	Product Code	Units on Back Order	Line Units	Line Price	Line Total
242	1	2	0	2	$20.00	$40.00
242	2	1	0	1	$44.00	$44.00
242	3	3	3	0	$0.00	$0.00
243	1	4	2	0	$0.00	$0.00
243	2	5	0	1	$28.95	$28.95

Next, use the cursor, which has changed its shape to reflect your **Subform/ Subreport** selection, to draw the subform shown in Figure 6.93 to create a space for the invoice form's invoice lines.

As you examine Figure 6.93, note that the subform is an unbound textbox, labeled **Child90**. (We have boldfaced the Access-generated **Child90** label and used a white font to make it more easily visible on the green background.) Because we created many other subforms to test the system we produced for this book, this

FIGURE 6.92
The Toolbox Subform/ Subreport Button

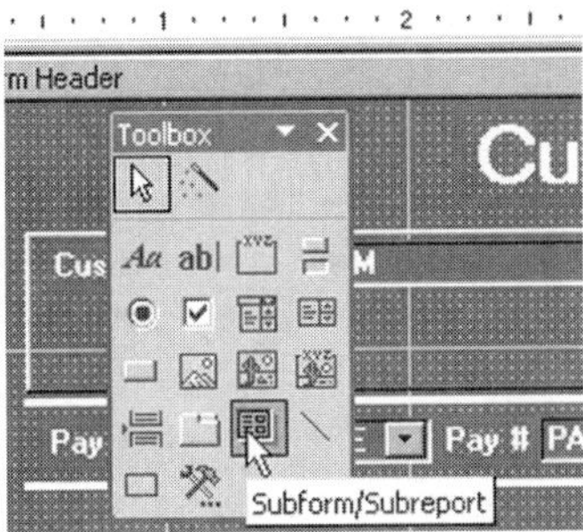

FIGURE 6.93 **The Subform Space on the Invoice Form**

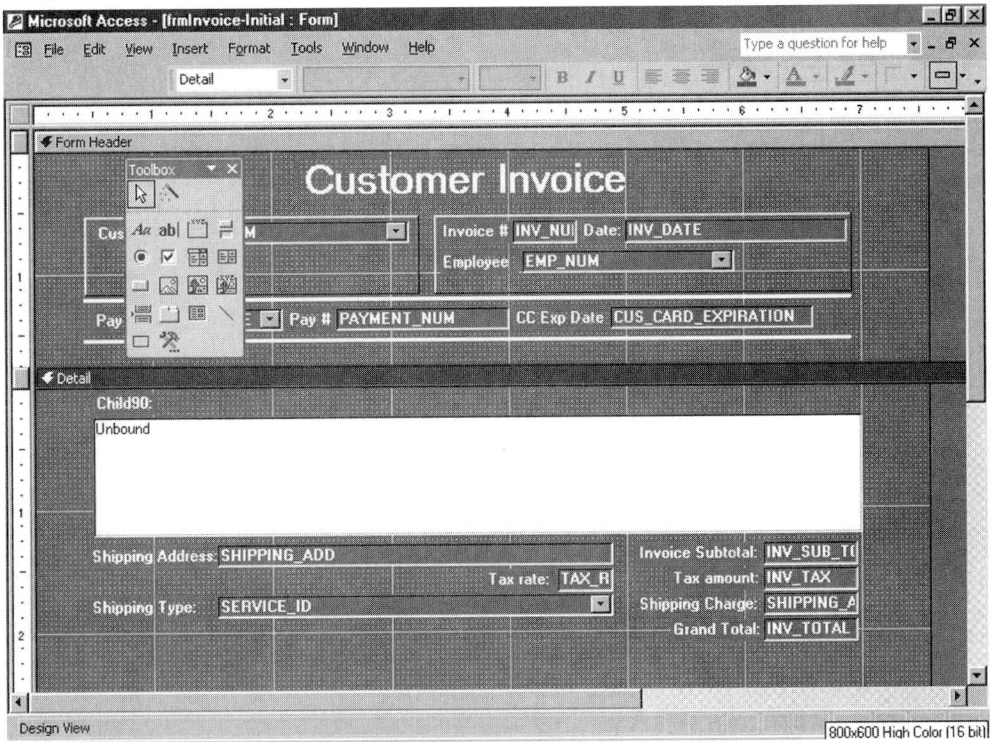

child number reflects those previous efforts. Your form will probably show a different child number. The "child" designation stems from the fact that the invoice is related to many invoice lines—the children—but that each of those invoice lines is related to only one invoice—the parent.

The subform (the child) is now ready to be linked to its parent, the invoice form. To create this link, use the subform's properties box and modify its contents as shown in Figure 6.94.

As you examine the subform's properties box in Figure 6.94, note that we have altered its line defaults as follows:

- We changed the default **Name** from **Child90** to **Invoice Subform**.
- The **source object** is the new subform, named **frmInvoiceSubform**.
- The invoice line (child) field is linked to the invoice via the INV_NUMBER. Therefore, we have typed INV_NUM in both the **Link Child Fields** and the **Link Master Fields** spaces. This link reflects the proper use of the foreign key (FK) in one table as the link to a matching primary key (PK) in the related table. In this case the INV_NUMBER is the FK in the INV_LINE table and points to the PK in the INVOICE table. Once again it is worth noting that our attribute naming

FIGURE 6.94
The Subform's Properties Box

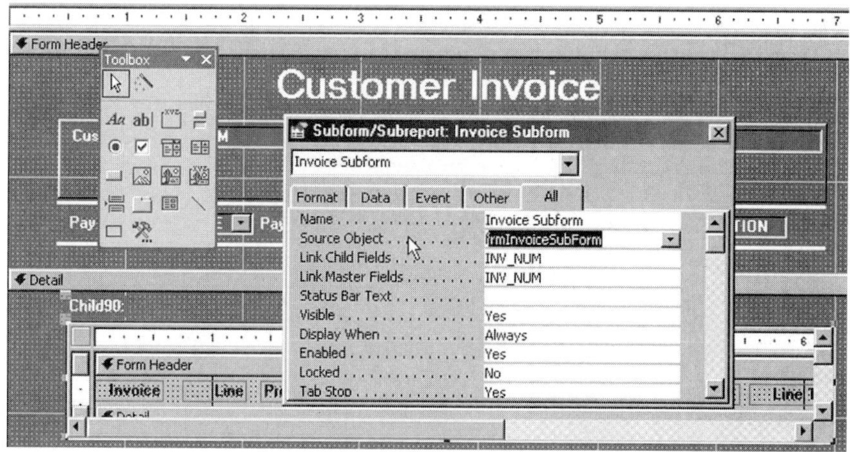

FIGURE 6.95 **The Completed Form/Subform**

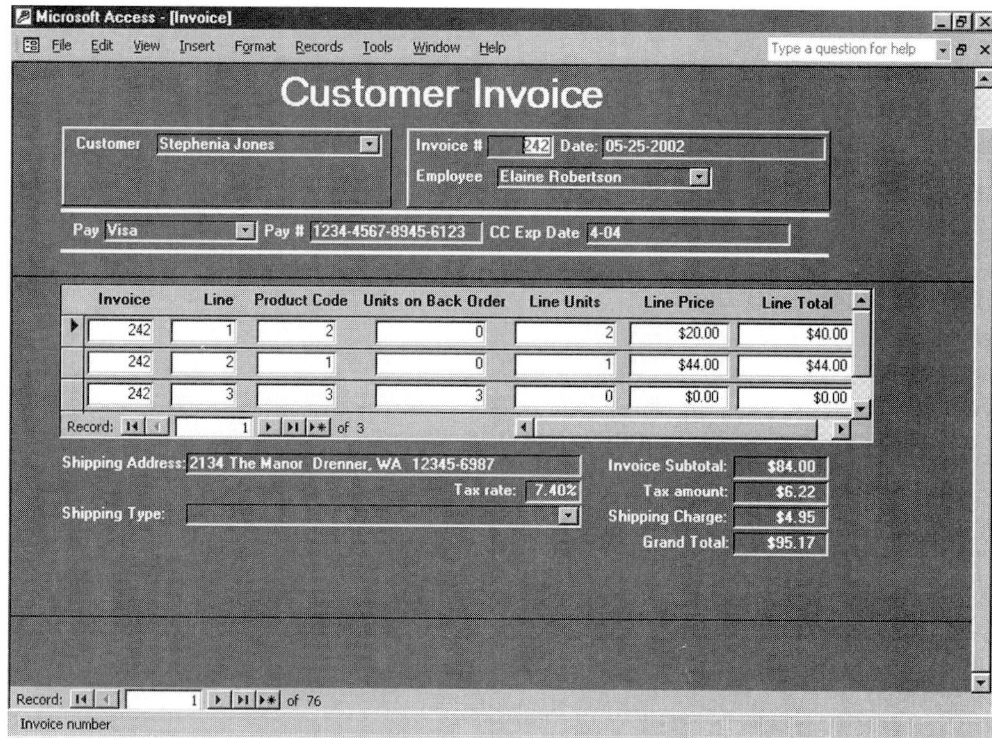

conventions make it easy to remember which attributes are used to properly link tables. Because we always use the same name for the FK and the PK, establishing the proper link is a simple matter of matching the parent and child field names.

After changing the property box default line values to match Figure 6.94 and after dragging the subform's limits to accommodate expected invoice line values, save the invoice form as **frmINVOICE** again and then open it to show the completed form/subform in Figure 6.95.

The invoice form/subform in Figure 6.95 contains quite a few handy features:

- The navigation buttons at the bottom of the invoice screen change the invoice selection. The subform's invoice lines will automatically change to reflect the selected invoice.
- The subform's record navigation buttons show you immediately how many lines each invoice contains, and you can scroll through these lines by using either

Note

If your subform does not quite match the space requirement illustrated in Figure 6.95, return to the **frmInvoice** form's design mode and drag the subform's limits to the desired size. Also, keep in mind that *any change you make in the form on which a subform is based will automatically be reflected in the subform.* For example, if you change the output spacing or the background and/or text colors in the **frmInvoiceSubform** (Figure 6.90), these changes will also show up in the **frmINVOICE** form (Figure 6.95). In short, you have a lot of control over how the subform's output is presented on the screen.

the record navigation buttons or the scroll bars located on the subform's right margin. Therefore, there is no real limit to the number of invoice lines that can be examined with this form/subform presentation.

- You can see the source of the invoice subtotal by examining the invoice line totals. (If the invoice form does not show all of its invoice lines, you can scroll down to examine each line as necessary.)
- Unless you have used the form's property box characteristics to present the form contents in "read only" mode by setting the edit values to **No**, you can use the form/subform to generate changes in both the INVOICE and the INV_LINE tables.
- Best of all, if you generate a new INVOICE record through the use of the form/subform, you can always preserve this record's link to its invoice lines. Entering INVOICE table records while forgetting to enter the associated INV_LINE records will thus become less likely. (After all, each INVOICE has at least one INV_LINE record.)

The invoice form shown in Figure 6.95, listed in your **CH06_POS_2nd** database as **frmInvoice-initial,** can easily be modified to become a primary component in a real-world database. For example, the **frmInvoice** shown in Figure 6.96 contains all the features that make this form practical. (You will learn how to

FIGURE 6.96 **The Edited frmInvoice Form**

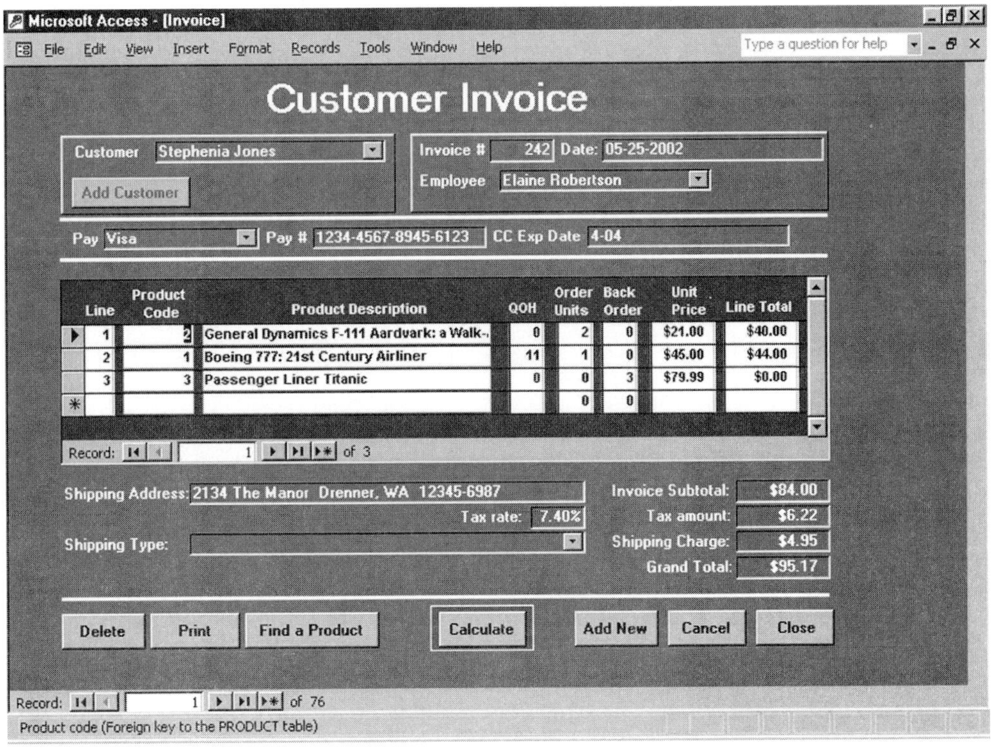

create the command buttons at the bottom of the form in the next section and you'll learn how to make them work in Chapter 8.)

6.6 DIALOG BOXES

In Chapter 5 you learned how to create parameter queries, and in section 5.2.5, Figure 5.26, you learned how to let Access produce dialog boxes to make the queries interactive. As useful as the Access-generated dialog boxes are, they use a format dictated by Access. Therefore, end users will not be able to use combo boxes and other devices designed to make input more intuitive and less prone to input errors. In addition, end users will have few prompting options. And, finally, the Access-generated dialog boxes are likely to disrupt the applications interface layout schemes, including color, placement, and size. The use of form-based dialog boxes is, therefore, attractive to applications developers.

To show you how to construct a form-based dialog box, we'll create the input requests for an employee search, using the employee number, last name, and first name. The input will be used to produce the segmented search illustrated in section 5.2.5, Figure 5.28A. But this time, we'll control the presentation format.

The form-based dialog box is based on a blank form, so its construction starts with the same design sequence that we used to produce the list box in section 6.4. Therefore, start by selecting **Design View** in the **New Form** dialog box without specifying a table or query as the data source. Next, click on the toolbox's **Text Box** button to select it and then draw the text box where you want it on the screen. The results of this procedure are shown in Figure 6.97. (We left the toolbox on the screen and placed the cursor back on the **Text Box** button so that you can see all the components. To save space, we captured only a small portion of the screen.)

After drawing the text box shown in Figure 6.97, we need to give it a label. Note that this text box's label defaulted to **Text0:**. Therefore, place your cursor in the text box label and type **Number:**. Repeat the process for the two remaining input requests: the employee's last name and first name. Then use the procedures you learned in the preceding sections to identify the form with a label, to format the labels and the text boxes, to group the input requests, and to produce the desired color layout.

Save the employee search form as **frmEmployeeSearch**; then return to the form in the design format to use the properties boxes for each of the form's components to make sure that the form is "clean"; that is, the form uses no scroll

FIGURE 6.97
Creating the Text Box on a Blank Form

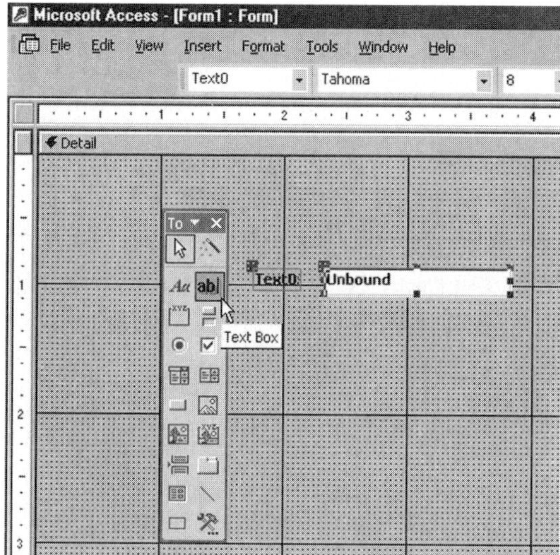

bars, no navigation buttons, no record selectors, no control box, no min and max buttons, and so on. After all, the form includes only labels and unbound control boxes, so there is no point in showing record selectors and navigation buttons. And you don't want the end users to control the form size and placement, so remove these options! (While you are working on the form, it is convenient to retain the **Close Button.** When you have completed all the editing on the form, you can set the **Close Button** property to **No.** You can still close the form via the menu bar by selecting **File/Close**.) Figure 6.98 shows the completed form. Note that we have set the **Grid X** and **Grid Y** properties to 24 to maintain a fine drawing detail. The 24 grid setting is probably your default setting, but if it is not, change it to 24. (Try changing the grid setting to 12 and see what happens to the detail grid. Then reset the grid to 24.)

6.6.1 Command Buttons and Query Modifications

The dialog box shown in Figure 6.98 cannot yet be used, because we must add two features:

1. After the input phase is completed, the form must be "told" that the input is to be used to begin a search. It is also a very good idea to give the user an option to abandon the procedure. We will use command buttons to get these jobs done. As its name implies, a **command button** is an object that will, when activated, cause a command—such as **open the form**—to be executed.
2. Once the search is activated, the form must trigger a query to find the employee records that match the form's input parameters. Therefore, the query that produces the segmented search output in section 5.2.5 must be modified to signify the use of a form. (See Figure 5.28A in section 5.2.5.)

To create a command button, open the form in the design format, activate the toolbox, and select the **Command Button** option. Then draw the command button as shown in Figure 6.99.

Note that Figure 6.99 displays a command button labeled **Command14**. Your command button label is likely to have a different number, because this is probably your first command button, rather than your fourteenth. Also, the command button number changes if you edit its name in its properties box. Regardless of what command button number shows up on your screen, you must edit the label to make it identify the command button's purpose. To edit the command button

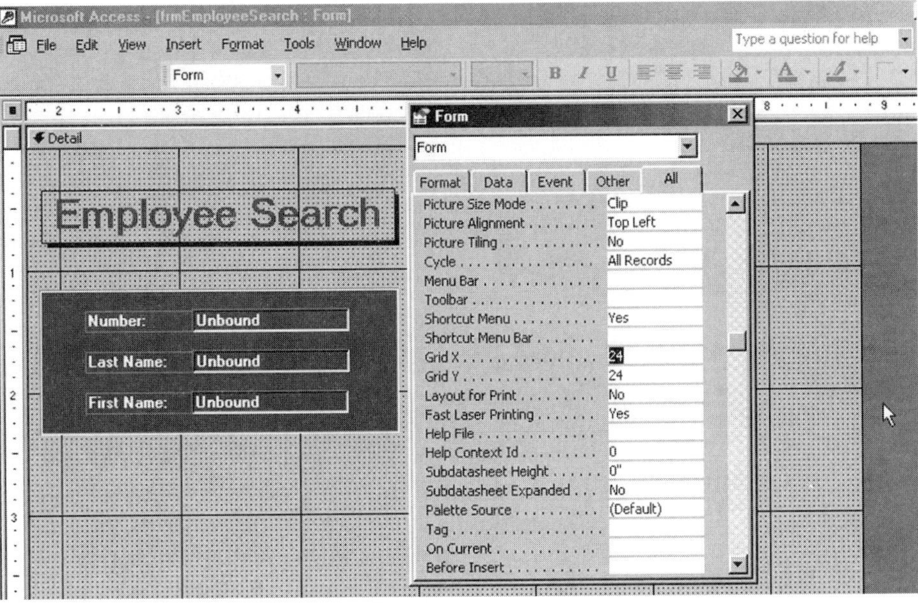

FIGURE 6.98
The Edited Employee Search Dialog Box in Design View

Note

There are two ways to make multiple command buttons.

1. You can click the toolbox's **Command Button** option each time you want to make a new command button. Because there are two command buttons in Figure 6.99, you must repeat the procedure.
2. Or if you have several command buttons to draw and you want to ensure their uniformity, select the command button you have just drawn, select the **Edit** option from the menu bar at the top of the screen, and then select the **Copy/Paste** option. Each time you click on the **Paste** option in edit mode, another copy of the command button is placed on the screen. Once all the command buttons have been created, drag them to their desired locations.

Keep in mind that Access conforms to all Windows procedures, so the **Edit/Copy/Paste** routine is always available for Access objects!

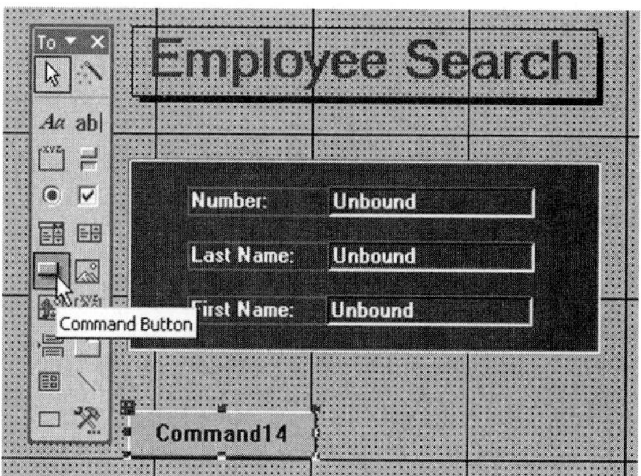

FIGURE 6.99
Creating a Command Button

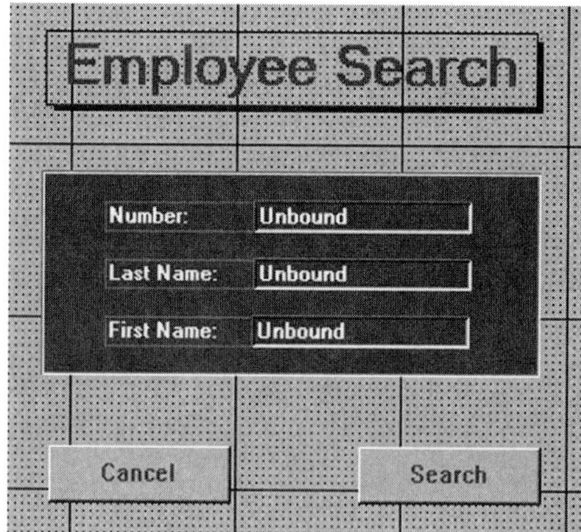

FIGURE 6.100
The Completed Command Buttons

label, select it and then wait just a second to click on it again. (If you double-click, you'll just open its properties box. That's what will happen whenever you select any object, so you can see that your design environment remains remarkably consistent. Such consistency is, of course, one of the many nice features in the Windows environment.) When you click the second time, the command button label is in edit mode, so you can change the label and format it. (You can apply boldface, change the font, the text color, and so on.) When you are done, your screen should resemble Figure 6.100.

Having created the form shown in Figure 6.100, make sure you check the properties of each object. We have named the three unbound text boxes **EmployeeNumberTextbox**, **Last Name Textbox**, and **First Name Textbox**, respectively. These names turn out to be important when we modify the

Note

To make the form's command buttons work, we must create the appropriate macros and attach them to those command buttons. We'll do that job in Chapter 8.

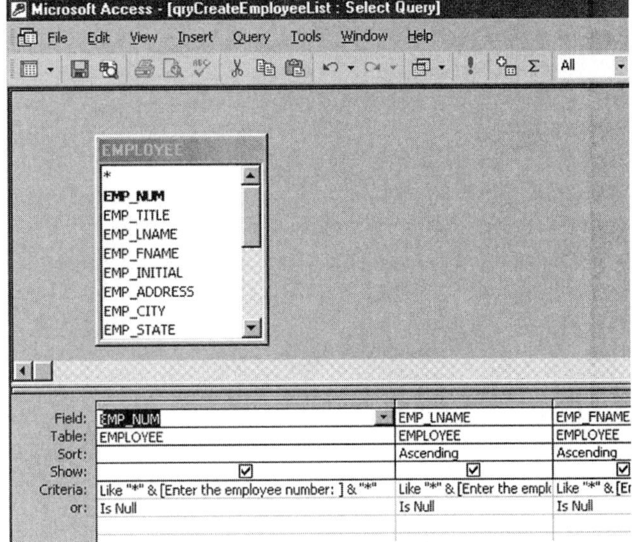

FIGURE 6.101
The qryCreateEmployeeList Parameter Query

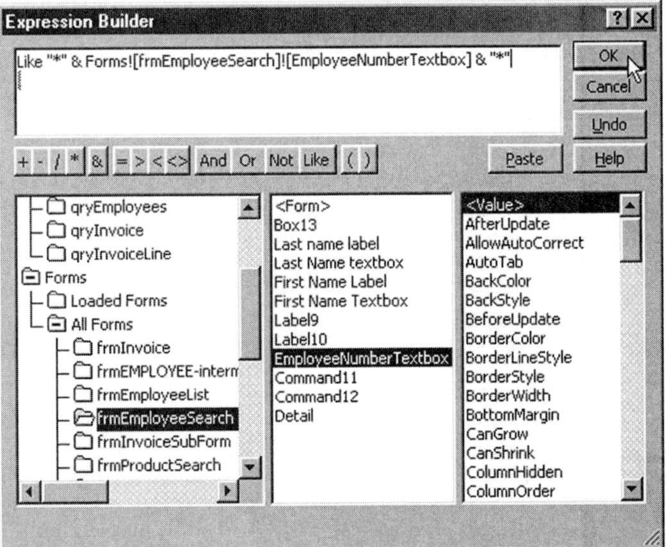

FIGURE 6.102
Modifying a Query Criteria Line with the Expression Builder

qryCreateEmployeeList query shown in Figure 101. We used that query as the Row Source when we created the **frmEmployeeList** form in section 6.4.

Because the **frmEmployeeSearch** form in Figure 6.100 will become the new input source for the **qryCreateEmployeeList** query shown in Figure 101, we must modify the query accordingly. Therefore, open the query in its design format as shown in Figure 101, delete the parameter criteria, and open the Expression Builder to create the new form-based criteria. The Expression Builder screen shown in Figure 6.102 reflects the changes we made in the **qryCreateEmployeeList** employee number's criteria line.

Note

Even if you don't use the **frmEmployeeSearch** form to trigger the query, it will still perform its task when opened. However, the parameter dialog boxes will indicate the form labels as shown in Figure 6.103. (We've shown only one of the three dialog boxes.)

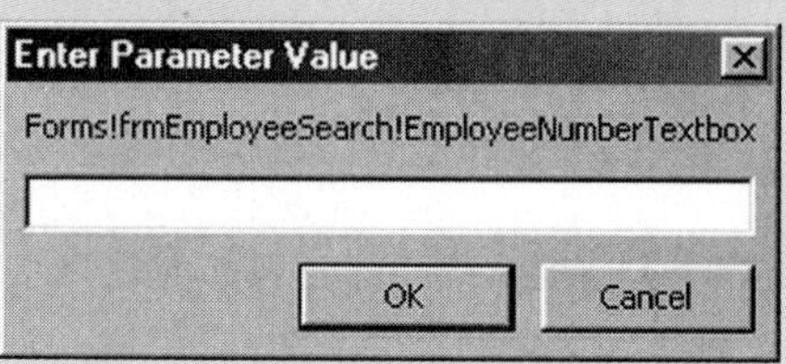

FIGURE 6.103
The First Dialog Box Prompt When the Form Is Not Used

Modify the remaining **qryCreateEmployeeList** query's last name and first name criteria, using the Expression Builder; then save the query again.

Using the query still opens the list box-based form we developed in section 6.4. Look at Figure 6.87 to remind yourself of the expected output format.

Note

At this point we have created the first portion of the database applications development process that will become an integrated system. This emerging system—thus far—contains three parts:

1. The **frmEmployeeSearch** form that receives the input.
2. The **qryCreateEmployeeList** query that uses the form's input to produce the output.
3. The **frmEmployeeList** form that presents the output.

However, although the small system's components are in place, it is not quite ready to function, because the **frmEmployeeSearch** form's command buttons are not active yet. To make the form's command buttons "hot," we must create the appropriate macros and attach them to those command buttons. We'll do that job in Chapter 8. In the meantime, we are all set to let the macros do their magic later.

Assignment

Use the just-completed employee searching system as the template to create a product search system. Use the product search form named **frmProductSearch** and a form-based query named **frmProductList** to produce the output in a list box format, using a form named **frmCreateproductList**. Use Figures 6.104 and 6.105 to help guide the development of this small system.

Remember that the command buttons will not work until you assign macros to them. You will learn how to do that in Chapter 8. Note that the **Search** button uses the control tip text **Find the product.** Use the **Search** button's Properties box and scroll down to the **Control Tip** option, then type the text you see in Figure 6.104.

FIGURE 6.104
The Product Search Form

Product Search
Number:
Class: Book
Type: Aircraft
Category:
Author:
Title:
Producer:
Cancel
Search
Find the product

FIGURE 6.105 **The Product List Box Form Sample Output**

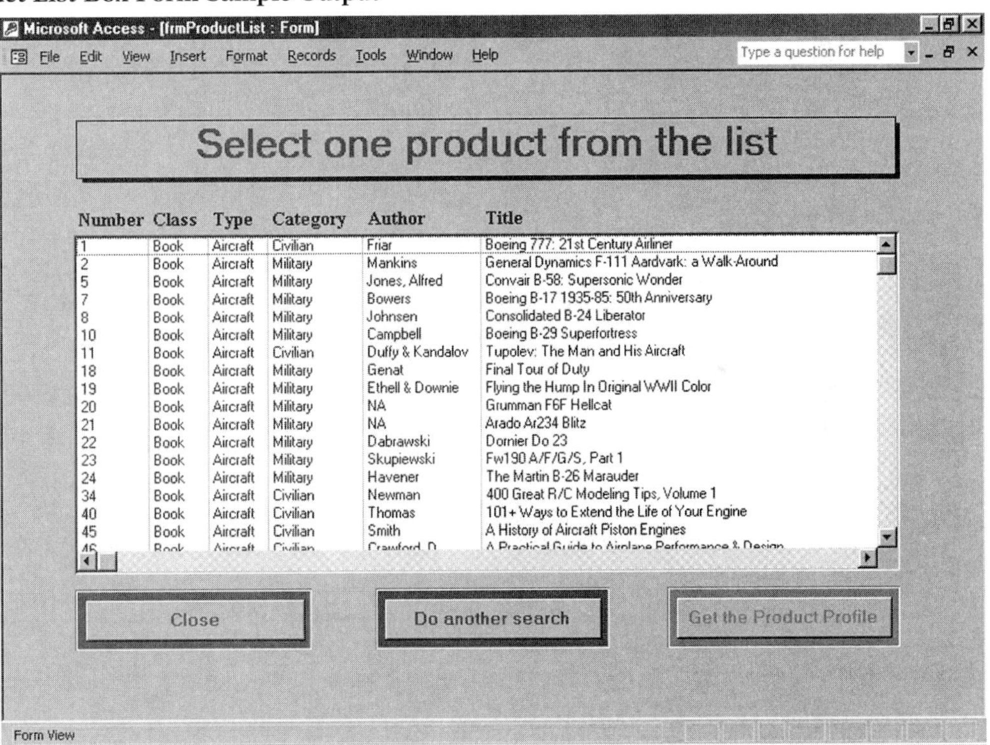

6.7 MENUS

Menus are used to create fully integrated database applications systems. Menu-driven systems are desirable because they

- Help make the database applications system user-friendly by eliminating the need to remember command languages. Menu-driven systems tend to be easy to learn and use, thus driving down training and end-user support costs.
- Control access by providing only those options that allow people to do their jobs efficiently, shielding the other database options and components from casual use. Although technically knowledgeable end users can easily defeat this aspect of most menu systems, at least the casual end user is less likely to accidentally

enter areas that are considered to be off-limits. Similarly, casual end users are not likely to do accidental damage to the database.

• Provide an environment in which system-level database security is easier to create and manage. Although you will learn in Chapter 10 how the database administrator can provide security through various Access security functions, menu systems make it easier to block off portions of the database and its applications. In fact, menu systems can promote reasonable levels of security even in the absence of administrative security measures. The menu systems can also augment administrative security measures by providing password-protected menu options.

• Create an environment that is tailored to specific types of applications and end users. For example, different departments of a business may use customized applications that are easily available only through menu systems. In fact, each department may even have its own menu system, and its end users may be unable to enter the menus of other departments without proper authorization.

In short, end users and database administrators like menu systems because they are easy to use, tend to be relatively goof-proof, and fit well into the database security framework.

6.7.1 Creating a Menu Form

Menus are basically forms that contain labels and command buttons. Therefore, use the blank form as a starting point. Then use the toolbox to add the tab controls to group the various menu components, colors, and so on. Naturally, remove the navigation button and record selectors options to produce a clean screen. Figure 6.106 shows a sample main menu for the POS system.

The main menu shown in Figure 6.106 contains three groups: transactions, data management, and additional menus. Once the menu form's buttons have been activated through the macros we'll develop in Chapter 8, each command button will open a form. For example, if you click on the **Transactions** tab and

FIGURE 6.106 A Sample Main Menu Form

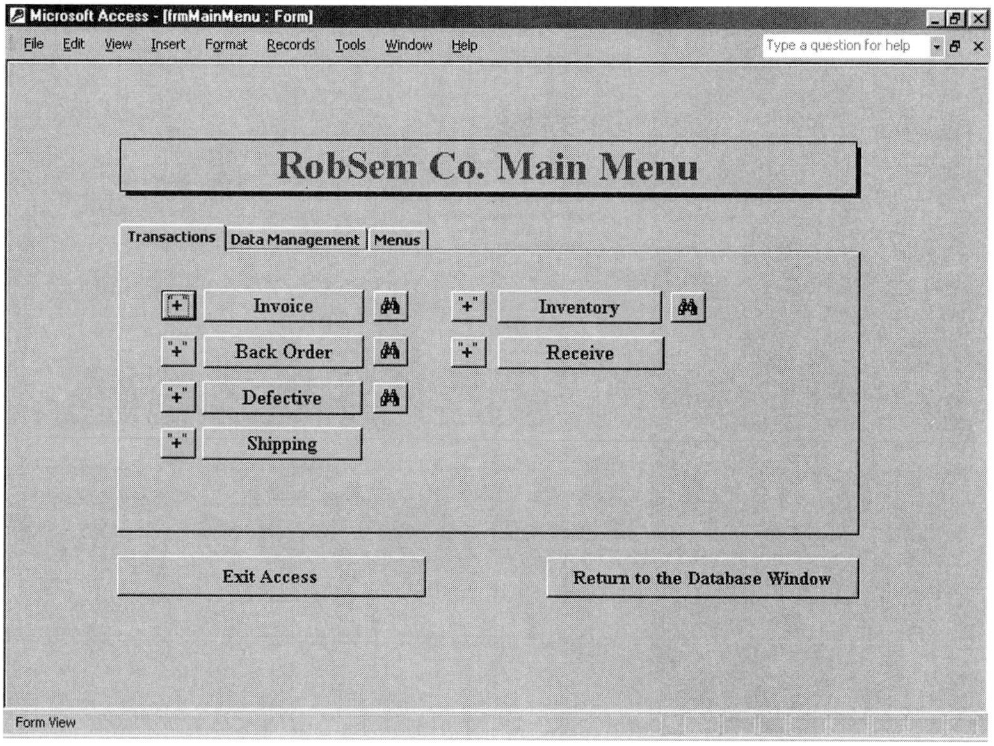

Note

Remember that this chapter focuses on form development. The macros that activate all of the command buttons will be developed in Chapter 8. Because the macros will reference the forms and their components, it makes sense to develop these forms before the macros are developed. We mention the macros in this chapter only to give you a sense of the application system's ultimate operation.

click on the **Invoice** button, the invoice form will be opened (see Figure 6.96). If you click on the **Add** button located to the left of the **Invoice** button, a new invoice form will be generated. And if you click on the button with the **Binoculars** on it, a search routine will be initiated to help you find a particular invoice: the search criteria may include a date range, a customer, a product, and so on. (The end user will help you establish what search routines are appropriate.)

Each **Data Management** option in Figure 6.106 is represented by a pair of command buttons: The button with + sign on the left represents the **Add New** option, and the button with the **Binoculars** image yields a search routine. The search routine is based on the segmented search procedure we created in sections 5.2.5 and 6.6.

To produce a tabbed menu form like the one shown in Figure 6.106, start with the familiar **New Form** selection at the database window's **Forms** option. Because the menu form is not bound to a table or query, we'll start with a blank form just as we did when using the dialog box forms. This time, select the **Tab Control** from the toolbox, then place the cursor on the form's detail and drag the basic menu form as shown in Figure 6.107. Note that, once again, we have made sure that the toolbox's **Wizard** button is turned off.

As you examine Figure 6.107, note that Access automatically produces two (default) tabs, labeled **Page1** and **Page2**. If you want to create additional tabbed menu pages, right-click on the menu object you have just drawn, then select the **Insert Page** option shown in Figure 6.108.

The **Insert Page** selection in Figure 6.108 will produce the additional page shown in Figure 6.109. (We right-clicked on the newly created **Page3** to generate the menu that enabled us to select its properties box.)

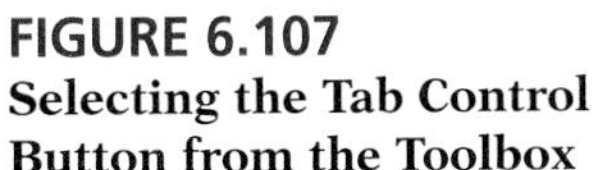

FIGURE 6.107
Selecting the Tab Control Button from the Toolbox

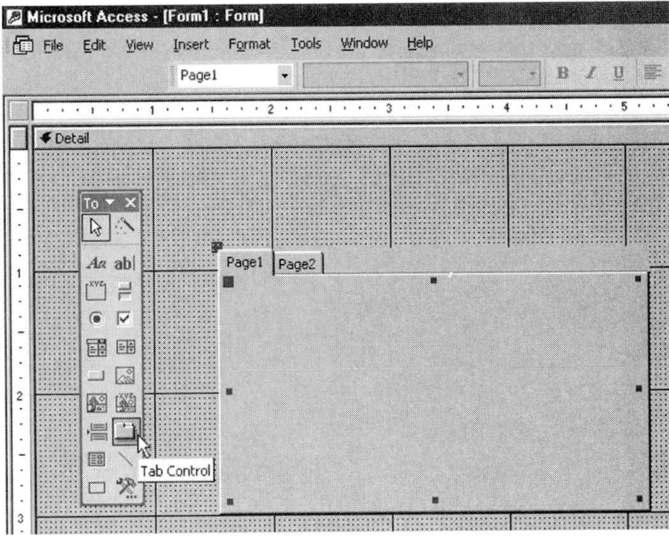

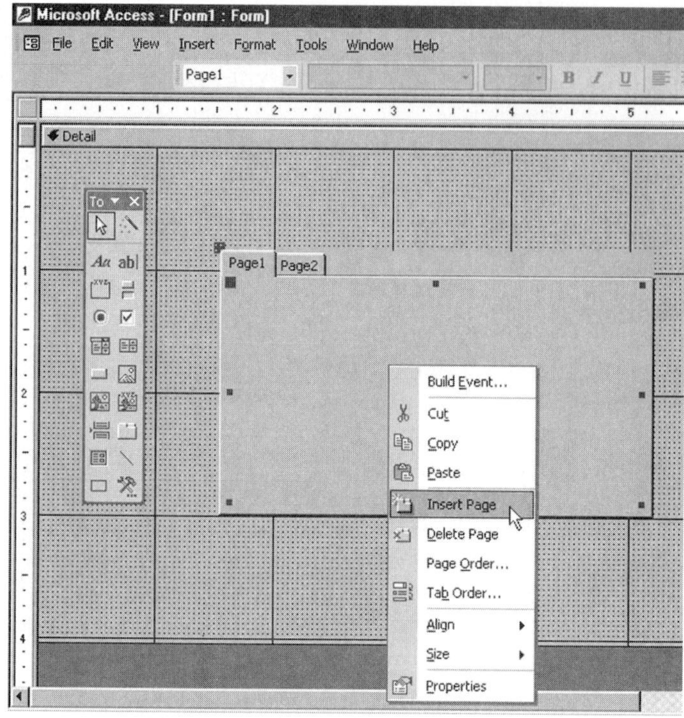

FIGURE 6.108
The Insert Page Option

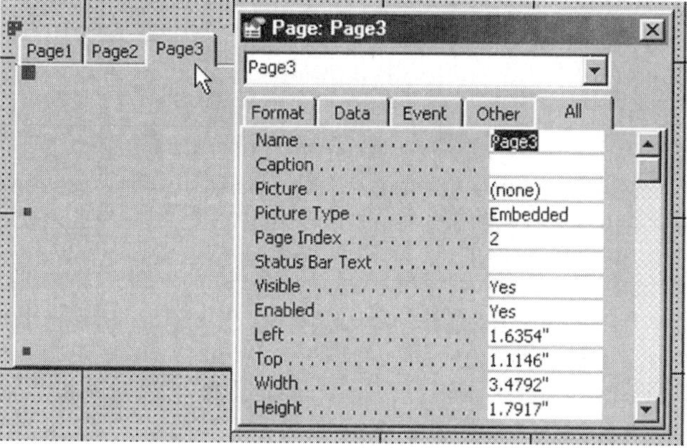

FIGURE 6.109
The Added Menu Page

To edit the tab text, you cannot simply select the tab and then type in the new text. Instead, select the **Page** properties box, select the **Name** option, and then type the text you want to see displayed on the tab. For example, if you want the first tab to be labeled **Transactions**, select **Page1**, select its properties box, and type **Transactions** in the Name slot. (A small segment of this activity is shown in Figure 6.110.)

If you close the properties box and open the form in its form view, you will see the **Transactions** label on the first menu page. (A small segment is shown in Figure 6.111.)

After getting the menu's basic page ready, use the menu form's properties box to remove the navigation buttons, the dividing lines, and so on. You can then add the command buttons and the other menu components to produce a clean-looking menu like the one shown in Figure 6.106.

To create the small binoculars shown on Figure 6.106's menu, first create a small command button and then open its properties box to assign a picture to the button. Figure 6.112 shows the properties box for the selected command button

Note

Make sure that you place the command buttons, and, for that matter, any page-specific objects, on the intended page. If you create a set of command buttons outside the menu limits and then drag them on the pages, you will discover that all the menu pages will inherit these buttons and their characteristics. For example, the Data Management page will inherit the **Transaction** buttons if you don't pay attention to this note! Of course, there are some instances that require the same object—such as a company logo—on each menu page. In that case, create the object outside the menu limits, then drag and drop it on the first page. Presto, all pages will inherit this object.

FIGURE 6.110
Editing the Tab Label

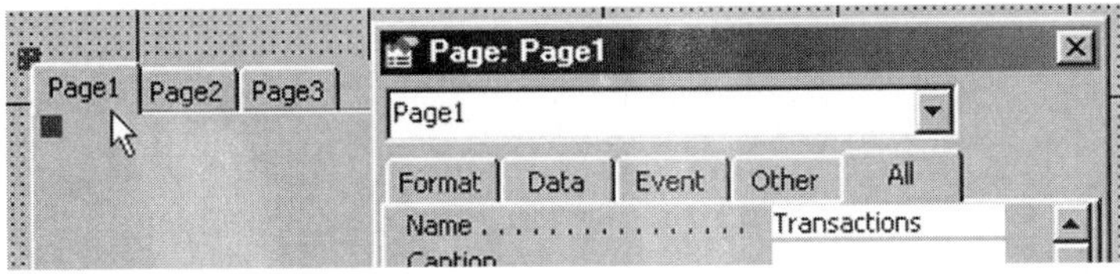

FIGURE 6.111
The Edited Tab Label

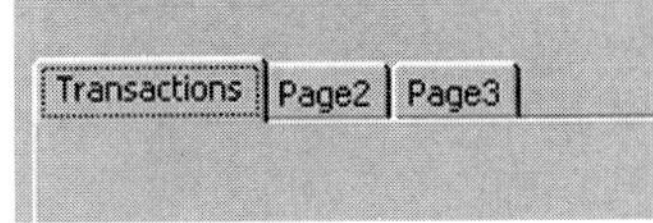

FIGURE 6.112
The Properties Box Picture Option

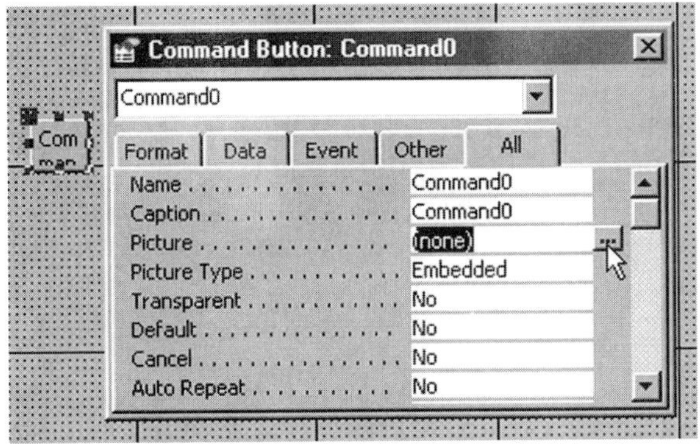

FIGURE 6.113
The Picture Builder Options List

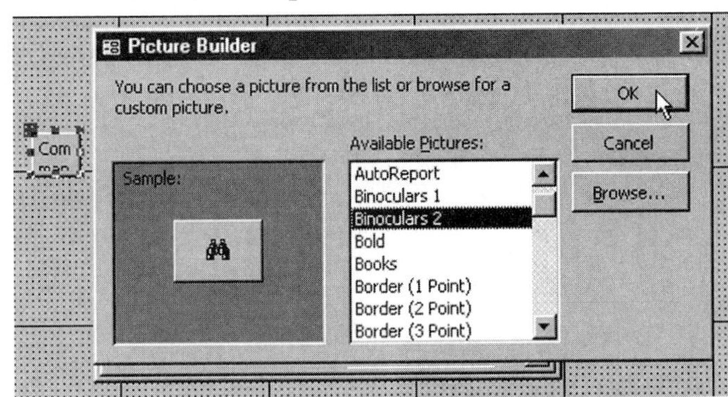

shown just to the left of the properties box. (We just created a new blank form to illustrate the process. That's why the default **Name** and **Caption** options are shown as **Command0.** Naturally, if we want to develop this form further, we would type in the appropriate command button name and caption.)

Figure 6.112 shows the **Picture** line's default value to be **(None).** Because a set of binoculars is a frequently used graphic to denote a search routine, we want to attach a binocular picture to the command button. (Note the use of such **Search** command buttons to the right of the various menu option buttons in Figure 106.) To place a set of binoculars on the command button shown in Figure 6.112, click on the **Builder** button on the **Picture** line to generate the picture options list shown in Figure 6.113.

As you can tell by looking at the options list in Figure 6.113, we scrolled down this list until we located the **Binoculars2** option. Click on the selected option to see the sample picture in the Picture Builder, and then click **OK** to place the selected picture on the command button. Figure 6.114 shows the results of this action. Note that the **Picture** property has changed to **(bitmap)** and that the selected Picture Type is classified as **Embedded**. We will explore the various picture options—embedded versus linked—in the next section.

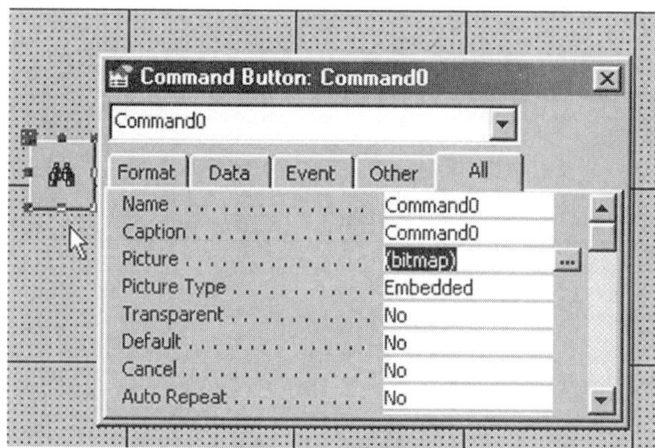

FIGURE 6.114
The Picture on the Command Button

6.8 EMBEDDED AND LINKED OBJECTS

The difference between object *linking* and object *embedding* is simple. A **linked object** is one that maintains its ties to the originating software. Therefore, if the original object is changed in the originating software, the change will automatically update all object copies that are attached to other objects. An **embedded object** is one that no longer has ties to the software from which it was generated. Therefore, the embedded object is not automatically updated when the object in the originating software is changed.

Because a linked object retains the ties to the originating software, it is always as up-to-date as the object in the originating software is. Therefore, if the object is *dynamic,* that is, it is subject to frequent change, object linking is probably a better choice than object embedding. However, the originating software must be available to the software in which the linked object resides. For example, if you link an Excel spreadsheet graph to an Access form, the Excel software must be available to the Access form. Similarly, if you link a picture file containing pictures of employees and products, the file must be available to the Access tables and forms that use them. If the path to the originating software is not defined, Access will generate an error message to let you know that the linked object is not available.

In Access terms, a linked object resides in a bound object frame. Therefore, if you want to create such an object on a form, open the form in the design format, select the toolbox, click on the **Bound Object Frame** button, and draw the bound object box. We've shown the sequence in Figure 6.115. (We have also generated the bound object box's **Properties** box; note that there is a control source line. We have not specified the control source because we did not want to tie you to a specific object set at this point.)

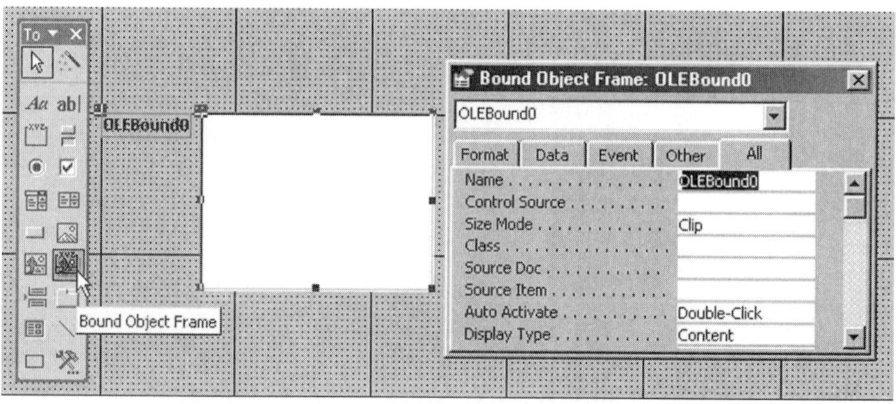

FIGURE 6.115
Creating a Bound Object Frame

Embedded objects are generally used when the objects are not likely to change often—if they change at all. Such objects are known as *static* objects. The advantage of the embedded object is that it no longer requires a link to the originating software. Therefore, you can copy the components that use the embedded objects without having to worry about maintaining the links.

In Access terms, an embedded object resides in an unbound object frame. Because the picture—perhaps a corporate logo placed on the main menu—is not likely to change often, we will place it in an unbound object frame. To create an unbound object frame, open the form in the design format, select the toolbox, and then click on the **Unbound Object Frame** button shown in Figure 6.116.

After selecting the **Unbound Object Frame** button in Figure 6.116, create the frame by dragging the cursor.

After you have dragged the cursor to create the unbound object frame, nothing seems to happen for a few moments. You will not even see the frame outline for the frame you have just drawn. Be patient, even though those few moments seem to last forever. Your patience will be rewarded when you see the **Insert Object** dialog box shown in Figure 6.117 pop up on your screen. Scroll down to the **Object Type** you expect to use on the form. As you can tell, we selected the **Microsoft Clip Gallery** as our object source. If you don't have this feature available, you can use some other picture source.

Click **OK** on the **Object Type** dialog box shown in Figure 6.117 to generate the **Microsoft Clip Gallery** window shown in Figure 6.118. Note that we have selected the (default) **Pictures** tab and that we have scrolled down to the **Transportation** category.

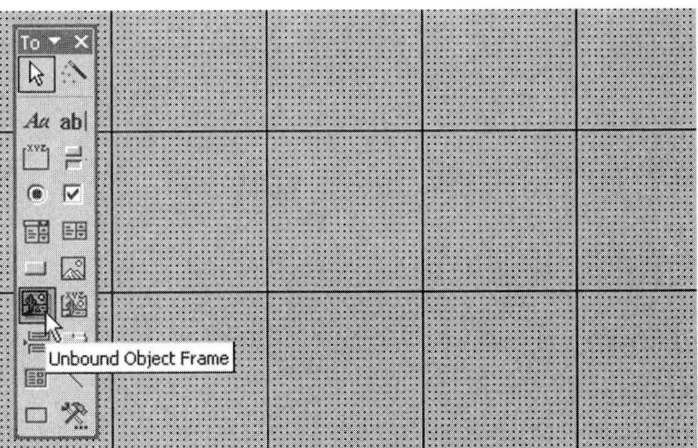

FIGURE 6.116
The Unbound Object Frame Option

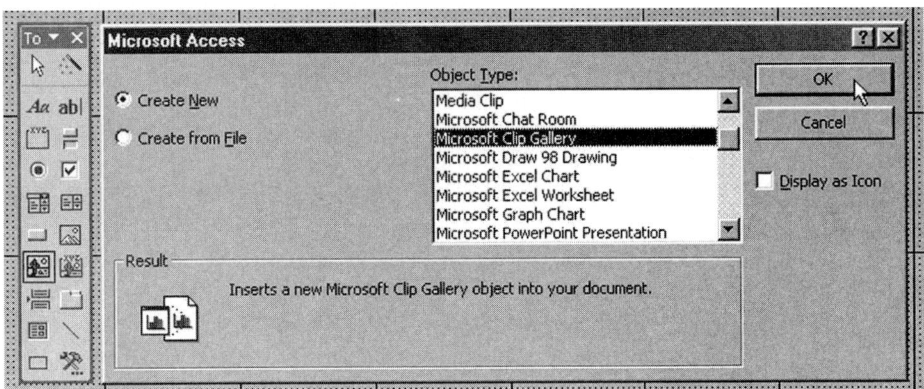

FIGURE 6.117
The Insert Object Dialog Box

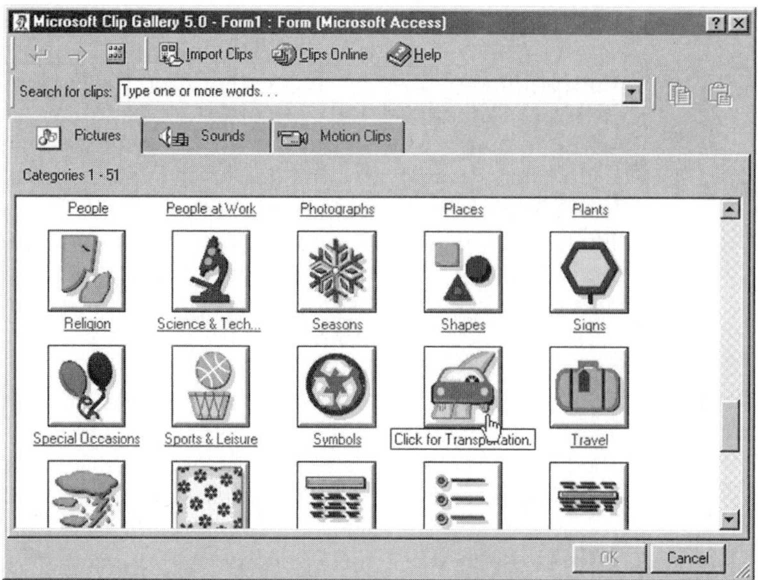

FIGURE 6.118
The Microsoft Clip Gallery Window

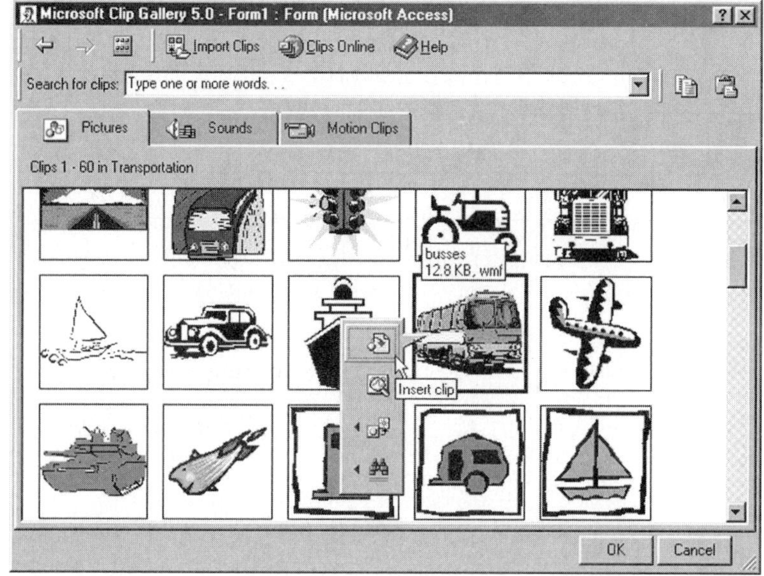

FIGURE 6.119
The Pictures within the Selected Category

By selecting the **Transportation** category in Figure 6.118, you will generate all the available pictures for that category (see Figure 6.119).

From Figure 6.119 select the picture you like and click on it. Then click **OK** or click on the **Insert** icon shown here next to the bus picture to get the picture on the form, as shown in Figure 6.120.

As you examine Figure 6.120, note that the picture's default **Size Mode** setting is **Clip**. Unfortunately, that setting shows only a portion of the picture because the object frame is smaller than the image it received. You can fit the picture to the frame by selecting the frame's properties box and then selecting the size mode's **Stretch** option, as shown in Figure 6.121.

Unfortunately, if you select a **Stretch** option and you draw the frame too wide for its height, you'll get the very flat bus distortion shown in Figure 6.122. If you draw the frame narrow and tall, you'll get a distorted vertical image. Therefore, if you select the **Stretch** option, you must draw frames that are reasonably proportional to the picture that you expect to fit into the frame.

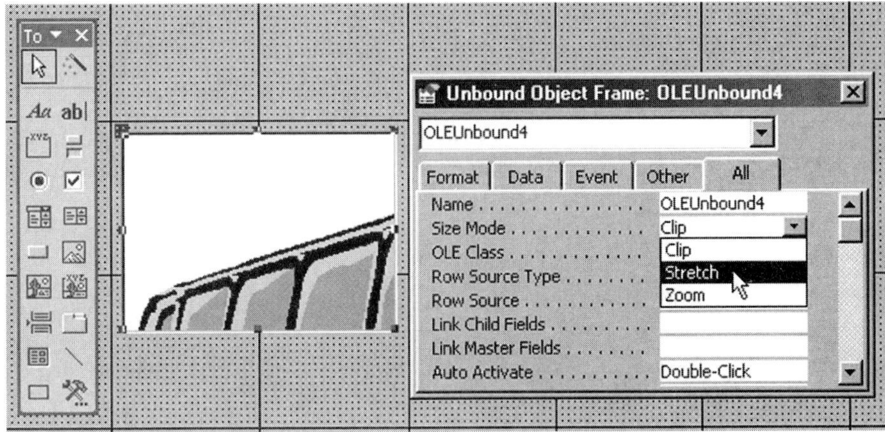

FIGURE 6.120
The Inserted Picture

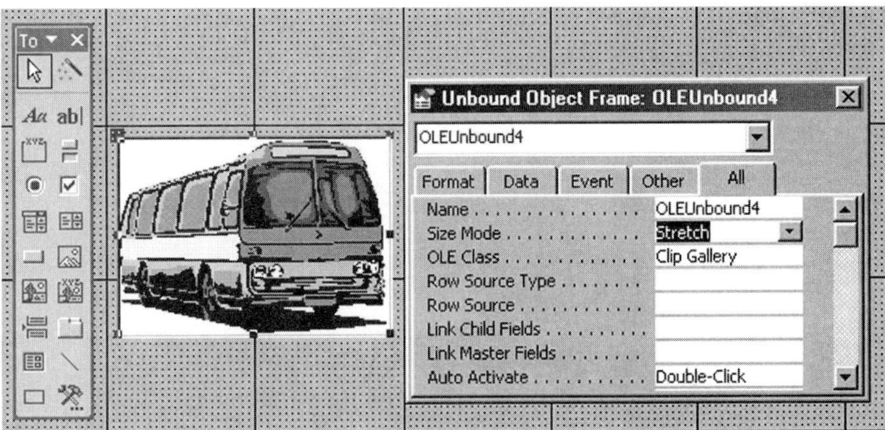

FIGURE 6.121
Sizing the Picture to Fit the Frame

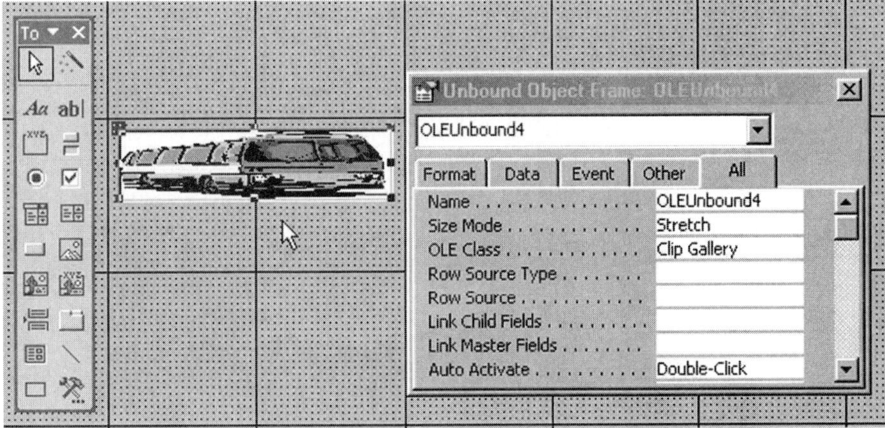

FIGURE 6.122
The Stretch Option in a Narrow Frame

Keep in mind that you can always alter the picture's fit by selecting a different **Size Mode** option via its properties box. The **Zoom** option will place the largest view of the picture that can be fit within the object frame—*without distortion.* You can then shape the frame that will give you the best view of the picture. For example, note the bus picture in Figure 6.123 in which the largest possible bus picture is limited by the frame height.

Because the picture is never distorted when the **Zoom** option is used, we prefer this option. Note that we have changed the frame size in Figure 6.124 and the

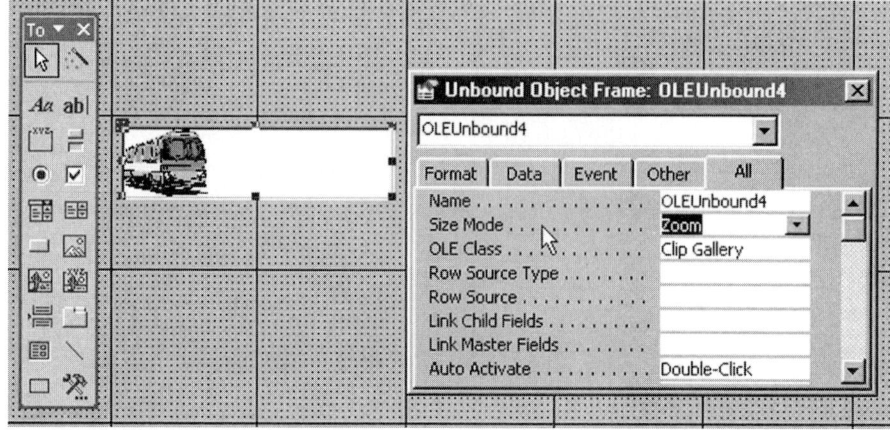

FIGURE 6.123
The Zoom Option View of the Picture

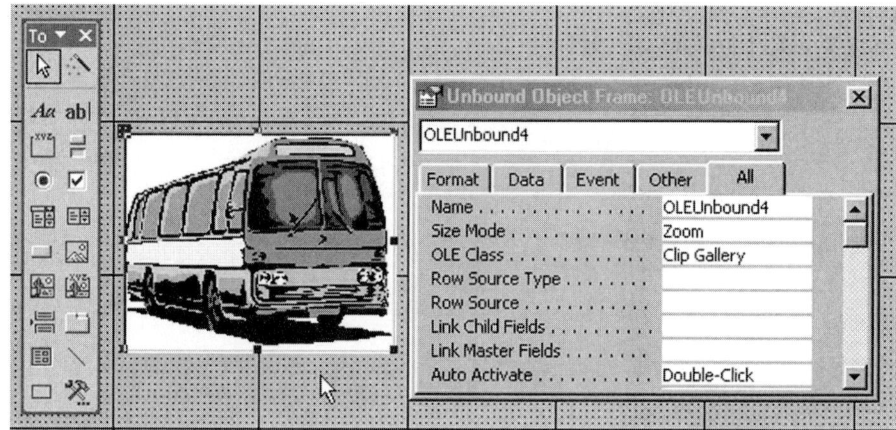

FIGURE 6.124
The Enlarged Picture

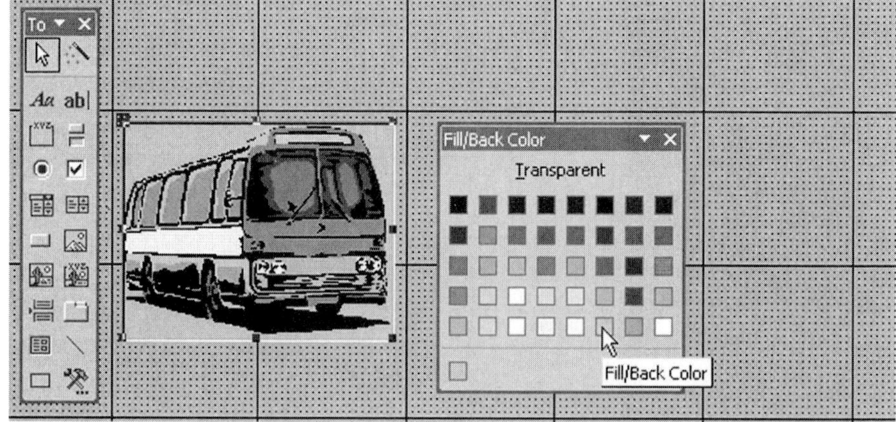

FIGURE 6.125
Selecting the Background Color for the Picture

bus picture automatically expanded to the largest possible size without distorting the image.

You can also change the bound object's background color. Select the frame in design mode; then click on the **Fill/Background** button—the paint can—and select the desired background color. We've shown this sequence in Figure 6.125.

Naturally, you are not limited to the use of the Microsoft Gallery; you can use corporate logos, the software development company's copyright, or any other unbound object within a frame. For example, note the following sequence in which

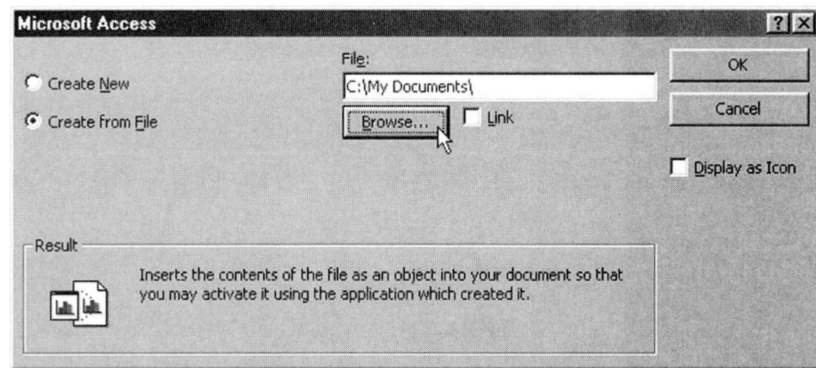

FIGURE 6.126
Browsing for a File Picture

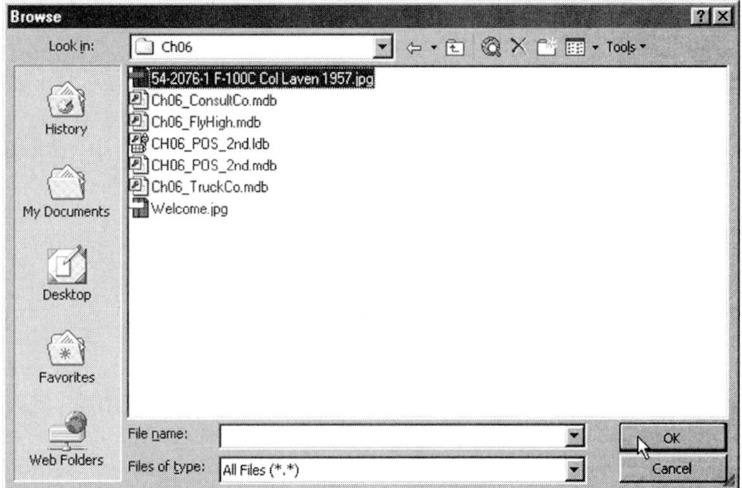

FIGURE 6.127
Locating the Picture

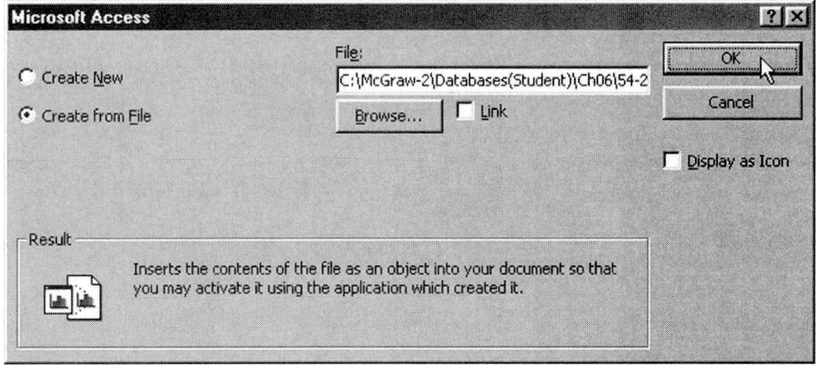

FIGURE 6.128
The Picture Is Ready for Insertion

we place a digital photo within an unbound frame. We start by locating the object, this time using the **Create from File** on the **Insert Object** window you first saw in Figure 6.117 to get to the screen shown in Figure 6.126. (Note that the dialog box changed when you clicked on the **Create from File** option.)

Figure 6.126 shows the default file location, **C:\My Documents**. Because the picture we want to insert is located in a different folder, select the **Browse** button to locate the picture. Our browsing produced the results shown in Figure 6.127.

We want to insert the .jpg picture named **54-2076-1 Col Laven 1957**, so double-click on that file or click **OK** after selecting the file to produce Figure 6.128. (Naturally, if you have copied the student databases from the CD to a

FIGURE 6.129
The Picture Displayed as an Icon

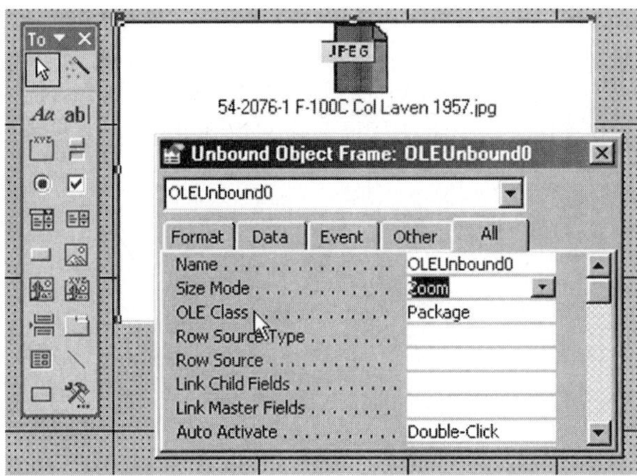

differently named folder in a different location, use that folder instead of the one we have used in this illustration.)

The path in Figure 6.128 shows that in this example the picture is located in the **C:\McGraw-2\Databases(Student)\Ch06** folder. Naturally, you should use the folder in which you stored the pictures. For example, if you copied the pictures in the **AC_Museum\AC_Pictures** folder from your CD to your computer's C: drive, the path designation would be **C:\AC_Museum\AC_Pictures**. Or perhaps you have copied the .jpg pictures to a 3.5″ diskette and placed them in a **\Pictures** folder. The path would then be **A:\Pictures**. In short, use whatever folder contains the pictures. Finally, if you want to be able to run the application from any drive, do not use the drive designator.

Clicking **OK** in the dialog box shown in Figure 6.128 yields the results shown in Figure 6.129. But the expected picture is not shown; instead, a .jpg icon shows up in the unbound object frame.

What happened to produce the unexpected result shown in Figure 6.129? The answer is quite simple: We used the academic version of the Access software, which did not permit us to use anything other than the Microsoft Clip Gallery's picture formats. Because you may have a similar problem, let's use the toolbox's **Image** button instead of its **Unbound Object Frame** button to get the job done. In fact, the **Image** button yields a much more flexible way to insert many different kinds of images. We'll even show you in Chapter 8 how to manage images as though they were saved in a database table, even though they are not.

FIGURE 6.130
The Toolbox Image Button

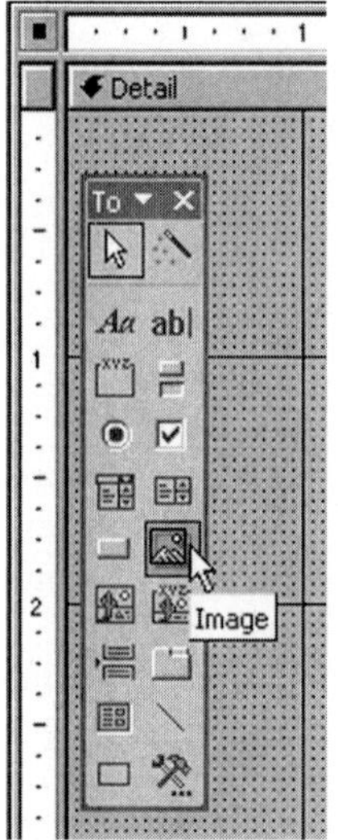

To place an image on a form with the help of the **Image** button, start—again—by creating a blank form, then open the toolbox and select the **Image** button as shown in Figure 6.130.

After selecting the **Image** button shown in Figure 6.130, move the cursor to the form and drag an image space just as you dragged one for bound and unbound frames. For just a few seconds, nothing seems to happen, and then the **Insert Picture** window pops up as shown in Figure 6.131. (Use the **Look in:** window to find the picture you want to use.)

After you have located the picture with the help of the **Insert Picture** window shown in Figure 6.131, double-click on it or click on it and select the **OK** button to produce the inserted image shown in Figure 6.132. (Note that we have already selected the **Zoom** option in the properties box's **Size Mode**.)

Use the properties box to remove the form's dividing lines, control boxes, and so on in order to clean up the form's appearance. Save the form as **frmAircraftImage**, and then open it to produce the results shown in Figure 6.133.

FIGURE 6.131 Using the Toolbox Image Button

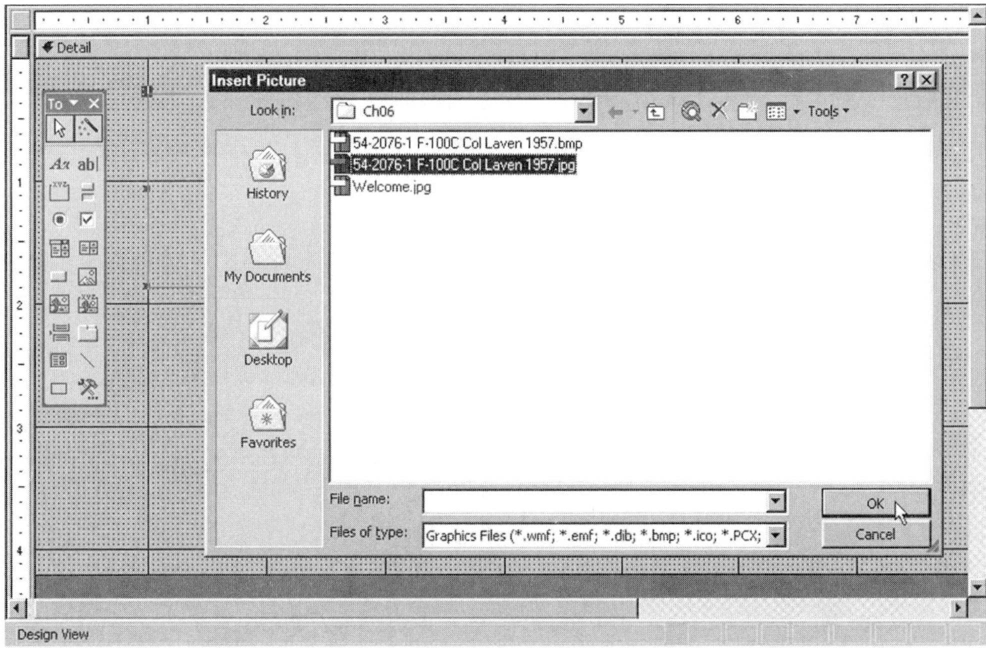

FIGURE 6.132 The Inserted Image

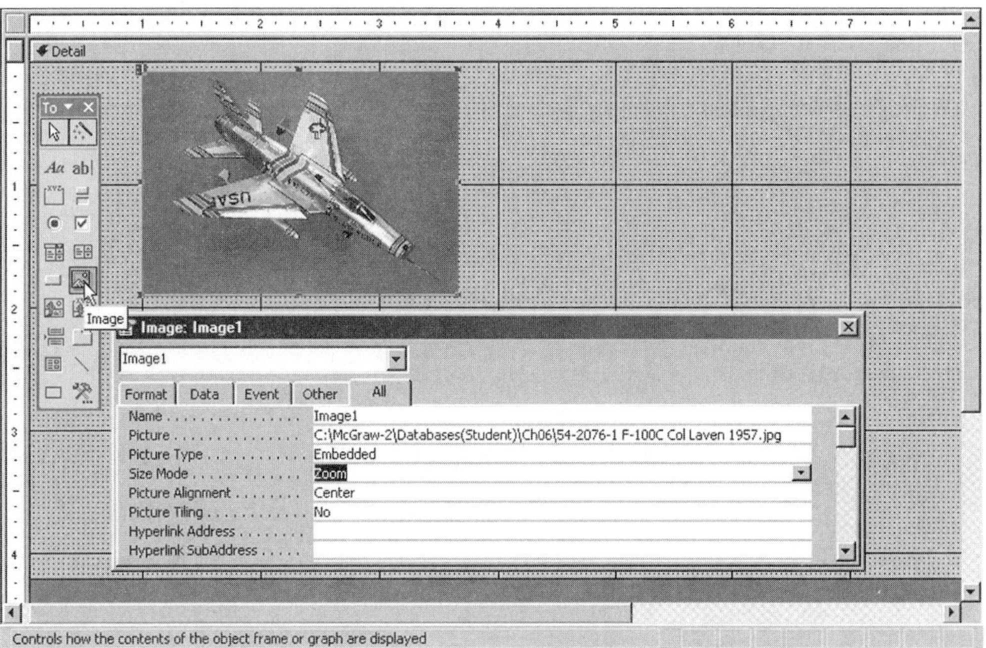

FIGURE 6.133
The Image in Form View

Problems

Note

The databases that are to be used to solve the following problems are located on the student CD that is included with this book. Copy the databases you want to use to your hard drive and uncheck the **Read-only** option from the file properties before you try to use those databases.

6.1 Use the **CH06_POS_2nd** database to modify the RobSem Main Menu shown in Figure 6.106 to match Figures P6.1 and P6.1A. (These figures illustrate the main menu's data management section (the second tab on the menu form) and the menu section (the third tab on the menu form). Remember to save the **frmMainMenu** form again when you have completed the modifications.

Note

Remember that none of the command buttons placed on your forms will work until you have created the macros that make them work. You will learn how to create such macros in Chapter 8. Just concentrate on the form layout in this chapter's problems.

FIGURE P6.1
The Data Management Section on the RobSem Main Menu Form

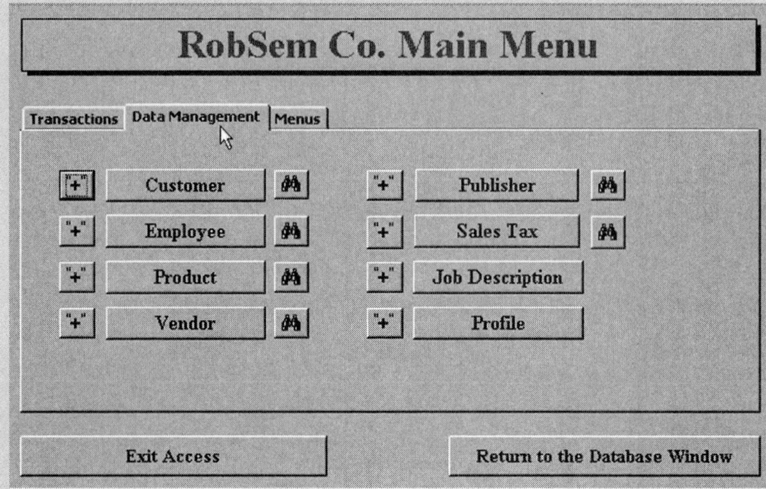

FIGURE P6.1A
The Menus Section on the RobSem Main Menu

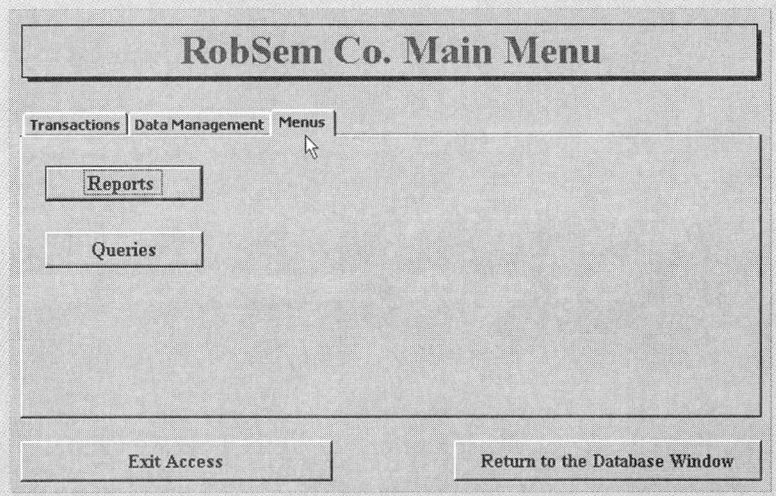

6.2 Use the **CH06_POS_2nd** database to create the customer profile form shown in Figure P6.2. Note that the form is based on a parameter query that requests the customer's last name as shown in Figure P6.2A. Name the form **frmCustomerProfile**.

FIGURE P6.2 The RobSem Customer Profile Form

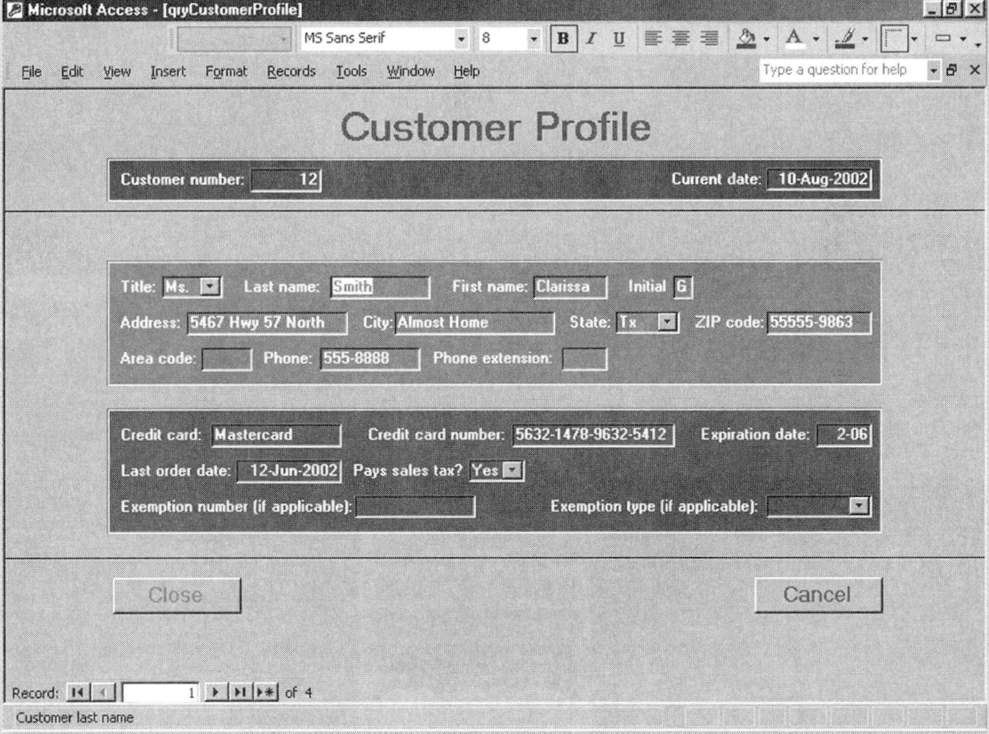

FIGURE P6.2A
The Last Name Parameter Request

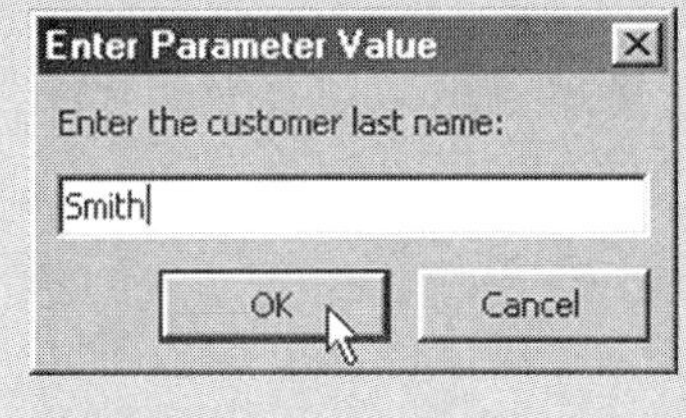

Enter Parameter Value

Enter the customer last name:

Smith

OK Cancel

6.3 Use the **CH06_POS_2nd** database to create the sales tax form shown in Figure P6.3. Name the form **frmSalesTax**.

FIGURE P6.3 The Sales Tax Form

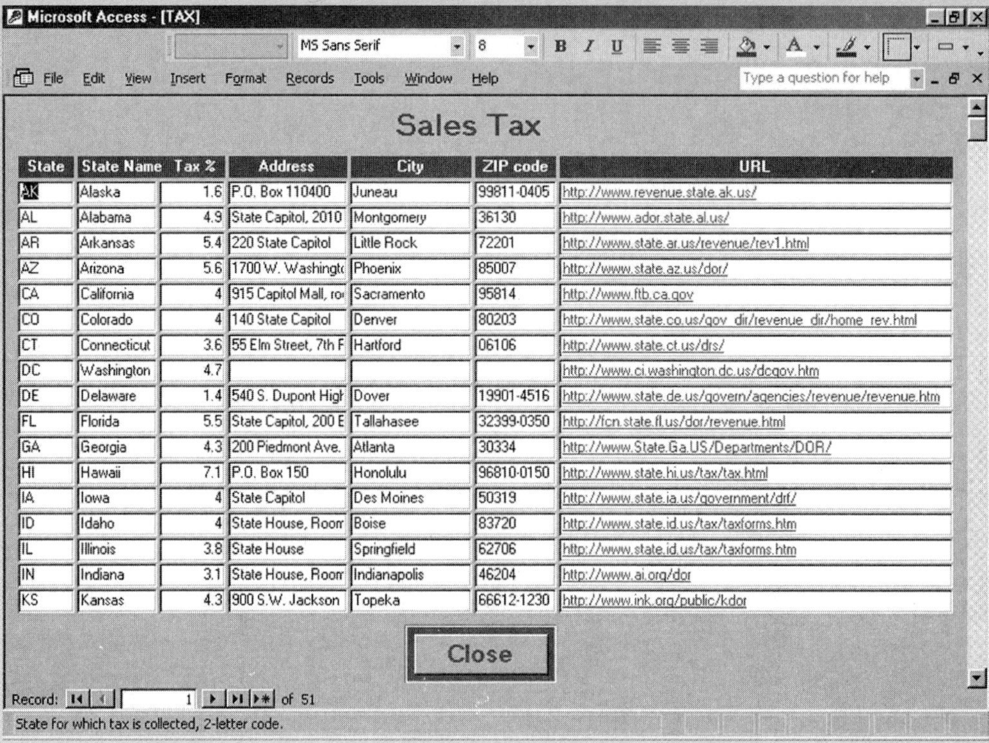

6.4 Use the **CH06_POS_2nd** database to create the report menu shown in Figure P6.4. Name the form **frmReportMenu**. (Note: Your ending date is the current date.)

FIGURE P6.4 The RobSem Report Menu

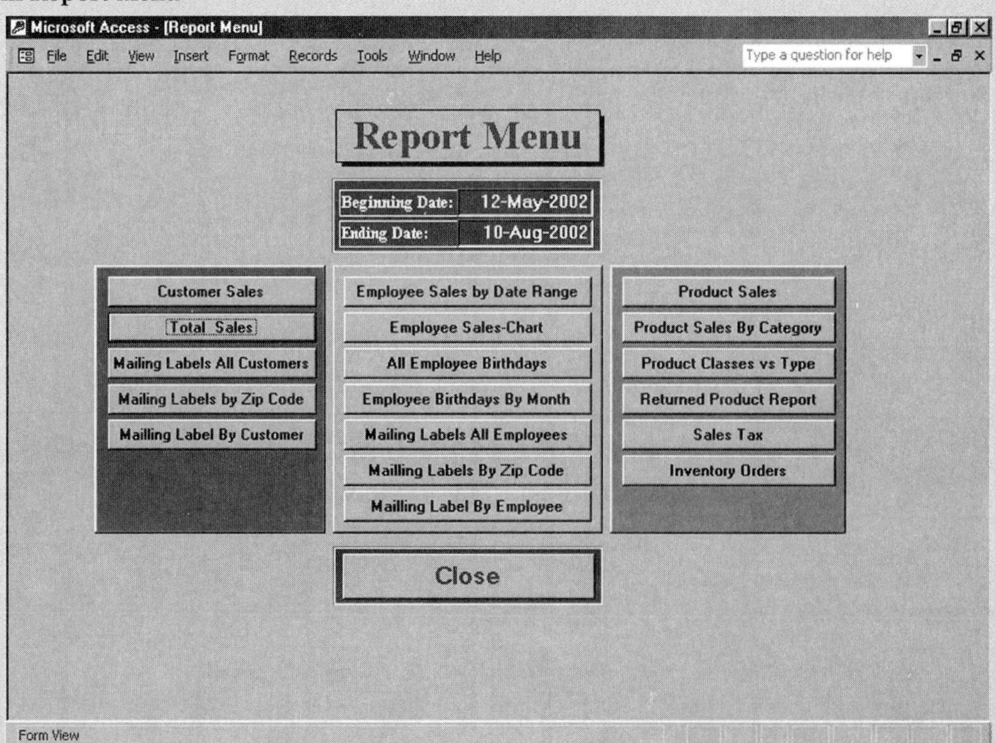

Note

The menu shown in Figure P6.5 is *not* a tabbed menu form like the one shown in Figure 6.106. Make sure that the **Pop Up** option in the form's properties box is set to **No**. If the form's **Pop Up** option is set to **Yes**, the form will be placed on top of the current object and the pop-up format will not enable you to close it at the form view level. (But you can still right-click on the pop-up form and select the design view to enable you to modify the properties and close the form from its design view.)

6.5 Use the **CH06_POS_2nd** database to create the query menu shown in Figure P6.5. Name the form **frmQueryMenu**.

FIGURE P6.5 **The RobSem Query Menu**

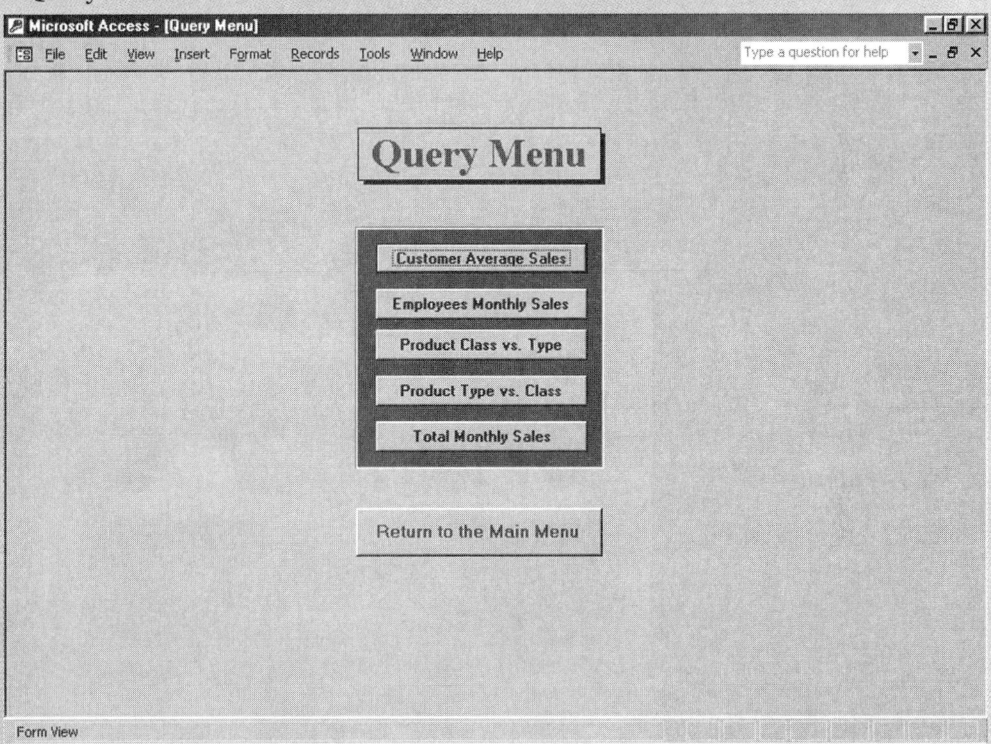

6.6 Use the **Ch06_TruckCo** database to create the employee search form shown in Figure P6.6. Name the form **frmEmployeeSearch**.

FIGURE P6.6
The TruckCo Employee Search Form

Employee Search
Last Name:
First Name:
Search
Cancel

6.7 Use the **Ch06_TruckCo** database to create the driver miles and hours update menu form shown in Figure P6.7. Name the form **frmDriverMiles&HoursUpdateMenu**. Then create the driver log menu form shown in Figure P6.7A and name it **frmDriverLogMenu**.

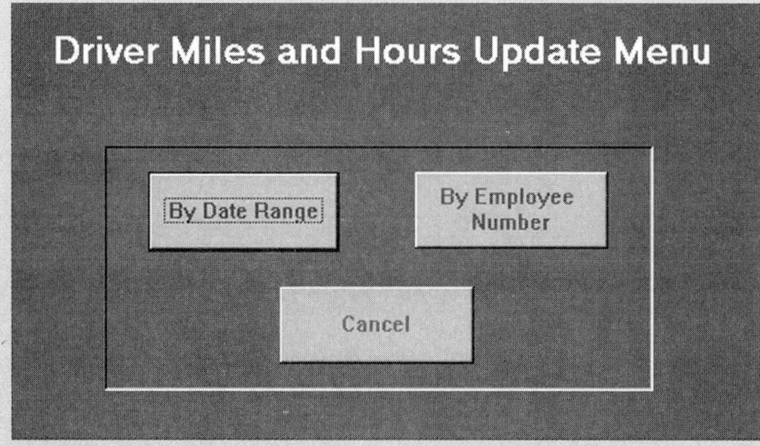

FIGURE P6.7
The TruckCo Driver Miles and Hours Update Menu Form

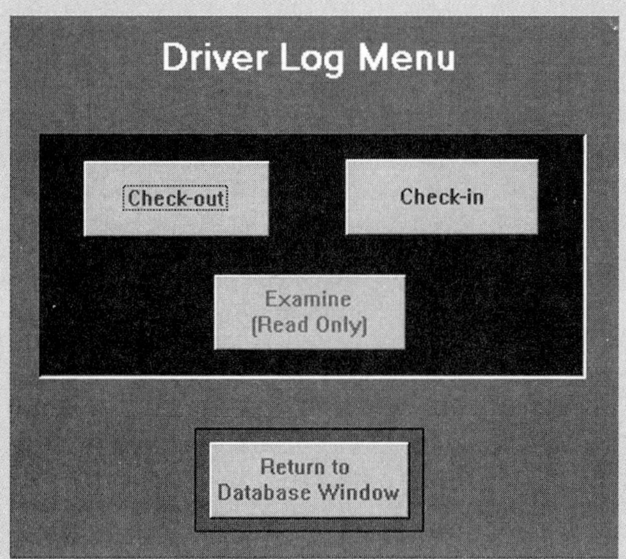

FIGURE P6.7A
The TruckCo Driver Log Menu Form

6.8 Use the **Ch06_TruckCo** database to create the driver log form shown in Figure P6.8. Name the form **frmDriverLog**.

FIGURE P6.8 The TruckCo Driver Log Form

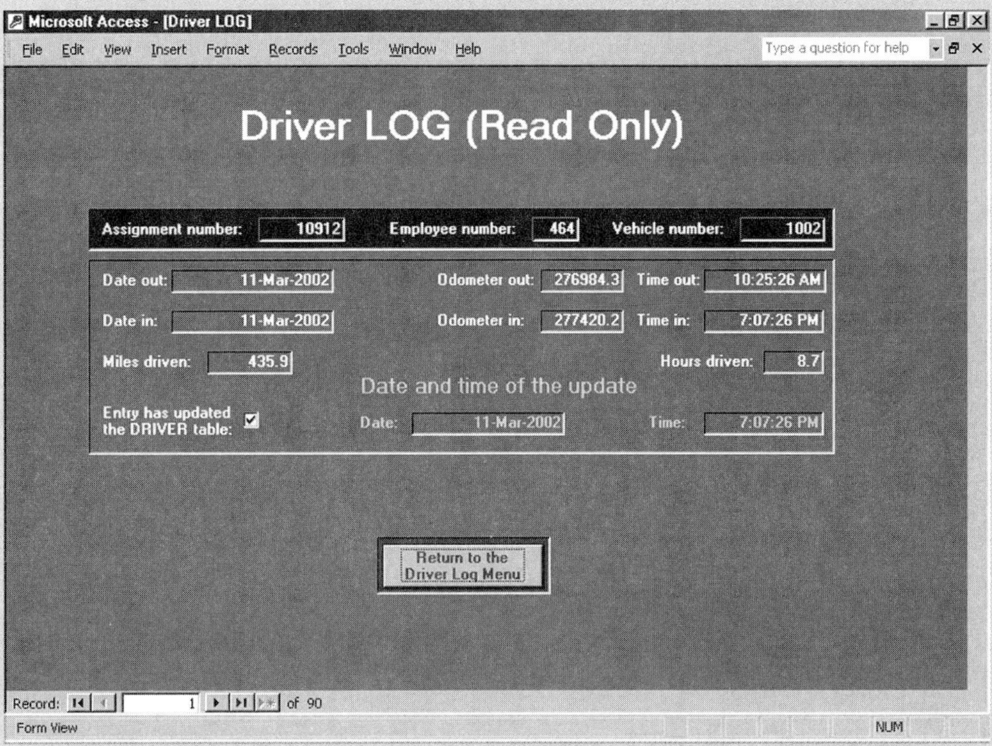
Microsoft Access - [Driver LOG]

File Edit View Insert Format Records Tools Window Help — Type a question for help

Driver LOG (Read Only)

Assignment number: 10912 Employee number: 464 Vehicle number: 1002

Date out: 11-Mar-2002 Odometer out: 276984.3 Time out: 10:25:26 AM

Date in: 11-Mar-2002 Odometer in: 277420.2 Time in: 7:07:26 PM

Miles driven: 435.9 Hours driven: 8.7

Date and time of the update

Entry has updated the DRIVER table: ☑ Date: 11-Mar-2002 Time: 7:07:26 PM

Return to the Driver Log Menu

Record: 1 of 90

Form View NUM

6.9 Use the **Ch06_TruckCo** database to create the maintenance form shown in Figure P6.9. Name the form **frmMaintenanceLog**. (The query that creates the data source is based on the table named MAINT_LOG. Note the use of subforms.)

FIGURE P6.9
The Truck_Co frmMaintenanceLog Form

Log number: 10132 TruckCo Maintenance LOG Form

Vehicle: 1015 Date in: 07-14-2003 Odometer: 154667.9 Logged in by: 101

Complaint: Transmission whines at speeds over 40 mph. Rough idling -- suspect clogged fuel injectors. Also, do oil change and brake system check.

Maintenance detail lines

Line	Task	Part Code	Part Cost	Parts Used	Time	Mechanic
1	Transmission fluid low, replaced 2 qts	AFT-QT	$7.35	2	0.6	445
2	Cleaned fuel injectors		$0.00	0	1.3	124
3	Oil change, 2 gl	ACD-1G	$20.60	2	0.4	124
4	Oil filter change	ASF-10	$9.65	1	0.2	451

Record: 1 of 5

Release date: 07-14-2003 Released for service by: 448

6.10 Use the **Ch06_TruckCo** database to create the maintenance form shown in Figure P6.10. Name the form **frmMaintenanceLog-Version A**. (The query that creates the data source is based on the table named MAINT_LOG_A. Note the use of subforms.)

FIGURE P6.10
The Truck_Co frm MaintenanceLog Form, Version A

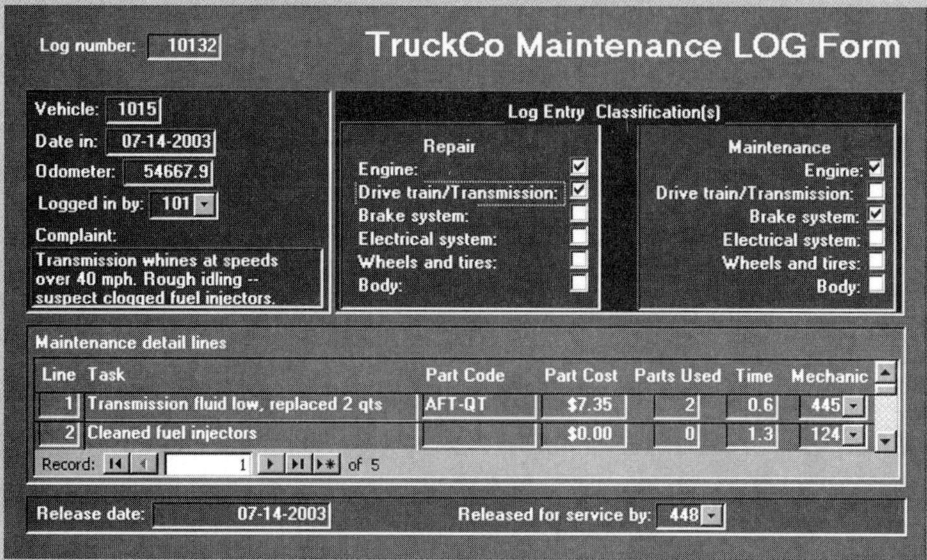

Use the **CH06_ConsultCo** database to complete problems 6.11 through 6.16.

6.11 Create a columnar form based on the PROJECT table. Name the **form frmProject-Initial**. The form's layout is shown in design format in Figure P6.11.

FIGURE P6.11 **The frmProject-Initial Design View**

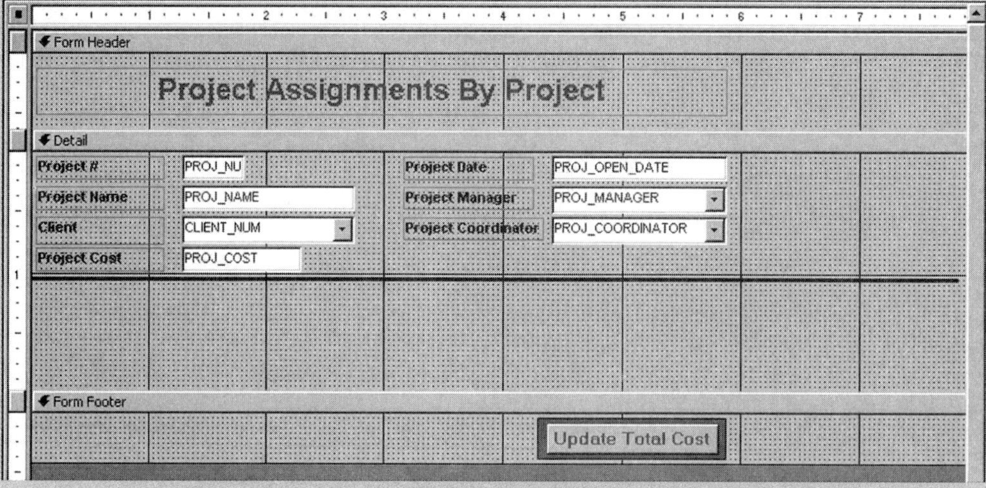

6.12 Create a query based on the ASSIGNMENT and JOB tables to be used as the basis for a form. Include all the ASSIGNMENT table fields and only the JOB_DESCRIPTION and JOB_CHG_HOUR fields from the JOB table. Name the query **qryProjectAssignment**. The query's design view is shown in Figure P6.12.

FIGURE P6.12 The qryProjectAssigment Query's Design View

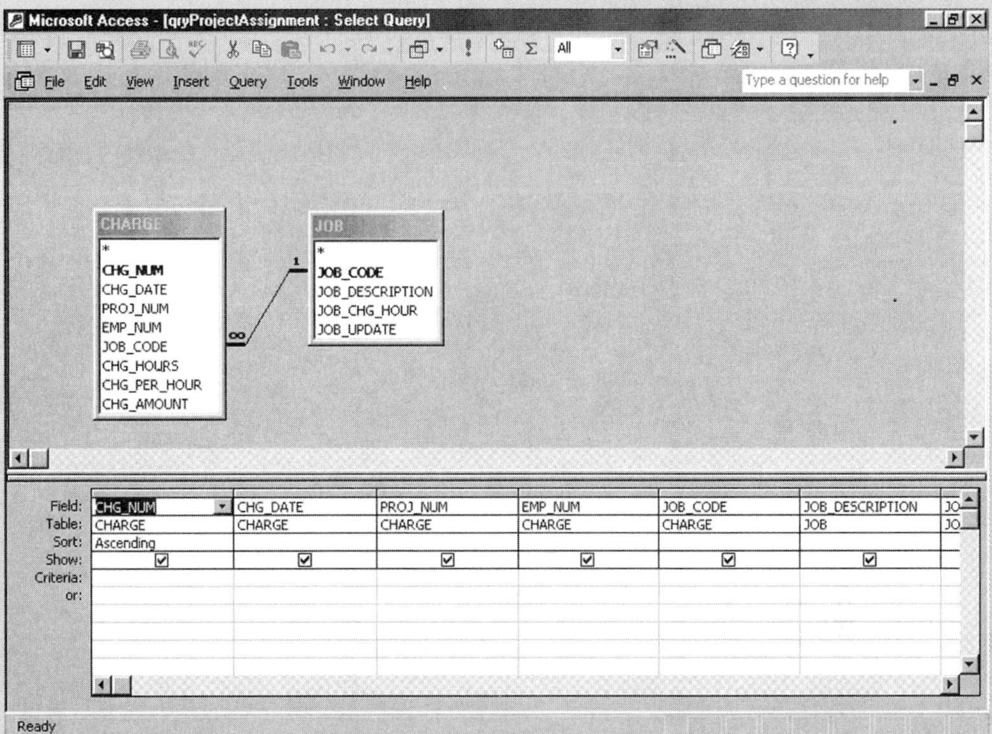

6.13 Create a tabular form based on the **qryProjectAssignment** query from problem 6.10. Name the form **frmProjectAssigment**. The form's design view is shown in Figure P6.13.

FIGURE P6.13 The frmProjectAssignment Form's Design View

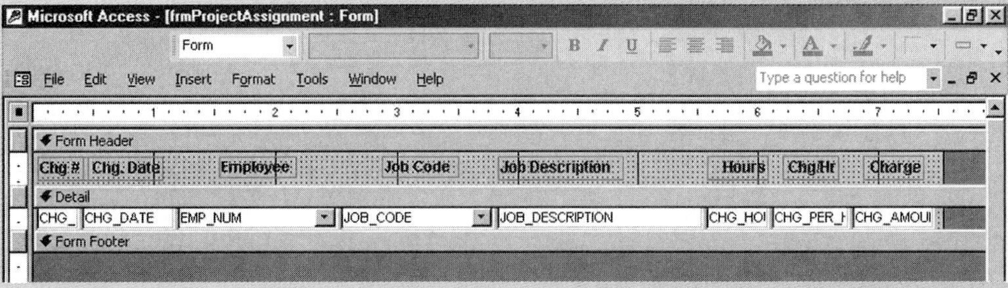

6.14 Save the **frmProject-Initial** form you created in problem 6.11 as **frmProject**, and then insert the **frmProjectAssignment** form you created in problem 6.13 into the **frmProject** form. (The frmProject form will be the main form and the **frmProject-Assignment** form will be its subform. Use the PROJ_NUM to link the child and master fields.) This main form/subform combination will retain its main form name. That is, the main form/subform combination will still be called **frmProject**. The form's design layout is shown in Figure P6.14. Note that the subform has been selected and that the properties box reflects this selection. As you examine the properties box, note that we have named the subform to distinguish it from the **Source Object** name. You will discover that using the **nm** prefix will make it much easier to reference the subform when you start using the macro builder in Chapter 8.

FIGURE P6.14 The frmProject Main Form/Subform in Design View

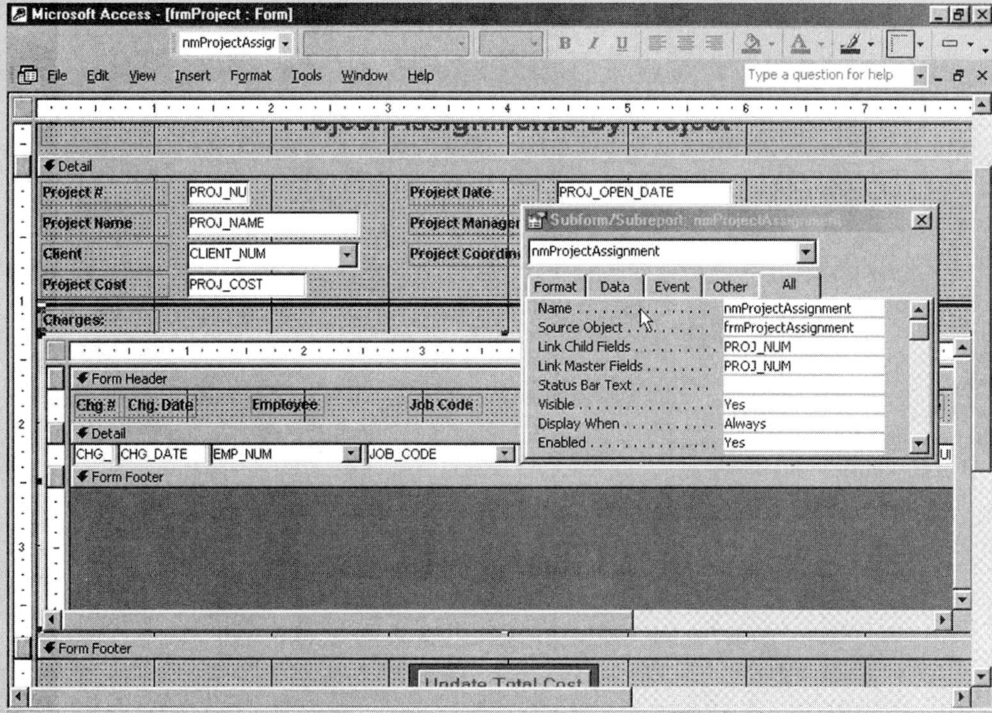

6.15 Open the form you created in problem 6.14 and navigate through the records to examine all the assignments made for each project. Your screen should resemble the one shown in Figure P6.15.

FIGURE P6.15 The frmProject Main Form/Subform in Form View

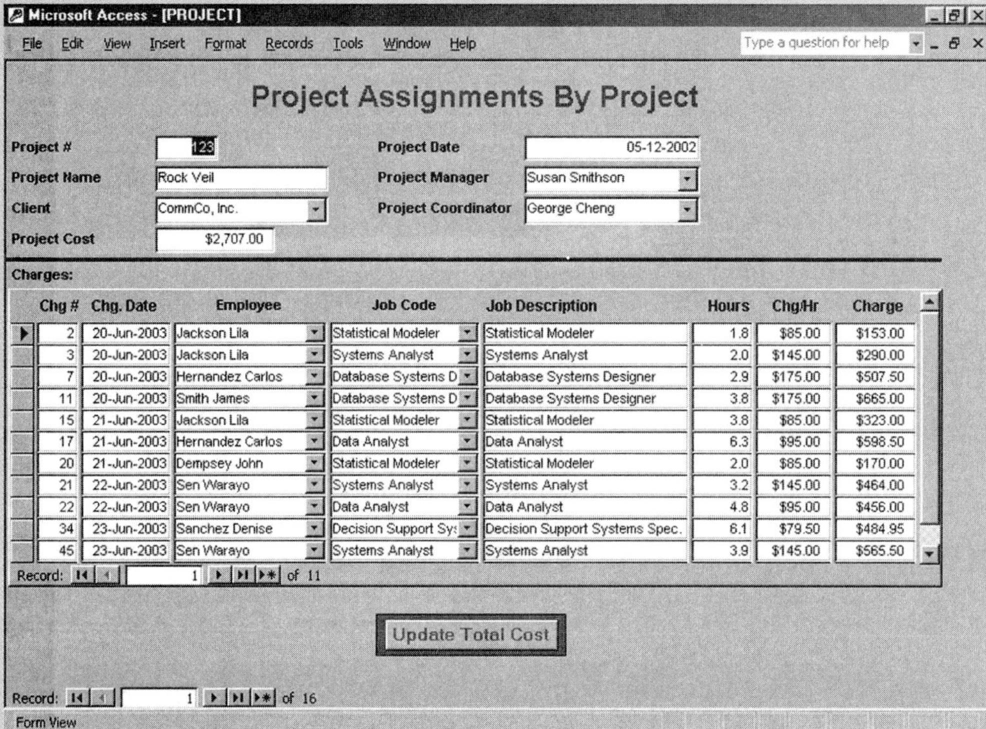

6.16 Use the **Ch06_JewelCo** database as the basis for the main form/subform shown in Figure P6.16. Use the same techniques that you used in problems 6.14 through 6.15. (Note that this main form has two subforms!) Name the subforms **frmSoldJewelry** and **frmUnsoldJewelry**, respectively. The main form name is **frmJeweler&Jewelry**.

FIGURE P6.16 The JewelCo Database's frmJeweler&Jewelry Main Form/Subform

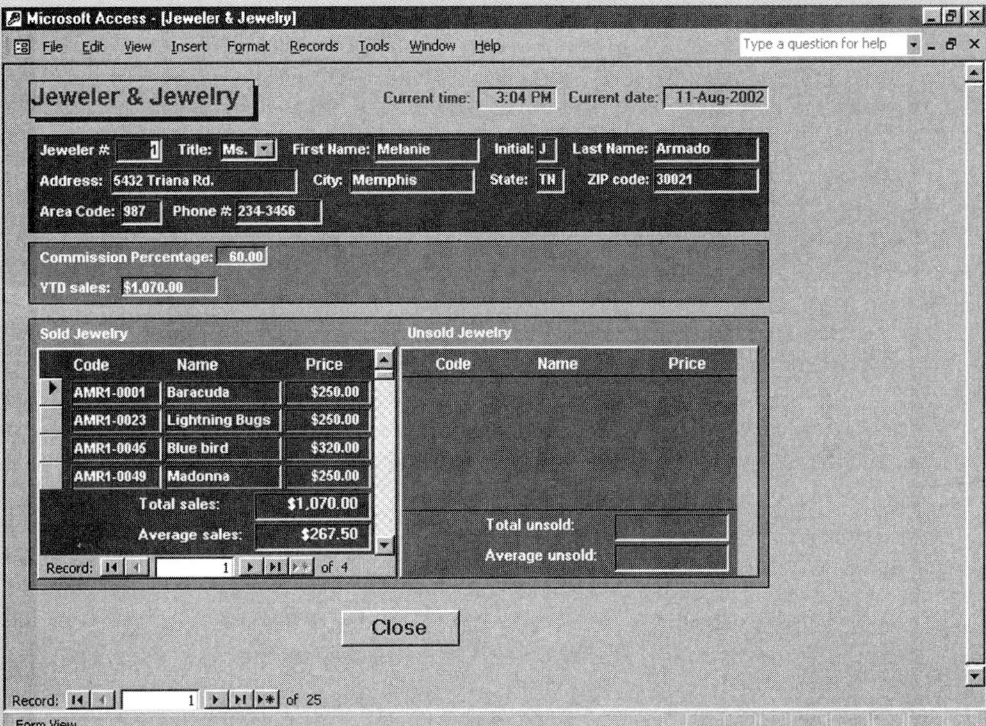

As you examine Figure P6.16, note that the total and average sales values are generated for both sold and unsold jewelry for each jeweler in the database. This first record indicates that jeweler 1 does not have any unsold jewelry in the JewelCo Company's inventory. (It's clearly time to contact this jeweler for additional jewelry.) Figure P6.16A shows you how the total and average values were generated in the **frmSoldJewelry** subform. (Look at the control source in the properties box for the selected **Total sales:** control. The same technique would be used in the **frmUnSoldJewelry** subform.)

FIGURE P6.16A The frmSoldJewelry Subform in Design View

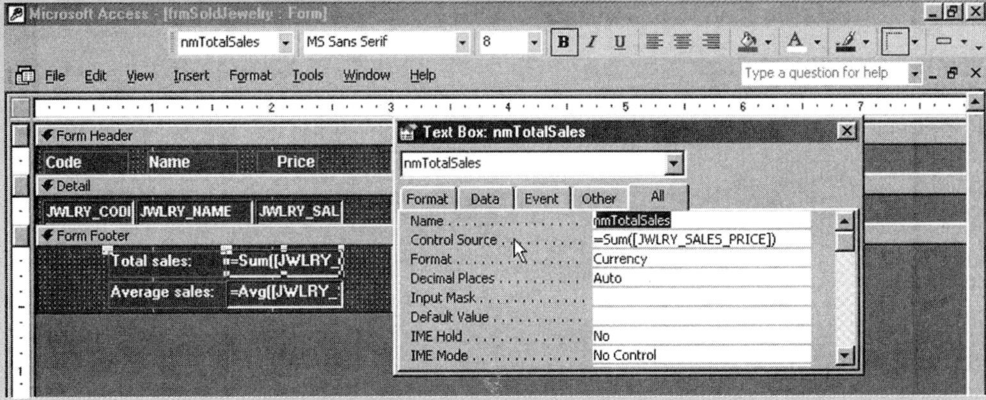

6.17 Create all the forms necessary to view and modify the tables in the **Ch06_POS_2nd** database. Include at least one main form/subform. Then create the menus that will be used to navigate through the applications. For example, the main menu selections must include a command button that will enable the end users to open the report menu. In turn, the report menu must include the command buttons required to select available reports and to return to the main menu. The main menu must also include a command button that lets the end user view all the forms. All submenus must have a command button that allows the end user to return to the main menu. If you create menus called from submenus, those menus must include command buttons that will enable the end user to return to the main menu or to the menu from which the submenu was called.

Use the main menu shown in Figure P6.1 as your menu design guide. (Naturally, your menu details will be different because each database will have different end-user requirements.) Use color groups to organize the menu layout logically.

Remember, your command buttons will not work until you have learned to write the appropriate macros in Chapters 9 and 10. However, you will at least be ready to attach those macros when you get to Chapters 8 and 9!

6.18 Given the requirements listed in problem 6.17, create all the forms, including menu forms, for the **Ch06_FlyHigh** database. Include complex forms in which parent/child (1:M) relationships exist.

6.19 Given the requirements listed in problem 6.18, create all the forms, including menu forms, for the **Ch06_ConsultCo** database. Include complex forms in which parent/child (1:M) relationships exist.

Reports and Labels

Preview

In Chapter 5 you learned to use queries to extract data from the database and to convert data into information. Although the queries performed their work well, Access controlled the presentation format and, to put it charitably, that presentation format was rather bland. End users expect more formal and attractive output presentation than the queries can deliver. In addition, it is impossible to let queries perform certain jobs, such as generate subtotals and totals within a single query to produce a single printed summary. Yet end users tend to find such summaries very useful and don't want to generate multiple queries to produce results that will then have to be cut and pasted. The Access reports are able to overcome these query shortcomings. Therefore, this chapter's report coverage is the virtual icing on Chapter 5's query cake.

Because reports are usually based on queries, the query coverage in Chapter 5 is a necessary prerequisite to this chapter's focus on report generation. In fact, many of the reports in this chapter are based on queries developed in Chapter 5 or on queries you produced when you completed the problems in that chapter's problem section. Your knowledge of queries should make report generation a simple task, especially because Access provides a very effective and simple-to-use collection of report templates and wizards.

After you have learned how to generate the basic report layout with the help of the Access report templates and wizards, we show you how to customize the report presentation format. We show you how to use the by-now-familiar Access tools such as properties boxes and toolbars to produce the polish that will yield high-quality, formal presentations of information. It is always useful to remember that the people who will look at your reports are likely to judge your professionalism on the basis of the report presentation quality, as well as its usefulness.

Sooner or later, any organization's managers contact customers, clients, or patrons by using form letters. Therefore, we show you how to use the report format to create such form letters. Business organizations typically generate invoices, shipping documents, and so forth. All these documents are, in effect, special reports. Therefore, we show you how to create such reports in this chapter.

Once the form letters, invoices, shipping documents, and other similar documents have been printed, they have to be mailed or shipped. Access places mailing-label generation within its report menus. Therefore, it is appropriate to examine in this chapter how to create mailing labels and how to customize them.

Objectives

When you have mastered the material in this chapter, you will know how to

- Use the templates and wizards to create reports.
- Use the Access tools to customize the report format.
- Produce mailing labels in a variety of formats.
- Create customized form letters.

Note

The examples in this chapter are based on the **Ch07_POS_2nd.mdb** database, located in the **Ch07** folder on the student CD. (After you copy the database from the CD to your drive, remember to uncheck the **Read-only** check box from the **Ch07_POS_2nd.mdb** file properties.)

7.1 CREATING A REPORT: SOME PRELIMINARY ACTIVITIES

Before you can create a report, you must know what its output is expected to look like. Therefore, the first step in creating a report is to define the output format. The low-tech pencil and a piece of paper still provide a good way to lay out the expected report format. Failing to do some basic planning makes report creation more of a challenge than it needs to be!

Our first report will yield a listing of all employee birth dates by month. You can get an idea of the expected report output from the segment of the report's screen presentation shown in Figure 7.1. Examine the output carefully because its format will guide our report development.

Figure 7.1 illustrates a few points that are worth emphasizing:

- The birth dates are organized by the birth month. We'll have to remember that the months are sorted in ascending order. However, text strings such as month names are sorted in alphabetical order, which places *A* before *B*, *B* before *C*, and so on. So if we sort by month *name*, April will show up before January, and July will occur before June. Therefore, sorting by month name will not yield the expected output shown here. Instead, we'll have to sort by month number, and then we'll hide the month number to avoid its appearance on the report.
- The birthdays are grouped by month. Therefore, we'll have to remember to select the group option when we create the report.

FIGURE 7.1
The Employee Birth Date Report Output Format

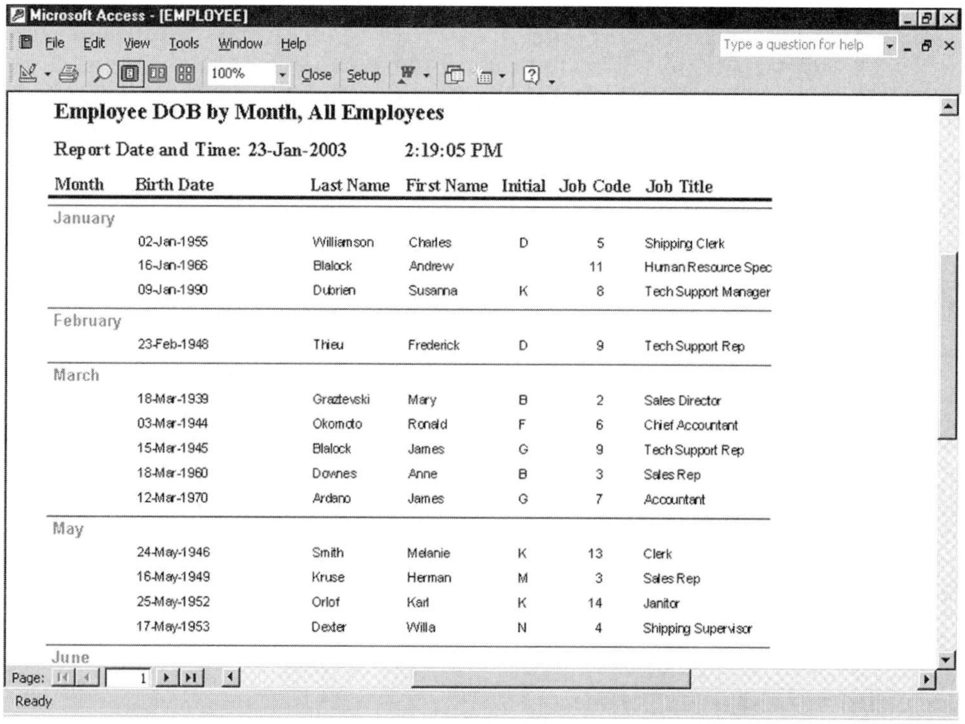

Microsoft Access - [EMPLOYEE]

Employee DOB by Month, All Employees

Report Date and Time: 23-Jan-2003 2:19:05 PM

Month	Birth Date	Last Name	First Name	Initial	Job Code	Job Title
January						
	02-Jan-1955	Williamson	Charles	D	5	Shipping Clerk
	16-Jan-1966	Blalock	Andrew		11	Human Resource Spec
	09-Jan-1990	Dubrien	Susanna	K	8	Tech Support Manager
February						
	23-Feb-1948	Thieu	Frederick	D	9	Tech Support Rep
March						
	18-Mar-1939	Graztevski	Mary	B	2	Sales Director
	03-Mar-1944	Okomoto	Ronald	F	6	Chief Accountant
	15-Mar-1945	Blalock	James	G	9	Tech Support Rep
	18-Mar-1960	Downes	Anne	B	3	Sales Rep
	12-Mar-1970	Ardano	James	G	7	Accountant
May						
	24-May-1946	Smith	Melanie	K	13	Clerk
	16-May-1949	Kruse	Herman	M	3	Sales Rep
	25-May-1952	Orlof	Karl	K	14	Janitor
	17-May-1953	Dexter	Willa	N	4	Shipping Supervisor
June						

Page: 1

Ready

Note

As you examine the query structure in Figure 7.2, note that the **Month#:** function uses a month format **"mm"** to ensure that the month *number* is returned in the format 01, 02, 03, . . . , 11, 12. If you don't use this format, the sort will yield incorrect results. For example, if you use the function **Month([EMP_DOB])**, the output will be 1, 2, 3, . . . , 10, 11, and 12, rather than 01, 02, and so on. Therefore, the sort routine will place month 12 (December) before months 2, 3, 4, and so on because the leading *1* in *12* is seen as less than 2, less than 3, and so on.

The same problem exists if you sort on the month names generated by **Month**. For example, because *A* occurs before *J*, sorting on the month name will place April and August before January.

7.1.1 The Query behind the Report

Because reports are usually based on queries, we'll first have to make sure that the query exists. We will base the report in Figure 7.1 on the employee birth date query. This query, named **qryEmployeeDOBbyMonth,AllEmployees**, is based on the query structure shown in Figure 7.2. (Because the report is based on this query, create the query before trying to create the report! Note also that we have used the **Field Properties** box to change the **Caption** to **Month #**. This caption makes a lot more sense than the **Expre1** caption—or some other **Expre** number—that would have been assigned by Access.)

Given the availability of the query on which the report will be based, start the report creation process by selecting the **New** option from the report folder in the familiar database window. This action will generate the **New Report** dialog box shown in Figure 7.3.

To take the work out of creating the report, we'll use a report template with a tabular option. Therefore, we've selected the **Autoreport: Tabular** option in Figure 7.3. Click on the data source window (above the **OK** and **Cancel** buttons) to display the list of available tables and queries. Scroll down the list until you find

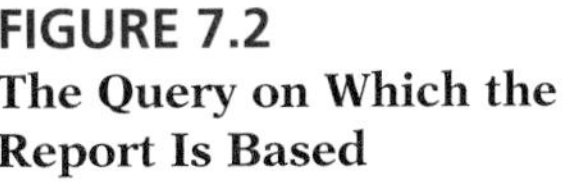
FIGURE 7.2
The Query on Which the Report Is Based

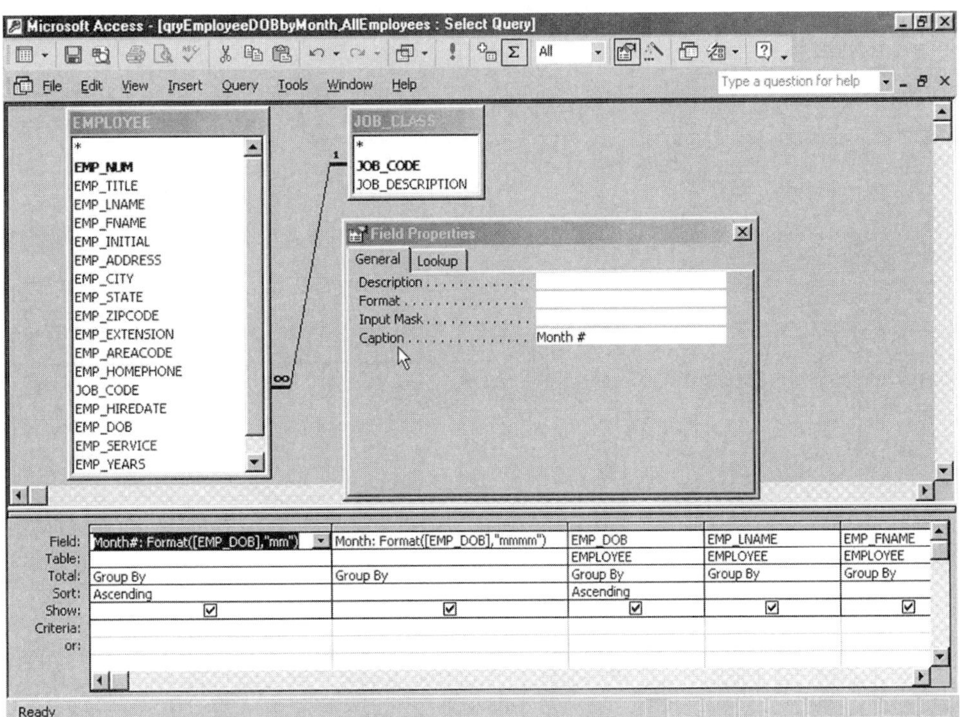

FIGURE 7.3
Selecting the Tabular Report Format Option

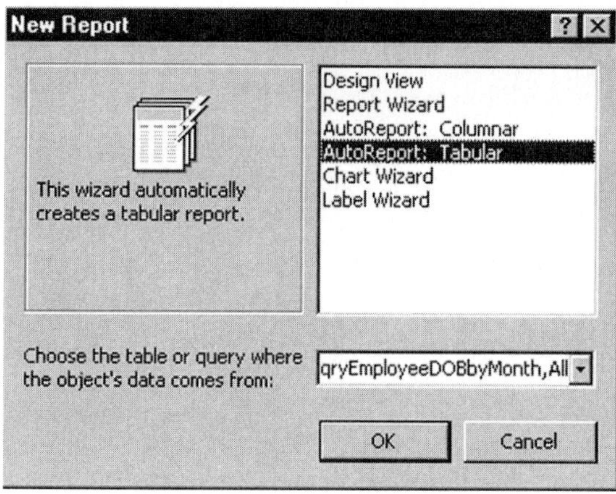

the **qryEmployeeDOBbyMonth,AllEmployees** query and then click on it to select it. Finally, click on the **OK** button to complete the process; then sit back and relax for a second or two while Access creates the report structure. Access displays the results of its efforts in the **Print Preview** format shown in Figure 7.4.

As you examine Figure 7.4, note that it does not (yet!) have the polished results shown in Figure 7.1. To match that output presentation, we'll have to do some serious modifying in the Access-produced report. However, before you make any modifications, save the just-generated report, using the name **rptEmployeeDOBbyMonth,AllEmployees**. Note that we follow these report naming conventions:

- The report's name carries the **rpt** prefix.
- The report name reflects its data source. In this example, the data source is the query named **qryEmployeeDOBbyMonth,AllEmployees**.

After saving the new report, you are ready to begin the modification process.

FIGURE 7.4
The Initial Print Preview Format

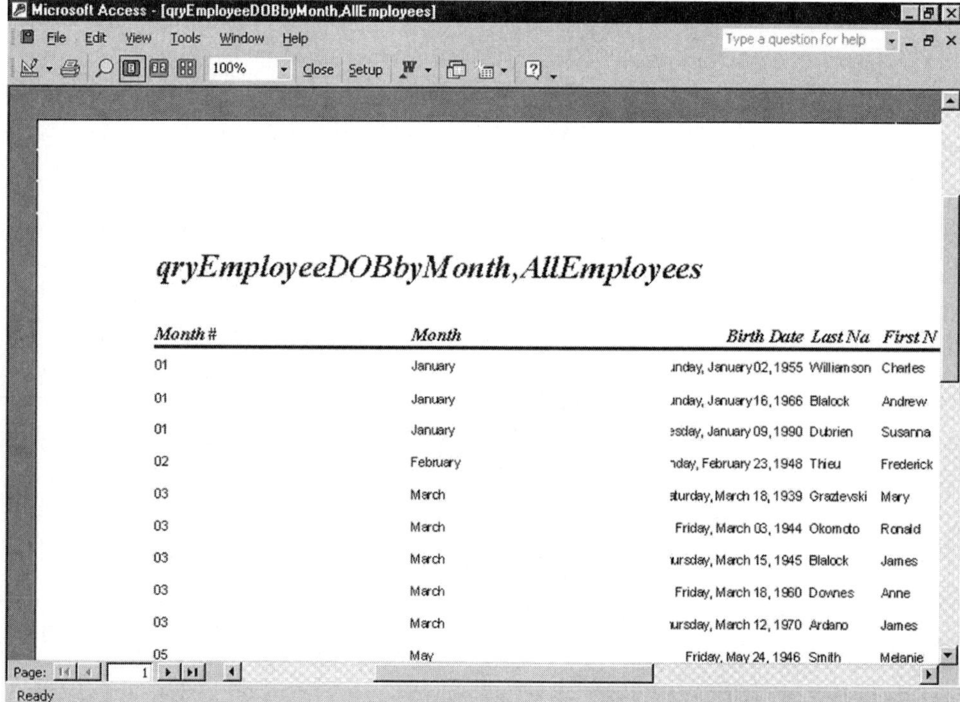

7.1.2 Modifying the Report Structure

Before you begin the report modification process, you must know what changes are to be made. Remember that the objective is to produce a report that will yield the output shown in Figure 7.1. If you compare Figure 7.4 to Figure 7.1, you'll note that you must

- Delete the **Month #** label.
- Hide the **Month #** values. Remember the note that accompanies Figure 7.2. Because the month number is used to sort the output, you do *not* want to delete the month number values, but you do not want to show them on the report.
- Change the **Month** name presentation to prevent its occurrence on each output line.
- Separate the month blocks with lines.
- Change the letter format from italics to standard but keep the bold type.
- Change the spacing to tighten up the output presentation.
- Change the header to reflect the report's contents and to show the date and time.

We'll make all of these changes in this section. The order in which the changes are made is immaterial. To modify the just-created and saved **rptEmployeeDOBbyMonth,AllEmployees**, open it in design mode. Next click on the **Month #** text box in the detail line and then open its properties box to produce the screen shown in Figure 7.5.

As you examine the properties box in Figure 7.5, note that the text box's default control source and its name are both listed as **Month#**. Also note that the **Visible** property is set to its default value **Yes**. Using Figure 7.5 as your guide, make these changes:

- To make a distinction between the control source and the name, change the name to **nmMonth#.** You will really appreciate this distinction when you start using the Macro Builder in Chapter 8. (Unless you make this change, which **Month#** should you select if you see a list that contains two of them?)

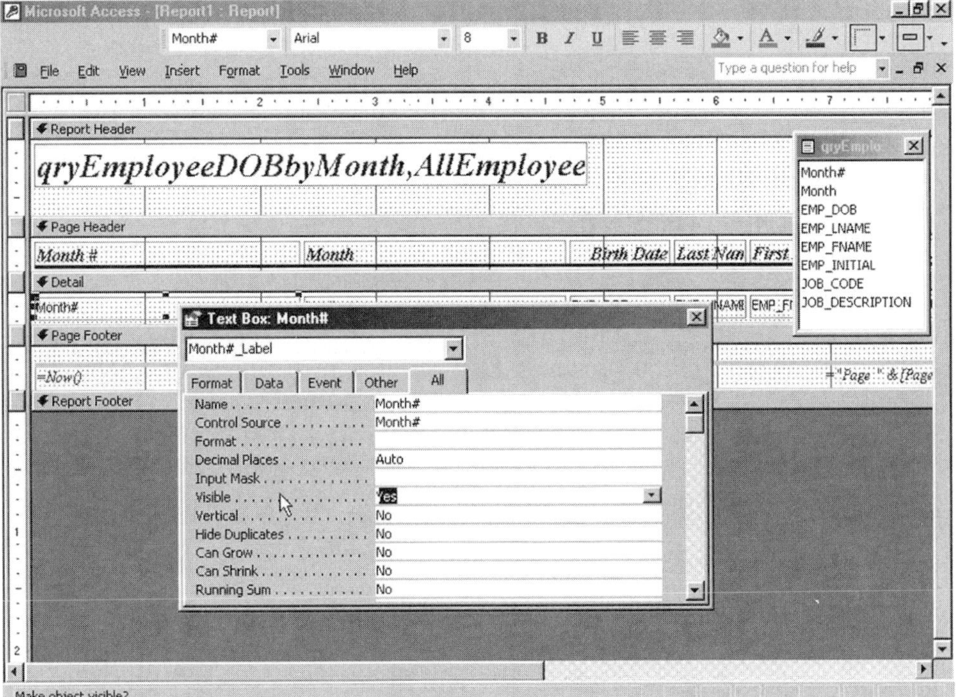

FIGURE 7.5
The Month # Text Box Properties Box

FIGURE 7.6
The Modified Report Design

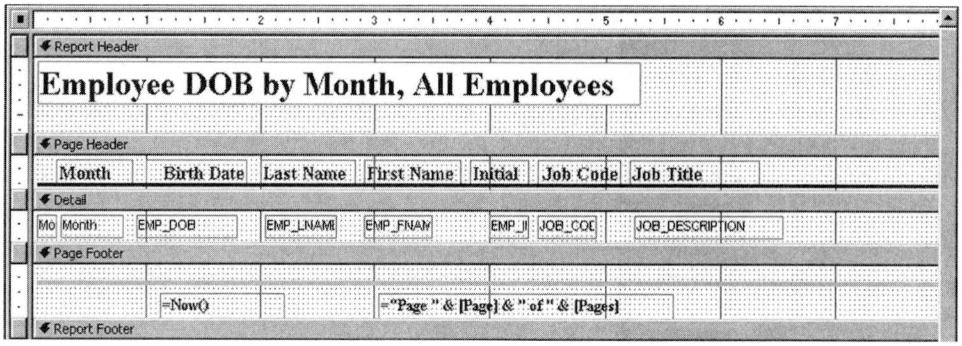

- To make sure that the month number **(Month#)** values do not show up on the report, change the **Visible** property to **No**. (But do *not* delete the **Month#** text box!)
- Close the **Month#** properties box.
- Move to the report header and modify the label to read **Employee DOB by Month, All Employees**. Change the font format to boldface. Note the dark blue font color.
- Move to the page header and delete the **Month #** label. Select all the other labels (**Month, Birth Date**, and so on) and then change their label format from italics to standard boldface. (Use the familiar button bar at the top of the screen.) Note the dark blue font color. Drag the labels to decrease the spacing between them.
- Move to the **Detail** line and drag all the text boxes to match the headers you moved in the preceding step.
- Move to the form's page footer, drag the components to center them on the page, and change the letter format from italics to boldface standard. Note the dark blue font color.

When you've made all these changes, the form's design screen should look like Figure 7.6. (Note that the **Month#** text box in the detail segment has been reduced—but *not* deleted—to accommodate the **Month** text box. Remember that the **Month#** values will not be shown because we set its **Visible** property to **No**.)

Save the report again. In fact, it's not a bad idea to save it after each round of modifications. As was true when you were working with reports and queries, you can always switch back and forth between the report's Design View and its screen presentation, named **Print Preview**, in the report mode. Therefore, to see the effect of the changes you've made, you can select the **Print Preview** option via the **Print Preview** button at the top of the screen to generate Figure 7.7. Naturally, you can always close the form and then open it by selecting the **Preview** button in the database window's report folder. However, we suggest you switch back and forth from the design stage to the preview stage via the **Print Preview** button. This procedure lets you check the output each time you make a design change, thus making it easier to fine-tune the changes.

Compare Figures 7.7 and 7.1 again, to see that the report header still requires modification and that the **Month** output still is repeated on each output line. Changing the report header requires the procedures you used to produce form headers. For example:

- Use the toolbox's label button to add the text box label (**Report Date and Time**).
- Use the toolbox's text box button to produce the date and time text boxes.
- Use the =**Now()** function to produce the date output and then select its properties box to set its format to **dd-mmm-yyyy**. (You may select **Medium Date**

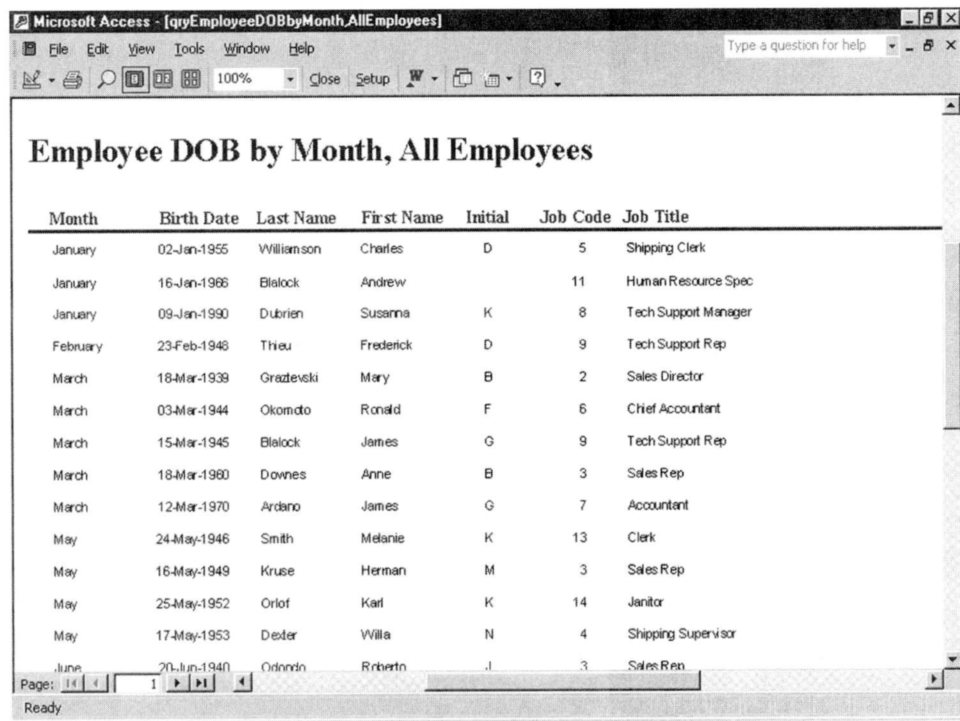

FIGURE 7.7
The Report's Preview Screen After the Initial Modifications

from the list or type **dd-mm-yy** if you want to limit the year format to its last two digits.)

- Use the =**Time()** function to generate the time output and then select its properties box to set its format to **Long Time**.

(You can skip ahead and check the results in Figure 7.11.) Controlling the month output takes a bit more effort, so we'll do that in section 7.1.3.

7.1.3 Creating Detail Line Headers (Subheaders)

Rather than showing the month each time it occurs, let's group the employee birthdays by the month in which they occurred. To get this job done, click on the detail segment header; its color will change to black when you do. Then right-click to generate the options list shown in Figure 7.8. (Note that we have placed the cursor on the **Sorting and Grouping** option to highlight it.) Select the **Sorting and Grouping** option shown in Figure 7.8 to produce the dialog box in Figure 7.9.

Because we want to use the month name as the subheader each time the month changes, make the dialog box selections shown in Figure 7.10. (Check Figure 7.1 again to see the intended effect.)

As you examine Figure 7.10, note especially these selections:

- Clicking on the **Field/Expression** yields the list of all available fields. Because we want to group the results by month number, we have selected the **Month#** option. If necessary, examine the query by expression (QBE) in Figure 7.2 to see the available month expressions. *Remember that we must sort on the month number, not the month name!*
- The **Group Header** selection is set to **Yes**. Note that this selection automatically opened a space between the detail line and the header. Because we selected **Month#** to be the field, this space is automatically labeled **Month# Header**.
- Because we want the month *name* to show up only when the month *number* changes, drag the **Month** text box to the **Month#** header as shown.

FIGURE 7.8
Selecting the Detail Section's Sorting and Grouping Option

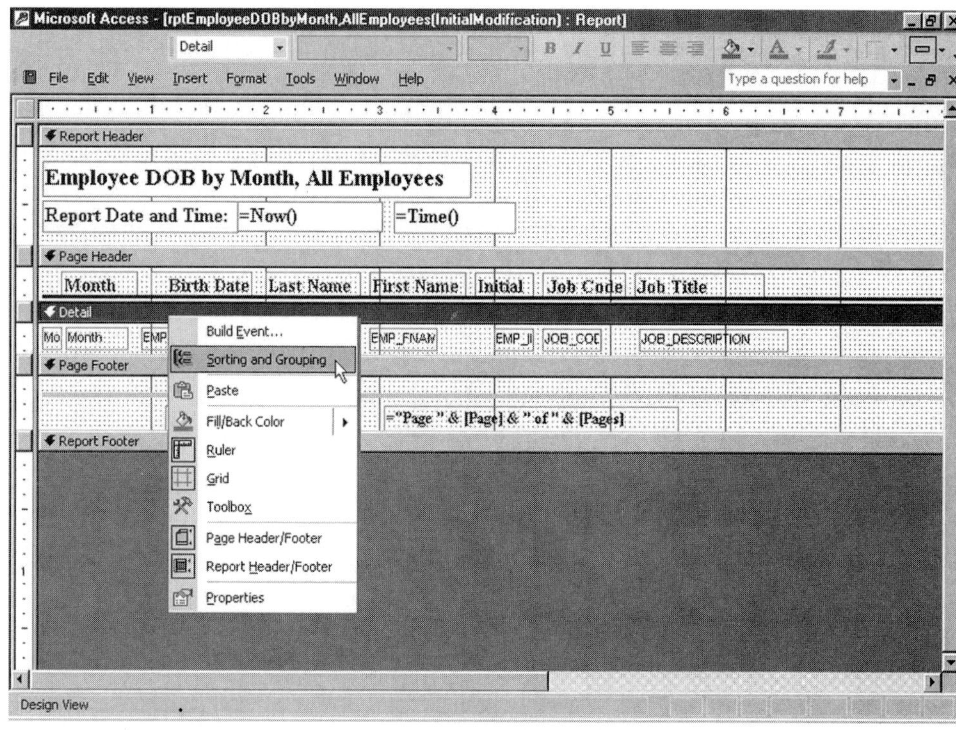

FIGURE 7.9
The Sorting and Grouping Dialog Box

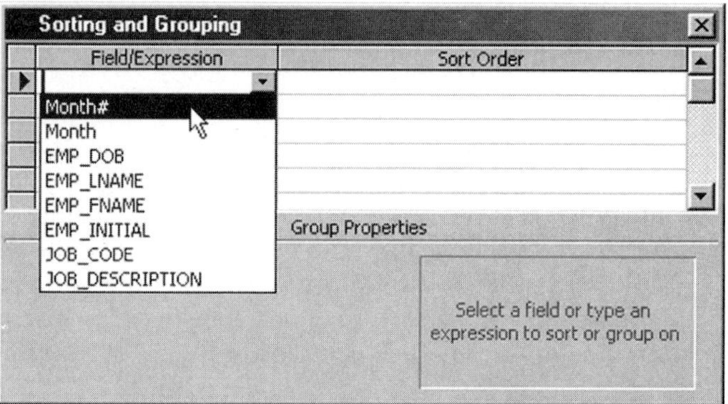

FIGURE 7.10
The Sorting and Grouping Dialog Box

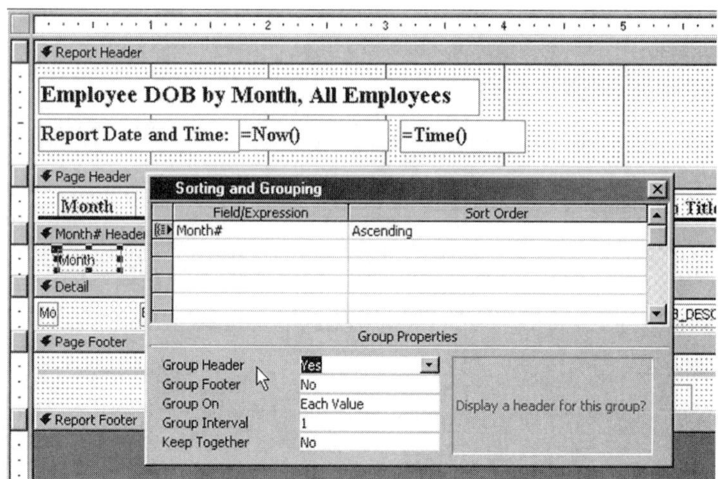

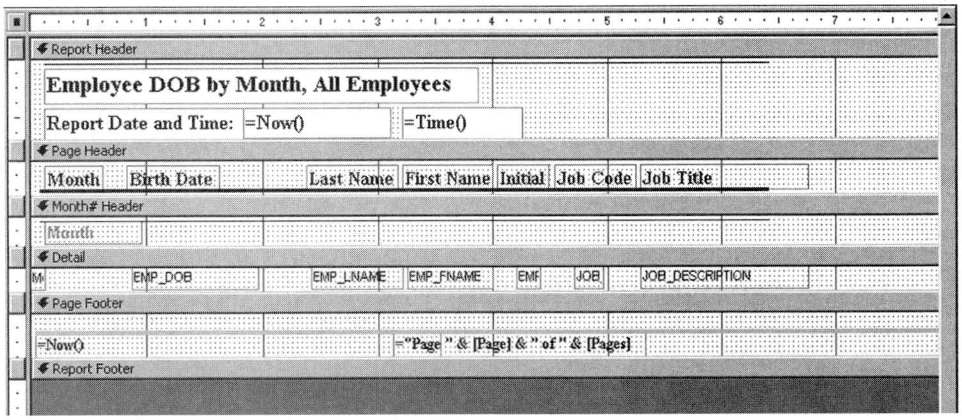

FIGURE 7.11
The Completed Report Design

- The **Group Interval** defaults to **1.** This value is appropriate because we want the month to be printed each time the month changes.

After making these entries, save the form again; then open it in design format to make the final report header changes shown in Figure 7.11 and to touch up the display format to match the output. (For example, we changed the font color in the **Month#** Header's **Month** text box to green and boldfaced it.) If you open the form in its **Print Preview** mode, you'll see that its output matches that of Figure 7.1.

7.2 CREATING A REPORT WITH SUBTOTALS AND TOTALS

One of the advantages of using reports is that they can provide activity summaries. Clearly, sales activities are of great interest to the RobSem Company. Therefore, various sales reports are generated periodically. One of the sales reports concerns the activity by RobSem sales personnel, so we'll create such a sales report. To provide a detailed summary of one aspect of the sales activities, we'll use sales subtotals for each employee, as well as the total sales for all employees. Figure 7.12 shows the report format. (Because the report is too long to fit on the screen, the grand total does not show up here, but it is part of the report. If you want to see the grand total values, just click on the "go to last page" slide control. The arrow-shaped cursor is located on it in the lower left corner of Figure 7.12.)

Figure 7.12 provides an appropriate map to guide the report's development activities. Note particularly the following features:

- Like the first report (Figure 7.1) in this chapter, this report uses subgroups. Instead of using Figure 7.1's subgroups by date, Figure 7.12's report uses subgroups based on the employee last name, EMP_LNAME. Therefore, the *detail* header will be based on EMP_LNAME.
- Each sales employee generates an invoice sales subtotal. (Peek ahead to the query in Figure 7.13 and, you'll see that each invoice line contains an INV_SUB_TOTALS field.) Therefore, both the detail header and the detail footer will be based on the EMP_LNAME.
- The employee names are concatenated. Concatenation is a process that "adds" strings. In this case, the first sales summary is written for Elizabeth Bahint. Therefore, we must add the EMP_FNAME value "Elizabeth" to the EMP_LNAME value "Bahint" to produce the detail header. Because we'll want to place a space between the first name and the last name, we can concatenate by using **([EMP_FNAME] & " " & [EMP_FNAME])**.

FIGURE 7.12
The Subtotal/Total Sales Report

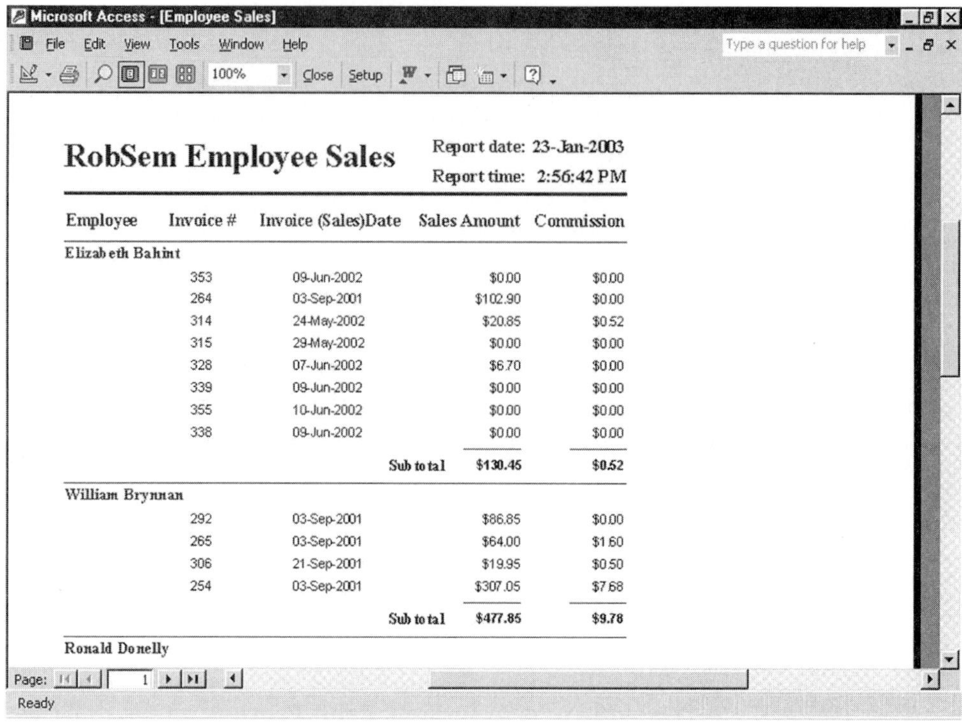

RobSem Employee Sales

Report date: 23-Jan-2003
Report time: 2:56:42 PM

Employee	Invoice #	Invoice (Sales)Date	Sales Amount	Commission
Elizabeth Bahint				
	353	09-Jun-2002	$0.00	$0.00
	264	03-Sep-2001	$102.90	$0.00
	314	24-May-2002	$20.85	$0.52
	315	29-May-2002	$0.00	$0.00
	328	07-Jun-2002	$6.70	$0.00
	339	09-Jun-2002	$0.00	$0.00
	355	10-Jun-2002	$0.00	$0.00
	338	09-Jun-2002	$0.00	$0.00
		Sub total	$130.45	$0.52
William Brynnan				
	292	03-Sep-2001	$86.85	$0.00
	265	03-Sep-2001	$64.00	$1.60
	306	21-Sep-2001	$19.95	$0.50
	254	03-Sep-2001	$307.05	$7.68
		Sub total	$477.85	$9.78
Ronald Donelly				

- The report's sales subtotal for each employee is the sum of his or her invoice subtotals. Therefore, if you group by employee, the employee sales subtotal will be calculated by using the sum function **Sum([INV_SUB_TOTALS])**, and this value will be placed in the subgroup's detail footer.
- The grand total, not shown in Figure 7.12, is the sum of the subtotals. You may also calculate this value by placing the **Sum([INV_SUB_TOTALS])** in the report footer.

FIGURE 7.13
The Query Structure for the Report in Figure 7.12

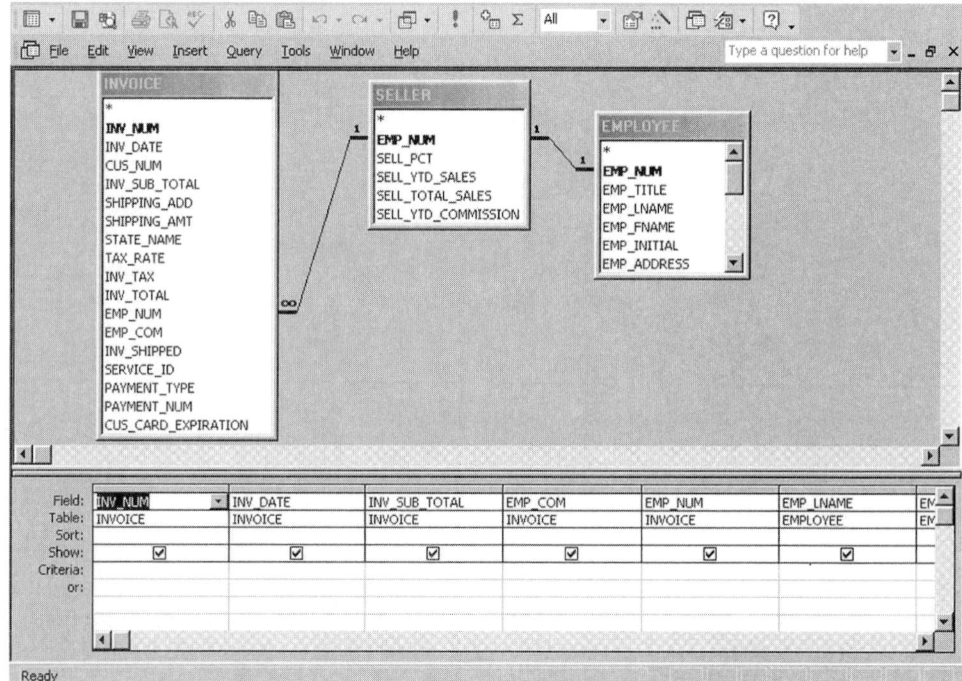

FIGURE 7.14
Selecting the Report Wizard

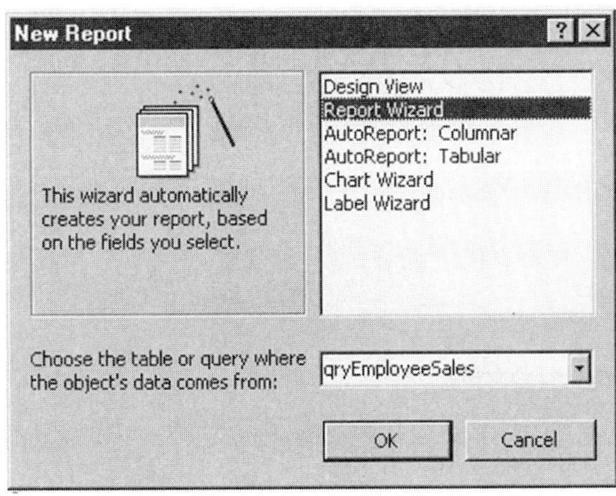

FIGURE 7.15
Selecting the Fields to Be Included in the Report

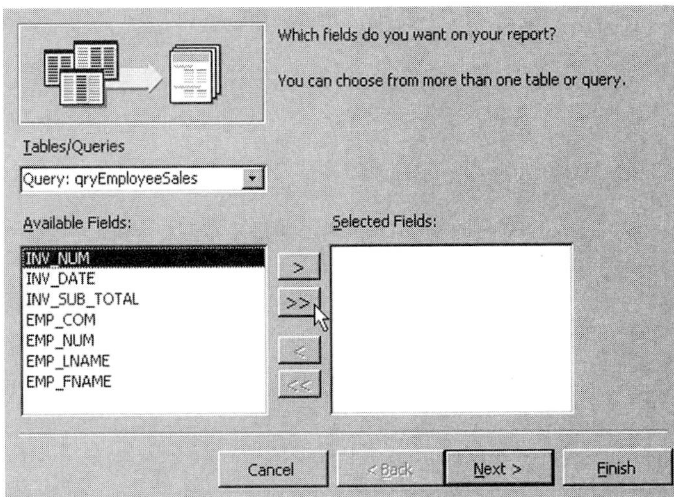

As you look at the query structure in Figure 7.13, recall that a report requires a data source. Let's now use Figure 7.13's query, named **qryEmployeeSales**, as the data source to create the report, to be named **rptEmployeeSales**.

7.2.1 Creating the Basic Report Structure with the Report Wizard

The simplest way to create the subtotal/total report is to use the Report Wizard, so select it from the **New Report** dialog box as shown in Figure 7.14. Note that we've also selected the query named **qryEmployeeSales** to be the data source.

Clicking the **OK** button in the **New Report** dialog box will produce the first **Report Wizard** dialog box, shown in Figure 7.15.

Note that this dialog box shown in Figure 7.15 gives you an option to change the data source by clicking on its **Tables/Queries** list box. However, our query selection is already appropriate, so we'll leave the selection as it is.

Because we'll use all of the query's fields in the report, click on the >> button to transfer all **Available Fields** to the **Selected Fields** box; then click on the **Next** > button to generate the dialog box shown in Figure 7.16.

FIGURE 7.16
The Subgroup Selection

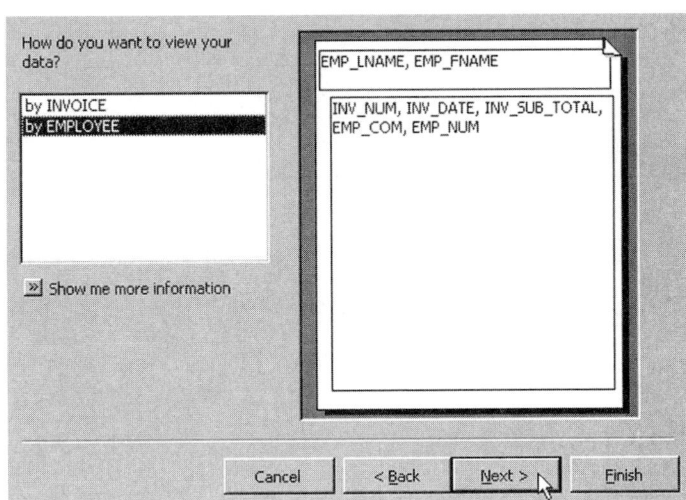

FIGURE 7.17
An Additional Grouping Level Option

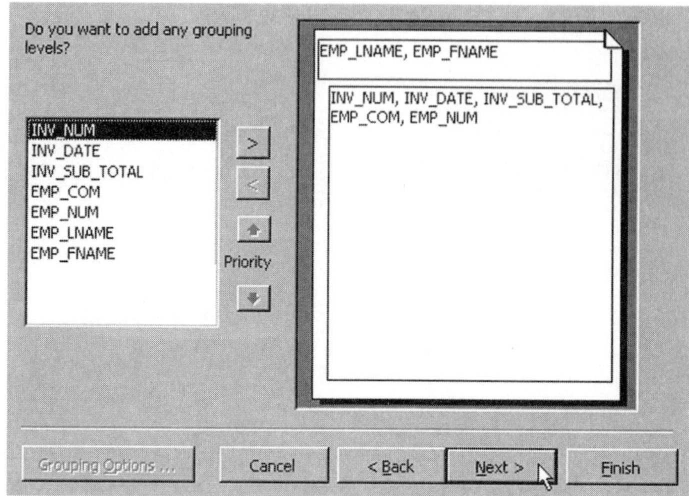

Because the report output (see Figure 7.12 again) groups and subtotals the sales by employee, select the **by EMPLOYEE** option in Figure 7.16, and then click on the **Next** > button to move to the dialog box shown in Figure 7.17. This dialog box allows you to pick the next subgroup level if you want one.

Because we do not need any additional subgroups, just click the **Next** > button in Figure 7.17 to generate the dialog box shown in Figure 7.18. This dialog box will allow us to select sort options for the report components. More important, the dialog box in Figure 7.18 provides a **Summary Options** box from which we can select the detail footer options.

Because the report output does not require additional sorting levels, leave the sorting options in Figure 7.18 blank. However, the **Summary Options** box in Figure 7.18 provides a powerful and flexible way to add detailed activity summaries to any report. Therefore, click on it to generate the dialog box in Figure 7.19 to let you select the detail footer and report footer options.

As you examine the field selections in Figure 7.19, note that both the INV_SUB_TOTALS and the EMP_COM fields have been selected. (The Access Wizard selected these two fields, because they were the only numeric fields available for calculations after we decided to use the EMPLOYEE as the subgroup in Figure 7.16.) Note also that we have selected the **Sum** option to calculate the totals and subtotals for the selected fields. The **Show** option indicates that the **Detail and**

FIGURE 7.18
Available Sorting and Summary Options

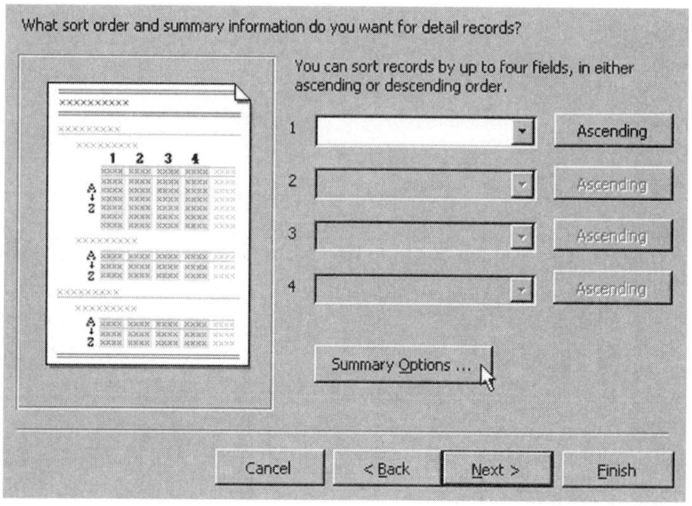

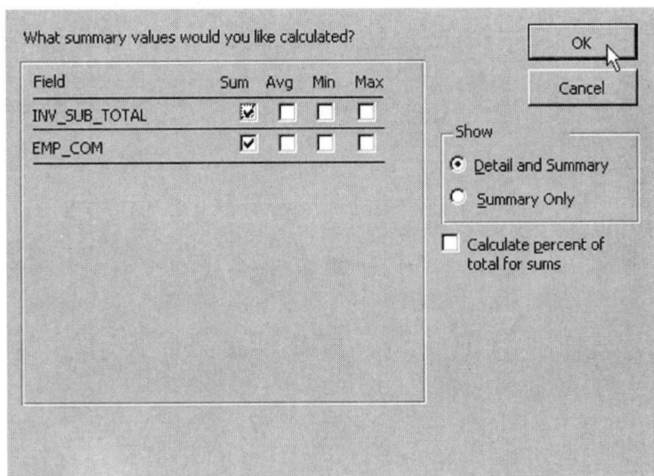

FIGURE 7.19
The Summary Options Selection

Summary selection has been made to ensure that both the subtotals (detail footer) and grand total (report footer) will be calculated and placed in the correct report section.

After making the selections shown in Figure 7.19, click on the **OK** button to return to the dialog box in Figure 7.18. Select the **Next** > button in Figure 7.18 to open the dialog box in Figure 7.20.

Figure 7.20 shows that we've selected the **Stepped** layout option to offset the subheader, thus making it more prominent. (After you've completed and saved the report, repeat the process and select the other layout options to see what their effects are on the report's presentation format.) We've also selected the **Portrait** option to print the report in a vertical format. (The **Landscape** option prints the report sideways. This option provides greater report width. However, the standard report presentation is the vertical [portrait] format, so that's the one you'll usually use.)

After making the selections shown in Figure 7.20, click on the **Next** > button to move to the dialog box in Figure 7.21.

You may select the default **Corporate** text format selection or any of the listed styles. (You can always change the text format later, using any of the design tools you learned about in the preceding chapters!) In this case, leave the style selection as it is and then click on the **Next** > button to generate the dialog box in Figure 7.22.

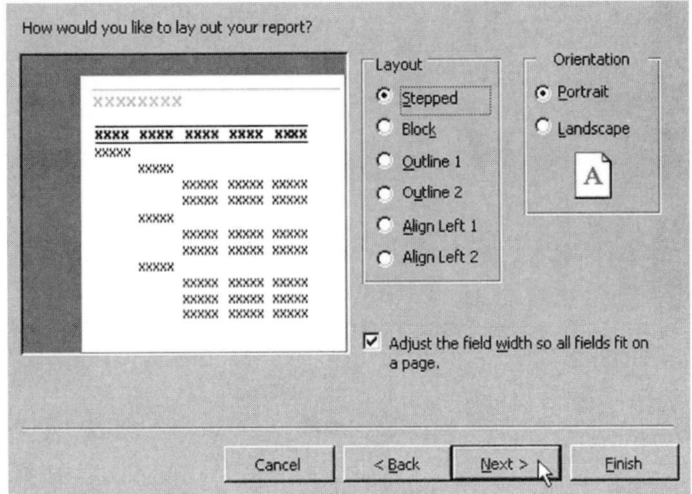

FIGURE 7.20
Report Configuration (Layout) Options

FIGURE 7.21
Report Print Style Options

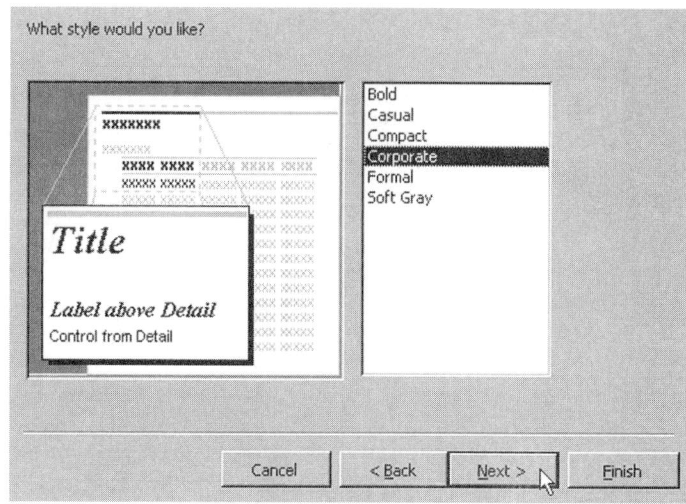

Figure 7.22's dialog box allows you to enter the report title. Note that the default title is **EMPLOYEE**, to reflect that this report is created to produce a sales report based on the EMPLOYEE subgroup selection we made in Figure 7.16.

Actually, the title entry in Figure 7.22 seems to be mislabeled. You might think that the entry asking for a report title would merely generate the report header. Instead, your entry creates the report header and it also identifies the report *name*. Therefore, type in the report name **rptEmployeeSales** to reflect its data source, the query named **qryEmployeeSales**. (We will edit the header later.) After entering the report name, click on the **Finish** button in Figure 7.22 to see the report output in Figure 7.23 and to save the report.

Because the report shown in Figure 7.23 leaves much to be desired in terms of both content and presentation format, place it in the design view shown in Figure 7.24 to begin the modification process.

Although the initial report output in Figure 7.23 is already superior to the unformatted query output, this first effort is not likely to fit your precise specifications. For example, if the report layout requirements must match those of Figure 7.12's report presentation, the format must be tweaked to yield a report that matches the desired layout. Such cleanup work is simple enough. Just open the report in its design view and then use the toolbox to produce the labels and text boxes that hold Figure 7.12's report header and other text details. You can also

FIGURE 7.22
The Report Title Option

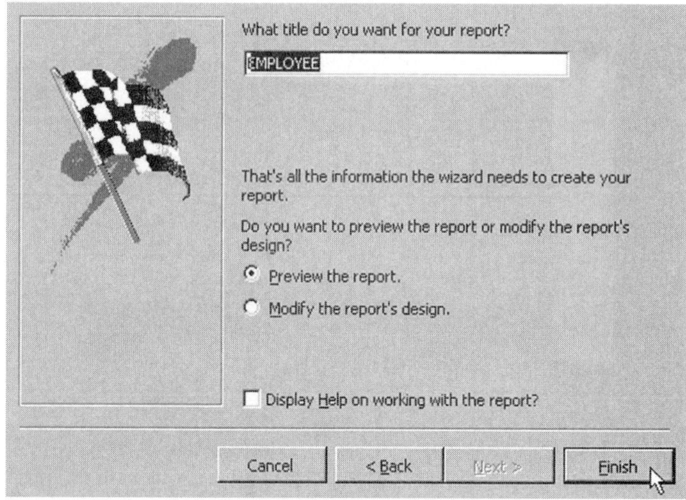

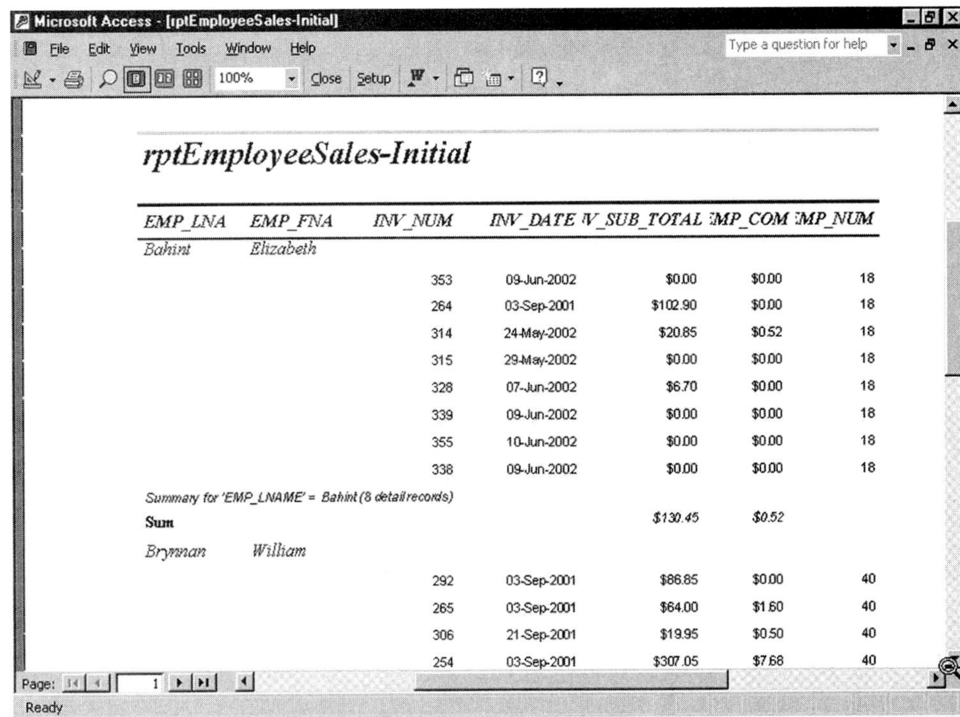

FIGURE 7.23
The Initial Report Output

edit the existing labels, move the text boxes and labels around to produce the appropriate spacing, and so on. If, for some reason, you want to change the data source, click outside the report's borders to bring up the report properties box and make the change. In short, all the tools you used to produce forms work just as well on reports.

Go ahead and make the changes in Figure 7.24's report structure to produce the output originally presented in Figure 7.12. When you are done, your report

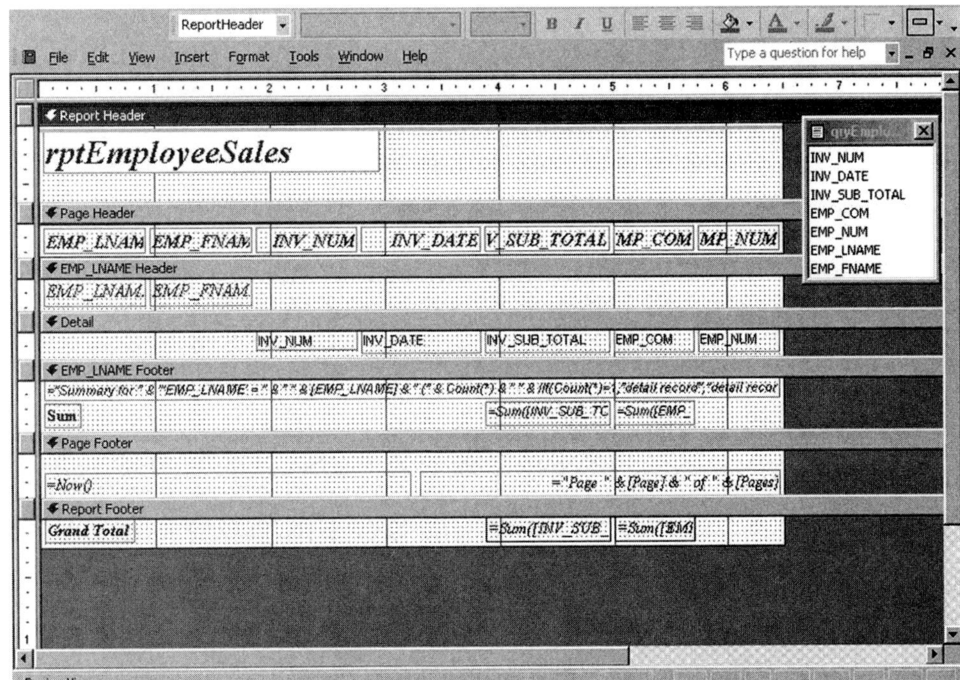

FIGURE 7.24
The Employee Sales Report in Design View

FIGURE 7.25
The Edited Report Structure

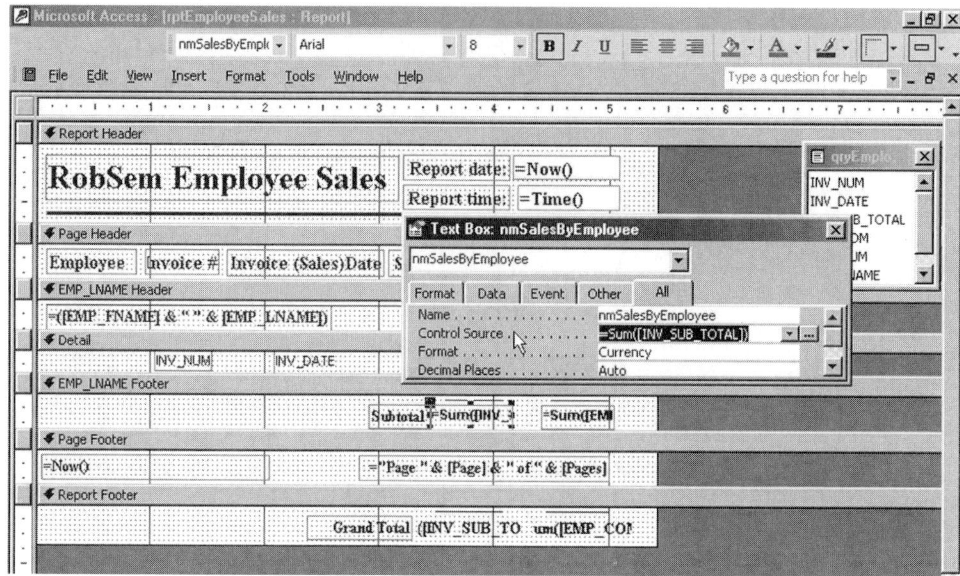

structure will match the one shown in Figure 7.25. (Note that the =**Now()** and =**Time()** text boxes can be "borrowed" from the report structure we showed you in Figure 7.11. You can always copy and paste labels and then edit them to suit your requirements. The **Edit/Copy/Paste** routines are always handy.)

As you examine Figure 7.25, note that we have generated the properties box for the first subtotal. Although Access automatically produced the subtotal and total functions, take a look at their structure. For example, the subtotals for the invoice amounts and for the employee commissions are calculated by
=**Sum([INV_SUB_TOTAL])**
and
=**Sum([EMP_COM])**.

The grand totals for the invoice amounts and for the employee commissions are computed by the same functions. The only difference between the subtotals and grand totals is their placement. The =**Sum()** functions produced subtotals when they were placed in the EMP_LNAME footer, but they produced grand totals when they were placed in the report footer. (The EMP_LNAME footer was created by Access when we decided to use the EMPLOYEE as the subgroup.) Knowing how the components work will help you edit existing reports and it will help you create complex customized reports. So take a good look at how Access generated the various components and see if you can generate a few reports from scratch. Finally, we need to give you a reminder to name the text boxes so that you will be able to distinguish between a textbox name and a text box control when you use various application builders. Note that we have named the textbox **nmSalesByEmployee.**

7.3 REPORTS BASED ON CROSSTAB QUERIES

Crosstab queries are wonderful tools that provide very useful summary results. Unfortunately, if you select row totals in the crosstab query, you cannot also select column totals, thus limiting the summarizing capability. You can overcome this limitation by using the crosstab query as the data source for a report. You can then create a report footer in which you use the **Sum()** function to generate the appropriate column totals. In addition, the report will provide the advantage of making the output conform to your presentation standards, rather than those imposed by the Access query layout.

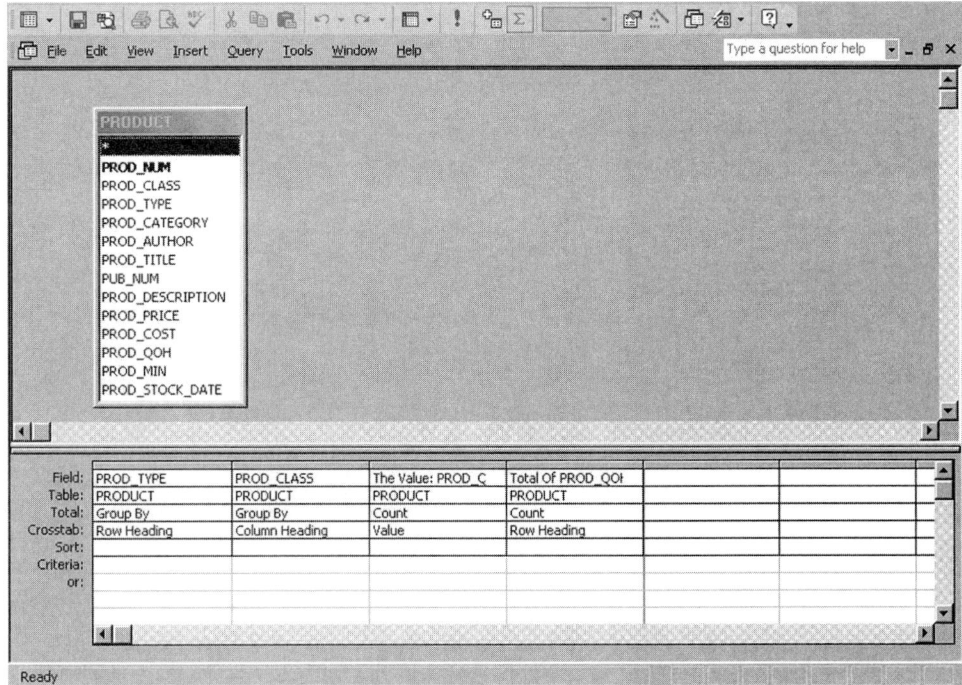

FIGURE 7.26
The Crosstab Query Structure

To demonstrate how such a summary report can be produced, use the Report Wizard exactly as you did in the preceding section. In this case, we'll use the query named **qryProductClassVsProductType** shown in Figure 7.26 as the report's data source. The query's output is shown in Figure 7.27. (If necessary, review section 5.3 in Chapter 5.)

As you examine Figure 7.27, note that the **Total Units** values are row totals that are found by adding the units for each product type: aircraft, cars, and ships. For example, the 84 units of the aircraft product type included 39 aircraft books, 17 aircraft CDs, 21 aircraft models, and 7 aircraft videos. However, the crosstab query cannot produce the column totals to answer a question such as How many books do we have in the inventory? It would be very helpful if we could generate an answer to that question (39 aircraft books + 5 car books + 4 ship books = 48 books) by letting the computer do the addition. Although the crosstab query cannot provide row and column totals simultaneously, we can generate the desired results through a report. We'll show how that job is accomplished in this section, using the basic crosstab query shown in Figure 7.26 as the report's data source.

The following report, to be named **rptProductClassVsProductType** to reflect the name of the crosstab query that helps produce its output, will be able to show that the inventory contains 48 books, 25 CDs, 29 models, and 26 videos. Create the report's basic structure exactly as you did in the preceding section. That is, use the Report Wizard and then select the **qryProductClassVsProductType** as the data source. Use all fields and then select the defaults for all the remaining dialog boxes. In other words, do not add grouping levels, do not select a sort order, leave the Tabular/Landscape presentation selection, and so on. When you

FIGURE 7.27
The Crosstab Query Output

File Edit View Insert Format Records Tools Window Help

Product Type	Total Units	Book	CD	Model	Video
Aircraft	84	39	17	21	7
Cars	22	5		4	13
Ships	22	4	8	4	6

FIGURE 7.28
The Initial Crosstab Report Output

rptProductClassVsProductType

Product Type	*Total Units*	*Book*	*CD*	*Model*	*Video*
Aircraft	84	39	17	21	7
Cars	22	5		4	13
Ships	22	4	8	4	6

are done, save the new report using the name we suggested earlier. That is, name the report **rptProductClassVsProductType**. The report output, shown in Figure 7.28, reflects Figure 7.27's crosstab query output precisely. (We'll modify the report to add column totals later.)

To add the column totals to the report output, begin by placing the report in the design view shown in Figure 7.29.

To add the column totals to the report structure shown in Figure 7.29, follow these steps:

1. Drag the report footer's edge down to make the report footer space.
2. Select the detail components named **Total Of PROD_QOH**, **Book**, **CD**, **Model**, and **Video**; then select **Edit/Copy**. (Note that the properties box shown in Figure 7.29 reflects the control source for the **Total Of PROD_QOH** text box.)
3. Place the cursor in the new footer space; then select **Edit/Paste** to place the detail components in the report footer.
4. Select each of the text boxes you just copied into the report footer and modify each by using the Sum function. In other words, the text box marked *CD* becomes =**Sum([CD])**, *Model* becomes =**Sum([Model])**, and so on.
5. Use the **View** button at the top of the screen to switch back and forth between the **Design View** and the **Print Preview** options to see the effect of each change.
6. Drag the new report footer text boxes to line them up with the detail line output.

That's it: The column totals will now be part of your report. All that's left now is the final cosmetic changes, so change the report header and other components to match the revised report structure shown in Figure 7.30.

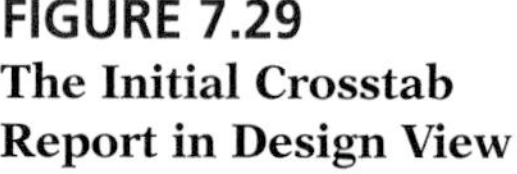

FIGURE 7.29
The Initial Crosstab Report in Design View

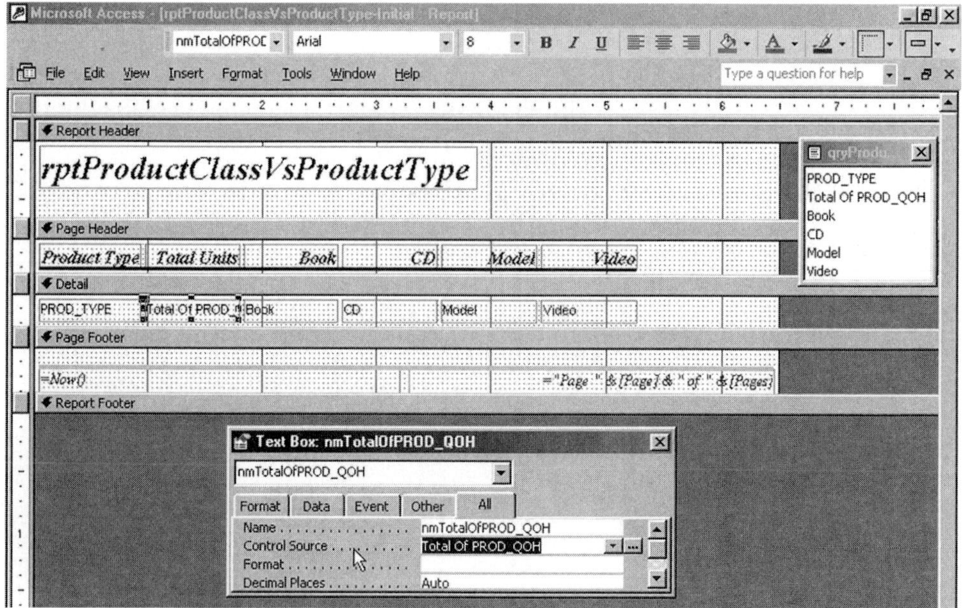

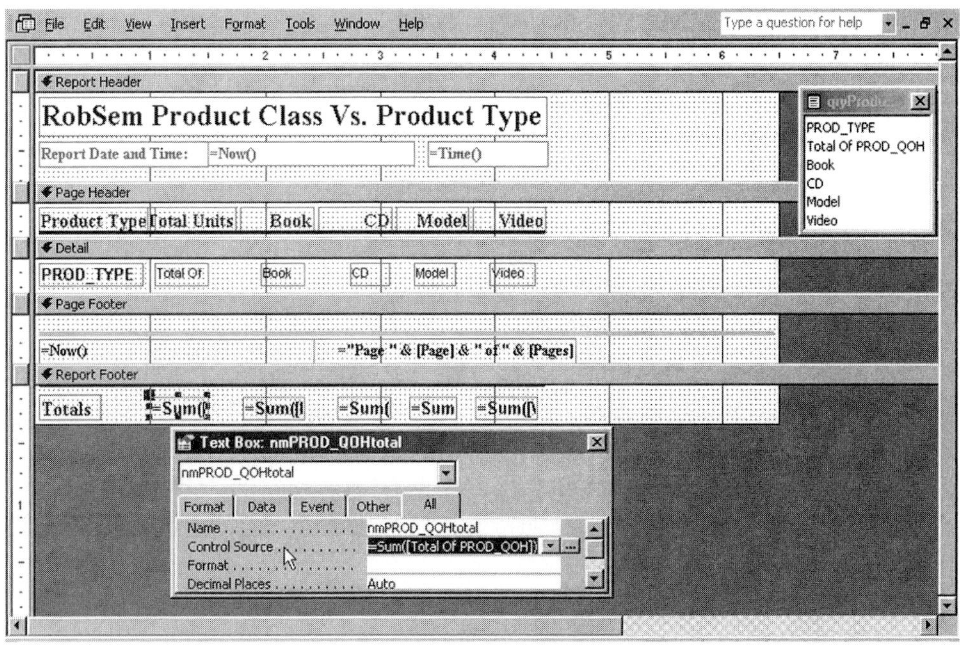

FIGURE 7.30
The Modified Crosstab Report Structure

Figure 7.31 shows the output from the crosstab-based report shown in Figure 7.30. Note that we have modified font sizes, changed spacing, and added lines to segment the report's output components.

7.4 USING REPORT GRAPHICS

Access makes it easy to add graphics to a report. All you need is a data source, which is usually a select query, and the Access Chart Wizard will handle the rest. To demonstrate the process, we'll add a bar chart in the header of Figure 7.31's report. The bar chart will show the column totals for Book, CD, Model, and Video.

Because the Chart Wizard works best with a select query, let's first create one to count the PRODUCT table's product types (PROD_TYPE = Aircraft, Ships, Cars) by their product class (PROD_CLASS = Book, Video, CD, Model). Therefore, the query design in Figure 7.32 reflects that we have grouped the products by their class and counted them within each product class by type. (Go ahead and create this query now. Name the query **qryCountOfProductTypeByClass** and

FIGURE 7.31
The Modified Crosstab Report Output

Microsoft Access - [Product Class Vs. Product Type]

File Edit View Tools Window Help

100% Close Setup

RobSem Product Class Vs. Product Type

Report Date and Time: 16-Aug-2002 11:52:33 AM

Product Type	Total Units	Book	CD	Model	Video
Aircraft	84	39	17	21	7
Cars	22	5		4	13
Ships	22	4	8	4	6
Totals	128	48	25	29	26

FIGURE 7.32
The Product Type Count by Class in Design View

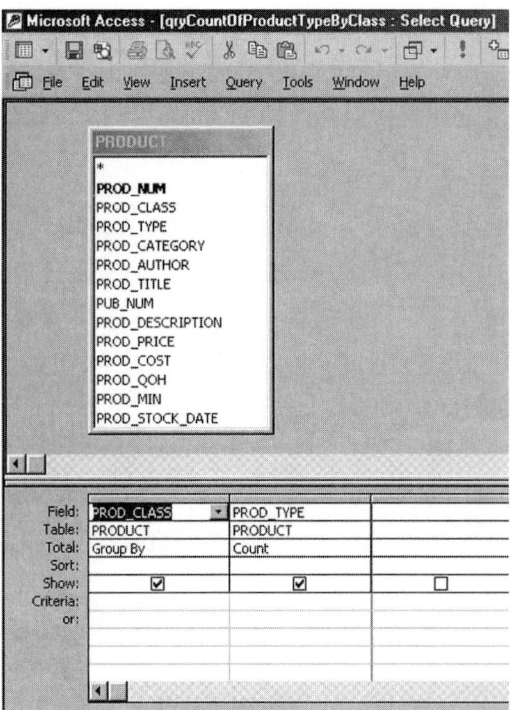

save it.) The query output is shown in Figure 7.33. Note that this output reflects the crosstab report summary results depicted in Figure 7.31.

The query structure shown in Figure 7.32 will be the data source for the graphics we'll insert into Figure 7.31's report header.

After creating the data source for the report graphics, open the **rptProduct ClassVsProductType** crosstab report in the design view that was shown in Figure 7.30. Drag the report's header space wider to make sure you have room to insert the graphics. After creating the necessary space, click on the **Insert** button located on the button bar at the top of the screen to produce the menu choices shown in Figure 7.34.

Click on **Chart** option shown in Figure 7.34 and then draw the chart space in the report header. As soon as you release the mouse button, the Chart Wizard will show up on your screen, as shown in Figure 7.35.

As you examine Figure 7.35, note that we selected the **Queries** option, because we will use the query named **qryCountOfProductTypeByClass** to serve as the graphics source. It's useful to remember that the graphics data sources are limited to tables and/or queries. We cannot use the report's column totals because those totals were created by the report, rather than by a query. And that's why we created the **qryCountOfProductTypeByClass** in the first place.

Before you click on the **Next** > button in Figure 7.35 to continue the chart-making sequence, you must have a clear idea about what the chart is expected to show and how the chart must show it. Therefore, define these parameters:

FIGURE 7.33
The Product Type Count by Class in Data Sheet View

Microsoft Access - [qryCountOfProductTypeByClass : Select Query]
File Edit View Insert Format Records Tools Window Help

PROD_CLASS	CountOfPROD_TYPE
Book	48
CD	25
Model	29
Video	26

FIGURE 7.34
Selecting the Chart Option from the Insert Menu

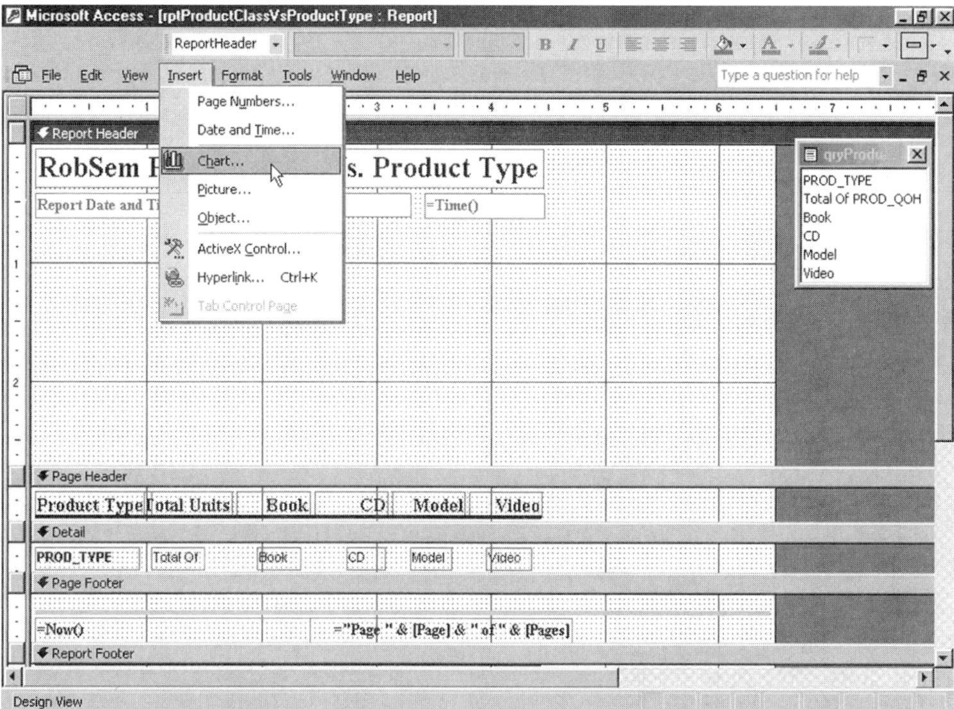

- Chart type: Bar chart.
- Chart Orientation: Sideways. (Remember, we opened a space for the chart in the report header, so it's a good idea to save some vertical space. This orientation allows us to show greater chart detail in less vertical space.)
- Chart X and Y axes: The X axis must show product *class* (Video, Model, CD, and Book), and the Y axis must show the count. Remember that the chart will be shown *sideways*, so the X and Y axes are located, respectively, at the left and bottom margins. Therefore, the expected graph output might look like Figure 7.36.

Now that you know what you want the graph to look like, go ahead and click on the **Next** > button shown in Figure 7.35. This action will open the next **Chart Wizard** dialog box, shown in Figure 7.37.

FIGURE 7.35
The Chart Wizard's Opening Screen

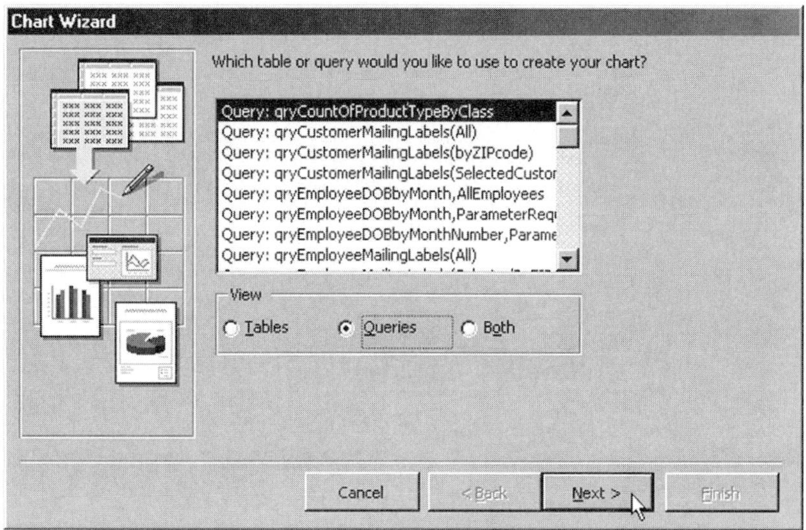

Note

If the Chart Wizard was not installed during the original Access installation process, you will see the message shown in Figure 7.35A. If you select **Yes** from the message box, Access will install the required components, *but you must have the original Office XP Professional CD available*. If you elect the **No** response, you will not be able to use the Chart Wizard to produce the graphics illustrated in this section.

FIGURE 7.35A Missing Chart Wizard Message

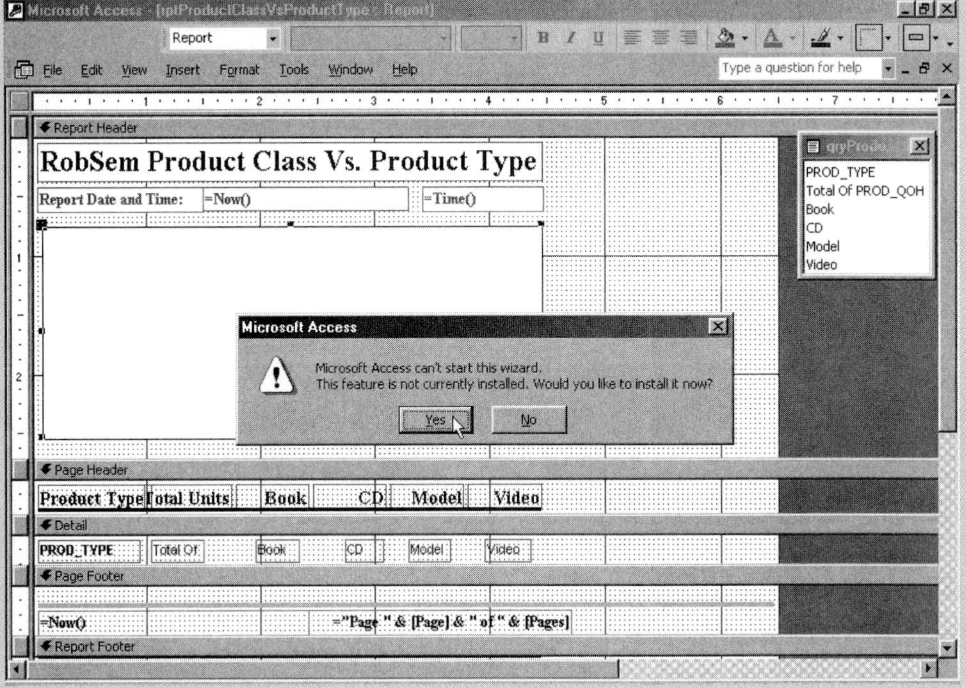

Because you'll need both the **PROD_CLASS** and the **CountOfPROD_TYPE** in your chart, click on the >> button shown in Figure 7.37 to move both fields to the **Fields for Chart:** box. Then click on the **Next** > button to open the dialog box shown in Figure 7.38.

Note that Figure 7.38 shows the sideways bar chart selection that matches the planned presentation layout shown in Figure 7.36. After making this selection, click on the **Next** > button to move to the dialog box in Figure 7.39.

Before moving on to the next dialog box, click on the **Preview Chart** button in Figure 7.39 to see what the chart will look like. Figure 7.40 shows the preview.

FIGURE 7.36 The Expected Graph Layout

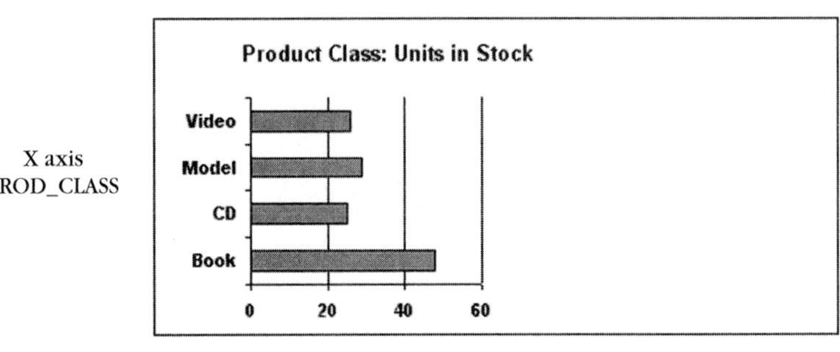

FIGURE 7.37
Field Selection

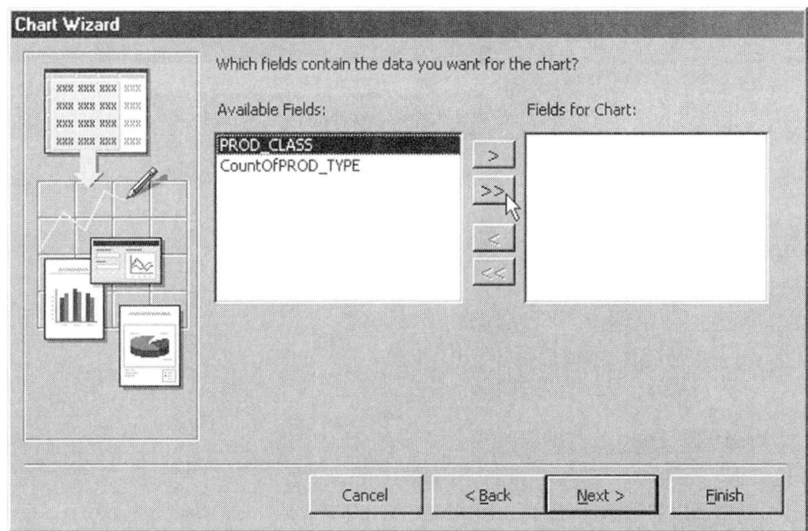

FIGURE 7.38
Selecting the Chart Type

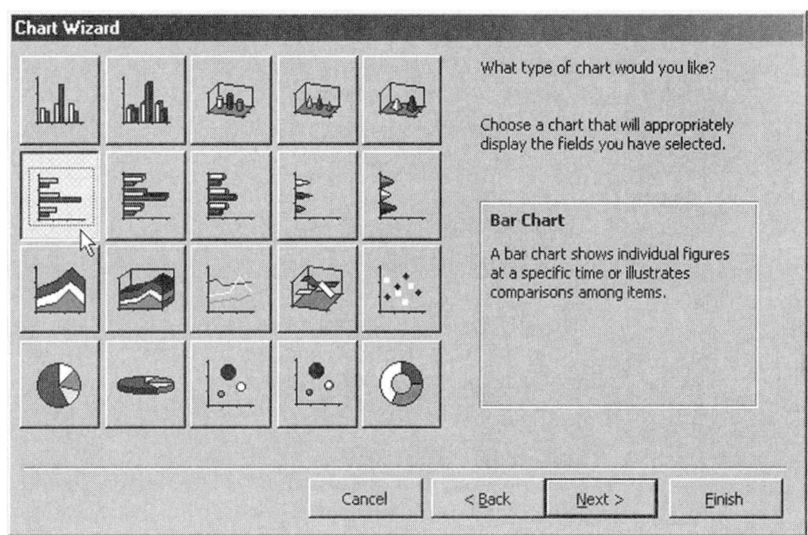

FIGURE 7.39
The Chart Data Layout

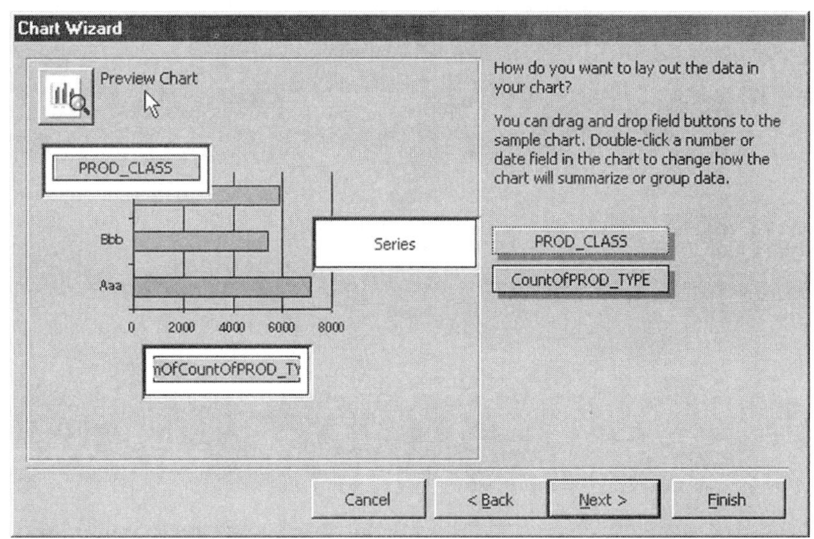

FIGURE 7.40
The Preview

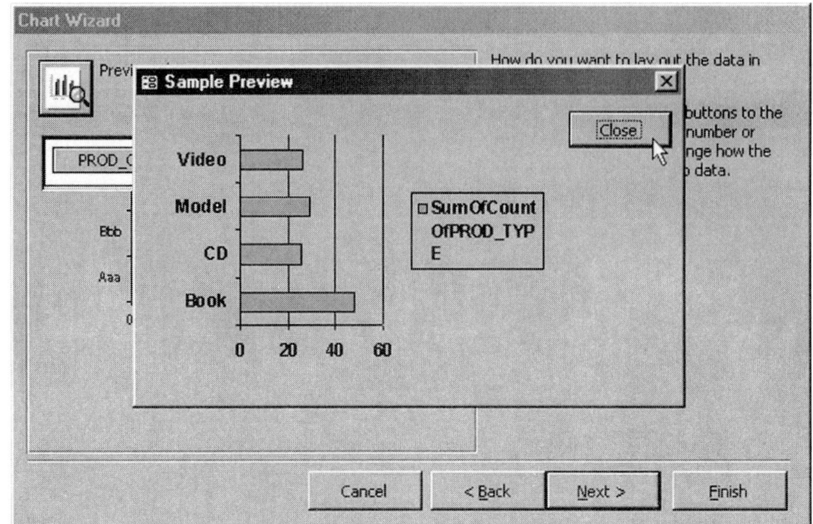

If you are satisfied that the preview matches your expectations, close it and then click on the **Next** > button to move to the dialog box in Figure 7.41. If you don't like the preview layout, click on the < **Back** button to return to the preceding dialog box. You can click on each dialog box's < **Back** button until you arrive at the dialog box that will enable you to make the necessary changes. For example, you may want to return to the dialog box in Figure 7.38 to select a different presentation style.

In this case, you do not want to use the option shown in Figure 7.41 to link the fields. (If you do, you'll get a different bar for each link.) Therefore, delete the report field's **TotalOfPROD_QOH**. After deleting this field, click on the **Next** > button to open Figure 7.42's dialog box to select the chart title.

Because the product class titles are already part of the query output, the use of a legend is redundant in Figure 7.42. So we have clicked on the **No, don't display a legend** option. Also, you will note that the chart title in Figure 7.42 defaults to the query name. Remember that in this example the chart is based on the query in Figure 7.32, named **qryCountOfProductTypeByClass**. And because the query name does not make a proper title header, replace it by typing **ProductClass: Units in Stock**. After typing the replacement title, click on the **Next** > button in Figure 7.42 to open the report's design view shown in Figure 7.43.

FIGURE 7.41
Linking Chart and Report Fields

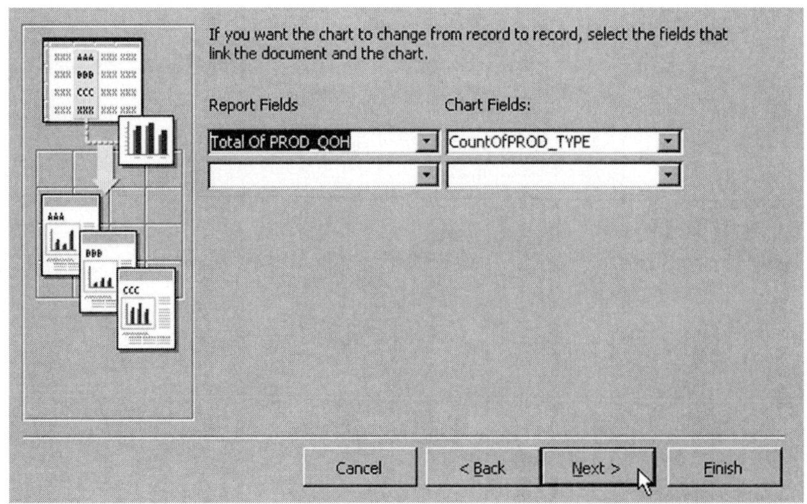

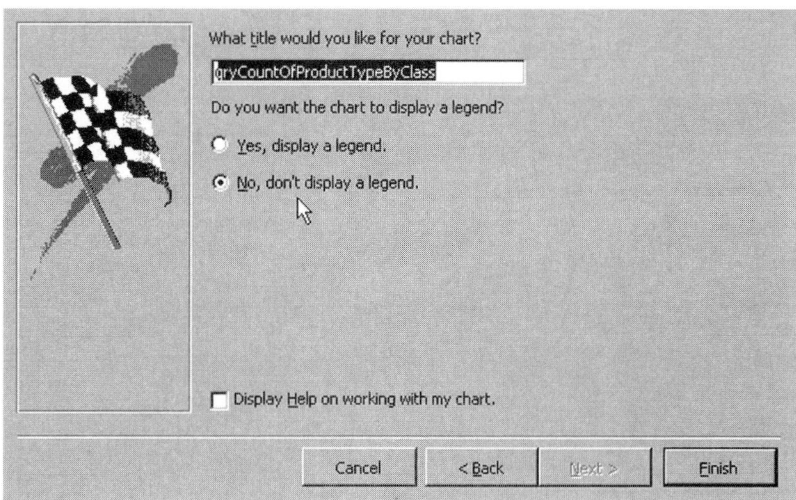

FIGURE 7.42
Selecting the Chart Title

As you examine Figure 7.43, you may be disappointed that the chart object doesn't look like the one you planned in Figure 7.36. That's because Access places a generic chart layout in the object box. If you select the report's **Print Preview** option, you'll see the planned output properly presented in Figure 7.44.

7.4.1 Editing the Report Graphics

You can return the report to its design view to drag the chart object's limits to line them up with the rest of the report output, as we have done. You can also edit the chart object by clicking on it and then clicking the right mouse button to select **Chart Object** to produce the **Edit** menu shown in Figure 7.45.

Using the **Edit** option shown in Figure 7.45 will produce Figure 7.46. As you examine Figure 7.46, note that we have clicked on the title label. You can use the standard editing functions to modify the **Chart Object**. Go ahead and experiment with them now.

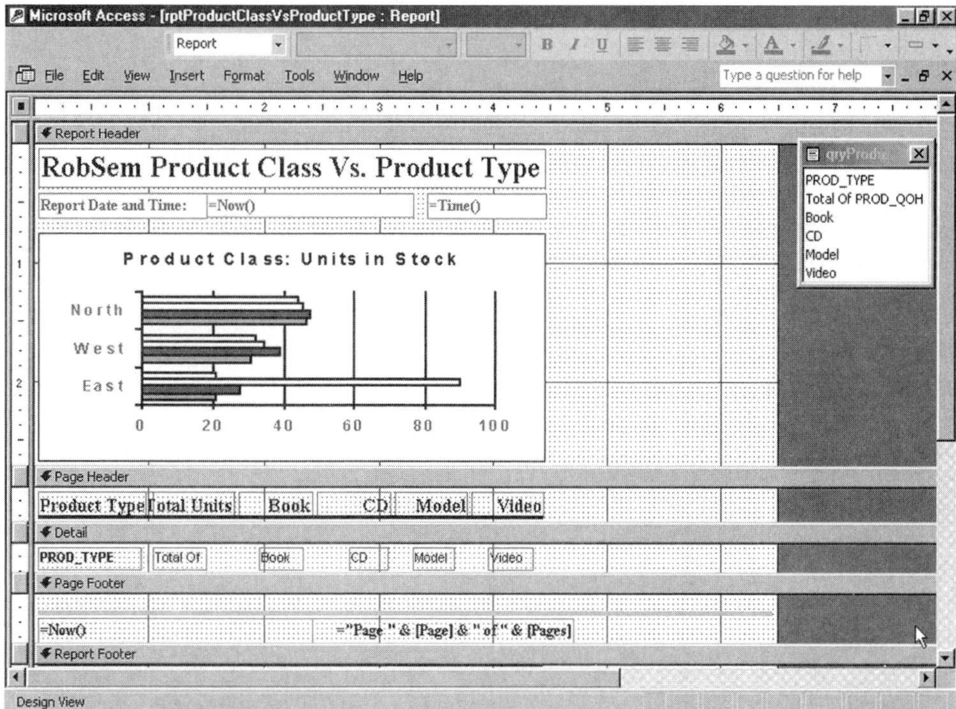

FIGURE 7.43
The Chart Object Box in the Report's Design View

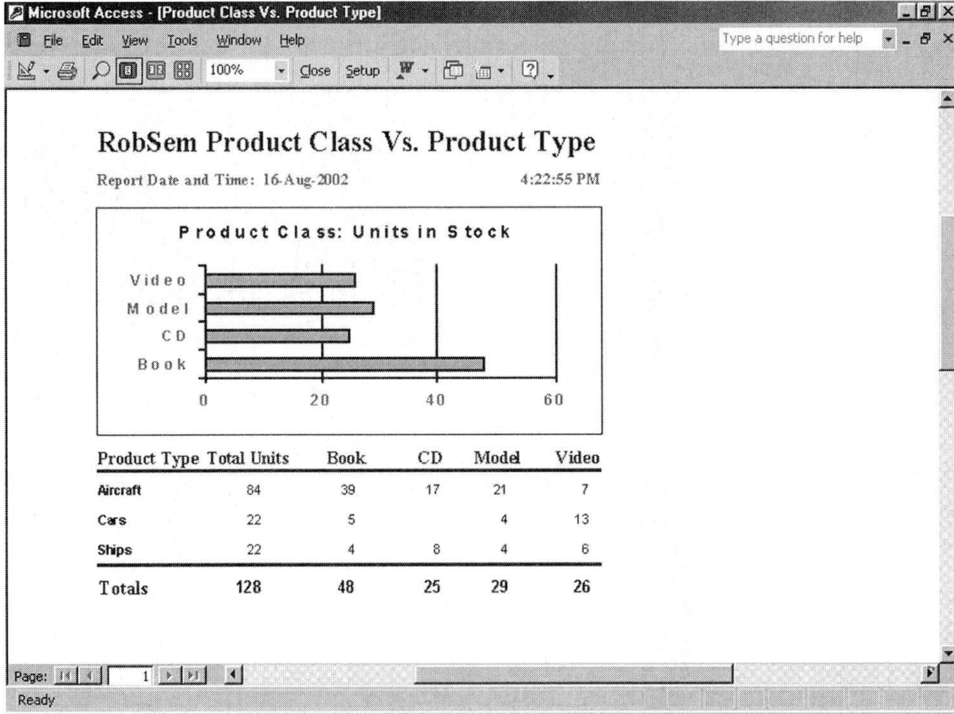

FIGURE 7.44 The Chart in the Report Header

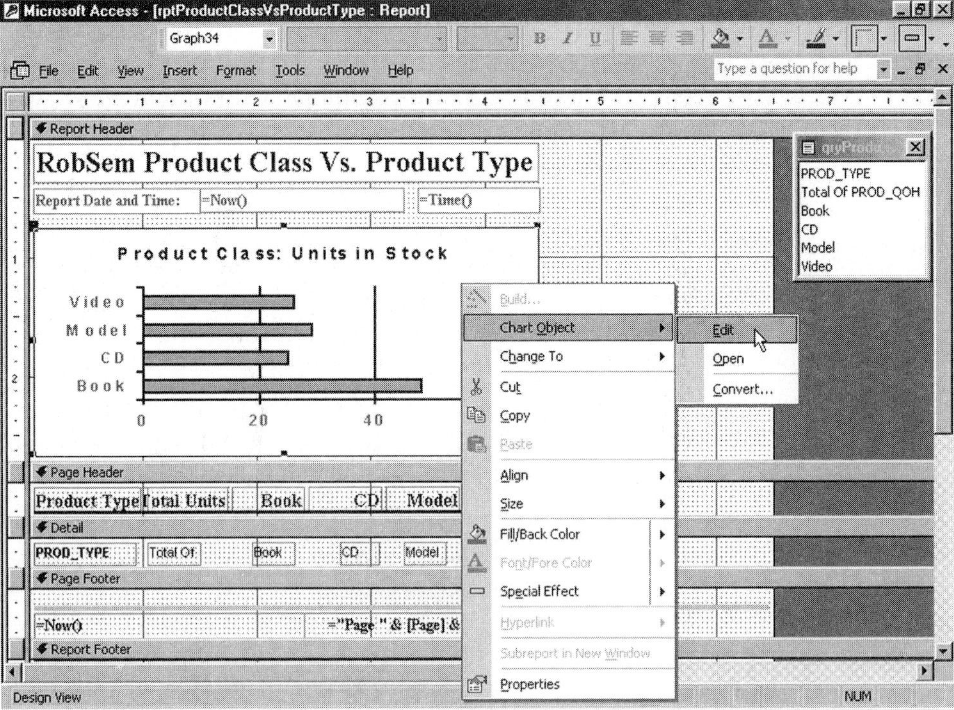

FIGURE 7.45 Generating the Chart Edit Menu

7.5 MAILING LABELS

Like paper clips and Post-it notes, mailing labels are very handy and, yes, they are taken for granted. Yet many daily business activities require frequent use of mailing labels. Just think of the RobSem Company's use of them. Products must be shipped, products must be ordered, vendors must be paid, customers must re-

FIGURE 7.46
The Chart Object in Edit Format

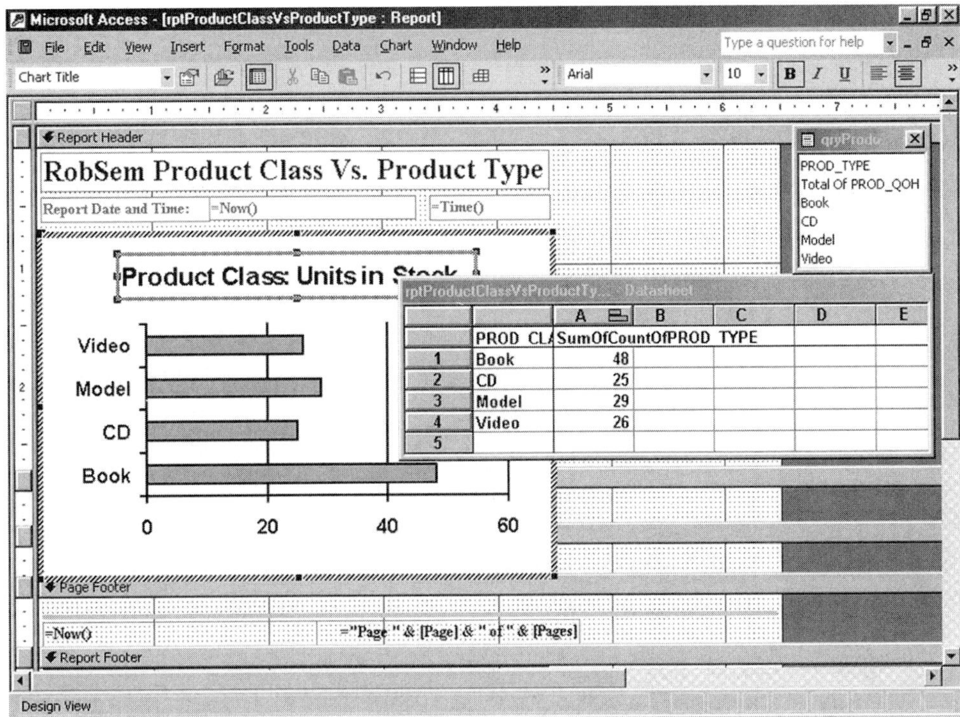

ceive notification of new products and/or special sales, employee notices must be mailed out periodically, and so on. Although most of these activities are now accomplished via the Web, the so-called snail mail still keeps the postal service busy. In any case, book, model, and similar product shipments cannot be done via the Web, so package mailing labels will remain an important applications development item for end users.

As common as mailing labels are, it's not surprising that Access has a special wizard for them. The Label Wizard is contained within the Report segment of the Access database application development software.

To create a mailing-label program, start at the database window's report folder and click on the **New** button to produce the **New Report** dialog box in Figure 7.47.

FIGURE 7.47
The Mailing Label's First Dialog Box

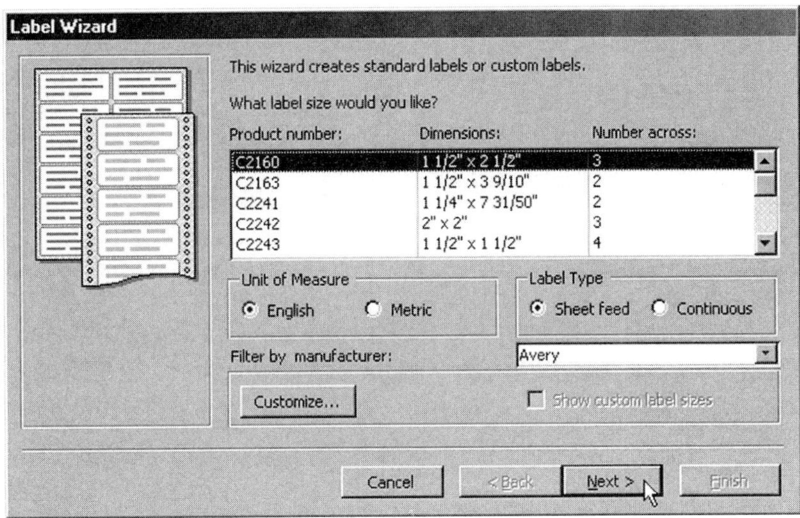

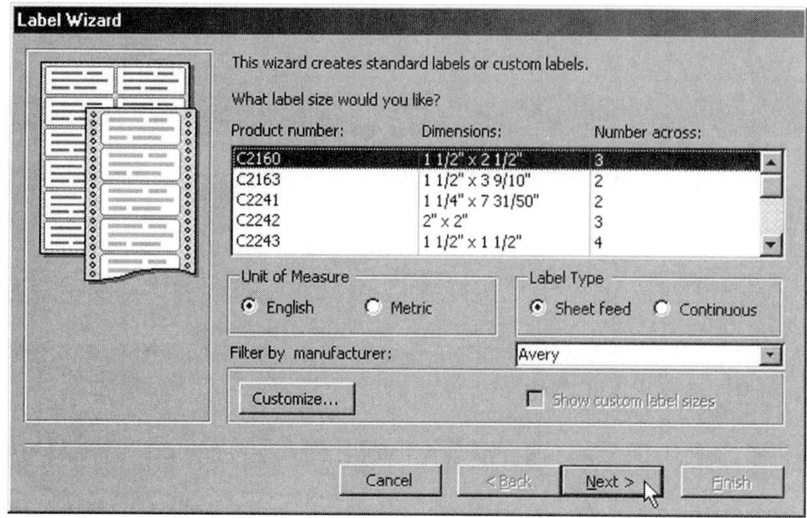

FIGURE 7.48
Label Type Selection

The mailing-label "report" requires a data source, so select one from the **New Report** dialog box. Because you will be creating the mailing labels for the Rob-Sem Company employees, select the **EMPLOYEE** table, make sure that **Label Wizard** is selected, and then click the **OK** button. This action produces the **Label Wizard** dialog box shown in Figure 7.48).

As you can tell by looking at the dialog box in Figure 7.48, many options are available. You may choose label dimensions, the number of labels printed across a page, label type, and so on. You can even customize the labels via this dialog box. And even this array of choices is expanded in the next dialog box, shown in Figure 7.49, generated by clicking the **Next** > button in Figure 7.48.

We'll select the default font shown in Figure 7.49, and we'll continue the mailing-label creation process by clicking the **Next** > button to generate the dialog box in Figure 7.50.

To transfer the fields from the **Available fields:** box to the **Prototype label:** box shown in Figure 7.50, click on each field to be transferred and then click on the > button to make the transfer. (You can also transfer a field from the **Available fields:** box to the **Prototype label:** box by double-clicking on it.) To complete the label's first line, you will need to transfer the EMP_TITLE, EMP_FNAME, EMP_INITIAL, and EMP_LNAME, *in that order*. When you have

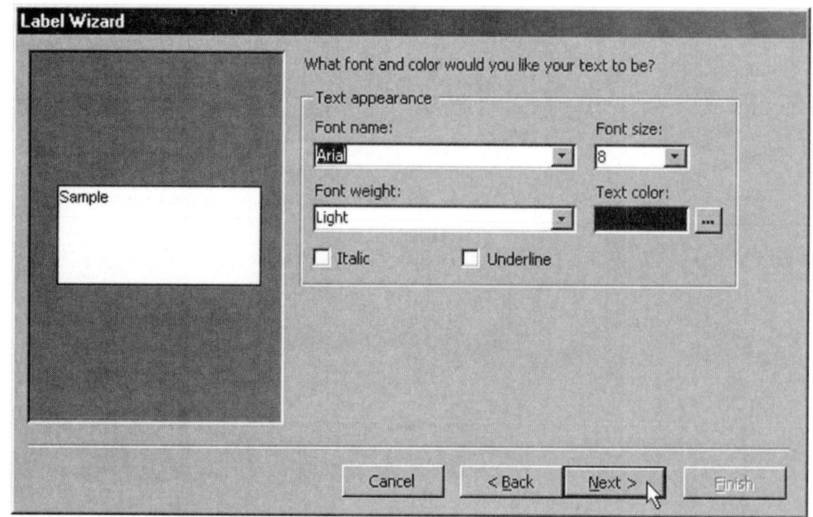

FIGURE 7.49
Selecting the Label Font

FIGURE 7.50
Selecting the Label Contents

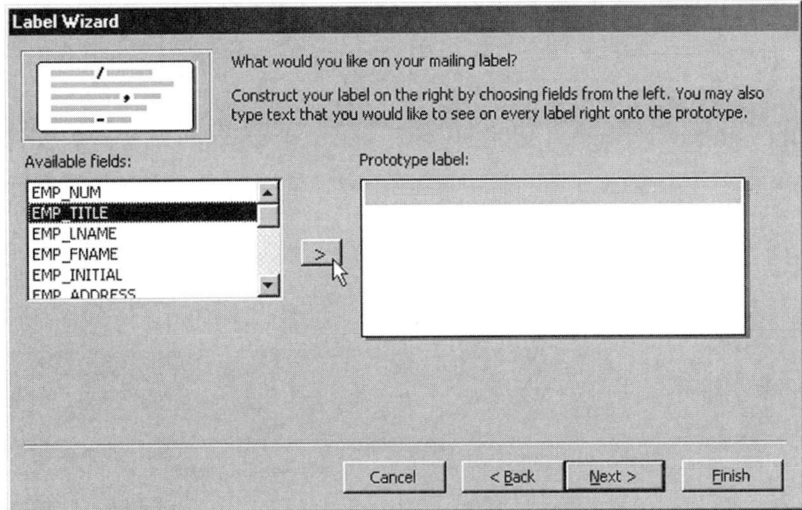

completed the first label line, use the keyboard's Enter key or the keyboard's ↓ key to move to the next label line, then transfer the EMP_ADDRESS field from the **Available fields:** box to the **Prototype label:** box. Finally, move to the third label line and transfer the EMP_CITY, EMP_STATE, and EMP_ZIPCODE to this third line. When you have transferred the fields, the screen should look like Figure 7.51. (Naturally, the longer first line has scrolled, so its contents are not shown in their entirety.)

When you have completed the label line entries shown in Figure 7.51, click on the **Next** > button to see the dialog box in Figure 7.52. To make it easier to find a given label in a large label output, we've made sure that the labels are sorted by last name, first name, and initial.

Click on the **Next** > button in Figure 7.52 to open the final Label Wizard dialog box, shown in Figure 7.53. The report name reflects the fact that the label output includes all employees. (Remember that Access Label Wizard resides in the *report* folder and that the label applications are treated as reports. Therefore, the **rpt** prefix is appropriate.) We have used the **(Initial)** name component to enable us to demonstrate the difference between the initial and edited label programs later.

FIGURE 7.51
The Completed Prototype Label

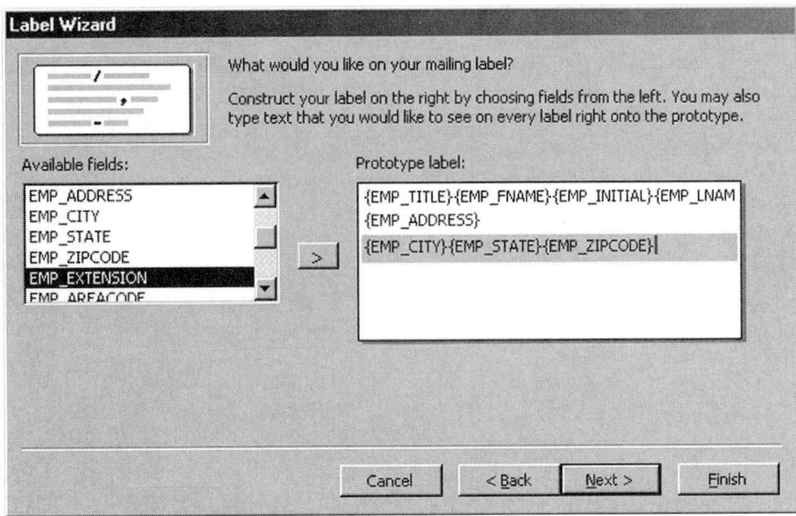

Note

The mailing labels can also be based on a query. For example, suppose you had created a query, named **qryEmployeeMailingLabel**, that contained the label fields. You could then have done the sorting at the query level. Therefore, if this query were used as the mailing label's data source, you could simply click on the **Next** > button in Figure 7.52 without having to select the sort fields shown here.

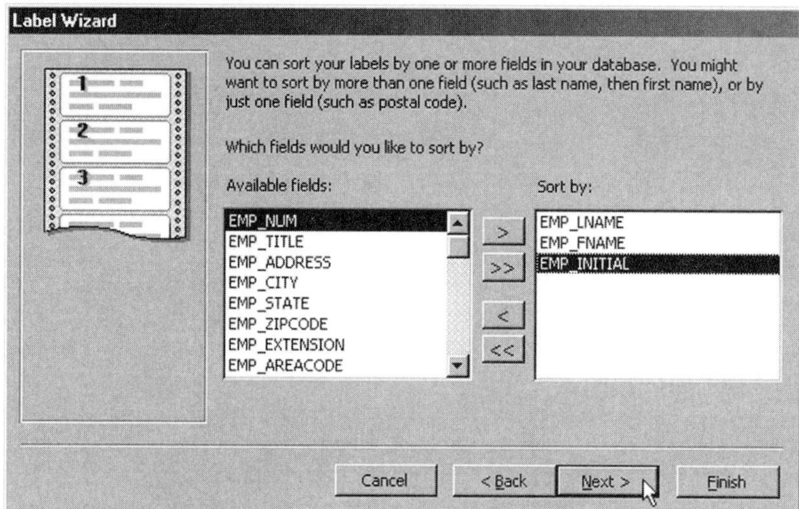

FIGURE 7.52
Sorting the Label Output

Click on the **Finish** button shown in Figure 7.53 to see the labels shown in Figure 7.54 on your screen. (Depending on the size of your screen, you may have to use the scroll bar to see the third label across.)

Although the labels shown in Figure 7.54 are serviceable, they don't measure up to high professional standards. For example, the field values are all pasted together, making them difficult to read. Fortunately, the mailing-label program is just a specialized report, so you can open it in its design format to make the desired changes.

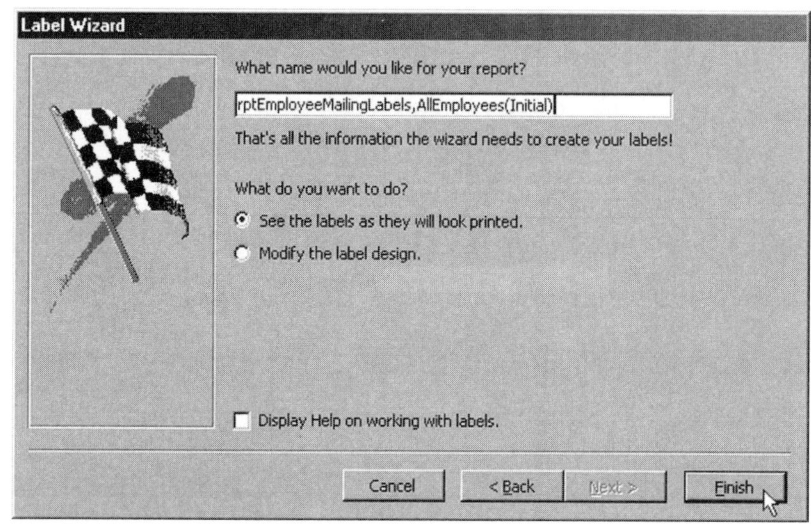

FIGURE 7.53
Selecting the Mailing Label Report Name

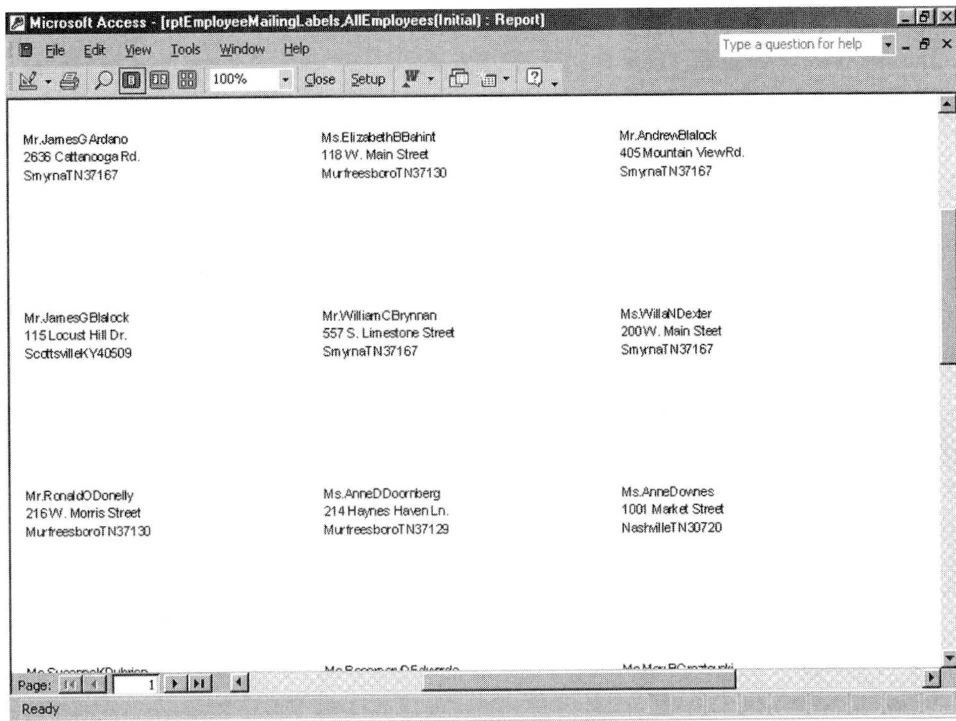

FIGURE 7.54
The Mailing Label Output

7.5.1 Modifying the Label Output Format

Before you modify the mailing-label report, think about how you want the fields to be spaced. Therefore, start by sketching the layout of a sample label that meets your requirements:

Mr. Xxxxxxxx Y. Zzzzzzzzzz
1234 Aaaaaaaa Street
Gggggggggg, UU 12345

Given the label layout, these features stand out:

- The first label line contains the fields EMP_TITLE, EMP_FNAME, EMP_INITIAL, and EMP_LNAME.
- To conform to the sample label layout, there must be a space after the title, a space after the first name, and a period and a space after the initial.
- Keep in mind that some employees do not have an initial, so you must use a logical condition to determine whether the initial needs to be printed and whether the period and the space have to be printed. (If you don't specify the logic that controls such conditions, an employee without an initial will have his or her first name printed, a space, a period, a space, and the last name.)
- The second label line contains only the EMP_ADDRESS. Therefore, there is no need for spacing between multiple fields, so this second line requires no modification.
- The label's third line contains the EMP_CITY, EMP_STATE, and EMP_ZIP-CODE. But there is a comma after the city name, followed by a space to separate the city name from the state. The two-character state code is followed by three spaces to make the ZIP code stand out.

Keep these layout requirements in mind as you make the changes in the label report.

To make the changes, open the mailing-label report in its design view. Once again, note that all the design tools and features used to modify the other reports

FIGURE 7.55
The Initial Mailing Label Report Design View

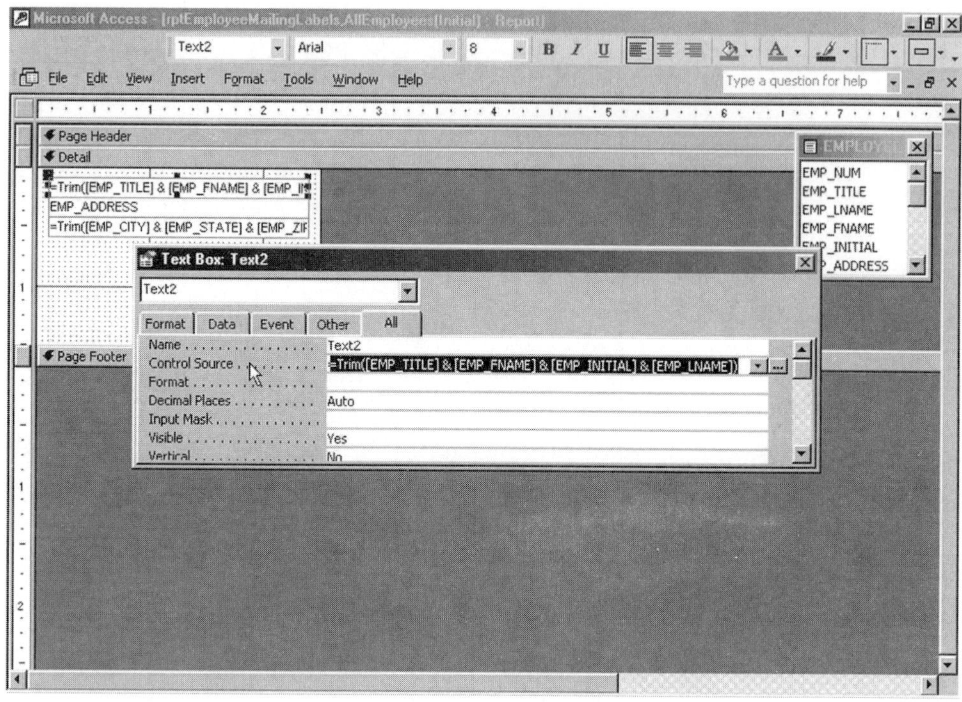

in this chapter work just as well on the mailing-label report! Your design view should look like Figure 7.55. (Note that we've clicked on the first label line to select it and that we've opened its properties box.)

Click on the **Control Source** builder button in the properties box to generate the **Expression Builder** shown in Figure 7.56.

As you examine the **Expression Builder** in Figure 7.56, note the following features:

- The **Trim** function is used to cut trailing blanks from the fields. This action allows us to control the exact placement of succeeding fields.
- You should recall that Access enclosed the fields in **{ }** when the label lines were created, yet it saved them as enclosed in **[ ]**. For example, when you originally placed the EMP_TITLE on the label's first line, it showed up as **{EMP_TITLE}**. Now you see that Access saved this entry with the familiar square brack-

FIGURE 7.56
The Expression Builder: First Mailing Label Line

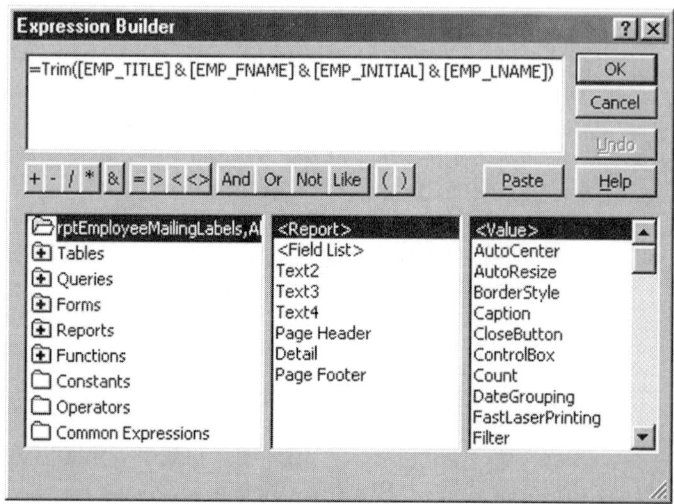

ets as **[EMP_TITLE].** That's just an Access quirk that has no bearing on the editing process.

- The ampersand (**&**) is used to add the line components. That is, the ampersand is used to concatenate the strings to produce the desired format.
- A space is a string entry created by tapping the keyboard's space bar. All strings that are not contained within fields as field values are enclosed in quotes. Therefore, adding a space between EMP_TITLE and EMP_FNAME requires the concatenation **[EMP_TITLE] & " " & [EMP_FNAME]**
- The logical condition follows this reasoning:

1. Check for a middle initial.
2. If—and only if—there is no middle initial, that is, EMP_INITIAL is null, a space must be inserted between the EMP_FNAME and the EMP_LNAME fields.
3. If the EMP_INITIAL is *not* null the EMP_INITIAL must be preceded by a space and followed by a space and a period and a space, and the EMP_LNAME.
4. The syntax that covers the logical requirements for points 2 and 3 is written as

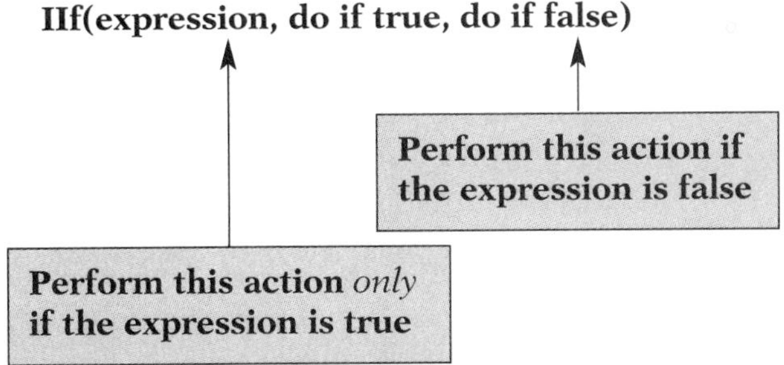

5. The combination of points 3 and 4 yields the "if and only if" statement

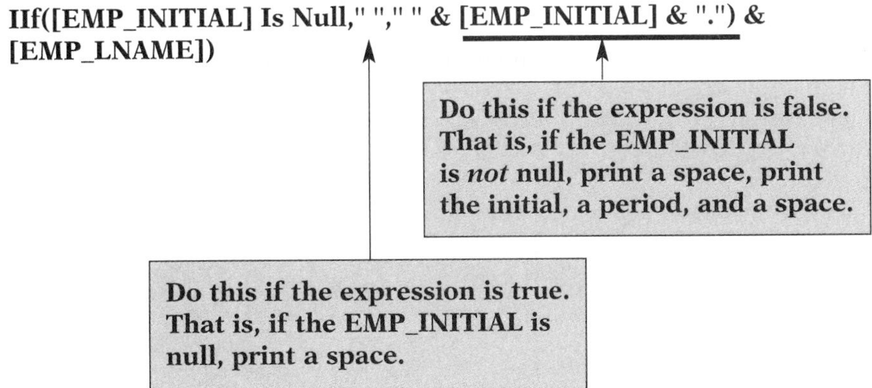

When you have completed the logical sequence, the Zoom listing for the first label line will look like Figure 7.57.

After editing the mailing label's first line, use the **Expression Builder** to edit the second line to read

```
=TRIM([EMP_ADDRESS])
```

and the third line to read

```
=TRIM([EMP_CITY] & ", " & [EMP_STATE] & " " & [EMP_ZIPCODE])
```

to make the labels more readable.

FIGURE 7.57
The Zoom Listing for the First Line Modification

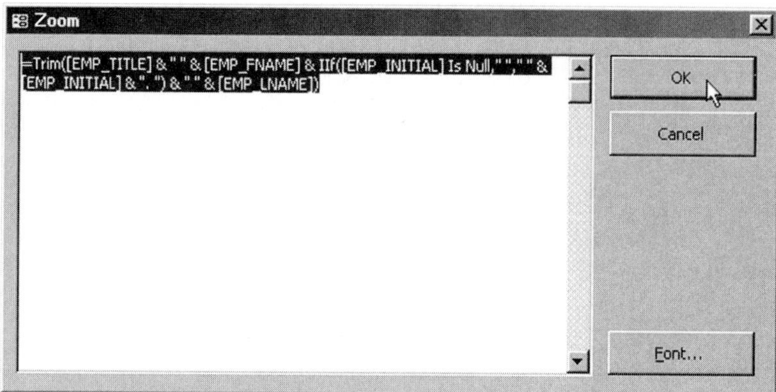

Make sure that you click **OK** when the Expression Builder's work is done, select the **Print Preview** option, and then remember to save the mailing-label report again. (But this time, use the **File/Save As** option to rename the modified report **rptEmployeeMailingLabels,AllEmployees** to distinguish the edited mailing label report from the **rptEmployeeMailingLabels,AllEmployees (Initial)** mailing label report. This action will enable you to compare the two versions later.

After you have saved the modified mailing label report, open it to see its labels. Figure 7.58 shows the completed label program output.

As you examine Figure 7.58's mailing-label output, note that we've scrolled the picture to the left to show that Mr. Andrew Blalock's label has, in fact, been printed correctly. That is, because Mr. Blalock does not have an initial, a space has been printed between the first and last names. The labels for employees with a middle initial show that the spaces were inserted properly and that the initial is followed by a period. With just a little effort, these labels broadcast the message that you carried the professional touch even when you had to deal with the

FIGURE 7.58
The Revised Mailing Label Output

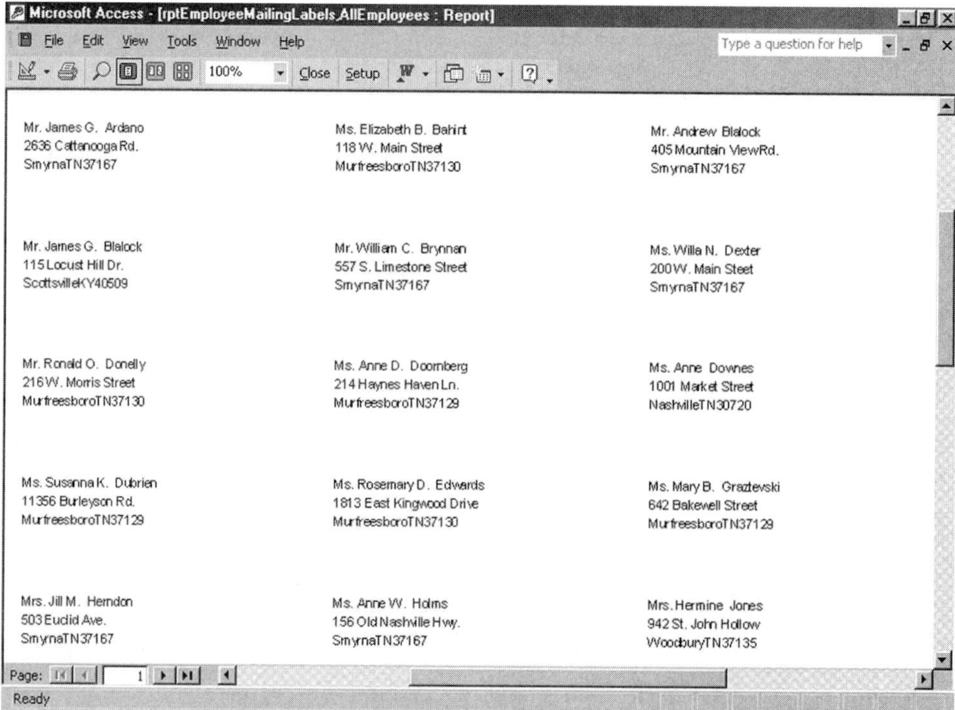

Assignment

Using the techniques you just learned, create the labels for the RobSem customers. First create a query named **qryCustomer MailingLabels(All)** and then use this query to serve as the data source for the label application. Name the label application **rpt CustomerMailinglabels(All)**.

application's minor components. (Now is a good time to put a space between the city and the state and two spaces between the state and the zip code.)

7.6 FORM LETTERS

Although using the mail-merge option in Microsoft Word may create form letters, they may also be made a part of the database itself. To create database form letters, use the **New** selection from the database window's report folder. The objective is to start with a *blank* report on which the letter can be typed. Therefore, select the **Design View** from the **New Report** dialog box and select the **qry CustomerMailingLabels(All)** query as your data source. (Because this query also is the source for the customer address labels, your letter's text boxes will match the mailing label text boxes.)

When the blank report format shows up on your screen, make the modifications shown in Figure 7.59. Therefore, starting with the blank report design, make these modifications to match the figure:

- Drag the report header to make it wide and tall enough to receive the letter header.
- Select the **Label** option **(*Aa*)** from the toolbox and type the letter header. Use one label per line. Boldface all letter header labels. The first line uses a 16-point format, while the remaining two letter header lines use a 12-point format.

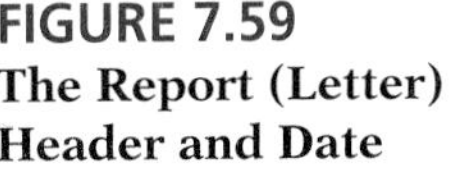

FIGURE 7.59
The Report (Letter) Header and Date

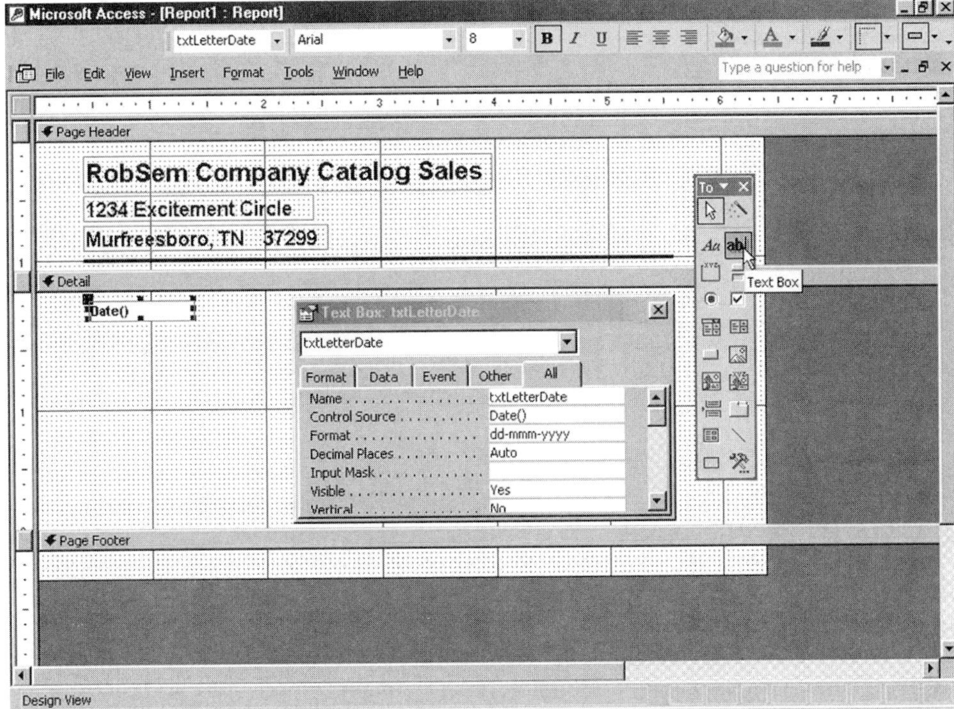

- Select the **Text Box** button from the toolbox to create an unbound control to receive the letter's date. After selecting the **Text Box** button—by clicking on it—perform the following actions:

  1. Click on the blank report's detail section to create the textbox. (Or you can drag a textbox space.) The resulting textbox will hold the date value.
  2. Delete the text box label. (The textbox label will have been generated by Access, which may show **Text(0)**. (The text number may be 0 or some other value, depending on how many other text boxes you have already created.)
  3. Open the text box's properties box, and then modify its entries to match Figure 7.59. Note that the letter date is the current date, **Date()**. The text box date is left-justified and boldfaced.

This form letter will announce a special sale to customers, so we'll use the customer data as the text box control. Therefore, continuing Figure 7.59's design view modification, perform the following actions, which are reflected in Figure 7.60.

- Create the text boxes to print the recipient name and address, using the bound text box format. The query named **qryCustomerMailingLabels(All)** was used to define the text box's control, and we've used the same logical formatting that was used in the mailing-label program to concatenate the title, first name, initial, and last name. Therefore, the first text box (customer name) line reads

```
=TRIM([CUS_TITLE] & " " & [CUS_FNAME] & IIF([CUS_INITIAL] IS
NULL," ", " " & [CUS_INITIAL] & ".") & [CUS_LNAME]).
```

- Note that you can "borrow" this text box format from the label application that we developed in the previous section. Just edit the line to match the **CUS** prefix shown here. If you completed the previous assignment, you already have the text box formatting done. In that case, just use the now-familiar Edit/Cut/Paste routine to produce the formatting for this form letter.

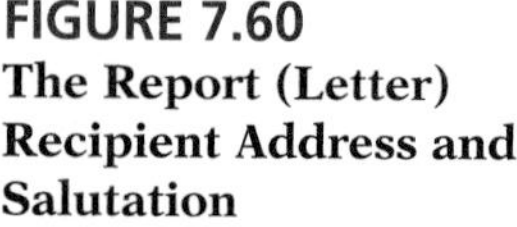

FIGURE 7.60
The Report (Letter) Recipient Address and Salutation

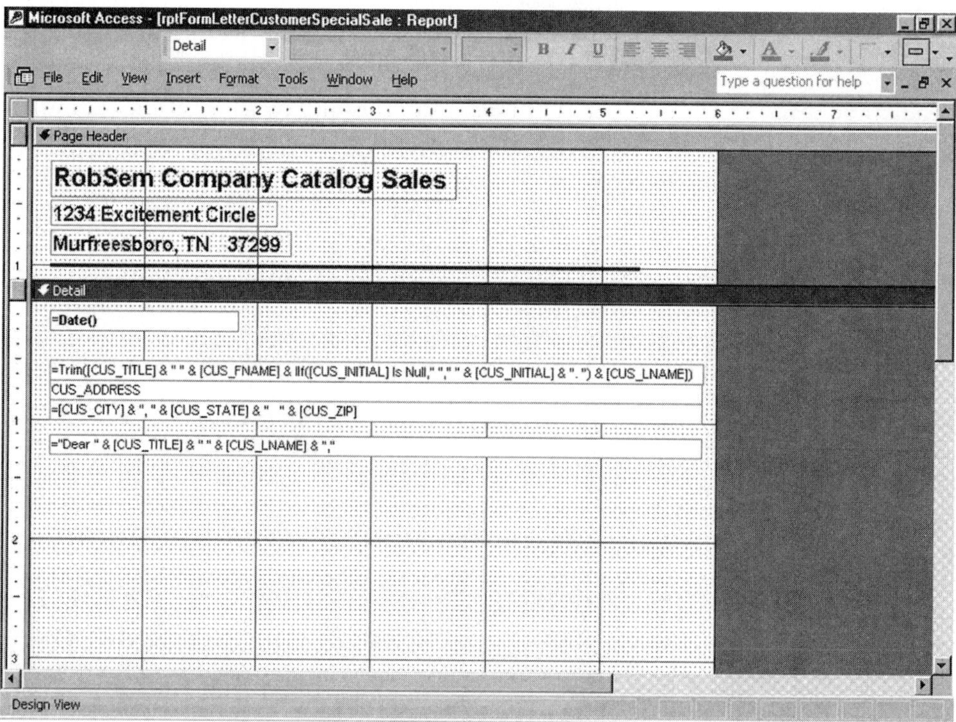

The second address line simply reads

```
CUS_ADDRESS.
```

The third address line requires the insertion of a comma and a space after the city name, the state abbreviation, three spaces, and the ZIP code. Therefore, the third line reads

```
=[CUS_CITY] & ", " & [CUS_STATE] & "   " & [CUS_ZIP]
```

to produce the desired results.

- Create a text box to receive the salutation. This text box will read

```
="DEAR " & [CUS_TITLE] & " " & [CUS_LNAME] & ","
```

to complete the letter's ties to the query.

Figure 7.60 shows the form letter's new text boxes. (We have dragged the text box limits to show you their contents.)

Next use the toolbox's **Label** button to draw a large label box and then start typing the letter you see in Figure 7.61.

Here are some things you should remember as you create the letter text shown in Figure 7.61:

- Pressing the keyboard's Enter key will cause you to exit from the text box, so *don't* use the Enter key to start a new paragraph or to skip a line.
- If you want to start a new line, press the keyboard's Ctrl key and, *while holding this key down*, press the Enter key. Use this same technique again to skip a line.
- Using the keyboard's Tab key causes Access to exit from the label box and to select the next available object in the report's design view format. Therefore, you cannot use the Tab key while you are in the label box. If you want to indent the discount message lines in Figure 7.61, use the space bar to move this portion of the text to the center.

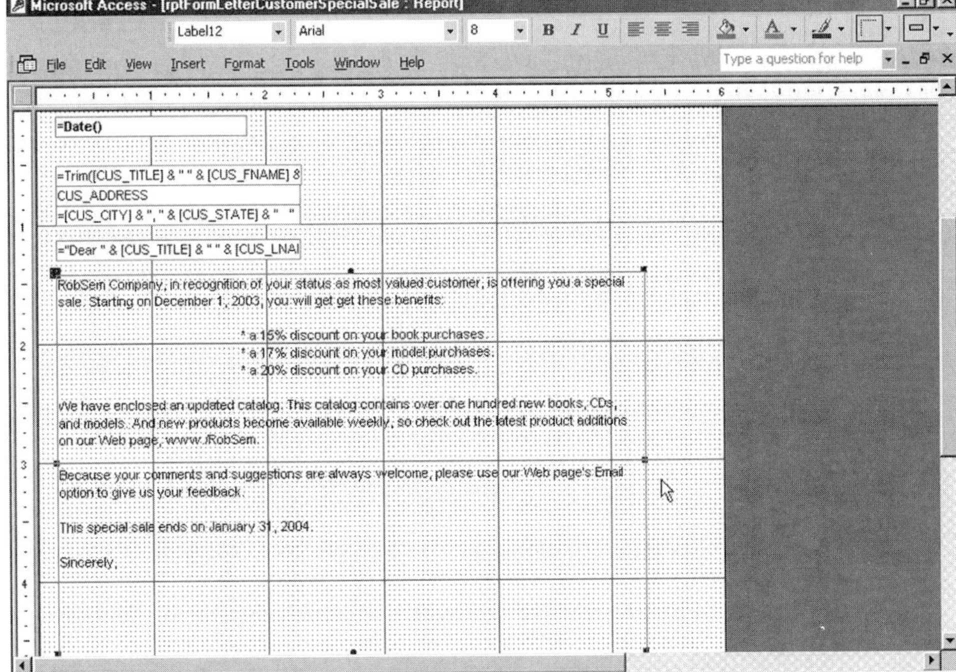

FIGURE 7.61
The Letter in the Detail Portion of the Report

FIGURE 7.62
The Page Footer Text

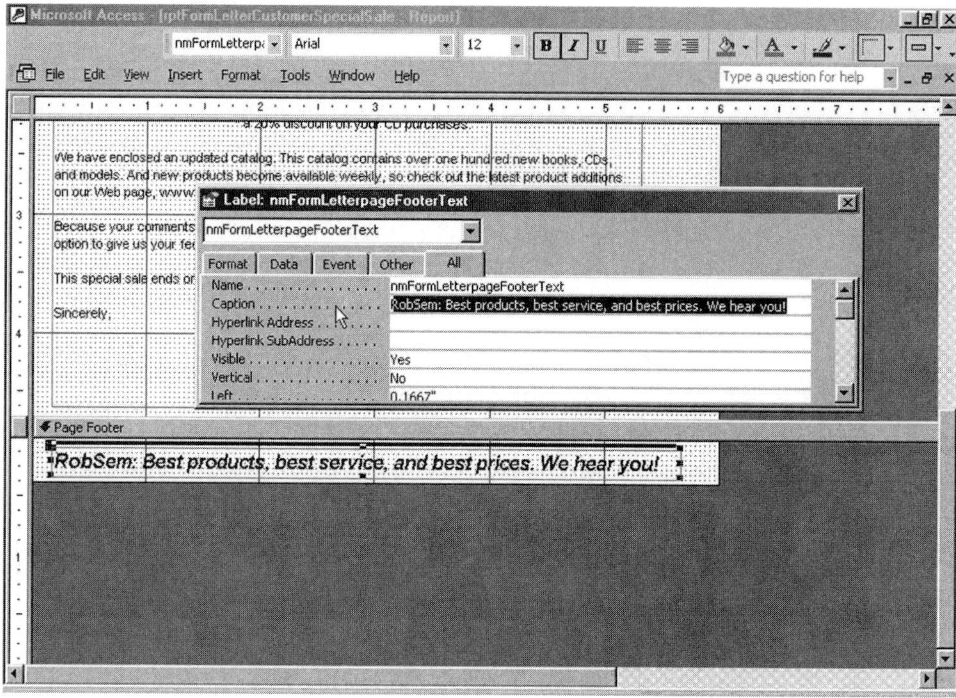

To round out the letter, drag the report footer to make space for a label box and then type in the text shown in Figure 7.62. As always, you can control the text format through the button bar at the top of the screen.

As you examine Figure 7.62, note that we have changed the label **Name** to reflect the label's purpose. Access creates a name such as **Label23** or some other numbered label, depending on how many labels you have already created. Unfortunately, a label name such as **Label23** will not mean much to you when you

FIGURE 7.63
The Completed Letter in Print Preview Format

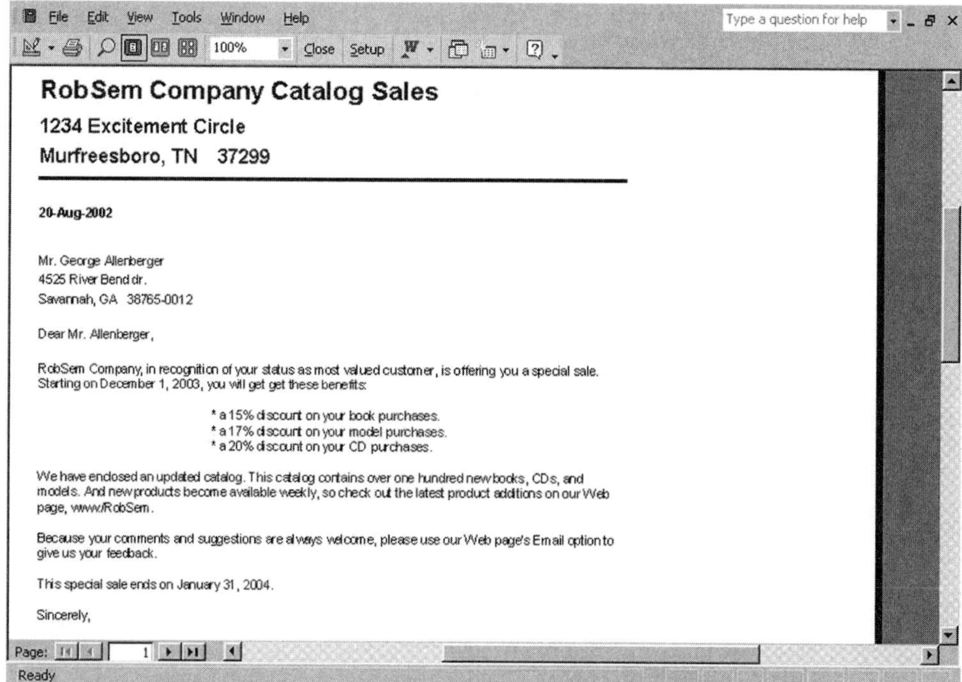

RobSem Company Catalog Sales
1234 Excitement Circle
Murfreesboro, TN 37299

20-Aug-2002

Mr. George Allenberger
4525 River Bend dr.
Savannah, GA 38765-0012

Dear Mr. Allenberger,

RobSem Company, in recognition of your status as most valued customer, is offering you a special sale. Starting on December 1, 2003, you will get get these benefits:

* a 15% discount on your book purchases.
* a 17% discount on your model purchases.
* a 20% discount on your CD purchases.

We have enclosed an updated catalog. This catalog contains over one hundred new books, CDs, and models. And new products become available weekly, so check out the latest product additions on our Web page, www.RobSem.

Because your comments and suggestions are always welcome, please use our Web page's Email option to give us your feedback.

This special sale ends on January 31, 2004.

Sincerely,

start writing the macros in Chapters 8 and 9. Self-documentation is a desirable quality in any application!

Use the toolbox's **Line** button to draw the line shown just above the page footer text in Figure 7.62 and then use the line's properties box to select its width. The completed letter is shown in Figure 7.63. (Because the letter is too long to fit on the screen, use the scroll bars to see the page footer's text.)

You can now print the letters, print the mailing labels, and let the customers know what a great deal is coming their way. By changing the query to one that yields an output by selected ZIP code, state, or city, you can fine-tune the customer selection.

Problems

Use the **Ch07_POS_2nd** database to work problems 7.1 through 7.8.

7.1 Create a report that generates the employee address labels by ZIP code. The input and output are shown in Figures P7.1 and P7.1A. A sample ZIP code input of **37130** is shown in Figure P7.1. (*Hint*: Use a **Like** function in your parameter query to ensure that you will generate an output for even approximate matches. Use an **Is Null** alternate to ensure that you will get all the ZIP codes if no input is made.) Name your report **rptEmployeeMailingLabels(SelectedZIPCode)**.

FIGURE P7.1
The Employee Labels ZIP Code Parameter Dialog Box

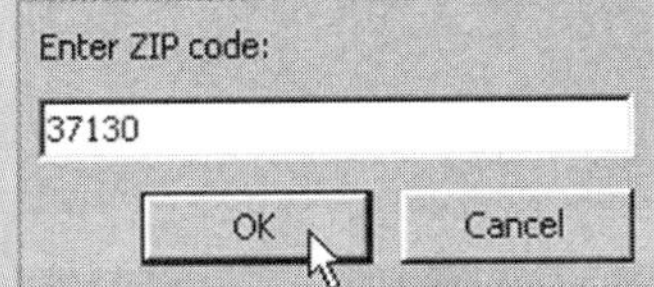

The ZIP code entry in the dialog box yields the results shown in Figure P7.1A.

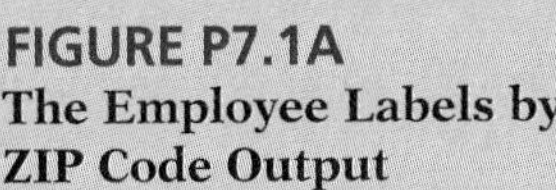

FIGURE P7.1A
The Employee Labels by ZIP Code Output

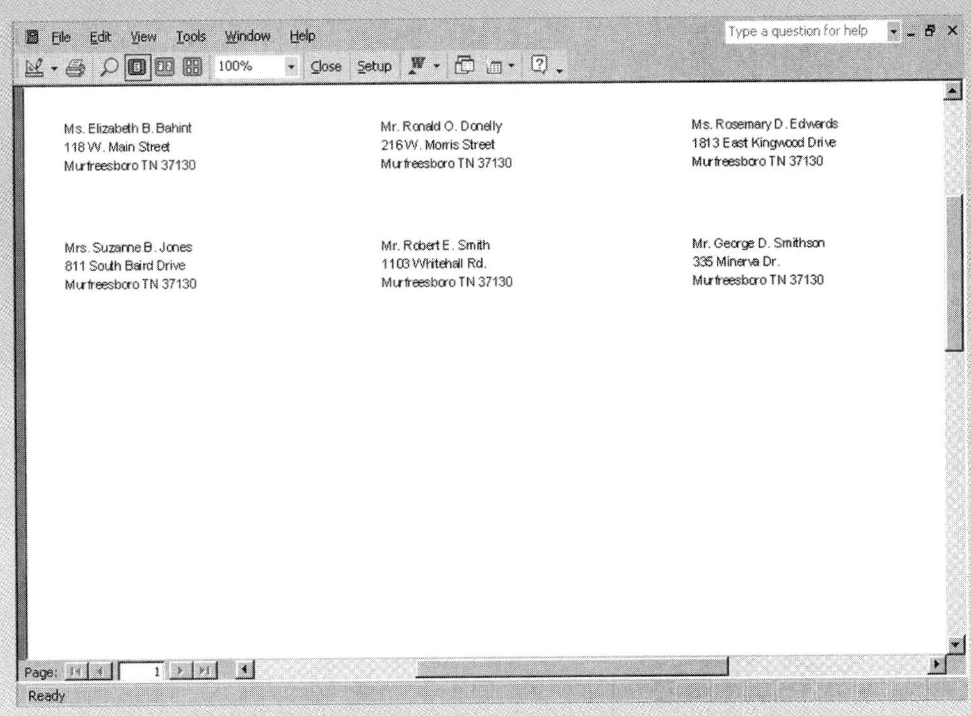

7.2 Create a report that generates the customer address labels by ZIP code. Use the same techniques that you used in problem 7.1. That is, use a parameter query based on the customer ZIP code. Name your report **rptCustomerMailingLabels(SelectedZIP Code)**.

Note

Use the databases on your CD as the basis for your work on all of the problems in this chapter. After you copy the databases to your computer's drive, do not forget to reset each file's properties to **Archive**. If you leave the file property as **Read Only**, you will not be able to make the necessary changes in the database contents!

7.3 Create a report that generates the employee address labels for a selected employee last name and first name. (*Hint*: Use a **Like** function in your parameter query to ensure that you will generate an output for even approximate matches. Use an **Is Null** alternate to ensure that you will get all the employee address labels if no input is made.) Incidentally, take a look at the EMPLOYEE table and note that a last name entry of **Smith** and a first name entry of **Robert** will yield several matches, because there are several employees named *Robert Smith*. You would, of course, have fewer matches if you included the employee initial. Name your report **rptEmployeeMailingLabels(SelectedEmployee)**.

7.4 Create a report that generates the customer address labels for a selected customer last name and first name. (*Hint*: Use a **Like** function in your parameter query to ensure that you will generate an output for even approximate matches. Use an **Is Null** alternate to ensure that you will get all the employee address labels if no input is made.) Name your report **rptCustomerMailingLabels(SelectedCustomer)**.

7.5 Create a report that will generate the output shown in Figure P7.5. (Hint: The Access-generated page count was moved from the footer to the header, using the familiar Edit/Copy/Paste routine.) Name the report **rptProductSales**.

FIGURE P7.5
RobSem Company Product Sales Report

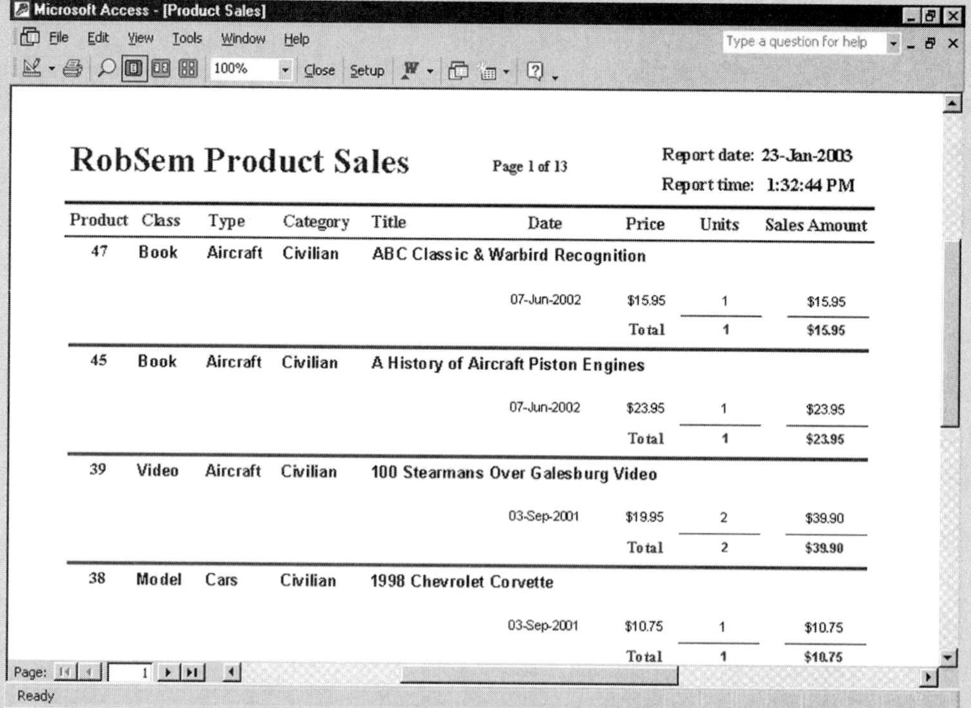

7.6 Create a report that yields a sales summary by customer (see Figure P7.6), using the format shown in problem 7.5. (Generate the subtotals for each customer and sum the customer subtotals to get the grand total.) Name the report **rptCustomerSales**.

FIGURE P7.6
A RobSem Company Customer Sales Summary

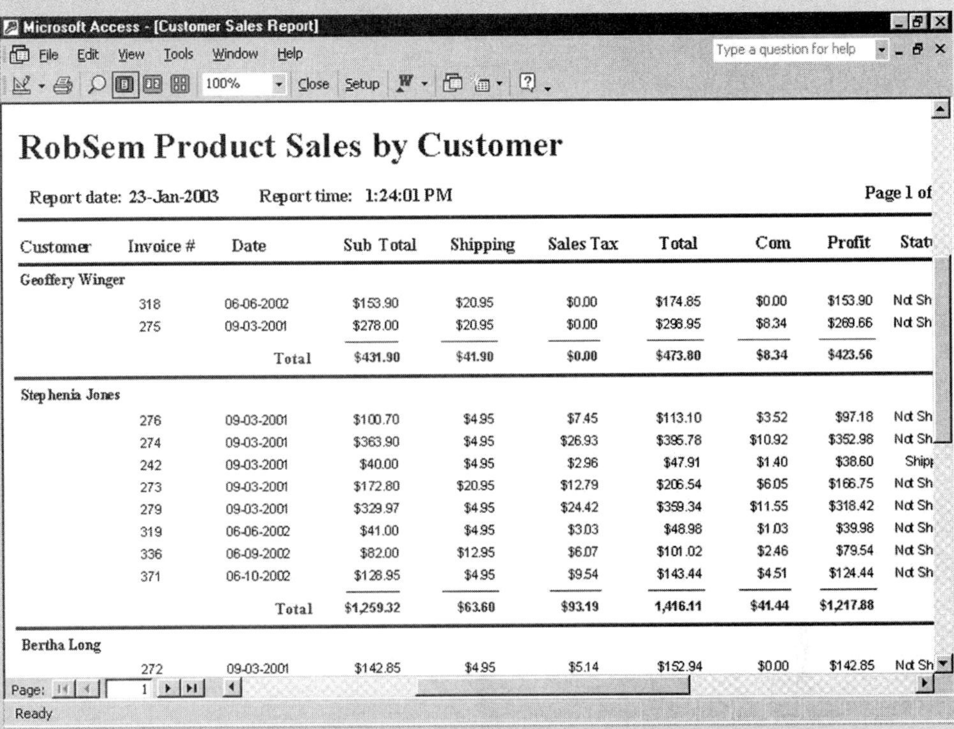

RobSem Product Sales by Customer

Report date: 23-Jan-2003 Report time: 1:24:01 PM Page 1 of

Customer	Invoice #	Date	Sub Total	Shipping	Sales Tax	Total	Com	Profit	Stat
Geoffery Winger									
	318	06-06-2002	$153.90	$20.95	$0.00	$174.85	$0.00	$153.90	Not Sh
	275	09-03-2001	$278.00	$20.95	$0.00	$298.95	$8.34	$269.66	Not Sh
		Total	$431.90	$41.90	$0.00	$473.80	$8.34	$423.56	
Stephenia Jones									
	276	09-03-2001	$100.70	$4.95	$7.45	$113.10	$3.52	$97.18	Not Sh
	274	09-03-2001	$363.90	$4.95	$26.93	$395.78	$10.92	$352.98	Not Sh
	242	09-03-2001	$40.00	$4.95	$2.96	$47.91	$1.40	$38.60	Shipp
	273	09-03-2001	$172.80	$20.95	$12.79	$206.54	$6.05	$166.75	Not Sh
	279	09-03-2001	$329.97	$4.95	$24.42	$359.34	$11.55	$318.42	Not Sh
	319	06-06-2002	$41.00	$4.95	$3.03	$48.98	$1.03	$39.98	Not Sh
	336	06-09-2002	$82.00	$12.95	$6.07	$101.02	$2.46	$79.54	Not Sh
	371	06-10-2002	$128.95	$4.95	$9.54	$143.44	$4.51	$124.44	Not Sh
		Total	$1,259.32	$63.60	$93.19	1,416.11	$41.44	$1,217.88	
Bertha Long									
	272	09-03-2001	$142.85	$4.95	$5.14	$152.94	$0.00	$142.85	Not Sh

7.7 Create a report that produces a summary for the five most frequently sold products. Use the format illustrated in Figure P7.7. Name the report **rptMostFrequentlySoldProducts**.

FIGURE P7.7
A Sales Summary for the Five Most Frequently Sold Products

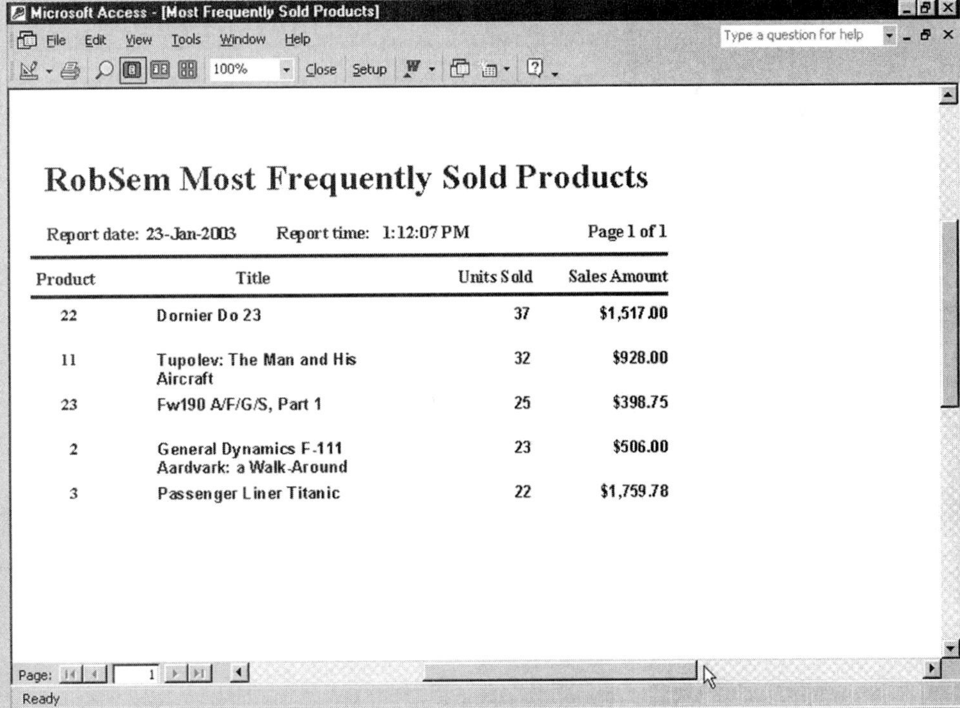

RobSem Most Frequently Sold Products

Report date: 23-Jan-2003 Report time: 1:12:07 PM Page 1 of 1

Product	Title	Units Sold	Sales Amount
22	Dornier Do 23	37	$1,517.00
11	Tupolev: The Man and His Aircraft	32	$928.00
23	Fw190 A/F/G/S, Part 1	25	$398.75
2	General Dynamics F-111 Aardvark: a Walk-Around	23	$506.00
3	Passenger Liner Titanic	22	$1,759.78

7.8 Create a report that produces an employee birthday list by requested month. The input and output are shown in Figures P7.8 and P7.8A. Name the report **rptEmployeeDOBbySelectedMonth**.

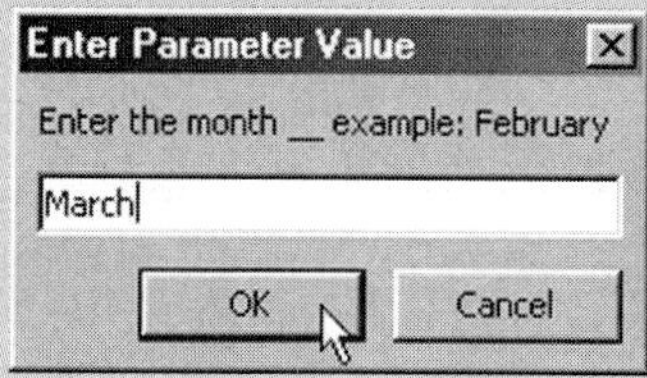

FIGURE P7.8
A Parameter Request for the Birthday Month

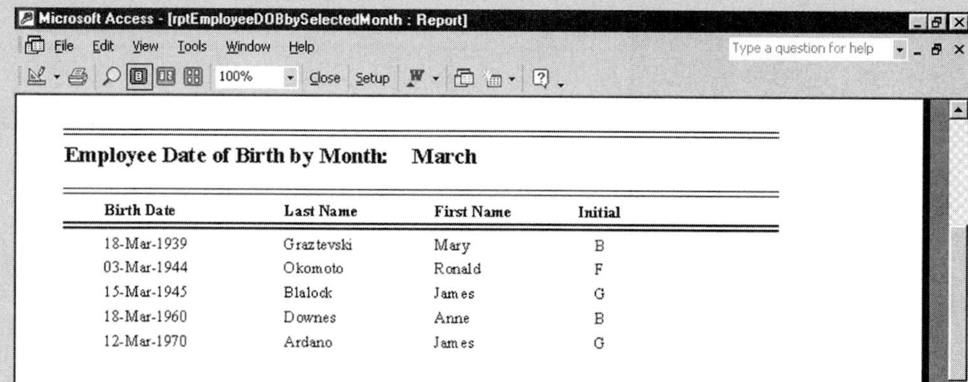

Microsoft Access - [rptEmployeeDOBbySelectedMonth : Report]

Employee Date of Birth by Month: March

Birth Date	Last Name	First Name	Initial
18-Mar-1939	Graztevski	Mary	B
03-Mar-1944	Okomoto	Ronald	F
15-Mar-1945	Blalock	James	G
18-Mar-1960	Downes	Anne	B
12-Mar-1970	Ardano	James	G

FIGURE P7.8A
The Employee Birthday List for the Selected Month

Use the **Ch07_ConsultCo** database to work problems 7.9 through 7.12.

7.9 Create a report to list the charges by project. Use the output format shown in Figure P7.9 and make sure that the grand total—not shown here—is shown on the last page of the report. The header must be repeated on each page. Save the report as **rptChargesByProject**.

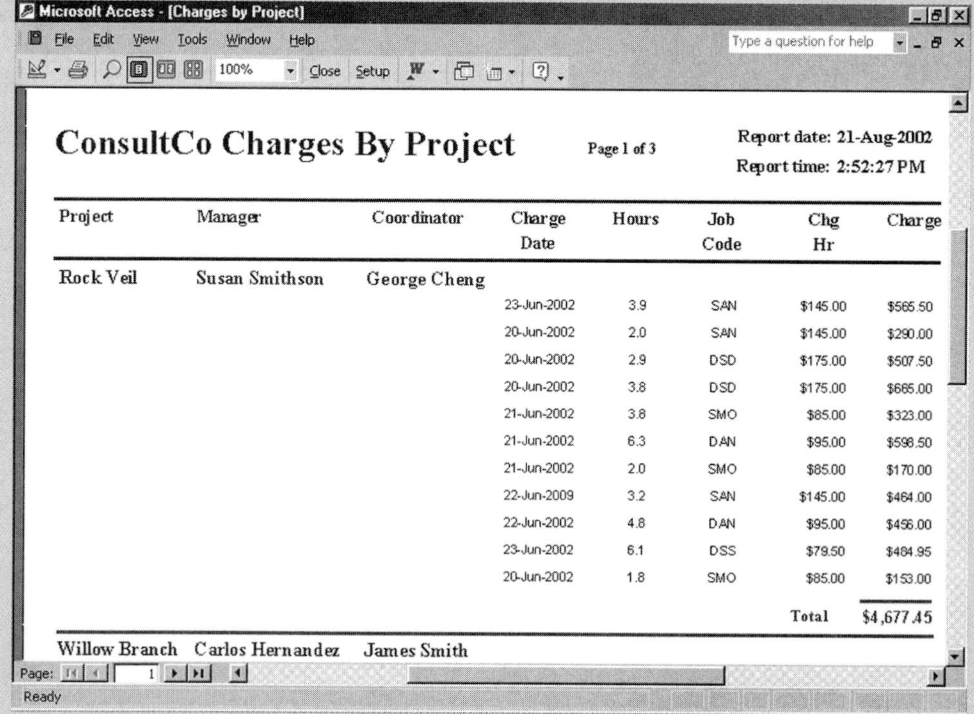

Microsoft Access - [Charges by Project]

ConsultCo Charges By Project — Page 1 of 3 — Report date: 21-Aug-2002 — Report time: 2:52:27 PM

Project	Manager	Coordinator	Charge Date	Hours	Job Code	Chg Hr	Charge
Rock Veil	Susan Smithson	George Cheng					
			23-Jun-2002	3.9	SAN	$145.00	$565.50
			20-Jun-2002	2.0	SAN	$145.00	$290.00
			20-Jun-2002	2.9	DSD	$175.00	$507.50
			20-Jun-2002	3.8	DSD	$175.00	$665.00
			21-Jun-2002	3.8	SMO	$85.00	$323.00
			21-Jun-2002	6.3	DAN	$95.00	$598.50
			21-Jun-2002	2.0	SMO	$85.00	$170.00
			22-Jun-2009	3.2	SAN	$145.00	$464.00
			22-Jun-2002	4.8	DAN	$95.00	$456.00
			23-Jun-2002	6.1	DSS	$79.50	$484.95
			20-Jun-2002	1.8	SMO	$85.00	$153.00
						Total	$4,677.45
Willow Branch	Carlos Hernandez	James Smith					

FIGURE P7.9
The ConsultCo Charges by Project Report

7.10 Create a report to list the charges by client. Use the output format shown in Figure P7.10 and make sure that the grand total—not shown here—is shown on the last page of the report. The header must be repeated on each page. Save the report as **rptChargesByClient**.

FIGURE P7.10
The ConsultCo Charges by Client Report

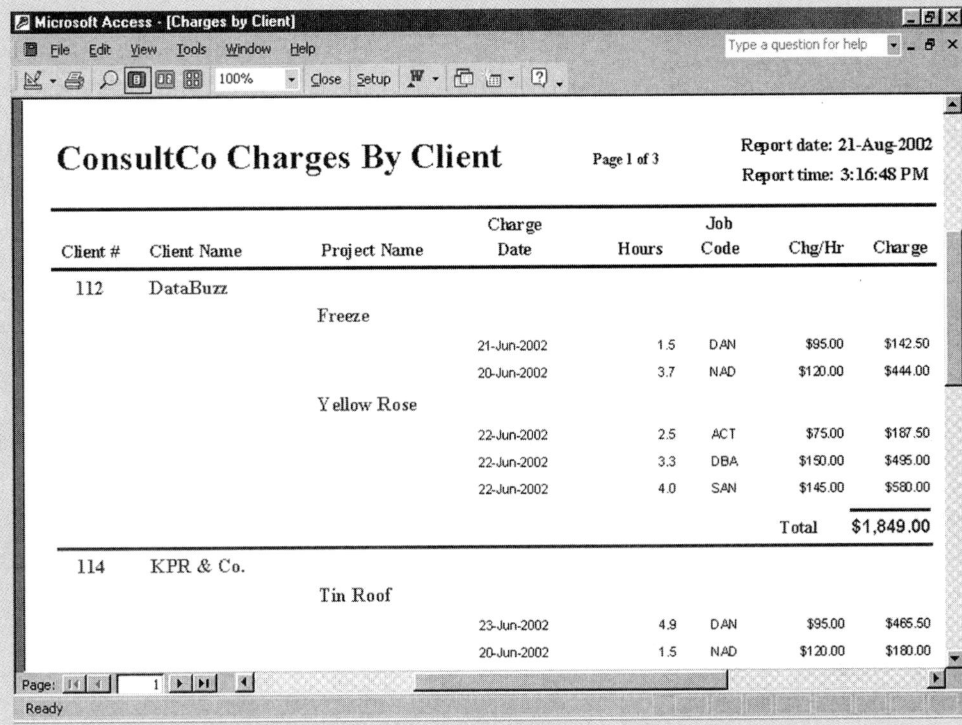

Microsoft Access - [Charges by Client]

ConsultCo Charges By Client

Page 1 of 3

Report date: 21-Aug-2002
Report time: 3:16:48 PM

Client #	Client Name	Project Name	Charge Date	Hours	Job Code	Chg/Hr	Charge
112	DataBuzz						
		Freeze					
			21-Jun-2002	1.5	DAN	$95.00	$142.50
			20-Jun-2002	3.7	NAD	$120.00	$444.00
		Yellow Rose					
			22-Jun-2002	2.5	ACT	$75.00	$187.50
			22-Jun-2002	3.3	DBA	$150.00	$495.00
			22-Jun-2002	4.0	SAN	$145.00	$580.00
						Total	$1,849.00
114	KPR & Co.						
		Tin Roof					
			23-Jun-2002	4.9	DAN	$95.00	$465.50
			20-Jun-2002	1.5	NAD	$120.00	$180.00

7.11 Create a report to list the charges by employee. Use the output format shown in Figure P7.11 and make sure that the grand total—not shown here—is shown on the last page of the report. The header must be repeated on each page. Save the report as **rptChargesByEmployee**.

FIGURE P7.11
The ConsultCo Charges by Employee Report

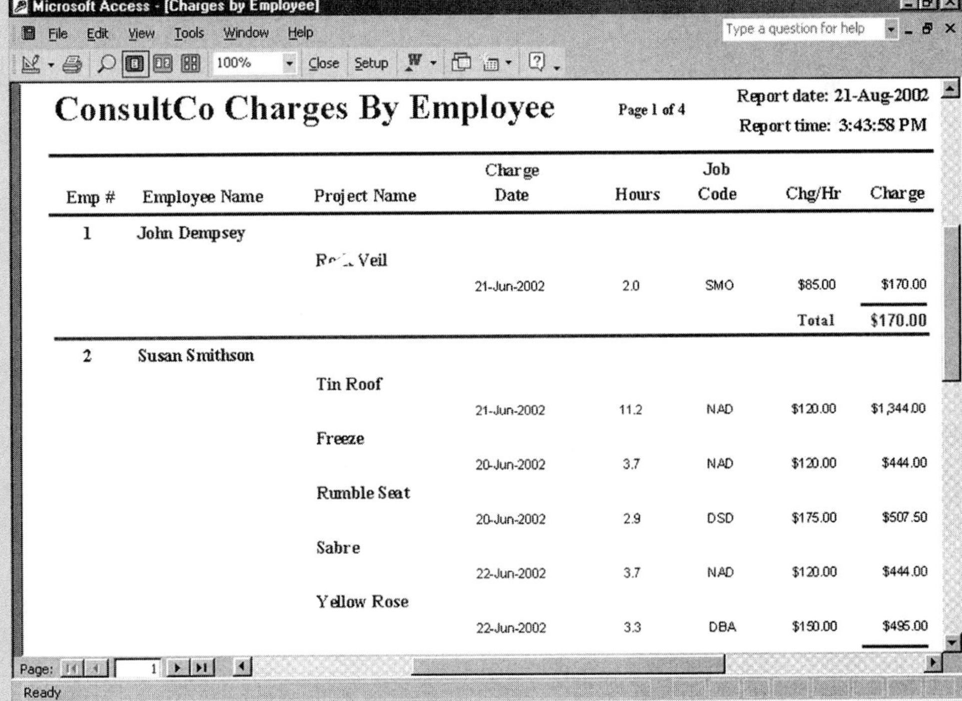

Microsoft Access - [Charges by Employee]

ConsultCo Charges By Employee

Page 1 of 4

Report date: 21-Aug-2002
Report time: 3:43:58 PM

Emp #	Employee Name	Project Name	Charge Date	Hours	Job Code	Chg/Hr	Charge
1	John Dempsey						
		R[illegible] Veil					
			21-Jun-2002	2.0	SMO	$85.00	$170.00
						Total	$170.00
2	Susan Smithson						
		Tin Roof					
			21-Jun-2002	11.2	NAD	$120.00	$1,344.00
		Freeze					
			20-Jun-2002	3.7	NAD	$120.00	$444.00
		Rumble Seat					
			20-Jun-2002	2.9	DSD	$175.00	$507.50
		Sabre					
			22-Jun-2002	3.7	NAD	$120.00	$444.00
		Yellow Rose					
			22-Jun-2002	3.3	DBA	$150.00	$495.00

7.12 Create a report to list the charges by job code. Use the output format shown in Figure P7.12 and make sure that the grand total—not shown here—is shown on the last page of the report. The header must be repeated on each page. Save the report as **rptChargesByJobCode**.

FIGURE P7.12
The ConsultCo Charges by Job Code Report

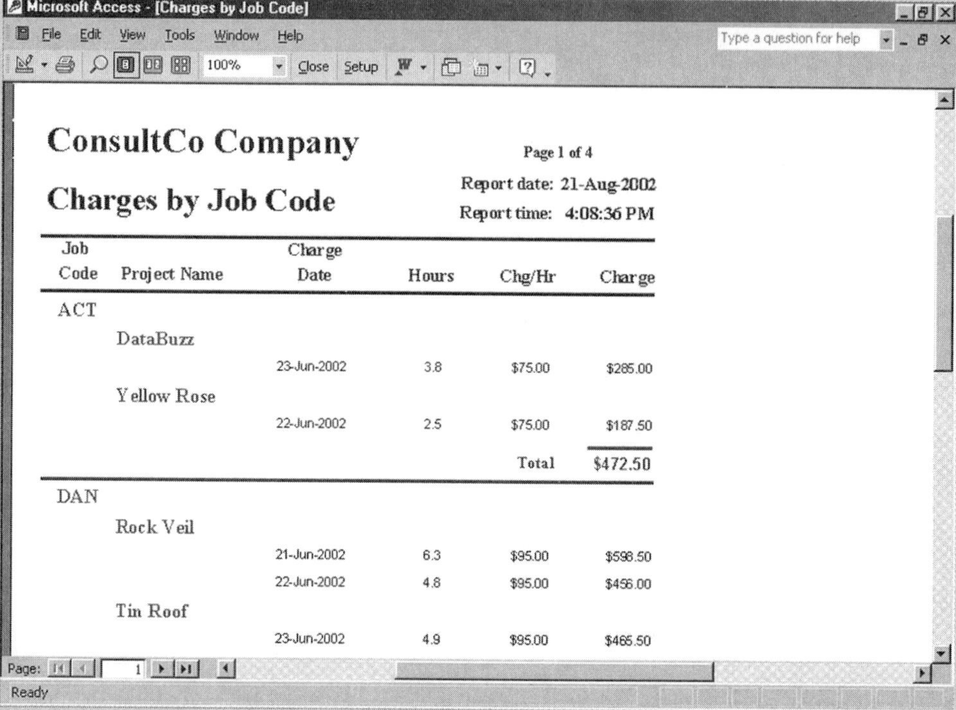

ConsultCo Company

Charges by Job Code

Page 1 of 4
Report date: 21-Aug-2002
Report time: 4:08:36 PM

Job Code	Project Name	Charge Date	Hours	Chg/Hr	Charge
ACT					
	DataBuzz				
		23-Jun-2002	3.8	$75.00	$285.00
	Yellow Rose				
		22-Jun-2002	2.5	$75.00	$187.50
				Total	$472.50
DAN					
	Rock Veil				
		21-Jun-2002	6.3	$95.00	$598.50
		22-Jun-2002	4.8	$95.00	$456.00
	Tin Roof				
		23-Jun-2002	4.9	$95.00	$465.50

Use the **Ch07_TruckCo** database to work problems 7.13 through 7.15.

7.13 Create a report to list the maintenance history of all of the company's vehicles. Use the output format shown in Figure P7.13. The header must be repeated on each page. Save the report as **rptVehicleMaintenance**.

FIGURE P7.13
The TruckCo Company Vehicle Maintenance Report

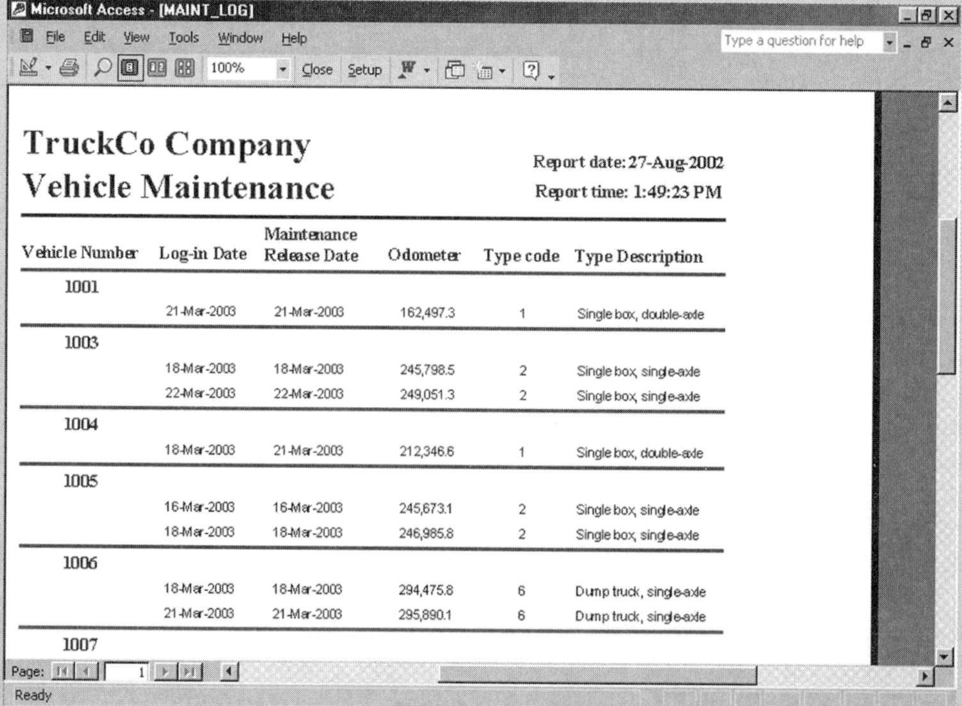

TruckCo Company
Vehicle Maintenance

Report date: 27-Aug-2002
Report time: 1:49:23 PM

Vehicle Number	Log-in Date	Maintenance Release Date	Odometer	Type code	Type Description
1001					
	21-Mar-2003	21-Mar-2003	162,497.3	1	Single box, double-axle
1003					
	18-Mar-2003	18-Mar-2003	245,798.5	2	Single box, single-axle
	22-Mar-2003	22-Mar-2003	249,051.3	2	Single box, single-axle
1004					
	18-Mar-2003	21-Mar-2003	212,346.6	1	Single box, double-axle
1005					
	16-Mar-2003	16-Mar-2003	245,673.1	2	Single box, single-axle
	18-Mar-2003	18-Mar-2003	246,985.8	2	Single box, single-axle
1006					
	18-Mar-2003	18-Mar-2003	294,475.8	6	Dump truck, single-axle
	21-Mar-2003	21-Mar-2003	295,890.1	6	Dump truck, single-axle
1007					

7.14 Create a report to list the base managers and the employee count for each base. Use the output format shown in Figure P7.14. Save the report as **rptBaseManagersAndEmployeeCount**.

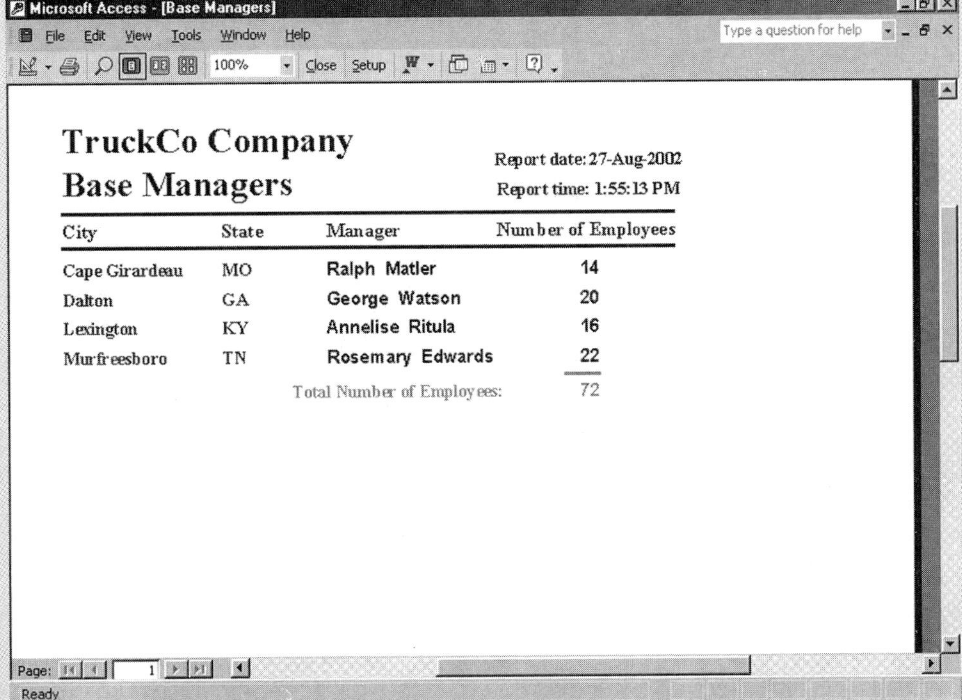

Microsoft Access - [Base Managers]

TruckCo Company
Base Managers

Report date: 27-Aug-2002
Report time: 1:55:13 PM

City	State	Manager	Number of Employees
Cape Girardeau	MO	Ralph Matler	14
Dalton	GA	George Watson	20
Lexington	KY	Annelise Ritula	16
Murfreesboro	TN	Rosemary Edwards	22
		Total Number of Employees:	72

FIGURE P7.14
The TruckCo Company Base Managers and Employee Count Report

7.15 Create a report to list the base managers and the employee phone list for each base. Use the output format shown in Figure P7.15. Save the report as **rptEmployeePhoneDirectoryGroupedByBase**.

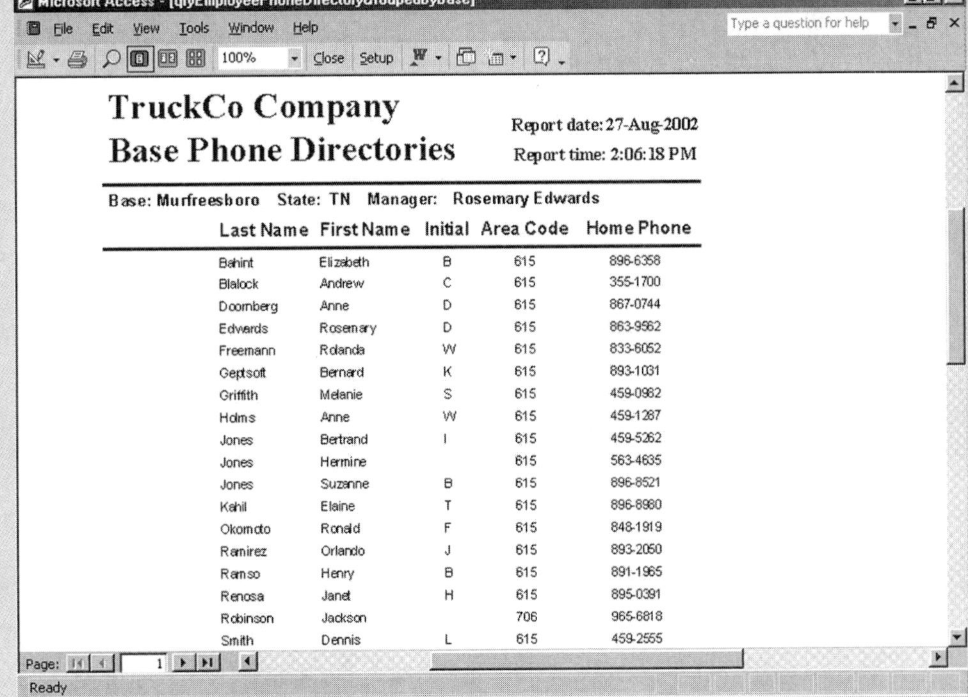

Microsoft Access - [qryEmployeePhoneDirectoryGroupedByBase]

TruckCo Company
Base Phone Directories

Report date: 27-Aug-2002
Report time: 2:06:18 PM

Base: Murfreesboro State: TN Manager: Rosemary Edwards

Last Name	First Name	Initial	Area Code	Home Phone
Bahint	Elizabeth	B	615	896-6358
Blalock	Andrew	C	615	355-1700
Doornberg	Anne	D	615	867-0744
Edwards	Rosemary	D	615	863-9562
Freemann	Rolanda	W	615	833-6052
Geptsoft	Bernard	K	615	893-1031
Griffith	Melanie	S	615	459-0982
Holms	Anne	W	615	459-1287
Jones	Bertrand	I	615	459-5262
Jones	Hermine		615	563-4635
Jones	Suzanne	B	615	896-8521
Kahil	Elaine	T	615	896-8980
Okomoto	Ronald	F	615	848-1919
Ramirez	Orlando	J	615	893-2050
Ramso	Henry	B	615	891-1965
Renosa	Janet	H	615	895-0391
Robinson	Jackson		706	965-6818
Smith	Dennis	L	615	459-2555

FIGURE P7.15
The Base Employee Phone Directory

Use the **Ch07_FlyHigh** database to work problems 7.16 through 7.18.

7.16 Create a rental report that shows the rental activity by customer. Use the output format shown in Figure P7.16 and make sure that the grand totals—not shown here—are shown on the last page of the report. The page header must be repeated on each page. Save the report as **rptRentalActivityByCustomer**.

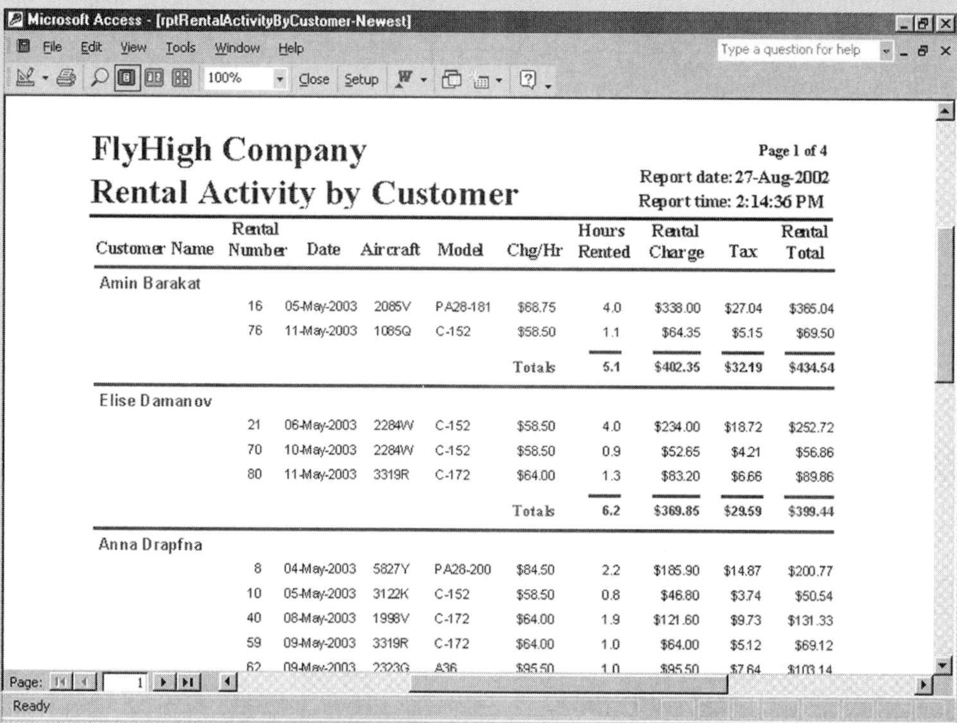

Microsoft Access - [rptRentalActivityByCustomer-Newest]

FlyHigh Company
Rental Activity by Customer

Page 1 of 4
Report date: 27-Aug-2002
Report time: 2:14:36 PM

Customer Name	Rental Number	Date	Aircraft	Model	Chg/Hr	Hours Rented	Rental Charge	Tax	Rental Total
Amin Barakat									
	16	05-May-2003	2085V	PA28-181	$68.75	4.0	$338.00	$27.04	$365.04
	76	11-May-2003	1085Q	C-152	$58.50	1.1	$64.35	$5.15	$69.50
					Totals	5.1	$402.35	$32.19	$434.54
Elise Damanov									
	21	06-May-2003	2284W	C-152	$58.50	4.0	$234.00	$18.72	$252.72
	70	10-May-2003	2284W	C-152	$58.50	0.9	$52.65	$4.21	$56.86
	80	11-May-2003	3319R	C-172	$64.00	1.3	$83.20	$6.66	$89.86
					Totals	6.2	$369.85	$29.59	$399.44
Anna Drapfna									
	8	04-May-2003	5827Y	PA28-200	$84.50	2.2	$185.90	$14.87	$200.77
	10	05-May-2003	3122K	C-152	$58.50	0.8	$46.80	$3.74	$50.54
	40	08-May-2003	1998V	C-172	$64.00	1.9	$121.60	$9.73	$131.33
	59	09-May-2003	3319R	C-172	$64.00	1.0	$64.00	$5.12	$69.12
	62	09-May-2003	2323G	A36	$95.50	1.0	$95.50	$7.64	$103.14

FIGURE P7.16
The FlyHigh Company Rental Activity by Customer Report

7.17 Create a rental report that shows the rental activity by aircraft. Use a parameter query to generate a report for a specific aircraft such as **2085V** (see Figure P7.17). If the end user does not make an entry and simply clicks **OK**, *all* the aircraft results must be shown (see Figure P7.17A). (*Hint*: Remember the **Like** function and the **Is Null** option?) Use the output format shown in Figure P7.17A and make sure that the grand totals—not shown here—are shown on the last page of the report. The page header must be repeated on each page. Save the report as **rptRentalActivityByAircraft**.

Enter Parameter Value

Enter Aircraft number:

OK | Cancel

FIGURE P7.17
The Aircraft Number Request

FIGURE P7.17A
The FlyHigh Company Rental Activity by Aircraft Report

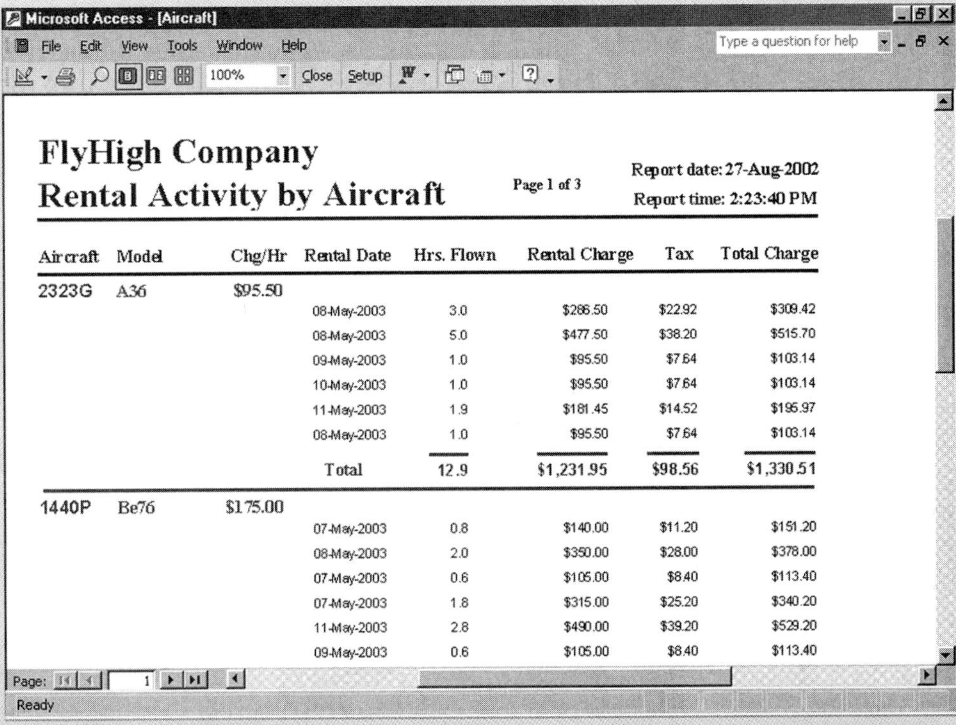

FlyHigh Company
Rental Activity by Aircraft

Page 1 of 3

Report date: 27-Aug-2002
Report time: 2:23:40 PM

Aircraft	Model	Chg/Hr	Rental Date	Hrs. Flown	Rental Charge	Tax	Total Charge
2323G	A36	$95.50					
			08-May-2003	3.0	$286.50	$22.92	$309.42
			08-May-2003	5.0	$477.50	$38.20	$515.70
			09-May-2003	1.0	$95.50	$7.64	$103.14
			10-May-2003	1.0	$95.50	$7.64	$103.14
			11-May-2003	1.9	$181.45	$14.52	$195.97
			08-May-2003	1.0	$95.50	$7.64	$103.14
			Total	12.9	$1,231.95	$98.56	$1,330.51
1440P	Be76	$175.00					
			07-May-2003	0.8	$140.00	$11.20	$151.20
			08-May-2003	2.0	$350.00	$28.00	$378.00
			07-May-2003	0.6	$105.00	$8.40	$113.40
			07-May-2003	1.8	$315.00	$25.20	$340.20
			11-May-2003	2.8	$490.00	$39.20	$529.20
			09-May-2003	0.6	$105.00	$8.40	$113.40

7.18 Create a rental report that shows the rental activity by model and aircraft. (This report is based on a crosstab query. Name the crosstab query **qryCrosstabRental ActivityGroupedByModel**.) Use the output format shown in Figure P7.18. Save the report as **rptRentalActivityByModelAndAircraft**.

FIGURE P7.18
The FlyHigh Company Rental Activity by Model and Aircraft

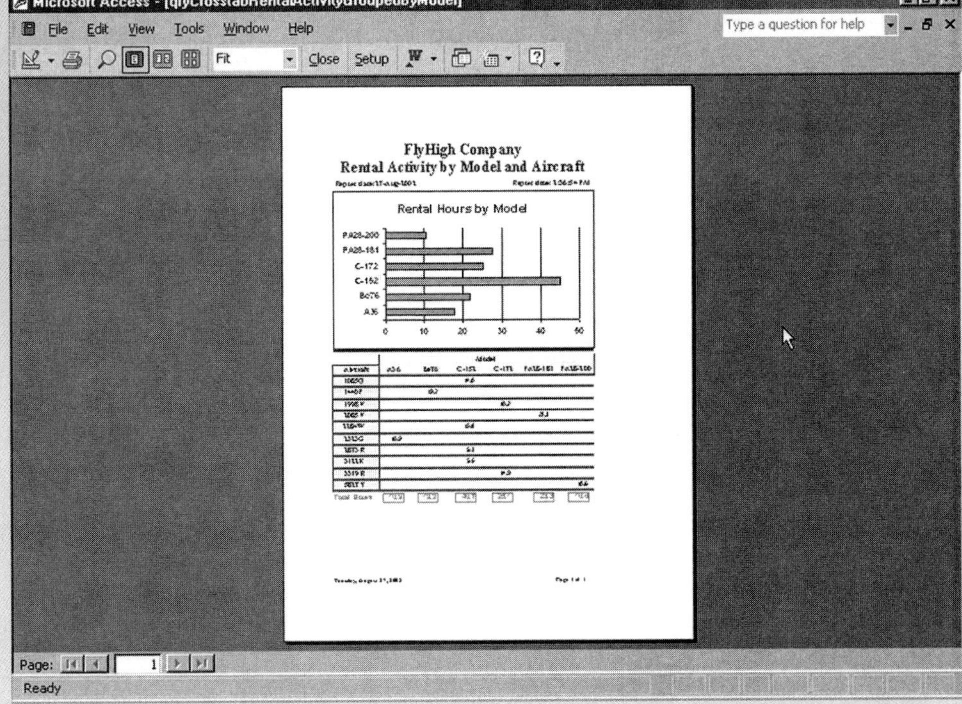

Use the **Ch07_JewelCo** database to work problems 7.19 and 7.20.

7.19 Create a sales report that shows all sales for each jeweler. Use the output format shown in Figure P7.19 and make sure that the grand totals—not shown here—are shown on the last page of the report. The header must be repeated on each page. Save the report as **rptJewelerSales**.

FIGURE P7.19
The JewelCo Company Sales by Jeweler Report

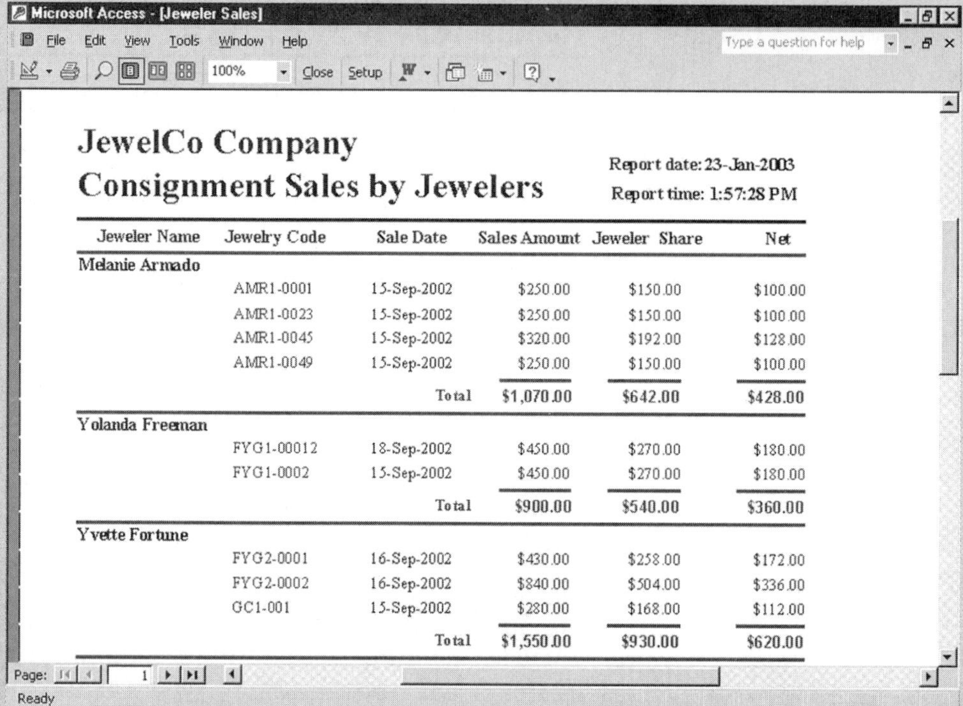

Microsoft Access - [Jeweler Sales]

JewelCo Company
Consignment Sales by Jewelers

Report date: 23-Jan-2003
Report time: 1:57:28 PM

Jeweler Name	Jewelry Code	Sale Date	Sales Amount	Jeweler Share	Net
Melanie Armado					
	AMR1-0001	15-Sep-2002	$250.00	$150.00	$100.00
	AMR1-0023	15-Sep-2002	$250.00	$150.00	$100.00
	AMR1-0045	15-Sep-2002	$320.00	$192.00	$128.00
	AMR1-0049	15-Sep-2002	$250.00	$150.00	$100.00
		Total	$1,070.00	$642.00	$428.00
Yolanda Freeman					
	FYG1-00012	18-Sep-2002	$450.00	$270.00	$180.00
	FYG1-0002	15-Sep-2002	$450.00	$270.00	$180.00
		Total	$900.00	$540.00	$360.00
Yvette Fortune					
	FYG2-0001	16-Sep-2002	$430.00	$258.00	$172.00
	FYG2-0002	16-Sep-2002	$840.00	$504.00	$336.00
	GC1-001	15-Sep-2002	$280.00	$168.00	$112.00
		Total	$1,550.00	$930.00	$620.00

7.20 Create a sales report that shows all sales for each customer. Use the output format shown in Figure P7.20 and make sure that the grand totals—not shown here—are shown on the last page of the report. The header must be repeated on each page. Save the report as **rptCustomerSales**.

FIGURE P7.20
The JewelCo Company Sales by Customer Report

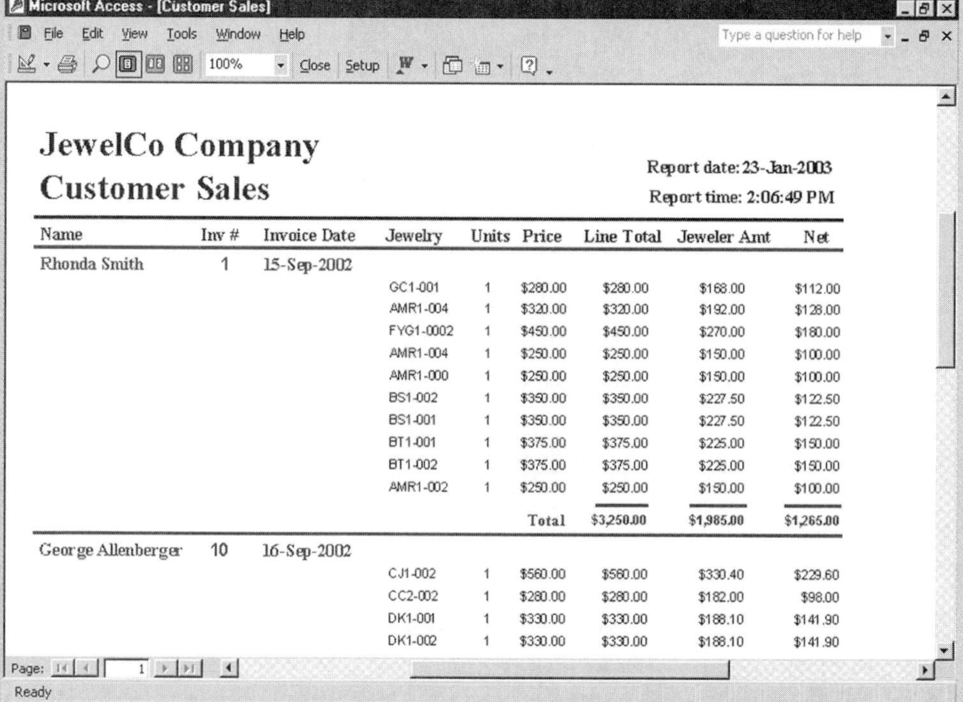

Microsoft Access - [Customer Sales]

JewelCo Company
Customer Sales

Report date: 23-Jan-2003
Report time: 2:06:49 PM

Name	Inv #	Invoice Date	Jewelry	Units	Price	Line Total	Jeweler Amt	Net
Rhonda Smith	1	15-Sep-2002						
			GC1-001	1	$280.00	$280.00	$168.00	$112.00
			AMR1-004	1	$320.00	$320.00	$192.00	$128.00
			FYG1-0002	1	$450.00	$450.00	$270.00	$180.00
			AMR1-004	1	$250.00	$250.00	$150.00	$100.00
			AMR1-000	1	$250.00	$250.00	$150.00	$100.00
			BS1-002	1	$350.00	$350.00	$227.50	$122.50
			BS1-001	1	$350.00	$350.00	$227.50	$122.50
			BT1-001	1	$375.00	$375.00	$225.00	$150.00
			BT1-002	1	$375.00	$375.00	$225.00	$150.00
			AMR1-002	1	$250.00	$250.00	$150.00	$100.00
					Total	$3,250.00	$1,985.00	$1,265.00
George Allenberger	10	16-Sep-2002						
			CJ1-002	1	$560.00	$560.00	$330.40	$229.60
			CC2-002	1	$280.00	$280.00	$182.00	$98.00
			DK1-001	1	$330.00	$330.00	$188.10	$141.90
			DK1-002	1	$330.00	$330.00	$188.10	$141.90

Use the **Ch07_DeptKey** database to work problems 7.21 and 7.22.

7.21 Create a report that shows the departmental key transactions (O = check-out, R = return) for each employee. Use a parameter query using the employee last name to generate a report for a specific employee, such as an employee named **Smith**. If the end user does not make an entry and simply clicks **OK**, *all* the employee key transactions must be shown (see Figures P7.21 and P7.21A). (*Hint*: Remember the **Like** function and the **Is Null** option?) Use the report output format shown in Figure P7.21A. The page header must be repeated on each page. Save the report as **rptKeyReport ByEmployee**.

FIGURE P7.21
The Employee Last Name Request

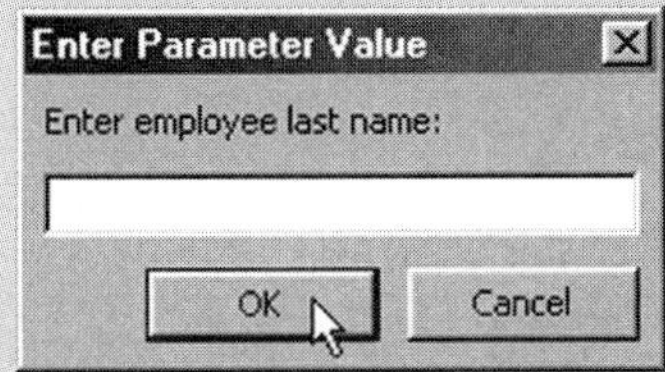

FIGURE P7.21A
The Key Transactions by Departmental Employees

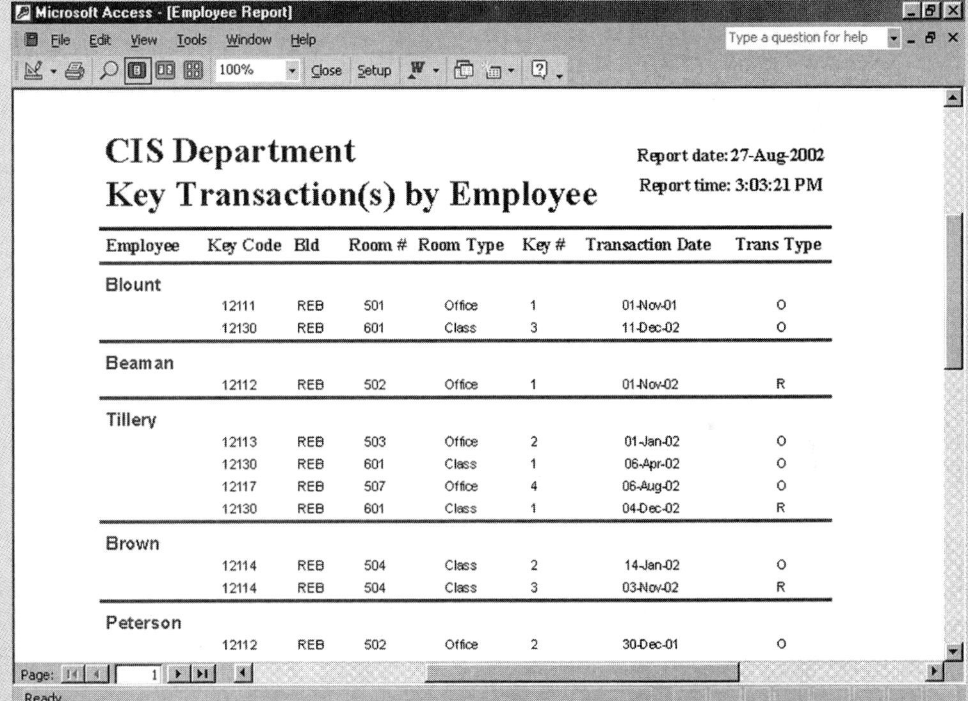

CIS Department
Key Transaction(s) by Employee

Report date: 27-Aug-2002
Report time: 3:03:21 PM

Employee	Key Code	Bld	Room #	Room Type	Key #	Transaction Date	Trans Type
Blount							
	12111	REB	501	Office	1	01-Nov-01	O
	12130	REB	601	Class	3	11-Dec-02	O
Beaman							
	12112	REB	502	Office	1	01-Nov-02	R
Tillery							
	12113	REB	503	Office	2	01-Jan-02	O
	12130	REB	601	Class	1	06-Apr-02	O
	12117	REB	507	Office	4	06-Aug-02	O
	12130	REB	601	Class	1	04-Dec-02	R
Brown							
	12114	REB	504	Class	2	14-Jan-02	O
	12114	REB	504	Class	3	03-Nov-02	R
Peterson							
	12112	REB	502	Office	2	30-Dec-01	O

7.22 Create a report that shows the departmental key transactions (O = check-out, R = return) for each key. Use a parameter query using the key number to generate a report for a specific key, such as **12112**. If the end user does not make an entry and simply clicks **OK**, *all* the employee key transactions must be shown (see Figures P7.22 and P7.22A). (*Hint*: Remember the **Like** function and the **Is Null** option?) Use the report output format shown in Figure P7.22A. The page header must be repeated on each page. Save the report as **rptKeyReportByKey**.

FIGURE P7.22
The Key Number Request

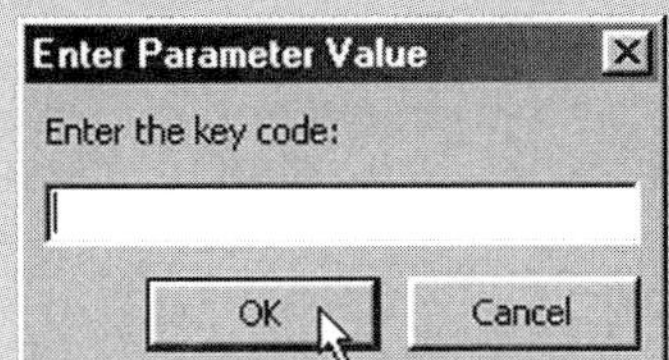

FIGURE P7.22A
The Key Transactions

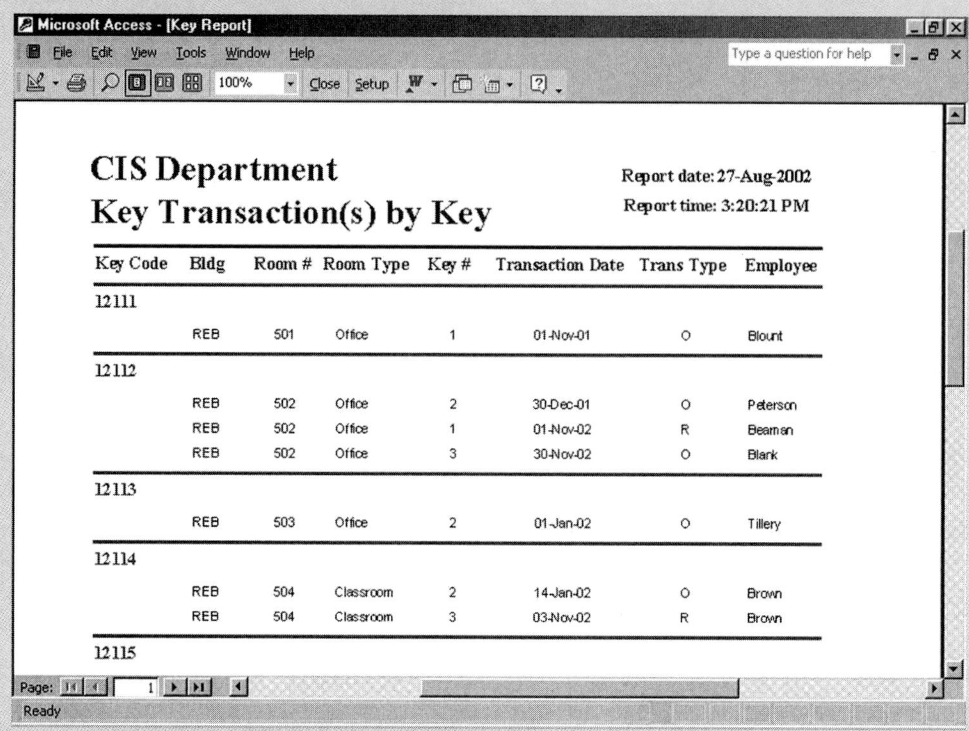

Microsoft Access - [Key Report]

CIS Department
Key Transaction(s) by Key

Report date: 27-Aug-2002
Report time: 3:20:21 PM

Key Code	Bldg	Room #	Room Type	Key #	Transaction Date	Trans Type	Employee
12111							
	REB	501	Office	1	01-Nov-01	O	Blount
12112							
	REB	502	Office	2	30-Dec-01	O	Peterson
	REB	502	Office	1	01-Nov-02	R	Beaman
	REB	502	Office	3	30-Nov-02	O	Blank
12113							
	REB	503	Office	2	01-Jan-02	O	Tillery
12114							
	REB	504	Classroom	2	14-Jan-02	O	Brown
	REB	504	Classroom	3	03-Nov-02	R	Brown
12115							

Chapter **Eight**

Macros and Macro Groups

Preview

In Chapters 1 through 3 you learned how to design databases, in Chapter 4 you learned how to implement databases, and in Chapters 5 through 7 you learned how to create useful and attractive end-user database applications. Although each database component works flawlessly at this point, end users would have a difficult time working in this database environment. First, end users would have to know how to work from the database window, and they would have to know which queries and reports to run. Because many queries serve as intermediaries to other queries and, worse, may lead to the unintended deletion or modification of records, making all the queries available to end users is a recipe for database disaster. Second, many forms serve as input to queries, which then are supposed to open other forms and/or reports. Unfortunately, this parameter-passing environment is anything but obvious to end users, so you would probably have to provide frequent and intensive end-user support. Finally, letting end users work in an unstructured and open database environment is very likely to lead to unintentional data corruption and security problems.

To make the database and its applications truly useful, you must create a structured *system* that ties the database's end-user applications together. Because you learned in Chapter 6 how to create menus and command buttons, you will now learn how the menu forms—and any other forms that make use of command buttons—can be tied together through macros. Therefore, you will learn how to activate all the command buttons on the forms to shift control from one form to another, opening and closing forms as needed. You will also learn how to use macros to trigger many different kinds of actions besides opening and closing forms. For example, you will learn how to create macros that hide or display different form components; change conditions from edit mode to read-only; write values to forms; trigger queries to update, modify, or delete records; and produce a host of other actions that make the end-user interface truly useful.

It is easy to produce a macro environment that is difficult to understand and, therefore, difficult to document and manage. You can avoid such problems by creating the macros within logical modules known as macro groups.

Objectives

When you have mastered the material in this chapter, you should know

- What a macro is.
- What macro actions, arguments, and conditions are.
- What a macro group is.
- How to create a macro group.
- How to create macros within the macro groups.
- How to use a naming convention to help make the macro environment self-documenting.

8.1 WHAT A MACRO IS AND WHAT IT DOES

A **macro** is an instruction or a set of instructions that triggers one or more actions. These actions include opening and closing forms; writing error messages; producing dialog boxes; changing tab orders; updating, modifying, and deleting records; processing input, and so on. Macros can also call up and execute other macros. Therefore, macros can be used to automatically perform the many actions that change a sometimes-bewildering collection of database components into an easy-to-use and comprehensive system.

Although the code that underlies the macros may be complex, creating and using macros is relatively easy. In effect, macros involve the use of a high-level computer language that hides the complexity of the actions from you. All you need to do is tell the computer what to do; you do not have to tell the computer how to do it. Access allows you to pick the various actions from a list, so you won't even need to remember the exact commands. (Of course, you will have to know what actions you need!) After you select an action, Access will even give you a list of appropriate action arguments. For example, if you select the macro action **Open**, a set of action arguments automatically appears. Because **Open** can involve different types of objects, Access will provide a list of possible objects, and each object type triggers its own object name options. Logical conditions can be created via the familiar Expression Builder. In short, although you will have to supply the logic of the system's actions, Access makes macro creation as simple as possible.

The reason for creating and using macros is simple: Macros can be used to hide the system's complexities from the end users. In short, the macro-based system can be used to guide end users to perform many different types of database tasks, without forcing these users to understand how the system works. Assuming that the system enables the end users to do their jobs more efficiently and intelligently, making the system easy to use is what helps make it such a powerful tool. To use an analogy, how useful would a car be to you if you had to know how to operate each of its components in order to drive? Just think of how difficult it would be to manage the engine's ignition sequences manually. Instead, you get in your car, turn the key, and expect the engine to work. Or suppose you had to know all about the hydraulic system to successfully activate its components manually? (We suspect that there would be many more accidents if drivers had to initiate a complex and lengthy set of actions manually to brake the car.) Fortunately, you simply press the brake pedal, and the rest happens automatically. In short, although the system's behind-the-scene activities may be complex and numerous, making the system easy to use is crucial to its success!

In the same vein, end users do not care about what macros are and what they do. What end users want is a system that is easy to use and one that helps them become more productive. In other words, the macros can combine all the components you have written thus far into a tightly controlled system that guides the end user to properly use the database environment.

8.1.1 Macro Groups

Macros are best placed in logical modules known as **macro groups**. Each of the modules defines the activities within a logically defined portion of the applications environment. For example, the main menu we developed in Chapter 6 (see section 6.7) contains many command buttons that transfer control to other forms and/or processes. The main menu also shows that the buttons are arranged in logical groups. These four button groups transfer control to four distinct functions: data management or maintenance, transactions, menus, and archiving.

Although no standards govern which macros must be stored in what macro group, it is absolutely necessary to create macro groups based on some logical footing. Ultimately, you must make professional decisions in answering questions such as

1. How many macros should be stored in a macro group? There is no hard and fast rule here, but too many macros in one macro group will make it hard to manage. If you put too few macros in a macro group, you'll wind up with too many macro groups. In the extreme case, if each of your macro groups contains a single macro, there is no point in creating macro groups at all. So here's some truly dangerous advice: Use common sense!
2. At what point do the transactions become sufficiently complex to warrant their own macro group? Once again, there is no hard and fast rule here. Clearly, if a transaction involves simple actions, such as merely opening and closing forms and performing a single data update, there is no point in putting it in its own macro group. On the other hand, if a transaction involves multiple steps and each step involves a complex process, it's ready to be placed in its own macro group. The answer to question 1 surely has an effect on the answer to question 2, and vice versa. And the advice remains the same: Use common sense.
3. Do you store all of the transaction macros in one transaction macro group, or do you break out each transaction type and create a macro group for it? The answer to this question is clearly influenced by your answer to questions 1 and 2. In turn, your answer to question 3 affects how you answer questions 1 and 2.
4. How, and to what extent, do you break down the logical processes? The answer to this question is clearly influenced by how you approached questions 2 and 3. And the answer to questions 2 and 3 are clearly influenced by the answer to question 4.

No matter what decisions you make on the basis of the preceding questions, do use macro groups. Do not use freestanding macros.

Putting macros within macro groups has several benefits:

- The macros will be easier to manage. If a macro malfunctions within a logically structured macro group, it will be easier to repair. Tracing a logical problem is much easier if the problem is contained within a logical sequence!
- Because macro groups conform to the system modules, it's easy to add similar modules later. The familiar **Edit/Copy/Paste** routine will greatly simplify your applications development process. For example, if you have multiple menu structures, first create a menu template form and its macros and then duplicate it with the **File/Save As** option. Finally, edit the duplicate to rename it and its components, and you have just saved yourself a lot of development time!

8.1.2 Macro Naming Conventions

Throughout this book we've emphasized the need to make the database environment as self-documenting as possible. We continue this emphasis during the macro development process. Therefore, we suggest the following naming conventions:

- Use the prefix **mcr** to identify macro groups. This naming convention makes it easy to distinguish between the form **frmFindEmployee**, the query **qryFind Employee**, and the macro group **mcrFindEmployee**.
- Use descriptive names. The name **mcrFindEmployee** indicates the macro's function. The name **mcrEmpTransFind2** leaves you wondering just what this thing might be, and a name like **mcrY3-TR98** leaves you completely baffled. Trying to figure out what some other developer had in mind when you are asked to repair or update an application is bad enough. Trying to figure out

what on earth you had in mind when you try to update your own work is positively humiliating.

- Use descriptive names that tie the macro to its transactions. For example, if the macro group contains macros that open a dialog box form named **frmFindEmployee** to trigger a query named **qryFindEmployee**, it would be useful to name the macro group **mcrFindEmployee**.
- Within the macro groups, use macro names that indicate their actions. For example, if a macro within the **mcrFindEmployee** macro group must open an employee search form, this macro might appropriately be named **Open EmployeeSearchForm**. Note that the macros within the macro group do *not* carry the **mcr** prefix. (The prefix would be redundant because the macro is contained within a macro group that already carries the **mcr** prefix.)

8.2 CREATING A MACRO GROUP

Copy the **Ch08_POS_2nd.mdb** from the CD to your drive. (After you have copied the database, remember to uncheck the **Read-only** option.) You are now ready to practice the skills you develop in this chapter.

To make the macro building and editing process as flexible as possible, Access lets you invoke the macro builder via many different sources. In fact, you can even create and/or edit a macro group by clicking on a form's command button—while the form is in its design mode—to use its properties box to open the macro builder. Such flexibility is particularly desirable when you want to edit an existing macro group. However, we'll build our first macro group via the database window from which we launched queries and forms. Therefore, start at the database window, select the macro folder tab, and select the **New** option to produce the macro builder screen shown in Figure 8.1. (Only the top portion of the screen is shown.)

As you examine Figure 8.1, note that the default presentation includes only two columns: **Action** and **Comment**. Because you will be creating a macro group to hold several macros, you'll need to add a **Macro Names** column, so place the cursor on the **Macro Names** button, as shown in Figure 8.1, and then click to select it. And because you'll occasionally need to specify the conditions under which a macro is executed, click the **Conditions** button that is located to the right of the **Macro Names** button. These two actions create the macro screen shown in Figure 8.2. (We've placed the cursor back on the **Conditions** button to show you what it looks like.)

FIGURE 8.1 The Initial Macro Builder Screen

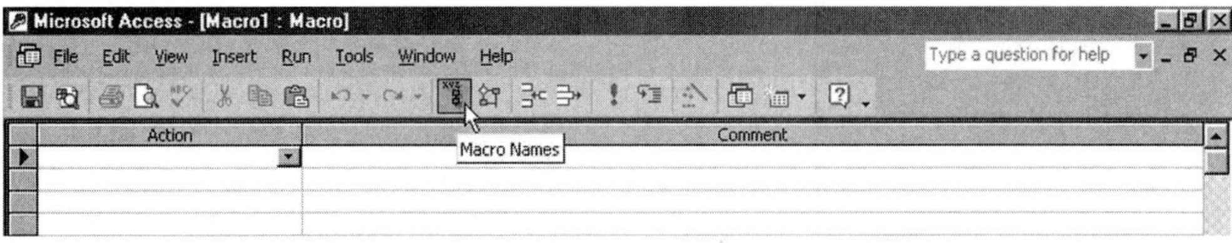

FIGURE 8.2 The Four-column Macro Builder Screen

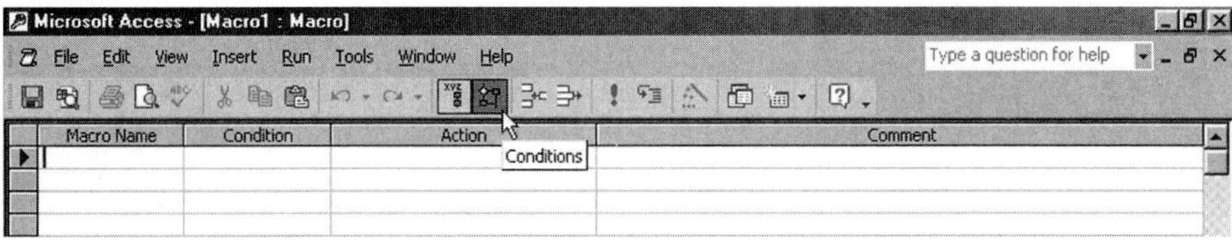

FIGURE 8.3
Saving the mcrQuery Macro Group

The four-column macro screen is the standard for all macro groups in this book. Although you have not yet created any macros in this screen, go ahead and save it as your first macro group, using the macro group name **mcrQuery,** as shown in Figure 8.3.

We'll start with the **mcrQuery** macro group for a good reason: It contains only a few simple macros that perform limited actions. Therefore, you'll gradually get used to the macro-building process.

8.2.1 Creating the Macros within the Macro Group

As its name indicates, the **mcrQuery** macro group will contain the macros that have to do with queries. Using the **Ch08_POS_2nd.mdb**'s menu system as the basis for your first macro group, note that the command buttons in Figure 8.4 allow you to select a query from a list of five available queries. In addition, the command button at the bottom of the menu enables you to close the query menu. Naturally, you must open the query menu to see the query menu in the first place.

In short, Figure 8.4 indicates that the **mcrQuery** macro group must be able to accommodate these actions:

- Open the query menu.
- Close the query menu.
- Open any of the five queries when a menu button is selected.

Therefore, we will place seven macros into the **mcrQuery** macro group.

Let's start by making sure that the query menu can be opened. Remembering that macros must be named to reflect their actions, take a look at Figure 8.5 and note that we have named the first macro **OpenQueryMenu**.

After typing the macro name in the first column of Figure 8.5, you must specify what action this macro is expected to take. Therefore, stay on the line containing the macro name, move to the **Action** column, and click to let Access generate the drop-down menu shown in Figure 8.5. Remember that the query menu in Figure 8.4 is a form, so the **OpenQueryMenu** macro must open the

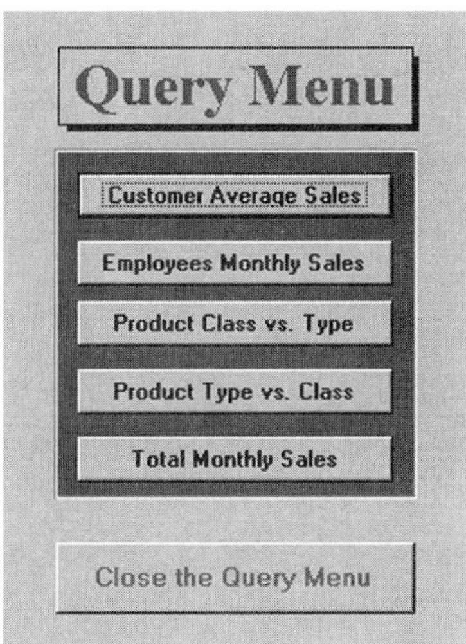

FIGURE 8.4
The frmQueryMenu Form Options

FIGURE 8.5 The First Macro in the mcrQuery Macro Group

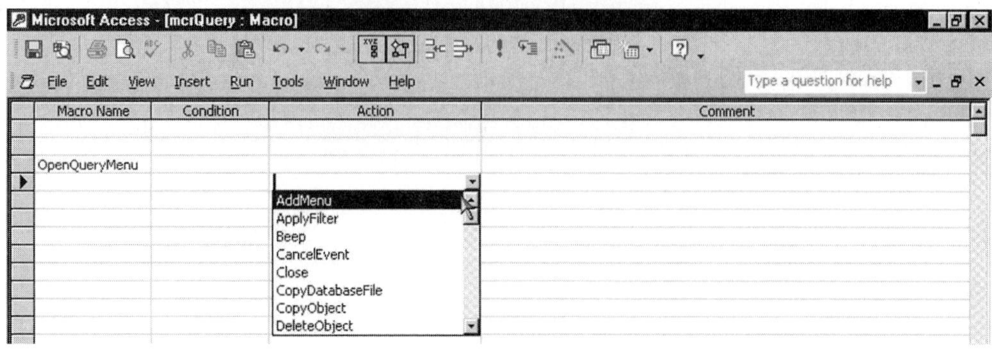

FIGURE 8.6 Several Macros in the mcrQuery Macro Group

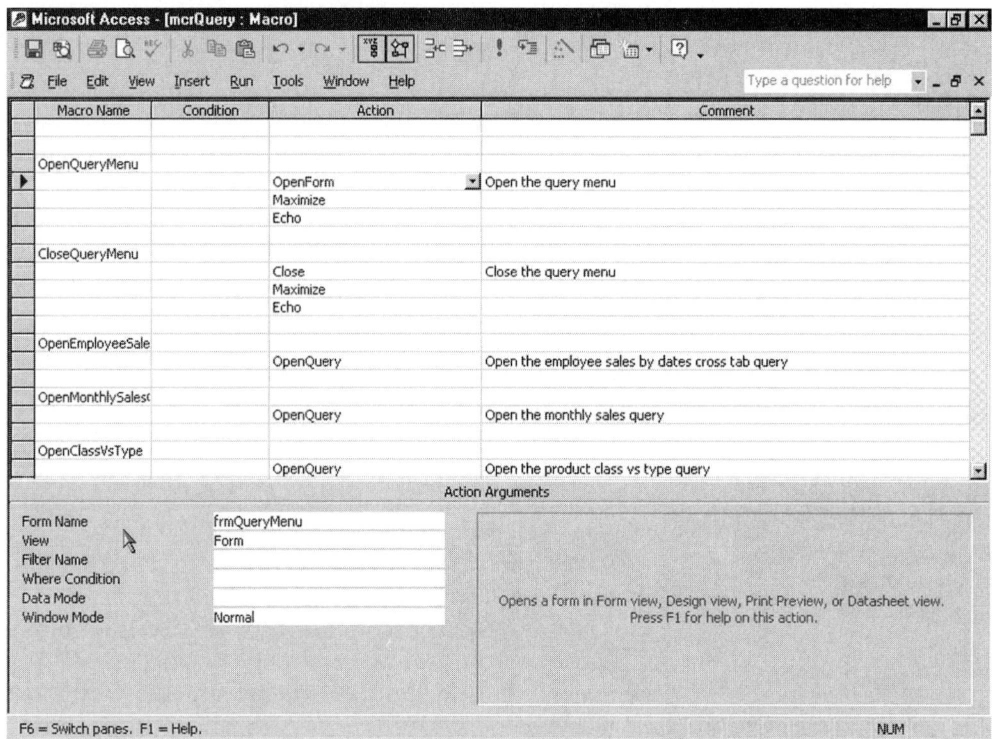

form. Therefore, use the scroll bar on the menu's right margin until you see the **OpenForm** option; then click on it to select it and move it to the action column. The results are shown on the first line in Figure 8.6.

As you examine the screen shown in Figure 8.6, please note the following features:

- For each macro, we have placed the initial macro **Action** one line below the macro name. This convention is very useful for two reasons. First, if you later want to insert a macro **Action** *above* an existing macro action, all you need to do is insert a line below the **Macro Name** and then select the desired action. Second, the offset makes it easier to distinguish the components of the macro group.
- We have written the first macro name a few lines below the first line to make space for a few **Comment** lines and/or additional macros.
- We have skipped a line between each macro's last **Action** and the next **Macro Name** to make it easier to read the macros later. In fact, to make each

Note

Once you have become familiar with the available actions, you may also type the action name. Usually, you'll only need to type a few characters before Access recognizes what you probably want to do. Then Access will automatically type in the remaining characters for you. For example, if you want to type in the action selection **Close**, Access will type the **ose** portion after you type **Cl**. But be sure to check what Access has selected for you. Sometimes Access misreads your intentions, and you'll have to type a few additional characters before it makes the proper selection.

Note

Access will automatically produce the appropriate options when you select an action. For example, if an action requires an argument, Access will automatically produce the **Action Arguments** screen segment shown in Figure 8.6. Access will also explain what actions you are expected to take, depending on where you clicked. Using Figure 8.6 as the example, we clicked on the **Macro Name** column, thus causing Access to write the message **Enter a macro name in this column**. Go ahead and click on several macro screen portions to see what prompts you'll get.

macro stand out, it may be useful to skip several lines between each macro's last **Action** and the next **Macro Name**.

Remember that you can widen each section of the screen by dragging the section limits. Looking at Figure 8.6, for example, you might want to drag the **Macro Name** section limit to make it wider so that you can read the fourth macro's complete macro name.

After selecting the **OpenForm** action shown in Figure 8.6, you must specify what form is to be opened. The clarification or augmentation of an action is accomplished by defining the action argument. In this case, the **OpenForm** action requires that you specify which form to be opened. Because you want the **OpenQueryMenu** macro to open the query menu form named **frmQueryMenu**, click on the **Form Name** option shown in Figure 8.6 and select the form name from the drop-down list.

Figure 8.6 also shows you that the **OpenQueryMenu** macro contains three actions: the **OpenForm**, **Maximize**, and **Echo**. You already know what the **OpenForm** does. As expected, the **Maximize** action maximizes the screen presentation. Therefore, the selected form will be expanded to fit the screen. The **Maximize** action requires no further clarification, so Access will not produce a set of action argument lines. However, if you leave the cursor on the **Maximize** action, Access will explain what it means by printing the message **Maximizes the active window so it fills the Microsoft Access window. Press F1 for help on this action**. The **Echo** action requires the action argument shown in Figure 8.7. By clicking on the **Echo On** option, you'll generate a drop-down list with the choices **Yes** or **No**. The explanation of the **Echo** argument is shown in the lower right corner of the figure.

As you examine Figures 8.6 and 8.7, you'll note that we have written some brief explanations on several of the **Comment** lines. Given the simplicity of the macros and their actions, these comments are unnecessary. In fact, we did not write comments to explain actions such as **Maximize** and **Echo**. However, as the macros and their actions become more complex, such comments become an

FIGURE 8.7 **The OpenQueryMenu's Echo Action Argument**

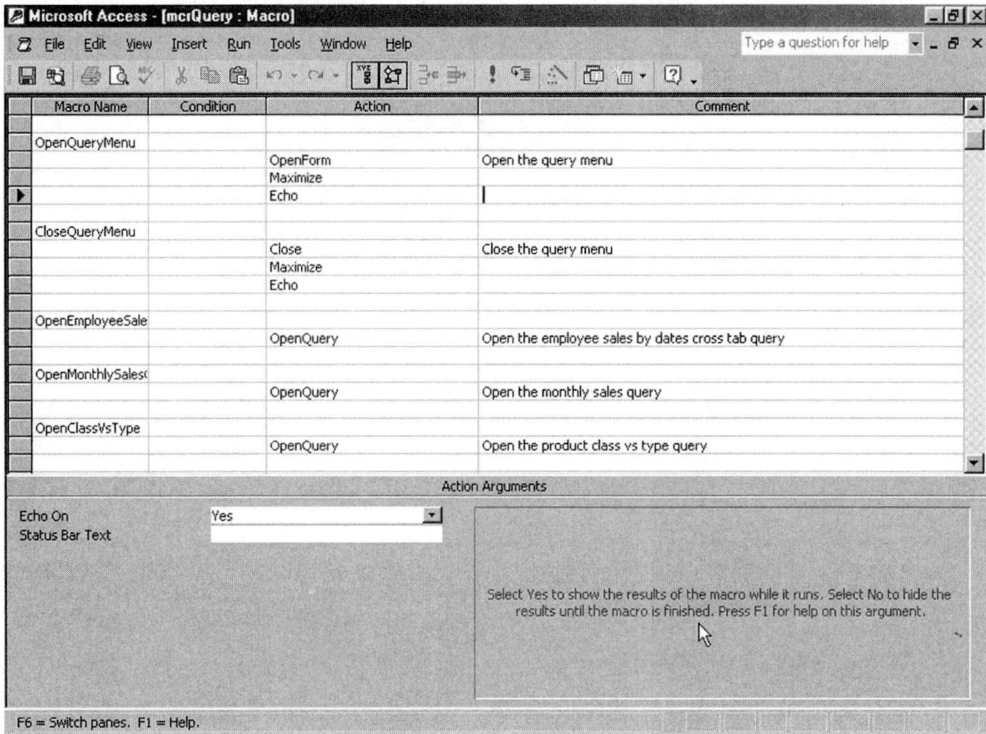

important part of the documentation process. Therefore, we suggest you start getting used to writing comments!

Thus far we've shown you two macros in the **mcrQuery** macro group. The first macro opens the **frmQueryMenu**, and the second closes it. You now must create the five macros that open the queries you want to call via the query menu shown earlier in Figure 8.4.

To open each of the five queries, all you need to do is write the five macros shown in Figure 8.8. Each macro uses an **OpenQuery** action that triggers an action argument to open the query in datasheet format. Note, for example, that the **OpenEmployeeSalesQuery** macro opens the **qryEmployeeSales** query. Similarly, the second macro, named **OpenMonthlySalesQuery**, opens the **qryMonthlySales**.

As you examine Figure 8.8, note that all the actions involve the **OpenQuery** command. Therefore, adding the prefix **Open** and the suffix **Query** to the macro names is probably not necessary. For example, naming the first macro **Open EmployeeSales** or even **EmployeeSales** would have been quite acceptable. We've left off the **Query** suffix in two of the macro names. In any case, use descriptive macro names, but keep them reasonably short. Proper documentation only requires that you can later identify the macro components and functions easily.

Note also that we have violated one of the macro design conventions we discussed earlier. Figure 8.8 shows that the **Macro Name** and the macro **Action** are written on the same line. Although the macros will execute properly even when you violate basic self-documentation techniques, we will show you in the next section how to edit the macro group contents.

8.2.2 Editing the Macro Group Contents

All the standard edit commands are available when you place the macro group in the design mode. The copy, delete, and paste options are your primary editing tools, and we suspect you'll use them often. In addition, you'll often find it useful

FIGURE 8.8 The Query Execution Macros

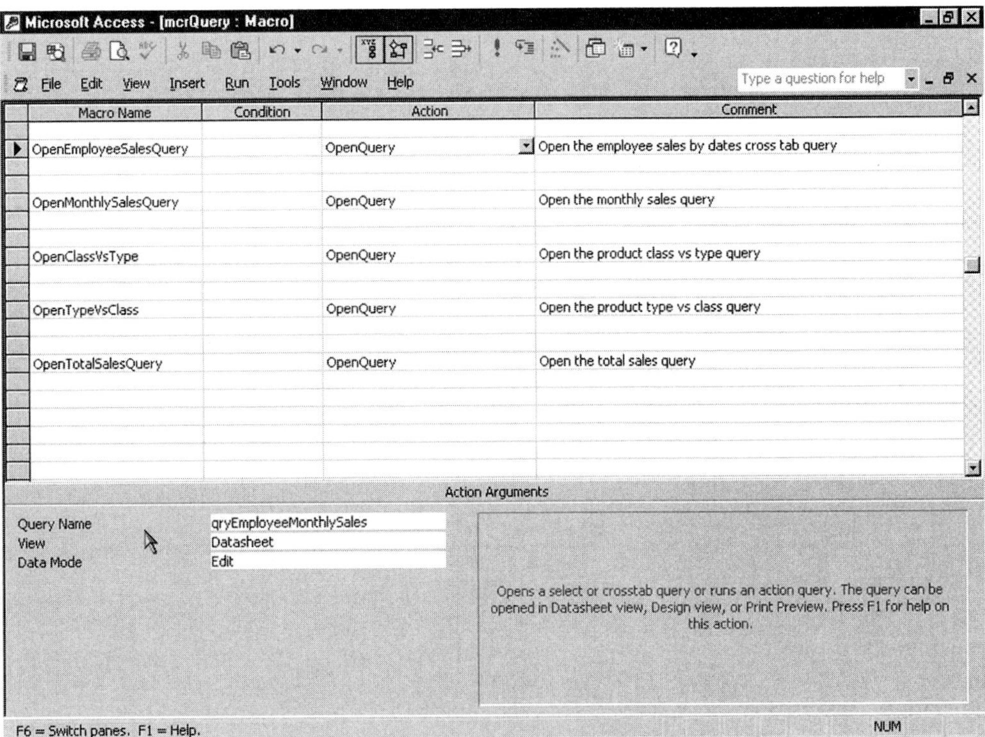

to insert lines between actions in order to add new actions. (The macro actions are executed in the order in which they are encountered. However, the macros themselves may appear in any order because they can be called in any order.)

To see how the editing options are used to format the macro group contents, start with Figure 8.8. Note that the first action following each macro is located on the same line. Given the discussion in the previous section, you already know that it is better to place the first action one line below the macro name. To produce this format for the **OpenQueryMenu** macro, mark the macro name and use **Edit/Cut** to place the macro name on the clipboard. Then click on the **Macro Name** line above the original line and use **Edit/Paste** to produce the results shown in Figure 8.9. (Note that we have edited all the macros in Figure 8.9.)

Changing an Action or an Action Argument

To change any action or an action argument, click on it to produce the Access-generated drop-down list and then make the appropriate selection from the list. Because all of the actions and action arguments shown in Figure 8.9 are correct, no changes are necessary.

Inserting and Deleting Lines

To insert a line, mark it by clicking on the line's left tab. (Note that the cursor shape changes to a thick arrow when you place it on the line's left tab.) This action will invert the line's screen presentation as shown in Figure 8.10. You can then right-click on the marked line to pop up the menu you see in Figure 8.10 and then click on the **Insert Rows** selection to insert a row. Or you can simply mark the line and then press your keyboard's insert key to get the same result. (The second approach is quicker and easier. As you can tell, we have pressed the insert key three times to insert several additional lines.)

If you want to delete a line, mark it as shown in Figure 8.10 and then press the keyboard's delete key to delete the line. (Or right-click on the marked line and use

FIGURE 8.9 The Revised Macro Name Locations

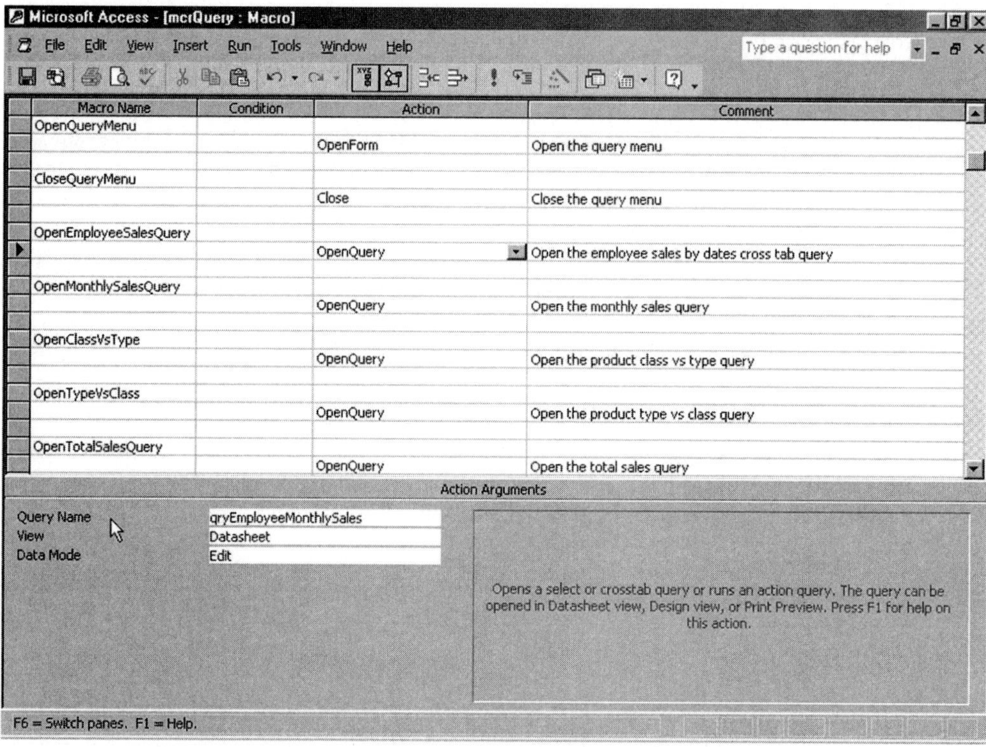

FIGURE 8.10 A Marked Screen Line

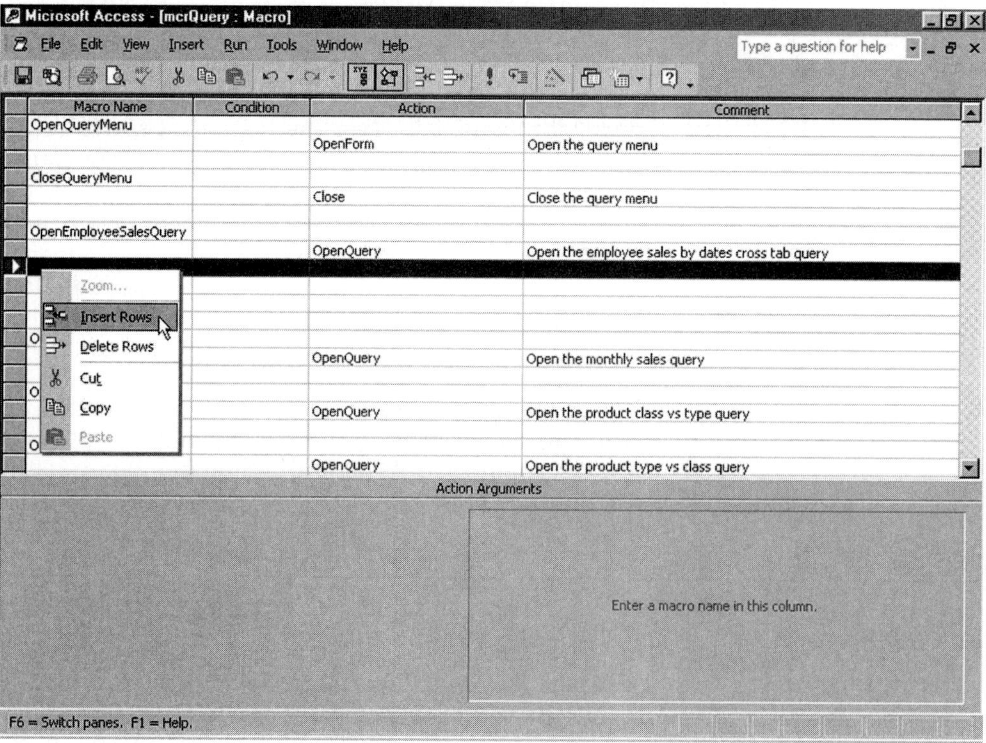

the pop-up menu's **Delete Rows** option.) Incidentally, it is always a good idea to leave a few blank lines before the first macro name line. The comment portion on the extra lines can then be used to write, if necessary, the macro group's

Assignment

Add the **Maximize** and **Echo** actions to the **OpenQueryMenu** macro, then copy and paste these actions to each of the macros in the **mcrQuery** macro group. The results are shown in Figure 8.10A.

FIGURE 8.10A The Edited Macros in the mcrQuery Macro Group

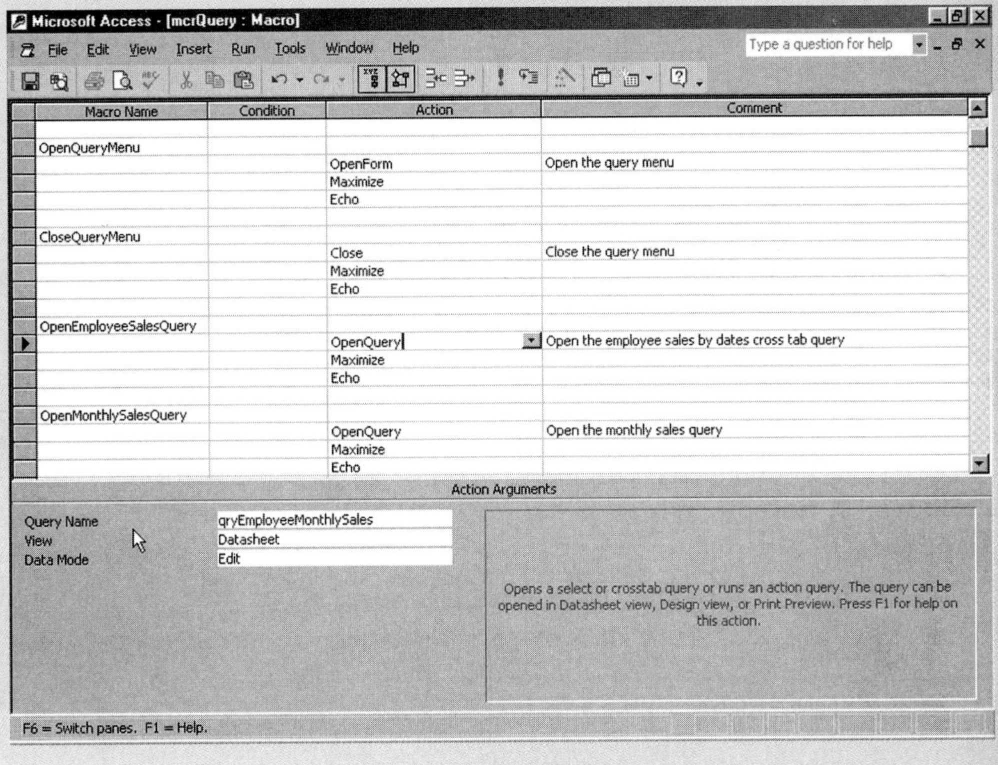

documentation. Placing a few extra lines between the macros within the macro group makes the macro group contents easier to read.

8.3 ATTACHING THE MACRO TO THE COMMAND BUTTON

From an end-user's point of view, macros don't perform their intended actions until they are connected to the form's command buttons. To illustrate how this is done, we will use the **frmQueryMenu** form first shown in Figure 8.4.

To attach the macros to any of the form's command buttons, complete the following steps. (We will use the **Close the Query Menu** button to illustrate the process.)

1. Open the form in the design mode. (As you can tell by looking at Figure 8.11, we have selected the **frmQueryMenu** form.)
2. Click on the object you want to attach the macro to. (Check Figure 8.11 to see that that we have selected the form's **Close the Query Menu** button.
3. Open the object's properties box—in this example, the **Close the Query Menu** button—and cursor down to the properties box's **On Click** property. (See Figure 8.11.)
4. Click on the properties box's **On Click** property line to generate a drop-down list of available macros within the macro groups. (See Figure 8.11.)

FIGURE 8.11 **Selecting the Macro to Be Attached to the Object**

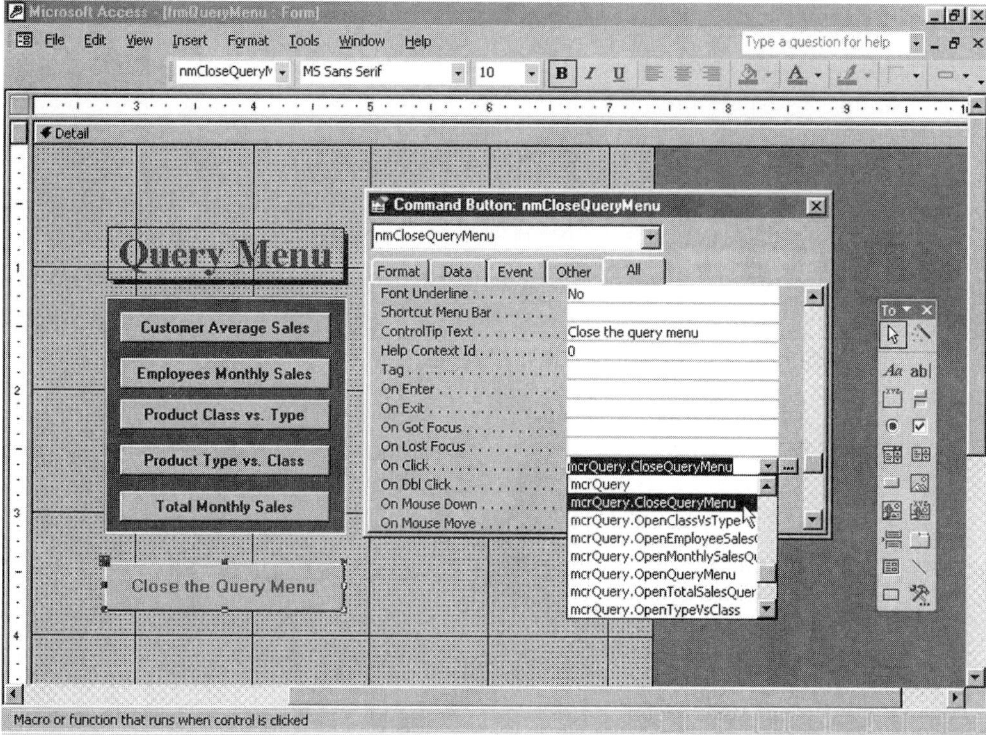

5. Cursor down the drop-down list of available macros within the macro group to find the macro you want to attach to the **Close the Query Menu** button object. (Check Figure 8.11 and note that we cursored down to the **CloseQuery Menu** macro in the **mcrQuery** macro group.)
6. Click on the selected **CloseQueryMenu** macro to write it in the **On Click** property line. (Figure 8.11 shows that we have already done that.)
7. Save the **frmQueryMenu** form again, which now has the **CloseQuery Menu** macro attached to the **Close the Query Menu** button object.

As you examine Figure 8.11, note that Access uses the macro group name as a prefix to the macro name. In this case, Access has labeled the selected macro **mcrQuery.CloseQueryMenu**. (Access uses a period to separate the macro group name from the macro name.) Given this Access naming convention, you can use the same macro name in other macro groups. For example, Access will reference the **CloseMenu** macro in the **mcrMainMenu** macro group as **mcrMainMenu.CloseMenu**. Similarly, the **CloseMenu** macro would be referenced in the **mcrReportMenu** macro group as **mcrReportMenu.CloseMenu**. This convention makes the documentation easier and allows you to use the same macro name in different macro groups.

Figure 8.11 also shows the familiar three-dot builder button next to the **On Click** property line. If you have already selected a macro, clicking on the builder button will automatically open that macro in its design format. At this point, you can edit all the existing macros within the macro group, add new macros, and so on. If you have not selected a macro from the drop-down list, clicking on the builder button will open the **New Macro** design option. Therefore, you can even build the macro groups and the macros within them at the query and form levels.

After completing the seven-step macro development and attachment process, open the form in its form view and then click on the form's **Close the Query Menu** button to see the macro work.

FIGURE 8.12 **The Exit Access Command Button on the Main Menu**

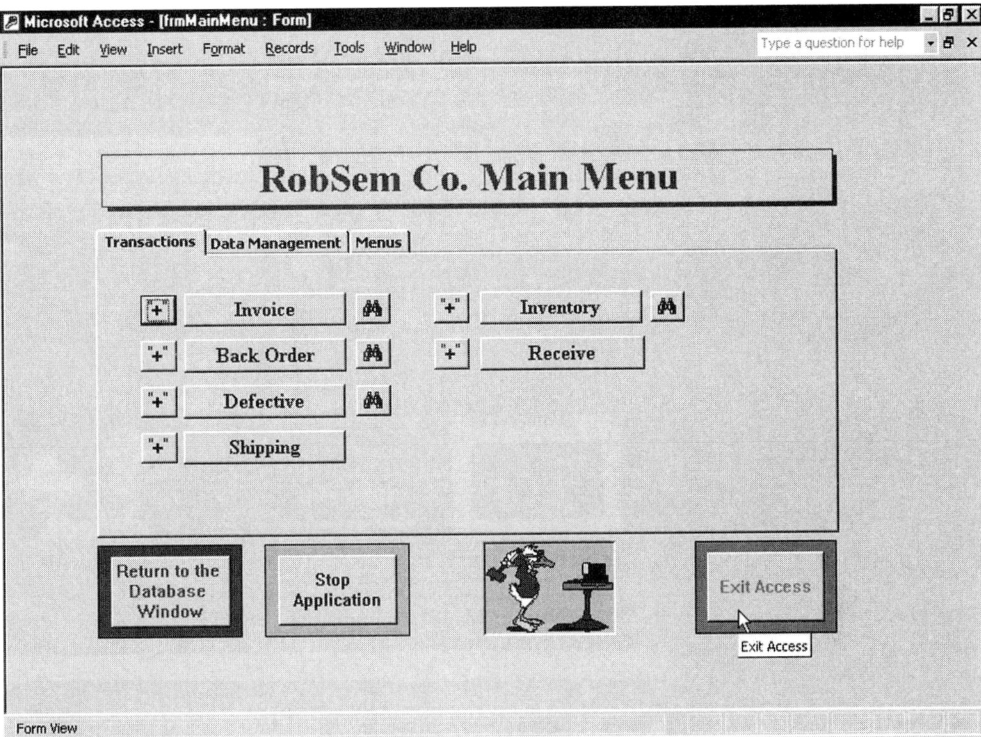

FIGURE 8.12A
The Confirmation Message Box

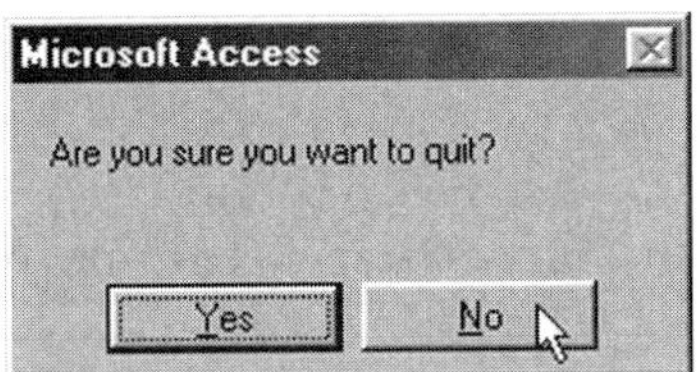

8.4 MANAGING THE INTERFACE

Each database application system has many options that can lead to unintended consequences. The simplest example involves a main menu on which an **Exit Access** command button is located (see Figure 8.12.)

If the end user clicks on the **Exit Access** command button in Figure 8.12, the application is terminated and the application is closed. But suppose the end user *accidentally* clicks on this button? It would be nice if your application software would confirm such a critical action before executing it. For example, you might want to design the interface so that clicking on the **Exit Access** command button produces the confirmation message box shown in Figure 8.12A.

To produce the confirmation window shown in Figure 8.12A, open the **Ch08_POS_2nd.mdb** database's **frmMainMenu** in its design view. To produce Figure 8.12B, the following steps must be completed:

- Click on the form's **ExitAccess** button.
- Open the **ExitAccess** button's properties box.
- Select the **On Click** option.
- Scroll down to **mcrMainMenu.ExitAccess** macro. (Note that we have placed the cursor on the builder button.)

FIGURE 8.12B
Attaching a Macro to the Exit Access Button

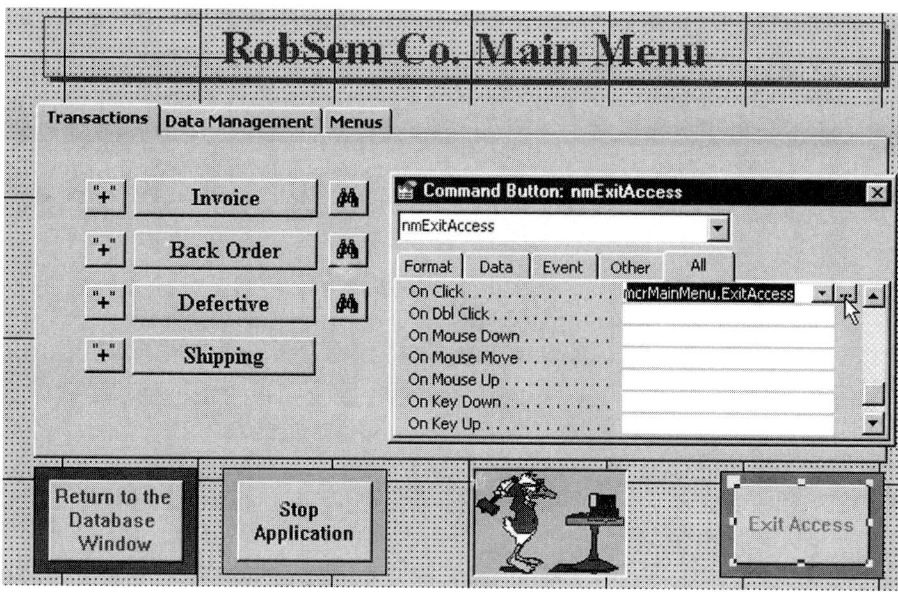

FIGURE 8.12C **The ExitAccess Macro in the mcrMainMenu Macro Group**

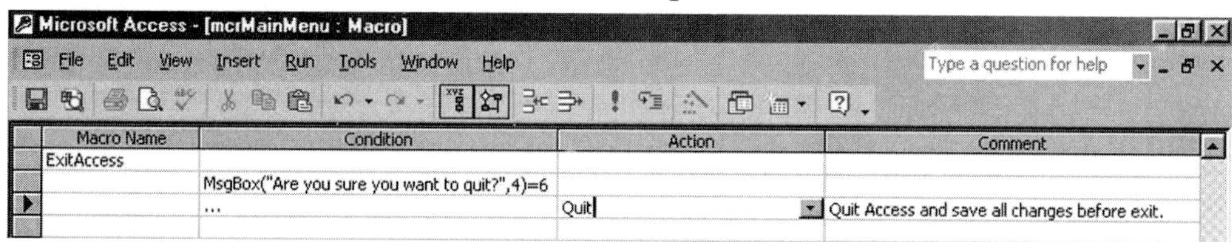

FIGURE 8.12D
The Yes, No, and Cancel Options on the Message Box

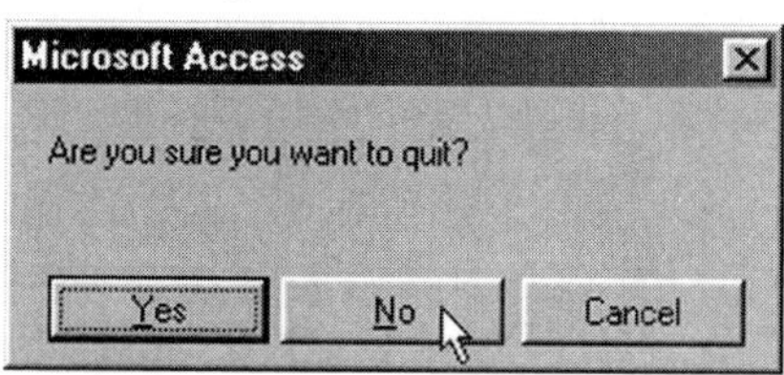

FIGURE 8.12E
The Warning Message Box

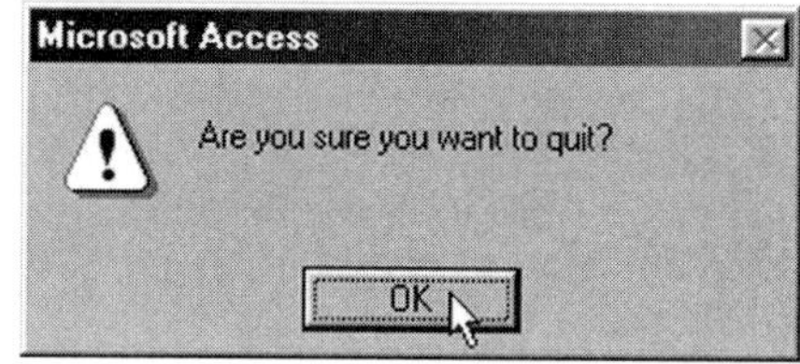

Click on the builder button shown in Figure 8.12B to select the **mcrMain Menu** macro's design view. Within the **mcrMainMenu** macro's design view, scroll to locate the **ExitAccess** macro shown in Figure 8.12C.

As you examine Figure 8.12C, note that the **Msgbox** to be displayed is located in the macro's **Condition** column. The **MsgBox** contains the message you want to display to the user and the numbers you see are used by Access to define the presentation and execution formats of the message box. For example:

- The number 4 is used to produce the **Yes** and **No** options shown in Figure 8.12A. If you substitute the number 3 for the number 4, the message box will have the **Yes**, **No**, and **Cancel** options displayed as shown in Figure 8.12D.
- You can control the message box type by using numerical codes. For example, the number 48 would have launched a warning message like the one shown in Figure 8.12E. (It does not make sense to use the warning message box in this case; we just want to show you what one looks like.)

TABLE 8.1 Sample Message Box Button Codes

Visual Basic Code	Value	Message Box Buttons
vbOKOnly	**0**	Shows an **OK** button
vbOKCancel	**1**	Shows **OK** and **Cancel** buttons
vbAbortRetryIgnore	**2**	Shows **Abort**, **Retry**, **Ignore** buttons
vbYesNoCancel	**3**	Shows **Yes**, **No**, and **Cancel** buttons
vbYesNo	**4**	Shows **Yes** and **No** buttons
vbRetryCancel	**5**	Shows **Retry** and **Cancel** buttons
vbCritical	**16**	Shows **Critical Message** icon on message box
vbQuestion	**32**	Shows **Warning Query** icon
vbExclamation	**48**	Shows **Warning Message** icon
vbInformation	**64**	Shows **Information Message** icon

Table 8.1 shows a few of the more common message box codes. You can use the Access **Help** function to find many additional options for the **MsgBox** function button settings.

- The **=6** in the **MsgBox("Are you sure you want to quit?",3)=6** function shown in Figure 8.12C defines which button on the message box will launch the macro. For example, **=6** launches the macro if you click **Yes** on the message box, while **=7** launches the macro if you click **No** on the message box.

If you want to see the other Access codes that govern message boxes, you can use the built-in **Help** function to generate the summary displayed in Figure 8.12E. (You can open the **Help** function with the F1 key or you can use the Access Assistant. In either case, use the search key message box to see the available options shown in Figure 8.12E. Scroll down to see additional options.)

Now that you have had a chance to examine the various message box codes, let's return to Figure 8.12C to see the macro's structure. The three dots under the message **Condition** are used to control the flow of the macro's components. *Specifically, the three dots signify that the next action in the macro will be executed only if the specified condition is met.* If the user clicks **Yes** on the message box shown in Figure 8.12A, all macros under the condition with three dots will be executed. If **No** is selected, nothing will happen. (Go ahead and make sure that the **ExitAccess** macro is attached to the main menu's **Exit Access** button and then open the form and then click on the **Exit Access** button to see the **ExitAccess** macro in action.)

The complete macro contents are shown in Table 8.2. Although you can print the macro contents directly from Access, we like to use the format in Table 8.2 to document our macros. Condition statements are always lined up—use left justification in the text—under the **Condition** header. Action statements are always lined up—use left justification in the text—under the **Action** header. Action argument statements are always lined up—use left justification in the text—under the **Action Argument** header. You can create a Word macro documentation template like the one shown in Table 8.2, then cut and paste the actual macro components into this documentation template. (You'll never have to worry about typing errors this way!) This documentation format makes it very easy to examine the contents

TABLE 8.2 The Macro That Controls the Exit Access Button Actions: Macro Group Name: mcrMainMenu

Macro Name	Condition	Action	Action Argument
ExitAccess	MsgBox("Are you sure you want to quit?",4)=6		
	. . .	**Quit**	Options: Save All

of even complex macros, because all of the macro's components are easily visible. If your macros yield errors, this format makes it much easier to find and fix those errors.

As you examine the macro shown in Table 8.2, note that the macro names conform to the button names. For example, the **ExitAccess** macro name matches the **ExitAccess** button name. This naming convention makes it easy to remember which macros control which objects. Clearly, macros are powerful tools that help applications developers help the end users!

8.4.1 The Startup Screen

When end users start an application, they should not have to know how to find the main menu, how to open it, and how to clean up the screen by removing unwanted menu bars. That's why application developers like to launch the applications automatically when the database is opened. There are two ways to get that job done. You can either use the built-in Access startup tools or write a special macro known as an **Autoexec** macro.

Using the Access Startup Tools

Use the menu bar at the top of the screen and then select **Tools/Startup** as shown in Figure 8.13.

When you make the selection shown in Figure 8.13, Access produces the dialog box shown in Figure 8.14. In this case, we have entered the form name **frmStartup** to ensure that this form, shown in Figure 8.15, is opened when the application is started. You can, of course, open the main menu or any other form you consider to be useful and appropriate.

Figure 8.15's **frmStartup** form may be closed to show the main menu, or if the end user does not select the **Close** button within a specified period of time, the form closes automatically and opens the main menu. The timing selection is made via the form's property box, using the **On Timer** and **Timer Interval** specifications shown in Figure 8.16. Go ahead and experiment by changing the **Timer Interval** values; then open the form to see the effect.

Although the **frmStartup** will automatically open the main menu, it is always a good idea to give the end user the option to close the form at will. Note, for example, that the form shown in Figure 8.15 has a **Close** button that will trigger a

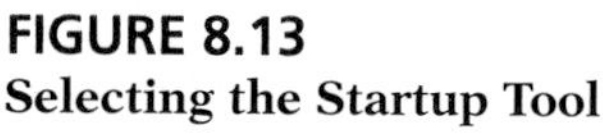

FIGURE 8.13
Selecting the Startup Tool

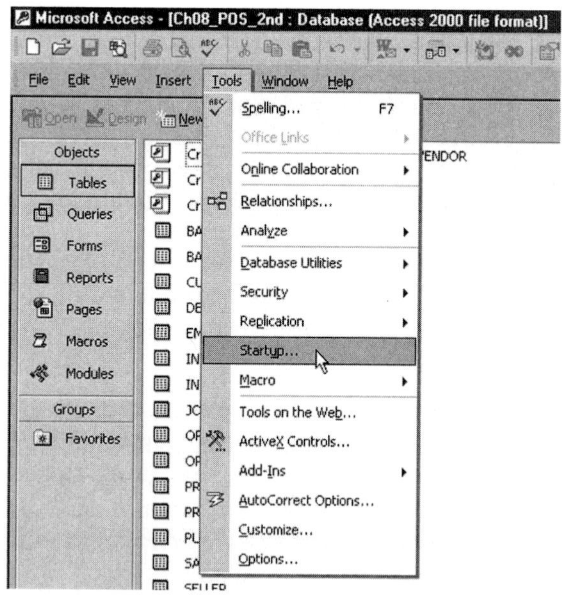

FIGURE 8.14 **The Access Startup Specification**

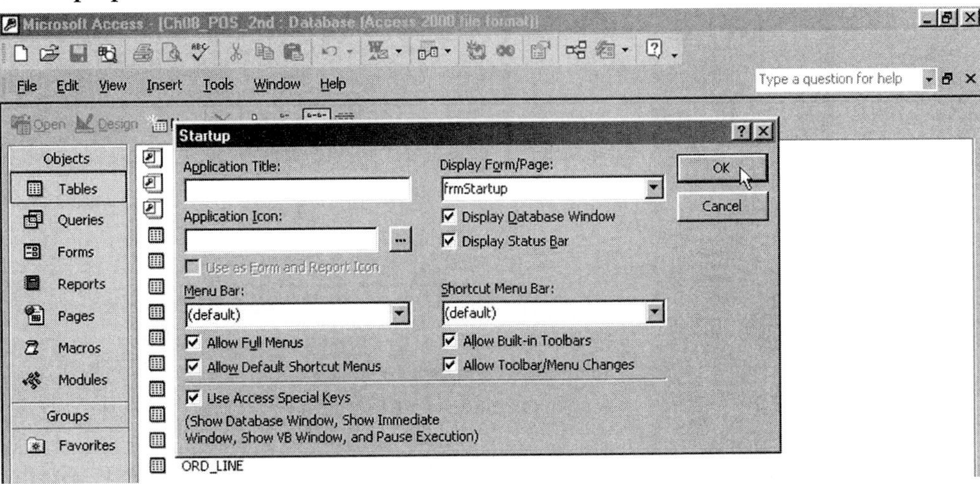

FIGURE 8.15 **The frmStartup Form**

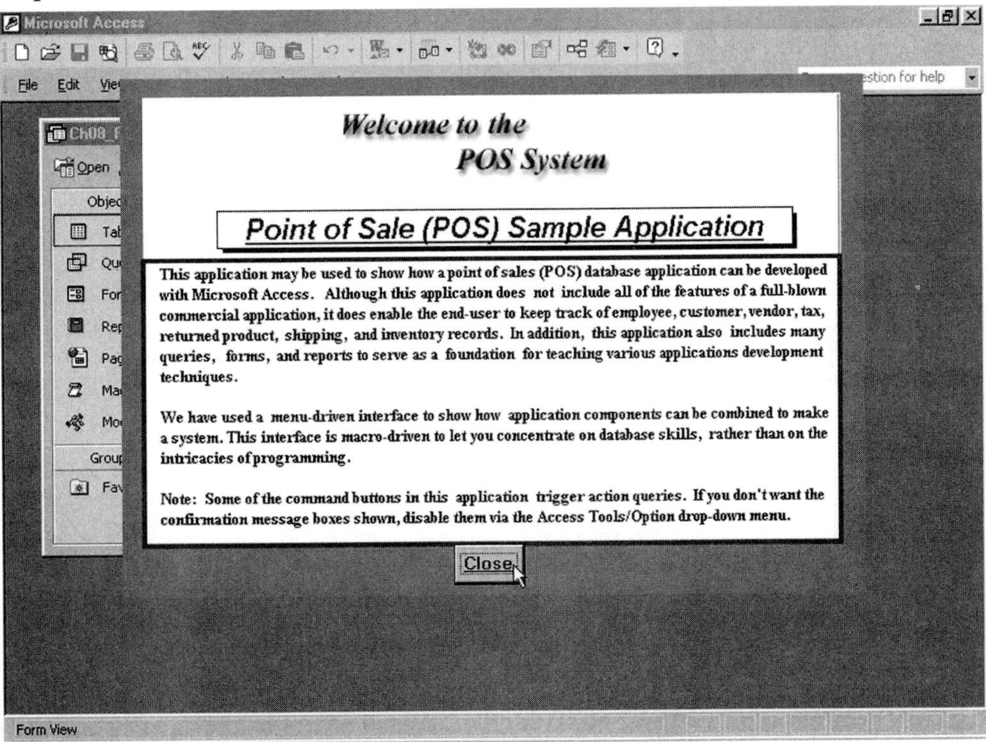

macro to open the main menu. (The **Close** button's **On Click** property will be **mcrStartup.CloseStartup**.)

The Autoexec Macro

Instead of selecting the startup procedures shown in Figures 8.14, 8.15, and 8.16, you may also create a special macro named **Autoexec**. This macro will be executed automatically when you open the database. Typically, the **Autoexec** macro will open a main menu or some other startup form. In addition, the **Startup** or the **Autoexec** macro (see Figure 8.17) may be used to remove unwanted button

FIGURE 8.16 The frmStartup Form's Timer Specification

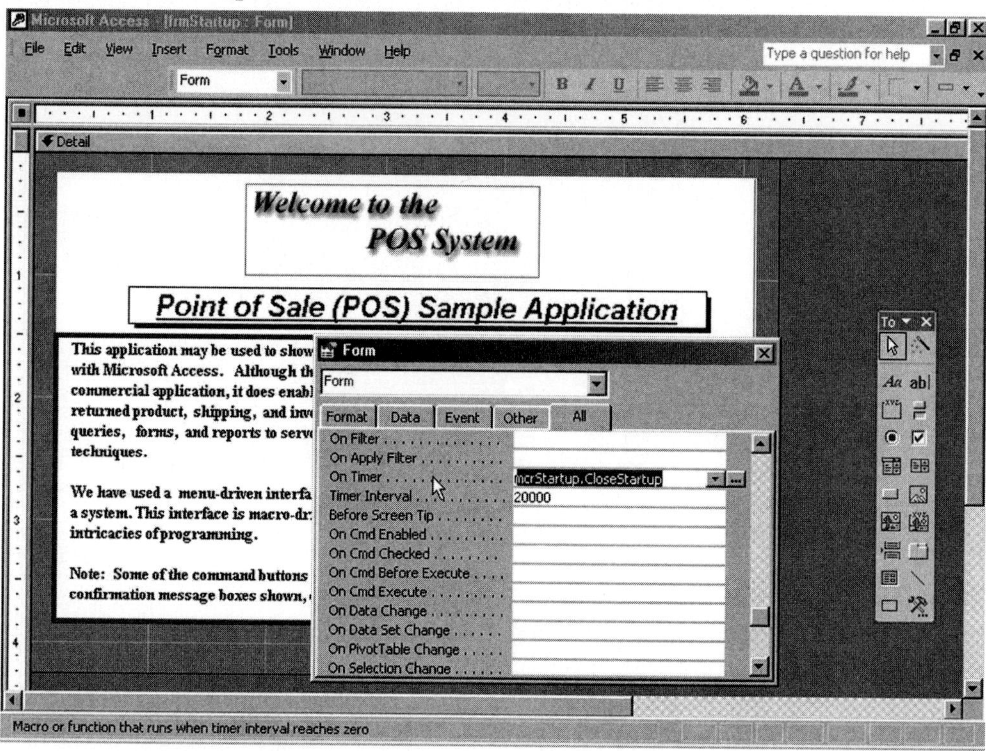

FIGURE 8.17 The Autoexec Macro

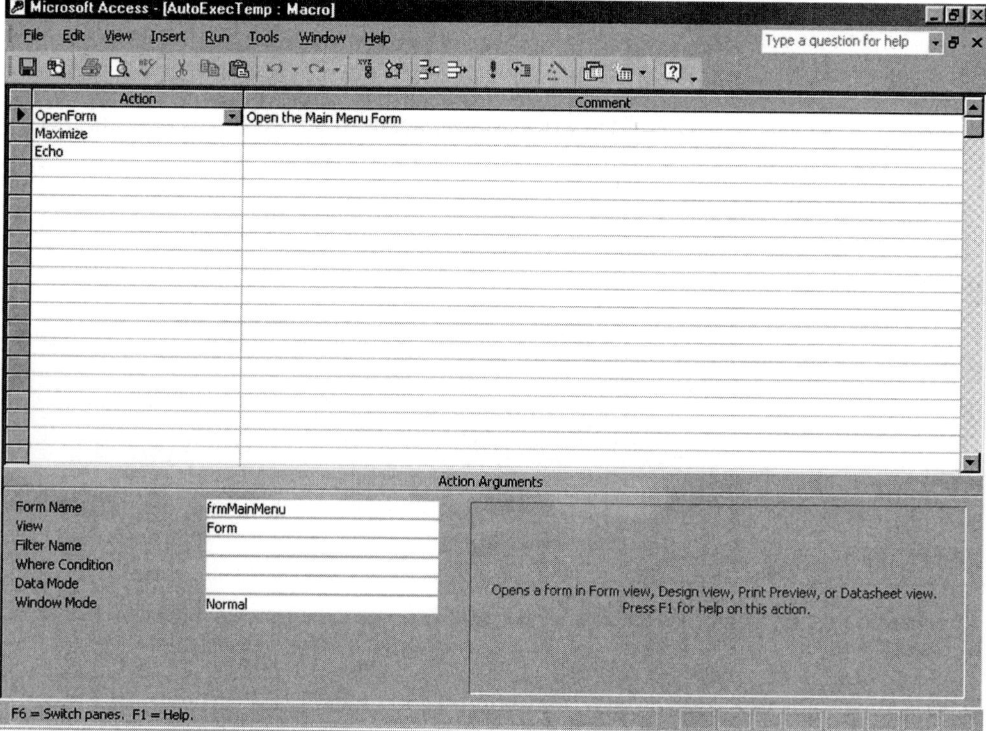

bars and/or menu bars. For example, if you use the **Startup** option, you can uncheck such choices as **Allow Full Menus** to the menu, while the **Autoexec** may be written to use a **ShowToolbar** macro to hide any toolbar(s).

Note

If you use the **Startup** option and the **Autoexec** macro in the same database, both commands are executed at the same time. For example, if you select the **frmStartup** in the **Startup** option and the **frmMainMenu** in the **Autoexec** macro, both forms will open on startup. That's why you should not use both options—either select **Startup** or use the **Autoexec** macro.

Because we have used the **Startup** option in the **Ch08_POS_2nd.mdb** database, we renamed the **Autoexec** to **Auto execTemp** in **Ch08_POS_2nd.mdb** to prevent both commands from running at the same time. You can rename the **Auto execTemp** to **Autoexec** to see how the various options work.

8.5 USING MACROS TO BUILD BASIC APPLICATION SYSTEMS

You now know how to create a macro group and the macros within it. But you've only seen macros that open a form, close a form, and open a query. Fortunately, macros are capable of doing far more than such simple tasks. For example, macros can be used to perform data entry error checks, dialog box operations, data management functions, and a host of other activities that will allow you to create a viable database end-user applications system from a collection of individual application components. With the help of macros, you'll also be able to hide the system's complexity from the end user, thus producing a user-friendly system that is less likely to produce input and output errors. Such a user-friendly system also keeps end-user training costs to a minimum.

There is no practical way to explore all the available macros. In fact, when you learned to create some simple macros earlier, you probably noticed that the macro action drop-down list contained a long list of possibilities. And many of these actions gave rise to a wide range of action arguments. (We hope that you were curious enough to select a few macro actions and action argument options and explore them with the help of the F1 key!) However, before you begin exploring the many possibilities, we'll use the following sections to illustrate a few macros that are particularly useful in applications development. For example, we will show you how to create macros that will be used to

- Detect data entry errors and to produce appropriate error messages to alert the end user to the problem.
- Transfer input from a form to a report.
- Perform a form-based data search that uses the segmented search process you learned about in Chapter 5.
- Find a customer on the invoice form you created in Chapter 6.
- Calculate the invoice totals.

If you understand how the macros work in these macro applications, you should be able to create simple menu-based application systems. And you should have a sufficient macro knowledge base from which to explore more extensive macros in Chapter 9.

8.5.1 Trapping Input Errors

Suppose you want to search for sales values within a date range by employees. The date range is supplied via a form named **frmReportMenu** (see Figure 8.18).

As you examine the date entry component on the **frmReportMenu** form in Figure 8.18, you recognize that the form must be able to

1. Accept two dates, a starting date and an ending date, as input. Therefore, we have created two unbound text boxes, named **nmBeginningDate** and **nmEndingDate**, respectively.

FIGURE 8.18 **A Date Search on a Form**

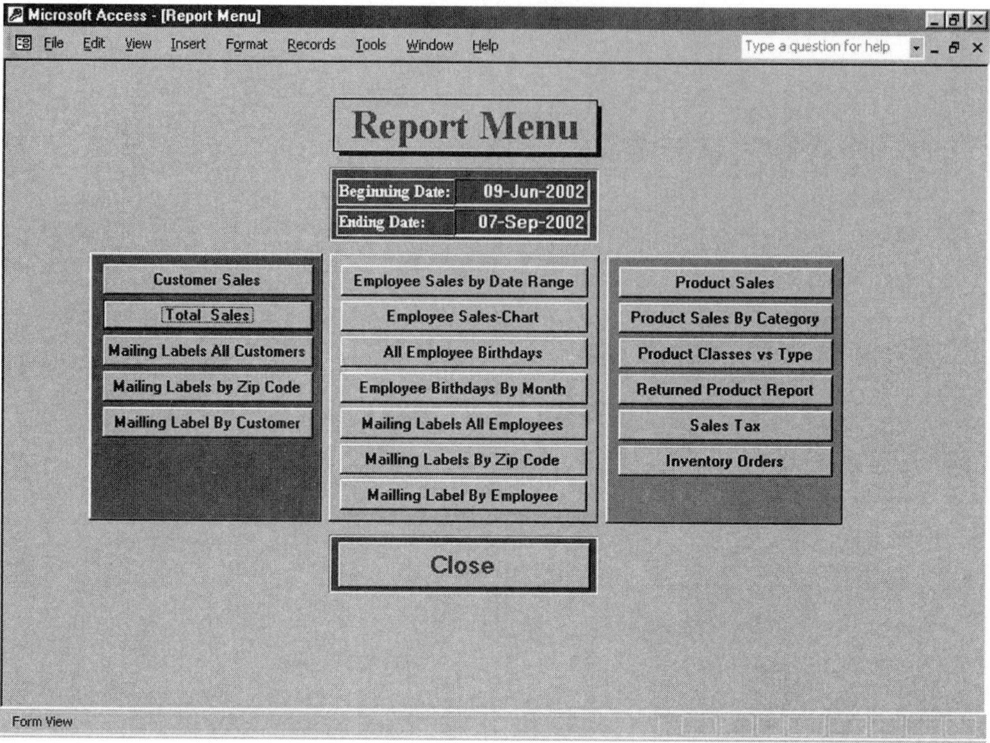

2. Ensure that the input dates conform to the desired format; you can set the date format to a **Short Date**, or a **Medium Date**, a **dd-mmm-yyyy** format for the two text boxes. If the end user makes a data entry format error, a message box must explain the error. (You do *not* have to specify the message box or its text; both are the result of date format you specify.)

Figures 8.19 and 8.19A show the format definition for the **frmReportMenu** form's **nmBeginningDate** text box and the message box triggered by an invalid date. We used the date entry **December 32, 2002**, to trigger the error. The same error message would be triggered by 6/39/03, because there is no such date. (The invalid date message is triggered by Access, so you do not need to write a macro to generate the message box.)

Note that the beginning date's default value in Figure 8.19 is defined by the current date minus 90 days. You can, of course, select another default value or no default value at all. This choice is one of many that are made after consultation with the system's end users.

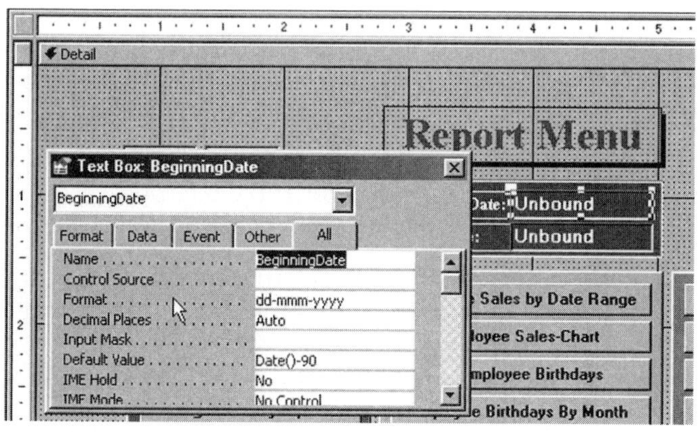

FIGURE 8.19
The Date Format for the Beginning Date's Unbound Text Box

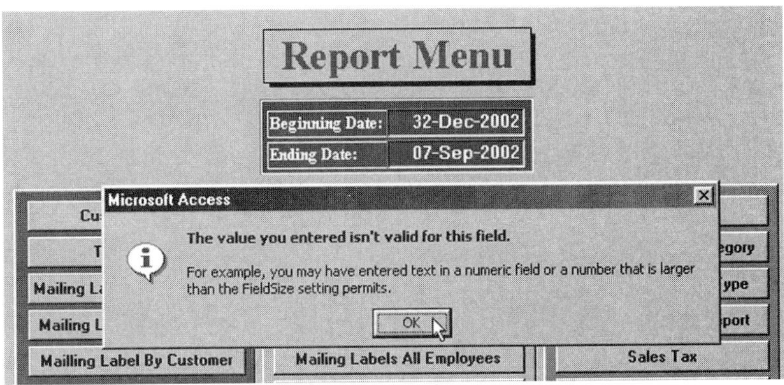

FIGURE 8.19A
The Invalid Beginning Date Entry

3. Prevent end users from entering an ending date that occurs before the starting date. For example, if the report's starting date is to be 05-Mar-2002, the ending date must be either 05-Mar-2002 or some date beyond it, such as 15-Mar-2002. If an error is made, you want the system to produce a message box that tells the end user what the problem is, and you want the end user to be able to correct the error. *This error trap requires a macro action.* (The sequence of events is shown in Figure 8.20.)

What happens if the date range meets the conditions, but there are no data for that date range? For example, let's suppose that you entered a beginning date of 1/15/02 and an ending date of 2/15/02. The date range is appropriate, because the beginning date is less than the ending date. Unfortunately, there are no sales records for that date range and—unless we trap this condition—the report will print an output that shows ######? in its text boxes. (The INVOICE table contains invoices for 5-Feb-2003 through 11-Feb-2003.) Such an output will either alarm the end user or lead to the conclusion that your application is not ready for prime time. Fortunately, such an error can also be trapped with a macro. For example, the system must be written so that it produces a message box such as the one shown in Figure 8.20A.

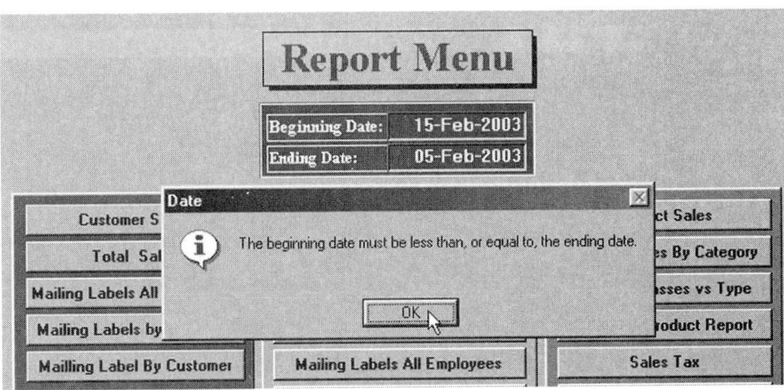

FIGURE 8.20
An Incorrect Date Range Entry

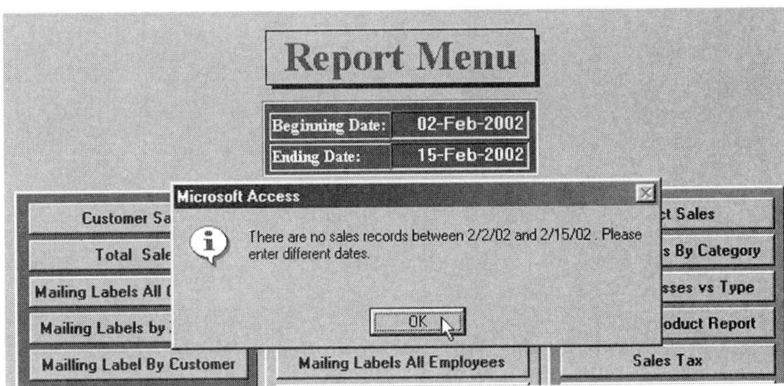

FIGURE 8.20A
No Records in the Specified Date Range

4. Return the cursor to the **frmReportForm**'s date entry box to enable the end user to make a corrected entry. When the end user clicks on the message box's **OK** button shown in Figure 8.20A, a macro will be used to set the value in text box back to a valid date, such as the current date in the **BeginningDate** and the current date plus **30** days in the **EndingDate**. *Placing the cursor on a selected portion of the form requires a macro action.* Figure 8.20B shows the correct date entries for the report(s) that are to be generated.

If the date range is valid and there are sales (INVOICE) records for the selected date range, place the date range on the report shown in Figure 8.21. This date range will be transferred from the form shown in Figure 8.20B. Note that we selected a date range of 5-Feb-2003 through 15-Feb-2003.

FIGURE 8.20B **The Corrected Date Entries**

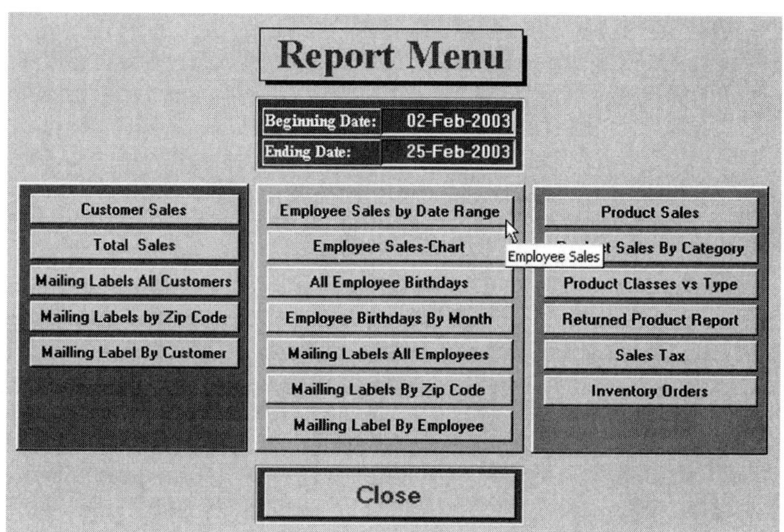

FIGURE 8.21 **The Selected Date Range on the Report Menu**

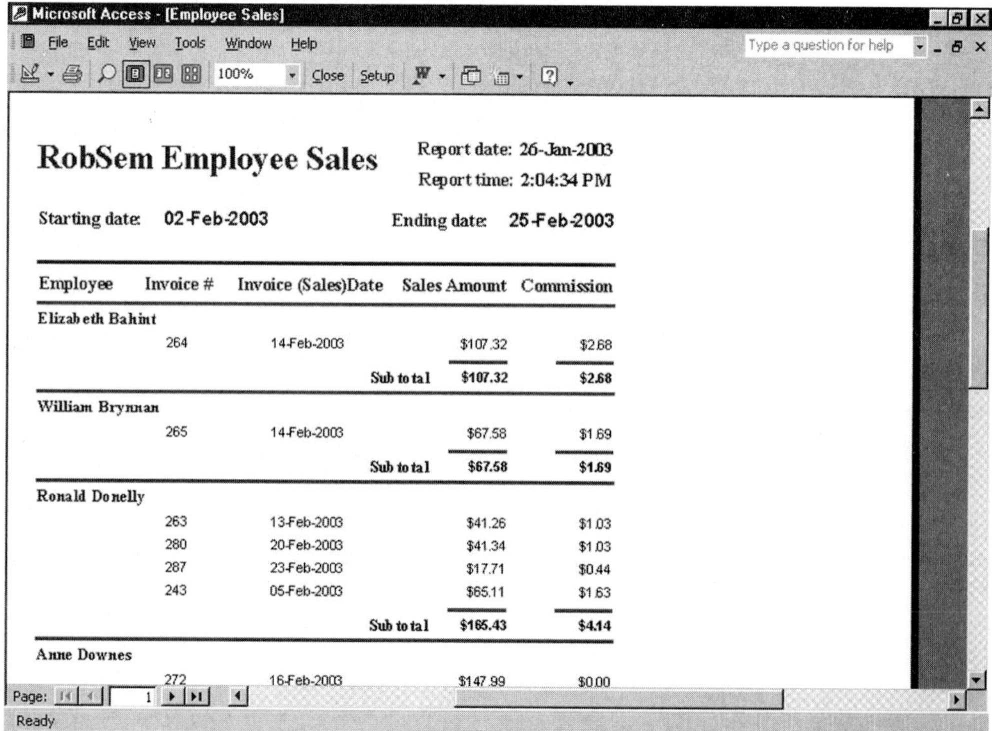

The report date range output shown in Figure 8.21A is based on the date text boxes used in Figure 8.18. Note that the report's beginning date is defined by the **Control Source** in its **Properties** box. Using the same technique, the report's ending date **Control Source** would be defined by **=[Forms]![frmReports Menu]![EndingDate]**.

The rest of the report shown in Figure 8.18 is based on the query shown in Figure 8.21B.

As you examine the query in Figure 8.21B, note that the query's **Criteria** specification now references the **frmReportsMenu** form. (In Chapter 5 you would have specified the date parameters by writing the query's **Criteria** statement as

FIGURE 8.21A
The Selected Employee Sales Report's Beginning Date

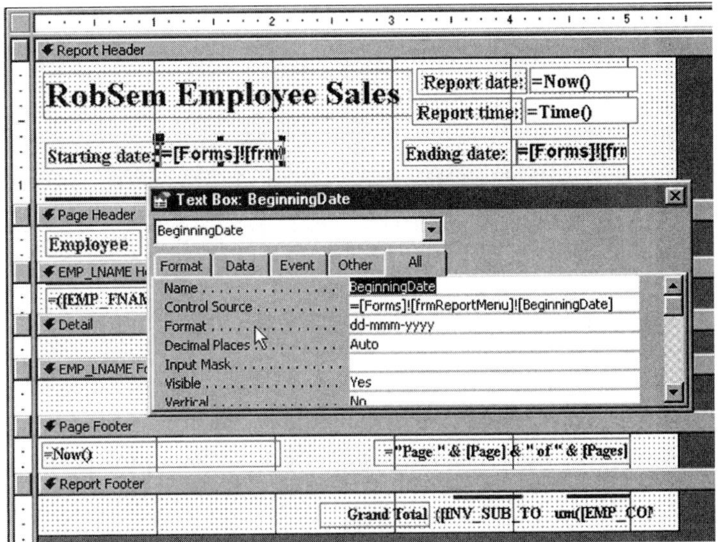

FIGURE 8.21B **A Query Generates the Report Output**

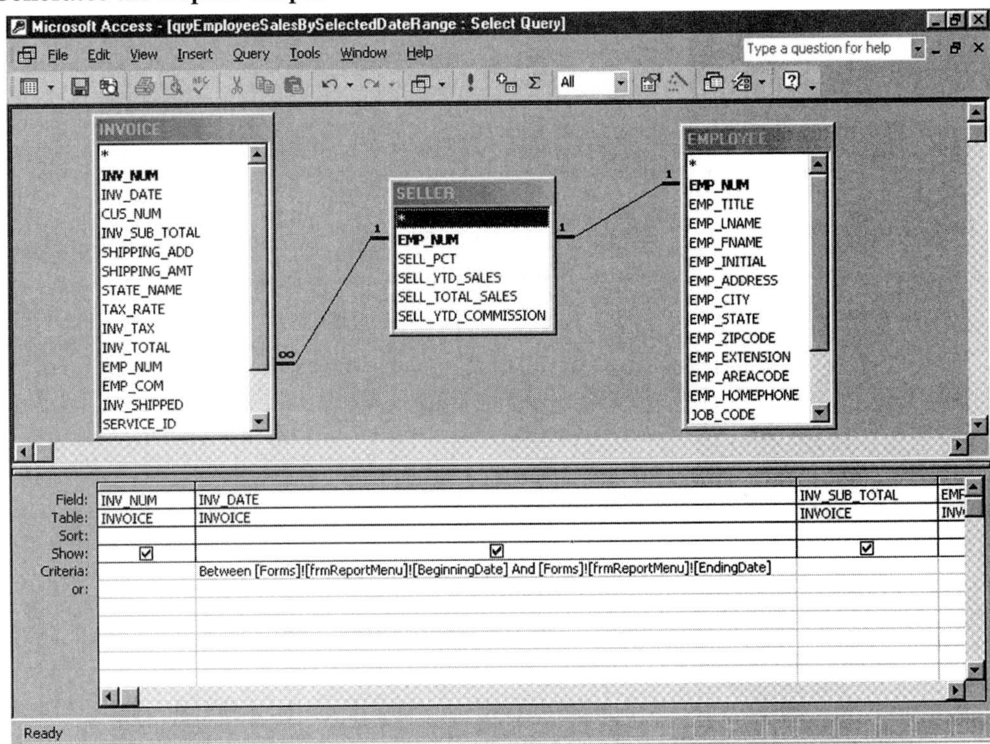

FIGURE 8.22 The mcrReport Macro Group

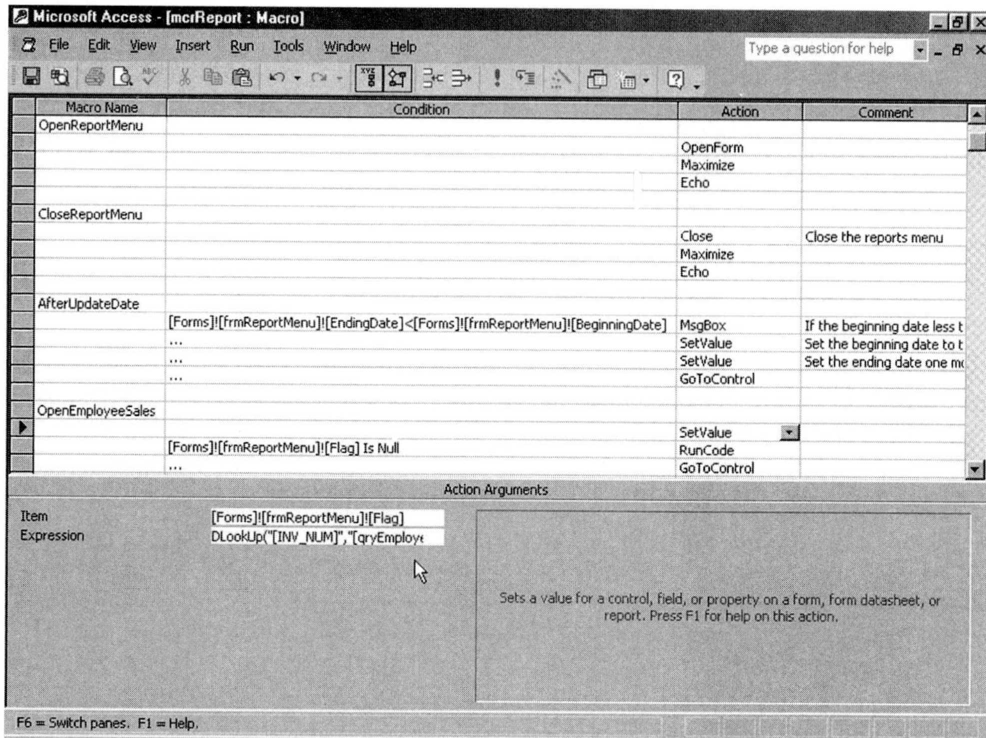

Between [Enter starting date] And [Enter ending date]. The macros make your criteria selection much more flexible because they will allow you to specify *any* data source in the **Criteria** statement.)

Now that all of the components and requirements are known, let's create the macro group and the macros within it. To keep the macro development process as simple as possible, we'll create a macro group based on the **frmReportMenu** form in Figure 8.18. The macro group is named **mcrReport** to reflect its origin and function. To make it easy to see which macro is associated with which action, we'll name the macros to match the button names. The macro group and a few of its macros are shown in Figure 8.22.

As you examine Figure 8.22, note that the **OpenReportMenu** and **Close ReportMenu** macros simply open and close the **frmReportMenu** form. The **Maximize** action ensures that the database window will be maximized. Keep in mind that the macro actions are always executed in sequence. For example, the **OpenReportMenu** macro performs these actions in sequence: open the **frm ReportMenu** form, **Maximize** the screen, and **Echo** the commands.

Writing the macro documentation is an important feature of any system development. Although Microsoft enables you to print the macro group contents, the print format is not always easy to read. Therefore, we suggest that you use the macro documentation format shown in Table 8.3 to give yourself a bird's-eye view of each macro's composition and function. You can use this format to plan the more complex macros, too.

Table 8.3 shows only part of the **mcrReport** macro group. You are already familiar with the open and close actions. However, the **AfterUpdateDate** and the **OpenEmployeeSales** macros deserve closer scrutiny. Let's start by examining the **AfterUpdateDate** macro details:

- We named the macro **AfterUpdateDate** to reflect the fact that its actions will be triggered *after* a date entry is made on the **frmReportMenu**. For example,

TABLE 8.3 Macro Documentation: Macro Group Name: mcrReportMenu

Macro Name	Condition	Action	Action Argument
OpenReportMenu		Open	Form Name: frmReportsMenu Window Mode: Normal
		Maximize	
		Echo	Echo on: Yes Status bar text:
CloseReportMenu		Close	Object Type: Form Object Name: frmReportMenu
		Maximize	
		Echo	Echo on: Yes Status bar text:
AfterUpdateDate	[Forms]![frmReportMenu]![EndingDate]<[Forms]![frmReportMenu]![BeginningDate]		
	...	MsgBox	Message: The beginning date must be less than, or equal to, the ending date
	...	SetValue	Item:Forms]![frmReportMenu]![BeginningDate] Expression:Date()
	...	SetValue	Item:Forms]![frmReportMenu]![EndingDate] Expression:Date() + 30
	...	GoToControl	Control Name: BeginningDate
OpenEmployeeSales			
		SetValue	Item:[Forms]![frmReportMenu]![Flag] Expression: DLookUp("[INV_NUM]", "[qryEmployeeSalesBySelectedDateRange]")
	[Forms]![frmReportMenu]![Flag] Is Null		
	...	RunCode	Function name:MsgBox("There are no sales records between " & [Forms]![frmReportMenu]![BeginningDate] & " and " & [Forms]![frmReportMenu]![EndingDate] & ". Please enter different dates.",64)
	...	GoToControl	Control name:BeginningDate
	...	StopMacro	
		OpenReport	Report name: rptEmployeeSalesBySelectedDateRange View: Print Preview Where Condition: Filter Name: Window Mode

the message box will pop up *only* if the ending date is less than the starting date. You could, of course, select any name that you think reflects the macro's intent appropriately. (Entering the same date twice would, of course, generate a report covering the activities of a single day.)

- If a condition triggers more than one action, the condition must be carried over to the next macro line. Access uses three periods (...) in the **Condition** column to signify that the actions are tied to the previously stated condition. For example, if you check the second **AfterUpdateDate**'s **Condition** statement, you'll see that *four* actions are required when the ending date occurs before the starting date:

1. Show a message to alert the end user that the ending date occurs before the starting date.
2. Set the beginning date equal to the current date.
3. Set the ending date equal to the current date plus 30 days.
4. Place the cursor back on the form's beginning date text box to enable the end user to correct the date entry. (You can place the control on either the **Beginning Date** or the **Ending Date**, whichever you think is appropriate. If you do

not control the cursor's position, you should give the end user the option to click on any text box on the form. And you could, of course, expand the message box's message to give additional directions to the end user.)

- We used the **SetValue** action in this example to show you how it can be used to control the cursor location and how you can write a value on a form. In fact, the **SetValue** action may be used to write values into or onto any object. Therefore, you'll use the **SetValue** action often and in a variety of circumstances.
- Access does *not* prompt you to let you know that a continuation (...) option exists. Therefore, if you need to continue actions based on some condition, click on the line below the initial condition specification and just type in the three periods. Use Table 8.2 as your guide.

The **OpenEmployeeSales** macro has a few additional features that you will encounter often, especially when you try to control processes such as invoicing and ordering.

- The first **SetValue** action uses the action argument **Item:[Forms]![frm ReportMenu]![Flag]**. The **Flag** is a hidden text box that we placed on the form to temporarily store a value that can then be used to check for a specified condition (see Figure 8.22A). In this case, we want to make sure that the date range values entered on the report menu actually contains records. If no records are found, we want to alert the end user of this fact, rather than print an "empty" report.

As you can tell by looking at Figure 8.22A, the **Flag** text box's **Visible** property is set to **No**, so the text box does not show up when you open the form in form view mode. Also, note that there are several other (hidden) text boxes on the form. You will use these hidden text boxes when you start managing the other reports that will be accessed through the **frmReportMenu** form.

- The first **SetValue**'s expression gets its value from the **DLookUp** function:

```
DLookUp("[INV_NUM]","[qryEmployeeSalesBySelectedDateRange]")
```

FIGURE 8.22A The Hidden Flag Text Box on the frmReportMenu Form

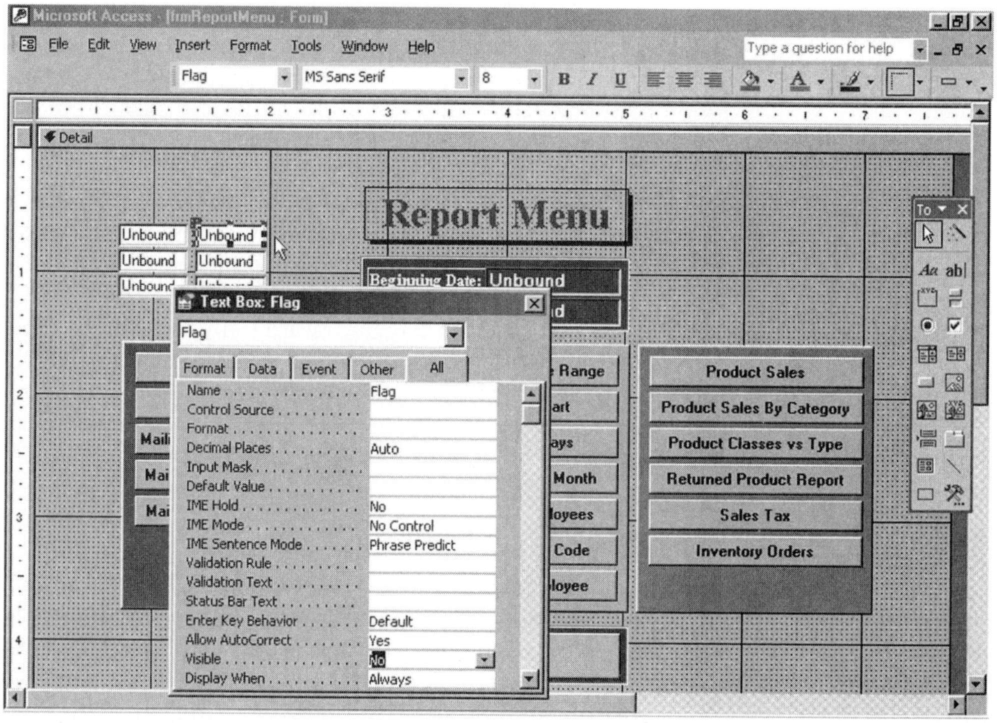

As its name implies, this function is used to look up specified values in a query, a form, or a table. In this case, we want to find an invoice number that is generated by the query for the specified date range. If an invoice number is found, the date range actually contains invoices. If no invoices are found for the specified date range, the INV_NUM will be null. We will make use of this when we decide whether or not to print the report.

• The results of the **DLookUp** function are used in the condition column in Table 8.2. If no records are found for the specified date range, that is, **[Forms]![frmReportMenu]![Flag] Is Null**, the **RunCode** action is executed. In this case, the code is used to produce a message box (see Figure 8.20A) that tells the end user that no records were found for the specified date range and that a new date input is required. When the end user clicks the **OK** button on this message box, the cursor must be returned to the **frmReportMenu** form's **Beginning Date** control. (Note the **GoToControl** action in Table 8.3.)

• If the **StopMacro** action is not included to terminate the conditional actions, the **OpenReport** action will be executed regardless of the condition. Unless the last action in the conditional column is also the last action in the macro, forgetting the **StopMacro** action causes the remaining actions in the macro to be executed. Please note that the three dots before the **StopMacro** action indicate that this action is still part of the conditional sequence!

• If the date range yields invoice records, the **SetValue** action in the **Open EmployeeSales** macro writes the invoice number in the report menu's **Flag** control. Therefore, the **Flag** control is not null and the macro prints the report for the specified date range. (The actions under the **Condition** are only executed if the **Flag** is null.)

8.5.2 Managing Processes through Macros

You learned how to perform segmented searches in Chapter 5 and how to create the end-user interface for such searches in Chapter 6. But you also discovered that there was no way to put the form-based components into a command button–based system until you learned how to use macros. We'll show you how to get that job done in this section.

In section 8.5.1, we developed a macro group based on a form in order to introduce you to the basics of the macro-building process. Although form-based macro groups are useful, more complex systems often rely on macro groups that are defined by processes, rather than by the system's forms.

If the macro groups are to be process-based, each process must be broken into a series of simple steps, each one of which would be governed by a macro. For example, invoicing is a process that may become the basis for a macro group named **mcrInvoice.** The macros within the **mcrInvoice** macro group would reflect process components such as

- Open the invoice form.
- Match the invoice to the customer.
- Write the invoice lines.
- Update the inventory.
- Calculate the total.

(The **mcrInvoice** macro group's development and many other complex macros will be discussed in detail in Chapter 9.)

If any process contains many components, it may be useful to break out each set of logically related components to become the basis of a new macro group. This technique helps control the proliferation of macros within a single macro group, thus making it easier to manage the macro-based system.

Any complex procedure, such as the segmented search you first saw in Chapter 5, can be presented as a process. In the following segmented employee search, we will begin by examining the interface. What forms will be used, and what options will each form provide? To answer these questions, begin with a pencil and a piece of paper and sketch the interface components. We'll begin with the search form shown in Figure 8.23. Note that this search form, appropriately named **frmEmployeeSearch**, contains two command buttons, each of which requires a macro.

If the end user makes no entry prior to clicking on Figure 8.23's **Search** button, all employee records will be listed. (This segmented search process is based on the **Like** function in the query's criteria statement. The **Like** function's details and uses were described in Chapter 5.) We have already entered the name **Smith** in the **Last Name** text box. Therefore, all employees whose last names include the string **Smith** will be listed, as shown in Figure 8.23A. (Note that the control tip text in this figure is displayed on two lines. You can get this result by opening the form in its design mode and then selecting its list box's properties box. Cursor

FIGURE 8.23
The Employee Search Opening Screen

FIGURE 8.23A An Employee List Output on the Employee Search Input

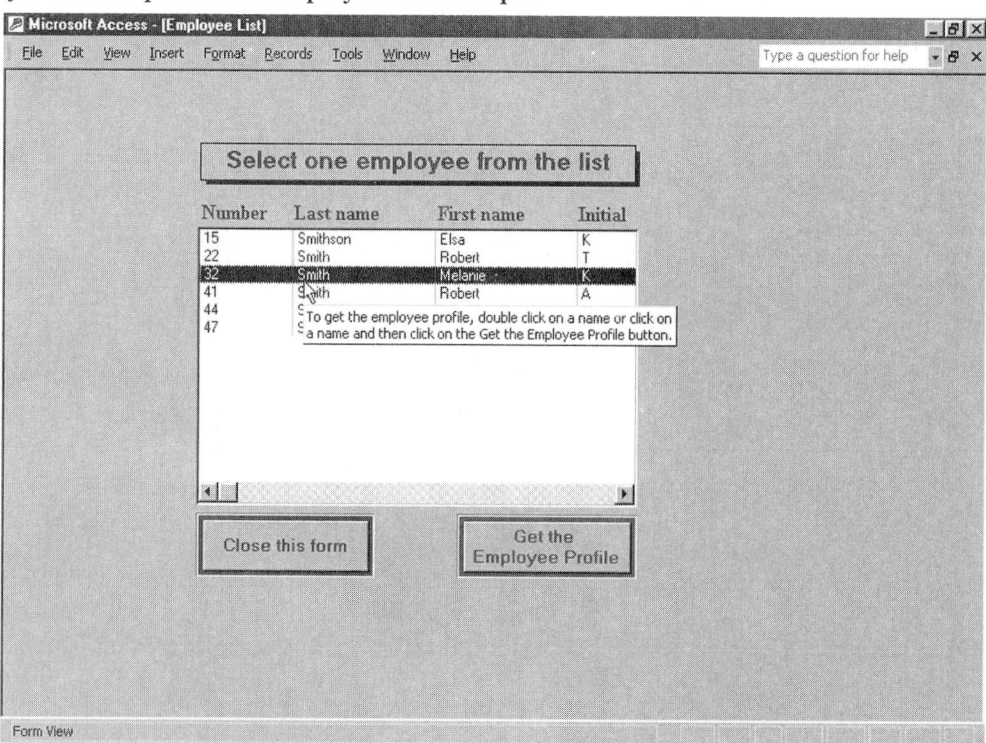

down to the **Control tip** text line, type the first line, hold down the keyboard's shift key and press the Enter key, and then type the second line.)

Figure 8.23A's form also uses two command buttons, thus requiring two additional macros. To get the complete employee profile, the end user must either double-click a selection, or click on a line and then click on the **Get the Employee Profile** command button. Failure to perform these search actions will generate the message box shown in Figure 8.23B.

FIGURE 8.23B **A Reminder to Follow the Required Procedure**

If the end user follows the appropriate procedure for the selection illustrated in Figure 8.23A, the employee profile form in Figure 8.23C is shown. Note that the record properly reflects Melanie Smith's employee data. (The sales percentages are based on a subform, which, in turn, is based on the SELLER records. Either Ms. Smith is not a salesperson or she is a newly appointed salesperson; all sales data values are zero.)

To complete the macro group's macros, note that the employee profile form in Figure 8.23C also contains three command buttons. Each of these three buttons must have a macro attached to it.

Now that you know what the interface components of the employee search process are, map out the process that generates the appropriate forms. Use your high-tech lead pencil and a piece of paper to do the mapping. (Check your map against Figure 8.24.)

From the interface process map, you'll note that the employee search process requires the six macros found in the **mcrEmployeeSearch** macro group shown in Table 8.4. The **MaxSize** macro is added so that future macros can call it to maximize the screen when necessary.

FIGURE 8.23C **The Employee Profile Form**

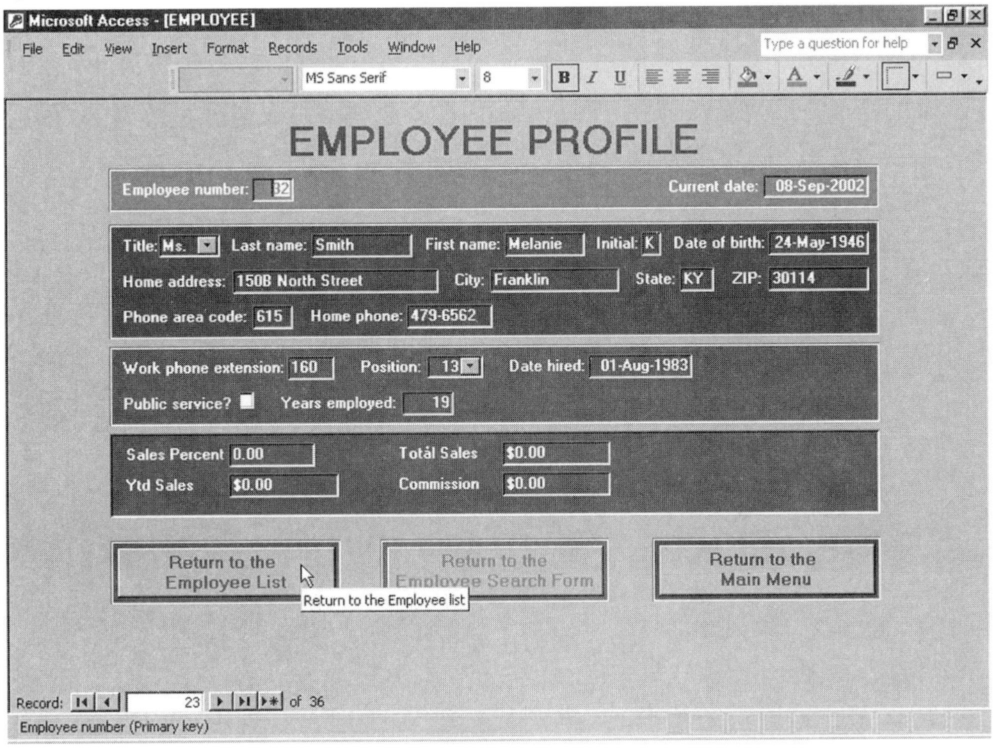

FIGURE 8.24
The Interface Process Map

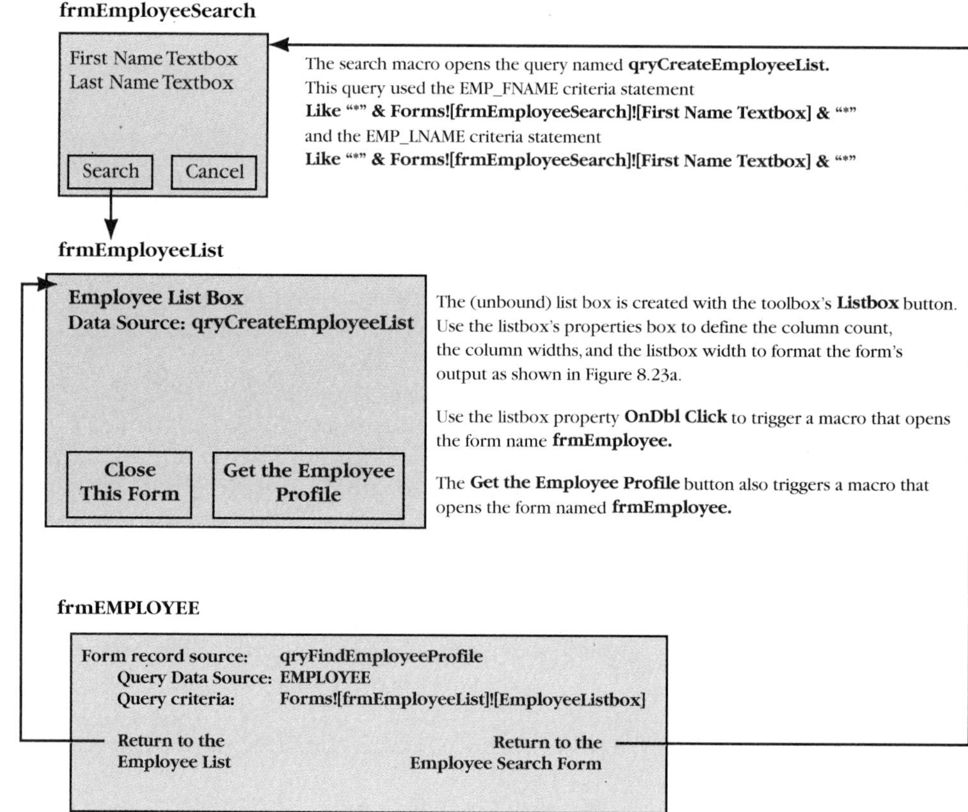

TABLE 8.4 The Employee Search Process Macro Group: Macro Group Name: mcrEmployeeSearch

Macro Name	Condition	Action	Action Argument
MaxSize		Maximize	
SearchButton			
		Close	Object type: Form Object name: **frmEmployeeList** Save: Prompt
		OpenForm	Form name: **frmEmployeeList** View: Form Data mode: Edit Window Mode: Normal
CancelSearchButton		Close	Object Type: Form Object Name: **frmEmployeeSearch**
		Maximize	
ReturnToEmployeeSearch			
		Close	Object type: Form Object name: **frmEmployee** Save: Prompt
		Close	Object type: Form Object name: **frmEmployeeList** Save: Prompt
		OpenForm	Form name: **frmEmployeeSearch** View: Form Window Mode: Normal
		Maximize	
		Echo	Echo on: Yes Status Bar Text:

Macro Name	Condition	Action	Action Argument
ReturnToEmployeeList			
		Close	Object type: Form Object name: **frmEMPLOYEE** Save: Prompt
		Maximize	
		Echo	Echo on: Yes Status Bar Text:
ReturnToMainMenu			
		Close	Object type: Form Object name: **frmEmployeeSearch** Save: Prompt
		Close	Object type: Form Object name: **frmEmployeeList** Save: Prompt
		Close	Object type: Form Object name: **frmEMPLOYEE** Save: Prompt
		Maximize	
		Echo	Echo on: Yes Status Bar Text:
FindEmployee			
	[Forms]![frmEmployeeList]![EmployeeListBox] Is Null		
		MsgBox	Message: Please select an employee from the list
	...	**GoToControl**	Control Name: **EmployeeListBox**
	...	**StopMacro**	
		OpenForm	Form name: **frmEMPLOYEE** View: Form Window Mode: Normal
		Maximize	
		Echo	Echo on: Yes Status Bar Text:
		GoToControl	Control Name: EMP_NUM
		FindRecord	Find What:=[Forms]![frmEmployeeList]![EmployeeListBox] Match: Whole Field Match Case: No Search: All Search As Formatted: No Only Current Field: Yes Find First: Yes
CloseEmployeeList			
		Close	Object type: Form Object name: **frmEmployeeList** Save: Prompt

As you examine the macro group in Table 8.4, note that the **FindEmployee** macro covers two possibilities:

1. If the **frmEmployeeSearch** form's input entries do not yield a matching record in the EMPLOYEE table through the use of the **qryCreateEmployeeList** query, the **frmEmployeeList** form's list box will be empty. Therefore, there is no way to select a list box value to open the **frmEMPLOYEE** form, which displays the EMPLOYEE record based on the results obtained from the list box. (In short, no list box value, no record, and no employee form output.)
2. The list box contains one or more rows, but none was selected. Once again, if no list box row is selected, the query based on the list box value cannot be

Note

Remember that all the forms, queries, and macros shown in the text portion of this chapter are also included in the **Ch08-POS_2nd** database found on your CD. If you have trouble following the discussion sequences, you can open your database, open each form, place it in its design view, and check the macros individually against the mapped summaries. This run/view/check/review routine has often produced those wonderful "I've got it!" moments for students.

executed. That's why we created an error trap to ensure that the cursor returns to the **frmEmployeeList** form's list box. In short, assuming that you are using the macro-based system, the **frmEMPLOYEE** form cannot be opened unless a record is selected from the **frmEmployeeList** form's **EmployeeListBox** control.

Because all macro lines are executed sequentially, the **FindEmployee** macro's **[Forms]![frmEmployeeList]![EmployeeListBox] Is Null** condition must be terminated by a **Stop Macro** action. If the **Is Null** condition does not exist, the macro condition's actions are bypassed and the **FindEmployee** macro's last two actions are executed.

Finally, forms must be opened and closed carefully and in the proper sequence. Suppose, for example, that you closed the **frmEmployeeSearch** form before you opened the **frmEmployeeList** form. This action will prevent the use of the **frmEmployeeSearch** form's input, thus producing an empty list box in the **frmEmployeeList** form regardless of your input. If you examine the **Find Employee** macro, you'll see that we closed the **frmEmployeeSearch** form—but not the **frmEmployeeList form**—before we opened the **frmEmployeeProfile** form. That's because the **frmEMPLOYEE** form requires the input from the **frm EmployeeList** form. In short, watch your form opening and closing sequences. Also, if you open a form based on some preceding I/O sequence, it's safest to close the form first and then open it again to ensure that only the most current I/O is used. That's why the **SearchButton** macro from Table 8.4 closes the **frmEmployeeList** form and then opens it again.

8.6 MANAGING IMAGES ON FORMS

In the previous sections, you learned how to create macro groups and the macros within them. You also learned how to produce macro-driven search routines and how to build and manage a basic menu-driven system. You can apply these same techniques to image management.

Images play a major role in the database systems environment. For example, many companies require their employees to use ID badges that contain the employee's photo. Security-conscious companies may require an employee check-in that compares the employee image on the photo ID to one stored in the database. Naturally, the images must be integrated into the database environment. After all, if an employee photo cannot be linked to the employee's data, the image is not particularly useful.

Organizations of all kinds and sizes use images to sell their products and services. That's why image management is a very important component of any real-world database design. We will, therefore, show you how to manage images—in our example, a set of aircraft photos—that may be inserted into forms, reports, or other database objects. What's particularly nice about the techniques that we will illustrate in this section is that they can be applied to any object, whether it is a picture, a video, or a sound track. And what's particularly nice is that these techniques are easy to learn!

Perhaps the first thing you should know is that you should *not* store images—or any nontext objects—in the database. If you try to use database storage to manage your images, you will discover that the database storage requirements and image management overhead tend to increase very rapidly. Fortunately, you can store your images outside the database. (In fact, we will demonstrate in this section that you can even store the images in a folder different from the one in which you stored the database.) Once you have decided on a storage space for your images, you can provide a macro-driven link to those images.

In this section, we will show you how to manage images on forms. Although you have already learned how to create queries, forms, and *static* images on those forms, we will provide a step-by step development guide to show you how to create an attractive form on which the image is *dynamically* linked to the database data through a macro. The material in this section will then be used in the problem section to let you create a simple, yet surprisingly sophisticated, small end-user applications system. (Look ahead to the picture series in problem 8.33 to see a small image-based system at work.)

Step 1

Copy the **AC_Museum.mdb** database from your CD to the root directory (folder) of your drive. Use the following directory (folder) structure:

Folder	Subfolder	Contents
\AC_Museum		
	\AC_Pictures	Aircraft photos
	\Database	**AC_Museum.mdb**

(Remember to uncheck the **Read Only** property for the copied database!) Open the database and check the PHOTO table contents. The results are shown in Figure 8.25.

Step 2

Create the query—name this query **qryAC_Photo**—that will be used to generate the form contents (see Figure 8.26).

As you examine Figure 8.26, note that the photo location must be prepared to accept the .jpg images to be used in the form. This job is done through the **Expr1:** created by you in the Expression Builder. Note that the **Expr1** label in Figure 8.26 indicates the modification of the PHOTO_LOCATION attribute's composition. (You should remember that the **Expr1** name is assigned by Access as you created the expression. If you have defined additional attribute modifications elsewhere, you may see some other assigned name, such as **Expr2**, **Expr3**, and so on.)

Perhaps you noticed that the expression in Figure 8.26 reads

```
EXPR1:PHOTO!PHOTO_LOCATION+PHOTO!PHOTO_ID+".jpg
```

FIGURE 8.25 **The PHOTO Table Contents**

Microsoft Access - [PHOTO : Table]

File Edit View Insert Format Records Tools Window Help Type a question for help

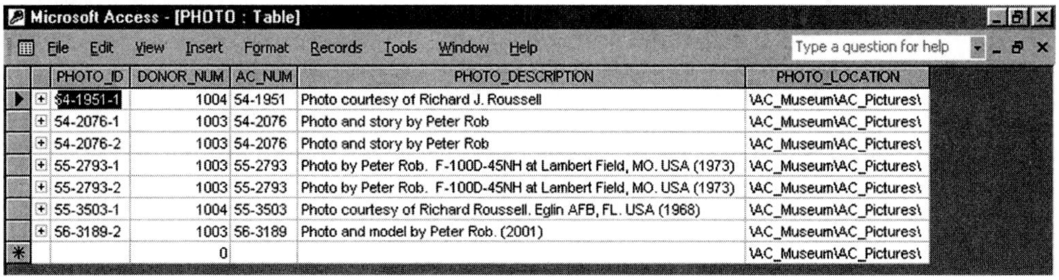

PHOTO_ID	DONOR_NUM	AC_NUM	PHOTO_DESCRIPTION	PHOTO_LOCATION
54-1951-1	1004	54-1951	Photo courtesy of Richard J. Roussell	\AC_Museum\AC_Pictures\
54-2076-1	1003	54-2076	Photo and story by Peter Rob	\AC_Museum\AC_Pictures\
54-2076-2	1003	54-2076	Photo and story by Peter Rob	\AC_Museum\AC_Pictures\
55-2793-1	1003	55-2793	Photo by Peter Rob. F-100D-45NH at Lambert Field, MO. USA (1973)	\AC_Museum\AC_Pictures\
55-2793-2	1003	55-2793	Photo by Peter Rob. F-100D-45NH at Lambert Field, MO. USA (1973)	\AC_Museum\AC_Pictures\
55-3503-1	1004	55-3503	Photo courtesy of Richard Roussell. Eglin AFB, FL. USA (1968)	\AC_Museum\AC_Pictures\
56-3189-2	1003	56-3189	Photo and model by Peter Rob. (2001)	\AC_Museum\AC_Pictures\
	0			\AC_Museum\AC_Pictures\

FIGURE 8.26 The qryAC_Photo Query Design

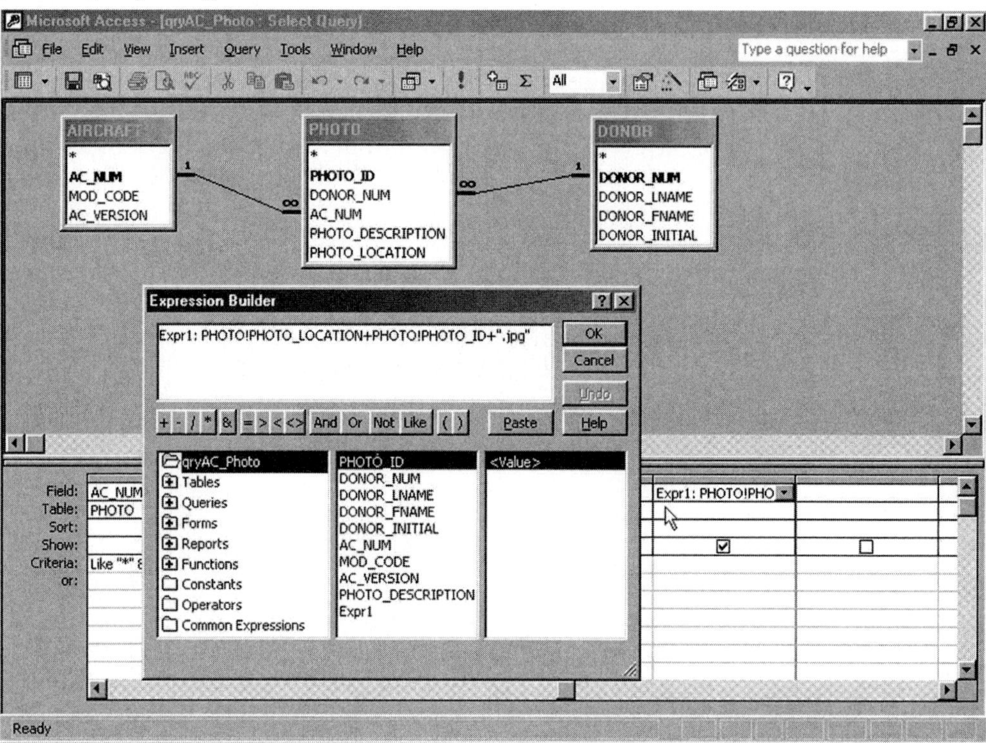

FIGURE 8.26A The qryAC_Photo Query Output, First Eight Fields

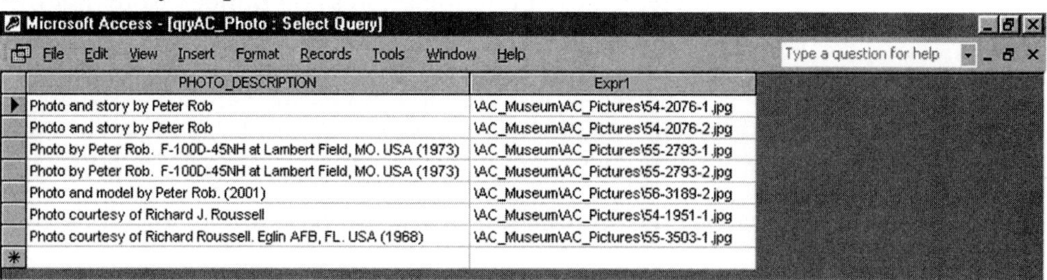

PHOTO_ID	DONOR_NUM	DONOR_LNAME	DONOR_FNAME	DONOR_INITIAL	AC_NUM	MOD_CODE	AC_VERSION
54-2076-1	1003	Rob	Peter		54-2076	F-100C	25-NA
54-2076-2	1003	Rob	Peter		54-2076	F-100C	25-NA
55-2793-1	1003	Rob	Peter		55-2793	F-100D	45-NH
55-2793-2	1003	Rob	Peter		55-2793	F-100D	45-NH
56-3189-2	1003	Rob	Peter		56-3189	F-100D	75-NA
54-1951-1	1004	Roussell	Richard	D	54-1951	F-100C	20-NA
55-3503-1	1004	Roussell	Richard	D	55-3503	F-100D	20-NA

FIGURE 8.26B The qryAC_Photo Query Output, Last Two Fields

PHOTO_DESCRIPTION	Expr1
Photo and story by Peter Rob	\AC_Museum\AC_Pictures\54-2076-1.jpg
Photo and story by Peter Rob	\AC_Museum\AC_Pictures\54-2076-2.jpg
Photo by Peter Rob. F-100D-45NH at Lambert Field, MO. USA (1973)	\AC_Museum\AC_Pictures\55-2793-1.jpg
Photo by Peter Rob. F-100D-45NH at Lambert Field, MO. USA (1973)	\AC_Museum\AC_Pictures\55-2793-2.jpg
Photo and model by Peter Rob. (2001)	\AC_Museum\AC_Pictures\56-3189-2.jpg
Photo courtesy of Richard J. Roussell	\AC_Museum\AC_Pictures\54-1951-1.jpg
Photo courtesy of Richard Roussell. Eglin AFB, FL. USA (1968)	\AC_Museum\AC_Pictures\55-3503-1.jpg

As you build an expression, Access *sometimes* fails to place the square brackets around the expression components. However, after the expression has been built and saved, the familiar square brackets show up as expected when you open the query in its design format and examine the expression again:

```
EXPR1:[PHOTO]![PHOTO_LOCATION]+[PHOTO]![PHOTO_ID]+".jpg
```

The query shown in Figure 8.26 yields the results shown in Figures 8.26A and 8.26B. Note that the **Expr1:** expression has been executed. Therefore, the photo locations now include the photo ID and the **.jpg** extension.

FIGURE 8.27 The Initial Form in Design View

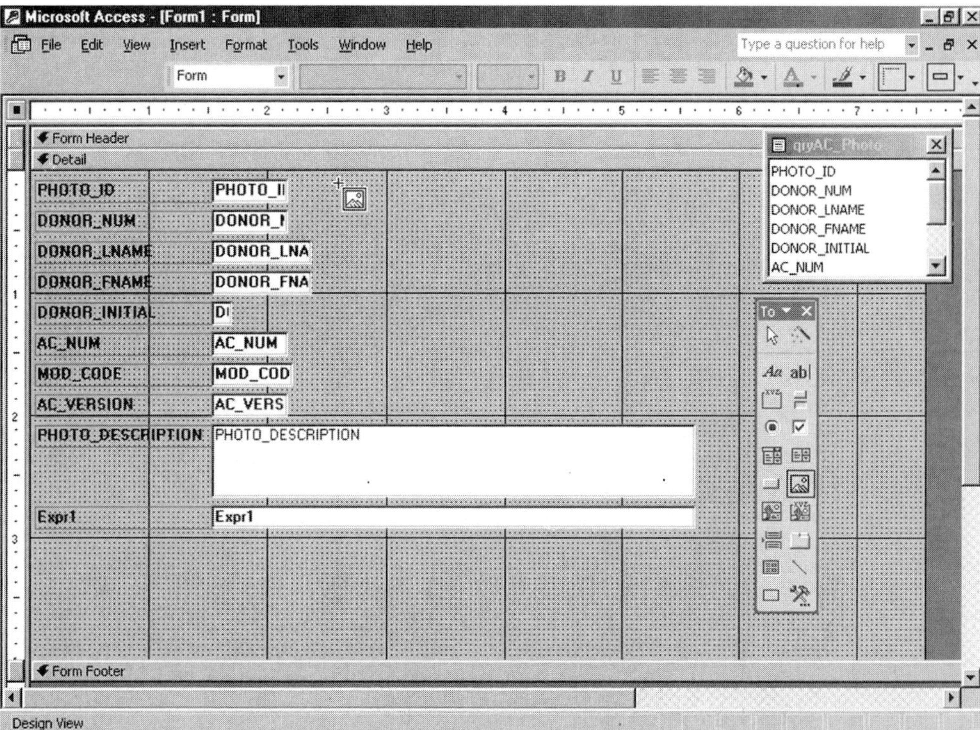

Keep in mind that you may have trouble remembering later what **Expr1:** indicates. Therefore, you should change the name using the properties box to one that you can easily identify. For example, **nmPhotoLocation** would work well. (In this illustration, the **Expr1:** label has been maintained; you can change it after you have completed the procedures illustrated in this document.)

Step 3

Create the form based on the **qryAC_Photo** query, leaving it in design view. Then click on the **Image** button in the toolbox and move the cursor to the intended image location (see Figure 8.27). Note that the cursor, which is located to the right of the PHOTO_ID text box, has changed its format to reflect the image selection when you moved the cursor over the form.

Using the image cursor, drag the cursor to create a rectangle to define the image borders. As soon as you have drawn the rectangle, Access generates the **Insert Picture** screen shown in Figure 8.28. (You will have to select whatever folder you stored your pictures in.)

Step 4

Using Figure 8.28 as your guide, leave the cursor on any of the .jpg files, then click **OK** to get the image insertion process started. Don't worry about which picture you're inserting. (You will later create a macro to match the pictures to their proper aircraft photo IDs.) The insertion action will generate the results shown in Figure 8.29. Note that the default **Size Mode** is **Clip** and that the picture doesn't fit the box you have drawn. (Only a portion of the aircraft photo shows up.) Note also that the default name of the image in this example is **Image20.** (You'll probably get a different image default value, because its number depends on how many times you have inserted an image. We ran 19 image insertion routines to ensure that the text reflects what happens on the screen, so we are at **Image20**.)

FIGURE 8.28 The Picture Source

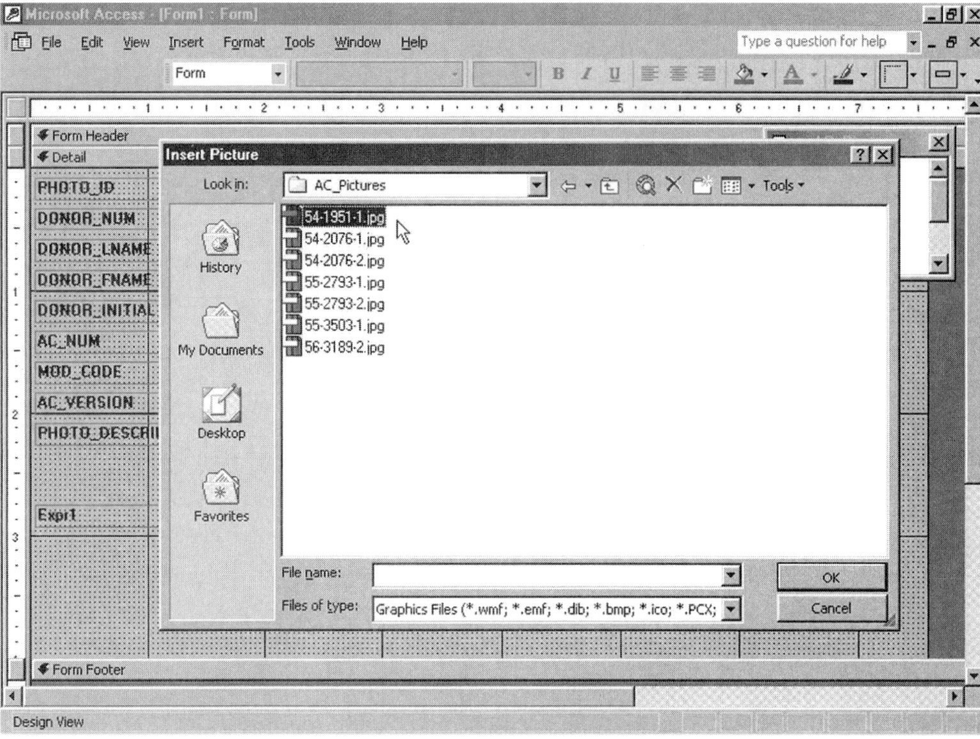

FIGURE 8.29 The Image Properties

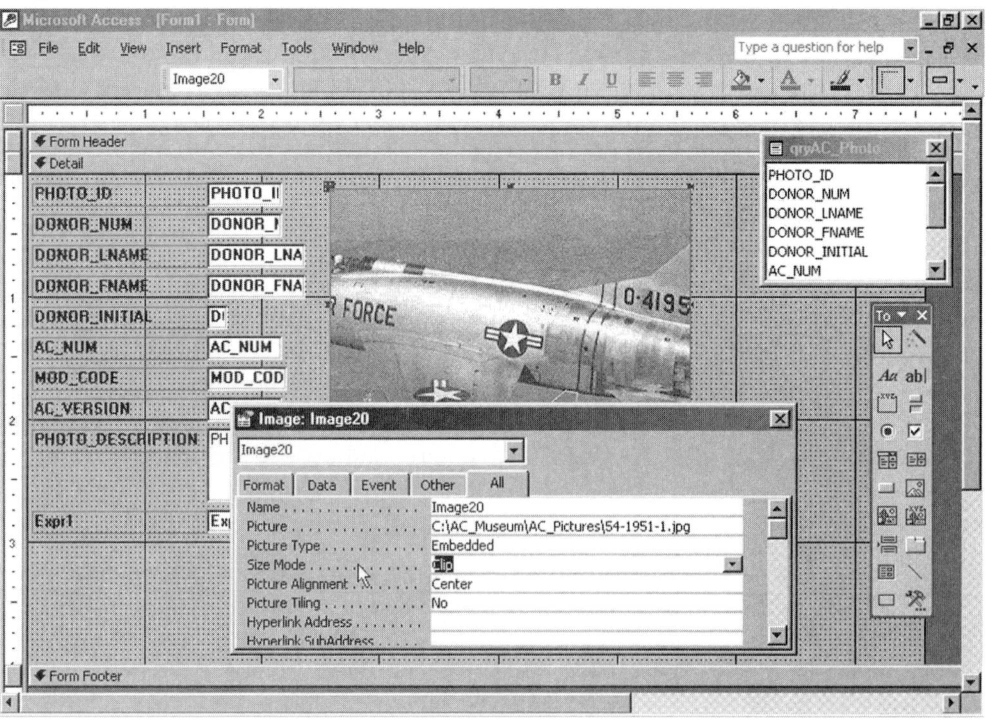

As you examine Figure 8.29, note that the picture location is, at this point, the first default value found in the picture location. In this case, that default picture is defined to be

```
C:\AC_MUSEUM\AC_PICTURES\54-1951-1.JPG
```

FIGURE 8.30 The Revised Image Properties

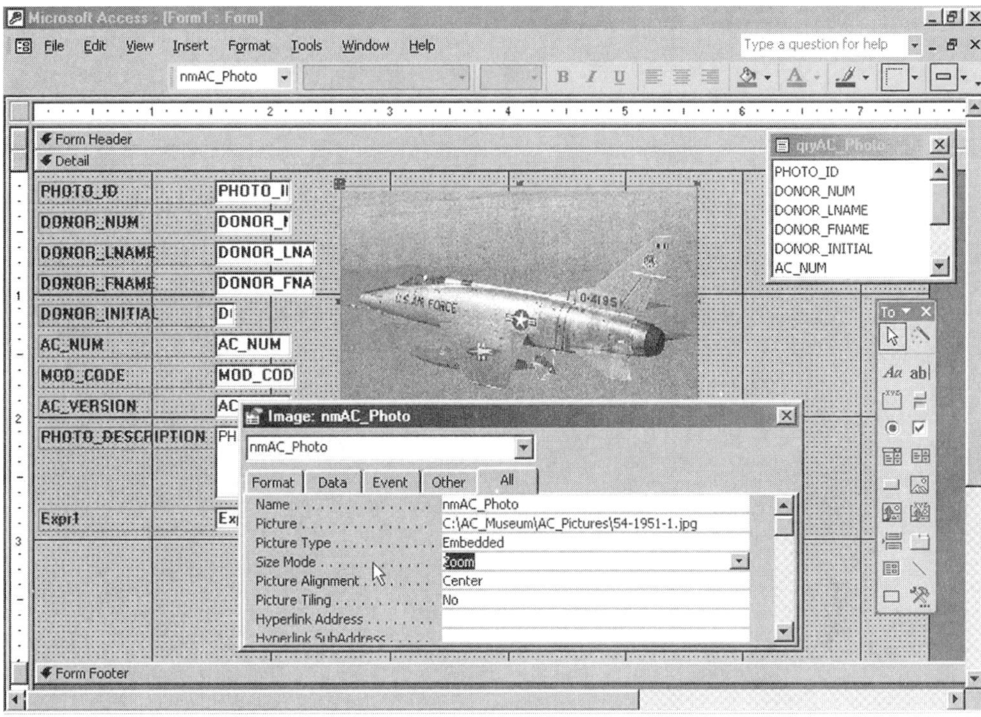

This picture may or may not match the aircraft number yet. But do delete the **C:** portion of the picture's location. The reason for this deletion is simple: If you do not specify a drive, you will be able to run this application from a floppy (drive A:), a ZIP drive (drive D:), or some other drive—as long as you always copy the entire directory (folder) structure that contains the pictures and the database to the root directory. (In this example, **\AC_Museum** was designated to be the main folder and **\AC_Pictures** and **\Database** were designated to be the subfolders.)

Save the form and name it **frmAC_Photos**. (It's a good idea to save the form again after you have made some changes in it that you'd like to preserve!)

Step 5

Change the **Picture Type** to **Zoom,** then size the picture and place it where you want it on the form. Clean up the form to enhance its presentation qualities. Note the results shown in Figure 8.30. Note also that the name of the image was changed from the default **Image20** (see Figure 8.29) to **nmAC_Photo**. This name will later be used in a macro, so it's important to take care of such details at this point.

Step 6

Make sure that the form's photo location is properly designated (see Figure 8.31). Note that the control source is the **Expr1:** that was created in the query in Figure 8.26. Also note that the **Name** was changed from the default name to **nmPhotoLocation**. It is worth repeating that this name will be later referenced in a macro, so take care of such details now.

Step 7

Create the macro group and name it **mcrACphotos.** Within this macro group, create a macro named **LocateAC_Photos.** The macro actions and its arguments are shown in Table 8.5. (Note that the **Status Bar Text:** action argument for the **Echo** action was left blank.)

FIGURE 8.31 The Photo Location Definition

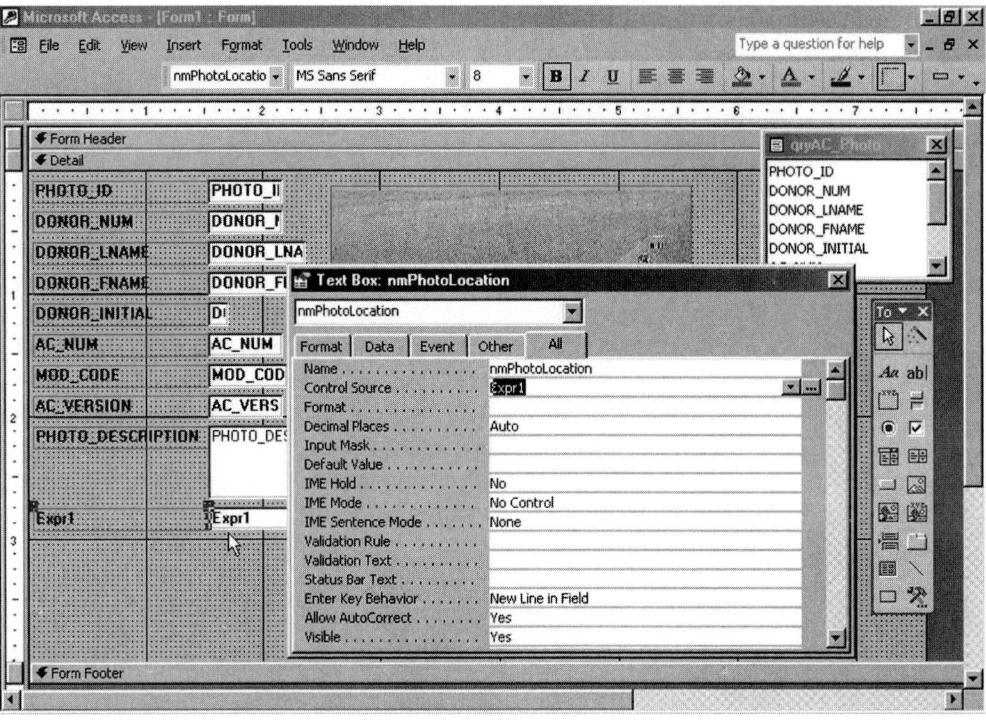

TABLE 8.5 The LocateAC_Photos Macro, Its Actions, and Its Action Arguments

Macro Name	Condition	Action	Action Argument
LocateAC_Photos			
		Hourglass	Hourglass On: Yes
		Echo	Echo On: Yes Status Bar Text:
		Set Value	Item: [Forms]![frmAC_Photo]![nmPhoto].[Picture] Expression: [Forms]![frmAC_Photo]![nmPhotoLocation]

Step 8

Open the form's properties box by clicking anywhere *outside* the form, and attach the macro to the form. Make sure that you select the **On Current** property (see Figure 8.32).

Using Figure 8.32 as your base, modify the form to match the presentation in Figure 8.33.

Step 9

Open the form to see the effect of your efforts in Figure 8.33. You will also discover that the picture will change to match the aircraft photo location and content when you use the navigation button to scroll through the photo records.

As you can tell by examining Figure 8.33, you can add command buttons to return to a menu or to repeat a search routine. The addition of a search routine requires that you'll have to modify the form's query to make it a parameter query that will let you select the pictures to be displayed. And, naturally, you can use this technique to track any number of images located anywhere in any folder in your computer's directory structure. (You'll have a chance to do that in problem 8.40!)

FIGURE 8.32 **The Form's Macro Connection**

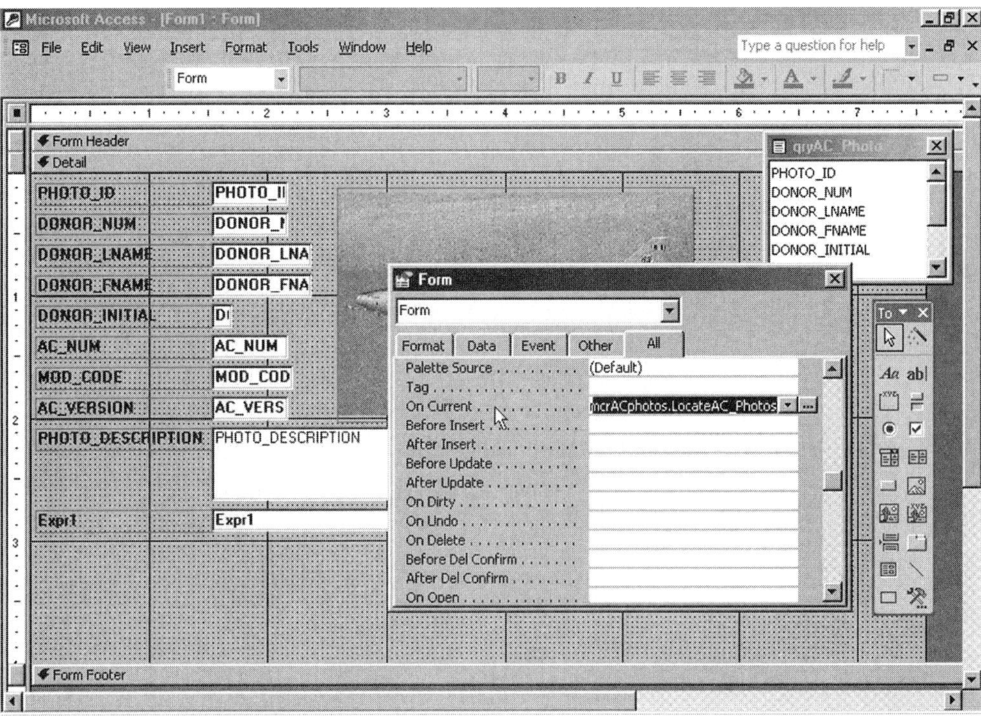

FIGURE 8.33 **The Completed frmAC_Photo Form**

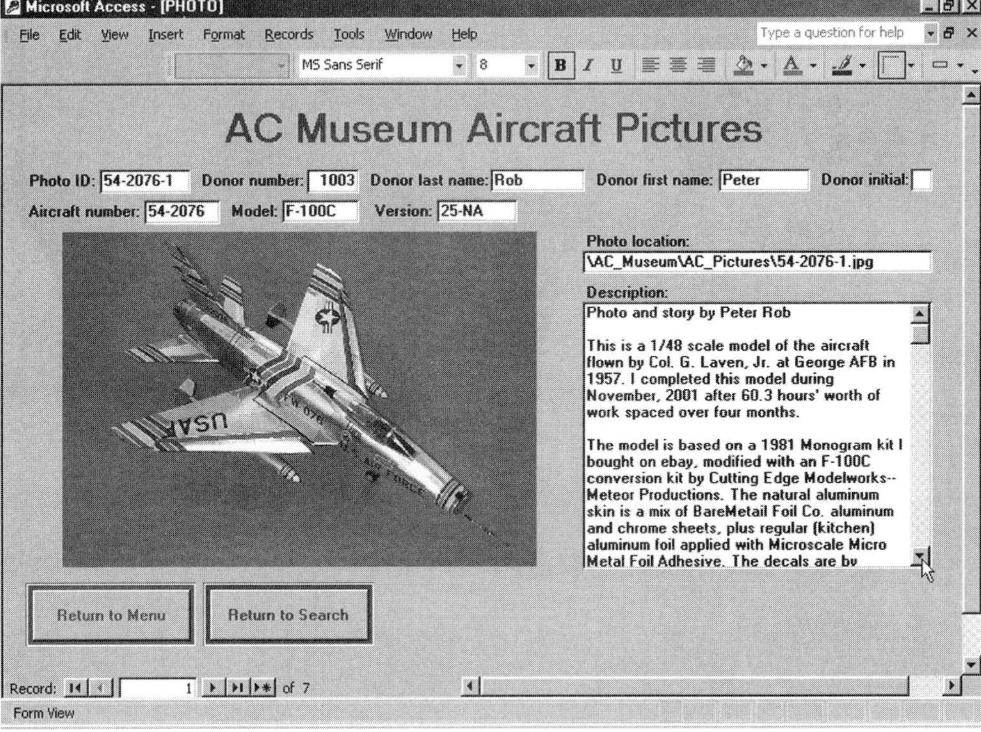

Finally, keep in mind that the description text is based on a memo field, so you can store a lot of text. If you click on the **Description:** box in Figure 8.33, you will discover that we have used its properties box to specify a vertical slide so that you can scroll through text that extends well beyond the text box.

8.7 MACROS AND VISUAL BASIC FOR APPLICATION

Because macros play such a vital role in Access applications development, we will show you how they can be applied to a fairly complex set of transactions in Chapter 9. But however useful macros may be, you should know that macros have limited transaction capability. Therefore, they are used primarily to facilitate rapid applications development and prototyping.

If you need more flexible database applications and you work with complex database transactions, you ought to explore contributions of Visual Basic for Applications (VBA) to the Access database environment. (Because this is not a VBA book, we do not cover VBA development.) However, once you know how to design and implement databases and you know how to prototype the applications, you'll find that detailed knowledge of VBA programming will become a very desirable tool in your applications development work. Of course, do keep in mind that VBA is not particularly useful until you know how to design and implement databases and how to design and implement an attractive, flexible, and user-friendly applications environment. That's why you selected this book in the first place!

Finally, in spite of our VBA praises, we do not mean to imply that macros lack functionality. Macros pay the proverbial freight by letting you produce applications quickly and efficiently. Therefore, macros are highly valued prototyping tools, and your macro skills will be very desirable. But keep in mind that you can move a thousand tons of sand more efficiently in a dump truck than in a pickup truck. However, that fact does not render a pickup truck useless.

Problems

Problems 8.1 through 8.13 are based on the **Ch08_POS_2nd.MDB** database found on your CD. Use the main menu screens shown in Figures P8.1 through P8.1B to serve as your guide to the development of the **mcrMainMenu** macros. *Note:* This macro group includes, but is not limited to, the macros that were developed in this chapter. (The macros developed in the chapter are also included on the student CD.)

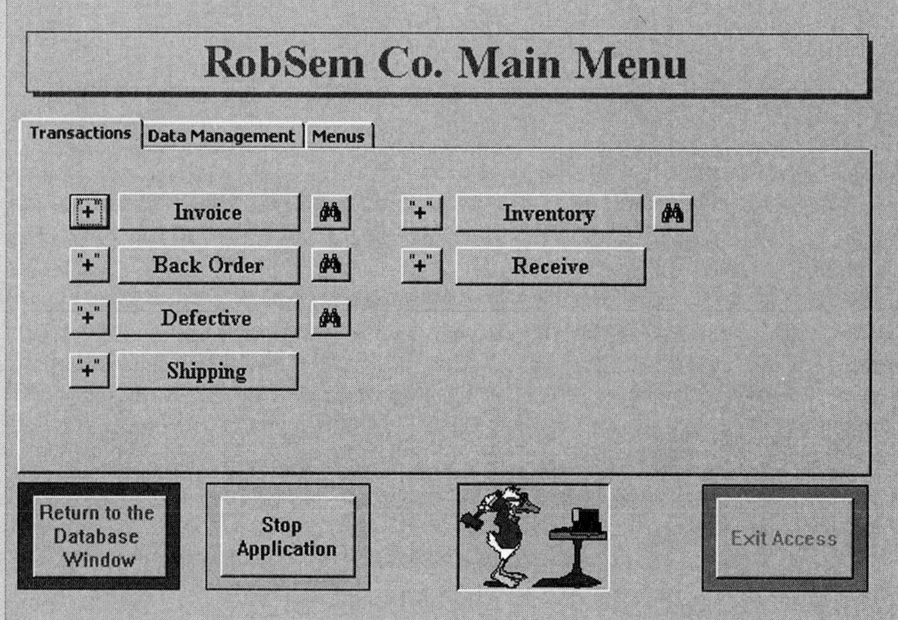

FIGURE P8.1
The RobSem Company Application's Main Menu Transactions Page

FIGURE P8.1A
The RobSem Company Application's Main Menu Data Management Page

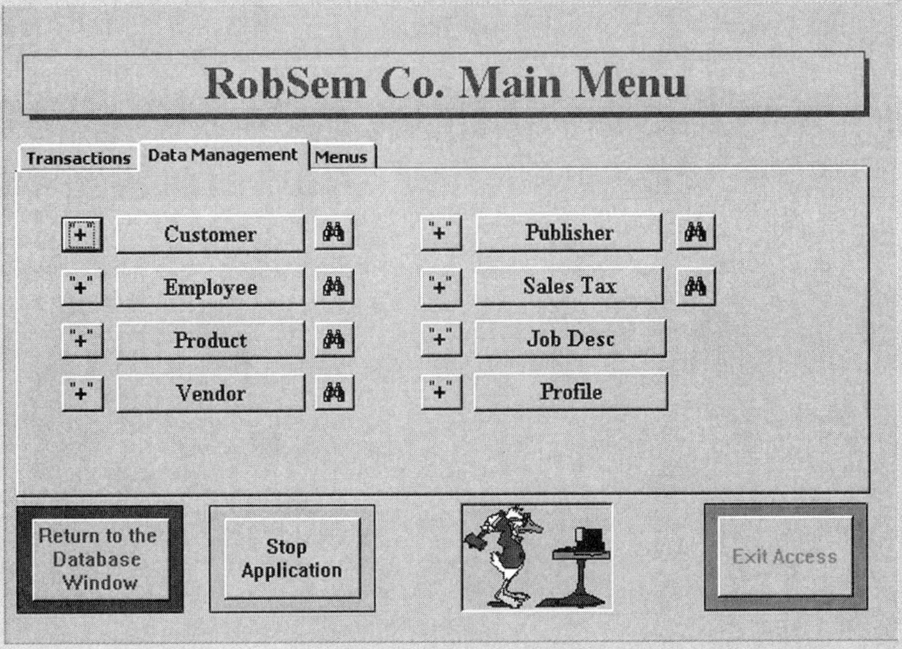

FIGURE P8.1B
The RobSem Company Application's Main Menu Menus Page

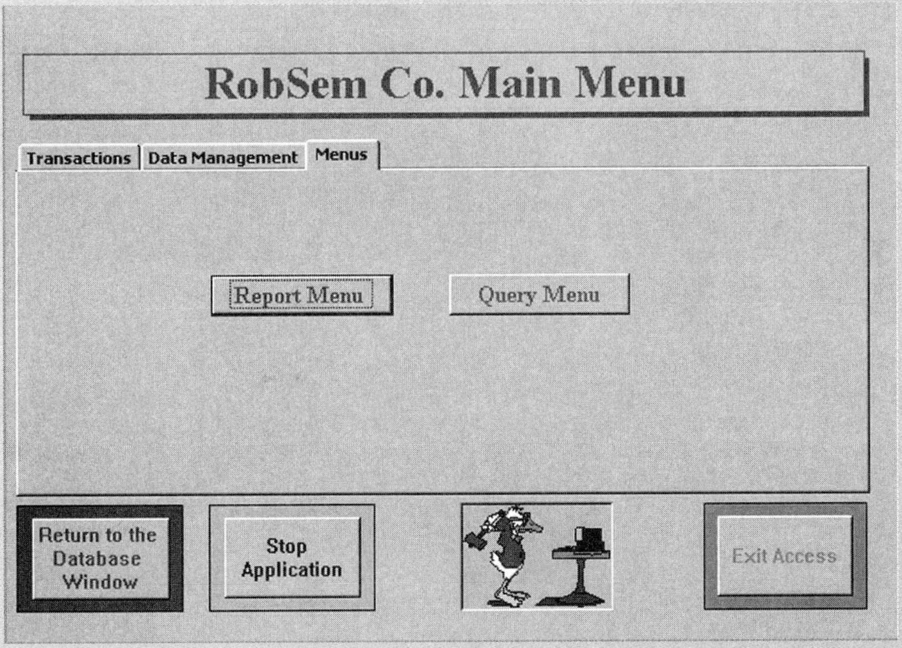

Clicking on the **Report Menu** command button produces the menu shown in Figure 8.18. Clicking on the **Query Menu** command button produces the menu shown in Figure 8.4. (The macros for the query menu are shown in Figure 8.10.)

8.1 Given the preceding menu structure information, create the main menu macro group's interface process map. Use Figure 8.24 as your development map's template.

8.2 Write a macro named **OpenMainMenu.** (*Note:* This macro will be called by clicking on the **Close** button in Figure 8.22's **frmStartup** form. Or if you elected to use an **Autoexec** macro, call the **OpenMainMenu** macro from the **Autoexec** macro.) As its name suggests, the **OpenMainMenu** macro will open the main menu screen shown in Figure P8.1. Remember to maximize the screen when the macro opens it.

8.3 Write a macro named **OnLoadMainMenu** and attach it to the main menu form's **On Open** property. The macro must maximize the main menu screen anytime it is opened. (Remember to turn on the **Echo**.)

8.4 When the main menu's **Stop Application** button is clicked, make sure that the end user sees two buttons named **Cancel Stop** and **Confirm Stop**, respectively. Write the macros that will make these buttons appear and disappear and that will enable or disable them when appropriate. Name the macros **StopApp**, **ConfirmExitApp**, and **CancelExitApp**, respectively. (To help you do this job, we have illustrated the sample procedures for the **Stop Application** command button in Figures P8.4 through P8.4C. The sample macros are shown in table P8.4. Study these examples carefully before you try to work this problem. Note that we have changed the presentation format of the command buttons and that we have inserted a picture. You may insert, within reason, any picture you like. (Some of our students insert a picture of their project team.)

FIGURE P8.4
The CancelStopApp On Click Property

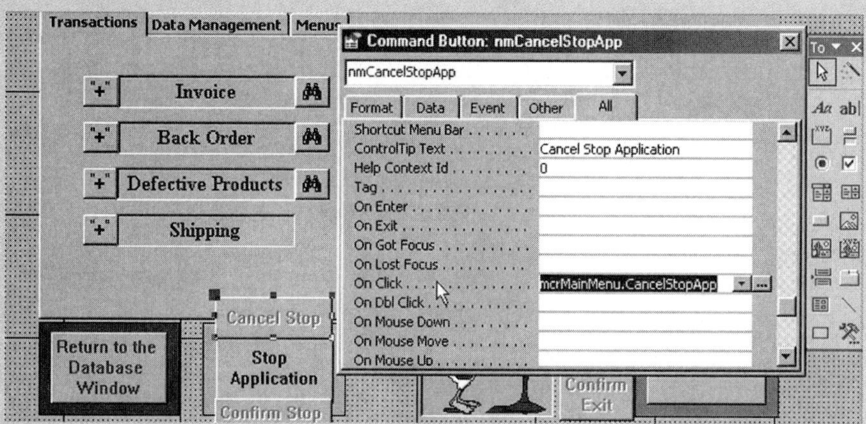

FIGURE P8.4A The CancelStopApp On Click Property

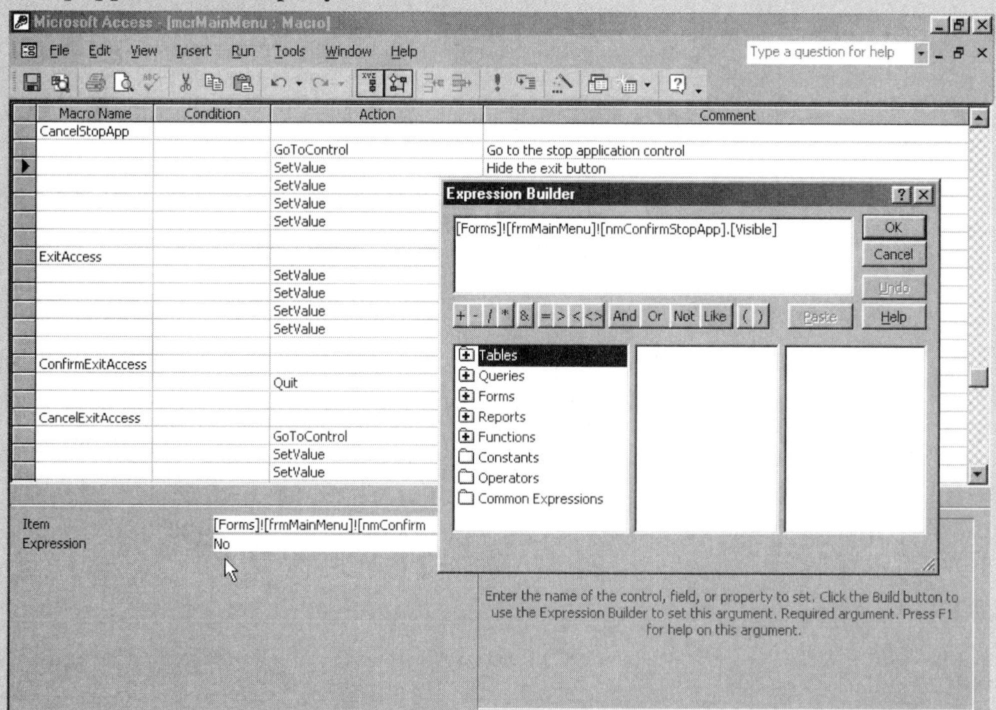

As you examine Figure P8.4A, note that the **CancelStopApp** macro's components and their structures. (The process starts by using **GoToControl** to place the focus on the **Stop Application** command button in Figure P8.4 when the macro opens.) The macro actions are displayed in Table P8.4.

TABLE P8.4 The StopApp and CancelStopApp Macros

Macro Name	Condition	Action	Action Argument
StopApp			
		SetValue	Item: [Forms]![frmMainMenu]![nmCancelStopApp].[Visible] Expression: Yes
		SetValue	Item: [Forms]![frmMainMenu]![nmCancelStopApp].[Enabled] Expression: Yes
		SetValue	Item: [Forms]![frmMainMenu]![nmConfirmStopApp].[Visible] Expression: Yes
		SetValue	Item: [Forms]![frmMainMenu]![nmConfirmStopApp].[Enabled] Expression: Yes
CancelStopApp			
		GoToControl	Control Name: nmStopApplication
		SetValue	Item: Yes [Forms]![frmMainMenu]![nmConfirmStopApp].[Visible] Expression: No
		Set Value	Item: [Forms]![frmMainMenu]![nmConfirmStopApp].[Enabled] Expression: No
		SetValue	Item: [Forms]![frmMainMenu]![nmCancelStopApp].[Visible] Expression: No
		SetValue	Item: [Forms]![frmMainMenu]![nmCancelStopApp].[Enabled] Expression: No
ConfirmStopApp			
		Close	Object Type: Form Object Name: frmMainMenu Save: Prompt

When you are done, remember to attach the macros to the command buttons. Figure P8.4B and 8.4C show the effect. (To save space, we have only shown the form's **Exit Access** command button and the effects of its use. If you click **Cancel Exit**, you will remain on the menu form. If you click **Confirm Exit**, the application and Access will be shut down.)

FIGURE P8.4B
The Exit Access Command Button in Form View

FIGURE P8.4C
The Result of Clicking the Exit Access Button

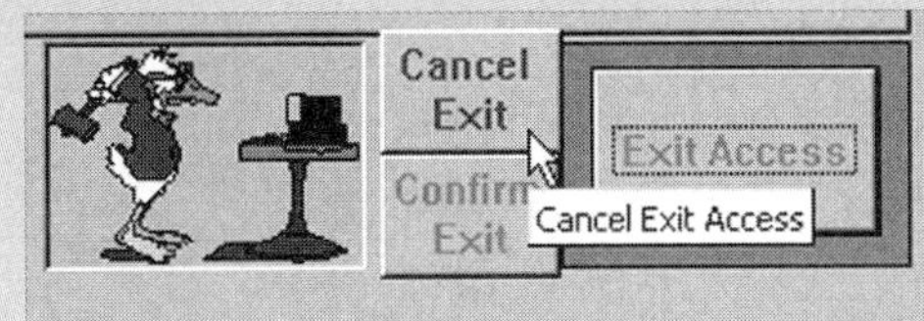

8.5 Write a macro named **ReturnToDatabase** to close the main menu and to show the database window. (*Hint:* Because the database window is never closed, the main menu simply lies on top of it. Therefore, if you close the main menu, you should see the database window again.)

8.6 Use the report menu options shown in Figure P8.6 to form the basis for a macro group named **mcrReport** in which all the macros governing all aspects of the reporting process will be stored. (This macro group should already contain the macros that were developed in this chapter! If it does not, create these macros first. The report menu includes a default date range that will be used by the reports that are called via this report menu. The end user must, of course, be able to change the default date range shown on the menu.)

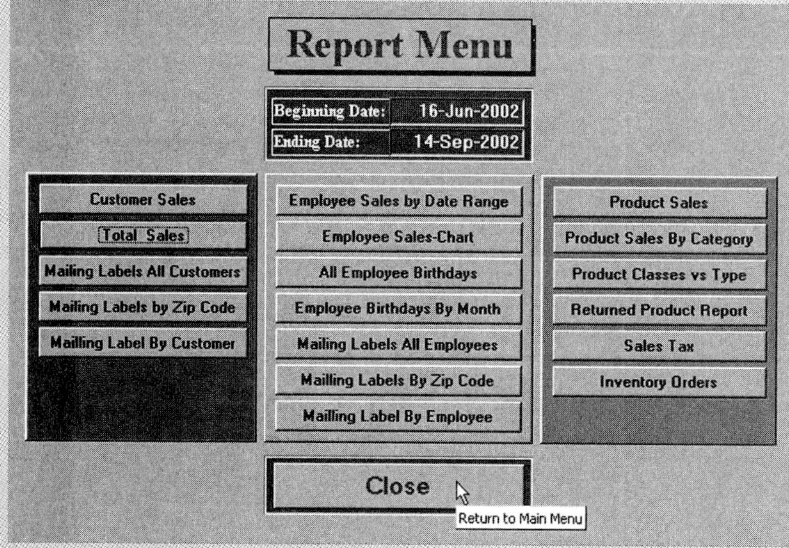

FIGURE P8.6
The Report Menu Options

8.7 Using the command button options shown in Figure P8.6, create the report menu interface process map. Use Figure 8.24 as your development map's template.

8.8 Create the **OpenReportMenu** and **CloseReportMenu** macros. As the names suggest, the first macro will open the report menu shown in Figure P8.6, and the second macro is executed when the end user clicks on the **Close** command button. Note again that the macro naming conventions we have used are part of the self-documentation process—a macro name must reflect its function! (The **Open ReportMenu** macro is called from the main menu, so it must be stored in the **mcrMainMenu** macro group. The **CloseReportMenu** must be stored in the **mcr Report** menu group because it is part of the reporting process.)

8.9 Using the command button options shown in Figure P8.9, create the query menu interface process map. Integrate this interface process map with the process maps you created earlier. Use Figure 8.24 as your development map's template.

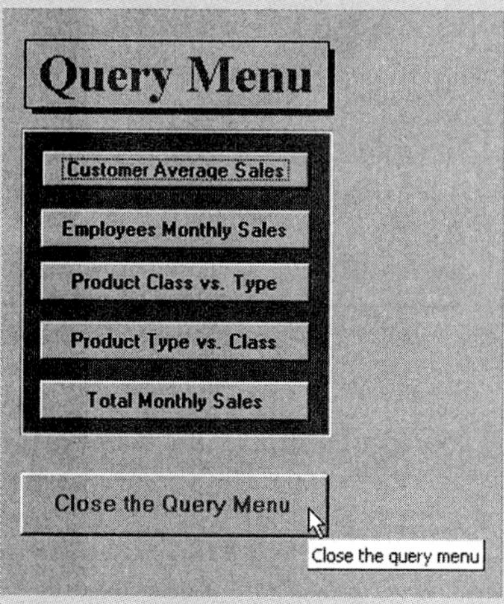

FIGURE P8.9
The Query Menu

8.10 Create the **OpenQueryMenu** and **CloseQueryMenu** macros. As the names suggest, the first macro will open the query menu shown in Figure P8.9, and the second macro is executed when the end user clicks on the **Close the Query Menu** command button. Note again that the macro naming conventions we have used are part of the self-documentation process—a macro name must reflect its function! (The **Open QueryMenu** macro is called from the main menu, so it must be stored in the **mcr MainMenu** macro group. The **CloseQueryMenu** must be stored in the **mcrQuery** menu group, because it is part of the querying process.)

8.11 Create a macro group named **mcrProductSearch**. After creating the macro group, create all the macros that will allow the end user to successfully complete the product search. The product search screen is shown in Figure P8.11. Note the use of combo boxes.

FIGURE P8.11
The Product Search Form

a. The search must lead to a product list that contains all possible product matches.

b. The selection of any product list line must produce the correct product profile. (*Hint:* Review the segmented search procedure in section 5.2.5 in Chapter 5. Also take another look in this chapter's section 8.5.2 to review how search routines are used. Chapter 6's section 6.4 will be a good source of a review for the creation and display of list boxes.)

Brief review: To generate a form-based segmented search, use the **Like** function in the query's criteria line for each of the attributes used in the search procedure. In general terms, the appropriate format would be

```
Like IIf(Forms![Form Name]![Control Name]is null,"*", Forms![Form
  Name]![Control Name]
Or Like & "*" Forms![Form Name]![Control Name] & "*")
```

The **Like IIf** function ensures that the query's execution will yield all records if no entry is made in the **Product Search** form. The second **Like** function allows you to search for the record using any combination of letters in that record.

Although the **Like IIf** function yields a stable and logically precise search, a simplified version of the form-based segmented search may be used, too. For example, the following query criteria would work on a segmented search based on a form named **frmEmployee Search** and its text boxes, named **nmEmployeeNumber**, **nmLastName**, and **nmFirst Name**, respectively. A complete form-based search, culminating in an employee profile form, might then look like this:

- Open a form named **frmEmployeeSearch**. This form contains a **Search** command button.
- The **Search** command button uses the **On Click** property to open a search macro named **mcrEmployeeSearch.SearchButton**.
- The search macro opens a form named **frmEmployeeList**. The form's list box row source is a query that derives its values from a query named **qryCreateEmployee List**. This query uses as its EMP_NUM, EMP_LNAME, and EMP_FNAME criteria the following limitations:

```
Like "*" & [Forms]![frmEmployeeSearch]![nmEmployeeNumber] & "*"
Or: Is Null
Like "*" & [Forms]![frmEmployeeSearch]![nmLastName] & "*"
Like "*" & [Forms]![frmEmployeeSearch]![nmFirstName] & "*"
```

- Select the employee from the list box to open the employee profile form. One way to open the employee profile form is to double-click on a selected list box line and then use a macro to open the employee profile. If the end user failed to select a list box line, use a macro to print a message:

```
Condition: [Forms]![frmEmployeeList]![EmployeeListBox] Is Null
MsgBox: Please select an employee from the list.
```

We hope that this quick review helps you in developing your macro-based search procedures.

8.12 If you examine the main menu in Figure P8.1, you'll see that each option on the **Transactions** tab (page) has a set of binoculars to the right of each option. These binoculars indicate a search command button. For the **Invoice** option, create the forms and the macros that are necessary to find an invoice for selected customers. As you click on the search button, the macro must open a form from which the customer can be selected. Because this initial action is taken from the main menu, store the action in the **mcrMainMenu** macro group and name it **FindInvoice**. (In other words, the macro is referenced as **mcrMainMenu.FindInvoice**.) The search for the invoice will be conducted from the form shown in Figure P8.12. Note that this form contains two list boxes, one showing all the customers and one showing all the invoices for that customer. We have cursored down to the customer named **Michael Brookshire**. (Remember that in our original design the INVOICE was optional to the CUSTOMER, because the RobSem Company included *potential* customers in its database.)

FIGURE P8.12
The Initial Invoice Search Form Based on List Boxes

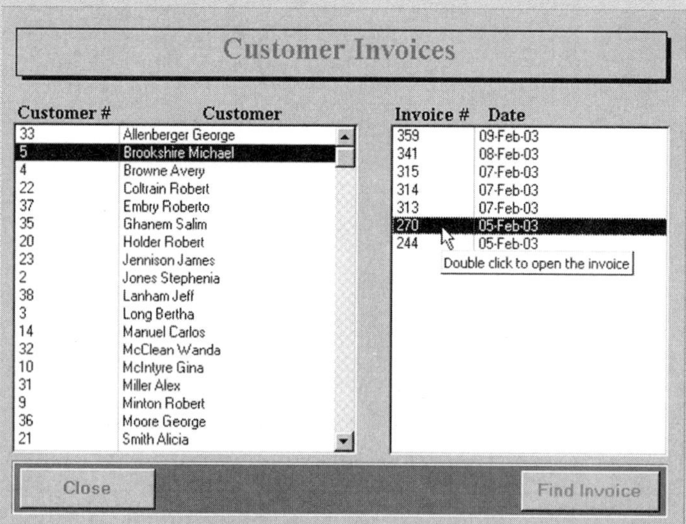

Before you try to work this problem, let's first examine some basics. You learned how to create list boxes in Chapter 5 and you saw an additional list box example in this chapter. However, this is the first time you have seen two list boxes on one form—and the second (invoice) list box output is generated by the first list box (see Figure P8.12A).

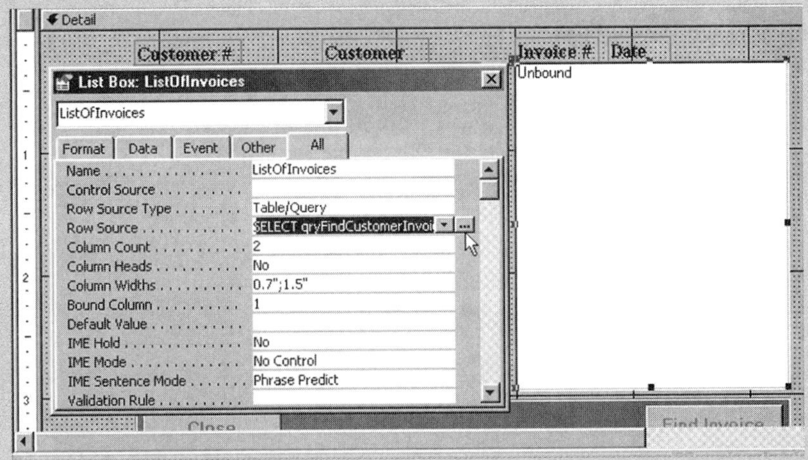

FIGURE P8.12A
The Output of One List Box Based on the Input of Another List Box

The **Row Source** in Figure 8.12A can be examined with the help of the **Zoom** option. (Right-click on the **Row Source** and select **Zoom**.) This action will generate the SQL statement shown in Figure P8.12B.

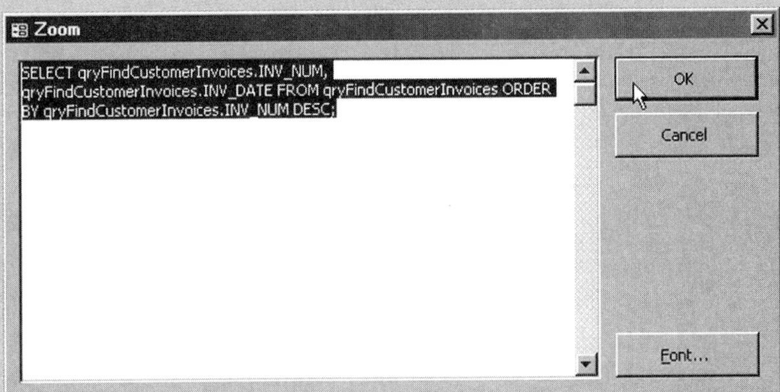

FIGURE P8.12B
The Row Source Select Statement

Keep in mind that you do not have to write the Select command in Figure P8.12B. Instead, select the **Query Builder (...)** option in Figure P8.12A and you will see a familiar QBE screen. Simply select the data input source as shown in Figure P8.12C.

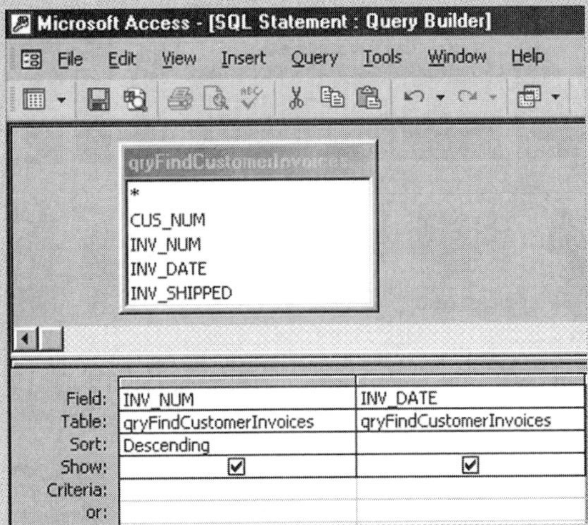

FIGURE P8.12C
The Row Source Query Builder Screen

The **qryFindCustomerInvoices** query output becomes the Row Source for the second list box. (Look at the **Criteria:** statement in Figure P8.12D.)

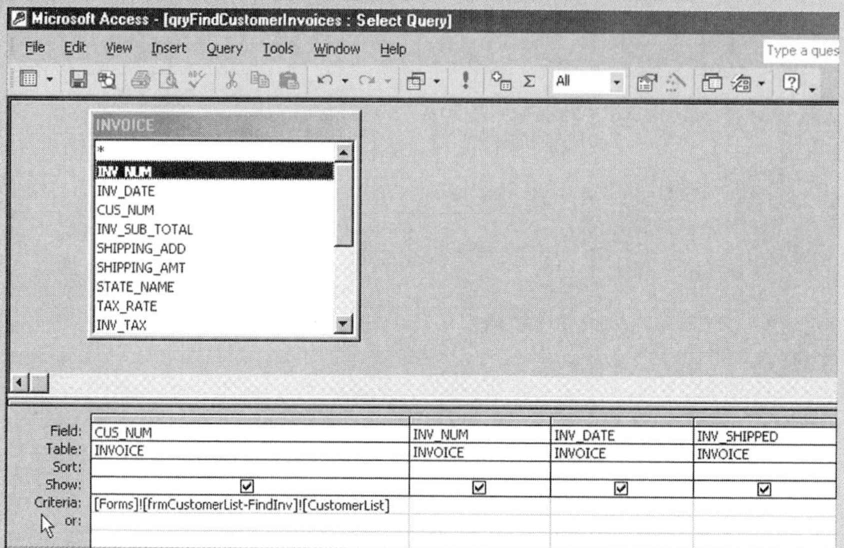

FIGURE P8.12D The Customer List Box as the Parameter in the Query

Assuming that you have created the queries correctly and that you have made them the source for the respective list boxes, the selection shown in Figure P8.12 will yield the results shown in Figure P8.12E. Make sure that the selection of the **Close** button will return you to the form shown in Figure P8.12. (Clicking on the **Close** button on the form shown in Figure P8.12 must return you to the main menu.)

FIGURE P8.12E The Found Invoice

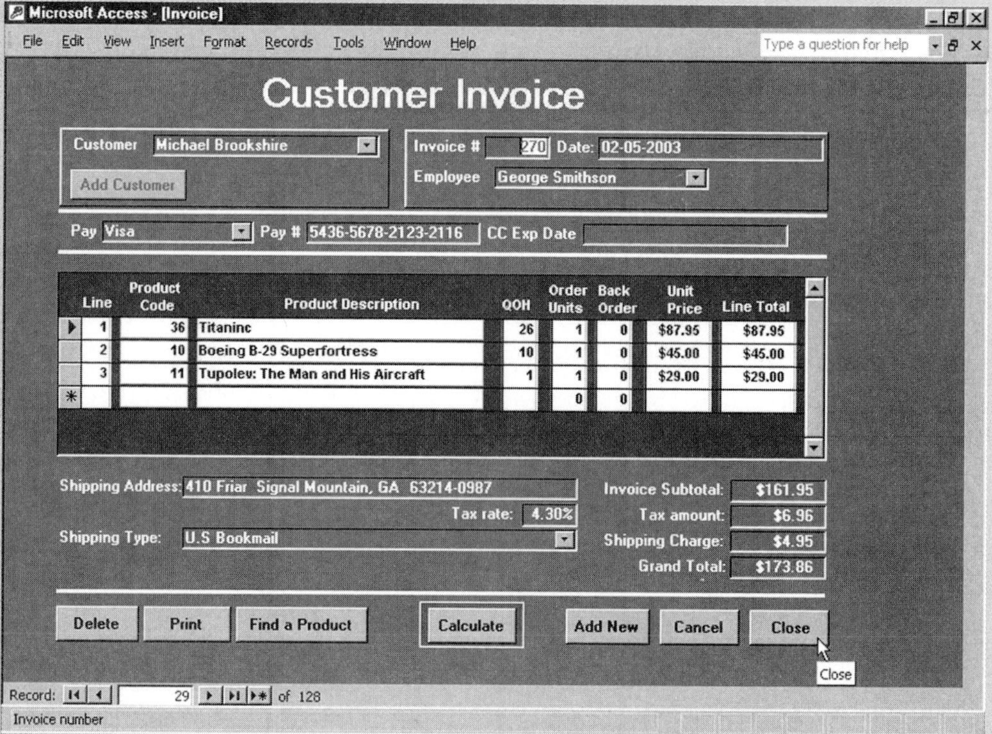

8.13 Write the search routines for the remaining options on the Main Menu's **Transaction** tab (page) shown in Figure P8.1.

Use the **Ch08_JewelCo** database to complete problems 8.14 through 8.37. These problems require you to create all the queries, forms, and macros you'll need to produce the solutions. When you have completed the problem set, you will have created a small, but already useful, database application system.

8.14 Create a search routine for the customers. The search routine begins with the form shown in Figure P8.14.

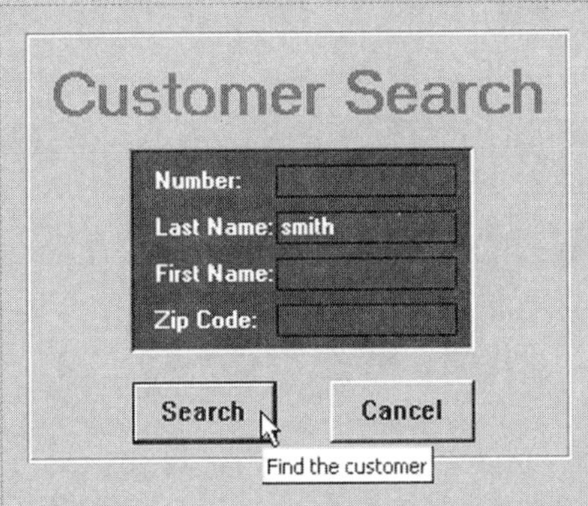

FIGURE P8.14
The frmCustomerSearch Form

8.15 The form you created in problem 8.14 must open the customer list box shown in Figure P8.15. Create this form and name it **frmCustomerList**. Write the macros that yield the customer list form after the **Search** button in the customer search form has been clicked.

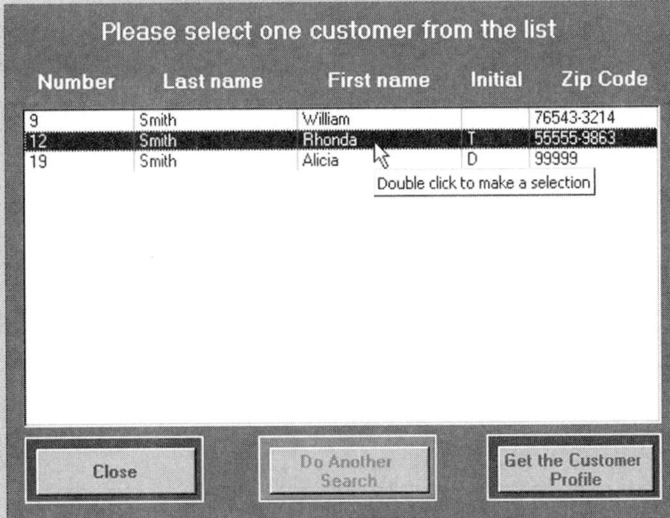

FIGURE P8.15
The frmCustomerList Form

8.16 Create—and attach—the macro for the **Get the Customer Profile** command button in problem 8.15. This macro must generate the customer profile form based on the list box selection in problem 8.15. (The results are shown in Figure P8.16.)

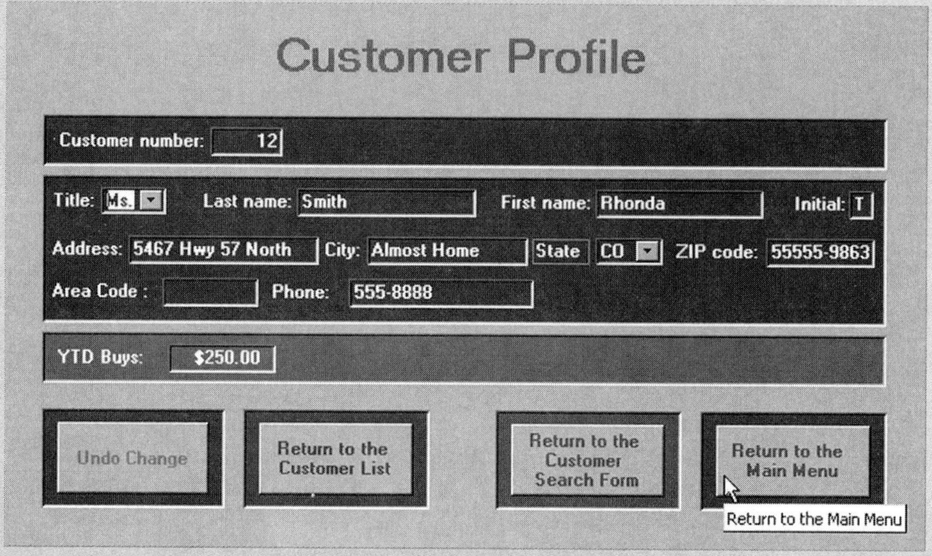

FIGURE P8.16
The frmCustomerProfile Form

8.17 Create all the macro groups and the macros in those groups that will allow you to use any of the command buttons shown on the forms shown in Figures P8.14 through P8.16. (As its name suggests, the **Undo Change** command button in Figure P8.16 lets you cancel any and all changes you have made on the customer profile form.)

8.18 Create the jeweler search form shown in Figure P8.18, then create the macro group for the search routine. The first macro in this macro group will, of course, trigger the search that yields the results shown in Figure P8.19.

FIGURE P8.18
The frmJewelerSearch Form

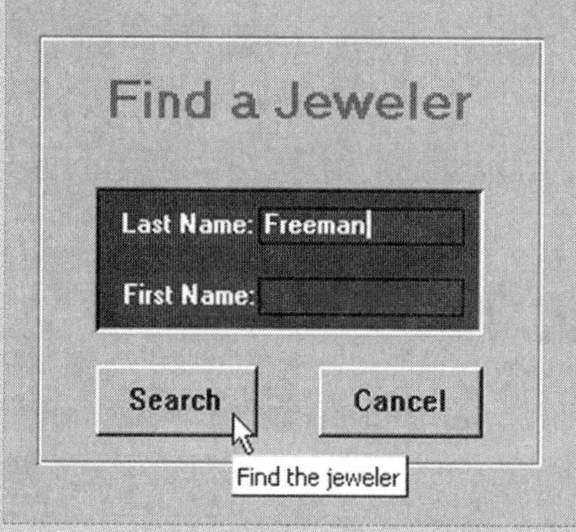

8.19 Create the form—and the macro(s)—that will produce the list box shown in Figure P8.19.

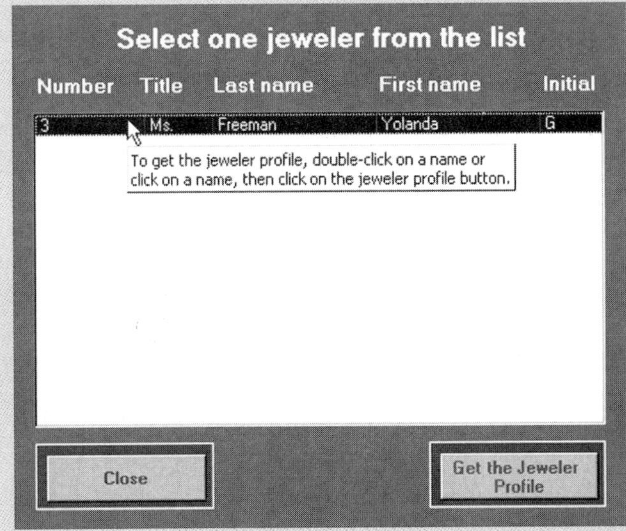

FIGURE P8.19
The frmJewelerList Form

8.20 Given the selection shown in the list box in Figure P8.19, open the jeweler profile form shown in Figure P8.20. Write the macros and place them in the proper macro group to accomplish all the tasks that are generated through the command buttons.

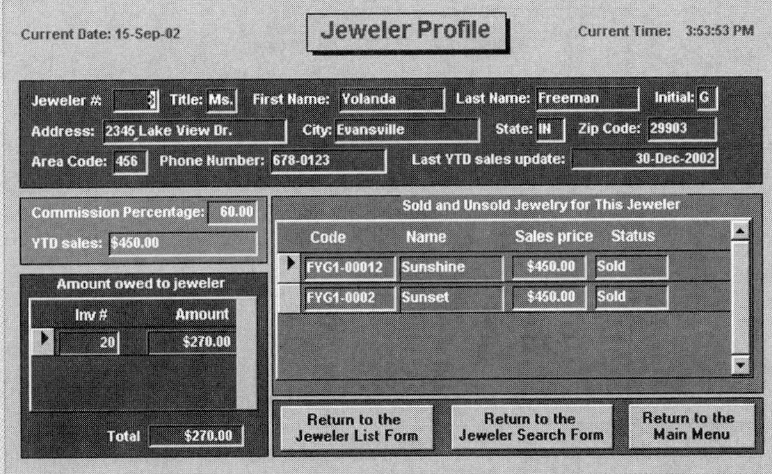

FIGURE P8.20
The frmJewelerProfile Form

8.21 Create the invoice form shown in Figure P8.21. (Note that the customer YTD purchases have not yet been updated; the current invoice total is already greater than the YTD purchases.)

FIGURE P8.21
The frmInvoice Form

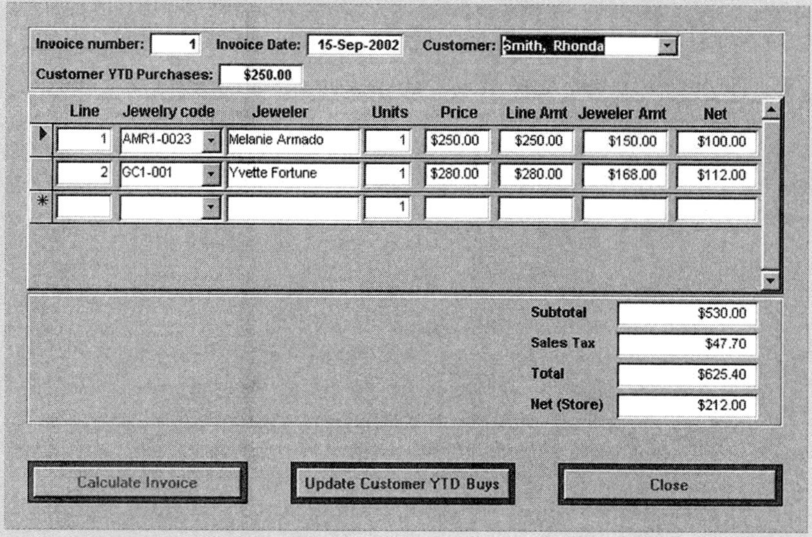

8.22 Given the invoice form format in Figure P8.21, make sure that the selected product code is matched to that product's price in the JEWELRY table, and then write that price in the subform's LINE_PRICE. To perform that task, complete the following steps:

a. Create a macro in the **mcrInvoice** macro group and name it **AfterUpdateJewelry Code**.

b. Attach the **AfterUpdateJewelryCode** macro to the **frmInvoiceLine** form's JWLRY_CODE **After Update** property.

c. When the JWLRY_CODE field is updated, that is, the cursor has left the JWLRY_CODE field, the macro's condition must be based on whether or not the field is null. In other words, use the condition

```
[Forms]![frmInvoice]![frmInvoiceLine].[Form]![JWLRY_CODE] Is
Not Null
```

d. If the JWLRY_CODE is not null, use **SetValue** to set the LINE table's LINE_PRICE equal to the JWLRY_SALES_PRICE, located in the JEWELRY table that is referenced by the **frmInvoiceline** form.

At this point, your macro should look like the segment in Table P8.22

TABLE P8.22 The Partially Completed AfterUpdateJewelryCode Macro

Macro Name	Condition	Action	Action Argument
AfterUpdateJewelryCode			
	[Forms]![frmInvoice]![frmInvoiceLine].[Form]![JWLRY_CODE] Is Not Null		
	...	SetValue	Item: [Forms]![frmInvoice]![frmInvoiceLine].[Form]![LINE_PRICE] Expression: [Forms]![frmInvoice]![frmInvoiceLine].[Form]![JWLRY_SALES_PRICE]

8.23 Assuming that you have completed the work in problem 8.22, make sure that the following line values are properly calculated after each line selection of the product and the units:

a. LINE_AMOUNT=LINE_UNITS*LINE_PRICE.

b. LINE_JWLR_AMOUNT=LINE_AMOUNT*JWLR_PERCENT

c. LINE_NET=LINE_AMOUNT−LINE_JWLR_AMOUNT

These three computations are performed and placed with the **SetValue** action, and they are governed by the condition used in problem 8.22. Therefore, do not forget the three-dot (...) continuation symbol in the condition column below the stated condition! For example, the line amount would be governed by the **SetValue** action's **Item** shown next:

```
[Forms]![frmInvoice]![frmInvoiceLine].[Form]![LINE_AMOUNT]
```

and its expression will be

```
[FORMS]![FRMINVOICE]![FRMINVOICELINE].[FORM]![LINE_UNITS]*
[FORMS]!
[FRMINVOICE]![FRMINVOICELINE].[FORM]![LINE_PRICE]
```

8.24 After you have completed the work in problems 8.22 and 8.23, use a **RunMacro** action—yes, the condition remains in force—to execute the **mcrInvoice.Calculate Invoice** macro. This macro will ensure that the invoice subtotal, tax, jeweler amount, and the net value are computed and placed on the form. Given this format, you will see a continuous update of these values as each invoice line is executed. This is a very desirable feature, because it lets the end user answer the customer's questions about the purchasing cost anytime during the invoicing process.

8.25 After completing the work for problems 8.22 through 8.24, create a macro named **UpdateCustomerYTDBuys** in the **mcrInvoice** macro group to open the update query that will update the CUS_YTD_BUYS attribute when the **Update Customer YTD Buys** command button in Figure 8.21 is clicked. The update query's structure is shown in Figure P8.25 and its data source is shown in Figure P8.25A.

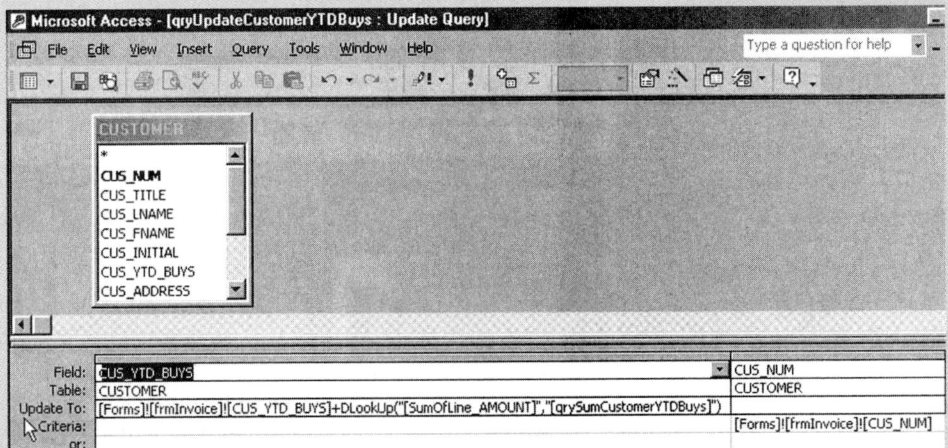

FIGURE P8.25
The qryUpdateCustomerYTD Buys Update Query

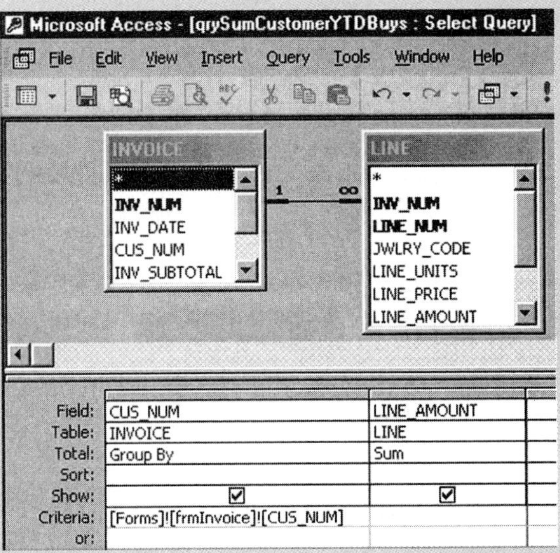

FIGURE P8.25A
The qrySumCustomerYTDBuys Query

8.26 Create a macro that uses the **Requery** action to refresh the JWLRY_CODE drop-down list each time it has the focus. Attach this macro to the JWLRY_CODE's **On Got Focus** property. (The macro refreshes the list to ensure that the query output is limited to the records that conform to the **Not Sold** status.)

8.27 Create a columnar form based on the JEWELER table. Save this form as **frmJEWELER**.

8.28 Create a query based on the LINE table, using the JWLR_NUM, the INV_NUM, the JWLR_PAID, and the JWLR_AMOUNT attributes. In the JWLR_PAID **Criteria** option, type **No** to limit the query output to unpaid JWLR_PAID records. Name the query **qryJewelerAmount**. Then create a tabular form based on the **qryJeweler Amount** and name this form **frmJewelerAmount**.

8.29 Create a columnar form based on the JEWELRY table. Name this form **frmJEWELRY**.

8.30 Insert the **frmJewelerAmount** and the **frmJEWELRY** forms on the **frmJEWELER** form and then link the **Child** and **Master** fields through the JWLR_NUM. Edit the form to produce the results in Figure P8.30. Note that the form includes three buttons: **Close**, **Paid**, and **Update YTD Sales**. (Note also that we have cursored down to jeweler number 3, Yolanda Freeman.) The source for the total amount owed to the jeweler is shown in Figure P8.30A.

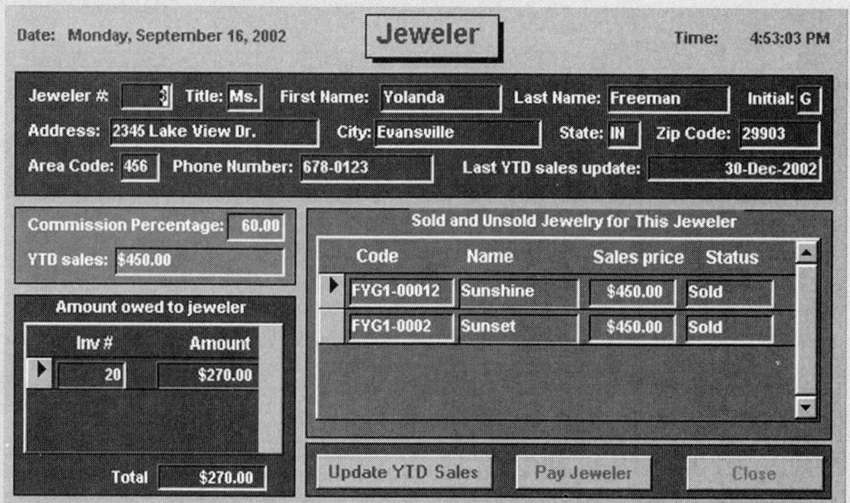

FIGURE P8.30
The frmJEWELER Form

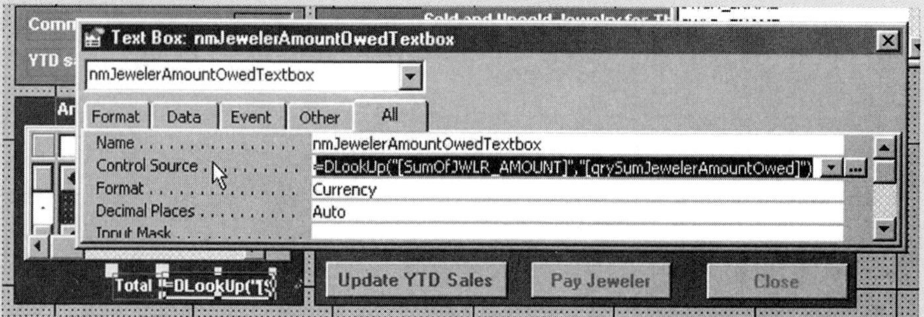

FIGURE P8.30A
The Total Amount Owed to the Jeweler

As you examine the structure of the query in Figure P8.30B, keep in mind that the **Name:** field—and, therefore, the JEWELER table—are not required to show the total in Figure P8.30. The inclusion of these two objects serves another reporting purpose.

Note also that the amount owed is not shown unless it is greater than zero. That is, the **Criteria:** statement shows **>0** for the **Sum.** Finally, note that the data source for the **Sum** is the query named **qryJewelryAmountOwed**. This query is shown in Figure P8.30C. Note that the **Criteria:** statement for JWLR_PAID is **"No"**.

FIGURE P8.30B **The qrySumJewelerAmountOwed Query**

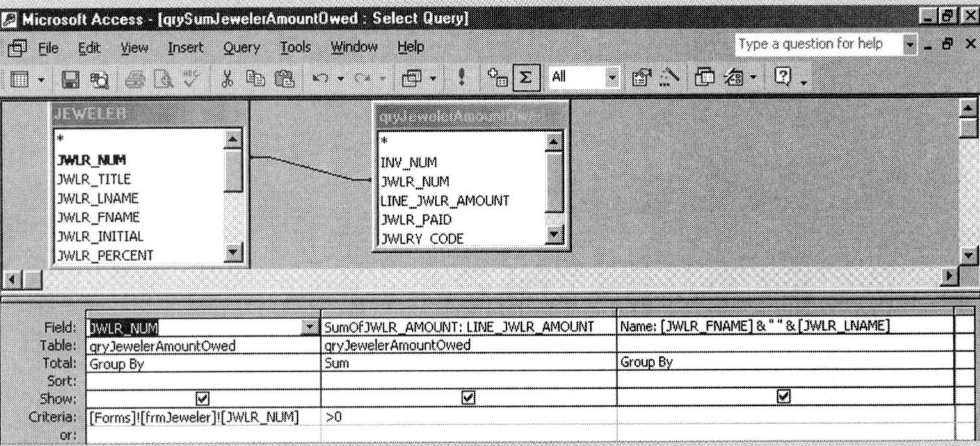

FIGURE P8.30C **The qrySumJewelerAmountOwed Query**

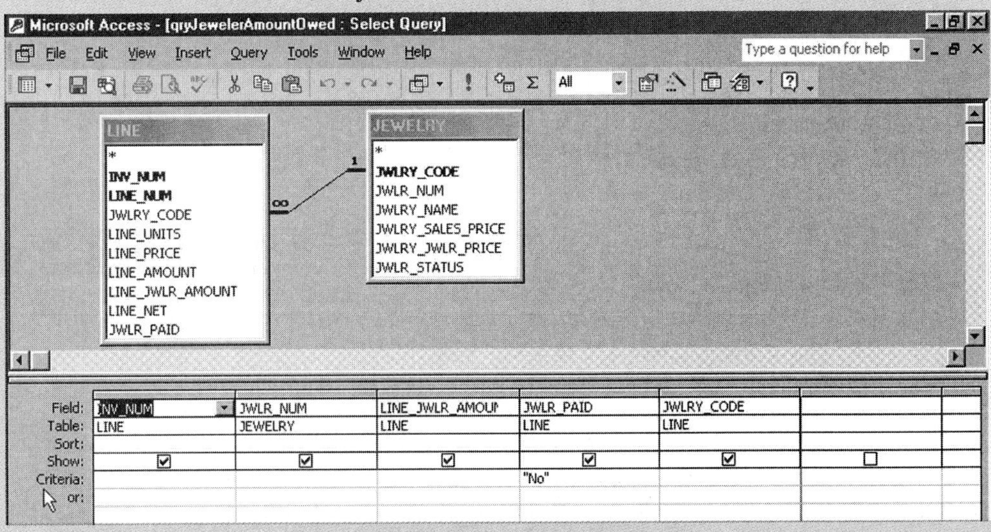

8.31 Create a new macro group named **mcrJeweler**. In the macro group, create a macro to close the **frmJEWELER** form and to maximize the screen. Attach the macro to the **Close** button shown in Figure P8.30.

8.32 Create an update query that will change the JWLR_PAID attribute value to **Yes.** The query is based on the LINE table, using only the attributes JWLR_NUM and JWLR_PAID. In the JWLR_NUM **Criteria** property, point to the **frmJEWELER** form's JWLR_NUM attribute to update only the records for which the form's JWLR_NUM is selected. Name the query **qryUpdateJewelerPaidStatus** (see Figure P8.32).

FIGURE P8.32 The qryUpdateJewelerPaidStatus Update Query

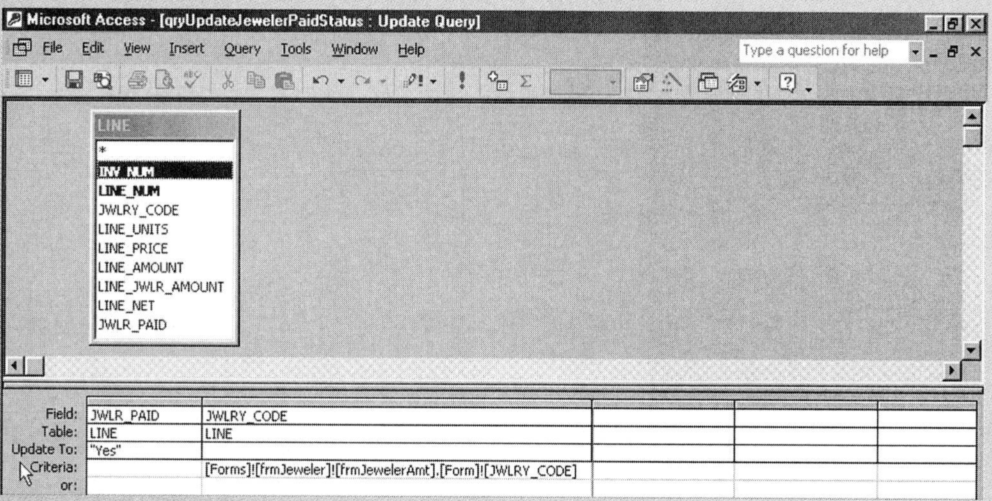

Keep in mind that it is probably not wise to update the jeweler's payment status at this point. After all, just because the item has been sold does not necessarily mean that the jeweler is paid at that moment. This update is done for update illustration purposes only. You can later create a form that allows the end user to "batch" update all the jewelers whose jewelry has been sold and who have not yet been paid.

8.33 Create a macro that will open the **qryUpdateJewelerPaidStatus** query when the **Pay Jeweler** command button is clicked on the **frmJEWELER** form shown in Figure P8.30.

8.34 Create a query based on the LINE table, **Group By** the JWLR_NUM, and **Sum** the INV_AMOUNT. In the **Criteria:** line for the JWLR_NUM, point to the JWLR_NUM on the **frmJEWELER** form. Name the query **qryJewelerYTDSales**.

8.35 Create a macro to write the JWLR_YTD_SALES on the **frmJEWELER** form. In the **Item** section, point to the JWLR_YTD_SALES on the **frmJEWELER** form. In the **Expression** section, use the **DLookUp** function to retrieve the sum of the INV_AMOUNT from the **qryJewelerYTDSales** query. (If the jeweler has no YTD sales, the field of the JWLR_YTD_SALES will be set to null, so use the condition limit to check for null values.) If a null value is encountered—that is, the null condition is **Yes**—set the field value to **0**. Attach the macro to the **frmJEWELER** form's **Update YTD Sales** button.

8.36 Create the Main Menu form shown in Figure P8.36. Name the form **frmMainMenu** and make sure that this form is opened when the end user opens the database. (Remember the **StartUp** option?)

FIGURE P8.36
The JewelCo Company Main Menu

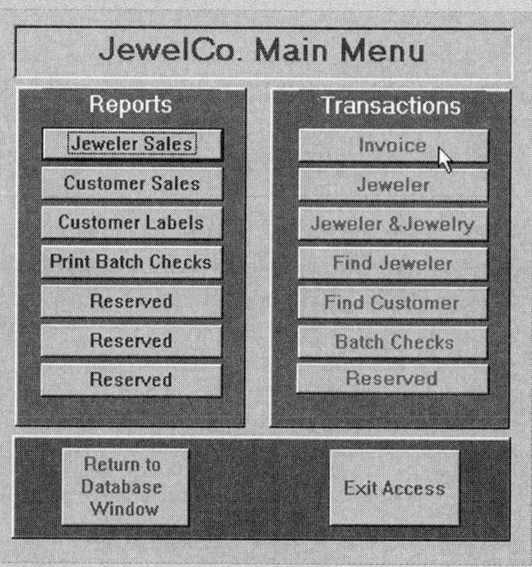

You have already created the **Invoice** and **Jeweler** forms, so go ahead and create the **mcrMainMenu** macro group and create the macros named **OpenInvoice** and **OpenJeweler**.

8.37 Write a macro that produces a message box such as the one shown in Figure P8.37 when the **Exit Access** command button on Figure P8.36 is clicked.

FIGURE P8.37
The Exit Access Options

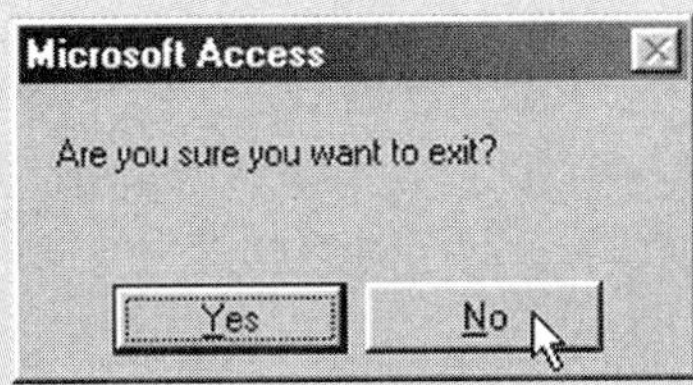

8.38 Create the **frmJeweler&Jewelry** form shown in Figure P8.38, and then write the macro to call it from the main menu shown in Figure P8.36. (Note that we have cursored down to jeweler number 7.)

FIGURE P8.38 The frmJeweler&Jewelry Form

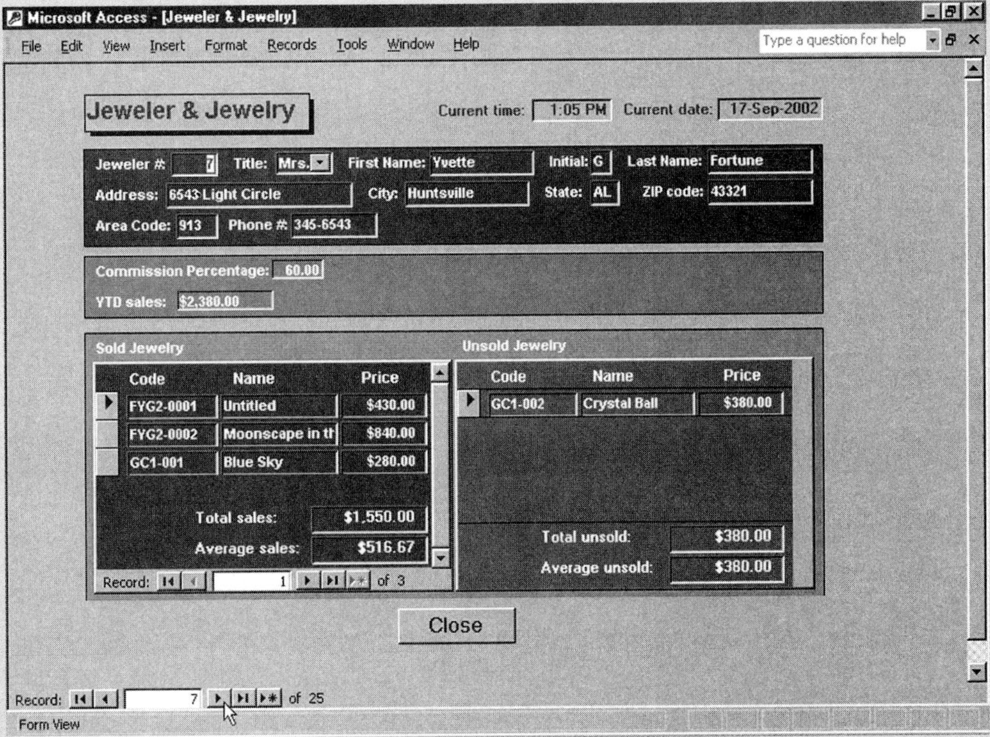

As you examine Figure P8.38, note that the form uses two subforms. Figure P8.38A shows one of those subforms. Note that the structure of the **Total Sales** text box's control source is specified to be **=Sum([JWLRY_SALES_PRICE])**. This is another way to sum a query's values within the form, but make sure that it is placed in the form's *footer*. (You should recall that the other way to sum the values and place them on the form is to use the **DLookUp** function we have used before.) The advantage of the approach shown here is its simplicity. The (minor) disadvantage is that it is part of the subform's footer. Therefore, if the subform contains a lot of records, you may have to scroll down the subform to find it. The advantage of the **DLookUp** function is that its results can be placed anywhere on the form. (We do have a bias toward simplicity, but you should know how to use either technique.)

FIGURE P8.38A The frmSoldJewelry Subform

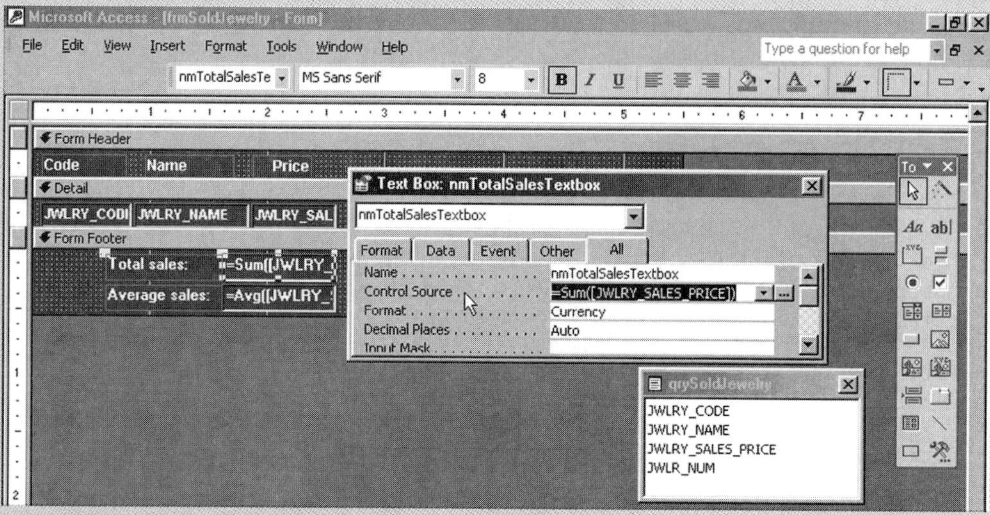

The record source for the subform shown in Figure P8.38A is the query shown in Figure P8.38B.

FIGURE P8.38B The qrySoldJewelry Query

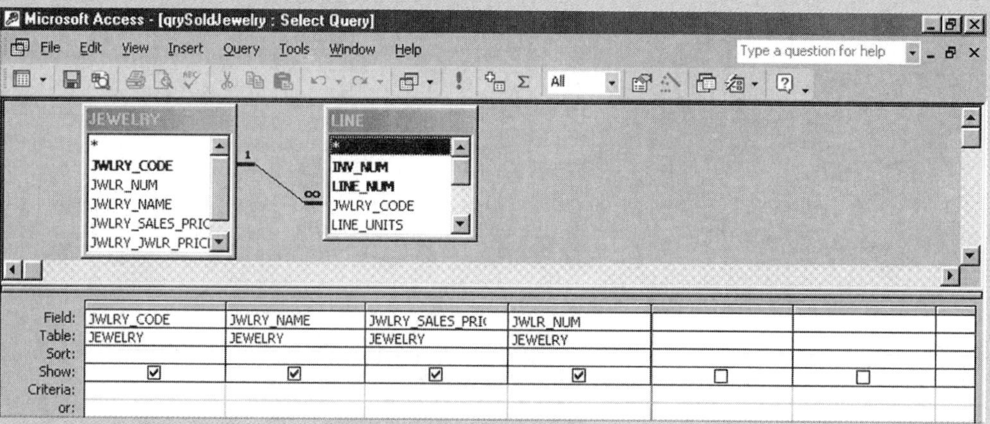

Incidentally, as you examine the **Average sales:** text box in Figure P8.38A, note that you can generate the average sales with the same technique that we used to generate the totals. (The only difference is that you use the **=Avg([JWLRY_SALES_PRICE])** function, instead of the **=Sum([JWLRY_SALES_PRICE])** function.) Now go ahead and create the unsold jewelry subform to match the structure of the sold jewelry subform. Remember to use the JWLR_NUM in both subforms as the link between child and master fields.

8.39 Create the additional forms and reports that can be accessed from the main menu shown in Figure P8.36. Use the segmented search routines illustrated in the chapter to find jewelers and customers. The report section on the main menu should contain at least some reports that will enable JewelCo managers to evaluate their business environment. (Sample questions: Which jewelers generate the most sales, and what are their sales amounts? What are the total sales and net sales over any selected date range? What is the total inventory value, listed by jeweler?)

Use the **AC_Museum** database to serve as the basis for problem 8.40. Copy the **AC_Museum** folder from your CD and place it on your disk. Figure P8.39 shows that we have moved the folder to the **C:** drive. The **\Database** subfolder contains the **AC_Museum** database that you will need to produce the applications for problem

8.40. (Make sure that you remember to remove the **Read-only** property from the database after you have copied it to your disk.) The **AC_Pictures** subfolder contains the **.jpg** files that are accessed by your database applications, so make sure that your **AC_Pictures** subfolder contains those pictures.

FIGURE P8.39 The AC_Museum Folder and Its Contents

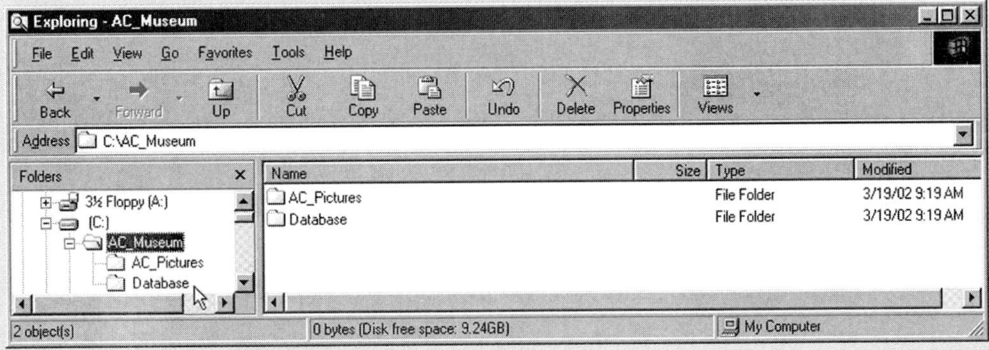

The most complex part of problem 8.40's applications involves the image management on forms. This component was completely developed in section 8.5. (See Figures 8.25 through 8.33.) In section 8.5 we explained that the dynamic linking required you to define a path to the pictures. Our examples assumed that the pictures were located in the **\AC_Pictures** folder. *If you change the picture folder names or locations, you must use an update query to modify the picture locations and/or names in the table that stores those locations!*

8.40 Create the queries, the forms, and the macros to produce the small system shown in the sequences in Figures P8.40 through P8.40E. Note that the figures illustrate a sequence of all of the system's features. Make sure that the main menu is loaded on **StartUp**. (We created the aircraft form in this chapter.)

FIGURE P8.40
The AC_Museum's Main Menu

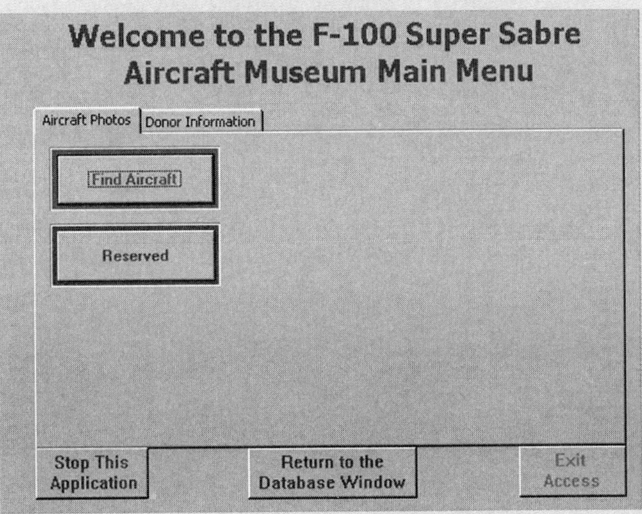

First, use a segmented search routine to find any aircraft. When you click on the main menu's **Find Aircraft** command button, the system should show the search form in Figure P8.40A:

FIGURE P8.40A
The Aircraft Search Form

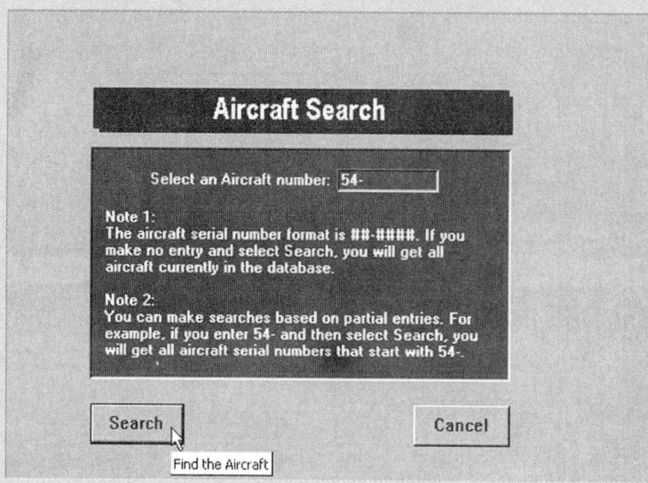

The input shown in Figure P8.40A will produce the aircraft form in Figure P8.40B. (Note that we have cursored down to the second record and that the navigation bar shows that there are three aircraft with serial numbers that include the **54-**value we input in Figure P8.40A.)

FIGURE P8.40B **The Found Aircraft**

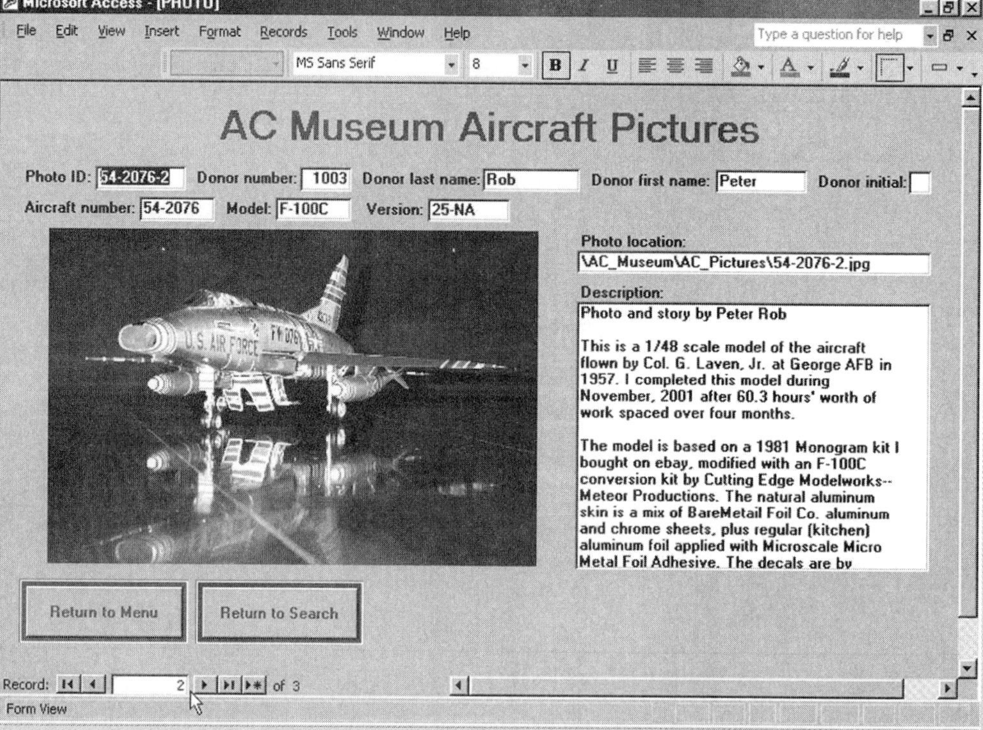

As you examine the output in Figure P8.40B, remember that all the aircraft data are dynamically linked to the picture, and vice versa. Note that you can either return to the aircraft search routine or to the menu. We have selected the **Return to Menu** option to return to the menu. We then selected the **Donor Information** tab (page) shown in Figure P8.40C to generate the dialog box shown in Figure P8.40D.

FIGURE P8.40C
Start the Donor Search

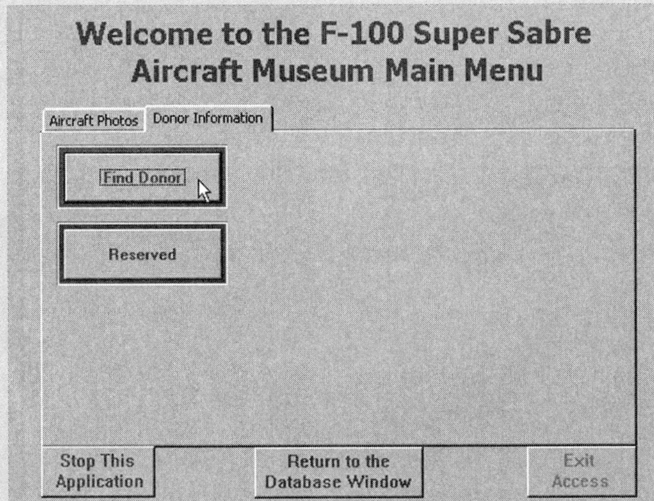

FIGURE P8.40D
The Donor Search Form

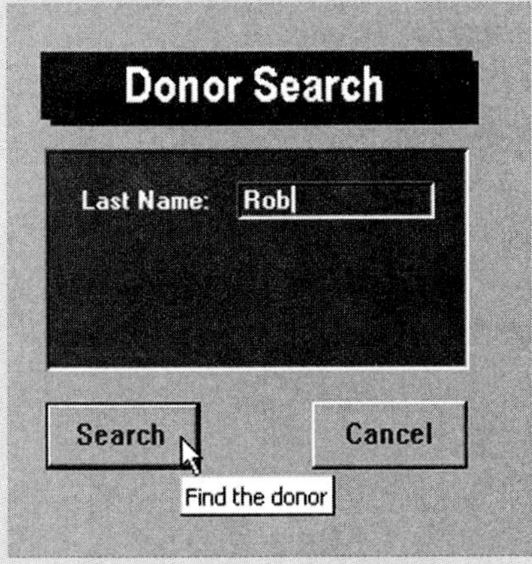

The search parameter (Rob) shown in Figure P8.40D will generate the output shown in Figure P8.40E.

FIGURE P8.40E **The Found Donor**

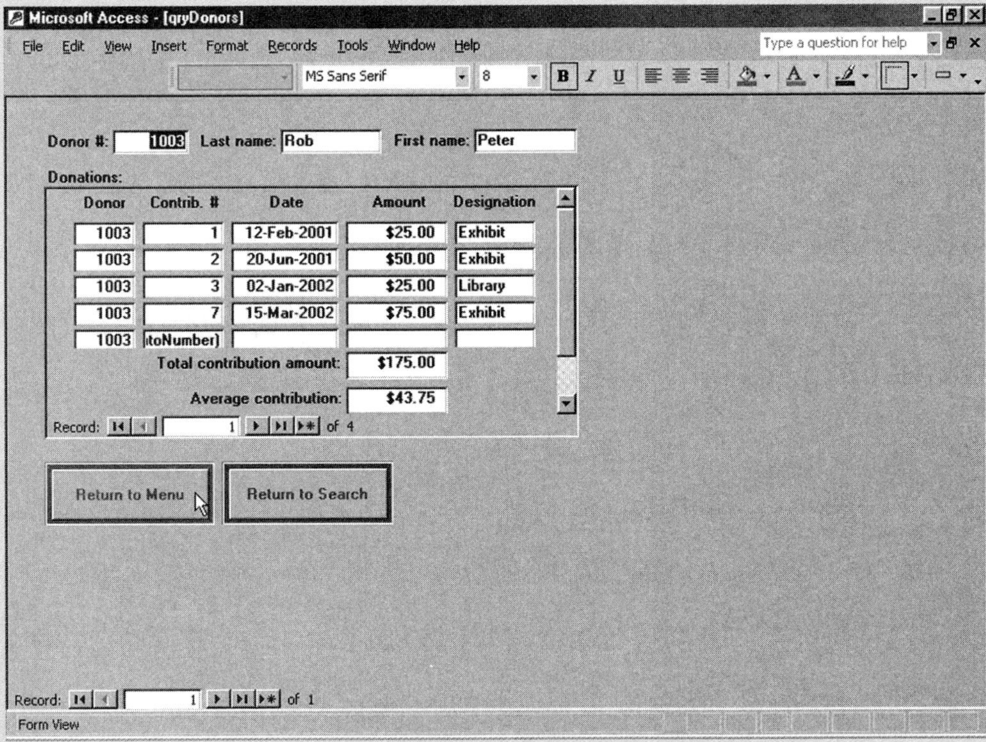

Chapter Nine

Access and the Internet

Preview

The Internet—more specifically, the World Wide Web, which is one of several services provided by the Internet—has become the foundation for economic interchange at all levels and in virtually all countries.[1] Even with minimal access to the electronic highway known as the Internet, today's consumers can interact with the world in a wide variety of new ways, using e-mail to communicate and using the Web environment to buy products and services and to expand their educational and social horizons. Given the competitive advantages provided by rapidly spreading Internet technologies and the rapid growth of a Web-savvy consumer base, many businesses have either augmented their traditional operations with Web-enabled buying and selling or they have become purely "online" businesses. In short, most businesses now conduct all or part of their operations electronically.

Businesses and other organizations may use the Web as a static medium, a dynamic medium, or a combination of the two. Static displays range from simple catalog listings to video-based presentations, but they do not permit customers to interact with the data. Dynamic displays are interactive, thus enabling the user to determine what is to be displayed through database queries. Clearly, sales transactions require a dynamic Web environment in which frequent data updates take place in customer charge accounts, product inventory, shipping accounts, and so on.

In this chapter, we will show you how to use Microsoft Access to create applications that can be used in a dynamic Web environment. Although we will show you some basic examples of the code that is used to generate the Web components known as *Web pages*, our focus is not on code generation. Instead, we will let the Microsoft code generators perform their magic for you so that you can create and use applications that interact with your databases without having to worry about the coding details.

Objectives

When you have mastered the material in this chapter, you will know how to

- Create a page, using the Access Page Wizard.
- Use a page to drill down into a record set to get an increasingly detailed view of the data.
- Create and use the Office Spreadsheet on a page.
- Create and use the Chart on a page to show information graphically.
- Create and use the Pivot Table on a page.
- Insert images and hyperlinks on a page.
- Create a small system in which the end user can navigate to the various application components.
- Identify and correct common errors.

9.1 AN INTRODUCTION TO WEB PAGES

From the end users' point of view, the **World Wide Web (WWW),** usually referred to as "the Web," is basically a worldwide network of Web pages. A **Web page** is a specially formatted document that may contain text, graphics, video, audio, and/or other objects such as spreadsheets. Each Web page has an address, known as an **URL** or **Uniform Resource Locator.** Most URLs use the prefix *http://* as part of their address. This **http** prefix, which is the acronym for **HyperText Transfer Protocol,** reflects the presentation and transmission format used by most URLs. (A **protocol** is a set of rules.)

Web pages are linked through **hyperlinks,** which are the visual elements on Web pages through which you can load the addresses of other Web pages into the browser. The **browser** is software, such as Microsoft Internet Explorer or Netscape Navigator, that enables you to navigate (browse) through the Web. Although the hyperlinks are the *visible* way in which Web pages are linked, those hyperlinks perform their linking magic through a standard communications protocol known as **TCP/IP (Transmission Control Protocol/Internet Protocol).**

In the recent past, developing a Web page required a lot of HTML coding. **HTML (HyperText Markup Language)** is a language that is used to define the Web page's display and use characteristics. (A **markup language** merely formats the elements of a Web page so that a browser can display it on a computer screen.) HTML is easy to learn; it is basically a collection of simple English language constructs. And it can easily be produced with even the simplest text generators such as Notepad. There are only two requirements for a basic HTML-based Web page: The HTML code must be written to conform to the **American Standard Code for Information Interchange (ASCII),** and you must save the document with an **.htm** or **.html** filename extension. Take a look, for example, at the html code in Table 9.1.

TABLE 9.1 **Sample HTML Listing**

```
<HTML>

<HEAD>
<TITLE>F-100-main</TITLE>
</HEAD>

<!- Color code "#a2a2a2" = gray           ->
<!- Color code "#00005a" = dark blue      ->
<!- Color code "#ff0000" = red            ->
<!- Color code "#50c0e3" = sky blue       ->

<BODY BGCOLOR="#50c0e3">

<CENTER>
<FONT COLOR="#00005A" SIZE="+1" FACE="Arial">
<STRONG>
<P>The Web Home of the North American F-100 Super Sabre</P>
</STRONG>

<IMG SRC="pics/54-2076-2.jpg" HEIGHT="370" WIDTH="540"
ALT="Photo of F-100C Super Sabre #54-2076">
</CENTER>

<P>F-100C, 435th TFS, 479th TFW, as flown by Col. G. Laven Jr.
at George AFB, California, 1957.
</P>
</FONT>
</BODY>
</HTML>
```

FIGURE 9.1
A Segment of Sample HTML Output

The sample code listing shown in Table 9.1 creates the segment headed by "The Web Home of the North American F-100 Super Sabre" shown in Figure 9.1. The U.S. and Tennessee flags and the hyperlinks shown on the left side of the picture are generated by another piece of HTML code that is not shown in this chapter.

The code shown in Table 9.1 was written with Microsoft Notepad, the text editor that comes with your Windows operating system. The listing is only used as an example; you need not learn HTML coding to do what we will explore in this chapter. However, because you are likely to encounter at least some of the basic terminology when you build Web pages, we do believe that the brief following listing and its brief discussion have a proper place in this chapter. In fact, you will see that the Access Wizard automatically creates HTML code—with an .htm file extension—in files stored outside your database as you develop Web pages within your database.

If you examine the HTML code in Table 9.1, you will notice that each HTML document contains a series of *tags.* A **tag** is an HTML key word that is enclosed in angle brackets. For example, <HTML> is a tag, as is <CENTER>. *Each tag must be closed after it has performed its job.* Closing a tag is accomplished with the help of a forward slash before the key word. For example, </HTML> is the closing tag for the HTML key word. Note that the following HTML segment opens and closes each tag.

```
<HEAD>
<TITLE>F-100-main</TITLE>
</HEAD>
```

HTML coding is easy to read, especially for English speakers. For example, IMG SRC indicates *image source,* CENTER means *center the text,* STRONG means *boldface the text,* and so on.

An HTML document, such as the one shown in Table 9.1, has at least these components:

<HTML>	Indicates the start of the HTML document
<HEAD>	The document header

Note

If you want to explore the development and use of data access pages, you must have a legal license to Microsoft Office controls. To view the data access pages on the Web, you need the Microsoft Web Components. If you do not have Office 2002 installed, you will see the message in Figure 9.2 when you try to develop a data access page.

FIGURE 9.2
The Data Access Page Notification

Data Access Page Notification

This page requires the Microsoft Office Web Components.

See the Microsoft Office Web site for more information.

Also, keep in mind that you can design a data access page quickly, but there is a limit to what the data access page designer can do for you. When you become familiar with the data access page, you can use the Microsoft Script Editor to edit the page created by the data access page designer. However, because the focus of this book is the database, we will *not* demonstrate the use of the Microsoft Script Editor—that part of the development is beyond the scope of this chapter.

Finally, data access pages can be seen with Internet Explorer 5.0. However, you should use Internet Explorer 5.5 and up if you want to enjoy the detail in the data access pages.

<TITLE>	The document title
<BODY>	The component that shows the page contents

Although the HTML code we have just shown you is simple, easy to produce, and adheres to a worldwide standard that enables all kinds of computers to read and translate the code, its main strength lies in the creation and display of static Web pages. As its name implies, a **static Web page** can only display a *predefined* set of pictures, a text-based listing, or other objects, but you cannot interact with those objects. In contrast, a **dynamic Web page** is one in which the end user can change the screen contents by interacting with the screen's components. For example, if you can select what objects that will be displayed on the screen, you are looking at a dynamic Web page. For example, if you buy a product online, you are interacting with the Web pages to select the product, enter your shipping address, and enter your credit card number.

Interacting with a Web page usually requires that some query be executed. (Sample query: Show me the books in stock for an author named Alice Smith.) You can create dynamic Web pages with a version of HTML known as **dynamic HTML.** Writing the dynamic HTML code can be quite a chore. Although you can insert SQL calls within HTML code, creating dynamic Web pages in an HTML environment turns out to be rather cumbersome.

Fortunately, Microsoft Access has made the development of dynamic Web pages simple through its use of data access pages. **Data access pages** are documents based on HTML and ActiveX controls. **ActiveX controls** use the **ADO** (**ActiveX Data Objects**) protocol to establish the connection between the user and the database. Therefore, data access pages make it possible for you to create dynamic applications that will enable your end users to access your database via the Internet to perform such actions as

- Finding a product or service.
- Placing an order.
- Checking out the status of an order.
- Paying online.

When you develop a data access page, Access displays that page in the same format that you see in your browser. When you develop a data access page and

> **Note**
>
> Make sure that you read the "Note about the Chapter 9 applications" on the CD before you begin your work on the **Ch09_POS_2nd** applications. If you cannot use the C: drive, use the drive that you *can* use. For example, if you store your applications on a ZIP drive that is designated as drive D:, use the path **D:\Rob-Semaan-2ndEdition\Databases(Student)\Ch09\Ch09_POS_2nd**.
>
> *You may also leave off the drive designation when you specify the data source for any application component.* However, if you move the application to another drive, Access will automatically append the drive designation to the path used by the initial page.

save it in an HTML file, you will be able to open it in your browser and use your PC to interact with the data. *However, if you want the public to access your pages on the Web, you must place the pages on a Web server.* (Microsoft Access hosts an instance of Internet Explorer.)

After you have developed a main page from which you can call the other pages in your system, you will see that Access created a main page folder. One of the components in that folder is an **.xml** file. **XML (eXtensible Markup Language)** is, in effect, a language that may be used to create other markup languages. Unlike HTML, XML is not limited to a predefined and fixed set of elements. Instead, XML enables you to define new elements and tags that are application-specific. Therefore, you can create an almost endless collection of versions of markup languages that, because they are application-specific, can be made very efficient at handling specialized information.

9.2 CREATING A DATA ACCESS PAGE USING THE DESIGN VIEW

To make sure that your work matches the presentation in this chapter, perform the following actions:

1. Create a new folder on your disk. Keep these points in mind as you prepare to create your folder:
   a. Although the folder location is a matter of choice, it usually is placed inside another appropriately named folder to keep the disk information well organized.
   b. To help us track our activities easily, we generally name the folder to match the database name. The database used in most of the chapter examples is named **Ch09_POS_2nd.mdb**. Therefore, we will name the folder **Ch09_POS_2nd**.
   c. In most of this chapter's examples, we will assume that the **Ch09_POS_2nd** folder's location is reached through the following path: **C:\Rob-Semaan-2ndEdition\Databases(Student)\Ch09\Ch09_POS_2nd**.
2. Copy the **Ch09_POS_2nd.mdb** from the CD attached to this book to the folder you have just created. (Do not forget to uncheck the **Read-only** property from the database properties box.)
3. Open the **Ch09_POS_2nd.mdb** database and click on the **Pages** tab as shown in Figure 9.3.
4. If you want to build all the pages shown in the text, delete all the page files. (Note that there are no pages shown in the **Pages** tab in Figure 9.3.)

If you examine the **Pages** window shown in Figure 9.3, note that you have three options.

1. Selecting the **Create data access page in Design view** option opens an empty page in design view. This option lets you build the page from scratch. That

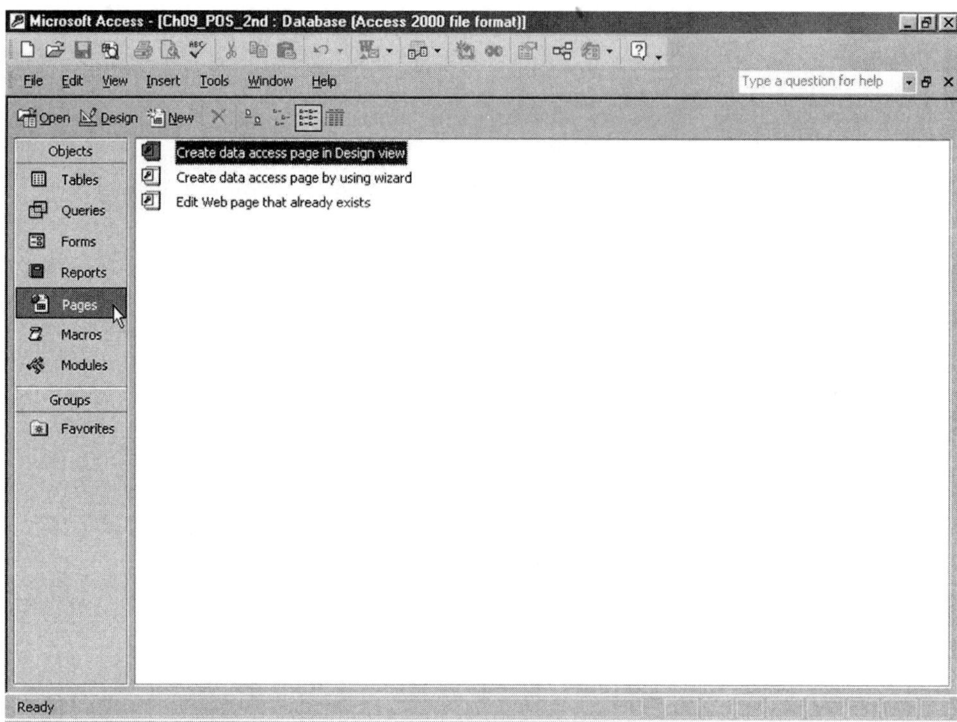

FIGURE 9.3
The Pages Window

is, you provide all the design elements to produce a data access page that matches your specific needs and interests.

2. Selecting the **Create data access page by using wizard** option creates the page for you. You can then modify the page that was produced by the wizard.

3. Selecting the **Edit Web page that already exists** option allows you to edit an existing page. If you import a page from a different database, this option allows you to make changes to the page *without changing the data source.*

Let's start by selecting the first of these three options. If you double-click on the **Create data access page in Design view** option shown in Figure 9.3, you will first see the warning message shown in Figure 9.4. (As the dialog box indicates, you can select the **Don't show this warning again** option to eliminate the warning. However, we prefer to be reminded of the Access 2000 limitation, so we'll leave the check box blank.)

Because you are already familiar with the Access interface, you already know that you can also select the **New** option and then select the **Design** view as shown in Figure 9.5. In either case, your selection will yield the warning shown in Figure 9.4.

Regardless of which of the two design options you select to create the new data access page, you will see the screen shown in Figure 9.6. (If you do not see the **Field List** on the right side of the screen, click on the **Field List** button shown in Figure 9.6.)

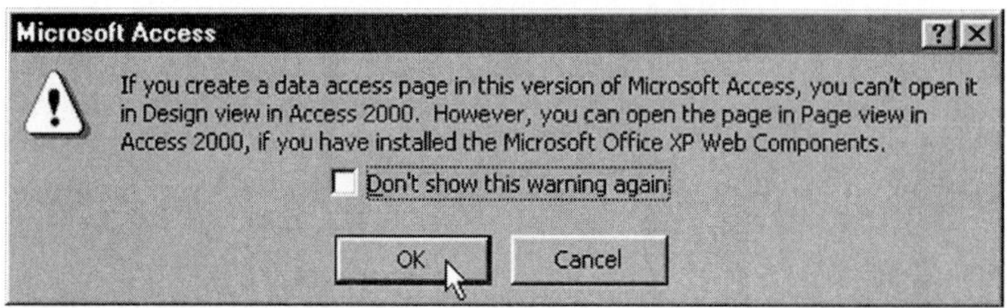

FIGURE 9.4
A Warning Message

FIGURE 9.5
The New Data Page Access Window

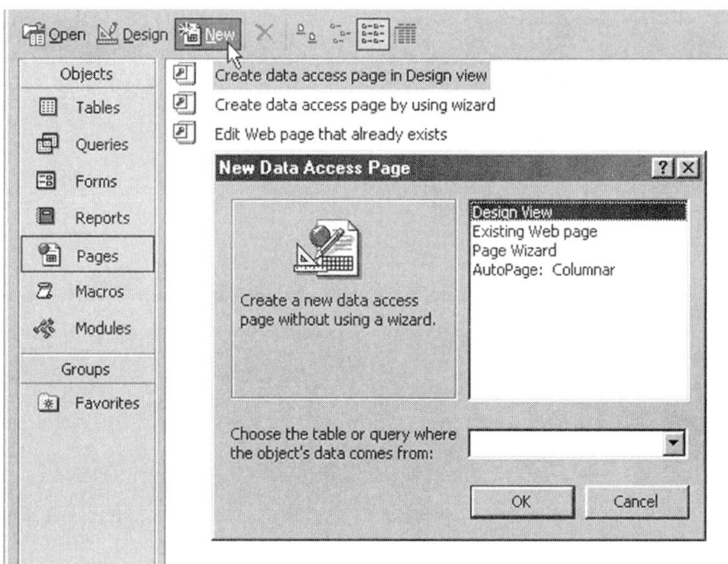

Before you continue with the page design, you must know what you want the page to display and what you intend to do with that page display. In short, plan ahead. Our purpose in this section is to create a page on which you can view—for any customer—all invoices and all the invoice lines that correspond to those invoices. Therefore, we will

- Place selected customer information, such as the customer number and name, on the page.
- Add invoices that are linked to the customer.
- Add invoice lines that are linked to the invoices.

As you examine Figure 9.6, note that the **Field List** displays all the tables and queries in the database. After selecting the **Field List**, click on the + sign next to

FIGURE 9.6
The Data Access Page in Design View

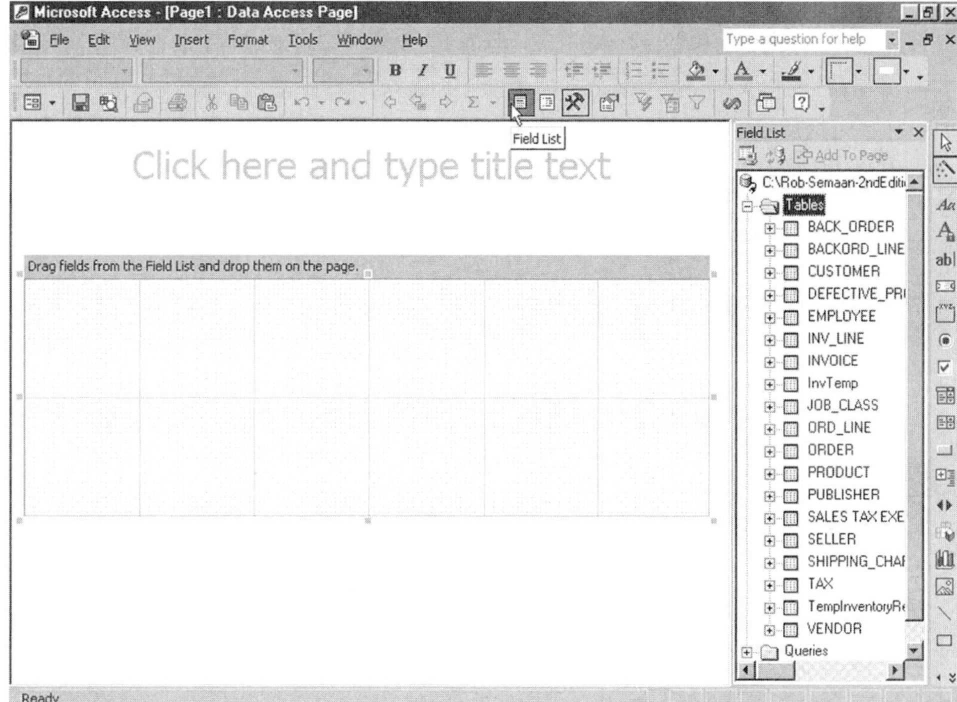

Note

You may see the initial data access page display as shown in Figure 9.6A. To change the data access page display shown in Figure 9.6A to the one shown in Figure 9.6, just click on the + symbol in front of the **Tables** folder. (The **Tables** folder in Figure 9.6 has a – symbol in front of it. If you click on the – symbol, the display will be reset to match Figure 9.6A.)

FIGURE 9.6A An Alternate Initial Field List Format

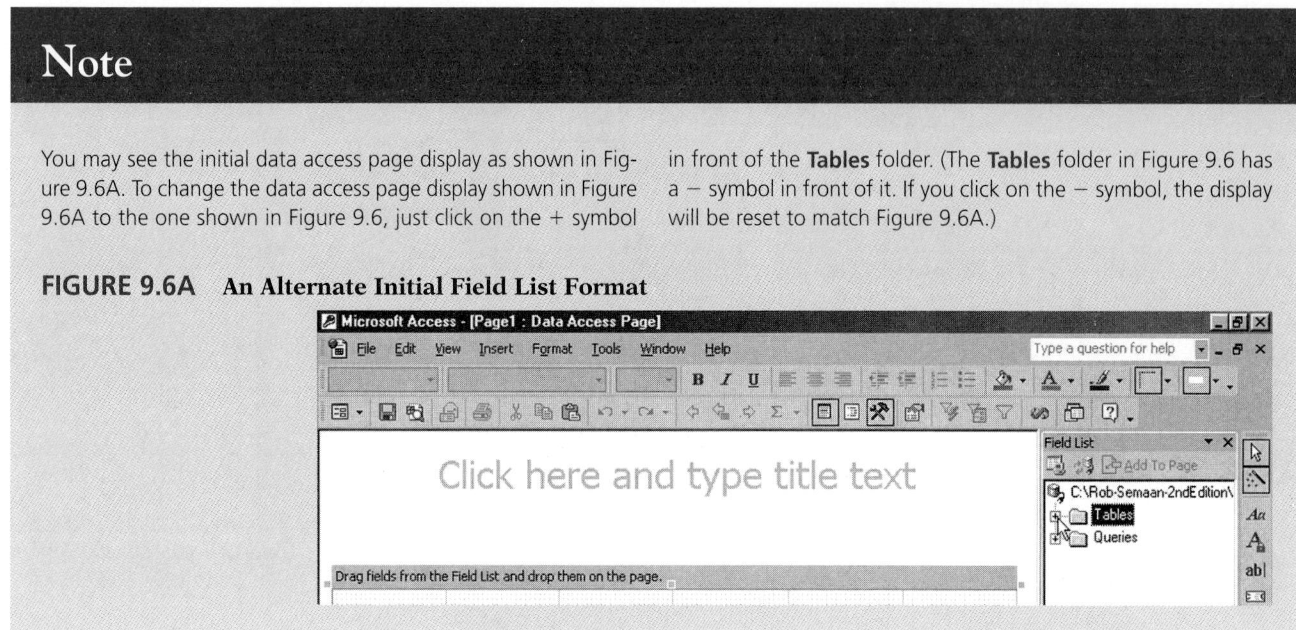

the CUSTOMER table to display all the fields in the CUSTOMER table as shown in Figure 9.7. (You can also double-click on the CUSTOMER table to see all of its fields.)

As you examine Figure 9.7, note that it contain a **Related Tables** folder. As its name implies, this folder contains all of the tables that are related to the CUSTOMER table. If you double-click on the **Related Tables** folder shown in Figure 9.7, or you click on the + symbol to the left of the folder, Access will generate Figure 9.8 to show you that the INVOICE table is related to the CUSTOMER through the CUS_NUM field. (Note the key symbol in front of the CUS_NUM.)

FIGURE 9.7 The CUSTOMER Table Fields

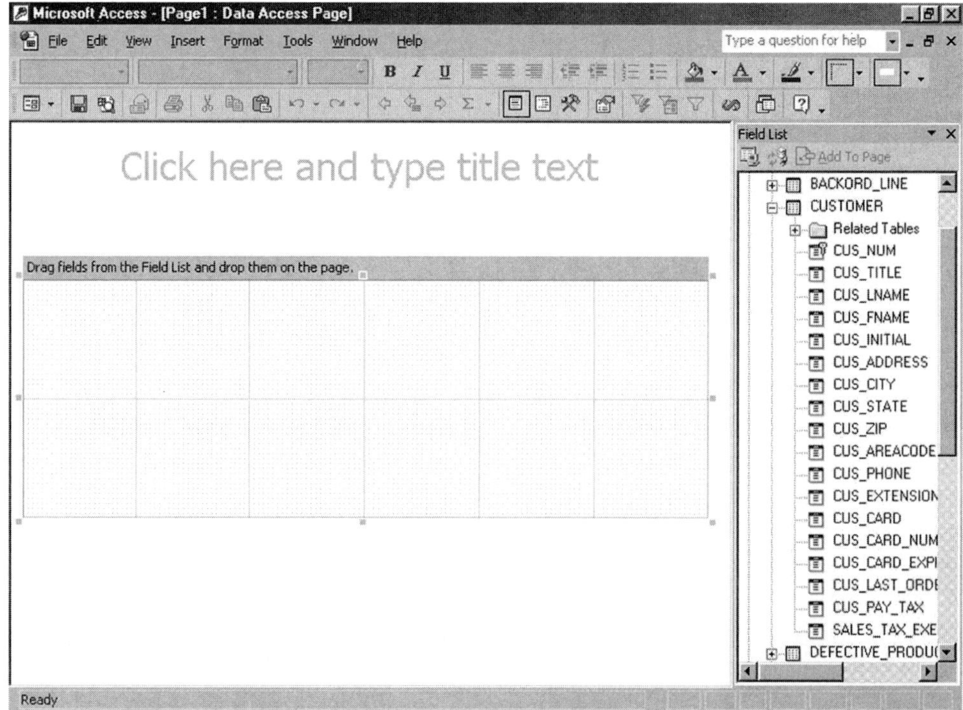

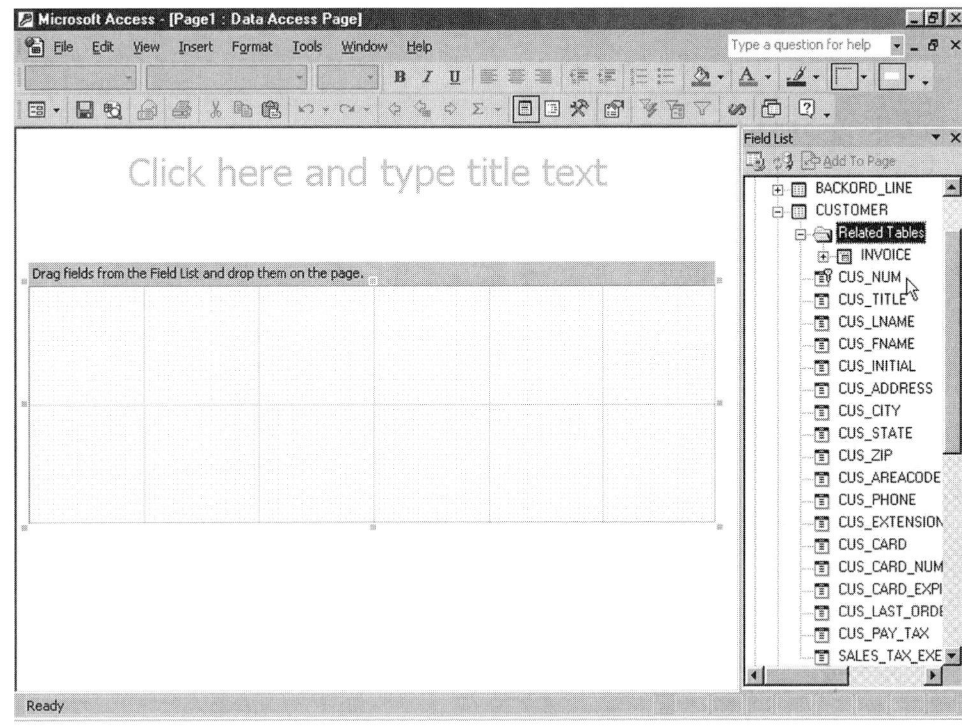

FIGURE 9.8
The Related Tables Folder

Make sure that the **Toolbox** has been selected—you will see the toolbar on your screen if it is—and click on the **Controls Wizard** as shown in Figure 9.9. In this illustration, the toolbar is located on the right side of the screen.

You have worked with the toolbox before, so you know that the button bars may be located on a different section of your screen. For example, the button bar on your screen may be located across the top of the screen and clicking on the

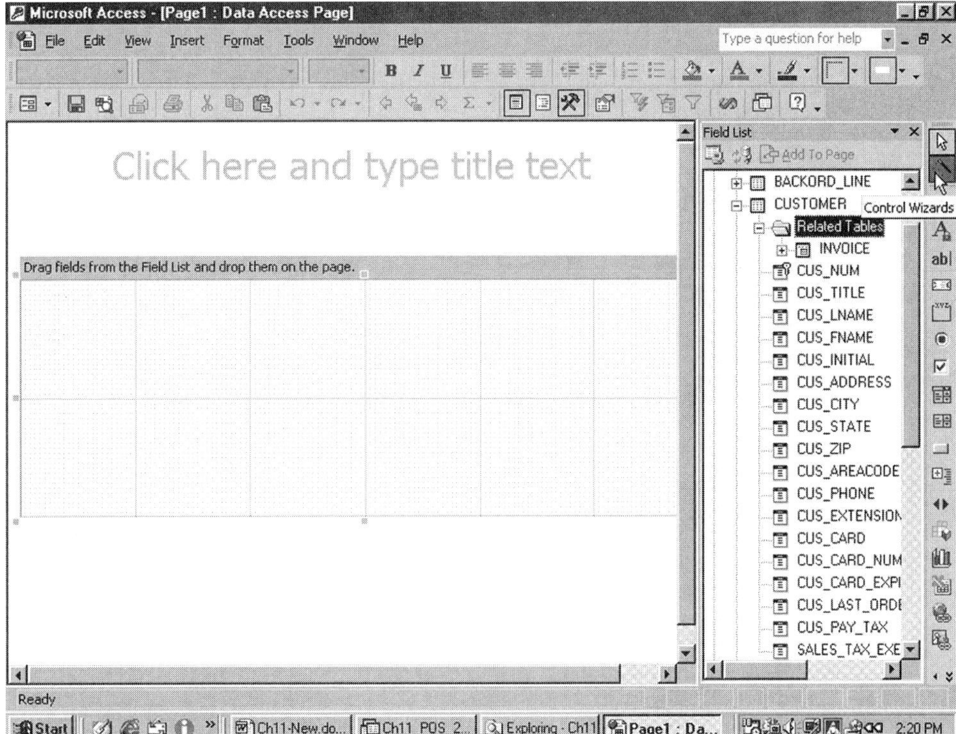

FIGURE 9.9
Select the Controls Wizard from the Toolbox

FIGURE 9.10
The Layout Wizard Window

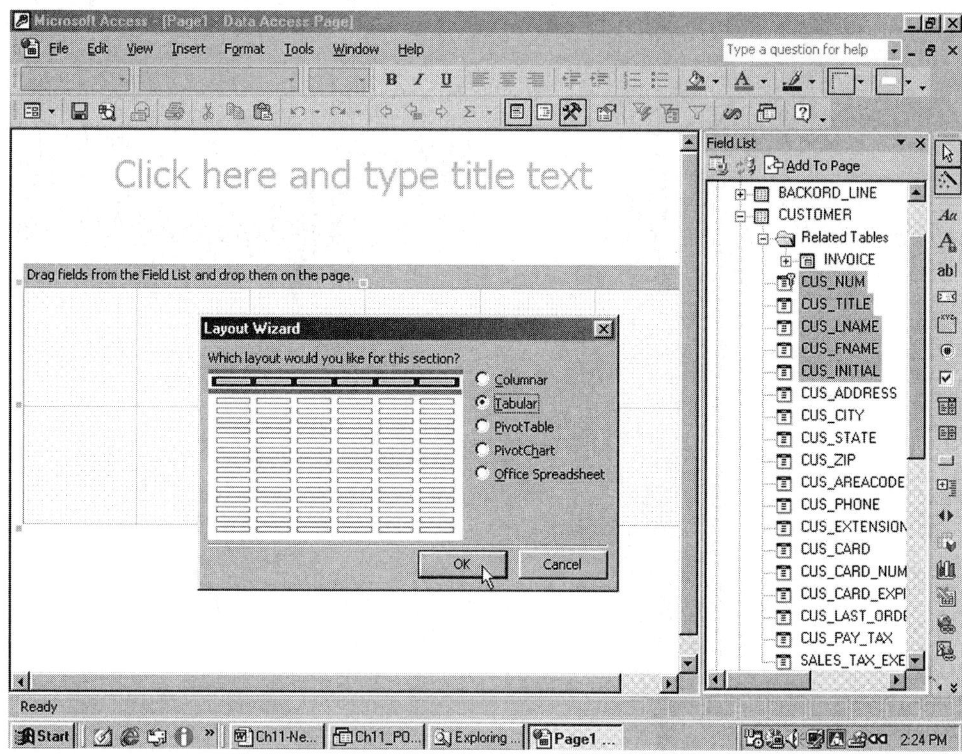

Controls Wizard button may put the results of this action on a portion of the screen different from the one shown in this illustration. You can drag and drop the button bars wherever you like!

After activating the **Control Wizards**, highlight the CUS_NUM, CUS_TITLE, CUS_LNAME, CUS_FNAME, and CUS_INITIAL fields shown in Figure 9.9, then drag and drop them inside the marked area—the page—to generate the **Layout Wizard** window shown in Figure 9.10. (The page header reads **Drag fields from the Field List and drop them on the page**. The page size may be changed by dragging its limits.)

Using the **Layout Wizard** window shown in Figure 9.10, select **Tabular** as illustrated. Next, click **OK** to generate the screen shown in Figure 9.11.

As you examine Figure 9.11, note that we have used the scrollbar at the bottom of the screen to show you the **Navigation** to the CUSTOMER table. This feature lets us navigate through the CUSTOMER table records. (Go ahead and slide the scroll bars back and forth to see all of the screen's contents.)

Now click on the + sign next to the INVOICE table shown in Figure 9.11 to display all of that table's fields. Highlight the INV_NUM, INV_DATE, INV_SUB_TOTAL, SHIPPING_AMT, INV_TAX, and INV_TOTAL. Drag the highlighted fields to the **Navigation: CUSTOMER** section shown in Figure 9.11 *and drop them on that section.* (As you drag them over this portion of the screen, you will see the highlighted segment titled **Create a new section below CUSTOMER** in Figure 9.12.)

If you have dropped the selected INVOICE fields in the drop zone shown in Figure 9.12, you will see the Layout Wizard again as shown in Figure 9.13.

If you click **OK** on the Layout Wizard shown in Figure 9.13, you will see the results in Figure 9.14. (We have again used the scroll bar at the bottom of the screen to show you the segment headers.)

Next, use the scroll bar on the screen's right margin to scroll down until you see the queries folder shown in Figure 9.15.

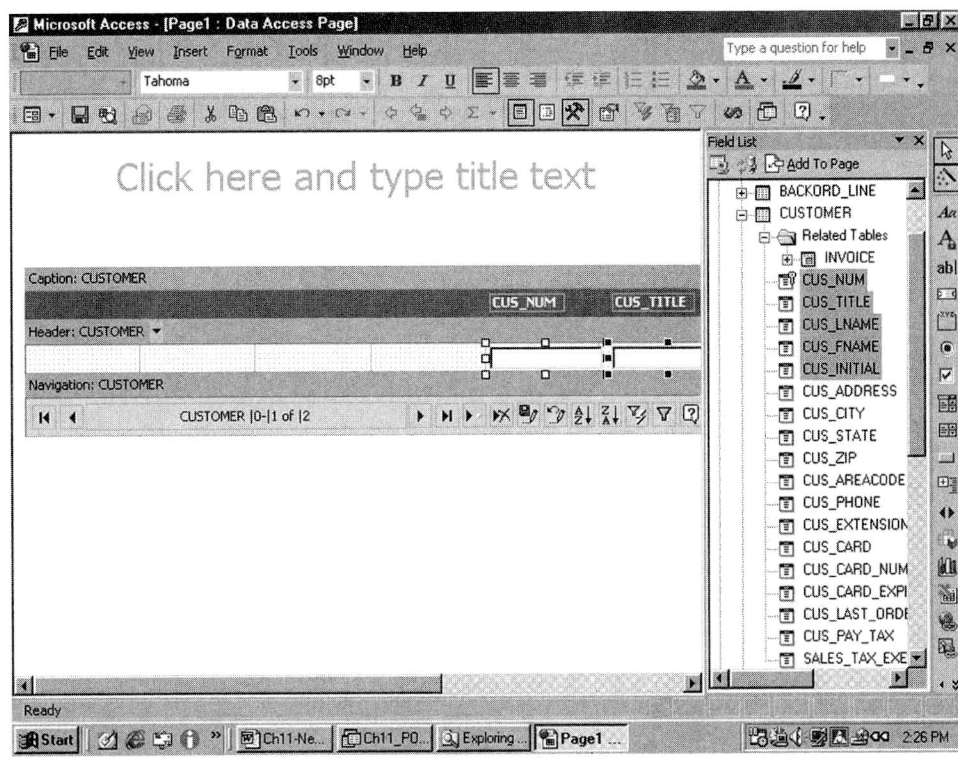

FIGURE 9.11
The CUSTOMER Fields on the Page

If you take a look at Figure 9.15, note that we have scrolled all the way down to the **Queries** folder. Next, we double-clicked on the **Queries** folder to see all the available queries. (Go ahead and perform this task now. When you have completed that task, select the **qryInvoivceLine** to show that query's output fields.

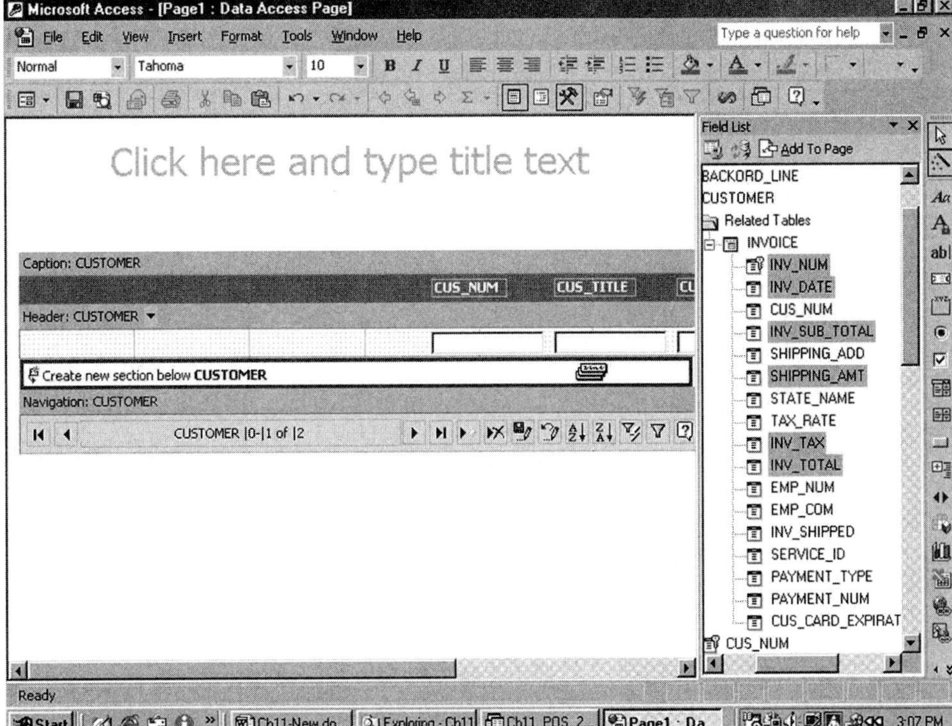

FIGURE 9.12
The Drop Zone for the INVOICE Fields

FIGURE 9.13
The Layout Wizard for the INVOICE Segment below CUSTOMER

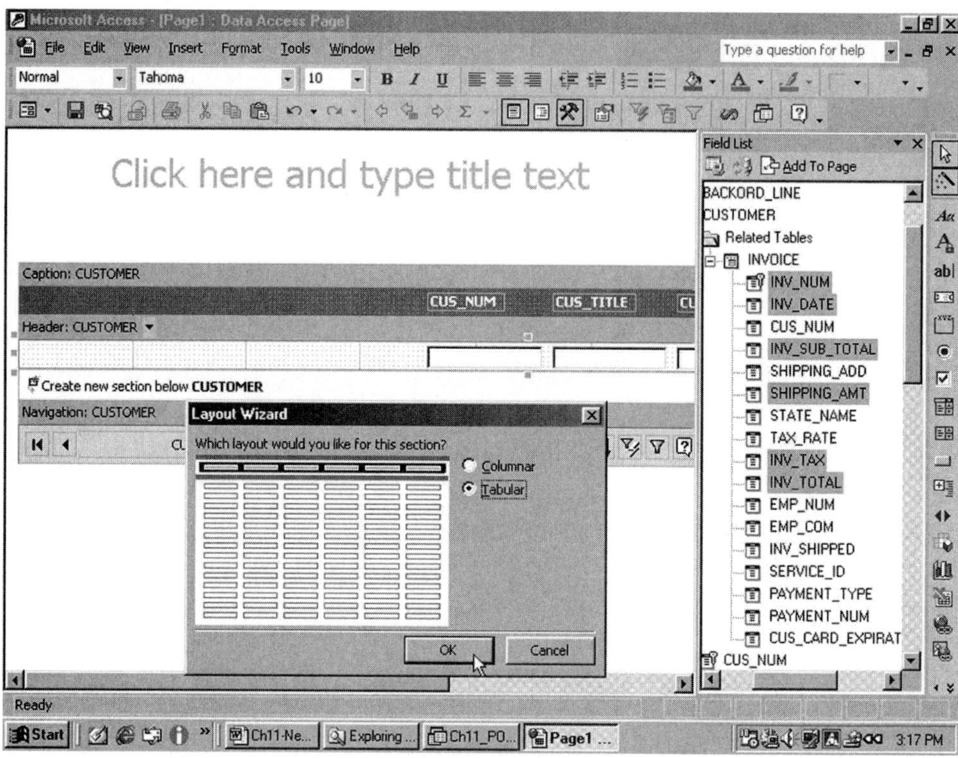

Highlight the INV_LINE_NUM, INV_LINE_UNITS, INV_LINE_PRICE, INV_LINE_TOTAL, and the PROD_TITLE. Drag these highlighted fields to the **Navigation: INVOICE** portion of the screen to generate the now-familiar **Layout Wizard** dialog box.)

FIGURE 9.14
The CUSTOMER and the INVOICE fields Inserted into the Page

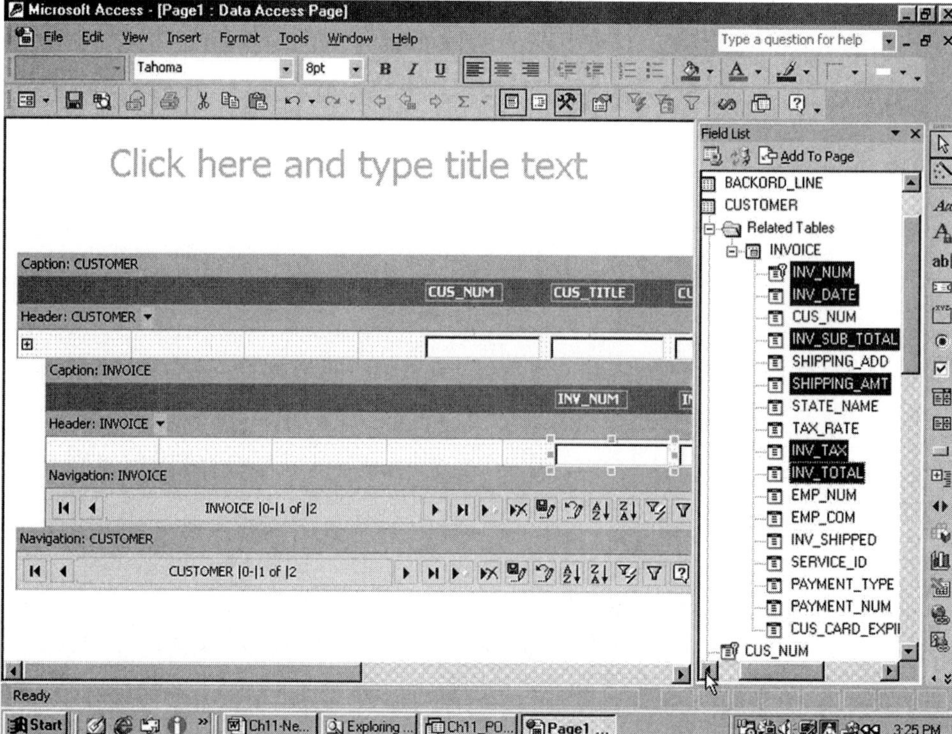

FIGURE 9.15
Inserting the Invoice Line Elements from a Query

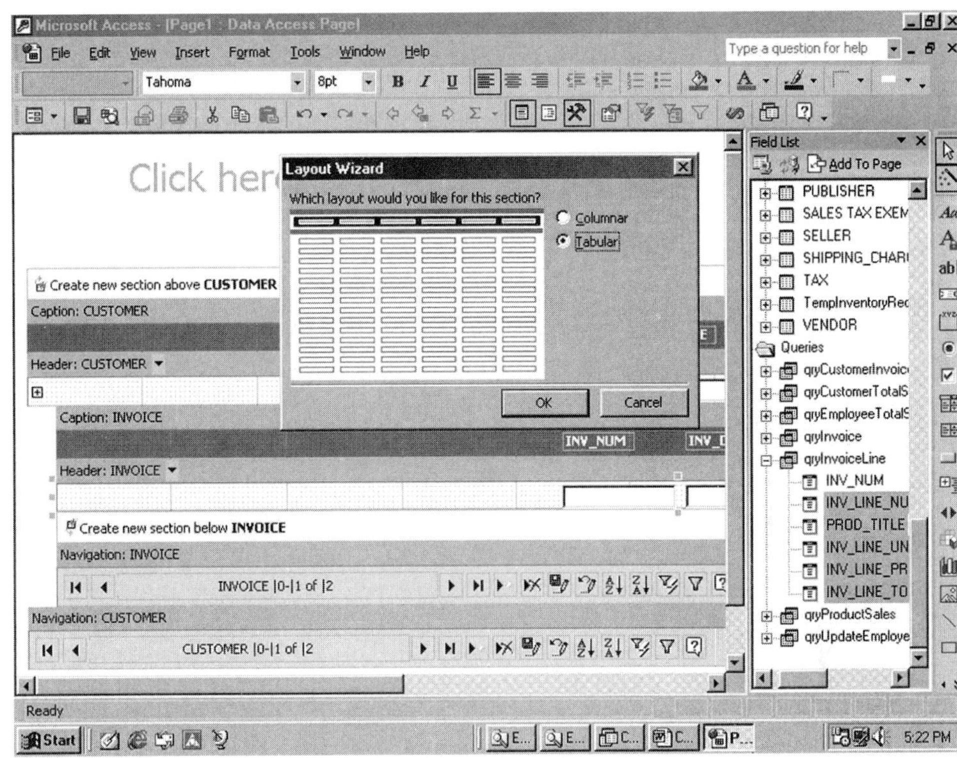

Select the **Tabular** option from the **Layout Wizard** dialog box shown in Figure 9.15 and click **OK** to generate the **Relationship Wizard** window shown in Figure 9.16.

As you examine the **Relationship Wizard** dialog box shown in Figure 9.16, note that the default selection is the INV_NUM. Also, the **Many records in 'qry InvoiceLine' match one record in 'INVOICE'** is checked to indicate the existence of a one-to-many relationship. Click the **OK** button on the **Relationship Wizard** dialog box shown in Figure 9.16 to generate the screen shown in Figure 9.17. (We scrolled down to show you the header section.)

FIGURE 9.16
The Relationship Wizard

Relationship Wizard

Choose a table to relate 'qryInvoiceLine' to: INVOICE

How do you want to relate 'qryInvoiceLine' to this table?

This field in 'qryInvoiceLine'... INV_NUM ⇔ Relates to this field in 'INVOICE'... INV_NUM

(•) Many records in 'qryInvoiceLine' match one record in 'INVOICE'

( ) One record in 'qryInvoiceLine' matches many records in 'INVOICE'

OK Cancel

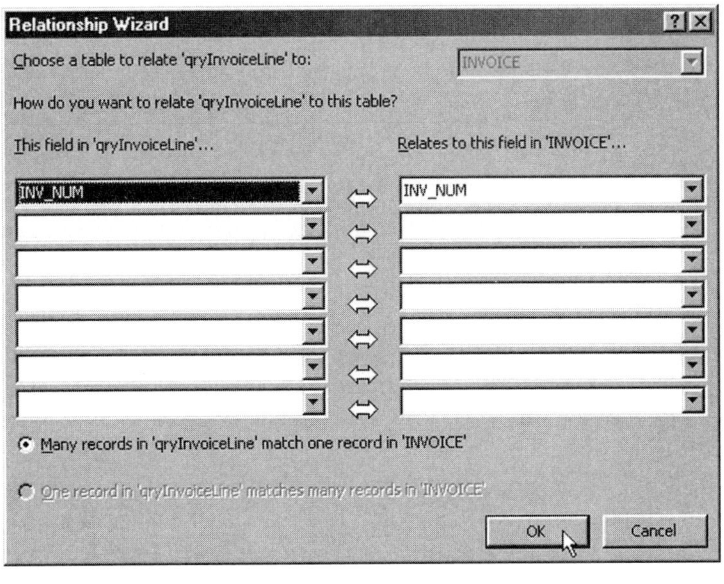

Note

The relationship between the INVOICE and INV_LINE tables is based on the INV_NUM field that is common to both tables. Access prompts you with the Relationship Wizard to define the relationship between the two tables. Building the relationship between the records on the page is like creating a link between the form and its subform or a report and its subreport. Such links are always created through the linked child fields and the linked master fields.

If you want to make the CUSTOMER and the INVOICE tables read-only, you must set *each one* to **read only**. (Making the page itself "uneditable" is not sufficient.) However, you can control the level and type of access to the tables by setting the page properties for those tables at the page level. To set the page properties for the customer data, right-click on the section just below the **Header: CUSTOMER** or click on the down arrow head next to the **Header: CUSTOMER**, and select **Group Level Properties** as shown in Figure 9.18. This action generates the screen shown in Figure 9.19.

Using Figure 9.19 as your guide, select **False** to **AllowAdditions**, **AllowDeletions**, and **AllowEdits** in the **GroupLevel** properties window of the page's CUSTOMER section. If you want to control the sort order for the page output by a selected field, you can set the **DefaultSort** to that field. As you can tell by looking at Figure 9.19, we selected the CUS_NUM field by typing it into the space.

We have done a substantial amount of work thus far, so let's save the data access page with the customary **File/Save** routine. (Or you can simply click on the **Save** button on the button bar.) Saving the data access page will cause the wizard to save the code that displays the data access page contents. This code is written in the .htm format, which is the default for any page you have built with the Access Page Wizard. However, it is always a good idea to make sure that the .htm

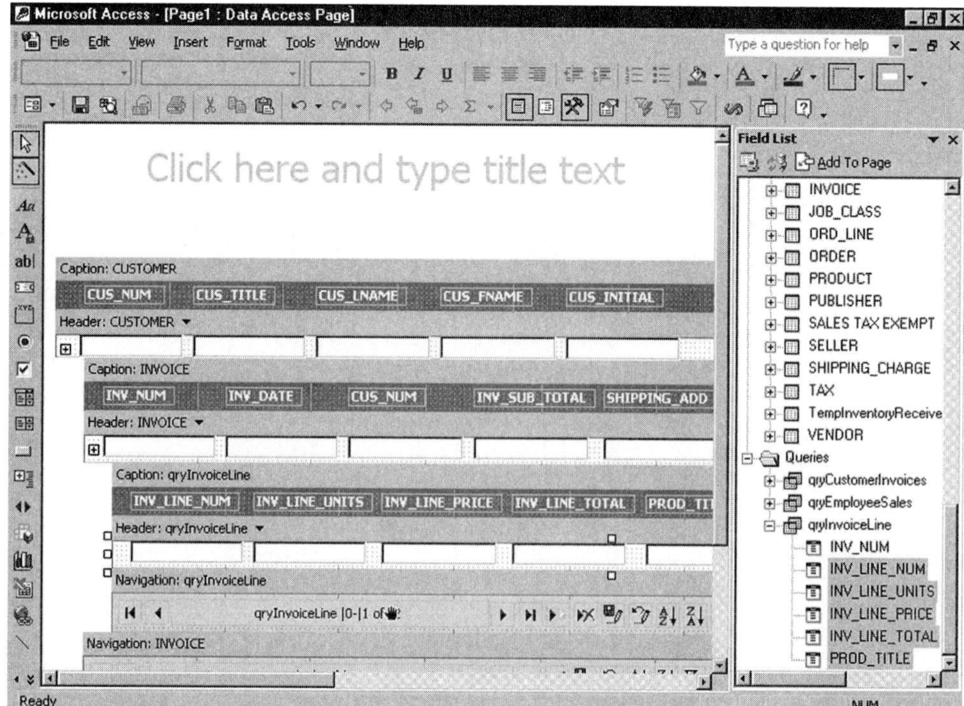

FIGURE 9.17
The qryInvoiceLine Fields Inserted into the Page

FIGURE 9.18
Selecting the Group Level Properties for the CUSTOMER Table

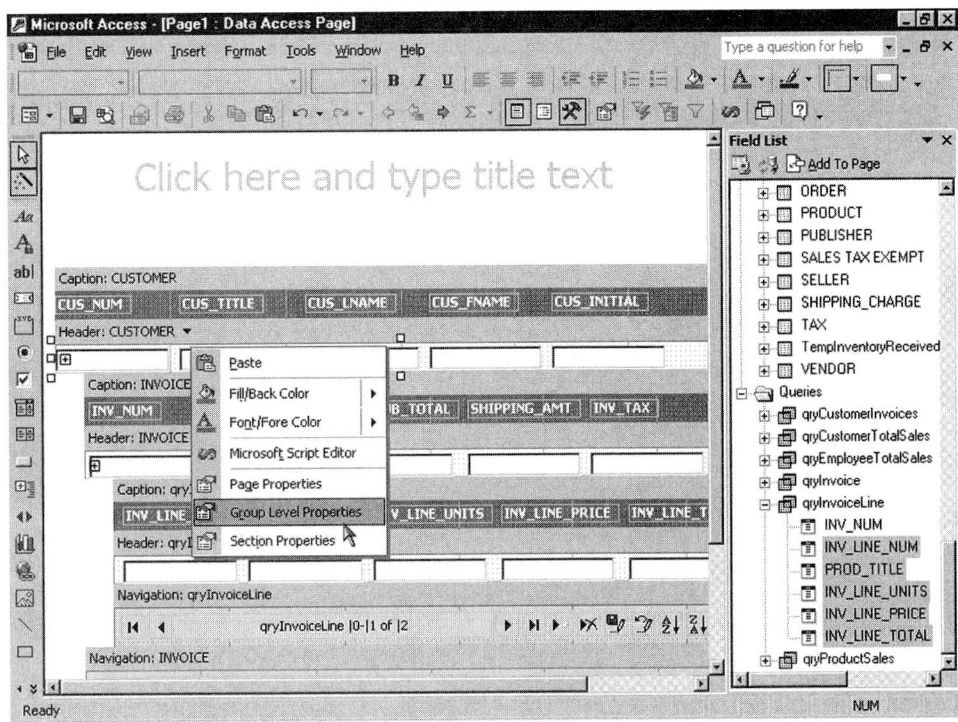

default format is maintained, so check the window you'll see in Figure 9.19A. Note that we will save the page as **CustomerSales**.

If you click on the **Save** button shown in Figure 9.19A, you will see the warning in Figure 9.19B. This is your first indication that the page you created within the database has a link to a corresponding .htm file located outside the database. If that file cannot be found, you will get a warning about the path to the required file. We will return to this point in detail in section 9.9.

Because you are developing this application on a stand-alone computer—or, if you are using a computer on a network, on a client computer—you can ignore the warning in Figure 9.19B. Therefore, just click **OK** on the button.

FIGURE 9.19
The Group-Level Window for the CUSTOMER Table

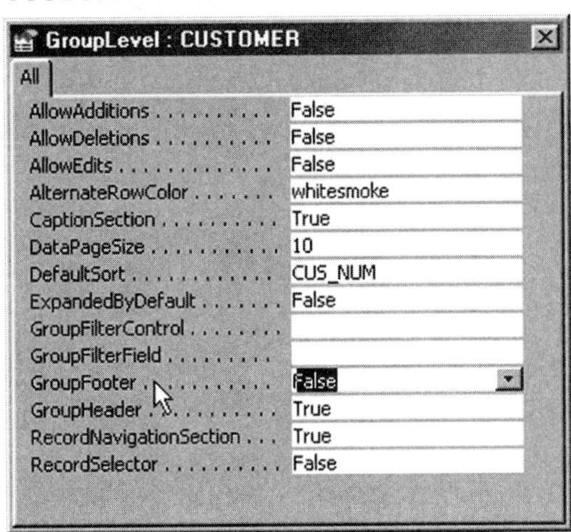

FIGURE 9.19A
Saving the Initial Page

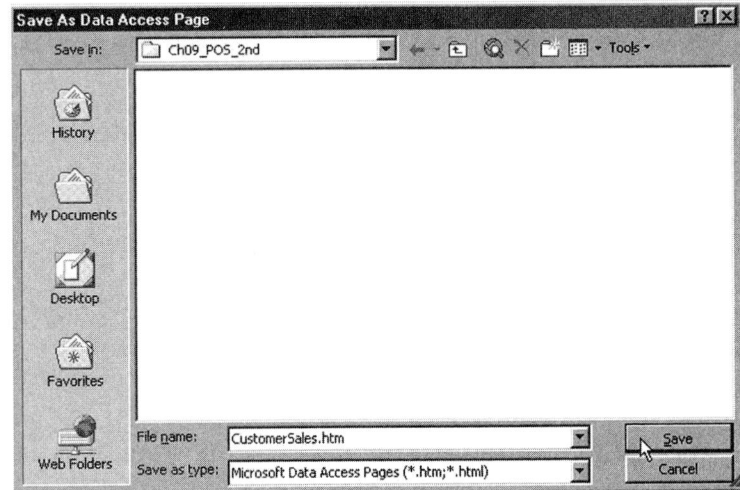

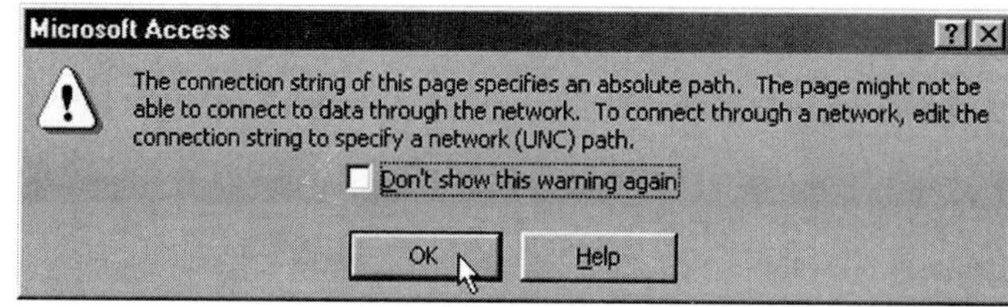

FIGURE 9.19B
The New Page Path Warning

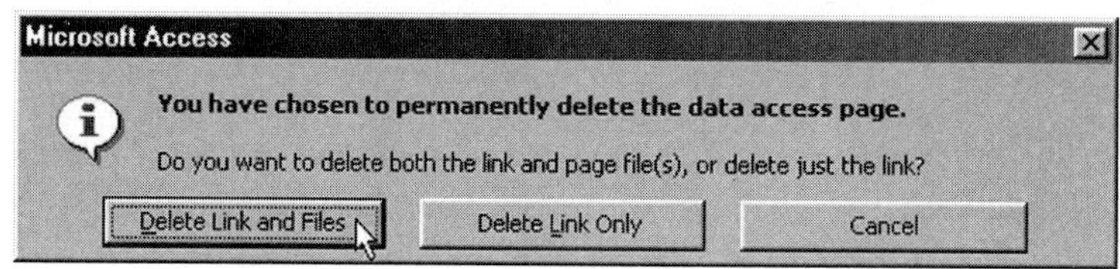

FIGURE 9.19C
The Page Delete Warning

Because there is a link—the access path—between the data access page inside the Access database and the related .htm file stored outside the database, you will also get a warning if you try to delete the data access page (see Figure 9.19C).

After saving the file in .htm format, let's continue the form's development. You can also control the presentation of various summary functions by setting the page properties. For example, to show the total value of the various invoice components for each customer, select **True** for the **GroupFooter** from the **GroupLevel** window of the CUSTOMER. The wizard automatically adds the appropriate footer to the page. First drag the INV_SUB_TOTAL to the footer as shown in Figure 9.20. The Access Wizard will automatically add the **SumOf** prefix to each field as you drop it in the footer. (We have dragged the limits of the footer to make it "tall" enough to receive the remaining fields.)

After dropping the remaining INVOICE table's SHIPPING_AMOUNT, INV_TAX, and INV_TOTAL one at a time, the footer section will look like Figure 9.20A.

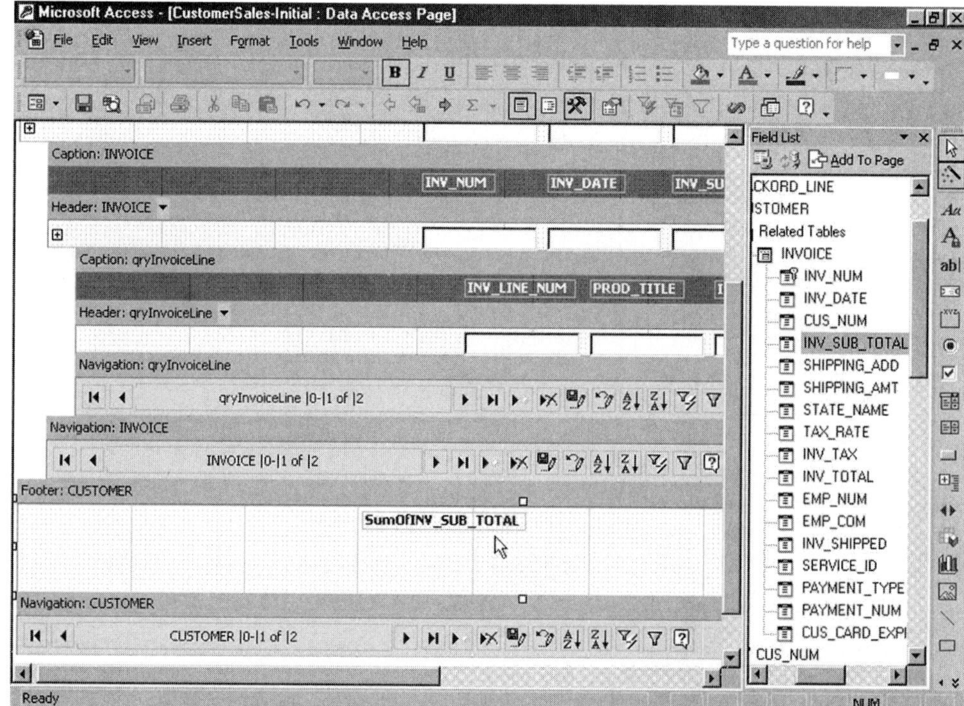

FIGURE 9.20
Adding the Invoice SubTotal to the CUSTOMER Footer

Note

We strongly recommend that you drag and drop the INVOICE table's INV_SUB_TOTAL, SHIPPING_AMOUNT, INV_TAX, and INV_TOTAL *one at a time*. If you mark them all and drag and drop them simultaneously in the footer, Access may lock up and place the process in an infinite loop. The only way to break out of that loop is to reboot the computer, which is annoying, to say the least!

FIGURE 9.20A
The Remaining Customer Invoice Summary Information

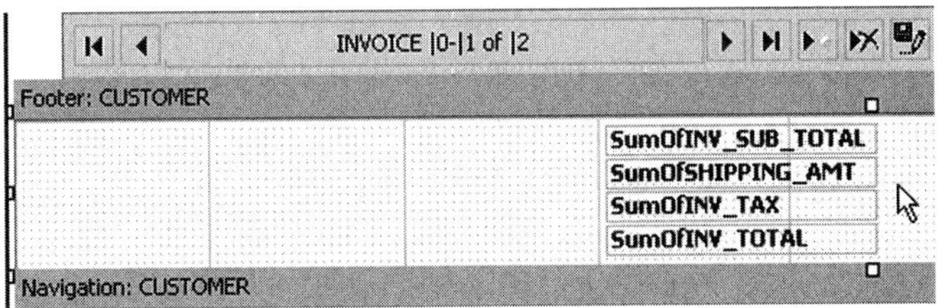

FIGURE 9.20B
Placing the Labels

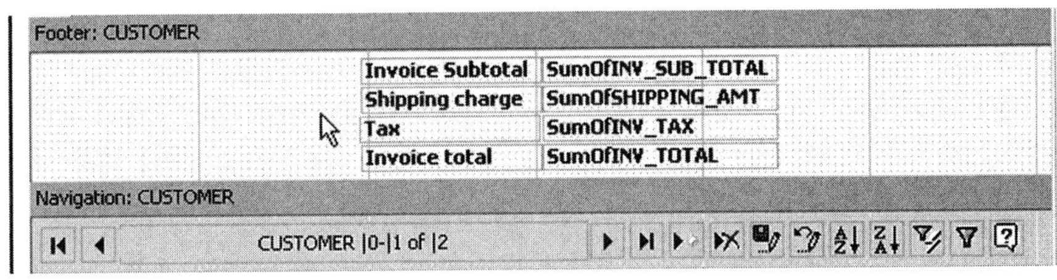

FIGURE 9.20C
Selecting the Page View

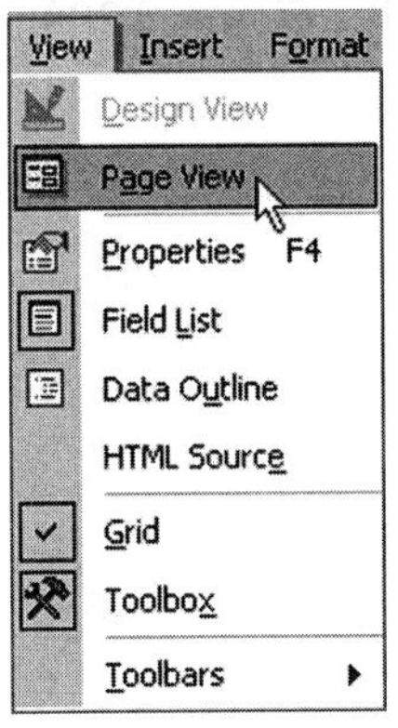

The text boxes shown in Figure 9.20A do have labels, but you may have to search for them. For example, we found the labels in the CUSTOMER header, so we dragged them to the CUSTOMER footer and then formatted them to produce the result shown in Figure 9.20B. (You are already familiar with the page label formatting procedures: They are identical to those you used to format form labels.)

You are now ready to see the initial results of the design efforts. Select the **Page View** option shown in the **View** drop-down menu shown in Figure 9.20C to generate the results shown in Figure 9.20D.

If you examine Figure 9.20D carefully, you will see that we have placed the cursor just below the + symbol at the first customer record's left margin. Click on this + symbol to get additional details about the invoices. Then click on the next + symbol to generate the invoice lines for the invoices. When you have clicked on all the + symbols shown in Figure 9.20D, you will see Figure 9.20E. Note that you now have the details of all of the customer invoices available. For example, you can see that customer number 1 generated one invoice (# 275) and this invoice has three invoice lines. Invoice number 275 had a subtotal of $278, the shipping charge was $20.95, the customer paid no tax, and the total paid was $298.95.

Naturally, you will want to clean up the output shown in Figure 9.20E to make its presentation more attractive. You already know how to do that: The procedures are identical to those we used in Chapter 6 when we explored the many options in form design. Place the form back in design view and you can move the text boxes, format their labels, select fonts, and so on.

You should recall that we have already made the CUSTOMER data read-only. To make the INVOICE read-only, follow the same steps that were just used to make the CUSTOMER table (recordset) read-only. Therefore, select the group level window for the INVOICE. (That window will look like Figure 9.19, but it will use the INVOICE properties, rather than those for the CUSTOMER.)

FIGURE 9.20D
The Initial Page View

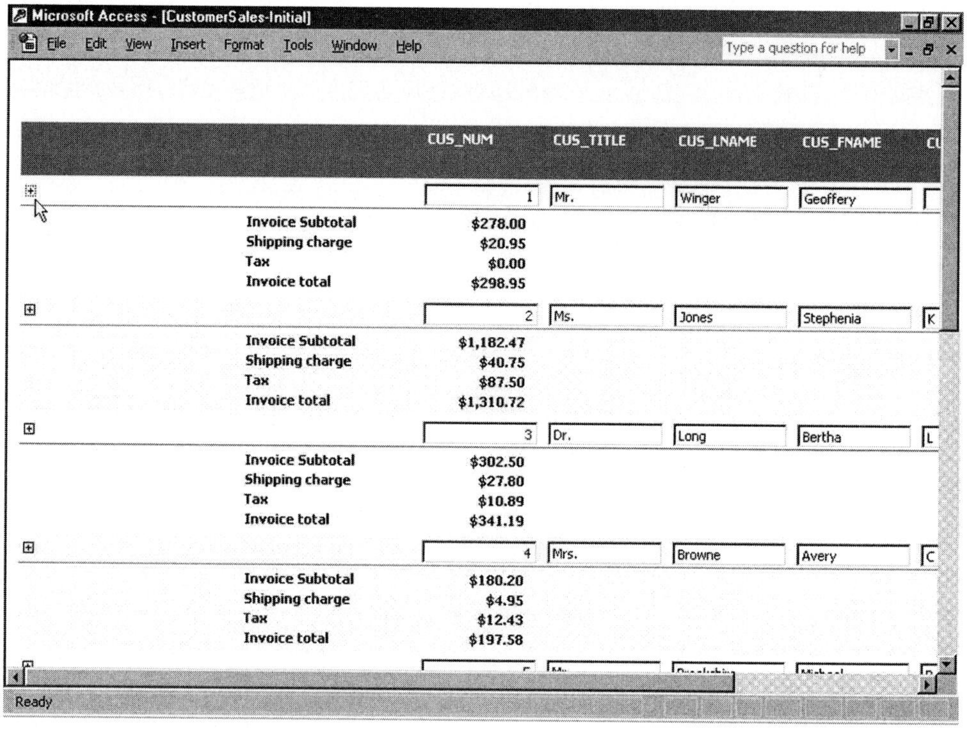

If you do not want the end user to see the form's navigation bars, you can accomplish that task by hiding those navigation properties. To select the CUSTOMER section navigation properties, right-click on the **Navigation: Customer** object on the page and then select its object properties as shown in Figure 9.21 to generate the screen shown in Figure 9.22.

Check Figure 9.21 and note that the entire navigation object was selected. Do not click on the center of the part that reads **CUSTOMER |0-|1 of |2**, because that

FIGURE 9.20E
The Customer's Complete Invoice Set

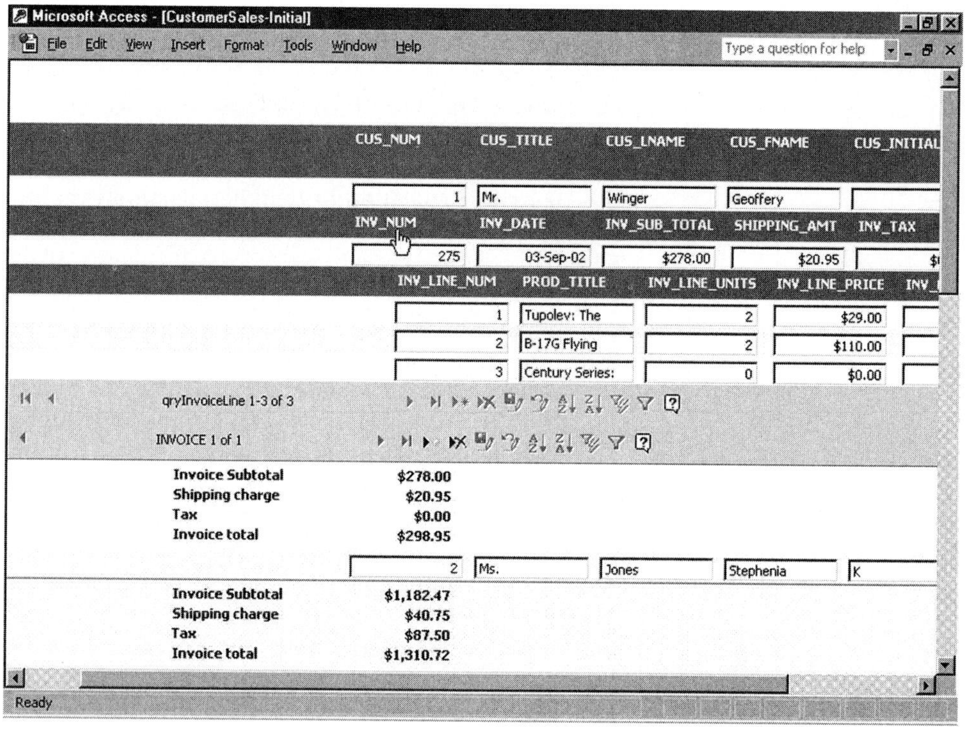

Note

You should recall that a record is, at least conceptually speaking, a row in a table. A **record set** is the complete collection of a table's records. Therefore, the words *table* and *record set* are often used as synonyms by database professionals. The label *record set* is often contracted to become a single word, thus becoming *recordset.* Microsoft Access adheres to that convention, so we will use *table* and *recordset* as synonyms. Incidentally, the *recordset* label is sometimes used to describe a query output. While this use of *recordset* is not quite accurate, it is common and you should be aware of its use.

is only a label. Do click anywhere on the bar left or right of the label or even just below or above the label's border. In any case, make sure that the small squares—the handles—surround the entire navigation bar, rather than just a component of it.

As you can tell by examining Figure 9.22, we selected the **Visibility** property. The default **Visibility** property is **visible**. Go ahead and change this property to **hidden**. (Now do the same thing for the **INVOICENavigation** and the **qry InvoiceLineNavigation** properties.) If you *do* want to see the navigation bar on the page, you can later reset this property to **visible**.

We are now ready to format the page the way we want it to look on the Web. To get that job done, click on the page's **Click here and type title text** and type **Customer Sales**. You can format each field by clicking on its label and changing the text and the font characteristics. Figure 9.23 shows an example of how we formatted the fields. We also changed the relative locations of the invoice and invoice line segments to offset them for easier end-user reading.

To save the page, you can simply click the **Save** button on the button bar or you can select the **File/Save As** option and then use the **Save As Data Access Page** window shown in Figure 9.24. We had already saved the page as **Customer Sales** during its early design stages. Therefore, the **Save As** routine generates the

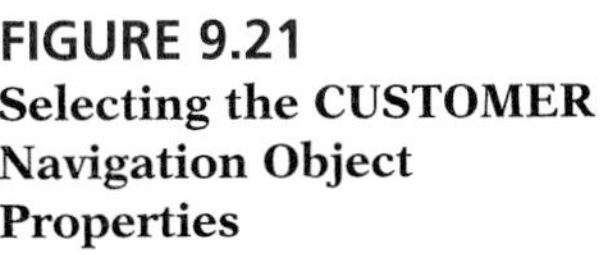

FIGURE 9.21
Selecting the CUSTOMER Navigation Object Properties

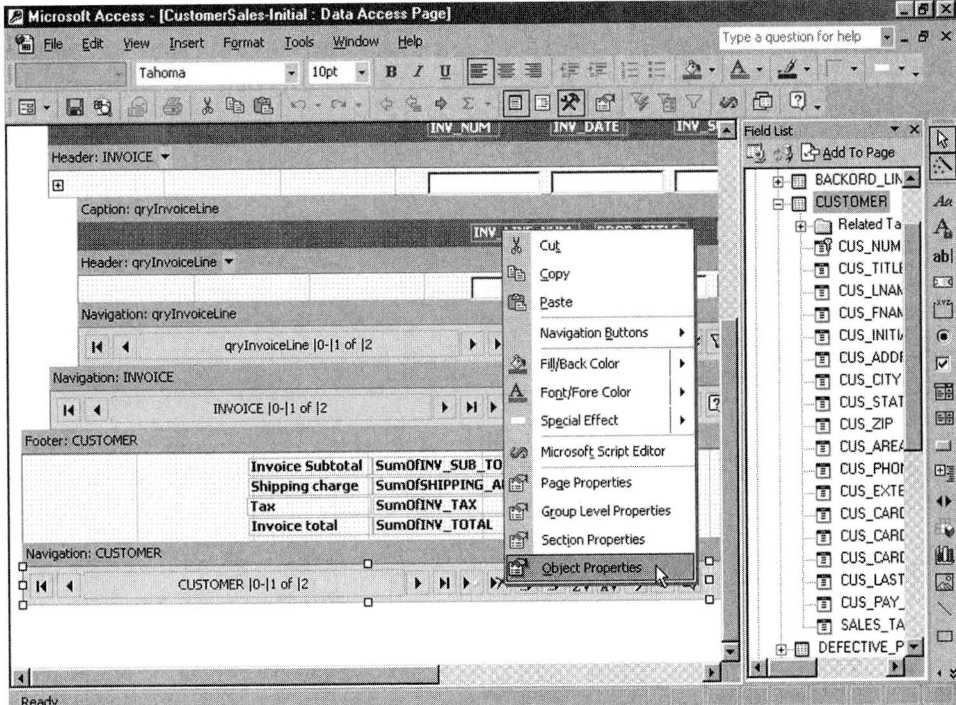

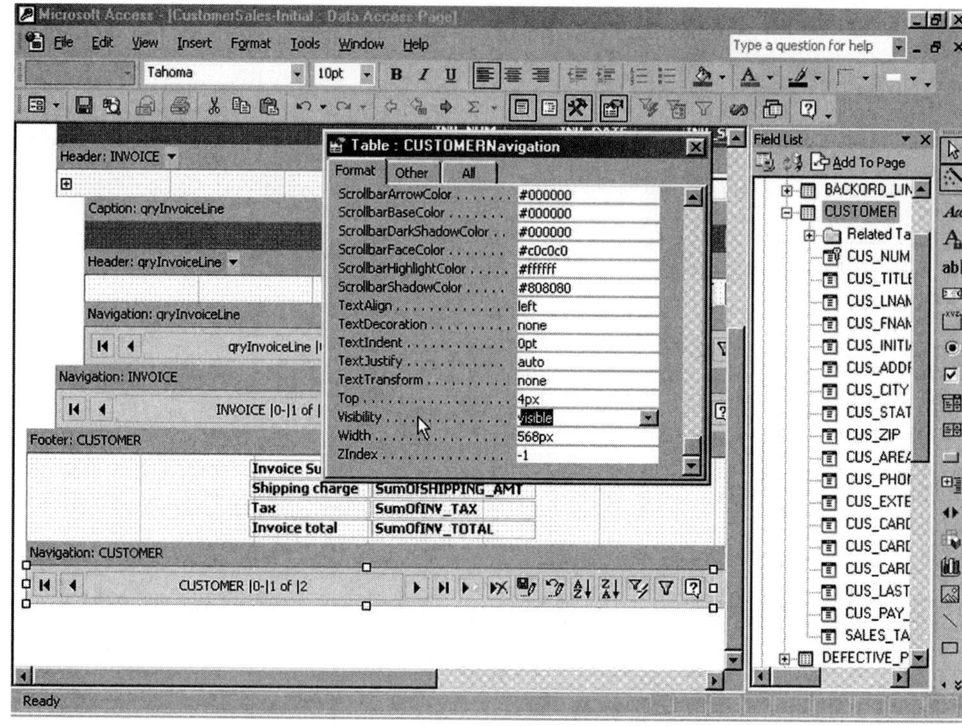

FIGURE 9.22
The CUSTOMER Navigation Properties Box

window shown in Figure 9.24. (If you have already saved the page as shown in Figure 9.19A, you can simply click on the **Save** button or repeat the **File/Save** routine. Because we saved the page earlier as a data access page, resaving it automatically retains the data access page format.) Regardless of which of the two techniques you use, we suggest that you save the page periodically as you work on it to avoid the accidental loss of your work.

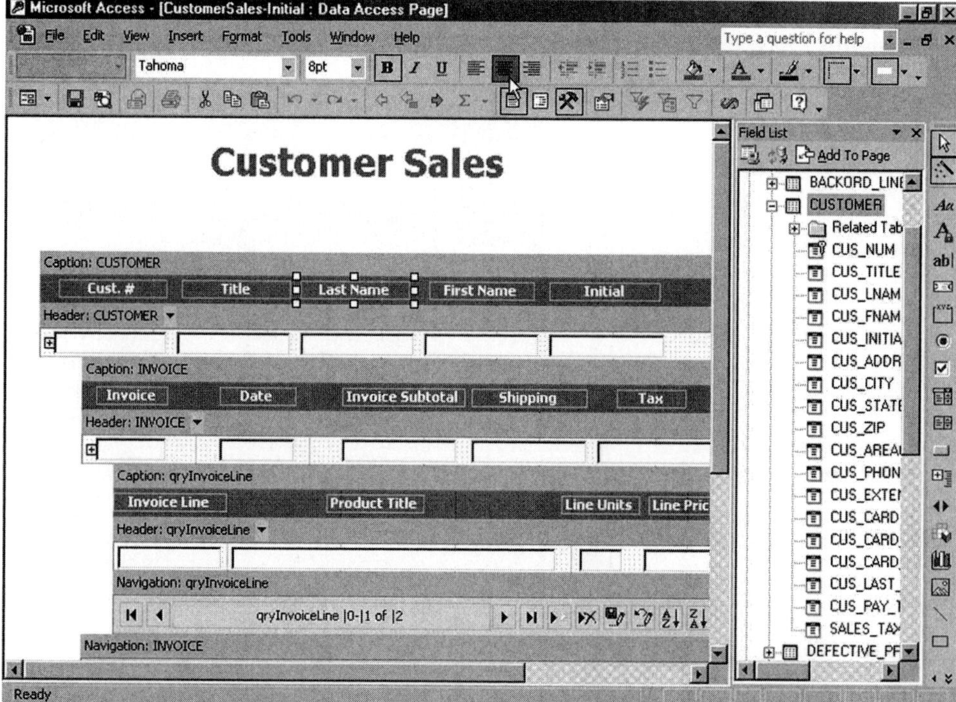

FIGURE 9.23
The Formatted CustomerSales Page

Note

If you want to change the section widths, move the text boxes *first.* You can then change the relative sizes of the sections that contain those text boxes.

FIGURE 9.24
Saving the Customer Sales Page in HTM Format

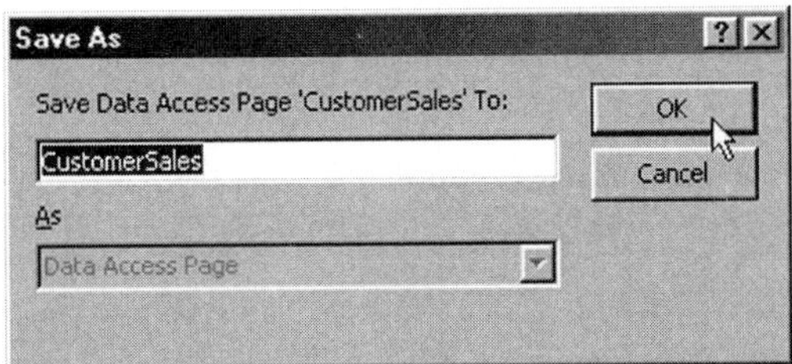

Because we started this page design in the POS_2nd database located in the Ch09 folder, Access saves the page in HTM format in the same folder that contains the database. After saving the HTM file, select **View/Page View** from the drop-down menu to examine the edited page shown in Figure 9.25.

Figure 9.26 displays the first level of the CUSTOMER recordset. To drill down into the invoices for that customer, click on the + sign next to **Cust #** to see all of the selected customer's invoices in Figure 9.26.

As you can see in Figure 9.26, the **Invoice Total** shows the sum total of all invoices for the selected customer. To drill deeper into the invoice detail, click on the + sign next to the **Invoice** number to generate the invoice details shown in Figure 9.27.

FIGURE 9.25
The Edited Customer Sales Page in Page View

Microsoft Access - [CustomerSales-Initial]

File Edit View Insert Format Tools Window Help

Type a question for help

Customer Sales

Cust. #	Title	Last Name	First Name	Initial
1	Mr.	Winger	Geoffery	
2	Ms.	Jones	Stephenia	K
3	Dr.	Long	Bertha	L
4	Mrs.	Browne	Avery	C

Cust. 1: Invoice Subtotal $278.00; Shipping charge $20.95; Tax $0.00; Invoice total $298.95

Cust. 2: Invoice Subtotal $1,182.47; Shipping charge $40.75; Tax $87.50; Invoice total $1,310.72

Cust. 3: Invoice Subtotal $302.50; Shipping charge $27.80; Tax $10.89; Invoice total $341.19

Cust. 4: Invoice Subtotal $180.20; Shipping charge $4.95; Tax $12.43; Invoice total $197.58

Ready

FIGURE 9.26
Drill Down into the Customer Records to See the Invoices

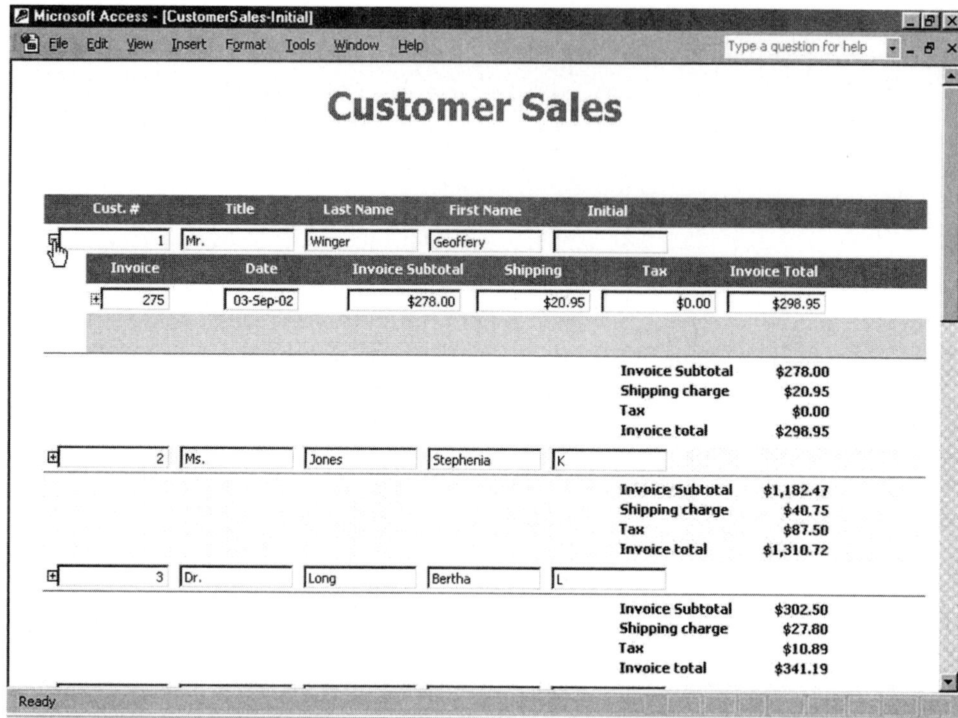

As you can tell by looking at Figure 9.27, we clicked on the + in front of invoice number 275 to display all of the invoice lines for that invoice. This presentation capability is truly spectacular, yet it was accomplished without writing a single line of code. (Those of us who labored in the complex coding environment of yesteryear are truly impressed. We hope that you are, too!)

As you examine Figure 9.27, note that the + symbols changed to − when you clicked on them. If you now click on the − symbol, you will restore the output's

FIGURE 9.27
Drill Down into the Invoice to See the Invoice Details

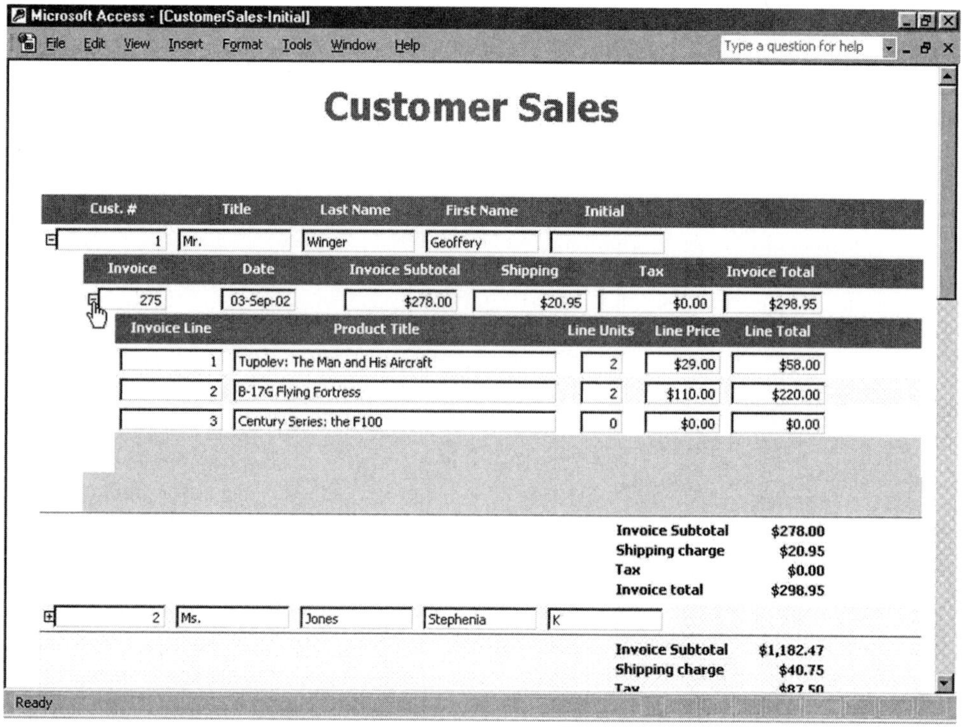

FIGURE 9.28
Selecting the CUSTOMER Table from the Page Wizard

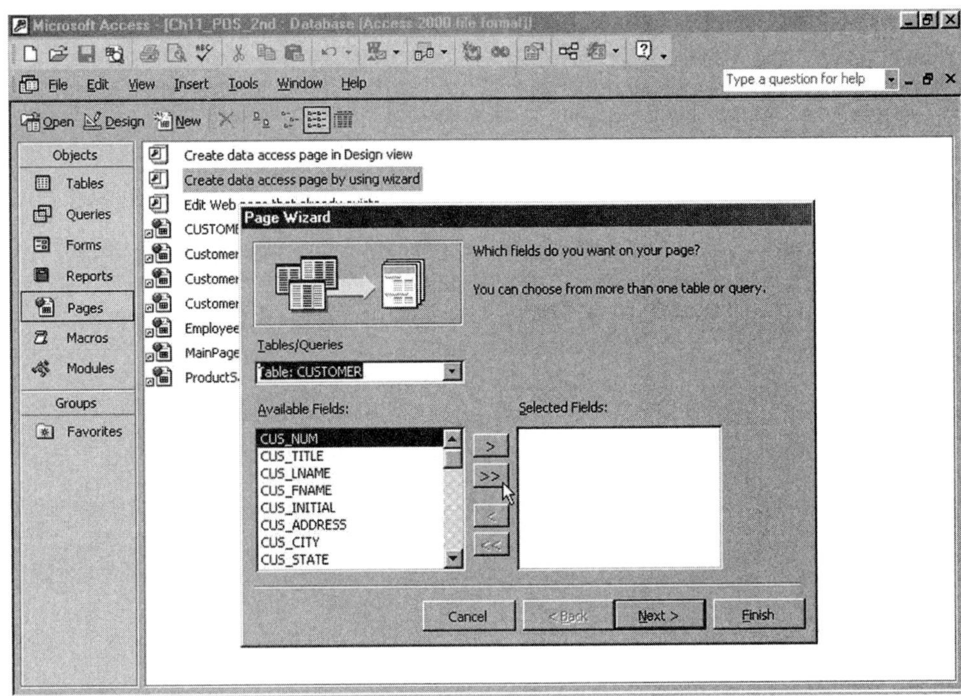

format to its original configuration. (Check just below the pointing hand in Figure 9.27.) If you want to see the navigation bar for this page, place it in design view and then set the **CUSTOMERNavigation Visibility** property to **Visible** (see Figure 9.22).

Quite aside from the fact that it is easy to generate operational details that are crucial to organizations of all kinds, we will show you later in this chapter how easy it is to add a link to other pages in the database. That's when you discover just how powerful a tool Access can be in helping you develop a small application system that can be viewed on the Web.

9.3 CREATING A DATA ACCESS PAGE WITH THE WIZARD

In this section, we will show you how to use the Page Wizard to create a data access page for the CUSTOMER records. Start by clicking on the **Create data access page by using wizard** option—the second option in the by-now-familiar pages window shown initially in Figure 9.3—to generate the data access page in design view as shown in Figure 9.28. Next, use the **Page Wizard Tables/Queries** option shown in Figure 9.28 to produce the drop-down list for the fields in the CUSTOMER table.

From the **Available Fields** window shown in Figure 9.28, select the fields you want to place on the page and then click on the > symbol to move the fields to the **Selected Fields** window. (If you want to include all the CUSTOMER fields, click on the >> symbol. If you want to remove a field—or remove all fields—use < or <<.) We will select all the fields, so our selection yields the results shown in Figure 9.29.

After selecting the fields shown in Figure 9.29, click on the **Next** > option to generate the screen shown in Figure 9.30.

As you can tell by looking at Figure 9.30, you can group the output by any available field. For example, if you are using a query based on the CUSTOMER and the INVOICE tables, the customer is likely to have multiple occurrences of the invoice results. Therefore, grouping by the CUS_NUM would be appropriate. However, since we are using just the CUSTOMER table, there is no point in

FIGURE 9.29
The Selected CUSTOMER Table Fields

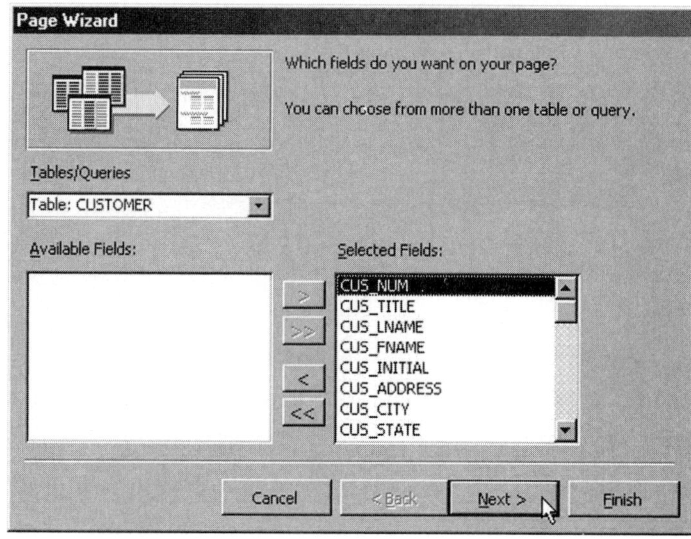

grouping on the CUS_NUM, because the CUSTOMER table does not contain duplicate records. Therefore, click **Next** >—without selecting a grouping level—to produce the screen shown in Figure 9.31.

You can select any sort field, of course. For example, Figure 9.31 shows that we want the output displayed in alphabetical order by the customer's last name.

You can select up to four sorting fields. For example, if you want to generate a telephone book, you would sort by last name, first name, and initial. If you select a multiple field sorting option, the sorting procedure is automatically cascaded, just as it was in Chapter 5 when you produced queries with multiple sort routines in them. If you examine Figure 9.31A, you'll see that we have elected to sort the output by the CUS_LNAME only. After making this sorting selection in Figure 9.31A, click **Next** > to produce the screen shown in Figure 9.32.

Using the dialog box shown in Figure 9.32, you can name the data access page to reflect the output. In this case, we have elected to keep the default name, **CUSTOMER**. After selecting a page name, you can select **Finish** to save the page. You can then open the saved page later or you can edit to modify its presentation or its structure. However, if you examine the dialog box in Figure 9.32, you see that there are two additional options: you can either select **Open the page** or

FIGURE 9.30
The Grouping Level

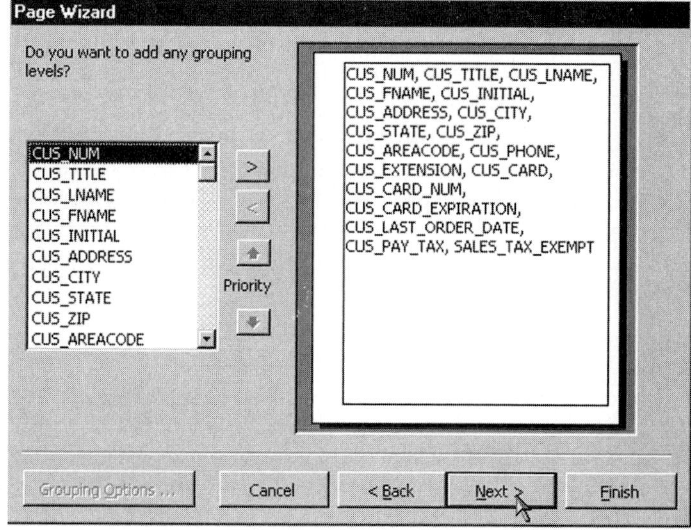

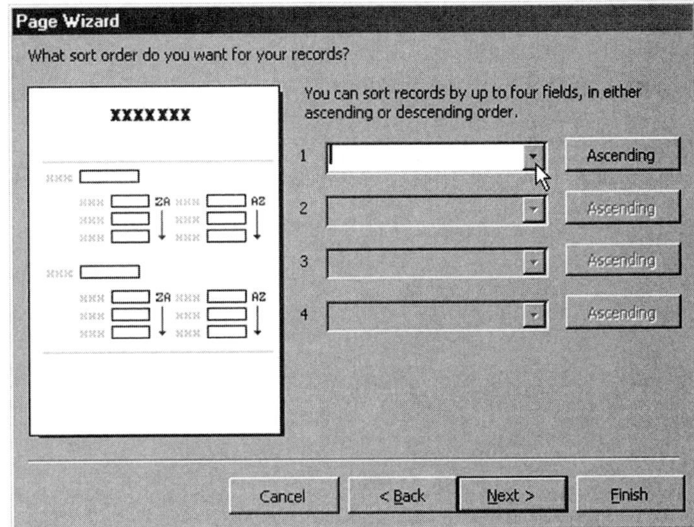

FIGURE 9.31
The Initial Sort Screen

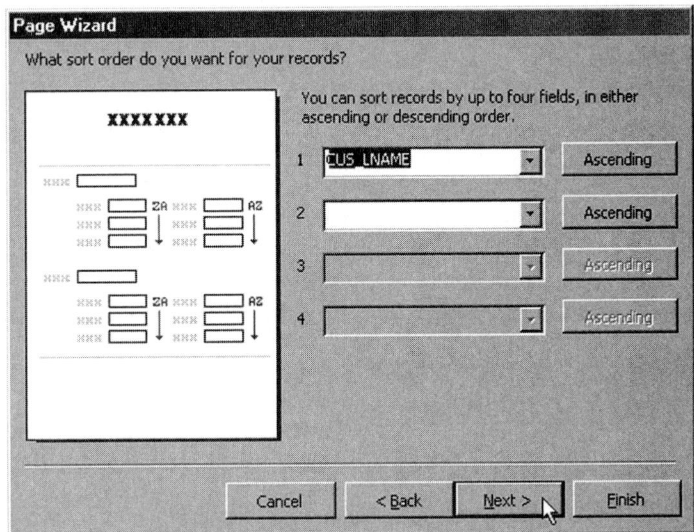

FIGURE 9.31A
The Selected Sort Option

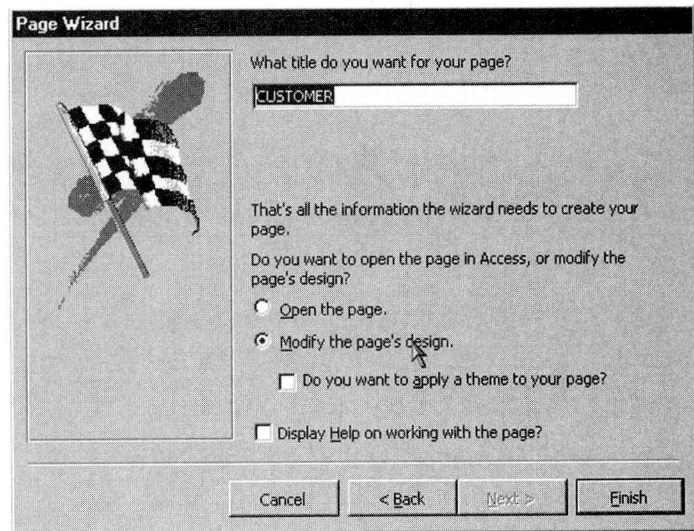

FIGURE 9.32
Name the Data Access Page

FIGURE 9.33
The CUSTOMER Page in Design View

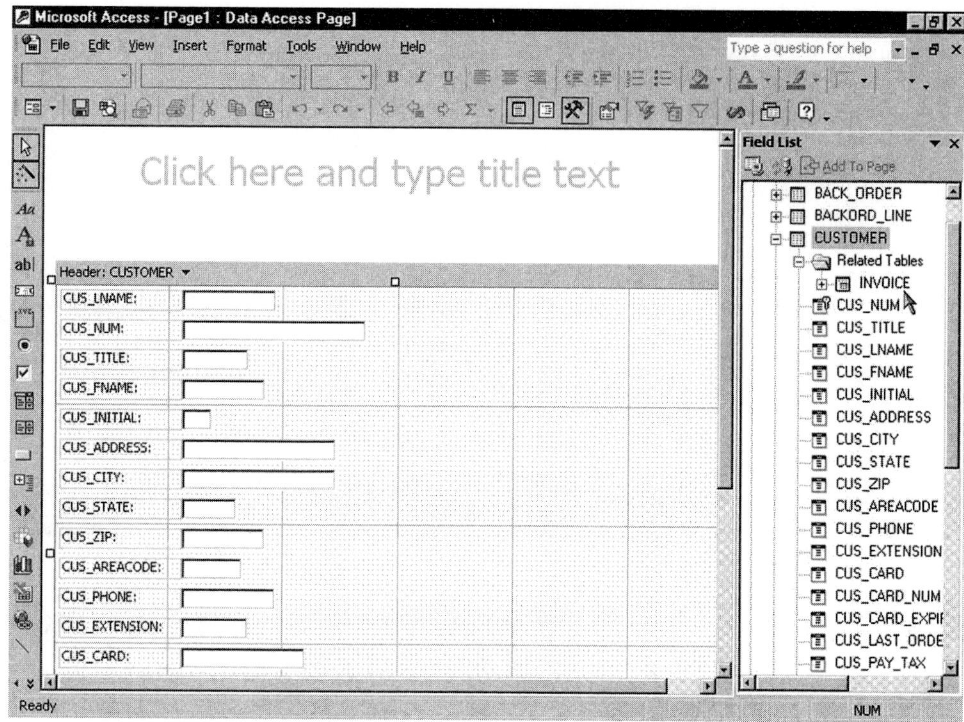

Modify the page's design. We will select the second option to modify the page design. This action will produce the screen shown in Figure 9.33.

Modifying the page design requires you to perform the same actions that you used in Chapter 6 to modify forms. For example,

- If you want to format the labels on the page, click on the label and then click again to edit the text. (Remember not to make the second click too fast; if you double-click, you get the properties window.)
- If you want add fields, click the **Field List** button and then drag and drop any field on the page.

And so on.

The page design does have a few extra features. For example, remember that the **Related Tables** folder contains all the tables that are related to the CUSTOMER table in the relationship. In this case, the CUSTOMER table is related to the INVOICE table through the CUS_NUM attribute. Also remember that the objective of the page design is to present information to the end user via the browser. Therefore, format the page the way you want it to look *in the browser.* (Figure 9.34 shows a sample customer screen in a very basic format.)

You can use the navigation object on the bottom of the screen to navigate, add a new record, or delete a record.

To find specific records, you can use a filter. To use a filter, first click on the field you want to be the filter key and then click on the **Filter by Selection** button. For example, suppose that you are using the CUSTOMER data access page shown in Figure 9.35. If you want to filter the customers' records to show only the customers located in TN, take the following three steps:

1. Find a customer in TN.
2. Click on the **State** field.
3. Click on the **Filter by Selection** button.

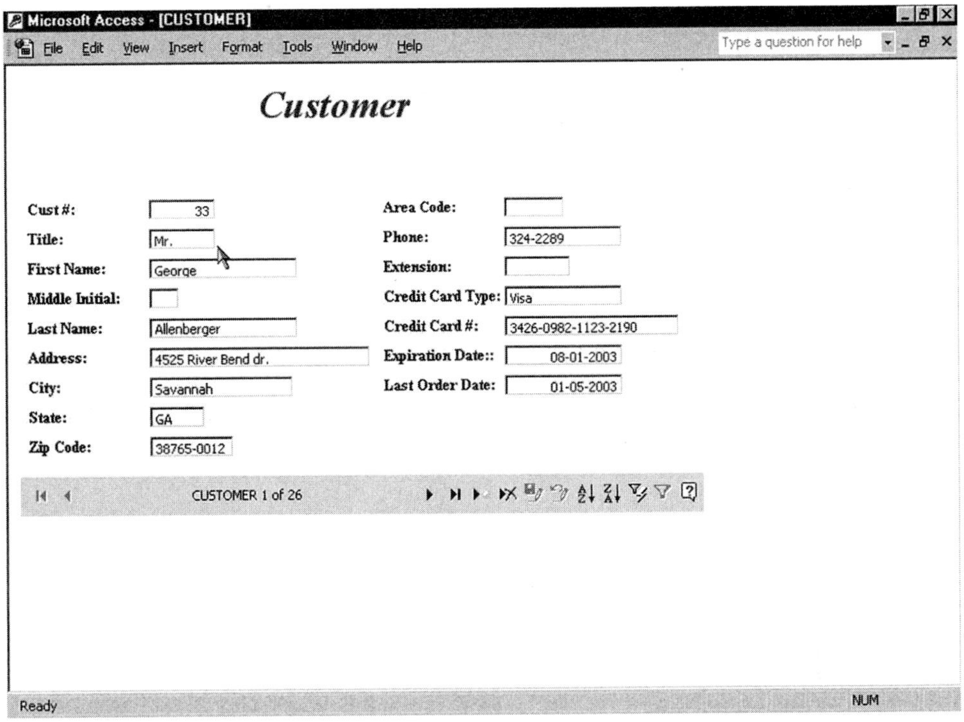

FIGURE 9.34
The Customer Output Page

To save the page, select **File/Save** from the drop-down menu to generate the screen shown in Figure 9.36. (Note that the previously saved **Customer Sales.htm** page shows up in Figure 9.36.)

You should remember from the previous section that you must save the HTM file in the same folder that contains the database. (Note the folder in Figure 9.36.) Save the page as **CUSTOMER.htm**.

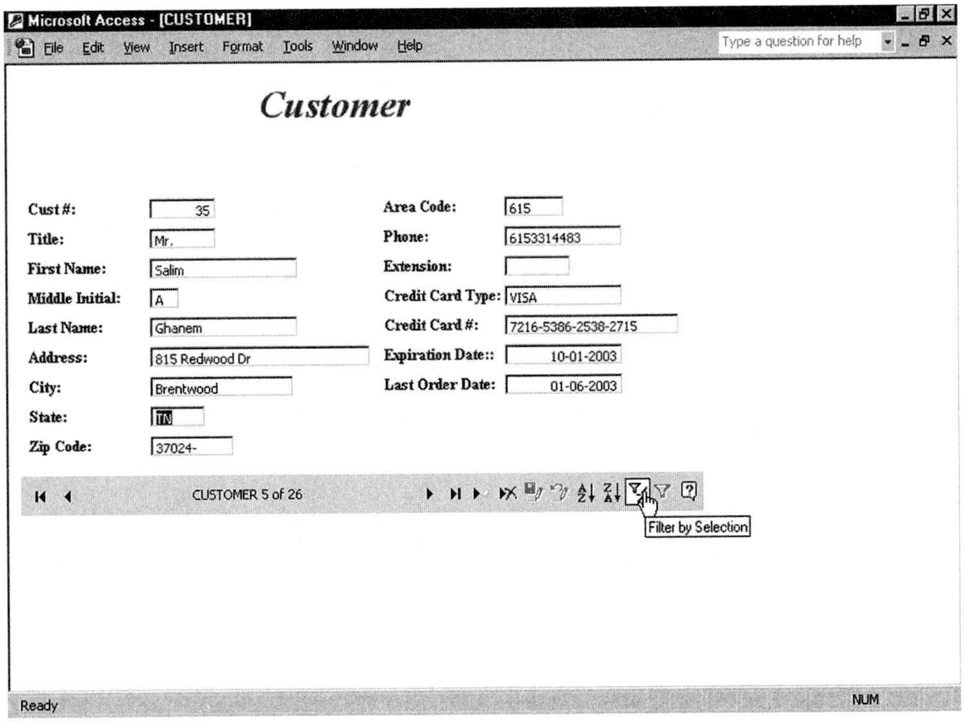

FIGURE 9.35
Filter by Selection

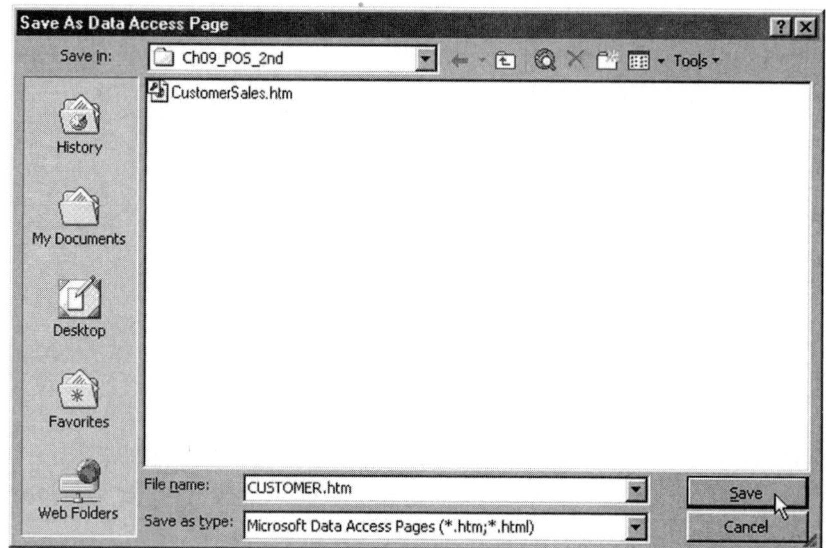

FIGURE 9.36
Save the Page in HTM Format

9.3.1 The Page Data Source

You will learn in section 9.8 that errors will be created if the page data source is incorrect. (We will also show you how to correct those errors.) Therefore, you should know how to find and verify the page data source. To see the page's data source, open the page in design view and then right-click on the **Page connection properties** as shown in Figure 9.37.

Clicking on **Page connection properties** opens the **Data Link Properties** window shown in Figure 9.38.

As you examine the screen shown in Figure 9.38, note that the **Data Link Properties** window contains four tabs: **Connection**, **Provider**, **Advanced**, and **All**. (Because the **Connection** tab is the default, we have listed it first.)

1. The **Connection** tab lets you verify, or change, the page's data source. If you click on the builder button next to the **Select or enter the database name:** op-

FIGURE 9.37
The Page Connection Properties

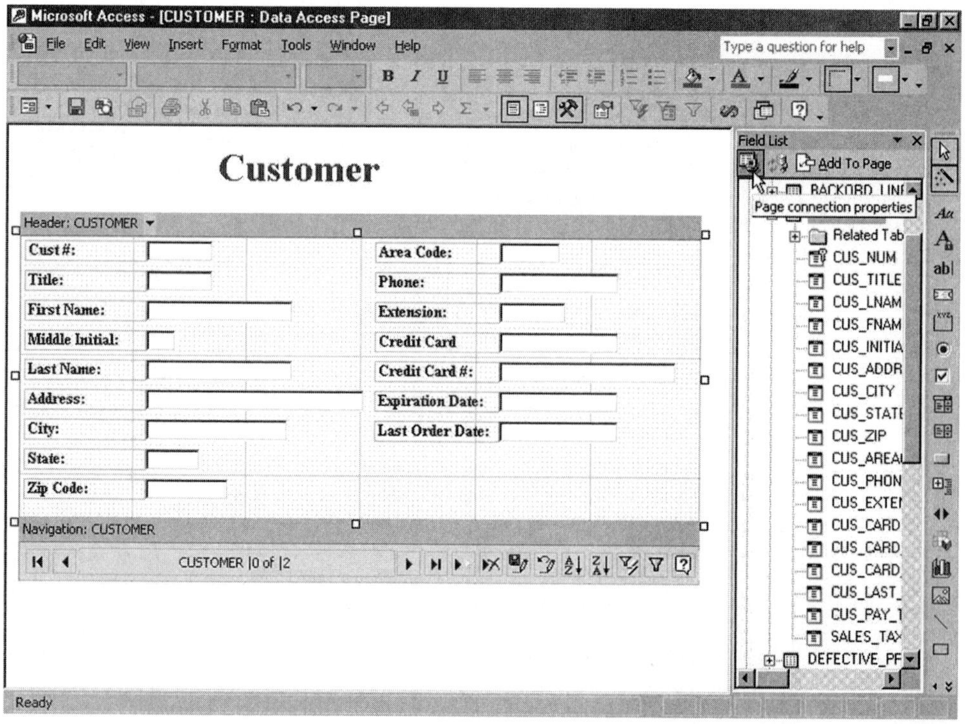

FIGURE 9.38
The Data Link Properties Window

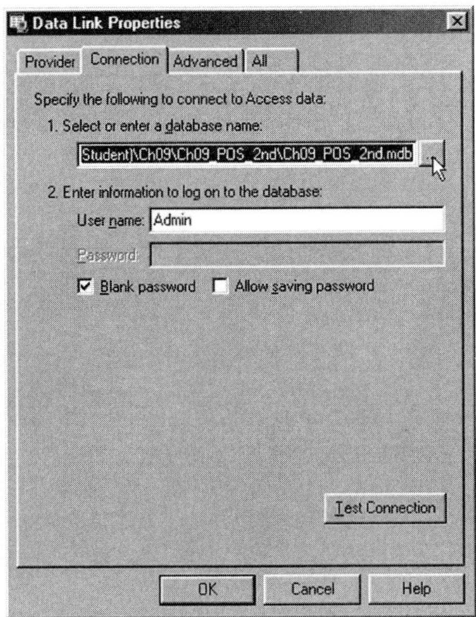

FIGURE 9.39
The Page Data Source

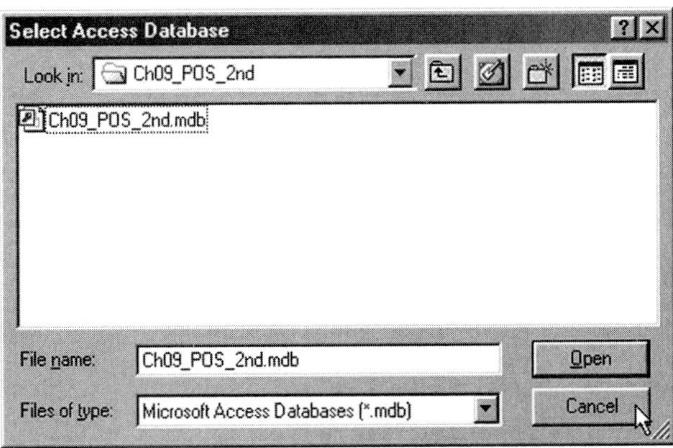

tion in Figure 9.38, you will see the window in Figure 9.39. If you like, you can start at the root and then click through the folder structure to reach the data source. (Because the data source is correct, select **Cancel** to avoid making an accidental change.)

2. The **Provider** tab in Figure 9.38 shows the available OLE DB Provider(s) providers that you can use to connect to an SQL Server database. Figure 9.40 shows the **Microsoft Jet 4.0 OLE DB Provider** to be the default connection type to an Access database. If you select the **Microsoft OLE DB Provider for SQL Server**, the connection tab changes to match the presentation in Figure 9.41.

FIGURE 9.40
The Provider Tab

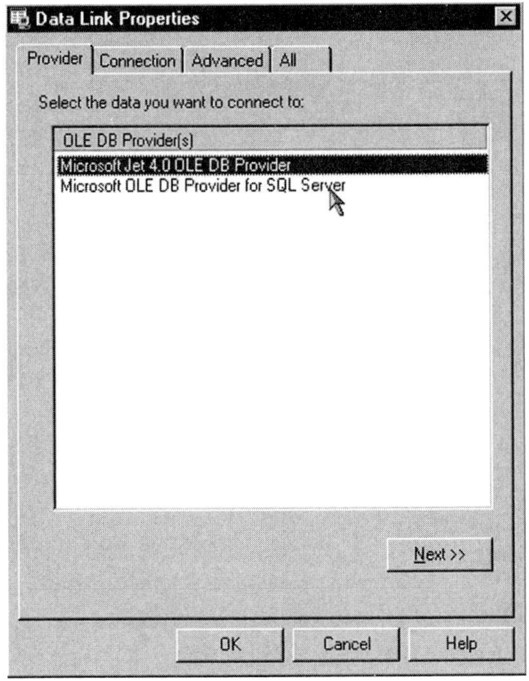

FIGURE 9.41
The Connection to an SQL Server Database

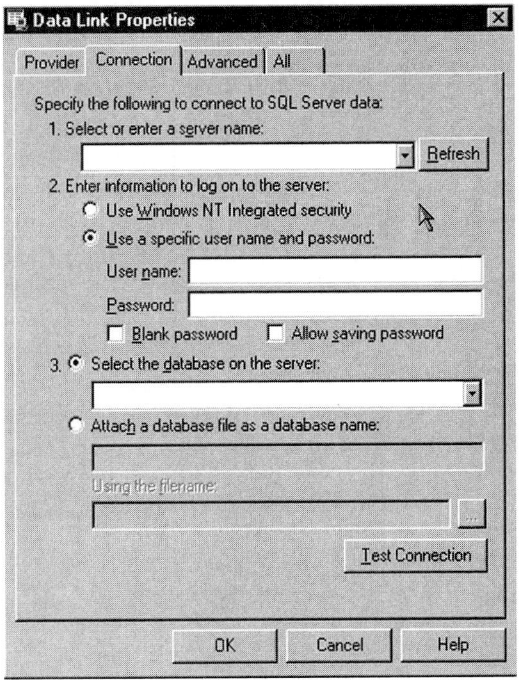

FIGURE 9.42
The Advanced Tab

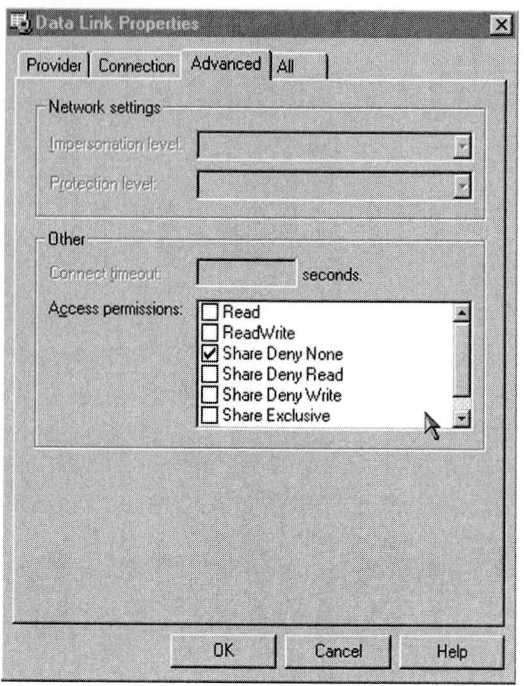

FIGURE 9.43
The All Tab

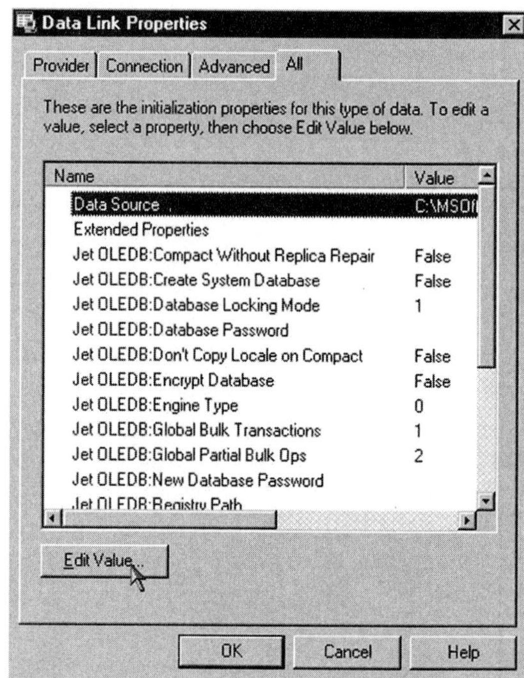

3. The **Advanced** tab shown in Figure 9.42 enables you to change permission to the database object(s). You will learn in Chapter 10 what a "permission" is and how you assign it. At this point, the **Advanced** tab is simply part of the data access familiarization tour, so do not make changes. (The **Cancel** button is a good option!)
4. The **All** tab shown in Figure 9.43 lets you edit the properties of the data connection. This option is useful to database administrators who want to secure the databases that are subject to their control.

9.4 CREATING A SPREADSHEET ON A DATA ACCESS PAGE

To create a data access page in a spreadsheet format, complete the following steps:

1. Click on **Create data access page in design view** from the database window first shown in Figure 9.3.
2. Enable the Control Wizards. (See Figure 9.9 again.)
3. Click on the + sign next to the **Queries** folder in the **Field List** section. This action will change the + sign to a – sign and it will show all the queries in the queries folder. Highlight the query named **qryTotalEmployeeSales**. (See Figure 9.44.)
4. Drag the **qryEmployeeTotalSales** query and drop it on the page to generate the screen first shown in Figure 9.10. (You will see the **Layout Wizard** window.)
5. Using the **Layout Wizard** window, select the **Office Spreadsheet** option, and click **OK** to generate the screen shown in Figure 9.45.
6. Expand the spreadsheet by clicking on its edge, and then drag each side to enable the end user to see all the fields.
7. Type ***Employee Sales*** in the title section and then save the file as **Employee Sales.htm**.
8. Finally, select the **Page View** option to see the results shown in Figure 9.46.

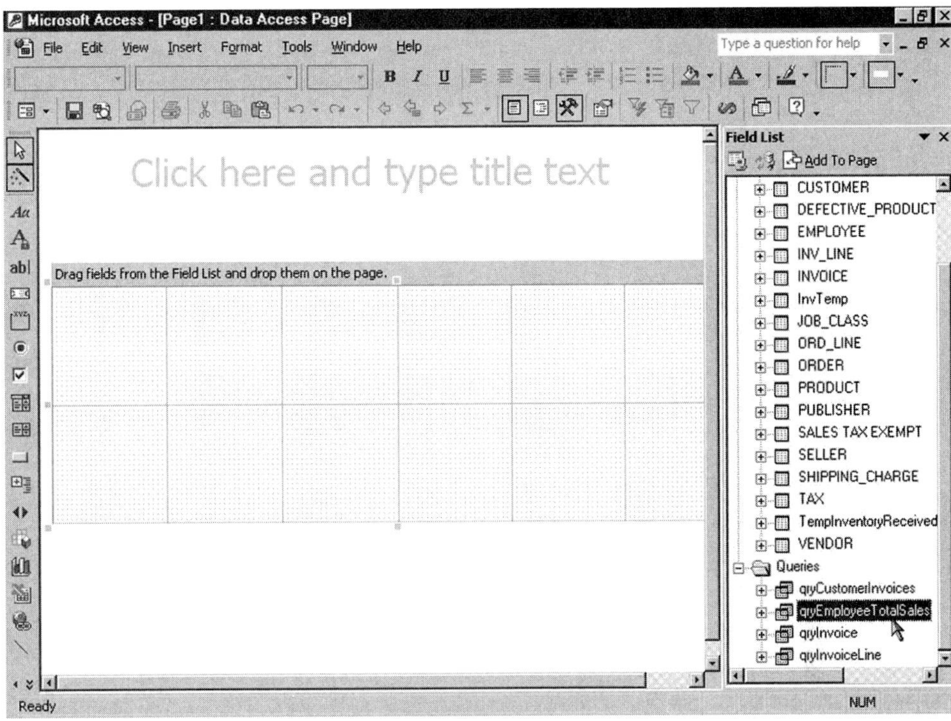

FIGURE 9.44
Selecting a Query from the Queries Folder

9.5 CREATING A CHART ON A DATA ACCESS PAGE

To create a data access page in a chart format, complete the following steps:

1. Click on **Create data access page in design view** from the database window first shown in Figure 9.3.
2. Enable the Control Wizards. (See Figure 9.9 again.)

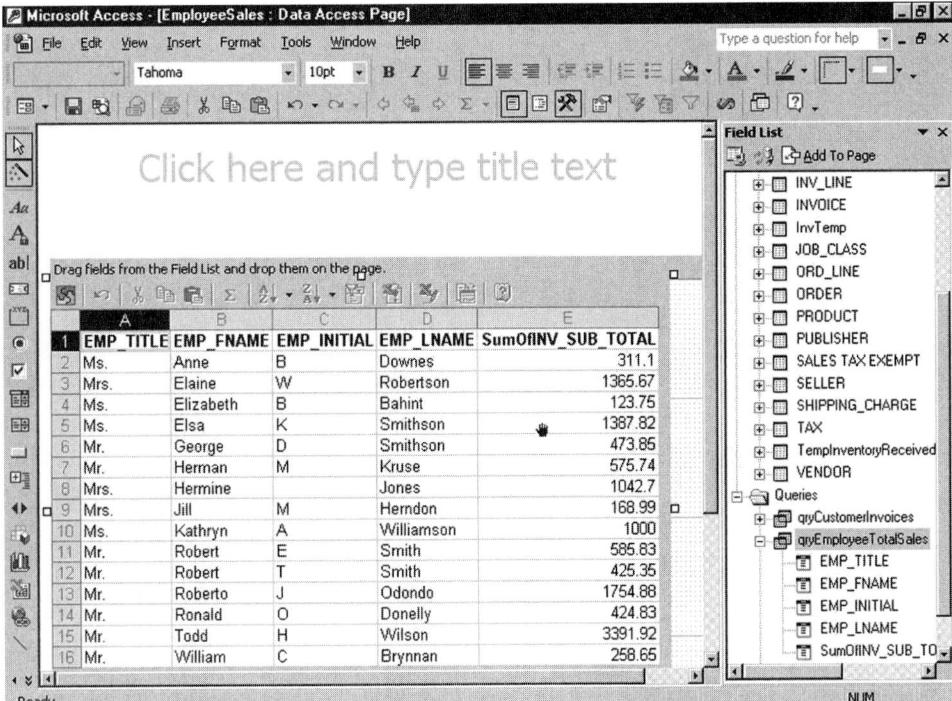

FIGURE 9.45
The Spreadsheet on the Data Access Page

Note

Even if the data are updatable *on the page,* the spreadsheet's underlying (database) data source remains unaffected. The spreadsheet is mostly used to perform calculations and to peruse "what if" scenarios. You can use the options on the spreadsheet header bar to sort, filter, and export the data to Microsoft Excel.

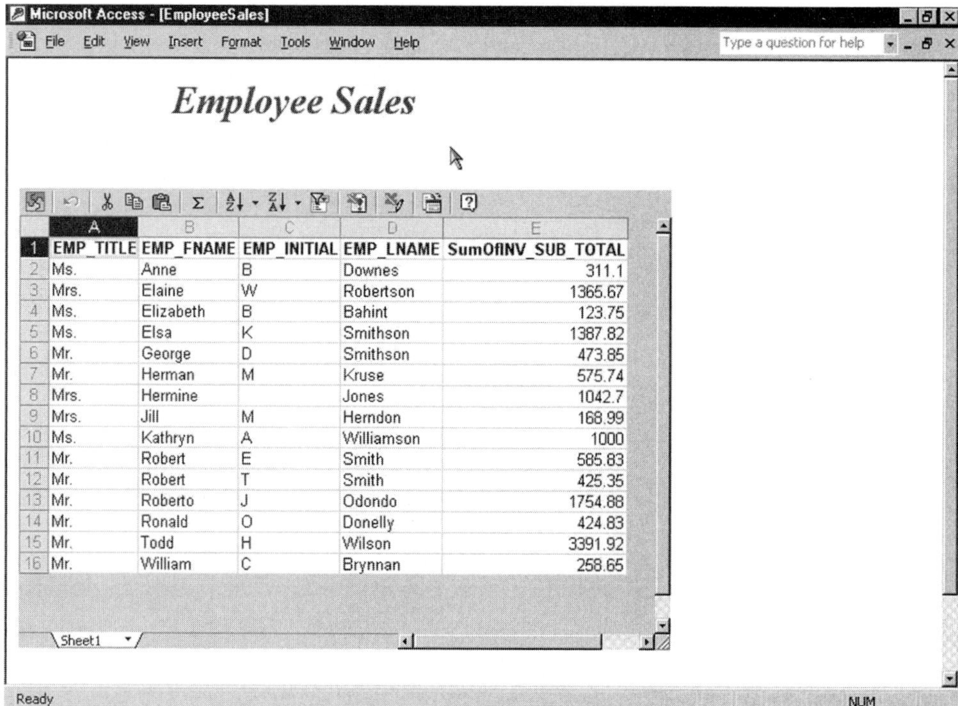

	EMP_TITLE	EMP_FNAME	EMP_INITIAL	EMP_LNAME	SumOfINV_SUB_TOTAL
2	Ms.	Anne	B	Downes	311.1
3	Mrs.	Elaine	W	Robertson	1365.67
4	Ms.	Elizabeth	B	Bahint	123.75
5	Ms.	Elsa	K	Smithson	1387.82
6	Mr.	George	D	Smithson	473.85
7	Mr.	Herman	M	Kruse	575.74
8	Mrs.	Hermine		Jones	1042.7
9	Mrs.	Jill	M	Herndon	168.99
10	Ms.	Kathryn	A	Williamson	1000
11	Mr.	Robert	E	Smith	585.83
12	Mr.	Robert	T	Smith	425.35
13	Mr.	Roberto	J	Odondo	1754.88
14	Mr.	Ronald	O	Donelly	424.83
15	Mr.	Todd	H	Wilson	3391.92
16	Mr.	William	C	Brynnan	258.65

FIGURE 9.46
The Spreadsheet in Page View

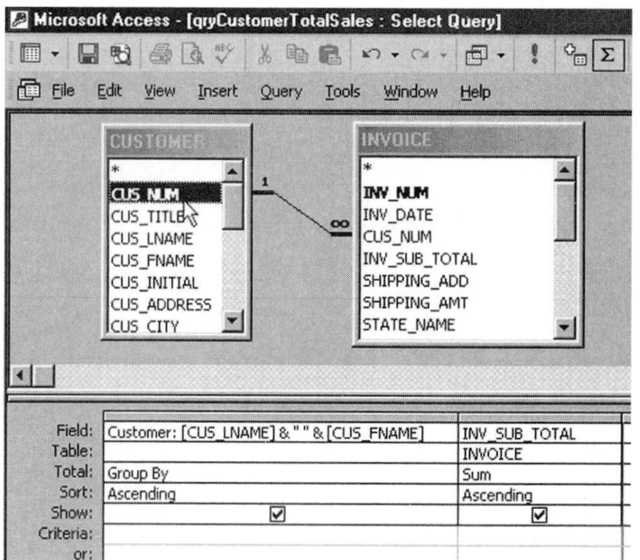

FIGURE 9.47
The qryCustomerTotalSales Query in Design View

Note

If you do not have a full installation of the 2002 edition of the software, you will *not* be able to produce the charts shown in this section. If you do not have the option to reinstall the full installation, skip this section.

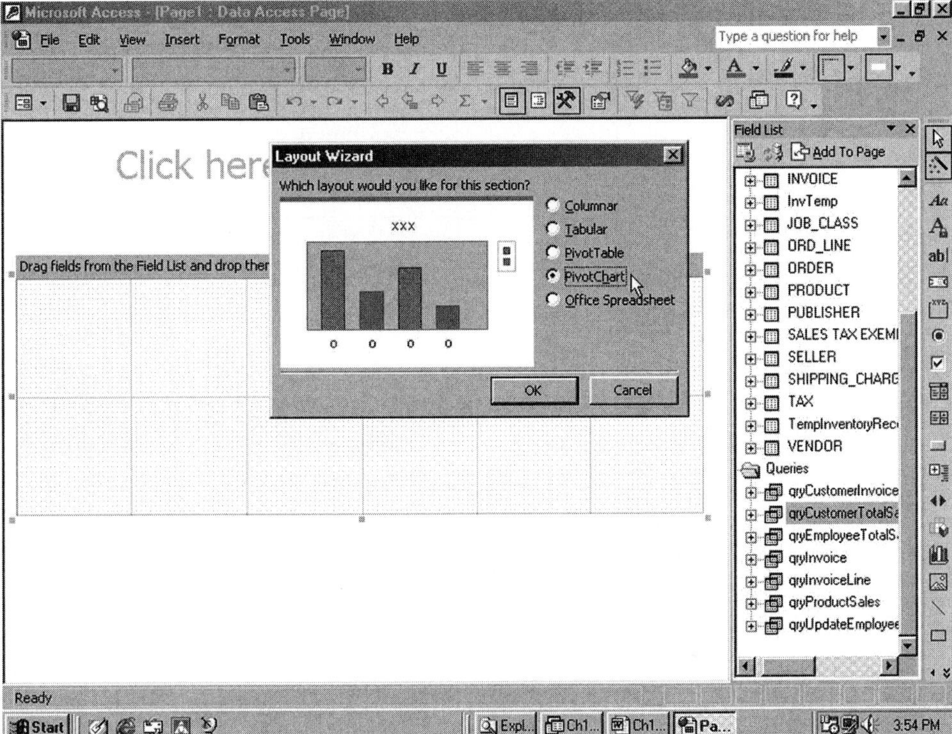

FIGURE 9.47A
The Pivot Chart Option

3. Click on the + sign next to the **Queries** folder in the **Field List** section.

4. Select the **qryCustomerTotalSales** query from the field list. The structure of this query is shown in Figure 9.47.

5. Drag and drop the **qryCustomerTotalSales** query on the page. This action generates the familiar **Layout Wizard** options first shown in Figure 9.10. Select the **Pivot Chart** option to produce the layout shown in Figure 9.47A.

6. After selecting the **PivotChart** option from the **Layout Wizard** window, click **OK** to generate the screen shown in Figure 9.48. (We have widened the page and chart limits by dragging them.)

7. Expand the chart size to fit on your screen.

8. Select the **Customer** field from the **qryCustomerTotalSales** query's fields and drag and drop it in the **Drop Category Fields Here**.

9. Drag the **SumOfINV_SUB_TOTAL** and drop it in the **Drop Data Fields Here** to generate the screen shown in Figure 9.49.

10. You can change the chart properties via its properties box. To open the chart properties box, double-click on the chart in design view to generate the properties box shown in Figure 9.50.

As you can tell by examining the screen in Figure 9.50, we have made sure that the field list is hidden from the chart display by selecting **False** from the **DisplayFieldList**.

FIGURE 9.48
The PivotChart Layout on the Page

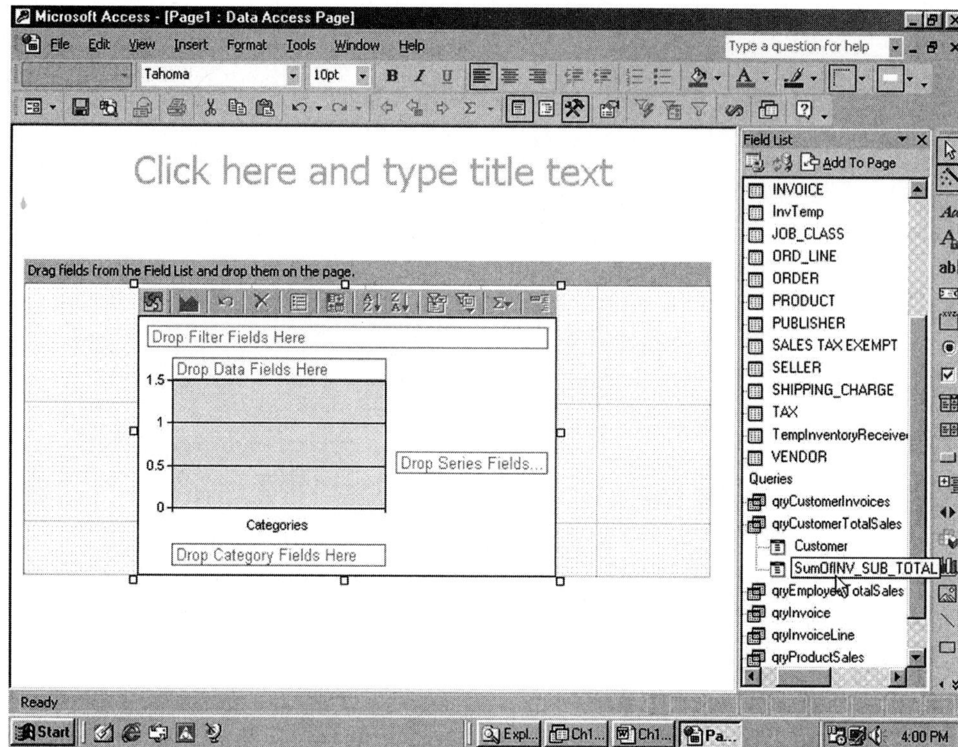

11. Type the chart header in the **Click here and type title text** section of the page and open the page in design view to examine the results shown in Figure 9.51.

If you want to change the appearance of the chart presentation, you can always select the chart object, and then select the **Command and Options...** from the drop-down menu shown in Figure 9.52.

FIGURE 9.49
The Chart in Design View

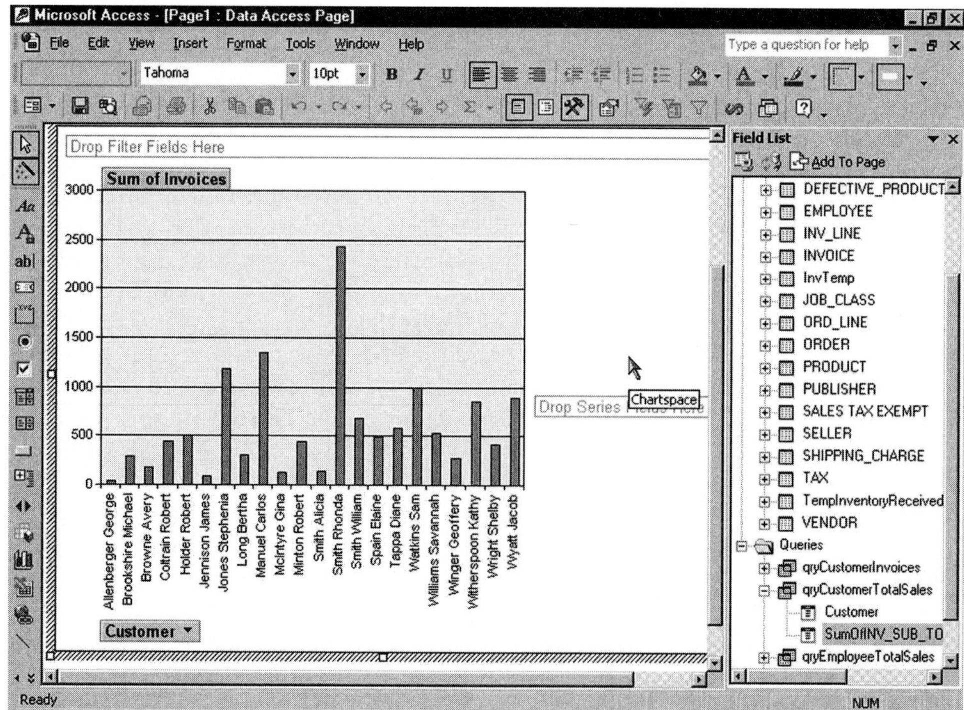

FIGURE 9.50
The Chart Properties

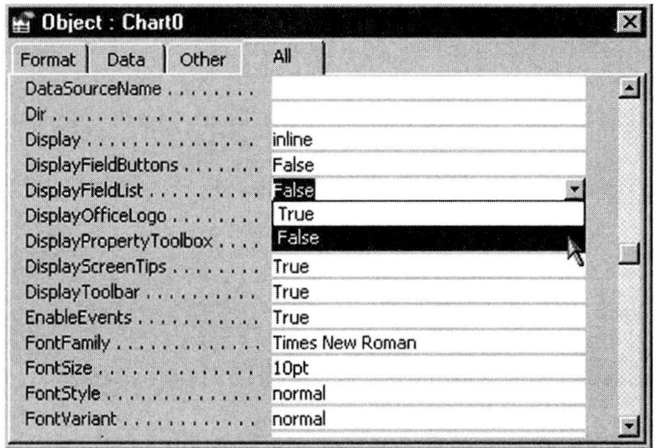

The selection shown in Figure 9.52 yields the choices shown in Figure 9.52A.

Although the presentation shown in Figure 9.51 does not lend itself well to chart formats such as pie charts, you do have those formats available. Several pie chart formats are shown in Figure 9.53.

9.6 CREATING THE PIVOT TABLE ON A DATA ACCESS PAGE

Inserting a pivot table on a page follows a familiar sequence:

1. Click on **Create data access page in Design view** from the database window.
2. Enable the **Control Wizards.**
3. Select the **Queries** folder from the **Field List**.
4. We will use the **qryProductSales** query as the data source in this example, so drag it to the page to produce the familiar **Layout Wizard**. (The query structure is shown in Figure 9.54.)

FIGURE 9.51
The Customer Sales Chart in Page View

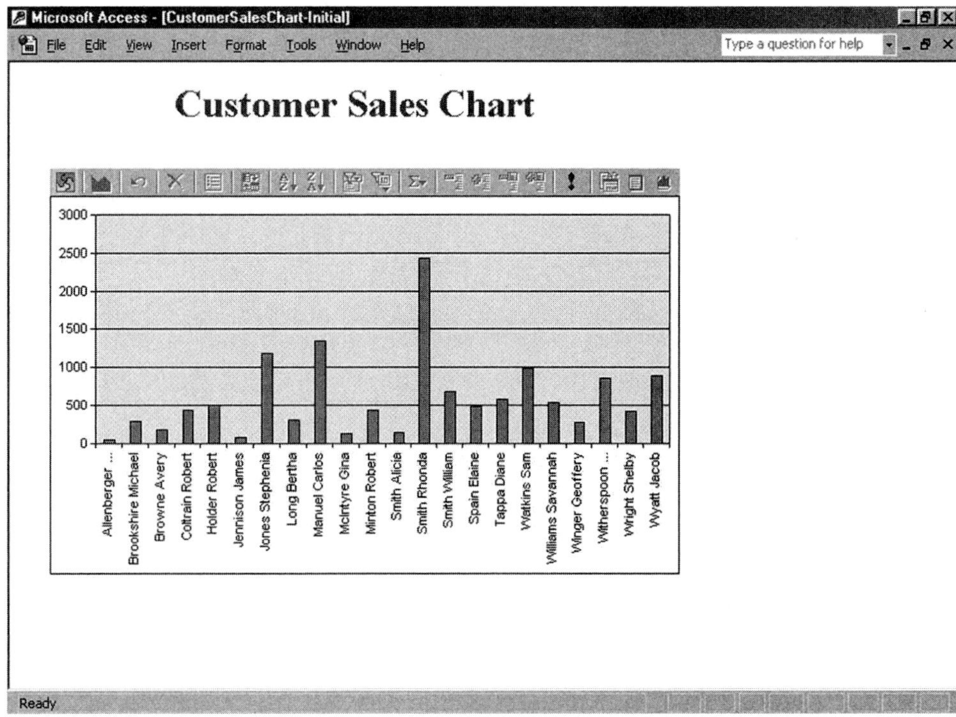

FIGURE 9.52
The Commands and Options Selection

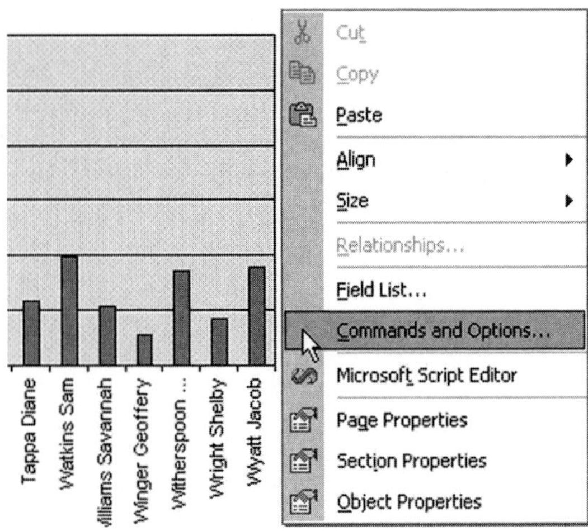

FIGURE 9.52A
The Chart Type Selection

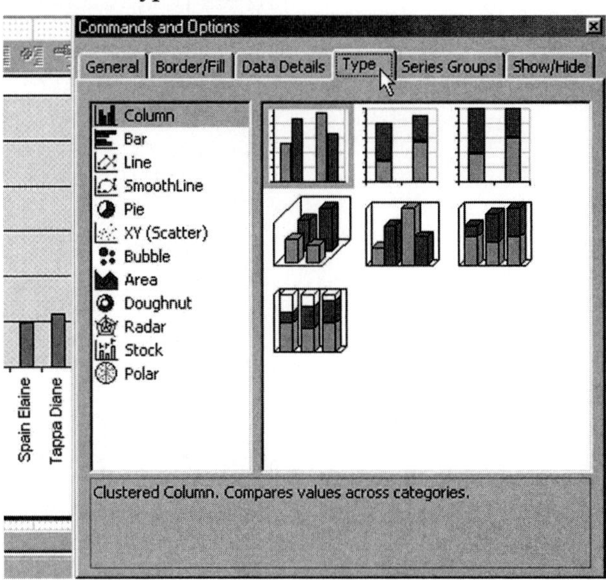

5. Select **PivotTable** from the layout wizard to generate the screen shown in Figure 9.54A.
6. When you click **OK** on the layout wizard shown in Figure 9.54A, you will see the initial page in its design view (see Figure 9.54B).
7. Type the page header **(Product Sales)** and format the text to display the header in blue with a font size of 24. Drag the limits of the page shown in Figure 9.54B to enlarge the area in which the pivot table will be displayed. Then drag the pivot table's edges to show all of the selected fields. When you are done, you will see the results in Figure 9.54C.
8. Open the page in **Page View** to generate the screen shown in Figure 9.54D.

FIGURE 9.53
Selecting a Different Chart Type

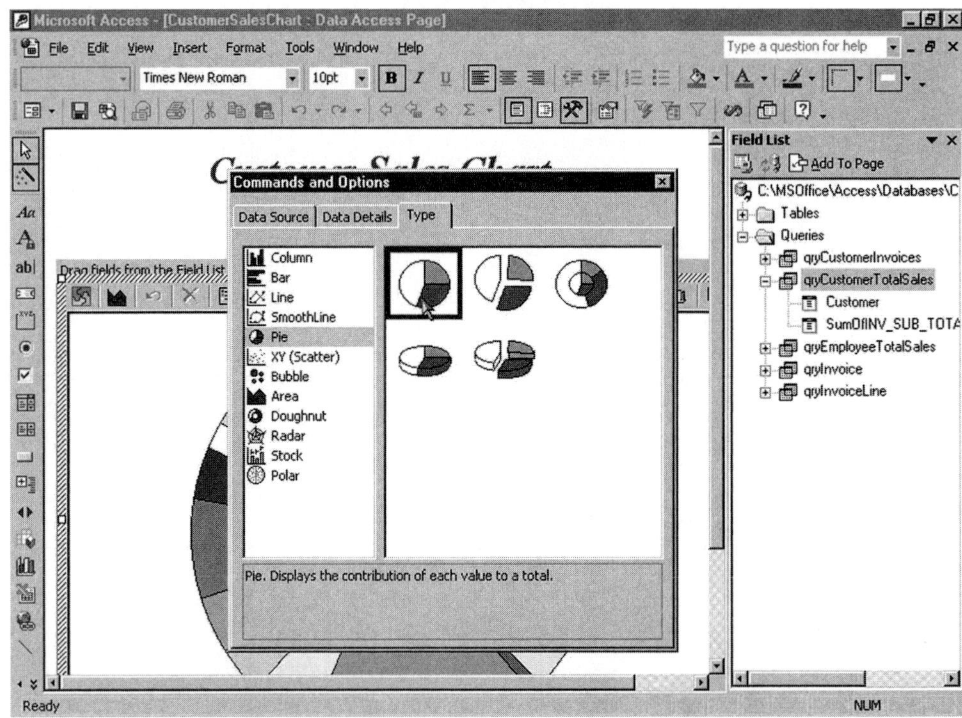

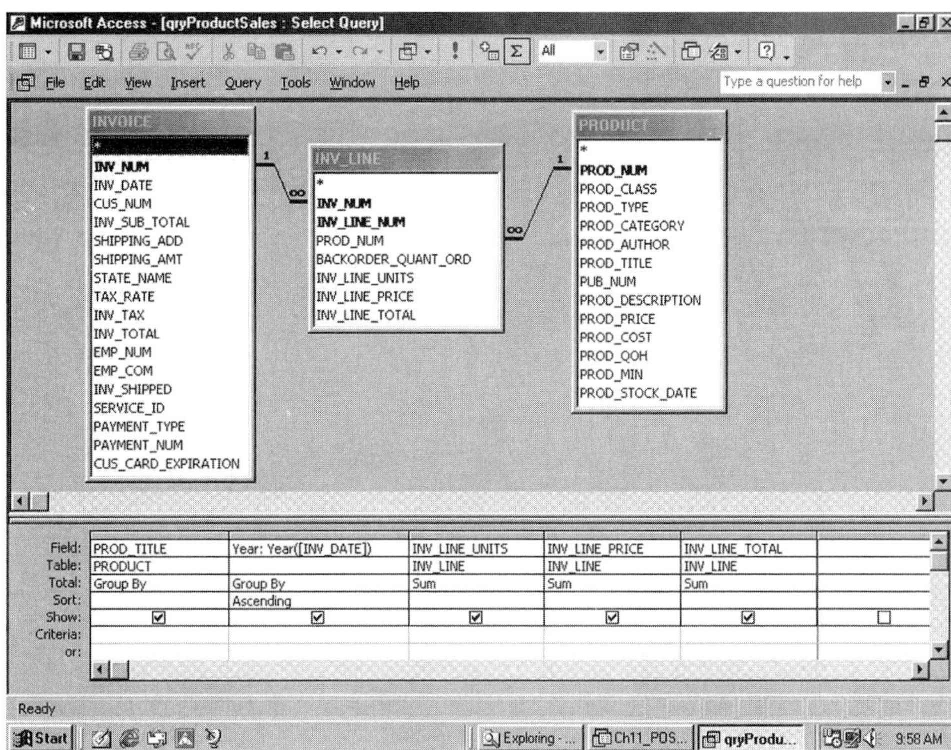

FIGURE 9.54
The qryProductSales Query in Design View

As you can see in Figure 9.54D, the arrow above each field—note the cursor location—allows you to see a list of the records for the fields. If you place your cursor on a record, you will see that the screen tip displays the full title of the product. If you uncheck a record displayed in the list of records and click **OK**, the record will be removed from the pivot table. To display the record again in the table, recheck the record from the drop-down list.

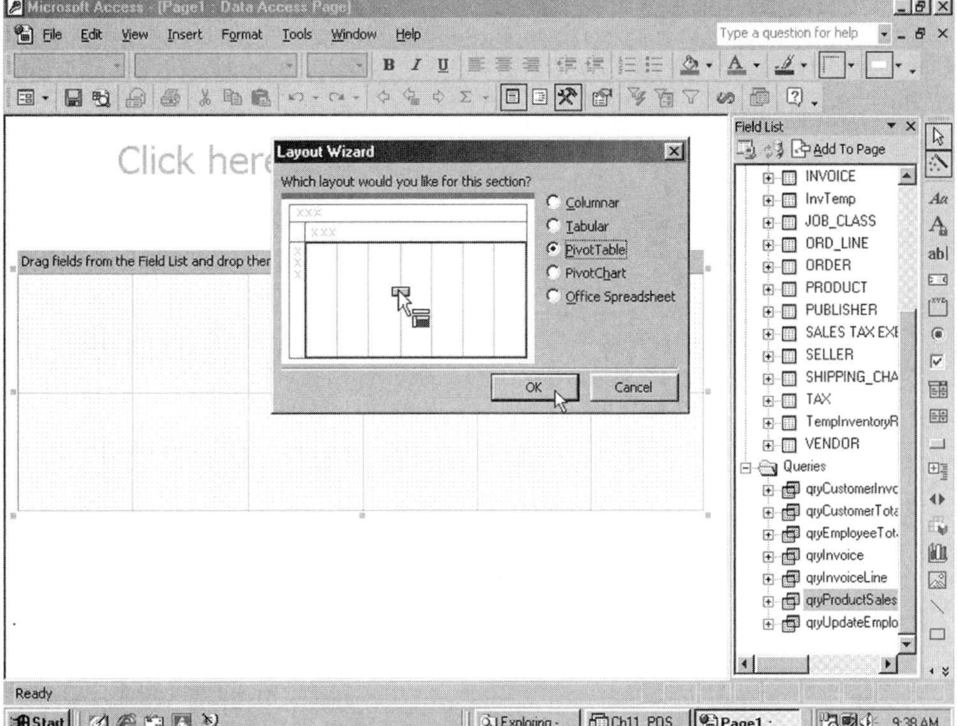

FIGURE 9.54A
Selecting the Pivot Table Option from the Layout Wizard

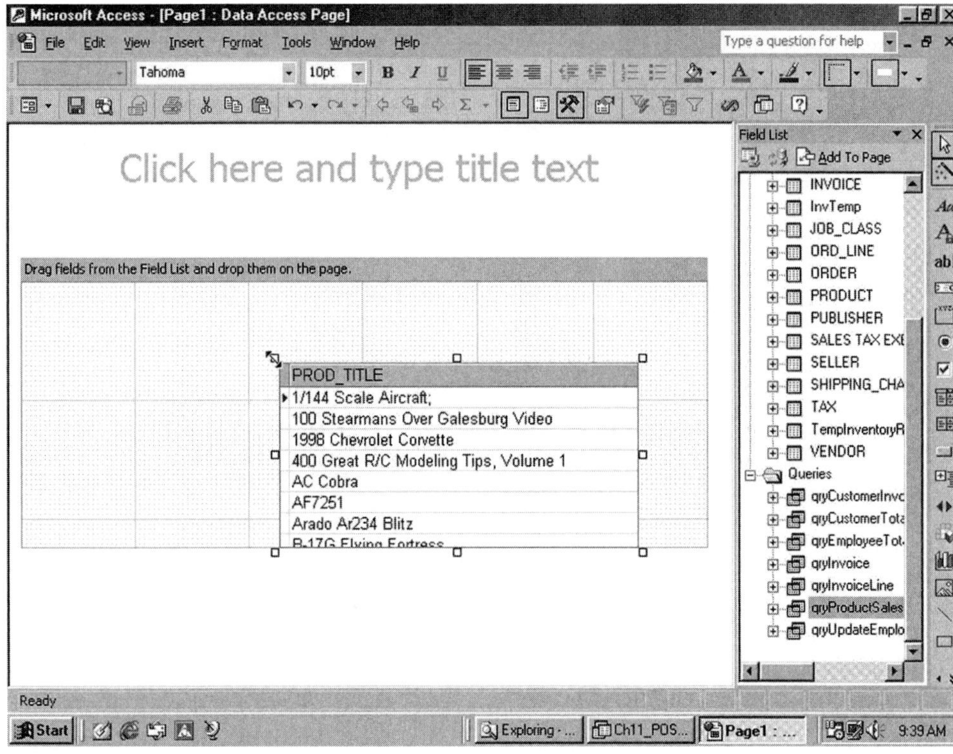

FIGURE 9.54B
The Initial Design View of the Pivot Table

9.7 CREATING THE MAIN PAGE

The main page is the first thing your end users are likely to see. That's why it is important to remember that you have only one chance to make a good first impression. Therefore, the main page must be user friendly, it must be simple, and it should contain only minimal information to maximize its access speed.

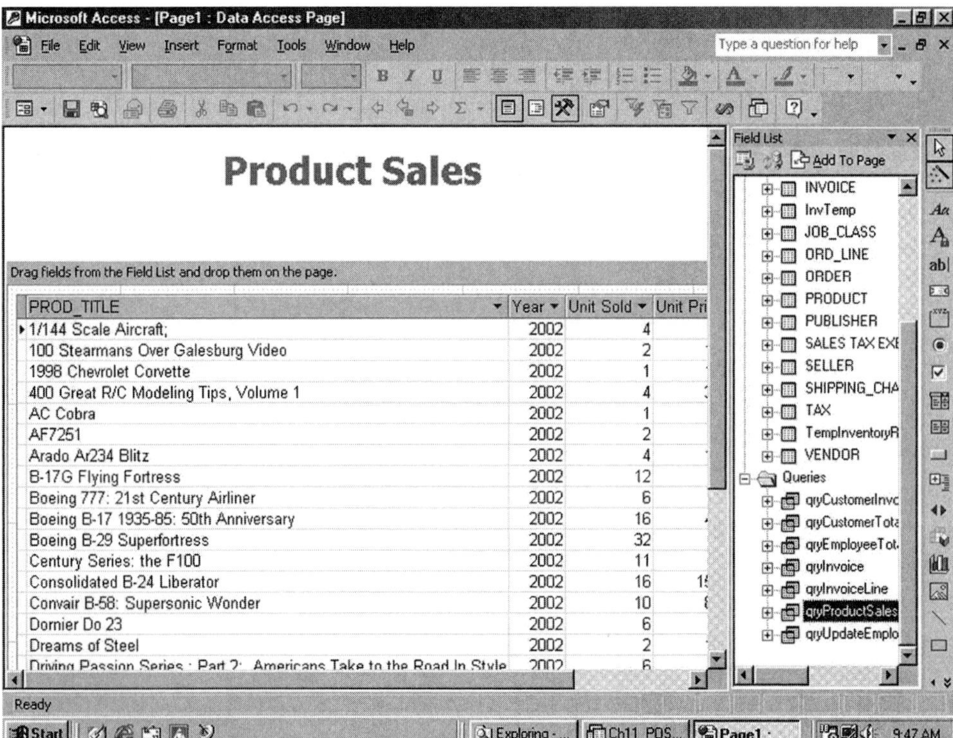

FIGURE 9.54C
The Modified Design View of the Pivot Table

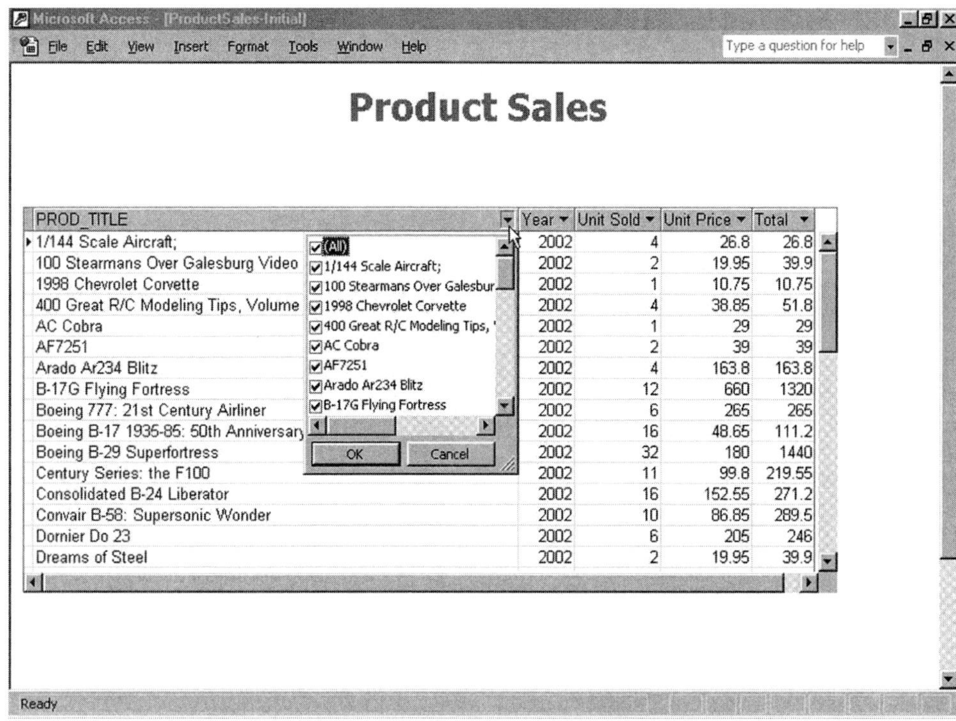

FIGURE 9.54D
The Product Sales Pivot Table in Page View

9.7.1 Inserting a Picture

Naturally, you can design your own main page. However, we'll give you a brief example to show you how easy it is to produce a main page. Let's start by clicking on the **Create data access page in Design View** option in the database window to produce the screen shown in Figure 9.55. (Note that we have *not* selected a data source, because a main page, like the main menu in Chapter 6, does not contain data.) Because pictures tend to grab a person's attention, let's begin by inserting a picture while we're in the design view.

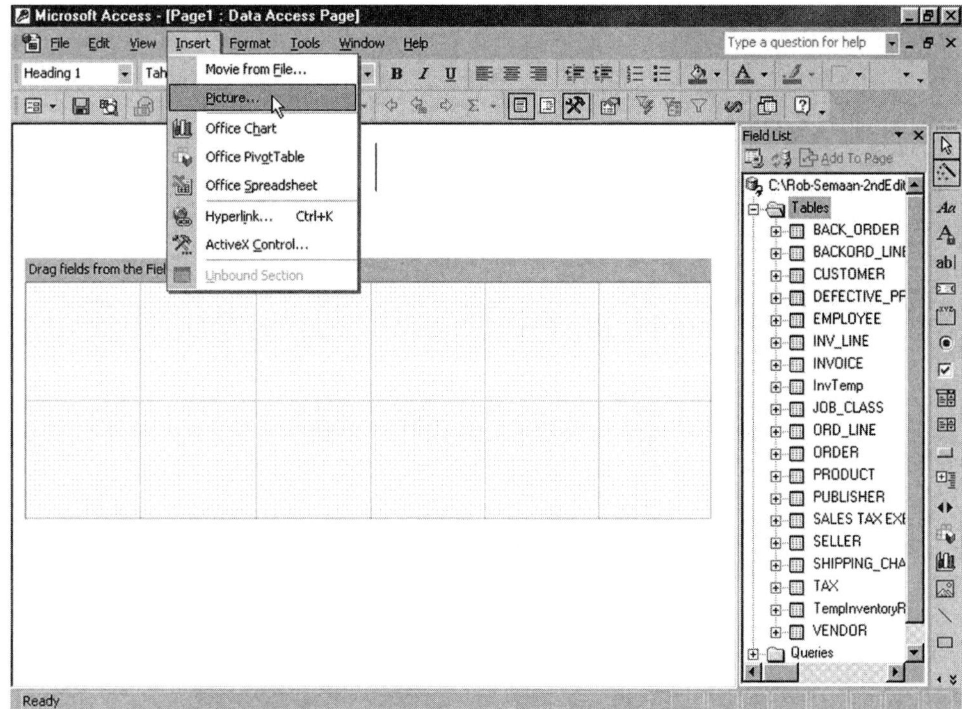

FIGURE 9.55
Selecting the Insert Picture Option

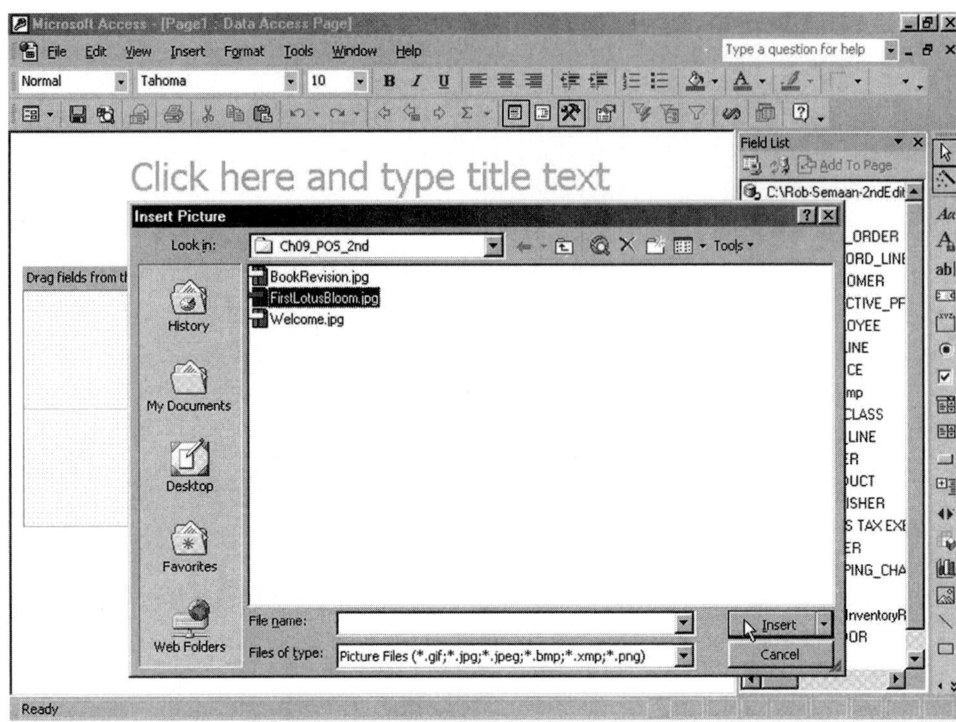

FIGURE 9.56
Selecting the Picture

We will start by putting a picture in the page header, so let's make sure that the cursor is placed on the page header portion of the page. After placing the cursor on the header, select the **Insert/Picture** option as shown in Figure 9.55.

As soon as you click on the **Picture** option shown in the drop-down list in Figure 9.55, the default storage location in Figure 9.56 will be displayed. The default picture location is the folder in which the database is stored. That default location is an excellent place to store *all* the pictures used by the database application. (The BookRevision.jpg file provides *some* visual evidence about the effort that goes into creating and editing the files from which this book was developed.)

As you examine Figure 9.56, note that we have clicked on the FirstLotusBloom.jpg file and placed the cursor on the **Insert** button. Clicking on the **Insert** button—or double-clicking on the file—will place the picture in the page header as shown in Figure 9.57.

As you examine Figure 9.57, note that we have placed the cursor on the **Field List Close** button. Because the main menu does not contain any data, the field list is not going to be used anyway, so go ahead and click on the **Close** button to make the field list disappear. Whenever you have a page in its design view, you can restore the **Field List** anytime by clicking on the button bar's **Field List** button.

After inserting the picture in the page header, it is clearly necessary to "size" the picture to fit properly into the page header section. You may have already decided that the picture insertion routine we used for the page header works just like the picture insertion routines we used in Chapter 6. However, there are some differences:

1. The inserted picture will fill the entire header. Therefore, you must scroll to find the picture's lower and right edge limits, and then drag those limits to control the picture size.
2. You cannot drag the entire picture to any location in the header. The picture's location is controlled through the text alignment button. (Note that we have selected **Align Left** to place the picture on the left side of the header.)
3. Unlike the picture routines in the Chapter 6 forms, you do not have an option to select a **Zoom** or **Clip** format, so size the picture's horizontal and vertical display to minimize distortion.

FIGURE 9.57
The FirstLotusBloom Picture Inserted in the Page Header

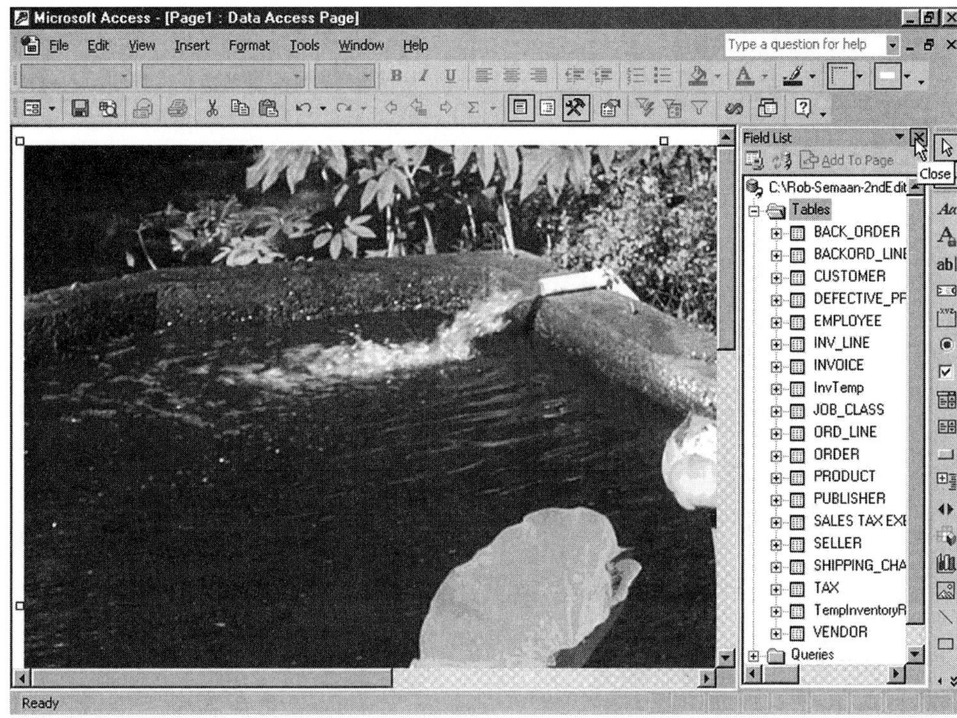

Keeping these three points in mind, we placed the picture in the header as shown in Figure 9.58.

9.7.2 Inserting a Line

Aside from inserting pictures, you can use the **Toolbox** options to insert lines, rectangles, and so on. For example, let's select the page—that is, the section under the header—in order to insert a line that will separate the main page's header from its main display section. To accomplish this task, select the **Line** option

FIGURE 9.58
The Sized Picture

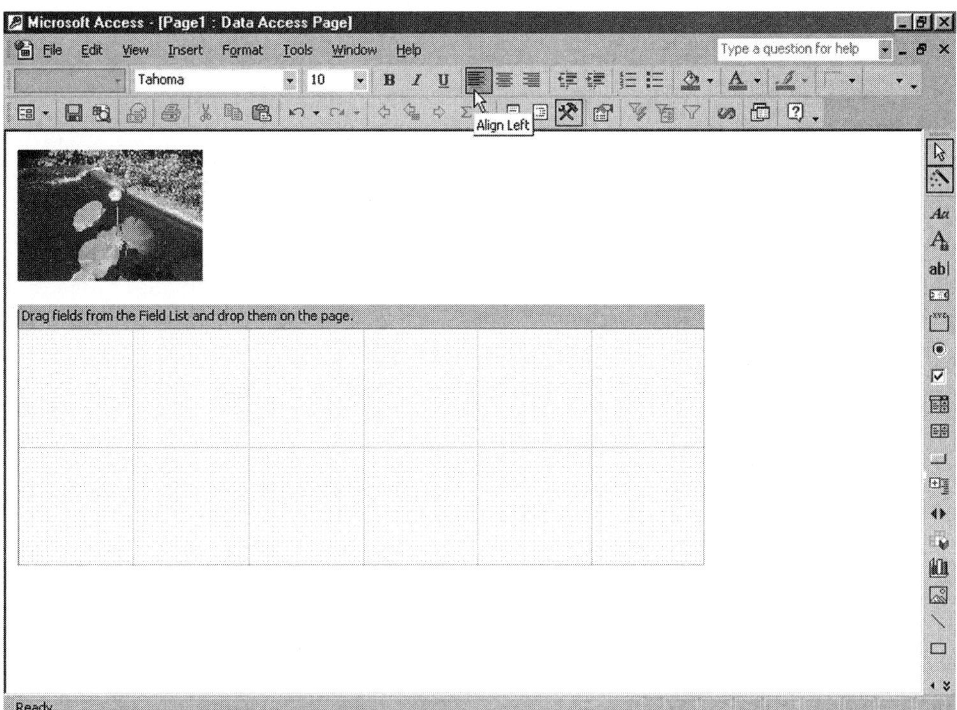

Assignment

The Welcome.jpg picture you see in Figure 9.56 is actually Word art that we have saved as a .jpg picture. Using this technique, you can exercise more control over the text display. Insert this picture and size it just as we showed you in Figures 9.57 to 9.58 to produce the results shown in Figure 9.59. (Note that we have restored the Field List.)

FIGURE 9.59 The Completed Main Page Header

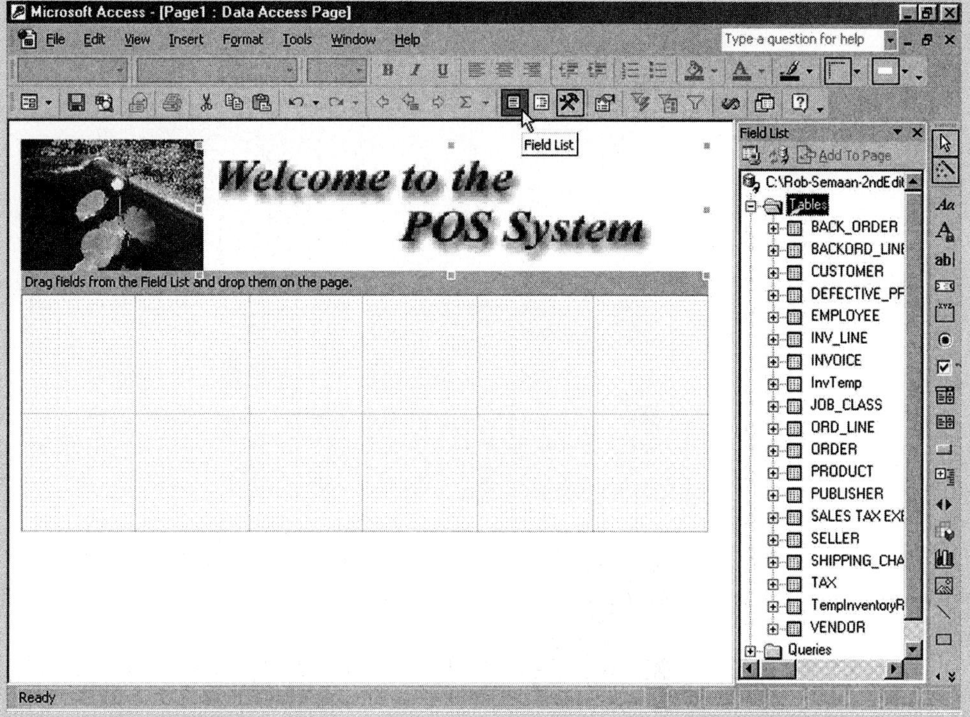

from the toolbox and draw the line by dragging the cursor. Note the result in Figure 9.60.

When you look at Figure 9.60, note that we used the line's properties box to control the line's characteristics. In this example, we selected the line color to be blue and the line width to be 15 pixels. You can also change the line thickness by using the familiar button bar options shown in Figure 9.60A.

We placed the line in the page itself, rather than in its header, because the page gives us most of the picture, label, and options that we had in form design. Better yet, if we work in the main page section, we are also no longer constrained by the text placement limits imposed in the header section. (For example, we could not drag objects in the header to any desired location; we had to use a text cursor and a text-alignment technique.) In short, while the header is an important segment of the page, the header has a limited function with limited capabilities. Therefore, most of the page's design and formatting activities will take place on the page, rather than on its header.

9.7.3 Inserting a Label

It is likely that you'll want to insert a label to explain to your users what is your site is all about. Inserting a label requires the toolbox again. (The **Label** option works just as it did when you created form labels in Chapter 6.) We have inserted a label to explain the POS system's purpose on the page shown in Figure 9.61. As

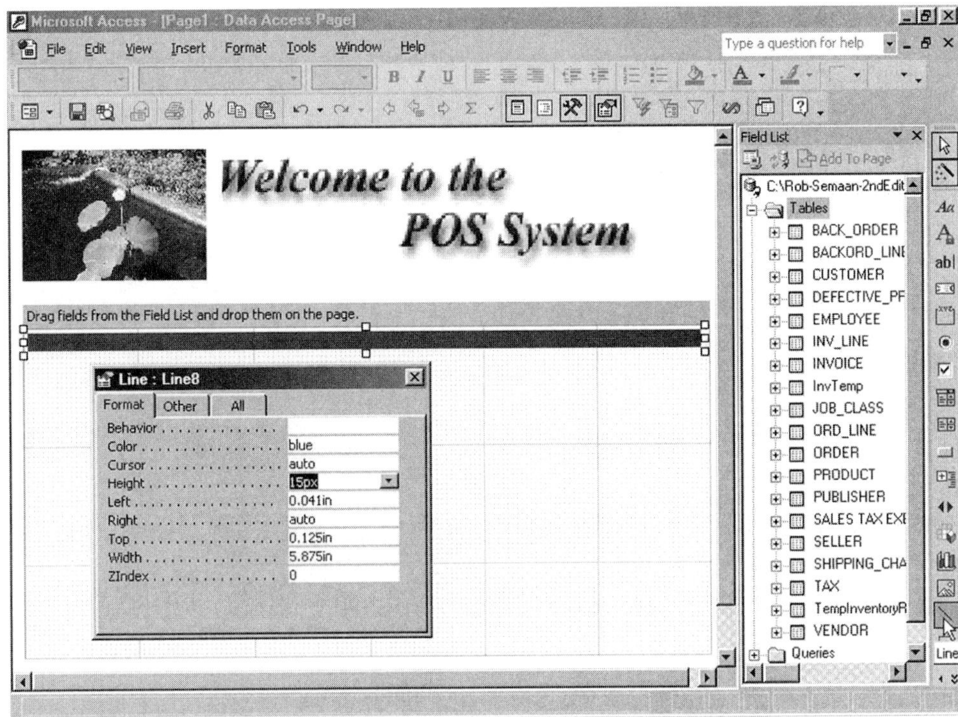

FIGURE 9.60
Inserting a Line

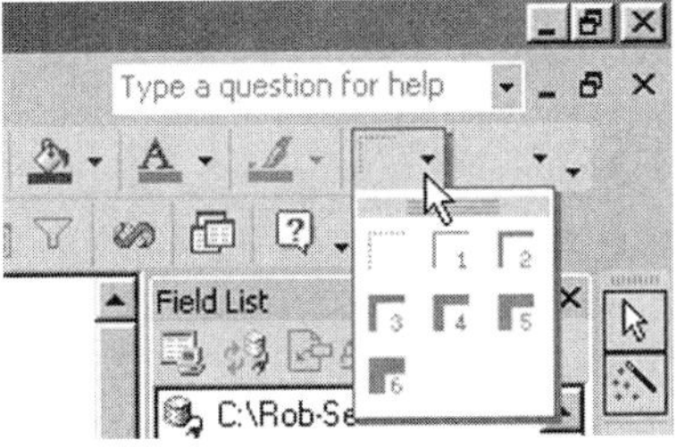

FIGURE 9.60A
Button Bar Options

you can tell, we also inserted a picture, the BookRevision.jpg, after we typed the label to serve as a background for the text.

As you examine Figure 9.61, note that we have typed the label, changed the font size and color, inserted the BookRevision.jpg picture, *and used the button bar's* **Format** *button to send the picture to the back to ensure that the label would not be hidden by the picture.* (Remember that all the label actions are identical to those used on a form. For example, to move the cursor to the label's next line, hold the Shift key down while you press the Enter key. To skip a line, press the Enter key twice. Use the button bar to center the text in the label. Perform all these chores before you insert the picture and send it to the back.)

9.7.4 Inserting Hyperlinks

If you want to have a system, you must be able to navigate from the main page to the various system components and back to the main page. In a Web environment, such actions are triggered by hyperlinks.

To insert a hyperlink on the page, select the **Insert/Hyperlink** option from the drop-down menu to generate the screen shown in Figure 9.62. (We have shown you only a small section of the screen. Note that we have saved the main menu as **MainPage.htm**.)

The selection of the **Insert/Hyperlink** option in Figure 9.62 generates the **Insert Hyperlink** window shown in Figure 9.63. Use this window to locate the application you want to display when the hyperlink is clicked. In this example,

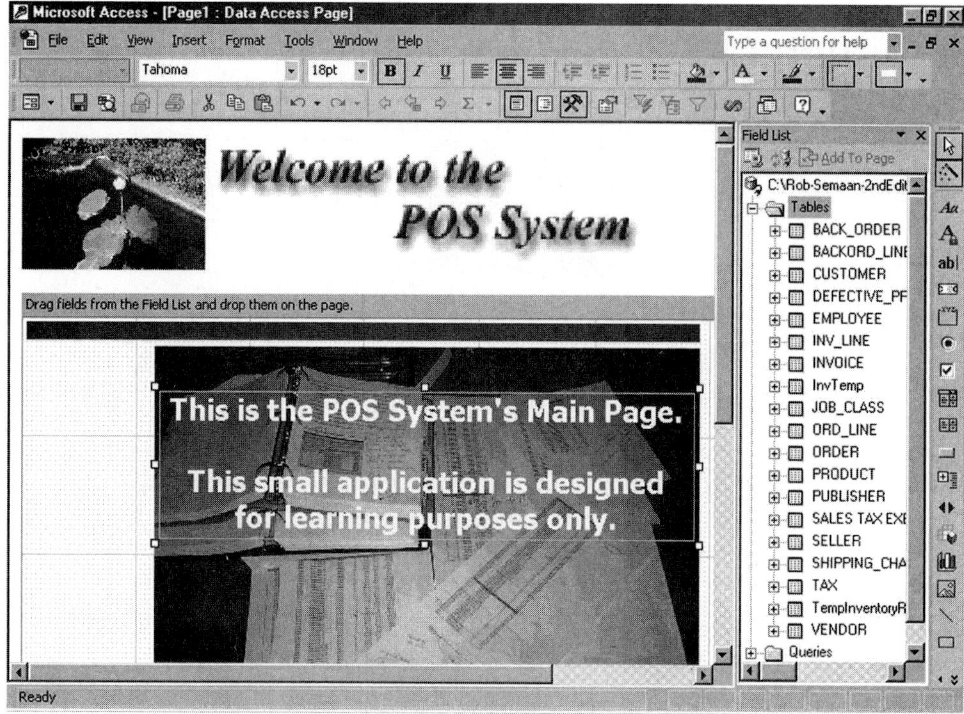

FIGURE 9.61
Inserting a Label

we want to open the CUSTOMER.htm page from the main page. Therefore, we have selected the **CUSTOMER.htm** page, located in the folder named **C:\Rob-Semaan-2ndEdition\Databases(Student)\Ch09\Ch09_POS_2nd**. In the **Text to display** field, type **Customer Information** as shown in Figure 9.63. Then select the **ScreenTip...** button to generate the **Set Hyperlink ScreenTip** dialog box and type **This link takes you to the Customer Information page**.

Finally, click **OK** on the **Set Hyperlink ScreenTip** dialog box and then click **OK** on the **Insert Hyperlink** window shown in Figure 9.63.

Save the **MainPage.htm** file again, and then position the hyperlink to the left side of the screen as shown in Figure 9.63A. (Note that the hyperlink text has also been formatted as boldfaced, left-aligned, and underlined. Look at the button bar selections along the top of the screen.)

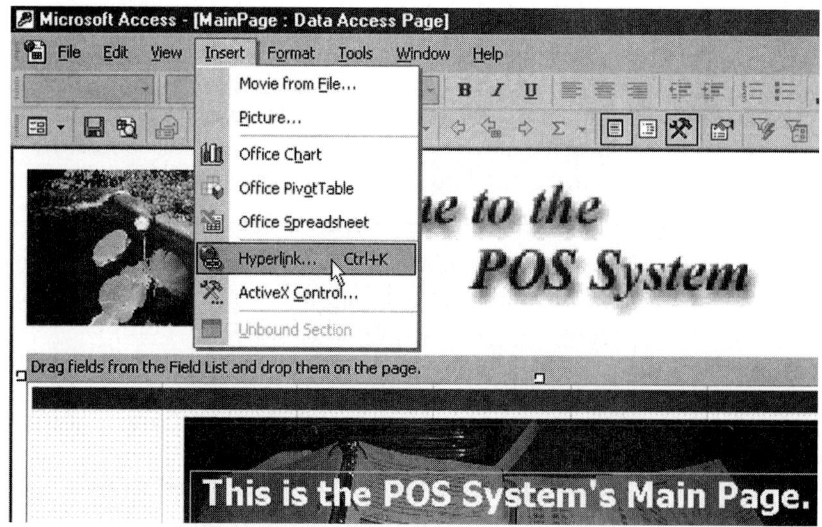

FIGURE 9.62
Inserting a Hyperlink

FIGURE 9.63
Select the Target Page and Type the Text to Be Displayed

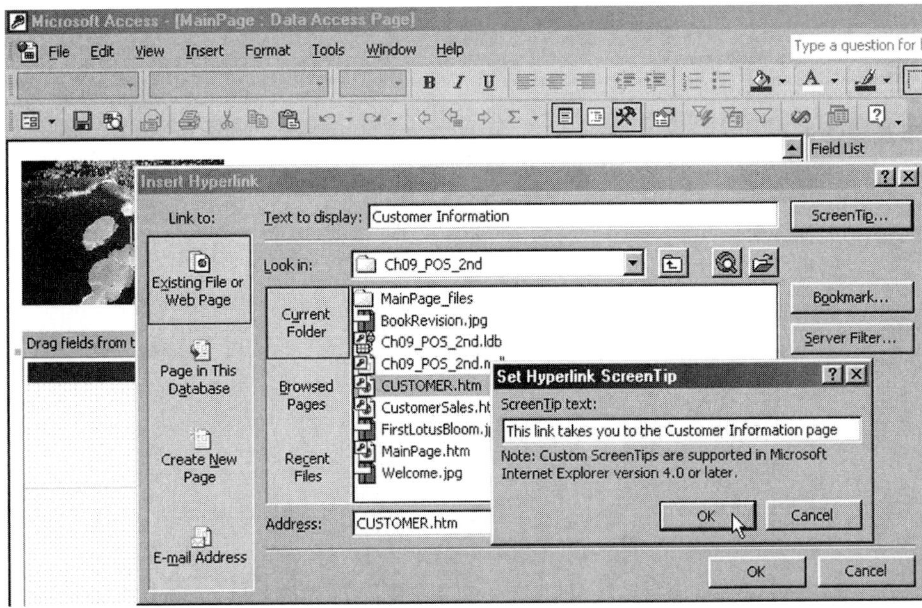

Keep in mind that you can always edit the hyperlink components. Just place the page in its design view, click on the hyperlink to select it, and then right-click to generate the drop-down menu as shown in Figure 9.64.

Select the **Edit Hyperlink...** option in the menu shown in Figure 9.64 to generate the dialog boxes in Figure 9.64A. (Note that we have generated the screen tip text in Figure 9.64A. We have not changed the text in this example, but we did want to show you that you have the option to do so.)

Screen tips are not only handy. If your Web display is publicly available—and that is a given in Web development—screen tips are actually required. The purpose of this requirement is simple: Screen tips enable other software to convert text into audio so that people with vision restrictions can use the Web displays more easily. That's why knowing HTML code is often useful; such knowledge enables you to edit the code to let you insert picture descriptions as screen text.

To create a distinct display section for the hyperlinks, use the rectangle tool in the toolbox to draw a rectangle around the hyperlink. Edit the rectangle to make

FIGURE 9.63A
The Placed and Formatted Hyperlink

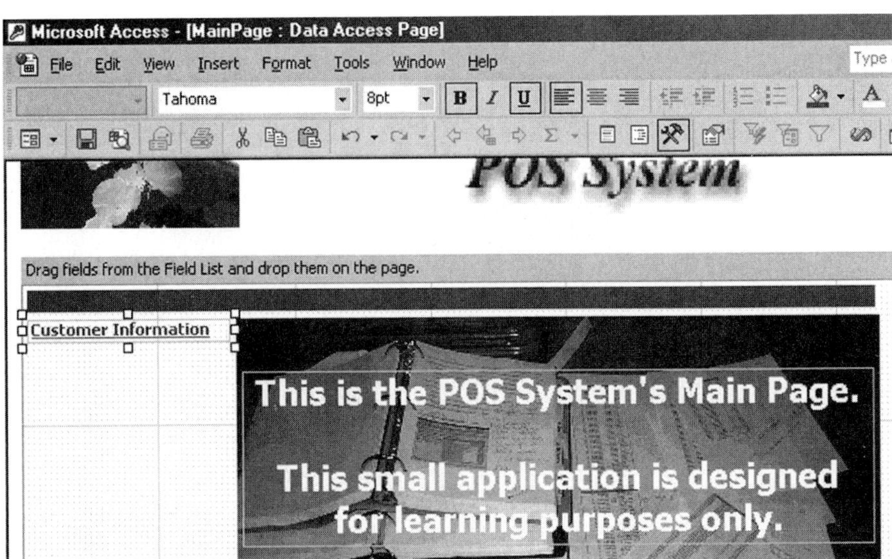

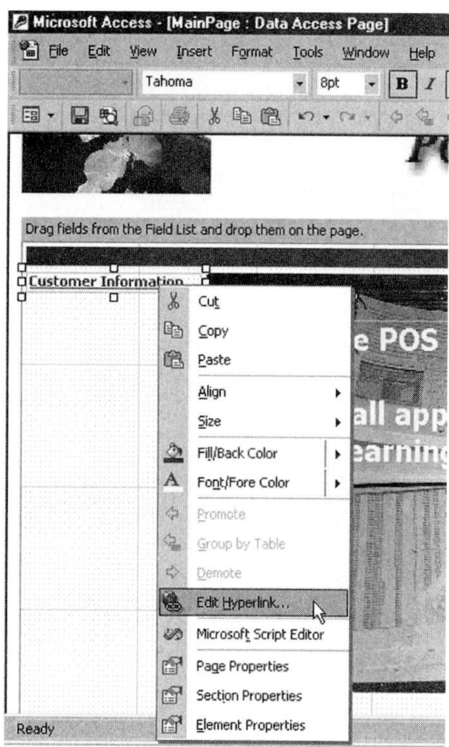

FIGURE 9.64
Select the Hyperlink Edit Option

it stand out as shown in Figure 9.65. (The **Toolbox** techniques you used in the form development in Chapter 6 still perform the same way. Note also that we have used the **Paint** button—look at the upper right corner of the screen shown in Figure 9.65—to select a line color and that we have used a line thickness setting of 2. Naturally, you can also set these properties from the rectangle's properties box.)

Save the page as **MainPage.htm** in the same folder with the other files. Open the main page in page view to see the results of the design work in Figure 9.66. (Note that the screen tip text is displayed.)

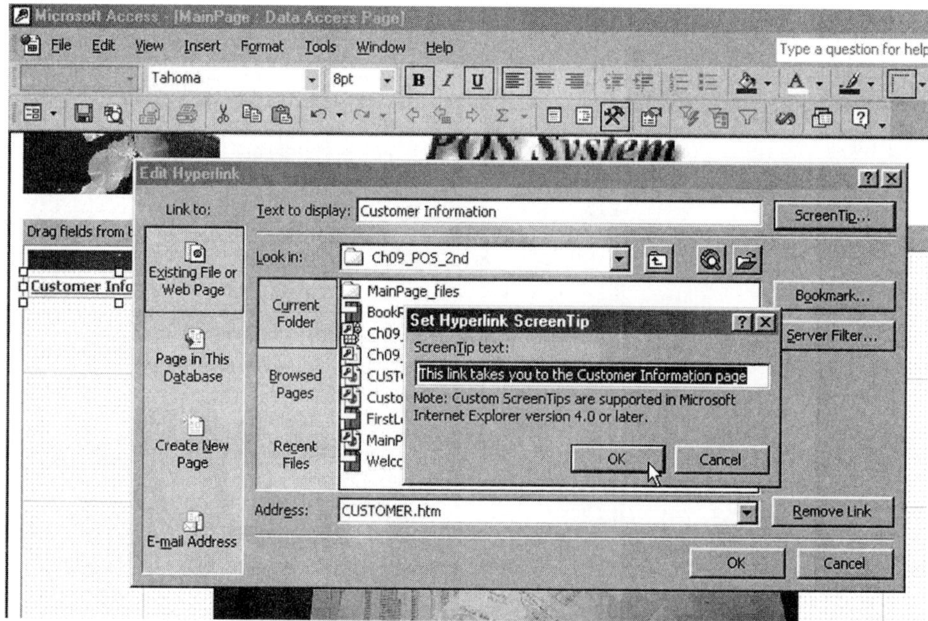

FIGURE 9.64A
The Hyperlink Edit Options

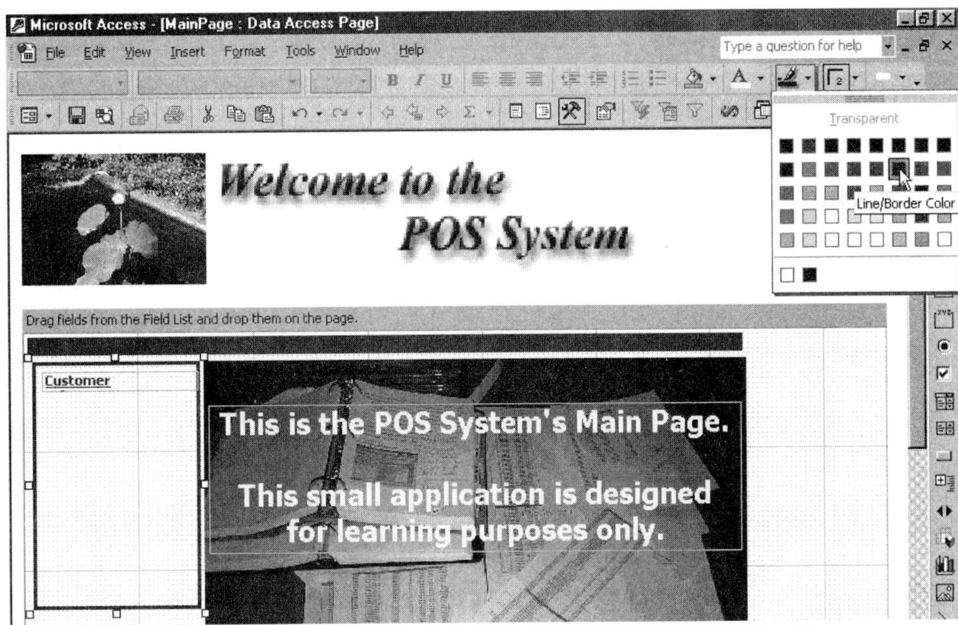

FIGURE 9.65
Delimiting the Hyperlink Segment on the Page

If you click on the hyperlink, you will see the customer page. As this point, you have a very basic system. Naturally, you should add a hyperlink on the **CUSTOMER.htm** page to select the **MainPage.htm** to complete the navigation circle. You will have the opportunity to create a more complete system in the problem section.

9.7.5 Editing the Page Components

You can still edit the links and the other page components after you have started to use the pages. For example, we showed you in the preceding section how to

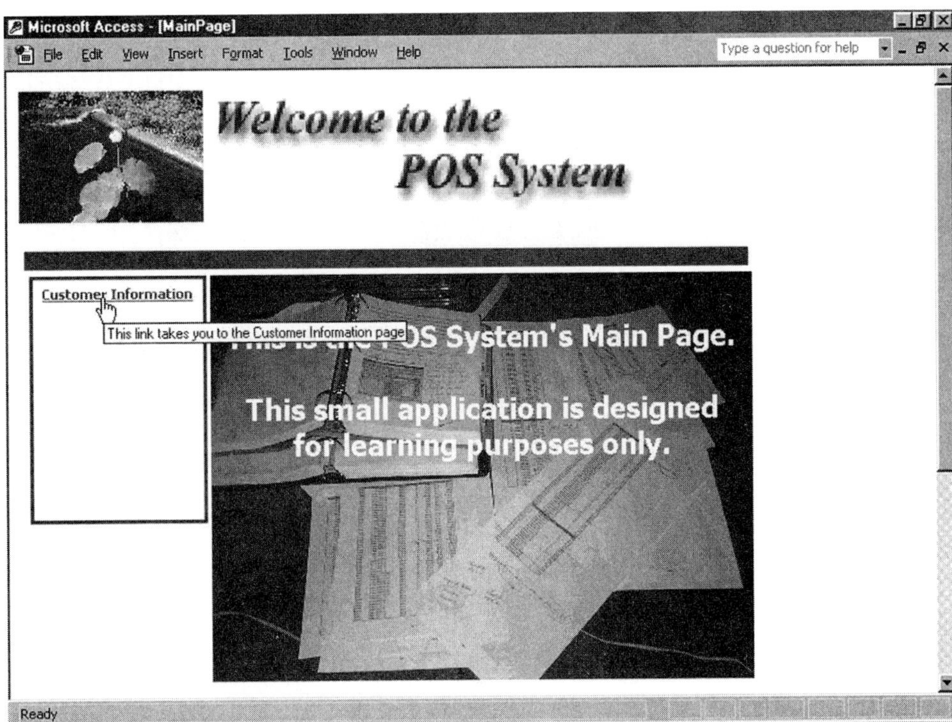

FIGURE 9.66
The Main Page in Page View

Note

Keep in mind that your computer's configuration controls the display of your pages. For example, if you do not have a local host installation, clicking on a link on any page will cause Access to try to open the page in the default browser. If you are not online, you will get an error message as shown in Figure 9.67. If you do *not* have a local host option on your computer, you must be online in order to use the link. You will see the same message if you click on a link that is not located locally. For example, if you place a link such as **www.microsoft.com** on your page, clicking on that link will produce the error message shown in Figure 9.67.

FIGURE 9.67
Unable to Open the Page

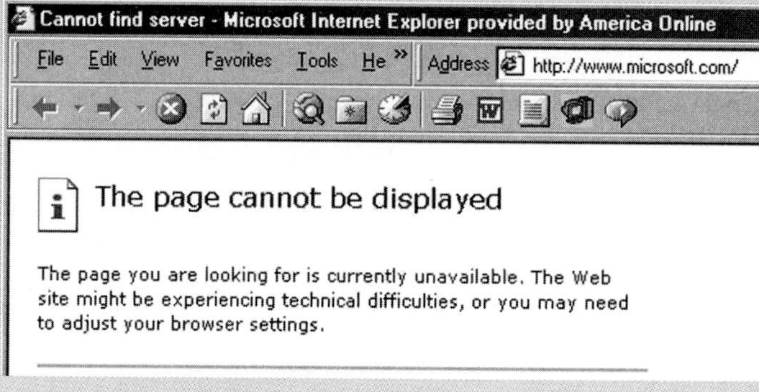

edit the hyperlinks. You can edit the other page components just as you edited the hyperlinks.

Remember how useful the properties box was when you designed and implemented forms in Chapter 6? That **Properties Box** option is still available, and it has an even greater range of choices in the page design environment. For example, if you want to change the rectangle around the hyperlinks to double-walled, you can follow this simple three-step process:

1. Place the page in its design view and select the rectangle we placed around the hyperlink.
2. Right-click on the selected rectangle to generate the drop-down menu shown in Figure 9.68 and select the **Element Properties** option.

FIGURE 9.68
Select the Element Properties

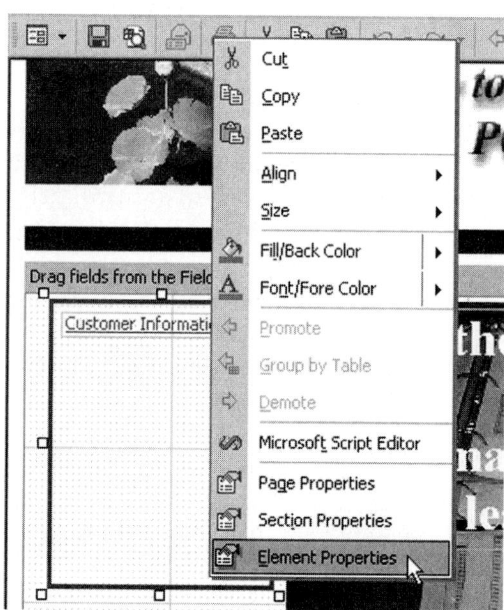

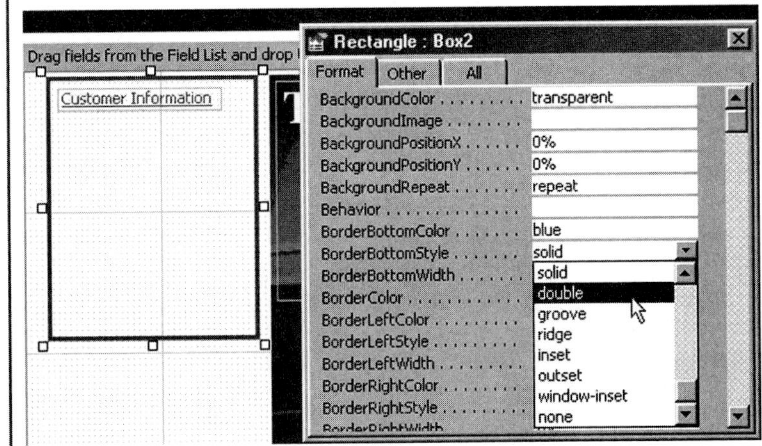

FIGURE 9.69
The Element Properties Box

3. Click on the **Element Properties** option shown in Figure 9.68 to generate the element **Properties Box** in Figure 9.69.

As you examine Figure 9.69, note that we have placed the cursor on the **BorderBottomWidth** to see its options. As you can tell, you'll have a wide choice of options from which to choose. Go ahead and cursor through the properties box to see how many options there are and what those options enable you to do.

In the preceding sequence, we edited an *element*—the rectangle—that was located in the *section* of the *page*. If you look at the menu in Figure 9.68 again, you will see that it includes options to edit the **Element Properties**, **Section Properties** and **Page Properties**. If you click on an empty spot in the page section, the menu options no longer include the element properties (see Figure 9.70).

Selecting the **Section Properties** option in Figure 9.70 will produce the properties box shown in Figure 9.71. Note that the properties box gives you the opportunity to control what the selected page section will look like. For example, if you click on the **BackgroundColor** option's builder button in Figure 9.71's properties box, you will see the color options shown in Figure 9.72

As you can tell by looking at the color options in Figure 9.72, you can even define your own custom colors. We selected the gray (silver) background color in Figure 9.72 to change the page's appearance to the display in Figure 9.73.

Finally, check the **Page Properties** option in the menu shown in Figure 9.70 and set the entire page's background to gray. Open the page and check the results. Go ahead and try various page and section options, then reset the page and section properties to their original configuration.

The **MainPage** menu does not have a *database* data source, so its page properties box does not show a **ConnectionFile** entry in Figure 9.74. However, it does have a **ConnectionString** entry that must match the location of the folder in which the **MainPage** is located.

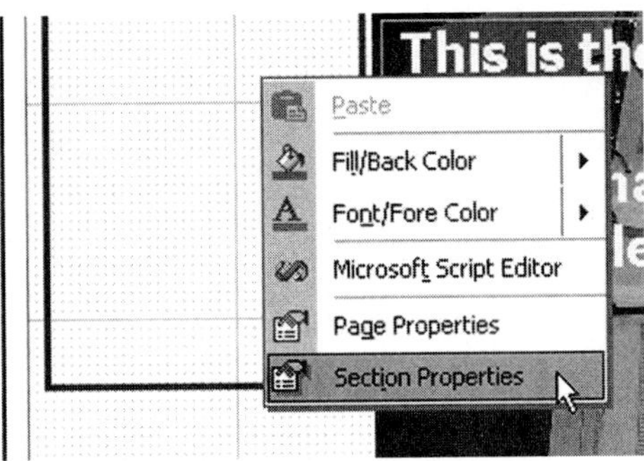

FIGURE 9.70
The Section Edit Options

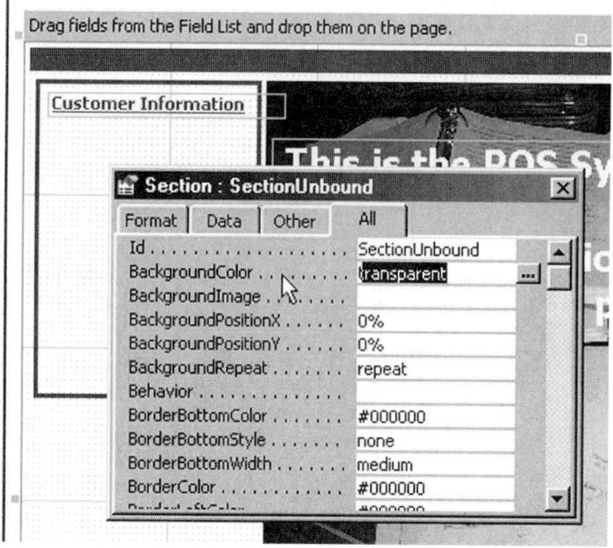

FIGURE 9.71
The Section Properties Box

Although the **MainPage** file does not have a data source in the *database* sense of the word, its *location* must be defined in terms of its location in a specific folder. Therefore, the *location* data source is the string you see after the **Data Source**= entry in Figure 9.74. If this location data source entry does not match the actual location of the **MainPage** file, opening the menu in its **Page View** format will yield an error message about improper data access. That's why moving the files in this environment can create quite a few errors. You will discover in section 9.9 what kinds of error messages will be generated and how you can correct such errors.

9.8 USING THE DATA ACCESS PAGES ONLINE

To use the data access pages online, you must first place your small system on a server. If you are a student, your college or university may let you use its server for educational purposes. If you are learning the material in this text as part of corporate training, your company may have a dedicated server available for educational purposes. If you are learning this material on your own, you can find (very limited!) server space at numerous commercial outlets, often even free of

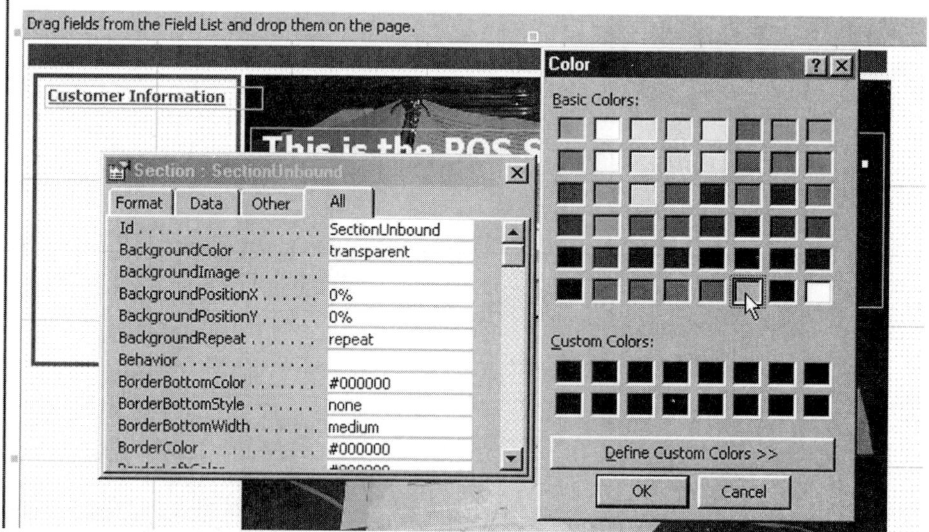

FIGURE 9.72
The Section Background Color Options

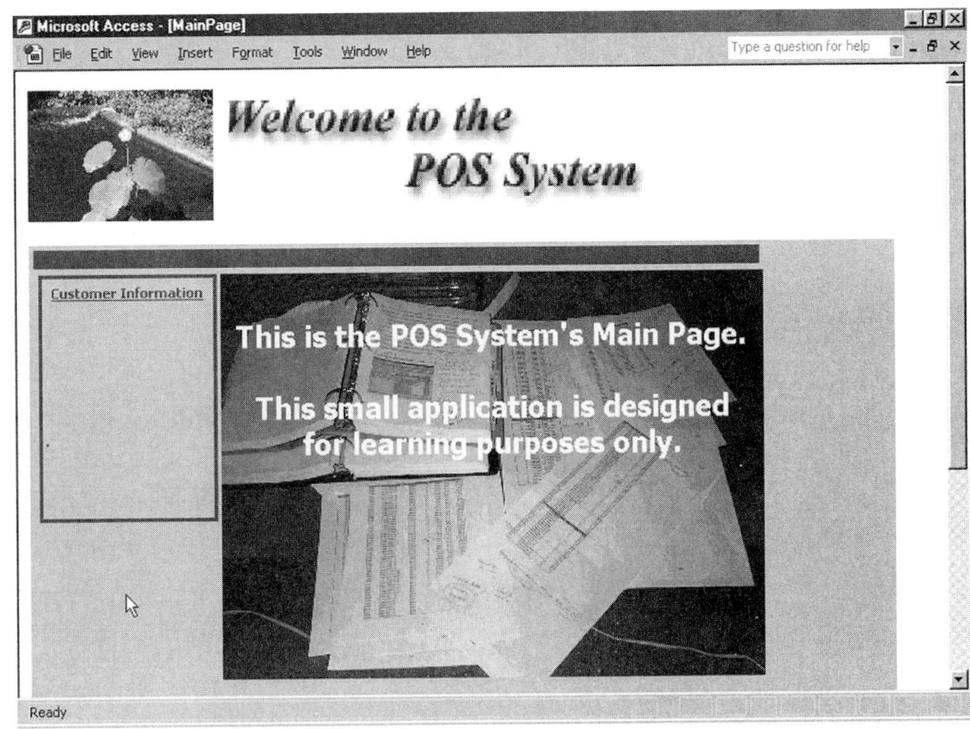

FIGURE 9.73
The Changed Page Section Background Color

charge. In any case, the server must support this Microsoft Access package. (The page format developed in Access 2002 is not universally compatible with other page formats.)

Once your small system is located on a server that supports your system's software requirements, you can access it as you would any website. That is, first get connected and then type your Web address in the browser address line. For example, if your work is located on a geocities server, you might type **www.geocities.com/mysystem/mainpage.htm** to see your work online. Naturally, you must know the server access path to your application in order to avoid the error messages we will examine in detail in section 9.9.

9.9 SYSTEM COMPONENT ORGANIZATION

To make the Web application work properly, all of its components must be available. Although you can place the components in different folders, such a decision will often make it difficult to control the application actions easily. *Therefore, we urge you to keep all of the components of your Web-based system in the same folder.* That is, to make the application system's management as simple as possible, with the least likelihood of errors, keep the database and the pages you developed

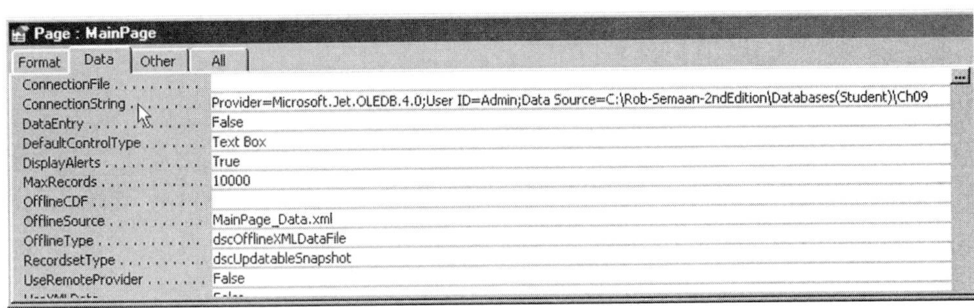

FIGURE 9.74
The Main Page Connection String

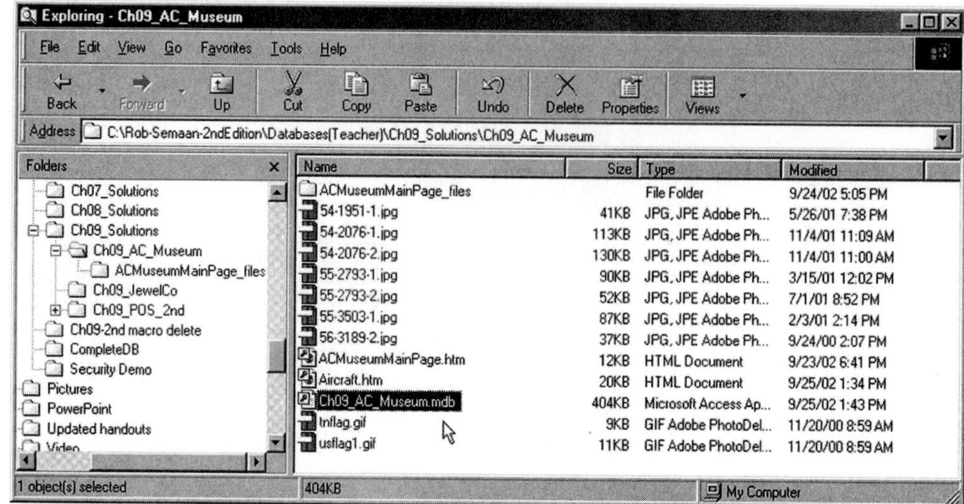

FIGURE 9.75
The Aircraft Museum Main Application Components

within that database, the corresponding page .htm files, and the components used by those files—such as .jpg files—in the same folder. Note, for example, the components located in the Figure 9.75. (This is a small system that you will create in problems 9.5 and 9.6. We will use the path to the database Web applications in the **Address** line shown in Figure 9.75 for illustration purposes. Naturally, you should substitute your own application path in the **Address** line if you want to trace the process explored in this section.)

As you examine Figure 9.75, note that this location contains

1. The database, **Ch09_AC_Museum.mdb**.
2. The .htm files that correspond to the main menu (**ACMuseumMainPage.htm**) and the single page (**Aircraft.htm**) called from that main menu.
3. All the image files used by the database application (the .jpg and .gif files)
4. A folder created and named by Access when the menu page is created in the database. (This folder is shown as the **ACMuseumMainPage_files** folder. This folder—shown in Figure 9.75 as the **ACMuseumMainPage_files** folder—contains the filelist.xml file shown on the Notepad page shown in Figure 9.76. The **ACMuseumMainPage_files** folder also contains all the image objects that were used by the database applications.

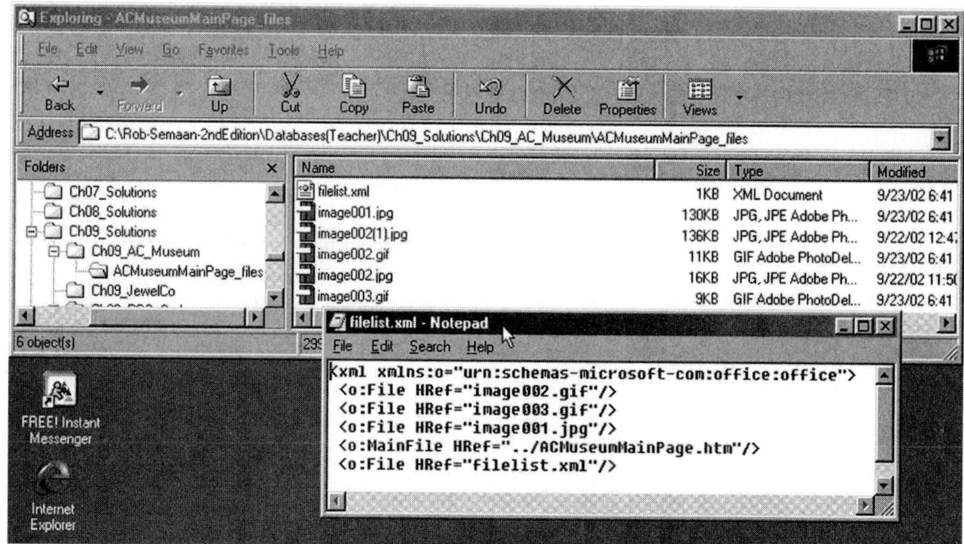

FIGURE 9.76
The Contents of the ACMuseumMainPage_files Folder

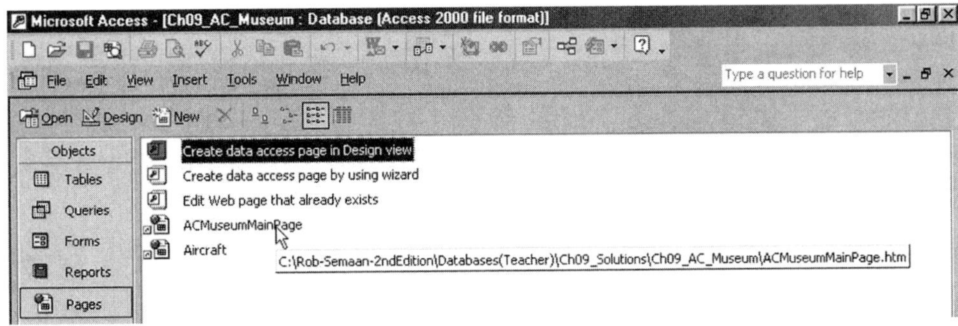

FIGURE 9.77
The Access Pages in the Database

If you open the **Ch09_AC_Museum.mdb** database shown in Figure 9.76, you will see the page contents in Figure 9.77. (Note that the two pages in the database are reflected in the two .htm files in Figure 9.77.)

9.10 COMMON ERRORS AND THEIR CORRECTIONS

Keep the pages in the database in the same folder as the .htm pages and vice versa. (If you examine Figure 9.77 again you will see that the path for the **AC MuseumMainPage** matches the location of the **ACMuseumMainPage.htm** file.)

If you move the database to a different folder, all of the components of that database—the database itself with all of its pages, the matching .html pages, the main page window, and all objects used by the database or any of its Web components—must be available to that database. Therefore, all the links and all of the connection strings must be edited to point to the correct objects in their correct locations. Even renaming an object, such as a page, also requires the same extensive editing for that object and for any link associated with that object. In short, we strongly recommend that you minimize location and object naming changes after you have created the Web version of the database.

Unfortunately, external requirements may force you to make occasional changes. For example, end users may request a different location for your applications, or you may have to make changes for application development reasons. If you must make changes, this section is written for you to show you what common errors can be expected and how you can correct those errors. Naturally, our list of corrections cannot be exhaustive. However, if you understand what caused these errors and what corrected those errors, you are likely to be able to think through errors that we have not anticipated in this book.

9.10.1 Correcting HTML File Link Errors

If the locations of the Access page and the corresponding .htm file are different, trying to open page in the database will generate the link error message shown in Figure 9.78. (To produce this error, we first placed the .htm file for the **ACMuseumMainPage** main menu in a different location to make sure that the path would not yield the required file.)

To fix the error indicated in Figure 9.78, click on the **Update link...** option to reset the path. This action will produce Figure 9.79. Select the proper access path through the **Look in:** list as shown in Figure 9.79. (Just keep clicking until you have found the **ACMuseumMainPage.htm** file at the end of the access path **C:\Rob-Semaan-2ndEdition\Databases(Teacher)\Ch09_Solutions\Ch09_AC_Museum**.)

After you have clicked through the proper path selection, select the proper .htm file—in this case, the **ACMuseumMainPage.htm** file—and click **OK**. As soon as you have accomplished that task, the main menu will properly open in its page view.

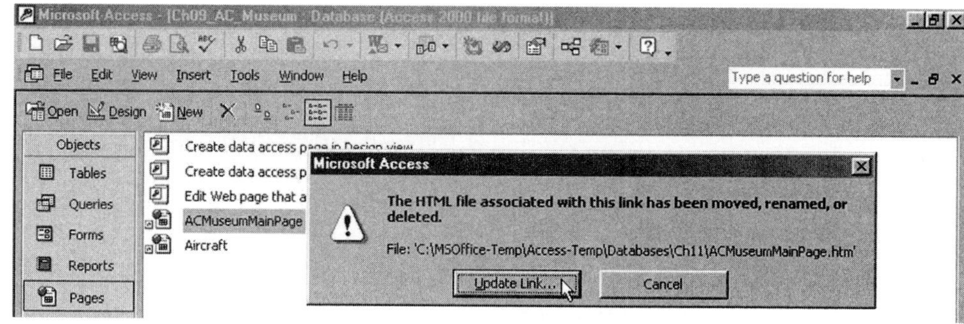

FIGURE 9.78
The HTML File Link Error Message

You can always double-check the page properties if you want to make sure that the correct path has been defined. Just right-click on the page filename to generate the menu shown in Figure 9.80 and click on that menu's **Properties** option.

If you double-click on the **Properties** option shown in Figure 9.80, you will see the dialog box in Figure 9.81.

9.10.2 Correcting Data Access Path Errors

The main menu did not use any data from the database. However, the page—Aircraft—called from that main menu is based on a query in the AC_Museum database. If that database is not located in the same directory or the path to it is improperly defined, you will see the error message in Figure 9.82.

As you examine Figure 9.82, note that the path reads **C:\MSOffice\Access\Databases\Ch11\Ch11_AC_Museum.mdb** rather than the correct path **C:\Rob-Semaan-2ndEdition\Databases(Teacher)\Ch09_Solutions\Ch09_AC_Museum**. If you click the **OK** button on the message box in Figure 9.82, the page will open, but none of the data components will be shown. (Note that the portion of the page shown in Figure 9.83 only indicates **#Name?** where data ought to be displayed.)

To correct the error in the data location for the page, close the page and return to the page window, then right-click on the page name to generate the menu from which you then select the **Properties** option to produce the dialog box in Figure 9.84.

Click on the builder button—note the cursor location in Figure 9.84—to redefine the path through the window in Figure 9.85.

After you have made sure that the entire path is correct, click **OK** in Figure 9.85 to generate Figure 9.86.

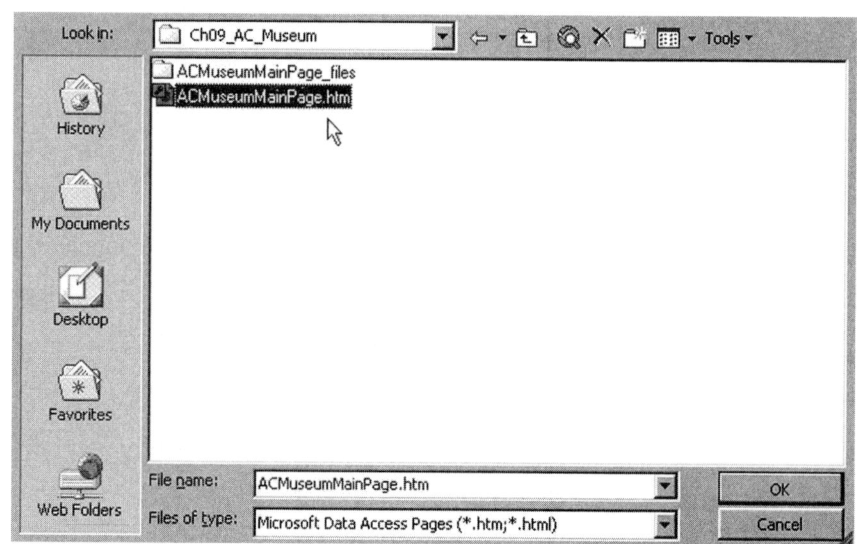

FIGURE 9.79
Defining the Correct Path to the HTM File

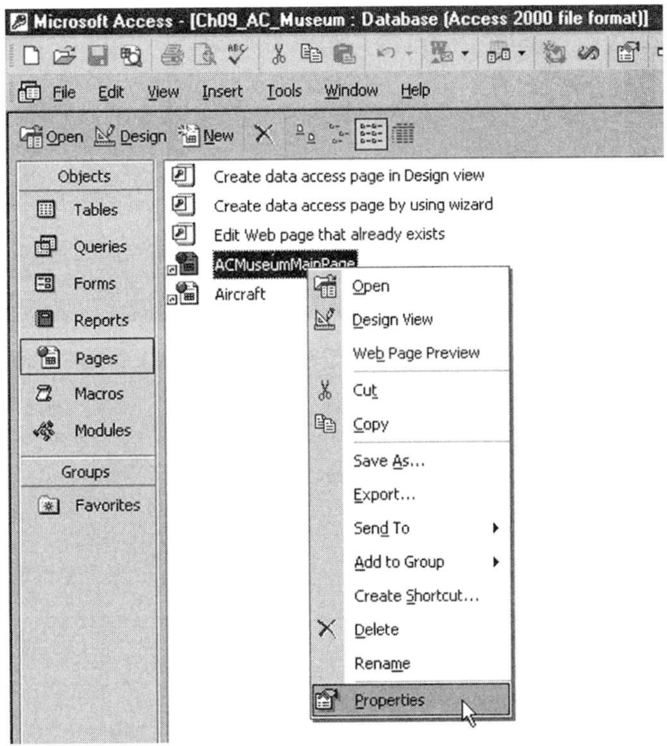

FIGURE 9.80
Select the Access Page Properties Box Option

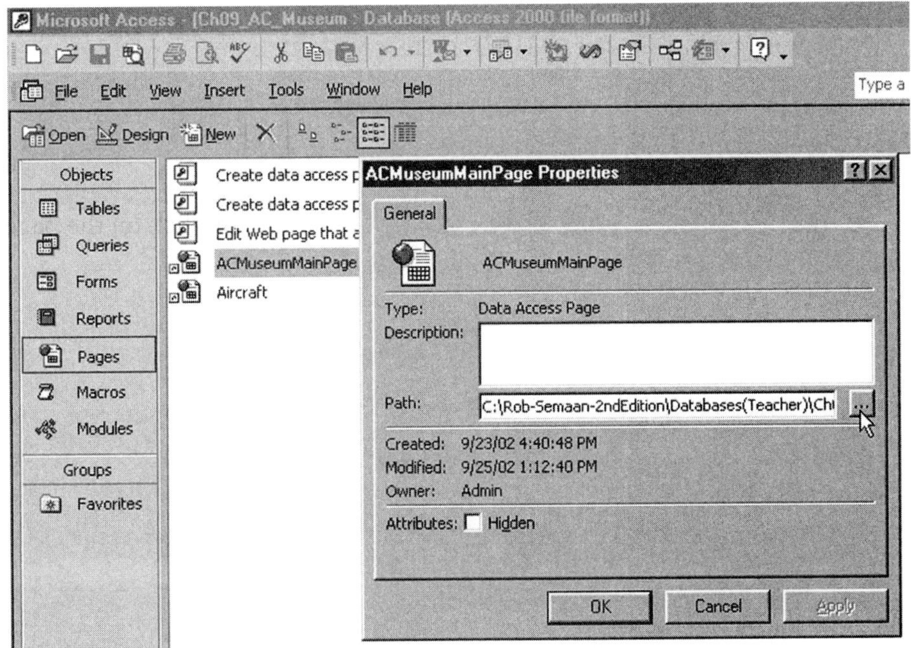

FIGURE 9.81
The Path in the Page Properties Option

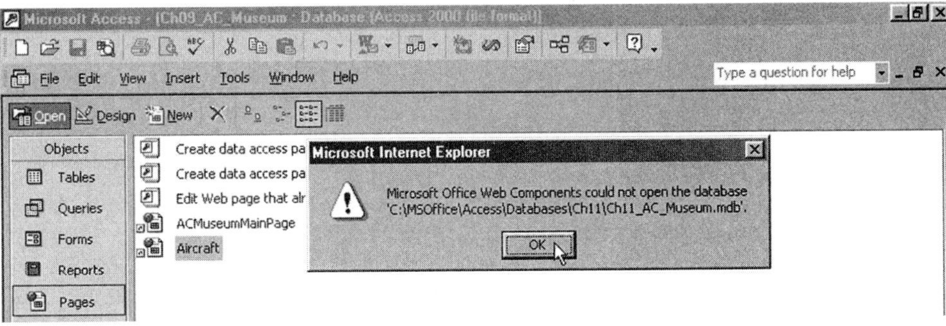

FIGURE 9.82
The Data Access Path Error

Note

If you have created all the page components discussed in the preceding sections and placed those components in a different folder, use that folder as your source, rather than the **C:\Rob-Semaan-2ndEdition\Databases(Teacher)\Ch09_Solutions\Ch09_AC_Museum** folder shown here. Instructors have access to the completed pages in the designated folder.

FIGURE 9.83
The Page without Data

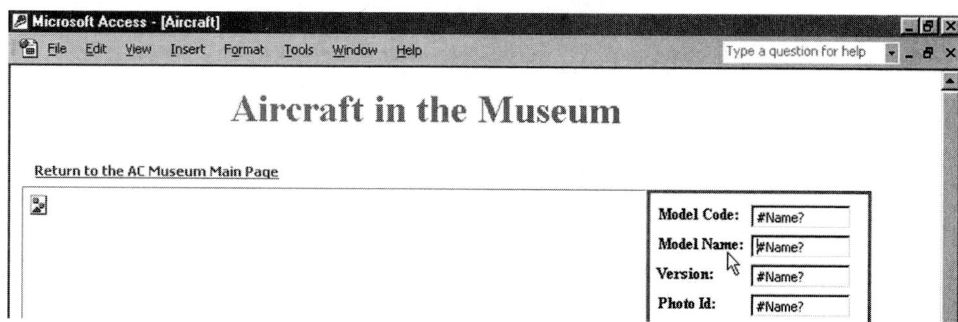

Click **Apply,** and then click **OK** to define the proper data access path. If you open the page again, you will see that it contains the appropriate data.

9.10.3 Correcting Connection String Errors

To illustrate set-up connection string errors, let's use the **Ch09_POS_2nd.mdb** database. The path to that database is defined by the string **C:\Rob-Semaan-2ndEdition\Databases(Teacher)\Ch09_Solutions\Ch09_POS_2nd.mdb.** (It is worth repeating that we have used the path shown here for illustration purposes. If your **Ch09_POS_2nd.mdb** database is located in a different folder, change the path shown here to match the one to your folder!) If the database—or any object within that database—is actually located in a different folder, the path to that database or its objects will be incorrect. The first indication of this problem is the error message displayed in Figure 9.87.

Click **OK** on the error message shown in Figure 9.87, and then open the page—in this case, the Customer Sales page—in its design view and right-click to pro-

FIGURE 9.84
Defining the Proper Path to the Page Data

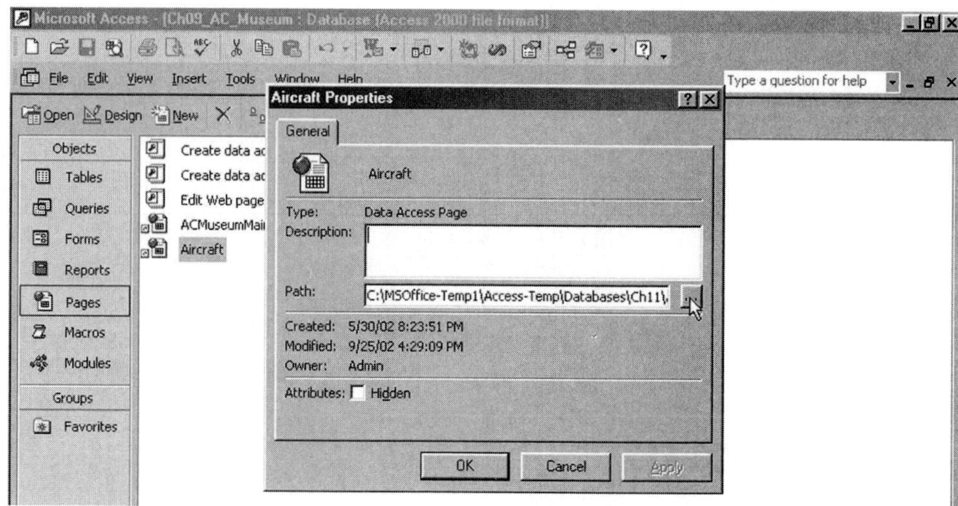

Note

Even if the file shown in Figure 9.85 *looks* correct, *go all the way back to the root and click through the entire path.* The window in Figure 9.85 does not show the entire path, and some components of that path may have been incorrect.

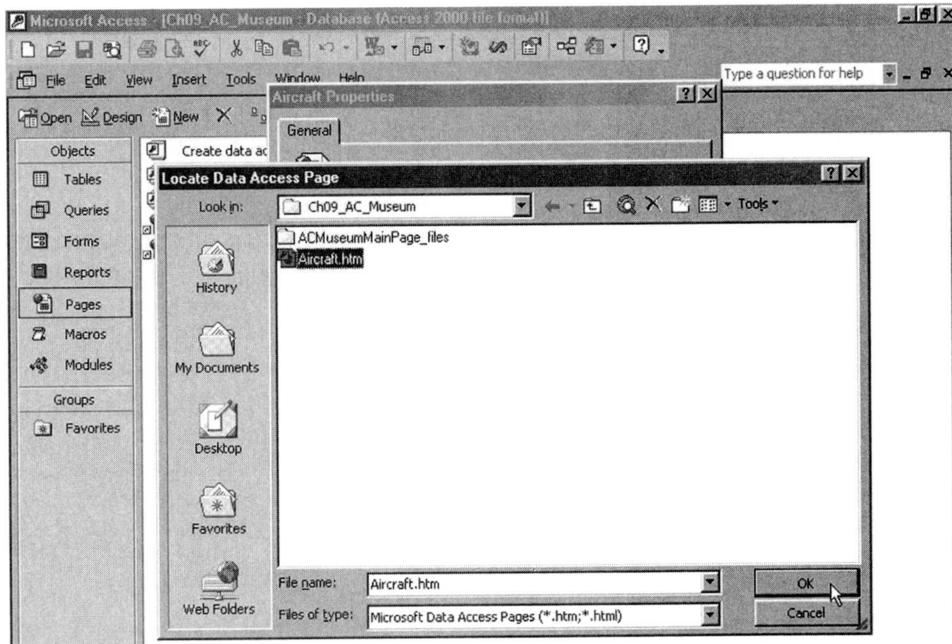

FIGURE 9.85
The Path Selection Window

duce the properties shown in Figure 9.88. (Make sure that you select the *page* level properties and that you select the **Data** tab to locate the **ConnectionString**.)

Click on the **ConnectionString Builder** button—the button with the three dots on it—to generate the **Data Link Properties** dialog box in Figure 9.89.

Clicking on the builder button in the **Connection** tab in the **Data Link Properties** shown in Figure 9.89 produces the window in Figure 9.90. Select the **Look**

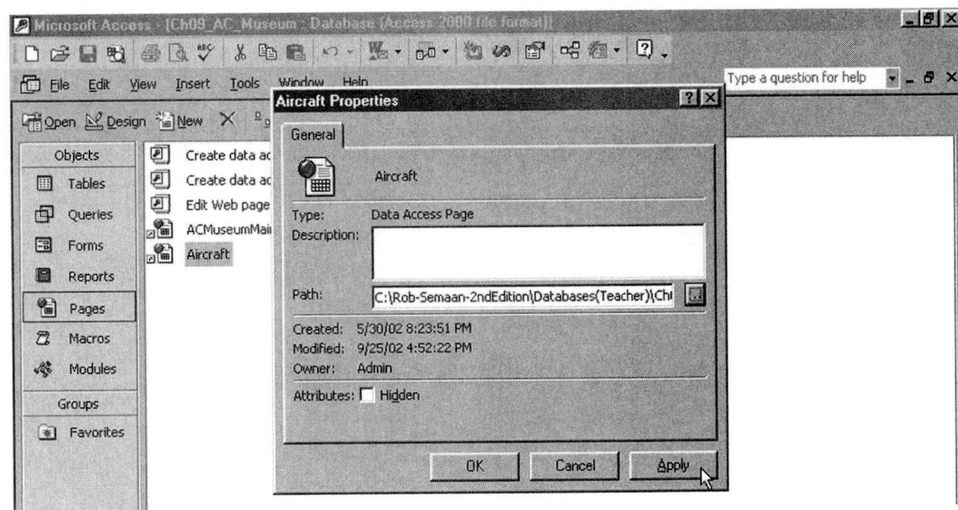

FIGURE 9.86
The Aircraft Data Access Path Selection

FIGURE 9.87
An Indication of a Connection String Error

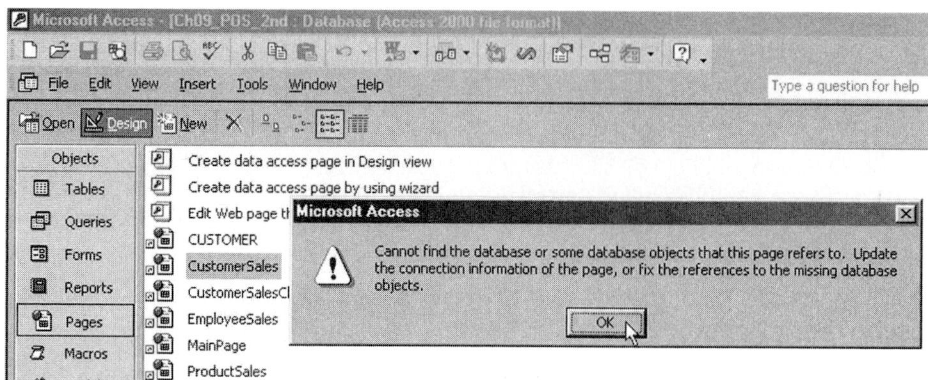

in: drop-down menu in Figure 9.90 to locate the correct database location. (In this case, the correct folder is the **Ch09_POS_2nd** folder.)

After selecting the **Ch09_POS_2nd** folder in Figure 9.90, double-click on the **Ch09_POS_2nd.mdb** database to insert it into the connection string. (See Figure 9.91. Do *not* use the **Open** button.)

Finally, close the properties box, save the page again to preserve the correction you have just made, and open the page in **Page View** mode. The page will now open correctly.

9.10.4 Correcting Hyperlink Failures

If you move the applications to another folder, you will discover that none of the hyperlinks that let you navigate from page to page will work anymore. To generate the error in this section, we set the hyperlink to a database that was not located in the path we had defined for it in the hyperlink. To see the effect of such

FIGURE 9.88
The Page Level Connection String

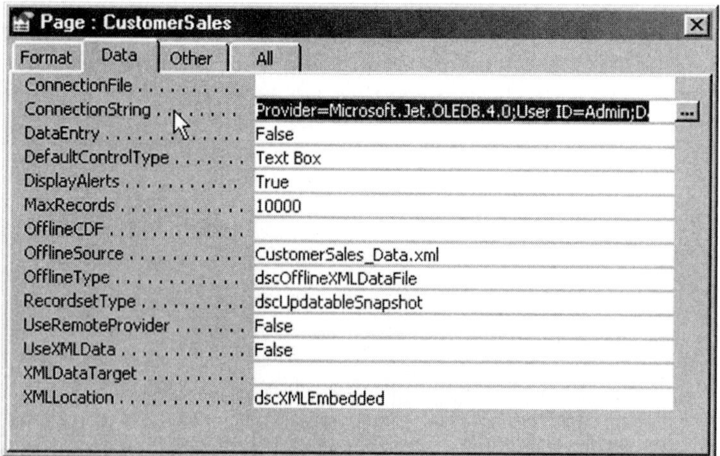

FIGURE 9.89
The Data Link Properties Dialog Box

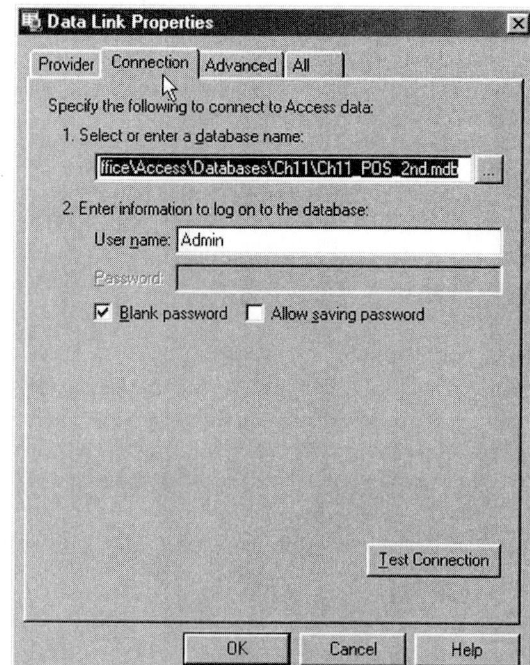

Note

Even if the file shown in Figure 9.90 *looks* correct, *go all the way back to the root and click through the entire path to reselect the* **Ch09_POS_2nd** folder. When the window in Figure 9.90 is first opened, it does not show the entire path, and some components of that path may have been incorrect. (The path shown in Figure 9.90 indicates that we clicked through the entire path.)

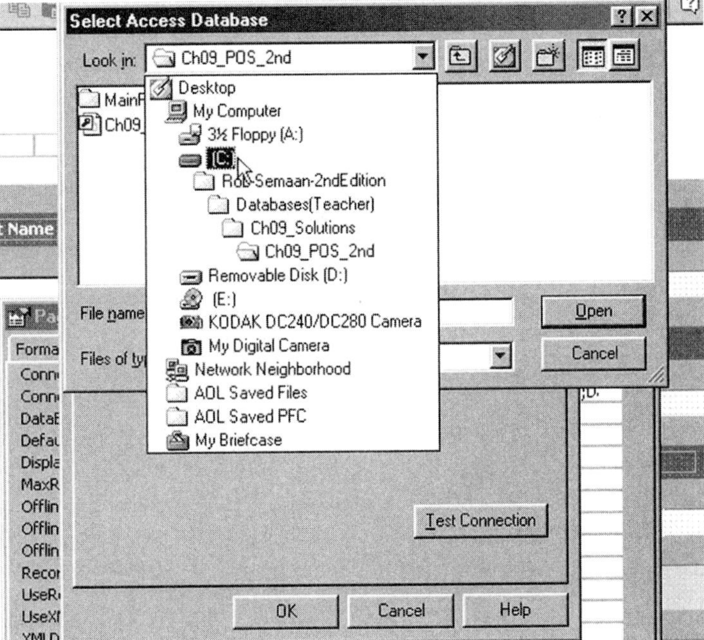

FIGURE 9.90
Finding the Correct Database Folder

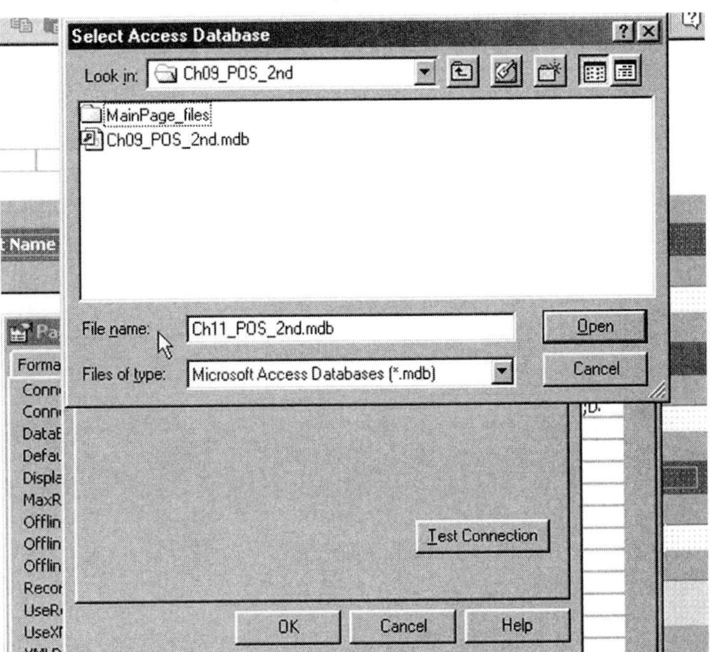

FIGURE 9.91
Selecting the Database for the Connection String

FIGURE 9.92
The Hyperlink to Nowhere

FIGURE 9.93
The Incorrect Path to the Aircraft Page

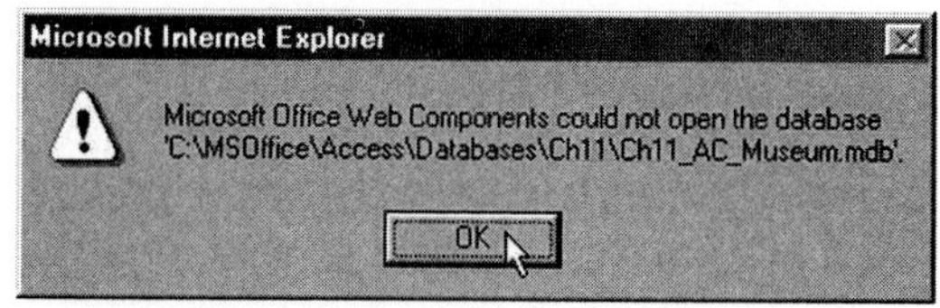

an error, let's start by selecting the **Aircraft in the Museum** hyperlink to the **Aircraft** page (see Figure 9.92).

When we clicked on the hyperlink shown in Figure 9.92, the error message box in Figure 9.93 was generated. Note that the path in the message box and the path in the Address window do not match the expected path, which is **C:\Rob-Semaan-2ndEdition\Databases(Teacher)\Ch09_Solutions\Ch09_AC_Museum\Aircraft.htm**.

Clicking **OK** on the message box in Figure 9.93 produces the Aircraft page generated by the **Aircraft.htm** code in Figure 9.94, but this page does not display the expected data. (Note the **#Name?** labels that are shown in the text boxes, indicating unknown fields.)

To correct this error, open the page in its Design format and select the hyperlink. Right-click on the selected hyperlink to generate the **Edit Hyperlink...** option shown in the menu in Figure 9.95. This action will produce the screen shown in Figure 9.96.

FIGURE 9. 94
Unknown Attribute Values

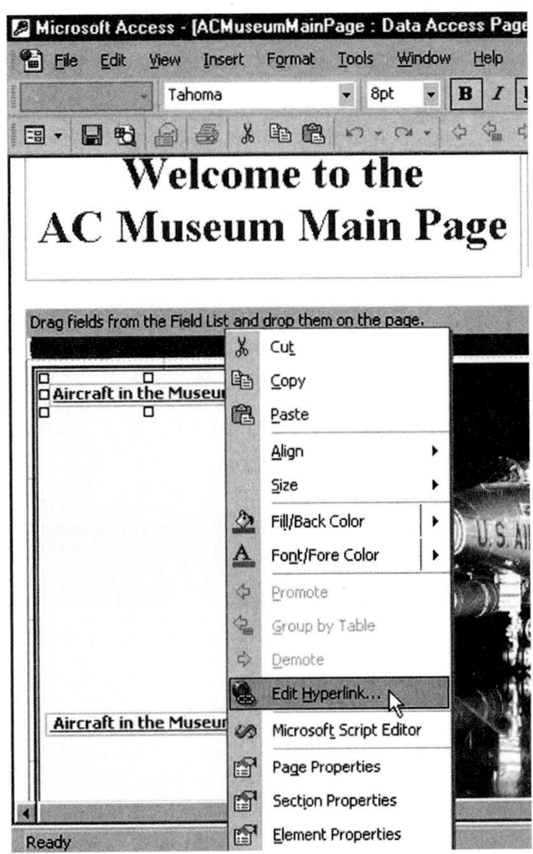

FIGURE 9.95
Select the Edit Hyperlink Option

Select the **Look in:** option in the **Edit Hyperlink** window in Figure 9.96 to select the proper path. (Only the last subfolder in the path is shown.) Note that we have selected the **Aircraft.htm** file to complete the correct path. As soon as you click the **OK** button on the window in Figure 9.96, the page will open with the correct data displayed on the screen.

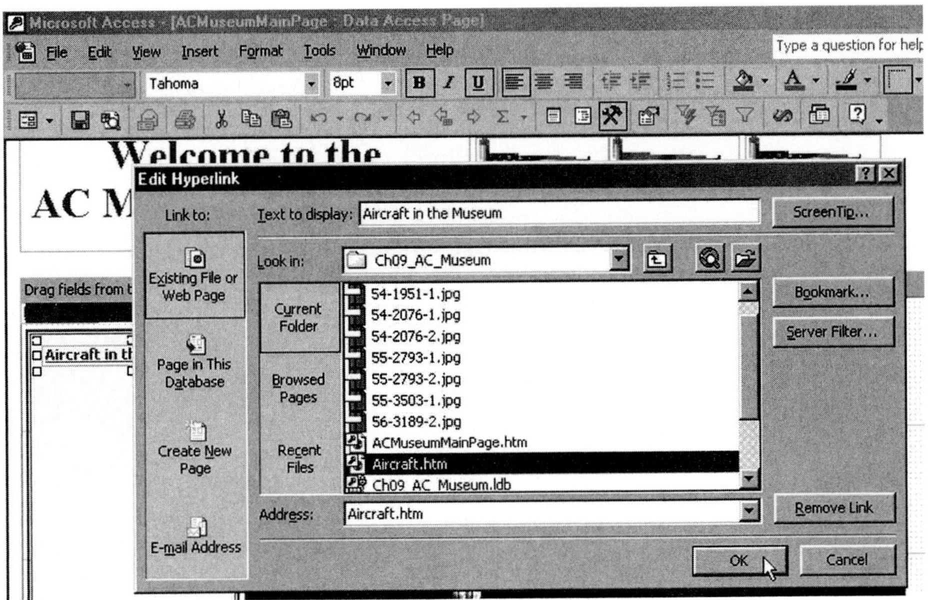

FIGURE 9.96
Find the Correct Hyperlink Path

FIGURE 9.97
Hyperlink Path Confirmation

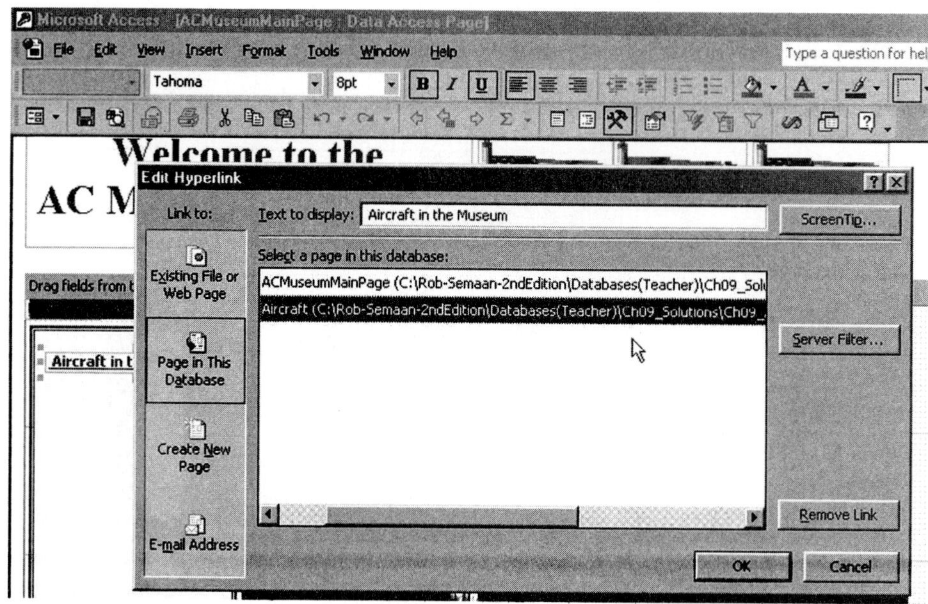

You can always right-click on a hyperlink—in the page design view, of course!—and use the **Edit Hyperlink** option to confirm the path. Note that Figure 9.97 shows the correct path, and the window is different from the one that showed up when the path was incorrect.

Please remember that you must edit all the hyperlinks in an application if you have moved any of the folders. Therefore, moving folders or changing the applications to a different drive will create quite a bit of work for you.

Problems

Problems 9.1 through 9.7 are based on the **Ch09_POS_2nd.mdb** database located on your student CD. Remember to uncheck the **Read-only** property after you copy this database from your CD to your computer.

9.1 Modify the main page to give it access to all of the pages developed in this chapter. That is,

- Insert a hyperlink to the **CUSTOMER.htm** page and name it **Customer Information.**
- Insert a hyperlink to the **CustomerSales.htm** page and name it **Customer Sales.**
- Insert a hyperlink to the **CustomerSalesChart.htm** page and name it **Customer Sales Chart.**
- Insert a hyperlink to the **EmployeeSales.htm** page and name it **Employee Sales.**
- Insert a hyperlink to the **ProductSales.htm** page and name it **Product Sales.**

Make sure that you have placed the appropriate hyperlink screen tips on each of the hyperlinks! Also, modify the rectangle around the hyperlinks to a double-walled format. The main page should look like Figure P9.1 when you are done. (Note that we have placed the cursor on the **Product Sales** hyperlink and that the screen tip shows up as expected.)

FIGURE P9.1
The Main Page after the Modifications

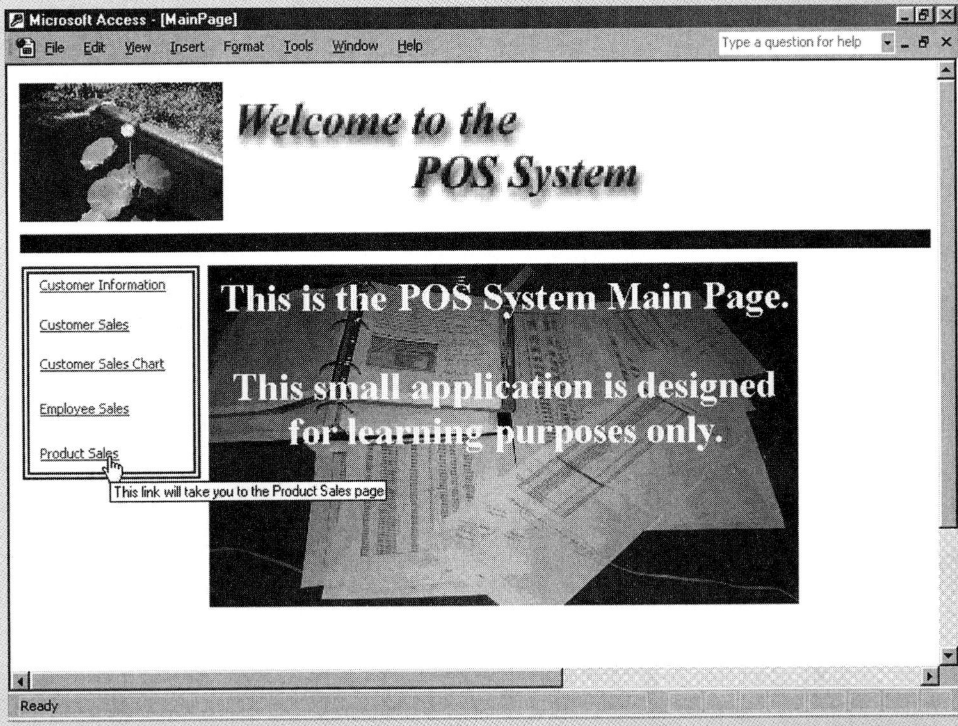

9.2 Modify the **CUSTOMER.htm** page to create links to all the pages in your system. When you are done, your page should look like Figure P9.2.

FIGURE P9.2
The Modified CUSTOMER.htm Page

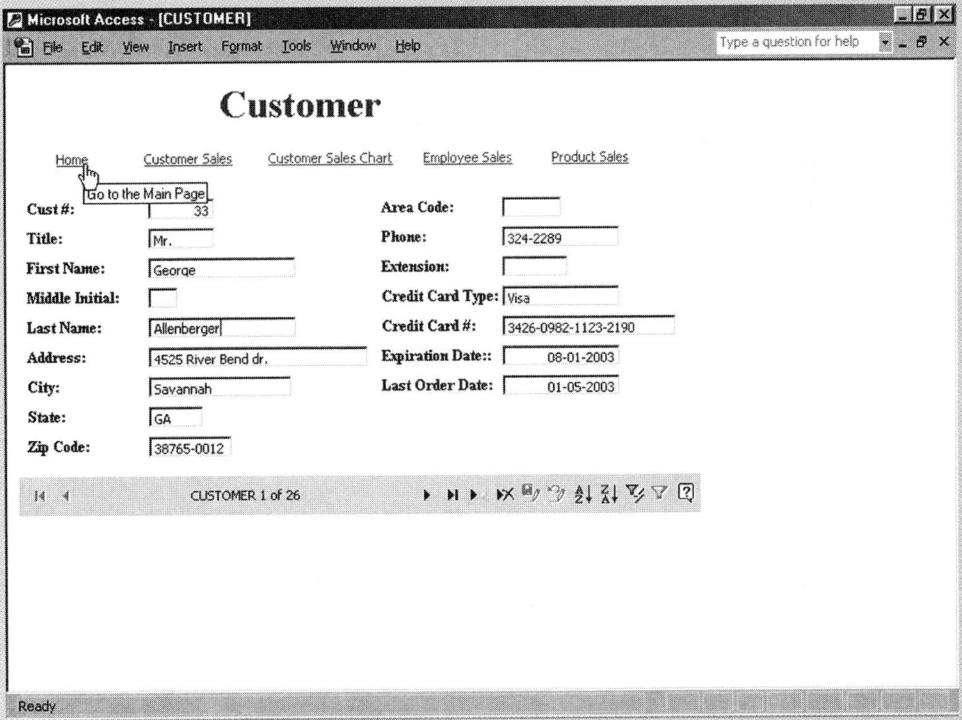

Microsoft Access - [CUSTOMER]
File Edit View Insert Format Tools Window Help
Type a question for help
Customer
Home Customer Sales Customer Sales Chart Employee Sales Product Sales
Go to the Main Page
Cust #: 33
Title: Mr.
First Name: George
Middle Initial:
Last Name: Allenberger
Address: 4525 River Bend dr.
City: Savannah
State: GA
Zip Code: 38765-0012
Area Code:
Phone: 324-2289
Extension:
Credit Card Type: Visa
Credit Card #: 3426-0982-1123-2190
Expiration Date:: 08-01-2003
Last Order Date: 01-05-2003
CUSTOMER 1 of 26
Ready

9.3 Modify each of the remaining pages that are accessed through the main page—see Figure P9.1—to place the links on them that allow you to navigate to all of the other pages. (One of those modified pages is shown in Figure P9.3.)

FIGURE P9.3
The Modified Employee Sales Page

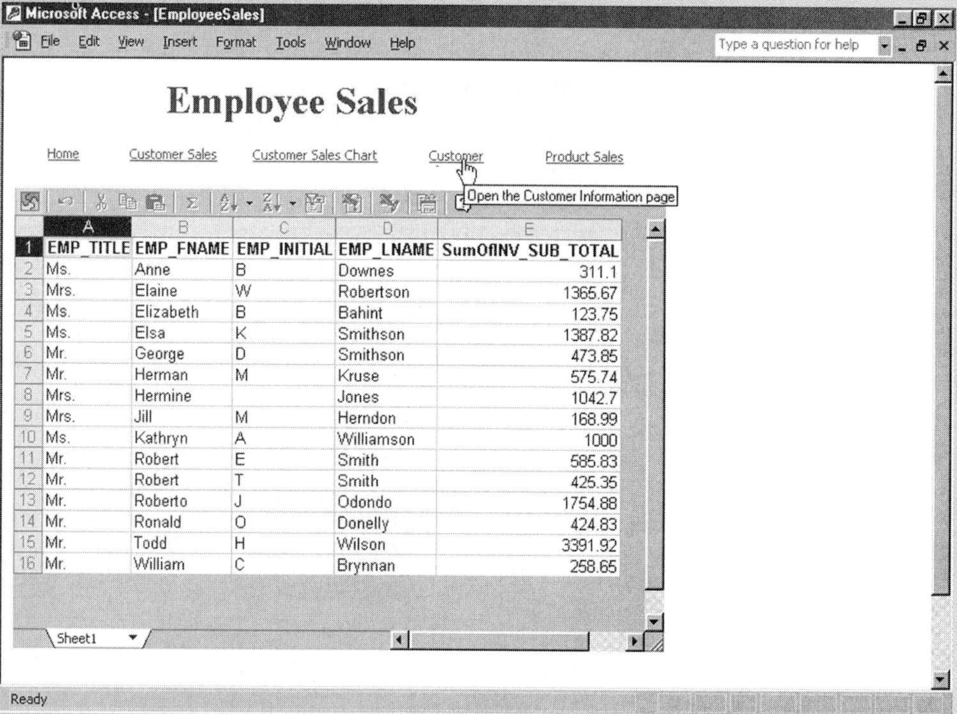

	A	B	C	D	E
1	EMP_TITLE	EMP_FNAME	EMP_INITIAL	EMP_LNAME	SumOfINV_SUB_TOTAL
2	Ms.	Anne	B	Downes	311.1
3	Mrs.	Elaine	W	Robertson	1365.67
4	Ms.	Elizabeth	B	Bahint	123.75
5	Ms.	Elsa	K	Smithson	1387.82
6	Mr.	George	D	Smithson	473.85
7	Mr.	Herman	M	Kruse	575.74
8	Mrs.	Hermine		Jones	1042.7
9	Mrs.	Jill	M	Herndon	168.99
10	Ms.	Kathryn	A	Williamson	1000
11	Mr.	Robert	E	Smith	585.83
12	Mr.	Robert	T	Smith	425.35
13	Mr.	Roberto	J	Odondo	1754.88
14	Mr.	Ronald	O	Donelly	424.83
15	Mr.	Todd	H	Wilson	3391.92
16	Mr.	William	C	Brynnan	258.65

9.4 Use the wizard to create an updatable data access page for the EMPLOYEE table.

9.5 To complete this problem, copy the **Ch09_AC_Museum.mdb** database and the .jpg files to the folder you will be using to store the page applications.

- Create a data access page using the design view and add all the fields found in the query named **qryAircraft.**
- Insert an image to the page and set the **ControlSource** of the image to the **PHOTO_ID** field in the **qryAircraft** query.

When you have completed these tasks, your page should look like the screen in Figure P9.5. Name the page **Aircraft.**

FIGURE P9.5
The Aircraft Page

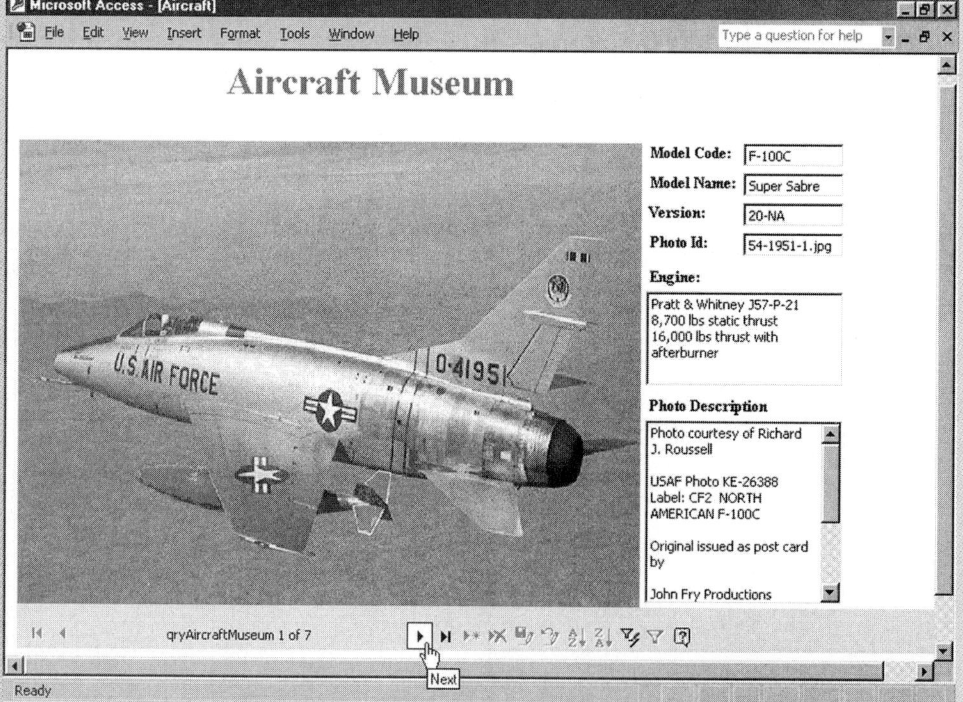

When you click **Next** twice on the navigation button, the picture should change as shown in Figure P9.5A. Note that this picture corresponds to the third record.

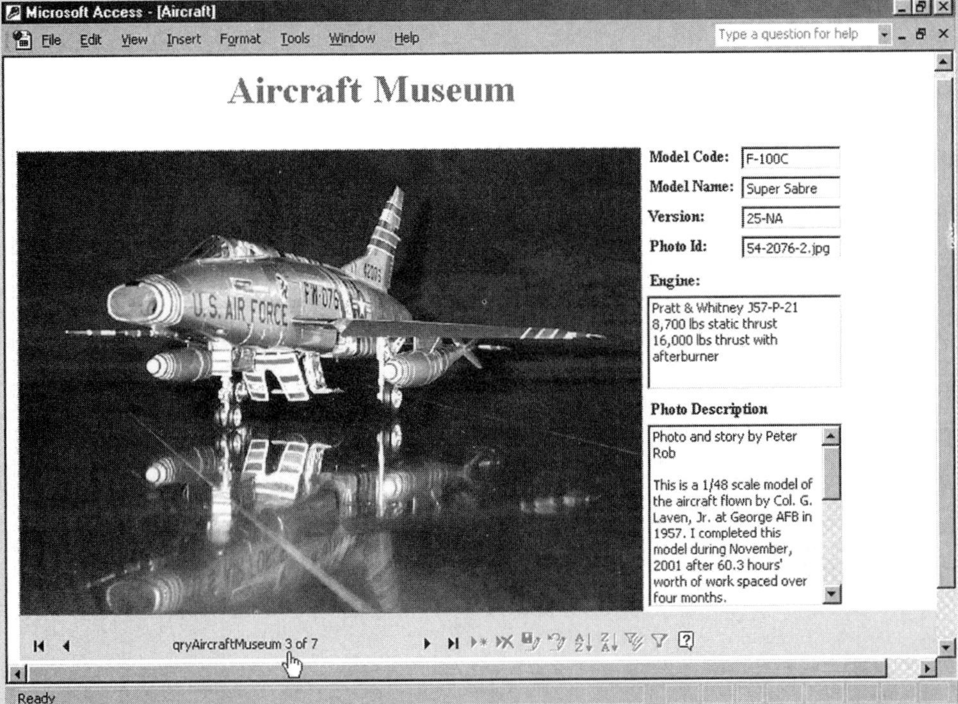

FIGURE P9.5A
The Third Record in the Aircraft Page

9.6 Create a main page for the **AC_Museum.mdb** database. The main page should look like Figure P9.6. (The U.S. and Tennessee flags are located on the CD as usflag1.gif and tnflag.gif; make sure you copy them into your folder.) Note that this main page has a link that allows you to access the page you created in problem 9.5. Save the main page as **ACMuseumMainPage**. (When you open the page, you'll see the flags wave thanks to the code embedded in the .gif files.)

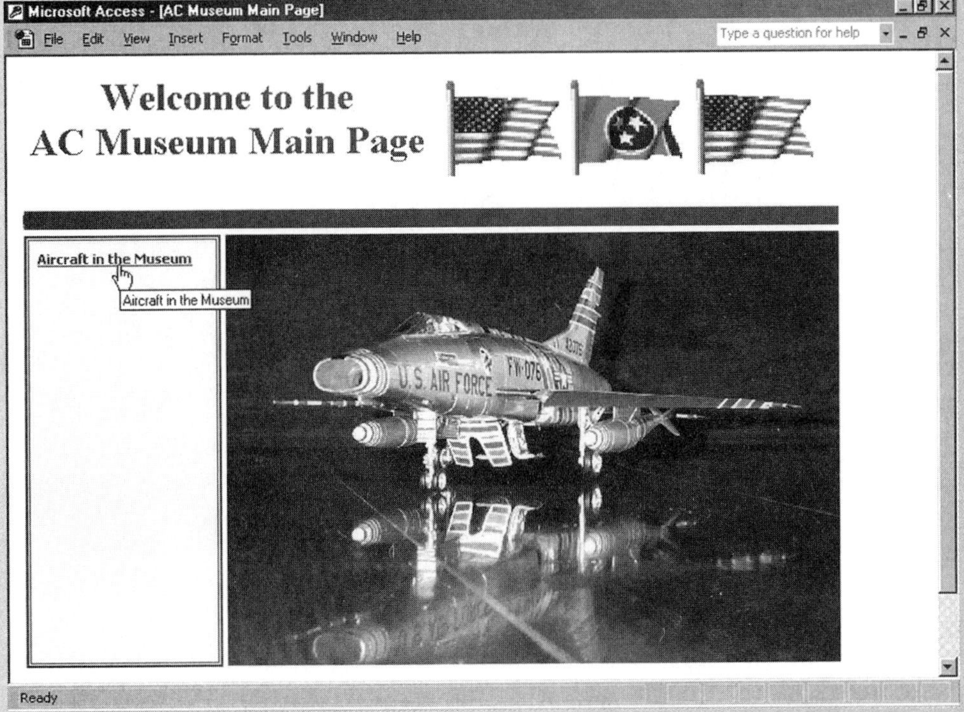

FIGURE P9.6
The AC_Museum Main Page

When you click on the **Aircraft in the Museum** link in Figure P9.6, note that the called page has been modified as shown in Figure P9.6A.

FIGURE P9.6A
The Modified Aircraft Page

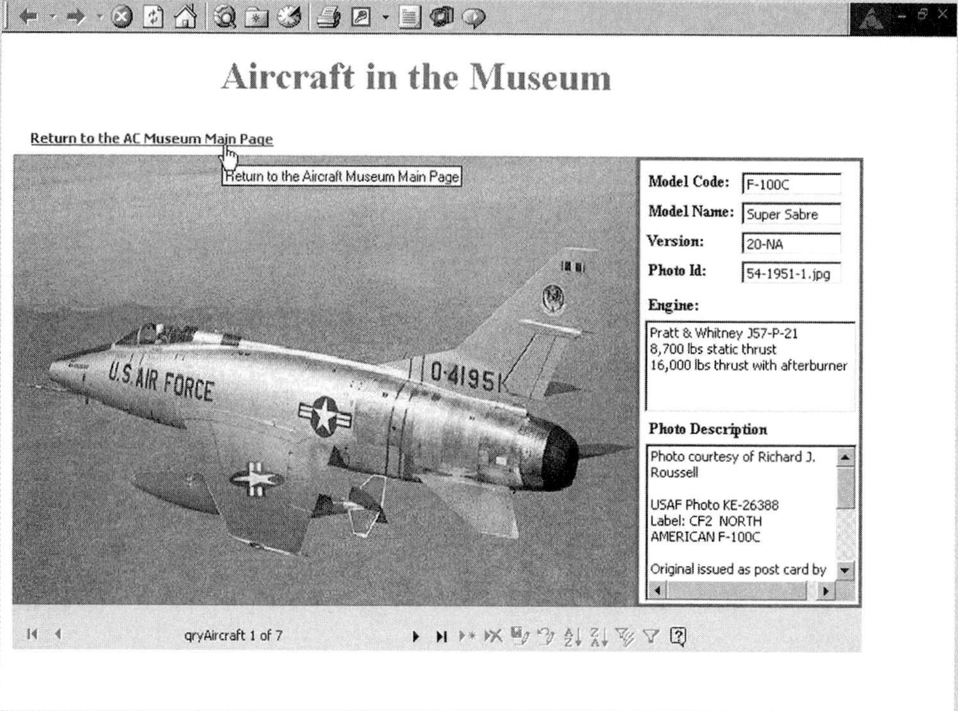

9.7 Create a set of Web pages to produce a Web-based system for the JewelCo database. (Use the **JewelCo.mdb** database on your CD.)

a. Create a main page with appropriate links to the other pages in the system. Use the Anne Rob-1.jpg , Anne Rob-2.jpg, and Anne Rob-3.jpg files to liven up your main page. Use the toolbox and the other available tools, such as the paint and font controls, to produce a colorful and attractive main page. A sample main page is shown in Figure P9.7.

FIGURE P9.7
The JewelCo Main Menu

b. Create a customer page with links to all other pages in the system.

c. Create a jewelry page showing all available jewelry. For each jewelry piece shown, include at least the jewelry price and the name of the artist who created the jewelry. Make sure that this page has links to all other pages in the system. Figure P9.7A shows an example. (Note that we have selected the second of 11 records.)

FIGURE P9.7A
Sample Jewelry Record

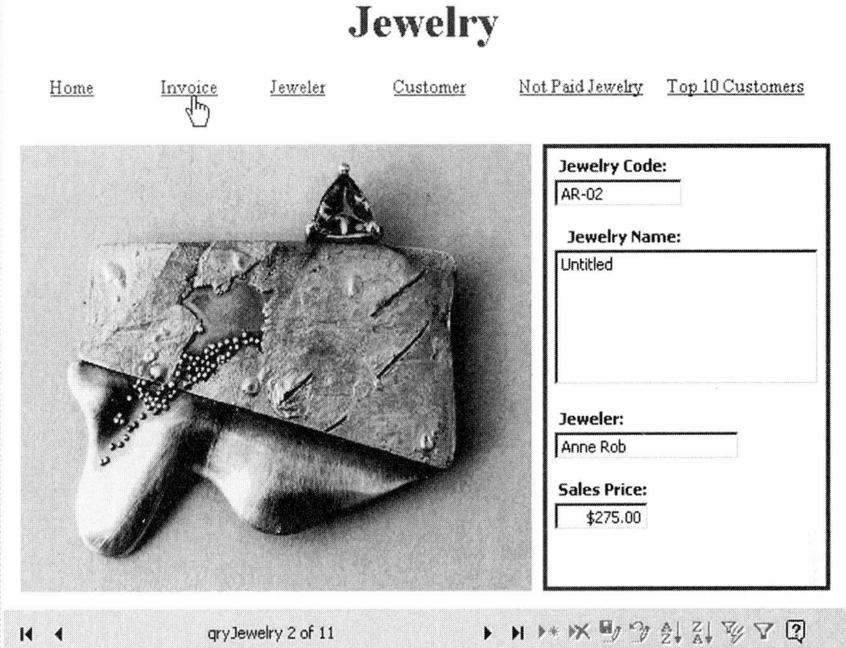

d. Create a sales summary page with links to all other pages in the system.

e. Create a summary of all payments paid to jewelers with links to all other pages in the system.

f. Create an invoicing page to let you sell jewelry and to display the contents of all invoices. Make sure that this page has links to all other pages in the system. Use a combo box to display the customer name for the customer who generated each invoice. (Read the following note to help you produce a page combo box.) Figure P9.7B shows a few records from the Invoice page. Note that we have drilled down into the first two invoices to show their invoice line contents.

FIGURE P9.7B
Sample Invoice Contents

Invoice

Home Jewelry Jeweler Not Paid Jewelry Top 10 Customers

Inv #: 1 Customer Smith Rhonda
Date: 15-Sep-2002

Line #	Jewelry Code	Unit	Price	Line Amt
1	AMR1-0023	1	$250.00	$250.00
2	GC1-001	1	$280.00	$280.00

LINE 1-2 of 2

Sub Total: $530.00
SalesTax: $47.70
Total: $577.70

Inv #: 2 Customer Browne Avery
Date: 15-Sep-2002

Line #	Jewelry Code	Unit	Price	Line Amt
1	AMR1-0045	1	$320.00	$320.00
2	FYG1-0002	1	$450.00	$450.00

LINE 1-2 of 2

Note

To create a combo box on page, use the same procedures that you used in Chapter 6 to create a combo box on a form. However, there is one small but important difference between a *form* combo box and a *page* combo box. When you create a *form* combo box, the wizard automatically binds the combo box source to that field on the form. In contrast, when you create a combo box on a *page*, you must *assign* the bound field of the combo box to the **ControlSource** of the page's **recordset**. If you forget to make this assignment, the record selected from the combo box will not be assigned to the record shown on the page. For example, if you examine Figure P9.7C, you will see that all of the displayed records show the same customer—George Allenberger—who is the first customer found in the combo box.

FIGURE P9.7C
The Effect of an Unassigned CUS_NUM

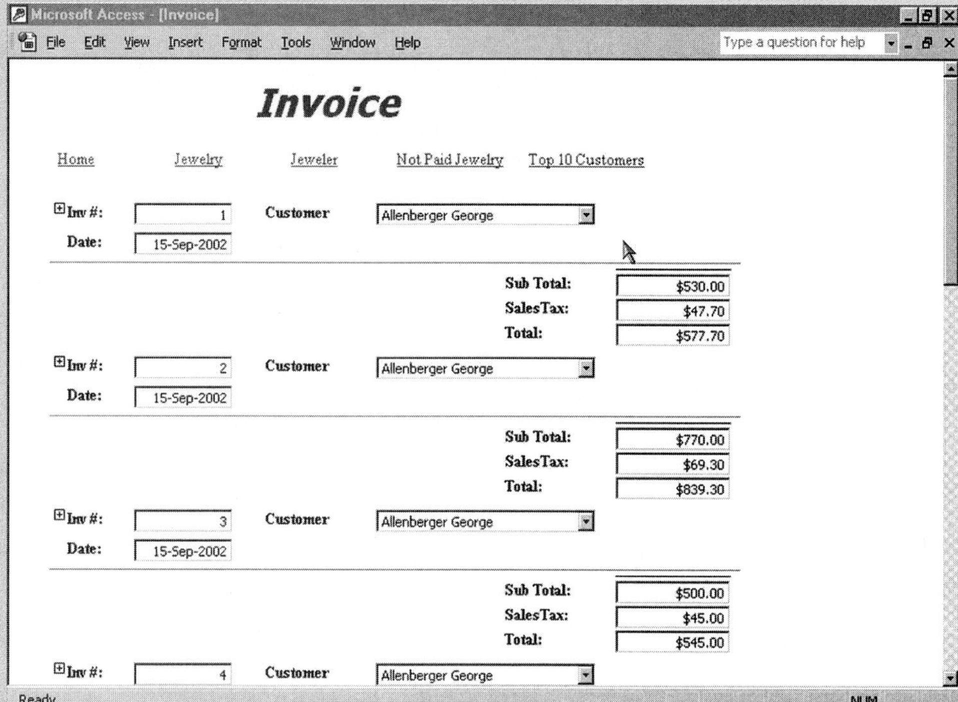

To assign the field to the control source on the page, right-click on the combo box and select **Element Properties** as shown in Figure P9.7D.

FIGURE P9.7D
Selecting the Combo Box Element Properties

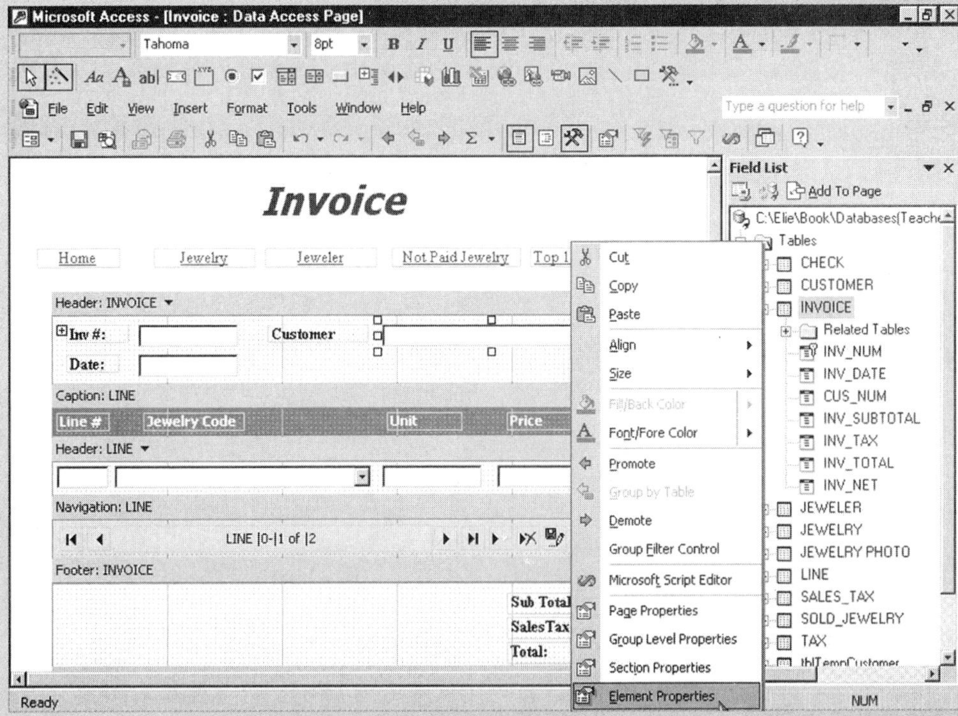

After selecting the **Element Properties**, open the combo box properties as shown in Figure P9.7E. Using the combo box properties shown in Figure P9.7E, click on the properties box **Data** tab and select the drop-down list for the **ControlSource** field. Select the field you want to assign to the combo box. Because each invoice is generated by a specific customer, select the CUS_NUM to be the bound field. Therefore, the CUS_NUM selected in the combo box must be assigned to the CUS_NUM on the invoice.

FIGURE P9.7E
Assigning the CUS NUM to the Control Source

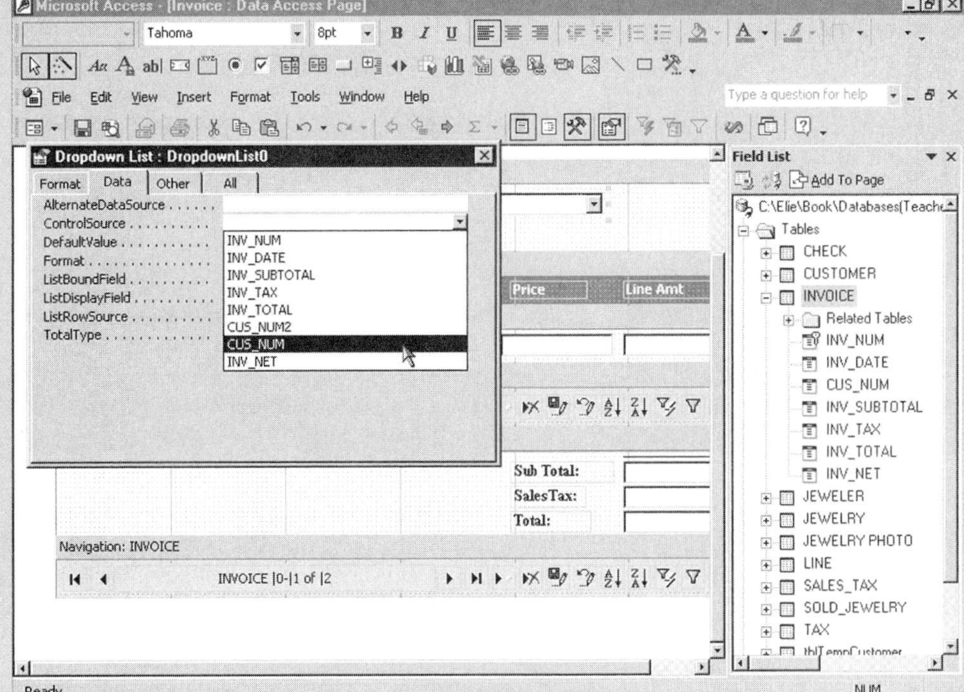

When you select the CUS_NUM from the **Dropdown List** shown in Figure P9.7E, Access adds a number to the field label as shown in Figure P9.7F. (Note the display of **CUS_NUM1: CUS_NUM**.)

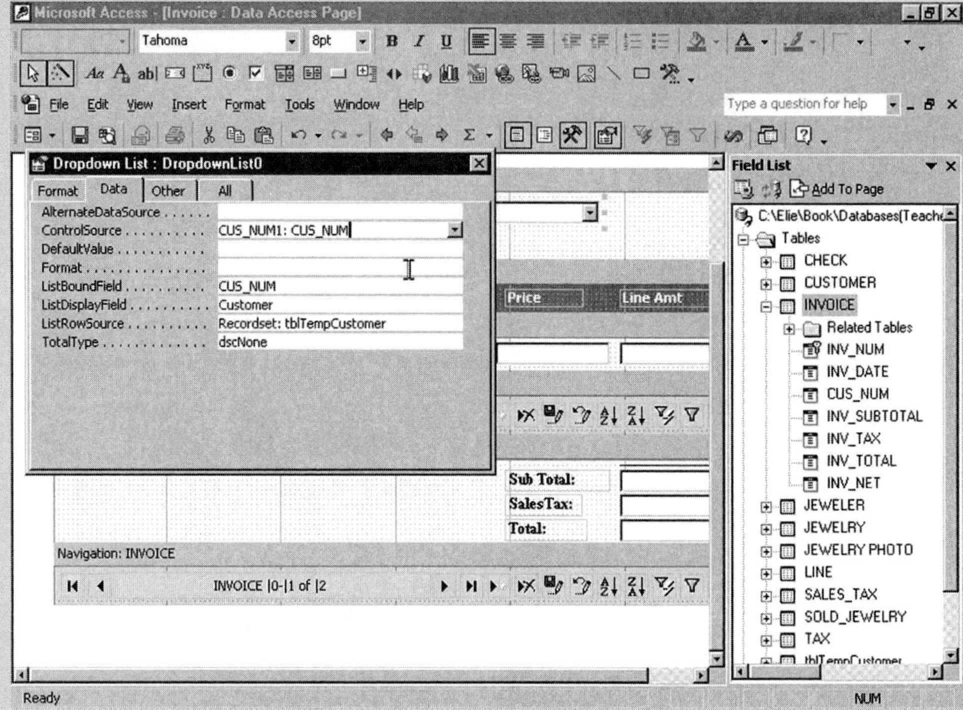

FIGURE P9.7F
Access Adds a Numeric Value to the Label

Close the page and save it. If you now open the page again, you will see that each invoice matches the customer who generated it (see Figure P9.7G).

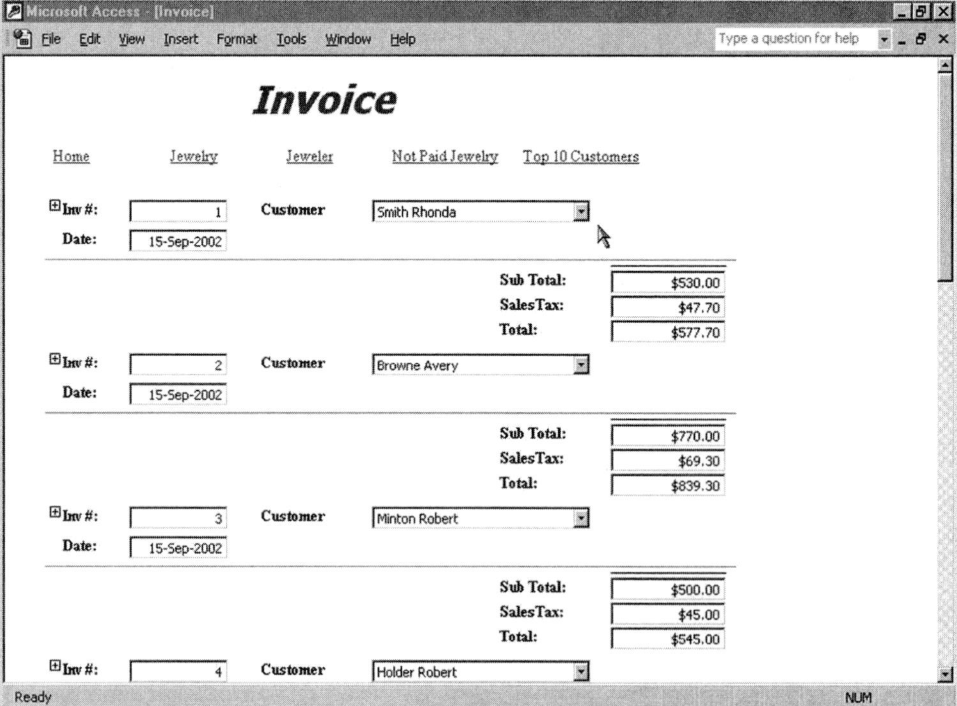

FIGURE P9.7G
The Bound Field Attached to the Control Source

Endnotes

1. Basically, the World Wide Web (WWW), usually referred to as "the Web," is a worldwide network of specially formatted documents that are linked through a standard communications protocol known as TCP/IP (Transmission Control Protocol/Internet Protocol). Although *Web* and *Internet* are often used as synonyms, the Web is only one of many services provided by the Internet. For example, the Internet also provides services such as FTP (File Transmission Protocol) and e-mail.

Chapter Ten

Database Security

Preview

Making the database secure is usually one of the major concerns to company managers. In this chapter, you'll learn several ways in which Access tools can be used to help secure database applications.

We will start by showing you how to protect the database through password protection. Next, you will learn how to create a more comprehensive database security environment through formal database administration. You will be the database administrator with full read/write permissions for all database objects. As the database administrator, you'll be able to create different levels of access for various types of database end users.

You will learn how to assign users to the groups, and you'll learn how to restrict database access to groups and to the end users in those groups.

We will show you how the database administrator can restrict database access through the use of permissions. These permissions range from read-only access to a small list of objects to full read/write access to all database objects.

You will also learn how database security can be enhanced through encryption. And we will show you how the security in a back-end database is carried even when the tables are linked to a front-end database. The back end will contain the database tables and the relationships between those tables. The front end will contain the queries, forms, reports, macros, and modules. By segmenting the database, you'll also be able to create greater data access flexibility. For example, you would be able to use a DB2, Oracle, or Microsoft SQL Server database as the database back-end and use Access to do all of the end-user applications development work at the database front-end.

Objectives

When you have mastered the material in this chapter, you will know how to

- Create and use database password protection.
- Use the database security vocabulary: Admin, user, group, permission, and object.
- Become an Access database administrator.
- Create new workgroup files or join an existing workgroup.
- Create groups and users.
- Assign permissions to workgroups and to the end users within those groups.
- Use database encryption to help secure a database.
- Segment a database into front-end and back-end components.

10.1 BASIC SECURITY OPTIONS

Because database security requirements are as varied as their applications, there are many different security options. For example:

- Using the developer edition of Access, you can create a runtime version of your Access database. This option allows you to run your database on a PC without requiring Access to be installed, and the user cannot make changes to your objects. Within this runtime version of the database, you can then design the security system to fit the end-user needs. The security system may be as uncomplicated as database password protection. Or it may include the full array of database administration security tools.
- You can create two Access databases, one classified as a *back-end database* and one as a *front-end database*. The **back-end database** is the database that contains the basic components of the database architecture such as the data dictionary, the tables, and the relationships between those tables. The **front-end database** contains the applications, such as queries, forms, and reports, that enable end users to access and manipulate the data. The back-end database tables may be password protected, or they may be protected with a full array of database administration security tools.

  The front-end database uses the back-end database's tables as *linked tables*. As the name implies, **linked tables** are tables in one database that are connected (linked) to applications that are located in another database. We will show you in this chapter how such links are created. The front-end database may have its own array of security measures.

  Separating the front-end and back-end databases enables you to use relational databases other than Access as the back-end database. For example, you can use an Oracle, an IBM DB2, or a Microsoft SQL Server database as the back-end database, and then link the tables in the back-end database to the front-end database through **ODBC (Open Database Connectivity)** drivers. Such back-end databases have far more sophisticated security tools than Access. *Unless you have proper authorization that specifies the full use of the back-end tables, you cannot make changes to the linked tables via the front-end database.*
- You can compile the Access database applications with an MDE file extension, rather than with an MDB file extension. A database with an MDE file extension compiles your **VBA (Visual Basic for Applications)** code to ensure that they cannot be viewed or edited. The MDE database will run exactly like an MDB database, but the applications—such as forms and reports—are more secure in an MDE database.

  Creating an MDE file does not require the creation of special authorizations to use the database. If you create an MDE file, Access will compact the destination file, remove all VBA source code, and save the database with an MDE extension. After saving your MDB database as an MDE database, you are no longer able to modify your forms, reports, or modules. However, you can still modify macros, queries, relationships, and tables.
- Using the **AutoExec** macro or the **Startup** option to run or to disable Access special keys may be useful. However, this security option yields only minimal security, because a savvy user can easily bypass the **AutoExec** macro or the **Startup** option by holding the Shift key while opening the application. On the other hand, to prevent an end user from holding the Shift key, you can create a module using VBA code to disable the Shift key bypass when the database is opened.

Although you should know what security options are available, many of these options are well outside the scope of this book. Therefore, we will not cover the use of the MS Access developer edition to create stand-alone applications, nor will we cover linking to Oracle, IBM DB2, or Microsoft SQL Server databases through the use of ODBC. For the same reason, we will not use the MDE option, nor will we use VB code. Therefore, we will limit our discussion to three ways in which the standard Access edition allows you to secure your database:

1. Secure a database through the use of a password while logging on.
2. Create a database security using the User-Level Security Wizard.
3. Create back-end and front-end databases.

10.2 DATABASE PASSWORD PROTECTION

To illustrate the procedures discussed in this chapter, we will use **Ch10_POS_2nd.mdb** database stored on the CD that is bundled with this book. We have stored this database in the **C:\Rob-Semaan-2ndEdition\Databases(Student)\Ch10** folder. (Go ahead and create the folder now and copy the **Ch10_POS_2nd.mdb** database from the student CD to that folder. Make sure that you remember to uncheck the read-only check box from the database properties after you have copied the database.) Naturally, you can create your own folder and substitute your folder structure whenever we show a security option that references the folder we have used.

To set a password for the database, first start Access, and then take the following actions:

1. Select **File/Open** from the menu bar to get the **Open** window shown in Figure 10.1.
2. Using the window shown in Figure 10.1, select the **Ch10_POS_2nd.mdb** database.
3. Click on the arrow next to the **Open** button shown in Figure 10.1 to produce the menu list.
4. Select the **Open Exclusive** option as shown in Figure 10.1.

After opening the database through the sequence illustrated with the help of Figure 10.1, you will see the familiar database window shown in Figure 10.2.

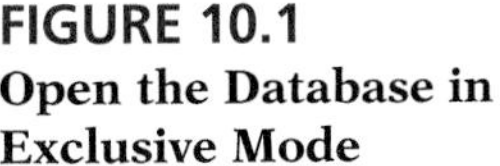

FIGURE 10.1
Open the Database in Exclusive Mode

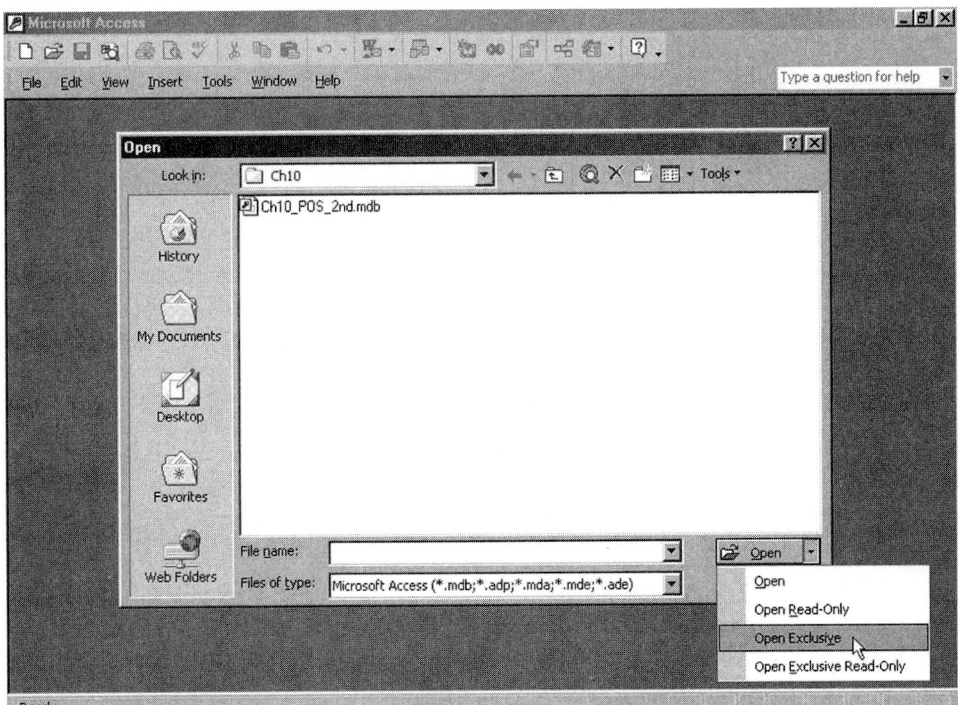

FIGURE 10.2
The Database Password Security Option

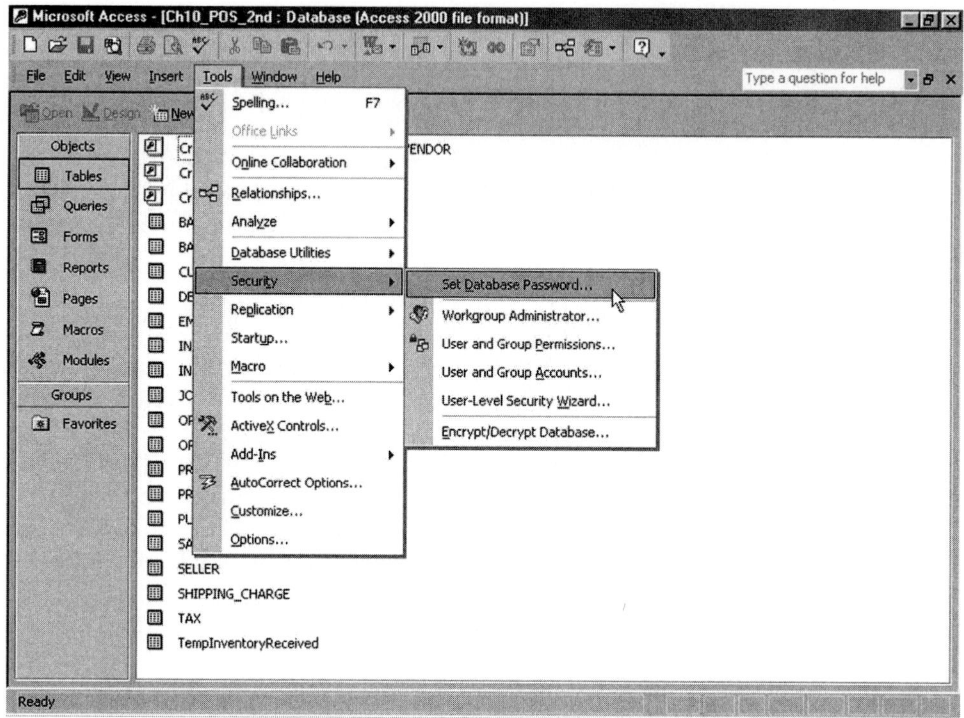

Using the window shown in Figure 10.2, click on the **Tools** tab and then click on **Security** to select **Set Database Password** option.

Enter the database password and verify it, using the dialog box shown in Figure 10.3. (Remember that passwords are case-sensitive!) Note that the password you typed shows up as a series of asterisks, one for each character you typed, including the spaces.

To see how password protection works, close the database and then open it again. Note that the database now requires the password entry shown in Figure 10.4.

If you enter the wrong password, Access rewards you with the message shown in Figure 10.5.

Click **OK** to acknowledge the incorrect password; then type the correct password when the **Password Required** dialog box opens again.

10.2.1 Removing the Password Protection

If you want to remove password protection, first open the database after selecting the **Open Exclusive** option shown in Figure 10.1, and then select the **Tools/Security** and **Unset Database Password** options as shown in Figure 10.6.

Because you must be authorized to remove password protection, Access requires that you first enter the correct password (see Figure 10.7).

FIGURE 10.3
Enter and Verify the Password

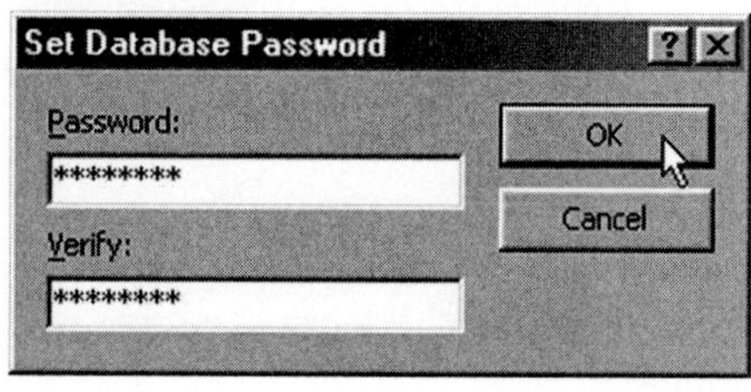

FIGURE 10.4
The Password Entry

FIGURE 10.5
Invalid Password

Note

Although this word of caution seems redundant, make sure you store the password in a safe place just in case you forget it. Access is very effective at locking you out of the database if you forget the password.

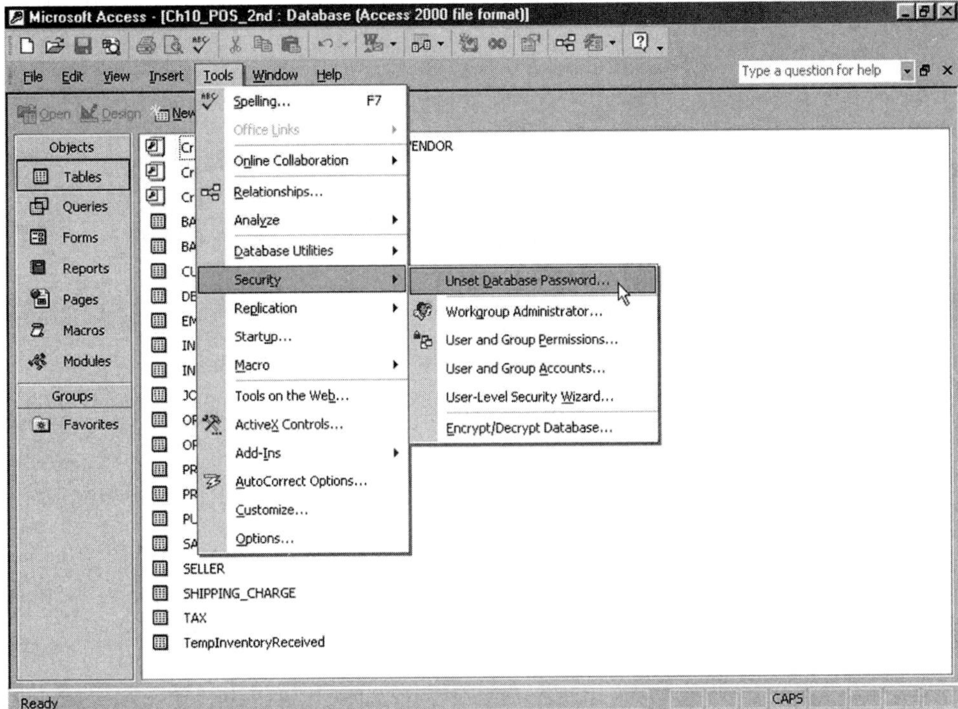

FIGURE 10.6
Removing Password Protection

Although database password security is better than no security at all, its use has quite a few limitations. For example, if you give out the password, those who have the password are free to use *and change* any database component. Such wide-ranging freedom tends to make database administrators nervous. That's why we'll take a look at other security options in the following sections of this chapter.

10.3 DATABASE ADMINISTRATION: BASIC SECURITY COMPONENTS

To create a database security environment to be managed by a database administrator, you must first know what the security components and actions are. Therefore, the following vocabulary is important. (The Access Security Wizard requires you to define and use these components, so you must know what they are!)

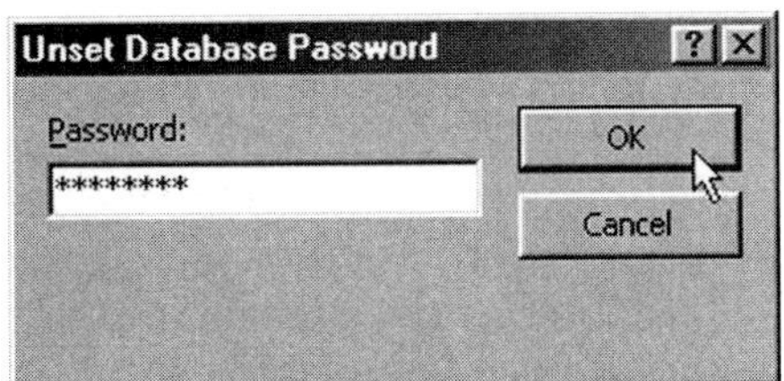

FIGURE 10.7
Password Required to Remove Password Protection

Note

If you did not use the **Open Exclusive** option when you opened the database, Access will produce the reminder shown in Figure 10.8.

FIGURE 10.8
Reminder to Open the Database in Exclusive Mode

- An **object** is any component of the database. That is, an object may be a table, query, form, report, macro, or a module in the database.
- A **permission** is the right to use an object. Note that the word *permission* may be used as a noun in the database context. Two types of permissions exist:
    1. An **explicit permission** is one that is granted to an individual user. An explicit permission assigned to one user will not affect any other user(s).
    2. An **implicit permission** is one that is granted to a specified group of users. Therefore, all users within that group have the same permission.
- An **operation** is any action that changes a database object. For example, operations include data updating, appending, or deleting. Operations also include modifying a table, query, form, report, macro, or module.
- The **Admins workgroup**, known as **Admins** in the Access security environment, is the administrative unit that contains the database system's administrator (**Admin**). The following points are worth emphasizing:
    1. Because the Admins workgroup must be managed by an Admin, the Admin is the default member in the Admins workgroup when that workgroup is created.
    2. The Admins workgroup is the core of the security system. Therefore, you cannot have a database administrative function without the Admins workgroup.
    3. The Admin manages the database security environment. Given this management function, the Admin is given full permissions on all objects in the databases by default. Because the security environment cannot be managed without the Admin, the Admin cannot be removed from the workgroup.
    4. The Admin is responsible for assigning any permission(s). A permission may or may not include the right to perform an operation on an object in the application.
    5. Each Admins workgroup must have at least one user, and all users in this Admins work group have the same rights as the Admin.
- A **User** is a person whom the Admin allows to use a specified object or a set of objects. The Admin assigns a specific set of permissions to use one or more objects to each user. Therefore, the Admin must create the user account and a set of permissions to use certain objects. When any user logs on, the user can assign a password to his or her user ID and must supply the password whenever (s)he opens the secure application. The Admin account is the default user account. *The user must be a member of a group, even if the user is the only member of that group.*

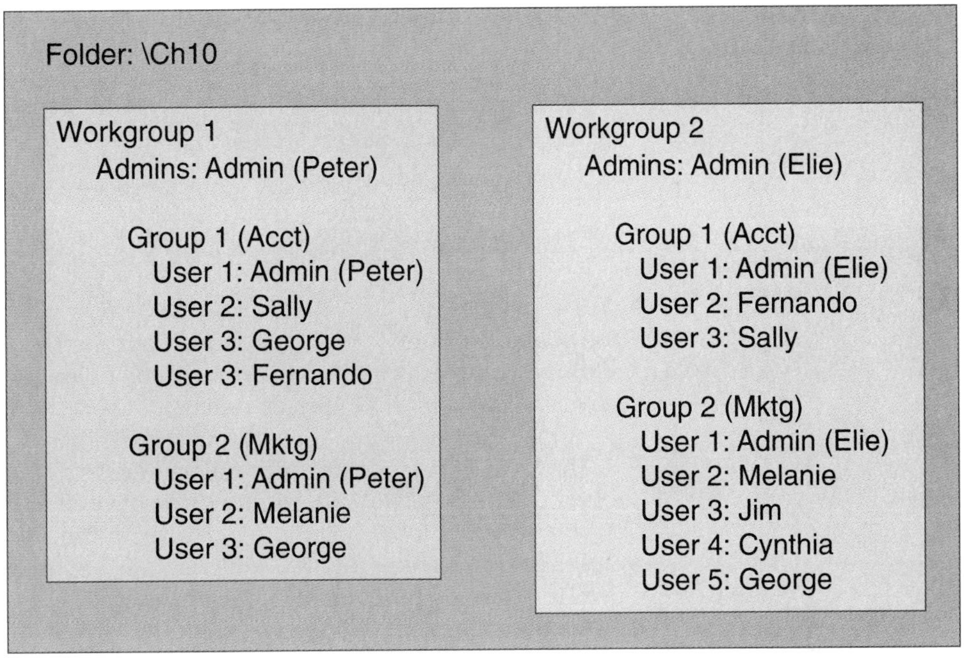

FIGURE 10.9
The Database Administration Environment

Folder: \Ch10

Workgroup 1	Workgroup 2
Admins: Admin (Peter)	Admins: Admin (Elie)
Group 1 (Acct)	Group 1 (Acct)
User 1: Admin (Peter)	User 1: Admin (Elie)
User 2: Sally	User 2: Fernando
User 3: George	User 3: Sally
User 3: Fernando	
Group 2 (Mktg)	Group 2 (Mktg)
User 1: Admin (Peter)	User 1: Admin (Elie)
User 2: Melanie	User 2: Melanie
User 3: George	User 3: Jim
	User 4: Cynthia
	User 5: George

- A **Group** is a database administrative unit that is composed of one or more users. The Admin can create a group account, assign permissions to a group, and then add users to the group. For example, organizational units such as accounting or marketing may become groups, and the employees in those departments will become the system's users. Permissions assigned to a group are inherited by all of the members of that group.
- The **Users group** is the default group created by Access. Access adds all users to this group. Therefore, if you want to secure an object, make sure you don't give this group a full permission to that object.

The preceding discussion of the database administrative environment is reflected in Figure 10.9. Keep this figure—and the preceding vocabulary—in mind as we develop a database security system in the following sections.

10.3.1 The .ldb File

Before examining workgroups and how they fit into the database's security framework, you need to know about the .ldb file. The **.ldb file** is a small file, created by Access, which contains basic database administrative data.

The .ldb file contains the user name in its first 32 bytes and the database security information in its second 32 bytes. The database administrator may use the information contained in the .ldb file to track all database users through their logon ID or through their computer name. The .ldb file also contains locking information. As its name implies, a **lock** is a device that prevents the use of an object. For example, if one user is performing operations on the EMPLOYEE table, a lock on that table would prevent another user from using that table until the lock is released.

When the last user closes the database normally, the .ldb file is deleted. However, if the database is corrupted, the .ldb file is not deleted when the database is closed. Instead, the .ldb file contents are used by the DBMS when it repairs the database.

Access helps manage the multiuser database environment by using a so-called *jet-locking protocol*. A **protocol** is a set of rules that governs a procedure or an action. The **jet-locking protocol** is named to reflect the fact that it is a set of rules created and enforced by the Access Jet Database Engine. The **Access Jet**

FIGURE 10.10
The Lock Table Message

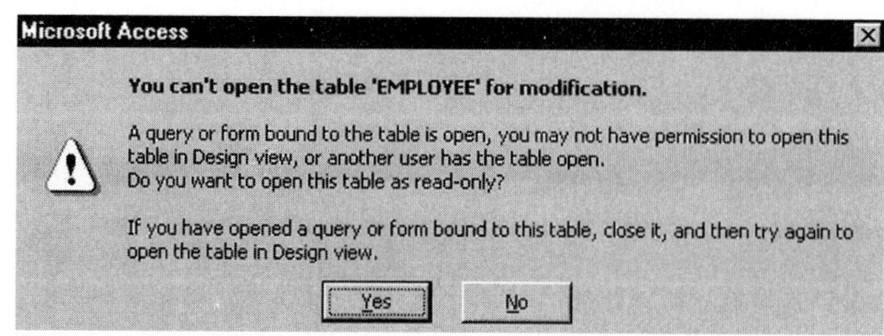

Database Engine is the software that powers the DBMS. This database engine automatically creates a lock whenever a database table is opened in a *shared database environment*. The lock is released when the last user closes the database normally, that is, without corrupting the database.

The locking protocol is, from the end user's point of view, simple and straightforward. For example, suppose you have opened a table in its design view. As long as you have the table open, the protocol stored in the .ldb file prevents another end user from modifying that table. Access will produce a message box (see Figure 10.10) to tell the second end user that the table is not available.

Access creates the .ldb file without intervention on your part. The .ldb filename will be the same as the database name as shown in Figure 10.11. In other words, the shared database **Ch10_POS_2nd.mdb** will have an .ldb file named **Ch10_POS_2nd.ldb.** (The .ldb and its associated .mdb file will always be located in the same folder.)

10.4 THE WORKGROUP FILES

The **workgroup file** stores information about the groups, the users, and the user passwords. When you launch a database, the workgroup associated with Access determines the permission on all the objects and data in the database. The Access Jet Database Engine is used to store and retrieve all data and objects from the workgroup information file. Therefore, when users start Access, it automatically maintains a link to the workgroup file in which the database security information is stored. The default name for the workgroup is **System.mdw.** However, you may use any valid name with an extension of .mdw to identify the workgroup file.

When Access was installed, it automatically created a workgroup file. Because the Access-created default workgroup files are identical in every Access installation, we strongly suggest that you create your own workgroup file or that you update the existing workgroup file to fit your specific requirements. You may define different levels and types of security for each workgroup file.

FIGURE 10.11
The .ldb File

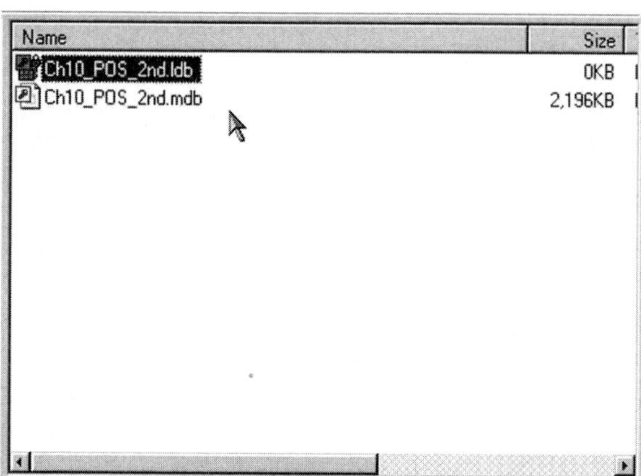

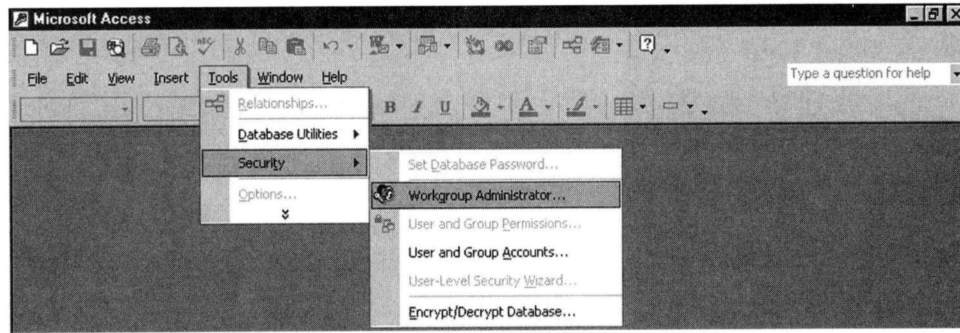

FIGURE 10.12
The Workgroup Administrator

To make sure that only database administrators can create workgroups, a unique **workgroup identification (WID)** must be created. This WID must be supplied whenever a new workgroup file is created.

To look at the current workgroup file, start Access and then select the two options shown in Figure 10.12. (Note that you do not see a database window in Figure 10.12, thus indicating that no database has been selected yet.)

Select the **Workgroup Administrator** to open the dialog box shown in Figure 10.13. The dialog box in Figure 10.13 contains the name under which the computer is registered, as well as the path to the workgroup file currently in use. Note that the default workgroup is named **System1.mdw**.

Before we continue the security creation process, let's pause to make sure that you understand the security structure. To exercise your duties and privileges as a database administrator, you must first become a workgroup administrator. That is, you must "own" a workgroup. After becoming a workgroup owner, you have the privilege of assigning groups and users within those groups. Finally, you may assign permissions to groups and to users within those groups.

10.4.1 Creating a Workgroup File

To create a workgroup file, follow these three steps:

1. Click on the **Create...** button shown in Figure 10.13. This action will produce the **Workgroup Owner Information** dialog box displayed in Figure 10.14.
2. Using the **Workgroup Owner Information** dialog box shown in Figure 10.14, enter the database administrator's **Name** and, if appropriate, the **Organization** name. If you already have a **Workgroup ID**, enter it. (Your workgroup ID must be unique, and it may consist of up to 20 numbers and letters.) If you do not have a workgroup ID or you want to create a new one, create it now. We suggest that you store your workgroup ID in a safe place, to be retrieved if you just

FIGURE 10.13
The Workgroup Administrator Dialog Box

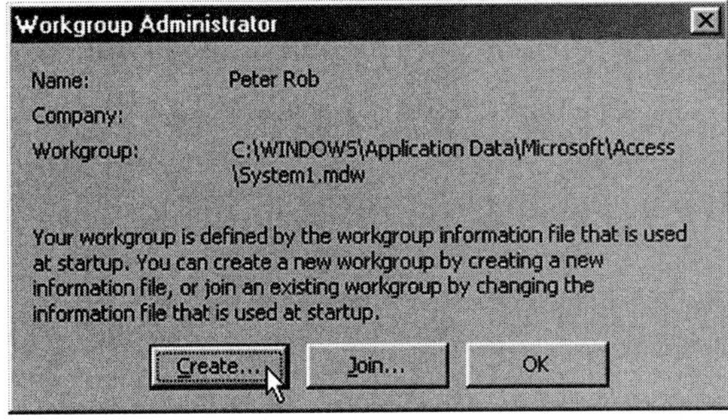

FIGURE 10.14
The Workgroup Owner Information Dialog Box

Workgroup Owner Information
The new workgroup information file is identified by the name, organization, and case-sensitive workgroup ID you specify.
Use the name and organization information below, or enter a different name or organization. If you want to ensure that your workgroup is unique, also enter a unique workgroup ID of up to 20 numbers or letters.
Name: Peter Rob
Organization: ACMuseum
Workgroup ID: SuperSabre
OK
Cancel

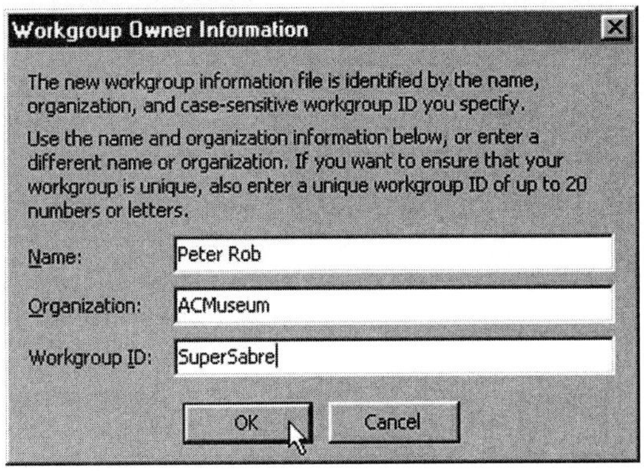

FIGURE 10.15
The Workgroup ID Notification

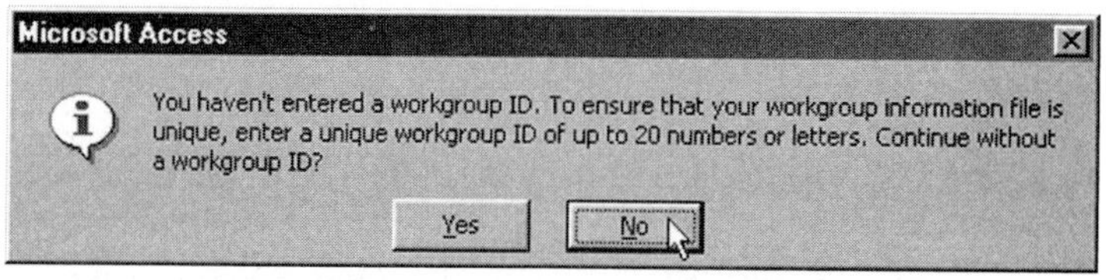

FIGURE 10.16
The Workgroup Information File Dialog Box

happen to forget it. (If you forget the workgroup ID, no changes can be made to the workgroup files). If you don't enter the workgroup ID, Access will generate a notification such as the one shown in Figure 10.15.

3. Assuming that you have entered the workgroup ID and clicked on the **OK** button in Figure 10.14, Access displays the Workgroup Information File in Figure 10.16, showing the current path. *The default path might change on a different computer*. (Never mind that Microsoft misspelled the "information" part of the instructions.)

4. As you look at Figure 10.16, note that the new file is named **System2.mdw** to preserve the default **System1.mdw** that was created when Access was installed. Click **OK** to generate the confirmation response in Figure 10.17.

5. If you are satisfied that the information shown in Figure 10.17 is correct, click **OK** to generate the confirmation message in Figure 10.18. Click **OK** to complete the procedure.

The confirmation message in Figure 10.18 shows that the .mdw file was successfully saved to the default **C:\WINDOWS\Application Data\Microsoft\Access** folder. We usually store the workgroup file in the same folder as the database. To show you how that task is accomplished, let's create a new .mdw file. (Because the security system's many components are required to interact outside the view and control of the application end users, you cannot simply copy an existing .mdw file to another folder.) Figure 10.19 shows that we are creating a new Workgroup ID for the ACMuseum organization.

Clicking **OK** on the **Workgroup Owner Information** dialog box shown in Figure 10.19 will yield Figure 10.19A.

FIGURE 10.17
Confirm Workgroup Information Dialog Box

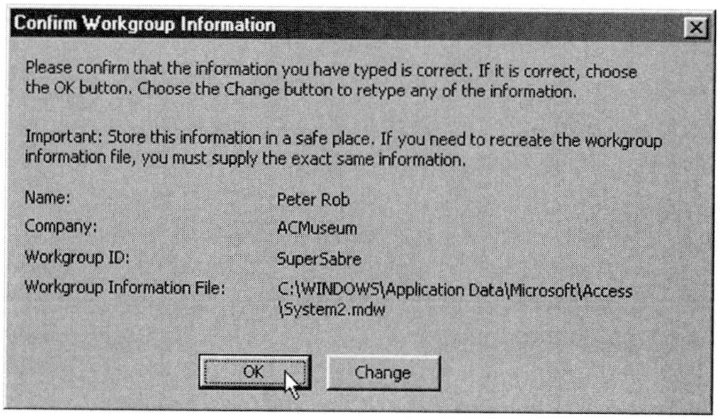

FIGURE 10.18
The Workgroup Administrator Message Box

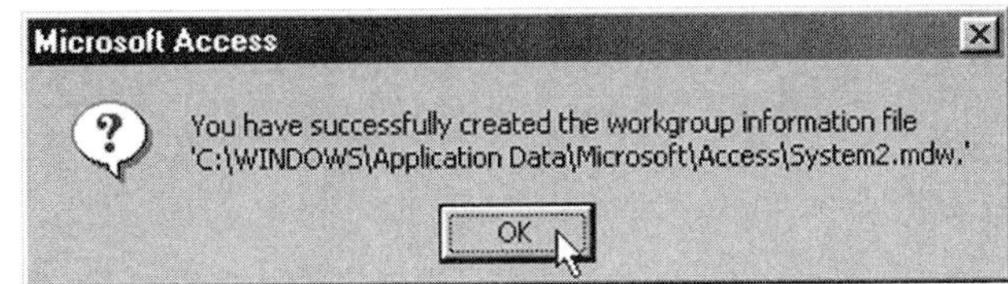

To store the .mdw file in your database folder, click on the **Browse** button in Figure 10.19A to generate the **Select Workgroup Information File** window shown in Figure 10.20. (We have used the **Save in:** line to find and select the **Ch10** folder.)

After you have found the folder—see Figure 10.20 again—in which you want to save the .mdw file,

1. Select the **System3.mdw** in the **File name:** line.
2. Click on the **Open** button in Figure 10.20 to transfer the folder location to the **Workgroup Information File** dialog box in Figure 10.20A.
3. Click **OK** on the dialog box in Figure 10.20A to generate Figure 10.20B
4. Because the information in the confirmation message box in Figure 10.20B is correct, click **OK**. You will then see the confirmation message boxes you first saw in Figures 10.17 and 10.18. (Naturally, these message boxes contain the information for the new .mdw file in its new location.) Click **OK** on each of these message boxes.
5. When you have completed step 4, confirm that the .mdw file is, in fact, located in the appropriate database folder. As you can see in Figure 10.20C, the .mdw file is located in the proper directory.

FIGURE 10.19
The ACM-F100 Workgroup Creation

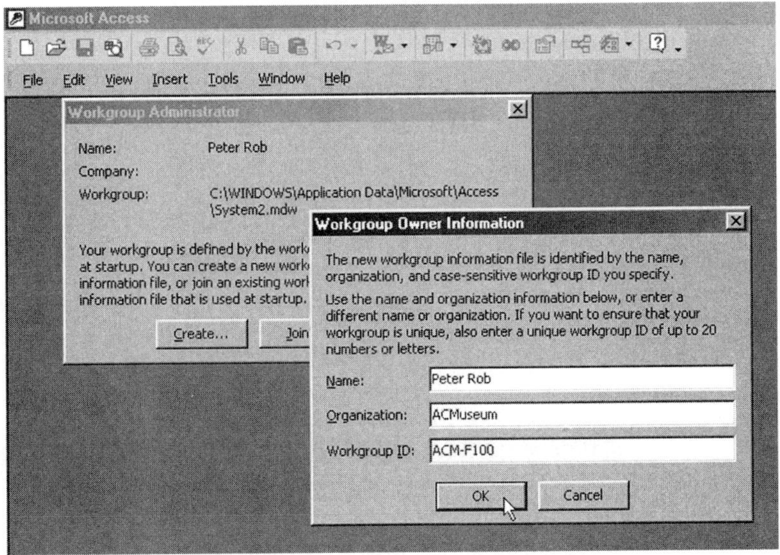

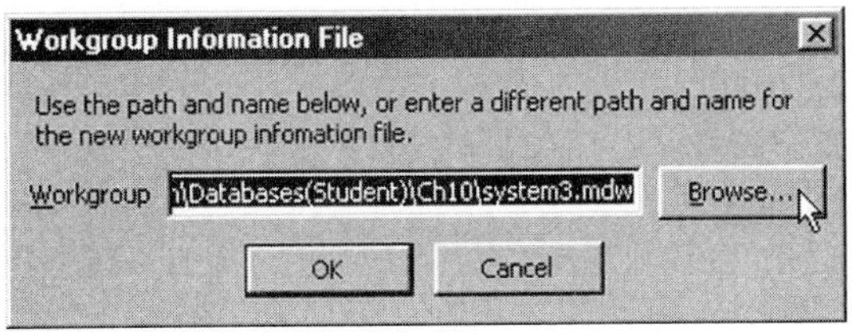

FIGURE 10.19A
The Browse Option in the Workgroup Information Dialog Box

Workgroup Information File

Use the path and name below, or enter a different path and name for the new workgroup information file.

Workgroup \Databases(Student)\Ch10\system3.mdw Browse...

OK Cancel

FIGURE 10.20
Select the Folder

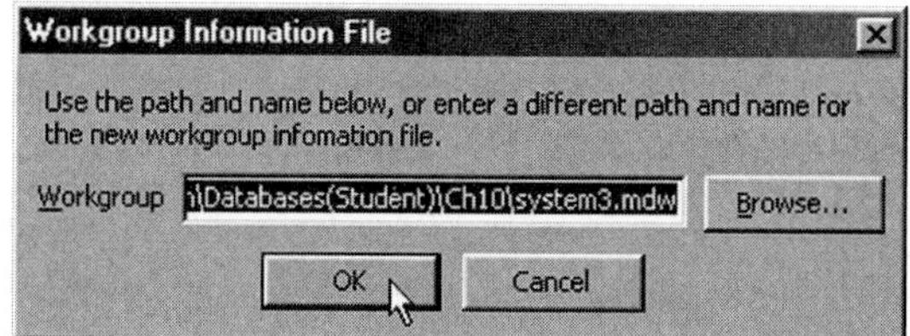

FIGURE 10.20A
The New Folder Selection in the Workgroup Information File Dialog Box

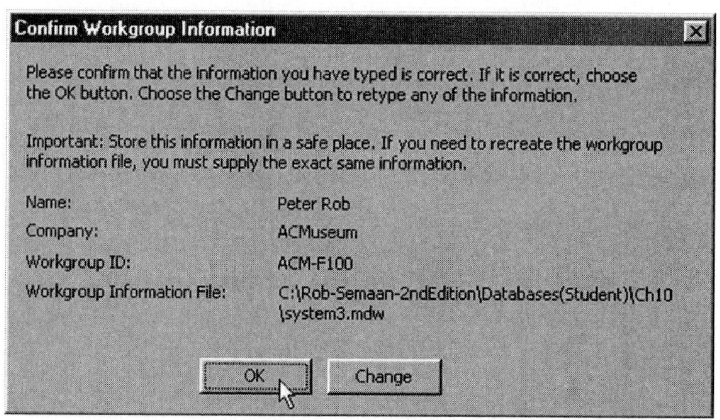

FIGURE 10.20B
The Confirmation Message Box

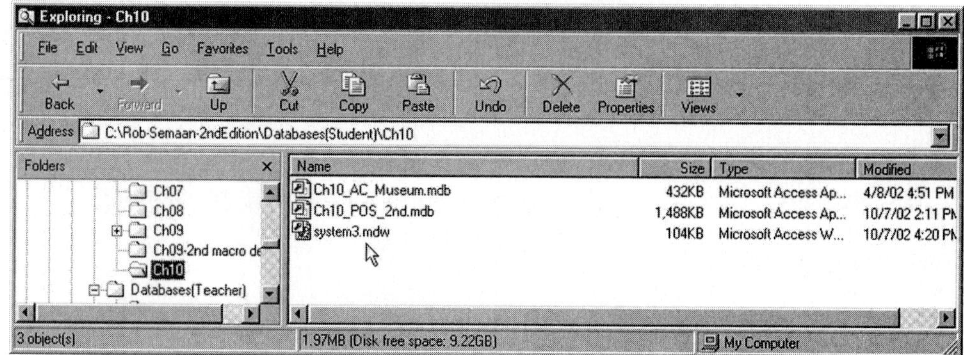

FIGURE 10.20C
The Relocated mdw File

Although you are likely to create a different workgroup file for each database, a workgroup file may be used by many different databases. (When you open a database, Access looks for its workgroup file, using the path specified in the Workgroup Information File.) Naturally, if a workgroup file is shared by different databases, each database requires different permissions to be assigned by the Admin to that database's users and/or to the objects within that database.

You can create many workgroup files and save them in one database folder. However, you can use only one workgroup file at a time. You should also remember that each workgroup contains its own users and groups with different security levels and permissions. By switching from one workgroup file to another, the security environment will change to reflect the newly selected workgroup. In short, all applications will be subject to the restrictions set in the currently available workgroup file.

The default **Users** and the **Admins** groups are identical in all Access applications, and the permissions given to these groups are identical in all Access applications. Therefore, we recommend that you create new groups, add users to these groups, and assign the appropriate permissions to the users and the groups.

10.4.2 Switching Workgroup Files

Figures 10.21 through 10.21D show the six steps that you'll need to complete to switch from one workgroup file to another. In this example, we'll switch from the current default (**system3.mdw**) workgroup shown in Figure 10.21 to the **system1.mdw** workgroup located in the **C:\WINDOWS\Application Data\Microsoft\Access** folder.

1. Select the **Tools/Security/Workgroup Administrator...** sequence you first saw in Figure 10.11 to generate the **Workgroup Administrator** dialog box shown in Figure 10.21. (Note that we have placed the cursor on the **Join...** button.)
2. Click the **Join...** button in Figure 10.21 to generate Figure 10.21A.
3. Click on the **Browse...** button in Figure 10.21A to produce Figure 10.21B. (Remember that you are trying to replace the current default workgroup file with the one that is located in the **C:\WINDOWS\Application Data\Microsoft\Access** folder. Therefore, click through the **Look in:** window shown in Figure 10.21B until you wind up with the folder in which the system1.mdw file is located.)
4. Click on the **Open** button in Figure 10.21B to generate Figure 10.21C.
5. Click the **OK** button in Figure 10.21C to produce Figure 10.21D.
6. Click the **OK** button in Figure 10.21D to complete the switch to the new workgroup file.

FIGURE 10.21
The Workgroup File Join Option

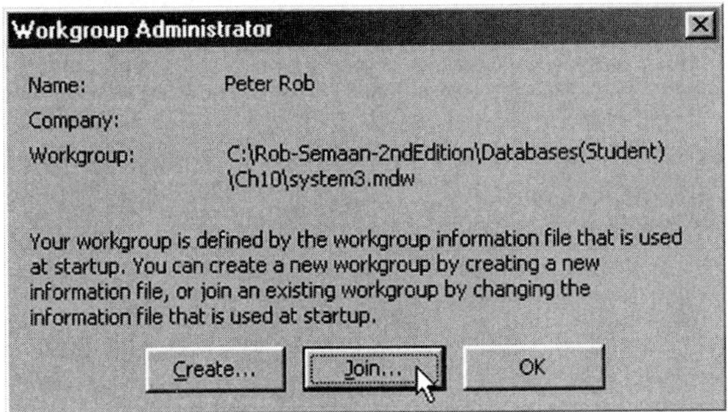

FIGURE 10.21A
The Current Workgroup File

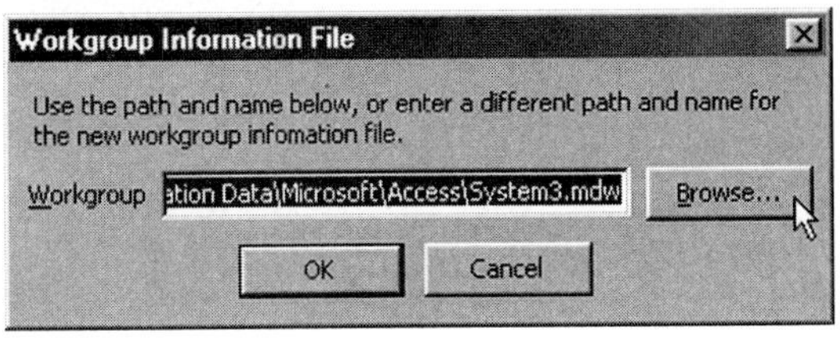

Workgroup Information File
Use the path and name below, or enter a different path and name for the new workgroup infomation file.
Workgroup ation Data\Microsoft\Access\System3.mdw Browse...
OK Cancel

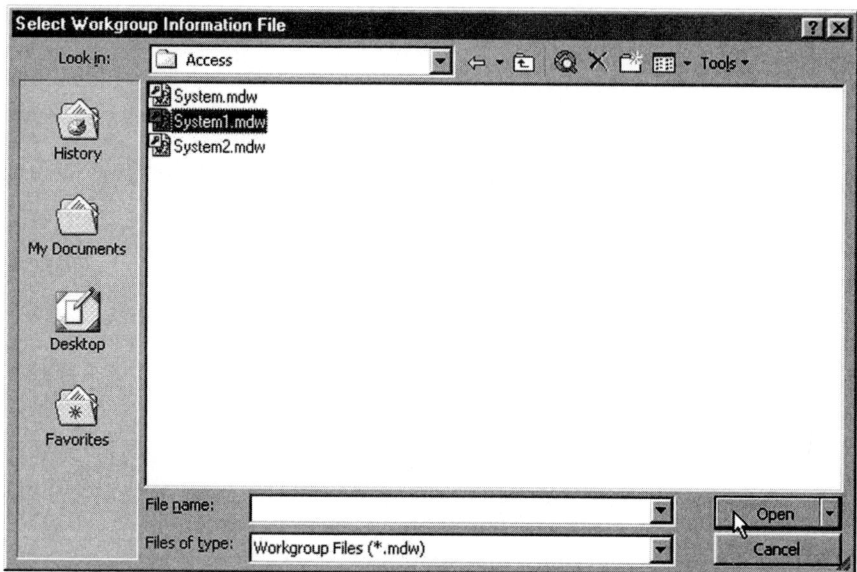

FIGURE 10.21B
The Available Workgroup Files

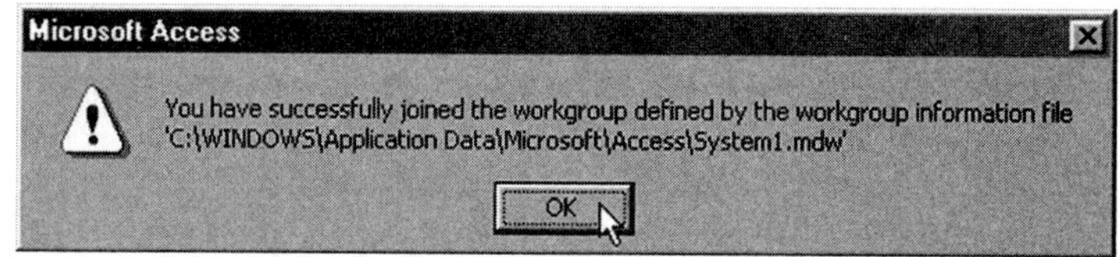

FIGURE 10.21C
The Successful Workgroup File Join

10.5 USER AND GROUP ACCOUNTS

The Access security system is based on user-level security, rather than on share-level security. The **user-level security** allows the logon user to access all objects based on the permission(s) given to that user. The **share-level security** subjects the user to a more restrictive environment that is based on an ID and a password. For example, a user might have one ID and a password to only *read* the EMPLOYEE table and another ID and a password to *update* the table. Each time the user wants to update the EMPLOYEE table, the user must supply the required ID and a password that matches that ID. Clearly, the share-level security option yields a more secure database.

In any case, if the database administrator wants to control access to and use of a database, he or she must set up group and user accounts. To create user and group accounts, start Access, select **Tools/Security**, and then select the **User and Group Accounts** option shown in Figure 10.22.

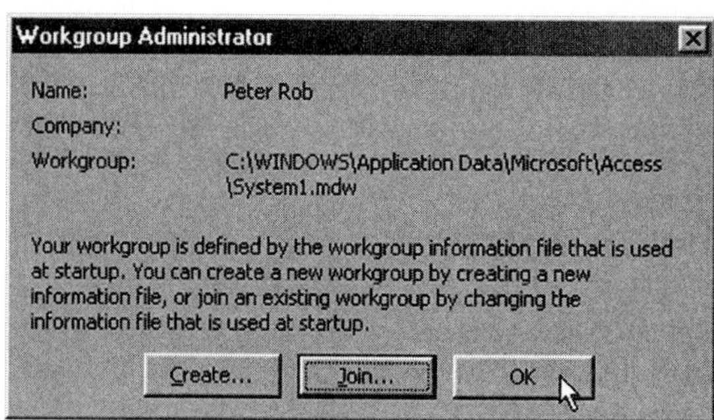

FIGURE 10.21D
Completion of the Workgroup Join Process

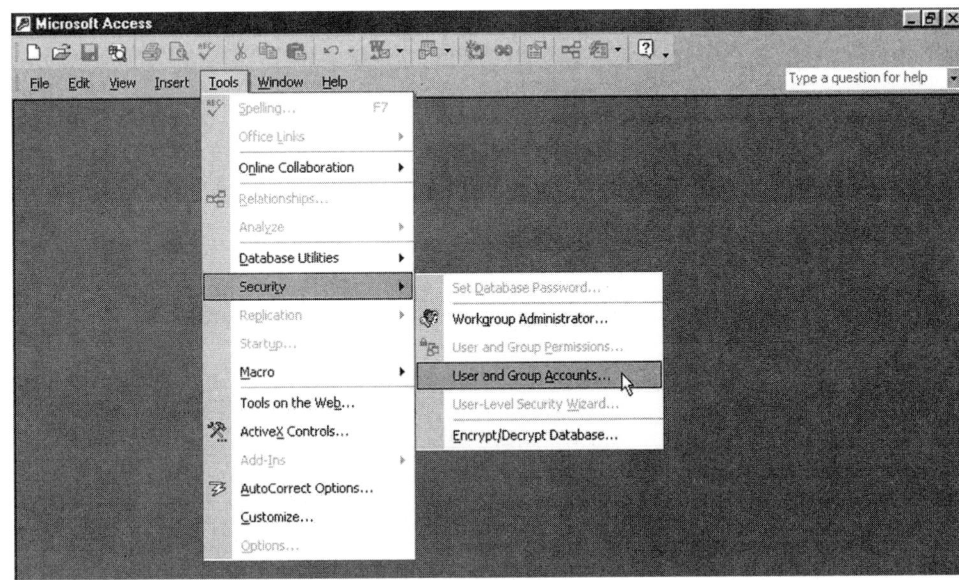

FIGURE 10.22
Select the User and Group Accounts

Given the selections shown in Figure 10.22, Access will display the **User and Group Accounts** dialog box in Figure 10.23.

As you examine Figure 10.23, note that Access has two default group accounts, one for the Admins group with an Admin user as default, and one for the Users group.

Once the database has an administrator to monitor and control its use, that administrator's first job is to create new groups and to create new users within those groups. After the groups have been created and the users are added to the existing groups, the administrator can add and/or delete users to and from the groups.

10.5.1 Admin Accounts

The first step in creating a security system is to assign a password for the Admin user. (Without an assigned Admin password, all database access is based on the same Admin logon, and this default logon does not require a password!) To create a password-protected administrative logon, first make sure that the **Admin** is selected from the **User Name** as shown in Figure 10.23. Next, click on the **Change Logon Password** tab shown in Figure 10.23 to generate Figure 10.24.

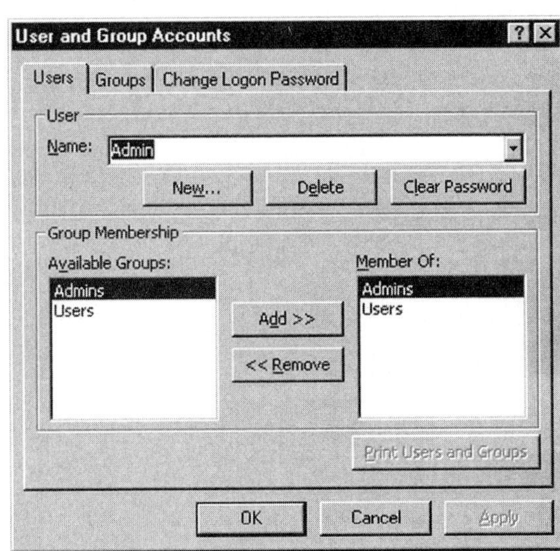

FIGURE 10.23
The User and Group Accounts Dialog Box

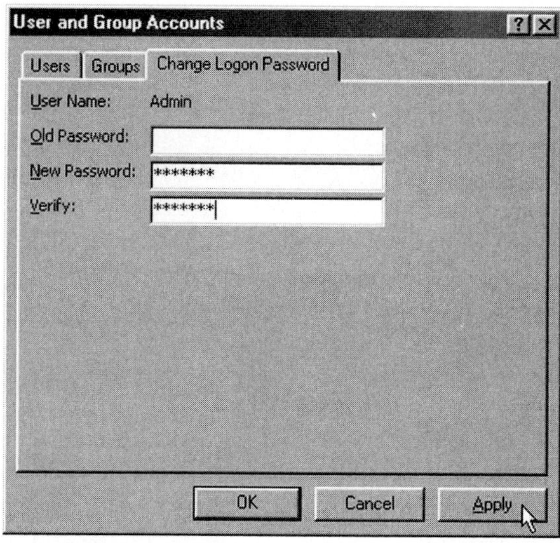

FIGURE 10.24
Assign Logon Password

As you examine Figure 10.24, note that we have left the **Old Password** blank, because no password exists at this point. (Remember, we are creating a brand new Admins environment in this example. If a password-protected Admins account already exists, you must, of course, supply the password for that account.) Next, enter the password in the **New Password** field, and confirm it in the **Verify** box. (We often use an easily remembered password—**LetMeIn**—to illustrate the procedure based on Figure 10.24. Naturally, you should use a more complex password if you want to ensure that the security system is not too easily compromised and, just as important, you should change it often.)

After verifying the password—remember that passwords are case-sensitive—click **Apply** and then click the **OK** button shown in Figure 10.24. (Do not forget to click the **Apply** button before you click the **OK** button!)

Exit Access and then start it again to generate the **Logon** dialog box screen shown in Figure 10.25. Note that the default name is **Admin.** If Admin is not the default name, type it in as shown in Figure 10.25 and enter the password into the **Password** field. Finally, click **OK** to complete the logon as the system's administrator.

10.5.2 Adding New Users to the Admins Group

First complete the **Tools/Security/User and Group Accounts** sequence in Figure 10.22 to generate the screen shown in Figure 10.23, then click on the **New...** button shown in that figure. This action will open the **New User/Group** dialog box in Figure 10.26.

Using the dialog box shown in Figure 10.26, enter the **Name** and the **Personal ID.** (Remember that you cannot use the same user or group name twice within the same workgroup. Also, keep in mind that the personal identification is required. This ID is *not* the password, it is case-sensitive alphanumeric, and it can be 4 to 20 characters long). Make sure you write down the **Personal ID** in a safe place in case the workgroup file is corrupted and you need to re-create it. A sample entry is shown in Figure 10.26A.

FIGURE 10.25
The Logon Dialog Box

FIGURE 10.26
The New User/Group Dialog Box

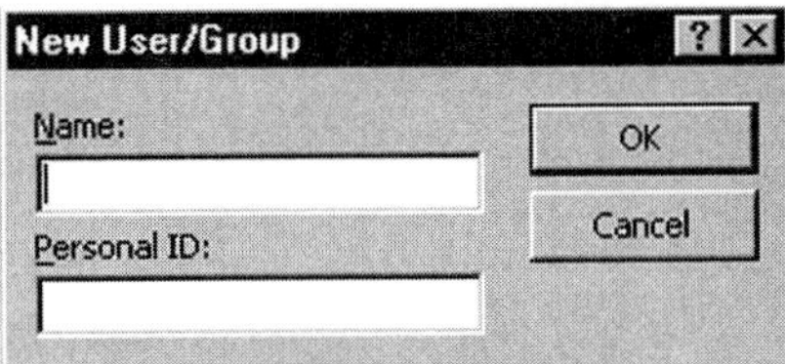

FIGURE 10.26A
The Completed New User/Group Dialog Box

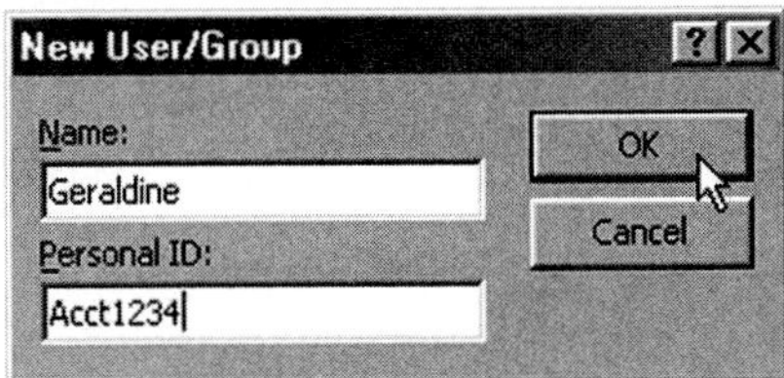

After you have completed the entries shown in Figure 10.26A, click on the **OK** button to ensure that Access adds the new user to the **Users** group account. This action will produce Figure 10.27, which shows Geraldine as a user in the **Name:** window.

To add the new user to the **Admins** group, make sure that the user name—in this case, Geraldine—is selected from the user drop-down list shown in Figure 10.27. After selecting the **Geraldine** user name,

- Select **Admins** in the **Available Groups** window.
- Click on the **Add**>> button located between the two windows.
- Click on the **OK** button.

At this point, the new user (Geraldine) is a member of both the **Admins** and **Users** groups (see Figure 10.27A). When you log on to Access again, Geraldine in the **Admins** group has the same privileges as the **Admin** user.

10.5.3 Deleting Users from the Admins Account

To delete a user, you must log on as **Admin**, select the user from the drop-down list, and click on the **Delete** button shown in Figure 10.27A.

10.5.4 Managing the User Groups

The Users group is an Access default account. Therefore, when you add a new user, the system automatically assigns the user to the Users group account. The Users group account cannot be deleted and it cannot be removed from the **Member Of:** window shown in Figures 10.27 and 10.27A.

To assign a password to a user, start Access to get the **Logon** dialog box in Figure 10.25. (We're assuming that you have already created all appropriate security

FIGURE 10.27
The New User

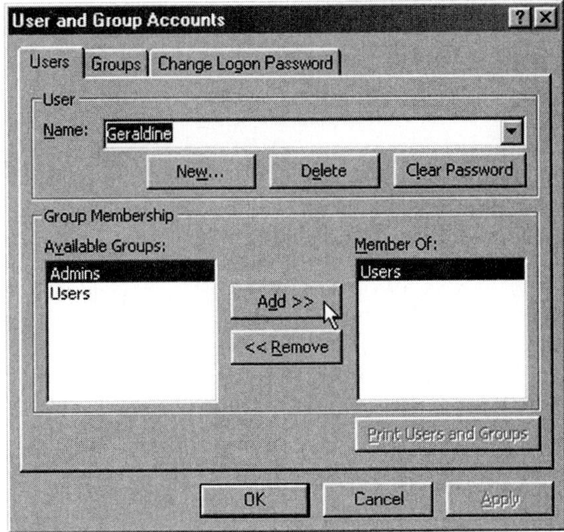

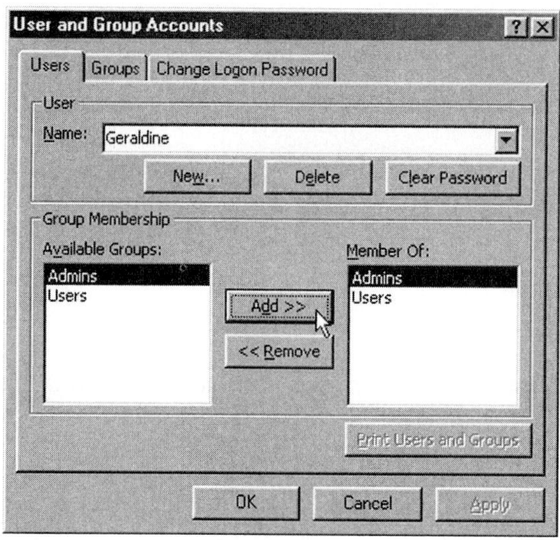

FIGURE 10-27A
The New User in the Admins Group

accounts.) In the name field, enter the user's name and leave the password blank. Next, open the **User and Group Accounts** dialog box shown in Figure 10.27. If you log on as **Admin,** all tabs are available. If you log on as a **User,** only the **Users** and **Change Logon Password** tabs will be available.

To manage the passwords, click on the **Change Logon Password** tab shown in Figures 10.27 and 10.27A to produce the screen shown in Figure 10.27B.

If you want to create a new password, leave the old password blank, enter the new password, and verify it. To change an existing password, first enter the old password, then enter the new one, and verify the change. To clear the password, enter the old password and then leave the **New...** and **Verify** fields blank.

10.5.5 Adding and Deleting Groups and Users within the Groups

In the previous sections, you learned that Access creates two group accounts as defaults: the Admins and Users group accounts. Given our discussion in section 10.5.1, you know that you should add your own groups and then assign users to those groups.

To create a new group, you must log on as an **Admin** and select the **Groups** tab from the **User and Group Account** dialog box (see Figure 10.28). Click on

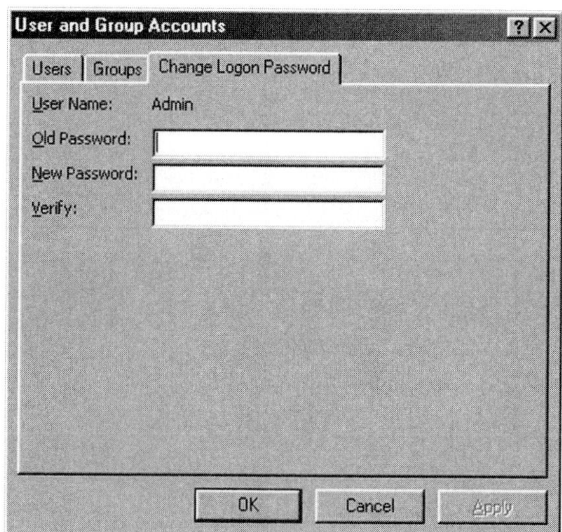

FIGURE 10.27B
The Change Logon Password Tab Options

Note

All users inherit the permissions from the group they are in. For example, if user Geraldine has no permission on the EMPLOYEE table and she has been added to a group that has a permission to the EMPLOYEE table, Geraldine automatically inherits the permission of the group and she has permission to the EMPLOYEE table. If Geraldine is removed from the group, she loses her permission to the EMPLOYEE table.

FIGURE 10.28
The Groups Tab

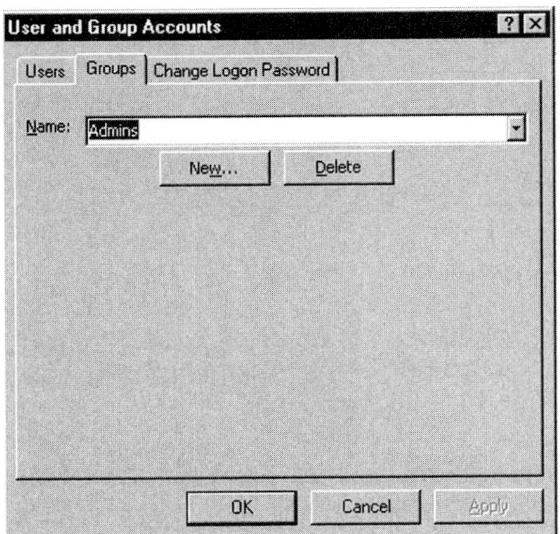

FIGURE 10.28A
The New Group Dialog Box

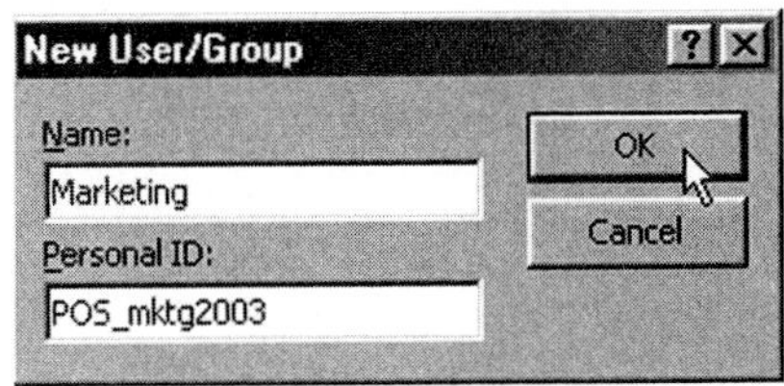

the **New...** button and enter the new group's **Name** as well as the **Personal ID** as shown in Figure 10.28A.

When you click **OK** on the dialog box shown in Figure 10.28A, you will see Figure 10.28B. Note that the new **Marketing** group is now shown in the **Available Groups:** window.

FIGURE 10.28B
The New Group

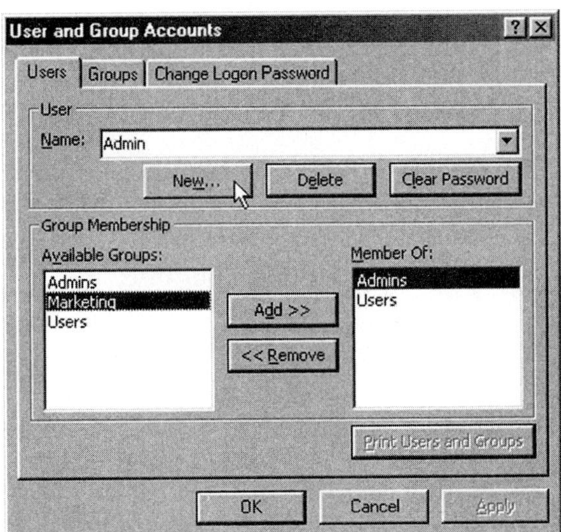

FIGURE 10.28C
Adding Users to the Group

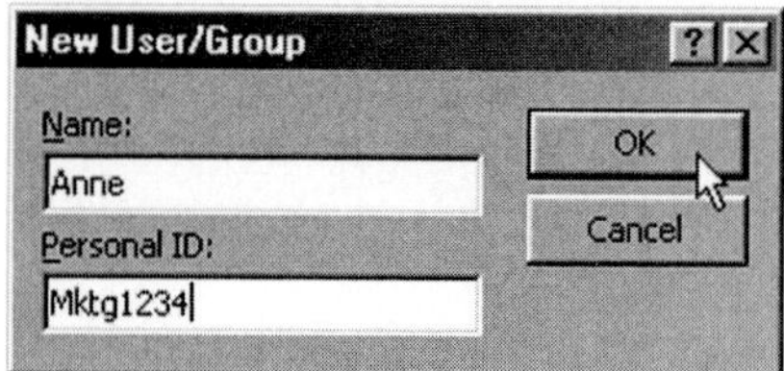

FIGURE 10.28D
The New User Entry

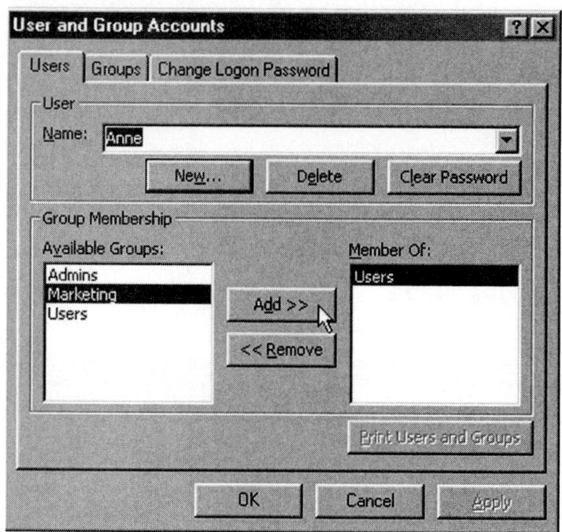

To remove a group, click on the **Delete** button in Figure 10.28B while the group name is selected from the drop-down list.

To add users to the new marketing group, select the **Users** tab from the **User and Group Accounts** dialog box in Figure 10.28B and then repeat the procedures discussed in section 10.5.2 to add users. For example, if you want to add Anne to the marketing group, make sure that **Marketing** is selected as shown in Figure 10.28B and then select **New...** in the **User Name:** window to generate Figure 10.28C. Type in the **Name:** and the **Personal ID:** as shown, then click **OK** to generate Figure 10.28D.

After adding a new user, make sure that the user is displayed in Figure 10.28D's **User Name** window. In the **Available Groups** window, highlight the group name—in this example, **Marketing**—you want to assign the new user to; then click on the **Add>>** button to move the group to the **Member Of:** window. Click **OK** to make the new user a member of the new group (see Figure 10.28E).

The next time you log on and select **User and Group Accounts...** as your **Security** option—see Figure 10.22 again—you will see the results shown in

FIGURE 10.28E
Move the New User to the Marketing Group

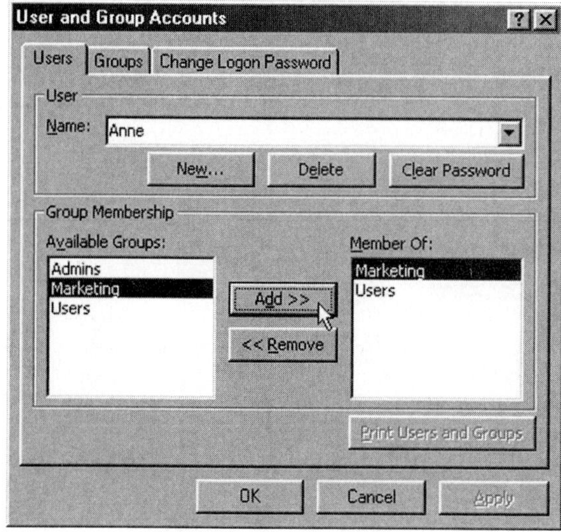

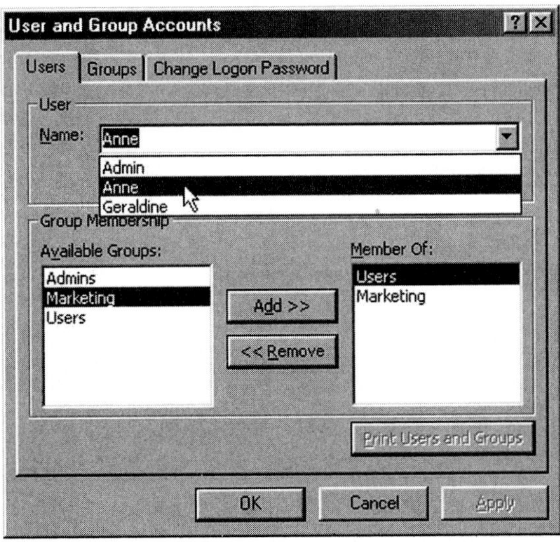

FIGURE 10.28F
The New User as a Member of the Marketing Group

Figure 10.28F. You may wonder why Geraldine is also shown. Remember that Geraldine was assigned as a member of the Admins group? Therefore, Geraldine in the Admins group has the same privileges as the Admin user. In short, Geraldine has access to all the groups that are part of her Admins group.

10.6 PERMISSIONS

The assignment and use of permissions is crucial to database security. Therefore, examine the permission summary in Table 10.1 carefully. It shows you which permissions can be granted to group and user accounts and what those permissions allow you to do.

TABLE 10.1 Access Permissions to User and Group Accounts

Permission	Allows the user to	Is used for
Open/Run	Open a database, form, or report or run a macro	Databases, forms, reports, macros
Open/Exclusive	Open the database exclusively	Databases
Read/Design	Open and look at any object in its design view	All objects
Modify/Design	View, change, and delete objects	All objects
Administer	Full access and assign permissions	All objects and the security system
Read Data	View data	Tables and queries
Update Data	View and change data without insert or delete	Tables and queries
Insert Data	View and add data without modify or delete	Tables and queries
Delete Data	View and delete data without modify or add	Tables and queries

10.6.1 Assigning Permissions

You can logon as an Admin and assign permissions to different groups and users, but it is easier and more reliable to use the User-Admin Security Wizard to perform these tasks. After the wizard has created the basic security structures, you can logon as an Admin to create your own groups, to assign users to those groups, and to assign permissions to groups and to users within those groups. To show you the full array of administrative functions, we will show you how to

1. Use the **User-Level Security Wizard** to create a secure database.
2. Logon as an **Admin** to create new groups and assign users to the groups.
3. Assign permissions to the groups and user accounts you created in step 2.

Note

If you completed the procedures in the previous sections, you should remember that the system1.mdw password is **LetMeIn.** (Passwords are case-sensitive!)

For a change of pace and to illustrate that the procedures we have demonstrated work in any folder environment, let's assume that you have copied the **Ch10_POS_2nd.mdb** database from its original folder to a new folder **C:\MSOffice\Access\Demos\Security**. After copying the database to this folder, you have renamed the database **POS_2nd.mdb**. Although we will use the **POS_2nd.mdb** database in this illustration, keep in mind that the same process can be used on any database.

To begin the process of assigning permissions, start by opening the database, in this example, the **POS_2nd.mdb** database. Two points must be kept in mind at this point:

1. To use the user-level wizard, the database must be opened in shared mode. If you try to open the database in exclusive mode, the wizard will inform you that you must use the database in shared mode, and it will give you the option to let it reopen the database in its shared mode.
2. No prior security was assigned to the database, or you are logging on as an **Admin**.

Assuming that you select the **Tools/Security** and **User-Level Security Wizard...** options in Figure 10.29, you will generate the screen shown in Figure 10.30. (Note that this wizard is activated at the database level.)

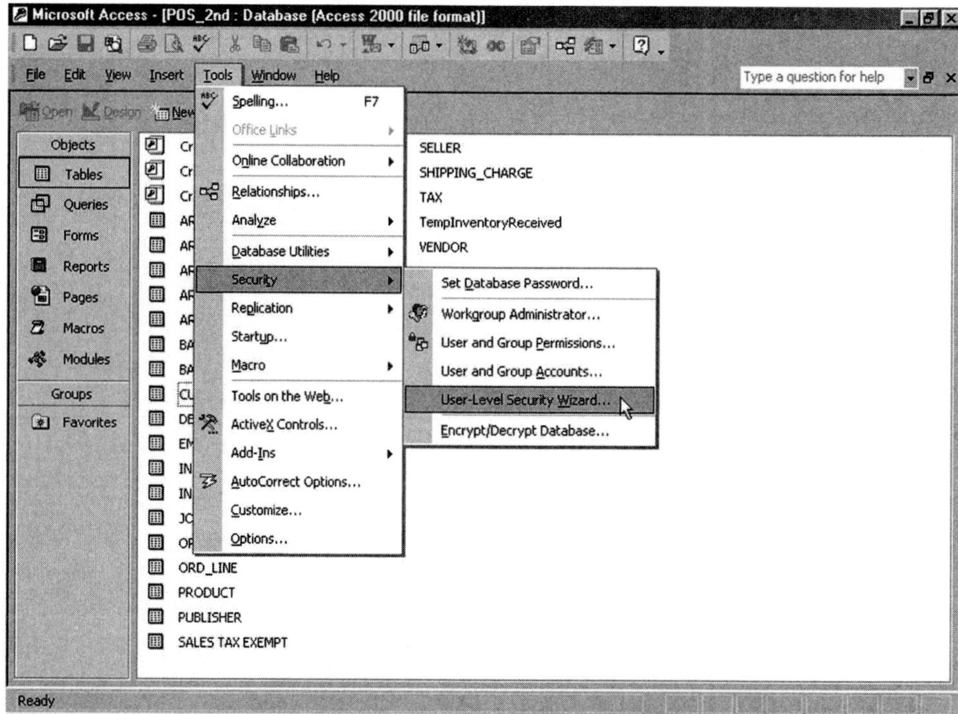

FIGURE 10.29
Starting the User-Level Security Wizard

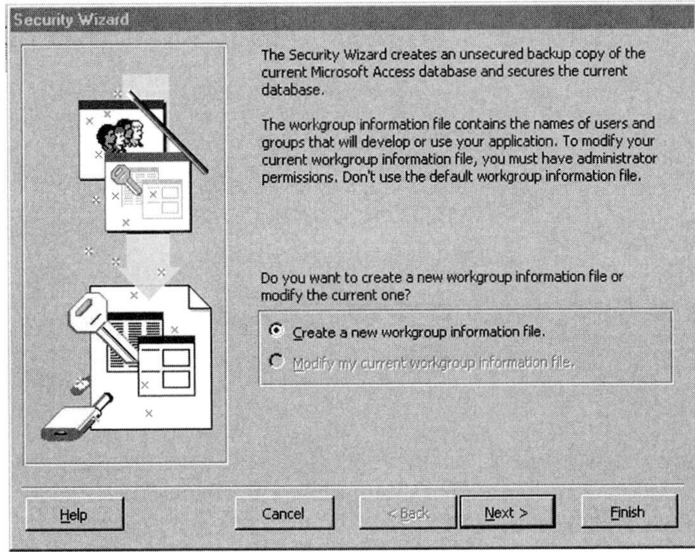

FIGURE 10.30
The Security Wizard

At this point, Figure 10.30 indicates that only the **Create a new workgroup information file** option is available. Note also that the screen in Figure 10.30 includes a brief description about the requirements that must be met to secure the database, so make sure that you read this description before continuing. After you have read the two paragraphs in Figure 10.30, click **Next** > to generate the screen shown in Figure 10.31.

As you examine the screen shown in Figure 10.31, note the following points:

1. Access automatically places the workgroup file in the same folder as the database.
2. Access assigns the default Microsoft Access name. You can change this name to suit your requirements.
3. Access automatically generates a Workgroup ID. You can change this ID to suit your requirements.
4. You can change the location of the Workgroup—use the **Browse...** button to select another location—and the Workgroup ID. (Make sure you write down

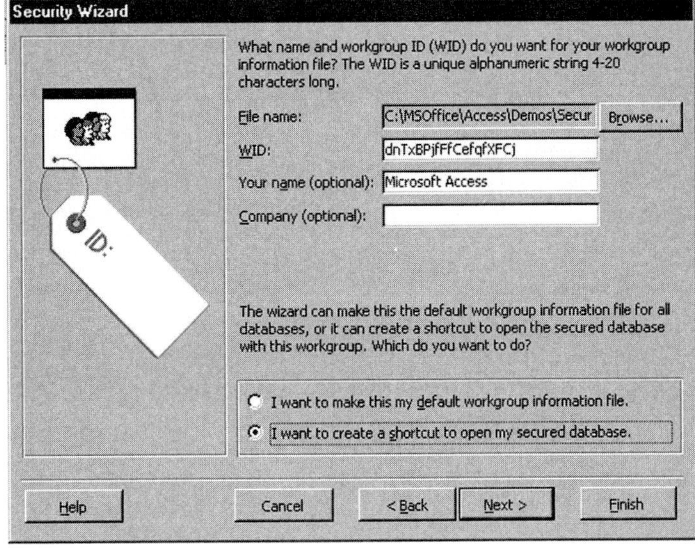

FIGURE 10.31
Creating the Workgroup

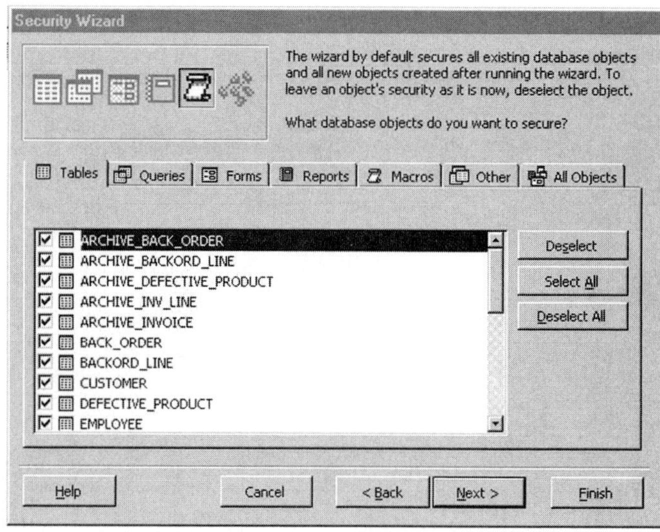

FIGURE 10.32
Selecting the Objects

the Workgroup ID so that you will remember its name when you want to modify it later.)

5. Two workgroup information file options are available: you can either check **I want to create a shortcut to open my secured database** to create a shortcut on your desktop or you can select **I want to make this my default workgroup information file** to make the Workgroup file a default in all your databases. We will select the first choice, because we don't want to use this workgroup as a default. (You will also discover later that Access makes your life as a database administrator a lot easier if you select the shortcut option. Therefore, we urge you to use the shortcut option.)

After you have made your entries and option selections in Figure 10.31, click **Next** > to generate the screen shown in Figure 10.32.

Using the screen shown in Figure 10.32, you can select the objects you want to secure. (We will use the **Select All** objects option.) Click **Next** > to generate the screen shown in Figure 10.33.

As you examine Figure 10.33, note that the Access Wizard creates a set of default groups. Each of those default groups has a group ID. If you want to examine a group, click on it and read its description in the Group Permissions. Each

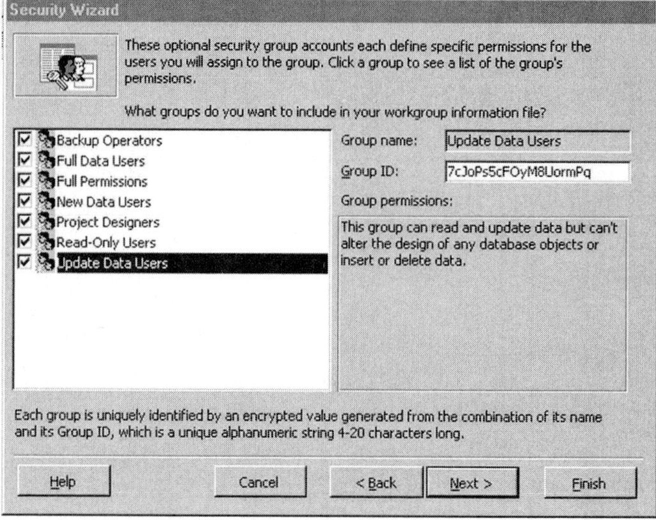

FIGURE 10.33
Selecting the Groups

FIGURE 10.34
Granting Permissions to the Users Group

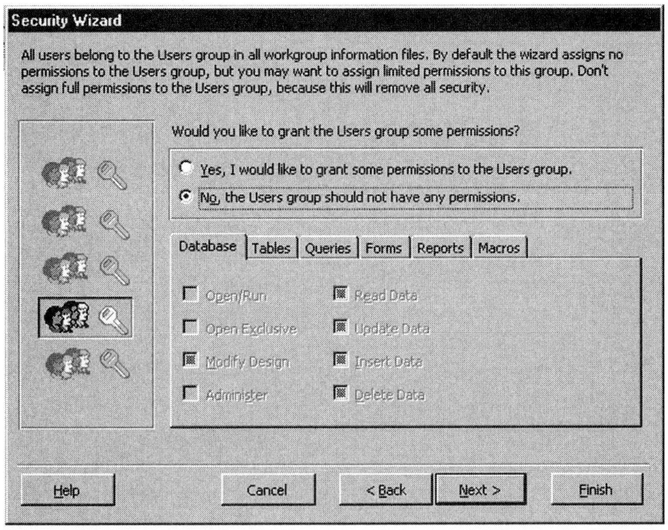

group you select will be added to the secure database. (We will select all groups, then click **Next** > to get to the screen shown in Figure 10.34.

As you examine Figure 10.34, you'll see that Access warns you about assigning full permission to the Users group because the default Users group has identical permissions in all databases. At this point, we will not assign any permissions to the Users group. Therefore, click **Next** > to get to produce the Users screen shown in Figure 10.35.

As you look at Figure 10.35, note that you can create users and assign them passwords. You can then assign these users to a group as shown in Figure 10.36. (The default Admin user is the one who is registered as the licenseholder on the current computer.) Type in your name in Figure 10.35's **User name:** and click **Add This User to the List** button. If you want to assign a password to your user name, select your name from the user list that is shown in Figure 10.35 and type it in the **Password** field.

As you can see in Figure 10.35, the Security Wizard automatically assigns a PID (personal identifier) to the user. Naturally, you can change this PID. When you are satisfied with the entries you have made and the options you have selected, click **Next** > to generate the screen shown in Figure 10.36.

FIGURE 10.35
The Users Screen

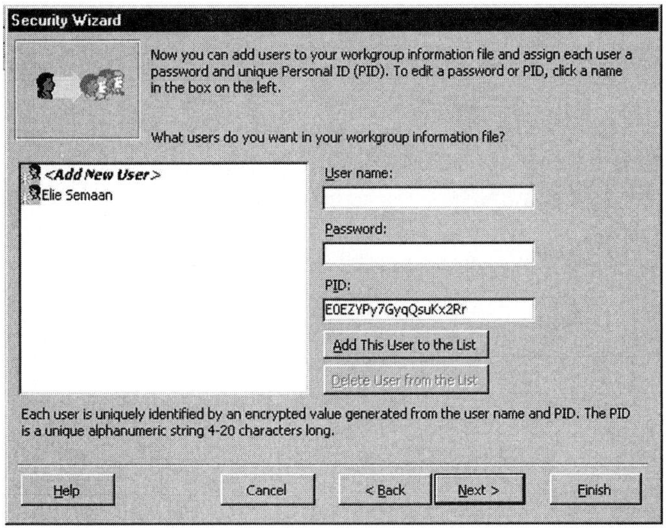

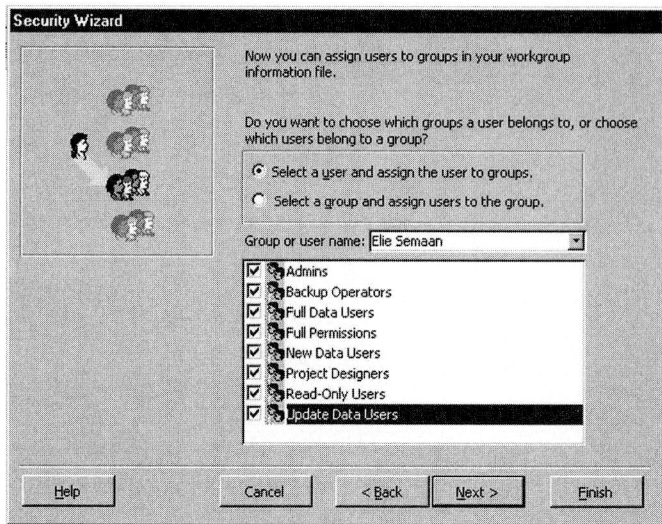

FIGURE 10.36
Assigning Users to Groups

Figure 10.36 indicates that you can assign users to groups. You can select the **Select a user and assign the user to groups** option or the **Select a group and assign users to the group** option. (We will select the first choice.) Select your name from the **Group or user name** drop-down list and check all the groups—or check only the Admins group—and click **Next** > to generate the screen shown in Figure 10.37.

Figure 10.37 shows the location of the backup database. (Access will assign a .bak filename extension to the backup database.) As a default, the database backup will be stored in the same folder as the secured database, but you can change the backup location by clicking on **Browse...** button. (Note that we have moved the location of the backup database.) If you are satisfied with the backup database location, click the **Finish** button shown in Figure 10.37 to complete the process of securing the database.

Given the warning message in Figure 10.38, click **Yes** to save the file to complete the process of securing your database. When the wizard completes securing the database, you will see the message in Figure 10.39.

Once the database has been secured, trying to launch the application through any means other than the shortcut created on your desktop by the Security Wiz-

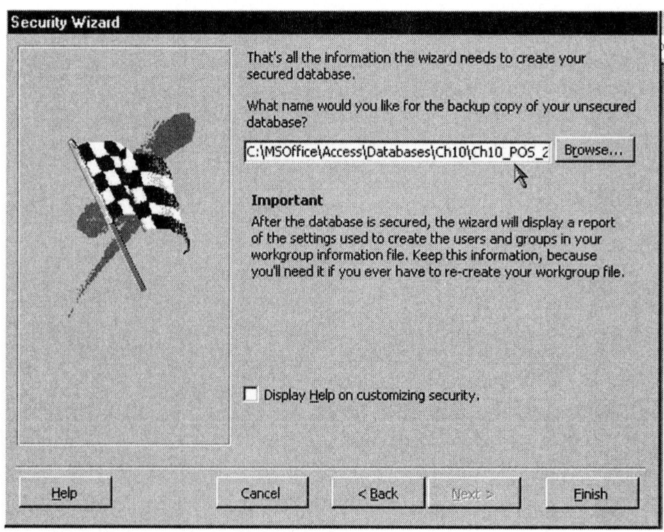

FIGURE 10.37
Naming the Database Backup

Note

The wizard generates a report that contains all the security information for the database. Because you are unlikely to remember all of the security information pertaining to the secured database, we urge you to print the report and to store it in a secure place. If you don't save the report, the wizard generates the warning message shown in Figure 10.38.

FIGURE 10.38
Warning Message

FIGURE 10.39
Completing the Security Process

Security Wizard
The Security Wizard has encrypted your database. To re-open your database, you must use the new workgroup file you have created, by closing Access and re-opening it.
OK

ard will produce the error message shown in Figure 10.40. *You must use the shortcut in order to associate the workgroup with your secure database.*

Click on the shortcut on your desktop to open the secured database, and then enter the user name and the password—assuming that one was assigned—as shown in Figure 10.41.

To assign permission to the groups and users you have created, select **Tools/Security** and **User and Group Permissions** from the database button bar to generate the screen shown in Figure 10.43.

Using the **User and Group Permissions** window shown in Figure 10.43, you can either select the **Users** or the **Groups** check box. At this point, we'll assign permissions to the Accounting group, using the following sequence:

1. Select **Accounting** from the **User/Group Name:** window.
2. Select **Database** from the **Object Type** drop-down list.
3. Select the **Open/Run** permissions.
4. Click on the **Apply** button.
5. Select **Table** from the **Object Type** drop down list.
6. Select **Read Data, Update Data, Insert Data,** and **Delete Data**.
7. Click on the **Apply** button.

While the selected group shown in Figure 10.43 is still selected,

1. Select **Query** from the **Object Type** drop-down list.

FIGURE 10.40
Opening the Secure Database without Using the Shortcut

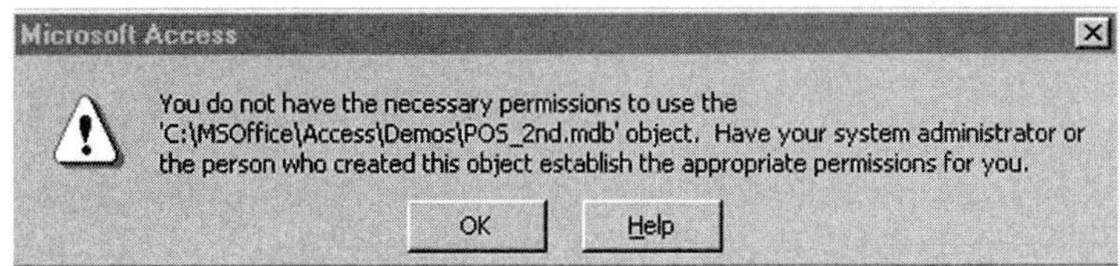

FIGURE 10.41
The Logon Screen

Assignment

Using the instructions provided in the preceding security sequence, create the Accounting, Personal, Technical, Sales, Shipping, and Management groups and assign users to them. When you have created the required groups, your screen should look like the one in Figure 10.42. (Given their location in the alphabetically organized group list, you cannot see the Personal, Technical, Sales, and Shipping groups—you will have to scroll down to see them.)

As you can tell by examining Figure 10.42, the groups you selected in Figure 10.33 are included in the Available Groups. Next, create users and assign them to these groups, or you can assign them to any other group(s) you have created.

FIGURE 10.42
The Available Groups

2. Highlight all queries in the **Object Name:** window.
3. Select **Read Data**, **Update Data**, **Insert Data**, and **Delete Data**.
4. Click on the **Apply** button.

While the selected group shown in Figure 10.43 is still selected,

1. Select **Form** from the **Object Type** drop-down list.

FIGURE 10.43
Assigning Permissions

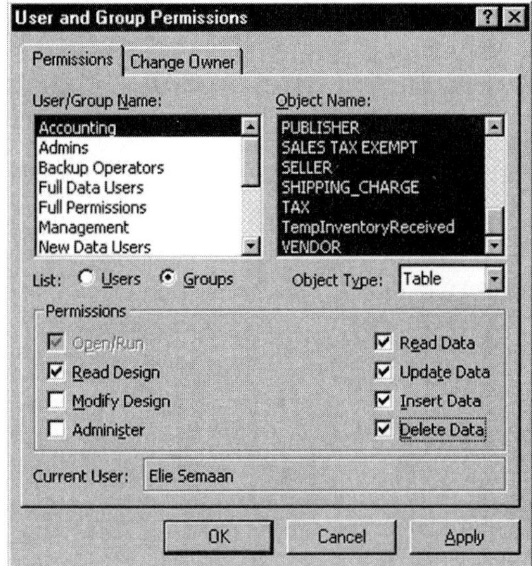

FIGURE 10.44
Logon as a User in the Accounting Group

2. Highlight all the forms in the **Object Name:** window.
3. Select **Open/Run** only.
4. Click on the **Apply** button.

While the selected group shown in Figure 10.43 is still selected,

1. Select **Report** from the **Object Type** drop-down list.
2. Highlight all reports in the **Object Name:** window.
3. Select **Open/Run** only.
4. Click on the **Apply** button.

While the selected group shown in Figure 10.43 is still selected,

1. Select **Macro** from the **Object Type** drop-down list.
2. Highlight all macros in **Object Name:** window.
3. Select **Open/Run** only.
4. Click on the **Apply** button.

You can follow the same steps to assign various permissions to the other groups. (Remember that all of the members of a group inherit the permissions assigned to that group. Naturally, you can change the permissions for the users within a group.)

Now close Access and run the database using the shortcut created by the Security Wizard on your desktop to get to the **Logon** screen shown in Figure 10.44. In the **Logon** screen, type in one of the users you assigned to the Accounting group as shown in Figure 10.44.

If Geraldine was not given permission to modify the EMPLOYEE table and she tries to open the EMPLOYEE table in design view, she would see the message in Figure 10.45.

There are two different way to secure a database without requiring the user to logon. One way to accomplish this task is by completing the following steps:

1. Open the database you want to secure and run the User-Level Security Wizard described earlier in Figure 10.28 and click **Next** > on the screen shown in Figure 10.30.
2. Click **Next** > on the screen shown in Figure 10.31 if you want to use the information created by the Security Wizard.
3. On the screen shown in Figure 10.32, click **Next** > to secure all the objects in the database.
4. In the screen shown in Figure 10.33, do not select any group and click **Next** >.
5. On the screen shown in Figure 10.34, check **Yes, I would like to grant permissions to the Users group** and do the following:

FIGURE10.45
No Permission Allowed on This Object

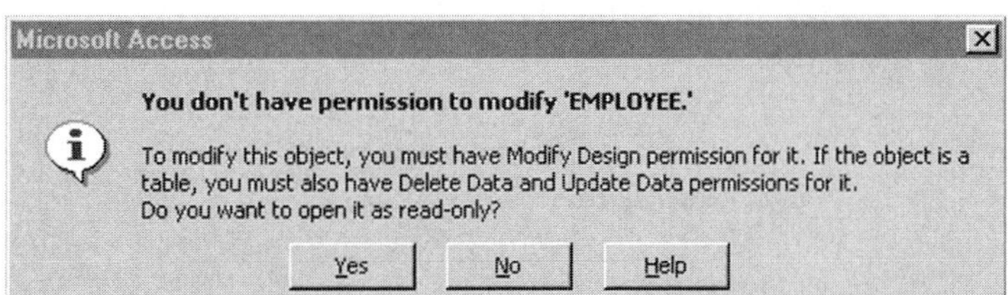

a. From the **Database** tab, check **Open/Run**.
b. From the **Tables** tab, check **Read**, **Update**, **Insert**, and **Delete Data**.
c. From the **Queries** tab, check **Read**, **Update**, **Insert**, and **Delete Data**.
d. From the **Forms** tab, check **Open/Run**.
e. From the **Reports** tab, check **Open/Run**.
f. From the **Macros** tab, check **Open/Run**.
g. On the screen shown in Figure 10.35, click **Next** > without adding users or assigning passwords.
h. In Figure 10.36, click **Next** > with the default selection.
i. Click **Finish** to complete the process.

After completing the security process, open the database *without using the shortcut*. You will see that there will be no logon screen. However, if you try to open any of the objects in design view, you will discover that your permission is denied. If you want to make changes to the database, open the database using the shortcut and logon with the admin user name created by the wizard.

The second way to secure a database without a logon is to complete the following steps:

1. Create secure database using the User-Level Security Wizard as described earlier, but do not assign a password to the Admin user.
2. Open the database and logon as an Admin as shown in Figure 10.41.
3. Select **Tools/Security** and then select **User and Group Permissions** from the database window button bar.
4. From the **User/Group Name** window, select **Admin**. No password should be assigned to the Admin user.
5. From the Object Type select **Database** and check the **Open/Run** permissions.
6. Select **Table** from the Object Type and select all tables as shown in Figure 10.43. Check **Read**, **Update**, **Insert**, and **Delete Data**.
7. Select **Form** from the Object Type; select all forms and check the **Open/Run** permissions.
8. Select **Report** from the Object Type; select all reports and check the **Open/Run** permissions.
9. Select **Macro** from the Object Type; select all macros and check the **Open/Run** permissions.

Now close the database and reopen it *without using the shortcut*. You can open Access and open the database from the Access menu. (You'll notice that you don't get the logon screen.)

Both ways can be used to develop a commercial application without requiring the users to logon every time they use the database. If you want to logon to the database as an Admin and make changes, you'll have run the database through the wizard-created shortcut created to make your changes.

10.7 THE OWNERSHIP ISSUE

An object's creator is the owner of that object. Therefore, if any user creates an object, that user can grant any permission for that object, regardless of the permission(s) given to that user. From a database administration point of view, such a state of affairs is not desirable. Therefore, the database administrator usually performs periodic checks to see what permissions are granted to which users. If the ownership of an object yields undesirable permissions, the database administrator must be able to change the ownership of that object.

To change an object's ownership, first logon as an Admin. Next, click on the **Change Owner** tab from the **User and Group Permissions** window as shown in Figure 10.46. From the **Object Type** drop-down list, select the object for which

FIGURE10.46
Change the Ownership of an Object

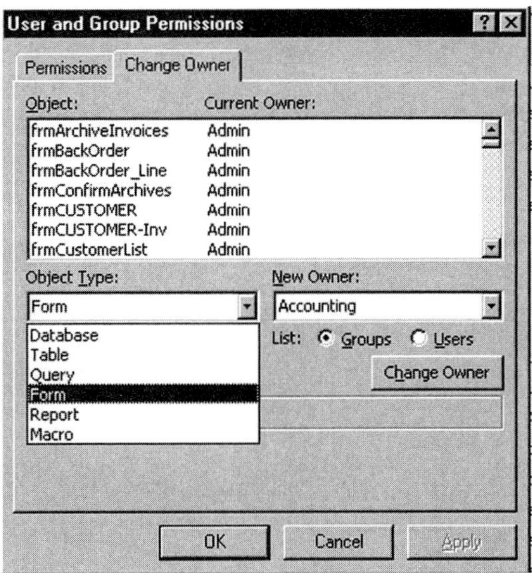

you want to change the ownership, select the user or the group from the **New Owner** drop-down list, and click on the **Change Owner** button.

10.8 REMOVING DATABASE SECURITY

If the database is in development as a prototype, maintaining the various administrative security levels may not be practical. One way to simplify the security procedures is to logon as an Admin, grant full permissions to all users, and remove the Admin password. While the database is still technically secured, the management of that security is now transparent to the user.

If you used the User-Level Security Wizard, removing the security structure is a little more complicated. (Remember that you can always go back to the backup database created by the security wizard. The backup database has a .bak filename extension, and it is located in the same folder as the secured database.) To remove the security from a secured database, follow these steps:

1. Open the secured database and logon as an Admin as shown in Figure 10.41.
2. Open the **Tools/Security** option, and then select the **User and Group Permissions** option.
3. Give full permission on all objects to all users and groups.
4. Remove all passwords from the Admin, the groups, and the users.

Close the secured database—in this example, **Ch10_POS_2nd.mdb**—and then create a new database in the same folder. (If you check the **File name:** entry in Figure 10.47, you will see that we named the new database **Ch10_POS_2nd New.mdb**. Naturally, you can select a different name for the new database, but you will find it easier to follow the procedures if your database name matches the examples.)

At this point, the new database (**Ch10_POS_2ndNew.mdb**) does not yet contain any tables, queries, or other database objects. Therefore, let's import these objects from the original **Ch10_POS_2nd.mdb** database. Using the new database, right-click on its database window and select **Import...** as shown in Figure 10.48.

The selection in Figure 10.48 yields the database **Import** window shown in Figure 10.49. Select the **Ch10_POS_2nd.mdb** database from this **Import** window.

FIGURE 10.47
Creating a New Database

FIGURE 10.48
Select the Import Option

Next, click on the **Import** button shown in Figure 10.49 to generate the **Import Objects** window shown in Figure 10.50.

Using the **Import Objects** window shown in Figure 10.50, click on the **Tables** tab and click on **Select All** button. Next, select the **Queries** tab and repeat the process. Select each of the remaining tabs for the objects you want to import—**Forms, Reports,** and **Macros**—then click on the **OK** button to import all of the **Ch10_POS_2nd.mdb** objects into the new **Ch10_POS_2ndNew.mdb** database.

After completing the import process, the **Ch10_POS_2ndNew.mdb** will be available to you without security.

10.9 ENCRYPTING AND DECRYPTING DATABASES

The **Encrypt/Decrypt** option produces an additional security blanket to ensure that only Access can open the database. For example, given an encrypted Access database, an Excel end user will not be able to access an encrypted Access data-

FIGURE 10.49
Selecting the Ch10_POS_2nd.mdb from the Import Window

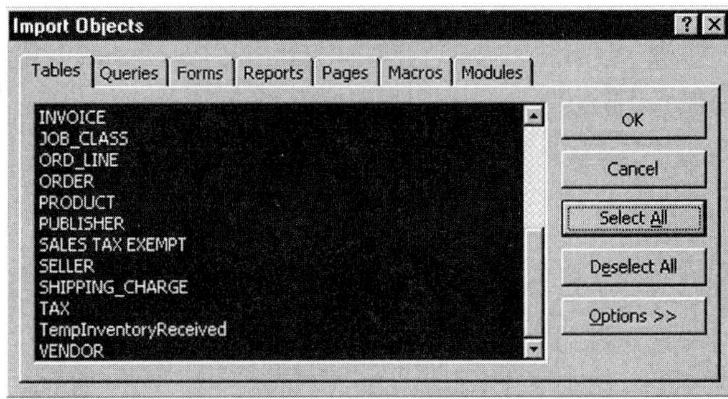

FIGURE 10.50 Selecting all Objects from the Imports Objects Window

base. The **Encrypt/Decrypt** option is particularly useful at the network level. Encryption decreases the performance of the database by about 15 percent, and it also prevents the database from being compressed.

To use the encryption option, follow these steps:

1. Open the database to be encrypted.
2. Select **Tools/Security** and **Encrypt/Decrypt Database** options as shown in Figure 10.51.
3. Give the encrypted database a new name as shown in Figure 10.52 and click on the **Save** button. (We have named the database to be encrypted **POS_Encrypted.mdb**. The default database name was **db1.mdb**.)

To decrypt the database, open the encrypted database and follow the same procedures you have followed to encrypt it. (If you have opened an encrypted database, Access will recognize the encryption. Therefore, even though the window will still be labeled **Encrypt Database As,** clicking on the **Save** button will decrypt the database.)

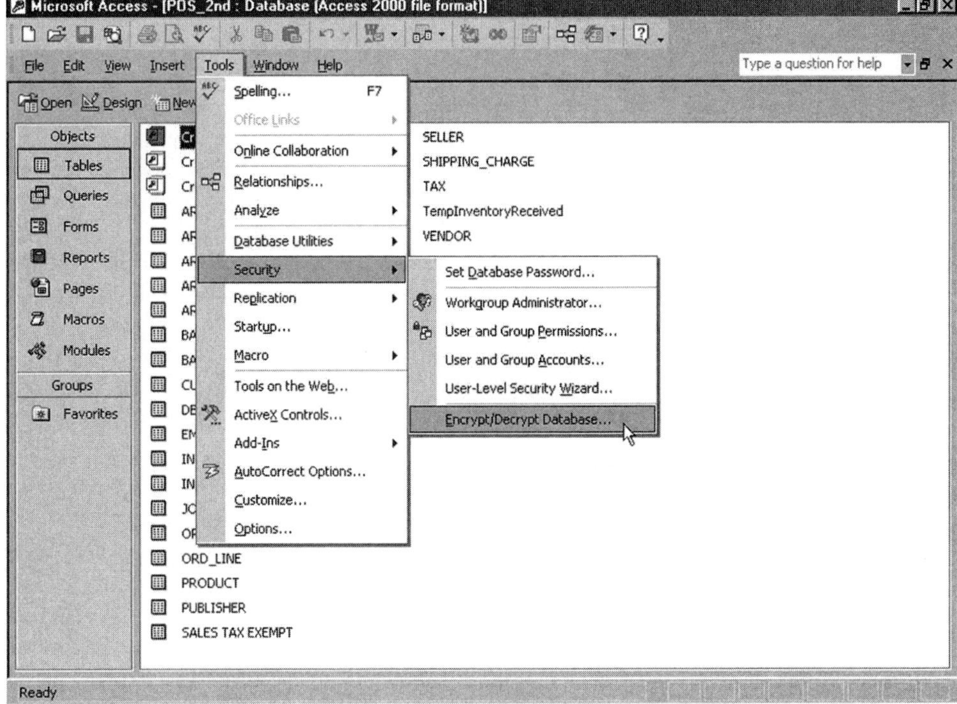

FIGURE 10.51 Selecting the Encrypt/Decrypt Database Option

FIGURE 10.52
Name and Save the Encrypted Database

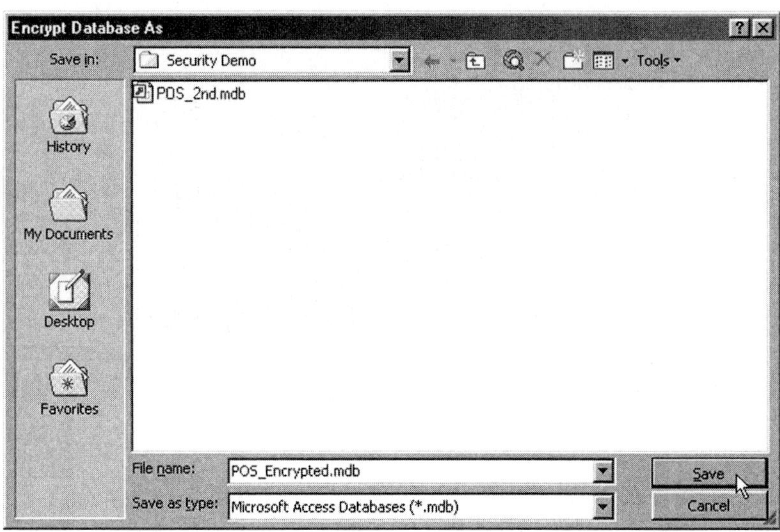

10.10 SEGMENTING THE DATABASE

You can add an additional measure of security by separating the database into two components: the database back-end and the database front-end. The back-end contains the tables and relationships, while the front-end contains all the end-user applications, that is, the queries, forms, reports, macros, and modules. The database front-end can then use the back-end database tables as attached tables.

The database back-end/front-end segmenting makes it possible to create a security system that requires unauthorized users to breach two sets of security walls. In addition, a front-end failure will leave the back-end intact. Similarly, a back-end failure will leave the front-end intact. Therefore, segmenting the database will add a measure of safety to the database operations.

Database segmenting has additional advantages. The use of a database back-end and its corresponding front-end enables developers to change the front-end applications without affecting the back-end database. For example, suppose that you are developing a database for a company. The company management has requested a change to the database applications, but it will not be feasible to accept an extended database downtime, because the database is crucial to the company's operations. If the database is segmented, you can make changes to the front-end database and replace it when you are ready, without losing data and without requiring an extended downtime. Also, because applications other than Access often use the same data stored in the database back-end, database segmenting makes the end-user applications environment more flexible. For example, if database tables are used as the data source for Microsoft Excel, there is no need to expose the Access queries, macros, and other application objects to the Excel applications.

One particularly desirable effect of database segmenting is that such segmenting makes it possible to use a different RDBMS as the database back-end, thus increasing the flexibility of the Access applications development environment. In fact, because Access applications development is so easy and flexible, Access may be used as a front-end to the back-end SQL Server databases.

10.10.1 The Database Back End

To show you how a database can be segmented, let's begin by creating a new folder—we'll name it **SegmentedDB**, but you can use any name that appeals to you. Within this new folder,

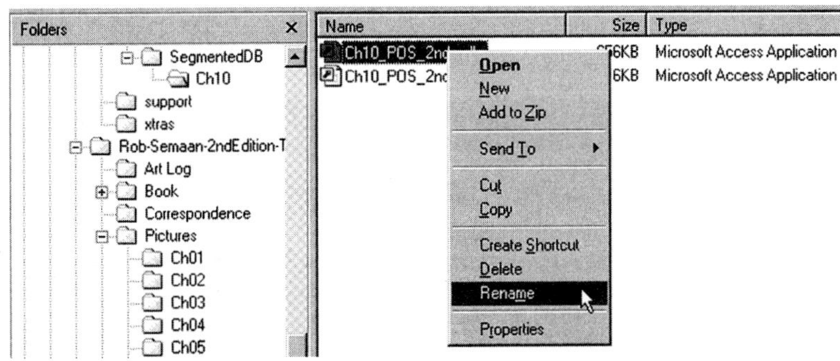

FIGURE 10.53
Rename the Ch10_POS_2nd.mdb to Ch10_POS_Frontend.mdb

FIGURE 10.54
Selecting the Link Tables Options

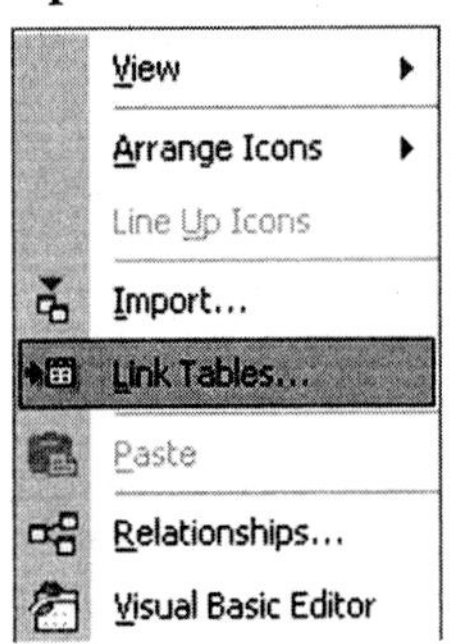

1. Create a folder named **Ch10**.
2. Create a new database named **Ch10_POS_2nd_Backend** and place it in the new **Ch10** folder.
3. Use the Access **Import** function to copy all the tables from the **Ch10_POS_2nd** database into the new **Ch10_POS_2nd_Backend** database. *(Because the back-end database will contain only the database tables, import only the tables, rather than all database objects.)*
4. Copy the entire **Ch10_POS_2nd** database to the new **Ch10** folder.

After you have completed steps 1-4, the **\SegmentedDB\Ch10** folder contains two databases, **Ch10_POS_2nd_Backend** and the copy of the **Ch10_POS_2nd** database.

10.10.2 The Database Front End

Using the Windows explorer, rename the **Ch10_POS_2nd.mdb** database in the **\SegmentedDB\Ch10** folder as **Ch10_POS_2nd_Backend.mdb**, as shown in Figure 10.53.

Now open the **Ch10_POS_Frontend.mdb** database *and delete all of its tables*. After deleting all the **Ch10_POS_Frontend.mdb** database tables, right-click on the database window and select **Link Tables...** option shown in Figure 10.54.

Selecting the **Link Tables...** option shown in Figure 10.54 will produce the **Link** window shown in Figure 10.55. Using this window, find and select the **Ch10_POS_Backend.mdb** and click on the **Link** button. This action will open the **Link Tables** window shown in Figure 10.56.

Using the **Link Tables** window shown in Figure 10.56, click on **Select All** button and then click on the **OK** button. This action will link all the tables shown in Figure 10.56 to the front-end database.

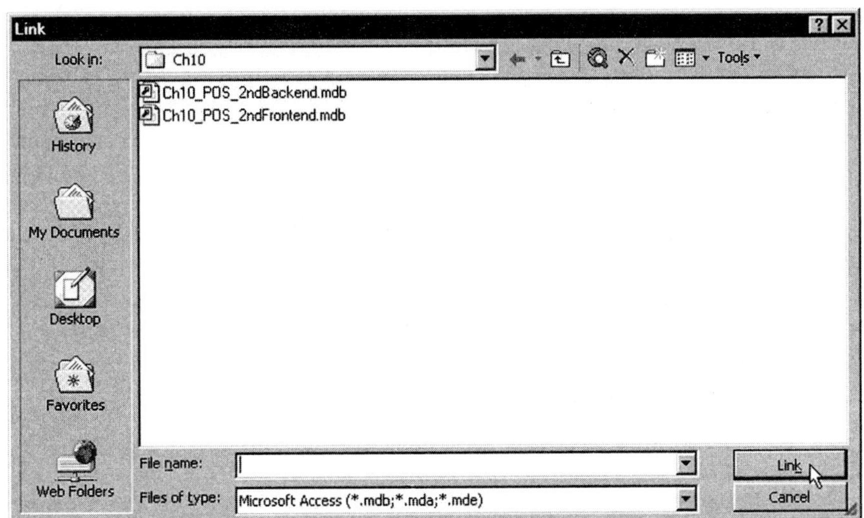

FIGURE 10.55
Selecting the Ch10_POS_Backend.mdb from the Link Window

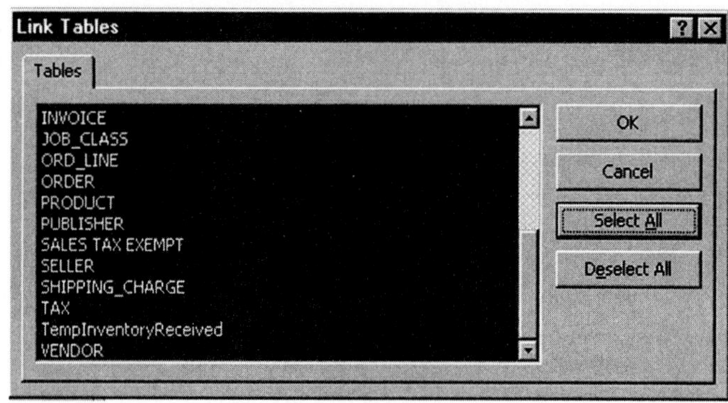

FIGURE 10.56
Click on Select All and Click on the OK Button

When you have completed the linking procedures, your front-end database window should look like Figure 10.57. (Note the link symbols—the small arrows—in front of each table to indicate that the tables are linked.)

To see the path used by the front-end database to its linked tables, select the **Tools/Database Utilities** and the **Linked Table Manager** options shown in Figure 10.58. (If the Linked Table Manager is not installed on the computer you are using, you must first install this option in order to use it.).

From the **Linked Table Manager** window you can see the path of the linked tables shown in Figure 10.59.

To refresh the linked tables, click on **Select All** in Figure 10.59 then click on the **OK** button.

If you want to link to tables in another database—perhaps one in the same folder or one in another location—you can accomplish that task without having to delete all the tables and then linking them all over again. To link to a new set of tables, click on **Always prompt for new location** in the Linked Table Manager as shown in Figure 10.59. Click on **Select All**, and then click **OK** to generate the **Select New Location** window shown in Figure 10.60.

Select the new location, then select the database and click on the **Open** button to change the path of the linked tables.

If you want to assign separate security options to the back-end and front-end databases, you can do so with the same security wizard that you used before. Starting with the **Ch10_POS_Backend.mdb**:

1. Open the **Ch10_POS_Backend.mdb** and run the User-Level Security Wizard as described in section 10.6.1.

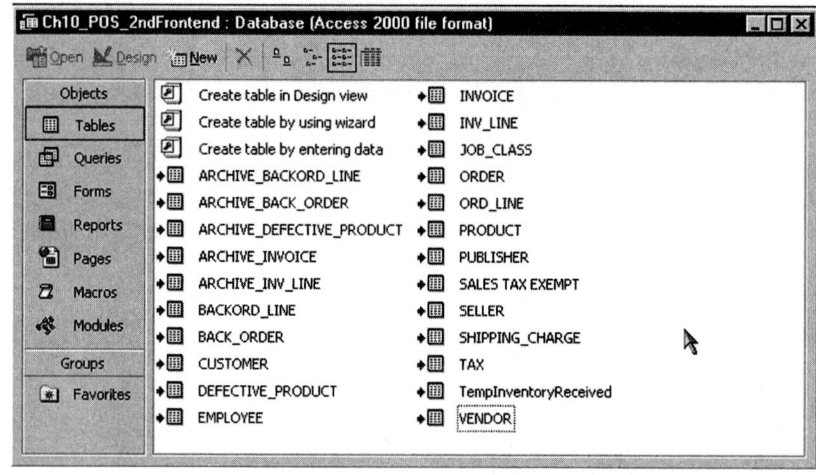

FIGURE 10.57
The Database Window with the Linked Tables

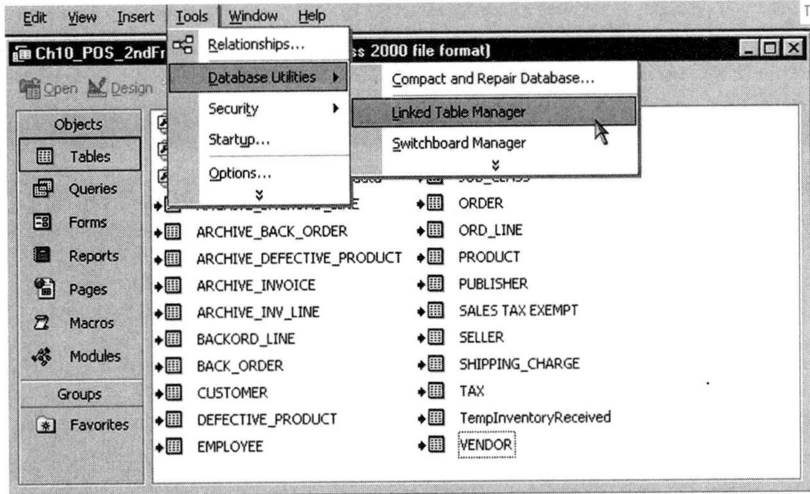

FIGURE 10.58
Select the Linked Table Manager

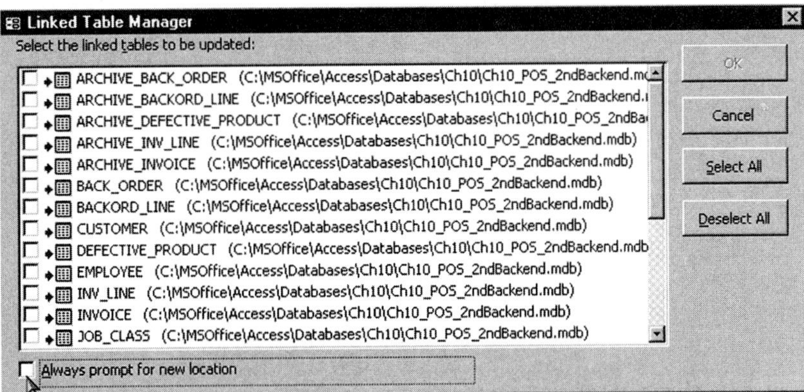

FIGURE 10.59
The Linked Table Manager Window

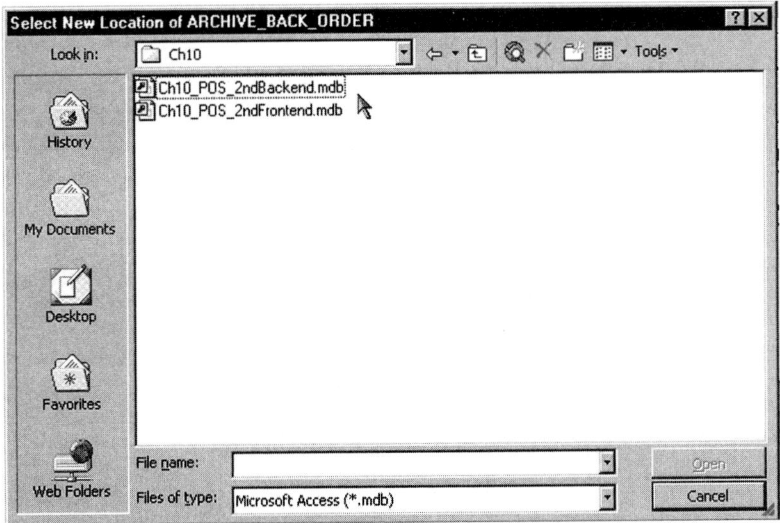

FIGURE 10.60
Select New Location Window

2. When you get to assigning permissions to the users group shown in Figure 10.34, check **Yes, I would like to grant some permissions to the Users group**, and do the following:
   a. Select the **Database** tab.
   b. Select the **Open/Run** permissions.

FIGURE 10.61
Permission Denied Message

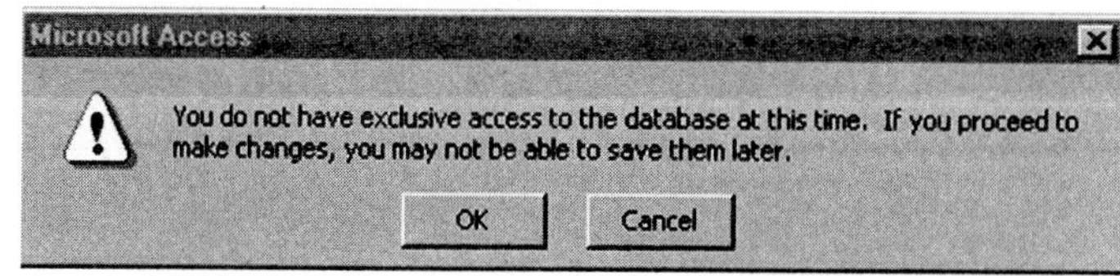

c. Select the **Table** tab.
d. Select the **Read** and **Update** permissions.

To secure the **Ch10_POS_Frontend.mdb** database, follow these steps:

1. Open the **Ch10_POS_Frontend.mdb** and run the User-Level Security Wizard as described in section 10.6.1.
2. When you get to assigning permissions to the users group shown in Figure 10.34, check **Yes, I would like to grant some permissions to the Users group** and do the following:
   a. Select the **Database** tab and check **Open/Run** permissions.
   b. Select the **Table** tab.
   c. Select the **Read**, **Update**, **Insert**, and **Delete Data** permissions.
   d. Select the **Forms**, **Reports**, and **Macros**.
   e. Select the **Open/Run** permissions.

Now you have two secured databases. In this example, we gave the Users group Read and Update Data permissions in the back-end database and we gave the Users group Read, Update, Insert, and Delete Data permissions in the front-end database.

Now open the **Ch10_POS_Frontend.mdb** without using the shortcut created by the Security Wizard; you'll see that you don't get the logon screen. If you try to open any of the objects in design view, you get a denied message as shown in Figure 10.61. (You were not given permission to the design view.)

If you open the EMPLOYEE table in Datasheet View, you will see that data insertions and/or deletions are not allowed (see Figure 10.62).

The reason for the inability to make changes in the EMPLOYEE table structure or its contents is found in the assignments of permissions. You should remember that, while using the Security Wizard, we assigned **Read, Update, Insert,** and **Delete Data** to the table objects in the **Ch10_POS_Frontend.mdb** database. However, we assigned only **Read** and **Update** data permissions when we created the security environment for the **Ch10_POS_Backend.mdb.** The permissions that were assigned to the back-end database are carried with the tables through the link to the front-end database. And if you create new tables in the front-end database, you will have **Read, Update, Insert,** and **Delete** data permissions to those tables.

FIGURE 10.62
Inserting and Deleting Data in the EMPLOYEE Table Is Not Allowed

File Edit View Insert Format Records Tools Window Help

EMP_NUM	EMP_TITLE	EMP_LNAME	EMP_FNAME	EMP_INITIAL	EMP_ADDRESS
31	Ms.	Page	Katheryn	D	312 Tennessee Street
32	Ms.	Smith	Melanie	K	150B North Street
33	Mr.	Kruse	Herman	M	304 Southland Dr.
35	Mrs.	Jones	Hermine		942 St. John Hollow
37	Mr.	Orlof	Karl	K	334 N. Frederick
39	Mr.	Okomoto	Ronald	F	2203 Riverland Drive
40	Mr.	Brynnan	William	C	557 S. Limestone Street
41	Mr.	Smith	Robert	A	601 Nashville Lane
42	Ms.	Zantaro	Sussette	A	114 S. Hamilton Street
44	Mr.	Smithson	George	D	335 Minerva Dr.
45	Mr.	Blalock	James	G	115 Locust Hill Dr.
47	Mr.	Smith	Robert	E	1103 Whitehall Rd.
49	Ms.	Doornberg	Anne	D	214 Haynes Haven Ln.
51	Mr.	Williamson	Charles	D	2535 E. Walnut Ave.
52	Ms.	Downes	Anne	B	1001 Market Street

Problems

10.1 Create a password protection for the **Ch10_POS_2nd** database.

10.2 Remove the password protection you created in problem 10.1.

10.3 Repeat the procedures to complete problems 10.1 and 10.2 for the **Ch10_TruckCo** database.

10.4 Using the **Ch10_POS_2nd** database, run the User-Level Security Wizard and add yourself as an Admin.

a. Logon to the secure database using the shortcut created on the desktop.

b. Create two new groups, one named **Accounting** and one named **Personnel**. Then add three users to each group.

c. Assign security permissions to each group. The permissions must include the following:

Read, Update, Insert, and **Delete Data** on tables.
Open/Run on **Forms, Reports,** and **Macros.**
Open/Run the database.

d. Now close the database and reopen it using the ID of one of the users you created in step b, and assign a password to the current user.

e. Try to open the tables, forms, and reports in design view. *You should not be able to open the design option of any of these objects.*

10.5 Segment the **Ch10_TruckCo** database into a back-end database, named **Ch10_Truck Co_BK**, and a front-end database, named **Ch10_TruckCo_FT**. *Hint*: First create a database named **Ch10_TruckCo_BK**. Open the **Ch10_TruckCo_BK** and use the **Import** option to import the tables from the **Ch10_TruckCo**. Next, rename the **Ch10_TruckCo** to **Ch10_TruckCo_FT**. Open **Ch10_TruckCo_FT** and delete all the tables. From within the **Ch10_TruckCo_FT**, establish the links to the **Ch10_TruckCo_BK** database tables.

10.6 Using another copy of the **Ch10_POS_2nd** database, run the User-Level Security Wizard and assign yourself as an Admin.

a. Logon to the secure database using the shortcut created on the desktop.

b. Open the **User and Group permissions**, and assign the following permissions to the Admin user:

Read, Update, Insert, and **Delete Data** on tables.
Open/Run Forms, Reports, and Macros.
Open/Run the database.

Now close the database and reopen it. *You should not see a logon screen.*

Try to make changes to the design of any of the objects in the database. *You should not be able to make any changes to any of the objects.*

10.7 Using another copy of the **Ch10_POS_2nd** database, run the User-Level Security Wizard and assign to the users the following permissions:

Read, Update, Insert, and **Delete Data** on tables.
Open/Run Forms, Reports, and **Macros.**
Open/Run the database.

Now close the database and reopen it without using the shortcut created by the wizard. *You should not see a logon screen.*

Try to make changes to the design of any of the objects in the database. *You should not be able to make any changes to any of the objects.*

Glossary

A

Access Jet Database Engine The software that powers the DBMS. This database engine automatically creates a lock whenever a database table is opened *in a shared database environment*. The lock is released when the last user closes the database normally, that is, without corrupting the database.

Admin A Microsoft Access database administrator who retains full permissions on a secure database used by a workgroup.

Admins workgroup (Admins) In the Access security environment, the administrative unit that contains the database system's administrator (Admin).

- Because the Admins workgroup must be managed by an Admin, the Admin is the default member in the Admins workgroup when that workgroup is created.
- The Admins workgroup is the core of the security system. Therefore, you cannot have a database administrative function without the Admins workgroup.
- The Admin manages the database security environment. Given this management function, the Admin is given full permissions on all objects in the databases by default. Because the security environment cannot be managed without the Admin, the Admin cannot be removed from the workgroup.
- The Admin is responsible for assigning any permission(s). A permission may or may not include the right to perform an operation on an object in the application.
- Each Admins workgroup must have at least one user, and all users in this Admins workgroup have the same rights as the Admin.

Anomaly Anything that fails to conform to the general rule. For example, if the general rule specifies that an employee has a last name, an employee without a last name would represent an anomaly. From a database perspective, anomalies cause the destruction of data integrity. Anomalies may be manifested as modification anomalies, insertion anomalies, and deletion anomalies.

ASCII American Standard Code for Information Interchange. A standard code used to identify character such as numbers, letters, or symbols.

Atomic attribute An attribute that is not further divisible into meaningful components. For example, a person's gender (M or F) cannot be further subdivided.

Attribute A characteristic of an entity. For example, a STORE entity is likely to have attributes such as a store identification code, a store name, and a store location. Similarly, an EMPLOYEE entity is likely to have an employee first name, an employee initial, an employee last name, an employee address, and an employee home phone number as its attributes.

B

Back-end database A database that contains the basic components of the database architecture such as the data dictionary, the tables, and the relationships between those tables. The tables of a back-end database are usually linked to a *front-end database* in which the application objects—queries, forms, reports, and macros—are stored.

Bound text box A text box linked to a field in a database table.

Boyce-Codd Normal Form (BCNF) A normal form that is a special case of the third normal form (3NF). A table is in 3NF when it meets the second normal form (2NF) requirements and contains no transitive dependencies. But a transitive dependency exists only when a non-key attribute determines another non-key attribute. However, it is possible for a non-key attribute to be the determinant of a primary key (PK) or part of a PK without violating the 3NF requirements. The BCNF eliminates this last possibility. See *transitive dependency, first normal form, second normal form, third normal form.*

Bridge table (composite table) A database table that is designed to connect or link two or more related database tables. Such a table uses at least the primary key components of the tables to be linked. For this reason, it is also called a composite table. For example, a composite EDUCATION table may use the EMP_NUM and the DEGREE_CODE to link the EMPLOYEE to the DEGREE to track the number and types of degrees held by each employee. A composite table may also include additional attributes, such as the institution from which the degree was earned and the date on which the degree was earned. See *composite table.*

Browser Software, such as Microsoft Internet Explorer or Netscape Navigator, that enables you to navigate (browse) through the Web.

Business rules Short and concise statements that establish the existence and composition of entities, attributes, relationships (expressed in terms of connectivities and cardinalities), and constraints. For example, the following declarations are business rules:

1. A customer may be assigned a sales representative.
2. No more than one sales representative can be assigned to a customer.
3. Each sales representative must be assigned at least one customer.
4. A driver may be assigned to many trips.
5. A driver may not drive more than 10 hours in any 24-hour period.

C

Candidate key Any attribute or combination of attributes that could serve the role as a primary key (PK) but that is not selected to be the PK.

Cardinality The minimum and maximum values for the entity occurrences that occur in a related table. For example, given a 1:M relationship between CUSTOMER and an optional INVOICE, the cardinality (0,N) written next to the CUSTOMER indicates that a customer may never have generated an invoice or may have generated many invoices. The cardinality (1,1) written next to the INVOICE indicates that each invoice references one and only one customer.

Client In any computer network, a computer that requests (through the end-users that use the computer) services such as data delivery, fax, printing, and so on from another computer (server) that delivers such services.

Command button An object that, when activated, executes a command such as *open a form, close a form,* or *print a file.*

Composite attribute An attribute that can be divided into meaningful components. For example, an employee's telephone number can be subdivided into the area code and the phone number itself. An employee's birth date can be subdivided into the year, month, and date.

Composite primary key Any primary key that is based on a combination of attributes. For example, if the EDUCATION table contains the attributes EMP_NUM and DEGREE_CODE, neither attribute by itself identifies each table row uniquely; that is, neither attribute can, by itself, serve as a proper primary key. But the combination of the EDUCATION table's EMP_NUM + DEGREE_CODE does yield a proper primary key.

Composite table See *bridge table.*

Connectivity The value of the relationship type, written by the entity box in an entity relationship diagram (ERD). For example, if you want to depict a 1:M relationship between CUSTOMER and INVOICE, the 1 is the connectivity for the CUSTOMER and the M is the connectivity for the INVOICE. See *entity relationship diagram.*

Control An object such as a text, label, or graphic or a command that can be used on a form to display data.

Crosstab query A query whose execution produces a (two-dimensional) cross-classification table. For example, a cross-classification table may be used to describe a group of people in terms of the two dimensions Age and Income.

Crow's Foot ERD An entity relationship diagram (ERD) in which the "many" side of a relationship is shown as a three-pronged symbol. The symbol resembles a bird's (crow's) footprint, thus giving rise to the name. The Crow's Foot ERD shows, in addition to the entities and relationships, each of the entity's attributes and the primary and/or foreign key designations.

D

Data Facts about people, places, things, or events.

Data dictionary A compilation of the data components, their names, and their characteristics.

Data redundancy A database condition in which a table contains *unnecessary* multiple values of the same attribute. (Multiple occurrences of foreign key values within a table are not redundant, because they are required to establish a relationship with another table.)

Data type The data characteristic that determines how the field values can be used. For example, an employee name is properly defined to be a text data type. You cannot perform arithmetic with a text data type. An employee's date of birth is properly classified as a (Julian) date data type. You can do (Julian) date arithmetic. For example, Date()—EMP_HIRE_DATE finds the number of days elapsed since an employee's hire date. Access lets you use many data types—text, OLE, numeric, date/time, logical, and so on—and many of the data types are available in different formats. For example, the date/time data type may be specified as long date, medium date, short date, long time, etc.

Data validation A process that verifies the proper data entry. The validation rule may be set at the table's attribute (field) properties box. For example, the validation rule (in "Mr.","Ms.","Mrs.") ensures that only these three entries will be accepted. To help the end user understand the data entry requirement, the validation rule is best accompanied by validation text that contains the message that the message box will produce.

Data warehouse A decision support system–oriented database that is primarily a data storage facility dedicated to using existing data to generate information. The data warehouse and its many variants rely on data extraction and loading, rather than on transactions, to generate the data stored within them. Much of the data warehouse's data are extracted from various production databases.

Database management system (DBMS) The DBMS manages the metadata in the data dictionary and automatically funnels all database activities through the database's data dictionary. The most important effect of this funneling activity is that it provides efficient access to the data within the database. The practical effect of the DBMS's existence is that it takes care of all physical storage details, data structures, relationships, and so on. See *metadata.*

Decision support system (DSS) database A database that is designed and used to focus on information requirements, rather than on the transaction requirements that characterize production databases.

Decomposition The process that breaks up the dependencies shown in a table's initial dependency diagram to form a new set of tables that exhibit dependencies indicating a higher normal form. For example, the decomposition of first normal form table structures yields second normal form or third normal form table structures.

Default value The attribute (field) value or characteristic that is assumed and executed without end-user intervention. Microsoft Access lets you define the default option in the field's property box. For example, if you enter Date() as a date field's default value, the result will be the current date. If you enter 0 as the default value for a numeric field, that value will show up automatically when you look at a record.

Deletion anomaly Given the existence of redundant data, the deletion of an attribute value or characteristic must be made in more than one place. Failure to completely delete the redundant data causes some of the "deleted" values or characteristics to continue their existence, thus producing the deletion anomaly.

Dependency A condition that is established when the value of one attribute is dependent on the value of another attribute. Putting it another way, the attribute X is dependent on the attribute Y if the value of attribute Y determines the value of attribute X. That is, Y is the determinant of X. This relationship is usually written as Y → X. If Z is also dependent on Y, the dependency may be written as Y → X, Z.

Dependency diagrams Structures that display all dependencies and their sources.

Derived attribute An attribute whose value is derived (usually calculated) from one or more other attributes. For example, a car mileage charge can be calculated by multiplying the miles driven by the charge per mile.

Determinant Exists when the value of attribute Y determines the value of attribute X. See *dependency.*

Dummy variable As used in a database environment, a variable that is used to store values that have no direct descriptive significance. For example, if a new customer does not yet have a sales representative assigned to him or her, the customer's sales rep number may be coded −9999 to indicate "no sales rep." (There is no sales rep with a number of −9999, so the number does not enable you to describe a real sales rep.)

Dynamic HTML An HTML file format that allows users to interact with a database via a Web server. Dynamic HTML must be used to ensure that end users can perform transactions on the database or generate information from the database through the use of a query. See *HTML.*

Dynamic Web page A Web page that enables the end user to change the page contents by interacting with the page components. For example, if you can select what objects will be displayed on the screen, you are looking at a dynamic Web page.

E

Embedded object An object that no longer has ties to the software from which it was generated. Therefore, the embedded object is not automatically updated when the object in the originating software is changed. For example, if a copy of an Excel spreadsheet is embedded in an Access form, the embedded spreadsheet will not be automatically updated when the original spreadsheet is updated in Excel.

Enhanced Chen ERD A Chen ERD in which the attribute names and functions (primary key or foreign key) are shown within each entity.

Entity A person, place, thing, event, or even a concept. It may be tangible or intangible. In short, an entity can be anything you want to keep track of. In a business environment, you are most likely to encounter entities such as employees, invoices, departments, customers, products, and vendors.

Entity integrity A condition in which each relational database table row is uniquely identified through a primary key (PK.)

Entity relationship diagram (ERD) A database modeling device that is used to develop database designs. The ERD uses symbols to indicate entity sets, relationships, and relationship types to produce an easily read, easily organized, and easily expanded database blueprint.

Entity set A named collection of related data. The data within an entity set are related through their classification. For example, the data in an EMPLOYEE entity set are related by the fact that only employee data are stored in this set. In other words, the EMPLOYEE entity set contains a collection of employee entities. You should not expect to find product entities in an EMPLOYEE entity set.

Equijoin A way to produce information by linking (joining) tables through common (equal) attributes. For example, you might produce a listing of all the employees who have a job classification of "accountant" by linking the EMPLOYEE and JOB tables through the common (accountant) job classification.

Existence dependent A condition that exists when one entity cannot exist without the related entity's presence. For example, DEPENDENT is existence dependent on EMPLOYEE. That is, a dependent cannot exist without an employee.

Explicit permission In the database security context, a permission that is granted to an individual user. An explicit permission assigned to one user will not affect any other user(s). See *permission.*

Expression A combination of operators, controls, properties, and field names that is used to define a single value.

EXtensible markup language (XML) A markup language that contains user-defined tags. XML (eXtensible Markup Language) is, in effect, a language that may be used to create other markup languages. Unlike HTML, XML is not limited to a predefined and fixed set of elements. Instead, XML enables you to define new elements and tags that are application-specific. Therefore, you can create an almost endless collection of versions of markup languages that, because they are application-specific, can be made very efficient at handling specialized information.

F

Field A database table column that stores attribute values. See *attribute.*

First normal form (1NF) A database table is in 1NF when these conditions are met:

- All key attributes are defined.
- Each row/column intersection contains only one value, rather than a set of values.
- All attributes are dependent on the PK.

Foreign key (FK) An attribute that establishes the relationship between the relational database tables. The FK in one table is an attribute that matches the primary key in the table to which it points.

Form A formatted data and/or information display or a formatted input device. Most forms display table and/or query contents in a predefined format. Some are designed to be dialog boxes, while others are used to receive input. In a Microsoft Access environment, forms can also be used as a basis for executing macro commands that open other forms, reports, or queries.

Form/subform A multi-component display that uses a main form and one or more subforms as (a) child(ren) of the main form. The main form and its subform(s) are linked through a common field. For example, an invoice may consist of a main invoice form and its subform, composed of the invoice lines. The invoice main form and subform are related (linked) through the invoice number.

Front-end database A database in which all application objects, such as forms, reports, and queries, reside. The front-end database does not contain the database tables used by its application objects. Instead, the front-end database's application objects derive their data from tables that are linked to a back-end database.

G

Group In the Access database administration context, an administrative unit that is composed of one or more users.

Group account An account that contains one or more user accounts in a secure database.

H

HTML (Hypertext Markup Language) A simple computer language that defines the format of the document contents to be published on the World Wide Web.

Hyperlink The visual element on Web pages through which you can load the address of another Web page into the browser.

HyperText Transfer Protocol (http) The protocol that defines the presentation and transmission format used by most URLs.

I

Implicit permission In the database security context, a permission that is granted to a specified group of users. Therefore, all users within that group have the same permission. See *permission*.

Information Processed data.

Inner join The default equijoin in Microsoft Access (see *equijoin*).

Input mask A device used to force a desired data entry format. For example, the entry .L,CCC in the employee title's field properties box will automatically capitalize the first character and will print all subsequent characters in lowercase format, regardless of how the end user types the values.

Insertion anomaly Given the existence of redundant data, the insertion of an attribute value or characteristic must be made in more than one place. Failure to make the same insertion in all of the places in which the redundant data occur causes different attribute values or characteristics to exist for the same attribute.

J

Jet-locking protocol A protocol (set of rules) that is named to reflect the fact that it is a set of rules created and enforced by the Access Jet Database Engine.

L

Label A control on an Access form or report that is used to display text material. However, a label can be unbound, or it can be bound to a field in a database table.

ldb file A small file, created by Access, which contains basic database administrative data. The .ldb file contains the user name in its first 32 bytes and the database security information in its second 32 bytes. The database administrator may use the information contained in the .ldb file to track all database users through their logon ID or through their computer name. The .ldb file also contains locking information.

Linked object An object that maintains its ties to the originating software. Therefore, if the original object is changed in the originating software, the change will automatically update all object copies that are attached to other objects. For example, if a copy of an Excel spreadsheet is linked to an Access form, the embedded spreadsheet will be automatically updated when the original spreadsheet is updated in Excel. (The copy maintains its links to the original.)

Linked table A table in one database that is connected (linked) to applications that are located in another database.

Lock A device that prevents the use of a database object. For example, if one user is performing operations on the EMPLOYEE table, a lock on that table would prevent another user from using that table until the lock is released.

M

Macro A preformatted instruction that performs a specified task. For example, OpenForm opens a form, and SetValue writes a value to a specified location.

Macro group Contains one or more macros to complete one or more task(s).

Many-to-many (M:N) relationship The M:N relationship exists when an entity can occur more than once on both sides of the relationship. For example, an employee may have earned many degrees: a BA, an MBA, an MFA, and so on. And many employees may have earned a BS or an MBA degree. M:N relationships should never be implemented in a relational database environment. Instead, they must be split into 1:M relationships.

Markup language A basic computer language that formats the elements of a Web page so that a browser can display it on a computer screen.

Message box A window that enables you to communicate with the end user through the display of a message. For example, if the end user fails to enter a required value, the message box might display the message "Please enter this required value."

Metadata Data about data. Includes the nature and types (1:1, 1:N, M:N) of relationships between the entities.

Modal A Microsoft Access property that defines the extent of an end-user's ability to perform actions. For example, a form set to modal will not allow the user to click outside the form.

Modification anomaly Given the existence of redundant data, the modification of an attribute value or characteristic must be made in more than one place. Failure to completely modify the redundant data causes different values or characteristics to exist for the same attribute, thus producing the modification anomaly.

Module A self-contained unit that performs a specified set of services. In Microsoft Access, a collection of Visual Basic (VB) declarations and procedures that are stored together as a unit.

Move handles Markers on an object's perimeter that indicate that the object may be moved by dragging on those handles.

Multivalued attribute An attribute that can have many values. For example, an employee can have many degrees, so the degree attribute is a multivalued attribute.

N

Non-key attribute An attribute that is neither a primary key (PK) nor a part of a PK.

Normal form A label that is used to indicate the nature of the dependencies that exist between the attributes within the entity.

Normalization The process that changes table structures to increase their normal form rating. Higher normal forms are required to minimize data redundancy. This process is most easily accomplished with the help of dependency diagrams.

Null Created by making no data entry at all, so a null denotes the absence of a value. A null is not a blank, because a blank, generated by tapping the space bar, has an ASCII value.

O

Object In Access, any component of the database. That is, an object may be a table, query, form, report, macro, or a module in the database.

ODBC Open Database Connectivity. A protocol that governs access procedures to all databases that meet ODBC standards.

OLE (Object linking and embedding) A protocol by which an object—such as a spreadsheet, a picture, video, sound, etc.—can be inserted into and used by an application.

One-to-many (1:M) relationship A 1:M relationship is found when an entity in one table may be related to many other entities in another table. For example, one customer can generate many invoices, but each invoice is generated by only one customer. Similarly, an employee may be assigned to only one department, but each department may have many employees assigned to it. The 1:M relationship is the most common of the three relationships. In fact, the 1:M relationship is the database design standard.

One-to-one (1:1) relationship A relationship in which one entity is related to only one other entity. For example, at least in the United States, one spouse can be related to only one other spouse. Although this relationship type is often the result of a failure to make a proper distinction between attributes and entities, it is a valuable tool in establishing proper supertype/subtype relationships.

Operation Any action that changes a database object. For example, operations include data updating, appending, or deleting. Operations also include modifying a table, query, form, report, macro, or module.

Optional relationship A relationship that exists when an entity occurrence on one side of the relationship does not require a corresponding entity occurrence on the other side of the relationship. For example, an employee may have one or more dependents, but we cannot require an employee to have dependents.

Optionality Shorthand for an optional relationship. In an entity relationship diagram (ERD), an optionality is indicated by writing a circle next to, above, or below any ERD entity box.

Outer join An outer join is a structured query language (SQL) operation that preserves unmatched rows from one or more joined tables. Which rows are preserved depends on the type of outer join used: left, right, or full. For example, a left outer join is one in which the unmatched rows from the left table are preserved. (The left table is the one on the left side of the JOIN statement.) Therefore, the unmatched rows in the PRODUCT table are preserved in the SQL command

```
SELECT*
   FROM PRODUCT LEFT OUTER JOIN VENDOR
   ON PRODUCT.VEND_CODE = VENDOR.VEND_
   CODE;
```

Access lets you select outer joins through its query by example (QBE) interface.

P

Page In Microsoft Access, a Web page that is used to display—either statically or dynamically—information over the Internet.

Partial dependency A dependency that is based on only part of the primary key (PK).

Permission The right to use a database object. Note that the word *permission* may be used as a noun in the database context.

Primary key (PK) An attribute, or combination of attributes, that uniquely identifies each row in a relational database table. Therefore, a PK cannot be null.

Production database A transaction-intensive database that uses frequent real-time data updates. The production database's use is characterized by frequent and complex transactions.

Protocol A set of rules. In a database context, a set of rules that governs database access and actions performed on the database.

Q

Query A question asked within the database environment. For example, a sales query might be: Which products sold in what quantity during what time frame?

Query by example (QBE) A technique that allows a user to generate a structured query language (SQL) command to generate an output for a database query without knowing the details of the structured query language.

R

Record A row (tuple) in a relational database table. An entity in an entity set.

Record set A complete collection of a table's records. For example, the customer record set would include all the records in the CUSTOMER table.

Recursive relationship A relationship that exists if an entity can be related to itself. For example, quite a few courses require one or more other courses as prerequisites. That is, the course entity is related to another course entity. In this case, the recursive relationship "course is a prerequisite to course" also happens to be an M:N relationship; after all, a course can have more than one prerequisite, and a course can be a prerequisite to many other courses.

Redundant data Data that are unnecessarily replicated.

Referential integrity A condition that exists when a relational database table's foreign key (FK) values either match the primary key (PK) values to which they point or are null. Referential integrity ensures that it will be impossible to point to PK values that do not exist.

Relational database A database whose structure and composition are based on the work done by E. F. Codd in 1970. Dr. Codd's use of the word *relation* stems from the mathematical set theory from which he derived his (relational) database model. What is especially important from the database professional's point of view is that, conceptually speaking, the data are stored in tables. This much-simplified conceptual view of data storage makes it much easier to model the data environment, eliminating the need to define data relationships at the physical level. The relational database is the dominant production database today.

Relational database management system (RDBMS) The software that manages the environment in which the relational database structures exist. The RDBMS takes care of the creation, use, and management of the relational database's very complex physical details.

Relational schema A diagram that shows how the entities in the entity relationship diagram (ERD) are related to each other by listing the attributes within each entity and connecting the entity foreign keys (FKs) to their respective primary keys (PKs).

Relationship type The nature of a relationship between entities, expressed by the number of their possible occurrences in the related tables. Three primary relationship types exist: one to one (1:1), one to many (1:M), and many to many (M:N).

Report A way to present information in printed format.

S

Second normal form (2NF) A table is in 2NF if

- All 1NF conditions are met.
- The partial dependencies have been removed.

However, a table in 2NF still contains transitive dependencies.

Secondary key A non-PK search key, which may not yield unique records. For example, the combination of a customer's first and last names may be a secondary key.

Selection markers Markers on an object's perimeter that indicate that the object has been selected. The selected object may then be manipulated through changes in its contents, location, or size.

Server In any computer network, a computer that provides services such as data delivery, printing, fax, and so on to computers that request such services.

Share-level security A security level that requires the user to supply both an ID and a password to access any database object. For example, a user might have one ID and a password to only *read* the EMPLOYEE table and another ID and a password to *update* the table. Each time the user wants to update the EMPLOYEE table, the user must supply the required ID and a password that matches that ID. The share-level security option yields a more secure database than user-level security.

Simple attribute See *atomic attribute.*

Single-valued attribute An attribute that can have only one value. For example, you only have one first name, only one birth date, and only one Social Security number.

SQL See *Structural Query Language.*

Static HTML The HTML file format that is used to display data without enabling end users to interact with such data. An example of a static format file is a product catalog.

Static Web page A Web page that can only display a *predefined* set of pictures, a text-based listing, or other objects, but you cannot interact with those objects.

Strong entity An entity that can exist without having a related entity. For example, an employee can exist without having a dependent, such as a child. (Employees are not required to have children.)

Structural Query Language A relational database language that enables users to create the structure of a database and all of its components, perform data manipulation and database administration, and query the database contents to extract useful information. SQL is a so-called third-generation language, defined as a language that enables the end-user to "tell the database" *what* to do without having to specify *how* to do it.

Supertype/subtype relationship A relationship in which the supertype is the entity set that contains common attributes and the subtype is the entity set that contains unique attributes. For example, although pilots are airline employees, they have many unique characteristics such as licenses, medical requirements, and training requirements. Therefore, these unique attributes are best stored in a (subtype) PILOT table, while the common attributes—such as names, addresses, and phone numbers—are best stored in an EMPLOYEE (supertype) table. The supertype/subtype relationship is usually used to avoid nulls.

Synonym A word that has the same meaning as another word. For example, the words "car" and "automobile" may be used to refer to the same object.

T

Tab order The procedure that controls the sequence of the cursor movements from one control to another on an Access form.

Table Conceptually, a matrix composed of intersecting rows and columns in which relational database data are stored.

Tag An HTML key word that is enclosed in angle brackets. For example, <HTML> is a tag, as is <CENTER>.

TCP/IP (Transmission Control Protocol/Internet Protocol) The standard Internet communications protocol. Although the hyperlinks are the *visible* way in which Web pages are linked, those hyperlinks perform their linking magic through TCP/IP.

Text box May be bound or unbound. A bound text box displays data from a table or a query, while an unbound control has no query or table link. Unbound controls are used to receive input.

Third normal form (3NF) A table in 3NF

- Meets all the 2NF conditions. See *second normal form.*
- Contains no transitive dependencies.

Toolbar A toolbar contains many buttons, controls, or menus that can be used on a database object such as a query, a form, or a report.

Toolbox A collection of Access tools that let you create or modify various controls placed on database objects such as forms and reports.

Transaction A logical unit of work that reads from or writes to a database. A transaction may involve a single action or consist of multiple actions. For example, a simple credit sales transaction requires at least three actions: the sale decreases the inventory by the number of units bought, adds the sales amount to the seller's credit sales total, and adds the sales amount to the customer's balance.

Transitive dependency A dependency based on an attribute that is not part of the primary key (PK).

Tuple A row in a relational database table.

U

Unbound control A control that is not associated with an existing data source.

Unbound textbox A textbox that is not associated with an existing data source. Such textboxes are usually used to provide input spaces or message boxes.

Uniform Resource Locator (URL) A Web address.

User In the Access database security context, a person whom the Admin allows to use a specified object or a set of objects.

User account An account created to identify a user in a user database.

User-level security A security environment that permits the logon user to access all objects based on the permission(s) given to that user.

Users group In the Access database security context, the default group created by Access. Access adds all users to this group.

V

VBA (Visual Basic for Applications) A programming language that is used to write Access application modules.

W

Weak entity An entity that meets two criteria:

1. It is existence dependent on a related entity.
2. Its primary key (PK) is at least partially derived from the related entity's PK.

However, there is no requirement for a weak entity to be optional. For example, an invoice line entity is weak, because it cannot exist without an invoice entity and its composite primary key includes the invoice's primary key. But the invoice line entity is not optional to the invoice entity, because each invoice must have at least one invoice line.

Web page A specially formatted document for use on the Internet's worldwide Web system. A Web page can contain text, graphics, video, audio, and/or other objects such as spreadsheets. Each Web page has an address, known as an URL or Uniform Resource Locator.

Workgroup file In the Access database security system, a file that stores information about the groups, the users, and the user passwords. The default name for the workgroup is System.mdw. However, you may use any valid name with an extension of .mdw to identify the workgroup file.

Workgroup identification (WID) The workgroup name. The WID must be supplied whenever a new workgroup file is created.

World Wide Web (WWW) Usually referred to as "the Web," it is basically a worldwide network of Web pages.

X

XML See *eXtensible markup language.*

Index